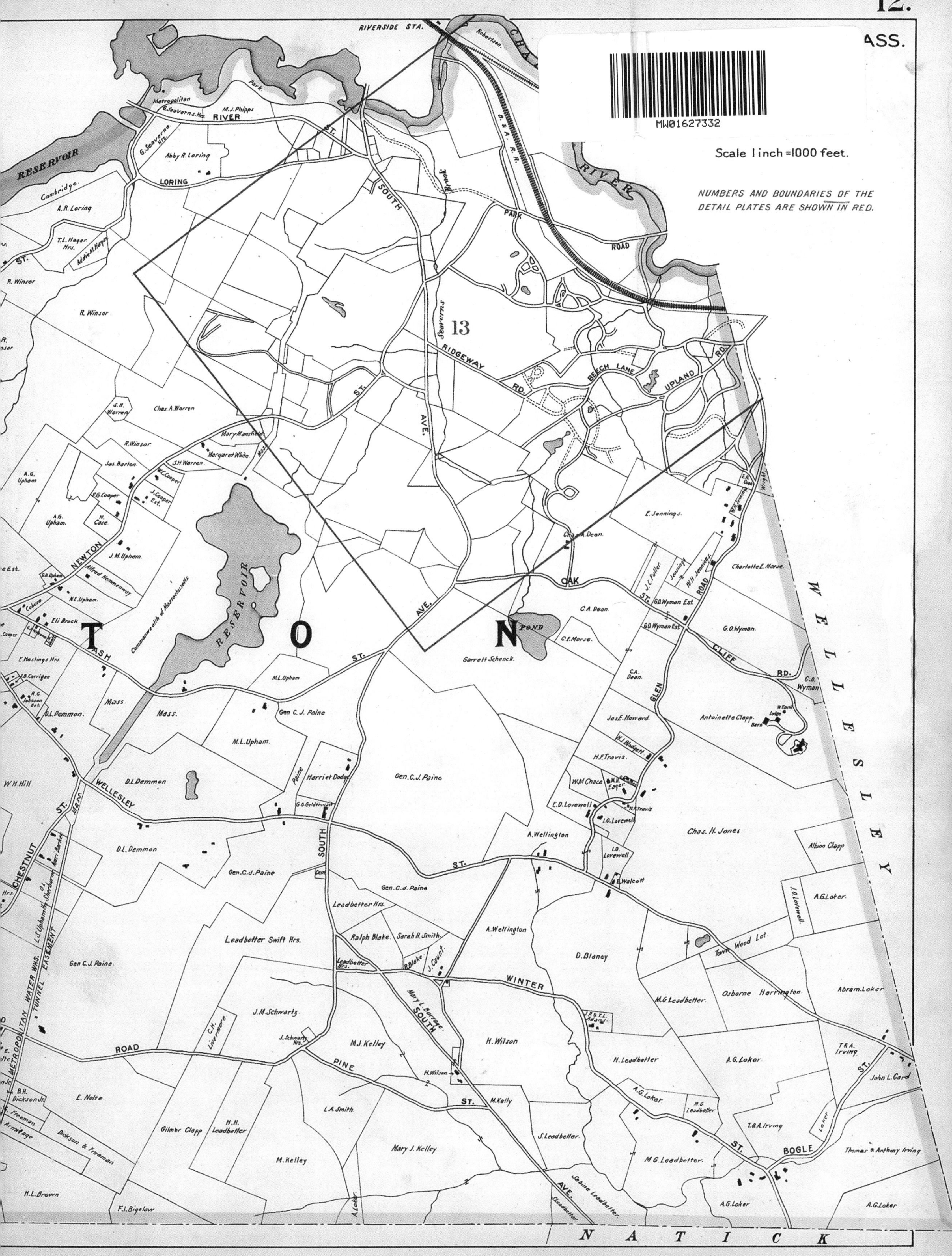
ASS.
MW01627332
Scale 1 inch = 1000 feet.
NUMBERS AND BOUNDARIES OF THE
DETAIL PLATES ARE SHOWN IN RED.
RIVERSIDE STA.
Robertson
Park
Metropolitan
G.Seaverns Hrs.
M.J.Phipps
RIVER
G.Seaverns Hrs.
Abby R. Loring
RESERVOIR
LORING
Cambridge
A.R.Loring
T.L.Hager Hrs.
Addie M. Hager
ST.
R. Winsor
R. Winsor
SOUTH
ST.
B. & A. R.R.
Brook
RIVER
PARK
ROAD
Seaverns
13
RIDGEWAY
RD.
BEECH LANE
UPLAND
RD.
ST.
AVE.
S.H. Warren
Chas. A. Warren
R.Winsor
Mary Mansfield
Margaret White
S.H.Warren
Jas. Barton
W.C.Cooper
A.G. Upham
F.G.Cooper
J.Cooper Est.
A.G. Upham
H. Case
NEWTON
J.M.Upham
Alfred Hemmenway
N.E.Upham
Coburn
Eli Brock
Commonwealth of Massachusetts
RESERVOIR
T
O
N
E.Jennings
Chas. A. Dean
J.C.Fuller
W.H.Jennings
Charlotte E. Morse
OAK
ST.
G.O.Wyman Est.
ROAD
C.A.Dean
G.O.Wyman Est.
G.O.Wyman
POND
C.E.Morse
Garrett Schenck
CLIFF
RD.
C.O. Wyman
W E L L E S L E Y
C.A. Dean
E.Hastings Hrs.
ASH
ST.
M.L.Upham
Gen C.J. Paine
Mass.
Mass.
Jas.E.Howard
Antoinette Clapp
Barn
H.F.Travis
M.L.Upham
D.L.Demmon
W.H. Hill
WELLESLEY
Paine
Harriet Dodge
Gen.C.J.Paine
W.M.Chace
E.D.Lovewell
I.O. Lovewell
H.F.Travis
G.O.Goldthwait
D.L.Demmon
A.Wellington
Chas. H. Jones
Albion Clapp
SOUTH
I.O. Lovewell
ST.
Gen.C.J.Paine
E.Walcott
CHESTNUT
Gen.C.J.Paine
Leadbetter Hrs.
I.O. Lovewell
A.G.Loker
ST.
Ralph Blake
Sarah H. Smith
A.Wellington
Leadbetter Swift Hrs.
Town Wood Lot
D.Blaney
Gen C.J.Paine
Leadbetter Hrs.
R.Blake
J. Cavot
WINTER
METROPOLITAN WATER WKS. TUNNEL EASEMENT
M.G.Leadbetter
Osborne Harrington
Abram Loker
J.M.Schwartz
C.H. Livermore
Mary L. Burrage
SOUTH
ROAD
J.Schwartz Hrs.
M.J.Kelley
H. Wilson
T.&A. Irving
PINE
H.Leadbetter
A.G. Loker
ST.
H.Wilson
John L. Card
B.H. Dickson Jr.
E. Nolte
ST.
M.Kelly
A.G. Loker
M.G. Leadbetter
L.A.Smith
Freeman
Armitage
Dickson & Freeman
Gilmer Clapp
H.N. Leadbetter
J.Leadbetter
T.&A. Irving
Loker
ST.
BOGLE
Thomas & Anthony Irving
M.Kelley
Mary J. Kelley
M.G.Leadbetter
H.L.Brown
AVE.
Sabine Leadbetter
F.I.Bigelow
A.Loker
Leadbetter
A.G.Loker
A.G.Loker
N A T I C K

Farm Town to Suburb

To Jake
Rudnitsky
with best wishes,
Pamela W. Fox
January 15, 2004

Figure A. The Weston Town Hall was built in 1917 as part of a sweeping town improvement plan that also created the present town green.

Farm Town to Suburb

THE HISTORY AND ARCHITECTURE OF
WESTON, MASSACHUSETTS · 1830–1980

by Pamela W. Fox
with Sarah B. Gilman, Photo Editor

Underwritten by
The Golden Ball Tavern Museum
Weston, Massachusetts

PETER E. RANDALL PUBLISHER
Portsmouth, New Hampshire

Printed in Hong Kong

Copies of the book can be obtained from:

Love Lane Press
98 Love Lane
Weston, MA 02493

or by writing to the

Golden Ball Tavern Museum
662 Boston Post Road
Weston, MA 02493

Peter E. Randall Publisher
Box 4726, Portsmouth, NH 03802

Design: Tom Allen, Pear Graphics

End leaves: from *Atlas of Middlesex County*, 1908

Library of Congress Cataloging-in Publication Data

Fox, Pamela W.
Farm town to suburb : the history and architecture of Weston, Massachusetts, 1830-1980 / by Pamela W. Fox ; with Sarah B. Gilman, photo editor.
p. cm.
"Underwritten by the Golden Ball Tavern Museum, Weston, Massachusetts."
ISBN 1-931807-01-9 (alk. paper)
1. Weston (Mass.)--History. 2. Weston (Mass.)--History--Pictorial works. 3. Historic buildings--Massachusetts--Weston. 4. Historic buildings--Massachusetts--Weston --Pictorial works. 5. Architecture--Massachusetts--Weston--History. 6. Architecture--Massachusetts--Weston--History--Pictorial works. 7. Weston (Mass.)--Buildings, structures, etc. I. Gilman, Sarah B. II. title.

F74.W59 F69 2001
974.4'4--dc21

2001051054

To Sarah Bates Gilman,
who believed in this book
and worked with me for four years to make it a reality

And to my husband, Michael,
and my children, Laura, David, and Danny,
with love

It is a noble faculty of our nature which enables us to connect our thoughts, our sympathies, and our happiness with what is distant in place or time; and, looking before and after, to hold communion at once with our ancestors and our posterity. Human and mortal although we are, we are nevertheless not mere insulated beings, without relation to the past or the future.... We live in the past by a knowledge of its history; and in the future by hope and anticipation.

—Daniel Webster, address at the 200th anniversary of the landing of the Pilgrims on Plymouth Rock, December 22, 1820

SPONSORS

The author and the trustees of the Golden Ball Tavern Trust gratefully acknowledge the support of the

Estate of Virginia Wellington Cabot

and the following contributors:

Historians

Polly Germeshausen
John and Ann Sallay
Dr. and Mrs. Harold S. Schwenk, Jr.

Benefactors

Friends of the Weston Public Library
Bill and Karen Gallagher
Tom and Robin Jackson
David and Winky Merrill and the Maple Hill Foundation
Alfred P. Pace and Family; Pace Builders
Mrs. William A. Whittemore

Patrons

Mary Gambrill Aydelott
The Bateman Family
Gerald T. Cameron Family
Lawrence and Gabriella Coburn
Oliver and Cynthia Curme
Mr. and Mrs. Albert P. Everts Jr.
Caroline and Walter Palmer
Daniel and Harriet Tolpin
Fred and Catherine Wiersema
Bill and Linda Wiseman

Supporters

Claudia and Robert Birnbaum
Christine Bishop and Paul Arkema
Alfred L. Aydelott
John G. Brooks
Cambridge Trust Company
Polly Carter
Barbara B. Clemson
Vangie and John P. Condakes
Arlena S. Cort (Mrs. Joseph C.)
The Country Garden Club of Weston
Dorothy M. and Lawrence B. Damon Jr.
Cheryl and Joe Dempsey
Brenton and Elizabeth Dickson
Barbara and Guy Dillaway
The Eastman Family
Ray and Pat Endreny
Gretchen and Edward Fish
Florentine Frames
Mr. and Mrs. Peter R. Gates
Gateway Medical Center
Elisabeth, Jeffrey, Grant, Reid and Ainsley Gilbard
Jan Gleysteen Architects, Inc.
Charles W. Hubbard III
Joan and Charlie Hunt
The Hyde Family
Donna and Hugh Kelly
Dorian Lightbown
Mary and John M. Lord Jr. and Family
Kay and John McCahan
Andy and Linda McLane
Mr. and Mrs. Francis Ware Newbury Jr.
Jim and Betsy Nichols
Omni Foods Supermarket
James Ricotta and Anne O'Neil
Julie and Howard Stagg
Margaret Winsor Stubbs
Bill and Anne Tierney
Hugo Uyterhoeven
Richard and Patricia Wayne
Mrs. Thomas H. West
Peter Wheeler
Mr. and Mrs. William M. Wilkinson
Women's Community League of Weston
Bella Wong and Steven Brand

Friends

Carol and Harry Azadian
Mr. and Mrs. Robert Billings
Joan and Harvey Bines
Mr. and Mrs. Benjamin Blaney
Douglas and Diana Bonner
Sandy and Ted Bowers
Mr. and Mrs. David H. Bradley
The Brewster Family
Sheila and Greg Burkus
Mr. and Mrs. John G. Callan
Martha and Marshall Campbell

IN MEMORIAM
William Anthony Whittemore
(1928–2001)

Chairman of the Golden Ball Tavern Trust
1981–2001
with gratitude for his encouragement and support

Gaynor D. Casner
The Chestnut Shop of Weston
Barbara F. Coburn
Kay and Frank Conrad
Philip A. Cooper
Dr. and Mrs. J. Holland Cotter
Robin Miller Peakes Coutts
Ari Curelop, Mark Curelop and Marioleni Mandelis
Terry L. Curl, D.D.S.
Tony and Alice Davies
Joanne and Lawrence DeAngelis
Mrs. Gail Whittemore Denman
The Detore Family
Sue and Jed Diehl and Family
Claes and Carin Dohlman
Jack and Marilyn Doyle
Joan and Dick Drury
Michael and Suzanne Eliastam
Stephen and Ellen Fine
Montie and John Fiske
Margaret and Woodie Flowers
Harriett Fox
Louis Fox
Mrs. Waldo Emerson Forbes (Sarah Cushing Paine)
Katherine L. French (In Memory of Mary Hubbard French)
Philip S. Gallagher
Elena and Joe Gardella
Jill and Steven Goldy
Bonnie Grad and Gary Wolf
Halcott and Cornelia Grant
Keith, Demie and Jessilee Gross
Cynthia Rich Grossman
John and Susan Gunderson
Brendan M. Harley Family
Mrs. Gordon T. Heald
In Memory of Ann C. Heffernon
Brooks and Katharina Helmick
Christian and Donna Hoffman
Mr. and Mrs. William O. Holleman
Nancy Willis Holmes
Dave Harmon and Karen Ingwersen
Elizabeth F. Jacobs
Mr. and Mrs. James T. Jensen
Harry and Jean Jones
Cynthia Kettyle
Keith and Debbie Kimball
Dennis and Valerie Kirshy
Bob and April Kiskaddon
Tina and Stan Kraus
Roger Lee and Gail O'Donnell
Leiby's Garden and Flower Shop
Helen E. Lennon
Elliot and Lenore Zug Lobel
Lodeiro Family
Anonymous
Jean E. MacQuiddy
Nicholas H. Madden
Betty Lou and Wes Marple
Judy Markland and Bill Saunders
Alice M. McDonald
John D. McKenzie Jr.
Daniel and Betty Ann Miller
Mr. and Mrs. James W. Moore
Caroline and Anthony Morse Jr.
Cheryl K. Nicholas
B.L. Ogilvie & Sons, Inc.
Drs. Lauren Oshry and Elias Reichel
Rita Nash Paine
Charles J. Paine II
John B. Paine III
Sarah C.M. Paine
Thomas M. Paine
Brooks and Gale Parker
Mr. and Mrs. Samuel R. Payson
Ron and Katie Pearson
Carol and Fred Perkins
Robert and Mary Perriello
Julia Lee Wakefield Proctor
Alison Sherman Randall, Dr. Sheldon Randall
Robin and Howard Reisman
Ted Romanow and Kim Redfield
William and Kathleen Rousseau
Ted and Betsy Rowe
Dr. Thomas and Cheryl Russo, Ashley, Ali, Elizabeth and Thomas
St. Julia Church
John McClean Sallay
Margaret Parks Sallay
James Watson Sallay
Michael and Natalie Sanders
Anne B. Schuknecht
Joyce Schwartz and Ed Lashman
Larry and Mary Shaw
Mary and Benjamin Smith
Barbara Spangler
Mr. and Mrs. Armstrong Stambaugh
Sherman and Jill Starr
Paul and Doris Sullivan
Lynn and Edwin Taff
John and Marsha Tucker
The Walpert Family
Weston Travel Service
The Whitledge Family
Nick and Sally Whitridge
Charles and Betty Williams

Figure B. Celebrations commemorating the United States Bicentennial included a Family Day parade on June 12, 1976. Horseback riders pass by the Golden Ball Tavern Museum on Boston Post Road.

CONTENTS

Figure B-1. G.W. Cutting & Sons general store in the town center was decorated with festive red, white, and blue bunting for the town's bicentennial celebration in 1913.

ACKNOWLEDGMENTS

Sally Gilman and I discovered our mutual interest in old photographs while taking a course in the Photo Shop computer program at Weston High School. For two years we worked together as volunteers organizing the extensive photo collection at the Weston Historical Society. When I began writing my book, Sally again volunteered to help. The two of us spent hundreds of hours copying, organizing, and selecting photographs for this history. Her enthusiasm, thoughtful advice, and darkroom expertise contributed enormously to the quality of this book and my enjoyment in producing it.

My second source of support over the years of writing has been the Golden Ball Tavern Museum, particularly Bill Whittemore, chairman of the board of the Golden Ball Tavern Trust from 1981 to 2001. Under Bill's leadership, the Golden Ball offered to help underwrite this book, providing much-needed institutional sponsorship and financial assistance. Sadly, Bill did not live to see the book completed. He died in March 2001, just as the draft was being submitted for publication. I would also like to thank current board chairman Bill Gallagher, Bill and Linda Wiseman, Beck Whittemore, Executive Director Joan Bines, and other members of the board of trustees who helped raise funds for this project.

I would like to thank Mary Lord for the time she spent redrawing many of the maps to make them clear and legible. George Bates, Stanley G. French Jr., Tom Paine, Ben Crouch, Harry and Jean Jones, Doug Henderson, and John Sallay spent many hours reviewing the first draft. Michael Steinitz and Brian Donahue contributed many helpful comments. Stanley French Jr., Tom Paine, and Julie Hyde enthusiastically shared extensive collections of family photographs and memorabilia. Ben Crouch provided invaluable information and photographs from his railroad and Weston Fire Department collections, Fred Campbell shared his recollections and photographs of the Dean estate, and Eloise Kenney was a cheerful and careful source who constantly delighted me with newly discovered pictures of her many Weston ancestors. Bob Pollock was a great resource for images and information on the Charles River and Riverside Recreation Grounds. Margaret Flowers rescued me several times when I experienced computer problems and made sure I really did have a back-up copy on the Zip disk. Herb Randle restored photographs that might otherwise have been unusable. I was fortunate to have the opportunity to consult two centenarians, Nelson McNutt and Raymond Washburn, and also the late Winsor Gale, who died just short of that mark.

The single largest source of photographs for this book is the Weston Historical Society. Over 200 of the more than 1,000 photographs and illustrations came from the society, which allowed me access to its fine collection. Among the board members who should be mentioned are Bill Martin, president, Doug Henderson, Vera Laska, and George Amadon. The second local institutional source was the Weston Historical Commission and its chairman Alfred L. Aydelott. I would like to thank the many helpful employees at Weston Town Hall and Elizabeth Drake and the dedicated staff at Weston Public Library; as well as Lorna Condon, librarian at The Society for the Preservation of New England Antiquities (SPNEA); Susan Abele, curator at The Jackson Homestead in Newton, Massachusetts; Sean Fisher, archivist for the Metropolitan District Commission (MDC); Barbara Coburn and the late Mary Maynard, archivists for First Parish Church; and the staffs at the Massachusetts Historical Society, Boston Public Library, Massachusetts Archives, Massachusetts State Library and Annex, Cambridge Historical Commission, Harvard University Archives, National Archives and Records Administration, New England Historic and Genealogical Society, Waltham Public Library (archives), and Frederick Law Olmsted National Historic Site in Brookline.

The following list does not exhaust the many Weston residents and out-of-towners who helped with specific chapters:

Chronological chapters 1–9: Brian Donahue; Ward Carter; Thomas Van Nuys; Guy Dillaway, archivist for the Friendly Society; Biz Paynter; Lorna Garron; David Fixler; Rick Wohlers; Hugo Uyterhoven; and Polly Germeshausen. Also David Johansen and Bill O'Neil of the Weston park and cemetery office.

Kendal Green: Harold Jr. and Jane Coburn; Jean Cahill Tierney and Jane Cahill Compton; Elsie Foote Cooke; Betty Rafuse; Norman, Jeanne, and Erica Saunders; Inge and Arthur Uhlir; Warren Vittum; Thelma Hanson; Ruth Fletcher; Marjorie Maxwell; Aimo Teittinen; the Hunt and Dumaine families; Jim Dolan; and Donna Ravn, librarian at the Cambridge School. Also, Scot Huntington and members of the Organ Historical Society Inc.

Church Street/Coburn Chapter: Edward "Ted" Coburn, the late Arthur L. "Bud" Coburn, Mary Coburn Hazard, Barbara Coburn, Edward Coburn, Martha Hutcheson, and Steena Jacobs. Also, Henry S. "Dusty" Reeder Jr., Grant Dowse, and other residents of Webster Hill.

The Northwest: Carl and Florence Coburn Smith; Winkie Merrill; Jean and Harry Jones; Mary Parker; Paul Nelligan, S.J. and the New England Province Archives at College of the Holy Cross; James W. Skehan, S.J.; Joseph Sheehan Jr.; the late Joseph Sheehan Sr.; Raymond Washburn; John Cronin; Clifford Harrington; and Dr. and Mrs. Joseph Gardella.

Boston Post Road East: Anna Melone, Alfred Aydelott, Polly Gambrill Aydelott, Eloise Kenney, Cindy and Bob Mosher, John Sallay, Katherine Peebles, Thomas Peebles, and the Cambridge Historical Commission. Also, Andrew Forest and the Massachusetts Broken Stone Company.

Sears Estate: Marjorie Harnish, Gale Parker, Mabel Richardson, and Elizabeth Hope Cushing.

Town Center: David Bradley, Melissa Burrage, David Colpitts, Rev. Robert Tyrrell, Patience Sandrof, and Wilmot Whitney. Also, the staffs at First Parish Church, St. Julia Church, and the Church of Christ, Scientist.

Boston Post Road West: Artemis Willis, Rev. Susan Crane, Lucy Carter, Gladys Clark, May Davidson, Jim Clark, Harry Lingley, Fred Perkins, Daniel Compton, Beth Hastings, Raymond Ogilvie, Ken Sutherland, Walter Mulcahy, and Golden Ball Tavern Museum Director Joan Bines and Archivist Dorothea Waterbury.

Love Lane: the late Edward Dickson, Polly Dickson, Lee Fernandez, John Kirk, Dick DiVito, Cheryl Dempsey, Mary Perriello, Jean Dowell, Mary Horne, and Dorothea Nolte Kelly.

Paine Estate/Chestnut Street: Thomas M. Paine, Charles M. Ganson Jr., Douglas Henderson, and Calvin Patriquin.

Case's Corner: Jeanne d'Arc O'Hare, CSJ, Regis College archivist. Also, the Arnold Arboretum library staff including Carol David.

Winsor Estate: Elise Winsor Palmer, the late Winsor Gale, the late Philip Trumbull, Carter Crawford, and Susan Graves Teare. Also Ray Heist, Weston Golf Club historian, and Gerhardt Krammer, Weston Golf Club manager.

Riverside: Susan Abele, Bob Pollock, David Kingsbury, and Sean Fisher.

Hubbard: Stanley G. French Jr., Katherine French, Elizabeth Jacobs, Charles Wells Hubbard III, Charles Hubbard Meigs, Harold and Paula Schwenk, and Virginia Scott.

Blake: Ruth Blake Oliver and Benjamin Blake.

Cutter's Corner: James Fraser, Harriet Elliston, Lelia Orrell Elliston, and Milton Theall.

Glen Road: Nelson McNutt, Mildred Balunas, and George Bates.

Peirce Estate: Tom Petrin, manager of Henderson House; Jean Mustard; and Robert Roche, archivist for Shepley Bulfinch Richardson and Abbott.

C.H. Jones Estate: Penelope Hare, Ruth Andrews, Paul Jones Jr., Jean D'Intinosanto Jones, Yola D'Intinosanto Colby, George Lombard, Mrs. John Wendall, Edward Abbott, and Halcott Grant. Their recollections are not always exactly the same, probably owing to changes over the history of the estate and their different ages and associations.

Dean-Byron-Norumbega: Fred Campbell, Garret Schenck, and Marcia Byron Hallett.

The Southwest: Roger and Wayne Mezitt, Santo Anza, Emanuel Benotti, Dorothy Cugini, and Emily Althausen.

Wellington/Blaney: Julie and Peter Hyde, Nina Danforth, Nicholas Danforth, Linda Cabot Black, John Sallay, Benjamin Blaney, and Thomas Denenberg, Associate Curator of American Decorative Arts, Wadsworth Atheneum.

INTRODUCTION

People needed to develop a deeper sense of place. . . . We needed to convince people that understanding the places where they lived, caring for the places where they lived, and having a practical connection with the places where they lived were worthwhile goals in life. The community's land had to be more than something to absorb effluent, and the community's history had to be more than something to absorb antiquarians.

Reclaiming the Commons, by Brian Donahue

When Col. Daniel S. Lamson sat down to write his *History of the Town of Weston* more than a century ago, he had a mission. He could see the town changing—and not for the better, in his opinion. He looked back to the rugged, fiercely independent early farmers and saw a moral fiber that had steadily weakened in succeeding generations. He wrote, "As the American people progress in wealth, comfort, and luxury . . . it is to be feared that the young men and women are losing sight of those sturdy moral principles which gave force and decision to the early settlers."[1] For Lamson, local history could function as a kind of moral compass to guide the way through a sea of material luxury and moral laxity.

I confess to idealizing my subjects, the men and women of Lamson's day, in much the same way that Lamson idealized his colonial forefathers. I am inspired by the goals and values of past town leaders. I admire the rich social fabric centered on churches, fraternal lodges, and the Grange. Weston residents at the turn of the 20th century seem rugged enough compared to the present day. Children were responsible for time-consuming and inescapable chores. When young people needed to go somewhere, they walked. Parents raised large families in houses the size of some present-day master bedroom suites.

But I did not write this history because I wish we could all be like our ancestors or because I find past history more interesting than present-day affairs. I wrote this history because I care about the present and future of the town. In an age of increasing diversity and a population always on the move, it is difficult for many Americans to have any effective sense of historical roots or commitment to the municipality in which they live. One of the purposes of this book is to help give Weston residents, present and future, a sense of connectedness to their current town's past. I would like everyone, not just those who grew up here, to understand the evolution of the town. I would like everyone to understand Weston's distinctive qualities and feel a responsibility for keeping it a good place to live.

All the things we take for granted in Weston—clean water, good schools, effective town government, conservation and recreational land—did not just happen. They are the result of generations of dedicated public service, much of which was and still is unpaid. The prerequisite for good town government is interested, knowledgeable, and committed citizens. In this book, readers will meet and, I hope, be inspired by the foresight and commitment of those who came before us.

This book has a second purpose, and that is preservation of community character. I moved to Weston in 1991. As a historic preservation consultant, I surveyed the town's historic resources in 1993–94 for the Weston Historical Commission. As an author of the 1996 *Open Space and Recreation Plan* and board member of the Weston Land Trust, I have been involved in land preservation. As a member of the Weston Planning Board for the past four years, I have watched the effect of "mansionization." New residents who come in with plans for their dream house often fail to see their individual building lot as part of a neighborhood and town with a particular character and sense of place that is different from other places. Not better, or more beautiful—just different, and unique.

Weston is unique because, like any other community, the town has its own history and its own architectural and landscape traditions. Early farmers cleared their fields and used the stone to build the walls lining our scenic roads. Estate owners resisted streetcars and built golf courses. Residents after World War II worked actively to conserve open space. Our environment was shaped in a certain way by those who came before us.

The past is prologue. Understanding the past allows us to see the present more clearly and make better choices for the future. George Kramer explained it this way in his essay "Why I Am a Preservationist":

> People move, places remain to define a neighborhood. A knowledge of our past breeds reflection and understanding of who we are and provides an opportunity to assess change. Where places reflect that past and rely on traditional building forms, we are most likely to act in moderate fashion, with care for the community at large. . . . In short, good places reinforce community. Good places make good citizens.

We are all temporary custodians of our buildings and our environment. I hope this book will provide the knowledge that breeds reflection. Conservationist Baba Dioum has been quoted as saying, "In the end, we will only conserve what we love, we love only what we understand, we will understand what we are taught."

This book is intended as a reference book that will also appeal to those with just enough time to look at the pictures. By writing about *really* local history—the history of individual neighborhoods and houses—I hope to reach those who will be mainly curious about their own "one square mile."

I would like to comment on what to some might be an overemphasis on the estates in Weston. I was able to collect a great wealth of original historical materials that I believe will be useful to scholars outside Weston who will someday write about men like John Charles Olmsted, Frederick Law Olmsted Jr., Arthur Shurcliff, Ernest Bowditch, and Joseph Everett Chandler. I also believe that the way estates were developed and later broken up was the major determinant of present-day land use. I do not mean to imply that it was the estate owners alone who made Weston what it is today. Throughout our history, the town has elected leaders from all walks of life who have volunteered their time and contributed their wisdom.

On a more mundane note, I would like to say something about the many footnotes in this book. Sometimes I have found that local history is like the children's game in which the first person is given a sentence and as each child whispers it in turn around a circle, the final garbled version barely resembles the original. Because it is just "local history," everyone who has lived in the town is, in certain ways, an expert and in other ways can be like the person who passes on the sentence not quite accurately. For this reason, I have tried to go back to primary sources whenever possible. Among my favorites are deeds, tax records, the annual town reports, and federal and state census records. I have relied whenever possible on memoirs, autobiographies, letters, diaries, and memorabilia to give firsthand accounts of life in Weston. I have used oral histories with some trepidation, knowing that people forget and that their words can be misinterpreted. Newspapers, too, have their problems, although they have been used often to convey the flavor of the period. I have footnoted all these sources, so that readers can decide for themselves how good the information is and go directly to the source for confirmation or additional details.

The list of buildings found at the back of each geographical chapter is not intended as a list of "significant" structures but rather a way to organize information that was too detailed or cumbersome to be included within the chapter itself. Many handsome and interesting houses have doubtless been omitted, particularly Modern examples from the postwar period.

I would like to invite readers to send their comments, additions, or corrections to me, to become part of the historical record that will be passed down to the next generation.

Pamela Wilkinson Fox
April 2001

Note

1. Lamson, *HTW,* 130.

Figure 1-1. The Allen House at One Chestnut Street, built about 1696, has long been considered the oldest remaining house in Weston. The original section had just two rooms, one above the other.

CHAPTER 1 · 1630–1830

Colonial and Federal Period: An Overview

English settlers in the 17th and 18th centuries laid the foundation for the town, a foundation that remained very much in evidence as Weston developed. Their church remained The Church. Their economic livelihood, farming, still sustained the community at the turn of the 20th century. Their Revolutionary War deeds became the basis for pageants and parades designed to instill feelings of patriotism and moral fortitude as the town moved farther and farther from its Puritan roots.

But this is not a book about the colonial period or the early republic. For 18th- and early-19th-century history, the reader is directed to Col. Daniel S. Lamson's History of the Town of Weston, 1630–1890. *Lamson records not only the town's ecclesiastical origins and civic development but also the "strong and sturdy lives" of her people. This book takes up where Lamson leaves off. It documents farm families in the next generations and immigrants who came seeking a better life. It tells of the estate owners who, with their money and vision, helped bring Weston into the modern era. This chapter will provide the necessary background for understanding the town's evolution in the 150 years from 1830 to 1980. It is the prologue to their story.*

Figure 1-2. In 1630, Sir Richard Saltonstall, prominent organizer of the Massachusetts Bay Colony, led a company up the Charles River to establish the settlement of Watertown, which included what is now Weston.

Topography and Pre-European Settlement

The Town of Weston lies 12 miles west of Boston. It measures about 5.5 miles from north to south and 3.5 miles east to west and contains 10,760 acres in a total area of 17.34 square miles. Brooks and streams on the north side empty into Stony Brook, the largest tributary of the Charles River. Weston is elevated above the adjacent countryside. The highest peak, Doublet Hill, is 360 feet above sea level. Farmers found Weston's soil rich but rocky. Picturesque hills and rock ledges, while not an asset to the early settlers, attracted later estate owners, who built their mansions to take advantage of panoramic views.

Early Weston historians wrote that there were no Native American settlements within the bounds of the town.[1] They theorized that the area was used as hunting grounds and that settlements were higher up the banks of the Charles and Sudbury Rivers. A more complete picture of pre-European inhabitants awaits further archaeological exploration. It is known that

Statistics	1765	1776	1790	1800	1810	1820
Population	768	1,027	1,010	1,027	1,008	1,041
Change		+259	-17	+17	-19	+33
Number of dwellings	105		132	135 (in 1798)**		

**In 1798, the U.S. government levied the Direct Tax, the first to list each dwelling with its owner and value.[2]

Charles H. Fiske's centennial oration gives the following statistics from 1773: number of polls (eligible voters) (218), slaves (16), horses (142), cows (535), oxen (167), sheep (279), and swine (225).[3] Slaveholding was not allowed in Massachusetts after 1781.

many early Weston roads were originally Native American trails. Only one attack on the settlement is recorded, in 1676, when Indians burned a barn on the Smith farm on Sudbury Road.

A Puritan Town

The first English settlement in Massachusetts was Plymouth Colony, established by Pilgrim separatists in 1620. A decade later, English Puritans arrived to found Massachusetts Bay Colony in the Boston area. They were seeking a simpler mode of worship, stricter discipline, and a purer church—hence the label "Puritans." Sir Richard Saltonstall and Rev. George Phillips led a company up the Charles River in 1630 to establish the settlement of Watertown, which included what is now Watertown, Waltham, Weston, and parts of Belmont, Cambridge, and Lincoln.

Figure 1-3. The dotted lines on this 1936 map show the boundaries of present-day towns originally part of the Watertown settlement.

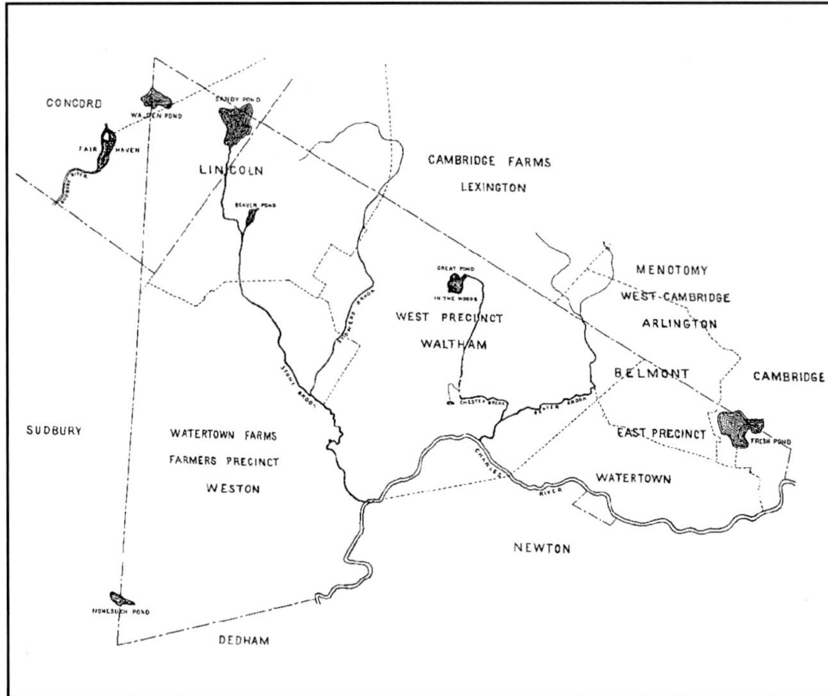

Figure 1-4. The Farmers' Burying Ground is the oldest cemetery in Weston. Pictured here is the gravestone of Rev. Samuel Woodward, minister at First Parish for 31 years.

Weston was known as Watertown Farms or the Farm Lands. Settlers receiving the first allotments of land used it primarily for grazing cattle. Bond's history of Watertown includes a list of the 1642 allotments, when 92 farms were laid out with a total of 7,674 acres.[4] The early settlement had no town green and no formal town center. Land was owned by private individuals rather than shared in a common field system. The original pattern of diagonal boundary lines known as squadron lines is still evident in the sharp bends of early streets such as Love Lane and Chestnut Street.

Until the late 17th century, the only church in the Watertown settlement was located in the more densely populated eastern section near Cambridge. Farmers who took up residence in what is now Weston beginning about 1673 had to travel nearly seven miles from the center of The Farms to the Watertown church. Estimated travel speed was four miles per hour, in good weather, for husband and wife sharing a horse. As Reverend Kendal remarked in his Centennial sermon, in making the trek "they manifested a zeal for the house and worship of God, not often found among their descendants."[5]

Weston farmers began building their own "Farmers' Meeting-house" in 1695. Three years later, the General Court granted their formal petition to establish a separate Farmers' Precinct, also referred to as the Third Military Precinct, the precinct of Lt. Jones's Company or the Westernmost Precinct. The name *Weston* is thought to come from its location at the extreme western end of Watertown.[6]

The first crude, unheated, 30-foot-square meetinghouse was used for services by 1700 and finally completed about 1710. It was replaced in 1721–22 by a larger building that looked much like a Colonial house.[7] Both the first and second meetinghouses were used for town meetings as well as worship services. In his *History of the Town of Weston,* Col. Daniel S. Lamson devoted his first chapter to the "ecclesiastical origin of the town":

> In those early days there was but one church, but one congregation, around which the settlers gathered, and paid their tithes for the support of the gospel. All things pertaining to the church were voted at town meeting . . . —as solid a union of Church and State, while it lasted, as ever existed in the old country.[8]

Weston was incorporated as a separate town on January 1, 1712. At that time, January was the 11th month of the year 1712; in later years January was considered the first month of 1713. Hence the date of incorporation is written as 1712–13 on the town seal. Land in the northwest corner became part of Lincoln when that town was incorporated in 1754. Otherwise, the boundaries of the town have remained largely unchanged.[9]

During the colonial period, community life centered on the church. Except for the brief tenure of the first pastor, Rev. Joseph Mors, ministers stayed for decades and were esteemed town leaders. When the first ordained minister, William Williams, accepted the call in 1709, the church had 18 male members.[10] Williams served until 1750, and his successor, the Rev. Samuel Woodward, from 1751 until his death in 1782.

One of the earliest acts of the town fathers was the establishment in 1703 of the Farmers' Burying Ground. By 1754 the town had three one-room schools, and by 1768 there were five "district" schools. Not until 1774 did voters agree to take over responsibility for all schoolhouses and pay back residents in the northwest and south districts who had been required to build and maintain neighborhood schoolhouses at their own expense.[11]

Transportation (1630–1830)

In 1673, the first post rider was dispatched from New York City to Boston, traveling over what were then mostly Indian trails.[12] His route, known over the years as the great country road or old post road, became the most important transportation corridor from Boston west to Worcester and then south to Hartford, New York, Philadelphia, and Washington.

The era of stagecoach travel began in 1772, when regular passenger service was initiated between New York and Boston. The uncomfortable journey took up to a week.[13] Stages stopped at taverns to exchange horses and allow travelers a frugal supper and a few hours of sleep before setting off in the early hours of the morning. Service was suspended during the Revolutionary War but resumed in 1783, when Levi Pease of Shrewsbury inaugurated a successful stagecoach line between Boston and Hartford, and later extended his route to New York City.

Between 1808 and 1810, the Worcester Turnpike Corporation constructed a toll road from Roxbury to Worcester through Framingham. This shorter course of travel, now Route 9, diverted some traffic, but the post road through Weston retained its importance for stagecoach transportation until the advent of the railroad.

Boston Post Road and North Avenue were major routes used by farmers from western Massachusetts, Vermont, and New Hampshire to transport products to Boston. Drovers brought cattle and hogs on foot to slaughterhouses in Brighton and Charlestown. Marketers hauled canvas-topped wagons loaded with produce. "Heavy teams" drawn by oxen carried wood, hay, cider, and apples.

Farming (1630–1830): A Brief Overview

As the town grew, the original diagonal allotment lines quickly disappeared. Colonial farmers needed a combination of meadow, tillage land, pasture, and woodlots to create a viable farm. They raised a variety of grains, vegetables, and fruits and maintained

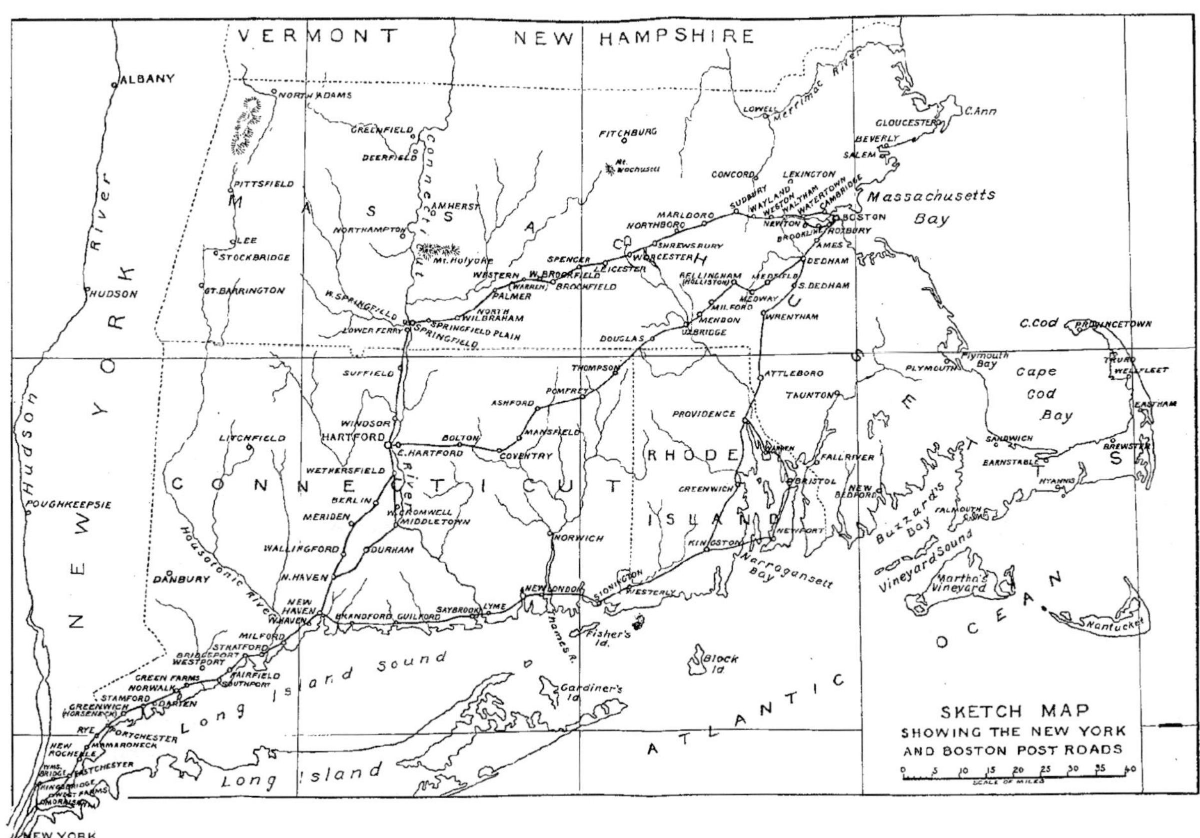

Figure 1-5. Weston was located on the 250-mile Upper Road, one of three "post roads" used by travelers between Boston and New York. For many years there was more travel on the upper road than on any other road leading out of Boston. In the 18th century, the trip to New York could take a week. By 1835–40, roads had improved and bridges were good, but travelers could still expect to spend at least two nights in wayside inns.

livestock. Farming was carried out not as a business but to satisfy the needs of the farm family. Recent rural historians have attacked the nostalgic myth of the independent, self-sufficient farmer. In *People of the Wachusett, Greater New England in History and Memory,* David Jaffee has written that "[t]he immense and intense effort to establish a family farm and wrest a living from the hard-scrabble soil of New England required commercial activity from the start of settlement."[14] The goal of entrepeneurship, however, was to secure necessities rather than accumulate capital.

Economic historians have documented critical changes in rural economic activity by about 1790.[15] Farmers traveled more to exchange produce, commodity markets emerged, and more farm laborers were being paid wages. Income from the sale of goods and services became more important for settling debts and acquiring new property. The farm household was still the basic economic unit of production. Those who did not have adequate land turned to commercial activities like shoemaking and other household manufactures as an adjunct to working the land.

As yarn mills and then textile mills were established in the 1820s, the domestic manufacture of homespun textiles declined. To buy goods they had previously made for themselves, farmers increased production of wool, pork, butter, cheese, cider, vegetables and other commodities that could be sold for cash. To avoid excessive reliance on fluctuating markets, many farmers steered a middle course between subsistence and surplus. They sought to preserve their ability to raise the variety of foods needed for their families while at the same time producing extra for sale in the marketplace.

Figure 1-6. Josiah Smith built the first part of his tavern (the west five bays) in 1756–57. An addition on the east side in 1763 included a second-floor ballroom. Smith's tavern was one of the most popular inns along the Boston Post Road. Josiah and his son Joel, who succeeded him as landlord, were both well-known "Liberty men." The tavern operated until 1838.

Commerce and Industry (1630–1830): A Brief Overview

Because of its location along the post road, Weston had a thriving tavern business.[16] The following is a list of the better-known examples:

Thomas Woolson Tavern, near 625 Boston Post Road. Operated from 1685 until about 1762 by Woolson and his descendants and subsequently by Capt. Samuel Baldwin. Ceased to be a tavern when purchased by Isaac Fiske in the 1810s. Destroyed by fire in 1890.

Josiah Smith Tavern, 358 Boston Post Road; built 1757; addition, 1763; used as a tavern until 1838.

Golden Ball Tavern, (Isaac Jones, tavernkeeper), 662 Boston Post Road. Built 1765–68, operated as a tavern until 1793.

John Flagg Tavern, near 725 Boston Post Road. Operated by Flagg from about the Revolutionary War until 1812, then by others until about mid-century. Destroyed by fire in 1902.

Benjamin Peirce Tavern. Originally located on a road through what is now the Sears conservation land. Later moved to the site that is now 293 Boston Post Road. Closed in 1785. Destroyed by fire in the 1790s.

Joseph Russell Tavern. Located on the southeast corner of North Avenue and Merriam Street. Operating by 1791 (possibly as early as 1773). Closed 1822 when Russell died. Later destroyed by fire.

Daggett Tavern. Located on North Avenue and Merriam Street. Built in 1821 by Milton Daggett and operated until about 1833. Unoccupied when destroyed by fire in 1844. Daggett was active in the nearby Methodist church.

Whitney Tavern, 171 North Avenue. Built about 1707; was a "common tenement" by the early 19th century.

Isaac Train Tavern, 465 South Avenue. Built 1802, operated as a tavern until about 1810.

According to Lamson, many houses of importance along the post road, including his own ancestral homestead, at one time served as taverns. Lamson describes the jovial social life, drinking, and card playing popular until the temperance movement and anti–card playing crusades began to have an impact in the early 19th century.

By the mid-1740s, Elisha Jones had a store, the earliest recorded in Weston, which for 30 years was an important trading post for the community and outlet for local products.[17] For those who needed to borrow money, Elisha functioned as the local banker.

Figure 1-7. The John Flagg Tavern was among the most important in Weston. George Washington stayed here in 1789. The building burned to the ground in 1902.

According to Lamson, the early industries, commerce, and trade of Weston from the date of settlement were quite extensive for so limited a population, and "almost every trade was to be found within its limits." Lamson enumerates the following to give his readers an understanding of the variety and extent of business interests before the introduction of railroads:

> . . . a brewery, or malt-house, numerous groceries, dry-goods stores, clock-makers, hatters, straw-braiders, grist-mills and saw mills, machine-shop, pottery, cabinet-making, wheelwrights, shoemaking, tannery, and apothecary shop.[18]

Lamson refers to the early 1800s as the "golden age of Weston retailing." The town was at the convergence of three major thoroughfares: the Great Country Road (Boston Post Road), the North County Road (North Avenue), and Old Connecticut Path, which connects with the Boston Post Road just over the town line in Wayland. Weston merchants supplied customers throughout the region until 1830–40. The increase in commercial activity led to the upbuilding of the village center. One Lamson ancestor owned a dry-goods store in the town center and in 1817 added a tailor shop so that prosperous farm wives could have their dresses made up as well. Stewart Holbrook, author of *The Old Post Road,* described Weston and other small towns along the Post Road when he wrote, "For a brief period, these waypoints knew an excitement, a prosperity and a measure of sophistication that many of them were never to know again. Then, they faded in the echo of the steamcars."[19]

The gristmill at Stony Brook, third in the Watertown settlement, was established in 1679 by Richard Child. Later a sawmill at the same location near the Waltham town line was used to saw timber for the early houses of Weston.[20] Lt. John Brewer's mill was established in the late 17th century on the headwaters of Stony Brook in what is now Lincoln, just over the town line.[21] Of regional importance were the Hobbs Tannery on North Avenue, established after 1730, and the Hews redware pottery on Boston Post Road, established in the late 1760s.

Figure 1-8. This oil painting of 1838 by Josiah Wolcott shows the Upham paper mill, built by Nathan Upham in 1802. The small, little-known mill was located on River Road on the Weston side of Stony Brook. After Upham's death in 1812, it passed to a series of owners, none successful. The Roberts brothers took it over in the mid-1830s and built a much larger mill on the Waltham side of the brook after this one burned down in 1840.

Architecture in the Colonial Period

The house long considered the oldest in Weston, the Allen house at One Chestnut Street, is thought to have been built about 1696 as a primitive 18-foot-square, two-story structure with an entry and stair and a massive chimney incorporating a smoke chamber. This type of early frame house, with one room on the first floor and one on the second, is referred to as having a one-over-one plan. Additions to the Allen house gave it the present saltbox profile.

Other early houses that probably began as one-over-one structures include the Harrington house at 555 Wellesley Street (c. 1710), William Smith house at 111 Sudbury Road (c. 1715), Mirick/Farnsworth house at 751 Boston Post Road (c. 1721), Whittemore/Coburn house at 153 Church Street (by 1726), and John Walker house at 118 Conant Road (c. 1740s). The Garfield house at 168 Summer Street, built sometime in the mid- to late 18th century, is the only remaining example not subsequently expanded to two-over-two.

Early one-story houses have all but vanished.[22] The Deacon Uriah Gregory house, pictured in Lamson's history, was an example with a central entrance, one window on each side, and a central chimney. Said to have been one of the oldest houses in Weston, it stood on Merriam Street until it was torn down in 1885.

The earliest two-over-two houses were constructed with a central chimney. Adding a one-story keeping room across the back gave them a "saltbox" profile in which the rear roofline sloped down from the ridgepole to the back of the keeping room. Because these houses were often expanded by raising the roof at the back to a full two stories, saltbox houses are now unusual. The form is best exemplified by the Whitney Tavern at 171 North Avenue (c. 1707) and the Allen and Walker houses.

Houses built during the colonial period and into the 1780s are often referred to as Georgian. This term is derived from the Renaissance classical houses popular during the reign of the English kings by that name. The architectural style is characterized by symmetry in the floor plan and facade. In New England towns like Weston, the most common form is the five-bay house with a gable roof and center entrance. The term *bay* is used here to refer to door and window openings on each floor. Windows often have small-pane sash and heavy lintels, and doors can be flanked by columns or pilasters and capped by a pediment, which in Weston is generally just a simple triangle. A few Georgian examples have corner quoins fashioned of wood in imitation of stone.

One of the finest mid-18th-century, center-chimney houses was built by Rev. Samuel Woodward at 19 Concord Road about 1752. It features remarkable Georgian raised-field paneling in both the first- and second-floor rooms, as befitting Woodward's important status as minister. The Upham house at 208 Newton Street would be a more typical example were it not for the flamboyant Connecticut River Valley doorway added about 1963. Other center-chimney houses include the Samuel Train house at 342 Winter Street (c. 1738) and the Jonathan Spring

Figure 1-9. The Upham family settled in Weston in 1719. Their venerable old saltbox stood on the west side of Ash Street until it was demolished in the early 1900s to make way for the open channel leading to the Weston Reservoir.

Figure 1-10. The tavern "at the sign of a golden Ball" was built by Isaac Jones in 1765–68. It has been called "the most beautifully proportioned example of Georgian architecture" in Weston.

house at 263 South Avenue (c. 1764). The Josiah Smith Tavern at 358 Boston Post Road (1757, expanded 1763), the only center-chimney example with a gambrel roof, was originally built with two front rooms and a large rear keeping room with cooking fireplace and beehive oven.

Appearing after mid-century are houses built with twin chimneys rather than a central chimney, a change that allowed for a gracious center hallway that could extend through to the back of the house. Significant four-over-four examples include the 1755 house built for wealthy merchant Elisha Jones and moved in the late 19th century to 22 Church Street, and the Golden Ball Tavern, built for Elisha's cousin Isaac at 662 Boston Post Road in 1768. Both are considerably more sophisticated than the average rural farmhouse.

Weston in the Revolutionary War

Incidents surrounding the War for Independence captured the imagination of Weston residents throughout the town's later history.[23] Often repeated in different versions is the story of two English spies, Ensign

Figure 1-11. Created in 1974 for the United States Bicentennial, this map shows landowners along the "Great Country Road," now Boston Post Road, in 1775.

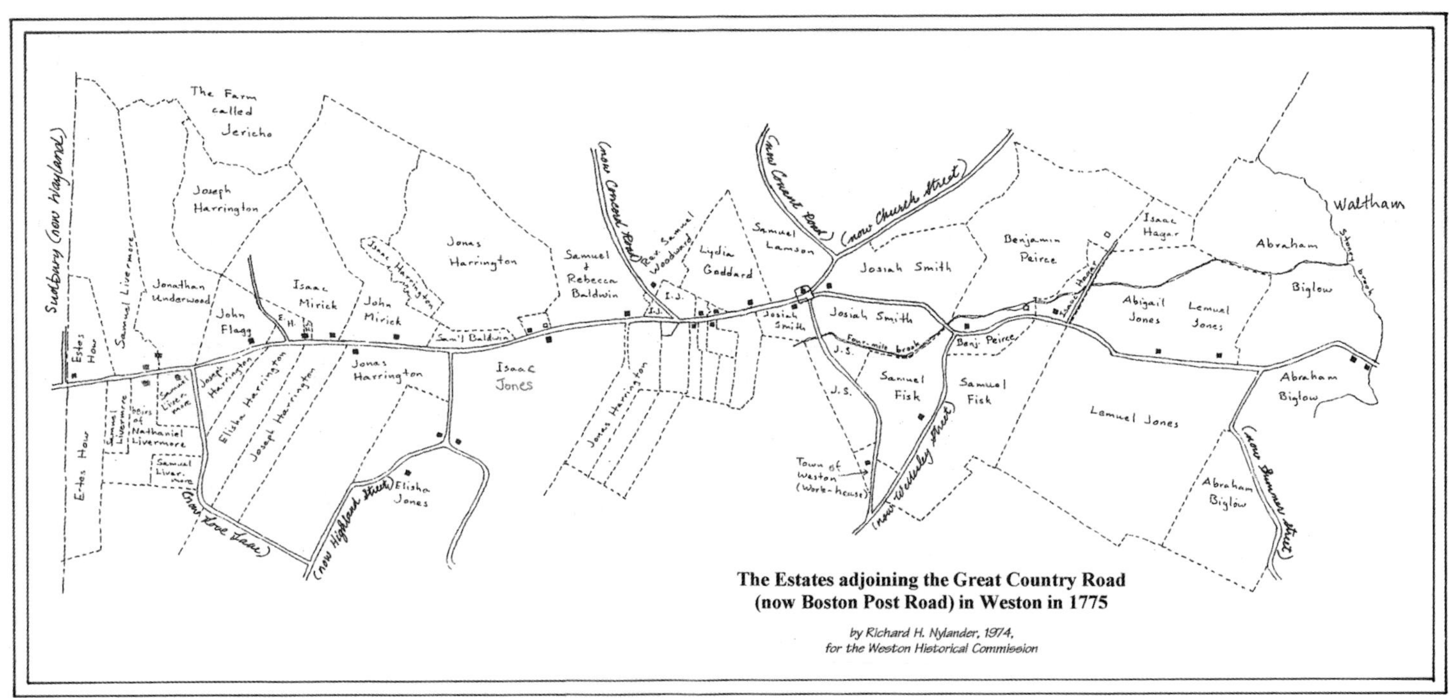

DeBerniere and Captain Brown, and their "man John." The spies were sent by General Gage from the British camp in Boston to Worcester to report on arms and ammunition in the hands of the rebels.[24] They stopped at the Golden Ball Tavern and found a "friend to government" in proprietor Isaac Jones. A later and more dramatic rendition of the story focuses on John Howe and his narrow escape from the hands of Liberty men. According to both versions, Gage decided that a force marching to Worcester would not make it back alive and chose to attack Concord instead.

On the morning of April 19, 1775, upon hearing that the British were marching to Concord, the Weston militia met at the house of Capt. Samuel Lamson in the town center. Among them was Rev. Samuel Woodward, who offered a prayer, then shouldered his musket and fell in with the ranks of the men. One hundred men and three officers set out to Concord and struck the British as they retreated back to Boston. During the war, Weston patriots also tended a military signal beacon placed in a tall elm tree on the Sanderson farm at the intersection of Highland Street and Love Lane.

Weston's most prominent patriot was Samuel Phillips Savage (1718–1797), a successful Boston merchant who retired to a farm in Weston about a decade before the war began. Savage maintained his contacts in the city, and in 1773 moderated the meeting at Old South Meeting House that led to the Boston Tea Party. He became head of the Massachusetts Board of War in 1776 and continued in this position until the board was dissolved in 1781.

George Washington traveled through Weston in 1775 on his way to Cambridge to take command of troops. Boston Post Road was also the route taken by Maj. Gen. Henry Knox in the winter of 1775–76 to deliver cannons from Fort Ticonderoga to General Washington in Cambridge. After the surrender of the British at Saratoga in 1777, hordes of General Burgoyne's defeated soldiers marched as prisoners over the Post Road, camping in Weston on their way to Cambridge. The "Burgoyne Elm" marking the site became Weston's symbol of liberty. The elm towered over the Fiske Law Office until it had to be cut down in the late 1960s.[25]

A final moment of glory in the town's 18th-century history was President Washington's visit on his journey to New England in the fall of 1789. He passed the night at Flagg Tavern and was welcomed the next morning by town leaders including Col. Thomas Marshall, who gave an address for the occasion. Washington kissed Hannah Gowen, then a child, and "it was for her a matter of great pride and glory as long as she lived."[26]

Census Data

In the 54 years from 1776 to 1830, population increased by only 64, or 6 percent. The 1820 Massa-

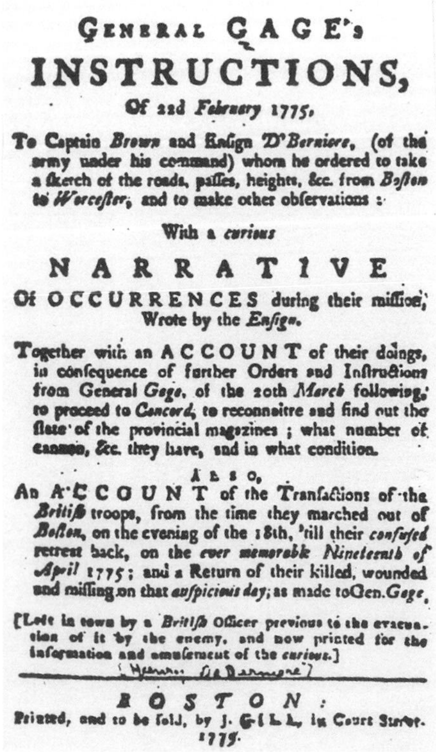

GENERAL GAGE's

INSTRUCTIONS,

Of 22d *February* 1775.

To Captain *Brown* and Ensign *D'Berniere*, (of the army under his command) whom he ordered to take a ſketch of the roads, paſſes, heights, &c. from *Boſton* to *Worceſter*, and to make other obſervations:

With a *curious*

NARRATIVE

Of OCCURRENCES during their miſſion, Wrote by the *Enſign*.

Together with an ACCOUNT of their doings, in conſequence of further Orders and Inſtructions from General *Gage*, of the 20th *March* following, to proceed to *Concord*, to reconnoitre and find out the ſtate of the provincial magazines; what number of cannon, &c. they have, and in what condition.

ALSO,

An ACCOUNT of the Tranſactions of the *Britiſh* troops, from the time they marched out of *Boſton*, on the evening of the 18th, 'till their *confuſed* retreat back, on the *ever memorable Nineteenth of April* 1775; and a Return of their killed, wounded and miſſing on that *auſpicious day*; as made to Gen. *Gage*.

[Left in town by a *Britiſh* Officer previous to the evacuation of it by the enemy, and now printed for the information and amuſement of the *curious*.]

BOSTON:

Printed, and to be ſold, by J. GILL, in Court Street. 1779.

Figure 1-12. This title page is from the only known contemporaneous report of General Gage's spy mission, published in 1779.

Figure 1-13. For his role in moderating the meeting that preceded the Boston Tea Party and presiding over the Massachusetts Board of War, Judge Samuel Phillips Savage has been called "Weston's most prominent patriot." He is buried in the Farmers' Burying Ground. This engraving is based on a portrait by John Singleton Copley.

Figure 1-14. Henry Knox, a bookseller before the war, was sent to Fort Ticonderoga to bring captured British cannons back to Boston. The heavily loaded carts were hauled by oxen over primitive, snow-covered roads. Knox passed through Weston in early 1776. A monument to his journey was placed in the town center in 1927.

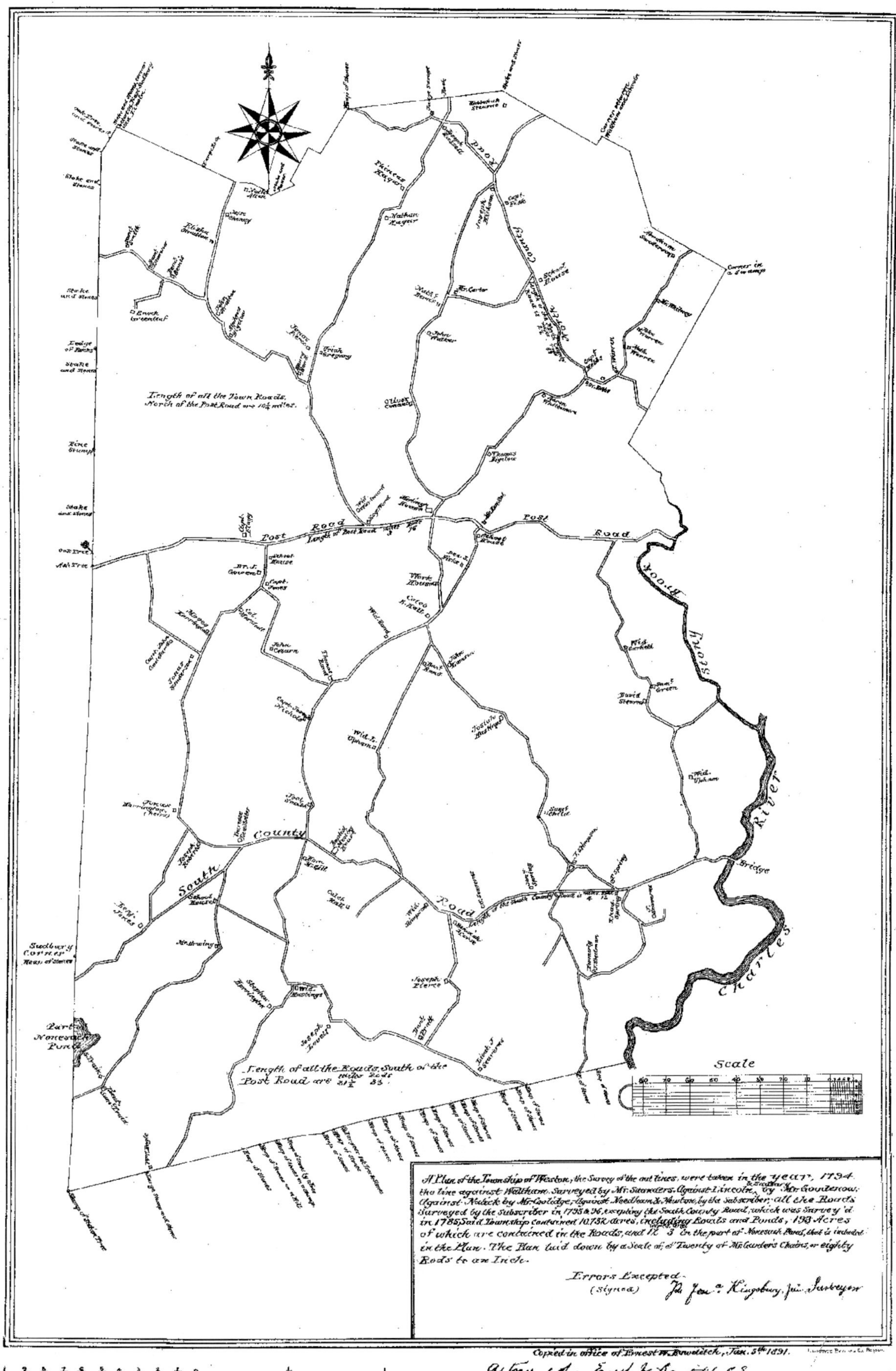

Figure 1-15. This map was made by Jonathan Kingsbury Jr. from surveys in 1785 and 1794–96. It was discovered among town records and copied in the office of Ernest W. Bowditch in 1891. A reproduction was inserted into each copy of the Town of Weston Tax Lists, *published in 1897. In the "Errata" section of that book, Mary Francis Peirce noted that "Dan'l Pratt" should read "Paul Pratt," that the southeast schoolhouse should have been shown on the east side of the triangle south of J. Stimpson, and that the house of Thomas Brown was omitted on the road northward from the widow Hastings. In other writings, Miss Peirce expressed her belief that the surveyor had omitted houses along Boston Post Road.*

Figure 1-16. Rev. Samuel Kendal, third ordained minister of First Parish Church, was over six feet tall, with a dignified and commanding appearance. Like his predecessors, he avoided theological conflicts that might have split the church. In 1799 the town budget of $2,100 included $300 for his salary. His centennial sermon of 1813 is of particular importance because it includes information from the first volume of town records, which was subsequently lost.

chusetts census lists three occupational categories for Weston males over age 16: agriculture (226 men, or 67 percent), commerce (10 men, or 3 percent) and manufacturing (88 men, or 26 percent).[27] Of the town's 1,041 residents, three were African-American and two were listed as foreign or naturalized.

Town Development in the Federal Period (1776–1830)

Settlement patterns continued as before, with population clusters on Boston Post Road and North Avenue. Two new burial grounds were established in 1790: the South Burying Ground on South Avenue and the Central Burying Ground on Boston Post Road.[28] By the late 18th century, the number of district schools had reached six—two on the north side, two in the center, and two on the south side. This arrangement continued for the next 100 years. In 1817 the town purchased an 80-acre farm on Conant Road near the Lincoln town line for use as a poor farm, replacing the earlier, more centrally located "work house" on School Street. [29]

The third ordained minister at First Parish, Rev. Samuel Kendal, held the office for 31 years, from 1783 until his death in 1814. Like his predecessors, Kendal was a moderate Calvinist who guided his flock without doctrinal controversy. He was succeeded by Rev. Dr. Joseph Field, who served from 1815 to 1865. Field presided over the final separation of church and town in 1824–25 and the construction of a new meetinghouse in 1840.[30]

Figure 1-17. The Methodist Society, established in 1894, was the third denomination in Weston. This frame Gothic house of worship was constructed in 1828 on North Avenue and burned to the ground on the last day of 1899. (1889 photo)

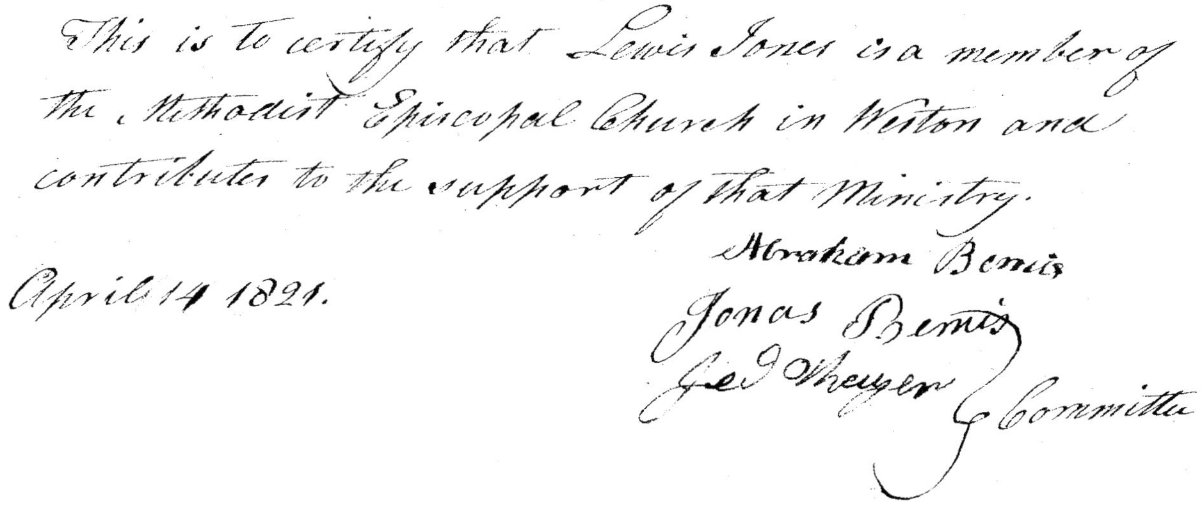

This is to certify that Lewis Jones is a member of the Methodist Episcopal Church in Weston and contributes to the support of that Ministry.

April 14 1821.

Abraham Bemis
Jonas Bemis
Geo Wheyer
Committee

Figure 1-18. Until the 1820s, Baptists and Methodists who wished to avoid paying taxes to support First Parish had to file for an exemption.

Two new religious groups were established in the late 18th century: the Baptist Society in 1776 and Methodist Society in 1794. The Baptist church was organized in 1789 and built its first meetinghouse on what is now South Avenue near Wellesley Street. This location proved inconvenient, and a new wooden church was constructed in 1828 on the Post Road. The Methodist church has always been located near the intersection of Conant Road and North Avenue. Town tax dollars supported the town church, now known as First Parish, until 1825, despite protests from both Baptists and Methodists.

Architecture in the Federal Period (1776–1830)
The early years of the new republic saw a continuity of architectural tradition. Many houses built in the late 18th and early 19th centuries are similar on the exterior to those built decades earlier. After the Revolutionary War, they are referred to as Federal in style, as the United States was no longer a colony. The stylistic term *Adam* is used to refer to decorative refinements introduced by the Adam brothers, who at the time had the largest architectural practice in England. The older brother, Robert, had traveled in Italy and popularized the swags, garlands, urns, and geometric designs he saw on his journeys.

Five-bay center-chimney and twin-chimney farmhouses continued to be built, such as the Nathaniel Bemis house at 216 Conant Road (c. 1785), Josiah Hastings house at 131 Newton Street (c. 1791), Isaac Train Tavern at 465 South Avenue (c. 1802), and Leadbetter house at 412 Highland Street (early 19th century). The Hastings homestead at 199 North Avenue (1823) and Bigelow/Coburn house at 161 North Avenue

Figure 1-19. By the early 19th century, John Dudley had built this house at 541 North Avenue and was taxed for a gristmill and sawmill. The low hip roof is typical of the Federal style. Otherwise, the exterior is similar to houses built decades earlier. (1940 photo)

Figure 1-20. Artemas Ward, Jr.(1762–1847) was an eminent lawyer. He practiced law in Weston from about 1789, when he bought the house now numbered 543 Boston Post Road, until he moved to Cambridge in the early 19th century.

Figure 1-21. Sophia Fiske, who was born in 1803, recorded information on her branch of the Fisk(e) family in this sampler, now owned by the Weston Historical Society.

(c.1823) demonstrate the continuity of architectural tradition through the 1820s.

Elements of changing fashion appear by the mid-1770s in the important house at 787 Boston Post Road (c. 1774–77), which combines Georgian exterior details such as corner quoins with up-to-date Federal features like the hip roof and entrance portico with delicate Adamesque fluted columns. Other important late Georgian houses include the Hobbs-Hagar house at 88 North Avenue (west end, c. 1786, east end after 1800) and the Artemas Ward Jr. house at 543 Boston Post Road (c. 1785), both of which also have wooden quoins that accentuate the corners of the building.

One distinctive characteristic of the Federal style is the low-pitched hip roof, as used in the John Dudley house at 541 North Avenue (c. 1795–1801), Fiske-Field house at 639 Boston Post Road (c. 1805), Luther Harrington house at 21 Crescent Street (c. 1812, a brick-ender), and Abraham Hews/Marshall Jones house at 510 Boston Post Road (remodeled to its present appearance c. 1824). Semicircular and elliptical fanlights were popular over the front door, as in the brick-end Abraham Hews Jr. house at 651 Boston Post Road (c. 1794). In 1827 wealthy lawyer Alpheus Bigelow built a late-Federal-style house at 863 Boston Post Road. While still using the traditional five-bay, side-gable form, the builder incorporated touches of elegance like leaded-glass tracery in the elliptical fanlight. Inside, rooms have high ceilings, generous proportions, and fine woodwork rare in a country town like Weston.

Notes

1. Lamson, *HTW,* 21, and Fiske, ibid., 11. A reconnaissance survey by the Massachusetts Historical Commission suggests that some potential for sites exists along the Charles River, around Nonesuch Pond, and along the Connecticut Path.

2. Tax collection records made on October 1, 1798, list all dwelling houses, along with owner, occupant, value, amount of land, and value of landholdings. The 1798 tax lists are reprinted in the *Town of Weston Tax Lists 1757–1827,* edited by Mary F. Peirce, 399–408. The following men owned houses valued at $1,000 or more: Robert Calef, John Derby, John Flagg, Enoch Greenleaf, Moses Gill, the Hobbs family, Isaac Jones, Isaac Lamson, Thomas Marshall, Joel Smith, and Artemas Ward (the highest value, at $2,000). Rev. Samuel Kendal's house was tax exempt.

3. Fiske, Charles H., *Oration,* July 4, 1876 (Weston, 1876), 27–28. Among the slaveholders were Weston's wealthiest and most prominent residents: Joseph Harrington (one), Braddyll Smith (two), John Flagg (one), Jonathan Bullard (one), Isaac Harrington (one), Samuel Phillips Savage (one), Josiah Smith (two), Elisha Jones (two), Joseph Gouldthwait (two), Isaac Jones (one), Josiah Starr (two).

4. The first order regarding allotments in The Farms was in 1638. See Bond, Henry, *Genealogies of the Families and Descendants of the Early Settlers of Watertown, Massachusetts . . . to which is appended The Early History of the Town . . . ,* second edition (New England Historic-Genealogical Society, Boston, 1860), 1027–28.

5. Kendal, Samuel, "A Sermon Delivered at Weston, January 12, 1813, on the Termination of a Century, since the Incorporation of the Town"(Cambridge: Hilliard and Metcalf, 1813), 19.

6. Gannett, Henry, *The Origin of Certain Place Names in the United States* (Washington: Government Printing Office, 1905), 321. See also *The Origin of Massachusetts Place Names of the State, Counties, Cities and Towns* (WPA, 1941) and Massachusetts Geographic Board (1927–1932), Massachusetts Archives.

7. The first meetinghouse was on land of Nathaniel Coolidge Sr., just south of the present church, approximately where the

parking lot is today. The second meetinghouse was across Church Street on the site later used for the first town hall.

8. Lamson, *HTW,* 17.

9. Residents in what is now Lincoln formed their own church in 1746, but the town was not incorporated until 1754.

10. Kendal, Rev. Samuel, D.D., "A Sermon Delivered at Weston, January 12, 1813, on the Termination of a Century, since the Incorporation of the Town" (Cambridge: Hilliard and Metcalf, 1813), 42.

11. For details, see "A History of Weston Schools," part of a survey report on Weston schools prepared about 1941, 4–5.

12. Holbrook, Stewart H., *The Old Post Road* (McGraw Hill, 1962), 1.

13. Jenkins, Stephen, *The Old Boston Post Road* (New York: G.P. Putnam's Sons, 1913), 22–24.

14. Jaffee, David, *People of the Wachusett: Greater New England in History and Memory, 1630–1860* (Ithaca and London, Cornell University Press, 1999), 5.

15. For a detailed discussion, see Christopher Clark's *The Roots of Rural Capitalism, Western Massachusetts, 1780–1860* (Ithaca and London, Cornell University Press, 1990), and Winifred B. Rothenberg's *From Market-Places to a Market Economy: The Transformation of Rural Massachusetts, 1750–1850* (Chicago and London, The University of Chicago Press, 1992).

16. See Lamson, *HTW,* chapter on taverns, 186–92.

17. For more on Elisha Jones, see *One Town in the American Revolution: Weston, Massachusetts,* by Brenton H. Dickson and Homer C. Lucas (Weston Historical Society, 1976), 36–43.

18. Lamson, *HTW,* 152.

19. Holbrook, op. cit., 13.

20. Lamson, *HTW,* 160.

21. In later years, it was operated by the Harrington family as a grist- and sawmill. See chapters 2 and 12.

22. The only surviving example may be a section of 120 Summer Street. See chapter 13.

23. Dickson and Lucas, *One Town in the American Revolution,* op. cit., covers the Revolutionary War in detail.

24. See Howard Gambrill Jr. and Charles Hambrick-Stowe, *The Tavern and the Tory,* 21–23, for information about DeBerniere and Brown. Lamson, *HTW,* 75–78 has excerpts from spy John Howe's journal, which researchers at the Golden Ball Tavern believe to be apocryphal. Howe's account, called "A JOURNAL kept by MR. JOHN HOWE, while he was employed as a BRITISH SPY During the Revolutionary War . . . ," was published at Concord, New Hampshire, by Luther Roby, printer, in 1827. See also "An Editor's Dilemma" in *WHSB,* March 1975, 2.

25. The following sign marking the site remains even though the tree itself has been removed: "Burgoyne Elm. After the Battle of Saratoga, Oct. 17, 1777, General Burgoyne's captured army on their way as prisoners to Winter Hill under the escort of General Glover camped under this elm and the two buttonwoods opposite while their officers were quartered in the tavern then standing on the knoll above." See also *WHSB,* May 1967.

26. Lamson, *HTW,* 112–13.

27. *Census of Massachusetts, 1820, Aggregate Amount of Each Description of Persons Within the District of Massachusetts* (Boston: B. Russell, 1821). The census breaks the population into ages. Of the 601 males, 366 were over 16. Of the 476 females, 326 were over 16.

28. *South Burying Ground:* Increase Leadbetter sold 0.5 acre to the town about 1789; first burial, December 1791. *Central Burying Ground:* 1.5 acres conveyed by Isaac Jones to town, January 1, 1790; first burial in May 1792.

29. The old poorhouse and land were sold to Samuel G. Derby for $230 and later became part of the James B. Case estate.

30. Regarding the separation of church and town, see *An Account of the Celebration by the First Parish of Weston, Massachusetts, of Its Two Hundredth Anniversary, 1898* (Weston, 1900), 173–74.

Figure 2-1. In the early 1850s, Weston built six new one-room schoolhouses. This photograph is labeled District School #6, which was later converted to a two-family residence and still stands at Brown and Winter Streets. The lintels over the windows and double-bracketed cornice are characteristic of the Italianate style.

The Early Industrial Period

In his History of the Town of Weston, Col. Daniel S. Lamson marks 1839 as the year the "ancient history of Weston closes" and 1840 as the beginning of a new era:

> The marvelous progress of our country in every walk of life, unparalleled the world over, may be said to date from 1840, when railroads came in and horse chaises began to disappear.[1]

Railroads brought with them a new period of material prosperity, as the American economy grew steadily and standards of living improved. Lamson mourned the change in values and increasing emphasis on "the pursuit of wealth and comfort."

The railroad spelled the end of the tavern business in Weston. Stagecoaches that once passed through regularly were abandoned in favor of train travel. Within decades the once hospitable town had no "abiding place for man or beast . . . outside of private hospitality."[2] As road traffic declined, so did Weston's retail business. Farm wives from neighboring towns took the train into Boston to buy dry goods. Enterprising merchants moved their stores to the city.

In less than two generations, New England farmers in the pre–Civil War era experienced the transition from comfortable subsistence to commercial agriculture and from household manufacture to the factory system. Nineteenth-century minister Horace Bushnell reflected on the dawn of the industrial age in a nostalgic speech at the Litchfield County centennial celebration in 1851. He called his speech "The Age of Homespun" because, to Bushnell, the making of clothes at home exemplified the spirit of an age already all but over.[3] Homespun had been replaced by a "dress of factory clothes, produced by machinery and obtained by the exchanges of commerce."

Bushnell believed that the Age of Homespun was being superseded by The Day of Roads. In his view, the isolation responsible for the backwardness of many farm communities was being eliminated by new networks of communication that would help to enlighten all who came in contact with them. Roads, railroads, steamships, and newspapers added up to a "Road for Thought."

Along this Road for Thought came a series of remarkable intellectual and social movements that stirred the hearts and minds of farmers and city dwellers

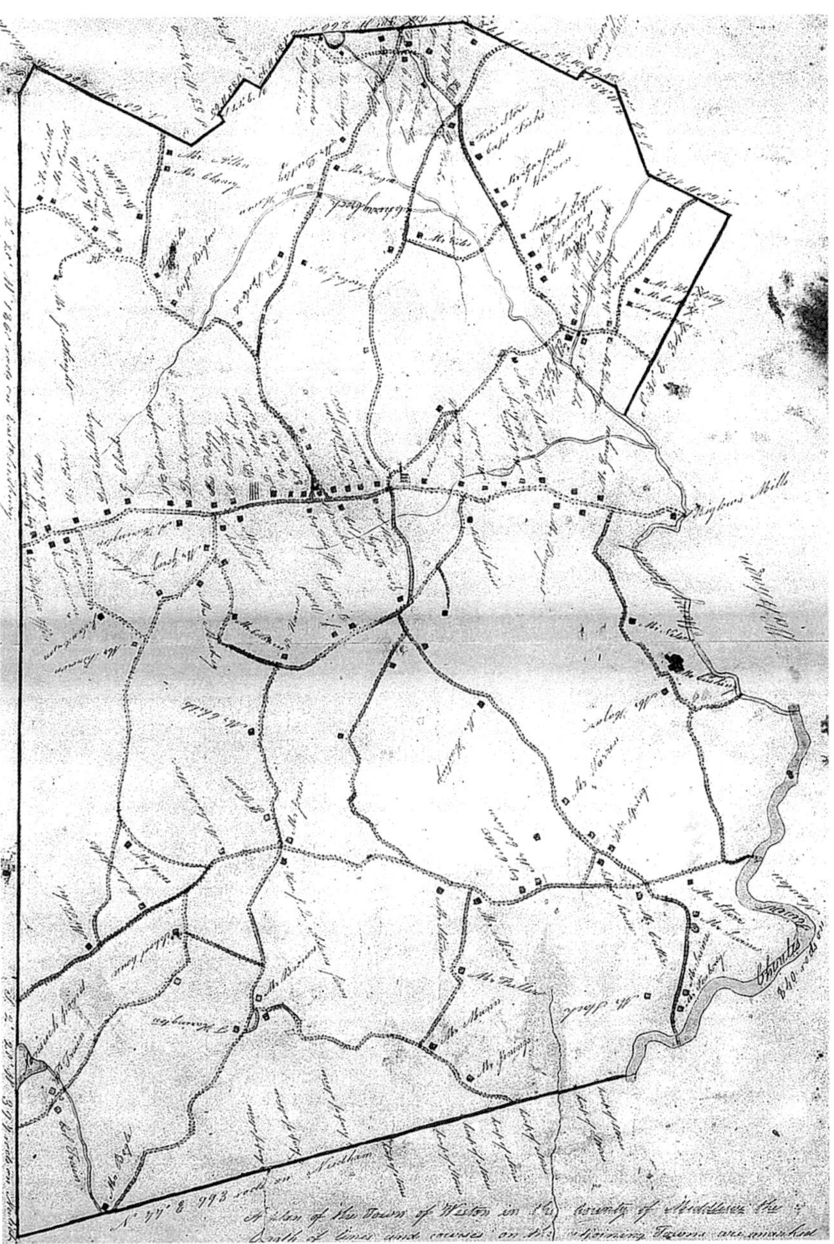

Figure 2-2. Surveyor Augustus Tower prepared this map of Weston in 1830.

Statistics	1830	1840	1850	1860
Population	1,091	1,092	1,205	1,243
Change	+50	+1	+113	+38
Number of dwellings	144		193	209

Figure 2-3. With construction of the Greek Revival–style First Parish Church in 1840 and Weston Town Hall in 1847 and the addition of the store at left in 1852, Weston's "town square" became the commercial and institutional heart of the community. This stereopticon view was taken before 1875, when a clock was installed in the church steeple.

alike. In religion, as Unitarians and Trinitarians struggled for control of long-established Congregational churches, First Parish in Weston moved quietly into the Unitarian fold. A vigorous temperance reform movement swept through rural communities and hastened the demise of Weston's tavern business. Finally, the antislavery struggle led by the men and women of Massachusetts foreshadowed the outbreak of the Civil War.

Town Development (1830–1860)

The mid-19th century was a period of major institutional growth. First Parish Church built a new meetinghouse in 1840 on the site of the present stone church, and Weston built a new town hall across the street in 1847. The triangle formed by the town hall, church, and Josiah Smith Tavern became known as the Town Square. Weston Public Library was founded in 1857 and occupied rooms in the town hall for about 40 years. The construction of new schoolhouses in the early 1850s and the founding of the first high school in 1854 are described below.

Streets were widened and straightened. State law mandated that "guide-boards" be erected at major intersections. In 1853, citizens gathered for a social event that raised $450 for cemetery beautification. According to a later report, this was "believed to be the first voluntary effort made by the [Weston] citizens unitedly, for ornamenting and beautifying the graveyards" with shade and ornamental trees.[4]

UNION BALL.

Sir.--Your Company with Ladies is respectfully solicited at the

TOWN HALL, WESTON,

on Tuesday Evening, Feb'y. 8th 1848.

Committee of Arrangements.

Samuel Hobbs,	Luke Brooks,	Leonard L. Brown,
S. H. F. Bingham,	Isaac Coburn,	John Coburn,
Nathan Hagar,	Benj. Peirce, Jr.,	J. Q. A. Harrington.

FLOOR MANAGERS.

George Smith, James H Wright, Benj. Peirce, Jr.

Dancing to commence at six o'clock.

Figure 2-4. The whole town was invited to the Union Ball, held in February 1848 to inaugurate the new town hall.

The best-known town doctor during this period was Otis E. Hunt, who settled here in 1848 and remained until 1864. Weston had three lawyers: Isaac Fiske, his son Augustus H. Fiske, and Alpheus Bigelow Jr.

Schools (1830–1860)

In 1827, the state legislature permitted local governments to support public schools for all children for 12 weeks a year. A decade later, Horace Mann was appointed the first head of a state Board of Education. Not until 1858 did the state mandate schooling for all children between 8 and 15.[5] The following year, the state began requiring that cities and towns print an annual school committee report. Much of the information on schools found in this and subsequent chapters is taken from these annual reports.[6]

Between 1851 and 1853, Weston built six new district schools to replace one-room schoolhouses dating from the 1790s and early 1800s.[7] The earlier schoolhouses had been constructed on lots barely larger than the buildings themselves, while the new ones were built on quarter-acre parcels deeded to the town for that purpose.[8] The 1859 school committee report comments with pride on the improvement:

> A few years ago, the committee were obliged frequently . . . to call attention to the dilapidated and uncomfortable condition of the school-houses. Now, instead of the rude buildings standing just on the edge of the road . . . without a foot of ground belonging to the district, except that covered by the school-house, you have airy, neat and tasteful buildings, affording ample room, and possessing almost every convenience to be expected or desired in a village school-house. You have in each district a good-sized yard and play-ground, which . . .

Figure 2-5. This photograph of pupils at one of the district schools shows the wide variety of ages in one classroom.

> may be ornamented with shade trees, shrubs and flowers; and when your children are there, in their innocent sports, shall present a most charming picture.[9]

In 1859 the highest number of students enrolled in each district school in any one term was as follows:

District School, No. 1 (East Centre School) (now 280 Boston Post Road): 49

District School, No. 2 (West Centre School) (BPR and Highland Street)[10]: 34

District School, No. 3 (North West School) (Concord Road and Merriam Street): 23

District School, No. 4 (North East School) (North Avenue): 47

District School, No. 5 (South East School) (South Avenue and Ware Street): 24

District School, No. 6 (South West School) (now 96 Brown Street): 21

Initially, only one of the district schools had a well. Students in the other schools had to go to neighboring houses for water.

In 1847 the school committee was asked to draft a plan for a high school but not until 1854 did it allocate $150 to fund it.[11] The 1859 school committee report describes the Centre School, which was the name used until 1860:

> A school has been established in the centre of the town, as a public school. At first it had but one session of three months.... Then it was tried for the fall and winter.... It proved itself to be a valuable acquisition . . . for by removing from [the district schools] the larger scholars that needed a male teacher, female teachers, who were better qualified to teach the younger scholars, could be provided. . . . Now the whole town enjoys the advantages of the Centre School for half the year and female teachers are competent for the districts.[12]

The town saved money because the women earned $17 to $20 a month compared with $50 to $60 a month for male teachers.

The Centre School was not strictly graded and students ranged in age from about 11 to 20. In 1859 the Centre School had 72 scholars in the second term, with an average attendance of 60, taught by a teacher and one assistant. Subjects were arithmetic, grammar, geography, algebra, geometry, natural philosophy, history, geology, reading, Latin, and bookkeeping. In 1859, school was in session 37 weeks a year.

Lamson records private primary schools and a school held in the "Jones tavern" in 1838 that was probably a high school. Here, for $3, some 50 students of both sexes could pursue the "common course" or for $4, "higher English and Latin."[13] The teacher, Mr. Dunn, was a strict disciplinarian who "applied liberally the essence of birch, sending the boys to the Willow Lane, so called, to cut and bring in to him the rods which were to be applied in corrective measures."[14]

Census Data

The 1840 U.S. census provides a picture of Weston's 1,092 inhabitants.[15] Male occupations were recorded

Figure 2-6. This engraving from an 1865 photograph shows the old Sudbury stage, which still stopped at Cutting's general store even after railroads brought the golden age of stagecoach travel to a close. The store used the image on its 1906 calendar.

in four categories: agriculture (227), manufactures and trades (95), commerce (6), and learned professions and engineers (5).

The 1850 U.S. census added more occupations and for the first time recorded country of origin. The town had 113 new residents, the largest growth since the census was first taken in 1790. Sixty-four percent of the men (258) were farmers, aided by 5 percent classified as laborers.[16] About 22 percent were skilled tradesmen, 2 percent were in the "learned professions," and the rest were engaged in commerce or held service positions such as coachmen and gardeners. More than two million people left Ireland during the disastrous famine of 1846–51, and their impact is recorded in the 1850 census. It lists 134 Irish immigrants in Weston, or about 11 percent of the town's population. An estimated 75 percent were under age 30. The second largest immigrant group came from Canada, particularly Nova Scotia and Prince Edward Island (12), followed by England (6) and Scotland (3).

Transportation (1830–1860)

Stagecoach travel reached its heyday in the 1830s. New toll roads, or turnpikes, between Boston and New York cut travel time to two days. In 1826, the first "Concord coach" began operating out of Boston. Made in Concord, New Hampshire, these stronger, lighter, more comfortable, and more decorative vehicles were popular in the Northeast and continued in use in the Wild West throughout much of the century.

The Eastern Stage Company, a syndicate that controlled coach travel in eastern Massachusetts, was formed in 1818 and favored the better taverns along the post road. In 1829, 77 stagecoach lines regularly provided service out of Boston in all directions. By 1832 this number had increased to 106.[17] In the mid-1830s, more than 2,000 mail and passenger coaches rolled in and out of Boston every week.[18]

In 1841, the first steam trains began through service from Boston to Albany and, three years later, to New York City. The stagecoach boast of "New York in Two Days" became a mockery. By the 1840s, die-hard conservatives were already bemoaning "the new and vulgar and dangerous mode of travel" by railroad and recalling the romantic era of the stagecoach.[19]

The Boston and Worcester Railroad was incorporated in 1831 and laid tracks through the southeast corner of Weston in 1834. Although the railroad never had a station in Weston, proximity to Wellesley Farms and Riverside Stations improved transportation on the south side of town. The railroad drew traffic from the Worcester Turnpike (now Route 9). Within a half dozen years, the corporation that ran the pike was forced out of business.[20] In 1867 the rail line merged with the Western Railroad to form the Boston & Albany.

The Fitchburg Railroad Company was formed in 1841 and opened its first section, from West Cambridge to Waltham, in 1843. The line was completed west to Fitchburg in March 1845 and east to Boston in 1848, opening up north-central Massachusetts to passenger and freight traffic.[21] In Weston, stations were located at Stony Brook, Church Street (Weston Station, later renamed Kendal Green), Silver Hill, and, beginning in 1888, Hastings. Company founders continued their push west with the goal of providing a second east–west route rivaling the Boston & Worcester. In 1869, the rail line was operating four weekday trains to Fitchburg, one to what is now Ayer, one to South Acton, and one to Concord.

The Agricultural Revolution in New England (1830–1860)

In the half-century before the Civil War, farmers gradually made the transition from comfortable subsistence to farming for profit. The industrial

Figure 2-7. Railroads furnished the cheap transportation essential to industrial change and helped break down the isolation of rural communities. The first railroad service in New England began operating in 1834 along a nine-mile stretch between Boston and Newton and was soon extended through Weston to Wellesley. The Meteor *was one of its first engines. There were never any Weston stations along the Boston & Worcester line.*

Figure 2-8. Oxen are heavier and more docile than the bulls they would have become. They were trained to work in pairs and were prized by Yankee farmers for their ability to haul heavy loads and work in rough and marshy ground. Gradually, lighter iron and steel plows allowed farmers to replace oxen with horses, which were faster and more versatile. This picture from the Weston Historical Society is labeled "Jones" and probably dates to the late 19th century.

revolution in New England was creating a new class of urban workers who were not producing their own food. As this population grew and farmers saw a market for their surplus, they showed increasing interest in agricultural improvements to boost yields. Farmers began to specialize in products suited to natural resources and location.

Increased use of rail transportation after mid-century influenced farm economics. As railroad networks expanded, midwestern farmers could sell wool, wheat, and pork at prices so low they discouraged local production. Midwestern farms were more competitive in growing grain, because land was cheaper, more fertile, and better adapted to the use of machinery. With the advent of the refrigerator car, western cattle ranchers eventually took over the market for beef. Rather than trying to compete, New England farmers living near cities increasingly turned to producing vegetables, fruits, and dairy products, where proximity to market gave them the advantage.

Beginning in the 1790s, organizations were founded to promote improved agriculture by holding exhibitions of livestock and farm produce. The Middlesex County Agricultural Society, founded in 1852, was one of 36 such Massachusetts societies established between 1792 and 1888. County fairs allowed farmers to compare their corn or cattle and learn about new methods of cultivation and breeding. Prizes brought attention to high-quality products and led to rivalries among progressive farmers. Papers on agricultural subjects were presented by specialists in a forerunner of later agricultural extension services. The state Board of Agriculture, founded in 1852, stressed scientific agriculture.

Development of stronger, lighter hand tools meant that farmwork could be accomplished more efficiently. Labor-saving machines like hay rakes were invented and continuously improved between 1820 and 1890. During the first quarter of the century, the change from wooden to cast-iron plows took place rapidly. Their lighter weight made it possible to substitute horses for oxen as draft animals. By 1840, the displacement of oxen was well under way in progressive communities.[22] New breeds of cattle and horses were introduced.

The older, more self-sufficient economy had emphasized self-reliance and independence, frugality, and thrift. It brought together all members of the family, young and old, male and female, in the production process. The market economy called for new skills such as shrewdness in buying and selling. Farming became a more speculative business, with price fluctuations bringing added risk. Historian Percy Bidwell expressed the change this way in a 1921 article, "The Agricultural Revolution in New England":

> Thereafter success in getting a living no longer depended on the unremitting efforts of the farm family, aided by Providence, but to a large extent also upon the unpredictable wants and labors of millions of persons in the industrial villages, and in the newer farms to the westward.[23]

Lack of business experience was a distinct handicap.

During this transition period, there was little uniformity. In a single county, one observer wrote of seeing "every system of farm management practiced that has ever been followed since the days of Noah."[24] In every community were progressive farmers and, often in close proximity, "common, irregular, ragweed . . . helter-skelter farming," with the majority between these extremes.

Figure 2-9. Clearing of land for fields and cow pastures led to widespread deforestation. Up to 85 percent of New England had been cleared by the mid-19th century. This photograph, taken looking south from Cat Rock, shows the three Coburn farms on Church Street and North Avenue. In the foreground, at right, is the Thomas Coburn house (161 North Avenue) and barn. In the center at a distance is the Coburn homestead (153 Church Street) and barn (154 Church Street), and to the left in the distance is the Edward Coburn house (171 Church Street) and barn. In the left foreground is the original Drabbington Lodge, which opened in 1897 in an old farmhouse. This building burned in 1898 and was replaced by the shingled hotel now used as a retirement home. Note also the fire tower, used to watch for fires started by cinders from coal-burning trains.

Farming in Weston (1830–1860)

Farming remained the foundation of Weston's economy. More than half the farms were under 80 acres. Hay became a cash crop, and for a time local farmers succeeded in draining low-lying marshes to create new hayfields.[25] Clearing of land for fields and cow pastures led to extensive deforestation.[26]

Statistics from the mid-19th century indicate that hay was by far the most important crop, followed by potatoes.[27] The town had 13,322 apple trees cultivated for fruit. Cutting firewood employed 50 men part time.[28]

The market for beef cattle produced in New England was not immediately undercut by the early railroads, as refrigerator cars had not yet been developed and shipment of live animals was expensive. In 1840, most of the cattle sold in the great livestock market in Brighton still came from northern Massachusetts and north-bordering states and was transported by hoof along roads such as North Avenue.

Product	1845	1855
hay	$16, 146	
English hay		$22,785
wet meadow hay		7,410
potatoes	6,460	15,450
fruit	6,271	6,471
butter	5,423	6,575
Indian corn	5,238	12,204
milk	not listed	5,600
firewood & lumber	4,830	5,500

Figure 2-10. This chart shows the value of Weston farm products in 1845 and 1855, as compiled from state records. Note that the 1855 list differentiates between English and wet meadow hay. The term "meadow hay" encompassed five or six native species of grasses that grew well in wet land. It was coarse and contained less protein than the more desirable, more expensive English hay. The latter was made up of domesticated grasses like timothy, red clover, and red top, which had to be sown in upland fields or other well-drained areas.

One important factor in the financial well-being of many farm families was supplementary income from household industry or secondary jobs. Weston farmers sewed shoes, made cider, or earned extra money teaming, contracting, or maintaining town roads.

Commerce and Industry (1830–1860)

As the golden age of Weston retailing and tavern-

Figure 2-11. Stony Brook, the largest tributary of the Charles River, was used to power Weston's most important group of mills, located just south of Boston Post Road near the Waltham town line. In 1845 the firm of Coolidge, Sibley and Treat was employing 40 hands in making machinery for the textile industry.

keeping came to an end, new businesses had to rely on local rather than regional patronage. George W. Cutting, who established his first store in the "town square" in the early 1830s, prospered by meeting the needs of local farm families. His general store carried tools, feed grain, groceries, and dry goods. By mid-century, the popular Cutting was the leading storekeeper in Weston. In 1859 he was appointed postmaster.

By the mid-19th century, an incredible variety of Massachusetts mills, large and small, were "energetically manufacturing everything under the sun."[29] The census of 1850 reported that Massachusetts, with less than one twentieth of the nation's population, contributed one seventh of the wealth gained from industry. The most important state industry was the manufacture of boots and shoes. Massachusetts was also producing about one third of the nation's textiles. The importance of this industry indirectly to Weston can be seen in the drop in the price of a yard of cloth from 80 cents in 1815 to 5 cents in 1861.[30]

While Weston did not have the waterpower to attract major industry, the town did have small local mills and "manufactories." Shoemaking was Weston's largest trade in 1837, when statistical tables were first published for Massachusetts industry. That year 5,606 pairs of boots and 17,182 pairs of shoes valued at $30,370 were manufactured by 58 men and 25 women.[31] The high number of workers reflects the fact that shoemaking was still essentially a home industry. Two machinery makers had 10 employees and products valued at $8,000. Another 15 men were employed tanning leather and making chaises, harnesses, pottery, and plows. Weston had a woolen mill that finished 12,000 yards of cloth and employed two hands.

By 1845, the town's largest industry, Coolidge, Sibley & Treat, was making cotton, woolen, and other machinery valued at $39,000 and employing 40 hands.[32] Shoemaking had dropped in value by almost half, to $17,110. In 1845, Weston had a cotton mill that employed 12 men and six women and made 62,400 pounds of thread valued at $11,608, along with 15 tons of cotton batting. The tannery was still in business, although the number of hides had dropped to 1,000. Small establishments made leather goods (saddles, harnesses, and trunks), locks, cutlery, wagons and sleighs, pottery, loom pickers, and plows.

In 1855 Sibley Mills was producing only $26,000 worth of machinery but was still by far the largest industry in Weston, employing 26.[33] Shoemaking had dropped to a third of its 1845 value. A new company had been formed to make chairs and cabinets and another to manufacture shovels, spades, forks, and hoes. The pottery, saddle, harness, and trunk manufactory and wagon makers were still in business, and seven men were employed making mechanics tools. Weston also had a bakery making $11,000 worth of bread and employing six.

The following list of mills and industries known to have been operating during the early industrial period includes the book chapter if they are further described. Post–Civil War industries are listed in the next chapter.

Early Grist- and/or Sawmills

Richard Child (later Bigelow). Boston Post Road at Stony Brook (chapter 13).

Brewer (later Harrington). Headwaters of Stony Brook in Lincoln and Weston (chapter 12).

Sanderson. Crescent Street (chapter 13).

Hobbs Tannery. 87 North Avenue (chapter 10). Established 1730 or after, closed 1862. Power from Hobbs Brook. Members of the family also produced shoes, boots, harnesses, cartridge boxes, and chaises.

Hews Pottery. Boston Post Road (chapter 16). Established between 1765 and 1768; moved to North Cambridge in 1871. Power came from oxen or horses; produced earthenware pottery.

Upham (later Roberts) Paper Mill. River Road (chapter 1). Established 1802, burned down 1840. A larger paper-making operation was built on the Waltham side of Stony Brook.

Cutter's Cider Mill. South Avenue (chapter 24). Established before 1804, closed about 1915. Produced cider, vinegar, some champagne cider.

Cutting's Grist and Cider Mill. West of Lexington Street. Established about 1820 by John W. Cutting, oldest son of John and Cynthia Warren Cutting. Appears on 1875 *Middlesex County Atlas* labeled as Grist and Cider Mill.[34] Power from Hobbs Brook. Operated in late 19th century by Marshall Cutting, 10th child of John and Cynthia Warren Cutting. Later history unknown.

Garfield (later Foote's) Mill. 290 North Avenue (chapter 10). Established about 1821, cider mill still in operation in 1950. Power from Stony Brook. Also used for blacksmithing, wheelwrighting, and later carriage making.

M. & J. Jones Paint and Harnesses. 510 Boston Post Road (chapter 15). Established mid-1820s, closed after 1875.

Coolidge, Sibley & Treat/ Sibley Mills. Boston Post Road at Stony Brook (chapter 13). Established 1831 at earlier mill site purchased from Abraham Bigelow. Owned solely by Nathaniel Sibley after 1850, closed in 1884. Machine shop, gristmill, mill for manufacture of cotton yarn machinery, powered by Stony Brook. Products included cotton machinery and looms, doorlocks, steel and iron hardware, wood-planing machines, and pencil sharpeners. Also located on the Sibley land was a furniture factory built in 1833, leased to Joseph H. Cummings and destroyed by fire about 1850.[35]

Hobbs & Hagar Shoe Factory. 88 North Avenue (chapter 10). Partnership formed 1834, closed about 1850. Produced boots and shoes.

Bingham's Machine Shop. 39 Crescent Street

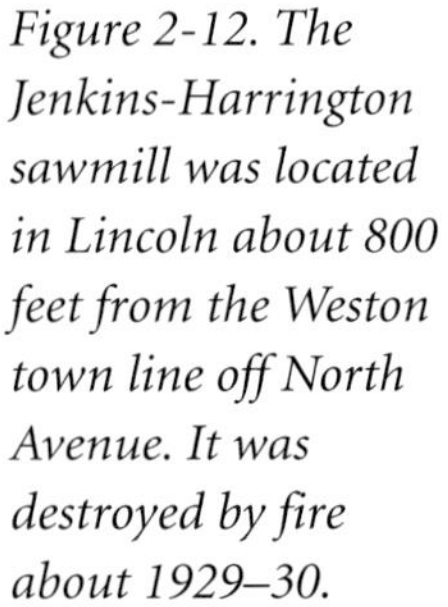

Figure 2-12. The Jenkins-Harrington sawmill was located in Lincoln about 800 feet from the Weston town line off North Avenue. It was destroyed by fire about 1929–30.

Counterclockwise from upper left.

Figure 2-13. No. 761 Boston Post Road, constructed for farmer Mark Sibley about 1840, illustrates the "temple-front" Greek Revival form and is notable for its handsome porch. Generally, when the triangular gable end of a house was oriented to face the street, the house was only three bays wide, rather than the five bays in this example.

Figure 2-14. Farmer Otis Train built this house at 137 Wellesley Street about 1847. Wide corner pilasters, wide-trim boards at the cornice line, and a porch with fluted columns create an updated Greek Revival version of the traditional pre-1840, five-bay house.

Figure 2-15. The 1854 house of mill owner Nathaniel Sibley at 104 Boston Post Road has fashionable Italianate paired brackets along the cornice, but the form is still the traditional five bays across. The wide-board trim is a lingering Greek Revival feature.

Figure 2-16. Characteristic Italianate features of 28 School Street include the central wall gable, round-headed window, and squared porch posts.

(chapter 13). Established about 1838 on the site of an earlier gristmill. Samuel H.F. Bingham produced machinery to make heavy woolen goods and the Bingham butter and cheese drill, also referred to as the Butter and Cheese Tryer. His heirs sold to machinist Henry Bowen in 1869. Later Charles A. Freeman screen factory. Power from Three Mile Brook.

Mill/Machine Shop. Behind 293 Boston Post Road (chapter 13). Appears on the 1875 map, probably dates to 18th century. Closed in late 19th century. Power from Three Mile Brook. Produced cotton batting and other products.

Mill (later E.A. Hall's Shoddy Mill). Church Street (chapter 10). Lamson says that Luther and Quincy Harrington had a machine shop here.[36] Labeled "Pencil"Fact[ory]" on the 1852 "Craigie" map and "wool mfy" on the 1875 *Middlesex County Atlas.* (See next chapter for E.A. Hall's Shoddy Mill.) Closed 1886. Power from Stony Brook.

School Furniture Factory. 27 Crescent Street (chapter 13). Established 1854 by Samuel Shattuck and later run by Oliver Kenney and others. Closed in 1917. Power from Three Mile Brook. Produced school desks and chairs.

Architecture (1830–1860)

Handsome Greek Revival houses testify to the town's relative prosperity during this period. Greek Revival was the dominant style of American domestic architecture from about 1830 to 1850 and appears in rural Weston in the late 1830s. Ancient Greece was thought to be an especially appropriate model for a young American republic struggling to free itself from British influence after the War of 1812. Some residential examples echoed the Greek temple form by facing the gable end to the street, an orientation that continued to be popular long after other elements of the style passed out of favor. In many examples, wide trim is used to outline the triangular pediment formed by the pitch of the roof. In keeping with the temple theme, Greek Revival houses were painted white. In Weston, many fine examples have a one-story porch across the front.

Mill owner Samuel H.F. Bingham built a well-detailed Greek Revival house at 39 Crescent Street sometime after 1839. Farmers and tradesmen in the next decade followed this popular fashion. Examples include the Mark C. Sibley house at 761 Boston Post Road (c. 1840), John Lewis Gourgas III house at 178 Boston Post Road (1842), Nathan Barker house at 101 Wellesley Street (c. 1843), Train-Milton house at 137 Wellesley Street (c. 1847), Jesse Viles house at 254 Conant Road (c. 1847–48), Albert Hobbs house at 820 Boston Post Road (c. 1848) and Cheney house at 455 Concord Road (c. 1850). Edward Coburn's house at 171 Church Street (1841) had unusual porch supports. The Horatio N. Fiske house at 11 Rolling Lane (c. 1839), Willard Rand house at 233 Ash Street (c. 1847), and Otis Train house at 138 Wellesley Street (c. 1855) are simple "temple-front" examples without porches.

Beginning in the 1850s, houses in Weston began to show the influence of the Italianate style, which dominated American domestic architecture between 1850 and 1880. Along with the Gothic Revival, which was rarely used in Weston, the Italianate began in England as part of the picturesque movement and represented a reaction against formal classicism. In affluent communities of the time, the style can be quite flamboyant, sometimes incorporating towers and ornate window and door detail. Weston examples give just a hint of the possibilities. Here the style is most easily recognized by the use of single or paired brackets at the cornice. Window and door hoods are sometimes supported by brackets as well. The columns popular in the Greek Revival years were replaced by squared or chamfered porch posts. Round-headed windows are common in the peak of the gable end or within a central wall gable used to break up the front facade. Window sash is often divided into two panes and entrances can have double doors. Narrow-trim boards replaced the wide corner pilasters and entablature of the earlier Greek Revival.

One of the earliest Italianate examples in Weston is the Dr. Otis Hunt–E.H. Sears house at 338 Boston Post Road (c. 1851), which has a central pavilion, round-headed windows, and double-bracketed cornice. Many of the 1850s schoolhouses have bracketed cornices. The Marshall L. Upham house (1853), now at 207 Newton Street, has robust console brackets supporting a central hood over the entrance. A central wall gable focuses attention on the entrance of the well-preserved Italianate cottage known as the George Smith house at 28 School Street (c. 1853). An earlier Weston farmhouse at 89 Sudbury Road was updated with the addition of a central peaked gable. The Henry J. White house (late 1850s) at 84 Wellesley Street has an L-shaped plan and the characteristic double brackets.

Also appearing during this period is the three-bay, side-gable house with center entrance. The Dennis Keefe house at 22 Summer Street (c. 1860) features a typical Italianate bracketed hood over the front door. The Andrew K. Brotchie house at 137 Boston Post Road (c. 1853 with later porch), Upham/Burrage house at 505 Boston Post Road (1856), and Manley Seaverns house at 119 Park Road (c. 1864) exemplify the straightforward mid-19th-century form.

Country Estates before the Civil War

Tamara Thornton's book *Cultivating Gentlemen: The Meaning of Country Life among the Boston Elite, 1785–1860* describes how merchants, financiers, manufacturers, lawyers, and politicians of Boston's upper crust established country seats and gentlemen's farms in the late 18th and early 19th centuries. Well-known examples include The Vale in Waltham, Codman Farm in Lincoln, and the Bussey estate in Jamaica Plain, which became the nucleus of the Arnold Arboretum. Prominent Bostonians searched for alternatives to the Old World concepts of aristocracy they had rejected for the new Republic. Rural pursuits were a "powerful means of self-characterization," according to Thornton:

> There was, however, no single image that country seat owners wished to project. In fact rural pursuits were so potent precisely because they acted as a rich and varied reservoir of associations, conjuring images laden with meanings of the aristocrat, the squire, the landed merchant, the yeoman, and the statesman retired from the world.[37]

In 1839 John Warner Barber wrote in his *Historical Collections*, "There are a number of beautiful country-seats [in Weston], where persons from Boston reside during the summer months."[38] In his 1846 *Gazetteer of Massachusetts,* John Hayward reported, "This pleasant town is so easily approached from the city, that it is fast filling up by citizens who love a country residence."[39] Neither Barber nor Hayward provides additional details, but some information is available about pre–Civil War country estates.

John Mark Gourgas (1766–1846), distinguished descendant of a noble Huguenot family, lived on what is now Boston Post Road from 1822 until his death in 1846 in the house now owned by the Gifford School. In his declining years, his brother, John James Joseph Gourgas, occupied half the house in Weston during the summers. The Gourgas family owned several large tracts of land along Boston Post Road, which they operated as a gentleman's farm.

Gen. Daniel G. Derby, described as "a man of mark in his generation, and of the Derby family of Salem," owned a Colonial residence on Wellesley Street where Case House is today. He was noted for his lavish hospitality and entertained prominent men like Commodores Perry, Decatur, and Bainbridge.[40]

After General Derby's death in 1843, the property was sold to Charles White. In 1851, White was one of six residents listed in the book *The Rich Men of Massachusetts* as having the largest fortunes: Alpheus Bigelow ($200,000), Augustus H. Fiske ($150,000), Isaac Fiske ($50,000), Josiah Quincy Loring ($150,000), James Paul ($75,000), and Charles White ($70,000).[41] White is described in the book as a retired apothecary who "started poor." He owned the property for about two decades before selling it to his niece Mrs. James Brown Case.

Another of the six Weston men listed in *The Rich Men of Massachusetts,* Josiah Quincy Loring (1819–1862), acquired about 100 acres in the 1850s on what is now Loring Road.[42] The son of Josiah Loring, one of Boston's well-known merchants, Loring is described by Lamson as "a thorough Latin and

Greek scholar [who] retained his love of classic literature throughout his life."[43] He bequeathed valuable books to Harvard College and assisted in founding Weston Public Library.

In 1856, Frederick T. Bush, importer and former U.S. Consul to Hong Kong, bought the Starr Farm on South Avenue near Cutter's Corner. In 1861 Bush was taxed for 75 acres and $21,971 worth of personal property. At that time, most Weston residents had no taxable personal property.

Notes

1. Lamson, *HTW,* 130
2. Ibid., 192.
3. Handlin, David P., *The American Home: Architecture and Society, 1815–1915* (Boston: Little Brown & Co, 1979), 6–7.
4. 1865 *TR,* 14.
5. Winship, Albert E., "Education (1820–1890)" in Hart, ed., *Commonwealth History of Massachusetts,* vol. 5, 175.
6. Weston began printing school reports as early as 1843, although many of the earliest annual reports have been lost. Reports from the treasurer and the library and school committees were first printed together under the title "Reports of the Town of Weston" for the year ending March 31, 1862.
7. In 1851 the town voted to build three new schoolhouses, in the northwest, northeast, and center-east districts, at a total cost of $4,111.92. In 1852 the West Center Schoolhouse was built. New schoolhouses were built in Districts 5 and 6 (on the south side) in 1853, at a cost of $3,198.68. See Lamson, *HTW,* 171–72, and also school records preserved in the town hall vault. School records show that a committee modeled the houses after one in the northerly part of Waltham built about 1850. That building was 40 feet by 28 feet. The committee felt the town needed two houses of this size, two a little smaller, and two a little larger.
8. Lamson records that Isaac Jones gave land 12 rods square for the schoolhouse on Highland Street and Dr. Kendal gave land on Wellesley Street, both in 1793. A new northwest school was built in 1796 and southeast school in 1812 (Lamson, *HTW,* 168–69).
9. 1859 "Report of the School Committee of the Town of Weston for year ending March 31, 1859" (Boston, Geo. C. Rand & Avery, City Printers, 1859), 4–5. A copy is bound with other town reports at Weston Town Hall. The 1863 School Committee Report also praises the design of the buildings and says that other towns in the Commonwealth followed Weston's model.
10. Moved to its present location at 700 Boston Post Road to make way for the Boston Post Road bypass.
11. Lamson, *HTW,* 134.
12. 1859 Weston School Committee Report, 5 (bound with early town reports, Weston Town Hall).
13. Lamson, *HTW,* 170.
14. Ibid.
15. U.S. census records on file at the National Archives and Records Administration in Waltham. Statistics in the next paragraphs were compiled by Pamela W. Fox.
16. These figures were obtained by looking at each occupational category as a percentage of the total 405 men whose occupation is listed.
17. Earle, Alice Morse, *Stage-coach and Tavern Days* (New York: The Macmillan Co., 1900), 272–74.
18. Holbrook, Stewart H., *The Old Post Road,* 13.
19. Ibid.
20. Hinchliffe, Elizabeth M., *Five Pounds Currency, Three Pounds of Corn: Wellesley's Centennial Story* (Town of Wellesley, Massachusetts, 1981), 27.
21. Bachelder, J. Leonard, *The Half Century Limited* (Massachusetts Bay Railroad Enthusiasts, Inc., 1984), 6–7.
22. Bidwell, Percy W., "The Agricultural Revolution in New England," *American Historical Review* 26, 1921, 687.
23. Ibid., 695.
24. As quoted in Bidwell, ibid., 698.
25. Drainage ditches are still evident in Jericho Forest off Concord Road, in the wetlands on town conservation land west of 555 Wellesley Street, and probably other places as well.
26. Shea, Lois R., "New England's not-so-colorful past," *Boston Sunday Globe,* October 4, 1998, B-1.
27. Palfrey, John G., Secretary of the Commonwealth, *Condition and Products of Certain Branches of Industry in Massachusetts for the Year Ending April 1, 1845* (Boston: Dutton and Wentworth, 1846).
28. DeWitt, Francis, Secretary of the Commonwealth, *Statistical Information Relating to Certain Branches of Industry in Massachusetts for the Year Ending June 1, 1855* (Boston: William White, 1856), 360–61.
29. Whitehill, Walter Muir, and Kotker, Norman, *Massachusetts: A Pictorial History* (New York: Charles Scribner's Sons, 1976), 11.
30. *An Account of the Celebration by the First Parish of Weston Massachusetts of Its Two Hundredth Anniversary, 1898* (Weston, 1900), 166.
31. Bigelow, John, *Statistical Tables: Exhibiting the Condition and Products of Certain Branches of Industry in Massachusetts for the Year Ending April 1, 1837* (Boston: Dutton and Wentworth, 1838), 41.
32. Palfrey, op. cit. The report does not give the company name, but Coolidge, Sibley & Treat has been inferred from tax records.
33. DeWitt, op. cit.
34. See also "A Family Reunion," probably *Waltham Free Press,* unknown date, Coburn scrapbook #4, 49.
35. Lamson, *HTW,* 160–61.
36. Ibid., 162.
37. Thornton, Tamara Plakins, *Cultivating Gentlemen: The Meaning of Country Life among the Boston Elite, 1785–1860* (New Haven and London: Yale University Press, 1989), 21–22.
38. Barber, John Warner, *Historical Collections* (Worcester: Dorr, Howland & Co., 1839), 442.
39. Hayward, John, *A Gazetteer of Massachusetts* (Boston: John Hayward, 1846), 306.
40. From obituary of Nathan Barker, who worked for General Derby, *WDFPT,* May 16, 1902.
41. Forbes, A. , and Greene, J.W., *The Rich Men of Massachusetts, Containing a Statement of the Reputed Wealth of about Fifteen Hundred Persons with Brief Sketches of More Than One Thousand Characters* (Boston, W.V. Spencer, 1851), 124–25
42. For major purchases, see MCRD 632/394 (1852, 58 acres from Leonard Cushing) and 785/515 (1858, 46-plus acres from Peter Renton). Renton, a Boston physician, was Loring's father-in-law. See also "Plan of Estate Owned by the Heirs of the Late J.Q. Loring," July 1874, MCRD Plan Book 31/ 44. Shows the location of the house, large barn, and henhouse.
43. Lamson, Daniel S., "Weston," in D. Hamilton Hurd, ed., *History of Middlesex County, Massachusetts* (Philadelphia, 1890), vol. 1, 506.

Figure 3-1. Weston native Edmund L. Cutter served in the 44th Massachusetts Regiment, Company 1. He was one of a dozen Weston soldiers who died in the Civil War. Cutter was 31 when he succumbed to battle wounds on April 25, 1863, in a Newbern, North Carolina, hospital.

CHAPTER 3 · (1860–1890)

Civil War and Post–Civil War Era

In the second half of the century, Massachusetts became the first truly industrialized state in the Union. The Civil War economy resulted in a 61 percent increase in the state's manufacturing output. But prosperity was not without a price. The rural landscape was giving way to urban industrial centers. By 1865, Massachusetts was the second most densely populated state in the nation. Many of the newcomers were foreigners and Roman Catholics, whose language and customs were strange to the native-born. In the 1830s and 1840s, it had been possible to believe that new factories would bring prosperity without ethnic and class struggles. This hope dimmed with each report of strikes and violence. Moreover, locally made goods could not compete with products put out by large and efficient factories. The decline of small-town mills and manufactories meant a loss of diversity for rural economies.

As industrialization and urbanization increased, towns that had been bypassed as unsuitable for large-scale water-powered industry proved attractive for other reasons. The "backwardness" of the countryside became its charm. As noted in the book Picturing Old New England, *writers heralded the change and "conspicuously disengaged themselves from the problems of social reform, retreating with astonishing speed into the quiet pleasure of country life."[1] Restful, out-of-the-way old villages like Deerfield and seacoast communities like Ogonquit, Provincetown, and Nantucket became tourist attractions or art colonies. Others, like Weston, appealed to those who fancied a farm landscape close enough to cities to allow convenient commuting to country estates and summer homes.*

Figure 3-2. Twenty-one of the Weston men who enlisted as "nine months' men" in 1862 were in the 44th Regiment Infantry, Company 1. They were among those photographed at Camp Meigs in 1863.

Weston in the Civil War

In the fall of 1860, "when the clouds were thickening over us," Capt. Daniel S. Lamson organized a home guard to prepare for war.[2] About 50 young men joined the company and practiced gun drills and marching. After the attack on Fort Sumter in April 1861, Weston residents took up a subscription to purchase a flagpole, which was erected on the common in front of First Parish Church.[3] In June 1861, Lamson was appointed major of the Sixteenth Regiment forming in Cambridge.

Initially, patriotism ran high and the town had more than enough volunteers to fill its assigned quota, as reported by the selectmen in 1862:

> The great and engrossing subject of public attention has been the war, and the raising of men and means for carrying it on; and it is with pleasure we are able to report that enough of our citizens and

Statistics	1860	1865	1870	1875	1880	1885
Population	1,243	1,231	1,261	1,282	1,448	1,427
Change	+38	-12	+30	+21	+166	-21
Number of dwellings	209	218	234	232	236	249
Total valuation	$1,016,605	$1,103,274	$1,069,867			$1,871,850

inhabitants have freely and patriotically volunteered . . . to fill the quota assigned to the town.[4]

As more soldiers were called for, residents voted to pay a bounty of $100 to each man enlisting in the Union Army, an amount later increased to $200.[5] In all, Weston furnished 126 men and paid bounties for 47. Residents contributed more than $5,000 for these bounties. Total war-related expenses came to $9,128 out of a total town budget of $13,710 for the year ending March 1863.[6] Added to money raised by voluntary subscriptions, the town spent a grand total, according to Lamson, of $18,070, "which must be admitted as a very liberal and patriotic showing for a population of about 1,400."[7]

Twelve men died, eight in action, three of wounds or disease, and one as a prisoner at Andersonville.[8] The bodies of those who could be found were brought home and buried at the expense of the town.[9]

On August 22, 1865, the citizens of Weston gathered to honor their dead and celebrate returning heroes. After memorial services at First Parish Church, soldiers and citizens marched to the town hall for a bountiful collation, "which showed the talents of the women of Weston."[10] Patrick Gilmore's brass band played for dancing. The following year, the town voted to build an addition to the town hall that would include a memorial hall and more space for the rapidly growing library. The marble Civil War monument commissioned for the new hall was later moved to the reading room of the 1899 Weston Public Library.

Town Development (1860–1890)

The annual printed reports from the 1860s to the 1880s concentrate on major budget items including schools, the library, poor farm, cemeteries, and roads. Post–Civil War growth of town government in other areas was fostered in part by new state regulations. In 1869 the Massachusetts legislature created the first state Board of Health in the country. Over the next decades, it took on issues like water purification, clean milk, communicable diseases, sanitary engineering, water and sewerage, and food and drugs. By

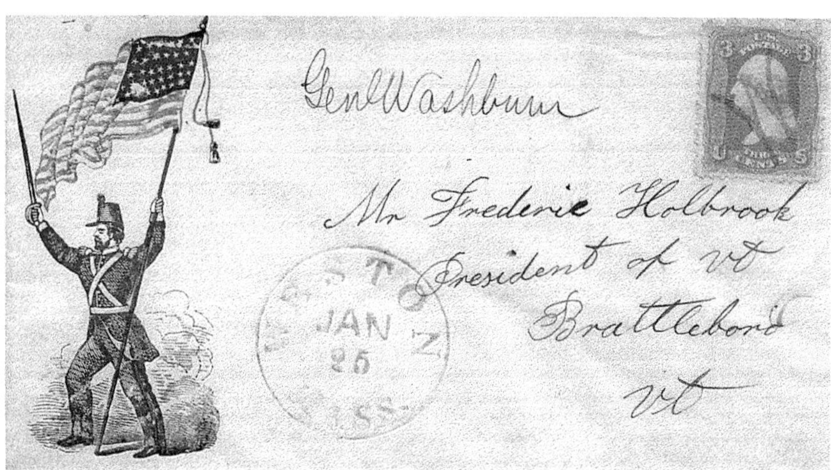

Figure 3-3. One of only two or three known Civil War patriotic "covers," or envelopes, this cover is stamped with the "Weston" postmark, meaning that it was mailed in Cutting's Store. Postmaster George W. Cutting Sr. canceled the stamp with a black letter W.

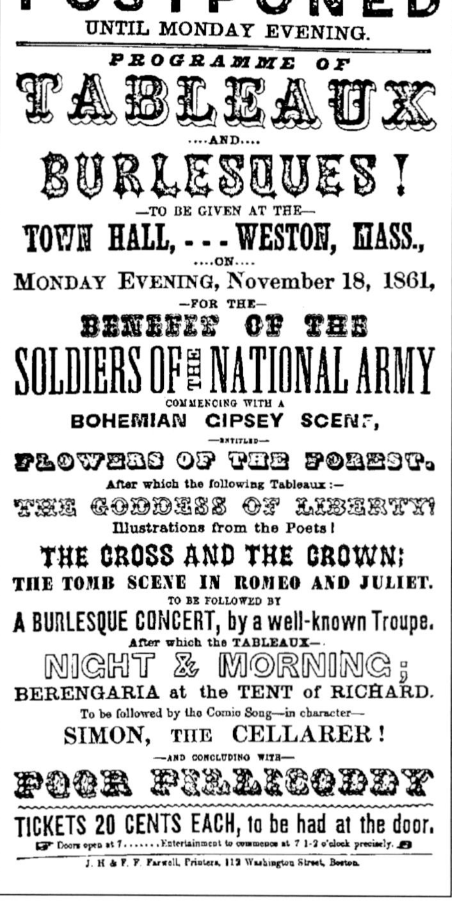

Figure 3-4. Twenty cents purchased a ticket for an 1861 benefit for Union soldiers, held at the town hall.

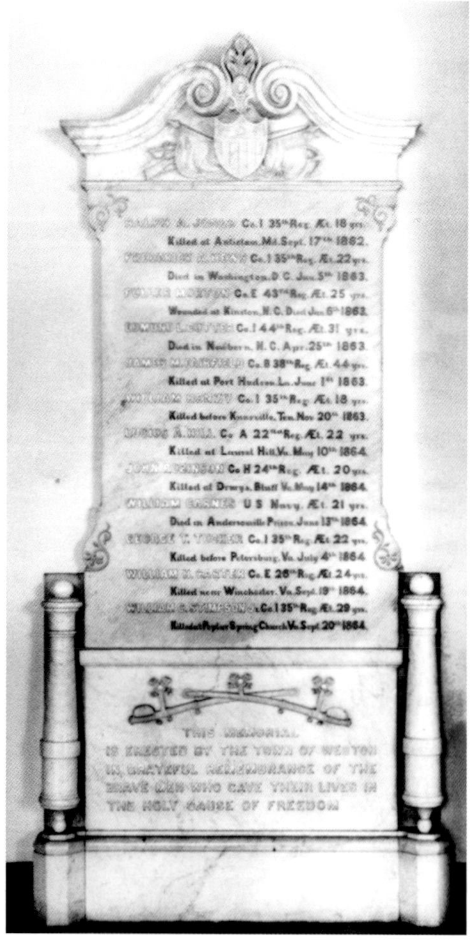

Figure 3-5. This elegant marble Civil War monument was relocated in 1899 from the town hall to the new Weston Public Library.

1875, birth and death statistics were being printed in town reports and helped determine the relative health of the community.[11]

In 1874 the selectmen established a "watering place" at the intersection of North Avenue and Church Street, with pump and stone trough, for the benefit of the traveling public. The following year, a private citizen established a similar public watering trough on Boston Post Road at the corner of Wellesley Street and presented it as a gift to the town.[12]

Weston celebrated the national centennial in 1876 with a daylong celebration on the Fourth of July. In

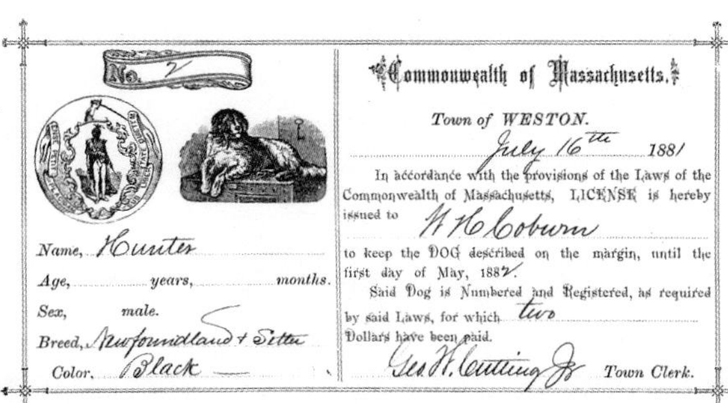

No. 2

Commonwealth of Massachusetts.

Town of WESTON. July 16th 1881

In accordance with the provisions of the Laws of the Commonwealth of Massachusetts, LICENSE is hereby issued to W H Coburn to keep the DOG described on the margin, until the first day of May, 1882. Said Dog is Numbered and Registered, as required by said Laws, for which two Dollars have been paid.

Geo W. Cutting Jr Town Clerk.

Name, Hunter
Age, years, months.
Sex, male.
Breed, Newfoundland & Setter
Color, Black

Figure 3-6. The issuance of dog licenses, which began in 1876, was part of state and local efforts to promote public health and safety.

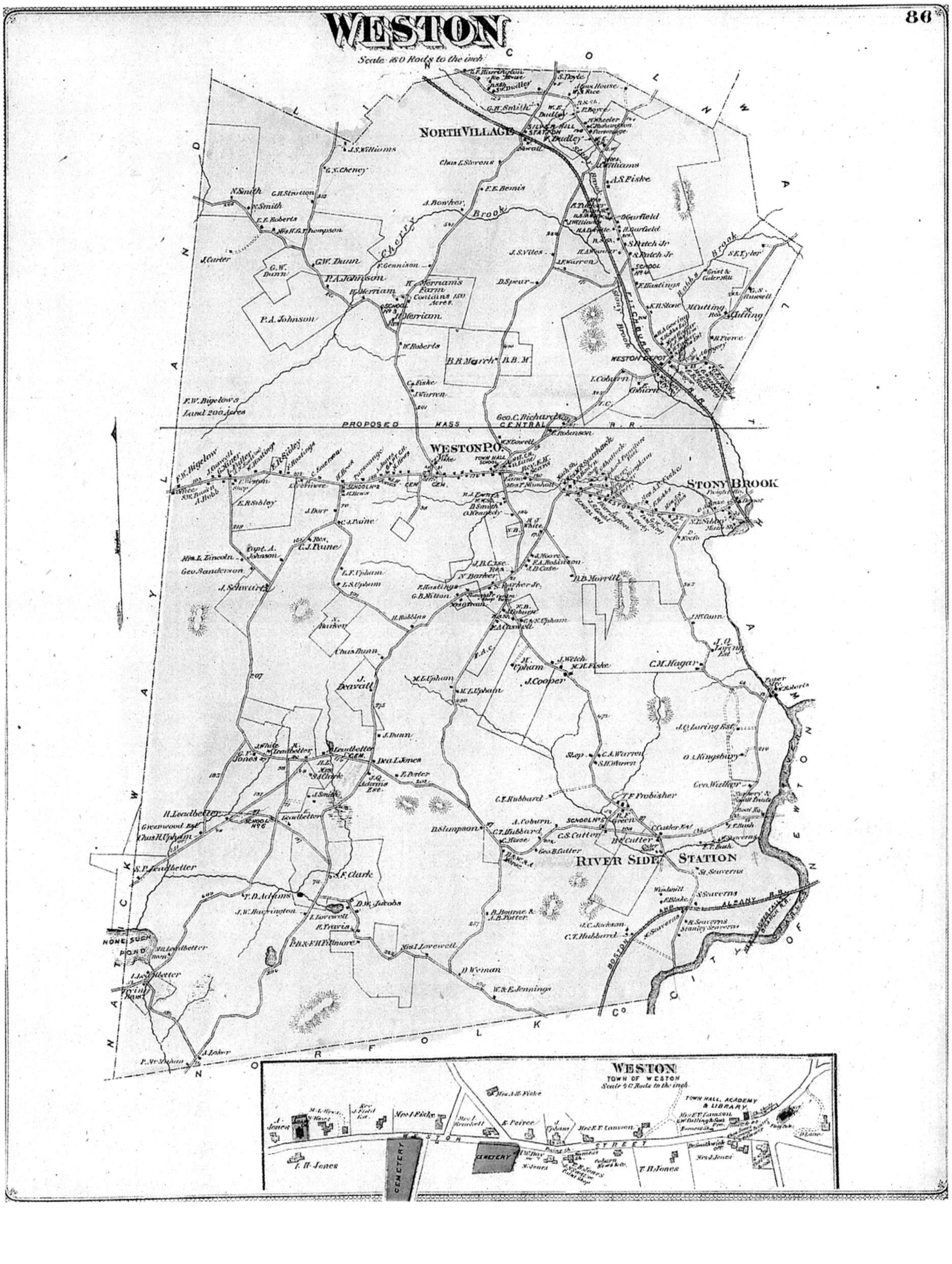

Figure 3-7. The 1875 Middlesex County Atlas *shows property boundaries for some of the town's largest farms—for example, the Fiske farm on North Avenue. The map records the further development of Boston Post Road and North Avenue and shows the location of numerous machine shops and small manufactories.*

Figure 3-8. In 1880 Miss Anna Coburn (center, rear) took over at District School #4 on North Avenue. In Miss Annie's classroom, "order prevailed and neatness enthroned itself."

the evening, there was "a brilliant display of Fireworks, with Music by the Weston Cornet Band, from their new stand on the Common."[13]

In 1882, a committee was chosen to select names for the town's principal roads. Many of the names are still used today, with the following exceptions: Central Avenue (now Boston Post Road), Forest Street (Conant Road), Elm Street (Love Lane), and East Newton Street (Park Road).[14] In 1887 the Town Improvement Society was reported to be erecting lampposts for streetlights.[15] These oil lamps were lit each evening.

The town adopted its first bylaws in 1882.[16] While most regulations had to do with management of town government, several fell into the category of "village improvement." Residents were forbidden to place rubbish, dirt, or wood where it would obstruct a road or sidewalk or mar its appearance. They were not to tie horses or wagons to street trees, drive nails into street trees, or deface trees, walls, fences, or buildings with posters or handbills. Other bylaws related to conduct; for example, "No person shall behave themselves in a rude or disorderly manner, or use any indecent, profane, or insulting language in any public place in the Town . . . or . . . remain upon any sidewalk [or] doorstep . . . so as to annoy or disturb any person, or obstruct any passage. . . ."

Figure 3-9. High school classes were held in the town hall until the first high school, shown here, was constructed in 1878. The wooden building was later used for lower grades and then torn down in the early 1930s to make way for what is now known as Brook School Building C.

Schools (1860–1890)

Beginning in 1862, students over age 12 were sent to the Centre School in Town Hall regardless of their academic performance. The older children, particularly the "dull older scholars," were thus removed from the district schools, allowing female teachers to give more attention to the younger children. The Centre School became both a grammar school, also referred to as an intermediate school, and a high school, with both groups housed in the same room. The intermediate school became an expedient alternative for students too old for district schools but unprepared for high school.

Establishing the intermediate school decreased the population of district schools. In 1875, enrollments were as follows: #1 East Centre, 35, with average attendance 24; #2 West Centre, 17, average 11; #3 North West, 14, average 11; #4 North East, 28, average 24; #5 South East, 24, average 14; #6 South West, 24, average 21. Although some of the schools were small, the committee felt that combining district schools would require children to travel too great a distance. Teachers often boarded with families.

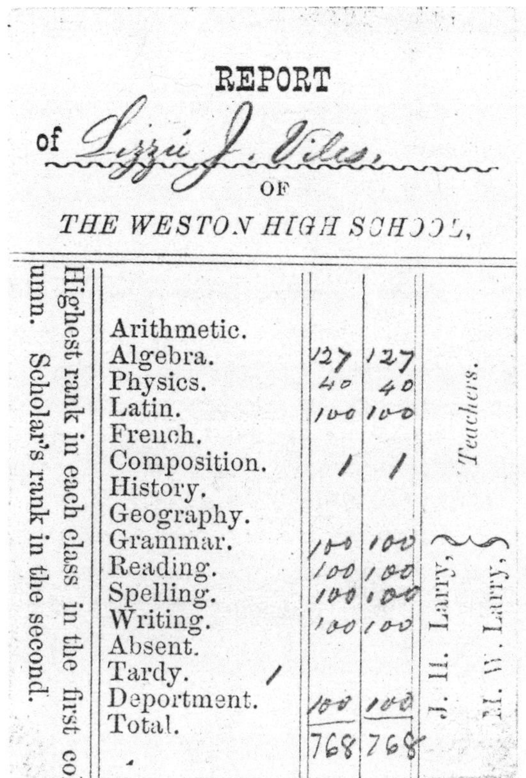

REPORT

of Lizzie J. Viles

OF

THE WESTON HIGH SCHOOL,

Arithmetic.		
Algebra.	127	127
Physics.	40	40
Latin.	100	100
French.		
Composition.	1	1
History.		
Geography.		
Grammar.	100	100
Reading.	100	100
Spelling.	100	100
Writing.	100	100
Absent.		
Tardy.		
Deportment.	100	100
Total.	768	768

Teachers. J. H. Larry, M. W. Larry,

Highest rank in each class in the first column. Scholar's rank in the second.

Figure 3-10. Lizzie Viles became one of the town's best-loved teachers. Her Weston High School report card from the late 1860s shows the highest score in the class in every subject.

John H. Larry, esteemed principal from 1866 to 1873, raised high school academic standards.[17] Admission was by examination. The school committee strengthened the curriculum, noting, "Hitherto the rule has been to take such studies as suited the taste or inclination of the scholars, without any regard to what would be for their permanent benefit."[18] The new three-year course of study included Latin, algebra, grammar and arithmetic, physiology, geometry, rhetoric and philosophy, chemistry, French, botany, mental philosophy, geology, and astronomy. The school began the systematic study of music with the goal that every student learn to sing. The first high school class of three graduated in 1868. The Weston High School Association was formed in 1871 and held its first reunion at the traditional March graduation the following year.

The high school quickly outgrew its quarters in Town Hall, but not until 1877 did the town finally vote to build a separate high school on School Street.[19] The building committee chose Boston architect Carl Fehmer, "whose reputation for elegance of style and mechanical skill needs no commendation."[20] The new high school was completed in 1878 and cost $10,000 to build and furnish.[21] It had space for 75 students and a second-floor hall seating 300.

In 1882, the report of the Subcommittee on Finance and Repairs urged the town to furnish textbooks:

> This wealthy town can easily afford to appropriate the sum asked for, thus relieving parents with large families of considerable expense . . . and making our schools "free" in fact as well as in name.[22]

Public interest in the high school declined over the decade, and by 1888 attendance had decreased to 28. For three years there was no graduating class.

Development of Linwood Cemetery

Efforts continued in the 1860s to beautify the Farmers', Central, and South Burying Grounds. Linwood Cemetery was established in 1873 with the purchase of nine acres from Marshall Hews.[23] A receiving tomb was built by 1876 for temporary use each winter. That year, the trustees wrote that they had visited

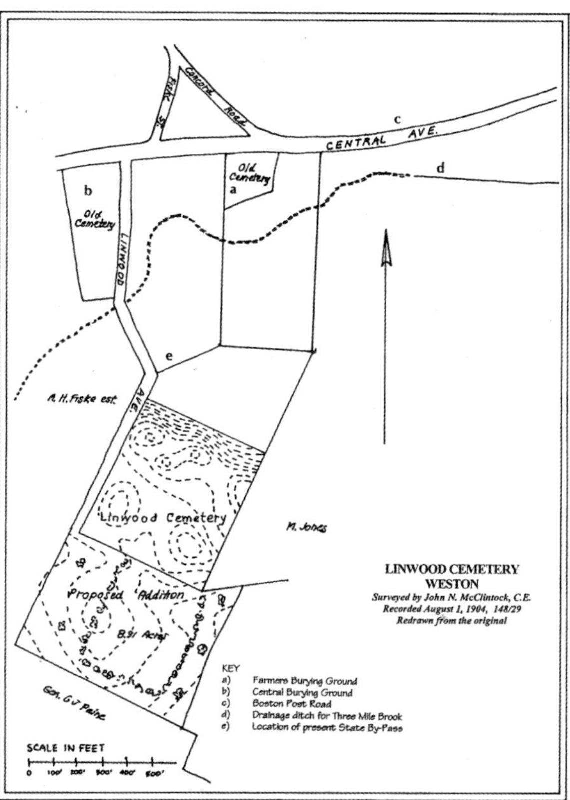

Figure 3-11. This map shows the first (1873) and second (1904) purchases of Hews land for Linwood Cemetery. The two earlier cemeteries are shown as well. Central Avenue is now Boston Post Road. The State Road Bypass, built in the early 1930s, now bisects this map.

Figure 3-12. This present-day photograph shows the Hobbs and Hastings family plot at Central Burying Ground, also known as Central Cemetery. By 1876 cemetery trustees reported that the custom of enclosing lots with granite curbing or iron fencing had passed out of fashion and was being replaced by the "landscape lawn" system, which was easier to maintain.

cemeteries in adjoining towns and "found that the plan of finishing lots by curbing with granite, or enclosing with an iron fence, has been almost entirely abandoned." The "modern" practice, which became known as the landscape-lawn system, allowed for more open lawn and easier maintenance by encouraging only one memorial for each plot and discouraging plot enclosures, paths, hedges, ironwork, urns and vases, and other such accessories common in early-19th-century cemeteries. The trustees added, "We are certain that it is less expensive, and, in the end, will give better satisfaction. . . ."[24]

Landscape gardener G.A. Parker was hired in the mid-1890s to study the grounds. He praised the undulating topography and layout and urged the trustees of burial grounds to formally adopt the "lawn cemetery" approach:

> The ideal cemetery of greatest beauty is what is commonly known as the "Lawn Cemetery," where different lots are not distinguished by independent grading . . . and where the lawn mower can be run without interference from different grades or lot lines between plots . . .
>
> It is the inharmonious grading of lots, the "fixing up" of one lot independent of all others, that gives cemeteries their patchy, disagreeable appearance. This, however, has not been done so offensively here as in many country cemeteries.
>
> The opportunity of making this a beautiful rural cemetery is seldom equaled. Nature has done much for the spot; it only requires that man shall work in harmony with her.[25]

Figure 3-13. About 1888, Sarah Kingsbury had this tintype made with her four children, Clara, Alden, Walter, and Emma. Sarah was the wife of farmer Otis Kingsbury.

Census Data: Occupations and Immigration

While Weston men were still predominantly farmers or farm laborers, the 1870 U.S. census records a wide variety of other occupations, from florist to real-estate agent. Approximate percentages were as follows: farmer or farm laborer (66%), tradesmen (17%), commerce (7%), professional (2%), manufacturers (1%), service occupations (2%), and miscellaneous (4%). [26]

Women's occupations were listed for the first time in 1870. One woman per household was generally designated as "keeping house" (71%). By far the largest number of paid women were in household service as domestics, cooks, nurses, and housekeepers, for a total of 22 percent. Twelve women (4%) were schoolteachers.

The 1870 U.S. census lists 181 residents, or 14 percent of the population, born in the following countries outside the United States: Ireland (101), Canada (48, including 29 from Nova Scotia), England (21), Scotland (7), Germany (3), and Russia (1).

A decade later, the 1880 federal census records a major increase in immigrants from Nova Scotia. For the first time, Canadians surpassed the Irish (113 to 110). Of the Canadians, 91 were from Nova Scotia and 8 from New Brunswick. Some found work in Weston mills. In 1880, seven immigrants in a large extended family from Nova Scotia were living together and working at the shoddy mill in Kendal Green, while another group lived in a boardinghouse and worked in an unidentified mill. Attitudes toward Nova Scotian immigrants can be inferred from items such as this in the "Weston" column of the *Waltham Daily Free Press* in the early 1890s:

> Those who made the disturbance at the dance undoubtedly came with that intention. There was considerable noise on the street before the dance and indecent language was used. . . . They are said to be from Nova Scotia.[27]

By the early 20th century, Nova Scotian immigrants like George and James Foote, Beriah Ogilvie, and Cyrus Clark were well established as small businessmen or

Figure 3-14. The Massachusetts Central Railroad was chartered in 1868. After many delays, it finally began operations in 1881, when this photograph was probably taken in Hudson. A few years later it was reorganized and renamed the Central Massachusetts Railroad.

Figure 3-15. Weston Station was one of two Weston stops on the Central Massachusetts Railroad. The handsome building, which still remains on Church Street, was constructed about 1881 in the Stick style. All the stations had wide overhanging eaves, decorative truss brackets, and vertical board-and-batten siding. This early-20th-century photograph shows the bustling depot around its peak years of operation, 1907–14.

farmers. Their stories are told in chapters 10 and 16.

The first immigrants from Scandinavia are recorded in 1880: five from Sweden and one each from Norway and Denmark. The number of Swedes increased to 45 by 1900, reflecting the national origin of many of the skilled employees at the Hook & Hastings organ factory, which moved to Kendal Green in the late 1880s.

By the time of the 1885 state census, there were 1,427 people in Weston. Eight hundred, or 56 percent, had two native-born parents and 462, or 32 percent, had two foreign-born parents.

Transportation: The Massachusetts Central/ Central Massachusetts Railroad

The Central Massachusetts, third of the train lines through Weston, was chartered in 1868 at the peak of railroad fever. It has been described as "a railroad that should never have been built" and "an anachronism before the first spadeful of earth was turned."[28] Historian Daniel Lamson failed to conceal his scorn for the entire operation:

> The Massachusetts Central Railroad, in its inception purely a speculative enterprise, has now come to maturity on a solid basis after twenty years of incubation. Not one of the original officers had personally any practical experience either in building or operating railroads. They went to work blindly, and began their road "nowhere," and ended it in about the same place, as regards being within the reach of business.[29]

The problem with the Central Massachusetts was that it was never more than 20 miles from two parallel, prosperous, and well-established lines: the Fitchburg to the north and Boston & Albany to the south. Wayland, a town of only 1,766 people in 1875, was the largest community with no other rail service. Promoters had hoped to reach west of New England but they were fortunate to make it to the Connecticut River. Other problems were the single track, with only occasional turnouts for trains to pass each other, and the meandering route.

As first incorporated in 1868, what was then called the Wayland and Sudbury Branch Railroad

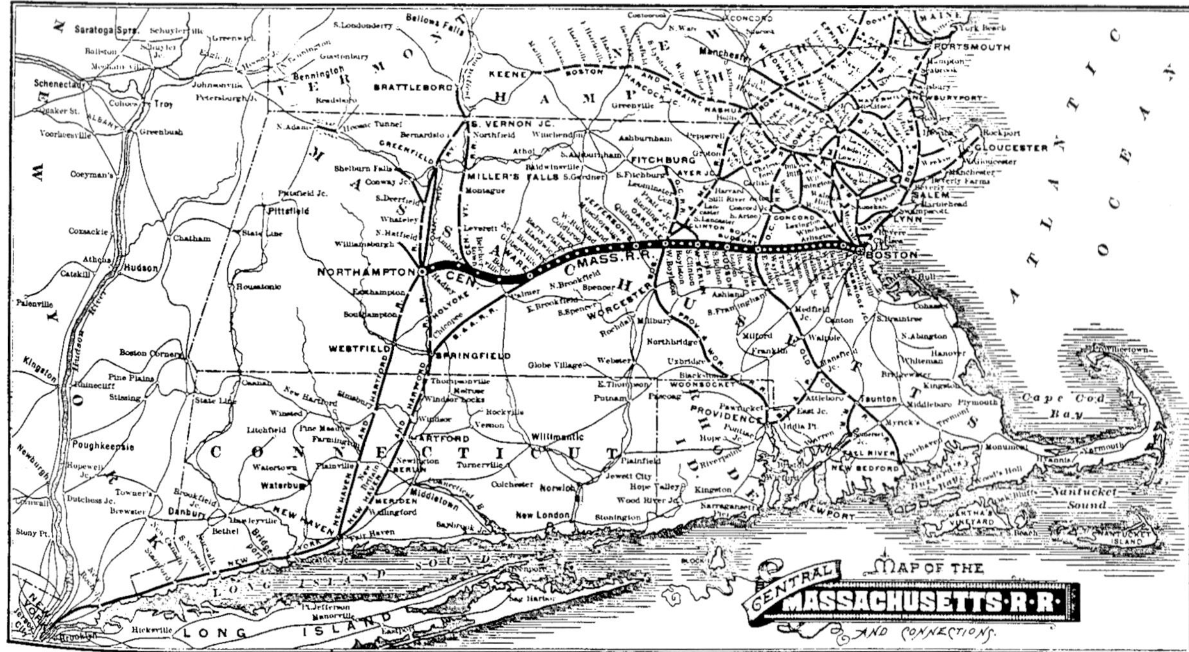

Figure 3-16. The Central Massachusetts Railroad and its connections as of July 1888.

was authorized to run 6.75 miles from Mill Village in Sudbury to Stony Brook, where it would join with the Fitchburg Railroad. After being expanded in scope and incorporated again as the Massachusetts Central in 1869, the company commenced work in 1870. It had problems with failing contractors and was for years in a "comatose condition," according to Lamson. Organizers had trouble raising money. Even in Weston, where the railroad would directly benefit the town, voters twice rejected resolutions to purchase stock with public funds. Work started again in 1878 and in 1880 stockholders ratified an agreement with the Boston & Lowell to lease the Massachusetts Central for 25 years.

After a decade of work and millions in expenses, the railroad opened in 1881 from Boston to Hudson, a distance of 28 miles. Weston Station was in place by the grand opening on October 1 of that year. By 1882 the line was complete to Jefferson, but the following year, operations were again suspended because of financial problems. Trees grew in the neglected roadbed.

The railroad was reorganized under the name Central Massachusetts Railroad and restarted in 1885. In 1886 the line was again leased to the Boston & Lowell, which in turn leased it to the Boston & Maine. Finally, in 1887, the first train reached Northampton, where connections could be made with other lines. By the turn of the century, the Central Massachusetts was being used by residents of the developing Pigeon Hill neighborhood and others to commute into Boston.

Agricultural Developments in New England (1860–1890)

In his chapter on Massachusetts agriculture in the 1930 *Commonwealth History of Massachusetts,* Arthur Gilbert lists the following contributors to agricultural progress during the years 1820 to 1889: 1) evolution of farm implements and farm machinery, with resulting increases in productivity; 2) increased production of crops best suited to local conditions; 3) livestock improvements and progress in a specialized dairy industry eventually concentrating on the production of fluid milk; 4) the constructive work of the State Board of Agriculture in encouraging agricultural progress; 5) the growth of agricultural education; 6) the work of the Cattle Commission in promptly stamping out contagious diseases in cattle herds and poultry; 7) the general improvement of farm living conditions.[30]

Living conditions improved with inventions like the iron cookstove, ice chest, and sewing machine and the introduction of home canning, which made possible a more varied winter diet. Still, farm wives had multiple responsibilities. During the last half of the 19th century, increasing numbers of farm households employed an immigrant girl as a domestic servant.

Government and voluntary farm-oriented organizations proliferated. During the early Civil War years, President Lincoln created the U.S. Department of Agriculture. In 1863, the Massachusetts Agricultural College was founded in Amherst. The State Agricultural Experiment Station, also located in Amherst, was established in 1882. These institutions, along with the state Board of Agriculture, county societies, and farmers' clubs, institutes, and Granges, helped disseminate information and improve farm productivity. Agricultural books and publications also had a stimulating effect. The Grange movement, a fraternal association of farmers that included both men and women, spread through the country dur-

Figure 3-17. Milk was Weston's most valuable farm product throughout the post–Civil War period. Productivity per cow more than doubled in the 20 years between 1865 and 1885. In 1885, 963 "milch" or milk cows produced more than 500,000 gallons of milk. This photograph shows dairy cows on the Glen Road farm of Edward Jennings.

NATHAN BARKER, JR.,

AUCTIONEER, BUTCHER,

CATTLE DEALER AND DROVER.

Auction Sales solicited and promptly attended to. Cattle pastured by the season at reasonable prices. Beef and Veal Bought or sold on commission. P.O. Box 23.

Residence, Wellesley St., near Newton St., Weston.

Figure 3-18. In the 1887 directory, Nathan Barker Jr. of Wellesley Street advertised cattle-related services including driving cows to pasture for the summer season, auctioning, and butchering.

Products	1865	1875	1885
Valued over $2000	**value in $**	**value in $**	**value in $**
English hay	47,205	36,098	39,807
milk	24,574	49,813	70,535
manure		16,930	20,339
meadow hay	12,251	6,933	6,008
Indian corn	10,981	2,285	3,203
potatoes	10, 330	14,494	8,054
beef, dressed	9,507	1,820	6,722
pork, dressed	9,545	7,011	5,929
market gardening	8,660	listed by product	listed by product
firewood (sale + use)	7,623	13,988	6,011
cider (sale + use)		7,912	816
strawberries		7,413	7,523
nuts and berries	6,910	listed by product	listed by product
butter (sale + use)	4,692	1,963	3,649
apples	3,913	6,949	3,330
cucumbers		6,298	3,821
cabbage		5,879	2,430
corn fodder		1,831	5,957
green corn		5,830	5,202
eggs	3,699	5,007	8,255
veal dressed	3,232	3,251	2,774
pickles	2,850		
oat fodder			3,119
asparagus			2,387
Animal Census			
milch cows	534	615	963
horses	208	320	297
swine, pigs, hogs	145	521	698
oxen (over age 4)	80	28	22
sheep	28	0	0
hens and chickens	not listed	5,002	7,591

Figure 3-20. This chart shows the value of Weston's agricultural products and also the animal census, based on state records. Notice the increase in the value of milk.

Figure 3-19. The number of pigs and hogs in Weston rose from 145 in 1865 to almost 700 in 1885. Farmer Otis Kingsbury poses with one of his charges.

ing the last quarter of the century.

The late 19th century was a period of specialization in crop management. Crops that did not show good profit were dropped by progressive farmers. An 1875 state census lists the yield and value of 19 crops, with those highest statewide in total value being potatoes and apples. The production of hay, New England's most widespread crop, increased with demand from dairy farmers and city dwellers. In 1886, the Boston Market Gardeners Association was formed for vegetable growers. As markets expanded and better varieties were developed, market gardeners increased production of strawberries. Once greenhouses came into use, local producers saw opportunities in growing flowers as well as vegetables. The Boston Flower Exchange was organized in 1892 to provide better sales facilities.

The importance of the dairy industry in Massachusetts during the late 19th century is evident from an 1885 census showing that one quarter of the agricultural products were dairy. To provide support, the state established the Dairy Bureau in 1892. Breeders set up national associations, many based in New England, and began to keep pedigree records of Devon, Jersey, Holstein, Ayrshire, Guernsey, and Brown Swiss cows.

Contemporary agricultural historians have termed this the "era of concentrated products" in New England. They point out that cheap midwestern grain, far from undercutting New England agriculture, was fed in great quantities to local cows and chickens and thus transformed into far more valuable milk and eggs. As an extra bonus, farmers could use their augmented supply of manure to fertilize market crops, corn fodder, and hay.[31]

New incubators and the relative cheapness of western grain encouraged New Englanders to increase the size of poultry flocks and develop specialized poultry farms. The American Poultry Association was founded in 1873 and the Boston Poultry Show held annual exhibitions. In the 1880 federal census, the first to list poultry separately, the six New England states held the nation's six top positions in egg yield.[32] In 1885, an estimated 35,000 to 40,000 Massachusetts residents were raising poultry on a large or small scale.

The period 1860–1890 saw increased concern with contagious diseases in cattle and other livestock. The state Cattle Commission was formed in 1860 after two imported Dutch cattle were found to be sick with an unknown disease. Later diagnosed as pleuropneumonia, it spread rapidly. Laws were passed to stop infection by slaughtering whole herds where a single sick animal was found. Foot-and-mouth disease made its appearance in 1878 and spread rapidly to 80 towns in Massachusetts, including Weston. By the 1880s, tuberculosis was widespread in cattle.

Although coal was increasingly preferred as fuel for factories and railroad engines, cordwood was used in ever larger quantities for home cooking and heating. Wood was used by tanners, shipbuilders, and carpenters. According to Howard S. Russell's study of New England agriculture, *A Long, Deep Furrow,* the decade of the Civil War "marked New England's high point for cultivated land and low point for its forest cover."[33] Roughly two thirds of Massachusetts land had been "improved." Late-19th-century paintings and photographs of Weston show large stretches of open space, broken by stone walls and the occasional tree.

The economic value of remaining forestland was threatened by the accidental introduction of the gypsy moth from Europe in 1868. Ten years later, widespread defoliation of trees in eastern Massachusetts brought the pest increasing public attention. In 1897 the brown-tail moth appeared, adding to the destruction. Large areas of forest and thousands of street trees were destroyed. Lead arsenate spray was introduced in 1892 to attempt to control the pests. To counteract the loss of street trees, village improvement societies began planting elms, maples, and oaks along the principal thoroughfares of Weston and elsewhere in New England.

Not all farmers adapted to market changes or took advantage of advances in agriculture. Prices of many staples, especially grain, went into continuous decline at war's end as midwestern grain flooded in. According to Russell, thousands of New England's poorer farms had gone out of production by 1870.[34] The next three decades were even more difficult. The panic and depression of 1873 hurt farmers. Young people abandoned New England farms for better opportunities in cities, on western farms, or in local industries. Those who stayed were generally those with fertile, well-located, and prosperous farms.

Farming in Weston (1860–1890)

At the time of the 1865 Massachusetts state census, Weston had 181 farms on 9,622 acres, for an average size of 53 acres.[35] Two hundred thirty men worked on farms, far more than the 30 "hands" employed in the six mills and blacksmith shops. The most valuable product was English mowing hay.[36] During these years, Middlesex County was the center of apple growing in Massachusetts. The 1865 census lists 16,312 apple trees in Weston cultivated for their fruit.

A decade later, in 1875, the most valuable farm product was milk, followed by English mowing hay.[37] In 1885 milk again topped the list.[38] Productivity per cow had more than doubled in 20 years, as farmers fed their cows more grain and extended the

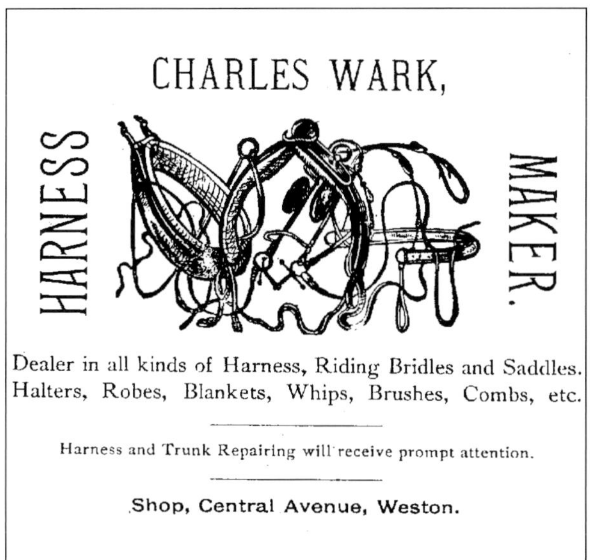

Figure 3-21. Charles Wark advertised his harness-making business in the 1887 directory. The photograph shows the shop on Central Avenue (now Boston Post Road).

milking period into the winter.

To earn extra income, some Weston farmers began taking in regular boarders or summer guests. Beginning in the mid-1870s, Willard Jennings took advantage of his location near the Wellesley Farms railroad station to develop the Glen House Hotel. Samuel Clarke, who owned the farm on Wellesley Street now known as Gateways, opened his farm to summer residents, and George H. Jones and his wife, Lettie, took in year-round and summer boarders at their Golden Ball Hotel.

Commerce and Industry (1860–1890)

The 1875 map of Weston in the *Middlesex County Atlas* shows more than 20 shops, mills, and factories. There were six blacksmith shops, four on well-traveled North Avenue alone, along with two machine shops, three paint shops, two harness shops, a carriage trimmer, two woodworking shops, two slaughter shops, a school furniture factory, and a woolen factory. The 1875 state census lists manufacturers and trades in Weston. The most important were butchering (value of goods $16,000), school furniture making ($12,000), and "wool carding" ($8,000). Also listed were harnesses and harness repair, machinery and tools, blacksmithing, carpentry, painting, wheelwrighting, and making butter and cheese testers. Total valuation of goods made and work done was $51,900, compared to $227,883 for agricultural products.[39]

A woolen factory, E.A. Hall's Shoddy Mill, was established about 1873 on what was already a mill site on Church Street at Stony Brook. The three-story wooden mill building was 119 feet by 36 feet and had two one-story wooden ells, a wool picker house, and a brick dyehouse. The company produced all-wool shoddy, a fabric made from reclaimed wool. The factory was destroyed by fire in 1884, rebuilt, and destroyed again in 1886.

A few other small manufactories were established in the 1880s or 1890s. In 1885, G.W. and Thomas Faber (later Thos. Faber & Son) established a rope-walk on North Avenue near the present No. 421 to make handmade linen window and dumbwaiter cord. The company closed in 1899 because of competition from machine-made cord.[40] The James Walton Woolen Knitting Mill, established in the 1880s near the corner of South Avenue and Pine Street to produce gloves and mittens, burned to the ground in late December 1891 but appears to have been rebuilt, as it is listed in the 1893 directory. Daniel Smith was making carriages beginning in the 1880s at his residence and shop on School Street and Daniel Garfield by the 1890s at a carriage shop on North Avenue. From the 1890s to about 1933, Charles A. Freeman operated a factory on Crescent Street that produced window and door screens and weatherstripping.

In 1889, the Hook & Hastings organ factory moved to North Avenue. This important industry, with its major impact on the north side, is discussed in detail in chapter 10.

Architecture (1860–1890)

The Civil War marked the end of Greek classicism. The Italianate style, first seen in Weston in the 1850s, continued to be widely used through the 1880s. A few houses were built with mansard roofs in a style known as Second Empire because it imitated the latest French building fashion. Examples include 179 Church Street, built by the Coburn family, the Horace Hews house at 687 Boston Post Road, and the George Stedman house at 237 North Avenue, which features the machine-made wooden ornament popular on city versions of Second Empire and Italianate houses. A mansard roof was added to the Cutter-Pushee house at 72 Church Street.

Also used occasionally in Weston during this period was the Stick style, a free adaptation of

Figure 3-22. The mansard roof was used extensively during France's Second Empire. In America, its short-lived popularity extended from the Civil War years to about 1880. In this example at 179 Church Street, the roof type was combined with an Italianate hood over the front entrance.

Figure 3-23. Teacher and Weston High School Principal Justin E. Gale built his Stick-style house at 15 Conant Road in 1879–80. Note how the prominent cornice brackets line up with the vertical "stickwork." Over the next decade, the Stick style was replaced by the closely related Queen Anne style discussed in chapter 4. The Gale house was probably the work of William N. Gowell, who lived next door.

medieval English building tradition that features wooden wall cladding interrupted by patterns of horizontal, vertical, or diagonal boarding known as stickwork. The style was first used for the Edward Fiske house at 215 Boston Post Road, which was the most expensive house in Weston when completed in 1867. The Albert Horatio Hews mansion at 699 Boston Post Road (1880) was pictured in an 1897 guidebook. Justin E. Gale built a well-detailed Stick house at 15 Conant Road in 1880. The style was used effectively for the picturesque 1881 Weston Station and the remodeled First Baptist Church, which was later demolished.

In contrast, the contemporaneous Shingle style was a quieter, uniquely American form that reached its highest expression in the seaside resorts of the northeastern states. Shingles were used to create a smooth and flowing surface that unified the exterior. Shingle-style houses are asymmetrical in massing and have irregular rooflines and, usually, extensive porches. The roof type can be gable, hip, or gambrel, with dormers of any shape. Decorative detailing is used sparingly. Embellishments are usually Colonial Revival in spirit, like classical porch columns and the occasional Palladian window. The Shingle style remained primarily a high-fashion, architect's style and was popular for the homes of estate owners such as Charles Townsend Hubbard, who built Ridgehurst at 80 Orchard Avenue (1883). The Francis H. Hastings house, Seven Gables, at 190 North Avenue (1885) demonstrates the sculptural possibilities. The James B. Case house, Rocklawn, at 89 Wellesley Street (1889), by Ernest Boyden, still has the dark brown shingles popular at the turn of the century. In 1891, architect Samuel Mead used the style for his own house at 50 Pigeon Hill Road, an important local example.

The Search for Country Homes

The first summer residents and gentlemen farmers moved quietly into Weston beginning in the 1820s. Newcomers in the second wave, from the Civil War to the early 1880s, also lived simply, often occupying existing farmhouses. The estate mansions were built in the third stage, between 1883 and 1915, when Weston's reputation as a location for country estates became known among well-to-do merchants and manufacturers.

The second wave began with James Brown Case, who bought property in 1863 and spent summers in Weston with his family, initially in the existing farmhouse. Charles Townsend Hubbard bought a farm on the south side in 1867 and used the old farmhouse as his country home until 1883. Gen. Charles Jackson Paine bought his farm in 1868 and kept the existing mid-18th-century house for years.

Figure 3-24. Estate owner Charles Jackson Paine bought the 18th-century Elisha Jones house and added the large addition at right. Twelve years later he gave the historic house to Charles H. Fiske with the stipulation that it be moved off the property.

Figure 3-25. Paine's America's Cup victories in the 1880s gave Weston increasing visibility. This newspaper cartoon by H. Popp dates from about 1893.

Paine's public celebrity after winning the America's Cup in 1887 focused media attention on Weston. This description of the town comes from a newspaper article that year:

> About 15 miles from Boston lies this quiet town of 1200 inhabitants, where General Paine has chosen to spend his summers. This is indeed a quiet place. A stranger cannot go to a hotel here and have a sumptuous supper spread out in his room. We have no hotels, nor sumptuous suppers either. Visitors must go for single meals to our one grocer-hardware-meat-gent's furnishings-variety and go-as-you-please-clerk store, lean up against a counter, gnaw on musty crackers and dried-up flour animals, washing it all down with fizzleless pineapple tonic for 15 cents. Cheap enough, to be sure, and General Paine need never fear that Weston will become a popular summer resort.[41]

Although the musty crackers and fizzleless tonic theoretically do not sound appealing, there is a certain cachet in newspaper coverage such as the following, which is a continuation of the above article:

> General Paine lives about a mile and a half from the center of the town. . . . He owns several hundred acres of valuable land, and lives in a spacious, colonial-shaped house on the summit of the hill. Here he keeps a score of easy driving horses, does some farming, and comes to rest after going off on a yachting cruise.

About a year later, a Boston newspaper published an article headlined: "A Massachusetts Town, Scenes in Cutting's Store at Weston. Citizens Who Have Honored the Town and Been Honored by It. Summer Home of General Paine and Many Leading Bostonians." This time the writer praises Weston's many attractions:

> What attracts rich people to Weston, do you ask? Well, in the first place, the natural beauty and healthfulness of the town; then the opportunity to purchase hundreds of acres of land at a moderate price; the retired nature of the locality, a yearning for their native homes, and countless other reasons. Last, but possibly not the least of these reasons, is the low tax rate, which this year is only $6, much less than one-half that of Newton or Boston. To those blessed with $100,000 worth of personal estate this makes a substantial difference. Boston does very well in winter, but the heated term, commencing the latter part of April, finds them punctually in Weston, ready to pluck Mayflowers and be plucked themselves.

During the period 1860–1890, three future estate owners came to the town as young men, well before they achieved the success needed to buy extensive property or build mansions. Francis Blake settled here in 1873 after marrying C.T. Hubbard's daughter Elizabeth. With the help of her father and grandfather, he built a house that, while not modest, was far from the showplace he developed two decades later. Horace Sears, son of the minister at First Parish Church, grew up in Weston and came back in the 1880s as a young adult to live with his widowed mother. Robert Winsor came to Weston in 1884 as a young Harvard graduate clerking for an investment banking firm and built a small frame house on less than two acres.

The role of these six families—Case, Hubbard, Paine, Blake, Sears, and Winsor—in the development of Weston cannot be underestimated. By the late 1880s, that role was already apparent in the erection of the new First Parish Church with the leadership and financial support of Horace Sears and the Paine, Case, and Winsor families. The remarkably fine fieldstone church was the first physical manifestation of the new wealth and sophistication that would radically change this modest country town.

Influence of Estate Owners on Road Improvements

The 1880 town report is the first to introduce a theme that would echo throughout the next two decades as the town considered what improvements were really

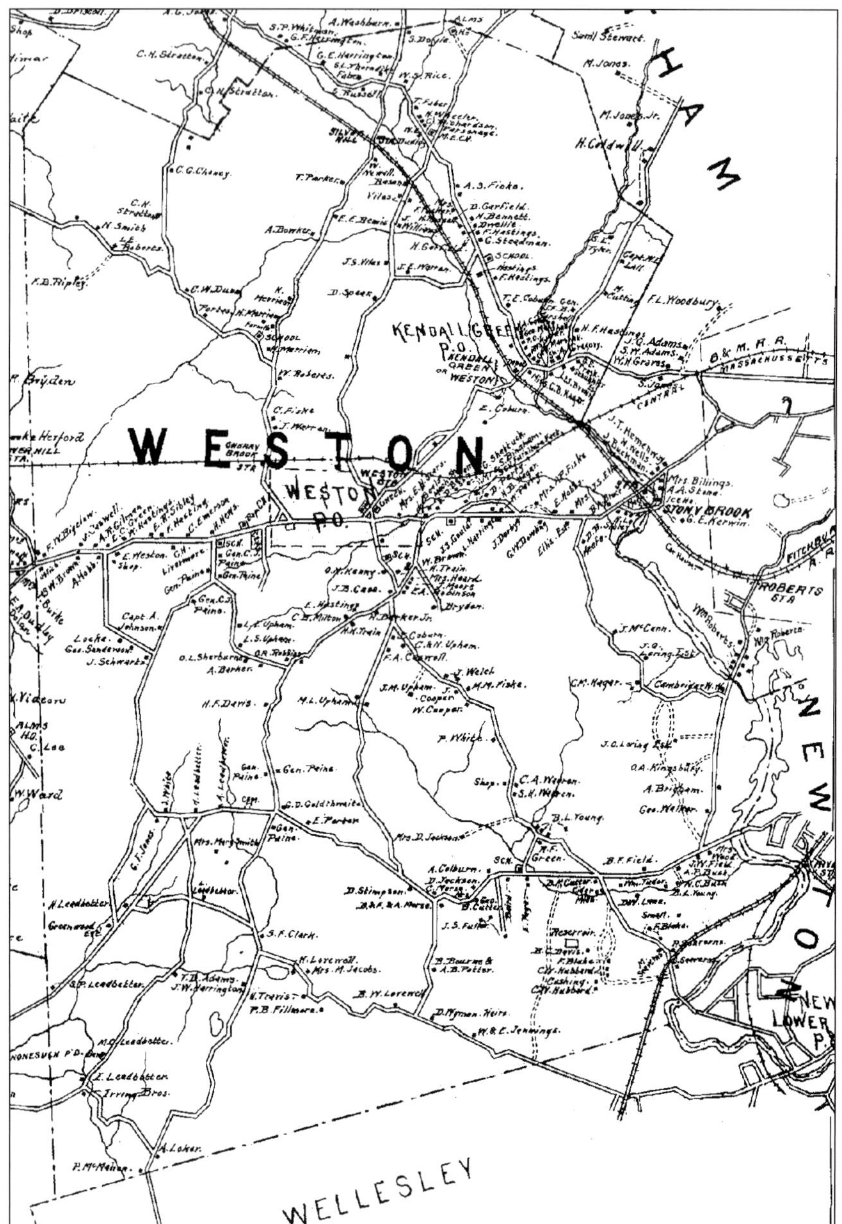

Figure 3-26. The 1889 Middlesex County Atlas *included this map and also a detail of Boston Post Road, which appears in chapter 15.*

"necessary." That year, the road commissioners wrote that "we believe all are convinced that nothing tends more to advance the material interest of the town than good roads."[42] The commissioners urged residents to do their part to make roads more attractive:

> In conclusion, we would suggest to all owning real estate abutting upon the highways that much might be done by cutting unnecessary wood growing on the sides, repairs of fences &c., not only beneficial to the roads, but would make our town much more attractive to those seeking places to locate a permanent home for themselves and families.[43]

The next year, the road commissioners made an even more explicit connection between good roads, summer residents, and the town's increasing prosperity:

> We would recommend liberal appropriations for highways, believing that good roads, more than any other means, will tend to the prosperity of the town, especially when we recognize the fact that two-thirds of our taxes are paid by a class whom we might style summer residents, and who are interested more in good roads and pleasant drives, than in any other town matters.[44]

At least one summer resident agreed. In 1882 General Paine donated a large sum for the purchase of crushed stone for the town's roads. Two years later, he donated a roller.

Again in 1883, the commissioners brought up the need for more improvements to an antiquated road system:

> . . . our increasing number of city residents, with our increasing valuation, demand that we should commence a system of improvements, to be continued from year to year, without excessive taxation. . . . But when we consider that of our 42 miles of highways, only our three main avenues . . . are of legal width, and that of the remaining 32 miles the necessary width only can be obtained by taking land of the abuttors, we may possibly realize what a herculean task we have before us.[45]

In 1887, General Paine served as president of the Town Improvement Society, which was called on for support and monetary assistance in beautifying Weston's main street:

> We would suggest . . . that the Town authorities and the abutters unite in striving to improve the avenue by uniform sidewalks and fences where desirable, believing that our Main street can be made second to none in the County of Middlesex in point of beauty and attractiveness, and also that our Town Improvement Society will cheerfully approve . . . and materially assist in so doing.[46]

Community Organizations, Churches, and Societies

Weston had three churches during this period: Unitarian, Baptist, and Methodist. Major church building projects were the reconstruction of the First Baptist Church in 1881 and construction of a new First Parish Church in 1888. One of the outstanding features of Weston life in the late 19th and early 20th centuries is the variety of activities centered on the churches. By 1887, First Parish had organized the Ladies Benevolent Society, which met monthly for charitable and social work; the First Parish Friendly Society, formed in 1885 to aid with fund-raising for the new church and increase sociability; and the Literary Union, which met every two weeks to discuss books. The Methodist church had a Ladies' Aid Society and Women's Foreign Missionary Society and the Baptist church also had several special-interest groups.

Two fraternal societies were formed in the 1880s. The Henry A. Upham Lodge, No. 52, in Weston was granted a charter in 1884 by the Ancient Order of United Workmen, Grand Lodge of Massachusetts. The purpose of the society was to encourage and support fellow members in sickness, distress, and unemployment and, in case of death, to secure for the family or heirs a payment of $2,000. Other objects were "the practice of Charity, the inspiration of Hope, and the Protection of all good and true brothers, and for the Education and elevation of our fellowmen."[47] The lodge met bimonthly and grew from 53 members in 1887 to 100 in 1899.[48] Beginning in 1901, the group met in the former library space in the town hall, which they remodeled into a lodge room.[49]

The second order was the Weston Commandery of the United Order of the Golden Cross. About 1888, the Waltham press reported that a widow had received a $2,000 benefit certificate from the Golden Cross Commandery, which by that time numbered about 50. The paper added "Fraternal insurance is working an immense amount of good in every community."[50] This group also met twice a month and sponsored literary and musical entertainments for its membership.

Figure 3-27. The First Baptist Church was extensively remodeled in the 1880s. The resulting dramatic wood-frame structure stood until the present church was constructed in the 1920s.

Figure 3-28. The Henry A. Upham Lodge of the Ancient Order of United Workmen was established in 1884. In 1898 the 19 original members gathered to have their picture taken at a Waltham photography studio. The arrangement of the men within the photograph is not known but their names and vocations are as follows: Nathan Barker Jr., cattle dealer; L.F. Upham, farmer; James M. Smith, janitor; E.W. Russell, master painter; E.O. Clark, provision dealer; John J. Brown, master builder; Elias King, carpenter; Charles A. Moody, blacksmith; Charles W. Wark, harness maker; J.J. Cowen, blacksmith; Merrill French, depot master; Edwin A. Newbury, farmer, Emery L. Bemis, sexton; William N. Gowell, master builder; M.J. Cutting, janitor; Thomas Coburn, street repairer; Oliver L. Sherburne, farmer; A.M. Upham, contractor; and C.A. Benson, provision dealer. During the first 14 years, the number of active members grew to 100.

Figure 3-29. The Weston High School Association was founded in 1871. This illustration is from the 11th reunion program of 1882, which featured music, poetry, and orations.

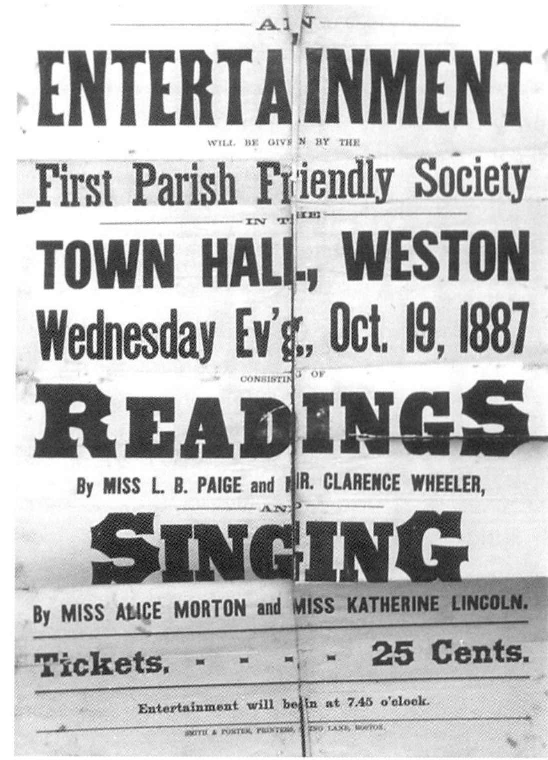

Figure 3-30. The First Parish Friendly Society was founded in 1885 to help raise money for the building of the new stone church. Highlights from the Friendly Society's first 30 years are included in the next chapter.

The Weston Temperance Club, also referred to as the Temperance Society and later reorganized as the Weston Prohibition Club, was started in the late 1880s and signed up 81 members in its first year. A newspaper article noted that Weston was already a "dry" town:

> There is throughout the village, a worthy desire to make this Club felt as a power in this community. It is an exceptional and valuable fact which should be published far and near, that there are absolutely no saloons in Weston, public sentiment being all one way.[51]

The 1887 directory also lists the Town Improvement Society of Weston, with Gen. Charles J. Paine as president; Gen. J.F.B. Marshall, Rev. Amos Harris, and Charles W. Hubbard as vice presidents; Andrew Fiske as secretary; and Miss Hattie Perry as treasurer. This group was reorganized in 1895 as the Village

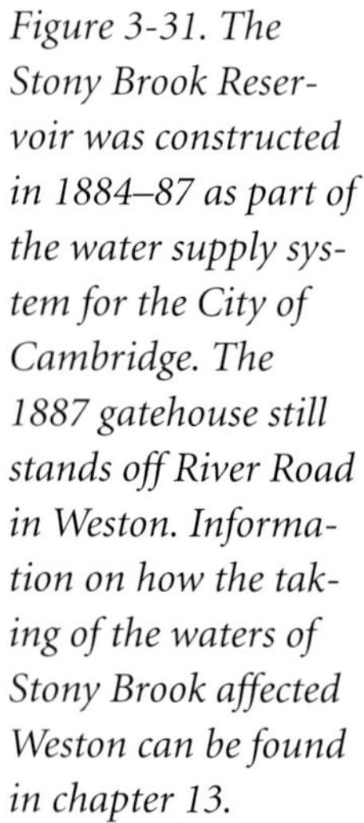

Figure 3-31. The Stony Brook Reservoir was constructed in 1884–87 as part of the water supply system for the City of Cambridge. The 1887 gatehouse still stands off River Road in Weston. Information on how the taking of the waters of Stony Brook affected Weston can be found in chapter 13.

Improvement Society and is discussed in chapter 5.

Notes

1. Brown, Donna, and Nissenbaum, Stephen, "Changing New England: 1865–1945," in Truettner, Wm. H., and Stein, Roger B., eds., *Picturing Old New England: Image and Memory* (National Museum of American Art, Smithsonian Institution and Yale University Press, 1999), 4.
2. Lamson, *HTW*, 137–38.
3. According to Emma Ripley in *Weston: A Puritan Town*, 16, the flag was first raised in a ceremony on May 3, 1861. It remained in this location until 1917.
4. 1863 *TR*, 3.
5. In 1863, as voluntary enlistments declined, 33 Weston men were drafted, although 28 were exempted, 2 found substitutes, and 1 paid a $300 "commutation" to avoid military service. Lamson's figures, quoted here as to number of men drafted, differ slightly from the figures in the town records (Lamson, *HTW*, 140). In May 1864, the town voted to pay bounties of $125 a man and a recruiting committee was directed "to go early into the market and secure the men before the price by competition should advance."
6. 1863 *TR*, 4–5.
7. Lamson, *HTW*, 143. Somewhat different figures are given by William Schouler in *A History of Massachusetts in the Civil War* (published by the author, Boston, 1871)vol. II, 471, as follows: Town expenditures related to the war $12,528.90. Donations from citizens to pay bounties: $5,104.95. Aid to soldiers' families (repaid by the Commonwealth): $2,358.66. Schouler also has a slightly different figure—131—for the number of Weston men who served.
8. The dead were Ralph A. Jones, James M. Fairfield, William Henry, Lucius A. Hill, John Robinson, George T. Tucker, William H. Carter, William C. Stimpson, Frederick A. Hews, Fuller Morton, Edmund L. Cutter, and William Carnes. Lamson's *HTW* provides details on page 142.
9. Schouler, op. cit., 471. Baptist minister Rev. Calvin Topliffe was appointed by the town to bring home the bodies and assist sick or wounded soldiers.
10. Kennedy, Donald G., "Return of Weston's Soldiers," *WHSB*, May 1983, includes this quote from a long account of the celebration in the Waltham press.
11. Weston Town Clerk's records of births, deaths, and marriages begin in 1848 and are available at Town Hall.
12. "The First Watering Troughs," *WHSB*, March 1974, 2.
13. Fiske, Charles H., "Oration Delivered before the Inhabitants of Weston" (Weston: printed by vote of the townspeople, 1876), 3–4.
14. 1882 *TR*, 36–38.
15. "Weston" column, *Waltham Daily Free Press*, early October 1887 (Coburn scrapbook #1, 233).
16. Printed in final form in the 1883 town report, 46–50.
17. Larry was not principal for one of the years during that time period.
18. "Report of the School Committee," 1868, 23. The debate about whether to use age or examination as the criterion for high school admission continues through the next decades.
19. Located on the site of Brook School Building C on School Street, on land purchased from Henry J. White in 1875 (MCRD 1343/413).
20. 1878 *TR*, 27. Committee members were George W. Dunn, Edward Coburn, Henry J. White, and William N. Gowell.
21. See Auditor's Reports, 1878 and 1879 *TR*, 14.
22. 1882 *TR*, 57–58.
23. MCRD, Book 1284/203 (Marshall Hews to Town of Weston), October 1873, $2,250. Regulations in town report of 1875.
24. 1876 *TR*, 32–33.
25. 1895 *TR*, 55.
26. Computed as percentage of men whose occupations are specifically listed.
27. Coburn scrapbook #3, c. 1892, 48.
28. Boston and Maine Railroad Historical Society, *The Central Massachusetts Railroad* (Boston: Thomas Todd Co., 1975), vii.
29. Lamson, *HTW*, 146–47.
30. Gilbert, Arthur W., "Massachusetts Agriculture (1820–1889)," in *Commonwealth History of Massachusetts*, Albert Bushnell Hart, ed., vol. IV, 398–99.
31. Donahue, Brian, *Reclaiming the Commons* (New Haven: Yale University Press, 1999), 64–65.
32. Russell, Howard S., *A Long, Deep Furrow: Three Centuries of Farming in New England* (Hanover and London: University Press of New England, 1982), 267.
33. Ibid., 276.
34. Ibid., 255.
35. Warner, Oliver, *Statistical Information Relating to Certain Branches of Industry of Massachusetts* (Boston: Wright & Potter, 1866), 414–15. Note that many of the 181 farms were small. The 1861 tax records list only 98 Weston properties more than 40 acres. Sixty-one were between 40 and 79 acres, 25 were between 80 and 119 acres, and 13 were more than 120 acres, with the largest three being the Boylston farm, owned by nonresident Charles F. Adams (419 acres, Wellesley Street and South Avenue, later part of the Paine estate), the Fiske homestead (248 acres, North Avenue), and the Slack farm (225 acres, southeast part of Weston, later part of the Hubbard estate).
36. Of the 9,622 acres belonging to Weston farms in 1865, 5,732 acres (60%) were considered "improved." Of this, 2,582 acres were woodland. The use of other improved land was broken down as follows, listed here in order of acreage: English mowing hay, 1,756 acres, 1,611 tons of English hay, $47,205 value; wet meadow or swale mown hay, 757.5 acres, 721 tons of hay, $12,251 value; Indian corn, 261.25 acres, 7,406 bushels, value $10,981; potatoes, 112.25 acres, 10,923 bushels, $10,330 value; market gardening, 71.75 acres, $8,660 value; barley, 48.5 acres, 679 bushels, $1,015 value; rye 45 acres, 555 bushels, value $841, cranberries, 14 acres, 34 bushels, value $170; oats, 13 acres, 335 bushels, $335 value; turnips, 9.25 acres, 1,410 bushels, $922 value; cabbage, 5 acres, $835 value; winter squash, 4 acres, $655 value; beets and other vegetables, 3 acres, 686 bushels, $295 value; carrots, 3 acres, 1,241 bushels, $643 value.
37. Massachusetts Bureau of Statistics, *The Census of Massachusetts, 1875*, prepared under the direction of Carroll D. Wright (Boston: Albert J. Wright, 1876), vol. III, 163–64.
38. Wright, Carroll D., *The Census of Massachusetts, 1885* (Boston: Wright & Potter, 1887), vol. III, 373–74.
39. *The Census of Massachusetts, 1875*, op. cit., vol. II, 109–110.
40. Dates based on town tax records, which list the rope walk from 1885 to 1899.
41. Probably *Boston Globe*, about October 26, 1887. "General Paine in Weston: Reception Tendered Him by His Townspeople: How the General Has Endeared Himself to This Rural Community" (Coburn scrapbook #1, 331).
42. 1880 *TR*, 29.
43. Ibid., 30.
44. 1881 *TR*, 36.
45. 1883 *TR*, 37.
46. 1887 *TR*, 40.
47. *WDFPT*, May 13, 1904.
48. "Nineteen Workmen," Coburn scrapbook #2, 420.
49. *WDFPT*, June 7, 1901.
50. Coburn scrapbook #1, c. 1888, 314.
51. Coburn scrapbook #1, 346.

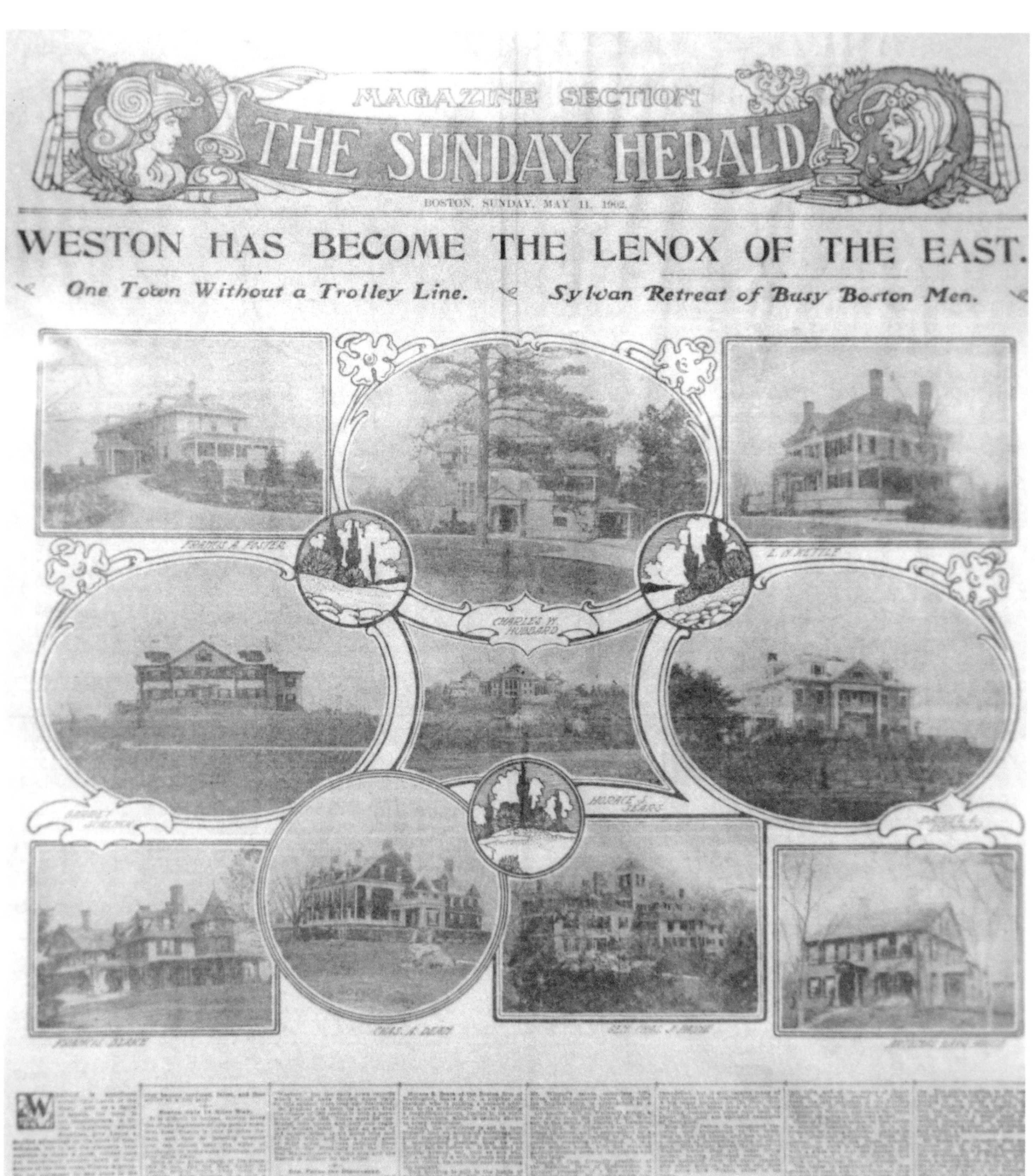

MAGAZINE SECTION

THE SUNDAY HERALD

BOSTON, SUNDAY, MAY 11, 1902.

WESTON HAS BECOME THE LENOX OF THE EAST.

One Town Without a Trolley Line. *Sylvan Retreat of Busy Boston Men.*

Figure 4-1. The Boston Sunday Herald *of May 11, 1902, proclaimed Weston the "Lenox of the East" and pictured nine estate mansions, most constructed within the previous decade.*

The Estate Era

Development of Country Estates

The period 1890–1915 is divided into four sections, each with its own chapter:

Chapter 4: Development of Country Estates (including Farming, Commerce and Industry, Architecture, Community Organizations and Census Data)

Chapter 5: Town Development in the Progressive Era

Chapter 6: Transportation: Trains, Trolleys, and the Automobile

Chapter 7: Patriotism and Nostalgia

By the 1890s Massachusetts was moving into the modern industrial age—an age dominated by the machine. Manufacturing processes traditionally performed by hand were yielding to human inventive genius. Modern machinery enabled factories to manufacture in great quantities. Large corporations were formed to promote efficient management and production. Financiers and executives poured their energy and financial resources into Massachusetts industries. The state reigned supreme in the area of fine textiles, woolens, boots and shoes, and high-grade writing paper.[1] Shrewd Massachusetts investors also recognized the need for better transportation, the usefulness of communication devices such as the telephone, and the increasing demand for heating fuel, electricity, and building materials. Many a new fortune was made in coal, steel, railroads, and mining.

The merchant princes and captains of industry were handsomely rewarded for their efforts. The turn of the century has been referred to as the "golden age of elegance" or the "era of excess," depending on one's point of view. These were the halcyon years before income taxes, world wars, depression, and inflation. In his book Crabgrass Frontier, *Kenneth Jackson has written, "The American nouveaux riches embraced the notion of conspicuous consumption in the form of ornamental real estate and decided that the most fashionable way to display great wealth was to invest in real estate of appropriately grand dimensions."[2] They sought out hilltops, shore fronts, and farms on which to build substantial estates. Their landholdings were developed in an era when domestic and garden labor was cheap and abundant.*

This chapter looks at country estates established in Weston in the late 19th and early 20th centuries. The movement of wealth into Weston took place not only because of the town's convenience and natural attractions but also because of carefully thought-out tax and spending policies.

Policies to Attract the Wealthy

Weston's country charms were well publicized by the 1880s, when Charles Jackson Paine's third victory in the America's Cup focused media attention on the town in which he maintained his country home. Dozens of Boston men of affairs followed Paine's lead. Some were attracted by the undulating

Statistics	1890	1895	1900	1905	1910	1915
Population	1,664	1,710	1,834	2,091	2,106	2,342
Change	+237*	+46	+124	+257	+15	+236
Number of Dwellings		344	383	425	462	509
Valuation	$2,191,080	$2,897,410	$4,435,527	$5,556,552	$6,924,245	$8,710,857
Tax Rate	$7.20		$8.00	$9.20	$11.20	$12.50

*change from 1885 to 1890

Chart showing changes in population, total valuation (combined real estate and personal property), and tax rate per thousand from 1890 to 1915. Population increased 41% between 1890 and 1915, while total valuation increased by almost 300%.

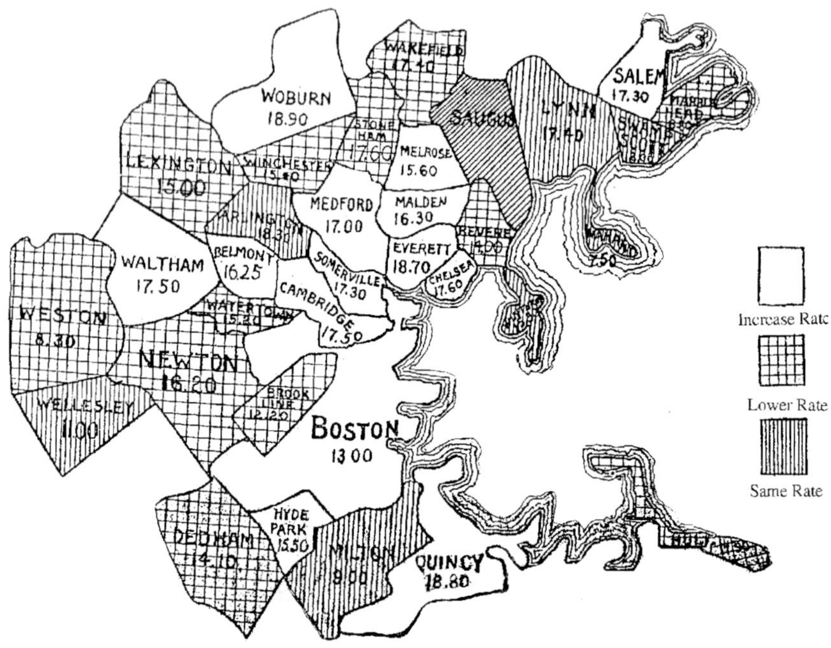

Figure 4-2. Tax rates were well known to those with major assets. This map from the 1897 Boston Herald *compares rates in various Boston suburbs. At $8.30 per thousand, Weston's was the second lowest.*

topography, picturesque scenery, and healthful air. Some valued convenience, with Weston just 12 miles and a half-hour train ride from their business or home in Boston. Three railroad lines with six stations provided connections to major cities throughout the East. Also appealing was Weston's low population density of only 1,834 inhabitants in 16.8 square miles in 1900.

Still others came to Weston as a result of town policies designed to attract wealth. One influential advocate of this growth strategy was Francis Blake, who in 1890 became the first estate owner elected as selectman. Blake's "liberal economy" meant spending money for improvements and at the same time keeping taxes down, as explained in this 1897 selectmen's report:

> The Board believes that the future prosperity of the town must depend largely upon the increase in real estate values. . . . If the belief is correct, it is obvious that a spirit of "liberal economy" should control the conduct of town affairs. In other words, there are many improvements, the cost of which might at first thought appear to be extravagant, but which ultimately would prove to be most profitable investments . . . it will probably be generally admitted that liberal expenditures for street-lights and sidewalks cannot fail to add to the prosperity of the town.
>
> On the other hand, it should always be borne in mind that a low tax rate, on a low valuation, is one of the strongest inducements to the class of persons from which it is most desirable that future additions to our community be drawn.[3]

At a time when individuals paid property taxes on both real estate and personal property, the tax rate was a critical pocketbook issue. In 1865, Boston had appointed an efficient assessor whose vigorous enforcement of the tax law had the unforeseen effect of driving wealth out of the city. Within five years, $14 million in taxable property had been transferred from Boston to eight suburban towns.[4] The shifting of assets continued for the next half century, with Weston among the favored recipients, along with Brookline, Cohasset, Dover, Falmouth, Groton, Hamilton, Lancaster, Lincoln, Manchester, Milton, Nahant, Wellesley, Wenham, and Westwood.[5]

Government studies of the money migration pointed out that assessors in small towns like Weston had every reason to underappraise property to attract and keep affluent residents. In May 1885, the Weston column of the *Waltham Free Press* noted, "The summer residents have moved in town this week to avail themselves of low taxes, which this town is noted for . . . *and a low valuation*." A 1902 feature story in the *Boston Herald* praised the beauties of the town and the "incompetence" of local assessors:

> . . . the fact [is] that the assessors are such poor mathematicians that when they get very high into the thousands in estimating the value of a man's property or in appraising his realty holdings, they become confused, falter, and then arrive at a full stop.[6]

A study by the Massachusetts legislature in 1908 reported that per-capita assessment on personal property in 14 suburban towns had risen from $432 in 1861 to $1,194 in 1905, while the rest of the state had seen a decrease from $247 to $219.[7] With municipal disparities growing ever larger, there was widespread support for the adoption of the state income tax on personal property in 1915. This was two years after passage of the 16th amendment to the federal Constitution allowing government to impose an income tax. Although intangible assets were no longer taxed at the local level, towns that had attracted wealthy residents in the years between 1865 and 1915 remained among the most affluent in the state.

Commerce and Industry (1890–1915)

While other communities viewed mills and factories as a source of needed employment, Weston leaders took the position that most such businesses were bad for the town. Their philosophy is clear as early as 1890, when the selectmen held a public hearing on the application of H.V. Partelow & Co. to expand its boatbuilding shop on the Charles River. Town residents protested vigorously that the operation was a source of physical danger to anyone crossing the South Avenue bridge and caused other problems including frequent roadway obstructions, escaping steam, and the noise of woodworking machinery.

Figure 4-3. Although the Weston selectmen generally opposed industry as "obnoxious to the pleasure of home life in the country," the Hook & Hastings organ factory was an accepted fixture on the rural landscape from 1889 to the mid-1930s. Weston native Francis Henry Hastings built the three-story wooden factory on his family farmland at North Avenue and Viles Street.

Furthermore, the shop was a "serious injury to the value of their estates and a drawback to the future growth of the town as a place for country homes."[8] The selectmen ruled against Partelow, who got the message and moved across the river to Auburndale.[9]

The selectmen's report on the hearing clearly sets out town priorities:

> . . . it is suggested that, if the present natural and municipal advantages of Weston are preserved, her future growth and prosperity must be largely due to the advent of persons seeking country homes in towns at a convenient distance from Boston. These advantages can be preserved only by a conduct of town affairs which shall ensure a low tax rate and a non-existence of business enterprises, which are obnoxious to the pleasure of home life in the country. Having regard to these facts, it is hoped that land holders will make their sales subject to such restrictions as will favor the prosperity of the town. [10]

H.V. Partelow & Co. was not the only business to leave town. A woolen knitting mill at South Avenue and Pine Street, a slaughterhouse on North Avenue, and a shoddy mill at Kendal Green all closed down in the 1880s or 1890s, in some cases after being destroyed by fire. In 1894 the board of health passed regulations designed to discourage or control businesses that were a danger to public health or emitted foul odors, including slaughterhouses and piggeries.

The Hook & Hastings organ factory appears to have been largely exempt from anti-industry bias. The widespread acceptance of the organ factory as good for the town can be attributed to its location on the north side, the high regard with which native son Francis Henry Hastings was held in the community, the factory's prestigious product, and its skilled workforce. Little controversy appears to have been generated by two small mills tucked out of the way on Crescent Street: the school furniture factory, which continued until 1917, and Charles Freeman's screen factory, which operated here from 1896 to the early 1930s. In contrast, the establishment of a quarry at Stony Brook was widely opposed, but efforts to purchase the land as a park were unsuccessful.

"Weston Has Become the Lenox of the East"

In early January 1897, the *Waltham Free Press* reported, "There seems to be little doubt that the land boom has reached Weston."[11] More than a dozen estate mansions were constructed in the 1890s and first three years of the 20th century. The most elaborate are pictured in a front-page story in the magazine section of the *Sunday Boston Herald* of May 11, 1902, headlined "Weston Has Become the Lenox of the East" and subtitled "One Town Without a Trolley Line" and "Sylvan Retreat for Busy Boston Men." This important article begins with a comparison with the Berkshire resort of Lenox:

> Weston is sometimes styled "The Lenox of the East," and as a figure of speech, the term is not inappropriate. A literal comparison would doubtless give Lenox a decided advantage on the score of magnificence, but in all the elements that make a quiet, retired (and yet convenient) country town of residences of the first class, Weston is probably not surpassed by any place in the state.[12]

Figure 4-4. Francis Blake's estate, Keewaydin, on the south side was pictured in several late-19th-century publications, including the 1890 History of Middlesex County.

The reporter refers to the street railway controversy, which had focused media attention on Weston:

> Weston isn't particularly prominent in the public eye. She seldom gets her name in the papers; unless some street railway company tries to invade her domain; then she protests with a vigor which emphasizes her conservative opposition to such innovations. She has an insular prejudice against such things, and a selfish desire (although a natural one) to keep her sylvan harmonies from the discord of clanging gongs and buzzing trolleys.
>
> "I believe in the principle of the 'greatest good for the greatest number,'" said one Westonite, "but Weston people are well supplied with travelling accommodations without having the street railways. There are so many places where a man can live if he wants to live on the line of a street railway, while there are so few places . . . if he does not want to live on . . . a street-railway."[13]

The reporter emphasizes the themes of quiet and convenience:

> It is difficult to believe, driving along the shady highways of this pretty town, that busy Boston is only 14 miles distant, and that by listening intently you can almost hear the whirr of machinery in wide-awake Waltham, only four miles away.
>
> Here is the great charm of the place. One is not, like the New Yorker at Lenox, several hours away from his business. From Weston it is only a little more than a half-hour ride, and at night, when a busy man returns to it the quiet seems to act as a balm to nerves drawn by business cares and by the manifold irritating noises of the large city.[14]

After describing the estates and central "village," the *Sunday Boston Herald* writer closes by giving credit to Francis Blake for Weston's up-building and lack of ostentation:

> He is the chairman of the board of selectmen, and as such has directed the affairs of the town in a manner to make it attractive to those who love a country life amid surroundings which are comfortable rather than magnificent, conservative rather than pronounced, beautiful rather than gorgeous.[15]

Estates in Weston: Overview

Some estate owners inherited their money. Others were self-made men who began work as clerks or errand boys right out of high school. Some were owners or managers of companies making shoes, paper, leather, textiles, and church organs; others were commission merchants who brokered textiles and bankers and investors in railroads, mines, and mills.

While the term "summer people" came to be used as a generic phrase referring to all wealthy newcomers, some estates were used every season except summer. Some were occupied year-round or used only as weekend and holiday retreats. In general, however, social life developed a seasonal rhythm marked by the arrival of the summer people each May and their departure after Thanksgiving. Their impact is expressed in this item in *The First Parish Calendar:*

> The city folk have nearly all departed, leaving behind only those whose homes seem as much here as elsewhere. The CALENDAR is sorry to see them go. They add vigor and color and joy to the town life, and existence is narrower and duller when they are gone.[16]

Owners spent winters in Beacon Hill or Back Bay town houses or traveled to Europe, Florida, or California.

Their houses ranged from Colonial farmhouses to the grand Italian villa built by Horace Sears atop a hill on Central Avenue. Most of the stylish new estate mansions were designed by architects from Boston. The following estate houses are listed in order of construction. Those still standing are marked with an asterisk.

Francis Blake (1873–75, Charles F. McKim, Queen Anne/Shingle style)

Charles T. Hubbard (1881–83, Francis Chandler, Shingle style)*

Francis Henry Hastings (1885, Hartwell and Richardson, Shingle style)*

James B. Case (1889, Ernest N. Boyden, Shingle style)*

Lorenzo N. Kettle (1892, Samuel Mead, Georgian Revival)*

Francis Foster (1895, James T. Kelley, Italian Renaissance)*

Garret Schenck (1898–1900, George F. Newton, Neoclassical)

Charles Dean (1898–1900, Hartwell and Richardson, Colonial Revival)

Brenton H. Dickson Jr. (1899–1901, A.J. Russell, Colonial Revival)*

Charles H. Jones (1901–02, J. Williams Beal, Shingle style/Colonial Revival)*

Robert Winsor (1901–03, attributed to A.J. Russell, Tudor)

Horace S. Sears (1900–02, Joseph Everett Chandler, Italian Renaissance)

Grant Walker (1910–12, Samuel Mead, Georgian Revival)*

Fannie Morrison (new facade, 1914, Samuel Mead, Georgian Revival)*

Mary Elizabeth Sparhawk Sears (1916, Samuel Mead, Neoclassical)*

Edward R. Peirce (1926–27, Coolidge, Shepley, Bulfinch and Abbott, Tudor)*

The architects of the following houses are unknown:

Bancroft C. and Anne Hubbard Davis (1882–83, Queen Anne)*

Benjamin L. and Charlotte Hubbard Young (c. 1885, Shingle style)*

William Munroe (1893, Shingle style)*

Daniel Ford (c. 1897, Georgian Revival)

Daniel Demmon (c. 1899, Georgian Revival)

Arthur Clapp (1902, Tudor)

Josiah Quincy Loring (date unknown)

Three existing farmhouses were restored by architects in the forefront of the historic preservation movement. Joseph Everett Chandler worked with Arthur Wellington, George C. Wales with Dwight Blaney, and Frank Chouteau Brown with Horace Phipps.

Sophisticated estate owners availed themselves of talented landscape designers who were among the pioneers in their profession. In the 1880s, Frederick Law Olmsted came out to Weston at the request of Gen. Charles Jackson Paine and Charles Townsend Hubbard to advise them on layout and plantings. His successor firm, Olmsted Brothers, laid out roads and the skating pond for the Winsor estate, designed Charles Wells Hubbard's Italian garden, and worked

Figure 4-5 (above). Many estate owners were self-made men who had no education beyond high school. Paper manufacturer Charles Dean ran away from home at age 16 to join the infantry in the Civil War and then began his career as a salesman. In this 1913 photograph, taken on his 69th birthday, he poses with his wife, Minnie; daughter Eleanor; and son-in-law Langdon Pearse.

Figure 4-6 (below). Arthur Wellington began work at age 14. He is pictured here with his three nieces, Linda (left), Margaret, and Virginia Wellington.

Figure 4-7. Estate life would not have been possible without inexpensive labor. The 1920 census lists 323 residents, or 14 percent of the town's population, as working for a "private family" or "private estate." This photograph is from the B.L. Young family album.

Figure 4-8. William Campbell (1889–1966) was the chauffeur and later caretaker for the Dean estate.

with Charles H. Jones for decades laying out roads and gardens and specifying plantings. Ernest W. Bowditch planned the Blake estate and its formal sunken garden, and Arthur Shurtleff (later Shurcliff) designed the Italian garden at the Horace Sears estate Haleiwa.

While the Sears and Blake estates, in particular, were known for their manicured grounds, most estate land in Weston was maintained in a more naturalistic style as fields, meadows, or woodland. Many properties were used as gentlemen's farms with all the necessary outbuildings and staff to keep livestock and take care of fruit trees and large vegetable gardens. The most unusual estate operation was Marian Case's Hillcrest Farm (later Hillcrest Gardens), which she began as a model farm using labor from a cadre of "Hillcrest boys."

The estate era in Weston and elsewhere would not have been possible without the inexpensive labor provided by immigrants from Ireland, Nova Scotia,

Wellesley Farms, Mass., is only twelve miles from Boston, and is reached by the express trains of the Boston & Albany Railroad in twenty-two minutes. Glen Farm is probably one of the most beautiful country spots in Massachusetts. It is interesting to note that such a thickly wooded country, so like the hills of New Hampshire, can be found in such close proximity to Boston.

Wellesley is considered by many of Boston's ablest physicians to be a very healthful place, it being situated in highlands and free from east winds. Glen House is situated on a high hill, and the rooms are naturally cool and airy.

GLEN HOUSE, GLEN FARM, WELLESLEY FARMS, MASS. Boston & Albany R.R.

Figures 4-9 and 4-10. To increase ridership, the Boston and Albany Railroad printed the brochure "Summer Homes," which described resort hotels along the B & A rail line. Glen House in Weston is listed under "Wellesley Farms" because of its proximity to that train station. (photo c. 1901–03)

The following chart lists "country places" over 25 acres established in Weston between 1848 and 1922. Some meet the definition of estate as "landed property usually with a large house on it." Farms are included when used as country homes by owners who were not dependent on agriculture for a living. Those with a succession of owners are listed only once, under the name of the first owner to purchase what was originally a farmstead.

Date Established*	Name	First Owner	Occupation	Approximate Size in Acres**	Later Owners	Main House	Book Chap.
1848		Augustus H. Fiske	lawyer	100–125	Andrew Fiske Gertrude H. Fiske Jr.	39 Concord Rd. (demolished)	16
1852		Josiah Q. Loring	gentleman	100	Abigail Loring	77 Loring Rd. (demolished)	2, 4
1856		Frederick T. Bush	merchant	75 by 1861	David W. Lane	72 South Ave. (demolished)	24
1863	Rocklawn	James B. Case	merchant, banker	121	Case sisters Arnold Arboretum	89 Wellesley St.	19
1867	Ridgehurst	Charles T. Hubbard	manufacturer	300 in 1900	Chas. W. Hubbard C. W. Hubbard Jr., Trustee	80 Orchard Ave.	22
1868		Gen. Charles J. Paine	lawyer, investor	658 in 1916	Paine Trustees (John B. Paine)	64 Highland St. (demolished)	18
1873	Keewaydin	Francis Blake	inventor	75	Benjamin S. Blake	44 Tamarack Rd. (demolished)	23
1873	Cherry Brook Farm	Herbert Merriam	gentleman farmer	170–230	Weston College	Concord & Merriam (demol.)	12
mid-1870s		Samuel G. Snelling	merchant	70	Samuel L. Thorndike Edward Merritt Beebe family	479 North Ave. 15 & 31 Round Hill Rd., Lincoln	12
1878		Edward J. Brown	merchant	60	Samuel Philip Miller	70 North Ave.	10
1878		Benjamin L. Field	merchant	35		99 South Ave (demolished)	24
early 1880s		Benjamin L. Young	businessman	114 in 1885 56 in 1900	B. Loring Young	4 Newton St.	24
1882	1. The Pines (home) 2. Ferndale Farm	Bancroft C. Davis Anne Hubbard Davis	lawyer	125 in 1891 213 in 1917	Pine Brook CC (farm)	59 Orchard (home)	22, 24
1889		Daniel Demmon	investor	179	Fannie Morrison Regis College	235 Wellesley St.	19
1891		Lorenzo N. Kettle	merchant	45	Walter H. Walker Francis P. Kirk	770 Boston Post Rd.	16
1891		James G. Freeman	investment banker	24 in 1900 46 in 1920	Trustees of C.J. Paine (Georgina Paine Fisher Howland)	55 Love Lane	17
1892	Doublet Hill	Francis A. Foster	merchant	49–58	Pine Brook CC	42 Newton St.	24
1893		William Munroe	broker	100	John M. Lilly William Renwick	10 Cherry Brook Rd.	12
1895		Francis Whitman	lawyer	65	Henry Whitman Francis Frazier Edward Collins	455 Concord Rd.	12
1896	Oak Ridge	Charles A. Dean	manufacturer	117	Walter Byron	67 Byron Rd. (demolished)	28
1897		Daniel Ford	publisher	120	Grant Walker Weston College	319 Concord Rd.	12
1897		George H. Nolte	broker/banker	70	G.H. Nolte children	Highland St. (demolished)	17
1897	Haleiwa	Horace S. Sears	manufacturer	55	Harry Bailey	327 Boston Post Rd. (demolished)	
1898	Chestnut Farm	Robert Winsor	investment banker	83 in 1898 472 in 1918	Weston Real Estate Trust	63 Winsor Way (demolished)	20

continued

1898		Garret Schenck	manufacturer	127	Hilbert V.N. Schenck	Bittersweet Lane (demolished)	28
1898		Theodore Dwight	librarian	56	Austin T. White Cambridge School	Lexington St. (demolished)	10
1899	Ivy Abbey	Brenton H. Dickson Jr.	cotton broker	28 in 1915	Edward M. Dickson	125 Highland St.	17
1901	Fillmore Farm	Charles H. Jones	manufacturer	270	Paul and Charles Jones Jr., trustees	458 Glen Rd.	27
1901		Arthur W. Clapp	manufacturer	85 in 1901 323 in 1927* *Weston and Wellesley	Edward R. Peirce Roger Babson	55 Westcliff Rd.	26
1907	Gateways	Arthur Wellington Louis Wellington	merchant broker	107	Danforth family	500 Wellesley St.	30
1908	The Old Elm	Dwight Blaney	artist	120	David Blaney	555 Wellesley St.	30
1909	Hillcrest Farm Hillcrest Garden	Marian Case	gentlewoman farmer	100	Arnold Arboretum	102 Wellesley St.	19
1909		A. Lincoln Filene	retailer	40		43 Coburn Rd. (demolished)	11
1911	Pine Rest	Horace Phipps Miss Alice Anthes	artist	33	Albert Speare	420 Concord Rd.	10
1921		Francis B. Sears Jr.	banker	66	Edwin and Rosamund Sears	21 Crescent St.	13
1922	Exmoor Farm	Marion Farnsworth	gentlewoman farmer	48 in 1925, 150 max	Lucy & Frank Carter	751 Boston Post Rd.	16

* "Date established" means date of original land purchase (not date of house construction)

**Approximate size. Because size of estates varied over the years, "approximate size" is an attempt to represent fairly the number of acres by either giving a date or choosing a number or range that stayed steady for many years.

Figure 4-11. One of Weston's early estate owners, Josiah Quincy Loring (1819–1862), acquired about 100 acres in the Loring Road area in the 1850s. Although his house at 77 Loring Road was demolished in 1956, the entrance into the property is still marked by granite posts and a well-crafted stone wall.

Italy, and elsewhere. Men worked as farm laborers, gardeners, hostlers, and coachmen while women were employed as chambermaids, cooks, nannies, and seamstresses. Many were dedicated to their employers and proud of their part in the smooth running of the estate. Employers in turn were kind to workers and their families. Although relationships were often cordial and long-lasting, they were based on a clearly defined class system.

Estate owners had a major impact on town government, schools, and private beautification efforts (described in the next chapter). They provided leadership and they provided money, in amounts large and small, for projects to enrich the town.[17] Commenting on the Bicentennial Pageant, which was free at a time when most towns were charging substantial admission fees, one outside observer described the sense of civic responsibility in this way:

> It would be difficult to suggest any other town where the fine spirit not merely of generosity alone, but of culture, refinement, idealism, artistic sense, [and] public and private obligation are so thoroughly pervasive or so handsomely exemplified.[18]

In addition to their public contributions, estate owners quietly took care of people in need and exercised a paternal benevolence.

Figure 4-12. J.Q. Loring's daughter Abigail was born in 1850. She never married and made Weston her home into the early 20th century. This photograph of her private study is one of a series documenting the fine interior furnishings of the Loring house.

While large estates were the most conspicuous sign of Weston's popularity for country homes, those with lesser pocketbooks also enjoyed its rustic attractions. There was a heavy demand for summer rentals, and families who summered at the beach often rented their Weston homes. Local farmers took in boarders. Two hostelries operated in the late 19th and early 20th centuries, the Glen House and the better-known Drabbington Lodge, which filled to overflowing each season with regulars from as far away as Minnesota.

Figure 4-13. After the Civil War, this 18th-century house at 168 Summer Street became part of the Loring estate and was occupied by John Martin (1849–1916), an Irish immigrant who worked as a tenant farmer. Martin's son Charles, pictured here holding the horse, later worked as the foreman for the Winsor estate. (Howes brothers photo, 1898)

Farming in Weston (1890–1915)

Agriculture remained the mainstay of the town's economy. Weston was the 193rd most populous town in the state in 1895 but ranked 52nd in agricultural production. That year, Weston had 143 farms broken down as follows: 104 general farms (average 64 acres), 13 dairy (average 76 acres), four egg and poultry (average 22 acres), four market gardens (average 22 acres), and three florists (average 1 acre), with the remainder classified as wood- or grass lots.[19] Ninety of the 104 general farms were still farmed by the owner. Agricultural products were valued at $245,704, the most important of which were dairy (34.5%) and hay (27%); followed by vegetables (11%); poultry (7.6%); animal products (5.86%); and fruits, berries, and nuts (4.55%).[20]

In 1905, the value of Weston's agricultural products was $335,663, with those contributing over 3 percent as follows: dairy (33.4%); hay, straw, fodder (19.5%); poultry products (11.8%); vegetables (9.95%); products from mines and quarries (9.6%); animal products (5.29%); and fruits, berries, and nuts (4.71%). Weston farmers produced 108,816 dozen eggs, the second highest of the 54 Middlesex County communities, and nearly 2.4 million gallons

Figure 4-14. John Martin worked the land owned by the Loring estate. His 16-year-old son, Charles, is hoeing at right. In the rear is the Martin house at 168 Summer Street. Route 128 now cuts through this farm field. (Howes brothers photo, 1898)

Figure 4-15. Ella Wyman McNutt picked strawberries on her family farm at the corner of Glen Road and Oak Street.

TELEPHONE 331-3 WALTHAM

JAMES BARTON

NEWTON STREET, WESTON

Market Gardener and Dealer in Live Poultry

Strawberry Plants for Sale

Figure 4-16. James Barton promoted his farm specialties in this 1909 advertisement.

of milk, the eighth highest.[21] Of note is the economic contribution of the new quarry later purchased by the Massachusetts Broken Stone Company.

The career of Samuel Warren exemplifies the trend toward specialized farms noted in earlier chapters. Warren lived his whole life on the family farm on Newton Street, which he took over in the mid-1850s at age 19. At his death in 1913 at age 78, his obituary in the *Boston Globe* called him a "recognized authority" on the cultivation of strawberries:

> He was one of the first men in this vicinity to see the value of specialization, and he has abandoned the other branches of truck farming to give almost his whole attention to the berries.[22]

One of his notable achievements was the development of fall-bearing plants. In 1905, the *Waltham Daily Free Press Tribune* reported that, at a late-summer exhibit at the Massachusetts Horticultural Society, veteran strawberry grower Samuel Warren showed some Pan-American strawberries that were "as delicious as if grown in June." In 1912 he reported picking 115 quarts after September 1, all of which found a ready market at a single hotel.[23] He added that, in some years, his plants bore ripe fruit as late as November 9, as well as producing as much fruit in June as any other variety. These accounts boosted another part of Warren's business, which was selling the plants themselves. In May 1911, the *Waltham Free Press* reported that "during the past three weeks, S.H. Warren has shipped the remarkable number of

60,000 strawberry plants to various parts of New England."[24]

Farmers continued to pasture their cattle over the summer in the area of Stow, Princeton, and Mount Monadnock.[25] It took about three days to herd the cattle out in spring and back again about November 1.

Deforestation continued into the 20th century. The *Waltham Daily Free Press Tribune* contains several reports in 1913 and 1914 of people buying woodlots and completely clearing them. Lots as large as 45 acres were purchased and woodchoppers would spend months cutting and sawing the lumber.[26]

Influence of Estate Owners on Agriculture

Estate owners varied in their approach to farming. At one end of the spectrum were men whose interest was limited to growing fresh vegetables for the dinner table and raising their children in a farm environment. At the other extreme were serious gentlemen farmers who focused their considerable intelligence and financial resources on raising purebred stock or improving yield and quality of market crops. Estate owners could afford to try new ideas and construct enormous state-of-the-art barns and outbuildings. They had the leisure and sophistication to keep up with scientific advances and the money to hire the skilled labor needed for a well-run farm.

Weston estate owners set about acquiring quality dairy stock, as indicated by notices such as this one in the *Waltham Free Press* in 1888:

> Ayrshire and Guernsey cattle of pure high grade, imported and registered, are a specialty at the Cherry Brook [Merriam Farm], . . . Case and Gen. Paine farms. No town in the vicinity of Boston, and some claim no town in the state, can exhibit more valuable and in every way desirable bovine herds than our own.[27]

About 1890, this article appeared in a Waltham newspaper extolling the virtues of General Marshall's new cow:

> If you have an eye to fine stock you can satisfy that curiosity by seeing the cow "Lucy" which has been lately purchased by Gen. J.F.B. Marshall of Kendal Green. She is of large frame, handsome as a picture, red and white, of Herford and Ayrshire grade, hair soft and silky with a bag which shows that three cans of milk per day can be produced, although the green field at present is very scarce, she is now milking at nearly that figure. The General has outdone his neighbors in this section who have some extra fine milkers and should be proud to own such a superior animal.[28]

Figure 4-17. With exhibits such as this, Marian Case's Hillcrest Farm (later renamed Hillcrest Gardens) was a perennial winner at Grange fairs and regional shows sponsored by the Massachusetts Horticultural Society.

By the early 20th century, dairying had become the most important branch of New England agriculture. Advances in production and milk safety favored those with money to invest. New tests made it possible to determine the butterfat content of milk from individual cows and to compare different breeds. Pasteurization required capital investment in expensive equipment, an investment most easily undertaken by larger dealers and a few serious estate owners.

In Weston, shoe manufacturer Charles H. Jones and lawyer Bancroft C. Davis both established model dairies incorporating the latest advances. Jones was a member and onetime president of the Guernsey cattle breeders association and was known for his champion bulls. He built his first dairy barn in 1903 and added a second, more up-to-date "testing barn" about 1914, where he housed pure-breed Guernseys and recorded their daily milk production. That year, Jones had 51 dairy cows and 12 bulls. Anne and Bancroft Davis developed the Ferndale Farm dairy. In 1910 they built a massive stone dairy barn furnished with state-of-the-art equipment and brought in farmer Frank Pope from Vermont to manage the operation. By 1915, Ferndale had more than 60 cows. By contrast, most Weston dairymen were small producers. As it became more difficult for them to process their own milk, they made increasing use of dealers who picked up milk cans at roadside collection points.

Both estate owners and general farmers were affected by the long and costly nationwide battle to wipe out tuberculosis in cattle, which involved the slaughter of animals by the thousands. In 1890, after he discovered his own small herd to be infected, Francis Blake delivered a paper on the public-health danger of drinking milk from infected cows. Other diseases also took a toll. In 1915, Herbert Merriam and his son, Charles, had to kill their entire herd of 60 prime cattle to prevent the spread of foot-and-mouth disease.

A few estate owners specialized in breeding horses. Francis Foster was a member of the New England Breeders Association, Charles Jones's daughters purchased and trained thoroughbred Kentucky bluegrass horses, and Ruth Dickson bred Morgan horses.

During this period, it was not uncommon for gentlemen farmers in Weston and elsewhere in New England to express concern about the comparatively low esteem in which agriculture was thought to be held, even by farmers themselves. They worried about the great number of young men leaving the family farm for other occupations. Marian Case sought to encourage interest in agriculture and prepare boys to be farmers by hiring them to work in the summer on her "experimental farm" and introducing them to the "scientific side of agriculture." Her "Hillcrest boys" kept journals and attended weekly lectures by well-known experts. Case's program was a mixture of hard work and education, with strong doses of idealism and patriotism. The boys were taught that "better help can be given to a nation with a plough than with a musket."[29]

Figure 4-18. Queen Anne was the dominant style of domestic architecture in Weston from the 1890s into the 1900s. No. 297 North Avenue was built for an employee at the organ factory. The variety of surface materials is typical of the style, as is the irregular massing and decorative porch detailing. (Photo c. 1900)

Figure 4-19. William N. Gowell, one of Weston's best-known builders, lived on Forest Street (now Conant Road).

Architecture (1890–1915)

The picturesque Queen Anne style spread throughout the country in the 1880s by way of pattern books and the country's first architectural magazine. The best Weston examples date from the 1890s. Queen Anne is one of the late-19th-century styles often referred to as "Victorian" because of its popularity during the long reign of the British Queen Victoria. Queen Anne houses have asymmetrical plans and irregular, steeply pitched roofs. Builders avoided plain, flat walls with liberal use of window bays, towers, recessed balconies, niches, porches and overhangs, and, for good measure, several different wall materials within the same plane. Window sashes could have decorative patterns or large single panes of glass. Spindle work, patterned shingles, and precut architectural details, all increasingly available because of expanded rail transportation, give the style its ebullient ornamental quality. Color was another essential element to the design. The variety of patterned surfaces is the distinctive feature of the George Stevens house at 297 North Avenue (early 1890s) and the Frank Murdock house at 302 Concord Road (c. 1894). The Henry Lewis Viles house at 300 Conant Road (1895) features a typical Queen Anne polygonal corner tower. Most examples of the style in Weston are simpler and can be identified by details such as spindle screens and turned porch posts. The shaped spindles have been called a product of America's love affair with the newly invented turning lathe.[30]

Shingle-style houses, first built in Weston in the 1880s, continued in popularity through the early 20th century. In the 1890s and early 1900s, many have gambrel roofs, for example, the William Munroe house at 10 Cherry Brook Road (1893), Drabbington Lodge at 135 North Avenue (1899), and Thurston "Cottage" at 153 North Avenue (1902). The Brenton H. Dickson Jr. house at 125 Highland Street (1900–01) and Charles H. Jones house at 458 Glen Road (1902–03) combine Shingle-style and Colonial Revival features.

Late-19th- and early-20th-century architects and builders drew on the full spectrum of architectural tradition for their creative inspiration. But while the Victorian era was characterized by a free mixing of styles, the subsequent Eclectic movement preferred relatively pure copies from each tradition as originally built in Europe or the colonies. The movement began in the late 19th century with fashionable houses built for wealthy clients by European-trained architects. Styles chosen by Weston estate owners included the Italian Renaissance, Neoclassical, Colonial Revival, and Tudor.

The Colonial Revival was popular not only for estate mansions but for all manner of smaller resi-

Figures 4-20 and 21. The Boston architectural firm of Hartwell and Richardson designed the main house (left), carriage house (below), and two other outbuildings for the Charles Dean estate, constructed in 1900–01. The gambrel roof and classical columns and balustrade on the porte cochere are typical of the Colonial Revival. (photo c. 1917)

dences as well. The general term "Colonial Revival" refers to the rebirth of interest in the early houses of the English settlements in the colonial (Georgian) and Federal (Adam) periods. Dutch colonial houses also provided prototypes. Interest was fueled in part by the 1876 U.S. Centennial and by the loss of important colonial landmarks like Boston's Thomas Hancock house, demolished in 1863. Americans looked back with nostalgia to the preindustrial age, but they also liked modern amenities like expansive interiors, flexible floor plans, interesting building shapes, and big porches. So in the late 19th and early 20th centuries, builders and architects borrowed freely from one or more early-American precedents to create their own eclectic mixtures. In Weston, Georgian Revival estate houses from the pre–World War I era include the Daniel Demmon house at 235 Wellesley Street (1900) before it acquired its new facade, the Lorenzo N. Kettle house at 770 Boston Post Road (1892), and the Grant Walker house at 319 Concord Road (1910–12). Also notable are architect Joseph Everett Chandler's houses for Abbie Andrews at 51 Church Street (1897) and Sarah Williamson at 98 Love Lane (1904).

The Tudor style is loosely based on late medieval English prototypes. Characteristic details include the high-pitched gable roof, facades with one or more cross gables, and decorative "half-timbering" usually executed in wood and stucco. The best early example, built for Arthur Clapp, burned in 1925. It was replaced by the house now known as Henderson House, which is a later version of the style as it evolved in the 1920s. One subgroup of Tudor, often referred to as Jacobethan, is patterned after late medieval buildings with Renaissance detailing. Weston has an excellent example, the Weston Public

Figure 4-22. The 1902 Arthur Clapp house had steep gables, half timbering, and diamond-paned windows characteristic of the Tudor style. It burned to the ground in 1925 and was replaced by a later Tudor example now known as Henderson House.

Figure 4-23. When it came time to build his own house in 1891, architect Samuel Mead (at right) chose a hilltop site on Pigeon Hill Road. Mead designed homes for estate owners and the emerging middle class.

Figure 4-24. Architect Harold S. Graves moved to Weston about 1900. He designed the stone tower for Fannie Morrison (now Regis College), remodeled Robert Winsor's barn for the Weston Golf Club, and planned many homes in the Meadowbrook Road area.

Library, completed in 1900 from designs by architect and local resident Alexander Jenney.

Samuel Mead and Harold Graves

Two versatile architects active in Weston in the Eclectic period were Samuel Walker Mead and Harold S. Graves. Mead (c. 1863–1946) never went to college and began his career in Boston as a draftsman for Ware and Van Brunt. He was introduced to Weston in 1883 when he designed a house for fellow Winchester native Robert Winsor at 309 Boston Post Road. After designing this relatively modest residence, Mead embarked to Europe for three years of travel and study as the second winner of MIT's prestigious Rotch Traveling Scholarship. On his return in 1887, he moved to Jamaica Plain and began a career with several well-known Boston firms including Cabot and Chandler and Cabot, Everett and Mead.

In the years after he settled in Weston, Mead fashioned estate mansions for Lorenzo Kettle, Grant Walker, Fannie Morrison (new facade), and Mary Elizabeth Sparhawk Sears. Three of his gracious Colonial Revival homes remain at 96 Church Street and 23 and 37 Webster Road. Mead's firm was responsible for the 1895 brick Weston High School, now Brook School Building A. More than 30 years later, Mead designed the yellow-brick Hillcrest barn at 135 Wellesley Street (1927). He also designed public libraries in Wayland and other suburban towns.[31]

Harold S. Graves (d. 1952) was a partner of James T. Kelley until the latter's death and also worked alone and with Thomas Epps. He moved to Weston about 1900 and built his own house at 23 Old Road about 1902. Like his contemporaries in the early 20th century, Graves was facile in many different styles including Italian Renaissance (for the theater at the Sears estate), Tudor (Regis Tower and 209 Meadowbrook Road), and Craftsman (143 Meadowbrook, which has touches of the Swiss chalet). He designed the distinctive English country cottage for Horace Sears's gardener at 23 Wellesley Street (1913) and notable small-scale Colonial Revival houses at 60 Wellesley Street and 10 Crescent Street.

Pre–World War I Subdivisions

Historians looking for the beginning of suburbanization often point to picturesque Llewellyn Park, New Jersey, designed by Alexander Jackson Davis in the 1850s, and to Riverside, Illinois, designed by Frederick Law Olmsted and Calvert Vaux in 1869. Up to that time, the trend had been for people to flock to the cities. Olmsted was among the earliest to write about the "clearly perceptible" reverse trend toward formation of suburbs, "especially affecting the more intelligent and more fortunate classes."[32]

Llewellyn Park introduced two new concepts designed to preserve rural character: the curvilinear road and natural open space at the center. The famous Olmsted & Vaux plan for Riverside also avoided the stiff and formal grid by using a system of curving roadways following the contours of the land. The plan aimed at creating a "village-like suburb with a sylvan domestic atmosphere."[33] The curvilinear street pattern, so unusual in its day, was chosen for a purpose, as explained here by Olmsted:

> . . . as the ordinary directness of line in town-streets, with its resultant regularity of plan, would suggest eagerness to press forward, without looking to the right hand or the left, we should recommend the general adoption, in the design of your roads, of gracefully-curved lines, generous spaces, and the absence of sharp corners, the idea being to suggest and imply leisure, contemplativeness and happy tranquility."[34]

Late-19th-century Weston was still a country town with little demand for this new type of suburban enclave. Neighborhoods like Maple Road/Wellesley Street, North Avenue, and the 600 block of Boston Post Road developed in linear form as landowners sold off lots on existing roadways or laid out short side streets to provide additional frontage.

In 1896–97, estate owner Horace Sears purchased 46 acres on Pigeon Hill and hired a Cambridge surveying firm to lay out Weston's first planned subdivision, using a curvilinear design of winding streets and culs-de-sac. Many of the original 17 generous-sized lots were sold to the town's slowly emerging professional class and to businessmen who took the Central Massachusetts Railroad into Boston. A simple loop road was used in laying out nearby Webster Hill, a similar neighborhood of handsome, solidly constructed homes that developed beginning in the 1910s.

Proximity to the Boston and Maine Railroad was a selling point in the town's second subdivision, Silver Hill, developed beginning in 1905. Here, capital was provided not by a single wealthy owner but rather by stockholders of more modest means who purchased shares in the Weston Land Association. A total of 89 lots were laid out along Silver Hill and Westland Roads, both semicircular streets with no through traffic. The effort to achieve a minimum lot size of at least 30,000 square feet reflects the vision of the developers rather than any town requirements.

Demand for house lots in Weston was not overwhelming, and one turn-of-the-century subdivision failed miserably. An 1898 plan for Glenfeld shows 80 lots along winding roads near the South Avenue bridge. Plans for street railways through the area, which might have increased demand, never materialized, and only a few lots were ever sold.

"Weston's Best Society"

In articles like this one from about 1890, the Weston column of the *Waltham Free Press* regularly described dances and social events given by the new elite:

> Mr. and Mrs. Robert Winsor entertained right royally at their residence on Central avenue. . . . A pavilion was erected for the occasion at the east of the house and was beautifully decked with ferns and Pine boughs and adorned with Chinese lanterns. Here the gay throng tripped the light fantastic far into the wee [small] hours of the morning to the entrancing melodies of Carter's orchestra. . . . Weston's best society was well represented.

In case readers did not know who Weston's best society might be, there followed a list of "distinguished guests." Newspaper items covered not only local parties but also Boston society events of interest to local readers. Some daughters of estate owners made their debut at age 18 and were feted at teas, parties, and debutante balls.

The town's inner social circle was well represented at the 1889 second annual Weston Tennis Club tournament on Labor Day at the courts of Horace Sears, Charles Kenney, and Robert Winsor. Sixteen couples entered, including members of the Paine, Fiske, Perry, Batchelder, and Coburn families. In the middle of the day a bountiful collation was served to players and enthusiastic spectators. The newspaper account added, "The costumes of the players were tasteful and appropriate, and rendered the scene one of rare beauty."[35]

In the early 20th century, fox hunts through Weston were conducted by the Middlesex Hunt Club, which had its headquarters in Lincoln. In one report of 1905, Charles Merriam II hosted a breakfast for 75 club members after the hunt.[36]

Community Organizations: Church, Fraternal, and Social Groups

Even a cursory reading of the Weston column in the *Waltham Daily Free Press Tribune* reveals a remarkable variety of festivals, social events, and

Figure 4-25. A production by the Weston Baptist Young People called "The District School" was held at that church during the pastorship of Rev. Harry Hinkley, about 1904–09.

entertainment. Leisure time had increased but automobiles were not yet available to provide easy transportation outside the community. As a result, church groups, lodges and secret societies, hospital aid societies, and clubs of all kinds flourished in the late 19th and early 20th centuries.

First Parish Church sponsored women's and men's groups as well as a literary club, which studied subjects like "the origin & development of the English novel" under the direction of Rev. Charles Russell.[37] Church suppers, called "Sociables," were put on by the Women's Benevolent Alliance monthly from September to June. Young people could not attend until they were in high school; then they could wait on tables and eat in the kitchen afterward. The June meetings featured strawberry shortcake or strawberries and cream for dessert and were usually held outdoors either at the Winsor, Sears, Case, or Francis Hastings house.

Beginning in 1891, the Young People's Union of the First Baptist Church sponsored regular programs at Town Hall. In less than a year, its membership increased from 18 to 70.[38] The 1894 series included stereoptican lectures on the Scottish highlands and the Catacombs. The Baptist Sabbath School held an annual picnic. By 1902, the Baptist church had a Men's Social Union, numbering 90 members, which met for lectures, debates, entertainment, athletic contests, and winter sleigh rides, all for the "mental and moral uplifting of Weston's young men."[39] The Ladies' Aid Society of the Methodist church was active at Kendal Green. Each Christmas season, all the churches and Sunday schools sponsored children's festivals, dramatic productions, and sales. The Methodist Society held "grand lawn fetes" with artistically arranged Japanese lanterns and ice cream and cake. The Epworth League of the Methodist church arranged community service projects. Beginning about 1911, the Weston Catholic Association began sponsoring occasional social events.

Hastings Hall, built by Francis Henry Hastings as a community center for organ factory workers and the Kendal Green neighborhood, was the location of concerts, lectures, and group meetings. The whist club gathered for card playing and the Shakespeare Club met every fortnight to study works like *Othello* and *Twelfth Night.*

Hook and Ladder #2 and Hose #1 held an annual supper of roast pig. Two fraternal orders, the Henry A. Upham and Pequod Lodges, sponsored literary and musical programs at regular membership meetings. The Firemen's Relief Association held fundraising events. For boys 15 and older, Edward B. Field and Alexander Jenney organized the Weston Boys' Club, which met at Field's house on the Post Road. They earned money to support the club by putting on programs at the Sears theater in Haleiwa, including a minstrel show and singing concerts. The high school had two troops of Camp Fire Girls.

Musical events included orchestral concerts at Weston High School, glee club concerts, piano recitals, vocals, and organ concerts. The Weston newspaper column lists a concert by the Wayland Military Band as well as a performance by the Weston Choral Union, with two soloists from Boston. The Choral Union was composed of the choirs of all the Weston churches and numbered about 50 voices.

The Weston Grange, Patrons of Husbandry, was formed in 1911 under the leadership of Edward P. Ripley, Master. Like the Upham and Pequod Lodges, the Grange conferred "degrees" in secret ceremonies attended only by members. Both men and women could join, with the women responsible for administering the "third degree." Grangers were predominantly farmers, although tradesmen, town employees, and some local professionals also belonged. Regular monthly meetings combined "wholesome entertainment" with education.[40]

Figure 4-26. The Ladies' Aid Society of the Methodist church sponsored concerts, church suppers, and lawn parties.

KENDAL GREEN M. E. CHURCH

LADIES' AID SOCIETY

Turkey Supper

WITH ICE CREAM AND CAKE

THURSDAY, JANUARY 18, 1906

6.30 to 8 o'clock. TICKETS 35 CENTS

Entertainment, Miss McLeod, Reader

Pinks and Candy For Sale

Weston M. E. Church,

CONCERT

Given by the CHOIR,

Assisted by Master CYRIL RAPER, Boy Soloist.

Wednesday Evening, Dec. 12th, 1906,

7.45 o'clock. Admission 25 cts.

LAWN PARTY

Weston Methodist Church

Kendal Green, Mass.

Tuesday, July 23, 1907, next night if stormy

ICE CREAM, CAKE, LEMONADE AND CANDY

Tickets 15 Cents.

Figure 4-27. In 1886, Friendly Society members with a theatrical bent formed the Norumbega Dramatic Club and toured neighboring towns. Standing: Miss Edith Coburn, Horace Sears, Arthur Milton, Will Coburn, Miss Elizabeth Viles, and Miss Alice Jones. Seated: Miss Ellen Jones and Mr. Anthony, the schoolteacher.

The Weston Grange socialized with Granges from nearby towns and held an annual fair each October. Newspaper reports describe the upper town hall decorated with potted palms from local greenhouses or autumn leaves and ears of corn. Lining the hall were booths with fine displays of fruits and vegetables. Tables were laden with jellies, canned fruits, cakes, and candy. Some years, there was a fortune-teller or a "fish pond." Suppers of cold ham, mashed potatoes, and apple pie with cheese were served in the dining hall, followed by an evening "peddlers' parade" or auction of vegetables.[41] Visitors could buy aprons and fancywork made by the Busy Bees, a group of about 20 Grange women who met weekly to sew for the fair.

Community Organizations: The First Parish Friendly Society

The most active and long-lived of these organizations was the First Parish Friendly Society, formed in 1885 "to promote friendly relations" and raise funds for building the stone church. At first membership was limited to members of First Parish and those "who attend its church services . . . and who are willing to be workers in its charities and social life."[42] By the 1890s, other Weston residents could also join in the fun, and the society continues today, although no longer under the auspices of First Parish.

The first president, Horace Sears, was the 30-year-old son of former minister Rev. Edmund H. Sears. When he achieved financial success, he built an estate mansion just east of the church that incorporated a theater used for Friendly Society productions. Sears and other founding members attracted men and women of varied social backgrounds, who contributed their energy and talent.

One of the first functions was a Fancy Dress Party held in the town hall in November 1886. Minutes of the society describe it as "the most brilliant party ever given in Weston." A newspaper account suggests the sense of excitement:

> Instead of the usual collection of nuns, fairies, undines and harlequins, the good people of the neighborhood assembled in the guise of characters taken entirely from American literature and history. Two hundred roles were given out by the indefatigable committee. . . . There followed desperate rummagings in garrets and trunks in search of ancient finery; and an overwhelming demand was made upon the distracted village librarian. Everyone had a part to study up, and a costume to arrange. When the eventful evening arrived, all the world of Weston stood on tiptoe. The well-known forms and faces as they entered the town hall and were announced by ushers, seemed strangely unlike themselves, and yet as strangely familiar. Like old friends whom we had known and loved, laughed and cried over, and yet had never expected to meet outside of the pages of the books in which they figured.[43]

Figure 4-28. Friendly Society productions were originally held in the old town hall, in the room shown in this 1899 photo. (Names listed with photo credits)

Processions and a series of tableaux from "The Courtship of Miles Standish" were followed by dancing and refreshments.

By 1891–92, the society was publishing an annual program listing twice-monthly entertainments such as plays, fancy-dress balls, lectures, variety shows, holiday parties, dances, and pencil games. The group put on spelling matches, slide shows, poetry readings, card parties, musicales, story readings, programs on travel, and debates on issues of local and national interest, such as "Shall Women Vote?" They discussed summer vacations, village improvements, missionary work, Arctic explorations, and Christmas in the olden days.

Figure 4-29. The theater wing at the Horace S. Sears estate, Haleiwa, was the first part of the Italian Renaissance mansion to be completed. A reported 150 to 200 neighbors and friends attended the formal opening on January 18, 1901, the approximate date of this photograph.

In the spring of 1900, the society put on a minstrel show. The Waltham papers provided a detailed account, including the apparent effort to utilize this form of entertainment without offending anyone:

> The striped coat, flapping straw hat, yawning carpet bag, umbrella and slipper; the cadaverous spectacles (which he looked over, instead of through, for fear he should wear them out); in short, the whole gaunt figure of the Rev. Slim Jim will never be forgotten. . . . The local touches and home brewed jokes were capital, accomplishing the sometimes difficult feat of combining fun and humor with delicacy and kindly regard for everyone's feelings. The minstrel introduction by "Eph" served to present the "colored brederen" to their appreciative audience.[44]

In one scene, Mr. Bingo Bink satirized the delicacy of the town's progeny "who have to be conveyed to school in barges to the tune of $3000 a year."

That fall, an imaginative dramatic program took its inspiration from advertising:

> About seventy persons were present, and they were well entertained for an hour and a half by twenty-one tableaux, illustrating advertisements that have been widely published during the last six months. The best of them were perhaps these:

> Queen quality shoes, Quaker oats, Fairy soap, Sozodont, Whitman's chocolates, Leibigs extracts, . . . and Dent's toothache gum.[45]

Like the minstrel show, the concept of a "poverty party" was not politically incorrect at the time. This Friendly Society party of 1905 was attended by 60 couples, including some of the town's wealthiest residents:

> Some of the characters were very unique. Mr. Jennie (sic) . . . the mechanical toy peddler was a decided hit, as was C.H. Fiske, Esq. as the ragman; Mr. Chandler as the vender of the Simple Life, A.H. Sibley as the Jew peddler, Mrs. Arthur Russell as the street musician; Miss Carrie Merriam as Salvation Army girl; Miss Ware in costume of newspaper; Mrs. W.H. Coburn as the pan holder woman; and Mrs. Jennie as the apple woman were some most appropriately costumed. Mrs. Charles Paine, Miss Florence Coburn, Miss Carrie Merriam and Miss Petty (sic) Lane received in rags. In one corner of the hall a jail had been arranged and anyone appearing in evening clothes was arrested. Mr. H.S. Sears and H.S. Bailey were thus treated but were later released on bail furnished by the ladies, 25 cents wooden money.[46]

After 1901, dramatic productions were held at Haleiwa, dances and parties at the town hall, and lectures at First Parish chapel. A sample annual program card for 1908–09 is representative of the schedule:

October 13: Reception and Dance, at Town Hall
October 27: Travels Abroad by Alfred W. Cutting, at Haleiwa
November 10: Vaudeville at Haleiwa
November 24: Old Weston Houses, at First Parish Chapel
December 9–10: Dramatics at Haleiwa
December 31: New Year's Eve, at Town Hall
January 12: Weston Home Journal, at chapel
January 26: "The Courtship of Miles Standish," at chapel
February 13: Hunt Ball, at Town Hall
February 23: Old Folke's Concert, at Chapel
March 9: Card Party at Haleiwa
April 1: April Fool, at Town Hall
April 13: Guessing, at chapel
April 28–29: Dramatics, at Haleiwa[47]

By 1914, membership in the Friendly Society had risen to 252. The increase in automobiles and telephones and the advent of movies and radio gradually changed social habits. The number of events and gatherings decreased, but what they lacked in frequency they made up in amount of work and preparation. The two annual dramatic productions became the major focus. In 1915 *A Nautical Knot* was the society's first venture into musical comedy, with a cast of 12 principals and a chorus of 21 mixed voices.[48] The success of this production marked the beginning of a new custom. The society presented musical comedies with multiple performances to raise money for Waltham Hospital, First Parish Church, and other organizations, beginning with the 1919 production of *The Red Mill*, discussed in chapter 8.

Figure 4-30. Ornate brackets frame the stage of the 200-seat theater at Haleiwa. For almost two decades, Friendly Society performances were given here or at Town Hall.

Figure 4-31. Dramatic and musical productions of all kinds were held at Haleiwa, many of them open to the public.

Census Data

The 1900 U.S. census reflects changing times. In the three decades from 1870 to 1900, the number of farmers (a category reserved for farm owners) decreased by 40 percent from 125 to 75. They were replaced in part by 21 men listed as "farm managers." Service occupations increased. The number of coachmen jumped from 5 in 1870 to 32 in 1900, with lesser rises in the number of gardeners, hostlers, and housekeepers. Trades like the making of boots and shoes, pottery, sash and blinds, and harnesses had disappeared in Weston by 1900, while new ones like plumber and electrician had not existed 30 years before. At least 35 Weston men worked at the organ factory, by far the largest single employer. Overall, the census reflects a remarkable increase in the variety of occupations, from about 50 different male jobs in 1870 to well over 100 in 1900, and from about 9 female job categories to 20. Women were working as teachers, clerks, landladies, librarians, factory workers, stenographers, bookkeepers, milliners, "typewriters," and artists, as well as domestic servants, the largest employment category.

The 1915 state census divides occupations into the following nine categories: agriculture (266 males, 1 female); extraction of minerals (20 males); manufacturing and mechanical industries (120 males, 11 females); transportation (66 males, 3 females); trade (86 males, 2 females); public service (21 males); professional service (54 males, 38 females); and domestic and personal service (41 males, 206 females); clerical (30 males, 26 females), for a total of 710 males and 287 females.[49]

Previous chapters have noted the influx of Irish immigrants into Weston by 1850 and immigrants from Nova Scotia and nearby Canadian provinces in the 1870s and 1880s. In 1895, 36 percent of Weston residents had two foreign-born parents, and 44 percent of residents had at least one.[50] The 1900 census records that about 27 percent of Weston residents were foreign born: 12% Canadian (217), 8% Irish (138), 3% Scandinavian (45 Swedish, 2 Norwegian, 2 Danish), 2% English (44), under 2% Scottish (30), and smaller numbers from Poland/Russia (11), Germany (5), Italy (4), France (2), Dutch Guiana (1), Hungary (1), and Armenia (1). Weston had 13 black residents in 1905.

The years 1900 to 1920 were dominated, on a national scale, by immigration from Italy. In 1900 Weston had only four residents who had been born in Italy. By 1920, that number had climbed to 25. In addition to the relatively small number of Italian residents of the town, Italian laborers were employed in all major public works projects in the early 20th century, including the building of the Weston Aqueduct and Reservoir and elimination of grade crossings at Weston and Cherry Brook Stations. Items in the Waltham papers point specifically to their nationality in items like: "A gang of Italians are at work on the Snake Rock property preparing to lay a spur track" and "A large Italian shanty has been built in the woods . . . to accommodate the workmen engaged on Grant Walker's new house."[51] In 1905 there was a brief strike among town cemetery workers, who protested the hiring of Italian workers to assist regular employees in getting the grounds into shape:

> Seven of the nine regulars refused to labor with the natives of sunny Italy and struck. They came around again the next day and Mr. Cooper told them they could go to work at once if they chose, otherwise they were done with the job so long as he was superintendent. They went to work again and all is peaceful.[52]

For many years, the only Italians living in Weston were those who came in the early years of the 20th century, many of whom worked on large estates. Later, according to one longtime resident of Italian descent, anyone with a foreign surname had trouble

Figure 4-32. Italian workers building the Weston Aqueduct and Reservoir were housed in shanties in the "Italian Camp" on Ash Street. This photograph was taken by the Metropolitan District Commission in August 1902.

buying property.

Notes

1. Hammond, John W., "Twentieth-Century Manufactures (1890–1930)" in *Commonwealth History of Massachusetts,* chapter XII, vol. V, 371.
2. Jackson, Kenneth T., *Crabgrass Frontier: The Suburbanization of the United States* (New York, Oxford: Oxford University Press, 1985), 88.
3. 1897 *TR,* 29–30.
4. Ecker, Deborah, "The Pocketbook Issue That Attracted Wealthy Boston Taxpayers to Weston in the Late 19th Century," *WHSB,* spring 1996.
5. Ibid., 4.
6. "Weston Has Become the Lenox of the East," *Boston Sunday Herald,* May 11, 1902.
7. Ecker, op. cit., 6.
8. 1891 *TR,* 27.
9. According to a letter in the Blake Papers (MHS, Box 64), the boat factory and its contents were totally destroyed in a fire on September 23, 1892.
10. 1891 *TR,* 27–28.
11. *WFP,* January 29, 1897. Two months later, the columnist wrote again that real estate was "in great demand," and "is the subject of considerable business." (*WFP,* March 12, 1897)
12. *Boston Sunday Herald,* May 11, 1902.
13. Ibid.
14. Ibid.
15. Ibid.
16. *The First Parish Calendar,* November 15, 1893, vol. I, no. 2.
17. Major benefactor Horace Sears contributed $20,000 toward the cost of the new town hall and added extra money for furnishings when the project went over budget. Francis Blake used his own money to construct a bridge over the Charles River to Riverside Station. Grant Walker, Caroline Case Freeman, and others gave large endowment funds to purchase library books. Francis B. Sears and Gen. Charles J. Paine helped set up the firemen's relief fund. The Paines and Winsors gave pictures to adorn the walls of the new 1895 schoolhouse, Charles J. Paine endowed a scholarship paying for freshman year at either Harvard or MIT, and Miss Marian Case gave substantial prizes for the best English themes. One year, Robert Winsor and Horace Sears gave money to provide each pupil with a year's subscription to a magazine fitted to his or her interests.
18. Adams, Warren P., *Journal of Education,* as quoted in *WDFPT,* November 6, 1914.
19. *Census of the Commonwealth of Massachusetts, 1895,* prepared under the direction of Horace G. Wadlin, (Boston: Wright & Potter, 1896–1900), vol. VI, 761.
20. Ibid., 266. Wood products, meats and game, greenhouse and nursery products, liquors and beverages, cereals and other food products each accounted for under 3 percent.
21. *Census of the Commonwealth of Massachusetts, 1905* (Boston: Wright & Potter, 1909), vol. IV, 57, and charts organized by product category.
22. *WDFPT,* October 3, 1913, as reprinted from the *Sunday Boston Globe.*
23. *WDFPT,* October 4, 1912.
24. *WDFPT,* May 9, 1911.
25. *WDFPT,* November 2, 1900.
26. For example, see *WDFPT,* February 20, 1914.
27. *WFP,* 1888 (Coburn scrapbook #1, 345).
28. The notice continues, "The purchase was made from John F. Dodge of South Lincoln, who prides himself on owning and selecting for other parties superior stock for milkers. The proof is in the sales made by him to Kendal Green residents."
29. Case, Marian, "The Third Summer at Hillcrest Farm," 1912.
30. Massey, James, and Maxwell, Shirley, *House Styles in America* (New York: Penguin Studio, 1996), 131.
31. His name appears in Whithey's *Biographical Dictionary of American Architects (Deceased),* which noted that Mead would be "... remembered for his work in the field of residence design" and planned "numerous suburban houses in the rambling and picturesque style of that period." Mead lectured at MIT's school of architecture from 1889 to 1915.
32. Newton, Norman T., *Design on the Land: The Development of Landscape Architecture* (Harvard University Press, 1971), 465. Newton quotes from "Riverside, Illinois," *Landscape Architecture,* 21 (July 1931), 257–91.
33. Ibid.
34. Ibid., 466–67.
35. *WDFP,* September 6, 1889.
36. *WDFPT,* late September 1905, October 29, 1909, and November 5, 1909.
37. Sears, Horace, "A Letter from Home—1883," reprinted in *WHSB,* March 1984, 4.
38. *WDFP,* January 1, 1892.
39. *WFP,* May 23, 1902.
40. *WDFPT,* May 2, 1919.
41. *WDFPT,* October 1913 and October 1919.
42. Friendly Society bylaws.
43. "Fancy Dress Party in Weston," unknown newspaper (probably *Waltham Daily Free Press*), November 3, 1886.
44. *WDFPT,* May 11, 1900.
45. *WDFPT,* October 26, 1900.
46. *WDFPT,* January 20, 1905.
47. Every member was entitled to two tickets for each event. Ticket distribution for dramatic performances was handled by the drama committee, and for all other meetings, guest tickets were limited to 25.
48. "Seventy-Five Years: A History of the First Parish Friendly Society of Weston, 1885–1960."
49. The Commonwealth of Massachusetts, *The Decennial Census, 1915,* prepared under the direction of Charles F. Gettemy (Boston: Wright & Potter, 1918), 278–79.
50. *Census of the Commonwealth of Massachusetts,* 1895 (Boston: Wright & Potter Printing Co., 1896), vol. III, 48.
51. *WDFPT,* April 1900 and June 16, 1911.
52. *WDFPT,* October 6, 1905.

Figure 5-1. When this photograph was taken in May 1908, the wooden former high school building on School Street was being used as a grammar school. Note the decorative detailing on the porch. Back row: Elizabeth McAuliffe, Margaret Leadbetter, Frederick Ryan, Daniel Compton, Mary Connors, Katie Belle Cameron, Mildred Barton, Mary Anderson, and Philip Connors. Middle row: Virginia Giles, Luella Hastings, twins Beatrice and Lagretta Lane, Pauline Coburn, Florence Washburn, Hazel Hobbs, Falconer McCullough, Evelyn Bartlett, A. Lenore Crouse, and Warren Eaton. Front row: Priscilla ___, Dorothy ___, Grace Ketchin, Isabelle___, C. Francis Whittemore, Carroll Harde, Spencer Whittemore, Edward Cain, Lewis Stevens, Helen Livermore, Lawson Foote, Crescenzo Sautianosua, Warren Foote, and Richard Upton.

The Estate Era
Town Institutional Development in the Progressive Era

During the 25 years from 1890 to 1915, often referred to as the Progressive Era, state and local governments tackled issues of public health, safety, and welfare. In 1890 Weston had no paid policemen, fire protection was in its infancy, and sanitary regulations were virtually unknown. Town expenditures totaled about $40,500. By contrast, the 283-page town report of 1915 contains the reports of the Superintendent of Moth Work, Swimming-pool Committee, Park Commissioners, Tree Warden, Board of Fire Engineers, Agent and Milk Inspector, Inspector of Slaughtering, Inspector of Animals, and Plumbing Inspector, all positions that did not exist 25 years earlier. The town had centralized its schools, redesigned the town center, and built two schoolhouses, a library, and two fire stations. Budget expenses in 1915 were almost $170,000.

During this period, the Weston Village Improvement Society was founded to work privately with local government to beautify the town and introduce modern amenities. Although one of its first goals was planting shade trees, the organization did not stop there. To provide water for sprinkling the streets and electricity for streetlights, private shareholders established the Weston Water Company and Weston Electric Light Company. Concerns about the appearance of the center culminated in the Town Improvement Plan of 1912, which created the town common. Always, town leaders balanced the cost of improvements against possible increases in the tax rate, which might scare off wealthy residents.

Figure 5-2. Alfred Leslie Cutting (1868–1926) was a selectman from 1900 to 1925.

Continuity of Leadership

By the mid-19th century, Weston had a tradition of choosing one selectman from the north side of town, one from the center, and one from the south. For decades, the north was represented by a farmer, the center by a middle-class businessman, and the south by an estate owner.

The period 1890 to 1915 was one of remarkable quality and continuity of leadership. North Avenue farmer Nathan Fiske, son of longtime selectman Alonzo Fiske, held the post of selectman for 25 years, from 1882 to 1884 and 1891 to 1912. When he retired, the town report had these words of praise:

> . . . he has displayed courage, independence, fairness, and good judgment. . . . It is a true and strong tribute to the official life of Nathan S. Fiske that he is not known to have a single enemy in the town.[1]

Henry J. Jennison of Boston Post Road was a selectman from 1889 to 1899. Jennison's Boston firm, Train and Jennison, was involved in real estate, insurance, and mortgages. He was followed by Alfred L. Cutting, who served until 1925. Cutting was the third generation of his family to operate the general store in the town center and was described as "progressive, zealous, and capable."[2]

South-side estate owner Francis Blake held the position for two decades, from 1890 until 1910, and was succeeded by his nephew B. Loring Young. When Blake resigned in 1910 due to ill health, the selectmen wrote: ". . . our splendid reputation throughout the Commonwealth is largely due to his ability in the administration of the affairs of the Town."[3]

Advances in Public Health

By 1886, the state Board of Health was responsible for control of epidemics, prevention of offensive trades, inspection of food and drugs, disposal of sewage, and protection of water supplies.[4] Weston had a local board of health beginning in 1888.[5] Its first annual report of 1890 begins with the boast that "Weston has always ranked as one of the healthiest towns in the State."[6]

By the 1890s, the germ theory of disease was fairly well established, and the Weston board began educating residents on the spread of germs through contaminated water supplies and contaminated milk. They traced a case of typhoid fever to a privy vault only 12 feet from the family well.[7]

By 1891, state law allowed local boards of health to regulate businesses hurtful to inhabitants or dangerous to public health. By 1894, the Weston Board of Health adopted rules to protect drinking-water supplies and minimize noxious odors. Swine had to be kept where they would not cause a nuisance. New slaughterhouses required a permit and established ones had to be kept free of offensive smells. Wastewater could not be emptied onto streets or sidewalks. Beginning in 1895, feeding city "swill," or garbage, to pigs was not permitted between May 1 and November 1 of each year.

Measures were introduced to improve the health of children. By 1893 the town was paying for any unvaccinated child to be protected against smallpox. Smallpox cases were rare; but after an outbreak in Boston, voters in 1899 required all Weston children entering school to be vaccinated.[8] Contagious diseases included diphtheria, measles, typhoid fever, scarlet fever, whooping cough, and meningitis. Schools were closed for weeks every year because of outbreaks. Infected houses were thoroughly fumigated with formaldehyde gas, "as approved by the highest authorities."[9] The board of health made continuing advances in early diagnosis, quarantining, and disinfection. In 1910, the board reported the first four cases of infantile paralysis (anterior poliomyelitis), a mysterious and much feared disease. There were no additional cases until 1925. The 1915 board of health report deplored that year's epidemic of measles, with 129 cases in a population of about 2,100. Four cases of diphtheria resulted in the death of one child at a Gypsy camp on Loring Road.

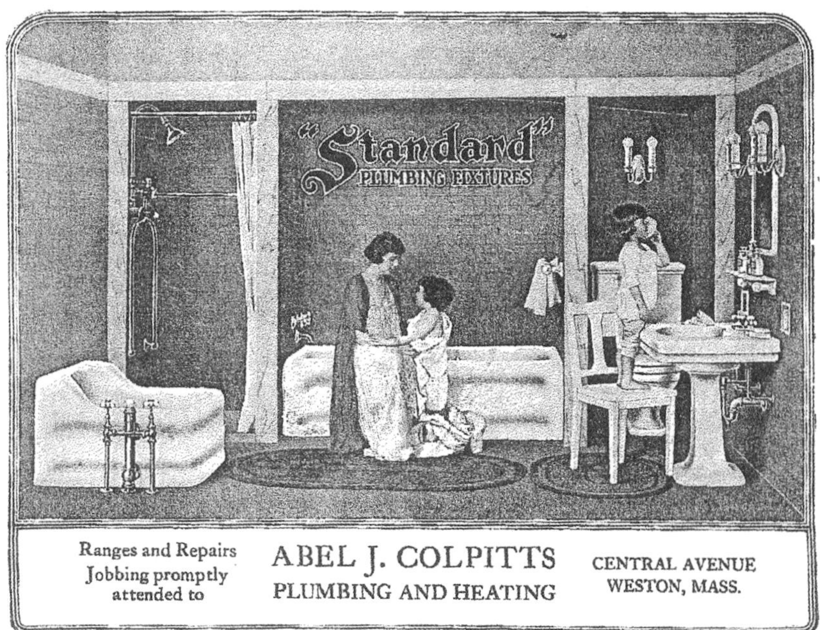

Figure 5-3. At the turn of the century, most Weston houses had no running water, no electricity, and no toilet facilities except outhouses. Arthur L. Hersum was the first plumber to be listed in town directories, in 1901. Abel J. Colpitts opened his business in the early 1920s.

In 1907 a teacher was assigned to inspect the sight and hearing of public school students. Many pupils were fitted with glasses for the first time. One year later, the school committee appointed local resident and town physician Frederick T. Hyde to act as school doctor in accordance with a new state statute. Soon the "universally condemned common drinking cup" had been replaced by drinking fountains. All schoolchildren were inspected for physical difficulties like tooth decay, bad nutrition, and poor eyesight and hearing.

In the second decade of the 20th century, demands on the Weston Board of Health increased steadily. Higher sanitary standards were adopted, as noted in the 1910 town report:

> Conditions that a few years ago went unnoticed have to-day, owing to our more enlightened view of things and higher standards of living, become important and objectionable.... There is a great deal of work to do in Weston in standardizing the homes, the barns and yards, and, greatest of all, the way of living of our families. [10]

The board initiated a campaign against flies and their breeding grounds. They began inspecting water closets, bathtubs, and sinks, which were becoming increasingly common in new and existing houses by the 1910s.

In another health-related decision, the town voted in 1896 to spent $250 a year to establish the Weston Free Bed at Waltham Hospital. Because of the subsidy and "valuable charitable assistance" from citizens of the town, the hospital agreed to care for all needy Weston residents who went there for treatment.[11]

Beginning in the late 1880s, local boards of health were required to monitor contagious diseases in animals, particularly pleuropneumonia and tuberculosis among cattle and glanders in horses. In 1897, the post of Inspector of Cattle and Provisions was created to examine the condition of barns and check cattle for disease. Inspector E.O. Clark reported positive results in 1900:

> I find a marked improvement . . . in the health of the cattle, and also in the sanitary condition of the barns. Owners of cattle realize more and

more that pure air, sunlight and exercise are as essential to the health of their stock as to that of human beings.[12]

Following passage of a state pure food and drug act, an Inspector of Dressed Meats began examining the carcasses of animals slaughtered for food.

In 1912, the Weston Board of Health voted to take advantage of a new laboratory system set up under the auspices of the Massachusetts Institute of Technology. The Cooperative Board of Health provided a milk inspector, bacteriologist, and plumbing inspector shared by eight communities. Each month, milk of licensed dealers was tested at random for richness and possible adulteration, filtered for dirt, and examined microscopically for bacteria.[13] Milk with a bacteria count of less than 10,000 per cubic centimeter was labeled "certified." In 1914, for the first time, the milk inspector recommended that milk fed to children be pasteurized to prevent spread of tuberculosis, "unless it comes from dairies where all cows are tuberculin tested at least once a year."

Other health dangers were not addressed during this period. Industrial accidents were commonplace, particularly at the Waltham Trap Rock Company but also at the chair and organ factories. Several laborers were killed during construction of the Weston Aqueduct. Train accidents and problems with runaway horses and overturned carriages were the cause of many, and sometimes fatal injuries.

Centralization of Schools

By 1891, the school committee reported that the six district schoolhouses had "seen their best days."[14] A lengthy study found that the Town of Concord had abandoned its scattered primary schoolhouses and built new schools in the town center. Children living beyond a certain radius were transported at the town's expense. Other Boston-area schools had made similar changes, in each case erecting "model buildings" equipped with the most up-to-date heating and ventilation systems.[15]

The study committee stressed the educational advantages of centralized schools:

> *First:* Equal advantages to scholars for all parts of the town.
>
> *Second:* More regular average attendance irrespective of the weather.
>
> *Third:* Better buildings, better ventilation, better equipment, better janitor service.
>
> *Fourth:* As a consequence, more enthusiasm, on the part of teachers and pupils, more efficiency, and the added stimulus which comes from increased educational life and energy.
>
> *Fifth:* Better facilities for superintendence and supervision.
>
> *Sixth:* Better grading and classifying.[16]

Figure 5-4. Advocates of centralized schools promoted the advantages of grouping children by grade. Of the six district schools, only #4 on North Avenue (shown here) and #5 on South Avenue continued in use after the 1893 reorganization.

A further impetus for change was the need for a larger school at Kendal Green, a need that could be eliminated if the centralized system were adopted. The 1892 town report addressed fears about young children being transported so far from home and about potential declines in property value.

The centralized system was implemented in 1893. By 1894, four of the six district schools had closed and the pupils were being transported to the 1878 high school on School Street.[17] School #4 on North Avenue and #5 at South Avenue remained in use for grades 1–6 because of strong neighborhood support. They were under the charge of two of the best-known and most respected teachers of the time, Miss Anna Coburn and Miss Elizabeth Viles.

School Transportation

With centralized schools, Weston began providing transportation for pupils living more than a mile away. Five-year-olds to high school seniors rode together in horse-drawn barges with open sides and two long seats facing each other. Unruly students were kept in line by teacher or student monitors.

In winter, transportation was by sleighs called pungs. In *Growing Up in Weston,* Phil Coburn recalled that the pungs had straw on the floor and heavy buffalo robes to put over the knees. Names painted on the side had no apparent meaning—for example, the one he rode in said HERE YOU HAVE IT in large letters. In his oral history, Jack Williams recalled what happened when there was not quite enough snow:

> . . . when they came to a bare spot in the road, the monitor would tell us little kids to get out and stand by the side of the road. The big kids would push the barge across the black spot, and when

BOSTON AMERICAN, SUNDAY, FEBRUARY 21, 1915.

THE SHAME OF THE TOWN

Weston's public school buildings and group of State wards who are obliged to walk to classes.

Gov. Walsh to Investigate Weston's Treatment of State Orphans, Who Are Compelled to Walk to School While Other Children Ride at Town's Expense

School was out, in Weston.

Barges were drawn up in front of one of the schoolhouses.

Children trooped out, laughing, playing, calling, last-tagging.

They piled into the barges, monitors reported that every place was filled, a teacher gave the word, and away went the two-horse rigs.

There were six children left—you will see them in the picture which accompanies this fact-story—and these six little ones cheerfully started to walk.

There was a boy among the six, and to him a reporter for the Sunday AMERICAN addressed a question:

"Why don't YOU ride?"

NOT ALLOWED TO RIDE.

The answer came from the six little throats in chorus:

"We are not allowed to!"

"Why not?" asked the reporter.

"Because," said the boy, "we are of the State."

"What does that mean?"

"We are State wards," said the boy.

Figure 5-5. This 1915 article in the Boston American *entitled "The Shame of the Town of Weston" tells of six orphans who were wards of the state and boarded with Weston families. They were not allowed to ride the horse-drawn school barges (shown in the picture) because the state would not pay its share of the transportation cost.*

we got back on the snow we'd all pile back in again.[18]

By 1903 barges covered eight routes from four to nine miles long.[19] Jesse Caunt owned his own barge. Every day he drove a nine-mile loop down Winter to Bogle Street in a two-horse barge seating 22.[20] L.E. Roberts owned and drove the barge that brought children from Sudbury and Concord Roads, a distance of about six miles. P.J. McAuliffe operated one- and two-horse barges on the other six routes.[21]

In 1908, eight barges transported 172 pupils who lived more than a mile from school. Another 122 students lived within a mile and had to walk. By 1914, two of the barges were motorized. The changeover was completed by the early 1920s and substantially reduced travel time. The 1922 town report remarked on the end of an era:

> Since 1893, Mr. Jesse Caunt has driven his horses over his route on school days, always careful, rarely late, and with never an accident. At Thanksgiving he gave way to motor transportation over the Wellesley Street route. The motorizing of the routes is now completed.[22]

"Auto barges" had their drawbacks as well. In January 1912, the *Waltham Daily Free Press Tribune* reported that P.J. McAuliffe's large auto barge had refused to climb Coburn's hill in the deep snow and the children had to walk to school. In the winter of 1920–21, snow was so heavy that motorized vehicles were put aside and horses hired at great expense to pull school barges.[23]

The high cost of transportation was a continuing issue with taxpayers. In 1902 the school committee reported that 274 cities and towns were providing some type of transportation but Weston's cost of $3,069 was the highest in the state.[24] A decade later, the committee wrote that transportation costs totaling more than 20 percent of the school budget were difficult to reduce given the extent of service.[25]

The 1895 Weston High School

In 1891, the school committee reported that for the third year in a row Weston High School had no graduating class.[26] It appealed to parents to keep their children in school:

> There does not seem to be a high ideal of education in our community—children are not required, not advised, and in some cases not even permitted, to take advantage of the opportunities for education that the schools offer. . . . Your Committee feel that parents wrong their children by permitting them to abandon school life as early as they do. The fate of the nation is bound up with that of the common schools. When the interest in education fails, then will our liberty begin to decay.[27]

In 1892, Justin E. Gale was hired as principal. Under his leadership, the number of high school students more than doubled and interest increased "in a most marvelous way."[28] The three-year course was increased to four, and for the first time, students began to prepare for college or the new Institute of Technology. A plea was made for larger accommodations. When Gale retired in 1895, just before a new high school was completed, the school committee wrote:

> He took the High School when it was at its lowest ebb; when there was not enough interest in education . . . to provide a graduating class. . . . It does not seem possible that the old indifference can ever return, and for this change the Town can never be sufficiently grateful . . .[29]

The new high school was designed by local resident Samuel Mead of the Boston firm of Cabot, Everett and Mead. Along with spaces especially designed for cooking, science, and manual training, there was an art room, assembly room holding 100 pupils, recitation room, and library.[30] Boys and girls had separate entrances. Walls were hung with "beau-

Figure 5-6. Weston High School pupils pose with principal Justin E. Gale in the early 1890s, before construction of the new brick schoolhouse.

tiful new classical pictures, matters aesthetic as well as practical having been considered."[31] The building cost $22,590.

Townspeople criticized the appearance of the new school, saying that it "would look better on a hill" and was "not handsome enough, etc."[32] The school committee responded that "justice to the taxpayers demanded that the building should be erected at as low a cost as would fully provide for the needs of the scholars," adding that the committee "never understood that the Town desired, or was willing to erect, a public monument for the adornment of the Town, and placed where it would make the greatest aesthetic impression."[33]

The new high school included space for manual training even though it was not yet part of the curriculum. An 1895 report argued that students should learn to use tools and be exposed to the kind of handcraftsmanship being lost in the age of machines. Written by Everett Schwartz, Weston native and principal of the Waltham Manual Training School, the eloquent report asserted that "the work of Manual Training helps to bridge the gulf between the existing ranks of society, and raises the intelligent workman to a higher plane of dignity."[34] The following year, the town voted money to establish a manual training course. In 1914 a new hall was added at the rear of the school, with manual training rooms in the basement.

Three courses offered only to girls covered cooking, advanced sewing and dressmaking, and advanced household matters. The latter included study of the price of food, care of plumbing, making of beds, purity of water and milk supplies, and avoidance of contagious disease. The superintendent's report of 1913 goes on to add, "Meanwhile, the boys are being considered—indeed they have been for years—in carefully planned science courses."

Figure 5-7. Architect and local resident Samuel Mead designed the second Weston High School (now Brook School Building A), constructed in 1895. Boys and girls had separate entrances. The walls were hung with "beautiful new classical pictures."

Primary and Intermediate School Facilities (1900–1915)

Beginning in 1902, sixth-grade pupils from the two remaining district schools were required to go to the central school, and by 1908 fifth-graders were transported there as well. The school committee awaited the day when residents of Cutter's Corner and Kendal Green would ask for all their children to attend the central schools, but that day was long in coming. Even after the number of pupils at School #5 decreased to 12, parents still pressed to keep it open.[35]

To accommodate pupils in grades 1–6 who formerly attended district schools, the hall on the second floor of the 1878 high school was divided into two rooms. When the high school moved into its

Figure 5-8. More than 50 primary school children are seated with hands folded on their desks in this photograph of a Weston classroom about 1893–94.

Figure 5-9. As the school population increased in the early 1900s, fiscally conservative town voters approved only this small, two-room schoolhouse for the four primary grades. Constructed in 1908, it had to be enlarged two years later by adding the brick first floor. (Now Brook School Building B)

new building, the old frame structure was devoted to the primary (1–6) and grammar (pre–high school) divisions. Within a few years it was again overcrowded, a situation chronicled with dismay in the 1905 town report:

> . . . the schools of the city of Boston have recently been declared degenerate because of fifty pupils in a room, and not only has our Grammar school averaged over that this fall, but our Intermediate room has had about that number. [36]

A proposal to build an eight-room central grammar school was rejected as too expensive despite the fact that the town was nearly free of debt and had experienced its highest increase ever in total property valuation. Also defeated was a proposal to buy land on North Avenue and build a new two-room schoolhouse, a vote signifying the town's commitment to centralized schools. Finally, in 1908, a two-room primary school designed by Boston architect J. Williams Beal was built between the existing grammar and high schools. Almost immediately, each primary grade needed its own separate room. Local architect Alexander Jenney was enlisted to enlarge the building by lifting it up and building two new classrooms underneath. Now known as Brook School Building B, the two-story version was completed in 1911.

Charles M. "Boss" Eaton

Charles M. "Boss" Eaton (1868–1949) came to Weston as principal in 1895, five years after his graduation from Harvard College. He took on the additional title of superintendent of schools in 1902 when that position was created by state law. He was also an outstanding teacher, whose favorite subject was Latin. Eaton was known for strict discipline and high standards of scholarship.

In the 33 years until his retirement in 1928, the dynamic Eaton implemented the change to centralized schools, developed the transportation system, and brought the program to "an enviable place among the systems of the State."[37] During the Eaton years, Weston was a community in transition. Before 1880, high school students pursued "cultural studies" in Latin and Greek, along with mathematics and some science. Those with "no distinct craving for an education" would drop out and begin contributing to family support. With the increasing wealth of the community, parents had less need of their children's assistance. High schools began getting children "who had no wish to improve themselves." Critics labeled the school a failure and demanded the teaching of mechanical arts, commercial courses, and business. As a small high school, Weston could not offer the diversity available elsewhere, but the super-

Figure 5-10. Charles Eaton devoted 33 years of his life to Weston schools, where he was known as "Boss Eaton" because of his high standards of discipline and scholarship. He was superintendent of schools, principal of the high school, and an outstanding teacher whose favorite subject was Latin.

Figure 5-11. Principal Charles Eaton stands in the back row of this photograph of Weston High School students in the first decade of the 20th century.

intendent and school committee did introduce the practical courses in manual training and home economics described earlier.

Eaton responded to criticism by pointing out the impossibility of meeting all the needs and desires of students, parents, taxpayers, and potential employers:

> Side by side dwell people of divergent views: the business man who wants the children in the public schools drilled into unthinking accurate machines for his employ . . . and in contrast with him, the idealistic mother, who sighs for more art, more poetry, more music.[38]

He wrote that "one hears from time to time of great achievements in the 'little red school-house' of the past, and unfavorable comparisons of our present schools," to which he responded that times had changed. For him, the important question was not what courses were taught but "what does each individual child get to make him more honest, more industrious, more self-respecting, and a better citizen when he is grown up?"[39]

Emphasis on character building is a constant theme in the Eaton years. In 1901, he wrote, "A small school is a good place for the building of character, and a good character is far more valuable than mere intellectual power." He decried the lack of ambition of certain children and tried to enlist the help of parents:

> Many parents to-day are so anxious to give their children the best of everything, to spare them pain or sorrow or toil, that they often forget that the power to bear some burden is one of the greatest needs and the finest things in life.[40]

He advised parents: "Lay upon your children some burden of responsibility—not too heavy—and see that it is carried well and proudly."[41]

Eaton was attentive to the physical well-being of his charges. He urged the purchase of gymnasium equipment so that the "superfluous bodily energies of the pupils might be directed . . . to useful exercises."[42] He encouraged boys to participate in "wholesome athletic sports" during the noon hour. He favored children walking to school in good weather and, in his 1898 report, requested money for an inexpensive shed to encourage those who wished to ride bicycles. During his tenure, public school children began to get swimming instruction at the new town pool. Because most pupils at centralized

Figure 5-12. Margaret Mosher (1896–1996) is pictured in the spring of 1916 in her graduation dress, holding her Weston High School diploma. Miss Mosher became Weston's first children's librarian, a position she held for 42 years, from 1920 to 1962.

schools could not go home for lunch, the superintendent arranged for hot soup and hot chocolate to be available for purchase at four cents a cup.[43]

The Teachers' Lodge

In the 19th and first half of the 20th centuries, custom dictated that female teachers be unmarried. In a town such as Weston, which offered limited housing opportunities, unmarried teachers with no local relatives faced serious obstacles in finding suitable boarding arrangements. In 1913 Horace Sears solved the problem by setting up a "Teachers' Lodge" across from his estate mansion. The gift was announced in the town report that year:

> Mr. Horace S. Sears placed at the disposal of the Committee a commodious dwelling on Central Avenue to be used as a teachers' house; and not only did he give the building for this purpose, but he gave it in perfect repair and completely furnished for living and housekeeping, even to silver and table linen, all without any charge whatever to the town. . . . The house has accommodations for eight teachers, besides the housekeeper, and for the first time it has been possible this winter for all to enjoy the pleasures and privileges of home life.[44]

Seven "lady teachers" boarded here the first year.[45] Sears assumed responsibility for the exterior and grounds and "cared for the place as if it were his own personal residence."[46] In 1917 he added an extensive ell with space for several more teachers. The town report noted, "The value of the 'Teachers' Lodge' to the efficient management of the schools cannot be overestimated."[47] This experiment in community housekeeping was continued by Sears's heirs until the 1950s, providing a home for Weston teachers even after they retired.

Figure 5-13. Pigeon Hill School students included members of the Paine, Winsor, Thorndike, and Bennett families. Miss Bridges, headmistress and teacher of the older children, is in the back row at the far right. When this photograph was taken, about 1906, the school had just two rooms. Children attended until they were old enough to go to Middlesex, Winsor, or other private secondary schools. (Names listed with photo credits)

Private Schools

The Pigeon Hill School had its origins in Waltham in 1890. It moved to Weston in 1905 at the urging of a group of Weston and Wayland parents who wanted their children to have a private school education, including Robert Winsor, John B. and Charles Paine Jr., and William and Arthur Coburn.[48] The location on Pigeon Hill Road at the foot of the hill was convenient to the Central Massachusetts Railroad, which transported some of the children to and from Wayland. In the first years, Miss Bridges, the headmistress, taught the older children and Miss Ware the three lower grades.[49] Madam Subelia taught French.[50] By 1914 the school included first to sixth grade, with three teachers taking two grades each.[51] First- and second-graders attended from 8:20 to 10:30 A.M. and older pupils stayed until 1:00 P.M., at a tuition cost of $150 a year for the older scholars.

In 1896 the first kindergarten was established in Weston. The private day school was originally located in the chapel-on-the-rock (the former District School #1) but was moved the following year to the Unitarian church parlor. Miss Lena Higgin-

Figure 5-14. This hook-and-ladder truck, the town's first piece of fire apparatus, was kept in a shed next to the Hastings cow barn on North Avenue. It was pulled by Tom Coburn's heavy farm horses, which were usually out in the fields when the whistle blew. (1895 photo, names listed with photo credits)

botham of Waltham was mistress of the school, and "Weston mothers may feel assured that their children, left in her charge, will receive a precious store of education combined with entertainment."[52]

Weston Fire Department

House and barn fires were serious problems in the late 19th century because they were nearly impossible to extinguish with the primitive equipment available. Brushfires were often started by cinders from wood-burning railroad engines.

In the fall of 1890, Weston took the first steps toward establishing a fire department.[53] That year, within a two-month period, 15 fires destroyed 50 acres of woodland and two barns. Arson was suspected. When the Isaac Fiske house (the former Baldwin Tavern) burned to the ground, a special town meeting was called to discuss the purchase of fire apparatus. A newspaper article advanced the following argument designed to win voter approval:

> That Weston owes it to its citizens, particularly to its summer residents who have made heavy investments in buildings in the town and whose money keeps down the taxes, to depart from the ways of a hundred years ago and get some means of protection from fires is a clearly evident fact.[54]

Organ factory owner Francis H. Hastings was appointed chairman of a committee that recommended the town buy three simple one-horse fire trucks equipped with ladders, hooks, pikes, axes, buckets, hand pumps, and hand chemical extinguishers. These were to be placed in each of the three sections of town as soon as fire companies were organized.

The first hook-and-ladder truck was stored in the Hastings barn on North Avenue near the organ factory. Sixteen men from the north side were appointed engine men. The selectmen's report explained that the protection would not be extended to other parts of town until it was certain that "any additional apparatus will be manned by an organization of men possessed of the same intelligence and public spirit, as . . . the members of Hook and Ladder Company No. 1." They added that "it is an axiom with fire experts that apparatus without organization is useless."[55] In 1891 Hook and Ladder Company No. 2 was organized to protect the town center. Equipment was housed in the basement of Town Hall.

Firemen were not paid until 1893, when the town voted to compensate the men 25 cents an hour for time spent fighting fires. That year the town offered a $500 reward for the arrest and conviction of the arsonist who set fire to a Concord Road house owned by Charles H. Fiske and to the town's largest business block two months later.[56] No one was ever convicted. A fire alarm system was installed, with wires initially strung from tree to tree.[57]

Figure 5-15. This 1900 photograph shows the original fire apparatus purchased for Hook and Ladder Company No. 2 in 1891. The equipment was stored in the first town hall, which had an above-grade basement at the rear. Horses were supplied by P. J. McAuliffe's livery stable on Church Street.

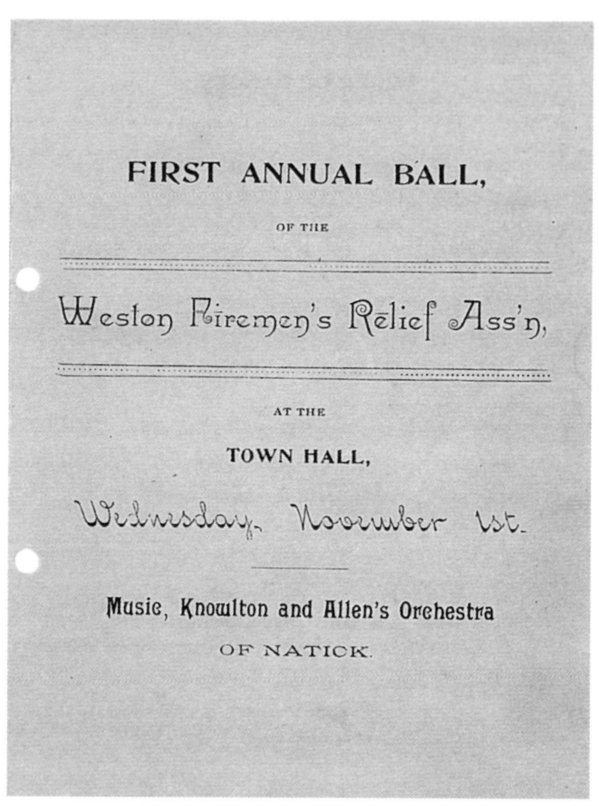
FIRST ANNUAL BALL,

OF THE

Weston Firemen's Relief Ass'n,

AT THE

TOWN HALL,

Wednesday, November 1st.

Music, Knowlton and Allen's Orchestra

OF NATICK.

Figure 5-16. This "Programme" cover was used for the First Annual Ball of the Weston Firemen's Relief Association, held in 1893 at the town hall. The event took place just weeks after fire destroyed three stores in the Coburn block. In the early years of the department, firemen from adjoining towns came to these balls to encourage their brother firefighters. The relief association was incorporated in 1906.

The town authorized the selectmen to install 20 fire hydrants, first used on a house fire in early 1899.[58] The importance of hydrants was apparent late that year when a house near a hydrant was saved while the Methodist church and Robert Winsor's barn, both far from any water supply, burned to the ground. In 1900 Weston ordered a new hose wagon "equipped with all the modern improvements, nickel plated trimmings, painted in a rich vermillion, gold letters and bordered with a pretty gold scroll."[59] The Weston Firemen's Relief Association, which had been started in the 1890s, was incorporated in 1906 with B.H. Dickson Jr. as president, H.F. Warren as vice president, Thomas E. Coburn as treasurer, and F.A. Sherburne as clerk. Mr. and Mrs. Francis B. Sears and Gen. C.J. Paine had previously contributed the money that became the nucleus of a fund.

Kendal Green and Weston Fire Stations

In 1908 the town built its first fire station, an all-concrete building that still stands on North Avenue. The station cost $9,315 and had space for three pieces of apparatus, quarters for a permanent man if needed, a social room, and a shower and bathroom.[60] No arrangement was made for keeping horses, which had to be borrowed from a nearby farmer.

In the 1908 town report, the building committee noted with pride the unsolicited praise for the Classical-style structure designed by Alexander S. Jenney. The *Boston Sunday Herald* printed a photograph of the Kendal Green Fire Station taken by a stranger who "seemed to consider it a thing of beauty." An article in the *Christian Science Monitor* called it "an illustration of the best of work in reinforced concrete" and "the only fireproof fire station in the United States."[61] The 1909 issue of *The Municipal Journal and Engineer* noted that "an effort was made to give [the new station] an appearance which would be sufficiently artistic for its surroundings . . . simple in outline but of attractive proportions."[62] The use of reinforced concrete made the building "practically uninflammable."

Critics responded that it was too low to the ground, too close to the street, and "in the worst place that could be found on North Avenue." In a letter to the editor, one writer enumerated more shortcomings:

> It has no tower for a bell and firemen seldom know what number of box has been pulled until they have inquired of the neighbors. The men's meeting room is down in the basement on the north side. Does Mr. Clark think the firemen are like groundhogs to meet underground?"[63]

In his unpublished history, fire department historian H. Bentley Crouch speculates on the reason for its location right on the road and its all-concrete construction:

> While the need for better quarters . . . for the apparatus . . . was undoubtedly one of the principal reasons for the erection of the new station there was another more obscure reason for building such an expensive structure. At the time there was considerable agitation among the residents of that district against the contemplated construction of a street railway line. . . . By placing the fire station at the narrow point in the road and

opposite the ledges it was felt that the street railway project would be blocked.[64]

The Kendal Green Fire Station was used for less than 10 years, until 1917, when it was closed to save money during the First World War. The use of motorized apparatus made the station unnecessary, and it never reopened.

The expense of the station was a source of contention and resulted in a dissenting "Minority Report of the Committee on Fire Prevention and Extinction," written by estate owner Charles W. Hubbard and printed in the 1908 town report. Hubbard wrote that he did not believe the department had ever extinguished a fire in any sizable building:

> In my opinion, more people would be kept out of the Town by the fear of unnecessary future expenditure on the Fire Department and increased taxes than would be kept out of the Town by further economy on a Fire Department which has never put out a house fire.

The Board of Fire Engineers printed its reply in the same report:

> We wish to refute the statements made in the open town meeting April 29, 1908 . . . that the Weston Fire Department has never saved a building after it has once caught fire—by giving this partial list of buildings which the members . . . have saved . . .[65]

Despite the rebuttal, the department acquired the irreverent nickname "The Cellar Savers."

Figure 5-17. The all-concrete 1908 Kendal Green Fire Station was completely fireproof and was praised as "sufficiently artistic for its surroundings . . . simple in outline but of attractive proportions." Used for only nine years, it closed during World War I as an economy measure. This 1910 photograph shows hose truck #2, the chief's car, and hook and ladder #1, along with Edward, Thomas, Albert L., Raymond, and Harold W. Coburn.

Figure 5-18. The second fire station, designed by local architect Alexander Jenney, was constructed in 1914 to serve the town center. Like the 1917 town hall, it was built as part of the town improvement plan and utilizes the same Georgian Revival style. Note the original double doors.

At Town Meeting in 1914, residents finally voted $16,500 to build a firehouse in the town center that could accommodate motorized fire trucks. Alexander

Figure 5-19. Once the new fire station was built, the department could finally purchase its first motorized vehicle. The four-cylinder White truck was partly paid for with a gift from Horace Sears. Call firefighters no longer had to borrow horses from McAuliffe's livery stable and could respond more quickly to alarms.

Figure 5-20. Patrick J. McAuliffe ran a busy livery stable next to Weston Station. He was appointed constable in 1901 and became Weston's first chief of police in 1908. His winning personality, keen sense of humor, and "heart as big as an ox" made him a much-loved figure. This photograph was taken in July 1911, at Mount Wachusett, where he had driven a group of Weston ladies on an excursion.

Jenney designed the three-stall brick building completed late that year. The town voted to purchase its first motorized fire truck, partially funded with a $3,000 contribution from Horace Sears. The four-cylinder White combination hose, chemical, and pump car cost $5,500. Chief Benjamin Parker requested a permanent employee and Reginald Stevens was hired in 1916 to spend each night in the fire station. A mechanized ladder truck was made by cutting in half a Corbin automobile donated by B.H. Dickson Jr. and adding ladder brackets and racks from an old horse-drawn truck. In 1922, the department purchased a fire alarm whistle that doubled as a no-school signal. Also that year, Benjamin R. Parker, the first fire chief, stepped down after 22 years. He was replaced by Franklin C. Mulock.

Weston Police Department

Weston had its problems with crime. Petty theft was commonplace. Items in the *Waltham Daily Free Press Tribune* record boys and automobilists stealing fruit, tramps milking cows dry, and thieves stealing pullets, bicycles, carriage blankets, and clothing off clotheslines. At the turn of the century, the town depended on local citizens appointed each year as constables or special police and paid for time served. In 1890 Daniel Lamson, whose farmhouse was in the town center, wrote a letter to selectman Francis Blake complaining, "There is rampant in the center of town a spirit of huddlism." He protested that residents could not go peaceably to the post office or library without being harassed, even in broad daylight, adding, "Stones are thrown, windows broken, property injured . . . Sign boards . . . defaced, broken & in some instances utterly destroyed & carried off—in fact a state of things unknown to neighboring towns."[66] Lamson complained that "our constables are of no account" and wanted a police officer to patrol the town center.

Selectmen appealed to public frugality to stop these "offences to the public peace." While some might have been committed by "evil-disposed persons passing over our highways at night on their way from Waltham to neighboring towns," the selectmen had no doubt that most were committed by Weston residents. They hoped such acts would stop so the town could avoid additional expenses:

> It is confidently believed . . . that sober thought on the part of the offenders, and exceptional vigilance on the part of all friends of good order, will make it unnecessary for the town to go to the expense of maintaining a paid police force.[67]

State police were brought in to handle the first murder in Weston, in 1894, when James Farrar of South Lincoln was killed while pursuing a burglar into Weston.[68] In 1902, during construction of the Weston Aqueduct and Reservoir, the town appealed to the Metropolitan Water and Sewerage Board for funds to pay special police officers. The 1902 report records arrests for drunkenness, assault, violation of the liquor law, larceny, and trespassing. By 1904, the town had seven constables and 25 police officers paid for the

Figure 5-21. In June 1905 an item in the Waltham Daily Free Press Tribune *noted that "Weston is one of the most beautiful towns in the environs of Boston and is celebrated for its fine old elm trees, which, for a long distance, form an arch over the broad road to Wayland." Many elms were planted after the Civil War as New Englanders worked to enhance village centers. They were prized for the distinctive branching pattern and rapid growth. This photograph was taken looking west from the town square and shows the small former tailor shop at right.*

hours they spent on duty. Patrick J. McAuliffe figured prominently in the Mabel Page murder investigation, as further described in the Cutter's Corner chapter.

P.J. McAuliffe is first listed as chief of police in 1908. In 1910 the *Waltham Daily Free Press Tribune* reported, "The Weston police are resplendent in their new uniforms. Chief McAuliffe is especially radiant."[69] In addition to his responsibilities as chief, McAuliffe ran a livery stable opposite Weston Station on the Central Massachusetts Railroad and was one of several town undertakers. Brenton H. Dickson III recounted many stories about his colorful personality, including this one:

> Everyone in town knew him, liked him, respected him and depended on him; in short, he was Weston's most unforgettable character. He loved to tell stories on himself, like the time he was driving a lady through Weston Center to look at a house she was considering renting for the summer. She pointed at the stone church and asked what denomination it was. "Unitarian," said Pat. "Are you a Unitarian?" "No," said his passenger, "I'm an Episcopalian." "Then," said Pat, "you might just as well rent a house for the summer in Hell as here."[70]

The police department had no town-owned vehicles until 1915, when the selectmen purchased one motorcycle.

The Origin of Village Improvement Societies

Improvements in public health, schools, and fire and police protection were undertaken as part of the expanded role of local government. Other improvements were initiated privately, through voluntary associations formed to beautify the town and add amenities not yet considered the responsibility of government.

In his book *The American Home: Architecture and Society, 1815–1915,* David P. Handlin discusses the idealization of the small town in the years after the Civil War. The growth of commerce and industry had created extremes of poverty and affluence, and immigration had increased ethnic and cultural diversity. According to Handlin, some theorists concluded that if everyone shared Christian home values, then social, economic, and political problems would resolve themselves. The growth of cities and resulting overcrowding, poor sanitation, and crime led many to idealize the small town as a healthy environment in which Christian values could best be maintained.

Many town improvers felt that beauty had strong moral and social value. They believed that beauty in domestic architecture exercised a beneficial influence on those who experienced it, and that harmonious surroundings reflected and helped to produce a harmonious community. Village improvements were often supported by wealthy people who took an interest in towns where they spent their vacations and wanted to help preserve the qualities that had attracted them to settle there.

In *The American Home,* Handlin explains one aim of village improvement societies across the nation:

> This fundamental goal was to make the town or village seem more town or villagelike. Such an

> end presupposed an image of an ideal community. The frequent use of the word "village" in itself was an expression of what the advocates of improvement had in mind.[71]

What many envisioned was the old New England town with Colonial houses framing a town green.

In towns like Weston that lacked a suitable town center, local improvement organizations worked to create one. Central spaces were cleared, cleaned up, or landscaped in a more attractive manner. For visual emphasis, a prominent building was sometimes set on the green, to be viewed across the open space. Village improvement societies frequently tried to save old buildings and coordinate the style of the buildings around the town green "to create an effect of architectural uniformity, an outward manifestation of the town's common purpose."

Because each town was interlaced with roads, village improvement societies made special efforts to improve their quality and appearance. They advocated better road surfaces and placed water troughs at convenient spots. Most important, they planted trees to create a "continuity of greenery" throughout the town. In some towns, the planting of trees was the major activity of the societies. Trees had practical value in relieving summer heat and improving the health of the environment. They embodied beauty and the associated ideals of moral and social harmony.[72]

Figure 5-22. The Village Improvement Society of Weston worked to beautify Central Avenue by planting street trees and promoting uniform sidewalks and fencing. The result is evident in this photograph of the Hews house, which once stood in the 600 block of what is now Boston Post Road.

The Village Improvement Society in Weston

Evidence of a Town Improvement Society in Weston appears as early as 1887, when the *Waltham Free Press* announced that the society was erecting lampposts.[73] Little is known of this organization, although the following item in the *Waltham Free Press* of 1893 indicates that it was working to beautify the town center:

> Now that fire has destroyed several buildings on the main road, it shows how much improved the street would be, if the building that may hereafter be erected were carried back . . . on a line with the dwelling house and the blacksmith shop. . . . [I]t seems a pity to have unpicturesque buildings crowding the street near the centre of the town, which so great an effort has been made to beautify.[74]

The 1892 town report contains the first comprehensive plan for laying out public and private buildings in the town square. A more complete discussion of this and subsequent plans is included in chapter 15. Of importance here is the interest in planning and concern for aesthetics as well as utility.

The Village Improvement Association of Weston, established in March 1895, appears to be a reorganization of the previous group. A four-page summary of goals, bylaws, and officers was inserted into the 1894 town report in a clear attempt by town officials to boost support. The constitution spelled out the purpose:

> The object of this Society shall be the preservation of the natural beauties of the town, the improving and ornamenting of the streets and public grounds of the town by planting and cultivating trees, the establishing and maintaining of walks, the establishing and protecting of good grass plots and borders in the streets and public squares, the providing of public drinking troughs, the lighting and watering of the streets, and generally the doing, in conjunction with the town authorities, whatever may tend to the improvement of the town as a place of residence.[75]

To become a member, residents had to "annually plant and protect a tree under the direction of the Executive Committee" or pay an annual membership fee of one dollar. Original officers were as follows: president, Justin E. Gale; vice presidents, Henry J. White and Francis H. Hastings; secretary and treasurer, Albert H. Hews; Executive Committee, Rev. Charles F. Russell, Miss Marian R. Case, Miss Edith Coburn, Howard L. Cooper, Charles H. Fiske, Nathan S. Fiske, Charles W. Hubbard, Mrs. David W. Lane, Miss Hattie S. Perry, Mrs. Louis E. Roberts, Horace S. Sears, Robert Winsor, and Mrs. Frederick T. Fuller.

In addition to planting and caring for street trees, the Village Improvement Society became involved in furnishing street lighting and watering streets in summer to keep down the dust. The privately owned

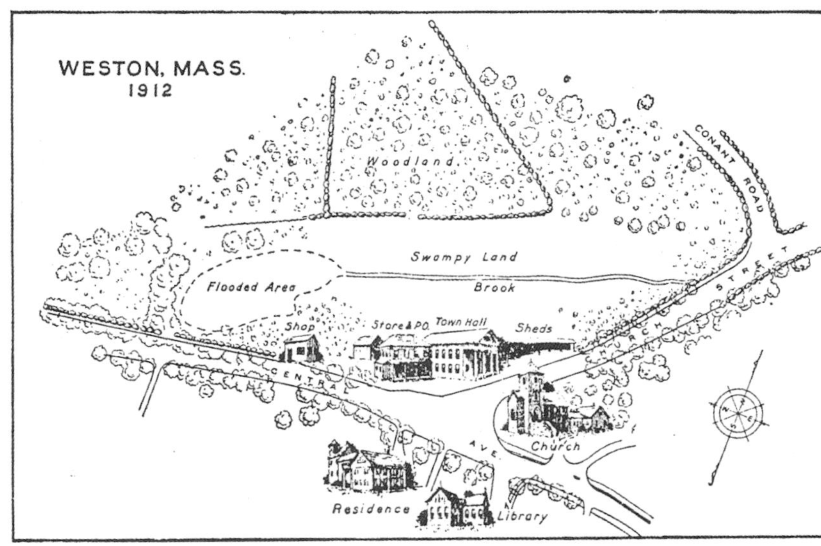

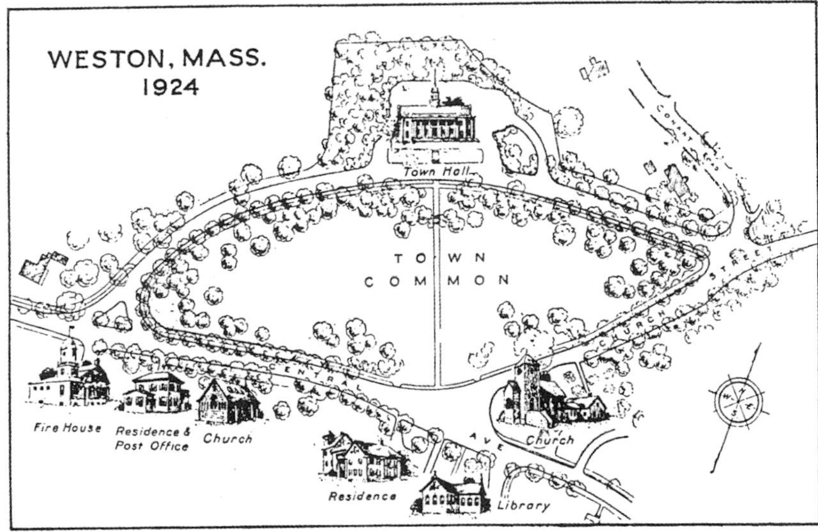

Figures 5-23 and 24. Weston's Town Improvement Plan, executed in the 1910s, is discussed in detail in chapter 15. These "before" and "after" sketches were included in a 1923 U.S. Department of Agriculture Farmers' Bulletin *encouraging rural towns to beautify their surroundings.*

Weston Water and Weston Electric Light Companies were established to carry out these projects.

The decorative metal watering trough in the town center was installed shortly after the water system was established in the mid-1890s. The trough was a coppery black color and had a water pipe up the middle and a grate at the bottom to drain the overflow. It was set next to the flagpole on a small circle of cobblestones level with the road surface. A twin trough was placed at the intersection of Church Street and North Avenue. Residents and teamsters regularly stopped to water their horses.[76]

As discussed in chapter 15, the major legacy of the Village Improvement Society was the Town Improvement Plan of 1912, which gave Weston its New England town green. So successful was this project that, in 1923, the U.S. Department of Agriculture featured Weston in an article in *Farmers' Bulletin* No. 1441. Called "Re-Planning the Rural Village," it encouraged "the farmer of the new day" to take civic action similar to that of Weston:

> The intellectual awakening of the twentieth-century farmer has made the man of the soil dissatisfied with the squalor of the old-time crossroads hamlets. In the thoughtful magazines that the rural mail carrier brings to his door, he sees how it is possible to beautify the surroundings of human life in city and village. Traveling in his automobile on vacation, he sees the results of an artist ferment that is working in American life. Perhaps a man from the city builds a country retreat near his farm. These are some of the influences that are lifting the American farmer out of the carelessness of the last century, encouraging him to beautify the surroundings of his house and buildings, and sometimes even to join in re-planning the villages.[77]

Weston Water Company

In December 1895, the *First Parish Calendar* contained an article on the Weston Aqueduct Company, predecessor to the Weston Water Company. The author, F.T. Fuller, began by explaining how the company was founded "for the public good, not [the] greed of private profit."[78] According to Fuller, early in the history of the Village Improvement Association the question was raised whether any escape was possible from the pervasive dust on the much traveled Central Avenue. A committee decided that the town needed a water supply system and that the expense, "while involving a yearly drain for some time to come upon the pockets of its promoters, would not be a heavier burden than they were willing to bear for so good an object."[79]

Money for construction was contributed by Horace S. Sears, Albert H. Hews, Charles J. Paine, George S. Perry, Robert Winsor, and Dr. F.W. Jackson. By late 1895 the company had laid about five miles of pipe and was supplying a limited area in the town center. A brick pumping station on Warren Avenue pumped water from nearby wells up to a reservoir on the highest point of the Highland Street hill, on land of General Paine.[80]

Fuller credits A.H. Hews for his energetic effort and liberal loan of teams, men, and supplies from his Cambridge factory. Fuller also speaks of the Italian laborers:

> I should also like to speak of the gratification of our citizens in finding the Italian laborers, whose coming was somewhat dreaded, such a quiet, industrious, civil, and well-disposed body of men. No complaints whatever regarding them have reached me; and I only regret that their inability to speak or understand English stood in the way of the efforts which would, otherwise, I doubt not, have been put forth for their good in religious and humanitarian directions, during their stay among us.[81]

At a special town meeting of 1895, the town voted

Figure 5-25. The Weston Water Company was funded by selling stock to civic-minded residents like Gen. C.J. Paine, whose purchase of 75 shares made him the largest stockholder.

to install 20 hydrants and rent them from the Weston Aqueduct Company for $25 each per year. To cover the cost, the town increased property valuations on those who lived close enough to benefit from a hydrant. It became the policy to extend hydrant service on the written request of individual property owners, who had to pay the major cost through increased taxes.

The Weston Aqueduct Company was supplanted by the Weston Water Company, which was incorporated in 1896 and issued stocks and bonds to pay off its predecessor.[82] The original incorporators were Charles J. Paine, Albert H. Hews, Charles H. Fiske, Fred W. Jackson, and Horace S. Sears, who served as treasurer until the company was purchased by the town more than 20 years later.[83]

Over the next two decades, town committees twice recommended against purchase of the Weston Water Company.[84] Residents were expected to make their own arrangements with the company or five other public or quasi-public sources: the City of Newton, Francis H. Hastings, Charles W. Hubbard, Weston Land Association (Silver Hill), and Keewaydin Water Works (Blake). Others relied on private wells.

The Warren Avenue wells were the only source of supply for Weston Water Company until 1910, when it acquired 18 acres off Church Street in Kendal Green and drilled six permanent supply wells from 18 to 25 feet deep. These became the major water resource for the town. In 1911, the Paine's Hill reservoir was repaired and concrete walls built up to provide storage of about 400,000 gallons.[85] When the Weston Water Company was taken over by the town in 1921, it was supplying an estimated 275 of the 547 buildings in Weston.[86]

The Weston Aqueduct and Reservoir was built in 1901–03 as part of the metropolitan Boston water supply system and is discussed in chapter 19. Even though this major public works project—and later the Hultman Aqueduct and Norumbega Reservoir—was located in Weston, the metropolitan system did not supply the town with water until the 1970s.

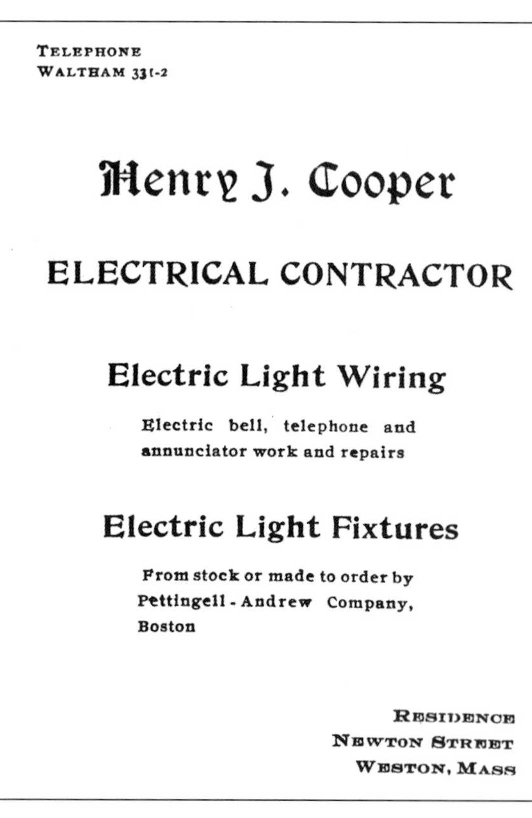
TELEPHONE
WALTHAM 331-2

Henry J. Cooper

ELECTRICAL CONTRACTOR

Electric Light Wiring

Electric bell, telephone and annunciator work and repairs

Electric Light Fixtures

From stock or made to order by Pettingell - Andrew Company, Boston

RESIDENCE
NEWTON STREET
WESTON, MASS

Figure 5-26. The Weston Electric Light Company was established in 1896, but few Weston buildings were wired for electricity until after the turn of the century.

Weston Electric Light Company

The Weston Electric Light Company was founded in 1896 and operated in conjunction with the Weston Water Company, with largely the same stockholders. Generating equipment was housed in the water company building and included a dynamo capable of supplying 1,000 incandescent 16 candlepower lamps.

The town, which had been maintaining about 180 oil lamps, contracted with the electric company to provide power for new electric streetlights.[87] The number was increased to 225 and reached 336 by 1903. Decisions on where to place new streetlights were based on two criteria: public safety and the amount of taxes paid by property owners who would benefit. Special treatment for the big taxpayers was openly acknowledged in town reports. The selectmen wrote that lighting should be installed only if "necessary for public convenience and safety" or, in special cases, "for the convenience of abutting landowners whose aggregate taxes may warrant the expenditures." In 1901, the selectmen recommended lighting Glen Road and Oak and Wellesley Streets, "which are now used by several large tax-payers of the town in approaching the Wellesley Farms station."[88] When Summer Street residents requested streetlights in 1903, the selectmen recommended against it because the public rarely used the street at night and the cost of lighting for one year would be more than the total taxes of abutting landowners.[89]

Electricity arrived in Weston homes around the turn of the century. The new Drabbington Lodge was illuminated when it opened in 1899. Estate owner Daniel Demmon was so eager to electrify his new home that in 1900 he put up a windmill with a powerful engine to generate his own electricity.[90] In September 1910 the newspaper reported, "The new engines are in operation at the electric lighting plant, and those who desire can have all-day lighting now." In early 1912, Weston Electric Light Company was sold to the Edison Electric Illuminating Company, which began furnishing the town's electricity. Thereafter, the Warren Avenue plant was used only by the water company.[91]

Introduction of Telephone Service

In 1875, the human voice was first transmitted over electrical wires and the telephone was born. Francis Blake, inventor of the Blake telephone transmitter, probably had the first phone in Weston, a distinction he achieved by paying to put up poles from his house to Newton Lower Falls in 1880. It was another decade before reports of private telephones begin to appear in the *Waltham Daily Free Press*, which regarded anything about the invention as newsworthy. In 1886 the newspaper reported that Cutting had removed the public telephone from his store, as he "could not stand the expense that the telephone company proposed to charge him for what was much more of a public than a private convenience."[92] In 1888 there was still no public phone in Weston. Residents petitioned the selectmen to revoke the license of New England Telephone and Telegraph Company to erect poles unless it provided a phone at Cutting's Store.[93] By 1890, telephones had been installed in the residence of Dr. Jackson and the Hook & Hastings organ factory. Robert Winsor had a phone by 1887, but James Case was still trying to get service in 1891.

Better telephone service meant more poles and wires. Town beautification advocate Edward Fiske voiced his vehement objection in an 1891 letter to the editor of the *Weekly Free Press:*

> The people of Weston are awakening to the fact that a great mistake was made by the selectmen in allowing telegraph poles and wires to be placed along Weston's beautiful Central avenue. The poles themselves are a great disfigurement to the avenue, being rough, unpainted and generally unsymmetrical. Great injury was done to the shade trees. . . . As the business . . . increases and the company puts up more wires, the evil will increase.[94]

Fiske pointed out that Central Avenue was being widened and straightened at great expense and when done "will be the finest street in the vicinity."[95] His suggestion to relocate poles to the Central Massachusetts right of way was never implemented, but the town did begin to exercise more control over their installation. By 1895, the company was required to maintain public telephones in the center and Kendal Green.[96]

Sidewalks

In the 1880 town report, the road commissioners admitted that "in one particular way we are very deficient":

> When we consider that a majority of our own citizens pass on foot to and from our Churches, Schools, Depots, Library, Post Office, &c., and when we see ladies tramping through the centre of our streets, in danger of coming in contact with every passing vehicle, we are led to believe that foot passengers have some rights . . .[97]

They recommended a small appropriation for sidewalks.

A decade later, Herbert Merriam requested a sidewalk for Concord Road, where many traveled on foot to Cherry Brook Station. In spring and fall, he wrote, the narrow road was very muddy and "particularly disagreeable for ladies."[98] In summer it was dusty, and pedestrians had to avoid cattle being driven over the road to pasture. Support for sidewalk construction was clearly expressed at Town Meeting in March 1890, when $4,500 was appropriated for roadways and $500 for sidewalks.[99]

Appointment of a Tree Warden, and the Battle against Gypsy Moths and Brown-Tail Moths

Beginning in 1899, state law required towns to appoint a tree warden to take charge of public shade trees.[100] As one of his first acts, Weston's first tree warden, Franklin G. Cooper, planted a row of shade trees from Cutting's Store to Weston Station paid for by Horace Sears and C.H. Fiske.[101] By 1912, orchardist and tree warden Edward P. Ripley was using public funds to plant trees. Forty rock maples were set out mostly along Central Avenue. Weston also passed laws to protect its trees by imposing fines for affixing advertisements or playbills on street trees ($50) and for wantonly injuring or defacing trees within the public way ($5 to $100).

The history of gypsy moths in Massachusetts goes back to 1869, when a French naturalist living in Medford was conducting experiments to cross native silk-spinning caterpillars with the European gypsy moth in hope of producing a hardy silkworm of commercial value.[102] The cages blew over in a severe windstorm and the caterpillars escaped. By 1880, the number of caterpillars in the immediate vicinity was noticeable. By the summers of 1889 and 1890, as they defoliated trees and swarmed over the sides of Medford houses, state legislators passed the first of many appropriations to abate the nuisance. By 1905 the insects had spread over such a wide area that the legislature allocated $300,000 and began requiring all infested towns to take over control work.

For 40 years, from 1906 until 1946, the task of battling gypsy moths and their sister scourge, brown-tail moths, was led by Edward P. Ripley. Control measures included brushing trees and egg clusters with creosote, burning caterpillar nests, protecting trees with burlap and tanglefoot, and spraying with arsenate of lead. In 1906 two crews scoured the town for gypsy moth egg clusters, which they had been able to keep under control on street trees and in orchards. In one 23-acre woodlot, the crew reported treating 700 egg clusters the previous winter and 25,000 the following year. In the fall of 1907, wooded areas were found to be so badly overrun that a special town meeting was called. An advisory committee was appointed consisting largely of estate owners, with Charles H. Jones, chairman, and members Benjamin S. Blake, William B. Clarke, Charles Merriam, Mrs. Francis H. Hastings, Miss Marian Case, B. Loring Young, and Edward Ripley, ex officio. [103]

In 1908, at the high point of the infestation, the town spent $19,326 on gypsy moth suppression, or 14 percent of its budget. This amount was equal to the entire school budget for that year.[104] By 1909 the town had purchased four spraying machines with the help of the state. Still, leaders despaired that it was beyond the resources of town and state combined to prevent deforestation of most of the town's woodlands. With the aid of foresters and entomologists, the town developed plans to control the moths by natural means using imported parasites and predaceous beetles.[105] Conditions improved gradually and the infestation was under control by the early 1920s, only to reappear in 1937 and again in 1945.

Parks and Recreation

Concerns about the environment, public health, urban crowding, and social conditions contributed to establishment of parks and recreational facilities throughout the Boston metropolitan area beginning in the 1890s. In Weston, estate owners led the way. The 1893 town report contains the first mention of the new Park Commissioners, formed to manage the gift of 19 acres on East Newton Street (now Park Road) from Charles W. Hubbard. The Park Commissioners "assumed that the Town would not wish to be called upon for an appropriation to expend on a park." They agreed that Hubbard could hay the property for three years, after which he would plant grass. Hubbard was asked to plant trees that would eventually hide the railroad embankment.[106]

Hubbard and his brother-in-law, Francis Blake, were strong supporters of the Metropolitan Park system proposed in 1893. By 1899, 77 acres in Weston had been taken to preserve the banks of the Charles River. In 1893 Francis Blake sold more than 20 acres to the Boston Athletic Association, which

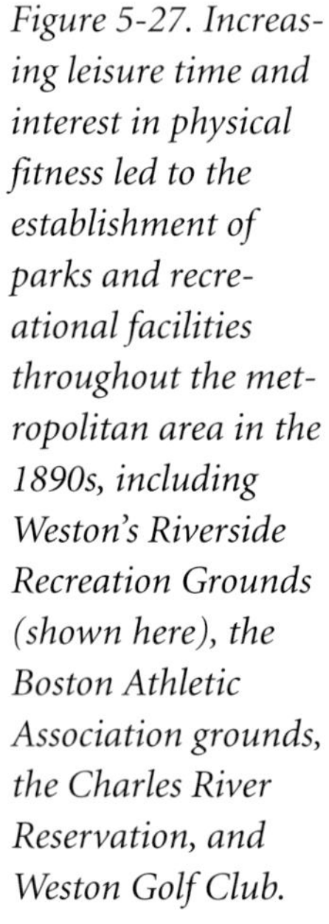
Figure 5-27. Increasing leisure time and interest in physical fitness led to the establishment of parks and recreational facilities throughout the metropolitan area in the 1890s, including Weston's Riverside Recreation Grounds (shown here), the Boston Athletic Association grounds, the Charles River Reservation, and Weston Golf Club.

established for its members a summer outdoor sports facility on the Charles River. In 1897 Hubbard established the nearby Riverside Recreation Grounds, which also provided facilities for land sports and boating. These three major recreational initiatives are discussed in chapter 21. Also in the 1890s, Weston Golf Club was established on Church Street near Kendal Green.

Figures 5-28 and 29. The Weston Athletic Association was formed in 1905 and sold shares of stock to fund construction of a town pool. The 20-foot by 60-foot concrete pool was located at the northeast corner of School Street and the present bypass and was used from 1906 to 1950. Boys and girls always swam at different times. These pictures were taken about 1915. The unidentified male diver at a boys swimming exhibition is pictured with Alice and Elinor Tyler.

The Town Pool

In 1902, a petition was circulated asking the Cambridge Water Board to build swimming pools for the boys of Weston, as the city had "preempted all the water courses and shut the boys out of their former swimming haunts."[107] Nothing came of this protest. In 1905, the Weston Athletic Association was incorporated as a stock company with the goal of building a town pool.[108] Horace S. Sears contributed land on School Street.[109] The concrete pool was 60 feet by 20 feet and an adjacent building contained showers and dressing rooms. The water was not heated.

At the 1906 town meeting, the town voted for the first time to allocate $500 for swimming instruction for schoolchildren. The pool was the only place in Weston where youngsters were taught to swim. Older residents recall being attached to the end of a pole like a fish during their lessons. At the end of the year, Weston Athletic Association held swimming and diving exhibitions, lifesaving demonstrations, and races, with winners awarded silver cups donated by local citizens. In 1912 the *Waltham Daily Free Press Tribune* estimated that nearly 200 people covered every inch of available space on the platform to watch.[110]

Regulations called for "quiet and gentlemanly deportment." Women and girls were always scheduled at different times from men and boys. At least through the early 1930s, the association required that all swimmers wear the bathing suits they provided, made of heavy duck cloth, "the kind you'd make a tent out of." Girls' suits were one piece and fastened in the front. Because of concerns about the spread of infectious diseases, Weston Athletic Association regularly employed a laboratory to investigate the sanitary condition of the water. Although the water was sometimes a grass-green color due to algae, the report in 1912 concluded "we see no reason why the use of the swimming pool should induce colds or coughs or be in any way injurious."[111] The 1915 town report again stressed high standards of hygiene:

> The pool, which holds 60,000 gallons of water, is emptied and cleaned every week. . . . A system of circulation through a filter is also used while the pool is in session. . . . Within the locker-building are soap, hot and cold shower-baths, and a laundered bathing suit, and a towel for everyone.[112]

In 1915, 4,108 visits were made to the pool. It continued in use until the present facility was created on Case land after World War II.

Notes

1. 1912 *TR*, 234.
2. *WDFPT*, March 15, 1901. (See also October 16, 1908.)
3. 1910 *TR*, 31.
4. The state board served as adviser to local boards, which were mandated beginning in 1894.
5. The 1888 board, consisting of Dr. Fred W. Jackson and the selectmen, is listed in the 1889 town report (for the year ending February 1889). The appointment of a board in Weston came after passage of an 1887 state law requiring local boards of health to supervise contagious disease in animals.
6. 1890 *TR*, 47. A later report cites the death rate of 11.11 per thousand, which "sustains Weston's high rank among the most healthful towns in the State" (1895 *TR*, 51).
7. 1891 *TR*, 36–37.
8. About 1820, in one of Weston's first public health initiatives, the town paid Dr. Benjamin James $50 to inoculate residents with cowpox. Cases of smallpox in Weston were very rare by the turn of the century. In 1902, a 62-year-old tramp at the almshouse came down with the disease. The high cost of his care, $544, was considered the responsibility of the Town of Arlington, where he was a legal resident. At that time, the care of any indigent person was considered the responsibility of his own town (see 1902 *TR*, 43, 113, and 1903 *TR*, 54).
9. 1898 *TR*, 77.
10. 1910 *TR*, 141.
11. 1896 *TR*, 29. Over the next decade the number of beds was increased to two and the cost per bed increased.
12. 1900 *TR*, 88.
13. The 1913 report is the first to list milkmen given licenses to sell milk, as then required by the state for dealers selling 20 quarts or more per day. The following eight dealers were licensed: Chauncy Andrews, B.S. Blake, Alfred H. Garfield, C.W. Hubbard, C.H. Jones, L.E. Roberts, C.H. Stevens, and Philip R. Spaulding. In 1914 the state began requiring the inspection and licensing of every dairy, even if it had only one cow. Three new dairies had licenses listed, F.H. Pope, H.L. Stone, and Henry L. White. In 1915 Arthur L. Coburn, Beriah L. Ogilvie, Joseph R. Roberts, G.H.D. Lamson, and Geo. W. Cutting & Sons were also licensed as milk dealers.
14. 1891 *TR*, 43.
15. See report of "The Committee Appointed to Consider the Tuition of Children Living on the Outskirts of the Town,"1892 *TR*, 45.
16. 1892 *TR*, 46–47.
17. In 1899, voters authorized the sale of the four unused schoolhouses.
18. Oral history, Jack Williams, interviewed by Betty Howard, July 9, 1986 (WPL).
19. For the complete route description, see 1903 *TR*, 70–73.
20. The other nine-mile route went down Newton and East Newton (now Park Road) to Glen Road. A two-horse barge seated 30.
21. Because of the long time required to get through the routes, some children were later required to walk to pickup points, and shelters were erected to protect them while waiting (1908 *TR*, 73).
22. 1922 *TR*, 57.
23. 1920 *TR*, 91.
24. 1902 *TR*, 57. The total number of cities and towns in the Commonwealth was 353.
25. 1912 *TR*, 80.
26. In 1892, the high school had its first graduating class since 1888.
27. 1891 *TR*, 44–45.
28. 1895 *TR*, 39.
29. 1895 *TR*, 39. Gale, in turn, praised school committee chairman Rev. Charles Russell, who handled the logistics of centralizing the schools and "put new life and spirit into the schools . . ." (Justin Gale to Francis Blake, January 31, 1893, Blake Papers, MHS, Box 64.910).
30. Newspaper article, unknown newspaper and date, Coburn scrapbook #3, 298.
31. *WDFP*, 1895 (Coburn scrapbook #3, 298).
32. 1895 *TR*, 42.
33. 1895 *TR*, 42–43.
34. 1895 *TR*, 49.
35. The number 12 was reached in 1911. For information about School #5 in the early 20th century, see Alice Fraser's "Growing Up in Weston: 1903–1920, part II," *WHSB*, January 1985, 1.
36. 1905 *TR*, 37.
37. 1949 *TR*, 161 (tribute to Eaton after his death).
38. 1908 *TR*, 61.
39. 1908 *TR*, 61–62.
40. 1913 *TR*, 60–61.
41. 1908 *TR*, 61.
42. *1895 TR*, 41.
43. This change was introduced in 1906. Students took turns serving and taking care of the dishes. After domestic science classes were initiated, students in the advanced class prepared the soup and cocoa.
44. 1913 *TR*, 73–74. The house is located at 334 Boston Post Road.
45. *WDFPT*, June 20, 1913 and November 6, 1914.
46. 1914 *TR*, 63.
47. 1917 *TR*, 59.
48. Robert Winsor purchased the school lot at 10 Pigeon Hill Road from Horace Sears in 1903 and owned it until 1918. MCRD, Book 3049/475 (Sears to Winsor, 1903), Plan Book 107/16, and Book 4212/376 (Winsor to John Bryant Paine, 1918). The early-20th-century school building was converted to a house about 1925–26 when the school moved to Meadowbrook Road.
49. Winsor Gale, interview with Pamela Fox, August 1998.
50. An account in the *WDFPT* says the new school had about 30 scholars (November 6, 1903).
51. Informational pamplet on Pigeon Hill School, 1914 (Edwin B. Sears collection, Weston Public Library).
52. *WFP*, December 25, 1896.
53. The town did not formally vote to establish a fire department until the town meeting of March 1894. This vote seemed to be largely a formality.
54. Baldwin Tavern burned August 22, 1890. *Waltham Daily Free Press* of August 27, 1890, contained notice of the September town meeting to discuss fire apparatus. See *WHSB*, "Fire Destroys Isaac Fiske House" (Baldwin Tavern), March 1974, and also 1891 *TR*, 28–29.
55. 1891 *TR*, 30.
56. This house, probably at 19 Concord Road, lost its rear ell. See 1893 *TR*, 19–24, and also chapter 15.

57. Signal stations were located at North Avenue and Viles Street, Church Street at the railroad tracks, and three locations along Boston Post Road. Call bells were at F.H. Gowell's in Kendal Green, Hook & Hastings organ factory, McAuliffe's stable, the chair factory, and the Baptist church.
58. *WDFPT,* March 10, 1899.
59. "A Handsome Hose Wagon Has Been Built," *Gardner (Maine) Times,* about November 30, 1900 (pasted into the WPL newspaper scrapbooks).
60. *WDFPT,* January 15, 1909, describing the dedication. Equipment housed here included a ladder truck, hose carriage, and 1,000 feet of 2.5-inch hose.
61. 1908 *TR,* 113.
62. "Weston's Concrete Fire Station," *The Municipal Journal and Engineer,* vol. XXVI, no. 7, New York, February 17, 1909, 249–51.
63. *WDFPT,* June 4, 1909.
64. Crouch, H. Bentley, history of the Weston Fire Department (unpublished manuscript), 14.
65. 1908 *TR,* 91.
66. Letter, D.S. Lamson to Francis Blake, November 14, 1890 (MHS, Blake Papers, Box 63.901).
67. 1891 *TR,* 31.
68. MHS Blake Papers (Box 64.913). Newspaper article of 1894 (undated, unknown newspaper).
69. *WDFPT,* November 11, 1910.
70. Dickson, Brenton H. III, "Travel and Transportation Through Weston: part III," *WHSB,* January 1970, 4.
71. Handlin, David P., *The American Home: Architecture and Society, 1815–1915* (Boston: Little Brown & Co.,1979), 96.
72. Ibid., 103. One important outgrowth of the village improvement movement after the turn of the century was the establishment of municipal planning organizations. The first National Conference on City Planning was held in 1909, and the first course in city planning started at Harvard University that year.
73. *WFP,* early October 1887 (Coburn scrapbook #1, 233).
74. *WFP,* 1893 (Coburn scrapbook #3, 127).
75. 1894 *TR,* inserted at the beginning of the book.
76. Research by Ellen Bennett for the Weston Garden Club.
77. "The Federal Government Describes Weston's Town Green," *WHSB,* October 1981, 4–5.
78. Fuller, F.T., "Weston Aqueduct Company," *The First Parish Calendar,* vol. III, no. 2, December 2, 1895. Note that the Weston Aqueduct Company was a small, local private enterprise and has no connection whatsoever to the later Weston Aqueduct on Ash Street, which was built as part of the metropolitan system.
79. Ibid.
80. According to the Fuller article, the reservoir was about 200 feet above the level of the pump house, giving a pressure of 87 pounds to the square inch. The standpipe was circular, 50 feet in diameter and 14 feet deep, with a solid stone-and-cement wall 2 feet thick, concrete bottom and shingled roof, and capacity of about a quarter of a million gallons.
81. Ibid.
82. Acts and Resolves passed by the General Court of Massachusetts in the year 1896 (Boston: Wright & Potter Printing Co., 1896), chapter 217, 157 ff.
83. Sears's financial statements for the Weston Water Company are printed in town reports. For example, see 1918 *TR,* 28.
84. See 1901 *TR,* 98, and 1908 *TR,* 80.
85. 1945 *TR,* 79.
86. 1920 *TR,* 49. See also 37–65.
87. A five-year contract was signed in 1897.
88. 1901 *TR,* 34.
89. 1903 *TR,* 34.
90. *WDFPT,* May 4, 1900.
91. *WDFPT,* February 23, 1912.
92. *WFP,* December 3, 1886.
93. This quote from the Weston column in the *WDFP* tells of a hearing the selectmen gave to parties who petitioned for a revocation of the license granted to N.E. Telephone and Telegraph Co. to erect poles:

> There is need of a public telephone in Weston and there are hundreds of times in the course of a year when it would be found exceedingly convenient. . . . To best accommodate the people the instrument should be located in Cutting's store. That is the center for all of that section. . . . As a matter of fact the telephone which was in there two years ago ought never to have been taken out. It was a piece of extremely short sighted policy on the part of the Telephone Co. to do so. The instrument would be kept there and the company should be satisfied with a fair proportion of its earnings. Such things grow on a community and it is only by use of them that the public learns of their convenience. (Coburn scrapbook #3, 26).

The following newspaper quote regarding the Cutting's store phone is from September 28, 1888:

> Nearly fifty telegraph and telephone wires run through Weston and yet there is no direct communication with the outside world. The people would agitate the matter and compel the telegraph and telephone company to do something!
>
> When there was a telephone station at Mr. Cutting's store it paid the corporation about $120 a year. This was enough and should have satisfied them. When they wanted Mr. Cutting to transact this business for nothing and pay them $50 a year besides, he very naturally concluded the 'game was not worth the powder' and the instrument was removed. If pressure is brought to bear in the right way we believe the people of Weston can have both telegraph and telephone service.

94. *Waltham Weekly Free Press,* May 20, 1891.
95. Ibid.
96. 1895 *TR,* 117.
97. 1880 *TR,* 30.
98. Letter, Herbert Merriam to Francis Blake and other selectmen (MHS, Blake Papers, 64.925).
99. *WDFPT,* March 28, 1900.
100. Chapter 330 of the Acts of 1899.
101. *WDFPT,* April 27, 1900.
102. 1945 *TR,* 58.
103. 1907 *TR,* 38–40.
104. 1910 *TR,* 10.
105. According to the 1945 town report, 58, this means of control was developed through use of federal funds appropriated to prevent the gypsy moth from spreading to other states.
106. 1893 *TR,* 94. Grass was planted in 1899.
107. *WDFPT,* June 6, 1902.
108. *WDFPT,* July 7, 1905. According to the article, a committee consisting of Livingston Cushing, Alfred L. Cutting, Charles M. Eaton, Nathan S. Fiske, Horace B. Frost, Francis H. Hastings, and Henry J. White solicited subscriptions to raise $6,500 at $10 a share, with each share entitled to a vote. The treasurer was Robert Winsor's brother-in-law, Lyman Gale.
109. Sears deeded this land to the association in 1915 with the stipulation that if it ceased to be used as a pool, it would revert back to his heirs.
110. *WDFPT,* August 9 and 30, 1912.
111. 1912 *TR,* 43, and *WDFPT,* September 20, 1912.
112. 1916 *TR,* 64.

Figure 6-1. After Nelson McNutt bought his first Model T in December 1919 for $750, his uncle built a shelter for it similar to the existing horse barn. The Model T, introduced by Henry Ford in 1908, was easy to operate, dependable, and simple to repair. The boxy exterior remained largely unchanged until production ceased in 1927. By that time, almost 16 million "Tin Lizzies" had rolled off Ford's revolutionary moving assembly line and the automobile had become an essential part of middle-class life.

The Estate Era

Transportation: Trains, Trolleys, and Automobiles

Until the second decade of the 20th century, most Weston residents traveled by public transit or walked. Most families could not afford a horse and carriage. For long-distance journeys, parlor, dining, and sleeping cars gradually made train travel more comfortable but not more flexible, as trains followed defined routes and strict schedules.

By the early 1900s, electric street railways offered a transportation system that was cheaper and more flexible. Trolleys ran frequently and an interurban network developed to link cities and towns in eastern Massachusetts. In 1902 Weston approved a street railway line to run along North Avenue from Waltham to Lincoln within an 81-foot-wide boulevard. The line was never built, and the town rejected other proposals that would have introduced the "discord of clanging gongs and buzzing trolleys."[1]

In the end it was the automobile, not the trolley, that provided the ultimate freedom from railway timetables. The period from 1893 to the 1920s saw the introduction of the motor car and the rise of motoring as both a means of travel and a social pastime. The motor car allowed greater flexibility in routes than either trains or trolleys, ensured privacy, and allowed for independence and individualism. Whereas trains symbolized standardization, centralization, group discipline, and technological mastery, the automobile represented emancipation.[2] *The driver was his own master. Little wonder that Americans developed a love affair with the automobile.*

In his book Random Recollections, *Brenton H. Dickson III recounts the trials and tribulations of early automobiling in Weston. His family's succession of cars included a Cadillac with kerosene lamps for headlights, an air-cooled Corbin that frequently overheated and caught fire, and a Peerless with a novel electric self-starter. Dickson recalls the blizzard of 1920, when the town was snowed in for 42 days and sleighs again reigned supreme.*

Attempts to control speeding on Weston roads date back to 1905, when Constable Charles A. Freeman clocked 351 out of 389 automobiles exceeding the speed limit of 15 miles per hour. Traffic quickly became an issue as the number of cars increased exponentially in the second decade of the century. Statistics printed in the 1914 Weston town report show total automobile registration in Massachusetts increasing from 43,435 in 1911 to 86,925 in 1914, an increase of more than 100 percent in four years. In citing these numbers, Weston's superintendent of streets noted that "Weston, located on the direct route from Boston to New York, receives its full share of this increase."[3]

Train Service (1890–1915)

In 1900, the Fitchburg Railroad merged with the Boston & Maine, and by 1906 three top-notch trains a day were leaving North Union Station in Boston for destinations west of the Hudson.[4] Bert Trask was in charge of Kendal Green Station. He wore a blue coat and a cap with a silver plate reading "Station Agent."[5] Trask operated the telegraph, sold tickets, and kept records of incoming and outgoing baggage. His hunting dog, a pointer, followed him to work and was taught to jump onto the settee in front of the station when the bell rang and to stay there until the gates were lifted. The raising and lowering of the gates was done by gate tender Harold Falk. Every day, Trask placed the mailbag on a holder next to the tracks, where it was scooped up by the 7 o'clock train. Local boys were paid ten cents a night to carry incoming mail and newspapers up to the post office on North Avenue.

Figure 6-2. The stationmaster at Kendal Green Station operated the telegraph, sold tickets, and kept baggage records. One tender was employed seven days a week to raise and lower the gates from 7 A.M. to 4 P.M., and a second man from 4 P.M. to midnight. At left is the freight house.

Figure 6-3. No one was killed in this November 20, 1904, train crash on the Boston and Maine Railroad Fitchburg Division main line near Stony Brook Station. To the right is the "wreck train" that was sent to help. Train-related accidents included frequent collisions at grade crossings.

For a few years in the early 1890s, the Central Massachusetts Railroad ran two important trains with parlor and dining cars from Boston to Washington or Harrisburg. Many commuters took the Central Massachusetts every morning to Boston. If you forgot your tickets, the conductor would let you bring them the next day. The three morning trains were irreverently nicknamed the "Worker" (7:03 A.M.), the "Clerker" (8:02 A.M.), and the "Shirker" (8:43 A.M.).[6] The Central Massachusetts reached its peak of operation during the period 1907–14. For a time, 12 trains a day ran in each direction.

Beginning in 1890, the state began working with railroad companies to abolish grade crossings, where scores of fatal accidents and injuries occurred each year. Plans to abolish the Central Massachusetts grade crossings at Church Street and at Concord Road were included in the town report of 1908, and the new bridges were opened for travel about 1913. Plans for the Stony Brook crossing appear in the 1912 report, but were not executed until 1930.

"One Town Without a Trolley Line"

About 1890, horse-car street railways in Boston began to convert some tracks to electric operation. The 1890s and early 1900s saw a dramatic increase in interurban electric railways, which were cheaper to build and maintain than steam railroads and consequently charged lower fares. By 1904, Massachusetts corporations owned more than 2,000 miles of electric railway routes, and the industrial eastern part of the state was crisscrossed with a web of closely knit lines. [7]

In October 1897, the Newton Street Railway Company petitioned the town of Weston to allow an electric street railway on Central Avenue (now Boston Post Road) from Waltham to the Wayland town line. This request appears to be the first in a decade-long series of petitions for street railway permits, only one of which was ever granted.

The debates over the street railway provide insight into politics, town values, and class differences at the turn of the century. In May 1899, selectmen considered the petition of the Waltham, Weston & Wayland Street Railway Company for Central Avenue. One hundred and forty-seven Weston residents signed a petition in favor. Opposition was led by Charles H. Fiske, Samuel C. Bennett, Rev. Charles F. Russell, and Robert Winsor, who submitted a list of 36 owners of real estate along the street who were against the idea. Town leaders analyzed the names of those who signed the petition and found that many owned no real estate in Weston or lived at some distance from the proposed railway. Only seven owned land on Central Avenue, valued at about $20,000. The 36 opposing Central Avenue signers owned real estate and personal property with a combined valuation of close to $475,000. Although the selectmen decided against the street railway, the directors of the company submitted the same petition the following year, with the same result.

In general, it was the "wealthy element" who did not want street railways, citing concerns about noise, safety, and aesthetics. These and other objections are cited in this printed missive of January 2, 1902:

> The arguments for and against admittance are more or less well known. . . . The more frequent service and ready communication with Waltham; the introduction into a peaceful town of disagreeable Sunday and holiday travel; the expense for the town and the danger to our citizens; the obstruction to travel, and the piling up of snow beside the track in winter; the possible benefit to small holdings of land immediately on the railway; the destruction of the market for the large holdings and for land off the line; that is, the loss of the character of the place and of the distinction which our town has for attractive residence free from the annoyances electric roads bring. Such a distinction has a decided value, and one fast increasing, for the towns near Boston still free from electric roads.[8]

Francis Blake, a selectman at the time, expressed another concern in a private letter to Alfred L. Cutting in May 1900:

> I . . . wonder whether you have considered . . . whether the establishment of a frequent, rapid and cheap method of transportation between our town and Waltham would not practically deprive us of the moral advantages hitherto derived from our yearly "no license" vote.
>
> My own well stocked wine cellar and daily habits do not permit me to masquerade as a "total abstainer"; but I am nevertheless, strongly of the opinion that grave evils to our community would result from a close connection between our rural village and the licensed bar-rooms of a factory city.[9]

Cutting replied the following day:

> Any good thing may be abused, and I hardly think it would be fair to deprive the many people who would use the Electric Cars . . . of their rights, simply because some might take this way of getting their drink. . . . I am inclined to believe that perhaps our interest as a rural residential community can best be preserved by keeping it away. Nevertheless, I believe that the wishes of a comparatively small number of our inhabitants who would not be damaged by an Electric Railway except from an aesthetic point of view; should not be given such weight as to deprive a much larger number of equally worthy inhabitants, of their right of cheap and rapid transportation.[10]

Figure 6-4. By 1910, more than 200 Massachusetts cities and towns were served by street railways, which greatly increased the mobility of the working man and were equated with progress and technological achievement. Weston estate owners opposed the introduction of streetcars into their quiet country town. In neighboring Newton, the Commonwealth Avenue trolley, shown here, provided transportation to Norumbega Park in Newton and Riverside Recreation Grounds in Weston.

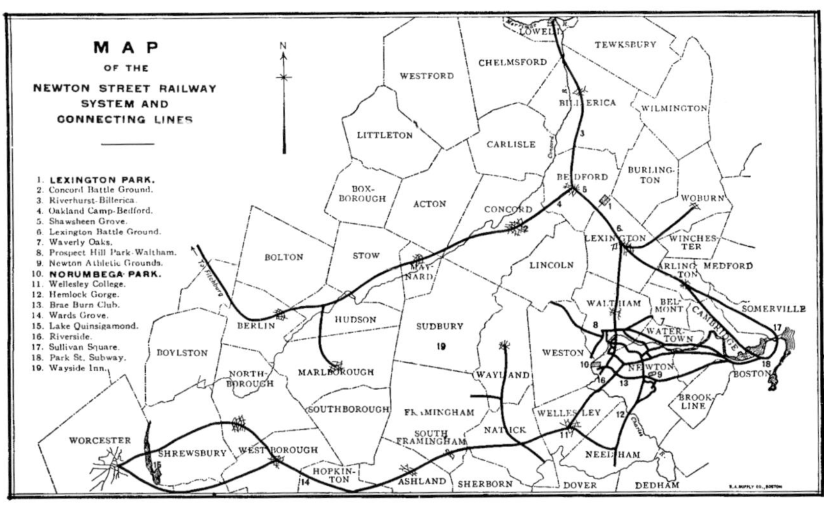

Figure 6-5. This map of the Newton Street Railway System and connecting lines was printed in a 1908 publication describing 40 excursions. The 47-mile trip from Park Square in Boston to Worcester cost 66 cents and took three hours and 42 minutes. The optimistic mapmaker shows a trolley line along North Avenue in Weston, an extension that was never built.

Street Railway Proposals

In 1901 and 1902, selectmen considered a petition from the Waltham Street Railway Company for a location on River Street, South Avenue, and East Newton Street, as well as petitions from the rival Waltham Street and Newton Street Railway Companies for a location on North Avenue. Regarding the South Avenue petition, resident Livingston Cushing presented objections signed by 24 of the 28 abutters, who together paid 98 percent of the taxes along this route.[11] To ensure that East Newton Street could never be used for a street railway, the town took some of the street as parkland, and in 1903 the name was changed to Park Road.[12]

The petition for North Avenue met with more favorable consideration. Because the majority of affected property owners favored the idea, the selectmen prepared a "boulevard plan" approved by vot-

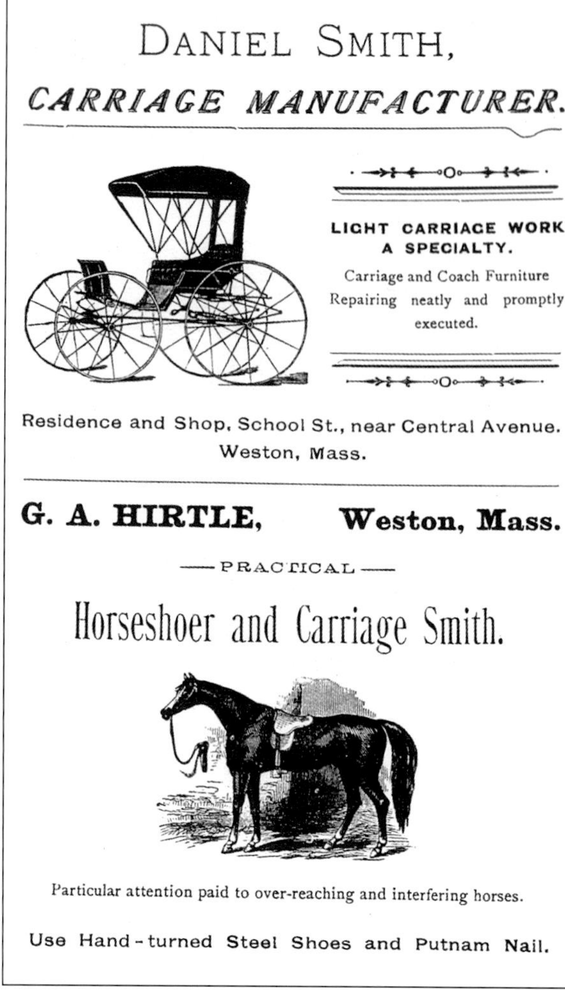

Figure 6-6. Daniel Smith advertised his carriage manufacturing business in the 1893 Directory of Wayland, Weston and Lincoln. *Horse-and-buggy-owners relied on men like G.A. Hirtle, who specialized in repairing broken carriages and shoeing "over-reaching and interfering horses."*

ers at the 1902 town meeting by a wide margin.[13] In December 1902, the selectmen granted the North Avenue location to the Newton Street Railway Company, subject to strict conditions.[14] The company had to lay out an 81-foot-wide boulevard that had sidewalks, two 20-foot roadways, and a 25-foot center strip for double streetcar tracks. They had to satisfy damage claims of abutters and pay all construction costs. The company agreed to charge no more than five cents a ride within Weston. The deal was accepted and the roadway laid out. The 1903 town report contains a full list of abutters whose land would be taken and their estimated damages.[15] Railway officials asked for an extension, noting that because of the weak stock market and financial obligations, they could not complete the project on time. The following year, the overextended company asked that the contract be annulled and paid the town $7,500 in damages.

Total mileage covered by streetcar lines grew slowly from about 1904 until World War I. After that, the overwhelming advance of the private automobile brought about a steady disintegration of the interlacing system of trolley lines, particularly interurban and suburban lines where traffic was not heavy. Weston remained "one town without a trolley line."

The controversy over public transit did not end there. In 1906 the state legislature passed an act requiring newly chartered electric railroad corporations to construct at least half their line on private property, which they were permitted to take by eminent domain.[16] This allowed the new electric railroads to travel at much higher speeds than could electric trolleys. In 1907 the Boston, Waltham and Western Company proposed two locations through Weston, one of which went right through the town square. While opposition was widespread, others like the writer of this 1908 letter to the editor strongly desired improved transportation and resented the way the town catered to its more affluent residents:

> . . . that [Weston residents] want some kind of conveyance to the east that will accommodate them much better than the Boston & Maine . . . is an absolute fact that cannot be brushed away. . . . The time is near at hand when some kind of a road will go through Weston. Whether it goes where it will do property the least harm and jar least on the nerves of summer residents is getting beyond the point where they can con-

Figure 6-7. Theodore Jones painted and trimmed carriages in the barn next to his house, the former Josiah Smith Tavern. He also made harnesses and sold fire insurance. Notice the water pump at left.

Figure 6-8. Estate owners traveled in style. This photograph, which dates from before 1887, was taken at Francis Blake's estate, Keewaydin, and includes Charles Townsend Hubbard in the backseat and his son, Charles Wells, next to the coachman.

> trol it. . . . The Railroad Commissioners will not long continue to let Weston and Weston alone stand in the way of electric interurban railways.[17]

But like street railways, plans for electric railroads fell out of favor with the increasing popularity of the automobile.

Carriages, Barges, and Pungs

Almost every town of any size had a wagon and carriage builder. At the turn of the century, Weston had two: Daniel Smith on School Street and Daniel Garfield on North Avenue. Theodore Jones painted and trimmed carriages in the barn next to the former Josiah Smith Tavern.

Horse-drawn vehicles came in all sizes and were designed for specific uses, road surfaces, and weather conditions. One four-wheel passenger carriage popular in Weston and elsewhere was the light, economical buggy, which had one seat fixed on a long, shallow tray and could be either open to the weather or covered with a top.[18] The shay or chaise was a two-wheeled vehicle with a folding top and a body suspended on springs. Coaches and coupes had side panels for better protection against the weather.

A carriage was a convenience out of reach to most residents of rural Weston, as the owner had to be able to feed and care for the horse and provide shelter for both horse and vehicle. For farmers, the one-horse farm wagon was a light, standard utility vehicle that often doubled as passenger transportation. Many people in town relied on P.J. McAuliffe's livery stable to provide carriages when needed.

Figure 6-9. Charles McNutt was employed as a "teamster" for Edward Jennings's Glen Farm and is shown here with a two-horse farm wagon.

Newspaper articles describing upcoming events often noted that barge transportation would be available from Kendal Green or other outlying areas. A barge was a two-seated wagon used to transport schoolchildren or other groups. It was covered on top and had open sides with black oilcloth curtains that could be lowered when it rained. The two seats faced each other along the length of the barge, which was entered at the rear.

When snow became too deep for carriages and barges, sleighs and pungs took over. Rather than plow streets, the highway department used a roller four to six feet in diameter to compact and preserve the snow for better sleighing. Some of the school

Figure 6-10. A pung was a large sleigh used for group transportation. This photograph of an unknown outing around the turn of the century shows the furs used to provide warmth.

Figure 6-11. In winter, rollers were used to pack down the snow for sleighs and pungs.

barges could be converted to pungs by taking off the wheels and adding runners; in other cases, barges were put away until spring and open pungs substituted. For warmth, passengers depended on a layer of straw under their feet and horse blankets or buffalo robes on their laps.

Bicycles

Bicycles have been called "the first cheap and practical means of private transport for the ordinary man."[19] In the 1870s and 1880s, manufacturers in England and the United States made important changes to high-front-wheeled models to improve stability, braking, and mounting. The so-called "safety bicycle" had two medium-sized wheels of approximately equal diameter and a chain drive to the rear wheel. The invention of pneumatic tires helped cushion the ride. By the early 1890s, the bicycle craze was in full swing, particularly in cities, where cycling in parks was especially popular.

Figure 6-12. Charles and Clara Kenney purchased bicycles for their five children, from left, Horace, Winthrop, Frederick, Elizabeth, and William. They are pictured in front of their home at 315 Boston Post Road about 1900.

In 1896 Robert Trask, station agent at Kendal Green, won a bicycle race from Haverhill to Providence and set a new record, going the distance of 200 miles in 15 hours and 20 minutes.[20] He was reported to have ridden his Warwick bicycle 5,000 miles that year. Evidence of the bicycle's increasing popularity in Weston can be found in news items such as this one from the 1899 *Waltham Daily Free Press Tribune:*

> For the first time since the incorporation of the Town the authorities have deemed it necessary to have the streets patrolled by a salaried police officer. This action has been taken on account of cyclists riding on the sidewalks. Notices have been posted in conspicuous places warning riders of this practice.[21]

Purchase of a new bicycle was often reported in the local news column. In March 1899 the newspaper noted that "Arthur Gilson of the Hastings factory expects to ride a Columbia chainless bicycle this year. It will be the first chainless machine owned in this vicinity." Charles Spear was reported to be rid-

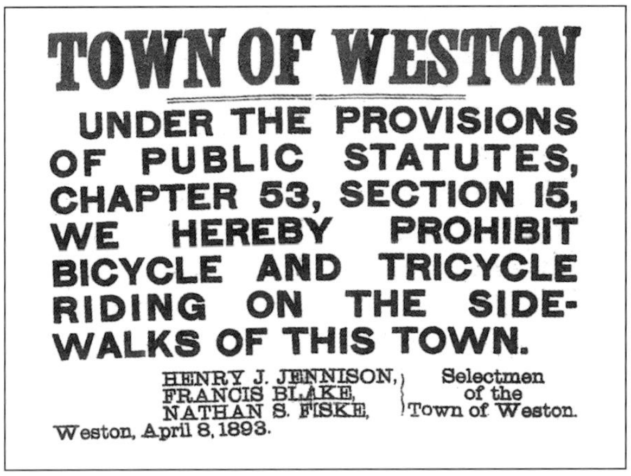

Figure 6-13. Posing at their noon lunch break is a group of Hook & Hastings organ factory workmen, two of whom have the new "safety" bicycles.

TOWN OF WESTON

UNDER THE PROVISIONS OF PUBLIC STATUTES, CHAPTER 53, SECTION 15, WE HEREBY PROHIBIT BICYCLE AND TRICYCLE RIDING ON THE SIDEWALKS OF THIS TOWN.

HENRY J. JENNISON, FRANCIS BLAKE, NATHAN S. FISKE, } Selectmen of the Town of Weston.

Weston, April 8, 1893.

Figure 6-14. The increasing popularity of bicycles made it necessary for the selectmen to ban them on sidewalks beginning in 1893.

Figure 6-15. The boy in the foreground is riding an early form of bicycle called a "dicycle." (Photo c. 1875–1887)

ing a new Waltham Comet bicycle. The 1899 library was planned with a bicycle room in the basement.

While not inexpensive, the bicycle was considerably cheaper than both the horse and buggy and the new "horseless carriage" that came into use by the turn of the century. Because of the relative cost, an article in the *Literary Digest* of 1899 confidently made this prediction:

> The ordinary "horseless carriage" is at present a luxury for the wealthy: and altho its price will probably fall in the future, it will never, of course, come into as common use as the bicycle.[22]

Early Automobiles in Weston

Automobiles made their debut in Weston in the early years of the century. The first documented car belonged to Gen. Charles Jackson Paine, who purchased a "double-seated motor carriage" from the Winton Motor Carriage Company in May 1900 for $1,500.[23] The car was shipped from the company's factory in Cleveland, Ohio, via the Boston and Albany Railroad. It was notoriously unreliable, according to the recollections of the general's daughter, Nina:

Figure 6-16. In this photograph of August 1904, an early automobile crosses the new Ash Street Bridge at the Weston Reservoir. Local residents complained frequently about excessive speeding. One newspaper item from 1905 reported that a touring car traveling at an unlawful speed had plowed into a herd of cows.

> [The Winton was] . . . very heavy and cumbersome, but considered the best kind in existence. . . . It arrived when we were . . . in Weston, and was immediately taken out on a trial spin. Papa couldn't be persuaded to go, but he told the boys to try it on a very steep hill near the old Weston golf course to see if it could make the grade. Of course it couldn't, and had to be towed home . . . [by] a team of hearse horses operated by the town's very colorful livery-stable operator Pat McAuliffe.[24]

Paine later got a letter from the Winton Company asking him for photographs of the Winton "in use," as it wanted to show General Paine's Winton in its advertisements. His daughter wrote, "It took quite a lot of self-restraint not to send photos of the Winton being towed by the hearse horses."

Figure 6-17. Eva Warren and Helen W. Cutting try out Percy Warren's first automobile.

For the first years of the century, automobiles were a novelty available only to the well-to-do, who kept their horses and carriages so as not to be dependent on the temperamental machines. Most cars during this period were driven by coachmen who doubled as chauffeurs. Engines had to be cranked by hand and required rest time to cool off. Every driver carried a tire repair kit, as early tires punctured easily. Many early cars had no headlights, tops, or windshields. The Weston column of the *Waltham Free Press* gleefully reported on automobile breakdowns and mishaps in items such as the following: "Mr. Robert Winsor's automobile failed him at Stony Brook yesterday morning, and he and his sister were obliged to take a train to Boston."[25] Because roads were not plowed, automobile travel was seasonal.

Weston's elite experimented with a variety of early automobiles. Livingston Cushing had a Stanley Steamer. In her memoirs, Alice Fraser recalls him driving down South Avenue and stopping in front of her house to build up steam before hissing down Park Road to Orchard Avenue. Horace Sears had a beautiful Locomobile, custom painted with vertical light and dark blue stripes.[26] Robert Winsor's first car was a green Lancia, an impressive car imported from Europe.[27] When Mrs. L.N. Kettle returned to her sum-

Figure 6-18. Carriages and automobiles shared the roads. This early-20th-century photograph is one of a series illustrating the narrow width of the bridge over the Charles River at South Avenue.

Figure 6-19. Many chauffeurs were former coachmen who learned to drive and repair temperamental early automobiles. This photograph is from the B.L. Young family scrapbook.

mer residence in Weston in 1911, she brought a fine Pierce-Arrow, one of the first enclosed limousines.

The spread of automobiles to the middle and working classes is chronicled with interest in the newspaper. This item appeared in 1906: "Percy Warren appears to be the latest owner in town of an auto. He is out with a Cadillac machine and wire and water repairs will now be quickly done provided the machine acts well."[28] In 1911, the *Waltham Daily Free Press Tribune* reported that Norman Jacobson, draftsman at the Hook & Hastings organ factory, had purchased a new Buick runabout.[29] In 1913 the

Figure 6-20. The "auto barge," an early form of bus, was in use in Weston by 1911. This one belonged to the Leadbetter-Sauer family on Highland Street. (1924 photo)

Figure 6-21. This two-cylinder Buick from about 1912–13 belonged to milkman Charlie Jennings, who is shown here driving. The curtains could be raised or lowered to provide some protection from the weather.

newspaper informed the town that "Dr. F.E. Wells has sold his trusty steed and got an automobile."[30] By 1917, workers from Silver Hill were commuting by car to the Waltham Watch Factory, and "They are said to be showing some speed."[31]

Businesses began to shift to motorized vehicles. G.A. Foote got an "auto coal truck" in 1911. Also in 1911, P.J. McAuliffe, owner of the local livery stable, bought a car and began renting it by the hour, day, or week, so anyone could "ride in comfort" in a first-class car with competent chauffeur. That same year, McAuliffe bought a "fine auto barge, one of the best in the state, all nicely carpeted, seating 45, and just the thing for parties of all kinds."[32] Beginning about 1914, McAuliffe ran auto barges to Waltham for people who wished to shop or attend theater on Saturday evenings and return before the late train. When Norumbega Park was open, the barge ran by way of the park, all for a 25-cent fare. The 1915 papers contain the first mention of "jitney buses," which ran regularly among Waltham, Weston, and Wayland.[33]

Figure 6-22. Concerns about the proliferation of gasoline stations, roadside stands, garages, and other automobile-related structures were part of the impetus behind zoning regulations of the 1920s. This advertising sign stood at Highland Street and South Avenue next to the Leadbetter farm. Note also the wooden "guide board," or street sign.

According to Elsie Foote Cooke, daughter of James Foote, her father had the first gasoline station in Weston at his blacksmith shop and cider mill on North Avenue. By 1914, licenses for the sale of gasoline had been granted to Foote, Benjamin R. Parker (Central Avenue), P.J. McAuliffe (Church Street), and G. Warren Broderick (North Avenue).[34]

For more than a decade, horses and horseless carriages shared the roads. Riders complained that their horses were badly frightened as automobiles began to roar over local roads. In *Once Upon a Pung,* Brenton H. Dickson III describes the scene at Cutting's Store when the occasional auto drove by:

> At mail time the hitching posts in front . . . were all occupied. . . . There was always a general shuddering among the equine contingent when an occasional automobile putted up behind them. Mufflers were in the early stages of development and the poor animals were slow in getting used to the frightening sounds of an internal combustion engine. Mr. John Paine had the first self-starter in town. . . . It was activated by compressed air and sounded something like a jet taking off. This, of course, drove any horse wild.[35]

Automobiles were a source of fascination for children and adults alike. When May and Wesley Jones were first married, in 1913, they would go to church on Sunday morning, eat their midday meal, and then carry chairs to the corner of Highland and Boston Post Road to watch the cars go by.[36] North Avenue resident Elsie Cooke remembers that as a child on North Avenue in the late 1910s, she and her friends would watch for cars and write down each license plate number. If they saw five cars, it was a big day.[37] In *Growing Up in Weston,* Philip Coburn, who was born in 1899, recalled boyhood afternoons of car-watching:

> On Sunday afternoons we were not allowed to engage in any form of sports, so we sat up on a rock ledge on Church Street across from our driveway and, equipped with a pad and pencil, would see how many makes of automobiles we could identify. We knew the makes of most of those that were owned by Weston residents.[38]

Automobiles were especially popular for Sunday drives. In 1902 the Waltham papers reported, "The automobiles are so thick on Sundays that they have driven the carriage driving people off Central avenue almost entirely."[39] Sunday car counts, by the day or hour, appear periodically in the newspaper, as in this 1909 item: "Sunday was a record day for automobile travel in Weston. Over 800 automobiles passed by on Central avenue."[40]

By the mid-1910s, Weston residents, like their counterparts across the country, were taking to the road on vacation. In her memoirs, Alice Fraser described her first automobile trip:

> In June, 1915, the Nashes took me on my first long auto trip. . . . The car was a seven-passenger Buick touring car. We drove to Deerfield and spent the night at the Deerfield Inn. Next morning we visited the old houses. . . . That afternoon we drove to Springfield and stayed in a hotel. . . . Dirt roads were bumpier, but we enjoyed every minute.[41]

Before long, Weston residents were motoring across the country. For example, a 1927 biographical sketch of coal and ice dealer George Foote notes that each year he "finds release from business responsibilities and cares" by taking long auto trips to Mexico, California, Florida or Canada. [42]

Proud owners who initially kept their automobiles in carriage houses or barns began constructing separate shelters. In 1904, the *Waltham Daily Free Press Tribune* reported that "Mr. George D. Pushee is building an automobile barn" and "Mr. George Downing is building an addition to his automobile stable."[43] In 1909 it reported that "George O. Hastings and his brother have purchased a barn near the Marshall Upham estate and will remove it preparatory to converting it into a garage. Rumor credits them with a new Buick machine."[44]

Speed Limits and Traffic

In 1902, the Massachusetts State Legislature passed the Automobile Bill, imposing speed limits of 10 mph in thickly settled areas and 15 mph elsewhere.[45] The bill required drivers to exercise reasonable precautions to prevent frightening horses. It was revised the following year to require registration of automobiles and licensing of drivers.[46] Towns were allowed to make special regulations on speed and to exclude automobiles from certain roads. Closing secondary roads to automobile traffic was advocated for both safety and budgetary reasons. Many roads were not wide enough for horse-drawn vehicles to pass big touring cars, which traveled at increasingly faster

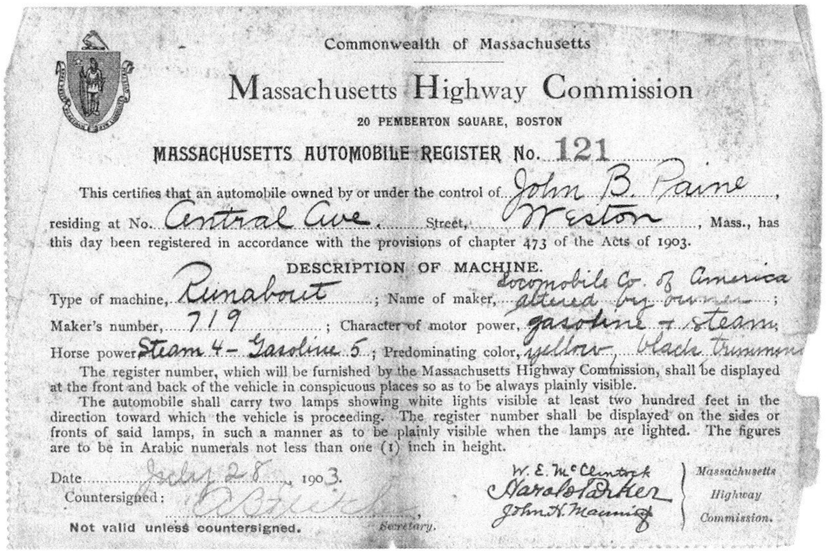

Figure 6-23. Descendants of early automobile enthusiast John B. Paine saved his license and registration from 1903, the first year these documents were required. His license number was 65 and his registration, shown here, was number 121. Paine's yellow Runabout with black trim was made by Locomobile and "altered by owner" to allow the engine to start without cranking. It was powered by both steam and gasoline.

Commonwealth of Massachusetts

Massachusetts Highway Commission

20 PEMBERTON SQUARE, BOSTON

MASSACHUSETTS AUTOMOBILE REGISTER No. 121

This certifies that an automobile owned by or under the control of John B. Paine, residing at No. Central Ave. Street, Weston, Mass., has this day been registered in accordance with the provisions of chapter 473 of the Acts of 1903.

DESCRIPTION OF MACHINE.

Type of machine, Runabout; Name of maker, Locomobile Co. of America altered by owner;
Maker's number, 719; Character of motor power, gasoline + steam;
Horse power Steam 4 – Gasoline 5; Predominating color, yellow, black trimming

The register number, which will be furnished by the Massachusetts Highway Commission, shall be displayed at the front and back of the vehicle in conspicuous places so as to be always plainly visible.

The automobile shall carry two lamps showing white lights visible at least two hundred feet in the direction toward which the vehicle is proceeding. The register number shall be displayed on the sides or fronts of said lamps, in such a manner as to be plainly visible when the lamps are lighted. The figures are to be in Arabic numerals not less than one (1) inch in height.

Date July 28, 1903.

Countersigned: ...., Secretary.

Not valid unless countersigned.

W. E. McClintock
Harold Parker
John H. Manning
Massachusetts Highway Commission.

Figure 6-24. Officer George Faber writes a ticket for a motorist caught speeding along Central Avenue in the late 1910s in his Model-T Ford Runabout. Behind the offending car is one of the Lamson houses, which was located just west of the present Christian Science church. In the upper left corner is the old Lamson tailor shop, which was moved into the commercial center after the town green was created.

speeds.[47] As more and more automobiles came into use, widening proved to be the only answer.

In 1905, because of concern with speeding cars and public safety, Weston selectmen decided to send notices to registered owners of any automobile clocked for excessive speed:

> The reckless, careless automobilist, who is a menace to every owner of an automobile as well as the general public, should have his license revoked, and it is with this end in view that we are gathering the records of the various automobiles passing through our streets.[48]

The selectmen reported that for a time, generous use of this notice produced fairly satisfactory results, but "a considerable number used our highways as a speedway." In the fall of 1905, an energetic anti-speeding campaign was conducted by Constable Charles A. Freeman, owner of the local screen factory. The town report printed his results:

> Of 389 automobiles carefully timed by stop watches over an accurately measured course 351 were exceeding the speed limit prescribed by law; 70 of the 351 were going at rates of speed varying from 22.5 to over 40 miles an hour and were summoned into court and paid fines aggregating over $600.[49]

The selectmen lamented that more-severe penalties were not available for those who continued to roar over local roads. Also of concern were drivers who opened their cutouts at night and tore through the town at such a rate of speed that "sleep is next to impossible."[50]

The corner of School Street and Central Avenue was particularly dangerous. Signs warned motorists to blow their horn when approaching the intersection. The 1912 *Waltham Daily Free Press Tribune* reported that nine out of ten drivers paid no attention, and Officer Sliney had succeeded in capturing dozens of offenders each week for breaking the law.

Complaints about traffic volume appear as early as 1905, when a description of the town from the *Boston Sunday Globe* was reprinted in the *Waltham Daily Free Press Tribune.* The article begins by praising Weston as one of the most beautiful towns in the Boston area, celebrated for its fine old elm trees and carefully preserved Colonial houses. The reporter waxes eloquent about apple blossoms, scarlet tanagers, and acres of wood violets, and then adds, "The only serious drawback to Weston is the never-ending procession of automobiles, which raise so much dust that driving is not as pleasant as it once was."[51]

Improving Town Roads

At the turn of the century, Weston had 42 miles of road, including 32 miles of "common road" and 10 miles of "avenues," North, Central, and South. Roads were divided into six districts assigned to three road commissioners, who were usually well-known farmers like Thomas Coburn, Marshall L. and Augustus Upham, A.S. Fiske, and Benjamin F. Cutter. In her recollections of growing up in Weston, Alice Fraser recalls her uncle Charles Cutter, who succeeded his father as road commissioner for the south side. Cutter used his own team of horses to grade, scrape, and plow the old dirt roads and sidewalks. To create smoother surfaces, he cut down steep hills and leveled the grades. In winter, Cutter rolled the snow to create a packed surface for sleighs. He was paid for his time and use of the horses.

Gradually, major roads were finished with

Figure 6-25. Crushed stone for town roads was hauled in stone-spreading cars. This photograph appeared on a postcard dated March 1915.

Figure 6-26. Weston's portable stone crusher was capable of crushing 150 tons of stone daily, according to a newspaper report of 1914. The storage bin was separated into four sizes. From there, stone was loaded onto self-spreading hauling cars and distributed on the streets, "changing the work of road building from drudgery into a pleasure and zest unknown before." The newspaper assured readers, "The outfit will easily pay for itself annually."

macadam, a hard gravel surface formed by compacting small crushed stones and binding them with a bituminous material. Church Street and Town House Square were "macadamized" in 1900. Other streets were finished with gravel. Better roads required better maintenance equipment. The town purchased its first snowplow in 1895 and seven more by 1908. A small vehicle storage building was constructed on Golden Ball Road to house the highway equipment.

In 1913, Weston changed to an elected Board of Road Commissioners, and Percy Warren was appointed the first superintendent of streets.[52] His challenge was to construct roads that could withstand motorized traffic and at the same time provide a safe surface for horses. Motor trucks were having an impact especially along North Avenue, where in the two years from 1911 to 1913, many teamers had started using trucks.[53] Warren recommended macadam for major roads but felt that the remaining 30 miles of town roadways could be maintained with gravel. To keep down the dust and prevent roads from raveling, Warren urged purchase of a road-oiling machine. He put down 70,000 gallons of road oil in 1915.[54] The new superintendent also recommended that the town finally purchase a stone crusher, which was in place by 1914 at the gravel pit owned by Weston Water Company at Kendal Green.

The 1915 town report includes the observation that the widening of streets tended to increase both the number of cars and their average speed, adding that "wide streets do not necessarily mean freedom from accident."

The State Highway System

The development of state highways is generally associated with the automobile, but "the bicycle was its godfather," according to Hart's 1930 *Commonwealth History of Massachusetts.*[55] In 1892, bicycle enthusiasts and other advocates of good roads secured passage of a law setting up a temporary commission to study the state's roadways. They

Figure 6-27. This photograph shows the town's watering wagon. Sprinkling dirt roads helped keep down the dust.

Figure 6-28. The shed at right, known to neighbors as the "steam roller house," was constructed on Golden Ball Road in 1907 for storage of road maintenance equipment like the watering cart, steamroller, road scrapers, and snowplows. (c. 1930s photo)

were found to be in "deplorable condition" outside municipal centers. The legislature established the Massachusetts Highway Commission in 1893 and the next year appropriated the first money for roadwork. Aid was to be spread throughout the state so each community could experience the benefits of good roads.

At a public hearing in late 1896, Weston residents debated whether to petition the state to accept Central and South Avenues as state roads, as they were used frequently by nonresidents. The financial advantage was that the state assumed the cost of macadamizing its roads and and keeping them repaired.[56] A typical state road consisted of a macadam bed 15 feet wide with a 3-foot gravel shoulder on each side, built at a cost of $10,000 per mile.[57] Central Avenue was accepted by the state and became an important link in a chain of highways connecting business centers of the Commonwealth.

Notes

1. "Weston Has Become the Lenox of the East," *Boston Sunday Herald,* May 11, 1902.
2. For an excellent discussion of these concepts, see *Americans on the Road: From Autocamp to Motel, 1910–1945,* by Warren James Belasco (Boston: MIT Press, 1979).
3. Statistics in 1914 *TR,* 45–46. By 1915, 113,895 cars were registered in the state.
4. The *Continental Limited* left every afternoon carrying a Pullman buffet, parlor car, and sleeping cars for the comfort of passengers traveling to Troy, New York, Chicago, and St. Louis. The *Chicago Express* departed at 4:30 P.M. on a different route and the *National Express* left at 6 P.M., also for Chicago and St. Louis. The trip to Chicago took about 29 hours.
5. Details in this paragraph from Philip Coburn's "Kendal Green Station," unpublished, undated typescript.
6. Dickson, Brenton H. III, "Part 3: Central Massachusetts," *WHSB,* May 1980, 5.
7. Cunningham, William J., "Transportation in Massachusetts (1890–1930)," in Hart, ed., *Commonwealth History of Massachusetts,* vol. 5, 425.
8. MHS Blake Papers, 65.943.
9. MHS Blake Papers, 65.936, May 14, 1900.

10. Cutting to Francis Blake, MHS Blake Papers, May 15, 1900.
11. 1902 *TR*, 24.
12. 1902 *TR*, 75–76, 1903 *TR*, 54.
13. 1902 *TR*, 25. The vote was 110 to 11.
14. 1902 *TR*, 26–30.
15. 1903 *TR*, 262.
16. 1907 *TR*, 29–35.
17. *WDFPT*, February 14, 1908.
18. Rittenhouse, Jack D., *American Horse-Drawn Vehicles* (New York: Bonanza Books, 1948).
19. Alderson, Frederick, *Bicycling: A History* (N.Y. and Washington: Praeger Publishers, 1972), jacket cover.
20. Coburn scrapbook #2, 3. According to the article, Trask would have covered the distance in 13 hours were it not for the pouring rain.
21. *WDFPT*, March 12, 1899.
22. *Literary Digest*, October 14, 1899, as quoted in Kenneth Jackson's *Crabgrass Frontier*, 157.
23. Bill for the car is in the Paine family papers belonging to Thomas Paine. Brenton H. Dickson III's book *Random Recollections*, 129, tells of the early Dickson cars. By 1903 or 1904, Dickson's father was already on his third automobile, a Cadillac.
24. Paine, Georgina, *Anec-dotage*, 1972, 59, as quoted in Thomas Paine's family history *Growing Paines*, 140. In 1905, the general bought a new car, a Surrey, made by the Waltham Manufacturing Company and reported in the newspaper to be a "handsome machine."
25. *WDFPT*, May 26, 1905.
26. PWF interview with Winsor Gale, September 2, 1997.
27. Ibid.
28. *WDFPT*, May 18, 1906.
29. *WDFPT*, April 1911.
30. *WDFPT*, April 11, 1913.
31. *WDFPT*, November 16, 1917.
32. *WDFPT*, September 29, 1911.
33. *WDFPT*, September 17, 1915.
34. *WDFPT*, November 13, 1914.
35. Dickson, *Once Upon a Pung*, 4.
36. PWF interview with Evan Levinson, November 11, 1997.
37. PWF interview with Elsie Cooke (b. 1910), May 21, 1999.
38. Coburn, Philip, *Growing Up in Weston*, 12.
39. *WDFPT*, June 6, 1902.
40. *WDFPT*, October 15, 1909.
41. Fraser, Alice, "Growing Up in Weston," *WHSB*, January 1985, 3.
42. *Middlesex County and Its People*, vol. IV, 368 (entry for George A. Foote).
43. *WDFPT*, April 8, 1904, and March 25, 1904.
44. 1909 newspaper clipping (undated, no newspaper name listed). Notes from scrapbook at First Baptist Church compiled by Rev. Harry E. Hinckley.
45. Acts and Resolves of 1902, Chapter 315.
46. Acts and Resolves of 1903, Chapter 473.
47. *WDFPT*, June 1, 1906.
48. *1905 TR*, 27. See also *WDFPT*, May 26, 1905.
49. 1905 *TR*, 28.
50. *WDFPT*, May 26, 1916.
51. Description from *Boston Sunday Globe*, reprinted in *WDFPT*, June 2, 1905.
52. The 1906 town report reprints a letter from the Massachusetts Highway Commission regarding improved methods of caring for highways, including this reorganization. Under the new system, the board oversaw a paid street superintendent who had no financial interest in doing the roadwork or in supplying gravel or teams. See 1906 *TR*, 80–81.
53. *1913 TR*, 53–54.
54. The 1917 town report, written after Percy Warren's untimely death at age 51, gives the following statistics on roadway composition:
   Miles of roadway: 47.5 (of which 3 were state highway)
   Bituminous macadam: 2.56 miles
   W.B. Macadam/Tarvia: 5.43 miles
   Gravel/Tarvia: 11.59 miles
   Gravel/Oil: 2.00 miles
   Earth & Gravel: 22.87 miles
55. Hart, ed., *Commonwealth History of Massachusetts*, 61.
56. *WFP*, December 25, 1896.
57. 1896 *TR*, 41. Newspapers reported the cost at $15,000 a mile.

Figure 7-1. This bird's-eye view of the 1913 Bicentennial parade was taken looking west from the First Parish Church steeple. The square was decorated with festive bunting and strings of red, white, and blue electric lights. The parade roster included the Waltham Watch Company and Bingville Horn Bands, fire department hook-and-ladder wagons, Indians and Pilgrims from the Bicentennial pageant, a stagecoach bearing George and Martha Washington, pony and goat carts, the Hillcrest fife-and-drum corps, decorated automobiles, and 18 floats and decorated wagons.

The Estate Era

Patriotism and Nostalgia

The previous chapters have concentrated on progress—progress in improving transportation and communication, progress in increasing farm and factory output, progress in advancing public health, safety, and education. As Americans rushed forward into the 20th century, many also looked back at what had been lost. They lamented the modern rootless society, the loss of local customs and traditions, and the lack of continuity as the new supplanted the old. Influential historians like Charles Eliot Norton, in his 1889 essay "The Lack of Old Homes in America," wrote about the disappearance of the "hereditary home" and the need for the "nourishment that the true home supplies."

Concerns about immigration and the resulting social upheaval fueled interest in preserving the past as the wellspring of "American" values like democracy, individualism, and self-discipline. These values were personified by the "sturdy, God-fearing, rugged-featured, strong-willed farmers" and "patient, sweet-souled New England mothers" of colonial days.[1] *Artists and writers established a glorious image of Massachusetts history that came to pervade American thinking. Thus began what Walter Muir Whitehill has called the state's "impassioned and sometimes obsessive love affair with its own past."*[2]

The late 19th and early 20th centuries saw a dramatic increase in the number of historical activities and organizations in Massachusetts and across the nation. Old homes were preserved as patriotic shrines, evidence of family lineage, and examples of handcraftsmanship increasingly valued in the machine age. Town histories were written. Historical societies were founded. Communities put their heart and soul into pageants reenacting important events in their own local history.

Weston residents were justly proud of their heritage. In his History of the Town of Weston, *Lamson wrote, "Few towns within a radius of twenty miles of Boston have preserved the old-time characteristics, both as regards population and customs, as has Weston."*[3] *In the historical address at the town's 1913 Bicentennial, Samuel Bennett addressed the challenge of preserving town character despite the influx of new residents:*

> *Only a few years ago, 40 years ago, there came into [Weston] any considerable number of persons of what are called summer residents, persons of large means, fortunes made otherwise than by farming . . . we all hope that that influx of persons will not in anywise change the character of this town, but that it may continue to be as it has been in the past, a fine old New England country town in every respect.*[4]

A Puritan Commonwealth

Massachusetts was "the last to welcome the immigrant," according to an essay in the 1927 *Commonwealth History of Massachusetts,* which added that the state "clung tenaciously . . . to the belief that it could keep its people substantially of English extraction."[5] When it entered the Union in 1788, the population of the "Puritan commonwealth" was almost entirely of British stock and the most homogeneous of any of the original 13 states. In 1849, the U.S. Supreme Court outlawed Massachusetts practices that restricted immigration, and for the next 30 years there was little regulation.

State residents worried about how to assimilate these less-than-welcome newcomers, who were not only poor but also alien in religion and outlook. Most of those entering the country between 1850 and 1890 were attracted by opportunities in expanding state industries. Mills eagerly accepted workers from Great Britain and Canada and later, as they expanded, sought additional workers from southern and eastern Europe.

After the Great Immigration of Irish during the mid-century potato famine and French Canadians in the late 1860s, the flood of immigrants increased in the 1890s and early 1900s, with the largest numbers entering in the years 1907 (85,583 immigrants to Massachusetts), 1913 (101,674), and 1914 (93,200). Both the vast numbers and change in country of origin worried Massachusetts residents. Before 1883, most immigrants were either English speaking or from Northern European countries. In 1907, at least 80 percent came from Austria-Hungary, Bulgaria, Greece, Italy, Montenegro, Poland, Rumania, Russia, Serbia, Spain, Syria, and Turkey. With them came a diversity of language, strangeness of customs, and perceived "lack of sympathy with

American ideals of government."[6]

In little over a century, a state that was once exclusively Protestant was profoundly altered by the influx of other religious groups, particularly Roman Catholics. Between 1866 and 1907, the number of Catholics in Massachusetts swelled from about 200,000 to more than 1,200,000.[7] The former Puritan colony became one of the largest centers of Catholic activity in the world. Religious antagonisms, legal discrimination, political battles, and social estrangement form an important part of the state's history in the late 19th and early 20th centuries.

Promoting Patriotism and Good Citizenship

Like other small towns across the nation, Weston celebrated the 1876 Centennial with a historical program highlighted by an oration. The speaker, distinguished lawyer Charles H. Fiske, introduced many of the patriotic themes repeated over the next half century. He expressed concern that "traditions handed down from father to son, from one generation to another, and growing dimmer and fainter . . . are frequently our only guide and light."[8] He bemoaned the destruction of valuable old documents and advocated collecting and transcribing information on "the character and customs of the people of the past time."

Figure 7-2. Col. Daniel S. Lamson (1828–1912) came from an old Weston family. He was appointed major of the Sixteenth Regiment Massachusetts Volunteers in 1861 and wears the number 16 on his hat. Lamson was always referred to as "Colonel," although he resigned from the military in 1862 because of ill health. He was the author of Weston's first history, published posthumously in 1913.

Why was the past so important? According to Fiske and his contemporaries, New England values formed the foundation of American democracy. The struggles of the early settlers in towns like Weston molded the so-called "New England character":

> To get at New England character, which is so potent in its influence upon the thoughts and lives of the people of this country, it is necessary to go back to the early settlement of New England, and see under what circumstances our forefathers came and settled here . . . what labors and struggles they underwent, and what courage they evinced to carry out their ideas of right and duty.[9]

According to Fiske, the New England town meeting, symbol of the right of local self-government, "formed the political framework of our country" by providing a pattern for other sections of the country to imitate in laying their foundations of government.[10]

Daniel Lamson, author of *History of the Town of Weston,* echoed Fiske in his concern for the nation's general moral and spiritual decline:

> As the American people progress in wealth, comfort and luxury, and enjoy all those appliances in every-day life which were unknown to our ancestors, it is to be feared that the young men and women are losing sight of those sturdy moral principles which gave force and decision to the early settlers.[11]

To Lamson, the shift of attention from the moral to the material had profound implications for local government:

> Families are not so large now, and perhaps we can say with equal truth that their virtues are less prominent. Time has become so valuable in the pursuit of wealth and comfort that it is thought wasted upon local affairs. . . . People throughout New England do not love the town meetings as they used to do.[12]

The struggle to preserve values and democratic traditions may have spurred Lamson to write his history of the town, which was praised for its "pronounced patriotic tone throughout."[13]

Local history was perceived as valuable in promoting good citizenship. For example, Weston native and organ factory owner Francis Henry Hastings organized lectures on the history of Weston aimed at making his immigrant workmen better citizens by "imbuing them with the spirit of the town in which they live which is full of revolutionary traditions."[14]

Writing the History of Weston and Collecting and Preserving Town Records

In 1884, Robert C. Winthrop, president of the Massachusetts Historical Society, sent a letter to Daniel Lamson asking him to write a history of the town of Weston, which was "the only town of any importance in the Commonwealth that had not its local history."[15] Although Lamson agreed to take on the project, he was concerned that more than 40 years of official town records, from 1712 to 1754, had been lost. At his suggestion, the selectman offered a $100 reward in 1891 for the return of the missing volume I, which, despite the financial incentive, was never found.

Lamson's chronicle ended with the year 1890. Some later information was added before the book was published in 1913, the year after his death. At that time, an editor was hired to organize the manuscript. Horace Sears paid the cost of printing and presented copies to 100 Weston households as part of the town's Bicentennial.

Lamson's difficulties with lost and inaccessible town records and his concern for the preservation of old documents were part of the impetus behind hiring retired teacher Mary Francis Peirce to organize town records. Chests and trunks full of records were collected from officers of the town and entrusted to the patient care of Miss Peirce.[16] Among the treasures unearthed in this process was a map of Weston made by Jonathan Kingsbury Jr. from surveys made in 1785 and 1794–96. A certified copy was produced and sent out with each town report of 1891.

Mary Peirce lamented that the old papers were "dropping to pieces from mould."[17] She recommended making a copy and preserving the originals, noting that other towns were doing the same. Given that a single handwritten copy would have cost $500, the selectmen decided to spend $890 to print 1,000 copies of the initial volume of town records, to be distributed free to each household. In all, four volumes compiled by Miss Peirce were eventually published by the town:

1893 *Town of Weston: Records of the First Precinct, 1746–1754* [now mostly the Town of Lincoln] *and of the Town, 1754–1803*

1894 *Town of Weston: Records of the Town Clerk, 1804–1826*

1897 *Town of Weston: Tax Lists 1757–1827*

1901 *Town of Weston: Births, Deaths and Marriages 1707–1850, Gravestones 1703–1900, Church Records 1709–1825*

In 1897, Arthur C. Goodell Jr., a leading authority on the preservation of state and municipal records, wrote to Miss Peirce:

Figure 7-3. Weston native Mary Francis Peirce (1831–1914) was a teacher at Cambridge Latin School. After her retirement, she spent her last 28 years collecting and organizing Weston birth and death records, tax lists, and government documents into four volumes published by the town. Here she sits by the fireplace in her historic 18th-century home at 543 Boston Post Road.

> . . . I believe that your work is, nevertheless, unique, and the most perfect work of the kind ever done in this state; and it gives me a sense of real satisfaction to know that the citizens of the small suburban towns of the Commonwealth are as intelligent and enterprising as their support of your labors prove them to be.[18]

Miss Peirce's reputation as the recognized historian and antiquarian of the town is confirmed in the 1902 *Boston Sunday Herald* article "Weston Has Become the Lenox of the East," which mentions how she had made her old house a "museum of interesting relics of other days."[19]

Remembering the Past

Memorial Day, or Decoration Day as it was sometimes called, was first celebrated in 1868, when May 30 was designated a date to decorate the graves of soldiers who fought in the Civil War. Memorial Day was a legal holiday in Massachusetts beginning in 1881, and by the turn of the century was a well-established event on the Weston seasonal calendar. Customary activities included speakers and a parade of schoolchildren and Civil War veterans from Town Hall to Linwood and Central Cemeteries, where veterans' graves were decorated with flags and flowers. In 1905 the parade was led by an 18-piece band, which returned to the center for an afternoon concert. In 1906, children began carrying small potted plants rather than flowers. Memorial Day observances during the World War I years were particularly elaborate.

When the 1840 First Parish Church was demolished in 1887 to make way for the present stone building, carriage maker Daniel Smith built models of the old church "for the benefit of those who desire

Figure 7-4. Schoolchildren participated in frequent patriotic celebrations designed to instill pride in American institutions and values. Memorial Day was a big event in the early 20th century, and all children were expected to be there.

mementoes." The writer of the "Weston" column of the Waltham newspaper predicted that "the time will come when these little models will acquire considerable value," adding that "many of the curiously and antiquarianly inclined have gathered relics, ranging from shingle nails to sticks of timber."[20]

In the mid-1890s, the Massachusetts Society of the Sons of the American Revolution designed an iron-and-bronze marker to place on the graves of soldiers who fought in the War for Independence. The town voted to appropriate $100 for these markers, which cost $1 each. Of the 187 men from Weston who served, organizers were able to find 63 graves.[21]

As part of the increased emphasis on local history, some place-names were changed at the turn of the century. Forest Street was renamed Conant Road at

Figure 7-5. A ceremony marking the dedication of the flagpole took place in the town square in 1890. In 1921, a new pole was erected at the present site next to the new town hall.

Figure 7-6. Mr. and Mrs. Marshall Cutting hosted this Warren-Cutting family reunion in 1881 at their home at 62 Lexington Street. A high point was the reading of a 22-stanza poem that began at Plymouth Rock with Richard Warren, who "signed our first great charter—Enrolled his name as a 'Mayflower' martyr."

the request of Justin Gale, who wrote that the name was both "euphonious & historical" and "carries the old local flavor."[22] A petition of 1902 asked the town to change the name of the oldest burying ground back to its original name, the Farmers' Burying Ground. Renaming of local streets continued into the 1920s.

The first documented historic house marker in Weston was installed at One Chestnut Street in 1911 by owner William H. Hill. The bronze slab was engraved as follows: "Oldest House in Weston Built A.D.–1696, Minute Men, Father and Son, Thomas Rand and Thomas Rand, Jr. went from this house and fought at Concord and Lexington, April 19, 1775."

Genealogy was another way to connect with Pilgrim forefathers. Those with money and an antiquarian bent, like Francis Blake, went so far as to hire professional genealogists to trace their roots in England as well. Family reunions emphasized links with the past. One example reported in the local press was a summer gathering in 1881 of about 70 descendants of John Warren, "one of the Pilgrims who landed at Plymouth."[23] Mr. and Mrs. Marshall Cutting gave the party, which was attended by family members from as far away as California. The wide hall of the Cuttings' Lexington Street home was decorated with flowers and evergreens and filled with tables loaded with rich delicacies. A reading of the family history in verse began like this:

Dear friends, go back in memory's view if you please,
To the time when the three Warrens crossed the seas
To land on Plymouth's rock-bound shore
And see their native land no more.[24]

Schools were enlisted to teach patriotic values. To cite one example, *The First Parish Calendar* commended

Figure 7-7. The Fusileer Veteran Corps of Boston formed part of the Sons of the American Revolution cavalcade that stopped in Weston on July 2, 1914. They dedicated a marker commemorating Washington's 1775 journey to Cambridge to take command of the Continental Army. The marker still stands just west of the Josiah Smith Tavern. Cutting's Store is visible in the background.

Figure 7-8. Selectman Francis Blake designed the town seal to incorporate the three most important dates in Weston's early history. His dilemma over whether to write the year of incorporation according to the "old style" or the contemporary calendar led him to redo the original design to read "1712–13."

Weston teachers for honoring George Washington's birthday in 1894:

> We cannot regret any labor which will arouse a higher and nobler spirit of patriotism in our children. While our great republic is amalgamating Teuton, Celt and Anglo-Saxon into one united American nation, no pains should be spared to inculcate in every child born on American soil, the fact that the success or failure of the great republican experiment depends in part on him.[25]

Washington and the Revolutionary War provided the focus for reenactments and historic markers. In 1914 the Sons of the American Revolution stopped in Weston on their pilgrimage from Philadelphia to Cambridge over the route traveled by the general in 1775. The party consisted of 14 automobiles decorated with flags and bunting, escorted by detachments from the Lexington Minutemen and other patriotic groups. They gathered in front of the Weston Public Library beside a slate marker newly placed there to commemorate Washington's journey.[26]

Designing the Town Seal

Selectman Francis Blake took charge of designing the town seal, still in use today. Blake wanted to familiarize residents with the three most important dates in Weston history: 1630, when Watertown (which included Weston) was established; 1698, when the settlers established their own Farmers' Precinct; and 1712–13, the year of the town's incorporation.

Blake consulted Daniel Lamson concerning the incorporation date, but after making up the die, he discovered that January 1, 1712, was calculated using the "old-style" calendar and was the equivalent of January 12, 1713. The reason is that before 1752, the year began in March, so January and February were the last two months of the previous year. December, as its name implies, was the 10th month. After 1752, the method of computing time was changed so that January was the first month. Eleven days were also added to the year, so that Weston's date of incorporation, January 1, 1712, computes to January 12, 1713.

Blake consulted a recognized authority, who gave him this advice:

> I should scarcely feel it necessary to change the date. Whatever you may do there will be some half-educated person who will try to give himself importance by criticizing. . . . But if you desire to change the die, in order to ward off all criticism, why not change the principal date to "1712–13" or "1712 O.S." . . . They look uglier, but make it clearer.[27]

Blake changed the town seal to read 1712–13.

Preservation of Colonial Houses

The preservation of Colonial houses and antique furniture, discussed in more detail in chapter 30, is yet another manifestation of nostalgia. The use of architecture to evoke the spirit of colonial America was promoted by men such as Weston resident Joseph S. Seabury. A real-estate broker with a specialty in country homes, Seabury's articles in early-20th-century issues of *House Beautiful* promoted renovation over new construction for both aesthetic and patriotic reasons. The old house resident would be "more closely in the spirit of characteristic country life" and would have a tangible link with antiquity that conferred the following benefits:

> There appears to be a distinct purpose in his surroundings and mode of life. He is continually reminded of early associations. It is a gratification to enter your door beneath a fanlight, designed

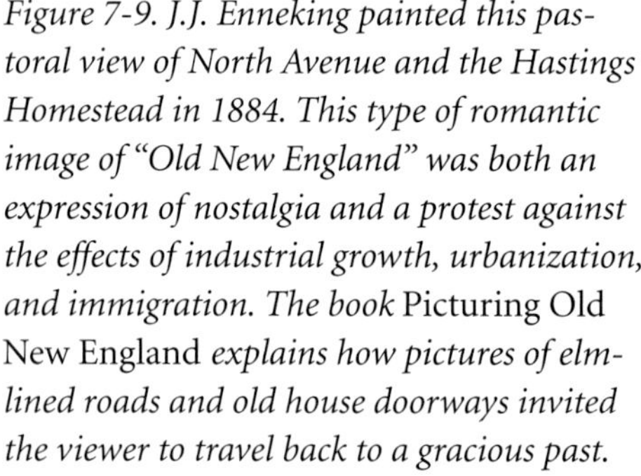

Figure 7-9. J.J. Enneking painted this pastoral view of North Avenue and the Hastings Homestead in 1884. This type of romantic image of "Old New England" was both an expression of nostalgia and a protest against the effects of industrial growth, urbanization, and immigration. The book Picturing Old New England *explains how pictures of elm-lined roads and old house doorways invited the viewer to travel back to a gracious past.*

Figure 7-10. William H. Hill (1838–1913), a prominent Boston banker, purchased One Chestnut Street as a summer residence in 1903 and named it Barberry Lodge. Hill's pride in its antiquity and Revolutionary War associations is expressed in the text of the historic marker he put up in 1911. Note the wild profusion of trumpet vines covering the venerable old saltbox. This popular turn-of-the-century convention evoked the uncontrived innocence of nature and the rural past.

> and constructed before even the Minute Men were heard of, and bring your guest into the reception-room, once the cozy sitting room, where a grandmother used to rock the windy winters through.[28]

In an article in the 1913 *House Beautiful* titled "Adding New Life to Old Houses," Seabury advocates preserving antique houses and their landscape setting because of their power to evoke the past:

> No house on a country road is so interesting or so charming as the old structure that grew up, as it were, with the elms that shade it, the apple orchard beside the barn, or the old inhabitant across the way. A new stucco dwelling with graded lawns and imported shrubbery and a neat garage is surely far from home on this country road of ours.
>
> Don't erect a new house in the old country. Modern dwellings—set and prim—greet our eyes at every turn; the old fashioned ones are rare and unique. They are fast disappearing. Preserve them before it is too late and they are all gone. There are many of us who love them, the stone fences and quiet pastures that go with them. They will forever bring to mind old days, strange customs and early hardships, and faithful folk who lived and died long years ago.[29]

Emphasis on the colonial era is also reflected in new buildings of the period. Public buildings like the red-brick town hall and fire station and churches like the Methodist (1900) and First Baptist (1924) rely on American Colonial architecture for their inspiration. The Colonial Revival has been by far the most popular house style in Weston from the turn of the century to the present day.

Figures 7-11 and 7-12. Real-estate broker, old-house enthusiast, and Weston resident Joseph Stowe Seabury wrote New Homes Under Old Roofs *in 1916. The book consists of "before" and "after" pictures of New England houses like this one at 420 Concord Road. Seabury praised the 1912 remodeling of the deserted farmhouse. In an article in* House Beautiful *in 1913, he wrote, "Modern dwellings—set and prim—greet our eyes at every turn; the old fashioned ones are rare and unique."*

Figure 7-13. Charles H. Fiske was Weston's first historic preservationist. He saved the 1755 Elisha Jones house by moving it from the Paine property on Highland Street to Boston Post Road in 1883 and then moved it again to its present location at 22 Church Street in 1888. This photograph was taken before 1916.

The Bicentennial of 1913

The celebration of Weston's Bicentennial was the most elaborate in the history of the town. A 200th anniversary committee consisting of Alfred L. Cutting, Arthur L. Coburn, Andrew Fiske, David W. Lane, and Edward B. Field, along with 15 subcommittees, took responsibility for planning and carrying out the three-day event on June 15–17, 1913. The occasion was marked by sports contests, exhibits, band concerts, children's entertainment, a major historical pageant and parade, and, on the last night, dancing under a tent and a spectacular fireworks display. The celebration was funded by a town appropriation of $4,000 over two years and generous donations of everything from food to fireworks[30]

The weather was perfect. Streets were oiled to keep down the dust. Strings of red, white, and blue electric lights encircled the town square and an electric banner with the inscription "1713–1913" was suspended across the square from telephone poles. The town hall, library, First Parish Church, and stores were festooned with red, white, and blue bunting. Festival-goers could buy official souvenir medals and red souvenir pennants for 25 cents each, or a souvenir poster designed by artist and local resident Gertrude Fiske. Nurses were available to baby-sit for small children in the schools.

The two-man Committee on Bell Ringing, Ralph F. Jones and Joseph T. Ayer, rang the bells at First Baptist and First Parish Churches each day at 7 A.M. and at sunset. On opening day, the official town crier, Robert H. Clark, arrived at the town square in an

Figure 7-14. The red felt pennant commissioned for the Bicentennial featured the Norumbega Tower.

old-fashioned chaise to announce this schedule of events, later printed in the 1913 town report:

Sunday, June 15
7:00 A.M. Ringing of church bells
9:45 A.M. TOWN CRIER at Village Square
Morning Anniversary services at the Catholic, Baptist, Episcopal, Methodist and Unitarian churches
4 P.M. UNION SERVICE with address by the Rev. William Lawrence, D.D., LLD., at tent on high school grounds
Sunset Ringing of bells at sunset

Monday, June 16
7:00 A.M. Ringing of church bells
8:30 A.M. ATHLETIC SPORTS and
10:00 A.M. BASEBALL GAME at estate of Robert Winsor
9:00 A.M. to 3:00 P.M. SCHOOL EXHIBIT, example of the work of Weston school children in drawing, sewing, manual training, and written work
9:00 A.M. to 6:00 P.M. HISTORICAL LOAN EXHIBIT at the house of the Misses Jones on the Village Square. Admission 15 cents
3:00 P.M. HISTORICAL PAGEANT on estate of Robert Winsor.
Ringing of church bells at sunset

Tuesday, June 17
7:00 A.M. Ringing of church bells
9:30 A.M. PARADE forming on Church Street, thence to Central Avenue to Concord Road, to Fiske Street, to Central Avenue, to Wellesley Street, to School Street, to Village Square
9:00 A.M. to 3:00 P.M. SCHOOL EXHIBIT, as on previous day
9:00 A.M. to 6:00 P.M. HISTORICAL EXHIBIT, as on previous day
10:30 A.M. CHILDREN'S ENTERTAINMENT at tent on High School Grounds. Admission by ticket
1:30 to 2:30 P.M. BAND CONCERT at High School Grounds
2:30 P.M. HISTORICAL EXERCISES at Tent on High School Grounds. Addresses by Mr. Samuel C. Bennett and by invited dignitaries. Admission by ticket
8:00 P.M. BAND CONCERT at High School Grounds
8:30 P.M. FIREWORKS at High School Grounds
9:00 to 11:00 P.M. RECEPTION AND DANCE in Tent at High School Grounds. Admission by ticket

Figure 7-15. Also produced for the Bicentennial was this medal, which repeated the Norsemen motif.

Day One: Sunday Services

On Sunday morning, worshipers at each of the town's churches were treated to musical programs and anniversary sermons recounting the history of their congregation. That afternoon, a reported 2,500 people attended a Union service in the tent at the high school, planned by First Parish pastor Rev. Charles F. Russell and his Committee on Sunday Services and enriched with music by the Bostonian Ladies' Orchestra and a choir of 100.

The sermon by Rev. William Lawrence, D.D., Bishop of Massachusetts, summarized in the anniversary edition of the *Waltham Daily Free Press Tribune*, is instructive for its theme contrasting country and city life. For his text, Bishop Lawrence chose the passage in which Jesus left the city and lodged in Bethany. He likened this to present-day Westonites who "engage in daily labor in the cities [and] return evenings to the peace and quiet of the country town" where they are refreshed by the country air, beautiful foliage, and quiet peace. Lawrence added, "The suburban towns have the opportunity to set the model of ideal life."

Lawrence admonished his listeners to work for civic betterment, not only for their village but also for the larger community of metropolitan Boston:

> Thousands of immigrants are coming into the port of Boston each year and they make their settlement in our community. Our self-interest compels us to feel that we must educate and uplift them.[31]

Lawrence urged those from the country to "bring to the city, the cheer, the glow and the character of life that surrounds you":

> Jerusalem is near Bethany and Weston is near Boston. You may go to the city daily, but you should ever try to spread the influence of that happy life that you enjoy in the country. . . . Pause then on this occasion to consider the opportunities and privileges that you enjoy, and let your thoughts go out to the thousands of people who in the crowded tenements of the large cities see little of the American liberty for which our forefathers fought and died. . . . [C]ome down from the hill . . . and go into the city, and make every sacrifice to uplift the people of our community.[32]

Day Two: The Pageant

The Weston Bicentennial pageant was one of hundreds held in New England and nationwide from about 1905 through the mid-1920s, during the heyday of American pageantry. In his book *American Historical Pageantry: The Uses of Tradition in the Early Twentieth Century,* David Glassberg examines these organized community spectacles, which improved on the old historical oration by dramatizing episodes from town history. Pageants were generally held outdoors in daylight with large casts of costumed volunteers and minimal props and scenery. They ranged in size from a cast of a few hundred, like that in Weston, to one in St. Louis in 1914 that had a cast of 7,000 and audiences of nearly 100,000 at each performance. In 1913, the American Pageant Association was formed to set standards, disseminate technical information, and, in general, protect the form from being misused.

Pageantry grew out of efforts by civic officials to create social unity out of a hodgepodge of classes, special interests, and immigrant groups.[33] The art form blended antimodernism and idealization of the past with the progressive goal of fostering civic pride. Progressives hoped pageants would help towns visualize solutions to their current social and economic problems while promoting "a unique local identity, sense of cohesion, and attachment to place."[34]

The Weston pageant committee, chaired by Sears protégé Charles O. Richardson, engaged Joseph Lindon Smith as director. The ingenious and versatile Smith was well known in pageantry circles and had staged productions in Milton and Lancaster. He was also a friend of Brenton H. Dickson Jr., who was instrumental in securing his services.[35] In *Random Recollections,* B.H. Dickson III describes Smith on the Dicksons' back porch constructing the pageant's enormous cornucopia out of heavy electric wire and papier-mâché.

The chosen site was a natural amphitheater on Robert Winsor's estate Chestnut Farm, complete with a pond for the Viking landing. An estimated 400 residents, about 20 percent of the population, took part, with many appearing in more than one scene.[36] Charles Richardson was pleased with the strong community support, which he felt would "prove of permanent value in the community and life of the town."[37] The production was funded with $1,500 from the town, plus private donations. Tickets were free to all residents. An estimated 2,300 people attended, according to the annual town report.

William Chauncy Langdon, one of the early promoters of the art, wrote that "the pageant is a drama in which the place is the hero and the development of the community is the plot."[38] As organized and directed by Smith, the Weston version consisted of a prologue, three historical episodes, and an epilogue. The prologue and epilogue were allegorical and starred a woman playing the part of Weston. The historical episodes were organized into six scenes as follows:

Early Times
- 1) The Indians 1000
- 2) The Coming of the Norsemen 1000
- 3) Settlement of the Western Precinct 1630

Revolutionary Times
- 1) English Spy 1775
- 2) March to Concord 1775

Washington's Visit 1789

The plot was printed in the newspaper to make it easier for residents to follow the story line, as there was little dialogue. The following brief summary is included to show how the town's history was portrayed in this landmark production. In the first two scenes, the Indians make camp and a young brave acts out a tale of stalking and killing an enemy. At its climax, as he pounces on the imaginary victim, the Indians are surprised and alarmed to hear a loud holler from the shore. Norsemen disembark from their boat, the Indians welcome them, and they eat together. The younger braves exhibit their skill with bows and arrows and the Norsemen with swords. The meeting comes to an end as the chief offers to guide the Norsemen up the river.

Six hundred years elapse, and in scene three, the Indians have been decimated by wars and pestilence. Puritans enter, singing a psalm of praise. Sir Richard Saltonstall persuades the Indians to trade money

Figure 7-16. Hundreds of historical pageants were held throughout the country in the early 20th century. By telling the history of a community, organizers hoped to promote civic pride and social unity in an age of increasing diversity. No Weston pageant would have been complete without a scene showing the patriotic farmers marching to Concord.

Figure 7-17. Well-known pageant director Joseph Lindon Smith produced Weston's pageant of 1913. Smith began in the year 1000 with Indians greeting the Vikings, who were thought to have settled along the Charles River. Some 400 town residents took part in the drama, held on the grounds of the Winsor estate.

Figure 7-18. Dramatic story dancing was pioneered by Isadora Duncan and incorporated into historical pageants like this one in Weston. Allegorical scenes allowed dramatic dancers to tell part of the story through their movements and props. These symbolic dances added variety and depicted abstract concepts that could not be easily acted. Women in the Weston pageant played parts like Present, Past, and Future.

and goods for land and John Eliot reads to them from the Scriptures. Two yokes of oxen accompany the Puritan farmers from Watertown who settle the western precinct.

Part II recounts the story of John Howe, the English spy, whose reconnaissance role for General Gage had by that time been transformed into legend. The next scene enacts the march of the Weston militia company to Concord, with feature roles for Weston's premier patriots, Samuel Phillips Savage, Capt. Samuel Lamson, and the gun-toting Rev. Samuel Woodward. In part III, Washington's visit to Weston in 1789, townspeople scurry around preparing for the president's visit. Washington dismounts from the coach, is greeted by Mrs. Lamson and Colonel Marshall, and, by tradition, kisses young Hannah Gowan.

In the prologue and epilogue, town residents play the parts of Weston, the Past, Present, and Future, the month of June, and the Hours of the day, along with Father Time with his scythe and dancers with great horns-of-plenty, garlands, and wreaths. At the end, these offerings are laid before an altar and the fruit poured out in a great heap on the ground. Weston and her companions leave the scene, Future holding a lighted torch, Present walking beside Weston, and Past, with shrouded head, following last.

Day Three: Weston on Parade

The Tuesday-morning parade was chaired by another Sears protégé, Harry Bailey. Participants lined up on Church Street under the supervision of Chief Marshall George H.D. Lamson.[39] The

Figure 7-19. The Ambler farm raised goats in Weston for a short time before moving to Maine in 1914. Its float reads "These kids raised on goats milk."

Figure 7-20. The Bingville Horn Band played for the Bicentennial parade and band concert.

Figure 7-21. Marian Case's "Hillcrest boys" formed a fife-and-drum corps that marched in the Bicentennial parade.

Waltham Watch Company Band and Company F of the Fifth Infantry Regiment of Waltham marched near the front, followed by members of the Weston Fire Department with hook and ladder and hose wagons. Next came the Bingville Horn Band, along with Indians and Pilgrims from the pageant. The town crier drove by in his ancient carriage, and a stagecoach carried George and Martha Washington.

Behind them paraded a cavalcade of ponies and pony carts driven by the young people of Weston, a young clown in a goat cart, and a team of goats pulling a float with the sign THESE KIDS RAISED ON GOATS MILK. The Hillcrest Farm Drum Corps marched next, along with the Hillcrest Farm wagons and auto decorated with flags and bunting.

There followed a series of floats representing various industries and secret societies of Weston. The Temple of Fraternity float represented the "principles of order" of the Henry A. Upham Lodge, Ancient Order of United Workmen. The Weston Grange had floats representing Spring (tilling the soil), Summer (girls in a bower of roses and flowers), Autumn (a husking bee), and Winter (a barn dance). Drabbington Lodge entered a four-seat wagon filled with people waving flags. Grocer G.W. Brodrick's wagon featured characters dressed like "living trade marks" for popular products like Gold Dust Twins scouring powder, deviled ham, and Quaker Oats.

The G.A. Foote Coal Company float carried Old King Coal and his court attendants surrounded by large blocks of coal. The Cushing Grain & Hay Co. and Jennison Express Company entered decorated wagons, as did plumber A.L. Hersum, whose float displayed a complete bathroom. Representing the Town of Weston was the moth department wagon and spraying machine decorated with flags and bunting. The Weston suffragette float bore the message VOTES FOR WOMEN. The parade closed with a column of decorated automobiles and two floats from the Hook & Hastings organ factory, the first carrying the keyboard and organist William H. Dolbeare, connected by electric cable to a second carrying the organ pipes.

The parade proceeded up Central Avenue (now Boston Post Road) to Concord Road, where it turned around via Fiske Lane and continued back on Central Avenue to Wellesley Street, School Street, and back by the school grounds to the town square. At the school grounds, prizes were awarded for floats (1st, Weston Grange; 2nd, Hook & Hastings Co.); for decorated automobiles (1st, Ferndale Farm; 2nd, I.W. Hastings); and for horses.

Bicentennial Exhibitions and Programs

On Tuesday afternoon, Alfred L. Cutting, chairman of the General Committee, presided over the historical exercises. Lawyer Samuel C. Bennett presented a detailed history of the town settlement. The lieutenant governor and elected officials from other cities and towns gave speeches.

Visitors could view the historical exhibit at the Josiah Smith Tavern and exhibits at the high school. The Historical Committee, chaired by Francis Blake's son-in-law, Stephen S. FitzGerald, restored and furnished three rooms of the former tavern. Items mentioned in the special anniversary edition of the newspaper include Chippendale, Sheraton, and Hepplewhite sideboards, chairs, secretaries, settles, and sofas loaned by members of venerable Weston families. Along with the mélange of oil paintings, deeds, Indian arrowheads, samplers, and pewter plates and porringers was the hallmark of such exhibitions, "kitchen utensils of Colonial days in great variety."[40] The most unusual contribution was C.H. Fiske's "old rubber galosh." Admission was 15 cents.

The Committee on School Exhibits, chaired by Superintendent Eaton, displayed examples of student academic work, drawing, and sewing. There were leather purses and belt bags made by girls in a special weekly class and Morris chairs, music cabinets, tables, and sleds made by boys in manual training.

Figure 7-23. The Weston Grange won first prize with four floats representing the seasons, including the autumn husking bee shown here. "Spring" showed tilling the soil, "Summer" had girls in a bower of roses and other flowers, and "Winter" depicted a barn dance.

Figure 7-23. The organ factory float took the second-place silver cup. The newspaper described it as "an impromptu affair" hurriedly assembled from a few hundred pipes and odd parts from instruments under construction. The organist and his keyboard traveled ahead in a separate wagon connected by an electric cable. Organist William Dolbeare played "familiar airs, folk songs, religious and patriotic, which were cheered and applauded."

Figure 7-24. G. A. Foote Coal Company entered the "Old King Coal" float in the 1913 Weston Bicentennial parade. The famous king is surrounded by court attendants and large blocks of coal.

Figure 7-25. G.W. Brodrick's Store in Kendal Green entered this "Living Trade Marks" float. The following people participated, although not all are in the photograph: Ralph Vittum (driver), George Brodrick (Deviled Ham), Mrs. George Brodrick (Dutch Cleanser), Harry Henderson and Harold Foote (Gold Dust Twins); Warren E. Vittum (Uneeda Biscuits), Harlan Berry (Quaker Oats), James Berry (Force), and Mrs. Brodrick's sister (Baker's Chocolate).

Figure 7-26. At the conclusion of the parade, prizes were awarded for floats and for decorated automobiles and horses.

A popular feature was a display of graduation programs, prize essays, and other memorabilia.

Horace Sears was in charge of the Committee on Reception, which hosted invited guests. Fellow estate owner and friend Robert Winsor chaired the Committee on Collation, which conducted a lunchroom and restaurant in the town hall on Monday and Tuesday. Another of Sears's inner circle, Charles C. Kenney, headed the Committee on Music, which engaged the popular Waltham Watch Company Band for the parade, band concerts, and Tuesday-night dance.

Committees not already mentioned included Transportation (Arthur T. Johnson, chairman); Sports (B. Loring Young); Information (William O. Kenney); Decoration, Illumination, and Badges (Charles A. Freeman); Printing and Publicity (Lyman

W. Gale); and Public Comfort (Sanford Orr, M.D.). The report of the anniversary committee concludes with this assessment:

> Your Committee feel that the celebration has been a splendid thing for the town. Our own townspeople have become better acquainted and more closely knit together because of the experience.[41]

Figure 7-27. This vast tent on the school grounds on School Street was the location of important Bicentennial events, including the Sunday "Union Service," historical exercises, and concluding reception and dance.

Notes

1. Preface to Lamson's *HTW*, vi.
2. Whitehill, Walter Muir, and Kotker, Norman, *Massachusetts: A Pictorial History* (New York: Charles Scribner's Sons, 1976), 253.
3. Lamson's *HTW*, 148.
4. Samuel Bennett's historical address at the 1913 Bicentennial, reprinted in *WDFPT* Special Anniversary Edition, 2.
5. Thayer, Mrs. Nathaniel, "The Immigrants (1830–1929)," in Hart, ed., *Commonwealth History of Massachusetts*, vol. IV, 142.
6. Ibid., 142–49.
7. Lord, Rev. Robert, "The Catholic Church in Massachusetts," in Hart, ed., *Commonwealth History of Massachusetts*, vol. V, 527–28.
8. Fiske, Charles H., "Oration Delivered Before the Inhabitants of Weston at the Town Hall, July 4, 1876" (Weston, printed by vote of the townspeople, 1876), 1.
9. Ibid., 6.
10. Ibid., 7.
11. Lamson's *HTW*, 130–31.
12. Ibid.
13. Editor's preface, Lamson's *HTW*.
14. *Boston Herald*, Sunday, July 13, 1890, as printed in Donald G. Kennedy's article "Francis Hastings' Labor Experiment," *WHSB*, January 1984, 5–6.
15. Report from Daniel Lamson about town records, c. 1890 (MHS, Blake Papers 63.901).
16. 1891 *TR*, 16. About the same time, the state legislature was also getting involved in what was being recognized as a critical problem and in 1892 created the position of Commissioner of Public Records.
17. 1891 *TR*, 19.
18. 1898 *TR*, 22–23.
19. *Boston Sunday Herald*, May 11, 1902.
20. Coburn scrapbook #1, 191. ("Weston" column, probably *Waltham Daily Free Press*). First Parish Church has a model that may be one of those built by Smith.
21. *1895 TR*, 67 (names listed in report).
22. 1901 letter from Justin E. Gale to Francis Blake (MHS, Blake Papers 65.940).
23. This phrase is from the first line of a printed account entitled "Weston, Mass.—Family Reunion," which describes the July 27, 1881, event and includes all 22 stanzas of the poem (author's files, from Eloise Kenney). Despite the claim, it appears that John Warren was not a Pilgrim and did not land at Plymouth Rock.
24. "A Family Reunion," newspaper account in Coburn scrapbook #4, 49.
25. *The First Parish Calendar*, February 17, 1894, vol. 1, no. 5, 1.
26. *WDFPT*, July 3, 1914. Selectman Alfred L. Cutting accepted custody of the marker on behalf of the town.
27. For complete information on the development of the town seal, see Blake Papers, MHS, Box 63.
28. Joseph S. Seabury, who was local representative for Poole & Seabury, Brokers in City and Country Houses, was responsible for moving the Artemas Ward Jr. house at 543 Boston Post Road back from the street. This quote from Seabury's article "The Reconstruction of Lynbrook Farm, the Country Home of Thomas P. Lindsay" in *The House Beautiful*, May 1914, vol. 35, 162.
29. Seabury, Joseph S., "Adding New Life to Old Houses," *The House Beautiful*, vol. XXXIV, June 1913, 2.
30. For the complete report, see 1913 *TR*, 116–24.
31. *WDFPT*, Weston Anniversary Edition, June 1913, 4.
32. Ibid.
33. Glassberg, David, *American Historical Pageantry: The Uses of Tradition in the Early Twentieth Century* (Chapel Hill & London: University of North Carolina Press, 1990), 185.
34. Ibid., 71.
35. Dickson, *RR*, 143–44.
36. As reported in the 1913 town report, the number of participants in each scene was as follows: prologue and epilogue (70), Indians (100), Norsemen (25), settlement of the Western Precinct (50), English Spy (8), March to Concord (75), Washington's visit (100).
37. 1913 *TR*, 120.
38. As quoted in Glassberg, op. cit., 71.
39. Description of the parade from Weston Anniversary Edition of the *WDFPT*, June 1913.
40. Ibid.
41. 1913 *TR*, 124.

Figure 8-1. All four sons of Charles and Clara Kenney served in World War I. From left: William, Horace, and Frederick were in the U.S. Navy and Winthrop was in the Army infantry. Daughter Elizabeth is in the center of this formal portrait taken about 1917.

CHAPTER 8 · (1915–1945)

World War I to World War II

Much has been written about the suburban phenomenon in books like Crabgrass Frontier *by Kenneth T. Jackson and* Borderland: Origins of the American Suburb, 1820–1939 *by John R. Stilgoe. Jackson defines the word* suburb *on the basis of function (non-farm residential), class (middle and upper status), separation (a daily journey to work), and density (low relative to older sections).[1] Beginning in the 19th century, influential publications encouraged the physical and social separation of the population into the male-dominated sphere of the business world, which was usually urban, and the female-dominated sphere of domestic life, preferably suburban. With each improvement in transportation, more and more business and professional men made the choice to work in the city and reside in the country. Away from the congestion of the city, they could breathe healthy air, find spiritual renewal in nature, and build the type of house that has remained the American ideal, the separate house surrounded by its own yard.*

In Weston, the transition from farm town to suburb was a gradual process that began in the 19th century with the the establishment of country estates. Around the turn of the century, the neighborhoods of Pigeon Hill and Silver Hill were developed within walking distance of railroad stations. The first "automobile suburbs," Meadowbrook Road and Chiltern Hundreds, were settled beginning in the 1920s, although Chiltern Hundreds still benefited from its proximity to rail transporation. Using Jackson's four criteria, Weston did not become a full-fledged suburb until after World War II, when the last farms were sold for development and major highway improvements greatly facilitated commuting.

New residents demanded better services. In 1913 the Town of Weston had no debt. It also had no adequate town buildings except the library, no town water system, few modern roads, and no zoning or building laws. Between 1913 and 1943, the town issued bonds totaling $766,000 to build the fire station, town hall, and new high school and to develop a municipal water system. By far the largest expense, $427,000, went for extending water service and finding new supplies.

The transition involved more than just new houses and improved infrastructure. At some point, a way of life came to an end. Some longtime residents point to the Depression as the break between old and new. The Depression changed traditional employment patterns and brought the town to an economic low point. Farmers and tradesmen, who had never been wealthy, lived hand to mouth. Remaining estate operations were largely curtailed. By the time the wartime economy brought Weston out of the Depression, the town had changed forever. As one resident put it, "After the war, the newcomers took over and it became a different town."

World War I

The outbreak of war in Europe on August 3, 1914, took Massachusetts by surprise. Few imagined that the United States would get involved.[2] President Wilson was reelected in 1916 with the campaign slogan "He kept us out of war." Young men from Weston who wanted to help the Allied cause enlisted with the Canadian forces, Foreign Legion, or hospital and ambulance service. Back at home, Weston held its first Fourth of July parade in 1916. Twenty young ladies dressed in white carried an American flag measuring 15 by 25 feet. Hillcrest Farm won first prize for its "Peace" float.[3]

After Germany began sinking American merchant ships, Massachusetts prepared for war by organizing a Committee of Public Safety and a Home Guard to take

Statistics	1920	1925	1930	1935	1940	1945
Population	2,282	2,906	3,327	3,848	4,375[4]	4,473
Number of Dwellings	564	652	773	858	962	1,019
Valuation	$5.411m	$7.377m	$8.981m	$10.055m	$10.625m	$10.733m
Tax rate	$14.00	$19.50	$20.50	$24.50	$21.00	$21.00

Figure 8-2. Joseph F. Lamson, son of Weston historian Col. Daniel S. Lamson, was a sergeant first class in the Motor Corps in World War I.

Figure 8-3. After the war, American Legion Post 214 sent questionnaires to returning soldiers asking for service data, photographs, and a "summary of your experiences." The photographs include this one of Roger Williams Bennett, son of Samuel C. Bennett. Another soldier who served in France as a private wrote, "One meal a day with starvation and cold."

the place of National Guard troops mustered into service. The United States declared war on April 4, 1917. The first Massachusetts troops were shipped overseas that fall and fought from February to November 1918. An estimated 147 men and six women from Weston served in the war, and six were killed in combat.[5]

During the war, Western grain normally used to feed New Englanders and their livestock was shipped overseas. Homegrown food and feed were needed to fill the gap, and home canning of vegetables flourished. Weston set up a Food Conservation Committee, chaired by Mrs. John B. Paine. To be sure no food was wasted, trained canners gave lectures and made home visits to provide instruction. A Community Canning Kitchen was established at Weston High School and staffed daily with a paid expert and volunteers. A census done in December 1917 counted a total of 24,000 jars canned that year.[6]

Rationing of food and other scarce commodities became necessary. The state initiated controls to prevent hoarding and profiteering and to secure uniform distribution of flour, sugar, and meat. Newspapers published pleas like this one asking citizens to substitute cornmeal and potatoes for bread:

> An army cannot have muffins and potatoes in the trenches. . . . Do not have toast for breakfast—HAVE CREAMED POTATOES. . . . Do not have bread for supper—HAVE SCALLOPED POTATOES. . . . The most important of all shipments to make abroad today is WHEAT.[7]

Coal shortages led to rationing, and gasoline shortages curtailed use of the newly popular automobile. The town closed District School #5 and stopped heating the Kendal Green Fire Station, which never reopened.

The war took away draftees from the farm and diverted other young men into war-related jobs. The Committee on Public Safety helped fund camps on the farms of Louis W. Dean, C.H. Jones, and C.W. Hubbard so that about 50 boys from out of town could live and work on Weston farms in the summer of 1917.[8] The committee arranged for plowing and harrowing to be done for almost 100 families. Land set aside for the new town common was cultivated for food.

Patriotic feelings ran strong. The town turned out in force for Memorial Day exercises in 1917. The dedication of the new town hall in late November 1917 became a celebration of democracy and freedom. B. Loring Young spoke eloquently of the Minutemen of Weston and fallen soldiers of the Civil War, adding, "We rejoice that men of Weston are again on the battle-line of democracy in the most righteous war yet seen on earth."[9] The banquet was omitted to conserve food. For Christmas 1917, the town sent silver medals bearing the town seal to all Weston servicemen.

In 1918, 81 percent of Weston households subscribed a total of $800,000 to the Liberty Bond drive, one of the highest rates per capita in New England.[10] The old town hall was fitted up as headquarters for the Weston branches of the Red Cross and American Fund for French Wounded. Volunteers prepared more than 20,000 surgical dressings, knit hundreds of sweaters and socks, and sewed over 3,000 pillow slips in 1917.[11] Estate owner Mrs. Austin White of Lexington Street gave a winter carnival that attracted 400 to 500 people for skating, tobogganing, dancing, and card playing, with proceeds of $400 going to the French wounded.[12] Schoolchildren collected war relief money to send to French children and Camp Fire Girls sold 960 chocolate bars, earning $20 for the relief of Belgian babies.[13]

In addition to the privations of war, the state was hit by an influenza epidemic in September 1918. Large gatherings were discontinued. In spite of public health efforts, 10,000 Massachusetts residents died in the month of October alone. Weston had an estimated 275 flu cases and four deaths.[14] Schools were closed for three weeks.

On November 11, 1918, the silence of the early-morning hours was broken by church bells announcing the signing of the armistice. Weston residents participated in an ecumenical service of thanksgiving at First Parish Church or headed over to Waltham for the largest parade in that city's history. Many soldiers were not discharged until the spring of 1919, when the town held a combination Welcome Home and Memorial Day celebration in their honor.[15]

On Memorial Day 1921, the town dedicated a flagpole just east of the new town hall, along with the boulder at its base bearing a bronze tablet inscribed with the names of those who lost their lives in the Great War.[16] The flagpole of Oregon fir was 101 feet long, 2 feet in diameter at the base, and was crowned with a golden eagle.[17] The following Memorial Day, the town dedicated two bronze tablets with the names of all men and women who served, to be placed in the main assembly room at Town Hall.[18] More elaborate ideas, such as building a memorial Community House with gymnasium, Scout meeting rooms, and an up-to-date swimming pool, reflected recreational needs not met until years later.

Town Development (1915–1945)

Weston continued its policies of progressive modernization and was blessed with dedicated and able men who served as selectmen for decades. B. Loring Young took the place of his uncle Francis Blake in representing estate owners and south-side residents. Except for two years when he was fully occupied as state representative, Young was selectman from 1910 to 1946. In addition to his leadership in creating the town green and town hall, Young was a member of the planning board when the first zoning laws were being considered. During World War II, he chaired the Committee on Public Safety in charge of civilian defense.

Figure 8-4. After World War I, the Fiske family gave the 1.25-acre Soldiers Field park at Concord and Boston Post Roads to the town in memory of 2nd Lt. Charles Henry Fiske 3rd (1896–1918). A monument designed by Harold B. Willis and erected by the family in 1931 reads, "He trained and served in many lands to find at last a death in France."

Young was known for his eloquent yet concise explanations of issues. His goals for the town were expressed in this speech at a special town meeting in December 1942, devoted in large part to the town's employment practices and employee benefits:

> Towns, like men, go forward or go back: they don't stand still. . . . Weston should not stand still, should not stay in a rut, however comfortable, complacent and self-satisfied we may be. Weston should be prepared for growth and change. We may not like the prospect, but we cannot help it. This town must prepare for the future. We can and should have the best budget, the most satisfactory building and zoning laws, the most loyal and efficient officers and employees, the best Town government to be found in Massachusetts. We must build our home, not for ourselves alone but for our children and our children's children in years and in centuries to come.[19]

Figure 8-5. Brenton H. Dickson Jr., Herbert "Bert" Tyler, and B. Loring Young served as selectmen for a combined total of 89 years. Weston artist Gertrude Fiske painted their portrait.

Figure 8-6. Fire Chief Frank Mulock is seated in the center of this Weston Fire Department photo of April 1939. At the far right is Erlon Merrill, the town's only full-time firefighter until the mid-1940s. Standing, left to right: Harold Stevens, Steve Colpitts, John Compton, A.J. Colpitts, John Lingley, Warren Vittum, Jerry Sliney, Dan Compton, Maurice Delong, Floyd Barbetti, C. Tebo, John Clark, Ralph Slayton, Fred Perkins, Jim Hanney, Murdock Cameron, Hugh MacDonald, John Cain, Harold Colpitts, Charlie Wheelock, Guy Akers, Charlie Stimpson, and Erlon Merrill. Seated: Winnie Martin, Frank Mulock, and Harold "Toe" Coburn.

Herbert E. "Bert" Tyler served as selectman for 36 years, from 1912 to 1948, including two decades as chairman of the board. Like his predecessor Nathan S. Fiske, Tyler spoke for farmers and north-side residents. When he retired, a resolution at Town Meeting noted his "scrupulous fidelity to duty, . . . New England farmer's sturdy common sense, and . . . keen perception of the wishes and needs of the townspeople." Appreciative citizens collected subscriptions and presented him with the keys to a new Ford truck.

Alfred L. Cutting, who had come onto the board in 1900, represented the center and the town's business interests and middle-class tradesmen. After Cutting's 25-year tenure, Brenton H. Dickson Jr. served 17 years, from 1926 to 1943. In addition, Dickson was town clerk from 1918 to 1943. Like their predecessors, Young, Tyler, Cutting, and Dickson continued the town policy of keeping down the tax rate. The 1942 town report noted that of 312 towns in Massachusetts, only 18 had a tax rate lower than Weston's.[20]

In 1917 the town hired its first permanent administrative employee, Miss Marion H. Upham, as clerk of committees. Elected officials like the selectmen and town clerk were paid for their duties, the highest paid being treasurer and collector at $1,000. Beginning in 1922, state law required that the town appoint a finance committee. Until 1921, the town still depended on constables and police officers who drew no regular salary but were ready to respond on call. In 1922, the town accepted a new state law providing for a full-time police department. J. Sumner Viles succeeded Patrick J. McAuliffe as chief in 1929 and served for almost three decades, until 1958.

Full-time police officers were needed in part

Figure 8-7. Dr. Fresenius Van Nuys (1876–1969), who practiced in Weston from about 1907 to 1951, has been described as "the epitome of the country doctor." In addition to an active practice, he was chairman of the board of health for 36 years and school physician for some 25 years. Older residents recall him standing by the classroom window every Monday morning with a stock of tongue depressors, as students filed by for a weekly throat inspection. He delivered most of the babies in town. Van Nuys was much loved for his kindness to young and old without regard for social position or country of origin. This 1929 painting by Gertrude Briggs was given to the town by his son, Thomas.

because of the increasing use of automobiles. The first police department report of 1922 lists 84 offenses for which arrests were made, 48 for automobile violations.[21] By 1925, automobile violations had increased to 198, including 135 arrests for operating under the influence. More than 100 car accidents were reported. These numbers decreased as Weston strengthened its police force. Police transportation was exclusively by motorcycle until 1929, when the department purchased its first car.

Over the next two decades, the town added permanent members to the highway, police, and fire departments and increased school staff. In the early 1940s, voters agreed to adopt modern employment practices set up under state statutes, including workman's compensation insurance, liability insurance, and employee retirement plans. Except for the chief, police officers were placed under civil service.

The period between the world wars saw major changes in treatment of the town's poor. Joseph Seaverns, the last inmate at the poor farm on Conant Road, died in 1915. Seaverns was 74 years old and had lived at the poor farm for 30 years. After his death, the farm was rented and then sold in 1922. The town continued to appropriate money for relief. In 1928, the name Overseers of the Poor was changed to Board of Public Welfare. Beginning in the Depression years, aid was divided into categories like "old-age assistance" and "mothers' aid." The federal government began supplementing town funds.

Advances continued in public health. By the 1920s, state law required every school system to have a school nurse. In 1927 the Public Health Nursing Service (incorporated in 1948 as Weston Visiting Nurse Association) was founded under the joint auspices of the town and the local chapter of the American Red Cross. The board of health and schools shared the services of a nurse who conducted physical examinations along with hearing, vision, and tuberculin tests. The board set up a school dental clinic beginning in 1930, and many children had their teeth repaired who otherwise would have been neglected. The board of health ran diphtheria immunization clinics to inoculate children not vaccinated by their private physicians. In 1943, the town marked its first decade without a diphtheria case. In the late 1930s, a clinic was started to immunize dogs against rabies. Immunization clinics for whooping cough were set up in 1943, and by 1945 combined vaccines could be administered for tetanus and diphtheria. Measles, mumps, and chicken pox remained the most prevalent contagious diseases. Weston had two cases of infantile paralysis in 1928 and two more in 1931.

In the 1920s, Weston acquired two small parks that added greatly to the beauty of the town center. The 1.25-acre Soldiers Field park was given in 1921 by the Fiske family and the 1.8-acre Lamson Park was taken by eminent domain in 1927. Soldiers Field was drained by opening a culvert under Boston Post Road.

In 1937, Miss Josephine Merriam of Minneapolis, Minnesota, offered the town $5,000 to erect a stone gateway to Central Burying Ground, where her parents and grandparents were buried. The Josephine Merriam Memorial Gateway was designed by local resident and architect Harold B. Willis. In a letter to B. Loring Young, Willis wrote, "We have made a serious effort to keep the gateway extremely simple and quiet, in harmony with that part of the Town, and are studiously avoiding anything highfalutin."[22] The memorial was constructed in 1938.

In 1920 the town was still providing bathing suits free of charge at the town pool on School Street.[23] By 1930, the pool was a quarter of a century old and in need of major repairs. The pool committee recommended that an indoor pool be included in plans for the new high school, but this suggestion was not adopted. In 1938 the committee reported, "Our old, shabby building and small pool still perform their usual service."[24] About 4,000 pool visits were made in 1935, or about 80 children per day in the summer months. Numbers increased during the war to 4,487 in 1944. By that date, the pool was part of summer recreation programs held on the playground and in the school gymnasium. In 1944 the town abolished the swimming pool committee and replaced it with an elected recreation commission and the stage was set for postwar changes.

By the mid-1930s, the town had three dumps, located at the present Church Street site and also on South Avenue and on Ash Street.

Schools (1915–1945)

Weston schools maintained their high standards under superintendent Charles M. Eaton, longtime school committee chairwoman Carolyn E. "Carrie" Burrage, and superintendent Carl T. Rhoades, who took over from Eaton in 1929. District School #5 on South Avenue, which the administration had wanted to close for years because of low enrollment, was finally shut down in 1917 as a wartime economy measure.[25] The North Avenue school, the last of Weston's one-room schoolhouses, remained open through the 1931–32 school year.

A special committee report of 1930 recommended that the existing system of centralized schools be continued, that students be divided into schools for grades 1–6 and 7–12, and that new facilities be built to accommodate a growing school-age population crowded into outdated facilities.[26] The committee concluded that the wood-frame building constructed in 1878 as a high school and then in use

Figure 8-8. On Flag Day, students stood around the flagpole while a boy in the senior class read from the Bible and led opening exercises. The handsome 1878 wooden building on the right was built as a high school and later used as a grammar school. It was torn down in the early 1930s.

Figure 8-9. Ralph Harrington Doane designed the Georgian Revival brick high school, completed in 1932 (now Brook School Building C; photo c. 1934).

as a grammar school was antiquated in design and a "fire menace." They recommended moving elementary students to the high school building and putting up a modern high school.

The new brick Georgian Revival high school was designed by architect Ralph Harrington Doane and completed in 1932.[27] Arthur Shurcliff was in charge of landscape design. In addition to classrooms, the building had a library, cafeteria, gymnasium, science and art rooms, general shop room for boys, and home economics unit. The latter had a food laboratory with kitchen equipment and a general-purpose room with stationary tubs, washing machine, electric ironer, hand iron, and sewing machines. A commercial department offering typewriting and book-

Figure 8-10. First grade, 1920–21.

Figure 8-11. Third grade, September 1934. (Names with photo credits)

Figure 8-12. Weston High School baseball team.

keeping was added in the mid-1930s. In 1941, a state supervisor inspecting the school wrote, "The Town of Weston is administering an efficient and modern high school that has been listed in the Class A group for many years."[28]

Physical education facilities, teams, and instruction time increased dramatically. The high school employed a full-time male physical education teacher for boys and a full-time female teacher for girls. In 1939, the grounds behind the central school complex encompassed about 20 acres, three times more than a decade earlier, with a football field, tennis courts, girls field hockey field, rebuilt baseball diamond, and skating pond used by schoolchildren and town residents. By 1943, the pond had been enlarged to include a hockey rink.

School lunches—a concept unknown at the turn of the century—went from hot soup and hot chocolate in 1906 to complete balanced meals by 1929. Milestones occurred in 1918, when the school began

Figure 8-13. Members of the Weston High School class of 1928 wore white graduation dresses, a tradition that has continued to the present day. (Names with photo credits)

Figure 8-14. Twenty-five students graduated from Weston High School in 1939.

a lunch program during the winter months, and in 1922, when milk was first provided at low cost to pupils in grades 1–4. In 1929, the Women's Community League arranged for equipment and began serving hot lunches at nominal cost. The school department took over the program two years later and hired a lunch coordinator. The third floor of the new high school building was devoted to a cafeteria for all 12 grades. Girls in the home economics department prepared some dishes as part of their cooking courses. By 1937, an average of 500 students a day chose lunch from a typical menu like vegetable soup (6¢), lamb in gravy on potato (10¢), lettuce sandwich (5¢), milk (5¢), and mock Indian pudding (5¢).[29]

The first public kindergarten opened in the central primary school in 1936. The Weston Parents Association was organized in 1937 by a group of kindergarten mothers who had been holding informal get-togethers. In 1951 the group changed its name to the Weston Parent-Teacher Association. They began a system of room mothers acting as liaisons between parents and school.

Two of the town's early preschools were formed during this period to provide educational opportunities for children aged 3 to 5. The Weston Nursery

Figure 8-15. In 1941, Weston High School had 176 pupils, eight full-time teachers, and six part-time teachers in drawing, music, physical education, home economics, and industrial arts. This photograph shows the faculty in 1942. Standing: ____, Constance Burrage, Lois Smith, ____, John Zorn, Aimo Teittinen, William Taunton, Ruth Smith, Rachel Speare, and Violet Golden (school nurse). Seated: Mildred Damon, John Proctor, Carl T. Rhoades (principal), Helen Green, Wallace Sawyer, and Helen Harding.

School was established in 1930 and, beginning in 1932, was owned and operated by Miss Elizabeth Parker at her home at 25 Conant Road. Miss Parker retired in 1971. The Red Barn Nursery School Inc. was formed in 1944–45 by merging the nursery groups of Mrs. Weston Blake and Mrs. Albert Speare, who became the first director. Incorporated as a cooperative in 1951–52, it was governed by a corporation of parents and interested town residents. The present facility at 724 Boston Post Road, completed in 1958, was the first separate building in Weston constructed as a nursery school.

In 1923–24, Weston's first private school moved from its original location on Pigeon Hill Road to a larger site on land belonging to estate owner Robert Winsor (see chapter 20). At that time the name was changed from Pigeon Hill School to Meadowbrook School. In 1931, the Cambridge School opened on Lexington Street in the Kendal Green area as a progressive private high school (see chapter 10).

Water Supply

In 1920, voters debated whether to purchase the Weston Water Company, which had been supplying water to a large part of the town since 1896. Dissatisfaction with service at Silver Hill appears to have prompted interest, at least in that part of town, in purchasing the company. Silver Hill did not have a sufficient water supply to make it safe from a serious fire hazard, and other parts of town were also far from the nearest hydrant. Opponents argued that if the town went into the business of supplying some of its inhabitants with water, others would naturally demand the same service, at great expense to the town. A lengthy committee report in 1920 recommended that Weston "take now the step it will undoubtedly take some day."[30]

Weston Water Company was acquired on July 1, 1921. With it came the services of Edmund T. Carver, who became superintendent of the new Weston Water Department and held that post until 1946. Over the next two decades, the town spent more than $400,000 improving an obsolete and inadequate system.[31] A major overhaul in 1928 involved the purchase of additional land at Kendal Green, drilling 18 additional wells, and laying large water mains to the town center, Silver Hill, and Wellesley Street/Meadowbrook Road.[32] By 1931 there were 50 wells around the Kendal Green Pumping Station, along with the earlier group of wells on Warren Avenue. As part of continuing improvements, a standpipe 52 feet in diameter and 49 feet high, constructed of steel with a capacity of just over 750,000 gallons, was constructed near the summit of Doublet Hill in 1931.[33] In 1937 the town took over the water system of the Weston Real Estate Trust in the Meadowbrook Road area, which served about 70 customers including Weston Golf Club.

In the late 1930s, the town began exploring for additional water supplies. At that time, about half the residents got their water from the public system and the remaining half from private wells or small private water companies. With the increase in population and possibility of continued drought conditions, the water department was concerned about reaching capacity. The town's three golf courses—Weston Golf

Club, Pine Brook, and Riverside (the present Leo J. Martin)—took about one fourth of water consumption in dry weather. Three expert seismologists from Weston College, Father M.J. Ahern, Father Daniel Linehan, and Father Thomas Smith, helped the town locate a water supply on the property of Mrs. Francis Blake. By 1941 a new pumping station next to Nickerson Field was supplying an extra million gallons a day.

In 1938–40, for a second time in its history, Weston was the site of a major water supply project serving the Boston metropolitan area. The construction of the Hultman Aqueduct and Norumbega Reservoir required lowering steel-reinforced concrete pipes almost 12 feet in diameter into a shallow trench. Details are included in chapter 28. The metropolitan system did not supply water to Weston until the 1970s.

Care of Street Trees

Annual reports from the tree warden chronicle the battles—won and lost—against insects, blights, and man-made hazards. Chestnut tree blight wiped out many of the town's roadside chestnuts in the late 1910s. A temporary reprieve from the gypsy moth scourge ended with the unusually mild winter of 1936–37, when most of the egg clusters survived, leading to widespread deforestation in 1937. Asking "Shall we economize and let the gypsy caterpillar destroy the beauty of the town?" the selectmen recommended an expenditure of $12,000, or an additional $1 on the tax rate, to wage a campaign.[34]

In 1937 the town experienced its worst elm leaf beetle infestation, which completely defoliated a large portion of the town's elms. The hurricane of 1938 left trees decimated. Tree warden Gilbert H. Upham warned that the thousands of dead elm logs scattered throughout woodlands were a breading ground for elm beetles, which had become the main carriers of the dreaded Dutch elm disease. At that time, Dutch elm disease had spread only as far north as Connecticut, but by the early 1940s, Massachusetts trees were also affected. On the positive side, in 1936 some 57 Norway maples were set out on Summer Street along the newly reconstructed road, paid for by a street tree fund established by Horace Sears.

Zoning and Planning

The theory of zoning—that no person who owns land should be permitted to use it in a manner harmful to the general welfare of the community—was an extension of long-standing laws to prevent nuisances. Designation of districts for specific uses first occurred in the 1880s but was not widely used until after the turn of the century.[35] The first major zoning ordinances were passed in Los Angeles in 1909 and in New York City in 1916. Zoning laws were used to establish and preserve the character of an area and tended to separate rich and poor. American planners recommended two types of legislation, the first to regulate building size and placement and the second to distinguish among different uses of land. Planners assumed that a particular type of building was most satisfactory when surrounded by others of its own kind in designated residential, commercial, and industrial areas.

Massachusetts was a leader in urging municipalities to create planning boards and regulate housing types. A first step toward establishment of zoning was taken in 1912, when the state legislature passed the tenement-house law. This act allowed communities to prohibit the erection of three-family frame houses known as three-deckers. In Weston, a special committee strongly supported the ban for reasons ranging from fire safety to the threat to real-estate values:

> The presence of three-deckers would be a serious menace to the future development of Weston. They are usually of the flimsiest construction and rapidly deteriorate, so that they soon become the dwellings of a class of tenants who add nothing to the revenues of the town, but who, on the contrary, become the cause of increased expense in all departments . . . . [Three-deckers] are terribly destructive of surrounding real estate values. Already in several towns the assessors have noted a great depreciation in neighboring properties.[36]

The committee report recognized the groundbreaking nature of this legislation: "For the first time in this country it is now possible for a town to protect itself against these evils and dangers by accepting the Tenement-house Act." After adopting the act, Weston appointed its first inspector of buildings, architect Alexander S. Jenney.

Weston's First Zoning Plan

As the town grew, the selectmen acknowledged the need for better planning in their 1921 report:

> Town planning is of value not merely for aesthetic reasons, but for practical business reasons as well. Proper location and width of streets, the location of municipal buildings, future problems of sewage disposal and water supply can be properly planned some years in advance.[37]

The planning board was organized by 1922, and as its first action, members recommended a comprehensive survey and master plan. They retained landscape architect Arthur A. Shurtleff (later Shurcliff), who had been responsible for the 1912 Town Improvement Plan, to draw a map showing existing land use.[38]

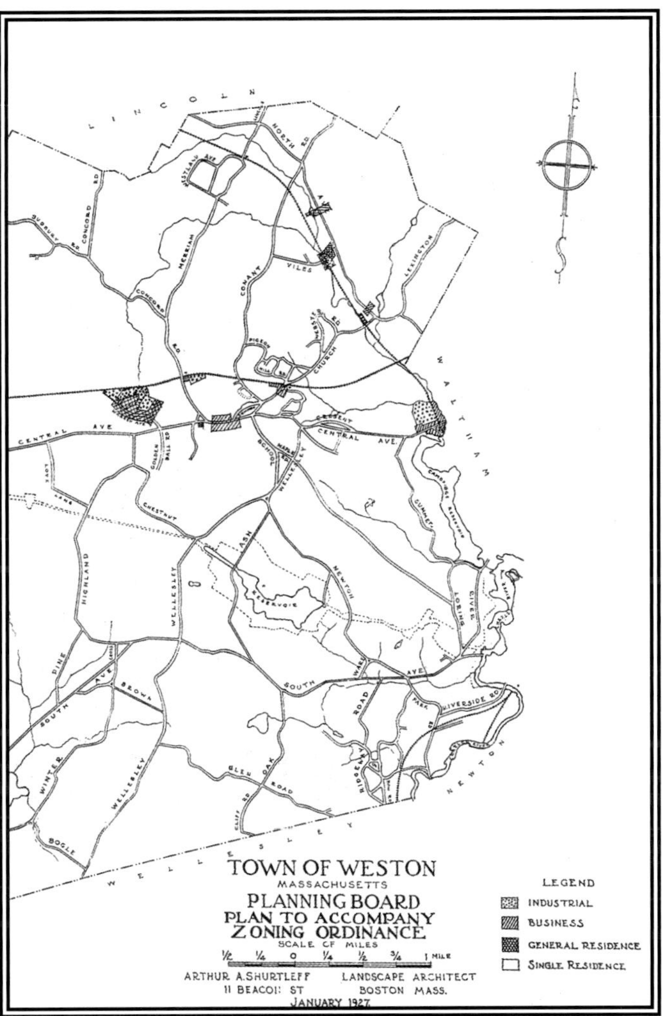

Figure 8-16. *Weston's first zoning map, prepared by planner and well-known landscape architect Arthur A. Shurtleff (later Shurcliff), was adopted in 1928. Most of the town was zoned for single residence only. This plan was the beginning of a consistent town policy to keep Weston residential and, as far as possible, rural or "green" in character.*

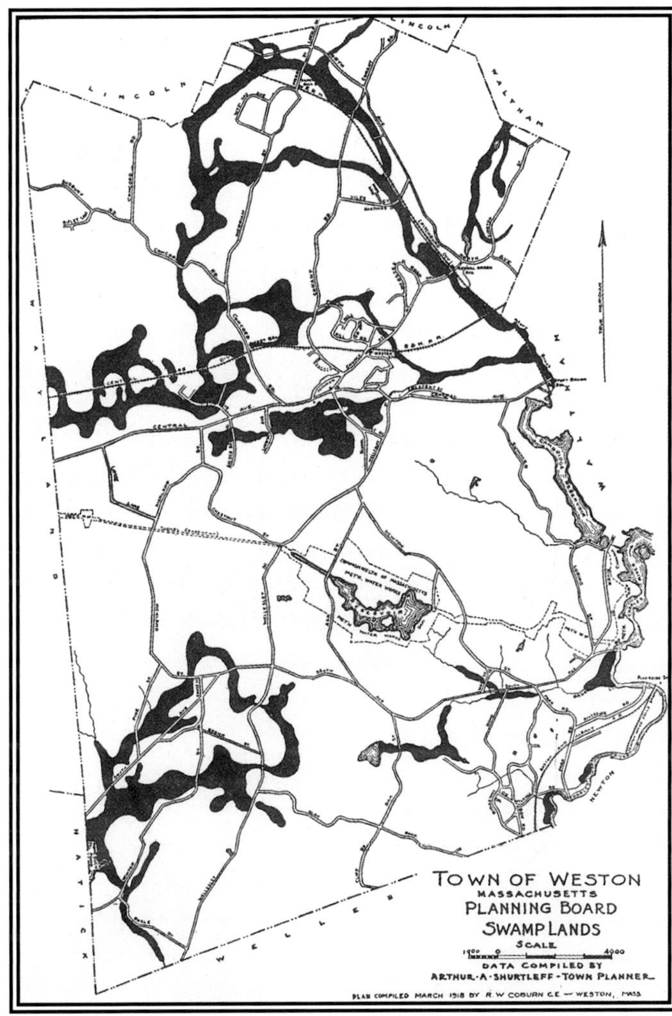

Figure 8-17. *The town's estimated 800 acres of swampland were mapped as part of the planning process directed by Shurtleff in the 1920s. The ecological value of wetlands was not understood at the time. Shurtleff suggested that building a highway through the swamp south of the town center would relieve traffic congestion.*

Under the direction of Shurtleff, who is referred to as the "town planner," the fledgling planning board prepared a list of problems and far-reaching solutions printed in the 1924 town report. The five members of the board, Edward B. Field, B. Loring Young, Alexander Winsor, George W. Bailey, and Raymond W. Coburn, had the full support of the selectmen, who alerted townspeople to the critical issues at stake:

> The Board has a most important work to perform if the future of Weston is to be properly safeguarded. . . . We are in the midst of a dangerous period and unless we exercise the greatest care, we may wake up too late and find ourselves in the same condition as many towns who have not been alive to the subtle changes taking place in their midst.[39]

The report pinpointed the characteristics that set Weston apart:

> Weston is a town of distinctive character. Many things permitted in other towns have not been allowed here. . . . A quiet, beautiful country village is becoming more and more rare, especially when situated as near a great city as Weston is. . . . Weston is distinctive because of its freedom from roadside stands, refreshment booths and Sunday selling . . . much of the charm of the town is due to the absence of these enterprises, so common in many rural communities where automobile traffic is large.[40]

Problems highlighted by Shurtleff in the 1924 town report included the following:

1. *Traffic congestion:* Traffic was number one on the list of problems. Congestion in the town center, Kendal Green, and south side near Auburndale had reached a point where public safety and convenience were compromised. Most of the vehicles were using Weston as a gateway to and from Boston. One

Figure 8-18. Traffic congestion was the most important issue addressed in Weston's first major planning study. Boston Post Road was eventually widened to accommodate parked cars on both sides. This photograph dates to the 1920s, when the Ginter Company was in business selling groceries in the Hersum Building in the 400 block.

proposed solution was widening main roads, particularly North, Central, and South Avenues.

2. *Swamps, ponds, and brooks:* The town had 800 acres of swampland, including more than 100 acres in the heart of the town. Shurtleff proposed that some of this "useless land" could be made valuable by draining it for future highway use. He suggested that the solution to traffic congestion in the town center lay in the nearby swamp.

3. *Schools:* Playgrounds were inadequate, and Shurtleff suggested studying swampland next to schools. He recommended that the town consider sites for future school buildings.

4. *Parks and playgrounds:* Shurtleff noted the need for playing fields and parks. He was well ahead of his time in suggesting that the town consider acquiring "lands of scenic interest" like those on high hills and along the borders of ponds, streams, and meadows:

> As the town builds up more closely, the question will arise to what degree the townspeople are willing to allow these landscapes to disappear as land is cut into house lots. . . . A step toward the preservation of one of these central landscapes was made in the acquisition of the Town Common. The triangle of land recently given at the junction of Concord Road and Central Avenue is a step in the same direction. . . . The question arises, will

Figure 8-19. This postcard of the G.W. Brodrick general store and post office on North Avenue, mailed in 1924, shows one of the town's early gas pumps. About this time, the fledgling planning board suggested that the time had come to stop granting any more licenses for garages and filling stations.

the Town be satisfied to allow the other open spaces in the vicinity to be closely built up?

5. *Cemeteries:* Shurtleff expressed concern about commercial development on the borders of the town's oldest cemeteries.

6. *Zoning:* Shurtleff cited problems caused by increased automobile usage:

> The automobile has forced most cities and towns of the Commonwealth to consider or to adopt zoning regulations to protect residence districts against property valuation depreciation through the construction of public garages, repair shops, storage yards and filling stations. Motors have also led to the erection in residence districts of food-vending booths, restaurants and rest rooms.[41]

Shurtleff noted that landowners had proved eager to adopt zoning to remove the uncertainty of haphazard growth.

In conjunction with the zoning study, another committee prepared bylaws regarding buildings, including requiring a building permit and setting out standards for height, setbacks, quality of materials, and construction. The new regulations required the use of septic tanks instead of the old-fashioned cesspool. These regulations were adopted in 1926 and the first Inspector of Buildings and Inspector of Wires, Franklin C. Mulock, was appointed.

In 1928 the town adopted the first zoning bylaws. Four districts were established: single residence, general residence, business, and industrial.[42] In general, the district map reflected actual land use at the time. Only a few small pockets were zoned for business, industry, or general residence, where double houses and boardinghouses were allowed. Minimum lot size was set at 10,000 square feet. The 1928 bylaw also established a ratio between building size and lot size.[43] Buildings had to be sited at least 15 feet from the street and lot lines. In 1934, minimum lot size was increased to 15,000 square feet in the single-residence district.

A sweeping zoning bylaw revision of 1937 broke the single-residence district into A, B, and C districts, with minimum lot sizes of 20,000, 30,000, and 40,000 square feet respectively. For the first time, street frontage was considered, with100 feet required in single-residence district A and 125 feet in districts B and C. In supporting the 1937 changes, the selectmen argued that overdevelopment would cost the town money as well as change its character:

> If the substantial land holdings in Weston are purchased by speculative builders for development purposes the whole character of Weston as a rural community will be changed and the town will become merely another crowded residential suburb. This would entail tremendous expense for additional water supply and for sewage disposal.[44]

Figure 8-20. The largest parcel zoned for industrial use in 1928 was owned by the Massachusetts Broken Stone Company. In addition to quarrying, the company produced asphalt "hot top" for road construction. The asphalt truck and the crushed-stone storage tower are pictured in this 1938 photograph.

Transportation (1915–1945)

In 1926, the *Minute Man* was added to the Boston & Maine schedule, although this popular train sped through Weston without stopping. The *Minute Man* carried coaches, parlor, and dining cars to Troy and a single sleeping car that was then picked up by the New York Central and carried on the *Lake Shore Limited* to Chicago, a trip that took 26 hours. It was the B & M's premier train for many years. A picture of the Revolutionary War Minuteman was adopted as the railroad's symbol.[45]

On the Central Massachusetts line, traffic was heavy during World War I and stable in the early 1920s. The increased use of automobiles and trucks eventually hurt train traffic. By 1927 there were only two passenger runs through to Northampton,

Figure 8-21. A freight train traveling nonstop from Mechanicsville, N.Y., to Boston speeds past Stony Brook Station with its wartime cargo in the winter of 1944–45.

Figure 8-22. In 1914 there were 85,407 motor vehicles registered in the state of Massachusetts. By 1939, that number had increased to more than a million. In this 1946 photograph, Marjorie Perkins Gibbs sits atop her 1941 Pontiac.

and in 1932 service to Northampton was discontinued. Train service revived during World War II with four trains daily between Clinton and Boston.

Small "jitney" buses operated off and on from the late 1910s into the 1940s. One bus traveled along Boston Post Road between Maynard and Waltham and another on North Avenue from Lincoln to Waltham. Residents of Kendal Green did more business in Waltham than in Weston town center because of the availability of public transportation. The jitney service was a great convenience at a time when many families still did not own a car. Drivers were very accommodating. Housewives could give Earl, the Boston Post Road bus driver, money for a few grocery items and then wait for him to drive back with their order. Teenagers with a quarter to spend could get to and from the Waltham theater for 10 cents, pay for the movie, and still have a nickel left for an ice-cream cone.

At the turn of the century, automobile ownership was a luxury. Early cars were expensive, costing in the range of $2,000 and up. Until 1906, high-priced models represented 43 percent of U.S. car sales. A decade later, these top-of-the-line automobiles had a market share of less than 2 percent, while one low-cost producer, Ford, had garnered 45 percent of the market.[46] Ford's rugged Model T appealed to prosperous farmers. Farm boys like Nelson McNutt on Glen Road could save their wages and buy a Model T for $750, giving them unparalleled freedom of travel.

By 1918, tires had improved and engines were more reliable. The construction of hard-surface roads not only tended to encourage auto traffic but also had a deterrent effect on horse-drawn traffic, as the harder surfaces were treacherous for the animals. The transition from horse-drawn to motorized transportation was largely complete in Weston by 1922. That year, the last horse-drawn school barge was replaced by a motorized bus. Eighty-five thousand gallons of tar and oil were spread on town roads to try to keep them in fair condition for automobile traffic. In the 1922 town report, the selectmen congratulated the road superintendent for his work in clearing snow, noting that "the expense is large, but with the almost universal use of automobiles it seems to be a necessary expenditure."[47] To improve automobile safety, the town's first "beacon light" was installed at Central Avenue (now Boston Post Road) and School Street in 1923.

In 1921, Raymond Coburn resigned as Weston's superintendent of streets because of his increased responsibilities as district engineer for the state highway department. He was succeeded by Augustus M. Upham (1854–1939), the second of three generations of Uphams to manage the town's roads. Augustus was first elected to the Board of Road Commissioners in 1899 to succeed his father, Marshall L. Upham. In 1936, because of ill health, he stepped down to assistant superintendent and his grandson Gilbert M. Upham was appointed superintendent.[48]

Both North and South Avenues were reconstructed in the 1920s. Work on the South Avenue project was done over five years, from 1926 to1930, at a cost of nearly $200,000 in state, county, and town funds. The old Worcester Turnpike, renamed Route 9, was also rebuilt in the late 1920s. While this diverted some through traffic from the tortuous Route 20, town officials continued to study ways to bypass the town center.

In his role as town planner, Arthur Shurtleff drew up a plan by 1926 for a roadway through the swamp south of the town center.[49] Because of wet soil conditions, many experts believed that the road, now known as the State Road Bypass, could not be built. By this time, Raymond Coburn was state construction engineer and had gained national recognition for his knowledge of road building. Coburn persuaded town and state officials to proceed. As part of the project, a bridge was constructed in 1930 over the Boston and Maine Railroad tracks at Stony Brook, abolishing one of the most dangerous grade crossings.

Between 1930 and 1933, Boston Post Road was reconstructed from the new bridge to Highland Street at a cost to the state of $350,000. The town was responsible for compensating 40 residents whose land was taken. The construction required removing thousands of cubic yards of peat. Two massive cranes worked around the clock digging and carting away the peat. Sand and gravel fill was trucked in to provide a solid underpinning for the new road.[50] The town had to install a pump to ensure continuous water flow along Three Mile Brook through the Crescent Street area. The pump is located near the intersection of the Post Road and bypass.

Farming (1915–1945)

In the second decade of the 20th century, Congress passed the Smith-Lever Act, which became the foun-

Figure 8-23. Orchardist Edward P. Ripley was the son of Civil War veteran Francis Ripley and brother of historian Emma Ripley. In 1920 he was appointed the first local director of the Middlesex County Bureau of Agriculture and Home Economics. (1911 photograph)

Figures 8-24 and 8-25. Beginning in the 1920s, county extension service agents were hired to help farmers increase productivity. Spray service cards were mailed to fruit growers telling them what pesticides to use and the best time for application. These undated photographs from the Ripley collection at the Weston Historical Society are thought to show spraying at the extensive Ripley orchard west of Ripley Lane.

dation of a county extension service to help farmers increase productivity. The professional agricultural and home demonstration agents proved their worth during World War I and gained the esteem of farmers and the general public.

In 1920, Edward P. Ripley was appointed the first local director of the Middlesex County Bureau of Agriculture and Home Economics, later renamed the Middlesex County Extension Service. The following year, Ripley reported that the bureau was "doing a real service in bringing back agriculture" by fostering market gardening and fruit growing.[51] Agents assisted fruit growers in orchard management, fertilization, pruning, and spraying. For poultry farmers, the bureau organized tours to study successful poultry farms and provided information on raising disease-free pullets and breeding poultry capable of high egg production.

Boys and girls clubs were organized around subjects like bread making, sewing, canning, poultry, pigs, and gardening. The 1922 town report noted that "Middlesex County continues to lead all others in the United States in the number of boys and girls enrolled in club projects."[52]

Dairying continued strong in Weston. Improvement in the quality of public milk supplies was one of the outstanding achievements of public health science during this period. Milk became cleaner, richer, and safer. Processors made increasing use of pasteurization. The 19 authorized Weston milk dealers in 1934 sold 39 grades of milk, only four of which were raw (unpasteurized) milk. After a reported case of undulant fever, the board in 1936 required all milk to be either pasteurized or certified as meeting standards of purity and quality. A comparison of milk from 1926 and 1936 showed significantly lower bacteria counts, no unsatisfactory sediments, and increased butterfat content.

Distributors purchased milk from area farmers and sold it locally or in Boston. In 1937, five dairies in Weston were licensed to pasteurize milk: Cedar Hill Farm Inc., John H. Clark, Wellesley Farms Dairy Inc., Ferndale Farm, and Cherith M. Foote. This number gradually decreased over the next decade. Wellesley Farms Dairy is last listed in 1939, Cherith Foote in 1940, and Cedar Hill Farm in 1941. The Clark and Ferndale dairies are still listed in the 1949 directory. J.H. Clark Dairy on Golden Ball Road is thought to have been the last to operate in Weston. Rising land values and consolidation within the industry contributed to the rapid decline of dairy farming after World War II.

Weston had three piggeries during this period: Walter Thompson's at the corner of South Avenue

Figure 8-26. Cedar Hill Farms advertised "Clean Milk from Clean Cows." In 1924, when this brochure was printed, its farm on North Avenue in Weston and two farms in Waltham sold certified milk for 26 cents a quart and "clean raw milk" for 18 cents.

CEDAR HILL FARMS
Established 1896

Announces the production of two grades of
CLEAN MILK FROM CLEAN COWS

PRICE LIST

Certified milk; single quart	26 cents
more than one quart, per quart	25 "
Grade A, clean raw milk, per quart	18 "
Cream, thick, per half pint	30 "
Cream, coffee, per half pint	22 "
Skim milk, per quart	8 "

PUBLIC INSPECTION
of our three farms is invited. Visitors are always welcome. The best hour for a visit is about four in the afternoon, since at that time the cows are being milked and the bottles filled.

and Winter Street, the Louis Dean piggery on Conant Road on the former poor farm property, and the Dean piggery on the Wayland-Weston town line. The latter was the subject of a 1932 complaint by Wayland and Weston residents because of the strong smell of manure applied to the land. The farm prevailed and the town report that year notes that "the [state] board of Health has felt that this is a legitimate practice in farming." [53]

Despite the efforts of the extension service, New England farming was on the decline between the two World Wars. Land fell out of agricultural production and was reforested, until by mid-century, about 65 percent of Massachusetts was again covered by trees.[54] It was this second-growth forest that greeted subdivison developers in the 1950s.

Livestock	1920	1925	1930	1935	1940	1945
Horses	253	176	170	166	189	112
Cows *(all types)*	652	688	545	400	415	314
Swine	403	70	133	529	298	577
Fowl	3,735	2,808	1,725	6,140	5,947	7,024

Subdivisions between the Wars

In the 1910s and '20s, two of Weston's largest estate owners, Robert Winsor and Charles W. Hubbard, created plans for developing their landholdings. Winsor hired the firm of Olmsted Brothers to lay out roadways through his estate that would be of value when he decided to subdivide. In 1918 Winsor turned over 422 acres to the Weston Real Estate Trust and sold 50 acres to the Weston Golf Club, which thrived in its new and larger site and added prestige and value to Winsor's farm fields. The trust had a small sales office on Meadowbrook Road and a marketing brochure touting the rural atmosphere and natural beauty. Most lots were more than an acre. No restrictions were placed on the size or cost of houses. The area developed slowly through the 1950s.

Hubbard's Chiltern Hundreds subdivision was laid out in the mid-1920s by Arthur Shurtleff, who was working at the same time as Weston's town planner. Shurtleff devised a plan of curvilinear streets clearly influenced by his years in the Olmsted firm. Lot sizes varied between about a quarter- and half-acre and were restricted by the developer to single-family use. The minimum cost of houses was initially set at $10,000. By the late 1920s, houses were under construction on Pembroke, Old Colony, Dean, and Locust Roads. The adverse economic climate of the 1930s and shortage of building materials in the war

Figure 8-27. Harvest-time in 1940 on Bert Tyler's farm, 178 Lexington Street. The farm ceased operation after Tyler's death.

CHILTERN HUNDREDS

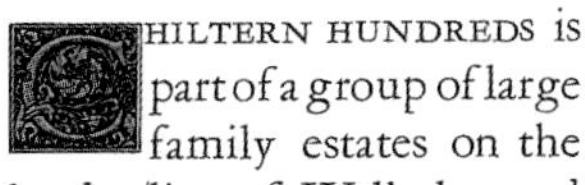

CHILTERN HUNDREDS is part of a group of large family estates on the border line of Wellesley and Weston, overlooking the Charles River valley. The owners of these estates are developing a tract of about 150 acres as a beautiful residential section, under certain social and building restrictions.

A FAMILY ESTATE

CHILTERN HUNDREDS is separated from the congested suburban districts by these large estates and by the Charles River Reservation of the Metropolitan Park, a river valley a mile and a half long.

EDGEWOOD

THE KNOLL

RIDGEWAYS

SOME OF THE HOUSES ON THE ESTATE

VALLEY OF THE CHARLES RIVER AND THE METROPOLITAN PARK

Wellesley Farms Station, on the B. & A. R.R. four track main line, has twenty trains a day each way, with numerous expresses, twenty-five minutes to South Station. All lots within half a mile of the station have gas, electricity and water, with frequent fire hydrants.

Figure 8-28. Estate owner Charles Wells Hubbard was the prime mover behind the Chiltern Hundreds subdivision in the southeast corner of Weston. Landscape architect Arthur A. Shurtleff laid out the winding streets in the mid-1920s. This 1926 brochure urged potential buyers of the "country homesites" to "motor out" or take one of 19 trains a day from Boston to Wellesley Farms Station. The houses illustrated were along Orchard Avenue and Oxbow Road and were not part of the subdivision.

years slowed development, and lots in Chiltern Hundreds continued to be available into the 1950s.

Sunset Road was laid out in the 1920s and Aberdeen, Pelham, Granison, and Legion Roads and Lantern Lane beginning in the 1930s. Developer J. Irving Connolly filed a plan for the 13-lot Irvington Court in June 1930. Later that same year, he filed a plan for Pinecroft, owned and developed by Connolly and his company, Country Homes, Weston, Inc.[55] This subdivision included about 93 lots on Pinecroft, Montvale, Fairview, and Conant Roads and Viles Street, ranging in size from 15,000 square feet on Viles to more than 65,000 square feet on Pinecroft. Homes were built in this area through the early 1960s. Connolly also developed Longmeadow Road, October Lane, and the east end of Baker's Hill Road in the 1950s.

Figure 8-29. The middle-class exodus from city to suburb was under way soon after World War I. Small "Cape Cod" houses like this one on Highland Street were popular in Weston, especially in the 1930s. Bankers and buyers of modest homes were convinced that new Colonials in traditional styles represented a solid investment even during troubled times.

Architecture (1915–1945)

The Colonial Revival maintained its popularity throughout this period. It was the most important of the revival styles used in new middle-class suburban developments. Unassuming Colonial-style houses filled pleasant neighborhoods where variety for its own sake was replaced by a "deeply satisfying traditionalism."[56]

Figure 8-30. One of the town's finest Georgian Revival examples was inspired by the 18th-century Westover plantation on the James River in Virginia. The architect of One Town House Road (1929) was local resident Harold B. Willis.

After 1915, there was a gradual movement toward more correct proportions and detailing based on documented American prototypes. The best examples in Weston of this more archaeological approach are by architect and town resident Harold B. Willis (1890–1962), who practiced with the Boston firm of Allen & Collens.[57] Willis moved to Weston in the 1920s after marrying into the Fiske family. He designed his own house at 49 Concord Road (1921), modeled after the 17th-century Parson Capen House, and the Parsons house at One Town House Road (1929), inspired by the 1729 plantation house Westover on the James River in Virginia. Like his contemporaries, Willis was versatile in a wide range of styles. He incorporated architectural fragments into many of his works, including his own home and the Sears Memorial Chapel (1930) at First Parish Church. He designed the original Meadowbrook School building (1924) and Weston High School (now Field School, 1949), and outside of Weston is known for his work on the Cloisters Museum in New York City, Hammond Castle in Gloucester, and Newton City Hall.[58]

Figure 8-31. The International-style house built in 1934 by Richard and Caroline Field at 74 Sudbury Road was "about as far out as anything could be," according to their daughter. It was originally painted shades of green in gradations from dark (at the bottom) to light, so the house would blend into the landscape. The architect was Edwin B. "Ned" Goodell.

Georgian Revival was used for important brick institutional buildings including the Weston Fire Station (1914), Weston Town Hall (1917), First Baptist Church (1924), and Weston High School (1932). Also notable is the brick Georgian house built for George W. Bentley at 8 Rolling Lane (1922), designed by Bentley's son-in-law, architect Clifford Albright.

Increased appreciation of Colonial architecture and the desire to own an authentic early house led to the moving of two 18th-century houses to Weston in the 1920s. The Burleigh House, an exceptional example of Georgian architecture, was moved from Newmarket, New Hampshire, to 100 Orchard Avenue in 1922–23. The house at 221 Ash Street was moved from Newburyport in 1923. Both were dismantled and rebuilt on the new site.

The Tudor style continued to be popular into the 1930s. The Edward Peirce house (now Henderson House Conference Center), Weston's last major estate mansion, was constructed in 1925–26 from designs by Coolidge, Shepley, Bulfinch, and Abbott, a firm with a lineage back to H.H. Richardson. New masonry veneering techniques allowed Tudor examples after World War I to mimic the brick and stone exteriors of their English prototypes. Notable brick Tudors from the 1910s and '20s include the Gordon Donald house at 33 Bullard Road (c. 1917), 163 Wellesley Street (1924: R. Clipston Sturgis, architect), and 99 Love Lane (1929).

The largest and most significant institutional building of the period is Weston College, now the Campion Center, at 319 Concord Road (1926). Designed by the nationally known firm of Maginnis and Walsh, the monumental brick seminary is Weston's only example of Beaux Arts classicism. The same firm planned the simple Gothic St. Julia Roman Catholic Church in the early 1920s.

In the 1930s, two International-style houses were built on Sudbury Road across from the Colonial farmhouses of earlier generations. This avant-garde style is rare, as Americans in general and Weston residents in particular favored period houses reflecting past traditions. The architect, Edwin B. "Ned" Goodell, was introduced to the modernist aesthetic on a trip to Paris in 1932. The Internationalists called the house a "machine for living," where superfluous ornament was stripped away and functionalism was

Figure 8-32. One of many inventions that made life easier was the electric refrigerator, which took the place of the old icebox. This picture of the kitchen in the Olive Thornton house was taken in 1939.

of prime importance. The house at 74 Sudbury Road was built by Richard and Caroline Crosby Field in 1934. Richard Field was a lawyer and professor at Harvard Law School who served as a Weston selectman and moderator for many years. Caroline, a Bryn Mawr graduate and early feminist, was very involved with the League of Women Voters at both the state and national levels and was known for appearing in Weston Center wearing blue jeans. Down the street, 102 Sudbury Road was built about 1938–40 for Hassler Whitney, a mathematics professor at Harvard University.

Recreation (1915–1945)

The growing popularity of golf in the first three decades of the 20th century is evident in the number of golf courses in town. The first nine-hole course, laid out by the Weston Golf Club on cow pastures in Kendal Green, closed in 1918 when the club moved to the Winsor estate. Its present 18-hole course was laid out by Donald Ross and built in two stages between 1918 and 1923. Land once belonging to estate owners Francis Foster and Bancroft and Anne Davis was sold in the mid-1920s to the Pine Brook Valley Golf Club, one of the first Jewish country clubs in the nation. Pine Brook also developed an 18-hole course. The 19-acre park on the south side donated to the town by Charles Wells Hubbard was transferred to Commonwealth control under a long-term lease and became part of Riverside Golf Course, now Leo J. Martin, which opened in 1930 as one of two public courses within the metropolitan park system. Its second nine holes were ready for use in 1932. Now-defunct courses of nine holes or fewer were developed at Drabbington Lodge on North Avenue (early 20th century), Trapelo Golf Club at North Avenue and Lexington Street (c. 1921–41), and the lesser-known Flagg Tavern course on Boston Post Road (1920s).

Three riding schools operated between the wars. The Weston Saddle and Bridle Club was incorporated in 1929 by Harry L. Bailey "to encourage horseback riding and other equestrian sports in the town of Weston."[59] Bailey served as first president; Lyman Gale as vice president; Charles Squibb as treasurer; and Mortimer A. Seabury as secretary. Although 1929 was the official incorporation date, the club appears to date back to the early 1920s, when the Baileys acquired the former Zollar property on Conant Road from Horace Sears.[60] The large dairy barn built for Sears's Colchester Farm became the club headquarters. Indoor and outdoor rings were constructed for horse shows. Annual dues were $50 and members could board their own horses for $10 a week or hire one of several dozen owned by the club. The club developed bridle trails and sponsored social events. Victor deBellefroid, the tall and austere Belgian riding master, ran a strict program for Wellesley College girls, who were required to appear in proper riding attire.

The Kendal Green Riding School was located on what was once the Edward Coburn farm at 171 Church Street. The barn was rented beginning in the 1920s to a riding school, which closed during the Depression and reopened in the late 1930s under

Figure 8-33. Thomas D. Cabot (right), a charter member of the Weston Saddle and Bridle Club, was one of 75 prominent Weston men listed in the "first year book" published when the club was incorporated in 1929. He is pictured here with his wife, the former Virginia Wellington, and their son, Ned, at Gateways Farm at the final meet of the Millwood Hunt in 1953.

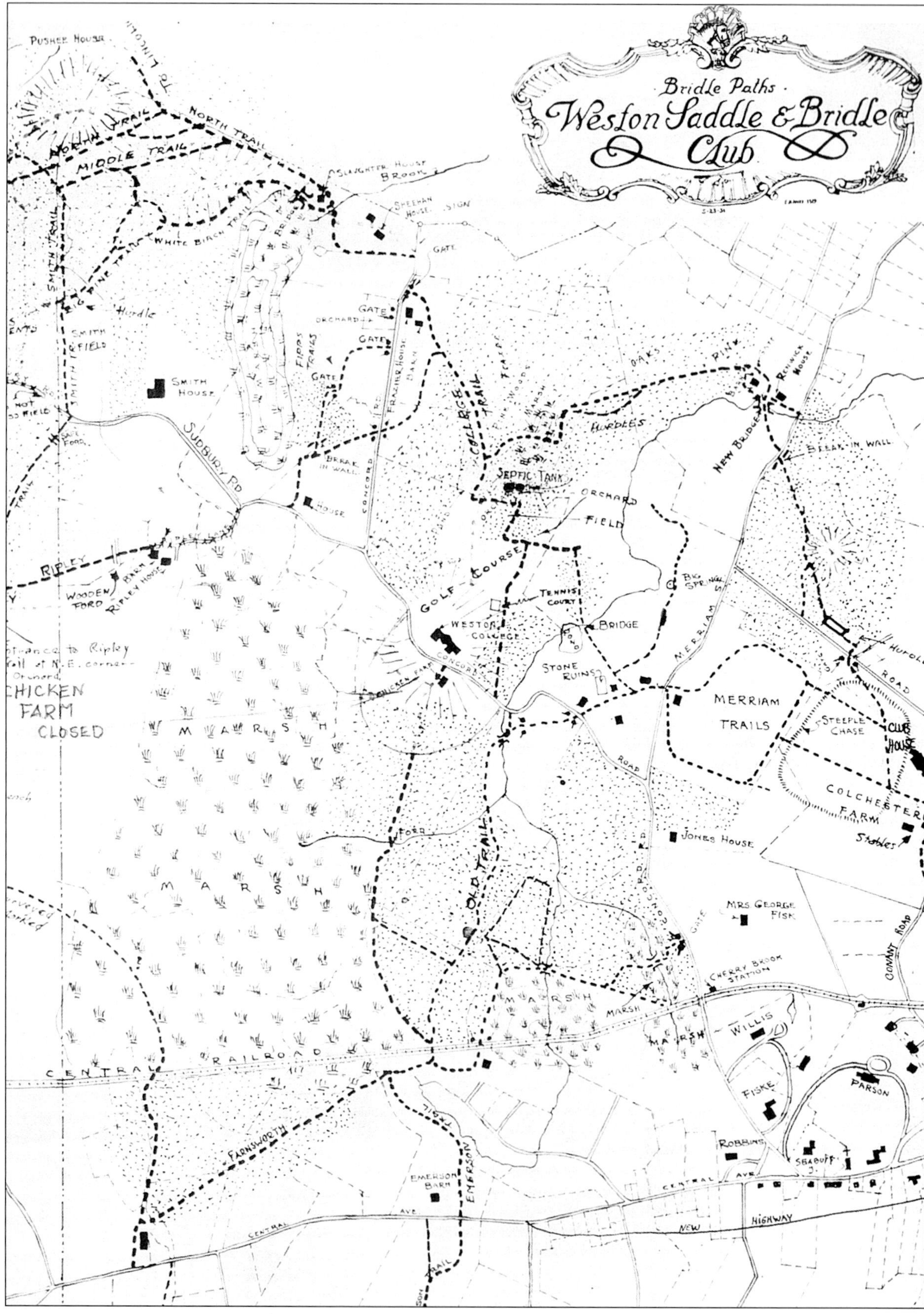

Figure 8-34. Members of the Weston Saddle and Bridle Club created and mapped bridle paths through Weston and surrounding towns. This map dates to about 1930 and shows the clubhouse on Conant Road (at right) and selected houses. Another part of the same map can be found in chapter 18.

the Kendal Green name. Until the barn was destroyed by fire in August 1954, the very Scottish proprietor, Miss Mary Barron, and the very Irish superintendent, Patrick McConville, lived on the property and rented out riding horses, gave lessons, and boarded horses.[61]

The South Avenue Riding Club was based at Ferndale Farm, where horses could be rented, trained, and boarded. In 1939 the club advertised large indoor and outdoor riding rings available day and night, as well as expert instruction.[62]

In 1919, estate owner Horace Sears decided Weston should have its own moving pictures "for the sake of producing clean and wholesome shows for

Figure 8-35. Weston suffragettes entered this red, white, and blue "Votes for Women" float in the town's Bicentennial parade in 1913. The first suffrage rally in Weston was held in June 1915. That year, more than 100 women registered to vote in town elections when Carolyn Burrage, the first female school committee member, was challenged by a male candidate.

the young people of the town."[63] Sears bought projection equipment, found a manager, and agreed to pay any deficits. Twice-weekly shows in the town hall, later cut back to once a week, included Pathé News and silent feature films like *Daddy Long Legs* with Mary Pickford, *His Majesty the American* with Douglas Fairbanks, and *Little Women,* played to piano accompaniment. Prices were 30 and 25 cents. The manager doubled as censor. In a newspaper article entitled "Weston Is Pioneer in Censorship of Movies by Citizens," he was quoted as follows:

> When you consider that our children and the young men and women of the town are attending these shows, it is absolutely necessary to keep them above the level of anything suggestive. Clean movies are the sine qua non of our plan.[64]

While as many as 350 residents reportedly turned out for popular films, attendance often failed to reach the average of 250 needed for economic self-sufficiency.

Figure 8-36. By the 1920s, increasing numbers of young women were continuing their education after high school and pursuing careers. Vina Macleod (left) worked as a bookkeeper for her father's business, B.L. Ogilvie & Sons. She is pictured here with fellow employee Beatrice Cahill in the company office.

Changing Status of Women and Women's Organizations (1915–1945)

The changing status of women is reflected in the weekly columns of the *Waltham Daily Free Press Tribune,* which increasingly mention women's educational achievements and occupations. More and more young women were attending college. By the second decade of the century, Weston women were training for jobs in teaching, business, physical education, social work, dietetics, and nursing. They worked in schools, libraries, factories, and offices and were opening and managing retail shops. Gertrude Fiske earned a reputation as the leading woman painter of Boston. Irene McAuliffe, daughter of Police Chief P.J. McAuliffe, staked her claim to the title of first woman policeman in Massachusetts.[65] Her sister, Elizabeth, drove the Weston school bus and continued her father's taxi service. Miss Catherine Filene, daughter of estate owner A. Lincoln Filene, was an energetic young feminist who was reported in 1920 to be compiling a book on careers for women.[66]

Like their counterparts throughout the country, Weston women were becoming more active in

Figure 8-37. Jane (Mrs. Lyman) Gale, shown here with her son Winsor, was the sister of estate owner Robert Winsor. Before World War I, she helped found and manage the Toy Theatre in Boston and in 1919 she managed the Friendly Society production of The Red Mill. *Her most lasting contribution to Weston was as a founder and first president of the Women's Community League, which was formed in June 1919.*

politics and women's social organizations. They were advocating for voting rights by 1913, when the Votes for Women float entered the town's Bicentennial parade. The first suffrage rally in Weston was held in the town hall in June 1915 under the auspices of the Weston Equal Suffrage League.[67] Weston women first registered to vote in large numbers in 1915, when Carolyn Burrage, the town's first female school committee member, was challenged by a male candidate. The *Waltham Daily Free Press Tribune* reported that within a few days, more than 100 women appeared before the Board of Registers and were added to the voter list.[68] The contest was resolved when another school committee member resigned, allowing both candidates to be seated.

In 1919, President Woodrow Wilson signed what would become the 19th amendment to the Constitution, allowing women full suffrage. Massachusetts became the eighth state to ratify it, in July 1920. That fall, state legislator B. Loring Young submitted a bill allowing women to hold any elective office, rather than being limited to school committee and overseer of the poor.[69]

Women took on leadership roles in volunteer causes during World War I and its aftermath. Hannah Bradford Fiske, daughter of Andrew Fiske and a debutante in the 1915 season, volunteered in France for more than a year as a refugee worker. She died of spinal meningitis a few weeks after returning home. Anna Hall, niece of Anna Coburn Hastings, headed the Weston branch of the American Fund for French Wounded. Under her supervision, 91 Weston women met regularly to sew refugee garments and prepare surgical dressings.[70] Mrs. A. Lincoln Filene was a tireless leader of Boston organizations aiding returning servicemen.

Before World War I, Jane Winsor Gale (Mrs. Lyman Gale) was a founder and manager of the Toy Theatre in Boston. She spent 11 months in France as a YMCA canteen worker during World War I. When she returned, she was described as "deeply impressed by the change in her fellow-townsmen. Their division into groups according to church affiliation had given way before a single strong community spirit, developed by their years of war work."[71] As she marched in the town's Memorial Day procession, she vowed to keep that spirit alive.

Within weeks, the Women's Community League was formed, in June 1919. The first Executive Committee consisted of Jane Gale, president; Mrs. Stephen Fitzgerald, secretary; and Miss Alice E. Jones, treasurer. Early committee heads included Mrs. F. Robins Mitchell (salesroom and headquarters), Mrs. A. Lincoln Filene (recreation), Mrs. Joseph E. Perry (membership and acquaintanceship), Miss Marian Case (education), and Mrs. Karl Andren (finance). Other founders were Mrs. Frank H. Brooks, Miss Mary Field, Mrs. Elmer Forbes, Mrs. Ralph Gray, Mrs. Frederick L. Kenyon, Mrs. David W. Lane, Mrs. Arthur H. Morse, Mrs. Phillip R. Spaulding, and Mrs. John B.E. Wheeler. Every woman in Weston was urged to join. By 1920, the original group of 15 had grown to include 174 women and 106 juniors.

The league motto, "For Happiness and Welfare," suggested their dual goal of providing wholesome good times and opportunities for education and community service. In its first years, the league sponsored Saturday-night community dances in the town hall and classes in social dancing for young people with Miss Mary Field.[72] By 1920, the league had established the Willow Plate Tea Room and "Food and Fancy-Work Exchange" in the Yellow Barn at what is now 494 Boston Post Road. Women who liked to cook, embroider, paint, or sew were encouraged to bring articles for sale at the tearoom, where others "too busy to do these things for themselves" would gladly buy them. The tearoom started off well, with 25 to 30 patrons a day, but success was short-lived. In the spring of 1921, the lease was taken over by Marian Case, who set up a market for Hillcrest vegetables.

The league's first current events lectures were held in 1921. The education committee sponsored appearances by notable Boston women and programs on child development for young mothers. From the beginning, the league welcomed opportunities to serve the community. The group sponsored construction of playgrounds and donated equipment to the town hall, fire department, and schools. By 1925 the league was supplying milk to undernourished schoolchildren, and the school cafeteria was begun under its sponsorship. The scholarship fund committee was appointed in 1928–29 to consider the financial needs of female Weston High School graduates at a time when all existing college scholarships were for boys.

The Women's Community League began a children's theater and workshop to provide Weston children with the opportunity to participate in dramatic productions. It funded free bus rides to Boston Symphony children's concerts, and camp scholarships for Girl and Boy Scouts. The league has sponsored square dances, Dancing on the Green, and fund-raising balls including the annual Chrysanthemum Scholarship Ball begun in 1966.[73] It began renting the barn at the Josiah Smith Tavern about 1975 and undertook a major refurbishing and expansion of the barn in the late 1970s.[74] The organization continues today as the town's largest and most active women's group.

In 1921, the Women's Community League organized a civics committee and became affiliated with the League of Women Voters of Massachusetts. A lecture course was offered on citizenship and legislative matters. The affiliation between the two organizations was soon discontinued, but it was from these roots that the Weston chapter of the League of Women Voters was established in March 1931.[75] Mrs. Royal G. Whiting served as first president. A report of first-year accomplishments lists active committees on efficiency in government, child welfare and laws relating to delinquent and neglected children, education, international cooperation to prevent war, and living costs and consumer issues.[76] By 1950, the Weston League of Women Voters had nearly 200 members.

Figure 38. Mary Ferranti and Amelia Benotti are pictured in front of St. Julia Church on Easter, 1946. The church was completed in late 1921. In the early years, the parish served immigrants from Ireland, Italy, and other Catholic countries.

The Weston Women's Christian Temperance Union (WCTU) was organized in November 1920.[77] Miss Laura E. Jones and Mrs. Bessie Jones, sister and wife of estate owner Charles H. Jones, conducted devotional exercises at the initial meeting at First Baptist Church, where Mrs. Charles E. Peakes was elected first president. Attendees were advised that, although the eighteenth amendment had been ratified, liquor traffic was by no means dead and much work had to be done before Prohibition

Figure 8-39. The first Boy Scout troop in Weston was organized in 1917. In this photograph, members of Troop 1 pause on their way to a Quebec jamboree in June 1935. The boys are, from left, Edward Edmunds Jr., Milton Theall, Guy Akers, Richard Kennedy, ___ Eldridge, Jack Ripley, and Charles Peterson.

Figure 8-40. Girl Scouting also began in Weston during the World War I years, when Helen Roberts and Edith Perry organized a troop in 1918. By the late 1930s, more than 100 girls were participating. Here they parade on Memorial Day in 1939.

became a fact. Illegal manufacture and sale of liquor did continue in Weston, as elsewhere in the country, until the amendment was repealed in 1933.

The Weston Garden Club was founded in 1940–41 "to stimulate the knowledge and love of gardening; to aid in the protection of native trees, plants and birds; and to beautify Weston."[78] During World War II, the club's emphasis was on service to patients at the Murphy Army Hospital in Waltham. Members provided fresh flowers and holiday wreaths for hospitalized veterans until the hospital closed in 1958. The Weston Garden Club became affiliated with the Garden Club Federation of Massachusetts in 1948, providing the opportunity to participate in statewide projects such as the Spring Flower Show.

Over the next half century, the Weston Garden Club has undertaken many beautification projects including installing plantings around the town hall, flagpole island, post office, police station, recycling center, Brook School apartments, and Merriam Village. Members maintain the Forbes wetland garden on Church Street and decorate town buildings for the holidays. The club began providing weekly flower arrangements for the library in 1949. Since Memorial Day 1948, they have planted seasonal flowers in the watering trough on Boston Post Road. They also plant the barrels at the Fiske Triangle and along Center Street near the supermarket. In the year 2000, the club had more than 100 members in three categories, regular, associate, and provisional. The latter is a young women's group established in 1957.

Other Community Organizations (1915–1945)

By 1907, Catholics in Massachusetts outnumbered all other religions put together.[79] The expansion of Catholic churches, schools, and seminaries throughout the state in the 1920s is unmistakable in Weston, where St. Julia Roman Catholic Church built its sanctuary in 1921, Weston College built its scholasticate in 1924–27, and Regis College opened its doors in 1927.

St. Peter's Episcopal Church built its first church in 1917–18 in the town center. First Baptist tore down its late-19th-century frame Gothic church and erected the present brick Colonial Revival building in 1923–24. First Parish Church constructed the parish hall and parlor in 1924 and the Sears Memorial Chapel in 1930.

The first Boy Scout troop was organized in Weston in 1917 by Rev. Dr. Joseph E. Perry, minister of First Baptist Church. In 1919 First Parish Church also started a troop. The original groups slowly lost membership but a new troop flourished in the late 1920s and 1930s under successive Scoutmasters Winfield Scott, Walter Dunham, Daniel Kennedy, Joseph Kohler, William R. Dewey Jr., and Gilbert Upham.[80] Cub Scouts under Cubmaster Austin Hale were meeting by 1938.

The first Weston Girl Scout troop was formed in the summer of 1918 under the leadership of Miss Helen Roberts and Miss Edith Perry.[81] The changing roles and perception of women and girls in the second decade of the 20th century are reflected in this newspaper account of a service project to earn money for a poor woman:

> The Girl Scouts . . . have been doing a stunt that will make the Weston boys take notice. Desiring to raise a sum of money for a kind purpose, they are cutting and splitting cord wood for a fair wage. The days when the only tool a girl could use successfully was a needle have gone by.[82]

Figure 8-41. The musical comedy The Red Mill *was performed in March 1919 at the Horace Sears estate for the benefit of Waltham Hospital. The production marked a turning point in Friendly Society history. It was the last major production at Haleiwa. Sears died just four years later, having provided the town with a performance space in the new town hall to replace his private theater.* The Red Mill *was one of the first large benefit musicals that gradually replaced the bimonthly lectures, theatricals, and social events that characterized the society up to that time. The play was managed by Jane Gale, assisted by her niece, Miss Mary P. Winsor (in black dresses in the bottom row). The cast photograph was taken at Haleiwa.*

Figure 8-42. The Friendly Society's first musical comedy was A Nautical Knot *(1915). In 1919 the group presented* The Red Mill, *and thereafter they produced a major musical comedy every three years.* Going Up *(1922) was followed by* Sweethearts *(1925),* Mlle. Modiste *(1928),* Hit the Deck *(1931), and* The Pirates of Penzance *(1934). During the Depression, the society decided to save royalties by writing original shows.* Many Happy Returns *(1937) featured book, music, and lyrics written entirely by members.* So Deep *(1940) was followed by five more original productions.*

Figure 8-43. Harry W. Patterson played the lead role of Richard, the Pirate Chief, in the 1934 Friendly Society production of The Pirates of Penzance. *Patterson performed in many Friendly Society shows and wrote the book and lyrics for* Many Happy Returns *and* So Deep. *He served as president of the Friendly Society in 1939 and was one of the original directors of the Weston Historical Society.*

Figure 8-44. Weston residents lined Boston Post Road in 1932 to celebrate the 200th anniversary of George Washington's birth. The cavalcade commemorated Washington's 1789 journey through New England.

Figure 8-45. A 1932 bronze plaque designating Boston Post Road as part of the George Washington Highway was attached to a boulder near the Fiske Law Office. In recent years, it was removed to the cemetery office for safekeeping.

Interest in Girl Scouting lapsed in the mid-1920s but revived in the early 1930s, at which time programs were organized for Brownie Scouts (1932) as well. By the later 1930s, there were more than 100 active Girl Scouts in Weston. At least two sites in Weston were used for camping: Pine Grove off Sudbury Road and Miss Anna Dickson's camp on Pine Street.

Weston Scouts Inc. was formed in 1938 to provide and maintain a suitable headquarters for both Boy and Girl Scouts.[83] Harold G. "Red" Travis was a founder and active trustee for more than 40 years and Josephine Sturgis Bidwell, the first president, served for 20 years, from 1938 to 1958. Incorporators were Julia G. Kellogg (Mrs. David), Gertrude G. Rhoades, Dorothy W. Grannis, Edith W. Ripley, and, for the Boy Scouts, "Red" Travis, William R. Dewey Jr., and Wilmot Whitney. Misses Louisa and Marian Case gave the land at School and Wellesley Streets.[84] Organizers raised funds with projects such as a minstrel show, giant rummage sale, and the cookbook *Treasured Recipes of Weston,* which sold about 1,000 copies. Architectural plans by Samuel Mead were scaled down by Mrs. Stanley Kellogg and the building was constructed in 1941 at a cost of just over $8,000.[85] That year, the Boy Scout national administration recommended that a cabin in the woods would be more suitable for the boys program and the Weston charter would be revoked if Weston's Boy Scouts used the proposed building in any way.[86] For this reason, it was used only by Girl Scouts for the first 30 years. Weston Scouts Inc. helped local Boy Scouts construct permanent cabins on Nobscot Reservation in Sudbury/Framingham in 1950.

The American Legion, an organization of U.S. war veterans, was founded in 1919 and formed Weston Post #214 by October of that year.[87] The first officers were Lawrence B. Page, commander; William J. Henderson, vice commander; Robert W. Bennett, adjutant; and Austin S. Hale, finance officer. Members visited hospitalized veterans, helped elderly residents, sponsored an annual high school prize for the best essay on the U.S. Constitution, and set up a college scholarship fund. They raised money with June strawberry festivals, annual chowder dinners, plays, minstrel shows, horse shows, masquerade balls, Washington's Birthday dances, Christmas tree sales, and antique auctions. For women, an American Legion auxiliary was organized in 1949.

Weston Post #214 fostered sports by sponsoring a Junior Legion baseball program, supplying uniforms for the baseball team, and working with Weston High School alumni to purchase sweaters for the football team.[88] Legion members were among the organizers of an enthusiastic community celebration in the fall of 1945 honoring Weston's veterans, as well as students and teachers of Weston High School.

The Depression Years

As the country sank into the Depression, private organizations in Weston came to the aid of needy families. According to a history of Weston Post #214 of the American Legion, there were "many, many families in Weston destitute of clothing, fuel and food" by 1930. The post's welfare committee quietly solicited funds from more-fortunate anonymous donors to provide necessities to poverty-stricken homes.[89]

Weston selectmen put off road reconstruction projects and increased the park and cemetery budget to give day work to men who otherwise would need poor relief. In 1933, as unemployment increased, Weston obtained its first federal grant from the Civic Works Administration. The CWA was replaced by the FERA (Federal Emergency Relief Administration, also referred to as ERA), another work program that provided federal money for labor and required towns to furnish materials and equipment. In 1934 the agency funded 17 projects employing an average of 45 town residents.[90] During the summer of 1935, an ERA garden was cultivated on three acres of land on School Street offered by Louisa Case, and more than 600 bushels of vegetables were distributed to needy Weston families. That year, the organ factory on North Avenue closed its doors, putting more men out of work. In 1935, the Works Progress Administration (WPA) replaced the ERA. Under the program, the town "endeavored to accomplish worthwhile things . . . that would have lasting value to the town, and not to simply provide work at jobs of no material benefit."[91]

Projects undertaken during the years of the CWA, FERA, and WPA, from 1933 to 1940, included installing a water main along South Avenue; relaying water pipes; building storm drains, catch basins, and culverts; and draining swampland. Workers painted the inside of the primary school, refurbished several rooms in the old high school, built a regulation tennis court and field hockey field on the school playground, and cleared land for a new athletic field. They painted the town hall, fire station, and town barn at Cutter's Corner.

Under the direction of the tree warden, workers applied creosote to gypsy moth egg clusters, trimmed street trees, and cleaned up after the hurricane of 1938. For the cemetery department, they built a 600-foot avenue through the cemetery, opening up an area for new lots. They inventoried, rearranged, and cataloged library books. Crews were put to work widening and straightening Summer Street and painting 10,000 feet of fences for beauty and preservation. WPA workers numbered all houses not previously numbered. In 1938 they surveyed 1,000 acres of the town. The information was used to prepare the assessor's maps of individual buildings and parcels that were completed by 1950 and are still in use today.

In the 1938 town report, the selectmen told their staunchly Republican constituency that they were "still of the opinion that the town has derived every considerable benefit from the WPA regardless of what we may think of it as a national program."[92] As the program was cut back in the late 1930s, the town initiated its own policy of requiring employable aid recipients to work for their relief on highway and cemetery projects. The building of the Hultman Aqueduct and Norumbega Reservoir in 1939–40 provided jobs for many former WPA workers. The town's last three WPA projects concluded in 1940; and in 1942 the Board of Public Welfare reported, "Defense industries seem able to employ all."[93]

Historical Activities and Celebrations (1915–1945)

George Washington and the Revolutionary War remained Weston's principal historical focus. In 1927, the Commonwealth of Massachusetts erected a monument in the town center commemorating the role of Gen. Henry Knox with the following educational text:

> Through this place passed General Henry Knox in the winter of 1775–1776 to deliver to General George Washington at Cambridge the Train of Artillery from Fort Ticonderoga used to force the British Army to Evacuate Boston.[94]

In 1931, the town appointed a committee to take charge of arrangements for the dedication of the George Washington Memorial Highway under the auspices of the Massachusetts George Washington Bicentennial Commission. The Weston Historical Committee was chaired by Gertrude Fiske and included Alice E. Jones and Edward P. Ripley. On June 10, 1932, Weston residents turned out to welcome a cavalcade on the first leg of a 115-mile trek commemorating Washington's 1789 journey through New England. The costumed general galloped into Weston on a white horse. Beneath the historic Burgoyne Elm, he greeted ladies in colonial gowns and gentlemen in long velvet coats and three-cornered hats.[95] The tradition of Washington kissing the young Hannah Gowen was reenacted. A reported 500 schoolchildren, accompanied by the school orchestra, sang songs known to the first president. Local dignitaries presented state officials with a bronze plaque that was affixed to a huge boulder under the spreading elm.[96]

In 1926 a committee considered renaming streets as a way to commemorate the town's heritage. The proposal to change Central Avenue to Boston Post Road received widespread support. The names of North and South Avenues were not changed back to North and South County Roads, although the committee argued that this would "restore continuity with the past to which the fathers of the Town belonged."[97] Neither was Ash Street ever renamed to commemorate the Upham family.

The Weston Historical Committee began to collect photographs and documents and to look for a

Figure 8-46. The 1938 hurricane devastated the New England landscape. Louisa Case lost trees around the family mansion, shown here. Her sister Marian recorded the destruction at Hillcrest Gardens as follows: 2,500 pine trees, 500 oaks, 250 maples, 74 apple trees, and 29 other fruit trees.

Figure 8-47. Many of the trees downed in the 1938 hurricane were taken to the Ogilvie sawmill.

permanent home. In 1936, on finding that the Cemetery Commissioners had extra space in the Fiske Law Office, the committee asked for an appropriation of $500 to fix up the front two rooms as its headquarters. In 1953 they moved to new quarters in the former Josiah Smith Tavern.

Hurricane of 1938

In a 1998 article called "Storm Warning," the *Boston Globe* describes what it was like in the days before satellite technology and sophisticated hurricane warning systems, when hurricanes had no names:

> Nobody knew it was coming. The morning of Wednesday, Sept. 21, 1938, dawned to cloudy skies and a forecast of rain, but nobody had the slightest clue that New England was about to get walloped by a hurricane that for decades would rank as the most damaging storm in the nation's history.

The *Globe* article cites some of the most dramatic statistics:

> For a few brief hours, some rivers reached record flood levels. A gust of wind at the Blue Hill Observatory in Milton was measured at 186 m.p.h.; for decades it was the second-highest wind speed ever recorded on this planet. Phone and electric lines—20,000 miles of them—were knocked down, leaving seven-eighths of New England's homes without power. . . . An estimated 275 million trees were snapped or uprooted. [98]

Weston was directly in the path of the storm. Linda Cabot Black, who was nine years old at the time, tells of saddling her pony after school and, knowing nothing of the impending storm, riding to a friend's house. She had to stay overnight because of the mounting wind. The next morning, she recalled, the countryside was transformed: "It seemed as though half of the trees of the town were down. The landscape looked like Jack Straws."[99]

Twelve men worked for a week on the WPA payroll to help clear the highways of fallen trees, which were taken to the town yard at Kendal Green to be cut up for firewood or timber. As many as 52 men at a time worked on the cutting. For the next two years, the wood was delivered by the highway department to families on relief. In the 1938 town report, the selectmen wrote: "It will be many years before the devastating effects of this hurricane dis-

Figure 8-48. "Step on it" was the slogan for tin can collection during World War II. Once a month, cans could be left in "Victory piles" at the curb, where they were picked up by town trucks. The cans had to be properly prepared by washing, removing the paper, cutting off both ends, and flattening them. In August 1942, Weston led the state with a collection of 3,470 pounds of tin cans.

"THE ALERT"

Published now and then by
The Weston Committee on Public Safety
September 10, 1942

SALVAGE ISSUE

TO ALL WESTON RESIDENTS

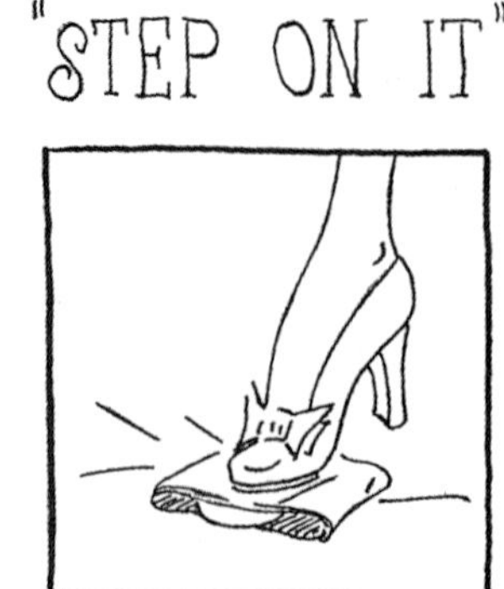

"STEP ON IT" is a good slogan not only for tin cans but for our whole war effort of which "Salvage for Victory" is a vital part. It is the first duty of every Weston citizen to get out every pound of scrap iron, steel, copper, brass, zinc, tin, lead, aluminum and rubber that can be found. Half of all steel production comes from scrap metal and Weston has tons and tons of it lying around. It is one of the most serious problems in our war effort. Don't forget we can lose this war unless we do our share.

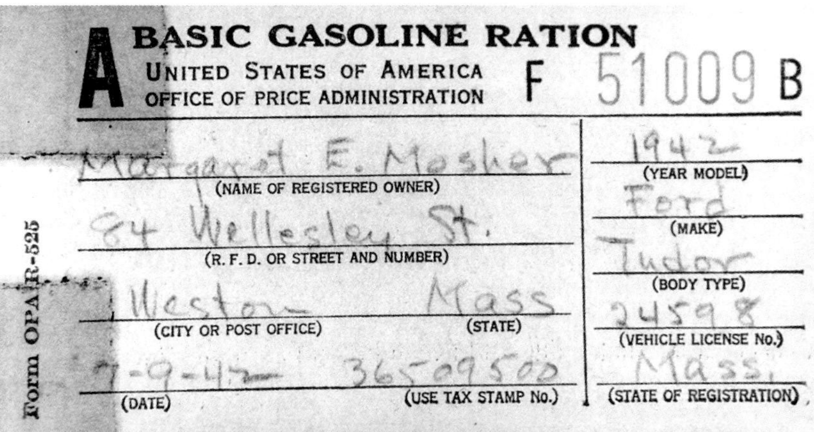
A BASIC GASOLINE RATION
UNITED STATES OF AMERICA
OFFICE OF PRICE ADMINISTRATION F 51009 B

Form OPA R-525

Margaret E. Mosher (NAME OF REGISTERED OWNER)	1942 (YEAR MODEL)
84 Wellesley St. (R. F. D. OR STREET AND NUMBER)	Ford (MAKE)
	Tudor (BODY TYPE)
Weston (CITY OR POST OFFICE) Mass (STATE)	24598 (VEHICLE LICENSE No.)
7-9-42 (DATE) 36509500 (USE TAX STAMP No.)	Mass. (STATE OF REGISTRATION)

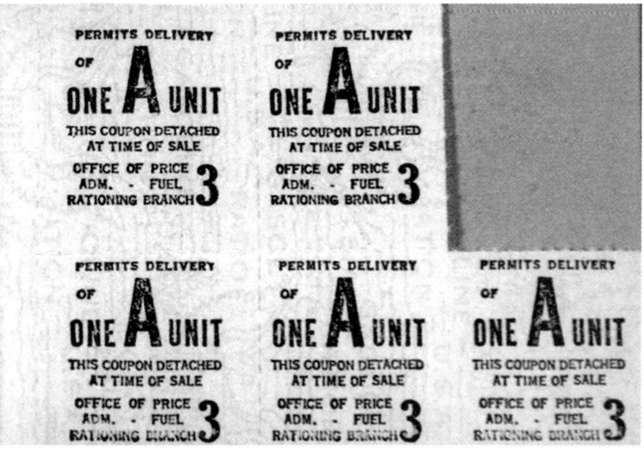

Figure 8-49. During the war years, the Weston Grange, Weston Garden Club, and Committee on Public Safety sponsored a fall Victory Garden Show at the town hall. First-year gardeners, amateurs, and professional farmers could compete for prizes in their respective classes.

Figure 8-50. Margaret Mosher of Wellesley Street saved her war ration books, which still contain unused stamps for purchase of foods like sugar, butter, and meat.

Figures 8-51 and 8-52. Each gasoline ration stamp allowed purchase of one "A" unit of gasoline, which could vary in amount depending on the demands of the war program. Supplemental B- and C-rations were issued if the car was needed for business or war work.

appear and it therefore behooves the town . . . to repair surviving trees and to plant new ones so that future generations may know the beauties we have enjoyed in the past."[100]

World War II: On the Home Front

Mobilization of the town was remarkable following the attack on Pearl Harbor in December 1941. The Weston Post of the American Legion assumed responsibility for maintaining an aircraft observation post at the Regis College tower manned night and day by members of the Weston legion. The Committee on Public Safety set up six divisions: Services and Supplies, Evacuation, Protection, Air Raid Precaution (ARP), Medical, and Health and Social Services. They were charged with providing food, water, temporary shelter, and medical assistance to residents and potential evacuees from Boston in the event of a bomb attack.[101] From 1942 to 1944, the committee published monthly issues of "The Alert" to keep the public informed on war-related issues.[102]

Civilian Defense eventually enrolled more than 900 volunteers. An impressive organizational chart can be found in the 1942 town report.[103] The Red Cross, American Legion, Women's Community League, League of Women Voters, and Boy and Girl Scouts cooperated on detailed plans. The town set up a center in the fire station attended round the clock to receive warnings of enemy planes. More than 300 men and women worked as air raid wardens. To comply with "dimouts" and blackouts, residents bought dark window shades and painted the top half of their headlights black.

The Women's Defense Committee collected and canned surplus food. Students in high school industrial arts classes made stretchers and splints. Red Cross volunteers gathered weekly to make surgical dressings and sew and knit clothing for refugees. Weston led the country in per-capita weight of tin

Figure 8-53. Austin Sherman Hale served in the Armed Forces in World War I. During World War II he wrote weekly letters to several hundred Weston servicemen, passing on town news and encouragement. He titled his letters "Here and There to Show We Care." Each week he received 25 or 30 replies from all over the world, many of which were published in the newspaper. Toward the end of the war, town residents helped fund "Victory dinners" for Hale's large extended "family."

Figure 8-54. Josephine "Jo" Sturgis Bidwell (pictured here on the bottom step of the Scout House) and her troop of Girl Scouts helped with Red Cross war work. Mrs. Bidwell was the first president of Weston Scouts Inc., a position she held for 20 years.

can collections and doubled its quota of metal scrap.[104] To stimulate interest in the "Salvage for Victory" scrap drive, Henry Davenport offered to give the town his original painting of Weston Town Hall when the quota was reached. Photographs in the 1942 town report show scrap metal heaps and an old windmill on the grounds of the Pine Brook Country Club being toppled to provide steel for the war. "The Alert" estimated that Weston had contributed almost a million pounds of scrap metal by April 1944.

The Weston Salvage Committee also collected newspapers, magazines, waste paper, and rubber. Butchers were authorized to pay four cents a pound for waste kitchen fats and grease, which were used to manufacture explosives. In 1944, Weston High School students collected 79,000 milkweed pods, enough to equip 66 servicemen with life jackets.[105] The Weston War Finance Committee ensured that the town surpassed its quotas for war loan drives.

Male teachers left their classrooms to enlist in the war effort. The school heating plant was converted to use coal rather than oil, and school officials struggled to maintain extracurricular activities despite gas rationing. Pupils sold more than $12,000 worth of U.S. War Savings Stamps and Bonds at school. The high school increased the time devoted to physical education activities like calisthenics, long-distance running, marching, and drilling.

The war effort left critical shortages at home.[106]

The federal Office of Price Administration (OPA) established rationing systems and controlled prices to curb runaway inflation. The original Weston rationing board, appointed in January 1942, consisted of Chairman Brenton H. Dickson Jr., Harry F. Warren, and Francis G. Goodale, who later took over as chairman. The minimal A-ration of gasoline was allocated to each passenger car, with supplemental B- and C-rations if the car was needed for business or war work. To cope with the gas shortage, residents organized joint shopping trips and ride sharing to trains, bus stops, and places of business. Heating oil was rationed and some households voluntarily converted to coal. Food coupons were issued for sugar, butter, fats, oils, meats, and peanut butter. Tires, bicycles, shoes, and typewriters were rationed.

The town put off capital improvements. Work requiring steel and asphalt had to be deferred, along with new equipment purchases. Town leaders saved unspent funds to avoid a steep tax rise after the war. The work of some departments was left undone because of labor shortages. Young men were no longer available for tree work. The highway department used high school boys for road maintenance and obtained tar to keep roads from deteriorating beyond repair.

In 1942, automobile traffic was cut at least 50 percent on weekdays and 80–90 percent on weekends because of the gasoline and rubber shortage and a ban on pleasure driving.[107] Police activity hit an all-time low. With so many young people serving in the Armed Forces and those left busy working in industry or the war effort, the 1943 police report observed that young people "don't have the time or the desire to get into mischief."[108]

Middlesex County farmers increased production by about a third over prewar years.[109] Enough local agricultural products were available to avoid food shortages in the county. The scarcity of labor was addressed by allowing men essential to farm production to remain on the farms, assisted by local help, foreign workers imported from Jamaica and Newfoundland, and prisoners of war. The extension service provided help to "Victory" gardeners and an annual Victory Garden Show was held at Town Hall. The Nutrition-Garden-Preservation Board assisted homemakers with preserving fruits and vegetables and the County Extension Service gave demonstrations on cooking vegetables and cooking with a minimum of sugar. Due to the severe shortage of new clothing, agents demonstrated how to sew and refashion clothing.

Figure 8-55. Memorial plaques from both World Wars were placed on a boulder outside Weston Town Hall. In the auditorium, bronze plaques list the names of all who served.

The Children's Exchange, predecessor to today's Clothing Exchange, was conducted by the War Services Division beginning about 1943, initially in the St. Peter's parish house and later in the basement of the town hall. In 1943 more than a thousand customers purchased 2,800 articles of clothing. The exchange kept a service charge of 10 percent. In May 1945 the exchange was taken over by the Women's Community League for the benefit of its education and welfare fund.

By 1943, Weston was anticipating war's end. Active Civilian Defense operations were suspended in November 1944. When the war ended in August 1945, the Weston Honor Roll, the official list of men and women serving in the Armed Forces, had reached 525 names. Twenty-one men gave their lives or were reported missing in action.[110] In 1949 the town installed a bronze plaque on the memorial boulder outside Town Hall bearing the names of those lost in World War II. The design was similar to the World War I plaque already in place on the same boulder. The town also voted to place a bronze honor-roll plaque in the upper town hall opposite a similar World War I plaque. In 1953, the Weston War Memorial Educational Fund, a scholarship fund for post-secondary education, was established as a memorial to citizens of Weston who served in the Armed Forces in all wars.

Notes

1. Jackson, Kenneth T., *Crabgrass Frontier: The Suburbanization of the United States* (New York and Oxford: Oxford University Press, 1985), 11. See also Stilgoe, John R., *Borderland: Origins of the American Suburb, 1820–1939* (New Haven and London: Yale University Press, 1988).
2. Information in this and the next paragraph was taken from John H. Sherburne's chapter "Massachusetts in the World War (1914–1919)," in Hart, ed., *Commonwealth History of Massachusetts,* vol. 5, 598. See also Edwin Conklin's chapter on World War I in *Middlesex County and Its People,* vol. II, 787 ff.
3. *WDFPT,* June 9 and July 7, 1916.
4. See 1941 *TR,* 28–29.
5. Soldiers who died in World War I were John Blanchard, Robert B. Denton, Lawrence Dwight, Charles H. Fiske III, Frederick W. Henderson, and Philip Winsor. 1918 *TR,* 30, 34–36.
6. 1917 *TR,* 44. The report adds that 60 families had canned but not counted their output, and 50 families had done no canning.
7. *WDFPT,* April 26, 1918.
8. 1917 *TR,* 38.
9. 1917 *TR,* 111.
10. *WDFPT,* 1918, and March 7, 1919.
11. A complete list of dozens of items is recorded on a "Summary of War Relief Work in Weston," January 1, 1918 (E.B. Sears Papers, WPL history room).
12. *WDFPT,* January 14, 1916.
13. *WDFPT,* May 11, 1917, and December 17, 1915.
14. 1918 *TR,* 86–87.
15. *WDFPT,* May 2, 1919, and following weeks.
16. 1921 *TR,* 32. See 1919 *TR,* 32 (insert), for architect Samuel Mead's drawing of a much more elaborate flagpole base, which was never built. In the 1960s, the flagpole was struck by lightning and Ralph Woodworth led a fund drive to replace it.
17. 1951 *TR,* 126.
18. 1922 *TR,* 42.
19. 1942 *TR,* 230.
20. 1942 *TR,* 12.
21. 1922 *TR,* 38.
22. Harold Willis to B. Loring Young, August 24, 1937. Correspondence and sketches, Town of Weston Cemetery Department. Miss Merriam's parents were Nellie and George Merriam. According to one of these letters, Miss Merriam had arranged to be buried in the family plot in Weston.
23. *WDFPT,* August 6, 1920.
24. 1938 *TR,* 90.
25. 1917 *TR,* 65.
26. 1930 *TR,* 313 ff.
27. "Weston High School Opened for Public Inspection on Holiday," *Waltham News Tribune,* April 22, 1932.
28. Quoted from *Handbook of the Weston High School Association,* no. VI, 1941.
29. 1937 *TR,* 79–80.
30. 1920 *TR,* 65.
31. The 1943 town report includes a complete analysis of income and expenses for these years.
32. 1929 *TR,* 42–45.
33. 1931 *TR,* 35.
34. 1937 *TR,* 22.
35. Handlin, David P., *The American Home: Architecture and Society, 1815–1915* (Boston: Little Brown & Co., 1979), 153–54. For a detailed account of the evolution of zoning, see Michael Holleran's *Boston's "Changeful Times," Origins of Preservation and Planning in America* (Baltimore and London: Johns Hopkins University Press, 1998). This book refers to New York City's zoning ordinance of 1916 as the first "comprehensive" American zoning ordinance.
36. Chapter 635 of the Acts of 1912. See 1912 *TR,* 43–44.
37. 1921 *TR,* 26.
38. 1922 *TR,* 50.
39. 1924 *TR,* 22. By 1924, 26 Massachusetts cities and towns had adopted zoning ordinances and another 26 were engaged in the process.
40. Ibid., 29–30.
41. Ibid., 68.
42. Business districts allowed certain by-right uses including hotels, restaurants, offices, banks, theaters, stores, public garages and stables, filling stations, and repair shops. Light industry could be permitted by the selectmen. The industrial district could not be used by industries that were offensive to the neighborhood because of cinders, odor, gas, fumes, dust, or chemicals. For text of bylaw, see 1926 *TR,* 86–98.
43. In the single-residence district, houses and ancillary structures could occupy no more than 40 percent of the area of the lot at the first floor and in the general-residence district, no more than 50 percent.
44. 1936 *TR,* 24.
45. Bachelder, J. Leonard, *The Half Century Limited* (Massachusetts Bay Railroad Enthusiasts Inc., 1984).
46. Ling, Peter, *America and the Automobile: Technology, Reform and Social Change* (1990), 82.
47. 1922 *TR,* 30. Compare this to 1920, for example, when motorized school barges broke down on snow-covered roads and horse-drawn pungs had to be substituted. (*WDFPT,* January 30 and February 13, 1920).
48. 1939 *TR,* 25.
49. "Town of Weston, Massachusetts, Compiled Survey of Meadow Lands in Vicinity of Center of Town," by Arthur A. Shurtleff, January 1926, shows path of new roadway (WHC).
50. Salvucci, Peter Jr., "I Remember Coburn," *Weston Town Crier,* letter to the editor, May 22, 1998.
51. 1921 *TR,* 65. The bureau also conducted field experiments in growing winter vetch and winter rye for enriching the soil and the effect of different applications of lime. Agents judged at the annual Grange Fair, which was held throughout this period.
52. 1922 *TR,* 67.
53. 1932 *TR,* 83
54. Donahue, Brian, *Reclaiming the Commons,* 247.
55. MCRD, Plan of October 1930 in Book 5513 (end), also June 1931 in Book 5570 (end) and February 1937 in Book 6101 (end).
56. Massey, James C. and Maxwell, Shirley, *House Styles in America* (New York: Penguin Studio, 1996), 186.
57. Later Allen, Collens and Willis and then Collens, Willis and Beckonert.
58. Kopl, George F., ed., *American Architects Directory,* 2nd edition (New York, R.R. Bowker Co., 1962). For Hammond Castle, see James F. O'Gorman, "Twentieth-Century Gothick: The Hammond Castle Museum in Gloucester and Its Antecedents," *Essex Institute Historical Collections,* vol. 117, no. 2, April 1981. A good source of Willis biographical material is Harvard University Archives.
59. "Weston Saddle and Bridle Club Inc. 1929." First yearbook with membership list and bylaws (Edwin B. Sears collection, WPL). The club was organized in September 1928 and incorporated in April 1929. Original incorporators were Harry Bailey, Charles G. Squibb, Mortimer A. Seabury, F. Manlius Sargent, Sinclair Weeks, Austin B. Mason, Lyman W. Gale, Harold B. Willis, Donald C. Watson, and Arthur H. Morse.
60. An editorial in the *Weston News Review* of May 28, 1936, said the club was now 15 years old. That year, the club was enlarging its horse show to meet the needs of horsemen throughout the area, with more than 200 entries.
61. PWF telephone interview with James Dolan. Kendal Green Riding School is listed in the 1949 Weston directory.
62. Advertisement in the *Weston News Review,* March 17, 1939.
63. *WDFPT,* November 26, 1920.
64. Ibid.
65. *WDFPT,* September 12, 1919, and March 26, April 2, September 1, November 17, and December 8, 1920.
66. *WDFPT,* October 22, 1920.

67. *WDFPT,* June 11, 1915. See also November 27, 1914.
68. *WDFPT,* March 12, 1915.
69. *WDFPT,* September 15, 1920.
70. On their last day of formal work in March 1919, Anna Hall was honored at a luncheon of her 91 volunteer workers and presented with bouquets of red, white, and blue flowers—the French national colors.
71. "History of Women's Community League Begins Today: Part I—1st 10 Years," *Weston News Review,* May 2, 1941. See also September 29, 1939.
72. *WDFPT,* July 11, August 8, 15, 22, October 24, 1919; and March 26, April 9 and 16, May 14, and September 3, 1920. See also December 8, 1920 (letter to the editor from Jane Winsor Gale summarizing the group's achievements). Miss Field's classes were held on Friday afternoons, and young people were charged an "exceedingly low" fee.
73. "Weston: A Twentieth Century Country Town," a "Know-Your-Town" handbook prepared by the League of Women Voters of Weston, March 1954. See also information submitted to Weston 2000 (WHS).
74. Marjorie Pierce, local architect and league member, helped design the addition, and the new room was named in her honor.
75. "Weston League of Women Voters," *The Town Reporter,* February 1950, vol. 5, no. 9 (insert).
76. *Waltham News-Tribune,* April 24, 1932.
77. *WDFPT,* December 1, 1920.
78. "Weston: A Twentieth Century Country Town," op. cit. See also information provided to Weston 2000 and "The Weston Garden Club," a short history at the back of Nancy Fleming's *Weston Town Common: A History.*
79. Lord, Rev. Robert, "The Catholic Church in Massachusetts," in Hart, ed., *Commonwealth History of Massachusetts,* vol. V, 527–28.
80. "Louisa M. Case Gives Land for a New Center," *Boston Evening Transcript,* May 11, 1938.
81. *WDFPT,* "Historical Sketch of Girl Scouts, Weston," January 30, 1920.
82. *WDFPT,* October 18, 1918.
83. For information in this paragraph, see histories and newspaper clippings compiled for the Girl Scouts and kept at the Scout House.
84. The deed for the 40,000-square-foot lot was signed by Louisa Case but the decision to donate the lot and adjacent park was made by agreement of both Case sisters, according to a letter of March 5, 1976, written by Harold Travis to his son, Robert (Girl Scout archives).
85. "Weston Scouts Incorporated Reports on History and Activities," *The Town Reporter,* 1942.
86. Travis, Harold G. "Red," letter to his son, Robert, March 5, 1976 (Girl Scout archives).
87. Jones, Harry, "Post History," Weston Post No. 214, American Legion Inc., Weston (unpublished typescript, March 1998).
88. Ibid., 20.
89. Ibid., 9 (a summary of activities of 1930–31).
90. 1934 *TR,* 46–47.
91. 1935 *TR,* 37.
92. 1938 *TR,* 29.
93. *1942 TR,* 39.
94. Text copied from the monument, which is located at the intersection of Boston Post Road and Town House Road.
95. "General Washington's Bicentennial Reenactment in Weston 45 Years Ago," *WHSB,* May 1977, 3, 6. Also "Weston Greets Cavalcade in Shade of Burgoyne Elm," *Waltham News Tribune,* June 10, 1932. Note that Weston High School graduation exercises that year also centered on the Washington theme.
96. Ibid. The bronze tablet is now stored by the park and cemetery department.
97. 1926 *TR,* 107.
98. Chandler, David L., "Storm Warning," *Boston Globe,* September 7, 1998.
99. PWF interview with Linda Cabot Black, 1996.
100. 1938 *TR,* 32.
101. 1942 *TR,* following page 34. The original eight divisions listed in the 1941 town report on page 41 were decreased to these six (the women's and publicity divisions were dropped).
102. Copies of "The Alert" were kept by one of Weston's great savers, Edwin Buckingham Sears, and can be found in his papers in the Weston Public Library history room.
103. 1942 *TR,* following page 34.
104. 1942 *TR,* 11.
105. "The Alert," November 18, 1944.
106. Weston War Price and Rationing Board report, 1943 *TR,* 129–135.
107. 1942 *TR,* 79.
108. 1943 *TR,* 80.
109. Middlesex County Extension Service report in the 1945 *TR,* 60.
110. Soldiers who died in World War II were Edmund Billings, Roland Bumpus Jr., George Burke Jr., Grant Conroy, Gordon Curtis Jr., Alexander Doyle, Townsend Doyle, Francis Guthrie, Harold Hanney, Paul Haynes, William Hitchcock, Theodore Hoague Jr., Philip Hughes, John Jones, J. Malcolm Macdonald, Stewart MacDonald, Ned McKrill, James Page, Frederick Peterson Jr., David Thayer, and Alexander Winsor Jr. See 1946 *TR.*

Figure 9-1. The class of 1952 was among the first to graduate from the new Weston High School (now Field School). Also shown in this composite picture are principal Julius Mueller and popular longtime mathematics teacher Helen Green. The tremendous growth in the school population after World War II is graphically illustrated by comparing this photograph, with 37 graduates, to the 1964 class photograph, with 160.

CHAPTER 9 · (1945–1980)

The Postwar Years: Managing Growth

The third quarter of the 20th century was the most extensive growth period in Weston history. After more than a decade of stagnation in the construction industry during the Depression and war years, housing was in tight supply throughout the region. The coming boom was acknowledged in the annual town report as early as 1945, when the superintendent of streets noted, "The Town of Weston is apparently on the verge of a post-war real estate development dwarfing by comparison anything ever seen before during normal times."

Despite high real-estate values and construction costs, the housing boom was under way by 1948, when 127 parcels of real estate changed hands and 64 permits were issued for new homes. That year, the town historian wrote, "Barring either continued inflation or an economic 'bust,' it looks as though Weston ten years hence will bear only a remote resemblance, physically, to the quiet country town it has been these centuries past."[1]

In the decade between 1950 and 1960, population increased 64 percent, the number of dwellings was up 68 percent, school population was up 143 percent (from 795 pupils to 1,932), total assessed valuation increased 110 percent, and school appropriations increased 288 percent, including debt service. The 1951 report of the selectmen summarizes the issues facing the fast-developing suburb:

> *Of the many problems which have confronted the town in the past year, the most important can be described in one word "GROWTH"—more houses, more families, more children, more roads, more school facilities, more public services and—more and heavier taxes.[2]*

Increases in tax revenue were accompanied by much greater increases in municipal expenses:

> *We can only express the hope that the many fine new neighbors who are constantly joining us will appreciate that if they demand all the services they received from the urban areas they deserted, we cannot afford to keep Weston the rural area which so attracted them.[3]*

Added to the financial strain of growth was the rise in inflation beginning in the early 1950s and continuing through the energy crisis of the early 1970s.

Why was Weston so popular? The town was known for its excellent school system, comparatively low tax rate, and reputation as a well-managed town. By the mid-1950s, Weston stood at the junction of two major highways, in close proximity to new technology companies in Waltham, Wayland, and along Route 128. The 1953 selectmen's report speaks of the town's "paradoxical position of a rural community in the ever-growing shadow of increasing urban development at its borders."[4]

This chapter chronicles the impact of population growth on town government, infrastructure, schools, recreation, and open space during the postwar years. Slowing down growth is the second major theme, as Weston sought to preserve its rural character by rezoning and purchasing land for conservation. In 1945, the town owned less than 50 acres of protected open space. Thirty years later, in 1975, an additional 1,300 acres had been preserved as town forest, recreation, and conservation land—a truly remarkable achievement.[5]

The 1960s and 1970s were also a time of social upheaval and political activism. The civil rights movement, antiwar and antiestablishment counterculture and the environmental movement all had an impact on Weston's institutional development. Socially conscious residents created a summer camp where children from Weston and Roxbury could play together, studied ways to build affordable housing, and formed a Youth Commission to give young people an alternative to boredom and drugs. In the process, they nurtured Weston's unique social experiment of the late 20th century, Green Power Farm.

Statistics	1950	1955	1960	1965	1970	1975	1980
Population	5,026	6,257	8,261	9,848	10,870	11,478	11,169
Dwellings	1,186	1,618	1,998	2,439	2,763	3,025	3,217
Valuation	$13.651m	$20.512m	$27.577m	$89.150m	$109.262m	$192.150m	$207.968m
Tax rate	$33.50	$40.00	$60.80	$30.00[6]	$50.00	$46.10	$48.50

Figure 9-2. As the town's first executive secretery, J. Ward Carter was in charge of day-to-day operations for 52 years, until his retirement in 2001. (1978 photo)

Figure 9-4. The Boston firm of Shepley, Bulfinch, Richardson and Abbott designed the new police station, completed in 1974.

Town Development (1945–1980)

Postwar growth required expansion of all town services, with a corresponding need for more personnel and larger facilities. Full-time employees were needed to coordinate the work of government and manage day-to-day operations. The 1949 town report records the positive response to the appointment of J. Ward Carter to the newly created position of executive secretary to the board of selectmen and town accountant:

> Every department head and every citizen of the Town who has had occasion to do business with the new Executive Secretary will testify to the fact that this was one of the best moves the Town had made in many years. Without exception, town departments have cooperated with him and made use of his services. . . . We look forward to a much more efficient administration of the Town's affairs with his assistance.[7]

The "Weston Plan of Executive Secretary and Selectmen" added to the town's reputation for being well run.[8]

Figure 9-3. In 1974, 13 Weston selectmen honored Ward Carter for 25 years as "the Dean of executive secretaries." Front: Douglas Mercer. Middle: Edward Langenbach, Harold Hestnes, Whit Smith, Bud Koester, and Joan Vernon. Back: Charles M. Ganson, Leonard Dowse, Peter Reiman, William R. Dewey Jr., Ward Carter, George Lovejoy, Edward M. Dickson, and Florence Freeman. Freeman was Weston's first female selectman and began her first term in 1964.

Figure 9-6. Weston Fire Department employees about 1964–65. Front row: Dave Giles, Lt. Al White, Ben Crouch, Lt. Charles MacLeod, Chief Wyman Johnson, Fred Lyons, Everett Schwartz, Louis Young, and Arthur Hallowell. Rear: John Thorburn, Bill Sinclair, John Ryan, Fred Perkins, Don Vautour, Phil Upham, and Lee Rafuse. Johnson was a Weston fireman for 30 years and chief for 13 years, until his retirement in 1976. John Thorburn succeeded him as chief.

Figure 9-5. Weston policemen in 1950. Front row: Frank Shaw, Robert Lazzari, and Harold Lingley. Back row: Robert Millen, Lawrence Cugini, Willard Frye, and Frank Woods.

At the turn of the 21st century, Carter was in his 51st year of service. In an intervew prior to his retirement in 2001, Carter recalled that when he first came to Weston, the town had only a small administrative staff including a full-time treasurer, one assistant in the treasurer's office, and two secretaries.[9] The Board of Public Welfare had a director. Charles Stimpson became the first town engineer in 1951. A practicing lawyer was paid an annual salary to serve part time as town counsel.

In addition to the pressing need for more schools, discussed later in this chapter, voters after the war were faced with constant pleas for new or expanded accommodations for the police, fire, and highway departments; library; and town administration. The police station in the basement of Town Hall had an office, lockup, windowless guard's room, and storage room commandeered for the chief's office. As early as 1945, the planning board was asked to find a suitable site for a new station. In 1964 the town made plans to expand the central fire station to include police headquarters. Proposed sites for the combined facility were held in abeyance for years pending approval of a town center septic system. Finally, in 1972, with the septic issue still unresolved, a portion of Park and Cemetery Department land next to the highway department garage was designated as a site for a separate police station. The Boston architectural firm of Shepley, Bulfinch, Richardson and Abbott was hired to design a new facility, completed in 1974.

Figure 9-7. Town meetings were held at the upper town hall (shown here) until 1965, when they were moved to the Weston High School auditorium.

Longtime police chief during this period was Frank O. Shaw, who held the position from 1958 to 1986.

The Weston Fire Department faced the need for a new south-side station and expanded central firehouse. Fire Chief Maurice L. Upham started his 17-year tenure in 1944 with one fireman and one piece of apparatus and built "an efficient unit of fourteen permanent men, twenty-two callmen, and six pieces of apparatus, a department that is in the forefront in fire fighting capability for towns of this size."[10] He was succeeded by F. Wyman Johnson, who oversaw construction of a new station at Ash Street and South Avenue in 1967, designed by Donaldson R. McMullin. John Thorburn became chief in 1976. Under his leadership, the central fire station of 1914 was finally enlarged in 1986–88. In another expansion of its responsibility, the fire department was charged with operating the town's first ambulance, purchased in the mid-1970s.[11]

In the late 1940s, the highway department was working out of obsolete garages on Newton Street, Golden Ball Road, and Kendal Green, with storage facilities in two additional locations. A new cement-block municipal garage, built in 1953, provided office space, a repair shop, storage for equipment and supplies, and employee locker rooms. Five more storage bays were added in 1964.

The Weston Public Library was remodeled in 1961 to accommodate additional stack space. Even after the renovations, the building was too small. The 1965 town report noted that the library had 45,000 volumes and was at capacity, meaning that "a book must be discarded for every new one bought."[12] The town voted to use Lamson Park, just

Figure 9-8. Denison Palmer simultaneously tosses three bags of trash into the town landfill in April 1978.

Figure 9-9. Recycling began in Weston in August 1971. Seventeen-year-old Heather Saunders was one of many high school students who volunteered to monitor the newly formed recycling center at the dump.

Figure 9-10. This early 1960s photograph includes, from left, Arthur F. Jones, superintendent of the water department.; Muriel Vittum Stimpson, secretary to the selectmen; F. Wyman Johnson, fire chief; an unidentified woman; Harold G. "Red" Travis; Frank O. Shaw, chief of police; Richard Bodge, librarian; and Daniel Compton Jr., highway department. Travis was frequently in charge of contacting town employees for the United Fund Drive.

Figure 9-12. Weston native Stanley Fabbri (1914–1976) headed the highway department for 28 years, from 1948 to 1976. (1972 photo)

The Town Reporter

WESTON · MASSACHUSETTS

Vol. 7, No. 6 | NOVEMBER, 1952 | EIGHT PAGES

No Matter What Your Affiliation May Be PLEASE VOTE

STATEMENT OF POLICY

"The Town Reporter" is an official publication of the Town of Weston. Its purpose is to disseminate information concerning the various Town Departments, and other activities which are of public concern and interest. "The Town Reporter" is published ten times a year, and each issue is delivered free of charge to every household in Weston.

Please address all communications to William T. Wolf, 46 Hill Top Road, Weston 93, Mass.

POLLS OPEN AT TOWN HALL TODAY, 7 a.m. - 8 p.m.; RIDES IF DESIRED

The Board of Selectmen wish to call the attention of every registered voter in Weston that no matter what his party affiliation is, it is his duty and privilege to vote on November 4th. It is not only the duty of each voter to vote but it is also his duty to be sure that all his neighbors get to the polls. The polls will be open from 7 a.m. to 8 p.m.

TRANSPORTATION TO POLLS

The Town Hall has been provided with telephone numbers of citizens who have volunteered to provide transportation for voters on November 4, 1952. If you wish transportation please call WA. 5-7320.

NO MATTER WHAT
Your Affiliation May Be
Please
VOTE

Figure 9-11. Weston took its politics seriously. In 1950 the town had 1,200 registered Republicans and 66 registered Democrats. Two years later, it had the highest record in New England and second highest in the nation in percentage of eligible voters who registered (91.5 percent) and cast a ballot (96.62 percent). The Town Reporter *was first published as the Civilian Defense publication "The Alert" during World War II and continued from 1945 to 1950 and then 1952 to 1956.*

west of Town Hall, as the site for a new library, a proposal that was rescinded in 1966 after strong opposition. Library reports from the early 1970s boasted one of the highest per-capita rates of book borrowing in the country. Not until 1994–95 was a new library finally constructed on town land next to the Field School.

Beginning in the early 1960s, the selectmen proposed an addition to Town Hall. The need for more space was postponed by reconfiguring the first floor and later by remodeling the basement into offices after the police department moved to its new headquarters.

The need for a town dump was first mentioned in the 1934 town report, which notes that such a public facility would do away with indiscriminate dumping on private land.[13] By 1952, dumps were operating on South Avenue near the Natick line and at Kendal Green. Location of the South Avenue dump on a main highway made control of its use more difficult than at Kendal Green. Identification stickers were first issued in 1960 to enforce prohibitions against outside dumping. Trash was disposed of by open burning. Because of the danger of air pollution and fire, pressure from the state

Figure 9-13. In the decade between 1950 and 1960, the school population in Weston increased 143 percent.

Department of Public Health led to development of a sanitary landfill in 1968. This solution proved to be both satisfactory and economical, although clearly time-limited. In 1971, the Federation of Weston Garden Clubs, League of Women Voters, and newly formed Youth Commission joined together to establish the Weston Recycling Committee. As pointed out in the 1971 town report, recycling not only benefited the environment but also prolonged the life of the landfill, which was expected to last only a decade.

Passage of the collective bargaining law by the state legislature in 1965 allowed municipal employees to form bargaining units to negotiate salary, benefits, and working conditions.

Figure 9-14. Junior high science students hold a large clamp used to make notepads out of recycled mimeograph paper. From left, back row: William Shotwell, Arthur Ulman, John Stasik (teacher), John Richardson, John Stubbs, Mark Pelsue. Front row: ____, John Crowley. (Early 1970s photo)

Schools

Throughout the postwar period, Weston schools were known for high standards and high cost. Schools routinely accounted for 60–65 percent of the town budget. Weston's per-pupil expenses were consistently high: $254 in 1948, for example, compared to a state average of $178. That year, of all the Massachusetts cities and towns with high schools, only Brookline had a greater per-pupil cost. In 1969, Weston's expenditure per student was again the second largest in the state. School administrators attributed these costs to comparatively small classes at the elementary level, a low student–staff ratio designed to individualize instruction, a high salary schedule, and a broad curriculum and small enrollment at the high school. In an era of teacher shortages, the school committee regularly increased teachers' salaries to attract and keep competent staff. The proportion of the budget devoted to special services like remedial reading and perceptual development also increased throughout the period. By 1969, 253 children received extra help within the system and 33 were enrolled outside the system.

The rapid rise in school expenses after the war was also the result of a tremendous increase in the number of pupils and the consequent need for new school buildings. In 1945 Weston had 635 pupils; by 1970 the number had grown to 2,937, an increase of 363 percent. By the end of the school building boom

Figures 9-15 and 9-16. Students pose at the entrance to the new Weston High School (now Field School) with English teacher Paul Mitchell in 1956–57. Seated, fourth from left, is future Weston teacher and coach Nancy Healey. The classroom photograph dates from 1957–58.

Figure 9-17. Students in the Weston High School business department practice for a Type-a-thon in March 1987.

Figure 9-18. Weston High School proms from the 1950s had a queen and her court. For their junior prom, the class of 1956 chose Judy Wetzel '56 as queen (seated). Standing, from left, Ellen Jo Connolly '55, Sue Wilson '56, Donna Cugini '56, Joanna Blake '56, Sylvia Tilly '55, Marian Larkin '56, Barbara Rushforth '56, and Cleo Styron '55. (1955 photo)

in 1970, Weston had spent more than $9 million building or remodeling schools.

In addition to strong academics, Weston schools offered a well-rounded physical education program. The 1958 town report claimed that "no public school system in the area had as large a proportion of its study body taking part in athletics and physical education as does Weston."[14] The program attracted considerable attention in professional circles and was the subject of an article in the *Physical Education and School Athletics Newsletter* in the fall of 1958.

After the war, the Parent-Teacher Association was formed to replace the earlier Weston Parents' Association and Weston Teachers' Club. The need for "an effective meeting ground for home and school" was one of 110 recommendations of 13 working committees that studied the Weston school system in 1944–45.[15]

Annual science fairs were held each year throughout the 1950s, with the winners often going on to attain regional and state honors. Russian was offered during the 1950s and 1960s, along with French and later Spanish. To provide additional curriculum options, Weston became part of a regional consortium to construct Minuteman Regional Vocational Technical High School, which opened in 1974.

The Roxbury-Weston connection began in the mid-60s, when the death of civil rights workers in Selma, Alabama, and the assassination of Martin

Figure 9-19. Music teacher Wendell Philips (right) directed the Weston High School band. (Photo 1956–57)

9-20. Weston High School drum majorettes pictured in the 1958 yearbook were led by Johanna Hoagland, in white. The squad, from left: Maribeth Manson, Deborah Lynch, Janet Tenneson, Marie Larsen, Anne Jones, and Barbara Wyman.

Figure 9-21. Weston High School field hockey team, 1958.

Figure 9-22. Weston High School girls basketball team, 1955. Standing: Margaret "Peg" Curtin and Terry Tighe. Seated: Sally Perkins and Anna Melone.

Figure 9-23. Weston High School football team, 1974.

Figure 9-24. The Weston High School mascot, shown here, is the wildcat. It was chosen in 1957–58.

Figure 9-25. Weston High School swimming team in 1984. Under coach Pete Foley (right), later joined by coach Claude Valle, the "Red Tide" won dual county league and state championships throughout the late 20th and early 21st centuries.

Figure 9-26. Weston High School began holding graduation ceremonies on the town green in 1963. Here, Ralph Morrison, Marjorie Quinlan, Margaret Vernon, and Stephen Condakes sing the National Anthem at the 1976 graduation.

Luther King Jr. brought together a small group of residents to discuss what Weston citizens could do to promote racial justice. Fifty children from Roxbury were bused to Weston, joining 50 local children for a summer day camp experience. Within two years, the camp developed into the Roxbury-Weston Preschool.

In 1967, five of the preschool students joined four other Roxbury children in Weston kindergarten classes in a program administered through the Metropolitan Council for Educational Opportunity (METCO). The voluntary desegregation program had begun a year earlier in seven other suburban communities.[16] Staff evaluation reported benefits to both Weston and METCO students, and nine more students were taken into the 1968 kindergarten class. By the 1975–76 school year, 161 METCO students filled an average of two seats per classroom in grades K–8. The METCO program continued to expand until 1979–80, when the first 10 METCO students graduated from Weston High School.

The Weston Education Enrichment Fund Committee (WEEFC) was created by Town Meeting in 1985 as a permanent subcommittee of the school committee. Its goal is to augment and enrich the Weston public schools by receiving tax-deductible donations that can be spent on projects not covered by the regular school budget.

School Building in the Postwar Years

After the war, the town embarked on an unprecedented 25-year school building program that resulted in a five new school complexes. In 1946 the town voted to build a new elementary school and appropriated funds for a building "of modern construction without 'useless decoration' " that could be expanded to accommodate at least 800 pupils. Land formerly belonging to the Case family was acquired from Harvard University's Arnold Arboretum at a cost of $10,000. The chosen architect was local resident Harold B. Willis of the Boston firm of Collens, Willis and Beckonert.

Just as the building was ready to go to bid in April 1948, Weston High School suffered a disastrous fire that gutted the inside of the 1932 brick structure. Two hundred ninety students were left without a school. The City of Waltham offered the use of its high school for afternoon sessions for the remainder of the school year. As a result of the fire, plans already prepared for the new elementary school were adapted to a 20-room high school for grades 7–12. The building committee added a gymnasium to the plan and found space for a cooking room, automotive shop, woodworking shop, and mechanical

Figure 9-27. On April 7, 1948, a fire at Weston High School set by a student raged for five hours in a spectacular blaze before being brought under control. The building was completely gutted, with damage estimated at $650,000.

Figure 9-28. The innovative design of the Country School won awards for architect Hugh Stubbins Jr. The building opened in February 1955, but will be demolished in 2001–03 to make way for a new elementary school. (2001 photo)

Figure 9-29. Woodland School, also designed by Hugh Stubbins Jr., was dedicated in January 1960. It is scheduled to be enlarged and reconstructed in 2001–03.

drawing room. Classes began in the new building (now Field School) on January 5, 1950.[17] The new high school cost $925,000 and was the largest public building in Weston. Furniture and equipment salvaged from the burned school were used wherever possible.

The former high school was reconstructed as an elementary school in 1948. The seven-month task fell to Collens, Willis and Beckonert in association with Donaldson Ray McMullin. In addition to reconfiguring classrooms, the major change was eliminating the lunchroom on the third floor and replacing the original gable roof with a flat roof. A school report observed, "The exterior of the building still has a colonial flavor but its simplified lines somewhat suggest contemporary design."[18] A newspaper reporter put it more bluntly: "All fripperies, like decorative urns, have been removed."[19] A new kindergarten room was added off the Case House in 1951. That same year, work began on renovating the 1895 brick former high school to create seven modern classrooms and fix structural weaknesses. Around the mid-1950s, this building became known as Building A, the primary school as Building B, and the 1932 former high school as Building C.

No sooner were these projects complete than another building committee was formed to plan an elementary school on the Case property, later named The Country School. The chosen architect, Hugh Stubbins Jr., taught for many years under Walter Gropius at Harvard's Graduate School of Design. He began his career designing crisp, modern houses and by the 1950s was busy with elementary schools for the baby-boom generation. Stubbins's design for Weston won the Boston Society of Architects prestigious Harleston Parker Award, given approximately annually since the 1920s to the most beautiful new building in the Boston area. Country School was one of the first modern buildings to receive the award and, according to one authority, was seen as a model for a new school type.[20] Work began in 1953, and the 20-room facility—complete with auditorium, gymnasium, administrative offices, and library—opened on Valentine's Day 1955.[21] The 1955 town report proudly noted, "School building experts from here and abroad have made much of it."[22] A fifth-grade student won a contest to choose the name.

Throughout the early 1950s, school administrators and town residents debated the merits of centralized vs. decentralized elementary schools. In 1952, the school committee outlined a program of expansion by building three six-year elementary schools, one each in the north, south, and central parts of town. The committee took steps to ensure that sites were available on the north and south sides. Although the planning board and town planning consultant favored decentralized schools, 1,380 residents attended a special town meeting in November 1956 and voted to continue centralization.

In 1958 the town acquired 32 acres by eminent domain from the Arnold Arboretum of Harvard University as a site for yet another elementary school.[23] In the interim, Building B was reactivated for use as classroom space. Woodland School was partially opened in November 1959 and completed in January 1960. Hugh A. Stubbins Associates was again chosen as architects, both for the first part of Woodland and for the six additional classrooms and multipurpose room added in 1964.[24]

The 1955–56 school year was the first in which the high school (grades 9–12) and junior high (grades 7–8) were in separate buildings, an arrangement that could be implemented after Country School was completed. The junior high was located in the 1932 former high school building known as Building C.

Figure 9-30. The $2.4 million Weston High School was dedicated in 1961. The building was completely remodeled in 1997–98. (1984 photo)

Figure 9-31. A 600-pupil junior high school was completed in 1969. Cambridge Seven Associates did the design. The building was remodeled in 1998–99. (2001 photo)

Another change at this time was that no new tuition students were sent to Weston from Lincoln after the 1954–55 school year because of the anticipated opening of the new Lincoln-Sudbury High School. In 1958, the last Lincoln student graduated from Weston High School.

As school enrollments continued to rise, the town in 1958 purchased 62 acres at South Avenue and Wellesley Street from the Paine Trust for a new high school.[25] The firm of Alderman & MacNeish of West Springfield was engaged as architect for the $2.4 million building, which was dedicated on December 2, 1961.

When the new high school opened in 1961, the 1950 high school became a junior high and Building C an elementary school. Continuing the Country-Woodland theme, Building C was renamed Brook School. While it was hoped that enrollments would stabilize, by the mid-1960s additional elementary and high school classrooms were needed. Extra rooms were added at Woodland School in 1964. In 1966–67, a major classroom and library addition increased the capacity of the high school to 1,100 students. In the mid-1970s, 225 students graduated from Weston High School, the largest number in the town's history up to that time.

In 1966 the town voted to purchase from the Paine Trust about 40 additional acres adjacent to the new high school on Wellesley Street. The sum of $3,600,000 was appropriated for a 600-pupil junior high, completed in 1969 from designs by another well-known firm, Cambridge Seven Associates Inc. The former junior high was remodeled and ready for occupancy as the elementary Field School by September 1970. Brook and Country Schools housed grades K–3 and newly established mixed-age classes. Field and Woodland were "intermediate" schools for grades 4, 5, and 6. Seventh- and eighth-graders were housed at the junior high and grades 9 through 12 at the high school.

School enrollment peaked in the early 1970s at more than 2,900 students, a figure that, as of the year 2001, has never been equaled. By 1974, enrollment predictions called for a 20 percent drop in school population over the next 10 years due to lower birth rates and a slowdown in housing starts. The era of Weston school building drew to a close. The three buildings comprising Brook School were closed in 1976 and Field School in 1981. Brook School was converted into housing for the elderly. Field School housed a variety of educational, civic, and recreational programs including the Weston wing of the Lincoln Community Children's Center, a day care center, and the Children's Center of Weston, an after-school program. The building was converted back to a school for fourth- and fifth-graders in 1995.

Water Supply

Major challenges facing the board of water commissioners involved improving existing water service in areas like Silver Hill and Conant Road, supplying water to scores of new homes, developing infrastructure, finding new water supplies, and deciding what to do about the town's remaining private water systems.[26] Water service on the north side was improved in 1947 with the construction of an 846,000-gallon standpipe on Cat Rock Hill. In 1959, a new one-million-gallon concrete tank was completed on Paine's Hill, replacing the earlier tank.

By the early 1950s, most of the town's water was supplied by the Nickerson Field well. Because of increased demand, a second well was drilled nearby on land donated by Agnes Fitzgerald. According to the 1954 town report, 72.4 percent of the town's 1,624 houses were supplied by the municipal water system. In 1960 the town voted to assume ownership

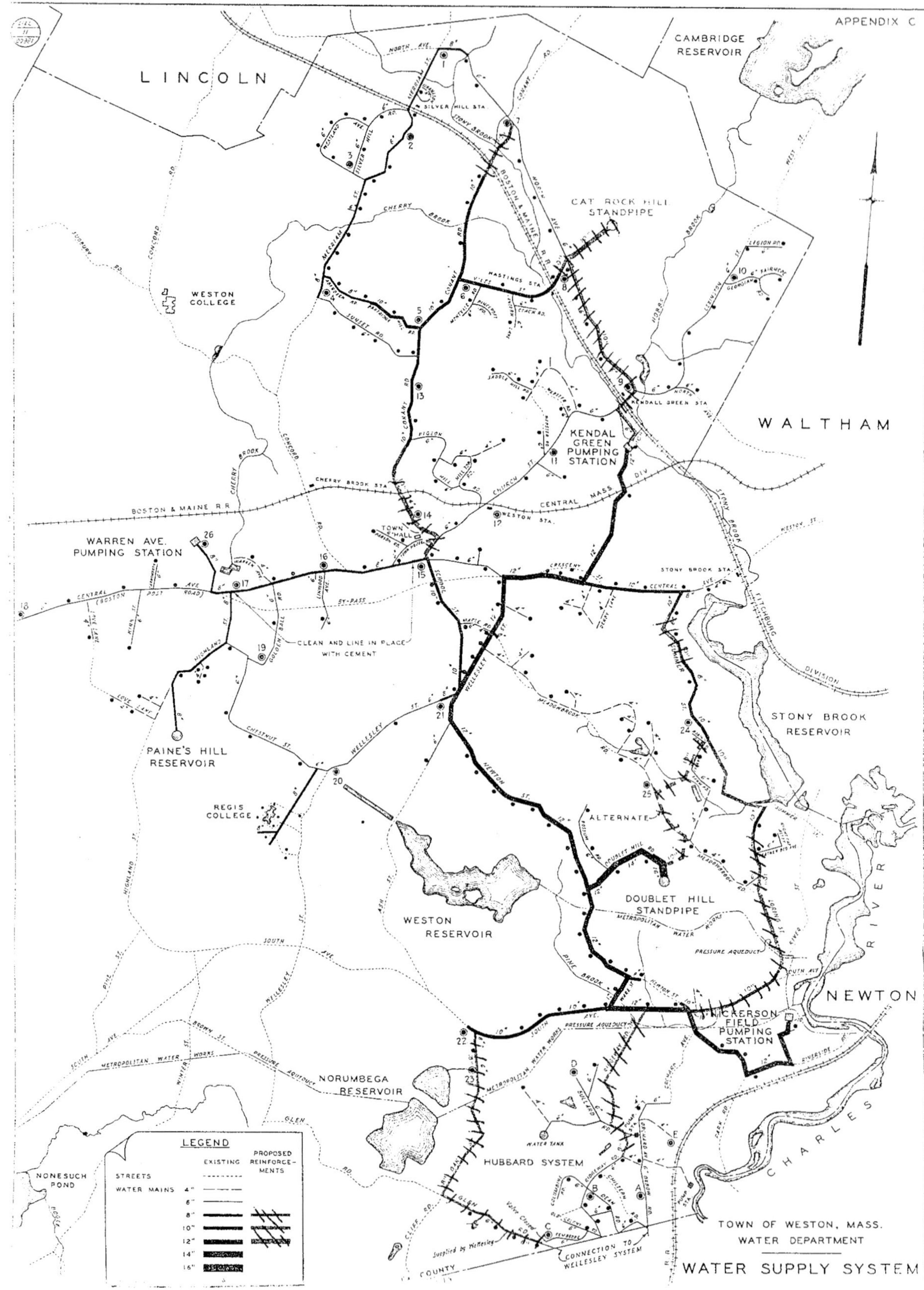

Figure 9-32. In its 1945 report, the engineering firm of Metcalf and Eddy proposed additions to the water supply system, marked on this map with cross-hatching.

and operation of the last two remaining private water companies, the Keewaydin (Blake) Water Works and the Hubbard Water System.

Also in 1960, voters authorized a professional study to seek additional water sources and reexamine the question of connecting with the metropolitan water system. Two years later, voters agreed to join the metropolitan system as the best solution to the need for a supplementary water supply.[27] In 1970 the Nickerson well, which was still the town's primary water source, was found to be severely contaminated with salt used to control icing on the Mass Pike and Route 128. The Kendal Green well was found to be contaminated from other pollutants in

1972, leaving the metropolitan system as the town's only water supply. In 1975 the town instituted suit against the Massachusetts Turnpike Authority and the Massachusetts Highway Department to prevent further contamination of the Nickerson Field well and to reimburse the town for damages. The suit was settled with a payment of more than $600,000, which was deposited in a special account. Since then, income has been used for water department expenses but the principal has been kept intact for possible future use in restoring the wells if appropriate technology becomes available.

Managing Growth: Planning and Zoning

The postwar period in Weston was characterized by proactive efforts to control and guide growth to create a certain kind of town. Concern for "preserving the rural character of the town" and "retaining rural atmosphere" is expressed frequently in town reports.

The planning board was primarily advisory in nature until 1943, when Weston adopted a new state law providing for an elected five-member board to oversee land development. Among its responsibilities, the new board had to approve subdivision plans, prepare an official map of the town, and prepare a master plan. By studying town resources and needs, leaders hoped to "avoid the evils of unrestricted, unoriented expansion apparent in many towns."[28] The board recommended acquisition of sites for town buildings as well as purchase of key parcels to protect the appearance of the town. Board members pushed for preparation of a set of assessors' maps to replace maps from 1903. The present town assessor's maps date from this period, although they have since been reduced in size and updated.

One strategy suggested to slow growth was to keep down the tax rate, on the theory that tax increases would force large property owners to sell to developers, with resulting loss of the "open fields, farms and woodland which we all enjoy at the expense of our larger property owners."[29] A high tax rate would lead to a "rapid conversion to low priced housing," requiring a further expansion in town services and another spiral of increased costs. But the low-tax approach, which had worked so successfully to attract and retain large estate owners at the turn of the century, was impossible to implement in the postwar economy, with its strong demand for housing and need for new facilities and services.

By the early 1950s, with the toll road under way and an extension planned into Boston within a decade, the selectmen recognized that development would focus on Weston. They initiated two important growth-control measures: a zoning bylaw increasing the amount of land needed to build and a land-acquisition policy reducing the amount of developable land by purchasing it for the town. The new bylaw was passed in 1954. It established four residential classes, A, B, C, and D, ranging in size from 60,000 down to 20,000 square feet, each with specific minimum street frontage and setbacks.[30] District lines were drawn to conform to existing neighborhood characteristics. The first town forestland was acquired in 1955, as described later in this chapter.

In the early 1960s, the planning board commissioned a master plan under the direction of Charles E. Downe, who summarized the town's basic goals as follows:

> To preserve and enhance the present general character of Weston as an outstandingly attractive suburban residential community and protect it from adverse effects of urbanization and nonresidential forms of land development.[31]

Among the nonresidential uses fiercely opposed during this period was the construction of a metropolitan sports stadium in the former Blake estate area in 1967.

Downe's results, available in 1965, indicated that the town had reached two thirds of its projected growth but was trying to cope with town facilities

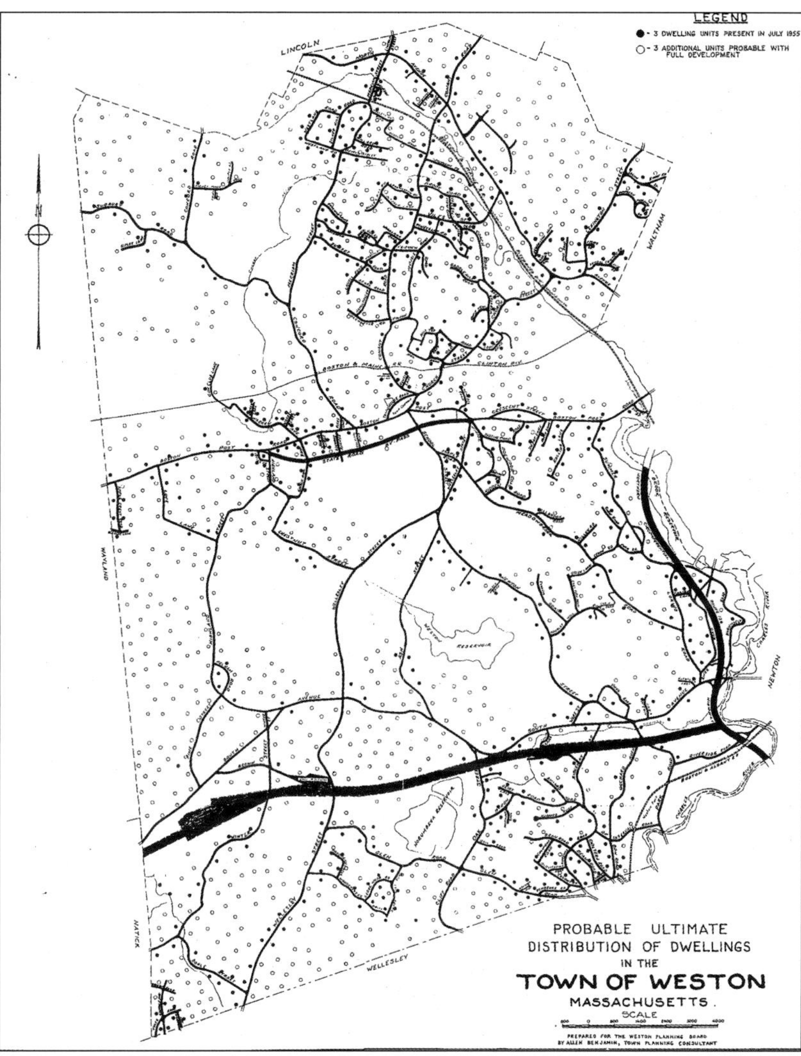

Figure 9-33. This map showing the "probable ultimate distribution of dwellings" was prepared for the Weston Planning Board in the mid-1950s. Each black circle represents three existing houses and each white circle represents the location of three potential houses, if the town were fully developed.

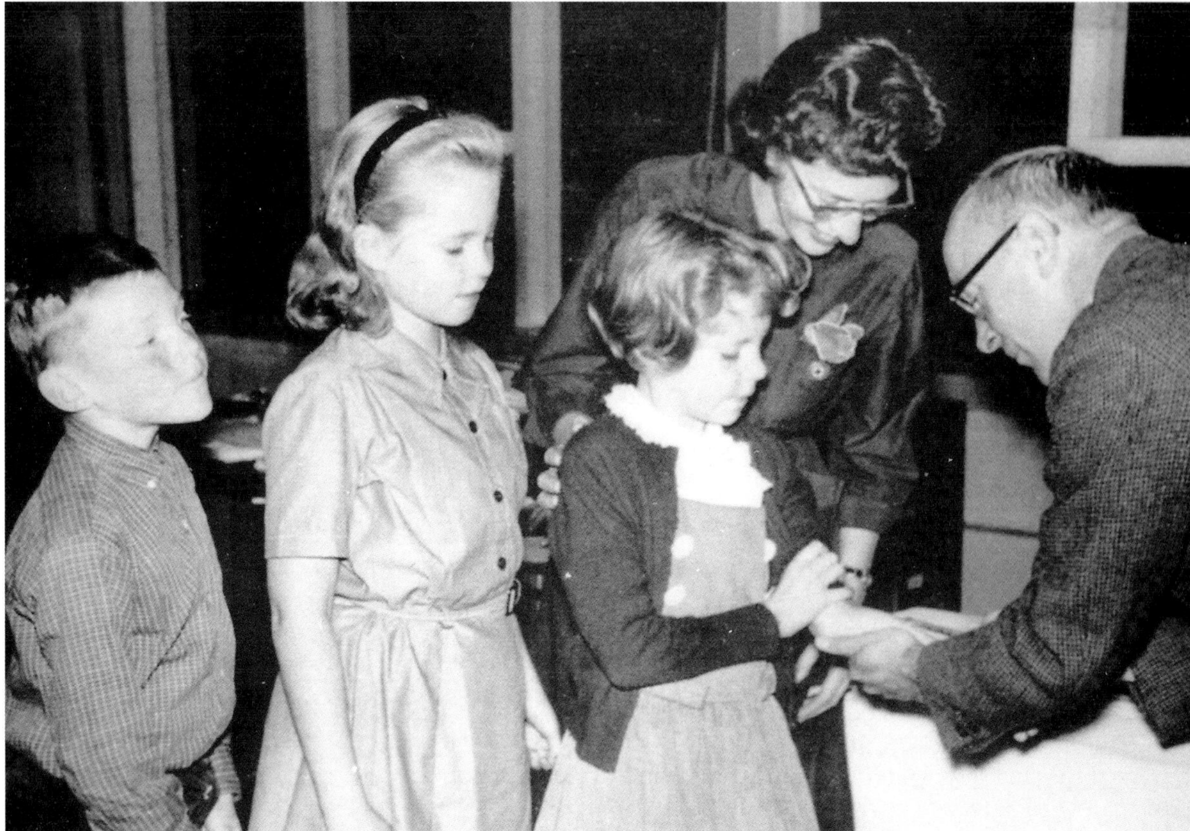

Figure 9-34. School nurse Jane Hosterman and school doctor David Reid administer the tuberculin test to elementary pupils in 1959.

planned for a much smaller municipality. The master plan identified the need for multiple dwellings for the elderly and affordable housing for town employees. It recognized the necessity of improving roadways and adding more sidewalks. One suggestion never implemented was for a north–south connector road to bridge the circulation barrier imposed by the State Road Bypass.

The Wetlands and Floodplains Protection District was created by vote of Town Meeting in 1975. Wetlands zoning gave the town the legal means to prohibit development in areas designated as wetlands and thus preserve land significant to water supply and flood prevention. A map delineating wetlands was created to define the boundaries of the district.

Public Health and Welfare Services

The board of health continued its emphasis on disease prevention. "Well Child" conferences, offered from 1951 to 1962, provided an opportunity for mothers to visit a pediatrician regularly for general health and vaccinations. The board launched the first program directed against a noninfectious disease, diabetes, in 1954. The first immunization clinics for polio were held in 1955, when school department officials cooperated with the board of health in administering the Salk vaccine. School opening was delayed throughout the greater Boston area because of continuing incidence of poliomyelitis. By 1956, more than 1,200 Weston children had been vaccinated. Also in 1956, Weston entered into an arrangement with Wellesley and Needham to share the services of a full-time health officer, to be employed by the Town of Wellesley.

In 1952, Dr. Fresenius Van Nuys resigned after 36 years on the Weston Board of Health, which under his guidance had a tradition of progressive community health work. Van Nuys was praised for his service as school physician and more than 40 years of active practice in the community.

The school dental clinic began applying sodium fluoride to children's teeth in 1947. Town committees studied the question of whether to add fluoride to the water supply to help prevent tooth decay, but it was not until 1973 that this was done. The caseload at the dental clinic dropped steadily in the late 1950s, until by 1959 it was only 40. Because equipment was deteriorating, the board of health discontinued the school clinic in 1960 and arranged with local dentists to provide services.

The late 1960s and early '70s saw the beginning of funding for drug counseling and treatment programs and shared resources for mental health including Human Relations Service in Wellesley and the Multi-Service Drug Center in Newton. A Drug Abuse Action Committee was appointed by the selectmen in 1970 to review the extent of the drug problem as it affected the youth in Weston and to recommend measures to educate the citizenry and prevent illegal use of drugs. A youth commission was established to provide activities for young people, in part because of concern that boredom was leading to drug problems.

Through the local board of public welfare, the town continued to administer state and federal money for old-age assistance, general relief, aid to dependent children (later aid to families with dependent children), and disability assistance. Medical assistance was later added. The town's agent worked as a professional social worker with those receiving aid. The 1954 town report states the town's philosophy toward aid recipients:

> All applicants who were able to do so were helped to help themselves to the limit of their capacities and encouraged to meet their problems in the most self-reliant way possible. Efforts are constantly made at rehabilitation. Regular visits to clients are, of course, required by law, but in a small community like Weston the human values derived from these visits go far beyond a routine check-up.[32]

Between 50 and 55 residents received public assistance in the early 1960s. Welfare administration and costs were taken over by the Commonwealth in July 1968.

Development of a Town Shopping Center

For many years, town officials wrestled with problems in the town center, particularly traffic congestion on Boston Post Road, a lack of convenient off-street parking, inadequate or nonexistent septic capacity, and concern for protecting aesthetic character. In 1955–56, Boston Post Road was widened in the commercial area by about 10 feet, allowing for more street parking and better traffic flow. The location of Center Street was debated for a decade and finalized in 1974. A proposed road linking Center Street to Colpitts Road never materialized, but a parking area was constructed behind stores on the south side of the Post Road. A natural buffer zone was established between the commercial district and State Road Bypass.

The lack of proper sewerage disposal was a problem dating back at least to the 1930s. It came to the fore in the 1960s when the board of health determined that pollution of the brook running under the town common came from a source in the business area. A study committee recommended building a sewerage disposal system serving the center and schools, with leaching beds within Jericho Town Forest. Opposition to use of town forestland for the effluent bed led to a renewed search for a suitable site. As plans were being made to vote on a second site farther within the forest, Regis College officials approached the selectmen to consider cooperative means of sewerage disposal. At the 1971 town meeting, voters authorized the sewer committee to proceed with linking the town center and Regis College to the Metropolitan District Commission (MDC) sewerage system in Waltham. Weston received approval from the City of Waltham and the state legislature. Concern that connecting with the MDC system would set a precedent and bring about more intense development throughout the town led to the abandonment of this proposal. Until construction of the solar aquatic greenhouse for sewerage treatment in the mid-1990s, many businesses in the center depended on holding tanks that had to be pumped several times weekly.

Affordable Housing and Other Housing Options

The shortage of affordable housing was not new to the town in the postwar period. By the mid-1920s, it had become increasingly difficult for people who grew up in Weston to find a place they could afford.[33] Weston increasingly attracted newcomers, which pushed up the cost of land, houses, and rents. The war greatly aggravated the situation because new construction lagged behind population increases. A 1947 report concluded that "every citizen knows that rental housing is substantially unprocurable and that houses can be bought only at grossly inflated prices."

The situation was particularly difficult for veterans, who returned to a competitive housing market with no vacancies in rental units. An advisory committee appointed to help returning vets look for housing, finance homes or businesses, and pursue education and employment recommended that houses be built to increase moderately priced housing stock.

The Veterans' Services Board obtained an option on land for the town to construct 20 homes to be rented to veterans and then sold at the end of the housing emergency. This proposal was turned down

Figure 9-35. The passage of a multiple-dwelling district bylaw in 1969 made it possible to build Jericho Village. The 22 buildings with 99 rental apartments were completed in 1973.

at Town Meeting, provoking this angry response from Austin Hale, director of Veterans' Services:

> Weston Veterans have not, and do not ask for charity, but assistance by the town would have made it possible for a number of them to establish normal family life. The indifference of the town to their need has embittered many service men.[34]

A second committee looked into more immediate and inexpensive solutions. The town converted the Cemetery House (the former Fiske Law Office) and a water department storage building on Warren Avenue into a total of three housing units and explored other ways to build new housing that veterans could rent and eventually purchase at cost. In 1950 the town funded the building of six houses scattered throughout the town.[35] Veterans paid rent of $50 a month but built up equity to enable them to purchase their home after five years.

Until the late 1960s, there was no provision in the bylaws for any type of new construction other than single-family houses. In 1969 voters passed new zoning regulations allowing for multiple-dwelling districts with "garden type apartments." At the same time, a Concord Road parcel owned by the Willis family was designated as a multiple-family district, allowing for construction of Jericho Village. This enclave of 99 apartments in 22 buildings was completed in 1973.

By 1970, Weston's estimated median family income was $29,600, the highest in the state.[36] A committee to study housing needs and possibilities, formed in 1970 to evaluate the need for affordable housing for the elderly and town employees, published the following statistics in the 1971 town report:

> 97% of Weston housing was single family
> Homes were expensive, with over 60% valued at over $50,000
> Basically no rentals and no apartments in Weston
> Less than 2% of households under 30 years of age
> Fewer than 10% of heads of household were not college graduates
> Land costs had increased 100% over the previous three years

One outgrowth was the passage of the accessory apartment bylaw, allowing for apartments to be created within existing dwellings under specified circumstances.

A housing action committee was appointed in 1975 to explore the development of elderly housing. Led by Victor Harnish and other concerned citizens, the nonprofit Weston Community Housing Inc. was formed to construct the first 30 Merriam Village apartments in 1977–78.[37] Harnish was the first president and Kenneth Fish the first treasurer. Land was donated by the town. To be eligible to rent the units, residents had to be 60 or older and have limited income.

The Town Forest and Conservation Commission

The town forest committee was established in 1953. Among the initial proponents were Selectmen William R. "Dick" Dewey Jr. and Charles M. Ganson. At that time, about 150 town forests had been established throughout the state. While such forests had been authorized under state general laws since 1882, it was not until after World War II that even the most farsighted Weston residents saw any need to purchase woodlands and open space that had always been abundant and free.[38] The study committee reasoned that a town forest would have recreational use and also lend a "country atmosphere." Four hundred acres in the Jericho area were identified as a priority.

In 1954, under the chairmanship of Dr. William Elliston, a new committee developed proposals to acquire land between Highland Street and Wellesley Street as well as in Jericho. Their report expressed what was to be the guiding philosophy behind purchase of conservation land in the town for the next decades:

Figure 9-36. In the mid-1950s, Dr. William Elliston spearheaded efforts to establish the town forest and the Weston Forest and Trail Association.

> . . . it has been found that the increase in value accruing to land abutting a town forest area is quite considerable. This allows an owner who retains his frontage land, to sell his back land for forest purposes at a lower price than would otherwise be possible.[39]

In 1955—a milestone year in the history of Weston land conservation—the town made its first purchase of 147 acres east of Highland Street from the Trustees of the Charles J. Paine Estate, at a cost of $51,500. General Paine's descendants donated an additional five-acre parcel with a view west to Mount Wachusett.[40] Marion B. Farnsworth donated 40 acres to begin the Jericho Town Forest.[41] The intention of town forest management was to care for the woodlands in accordance with accepted forestry practices. Trees were cut and thinned. In 1959, 3,000 white and red pine seedlings were planted. The following year, the Massachusetts Forest and Park Association awarded the town a plaque in recognition of good forestry practices.

Also in 1955, the Weston Forest and Trail Association (WFTA) was founded to protect open space, develop and maintain a trail system, and encourage the study of nature and conservation. WFTA was one of the pioneer organizations in Massachusetts dedicated to the preservation of land. Dr. William A. Elliston served as first clerk and the "heart of the organization for nearly thirty years."[42] Other founding members were Marie E. Lewis, president, and Henrietta N. Paine, treasurer, along with Thomas Cabot, Roger Ella, Florence Freeman, Stanley French, Francis Goodale, Victor Harnish, Ellen Lempereur, John B. Paine Jr., and Harrison Ripley. The association has helped the town acquire land and, as of 1997, owned 134 acres and held 14 acres of conservation easements and 15 miles of trail easements. To help educate residents on the values of maintaining land, Weston Forest and Trail Association sponsors monthly trail walks and educational programs.

The town regularly appropriated amounts from $10,000 to $25,000 annually during the 1950s and early 1960s to purchase additional town forest not only at Highland and Jericho but also anywhere backland could be obtained at reasonable prices.[43] In 1960 the town bought 48 acres off Sudbury Road from the family of Beriah L. Ogilvie to begin Ogilvie Town Forest, the third largest.[44]

The Weston Conservation Commission was formed in 1961 with powers newly granted by state statute.[45] Among its responsibilities was the management of wetlands. To avoid chronic drainage problems, the commission recommended acquiring rather than building in wet areas. Not until 1965 did the Hatch Act prohibit filling or dredging land bordering on inland waters without permission. The importance of streams, marshes, ponds, and swamps

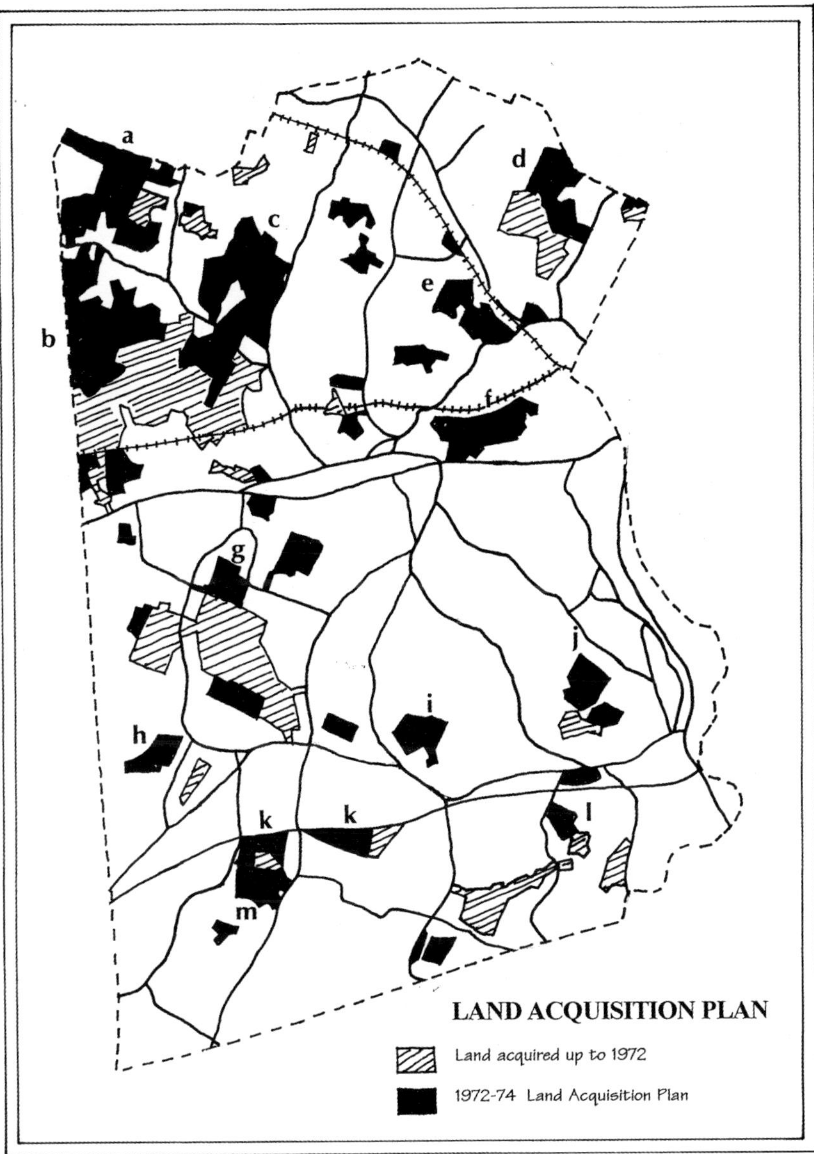

Key

Map letter	Conservation Area	# Parcels added	Beginning acreage	Acres added	Total in 1977
a	Ogilvie Town Forest	9	67	127	194
b	Jericho Town Forest	12	279	268	547
c	Weston College		0	146	146
d	Cat Rock Reservation		64	65	129
e	Coburn Meadow		0	45	45
f	Sears	3	0	82	82
g	Highland Town Forest	5	197	88	285
h	Pine Street Hilltop		0	21	21
i	Weston Reservoir area		0	31	31
j	Doublet Hill		0	60	60
k	Danforth		WFT 13	23	36
l	Ridgeway		WFT 5	15	20
m	Blaney		14	48	62

Figure 9-37. This map shows conservation land acquired by the town and the Weston Forest and Trail Association before 1972 (763 acres) and from 1972 to 1974 (1,115 acres) as part of an intensive land-acquisition program.

Figures 9-38 and 9-39. Hugo Uyterhoeven, a Harvard Business School professor, and Kenneth Germeshausen, an MIT graduate and founder of EG & G Inc., set a goal of doubling the amount of conservation land and persuaded the town to vote a total of $5.1 million to purchase it.

Figure 9-40. Weston's first "Green Map" was published in 1958 by the newly formed Weston Forest and Trail Association. In 1977 the WFTA issued four separate quadrant maps. In 1988 these were combined into one, largely through the efforts of George Bates, who is shown here checking the trails. Bates moved to Weston in 1958 and quickly became an active Forest and Trail member. He and Hugo Uyterhoeven established about half of the present 65 miles of trails.

in conserving water supplies and preventing flooding had finally been recognized.

Between 1955 and 1966, Weston purchased about 600 acres for $210,000. According to the 1960 town report, public acceptance was increasing: "It is becoming steadily more and more apparent that sensible preservation of the natural assets of a residential town can result in substantial appreciation of residential values, to the advantage of both developers and taxpayers."[46] But by 1967, skyrocketing land values were bringing conservation purchases to a virtual standstill.

In the 1970s, Weston College announced its intention to sell its seminary building and land, one of the town's largest remaining privately held parcels. A special committee headed by Kenneth Germeshausen was appointed to recommend priorities for acquiring some of the 300-acre property. According to committee member Hugo Uyterhoeven, public concern about the sale got people thinking about conservation and showed that they were willing to spend money to buy land.

Uyterhoeven and Germeshausen went far beyond the Weston College question in recommending a major program of land acquisition based on an exhaustive analysis of the town's remaining open land. They reported that, with development proceeding at a rate of some 200 acres a year, all of this open space could be gone within a decade. They argued that new houses would cost the town more in services than they paid in taxes and that the town could no longer rely on gifts or below market sales. Furthermore, the previous piecemeal approach of bringing each parcel to a town meeting vote should be replaced by a broad and large authorization. They maintained that "the opportunity to purchase undeveloped green areas is limited by time factors, and a more straight-forward and business-like method of acquisition should be devised."[47] Uyterhoeven was later to write, "We asked for a checkbook to compete head-on with the developers, who rapidly were buying up the remaining land."[48]

Uyterhoeven and Germeshausen made their case for a more aggressive approach to conservation at the 1972 Town Meeting. By unanimous vote, residents authorized a bond issue of up to $2.8 million with the dual goal of linking existing conservation land and achieving broader neighborhood distribution of green space. In addition to Uyterhoeven and Germeshausen, William Elliston, Harold "Bus" Willis Jr., and Herman "Bud" Koester Jr. were leaders in the land-acquisition process.

By 1974, three quarters of the money had been spent to create a "Green Belt" from the northwest corner south through the Jericho Town Forest and former Paine land and then easterly to link with the Weston Reservoir. Some of the money was used to acquire outlying Weston College land on Concord and Merriam Streets, but the key central portion remained elusive. The conservation commission continued its general policy of concentrating on backland to maximize acreage. The commission did negotiate pioneering conservation restrictions for one parcel to create a wooded buffer between South Avenue and new houses on Trailside Road. The town had a per-acre limit on the amount that could be spent. When the price got too steep, private money was raised through the Weston Forest and Trail Association to buy the land at the asking price and sell it back to the town at the allowed per-acre limit.

In 1974, the town voted an additional $1.3 million for the conservation commission to purchase more land in accordance with the 1972 town meeting vote. That same year, more than a million dollars was appropriated to buy much of the remaining Weston College land, to be matched by a state grant. This acquisition finally took place in 1977 and preserved 146 acres, including the athletic facilities and College Pond.

With the 1977 Weston College purchase, the goals of the land-acquisition plan were largely fulfilled. Between 1972 to 1977, the conservation commission made close to 60 transactions and acquired a total of about 1,115 acres. This included 970 acres purchased at a cost of $3.8 million and the 146-acre, $1.3 million parcel of Weston College land, purchased with a separate appropriation. In all, $5.1 million was spent for land acquisition.[49] When the effort began, the town had 763 acres of public and privately held land in conservation, or 7 percent of its total acreage. Five years later, the town had 1,878 protected acres, or 17 percent.

The $5.1 million was used to expand Highland Town Forest from 197 to 285 acres, Jericho Town Forest from 279 to 547 acres, and Ogilvie Town Forest from 67 to 194 acres. The town created the 45-acre Coburn meadow conservation area on Church Street, established the 82-acre Sears conservation area north of Crescent Street, and added to the Cat Rock recreation area. Topographical high points were purchased at Doublet Hill and at Pine Street. Land was purchased on the more densely developed south side including the Blaney meadow, Danforth land, and parcels between Orchard Avenue and Ridgeway Roads and south of Glen Road.

In her speech at the town's 275th anniversary in 1988, Jeannette Cheek summarized the importance of these two decades in Weston conservation history:

> Weston is fortunate in having individuals in the post-war period who were ready to give leadership to the idea of having the Town acquire land while it was still available and saving it for future generations to enjoy and be nourished by. . . . In the 1980s this would have been nigh impossible because development had gone too far. . . . [W]e should warn those who are new to Weston, and take the Green Belt for granted, that this did not come easily or all at once, but step by slow step. Vision of the goal, the education of an unaware public, and effective action by caring individuals were and are the key to conservation in Weston.[50]

Youth Commission and Green Power Farm

In 1971, town leaders created a youth commission "to support programs and projects arising from the expressed needs and desires of the young people."[51] The first coordinator, Donald Dunbar, spearheaded mental health counseling. Project Director William McElwain had a unique ability to inspire enthusiasm and old-fashioned hard work among young and old.

Figure 9-41. Bill McElwain (background, left), long-time project director for Green Power, supervises a produce stand in front of his house. He has been described as an "irreverent and joyful figure" and "a kind of farming Pied Piper for the youth of Weston."

Figure 9-42. Among the first signs of spring in 1978 were members of the Youth Commission hanging sugar buckets.

Figure 9-43. Brian Donahue served as Green Power director and helped found Land's Sake. An environmental historian, Donahue chronicled their story in his 1999 book Reclaiming the Commons.

Programs included the Green Power community farm, high school observatory, youth drop-in center, recycling at the town dump, job bank, and weekend bicycle trips.[52]

In his book *Reclaiming the Commons,* environmental historian and onetime Green Power director Brian Donahue gives this description of McElwain and his suburban farm in 1975:

> Bill was then in his mid-fifties, a vigorous man with sharp, grizzled features, a hawk nose, piercing blue eyes, and sparse white hair. Bill was and still is a blithely positive anarchist whose operating philosophy in dealing with obstacles to farming in the suburbs was, "It is easier to gain forgiveness than consent." The name Green Power itself was emblematic of the farm's era and purpose: this was a farm devoted to radical social and environmental change.[53]

By 1975, Green Power Farm had 20 acres under cultivation and employed 35 Weston youth in producing 100 tons of vegetables. These were distributed in Roxbury and Weston at reasonable prices, which helped the farm to be self-sustaining.[54] Donahue writes that McElwain "managed to get kids from Boston's most affluent and exclusive suburb growing fresh food for the inner city," a fact that "just blew people's minds."[55] He was also the prime mover behind Weston Community Gardens, which by 1975 involved 50 families in cultivating vegetables on small plots of Green Power land along Merriam Street.

Each fall McElwain and his youthful helpers collected apples and pressed them into cider. Beginning in the spring of 1973, adults and children collected sap from sugar maple trees and boiled it down to maple syrup in a "Sugar House" that McElwain built on grounds of the junior high school using lumber from trees cleared for the new police station. Besides the chance to eat maple sugar on snow, Donahue points to another reason sugaring was so popular:

> In the early years of the project we would hang more than a thousand buckets every spring. . . . The sap buckets made Weston feel like the traditional New England town that people liked to think they inhabited, a survival of something deep. The truth is, as far as I can discover, maple syrup was never made in any quantity in Weston before Green Power.[56]

Sugaring peaked in 1980 at about 1,500 buckets.

In the end, Donahue writes, "Green Power was a bold pioneer but not the most sustainable model for a community farm."[57] The program was transferred to the conservation commission about 1983 and the youth commission was disbanded in 1985. The Green Power summer farming program was eventually turned over to the nonprofit Land's Sake, formed in 1980 to help manage the town's conservation land and involve residents in its productive use.[58] Organizers including Donahue, Douglas Henderson, Martha Gogel, Robert Crockett, and Patricia Siek took up the mission of engaging Weston youth with the land.

Park and Cemetery, Tree Warden

The town continued its policy of acquiring small pocket parks at key intersections. Case Park (1.5 acres at Wellesley and School Streets) was a gift from the Case sisters in 1946 and Children's Park (1.25 acres at Boston Post Road and the State Road Bypass) a gift of Charles O. Richardson in 1949.

In 1962 the town acquired Anniversary Park East (11,800 square feet at the northeast corner of School Street and Boston Post Road) as part of beautification efforts inspired by the town's 250th anniversary. This allowed the town to remove a long-standing eyesore, the old swimming pool building and locker building. Anniversary Park West, of similar size, was acquired in 1963. The small triangular South Park (169 square feet) at the intersection of Newton Street and South Avenue was donated in 1967. The report that year notes that "we continue our efforts to acquire . . . areas for future parks at strategic spots . . . so that even in the 21st and following centuries, Weston will give its historic impression of being a community of natural beauty and charm."[59] In 1948 the town acquired 27 acres just east of Linwood Cemetery from the Marshall Jones family, an addition that more than doubled the size of the cemetery.

Turn-of-the-century photographs show the magnificent elm trees that once graced Weston's roadways and yards. It was with great apprehension that the town's tree warden each year reported the progress northward of the dreaded Dutch elm disease, which was first discovered in Weston trees in 1951. All nine of the first infected town-owned trees, most from North Avenue, were taken down and burned at the town dump. Six years later, 115 infected trees were removed. The battle with Dutch elm disease was spearheaded for 18 years by Tree Warden John L. Duffy. In 1963 Duffy wrote, "If Weston can continue to carry on a well-rounded maintenance program designed to preserve the public shade trees, we shall make a substantial contribution toward the preservation of the rural character of the Town." Spraying of all trees except the town's specimen elms was discontinued in the 1970s due to environmental hazards.

Figure 9-44. A spring-fed pond on former Case land was dredged for swimming and opened in 1951. Sand was brought from Crane's Beach in Ipswich.

To counteract the loss of the elms, the town planted hundreds of trees during the 1950s and 1960s, including European little-leaf lindens, sugar maples, thornless locust, flowering crabs, and dogwoods. Two hundred white dogwoods were planted in 1975 in honor of the nation's Bicentennial.

Recreation Commission and Memorial Pool

Although suggestions for building a recreational center as a World War II memorial were never implemented, the postwar period saw a steady expansion of summer and year-round athletic programs, crafts, recreation, and social events for all ages. In 1944 the swimming pool committee was replaced by an elected recreation commission. The newly formulated commission began a nine-week summer program that included not only swimming at the old School Street pool, which had been offered for decades, but also supervised playground time, organized games, and evening programs three nights a week at the youth center in the school gym. Over the years, the recreation commission offered baseball and basketball leagues, teen nights at Case House, summer evening movies, picnics, square dancing, tennis instruction, shop and handicraft classes, field days, Saturday morning year-round sports, and adult evening basketball in winter.

The Weston Memorial Pool opened in 1951. The natural spring-fed pool was created by dredging the

Figure 9-45. In this 1981 photograph, Weston senior citizens make holiday crafts at the Drop-In Center at Brook School Apartments.

Figure 9-46. The Cat Rock skiing facility had a 1,200-foot rope tow and a warming hut at the foot of the hill.

bottom of an existing pond on the Case land and bringing beach sand from Crane's Beach in Ipswich to spread four inches deep over the entire bottom. Walls were painted cement. A large boulder was used for diving until it was declared unsafe. The new pool was an immediate success. Forty percent of the town's population bought badges for 25 cents each. Total attendance for the year was 28,898, or an average of 411 per day, compared to summer attendance of about 4,000 at the old pool in 1950. In 1966, attendance reached 46,602 for the season. Water carnivals in the 1950s attracted hundreds of spectators.

Although the purity of the water was pronounced "unquestionable," algae could be quite thick. The problem of turbidity came to the fore in the late 1960s when the state passed regulations requiring a minimum visibility of four feet. As a result, voters approved construction of a concrete pool on the site of the natural pond. Classified as the largest outdoor pool in New England, the new facility opened in the summer of 1973 and again attracted residents in record numbers.[60] To bolster its playground program in 1972 when the concrete pool was under construction, the recreation commission started a day camp.

The commission also initiated programs for senior citizens. The Council on Aging was established in 1974 to identify the needs of the town's elderly population and to design and promote services to fill these needs. Programs in place by 1975 included a monthly blood pressure clinic and senior mini-bus operating within Weston.

To ensure that the town had enough playing fields for future organized sports programs, the recreation commission hired the firm of Shurcliff and Shurcliff to help predict future growth areas and select potential sites. The town already had title to the Jennings property near Glen Road, where a baseball field was created in the late 1950s. In 1952, the town accepted a two-acre parcel at the corner of Viles Street and Brook Road, since used extensively for recreation. A Little League baseball field was built on the Cat Rock land in 1958, the same year the town voted to purchase eight acres of the Renwick estate for the present Cherry Brook Road playing field. In 1961, the town voted to purchase four acres on Bogle Street, where a playing field was built in 1968. In 1976 the Weston Baseball League was formed to provide opportunities for boys and girls to participate in organized baseball and softball.

Even before the days of planned recreation, winter sports in Weston had always included skating on local ponds, particularly Foote's Pond and the Winsor skating pond. Over the years, skating areas were created behind the 1932 high school, at the new Memorial Pool, and, in 1963, on the property of the new high school. In the late 1960s, Foote's Pond was developed for skating, and a warming hut and lights were added by 1971. College Pond became available after purchase of Weston College land in 1977.

Figure 9-47. The Cardinals were Weston's Minor League Baseball champs in 1967. (Names with photo credits)

With the new popularity of skiing, the nonprofit Cat Rock Ski Club was formed in 1947. Membership was limited to Weston residents and fees were used to operate the rope tow at Cat Rock on weekends and holidays. In 1956, the town purchased 63 acres belonging to the Cat Rock Trust as recreational land, including the ski hill and future Little League field. The town operated the ski tow from 1957 to the late 1970s. The operation was dependent on natural snow. In 1958 it operated only six days and in 1959 only two days. One of the most successful seasons was 1964, when 500 family memberships were sold at $10 each and 600 individual buttons at $5. A daily ticket was $1.

Figure 9-48. Route 128 was built across Stony Brook Reservoir (1950 photo, looking north).

Figure 9-49. Route 128 in the Waltham-Weston area opened in 1951 with a celebration.

Transportation (1945–1980)

Route 128 dates back to the early 1900s, when a series of roads were connected in a network from town center to town center known as the Great Circumferential.[61] By the 1930s, the route had a number and was so choked with traffic heading for the North and South Shores and Cape Cod that communities had to hire extra police on weekends.

The first link of a new state highway was under construction from Peabody to Lynnfield in 1936. The controversial "ring road" built over the next three decades was damned as an extravagance of the politicians. Among its nicknames were The Road to Nowhere and Callahan's Folly, after Public Works Commissioner William F. Callahan.

The town report of 1940 mentions the possibility of Route 128 being built through Kendal Green, but the road's progress stalled during wartime. After the war, spurred on by growing traffic congestion in Boston and the suburbs and by the 1944 Federal Aid Highway Act, which encouraged regional highways, the state's master plan of 1948 endorsed continuation. Legislators voted funds for the Lynnfield to Route 9/Wellesley segment. Weston selectmen wrote, "The state is ramming through Route 128, arbitrarily rearranging town ways without even a courteous reception of reasonable requests to cooperate in our overall plans."[62] Approximately 41 acres in Weston were taken for the construction, including about 13 acres on the tax rolls.[63]

In 1950, the town historian reflected on the present disruption and future utility of the highway:

> 1950 in Weston was a year of earth-moving—of grades and cuts, detours, by-passes, budding cloverleaves and wooden railroad trestles; for in 1950 Route 128 really came to our Town. . . . Everywhere signs blossomed, asking pardon for the inconvenience, pointing with pride to this new link in the State's great network of highways. And over all hung a heavy pall of dust. A present headache—a future boon—to those who want to go places in a hurry, the new Route 128 appears to be here to stay.[64]

Opening ceremonies for this section of the "beautiful and completely modern highway" were held in November 1951.[65] The road was completed to Braintree in 1958 and widened and reconstructed over the next six years from its initial two lanes in each direction. Between 1953 and 1961, certain industrial sites appreciated in value by 500 percent as technology firms flocked to the Route 128 corridor, drawn by convenient, cheap, and newly accessible land. Cities and towns along 128 experienced explosive growth. The roadway "spread the development system out, made it more auto dependent," resulting in daily congestion.[66] Traffic in the Weston section of Route 128 rose from 60,000 cars a day in 1963 to 92,000 in 1974 and 163,000 two decades later.

The dust had barely settled when, in 1952, Weston got a hint of plans for a new toll road to pass either

Figure 9-50. The intersection of South Avenue and Route 128 was originally engineered with a rotary.

through Weston or south of Route 9. Initial routes through Weston were located just north and south of Weston Reservoir and Doublet Hill. At the 1953 annual town meeting, voters unanimously voiced their opposition to the proposed east–west toll highway "because of the great damage to property in the Town of Weston . . . in addition to the damage already sustained . . . by the location of Route 128."[67] A citizens committee urged consideration of routes southwest out of Boston or the termination of the toll road in Framingham rather than at Route 128, which was already at capacity at certain times. The committee argued that the future feeder road through Newton would be very expensive to build. Critics charged that the toll road was being built for the convenience of commercial truckers and wrote, "No figures have been made public justifying the need for an East–West Toll Road."[68]

Figure 9-51. This house was moved out of the way of the Massachusetts Turnpike, which required demolition or relocation of more than a dozen homes.

In the 1954 town report, the town historian wrote of the lost battle:

> Despite the very vocal opposition of practically every Weston resident, it appears certain that the new East–West toll road is going to slice right through the heart of our Town's beautiful South Side. Well—it was a stubborn battle, valiantly fought, and Weston went down with flags flying, which is cold comfort for those who live near the projected right-of-way.[69]

The interchange with Route 128 and Commonwealth Avenue required a larger area than was originally anticipated and the selectmen wrote, "It is regrettable that so-called 'progress' has laid waste such an extensive and choice area."[70] The town negotiated for the relocation of Park Road as a through route between South Avenue and Newton Lower Falls. Loss of taxable property taken for the Mass Turnpike was $241,420, or about 1 percent of the town's total assessed valuation. The 123-mile section from the

Figure 9-52. Route 128 is pictured here in the "Blizzard of '78." The National Weather Service called the savage blizzard of February 6–7, 1978, "the worst [storm] of the century" in southern New England. A record 23.6 inches of snow fell in a 24-hour period. The storm total was up to four feet, on top of 21 inches that had fallen only 18 days previously. Almost all roads, including the Massachusetts Turnpike and Route 128 (shown here), were impassable. Gov. Michael Dukakis ordered a state of emergency and mobilization of the Massachusetts National Guard.

New York state line to the Weston tolls opened in May 1957 and the extension into Boston in early 1965. The extension provided easy access to jobs in the city and increased development pressure on Weston.

Meanwhile, growth generated by Route 128 brought a "real plague of traffic to the Town."[71] In 1955 Lexington Street carried an estimated 500 cars per hour in the morning and evening rush hours and Boston Post Road carried about 350 cars per hour.[72] In 1960 police estimated that 80,000 cars traveled Weston's roads on an average day. Selectmen commented on "the ever-present conflict between preserving the aesthetic values of the Town and improving the highways in the interest of public safety."[73] About 1967, because of increased traffic and concern for the safety of pedestrians, the town initiated the building of footpaths outside the road right of way, requiring easements over private land. The first such footpath was constructed along Conant Road in the late 1960s.

Despite increased traffic, commuter options decreased. Trains on the former Central Massachusetts Railroad line were eliminated one by one after the war, until only a single train carried a dwindling cadre of loyal commuters between South Sudbury and Boston once a day in each direction. In 1971 the MBTA announced termination of passenger service. Towns along the route negotiated an extension of service, but despite a vigorous campaign that significantly increased ridership, the deteriorated condition of the roadbed led to slowdowns, derailments and delays, and, ultimately, termination of service.

Figure 9-53. Regular gasoline cost 39 cents when this photograph of Ed Abbott's gas station was taken around the 1960s.

Farming (1945–1980)

Nonprofit community farming began in Weston about the time that agriculture as an occupation had all but disappeared. In 1947 the board of health conducted its yearly inspection of livestock at 47 farms

Figure 9-54. Suburban developments that sprang up around American cities after World War II represent the fulfillment of the American dream of home ownership and material well-being. This house on Pollywog Lane is typical of the Colonial Revival homes constructed in the 1960s by Edward B. Sweidler, the largest builder in the area.

and reported 438 cattle, 433 swine, 96 horses, and 17 sheep.[74] Poultry farmers were keeping 4,893 fowls. The Middlesex County Extension Service was still serving farmers interested in dairying, market gardening, and poultry. It provided spray service for fruit growers and market gardeners. Increasingly, the extension service was also answering requests from new home owners for information on flower gardens and lawns. By 1962 the board of health annual animal census listed only 17 dairy cows, along with 303 swine, 80 horses,18 sheep, and seven goats. In 1975 the board of health was still issuing two licenses for piggeries at unnamed locations.

Architecture and Subdivisions (1945–1980)

In the more than two centuries from the town's founding until 1945, the number of dwellings in Weston grew to 1,019. It took only 16 years for this number to more than double, to 2,082, by 1961. To ensure that subdivision infrastructure such as pipes, drains, and roadways were properly located, the office of town engineer was created in 1951. Beginning in 1952, the board of health had to approve septic arrangements.

Edward B. Sweidler was the largest builder in the area. According to one real-estate agent's estimate, Sweidler built more than 400 single-family residences in Weston and Wayland, including homes on Cherry Brook Road, Round Hill Road, the Black Oak/Nobscot/Country Drive neighborhood, and the former Blake estate. Sweidler and his designers favored a traditional Colonial exterior with up-to-date interior features like family rooms. Their efficient organization kept costs down. Prospective buyers could select a floor plan and choose wallpaper and paint colors but were not allowed to design their own house or hire their own contractor.[75] Typical houses were 3,000 to 3,500 square feet.

The one-story ranch and its close relative, the split level, were widely used in Weston developments of the immediate postwar period. Examples abound in the subdivision of the former Charles Jones estate on Woodchester and Ledgewood Roads and of the former Charles Dean estate on Byron Road.

Many architect-designed houses of the 1950s through the early 1970s were built in the Modern style. The young academics, scientists, and technology professionals who commissioned them were looking for not only a simple, functional new aesthetic but also a new way to live. Modern houses typically offered open floor plans and were open to the environment. Architects sought to minimize the impact on the land and maximize passive solar potential. They built houses that fit with existing topography and blended easily into the natural landscape. In Weston, this style flourished on the north side in the avant-garde Kendal Common and throughout the King's Grant neighborhood. King's Grant features a wide range of contemporary design, from the early-1950s Techbuilt modular houses to later examples with low-pitched roofs, wide overhangs, and large plate glass windows.

The movement back to traditional styles began slowly in the 1960s and has continued to the present day. The term *Post Modern* has been applied to houses that combine some features of postwar modernism with traditional architectural details, often reinterpreted in novel ways. Neo-traditional houses, which can be eclectic or overscaled versions of popular historical styles, are referred to according to their source of inspiration, as in Neo-Colonial, Neo-Tudor, and Neo-French.

Following is a list of the approximate dates of principal subdivision roads built from 1945 through 2000. Subdivision dates can vary, depending on whether one is looking at the plan date, approval date, or date that houses were actually built. Streets may be listed more than once if developed in stages. Brief historical information and/or chapter references are included in parentheses.

1945–1950

Byron Road, Hawthorne Lane (Dean/Byron estate, chapter 28)
Coburn Road (Filene estate, chapter 11)
Colchester, Sears, Laurel, and Hamilton Roads (Zollar Farm, chapter 14)
Kendal Common; Ellis and French Roads (Trapelo Golf Club, chapter 10)
Rolling Lane
Winsor Way extension, Dogwood Road (Winsor estate, chapter 20)

1950–1954

Apple Crest Road, Blossom Lane (chapter 16)
Glen House Way (Glen House Hotel property, chapter 25)

Page Road
Brook Road extension and Valley View Road
Golden Ball Road extension
Hubbard Road extension (Hubbard estate, chapter 22)
Woodchester Drive, Pond Brook Circle, Ledgewood and Shady Hill Roads (Jones estate, chapter 27)
Baker's Hill and Longmeadow Roads; October Lane
Gail Road
Drabbington Way (Drabbington Lodge property, chapter 10)
Cart Path, Dellbrook, Hidden, and Robin Roads; Green Lane (Winsor estate, chapter 20)
Bradyll and Hallett Hill Roads
Spring Road
Spruce Hill Road (Fiske Homestead/Cedar Hill Farm, chapter 10)

1955–1959
Perry Lane
Corwood Drive
Overlook Drive
Blueberry Hill and Hickory Roads; Holly Circle, Driftwood Lane
Radcliffe Road
Robin Road extension
King's Grant, Bradford, Plymouth, Indian Hill, Bay State and Myles Standish Roads; Winthrop Circle (Fiske Homestead/Cedar Hill Dairy, chapter 10)
Baker's Hill extension and Arrowhead Road
Drabbington Way extension
Beaver and Walnut Roads; Sylvan Lane (small segment)
Cherry Brook Road; Pollywog and Buttonwood Lanes (Munroe/Lilly/Renwick estate, chapter 12)
Cart Path Road extension and Possum Road extension (Winsor estate, chapter 20)
Montvale Road, south end

1960–1964
Sherburn Circle
Tyler Road
Black Oak, Nobscot, and Lawrence Roads; Country Drive; Surrey and Deer Path Lanes
Westcliff, Falmouth, Hickory, and Scotch Pine Roads (Peirce estate, chapter 26)
Fields Pond Road
Woodridge Circle
Hobbs Brook and Forest Ridge Roads (Brown estate/Miller farm, chapter 10)
Bittersweet Lane, Stillmeadow Road (Schenck estate, chapter 28)
Round Hill and Stony Brook Road (Thorndike/Beebe estate, chapter 12)
Stonecroft Circle

1965–1969
Buckskin Drive, Westerly Road (Dean Dairy, chapter 16) The Dean Dairy subdivision involved the largest remaining privately owned, contiguous parcel of land in Weston—92 acres with 52 potential house lots.
Whitney Tavern Road
Autumn Road
Beech Road
Colonial Way
Walnut Road extension
Hancock Road
Chadwick and Walker Roads, Baldwin Circle
Blake and Tamarack Roads; north end of Orchard Avenue (Blake estate, chapter 23)
Cherry Brook Road extension, Juniper and Aspen Roads
Driftwood Lane, Rockport and Rocky Ledge Roads, Wit's End (Peirce and Jones estates, chapters 26 and 27)
Greenridge and Terrace Roads
Sylvan Lane extension (Blaney estate, chapter 30)

1970–1974
High Meadow Road (chapter 29)
Hillcrest Road
Laxfield Road (George Fiske estate, chapter 16)
Trailside Road

1975–1979
Audubon Road
Chandler Circle
Davenport Road

1980s
Bayberry Lane
Brenton Road
Claridge Drive (Kettle/Kirk estate, chapter 16)
Colchester/Laurel Road extension
Elliston Road
Sutton Place
Wild Flower Lane

Figure 9-55. Architect Henry Hoover, like many of his modernist contemporaries, sought to "build with the land." He designed this 1958 house on Highland Street to complement existing topographical features. The vertical wood siding is finished in a natural color that blends with the forested landscape. Modern houses of the postwar period were generally oriented to the site and to the sun, which provided passive solar heat in winter.

1990s
Bass Pond Lane
Candleberry Lane
Carroll Circle
Dickson Lane
Graystone Lane
Harrington Lane
Hastings Lane
Hitching Post Lane, Lower Field Road (Coburn, chapter 11)
Lane's End
Nottingham Lane (chapter 12)
Prescott Lane (chapter 21)
Sanderson Lane (chapter 17)
Whitehouse Lane (chapter 24)

Recreation: Horseback Riding

Love of horses and the sport of riding is a tradition in Weston going back to the estate era, when horseback riding was a favorite summer pastime of families like the Paines, Wellingtons, and Hubbards. In the period between the wars, horses could be boarded or rented at the Kendal Green Riding School and the Weston Saddle and Bridle Club, both of which closed in the 1950s.

The Weston 4-H Horse Club, founded in 1949 under the auspices of the Middlesex County Extension Service, was the oldest 4-H horse club in the state. The club was open to young people between the ages of 10 and 21 who had major responsibility for the care and exercise of a horse. Important annual events included the fall trail ride and the spring horse show, which in the 1950s took place on Conant Road at the Saddle and Bridle Club ring. In 1963, a new 4-H Riding Ring in the Jericho Forest off Concord Road was dedicated to the memory of Ruth Dickson (Mrs. Brenton H. Dickson Jr.), an avid rider and horse breeder.

The 1747 Farm Horse Show was one of the largest in Weston during this period. The show was started as a birthday present for Barbara Woodworth and was first held on the Woodworth property at 412 Highland Street, known as the 1747 Farm. When the annual show outgrew this location, organizers arranged with Regis College to lease land on the east side of Wellesley Street, where they developed two riding rings. In its heyday in the 1960s and 1970s, the three-day show had night classes under spotlights and master riders in the finest equestrian attire.

The Jericho Forest Pony Club was founded in the 1970s to teach riding and provide opportunities for competition in dressage, show jumping, and cross country. The name was chosen because Jericho Forest extends into both Weston and Wayland, the two towns from which original members were drawn. As a branch of the U.S. Pony Club, Jericho allowed young people aged 9 to 21 to advance through a prescribed series of skill levels. Several members went on to national and Olympic competition. Pony Club members also learned the complexities of horse care from veterinary medicine to growing hay. The club used the Regis College ring and later took over the lease.

One founder and longtime Pony Club director recalled with nostalgia the horse culture of the postwar period:

> In those days, most of our members had their own horses in their backyard or a neighbor's yard. That's the big change. Land is so developed now that the backyard horse in Weston is passé—which is kind of sad. Kids learned a lot from being responsible for the daily care of their horse. Now, they are often overextended with school sports and lessons and rely on a stable to take care of routine chores.[76]

Community Organizations (1945–1980)

Growing out of a 1945 victory celebration and previous work of Weston Post #214 of the American Legion was the Weston Boosters, formed in 1946 to

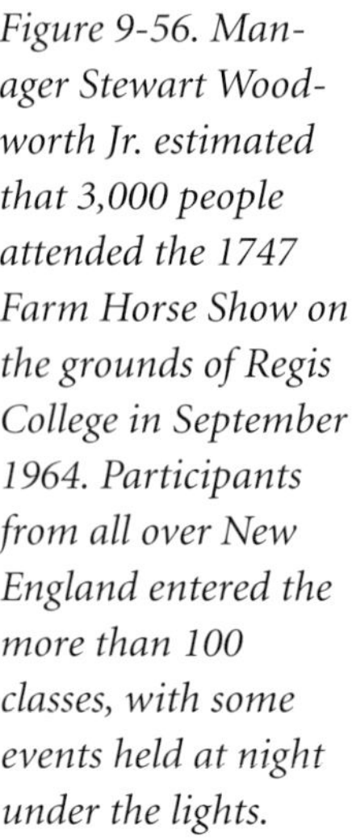

Figure 9-56. Manager Stewart Woodworth Jr. estimated that 3,000 people attended the 1747 Farm Horse Show on the grounds of Regis College in September 1964. Participants from all over New England entered the more than 100 classes, with some events held at night under the lights.

Figure 9-57. After World War II, the Friendly Society continued producing original musicals, including Escape on the Cape *(1950),* Never Walk Alone *(1953), and* All Kidding Aside *(1956). Competitions were held, and for years no fewer than four complete, full-length musical shows were submitted. Brenton H. Dickson III wrote the book, lyrics, and music for* Jericho *(1959) and collaborated on* On the Fence *(1962, shown here) and* Down to Earth *(1965).*

Figure 9-58. On its 75th anniversary in 1960, the Friendly Society had 950 members. Among them were the following stalwarts: from left, Beryl Field, Elizabeth Kenney, Connie Pooler, Dick Crouch, Anna Hall, Alice Perry, Helen Wheeler, Alice Fraser, Natalie Coburn, Rebecca McKenna, Marion Coburn, Pete Rowan, and Phil Coburn.

Figure 9-59. The all-male singing group the Weston Aires perform about 1961.

Figure 9-60. Weston Drama Workshop was incorporated in 1963. Principal characters in the 1967 production of *Toad of Tea Hall* were, from left, Maureen Ward, Martha Cochran, Chris Richardson, Ted Everett, and Jack Simons.

Figure 9-62. To announce the 15th season of the Country Evening Concert Series in 1965, the *Town Crier* published several photographs, including this one of Mrs. Edward (Polly) Dickson and the group's treasurer, Thomas J. Scott.

Figure 9-61. Performers in the "Golden Jubilee," the annual revue of the Couples Club of the Weston Methodist Church, in May 1958. Kneeling: Phyllis Law, Elaine Sinclair, Alvin Whitmore, Ruth Moller, and Ina Mills. Standing: Aimo Teittinen, Jerry Sinclair, Ken MacRae, Joe Campobasso, Dick Rice, Walter Maron, Warren Sinclair, and Bob Millen.

Figure 9-63. The Weston Rotary Club met for many years in the Weston High School cafeteria, located in the basement of the building now called Field School. (1951 photo)

recognize student achievement in scholarship, character, citizenship, and athletics. Theodore Chandler was the first president. Another founder was David A. Perry, a member of the Weston School Committee from 1933 to 1942, who worked for years to obtain the best coaching, athletic equipment, and facilities for the town. Also involved was Austin Hale, who turned his attention after the war to "boosting" Weston and Wayland sports by sponsoring annual dinners for teams and coaches. Wilmot Whitney, Harold Martin, Judge Frederic A. Crafts Sr., Frank Hitchcock, and Harold G. "Red" Travis were among the other early Boosters. The group held its first spring sports night in 1947, with dinner, speakers, and presentation of sweaters to members of athletic teams. Since then, it has provided athletic awards, helped with equipment purchases, funded the David A. Perry Memorial Scholarship, and sponsored the Ted Chandler Award for "the outstanding boy and girl in the graduating class of Weston High School."

The nonsectarian Men's Club of Weston was organized in 1945 and held monthly meetings at the Methodist church and later Field School. Speakers generally focused on local politics and current events. For the final event of the season, the ladies were invited to a catered dinner and dancing at Pine Brook Country Club. The group disbanded in the late 1960s.

Fostering the arts was the goal of several new postwar organizations. The Community Chorus of Weston, Wayland, and Sudbury was founded in 1947 to sing fine choral music. Conductor Chester W. Williams was from the New England Conservatory. The Country Evening Concert Series, begun in 1951 to bring professional music to the Weston area, sponsored concerts held at the town hall and Country School auditorium into the 1960s.

In 1962, a summer theater workshop was initiated at the request of a newly formed arts group. From this developed the Weston Drama Workshop, incorporated in 1963 as a nonprofit organization open to any student in the 5th to 12th grades. A program that began with 25 students grew in the early 1970s to 230. Its first musical, *The King and I*, was produced in 1966.

In 1950, Harry Starr and William Rinehart formed a Weston chapter of the Rotary International Club, with its traditional focus on community service. Over the years the Weston chapter has raised funds to send a handicapped child to camp each year, sponsored a chest X-ray program, and donated a scoreboard to the Weston High School football team. They worked to beautify the grounds at Merriam Village, helped the Council on Aging purchase two mini-buses, and contributed to building Tavernside Park.

Weston Post #2596 of the Veterans of Foreign Wars was established in 1953 to promote the best interests of the town and help disabled veterans and their families. The group was never as active as the older American Legion post.

Weston Post #214 of the American Legion, founded after World War I, was energized after the Second World War when young veterans joined in large numbers. In the postwar period, legionnaires

Figure 9-64. After World War II, the old horse watering trough in front of First Parish Church was adapted as a fountain. It was expensive to operate, and in 1948 the Weston Garden Club began planting flowers in it. At some point it was painted white. In 1975, the rusty trough was sandblasted, repainted, and reset on a new cobblestone traffic island.

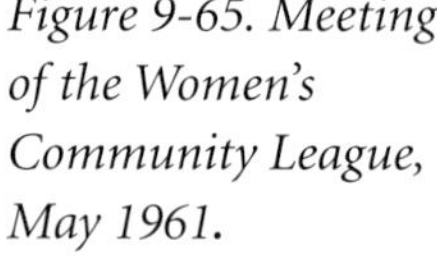

sponsored plays and events to fund a college scholarship and held an annual Washington's Birthday Ball. Membership declined beginning in the 1960s due to deaths and the inability to obtain new members in substantial numbers from the Korean, Vietnam, and Gulf wars. Membership had dropped to 15 in 1996, when Weston Post #214 was dissolved after 77 years. The scholarship fund was turned over to the Weston War Memorial Educational Fund, established in 1953 and administered by the town.

The Weston Garden Club, founded in 1940 and discussed in the previous chapter, organized the Provisionals in 1957. This "junior group" originally consisted of daughters and daughters-in-law of club members but was later broadened to include other young women.

The Country Garden Club of Weston was founded in 1954 and joined the Garden Club Federation of Massachusetts in 1955. The objective of the club is to "encourage an active interest in horticulture and conservation among amateur gardeners . . . and to further the knowledge of beautifying town and home." Since 1965, the Country Garden Club has helped landscape the grounds of the Golden Ball Tavern Museum, including planning, planting, and maintaining the herb garden.

The Community League Garden Club of Weston was also founded in 1954 and federated in 1955. Among its stated goals are promoting appreciation and enjoyment of plants and flowers, advancing the art of gardening and study of horticulture, aiding in protection of natural resources, and promoting civic beauty and roadside improvement. The Community League Garden Club maintains the perennial garden and plantings at the Josiah Smith Tavern and Barn and the landscaping of the Fiske Memorial at Concord and Boston Post Roads. Together with two other garden clubs, they help plant and maintain Case Park.

The Weston Arts and Crafts Association (WACA) was established in 1960 to promote and encourage appreciation for and participation in the creative arts and crafts. One of the original goals of founder Eunice Sawyer was to offer art instruction to town residents. WACA currently organizes three art shows a year: a juried event in the spring, a December holiday show, and Art on the Green in late September.[77]

In 1965, the Friends of the Weston Public Library was formed "to make the residents of Weston more aware of the public library, its services and its potentialities, to encourage the development of a strong and active public library . . . and to help provide, where necessary, items not otherwise provided."[78] The first officers were Mrs. Theodore Guild, president; Mrs. John Stubbs, vice president; Lawrence Pexton, treasurer; and Mrs. Eugene Ritvo, secretary. By

Figure 9-65. Meeting of the Women's Community League, May 1961.

Figure 9-66. The Weston Arts and Crafts Association sponsors art exhibitions and the annual Art on the Green, featuring local artists like sculptor Wendy Wrean.

1983, the Friends were sponsoring book sales each spring and fall to raise money for library projects.

The Weston Senior Citizens Club was organized in 1971 to promote the social, educational, and recreational interests of its members. The group organizes meetings, day trips, and special events. A decade later, the Weston Community Children's Association (WCCA) was formed to support families with young children. Its first major community project was Tavernside Park, a playground specially designed for younger children.

The Weston High School Association, founded in 1871, always held its annual meeting on the night of the high school graduation. Everyone in the graduating class was expected to attend. In the early 20th century, the celebration was a formal affair where girls in white dresses and boys in white pants and blue blazers were inducted into the venerable association. The group raised money for the schools by holding bake sales, dances, and plays directed by teacher John Zorn. As graduation classes became larger and larger after World War II, the task of keeping track of alumni became unmanageable. The association held a final gala in May 1971 to celebrate its 100th anniversary before formally disbanding. Since then, individual classes have sponsored their own reunions.

Civil Defense, the Korean War, and the Cold War

The 1950 town report includes this warning from the town's newly appointed director of Civil Defense:

> The aggressive action of the North Koreans last June brought into sharp focus once again the purpose of the long range strategy of the Soviet Union. It also became apparent that our nation was highly vulnerable to a devastating atomic bombing attack.[79]

Figure 9-67. In 1981, Donna Wheelock led a fund-raising campaign to fix up and endow the Scout House. Pictured here, from left, are Andrew Wheelock, Seth Morrison, Sara Morrison, Donna Wheelock, Christy Travers, and Fred Coburn.

By the end of 1950, more than 50 Weston young men had been drafted into the Armed Forces as part of a national mobilization. That fall, residents were asked to volunteer for any of 28 activities needed in case of a bomb attack. A general mobilization exercise was conducted on May 15, 1952. The national paranoia that characterized the McCarthy era led to the demotion of at least one popular Weston teacher. In 1957, the Civil Defense director discussed the latest thinking on protection of metropolitan residents

Figure 9-68. Red Cross volunteers serve coffee to firefighters at the 1948 high school fire. A Red Cross chapter was active in Weston by World War I, if not before. Over the years, the chapter helped with disaster relief, blood collection, volunteer services, first-aid training, water safety, and aid to veterans and their families. At times, a Red Cross Youth Club was active in the high school.

through evacuation or construction and use of bomb shelters. In the early 1960s, the town set up an advisory committee that discouraged construction of private shelters in favor of town-financed neighborhood versions, an approach that local leaders later decided was beyond the authority of the town.

At the same time residents were preparing for the possibility of another war, they voted in 1950 to establish an affiliation with the town of Rombas, France.[80] The selectmen wrote, "Any move within reason that may help the world get away from a bad case of pre-war jitters we support wholeheartedly. Incidently, all it costs is a little time and a few postage stamps."[81] The Rombas resolution begins "Whereas we, the citizens of the Town of Weston . . . desire to participate to the limit of our abilities in any genuine attempt to promote a just and lasting peace throughout the world. . . ."[82] The moving spirit was Henry M. Fiske, whose enthusiasm helped launch the program in the first decade. In 1960, the Weston-Rombas Affiliation expanded to include an exchange with Porto Alegre, Brazil.

Throughout the 1950s, Weston annually celebrated United Nations Day. The 1957 resolution states: "That the Town, recognizing the worth of the United Nations as a valuable instrumentality in the universal quest for world peace, approves the public observance of United Nations Day in 1957."[83] The United Nations Committee sponsored a yearly potluck supper with a noted speaker on U.N. activities.

Historical Activities and Celebrations (1945–1980)

In the early 1950s, the Misses Alice and Ellen Jones bequeathed their family home, the former Josiah Smith Tavern, to the Society for the Preservation of New England Antiquities (SPNEA). The society, in turn, leased the tavern to the town for a period of 20 years. A tavern committee was formed to raise funds and restore the 200-year-old structure, which was ready for occupancy in 1953. The town historical committee and several town departments occupied some of the rooms as offices, and the rest of the space was available for public and private gatherings. The Women's Community League donated money for the renovation and moved its Children's Exchange from the town hall to the tavern. A controversy arose over whether the porch should be removed because it was not original or be retained as an important addition. Compromise was reached by removing the porch from the older section of the house. The Women's Community League renovated the barn as its contribution to the nation's Bicentennial. In 1983, SPNEA turned over the Josiah Smith Tavern to the town, subject to preservation restrictions.

Weston celebrated its 250th birthday in 1963. Fifteen general committees and 35 subcommittees organized more than 60 events and ceremonies, focused during the four days from May 30 to June 2, 1963. As a result of the anniversary observance, a successful start was made to upgrade and beautify the town center. The Weston Garden Club worked to improve the town hall grounds and planted dogwood trees. One outgrowth of the celebration was the formation of the Weston Historical Society.

On August 21, 1967, the limbs of the historic Burgoyne Elm, estimated to be almost three centuries old, were cut off, leaving a mammoth trunk 18 feet high and 25 feet around the base. The historical society searched for a way to preserve the trunk from

Figure 9-69. The Weston Historical Society was founded in 1964 as an outgrowth of the 250th anniversary. Pictured at a society open house at the Josiah Smith Tavern (also known as the Jones House) in 1964 are, from left, Mrs. Edmund U. Ritter, archivist; Mrs. Henry W. Patterson; Mrs. James E. Fraser, curator; Harold G. Travis, president of the society; and Mrs. F. Leslie Ford.

Figure 9-70. The historical society was originally headquartered in the Fiske Law Office but later moved to the Josiah Smith Tavern, where this photograph was taken about 1987.

Figure 9-71. Ben Crouch (right) and Don Vatour in the combination truck No. 1 at the 1963 celebration of Weston's 250th anniversary. The truck was subsequently restored and now belongs to the Weston Firefighters Relief Association.

Figure 9-72. The Burgoyne Elm on Boston Post Road was a focal point of town historical celebrations in 1932 and 1963 (shown here).

deterioration. At the time of the nation's Bicentennial, the trunk was cut down to a height that would allow important historical dates to be burned into the elm's age rings. A large portion of the trunk was taken to a "secret hiding place" where "it will be kept ready to supply the 21st century a replacement slab."[84] Dr. Donald Wyman, then director of the Arnold Arboretum, propagated healthy scions to try to ensure that there would always be a Burgoyne Elm in Weston.[85]

In December 1968, the Weston Historical Commission was established, replacing the historical committee set up in 1931.[86] Under new state legislation, the commission was empowered to acquire and manage historic properties and inventory historic resources. As its first major project, the commission organized volunteers to conduct a survey of significant buildings. In 1975 voters defeated a proposal to create a local historic district along Boston Post Road that would have required review of exterior architectural changes. In the early 1980s, Boston Post Road was listed on the National Register of

Figure 9-73. Anniversary plate made for the 1963 celebration of Weston's 250th anniversary.

Figure 9-74. The significance of the Burgoyne Elm goes back to 1777, when captured British troops under Gen. John Burgoyne camped in the area for one night. In 1967, the limbs of the three-centuries-old tree had to be removed. In 1976 the trunk was cut down to a height that would allow important historical dates to be burned into the age rings. Today, only the historic marker remains to commemorate one of Weston's most cherished patriotic symbols. On the boulder is the bronze plaque of Gen. George Washington placed here in 1932.

Figures 9-75 and 9-76. The national Bicentennial was celebrated with a parade on Family Day, June 12, 1976.

Historic Places, an honorary designation that does not involve architectural review. In 1993, Crescent Street became Weston's first, and so far only, local historic district.

The opening event commemorating the U.S. Bicentennial was a reenactment on March 28, 1974, of the "Tea Raid" at the Golden Ball Tavern. Plaques were dedicated at Lamson Park (1975) and Sanderson Hill (1976) in memory of the march to Concord and the Revolutionary War signal beacon. A Bicentennial Family Day on June 12, 1976, was celebrated with a two-mile-long parade, picnic lunches and activities at Lamson Park and the town green, and evening entertainment in the high school auditorium.[87] *One Town in the American Revolution* was published, the library began an oral history project, and Rivers School made an original color sound movie, *The Journal of John Howe, British Spy.* In a continuation of town beautification efforts, the watering trough opposite the library was sandblasted, repainted, and set on a new cobblestone traffic island.

Figure 9-77. In the winter of 1775–76, Maj. Gen. Henry Knox traveled through Weston to deliver artillery to General Washington in Cambridge. The arduous journey from Fort Ticonderoga was reenacted in January 1976. Weston residents got a close look at the teams of Belgian horses, cannons, and antique oak sleds on the town green. The trekkers slept overnight in the Josiah Smith Tavern barn.

Statistics, 1960s

From *City and Town, Town of Weston Monograph,* Massachusetts Department of Commerce and Development, revised June 1968

Racial Data, 1960		
White	8,217	99.5%
Black	21	.3%
Other	23	.3%
"Foreign stock"	2,149	29.3%
Foreign born	520	6.3%

"Foreign stock" denoted ancestry. Of the 2,149 persons so labeled, 33.8% were Canadian, 13.4% Irish, 11.3% United Kingdom, 8.8% Italian, and 5.9% German.

Education (persons 25 years and over, 1960)	
Median # of school years completed	14.8
Completing less than 5 grades	1.3%
Completing high school or more	83.8%

Politics, Party Affiliation, 1966	
Total registered voters	5,194
Registered Democrats	11.2%
Registered Republicans	42.2%
Unenrolled voters	45.6%

Incomes of Families, 1960	
Incomes under $3,000	5.6%
From $3,000 to $5,999	7.6%
From $6,000 to $9,999	18.2%
$10,000 and over	68.6%
(Median income: $13,703 compared to $6,687 for Boston)	

Housing		
1 unit	2,089	99.9%
2 units	11	.5%
3 and 4 units	11	.5%
5 or more units	0	
(Median value of a house was $32,500.)		

New Dwelling Units Constructed			
1950–54	460	1965	84
1955–59	290	1966	73
1960–64	460	1967	67

Notes

1. 1948 *TR*, 145.
2. 1951 *TR*, 16.
3. 1951 *TR*, 16.
4. 1953 *TR*, 16.
5. Additional purchases brought conservation land to 1,740 acres by 1996. At that time, Weston Forest and Trail Association owned an additional 120 acres, town-owned recreation land totaled 107 acres, parks totaled 30.88 acres, and additional land was protected as cemeteries and by the City of Cambridge (Stony Brook Reservoir). Ref: Open Space and Recreation Plan, Town of Weston, Massachusetts, fall 1996.
6. Lower rate based on reevaluation in 1963.
7. 1949 *TR*, 16.
8. By 1955, this form of administration had been written up by several statewide organizations and "recently has been given recognition by action of the legislature making it possible for towns generally to establish the plan." See 1955 *TR*, 15.
9. PWF interview with Ward Carter, September 29, 2000.
10. 1963 *TR*, 181.
11. For the previous 40 years, emergency transportation service had been provided by the police department.
12. 1965 *TR*, 160.
13. 1934 *TR*, 78.
14. *1958 TR*, 159.
15. "Weston Studies Its Schools," summary booklet published by the Town of Weston, 1946.
16. Sayer, Gus A., "The History of METCO in Weston," *WHSB*, March 1985 (issued January 1987), 6. See also "METCO: Where It's Been, Where It's Going," *Weston Town Crier* special supplement, August 27, 1987.
17. Dedicated on March 25, 1950. See "1300 Tour Building at Dedication of New Weston High," *Waltham News-Tribune*, March 27, 1950.
18. 1948 *TR*, 130. Proceeds from insurance fell short of the approximately $230,000 needed for the reconstruction.
19. "Fire-Ruined Weston School Turned into Modern Building," *The Christian Science Monitor*, December 6, 1948.
20. Information provided by architect David Fixler.
21. Dedication in March 27, 1955. The cost was $975,152 plus equipment and furnishings.
22. 1955 *TR*, 118.
23. The damage settlement for the land totaled $39,500. Woodland School was built at a cost of about $670,000.
24. "Hugh Stubbins Is Weston Architect," *The Town Crier*, May 2, 1957, 9.

Figure 9-78. This medal was issued for the town's 275th anniversary in 1988. On the reverse side is the town seal.

25. Purchased from the Paine Trustees at a cost of $85,000.
26. 1943 *TR*, 95–97.
27. Weston was admitted to membership in the Metropolitan Water District in 1963. The town was assessed an initial fee of $79,000, payable over 10 years, and had to construct a pumping station to connect with water distribution mains.
28. 1945 *TR*, 50.
29. 1946 *TR*, 39.
30. District A: 60,000 square feet (street frontage of 200 feet); District B: 40,000 (150 feet); District C: 30,000 (125 feet); and District D: 20,000 (100 feet).
31. 1969 *TR*, 123.
32. 1954 *TR*, 112.
33. 1947 *TR*, 142 ff.
34. 1947 *TR*, 141.
35. Veterans' names and sites were as follows: Albert J. White, 337 Conant Road; Wyman Johnson, 55 Sunset Road; Richard Hosterman, 325 Merriam Street; Thomas W. Shepard, behind 208 Boston Post Road; Everett Schwartz Jr., 39 Sunset Road; Parker W. Hastings, 128 Wellesley Street. Ref: *The Town Reporter*, March 1950, vol. 5, no. 10, 3.
36. The *Wayland/Weston Town Crier Special Anniversary Edition, 1951–1971,* September 11, 1971, 39.
37. Risher, Jo Ann, "It's Happy Birthday for Merriam Village," *Town Crier*, October 20, 1988.
38. Town forests allowed under Chapter 255 of the Acts and Resolves of 1882.
39. 1954 *TR*, 140.
40. In 1975, a grant was received from the state bicentennial commission to complete the opening of the view of Mount Wachusett and place a bronze plaque on the east side of Highland Street, commemorating the Bicentennial and the 1955 Paine gift.
41. 1955 *TR*, 145. The gift of this 40 acres was made over more than one year. In 1957 the town purchased 100 acres from Blanche T. Bigelow, and by 1958 Jericho had reached 200 acres.
42. Jones, Elmer E., *Walks on Weston Conservation Land, Weston, Massachusetts: A Guide* (Weston: Weston Forest and Trail Press, 1999), 240.
43. 1958 *TR*, 151.
44. 1960 *TR*, 28. Price was $15,000.
45. Chapter 223, Acts of 1957, and Chapter 517, Acts of 1960. The Conservation Commission succeeded a broadly based Open Areas Committee in existence from 1960 to 1961.
46. 1960 *TR*, 163.
47. Report of the Conservation Commission, 1971 *TR*, 48.
48. Hugo Uyterhoeven, speech at the Weston special town meeting, December 1997. See also "Decision Time: Town Meeting," *Town Crier*, January 20, 1972, and 1977 *TR*, 162.
49. Figures provided by Hugo Uyterhoeven to PWF, February 2001. In some cases, money and acreage figures differ somewhat from those printed in the town report, depending on how recreation and Weston Forest and Trail land is counted and what time period is being considered.
50. Cheek, Jeannette, "Weston: A Community," *WHSB*, December 1988, 4.
51. 1971 *TR*, 44.
52. 1973 *TR*, 47, and Cheek, op. cit., 4.
53. Donahue, Brian, *Reclaiming the Commons,* 12.
54. Statistics from 1975 *TR*, 45 (Report of the Youth Commission).
55. Donahue, op. cit., 19.
56. Ibid., 165.
57. Ibid., 27.
58. For a firsthand account of the early years of Land's Sake, see *Reclaiming the Commons* by Brian Donahue, a founder and moving force behind its creation.
59. 1967 *TR*, 169.
60. 1973 *TR*, 125.
61. Information in the following paragraphs largely taken from Alice Hinkle and Diana Brown, "Route 128: 60 Years of Stop and Go," *Boston Sunday Globe, West Weekly*, February 25, 1996.
62. 1949 *TR*, 19.
63. *The Town Reporter*, December 1949, vol. 5, no. 7, 2.
64. 1950 *TR*, 125.
65. *The Wellesley Townsman*, November 1951, vol. 46, no. 20.
66. Quote from David Soule, executive director of the regional planning council, in Hinkle and Brown, op. cit.

67. 1953 *TR*, 161.
68. *The Town Reporter*, vol. 8, no. 4, September 1953. This issue includes a map with the toll road route in its present location and a list of properties to be taken.
69. 1954 *TR*, 161.
70. 1955 *TR*, 16.
71. Ibid., 142.
72. Ibid.
73. 1964 *TR*, 33.
74. 1947 *TR*, 108.
75. PWF interview with David Bradley, August 1999.
76. Interview with Lorna Garron. Weston founders of the Jericho Forest Pony Club included Doug and Lorna Garron, Mary Cressy, Polly Gates, Nancy Baer, Caroline Cameron, Anita Frank, Joan Weissbecker, Marsha Miller, and Mary Jo Rines.
77. Sherwood, Susan, "Club Caters to Crafty Folk," *The Weston Town Crier*, December 21, 2000.
78. *The Town Crier*, August 26, 1965, 2.
79. 1950 *TR*, 91.
80. The foreign student exchange program, arranged through the Weston-Rombas Affiliation Committee, began some years later.
81. 1949 *TR*, 18.
82. 1950 *TR*, 136.
83. 1957 *TR*, 158.
84. *WHSB*, May 1975, 1, 4.
85. The author was unable to find anyone who knows for certain whether any noble scions survived.
86. Established under state General Laws Chapter 40, section 8 D.
87. "Highlights and Sidelights: How Weston Observed the Bicentennial," *WHSB*, January 1977, 3.

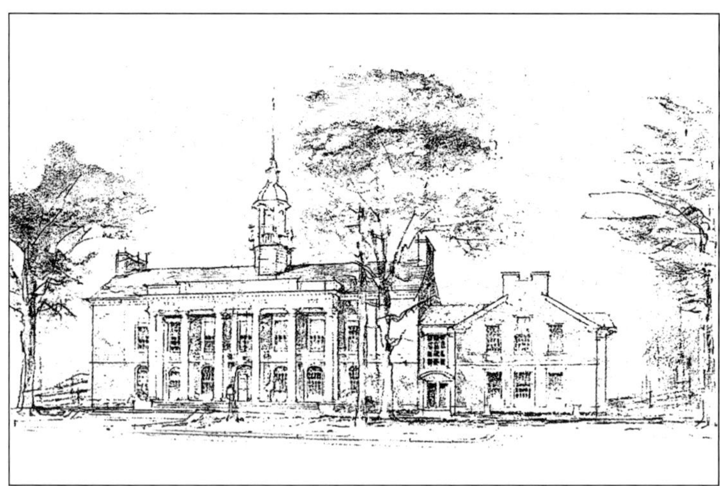

Figures A-1 to A-4. At the turn of the century, Weston had a population of 11,555. The per-capita income of $76,269 continued to be the highest in the state. Fifty percent of households earned $150,000 or more. The town had 3,348 dwelling houses and 2,149 children in the public schools. Eighty-nine percent of residents were white, 8 percent were Asian, 2 percent were Hispanic, and almost 1 percent were black. (Statistics from Town of Weston Annual Report 2000 *and* The Comparative Guide to American Suburbs, 2001.)

In addition to renovating the high, middle, and elementary schools, Weston residents in the 1990s and 2000 approved the building of a transfer station (1994, top left), new library (1995, top right, Galliher and Baier, architects), community center (2001, lower left, Claude E. Menders Architects Inc.), and an addition to the town hall (under construction, lower right, Ann Beha Associates Inc.).

AFTERWORD

In another hundred years or so, residents of Weston will look back on the late 20th and early 21st centuries with the perspective of time. They will see how decisions made in the years after World War II shaped the town for half a century or more. They will note the continuing strong support for the public school system and the tremendous expense in the 1990s and early 2000s of rebuilding and remodeling a succession of schools all built within a few decades after World War II. They will chronicle the building of new town facilities like the transfer station (1994), library (1994–95), community center (2000–01), and town hall expansion (2001–02). They will assess the outcome of decades of controversy over construction of an office building on the Massachusetts Broken Stone site. They will note the increasing diversity of the town's population, as families of many nationalities, races, and religions make Weston their home.

A history of the late 20th and early 21st centuries will probably take up a theme that has been a constant thread throughout this book—efforts to preserve community character. At the turn of the 21st century, Weston is using the same tools developed after World War II: zoning and purchase of conservation land. Zoning changes have allowed for increased oversight of new construction so that new houses will fit in with Weston's "semi-rural" atmosphere. Land-acquisition efforts have begun to focus on frontage parcels of scenic value visible from the roadway. Historians of the future can report on whether Weston successfully preserved the rustic, naturalistic quality of its scenic byways or embraced a more suburban ethos characterized by formal landscaping and lots of mulch.

Architectural historians will look at the way the size and cost of houses in Weston and across the country have increased with each decade until finally a new word, mansionization, *was coined to describe the phenomenon. They will note the continuing popularity of the Colonial Revival and the revival of the Shingle style as a way to accommodate the bulk of these new houses and the desire for individually tailored floor plans. Social historians will analyze the effects of wealth on community values, ideals, and patterns of living.*

Decisions made over the next decades will determine the direction we take as a community. Will we continue to address the issue of affordable housing? Will we accept empty-nester housing, condominiums, or additional rental housing to meet the needs of residents who no longer wish to own single-family homes? To what extent will Westonites of the 21st century embrace the goal of preserving the town's architectural fabric? How will we resolve our simultaneous desire to accelerate our own trips through town, slow down those speeding through our neighborhoods, and preserve the character of our scenic roadways? Will residents continue to participate in town government, volunteer in the classroom, coach soccer, lead Scout troops, plant flowers in the center, provide support services to the elderly, and attend to the hundreds of other volunteer jobs that keep a community strong?

Figure 10-1. The Hook & Hastings organ factory moved to Weston in 1889 and was a major influence on the development of Kendal Green for the next four decades. Many houses in the area were built for employees. Hastings Hall was the center of social and cultural life. Workers attended the revitalized Methodist church and their children were educated at the one-room District School #4. This 1898 image was taken by the Howes brothers, itinerant photographers.

CHAPTER 10

Kendal Green

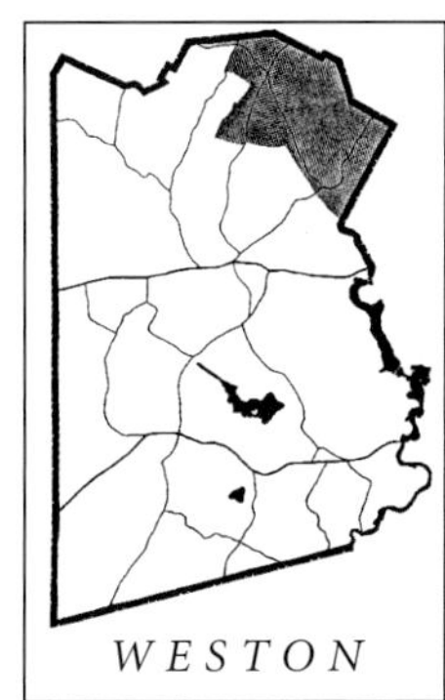

The place-name Kendal Green was coined in the mid-1880s by the distinguished Gen. James F.B. Marshall, who suggested it for the new post office near his home at North Avenue and Church Street. The part of town served by that post office, including Lexington Street, upper Church Street, and most of North Avenue, came to be known as Kendal Green.

North Avenue was "the great thoroughfare" between Boston, New Hampshire, and Vermont and into Canada in the early years of town history. In old deeds, it had many names: North County Road, Concord Road, Lancaster Road, Lancaster Turnpike, the Great Road, and "the road leading to Waltham." Farmers drove their cattle and hogs along North Avenue to slaughterhouses in Brighton and Charlestown. Stagecoaches passed this way. The construction of the Fitchburg Railroad in 1843–45 further stimulated growth.

One historical theme of this chapter is the development of businesses and services for travelers and residents. Early taverns provided rest and refreshment. In the 18th and 19th centuries, blacksmiths and wheelwrights set up small shops. In 1874 the town placed a water pump and stone trough at the intersection of North Avenue and Church Street, "for the benefit of the traveling public."[1] Local entrepreneurs established small grocery stores, and eating places including Brodrick's, Foote's, and the Cedar Hill Dairy Bar. Weston's first gasoline station was located on North Avenue.

Two major industries flourished in Kendal Green during different time periods. The waterpower of Hobbs Brook was harnessed early in the 18th century for the Hobbs Tannery, one of the first tanneries in the state. The tannery operated for more than a century and encouraged related industries like shoe and boot making. At the end of the 19th century, Francis H. Hastings, grandson of a North Avenue farmer and bootmaker, moved the Hook & Hastings Company from Roxbury to Weston. Hook & Hastings was one of the most important 19th-century organ manufacturers. An estimated 1,500 organs, including some of the most famous in the country, were constructed in Weston between 1889 and 1935, when the company closed its doors. For almost half a century, Hook & Hastings was the town's largest employer. Its influence extended well beyond the workplace, as Hastings worked to build a "Community of Labor."

Figure 10-2. Stony Brook, shown here with North Avenue and the Fiske house in the background, is the most important tributary of the Charles River.

Turn-of-the-century residents of Kendal Green were justly proud of their village, which rivaled Weston center in population, entertainments, and services. Their correspondent to the Waltham Daily Free Press Tribune *took full opportunity to gloat when the center was paralyzed by a major snowstorm. The storm halted the single-track Central Massachusetts railroad and brought town center dignitaries to Kendal Green to get mail or take the Fitchburg line into Boston:*

> *Kendall (sic) Green is especially favored not only in choice of scenery, society and sociability, but in equipments, conveniences and methods of coping with what to other parts of the town proves a menace to their comfort and business. What is known as Weston [Center] . . . is inconvenient, and . . . far removed from the real center of the life and business pulse of the town which is to be found at Kendall Green.*[2]

Early Settlers: The Fiske and Warren Families

The Fiske farm, said to be a mile square, was always one of the largest in Weston and was a "pleasing landmark to the stage passengers" on their way to Fitchburg or Groton.[3] Lt. Nathan Fiske bought the original 220 acres from his relatives in 1673 for 10 pounds. The land was located on the north side of North Avenue between about Conant Road and

Figure 10-3. The Fiske farm was one of the oldest and largest in Weston. Alonzo S. Fiske built this house on North Avenue in 1845 to replace the original homestead. It stood near the present Dairy Joy until the 1950s.

Figure 10-4. After the death of Alonzo Fiske in 1893, the town report printed two pages of resolutions in his praise, including this one: "He worked early and late upon committees, and . . . threw himself with heart and soul into almost every matter which concerned the town."

Figure 10-5. The Warren family was one of the first to receive an allotment of land in Watertown Farms. By 1794 there were three Warren houses on Lexington Street, including this one, which still stands at No. 71.

Viles Street.[4] It was passed, undivided, from father to son for six generations, until the last Nathan died a bachelor in 1912, leaving more than 260 acres.[5]

In the early 19th century, Capt. Sewall Fiske (1792–1868) realized that the location on the great highway "gave many opportunities for speculation." The family genealogy relates how, in addition to farming, Fiske and his partner kept a store:

> That was before the days of railroads, and they made a great deal of business by buying out countrymen who were on their way to Boston loaded down with poultry, geese, ducks, chickens, etc. They came in droves in the winter time, utilizing the sleighing. . . . In the fall [Fiske] would remain in Boston from Monday morning to Saturday night engaged in disposing of this produce.[6]

In 1845 his son, Alonzo Sewall Fiske (1818–1893), built a new farmhouse on North Avenue to replace the ancestral home. The family genealogy boasts that for many years Alonzo was "in charge of most of the town business of Weston," serving as assessor and tax collector, justice of the peace, selectman from 1858 to 1871, and state representative in 1878.

The second large north-side landholding dating back to the 17th century was the Warren farm, located at North Avenue and Lexington Street. John Warren came to Watertown in 1630 and was allotted 162 acres in the 1642 division of The Farms.[7] The tombstone of his grandson, Ensign John Warren

Figure 10-6. Five generations of the Hobbs family operated the Hobbs Tannery and branched out into making harnesses, shoes, and other leather goods. In the mid-18th century, Isaac Hobbs Sr. added the section at the right of this photograph to create the double house at 87 North Avenue. His grandson Samuel Hobbs married Abigal Kendal, who lived here until her death in 1883. She left the property to her nephew Gen. James F.B. Marshall. The well-known educator added the central wall gable and porches and called his country retirement home Kendal Green.

(1665–1703), is the oldest in the Farmers' Burial Ground. By 1794 there were three Warren houses on Lexington Street.[8] One of Ensign John's descendants, Cynthia Warren, married John Cutting Jr. in 1799. Their 11 children included John Warren Cutting (1800–1873) and Marshall Cutting (1818–1889), who were still farming on Lexington Street until the late 19th century.

Hobbs Tannery and Other Early Industries

At the intersection of North Avenue and Church Street, once known as Hobbs' Corner, is a cluster of important early houses associated with the Hobbs family and Hobbs Tannery. Tanning hides was an important colonial industry, as the tough, strong leather material was indispensable for use in harnesses, saddles, and shoes. Making leather required an abundant water supply. Hides had to be washed and soaked in vats of lime solution to loosen the hair, then scraped, smoothed, and tanned in pits of water containing ground-up bark, which produced tannin. The tannin slowly penetrated the hides and turned them into leather, a process that took 12 to 18 months. The leather was pounded to make it flexible and "dressed" by curriers, who stretched the hides and kneaded them in oil.

The Hobbs Tannery may have been established as early as 1730, the year after Josiah Hobbs (1684–1779) bought 122 acres in Weston and Waltham.[9] The tanyard was located on what is now town conservation land just west of Hobbs Brook, which provided the necessary water. The business became so well known that, according to Lamson's history, "it was the custom throughout the State, in early days, to locate houses and people in Weston by the distance from the tannery."[10]

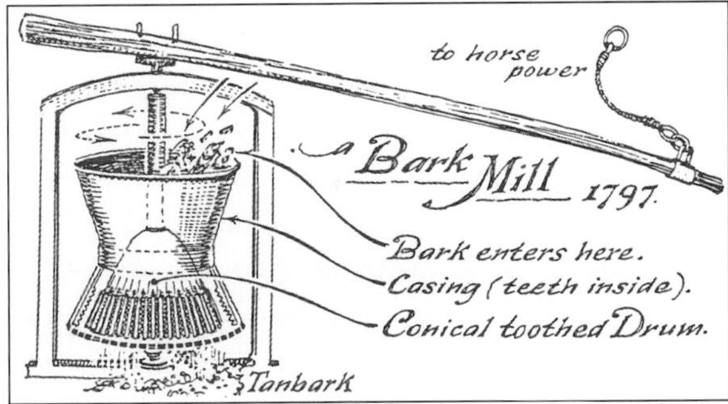

Figure 10-7. One of the essential ingredients in transforming hides into leather was ground bark, which was soaked in water to produce tannin.

Five generations of the family operated Hobbs Tannery for more than a century, until the Civil War. They branched out into related enterprises like slaughtering cattle and making harnesses, carriages, whips, leather cartridge boxes, belts, boots, and shoes. An appraisal at the death of Isaac Hobbs Jr. (1765–1834) reveals the extent of the business:

> . . . a tanyard containing about 60 vats, bark houses, currying shop and all the necessary buildings for doing an extensive business with sufficient water power for grinding the bark, pulling hides, and rolling leather with mills for same.[11]

The probate inventory lists several thousand skins and hides and more than 2,000 finished boots, bootees, shoes, slippers, pumps, and brogans, along with large quantities of shoemaking supplies stored in the "shoe shop."[12]

After Isaac's death, his son-in-law, Nathan Hagar Jr., formed the partnership of Hobbs & Hagar for the manufacture of shoes. According to one source, boots and shoes were the principal articles produced

Figure 10-8. The Hobbs-Hagar house at 88 North Avenue was built in two sections beginning in 1786. The corner quoins and heavy window caps are typical Georgian features. All the house lots in this photograph have fences or stone walls in front to keep out cattle and swine being driven to market along North Avenue. The animals drank at the stone watering trough, seen in the center of the photo. In 1903, residents worried that proposed road widening for a streetcar line would require taking down the elm trees in front of Miss Hagar's house. An item in the newspaper noted, "These trees are the largest in town, two of them measuring five feet in diameter and the other two only a little way behind. It would be a sin to cut these trees down . . ." (Photo c. 1894)

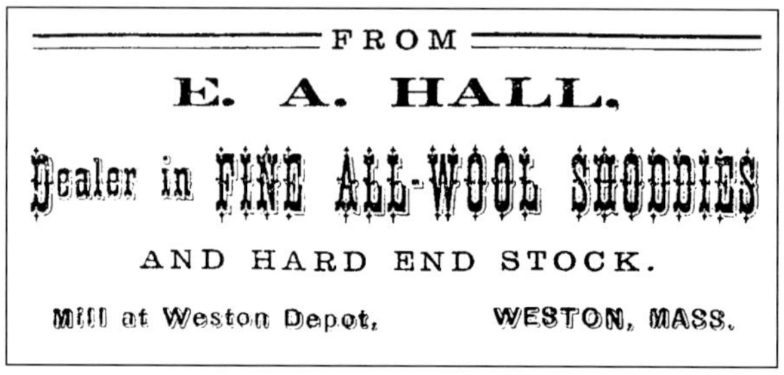

FROM

E. A. HALL,

Dealer in FINE ALL-WOOL SHODDIES

AND HARD END STOCK.

Mill at Weston Depot, WESTON, MASS.

Figure 10-9. E.A. Hall's mill on Church Street at Stony Brook produced "shoddy," a fabric made from reclaimed wool. The mill burned down for the second time in 1886 and was not rebuilt.

in Weston at this time. In 1837, 5,606 pairs of boots and 17,182 pairs of shoes were made in Weston.[13] This date was probably near the peak of the leather industry, as Hagar's shoe factory closed around 1850 and the tannery in 1862.[14]

Nineteenth-century maps show a mill on the east side of Church Street just south of the Fitchburg Railroad tracks. In the 1870s and 1880s, E.A. Hall operated a large shoddy mill here. The term *shoddy* refers to a fabric manufactured from reclaimed wool such as rags.[15] Power was provided by damming Stony Brook, creating a millpond across the street.[16]

The Poor Farm

In 1817 Weston purchased 80 acres on Conant Road straddling the Lincoln line for a poor farm, replacing an earlier work house at the south end of School Street.[17] Here, under the direction of the Overseers of the Poor, the town carried out its obligation to take care of indigent people lawfully settled in the town.

Not everyone was pleased with the location. In 1860, a committee considered the question of moving the poor farm and recommended construction of a new house instead:

> We have considered it a settled policy of the town to support their poor upon a farm of their own. We believe they should be provided with a warm and comfortable shelter, with wholesome food and proper raiment. We do not feel that it would be wise or politic for the town to exchange the present location for another one. We believe a building might be erected at an expense not exceeding $2,500.[18]

The resulting structure was "a plain, solid substantial house . . . well calculated for its design."

In 1871 it was again proposed to sell the poor farm and purchase a smaller place in a more central location. According to Lamson's *History of the Town of Weston*, "It was thought at the time that the people of the north side wanted to get rid of it in their neighborhood, and an effort was made to have the house located in the center of the town."[19] No action was taken.

The town subsidized the difference between expenses and income from farm sales. When the farming season was good and the caretaker efficient, the farm sometimes needed only a small subsidy from the town. The caretaker's wife kept the almshouse clean, cooked meals, and cared for the sick. Poor farm residents were expected to help, but at least one annual report, in 1867, noted that "the amount of labor they are able to perform is but trifling." The number of people residing permanently at the almshouse varied between one and six. They were generally older, with an occasional teenager. The record for the longest stay probably goes to Cooper Garfield, who died at age 100 after 35 years at the poor farm.[20]

The number of travelers and tramps given food and temporary shelter varied widely from year to year. For example, the number was 63 in 1870 but increased to 578 in 1878 and 1,140 in 1880, the years that the Massachusetts Central Railroad was under construction. A small outbuilding just north of the main house had a cement floor and was used extensively as a "tramp house." The 1878 report gave this assessment of the transitory occupants:

> These tramps say that they are seeking employment. They are mostly young men, and some of them, no doubt, are honest and would be glad to work if they could find employment; but a majority of them make tramping their business.[21]

In 1897, construction of the nearby Cambridge Reservoir brought another upsurge in the number of tramps. The town fed and temporarily lodged 1,270 men that year. The Overseers of the Poor tried having them work on the farm, "but in order to get anything out of them a man must stand constantly on watch and even then but little is done; furthermore, when they are worked they must be better fed."[22] The board concluded that "after a lodging it is best to give tramps crackers and water and let them go."

The poor farm operated on Conant Road from 1817 until 1915, when the last inmate died. The Overseers of the Poor sold the property in 1922.[23]

General James F.B. Marshall

The Hobbs land at the intersection of North Avenue and Church Street stayed in the family into the late 19th century, when it was inherited by Gen. James Fowle Baldwin Marshall (1818–1891). Though born in Charlestown, Marshall had Weston roots on both sides of his family.[24] His grandfather, Col. Thomas Marshall of Highland Street, was colonel of the Massachusetts Tenth Regiment.[25] His mother, Sophia Kendal Marshall, was a daughter of First Parish minister Samuel Kendal. The Reverend Kendal's other daughter, Abigail, married Samuel Hobbs in 1834 and moved to 87 North Avenue, the house where J.F.B. Marshall would live in retirement.

Marshall entered Harvard College as a young man but was forced to drop out during his second year because of poor eyesight, a lifelong problem. He moved to Honolulu, Hawaii, in 1838 and eventually became a partner in one of the islands' largest trading firms. He was elected to the legislature and worked actively on behalf of native rights, agricultural improvements, and temperance. Just before the outbreak of the Civil War, Marshall and his wife, Martha, returned to Boston with a modest fortune. During the war, Marshall served as paymaster general of the Massachusetts militia. Although his eyesight was never good enough for him to carry a gun or command troops, he was referred to in later years as "the wise, gentle General."[26]

At the close of the war, Marshall became an incorporator and trustee for the Hampton Normal and Agricultural Institute in Virginia, founded by his former Honolulu Sunday school pupil Samuel Chapman Armstrong, for the education of black teachers, male and female.[27] Initially, Marshall helped raise funds from the Boston community. He visited Hampton for the first time in 1870 and was so impressed that he agreed to move to the Virginia school and take on the roles of treasurer, acting assistant principal, and bookkeeping teacher. Twenty-four-year-old Horace Sears worked as Marshall's assistant treasurer for two years, from 1879 to 1880, and probably learned many of his business skills at Hampton. Sears remained a lifelong supporter of the school.

Figure 10-10. Gen. James F.B. Marshall (1818–1891) was a founder, original trustee, and teacher at Hampton Institute in Virginia, a school for the education of black teachers. His best-known pupil was Booker T. Washington, who visited the general in 1890 and spoke at Weston Town Hall.

Marshall's best-known pupil, Booker T. Washington, went on to become the first head of the newly formed Tuskegee Institute, which Marshall referred to with great pleasure as "Hampton's proudest monument." Washington sought Marshall's advice on how to begin the school and requested money from Hampton to buy land for a campus. Marshall loaned him the down payment from his own funds, the first of many such loans and gifts. He continued a steady stream of correspondence in which he advised Washington on accounting and fund-raising.[28]

Marshall remained at Hampton for 14 years. In 1883 his aunt "Nabby" Hobbs died, and Marshall retired to her home on North Avenue the following year. The property included several houses and 30 acres of former tannery land.[29] General Marshall enlarged and remodeled the 18th-century Isaac Hobbs house, adding a central gable and entrance porch. He called his North Avenue property Kendal Green.

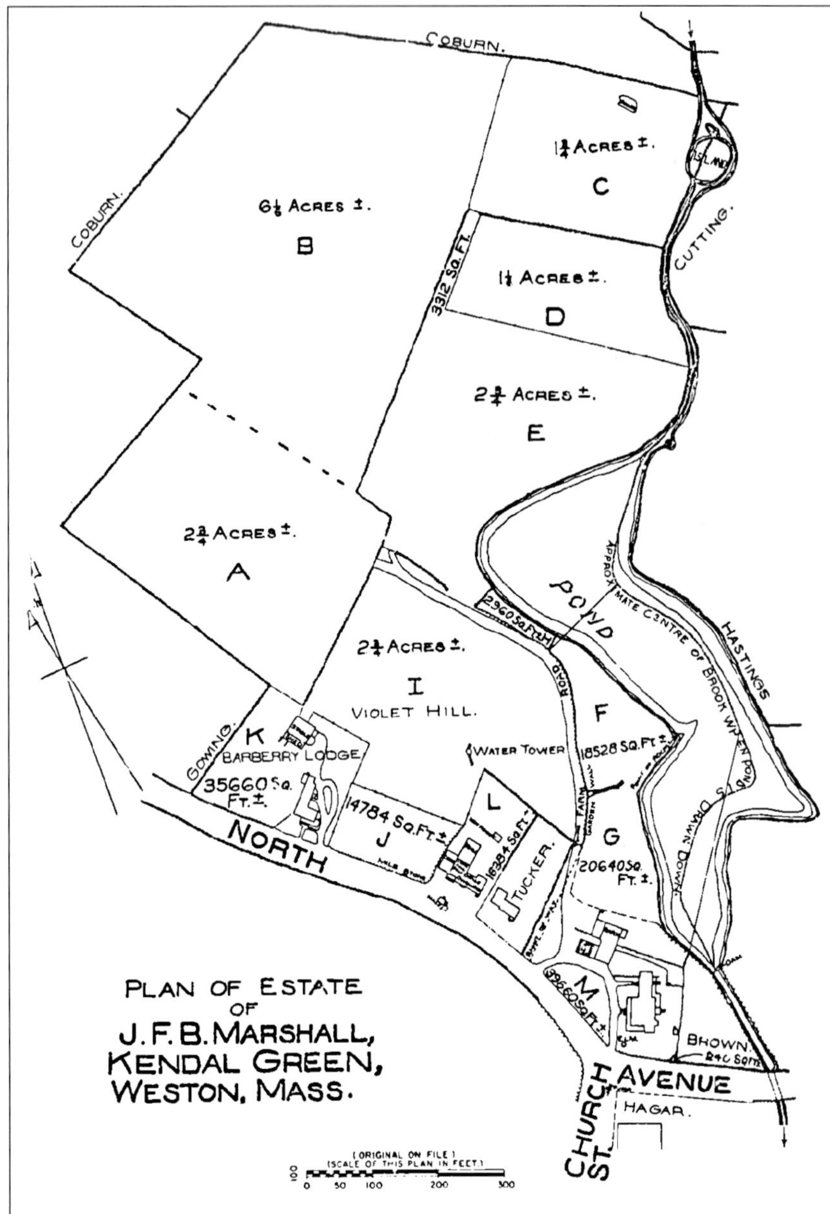

Figure 10-11. This 1889 plot plan shows the main house at 87 North Avenue (M), the general store and post office at 107-109 North Avenue (L), and the Ebenezer Hobbs house at 121 North Avenue (K), all owned by General Marshall.

As a well-known educator, Marshall received many letters. Not coincidentally, the postal service opened an office two doors down from his home in January 1886.[30] Marshall suggested the name Kendal Green as being "of pleasant sound and significance," as he explained in a letter of December 1885.[31] "Kendal" commemorated Marshall's grandfather, the "last of Weston's colonial pastors." Kendal Green was the name of a green cloth manufactured in the English town of Kendal and adopted as a uniform by Robert, Earl of Huntington, when he was outlawed and took the name of Robin Hood. Shakespeare immortalized the cloth in *King Henry IV* when Prince Hal asks Falstaff, "How couldst thou know these men in Kendal Green, when 'twas so dark thou couldst not see thy hands?" By 1886, the Kendal Green Post Office was in operation along with a small general store. The nearby railroad station adopted the name and the neighborhood came to be known as the village of Kendal Green.

During the seven years before his death in 1891, Marshall regularly took the train into Boston. He was an active officer of the American Unitarian Society, serving as the association's Secretary for Southern and Indian Educational Work. He retained his ties with Hampton and Tuskegee. In November 1890, Booker T. Washington visited the Marshalls on North Avenue and spoke at Weston Town Hall. Both Marshall and his wife died suddenly of flu-related pneumonia the following spring. The report of the Hampton Institute that year includes this tribute:

> . . . the good condition of our business affairs is largely due to him. But his influence and value extended far beyond his office duties. He gave tone to the entire work, and impressed his noble, kindly character on hundreds of students, who will always look on him as a father and true friend. . . . He will be remembered and mourned by many in this and other lands.[32]

Hook & Hastings Company: Early History

The decade of the 1880s also saw the establishment of the Hook & Hastings organ factory, by far the largest of the town's 19th-century mills and industries. At a time when the population was about 1,700, the factory employed more than 70 workers; and its presence influenced not only Kendal Green but also the economy of the town as a whole.

The organ factory had its beginnings in 1827, when Elias Hook (1805–1881) and his brother, George G. Hook (1807–1880), formed the organ-building firm of E. & G.G. Hook. In 1853 the brothers moved to a new factory on Tremont Street in Roxbury Crossing along the tracks of the Fitchburg Railroad. In this factory, said to be the largest in the country at that time, they built some of the century's greatest church and concert hall organs.[33]

Francis Henry Hastings (1836–1916) began working for the company as a draftsman in 1855. Hastings had grown up on North Avenue in the family homestead built by his grandfather Jonas Hastings (1784–1865) and grandmother Betsy Warren Hastings and passed on to his father, Francis (1809–1889). Both Jonas and Francis were bootmakers as well as farmers.

Young Francis Henry hated farming and apparently was not fond of school either. At age 14, he ended his formal education at District School #4 and went to work as an apprentice in a machine shop in Boston, making tools. One of his employers gave him this enthusiastic reference: ". . . for honesty, integrity, and industrious habits and good moral principles I would cheerfully recommend him."[34] He was 19 when he joined E. & G.G. Hook and 30 when he was taken into partnership in 1866.[35] An 1871 agreement changed the name of the firm to E. & G.G. Hook & Hastings.

Figure 10-12. Jonas Hastings built the Hastings Homestead (now 199 North Avenue) in 1823. He and his son Francis were bootmakers and farmers. Shoemaking was an important cottage industry in Kendal Green because of the tannery.

Figure 10-13. Elias Hook, left (1805–1881), and his brother George formed the organ-building firm of E. & G.G. Hook in 1827. Weston native Francis Henry Hastings joined the brothers in 1855.

Figure 10-14. Francis Henry Hastings (1836–1916) was born at 199 North Avenue and educated at the nearby district school. When he became head of Hook & Hastings, he moved the prestigious organ-manufacturing company to the farm fields across from his family homestead. On his death it was written, "The village of Kendal Green . . . is practically a monument alike to his enterprise and to his love of the place of his nativity."

Figure 10-15. Francis and Mary Cooley Hastings, parents of Francis Henry Hastings, celebrated their 50th wedding anniversary on June 20, 1883.

According to the publication *The Hook Opus List, 1829–1916 in Facsimile,* the firm was already using modern methods of mass production by the time Hastings became a partner.[36] He introduced stock models available by catalog and greatly increased advertising as a marketing tool. His artistic and mechanical skills and good business judgment ensured the company of a continuing period of prosperity that extended well into the next century.

One of the best-known organs built at the Roxbury factory was for the Church of the Immaculate Conception in Boston in 1863. It remains the largest surviving E. & G.G. Hook organ and "one of the finest examples of nineteenth century organ building."[37] Also outstanding were the 1875 organ for Holy Cross Cathedral in Boston, which at the time was the largest ever built by an American firm, and the organ for the 1876 Centennial Exposition in Philadelphia, which judges gave the "highest rank in its class." In 1877, the company's monumental Cincinnati Music Hall organ, with its four manuals, 96 speaking registers, and 6,237 pipes, took over the national record for size and remained the largest ever built by the firm. The Cincinnati organ was 50 feet wide and 30 feet deep and its pyramid of pipes rose 60 feet in the lofty hall. The pipes ranged in size from half an inch to 32 feet. In 1897, it was listed as the 18th of the 22 biggest organs in the world.[38]

These grand instruments attracted widespread public attention, and the firm's ability to handle the problems of producing and installing them contributed to its fame. The Hook factory reached peak production during the 1870s and 1880s, when it averaged 46 organs per year or nearly 1 per week. By 1880 the company had produced 1,000 organs.

In 1880 and 1881, the Hook brothers died and Francis Hastings purchased their share of the business. The company increased production of small stock organs while continuing to build large custom instruments. The name remained the same until 1893, when it was reorganized as a corporation and renamed the Hook & Hastings Company. Hastings maintained not only the prestigious Hook name but also its superior standards of craftsmanship. As one writer noted in the *Church Music Review,* "It is indeed seldom that a firm remains at the head of its profession continuously for so many years with uninterrupted success."[39]

"A Community of Labor"

In 1885, at age 49, Francis Henry Hastings built himself a Shingle-style house, Seven Gables, across the street from his boyhood home. It was designed by the Boston architectural firm of Henry W. Hartwell and William Richardson, who are also thought to be responsible for the stable across the street. This noted firm achieved particular success in the 1880s and 1890s. Architectural historian Susan Maycock Vogel analyzes the partnership:

> . . . it is in this light, as followers rather than innovators, that Hartwell and Richardson must be considered. Nevertheless, they were extremely popular architects, and their work, especially in the 1880s,

Figure 10-16. In 1885, Francis Henry Hastings built Seven Gables (now 190 North Avenue) almost directly across from his childhood home. The fashionable Shingle-style house was designed by the noted Boston architectural firm of Hartwell and Richardson. Characteristic of the Shingle style is the asymmetrical massing, sculptural quality, and uniform shingle cladding.

provides an excellent example of both popular architectural taste in Boston and the influence of H.H. Richardson on his contemporaries.[40]

In the Hastings house, the architects used one of their 1880s trademarks, diamond shingle patterns in the gable.

Many reasons have been suggested as to why Hastings moved his home and then the factory to Weston. He may have wanted to spend more time with his aging parents, who both died in the late 1880s. The family farmland was conveniently located on the rail line and available for new uses. Hastings's only child, Francis Warren, had left Harvard College in 1884 because of failing health; his father may have hoped that the country air would improve the young man's health.

Labor unrest in other industries and the rise of the labor movement may have inspired Hastings's effort to create a harmonious workplace and community at Kendal Green and thus avoid costly strikes.[41] The mid-1880s were years of often violent railroad strikes. In 1886 an anarchist exploded a bomb in Chicago's Haymarket, and that same year the American Federation of Labor was organized. Hastings's "community of labor" at Kendal Green should be viewed in the context of well-publicized strikes at Carnegie's Homestead steel mill near Pittsburgh in 1892 and at the Pullman factory in 1894.

The following chronology, compiled from the diary of Francis Henry Hastings and from deed records, summarizes the land purchases of Francis Henry and his son, Francis Warren Hastings, and their major construction projects between 1884 and 1895:[42]

1884: Purchased two parcels of land on North Avenue formerly part of the Hastings Homestead: one acre on the north side and five acres on the south side of the road. [43]

1885: Built main house, Seven Gables, and stable on North Avenue [#190, 191].[44] Finished and moved in. Purchased 15 acres of Hastings Homestead on north side of North Avenue.[45]

1886: Purchased rest of Hastings Homestead [for a total of 45 acres].[46] Purchased Warren Farm on Lexington Street [150 acres].[47]

1887: Purchased the Buttrick place [3.5 acres on north side of North Avenue].[48] Purchased Warner property [just under one acre on west side of Viles Street, including existing tenement].[49] Commenced west wing of factory. Built two double cottages on Viles Street [#126, 130]. Finished three Lexington Street double cottages [#17–19, 21–23, 27].[50]

1889: May 1, finished factory and moved business to Kendal Green. Built storehouse and Hastings Hall.

Figure 10-17. In 1899, newlyweds Francis and Anna Coburn Hastings sent this Christmas card showing the interior of Seven Gables.

Figure 10-18. The organ that Hastings designed in 1905 for his own residence had a player attachment enabling him to enjoy the best in organ music at home.

1891: Built east wing of factory. Built gardener's cottage behind the stable [189 North Avenue]. Built water reservoir in the woods on the west side of Cat Rock Hill. Equipped factory with automatic sprinkler and electric fire signal. Enlarged Hastings farmhouse by adding west-wing apartment.

1893: Sold Warren farm on Lexington Street to George H. Ellis. Built three cottages on North Avenue

Figure 10-19. In 1891, Francis Henry Hastings built this house at 189 North Avenue for his caretaker/gardener. It was one of the first in the neighborhood to use the "cross gambrel" roof arrangement. The shingles were originally brown.

[#225, 227, 231]. Built one cottage, No. 6, on White Lane (now the east end of Brook Road). Commenced two other houses on White Lane. Formed business into corporation.

1894: Finished the two cottages on White Lane (now Brook Road) begun in 1893. Built another cottage on White Lane.

1895: Bought Andrews house on White Lane and Gowell house at 266 North Avenue.

Postcards and photographs document the appearance of the huge wooden factory. A fixture on the landscape until its demolition in 1936, the building was more visible than it would be today because of the deforested landscape. As the town had no zoning regulations, nothing prevented construction of a factory amid farm fields, nor did local residents seem to object.

The factory had a center section that was 80 feet long, 40 feet wide, and four stories high, and two wings, each 100 feet long with three stories and a raised basement level. It was located just north of the Fitchburg Railroad tracks on the east side of Viles Street. A spur line led into the factory yard, so that

Figure 10-20. In 1887 Hastings began building the west wing of the new organ factory on Viles Street just north of the railroad tracks. Because the town had no zoning regulations, nothing prevented construction of a factory in this rural setting, nor did local residents seem to object. The company moved to the new building in 1889 and the east wing was added in 1891. Cat Rock Hill is in the background.

Figure 10-21. This photograph was taken about 1892, before construction of three worker houses on North Avenue. At the rear is the North Avenue School, and Hastings Homestead and barn, F.H. Hastings stable, and F.H. Hastings house, Seven Gables. In the middle ground is the tenement house, Hastings Hall, organ factory, and Hastings Station. White Lane (now Brook Road) is in the foreground and connects to Viles Street at right. The factory worker houses on White Lane had not been constructed.

lumber, coal, and other materials could be brought directly onto the property and finished organs loaded onto railroad cars for shipment. In its brochure of 1889, the company touted its new machinery, large lumber houses, dry rooms, and labor-saving devices and concluded that "we consider our large new factory the best equipped of any in the country, if not the world, of its kind."[51]

The size, materials, and "voicing" of pipes determined the quality of tone. Pipes could be as short as one inch or as long as 32 feet. Wood pipes were manufactured and assembled in the Wood Pipe Room, where the finest seasoned woods were specially treated to withstand extremes of temperature and humidity. In the Metal Pipe Room, pipes of graduated sizes were made according to

Figure 10-22. In the voicing room, employees perfected the distinctive sound of each organ stop and their proper blending to achieve "an enduring artistic creation." Each pipe had a different tone, depending on the size and material. William H. Dolbeare is pictured here with his son, Herman.

Figure 10-23. Hook & Hastings was the largest factory ever built in Weston. The three-story wooden structure had two 100-foot wings and an 80-foot center section. Notice the name of the factory on the ground.

Figure 10-24. Hook & Hastings made all parts of its organs except the keys. The company had special formulas for the composition of pipes produced in this metal pipe-making room.

specifications for size and type of metal, using a system of scales and gauges developed over the lifetime of the company. Materials used in each organ were subject to severe tests conducted in the Action Rooms. In the Voicing Room, employees called voicers devoted their attention to the individual sounds of each stop and the proper blending of the whole.

The Mill Room contained lathes, band and circular saws, planers, sanders, and other woodworking machinery used to create the fine-quality cabinetry that characterized Hook & Hastings instruments. When one of the large organs was completed, it was often set up in the central hall, called the finishing or erecting room. As many as 300 people would enjoy an informal evening's entertainment of singing and instrumental music before the organ was dismantled and crated for shipment.

The most important instruments often took years to build and were designed to coordinate with the church or hall in architectural style and color. This description of the organ built for the First Church of Christ, Scientist, Boston, in 1906, conveys the grandeur of these masterworks:

> The beautiful exterior, filling the great 60' arch, comprises many groups of large, gold speaking pipes, supported by casing of elaborately carved stone. There was a total of 126 stops, many thousands of pipes, the largest 32 feet long. This

Figure 10-25. Well-known Boston organs made by the Hook or Hook & Hastings firm over more than a century include the 1906 organ for the First Church of Christ, Scientist, shown here.

Figure 10-26. The Hook & Hastings Company gave this advice to those charged with purchasing a church organ: "When making your selection, DO NOT regard your organ as so many stops, so many pipes . . . but consider it solely as the most majestic of musical instruments and choose it for what it Creates, *DIVINE HARMONY. . . ." This cover was used for a hardbound promotional catalog of 1917.*

> Grand organ, by its immense size, extraordinary conception and masterly execution is unique and unsurpassed.[52]

Hook & Hastings also made moderately priced organs for chapels, schools, and residences. A pamphlet from the early 1880s shows six small, ready-made models.

In the mid-1860s, E. & G.G. Hook built some of the first American instruments to use pneumatic action, which enabled the player to bring out the power of the organ with less physical pressure on the keys.[53] Hook & Hastings Company later pioneered experiments in applying electric action to pipe organs. Its first organ with electric action was built about 1895–96 using platinum as the main contact for key and coupler actions.[54] Its last mechanical action organ was built in 1924 for St. John's Roman Catholic Church in Millers Falls, Massachusetts.[55]

The company's attention to quality and detail did not end with installation, as organs had to be carefully maintained and tuned. The company advertised that it had "competent and experienced tuners who are continually passing through various parts of the country" who could be called upon to service a Hook & Hastings organ.[56]

In 1906 the Hook & Hastings company had 70 employees, about half of whom lived in Weston.[57] The manufacture of organs required a variety of skilled tradesmen. Hastings once remarked that he needed "every branch of mechanics . . . workmen in wood, in metal, in leather, knowledge of music and acoustics, architecture, electricity, pneumatics, hydraulics . . ."[58] Hastings maintained

Figure 10-27. In busy times, the men worked 10 hours a day, six days a week, and shipped out approximately one organ a week.

relationships with European organ builders and employed experts trained in their factories. Scandinavians, particularly Norwegians and Swedes, were well represented in the workforce. Many of his employees worked at the factory for 30, 40, even 50 years and more.

"A Neighborhood Like a Family"

An article in the *Boston Herald* of Sunday, July 13, 1890, outlined Hastings's plan to create a harmonious workplace and community at Kendal Green.[59] The story, entitled "A Community of Labor" and subtitled "An Object Lesson for Employers and Employed—The Labor Experiment at Kendal Green . . . A Neighborhood Like a Family," begins, "One of the vital questions of the day is the labor question." The author praises Francis Henry Hastings for his thoughtful efforts to plan a community "so united in its aims and its work that it represents almost the ideal of relations between man and man."

Figure 10-28. Among the first organ factory worker houses were these three double cottages on Lexington Street, completed in 1887.

One way Hastings built his community was by providing a variety of housing options, including both rental and ownership, to employees who wished to move to Weston. An article in the *Danvers Mirror* explains the transition from city to country:

> The workmen at first nearly all lived in Boston, coming out to their task daily. But the city was close and stuffy. Kendal Green was sweet and country-like. Soon the absurdity of sleeping in the city in tenement rooms dawned on the mechanics. One after another they began to rent cottages at Kendal Green. . . . Gradually, a whole community of clean, self-respecting, intelligent mechanics sprang up around that organ factory.[60]

Hastings had anticipated the need for housing and built workers cottages on Viles and Lexington Streets even before the factory opened. Because he and his son owned three farms in the area, he was able to deliberately scatter the housing in different locations to avoid the appearance of a factory town.

Hastings rented some cottages by the year. He also encouraged his men to buy their own land and build their own houses, "and thus become landed proprietors." The 1890 *Boston Herald* article describes the development of White Lane, now Brook Road:

> A street is to be laid out on the opposite side of the railroad from the factory, and already the house lots have been marked off and sold. A moderate price was asked for the land, and the only provisions were that the houses were to be

Figure 10-29. Hastings scattered factory housing throughout Kendal Green to avoid the appearance of a company town. The two double houses at 126 and 130 Viles Street (right) were among the first to be built, in 1887. The third house from the right (since demolished) was an existing tenement with four apartments. At left is Hastings Hall (since demolished). In the background are the two original houses on White Lane, now Brook Road. By 1895, Hastings had built four more houses on White Lane for his employees.

> built within two years and that none were to cost less than $1,000. . . . It is Mr. Hastings' idea that the better the house is, the more highly the owner will value it, and the more pains he will make to keep it in good repair.[61]

Although homeownership many have been the original intention for the White Lane houses, they were, in fact, rented rather than owned by employees. Hastings and his son, Warren, did provide mortgages to workers who built homes on North Avenue, Merriam Street, and elsewhere in Weston.

The *Boston Herald* reported that Hastings took a personal interest in all his employees and regarded them as part of his family:

> Every man feels that he has a friend in his employer. If there is any trouble coming, if there is sickness in the family . . . the one to whom they all turn for help, for sympathy, for comfort, is the head of the concern. He knows personally every man in his employ.[62]

In answer to the question whether he had ever had any strikes, Hastings replied that he never had "the least word of difficulty." The *Herald* reporter speculated that the "atmosphere of friendliness and contentment" at Kendal Green was due in part to the class of men employed at an organ factory, with its "refining influences":

> There is no doubt that one's occupation does stamp the worker, and nothing could be more directly softening than the work on the fine organs in the midst of beautiful surroundings. It must call into life all that is best about a person, and make him finer and more true in spite of himself.[63]

The *Boston Herald* reporter speaks of the positive influence of country life on morals:

> To some of the men this life comes as a relief from temptation: the young men in particular are not in the way of the snares that are set at every corner in the city. They come to feel that intemperance and vice are out of harmony with the life about them.[64]

This statement exemplifies the strong anti-urban, anti-industrial sentiment that swept through the heavily industrialized state of Massachusetts in the 1890s and into the 1900s. Many believed that the small rural town was a healthy environment in which traditional values could best be maintained.

Figure 10-30. This picture, probably dating from the early 1890s, is taken looking northwest at the section of North Avenue numbered 263 to 331. The Gothic Revival house on the left side of the road is No. 272. At the right foreground is 263 North Avenue, built about 1875 by Samuel Patch Jr. The barn burned to the ground in the 1930s but the shop remains.

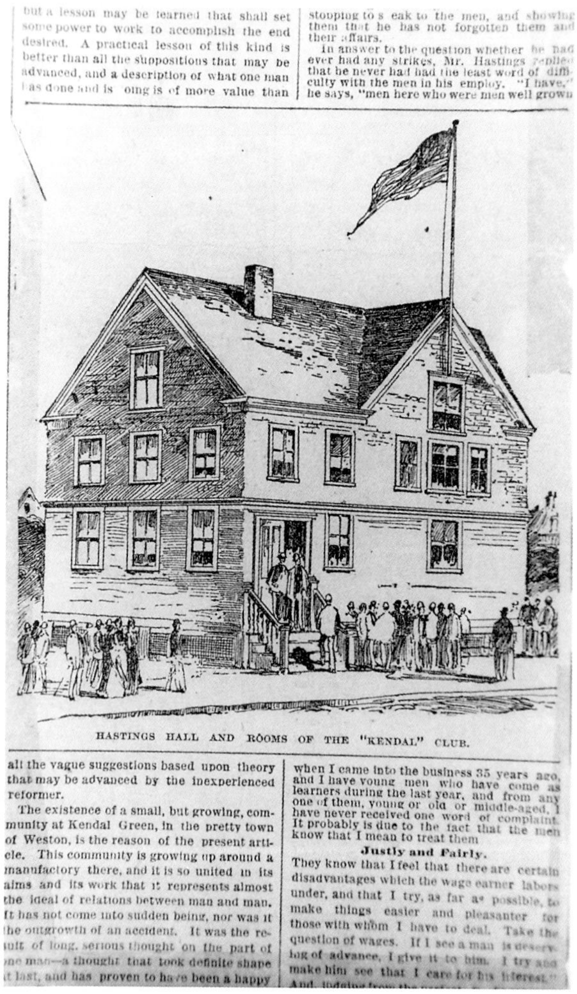

but a lesson may be learned that shall set some power to work to accomplish the end desired. A practical lesson of this kind is better than all the suppositions that may be advanced, and a description of what one man has done and is doing is of more value than

stooping to speak to the men, and showing them that he has not forgotten them and their affairs.

In answer to the question whether he had ever had any strikes, Mr. Hastings replied that he never had had the least word of difficulty with the men in his employ. "I have," he says, "men here who were men well grown

HASTINGS HALL AND ROOMS OF THE "KENDAL" CLUB.

all the vague suggestions based upon theory that may be advanced by the inexperienced reformer.

The existence of a small, but growing, community at Kendal Green, in the pretty town of Weston, is the reason of the present article. This community is growing up around a manufactory there, and it is so united in its aims and its work that it represents almost the ideal of relations between man and man. It has not come into sudden being, nor was it the outgrowth of an accident. It was the result of long, serious thought on the part of one man—a thought that took definite shape at last, and has proven to have been a happy

when I came into the business 35 years ago, and I have young men who have come as learners during the last year, and from any one of them, young or old or middle-aged, I have never received one word of complaint. It probably is due to the fact that the men know that I mean to treat them

Justly and Fairly.

They know that I feel that there are certain disadvantages which the wage earner labors under, and that I try, as far as possible, to make things easier and pleasanter for those with whom I have to deal. Take the question of wages. If I see a man is deserving of advance, I give it to him. I try and make him see that I care for his interest."

Figure 10-31. Hastings Hall was built in 1889 and stood on Viles Street until 1944. Over the years, it was the center for every kind of community event, from whist parties to discussions of Shakespeare's plays.

Hastings provided for recreation and social activities, which were undoubtedly much needed in rural Weston:

> As the little community grew, there was found a need of better means of social intercourse. Family visiting was all very well, but family visiting often degenerated into gossip and mischief-making.... So the thing to do was to make a hall and clubhouse.[65]

Hastings helped employees organize the Kendal Club, which met at the factory until Hastings Hall was built in late 1889. This simple wooden structure was located on the west side of Viles Street. It contained a hall seating 300 for entertainment and lectures, as well as a library, reading room "with all the daily papers, many of the weeklies, the leading scientific journals, and the popular magazines of the day," and a game room, "where the younger men pass many of their winter evenings."[66]

Although built for employees, Hastings Hall was used extensively by all local residents. Judging from turn-of-the-century Kendal Green columns in the *Waltham Daily Free Press*, it was the scene of more social events than the town hall in Weston center. The Kendal Club sponsored spirited debates on public issues, concerts, plays, dances, suppers, and lectures. Gen. James Marshall lectured here on "the Indian question." A separate Ladies' Club sponsored literary and social events.

Figure 10-32. In 1893, Francis Henry Hastings built the three cottages at 225, 227, and 231 North Avenue (left). At right is District School #4. The one-room schoolhouse had two entrances, one for boys and one for girls, as well as two coatrooms and two outhouses. A woodstove in the center of the room was kept stoked by the boys.

The company maintained a playground on Viles Street used by young children and by the organ factory baseball team. The annual baseball game against the Waltham Watch Company drew large crowds.

Some employees commuted by train to the Hastings railroad stop. A newspaper article from about 1893 provides insight into the life of the flagman, whose job was to signal the train if a passenger was waiting:

> It is a shame that the Fitchburg railroad does not provide the flagman at Viles Street (Hastings) with a suitable house. Mr. Foss is obligated to be on hand at 5:30 am and stay until 9 pm, or until [the] 35 goes down, every day of the week. He has, no thanks to the Fitchburg railroad, built himself a shanty and is now enlarging the same, in which he has a coal stove. On a cold morning or evening, it is no pleasure to wait in the waiting-room at Hastings for a train, which may or may not be on time, which is heated only by that generated by the benumbed passengers themselves and what of the sun's rays that can penetrate the building. What is needed at Hastings is more trains and a warm waiting-room. Later, we want a regular depot.[67]

In 1906, the railroad built a small but completely enclosed and heated station and a "crossing tender's shanty."[68]

In 1904 employees from Waltham who were dissatisfied with the train service hired a barge from McAuliffe's stable to convey them to and from work every day. According to the newspaper, "The very poor accommodation afforded them by the Boston and Maine RR Co. have driven them to adopt the barge plan, which is working nicely."[69] About 40 employees used the barge daily.

To protect the huge wooden factory building from fire, Hastings's insurance company demanded that he install a sprinkler system and fire hoses and organize a fire department.[70] In the fall of 1890, the Hook & Hastings Company purchased a hook-and-ladder truck and donated it to the town, which voted an appropriation for equipping and manning it. Acquiring fire apparatus for the north side and appointing 16 "engineers" for Hook and Ladder #1 were among the first steps in establishing the Weston Fire Department.[71] The fire truck was kept in a shed next to the Hastings cow barn. When the fire whistle blew, Thomas Coburn's heavy workhorses would be brought in from the fields and hitched to the fire truck.[72]

For 18 years, Francis Henry Hastings stored fire apparatus for the north side in a shed on his property. Finally, in 1908, the town built the Kendal Green Fire Station, an all-concrete, Classical-style building designed to be both functional and attractive.[73] The station was used only until 1917, when it was closed as a wartime economy measure.

Figure 10-33. This 1930 photograph shows the small Hastings Station in front of the organ factory. It was built in 1906 to replace an earlier unheated shelter.

Organs Built by Hook & Hastings Company

In its 108 years of operation, E. & G.G. Hook and Hook & Hastings produced an estimated 2,614 organs ranging in size from 8 to 80 feet and costing from $900 to $40,000 or more.[74] The company made 650 organs for churches and halls in Massachusetts, including instruments for Tremont Temple (1845, 1853, 1880); Berkeley Street Congregational (1861); West Church (1861); Church of the Immaculate Conception, Boston (1863); Mechanics Hall, Worcester (1864); Shawmut Congregational Church, Boston (1866); Cathedral of the Holy Cross, Boston (1875); Church of Immaculate Conception (reconstruction), Boston (1902); First Church of Christ, Scientist,

Figure 10-34. In its 108 years of operation in Boston and Weston, the Hook brothers and Hook and Hastings produced an estimated 2,614 organs ranging in size from 8 to 80 feet. Their works were known for superior craftsmanship and are considered among the finest examples of 19th- and early-20th-century organ building. (1893 photo, location unknown)

Entertainment

Celebrating the Completion of the 2000th Organ

built by

Hook-Hastings Co., Kendal Green, Mass.

Thursday, March Third, Nineteen Hundred Four.

Banquet, Hastings Hall, 6.30 P. M.

Organ Recital, Organ Factory, 7.30 P. M.

Admit Mrs. C. Fredrickson

Present this at the Door.

Figure 10-35. In 1904, when the 2,000th organ went to Washington, the occasion was observed by a recital and banquet.

Figure 10-36. When one of the great organs was completed, it was set up in the high-ceilinged "erecting room." As many as 300 employees and neighbors would enjoy an informal evening of singing and instrumental music. The organist in this photograph has been identified by members of the Organ Historical Society as Moritz Baumgarten, a German hired by Frank Hastings as head voicer about 1881. Under his influence, the voicing of Hook & Hastings organs became less bold and more mellow. The picture is thought to have been taken at the Weston factory before Baumgarten's departure in the early 1890s. After he left, the firm returned to its more traditional tonal roots.

Boston (1906, 1928); Perkins Institute, Watertown (1912); First Parish Unitarian, Dedham (1913); First Church of Christ, Scientist, Roxbury (1915); Central Congregational Church, Fall River (1916); and St. Paul's Cathedral, Boston (1921).[75] Where Hook & Hastings organs still remain, they are highly prized. For example, in raising funds to restore the 1863 organ at the Church of the Immaculate Conception in 1999, speakers called it "not just one of the finest 19th century organs in America, but perhaps the best 19th century organ in the world."[76]

In the Weston area, the company made organs for four churches in Concord (Unitarian church in 1871, Trinity Episcopal in 1923, St. Bernard's Roman Catholic in 1875, and the Orthodox Congregational in 1860), as well as the Unitarian church, Lincoln (1901); First Baptist and Trinity Episcopal, Newton Center (1901, 1915); First Unitarian, West Newton (1871, 1911), and many other Newton churches. They made organs for First Parish, Waltham (1867); First Trinitarian Congregational, Waltham (1870); St. Mary's Roman Catholic, Waltham (1900), and several other Waltham churches; First Parish Church, Weston (1887, 1917, and the Memorial Chapel of 1930); residence of Francis Henry Hastings, Weston (1905); Weston College chapel (1926); St. Peter's Church, Weston (1931); Wellesley College (1878); College of Music, Wellesley (1881); and Unitarian church, Wellesley Hills (1925).[77]

Francis Henry Hastings: "A Recognized Leader and Wise Counsellor"

In his history of the organ factory published in the 1983 *Weston Historical Society Bulletin,* Philip Coburn calls Francis Henry Hastings "a typical New Englander with strong puritanical ideas of the right."[78] He was a student of nature and fond of good books, especially books on history, art, and science. He enjoyed horseback riding and driving. His inventive talent earned him two patents, one in 1872 for improvement in the swells for pipe organs and another in 1897 for electro-pneumatic organ action. Hastings was a Republican and staunch Unitarian who supported First Parish Church and the American Unitarian Association. He was interested in Weston history and in 1894 compiled a history of the oldest houses for the Friendly Society. He arranged for about 20 of these houses to be photographed, and two decades later the pictures were used to illustrate Lamson's *History of the Town of Weston.*

Little is known of Hastings's first wife and the mother of his only child, Francis Warren Hastings (1862–1903). Warren worked with his father as an officer in the corporation. As his health grew steadily worse, he moved to Bermuda, where he became a permanent resident in 1895 and died of consump-

Figure 10-37. Anna Coburn Hastings (1853–1950) was photographed here with her niece Anna Hall (1877–1978), who lived with Mrs. Hastings after her husband died in 1916. Miss Hall stayed on at Seven Gables until her death at age 101.

tion in 1903. After his death, Arthur Leslie Coburn, who had joined the company in 1897 as secretary of the corporation and superintendent of the factory, was elected president. By that time, Coburn was also related to Hastings by marriage. In 1899 Francis Henry Hastings, then age 62, had married Coburn's sister, Anna, the schoolmistress at North Avenue School, who was 46.

On March 3, 1904, the company sponsored a banquet and organ recital at Hastings Hall to celebrate the completion of its 2,000th organ. Employees and their families, numbering about 150, were present by invitation. Newspapers described it as a happy gathering, where "the friendship that has long existed was manifested in many ways."[79]

In 1906, when Hastings was 70 years old, his employees gave him a party. About 300 friends and neighbors gathered at Seven Gables, which was "brilliantly lighted with Japanese lanterns festooned from tree to tree." Strauch's Waltham orchestra played on the piazza. Seventy-one employees signed an engraved testimonial praising his energy, perseverance, and able administration:

> Whereas, We recognize in you not only one whose powerful influence is of great gain to the community in which you live, but one whose name is recognized throughout the width and breadth of the land among musical people as the head of his profession—that of The Art of Organ Building—and rejoice greatly in the fact that you are . . . among us, a recognized leader and wise counsellor.[80]

Hook & Hastings Company: The Last Two Decades

Francis Henry Hastings died in 1916 at age 80. Management of Hook & Hastings passed to Arthur Coburn as president, Norman Jacobsen as vice president and supervising designer, and Alfred R. Pratt as secretary and superintendent, all associates of Hastings for decades. In the late 1920s, the company built its most famous modern instrument, the Rockefeller organ for the Riverside Church in New York City. It required one year to construct at the factory and nine months to install the 20 truckloads of parts. The organ contained 167 stops, 2,900 magnets, and 22,000 contacts; and the wires, if placed end to end, would extend a distance of more than 100 miles.[81] The following accolade was written by the organist and choir director after the job was completed in 1931:

> It has been four years now since we began to plan for the organs in the Riverside Church and now that the instruments are in active use, it is a pleasure to look back over the delightful association. In this age of mass production and a constantly increasing mechanization of life, it is encouraging to find at least one group of highly skilled artisans such as your company has, who put into their work the best that is in them, and who obviously regard the construction of an organ as a work of art and not merely a commercial job.[82]

The writer adds, "I hope that the Hook, Hastings Company will remain true to the artistic ideals which made the name famous in years past."

Although the Rockefeller organ marked a musical high point, the factory was nearing its end. "Talkies" replaced silent movies, eliminating the need for organ accompaniment. Radios and phonographs provided a new way to hear symphonic favorites. Municipal music programs were cut during the Depression and church budgets drastically reduced. Orders for residential organs declined. After A.L. Coburn died in 1931, the company continued for a few years under Alfred Pratt, but the business was clearly changing.

Anna Coburn Hastings has been quoted as saying, "The company motto was 'Quality First—and Always.' My husband always quoted quality. He never quoted price. Today organ makers are quoting price and I decided it was time to tear it down!"[83] Hook & Hastings closed its doors in 1935. In June 1936 a contract was signed with the Mystic Building

Figure 10-38. By the late 1890s, District School #4 was used for grades one to six. In 1900 teacher Lizzie Viles had an average attendance of 38 pupils. Beginning in 1902, sixth-graders were required to go to the central school, and by 1908, fifth-graders also. Many of the children had fathers who worked at the organ factory.

Wrecking Company of Chelsea to demolish the factory, lumber shed, tenement block on Viles Street, and railroad spur line. The buildings were taken down board by board and the lumber salvaged. The company was officially dissolved in April 1937. Hastings Hall survived until the mid-1940s, when it was damaged by fire and then torn down.

Many local residents recall the factory whistle, which blew every morning at seven o'clock, at noon and one o'clock to signal the beginning and end of the lunch break, and then at five o'clock at the end of the nine-hour workday. When the factory closed, everyone missed the whistle. The sound had marked time for the community—time for work, time for lunch, time for the children to come in from play. When the whistle stopped, it was the end of an era.

The Neighborhood: District School #4

Children of factory employees attended District School #4 on North Avenue, a frame one-room schoolhouse built in 1852. Teacher Anna Coburn guided her pupils with a firm hand and was an active member of a women's club that met at Hastings Hall. The 1890 *Boston Herald* article called Coburn "a young woman who more than any other except Mr. Hastings himself, exercises a moral influence in the community."[84] She retired from teaching in 1899 to marry Hastings.

The North Avenue School was part of what made Kendal Green a cohesive community. Older residents recall the separate entrances and cloakrooms for boys and girls, as well as the separate outhouses

School Reunion, Kendal Green, (Weston) Mass.

JUNE 24, 1893.

PROGRAMME.

2.00 to 3.30—Reception at the Schoolhouse by
Mrs. Maria A. (Warren) Pierce, Mrs. Mary J. (Hastings) Giddings, Miss Annie C. Coburn, Miss Alice Tucker, Mr. Alonza S. Fiske, Mr. F. H. Hastings, Mr. Arthur L. Coburn.

3.30 to 5.00—Social Intercourse, Rambles, Games, Etc.,
At the Ball Ground, at the Tennis Court, at the Residence of Mr. F. H. Hastings, and in the woods and fields; and at Hastings Hall.

5.00 to 6.00—Supper at the Large Tent.

6.00 to 6.30—Brief Exercises at the Large Tent.
1.—A History of the Old School, prepared by Miss Elizabeth S. Gowing and Miss Mary Frances Pierce; read by Arthur L. Coburn.
2.—Short Addresses by Rev. C. F. Russell and others.
3.—Poem, Whittier's "Reunion," read by Wm. H. Coburn.
4.—"Auld Lang Syne."—All Singing.

Figure 10-39. Francis Henry Hastings was the driving force behind major community social events including the 1893 reunion at the North Avenue School. For the reception, the little schoolhouse was handsomely decorated with ferns and flowers.

Figure 10-40. Former students and teachers gathered on Francis Henry Hastings's front lawn and later enjoyed a catered supper served under a large tent next to the Hastings stable. Notice the badminton net.

in back, with a fence between them. Flushing toilets came to the school and to area houses only after 1922, when town water pipes were installed along North Avenue. The schoolhouse was heated by a wood-burning stove.

Hastings was the moving spirit behind the 1893 reunion at the Old North School. Visitors played badminton on his lawn and assembled in front of the schoolhouse for group photos. One reporter wrote that, to out-of-towners, "the modern Kendal Green with its organ factory, its pretty cottages and its handsome mansion was quite a revelation."[85] Supper, served in the large tent erected by Hastings, was catered by Dill of Waltham, which reported that fully 500 were seated. Postprandial exercises included "an exceedingly interesting historical sketch of the school," followed by dancing.

The North Avenue School continued in use until the end of the 1931–32 school year, more than 30 years after most of Weston's one-room schoolhouses had been abandoned in favor of centralized schools.[86] It was demolished in the 1940s.

Figure 10-41. Schoolmates posed for group photographs at the 1893 North Avenue School reunion.

The Neighborhood: Weston United Methodist Church

The Methodist church on North Avenue was the house of worship for many organ factory employees and an important social center for the Kendal Green community. Methodism in Weston had its beginnings in 1789, when farmer Abraham Bemis was inspired by one of the early Methodist circuit riders who was speaking at a produce market.[87] The first formal Methodist worship service in Weston was held in August 1790. The open-air meeting took place near the corner of Conant Road and North Avenue, a central location easily accessible from surrounding towns. The preacher stood on a small hill and spoke to a reported crowd of 200 who gathered to listen. This circuit rider is thought to have been Rev. John Hill, who became the first pastor when the congregation was organized in 1794.

Figure 10-42. Dedicated in January 1901, the new Methodist church building was Colonial Revival in style and measured just 50 by 35 feet, with a vestry beneath. The church had 88 members. (1911 photo)

Figure 10-43. Not until 1917 was the Methodist church able to purchase this five-year-old, two-manual pipe organ, which had belonged to a wealthy Cambridge resident.

The Weston church was one of the oldest Methodist churches in New England.[88] The original Methodist society consisted of a dozen members, seven of whom bore the last name Bemis. Eight were women. The first trustees were Abraham Bemis, Habakkuk Stearns, Jonas Bemis, John Viles, and Daniel Stratton. The early members had to support the church and pay taxes to support the town church as well. For decades, Methodists joined Baptists in protesting what they considered an illegal assessment.

The first Methodist meetinghouse, built in 1797, was a modest structure, unpainted and unplastered, with neither pulpit nor pews.[89] There was no stove to warm the devout worshipers in winter. In 1828 the congregation purchased the present lot from Nathan Fiske and built a white clapboard church of simple Gothic design. The church prospered in the next decades, founding a Sabbath school in 1831 and the Methodist Female Benevolent Society in 1838.

As a policy of the denomination, pastors were limited to two years at the same church. In its first hundred years, the parish had 107 preachers. The first full-time pastor was Amos Binney, who served from 1833 to 1834 for a first-year salary of $143. In 1850 the church built a parsonage on land also purchased from the Fiske family.

By 1881, church ranks had dwindled as members died or moved away. The building of the organ factory brought new members and new vitality. The church even received the gift of a Hook & Hastings organ.[90] But on the last night of the century, December 31, 1899, the 1828 building was destroyed by fire, along with the organ, which was not insured. It was the darkest hour in the church's history. With only $2,000 in insurance and few financial resources, the trustees nevertheless voted to begin raising money to rebuild. Religious services were held at Hastings Hall until a new white Colonial Revival church, with a tall steeple, was completed in January 1901 from designs by architect George E. Strout.[91] In 1907, six maple trees were planted on the grounds and named in honor of six men who had labored to keep the church active and alive: John Tasker, Rev. John S. Day, Rev. J. Alfonse Day, Albert Washburn, George Harrington, and T.C. Richardson. Alfonse Day was pastor from 1901 to 1907, up to that time the longest tenure of any pastor in the church's history.

In 1917 the congregation was finally able to replace the organ with a five-year-old Hook & Hastings model. The 1901 church stood for 70 years, until its demolition in 1971 to make way for a new building of contemporary design.

Summer Residents: The Brown Estate

Late-19th-century photographs show the organ factory set within a landscape of rolling hills and open fields divided by stone walls. Stately elms lined North Avenue, but elsewhere most of the trees had been cut down, opening up picturesque vistas in all directions. Beginning in the early 19th century, this landscape attracted vacationers and summer residents to Kendal Green.[92]

Figure 10-44. This 1890s photograph of Weston United Methodist Church members on the steps of the 1828 church on North Avenue includes many of those who worked hard to rebuild the church after the disastrous fire. Top row: Mary Washburn, Alisha Harding, Rachel Washburn, Edith Whitney Flint, Sadie Rand Abercrombie, Howard Richardson, Effie Richardson, Eliza Whitney, Emma Viles Stedman, and George Rand. Bottom row: Mabel Washburn, Arthur Wheeler, Herbert Lewis, Emma Wheeler, Harry Harding, T. Colburn Richardson, and Louis Whitney.

Figure 10-45. Elms lined North Avenue at the turn of the century. The pastoral landscape attracted summer visitors, who rented houses or stayed at the Drabbington Lodge. This view is looking east from the intersection of Church Street.

In the late 1870s, Boston wool merchant Edward J. Brown and his wife, Mary, began purchasing land on the south side of North Avenue for a country home. The Browns' 60-acre estate extended to the railroad tracks and Waltham town line and included the former Hobbs tanyard and part of the pond across the street. Brown built a large clapboard Italianate house and laid out private roads through the woods and fields where the family could take guests on carriage rides without being inconvenienced by traffic.[93] Although the Browns returned to Cambridge each winter, local residents used "Brown's Pond" for skating and cutting ice.

Henry A. Gowing (1834–1894) was a prosperous Boston shirt manufacturer who used his family homestead on North Avenue as a summer residence.[94] In the late 1880s, he held a family reunion attended by 200 Gowing descendants, who wandered the extensive grounds with its "attractive walks, nooks, arbors [and] beds of flowers" and enjoyed an extended view of the countryside from an observatory on a nearby hill. After a dinner catered by Dill of Waltham, guests gathered in the "tastefully decorated" barn, amid flags and pine boughs, where Gowing gave a sketch of the family genealogy and one of the young girls read an original poem, "Ye olden time."[95]

Figure 10-46. The Gowing farmhouse on North Avenue was purchased in 1897 by George and Sarah Thurston, who opened the Drabbington Lodge. This photograph was taken in 1898, the year the house and barn burned to the ground.

Drabbington Lodge

In the spring of 1897, George and Sarah Thurston purchased the Gowing property and opened a boardinghouse for about a dozen guests. After two summers they made plans to enlarge and remodel the farmhouse for 40 guests, but a major fire destroyed both house and barn in November 1898.[96]

The Thurstons quickly rebuilt. Their hostelry, the Drabbington Lodge, was named after Sarah's birthplace in England.[97] The Shingle-style design was the work of Boston architect Frank Weston.[98] A newspaper article at the time of the opening in 1899 called it "one of the best of suburban hotels."[99] For city dwellers who could not afford their own country place, the lodge offered the perfect summer escape. The reception hall was "large and inviting," with fireplace and cushioned window seats. At one end was a writing room and a large parlor with mahogany and wicker furniture, a Hallet and Davis grand piano, and Japanese and Dresden urns. There was "artificial light at night," thanks to the recent availability of electrical service.

The dining room seated 60. Next to the billiard room was a smoking room furnished in green and red with mahogany furniture and "hair-seated chairs." The 32 sleeping rooms on the second and third floors were "beautifully furnished, according to the price paid for their occupancy. Iron and brass bedsteads are numerous . . . every sleeping-room has

Figure 10-47. After the fire, the Thurstons built this Shingle-style hotel, which was painted a wood-brown color with white trim and a green roof. Three years after it opened, the press reported, "Drabbington Lodge is more popular than ever this season. There is a constant stream of arrivals and departures, and the guests are among the best society." The building is now a retirement home at 135 North Avenue.

Figure 10-48. The Drabbington Lodge was probably the first major building in Weston to be wired for electricity, which was introduced into Weston about 1897.

a mantel and at least one closet. The floors are all of hardwood, and three or more rugs adorn the floor of every room."[100] New hair mattresses and feather pillows ensured sleeping comfort, and guests enjoyed the luxury of two bathrooms per floor. Servants' rooms were in the basement, along with the kitchen, vegetable cellar, and laundry.

Behind the lodge was a tennis court and a seven-hole golf course. A landscaped footpath originally led west to the summit of a rocky knoll, where an observatory offered views of the countryside. In 1900 the Thurstons built a stable across the street with a 50-foot-long carriage room and space for 18 horses.[101] In 1901–02, they built a "cottage" on the knoll, designed by architect George Strout.[102] Newspaper articles said that Mrs. Thurston was "strongly attached to this estate, and is building this house for her home"; but it was rented when completed and for many summers thereafter. To provide more space and further enhance the resort atmosphere, Strout designed a log "bungalow" behind the cottage in 1904, labeled on postcards as the Drabbington Annex.[103] At the height of the season, all three buildings were "constantly filled to overflowing."

The location of the Drabbington Lodge combined all the advantages of the country within easy commuting distance of the city. The lodge was "delightfully located on high land, where cool breezes blow in the summer and a charming view may be had all the year around." There was "every opportunity . . . for golf, tennis, croquet and other amusements." One advertisement describes it as "a 7-Gabled English Inn on estate of 27 acres, largely devoted to Golf, Home Cuisine, open wood fires, hot-water heat, garage, George A. Thurston Estate."[104]

The much lauded garden just west of the bungalow added to the picturesque quality of the resort, as indicated in this 1908 account:

Figure 10-49. The Cottage at 153 North Avenue was built in 1902 by the Thurstons, who often rented it to one family for the summer. (2001 photo)

> Mrs. Thurston has probably the most beautiful flower garden in Weston. . . . The grounds are radiant with the blooms of hundreds upon hundreds of flowers among which are phloxes in greatest variety of coloring, hydrangeas, gladioli, dahlias, golden glow and hollyhocks. It is a delightful sight and adds much to the attractiveness of grounds already charming.[105]

A 1913 newspaper columnist wrote that "next to his wife and baby Landlord Thurston's affections are centered on his beautiful garden. . . . Roses, roses and more roses in almost endless profusion."[106]

Newspaper clippings from the turn of the century give the names of families arriving each week from as far away as Indiana, Ohio, Kansas, and Minnesota, with children, nurses, chauffeurs, and governesses, for indefinite stays. Many "permanent guests" returned season after season and regarded the lodge as a second home.[107]

In *Once Upon a Pung*, B.H. Dickson III describes "well-to-do people [who] would spend several weeks there rocking on the porch, playing golf, or walking

Figure 10-50. The Thurston Bungalow at 147 North Avenue was built in 1904 as an annex to Drabbington Lodge. Early-20th-century bungalows came in all sizes, with details inspired by exotic architecture from the Japanese teahouse to the Swiss chalet. The Thurstons used the word bungalow *to suggest a retreat or summer house in the Adirondack rustic tradition. It was built of round logs that were probably early telephone poles, notched at the corners.*

along the shaded lanes in the neighborhood."[108] The Kendal Green column of the *Waltham Free Press* in 1898 tells how Mrs. Thurston's boarders and three dogs set out on a coon hunt and returned for a midnight supper.[109] Other articles describe a "hurdy-gurdy" party, Halloween festivities, book contests, and whist and progressive euchre card games. The ladies of the lodge had dancing parties on the spacious piazzas and formed a Thursday-morning circle that sponsored lectures and literary reviews by guests, followed by sewing of sheets and diapers for the Waltham Baby Hospital. Some years, Drabbington Lodge was open during the winter, with coasting, snowshoeing, and sledding as favorite activities. On winter evenings, guests gathered in front of the fire for games and storytelling.

The Thurstons celebrated their 25th wedding anniversary at the bungalow in 1906, attended by many of Weston's best-known residents. The rest of the town was provided with a complete list of "beautiful and valuable gifts" and who gave them, printed in the newspaper for all to evaluate.[110] When she died in 1910, Sarah Thurston was described as "a woman not only of rare executive ability but of a most kindly and sympathetic nature. Under exceedingly efficient management, the Lodge has become one of the most favorably known of suburban family hotels."[111]

A year later George, who was then 58, married Lenore Allen, a 30-year-old nurse originally from Nova Scotia. The couple had one child. The lodge was leased in 1920 to a "well-known hotel man" who kept it open in winter. Lenore Thurston remained involved in the management of the Drabbington Inn from the time of her husband's death in 1923 until about 1935, when it was leased to the Posse-Nissen School, also referred to as the Posse Institute. This girls college of physical education added a 45-foot by 100-foot portable wooden gymnasium to the existing recreational facilities.[112] About 75 students lived in the former lodge at least until 1940.[113] Some years later it was leased to the Sargent College of Physical Education at Boston University for use as a dormitory. In the mid-1950s, the facility operated as the Weston Inn. It was subsequently readapted as a retirement home.

Brodrick's Store

The post office and general store that General Marshall helped to establish in 1886 soon became an integral part of the Kendal Green neighborhood. Alfred Leslie Cutting, son of George Warren Cutting Jr., was running the store in 1888 and was appointed postmaster at Kendal Green in 1889, when he was just 21.[114] The *Waltham Daily Free Press* occasionally noted the bargains available at A.L. Cutting's in short promotions inserted between local

Figure 10-51. Drabbington Lodge closed during the Depression and the building was leased to the Posse-Nissen School, where girls were trained in physical education. This photograph of a May Day celebration was probably taken in the late 1930s.

Figure 10-52. George Warren Brodrick took over the Kendal Green general store and post office in 1899 and ran it for half a century. By 1897 the town had installed a scale for weighing coal and farm produce (right foreground), and by the mid-1920s Brodrick's had a gasoline pump.

Figure 10-53. Members of the Hersum family owned 99 North Avenue, next to Brodrick's store, for more than a century. This photograph was taken in 1898 by the Howes brothers, who were itinerant photographers. Notice the fashionable watermelon-shaped sleeves on the dress at right.

news items—for example, "Have you seen those 10 cent [per pound] raisins at A.L. Cutting's, Kendal Green."[115] In 1897 the town installed a scale out front for weighing coal and farm produce. After a few years on the north side, Cutting joined his father and brother-in-law in managing the family store in Weston center.

In March 1899, the *Waltham Daily Free Press* reported that George Warren Brodrick (1872–1952), the new proprietor of the grocery store, "is surprising everybody by his display of goods."[116] By 1901, the store was wired for electric lights and had a soda fountain. Brodrick was a stocky man who paid close attention to business. He sold grocery staples, newspapers, hardware, harnesses, a limited supply of dry goods, fishing equipment, lard, sour pickles from the barrel, doughnuts, penny candy, and five-cent bottles of cream soda, birch and root beer, and orange crush. Groceries could be ordered on the telephone for delivery. He carried seasonal items. For example, in December 1903, the newspaper reported that he "has just received a full line of hockey sticks, puts [sic] and balls, anticipating a long hockey and polo season."[117]

Neighbors came to the post office for their mail and lingered to exchange gossip or debate politics. In 1930 a "tea room" was added where hungry customers could buy simple fare like soup, beef stew, sandwiches, and ice cream. By the mid-1920s, Brodrick's had a gasoline pump. The post office closed in 1943 and the store by 1946.

The Garfield and Foote Families

Farther along North Avenue, in the area of the present convenience store and service station, the Garfield family ran a blacksmith shop and cider mill for much of the 19th century. George W. Garfield settled on North Avenue in 1821 on land purchased from the Fiske family. He built a large barn on the south side of the street across from his house. An undershot waterwheel on the lower level was powered by Stony Brook and used to turn the presses for

Figure 10-54. George Garfield's barn and cider mill were across from his house. The cider press had an undershot wheel powered by the waters of Stony Brook. Garfield was a blacksmith and one son branched out into carriage making. (1889 photo)

making cider. His three sons carried on the businesses. George (1820–1905) was a wheelwright; Hiram (1829–1889), a blacksmith; and Daniel (1833–1905), a carriage maker, cider and vinegar manufacturer, and blacksmith.[118]

In 1901 the property was purchased by William Foote and two years later by his brother James Thomas Foote (1869–1953), who continued the Garfield operations.[119] The Footes came from a Nova Scotia family of eight brothers. The blacksmith shop was a busy place in its day. Locals recall how the hired man on Thomas Coburn's farm would leave horses to be shod. When Foote was finished, he would give the horses a clap on the rump and they would trot a mile back down the road to the Coburn barn.[120]

Foote expanded the Garfield cider business, earn-

Figure 10-55. William Foote bought the blacksmith shop from the Garfield family in 1901 and sold it to his brother James in 1903. Pictured, from left: unknown man, Jerry Hennessy (a workman on Thomas Coburn's farm), William Foote, and James T. Foote with horse.

Figure 10-56. The family of James T. Foote: Earle, James (father), Elsie Ann, Gladys, Roy, Wiley, Maria (mother), and Harold.

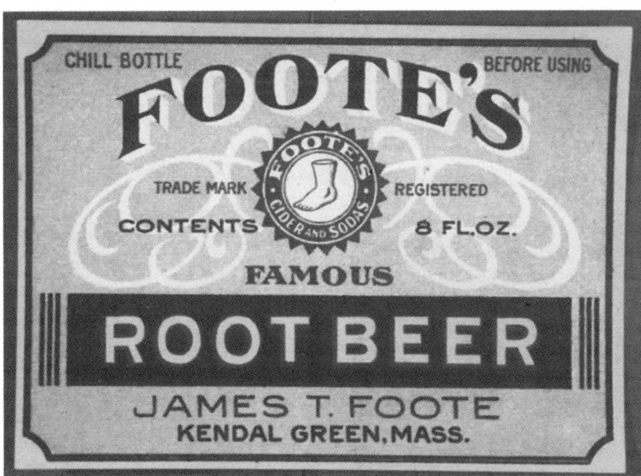

Figure 10-57. James T. Foote made his own soft drinks. His popular cider had a 20% alcohol content.

Figure 10-58. When automobiles made their appearance, James Foote kept up with the times. He tore down the blacksmith shop around 1915 and built a general store and cider mill nearer the street. He installed the first gasoline pump in Weston, according to his daughter Elsie. She remembers turning the handle to pump one, two, three, or five gallons for a customer. The house at left was built by James Foote in 1903.

ing the nickname "the Cider King." In December 1904 the newspaper reported that "Mr. Foote's cider has a great reputation" and he had received an order for 1,000 barrels.[121] One of the reasons for its popularity may have been the 20 percent alcohol content.[122]

With the advent of the automobile age, Foote tore down the blacksmith shop and built a small general store; a modern, well-equipped cider mill; and a service station with a Socony gasoline pump.[123] He began making his own ice cream and soft drinks including ginger ale, sarsaparilla, and orangeade. One of Foote's creations, called Wello—the Health Drink of America, tasted something like root beer.[124] He had a mill for making peanut butter. The combination of automobile service, grocery staples, and homemade ice cream and soda proved to be a great success, attracting locals, tourists, and residents of

THE "THINKING MAN" GOES TO

FOOTE BROS.

ICE CREAM — GROCERIES

SOFT DRINKS

292 NORTH AVENUE — OPEN YEAR ROUND

HOT DOGS — HAMBURGERS

Figures 10-59 and 10-60. Harold "Big Foote" (at right) and Earle "Little Foote" built their own store beside their father's cider mill and sold finger food, coffee, tea, ice cream, and groceries. Foote Brothers served as a neighborhood meeting place. (1967 photo, above, and 1961 Weston High School yearbook advertisement, at right)

nearby towns.[125] In 1915, the *Waltham Free Press* noted, "The endless string of high class automobiles coming and going at the mill is high testimony to the class of goods he sells."[126]

For years Foote battled with Weston selectmen over Sunday sales. Arguing that sweet cider should be drunk within 24 hours of its manufacture, Foote testified in 1915 before the state legislature in support of a bill making it lawful to sell sweet cider on Sunday.[127] In a letter to the editor in 1919, Foote wrote: "The Big Fellows of Weston can play golf or do anything they wish on Sunday, but if I sell soft drinks or Ice Cream or fruit they Summons [sic] me to Court."[128] After Chief McAuliffe issued a stop order in 1920, the Weston newspaper columnist wrote: "The thirsty autoist can no longer break the drought of the dusty Sunday trip by a gallon of Foote's popular beverage," and added the following commentary on Sunday customs:

> The effect of the order will be not only to deprive the farmers of their best day in the week but to disappoint hundreds of Waltham people who make a practice of planning their Sunday auto trip through Weston carrying a jug under the seat.[129]

After World War II, Foote's sons Harold and Earle built a grocery and ice-cream store called Foote Brothers. The store served for years as a meeting place for neighbors and North Avenue commuters, who gathered at the counter for coffee every morning at 10 o'clock.

The Tyler, Coburn, Miller, Viles, and Dean Farms

The Kendal Green area probably had more cows per square mile than any other part of town. Through the 1950s, farmers planted fields of corn to send to market, keeping the stalks to feed their herds.

Farmer and dairyman Sidney E. Tyler settled in the 1870s at the north end of Lexington Street, where he purchased 92 acres that had belonged to John Warren Cutting.[130] In 1904, the Kendal Green column in the *Waltham Daily Free Press Tribune* reported that Sydney had 10 acres in sweet corn and "has been long known in the Boston market for this crop." That year he harvested 1,500 bushels "more than a week ahead of anybody in this section" and was dubbed the Corn King.[131] Sidney's son Herbert kept about a dozen cows, raised chickens, maintained an apple orchard, and grew vegetables, which he sold at market or from a stand in front of the house. "Bert" Tyler served for 36 years as a Weston selectman and spokesman for the farmers.

In 1881, Edward Coburn settled his son Thomas on a 70-acre working dairy farm on North Avenue purchased from Kendall H. Stone. The property included the house at 163 North Avenue and a

Figure 10-61. Four generations of Coburns—Hannah Bennett Coburn (Mrs. Edward), Thomas, Edward, and Elizabeth—are shown in this picture, probably taken about 1917, the year Hannah Coburn died just short of age 87.

Figure 10-62. This view looking northwest on North Avenue shows the Whitney Tavern and part of the Thomas Coburn barn (since demolished). The land on the left side of the street was all Coburn cornfields until after World War II. In the distance is the Francis Henry Hastings house.

Figure 10-63. No. 161–163 North Avenue was built by farmer Converse Bigelow in the 1820s and became the home of newlyweds Thomas and Harriet Sherman Coburn in 1881. They added the ell at the back and Thomas took over the working dairy farm. He kept 25 to 30 cows in the main barn and five or six horses in the west wing. Milk was stored in the small shed attached to the east end of the barn. The house is still owned by his grandson and the stone wall and stone piers still remain. (1898 Howes brothers photo)

Figure 10-64. The Whitney Tavern (171 North Avenue) is traditionally dated to 1707 and retains its original saltbox form. A brief caption in Lamson's history says that Mr. Whitney once kept the famous Punch Bowl tavern in Brookline. The young man is Ed Stone. The Stone family lived next door and ran the farm later taken over by Thomas Coburn. The former tavern was used to house Coburn's farmhands. (1880s photo)

Figure 10-65. Mildred Elizabeth Coburn [West] (1895–1986) was the youngest child and only daughter of Thomas Coburn. The doll was a gift from her aunt Florence M. Coburn.

monumental barn with space for more than 30 cows and five or six horses. The old Whitney Tavern next door housed the hired men. Coburn's operation was large enough to support three or four regular employees. Thomas advertised in Weston directories as a contractor who could furnish teams and men at short notice and take care of cesspool cleaning. He was also a road commissioner for nearly a quarter of a century. When Thomas died in 1916, the farm was taken over by his second son, Harold, who ran it for 30 years. When Harold retired after World War II, the farm was leased and continued in agricultural use until a few years after his death in 1953.

Darius B. Vittum, a farmer and milk dealer, took over the farmstead of his father-in-law, M.J. Cutting. The former Warren property was still in the original family, having passed by marriage from Warren to Cutting to Vittum. The extent of his operation is indicated by the newspaper report of a disastrous fire that destroyed his barn in September 1897.[132] Two driving horses, two horses used on the milk route, and four workhorses all perished, together with seven cows, one of which was a valuable Holstein. Six cows were saved. The annual production of the family cider mill on Hobbs Brook had to be delayed.

The Viles family settled in Weston about 1790 at the corner of Conant Road and Viles Street in a house that burned in 1908. When Jesse Sumner Viles (1819–1906) married in 1847, his father gave him a piece of land on Conant Road where he and his wife, Lany Ann, built a house and raised a family of nine.[133]

Their daughter Elizabeth, or Lizzie, was the mainstay of the family. She began teaching at District School #5 on South Avenue immediately after graduation from Weston High School. Because of the distance from home, she boarded with Abijah Coburn during the week. When Anna Coburn retired to marry Francis Henry Hastings, Lizzie Viles took over the North Avenue School and was able to live at home. At her retirement reception, former pupils came from distant states to celebrate her "long years of loving patience" as an elementary school teacher from 1872 to 1919. Among the six pages of tributes in the 1919 *Town Report* is this quote from Superintendent Eaton: "New England has put her stamp upon the nation through such characters as yours."[134]

The sixth child of Jesse Sumner and Lany Ann Viles, Henry, decided early to become a milkman. He built his own house on Conant Road in 1895, along with a large dairy barn and milk house for processing.[135] He produced his own milk and paid other Weston farmers for theirs, which he delivered door to door in Waltham for 25 years. Henry hired as many as five men, some of whom lived in the two-family house just up the street. Viles continued in the dairy business until the 1940s. His son J. Sumner Viles became Weston's chief of police.[136]

Samuel Philip Miller (c. 1882–1956), a native of Prince Edward Island, came to Weston in the early 20th century and worked as a farmer on North Avenue. By about 1917, he had enough money to buy a small lot and build his own house. In 1921 he purchased most of the Brown property from Edward Brown's two unmarried children, Frederic and Alice. Alice was a physical education teacher who stayed on in the family home. By 1928, Miller had 22 dairy cows. His large cow barn, located opposite the end of Hobbs Brook Road, was a fixture on the landscape until it burned in 1963. Coburn, Tyler, and Miller all sold milk to H.L. Stone, a large Waltham dairy that did the pasteurizing and bottling.

In 1922, the town sold the 80-acre poor farm on Conant Road to Arthur Woodward, who was one of the Overseers of the Poor. Three years later, Woodward sold the 60 acres on the west side of Conant Road to Louis Dean.[137] Dean, who also operated the Dean Dairy on Boston Post Road, raised heifers here. A large barn was leveled in an incendiary fire of

Figure 10-66. This barn was probably built by the Brown family. It was located on what is now town conservation land on North Avenue approximately opposite Hobbs Brook Road. Farmer Samuel Philip Miller kept dairy cows here until the 1950s. The barn burned down in 1963.

1929, "largely remembered for the difficulties encountered with the 500 odd pigs that were kept in and about the barn."[138]

Development of the Fiske Homestead: Charles Cahill and Cedar Hill Farm

When Nathan Sewall Fiske died in 1912, the Fiske homestead with 250 acres was sold to William F. Schrafft, whose family was in the candy and restaurant business in Boston.[139] Schrafft evidently fancied the life of a gentleman farmer and made improvements including building new barns. His wife, on the other hand, didn't like the country and wouldn't move to Weston. In January 1923, Schrafft sold the farm to Charles J.R. Cahill and Joseph H. Beale, who established the largest dairy farm in Weston.[140]

Charles John Read Cahill (1869–1945) was born in Kings County, Nova Scotia, and emigrated to the United States in 1885 at age 16. He married another Nova Scotian, Lois Bennett, in 1890. A few years later, he secured a position as manager of the Cedar Hill Farm in Waltham, to which he gave his full energy and attention for 29 years. After years of working for others, Cahill formed an association with Joseph F. Beale, a professor at Harvard University. Together they purchased the Schrafft property in Weston and Cedar Hill Farm in Waltham, under which name their company was incorporated.

Cahill was treasurer and manager of the Weston property, which he developed as "one of the most up-to-date dairy farms in this section of the country," according to a biographical sketch in *Middlesex County and Its People.*[141] Tax records show that by 1928 Cahill had 102 cows and 40 yearlings. The modern cement cow barn had feeding racks for each cow, with the cow's name above. A second barn housed the two bulls and was used for hay storage. The third barn, known as the milk barn, was used for milking, pasteurizing. and bottling. Cows were bathed twice a day before being milked, and the inside of the milk barn was cleaned and whitewashed every week. An early advertisement announced "Two Grades of Clean Milk from Clean Cows," at prices ranging from 18 cents for "clean raw milk" to 26 cents a quart for "certified."[142]

The Cahills built a house on the hill overlooking the farm. Their four children, John, Reginald, Paul, and Charles, were young adults when the family moved to Weston in the 1920s. Paul and his new bride, Bernice, lived in the old Alonzo Fiske house, where Bernice cooked for the farmworkers who boarded there. In 1927 Cahill built a sales stand and luncheonette serving hamburgers, hot dogs, homemade chicken pies, and homemade ice cream.[143] Within the enclosed porch, customers could sit at small tables lighted with lamps made from Cedar Hill cream bottles.

Cedar Hill Farm after World War II: The Dairy Bar and Techbuilt

Despite Cahill's experience and hard work, the Waltham Savings Bank foreclosed on Cedar Hill Farm in 1941. Cahill's financial problems stemmed in part from the Depression. Although many of his

Figure 10-67. Cedar Hill Farm, established in 1923 by Charles J.R. Cahill, was one of the largest dairy farms in Weston. This photograph shows the complex of barns, which housed more than 100 cows, plus pasteurizing and bottling operations.

Figure 10-68. Charles J.R. Cahill (1869–1945) managed Cedar Hill Farm in Waltham for 29 years before starting a second dairy of the same name on North Avenue in Weston. (1930 photo wth his wife, Lois)

customers could not pay their bills, Cahill kept delivering milk because he felt their children needed it.[144] After the war, the property was sold to Kendal Green Realty Trust, which kept the 250-acre farm complex intact. They rented the barns to Watertown Dairy, which kept cows there until the end of the decade.[145] The trust rented the old Cahill dairy bar to Aimo Teittinen and Wallace "Pop" Sawyer, two teachers at Weston High School, who opened Cedar Hill Dairy Bar in the summer of 1946. Although the area was zoned residential, the business was allowed to operate because the use predated local zoning regulations. Teittinen and Sawyer sold hard ice cream for a nickel a cone, as well as hot dogs, hamburgers, cigarettes, and, in later years, pizza.

On October 22, 1949, less than a week after the last 40 head of dairy cattle were removed from the farm, the abandoned buildings burned to the ground in a spectacular 3:30 A.M. fire reportedly set by a disgruntled ex-employee.[146] Eyewitnesses reported flames shooting more than 100 feet in the air. "Adding to the visual effect," according to one newspaper account, "was the loud roar of the flames as they devoured the familiar Weston landmark."[147] Damage was estimated at $25,000.

Kendal Green Realty Trust held the land until November 1954, when they sold it to Techbuilt Inc., a Cambridge corporation.[148] The company designed modern-style structures based on the Techbuilt Idea, described in company literature as "a design for living" that "frees the family from the confines of space designed for the statistically *average* family and affords instead an opportunity to enjoy an expression of individual living requirements."[149]

The prototype Techbuilt house, built in 1953, reflected a decade of concentrated work and experimentation by Carl Koch, one of the leading modern architects of the postwar period. Koch received his architectural degree from Harvard and set up an office practice in 1939. His interest in new housing types led to his work from 1946 to 1949 on the Acorn House, a factory-fabricated home delivered to the site from the company in Concord, Massachusetts.

Figure 10-69. Twins Dean and David Cahill, grandsons of Charles Cahill, were born about 1937. Behind the carriage is the original Cedar Hill Farm sales stand and luncheonette, since remodeled and now known as the Dairy Joy.

Figure 10-70. Weston High School teachers Aimo Teittinen and Wallace Sawyer operated Cedar Hill Dairy Bar from 1946 to the early 1960s.

Beginning in 1952, he designed a series of low-cost, semi-factory-built, one- and two-story house plans for Techbuilt Inc.

Techbuilt houses were developed with a system of modular components that could be interchanged to provide design flexibility. Because the weight of the structure was borne by the outside walls, beams, and columns, the space inside could be divided to suit the needs of each family. Houses were often split level, with wide expanses of glass.

In late 1954, the Techbuilt corporation laid out 40 lots along North Avenue, the lower end of Cahill Road, (now King's Grant Road), and Spruce Hill Road. The first Techbuilt homes were constructed between 1955 and 1957. Because of their nontraditional design and modular construction, many Weston residents opposed the development. A group of local investors formed the Weston Land Company and bought the land in 1958. They gradually subdivided it into more than 100 lots on King's Grant, Myles Standish, Bradford, Indian Hill, Hancock, and Bay State Roads. Buyers purchased the land and hired their own architects or builders.[150]

Techbuilt continued to build modern modular houses in Weston, although prospective buyers had to find their own lots. In the late 1960s, Techbuilt maintained a district manager in a model home on Hobbs Brook Road just off North Avenue.[151] Customers could choose from a variety of standard house plans at a price that included the prefabricated components as well as materials and labor supplied by a local franchised builder. The 40 models listed in a company letter of 1968 ranged from the Montauk (576 square feet, $10,900 approximate cost) to the Marblehead (3,552 square feet, $57,000).

Aimo Teittinen and Wallace Sawyer purchased the Cedar Hill Dairy Bar and demolished the dilapidated Fiske farmhouse. In the early 1960s, when Sawyer became involved in Sputnik-inspired summer science programs and Teittinen became principal of the new junior high school, the partners sold to the Dennis Maxwell family. The Maxwells added French fries, onion rings, and fried clams to the menu and have operated the Dairy Joy ever since.

The Dwight Estate and Trustees of Trapelo

In 1898, Theodore and Sally Dwight bought 56 acres and developed a small country estate on the east side of Lexington Street where the Cambridge School is today.[152] This land had once been part of the Whitney Farm and included a Colonial house set close to the road, later known as the White farmhouse. Theodore Frelinghuysen Dwight (b. 1846) came to Boston as librarian of Boston Public Library in 1892 but stepped down after only a few years because of ill health.[153] He was quickly enlisted as a member of the building committee for the new Weston library. A letter written to Selectman Francis Blake in 1899

Figure 10-71. The Cedar Hill Farm property was sold in 1954 to Techbuilt Inc., a Cambridge corporation that designed nontraditional houses in modular units. The first Techbuilt houses in Weston were on Spruce Hill Road and the lower end of Kings Grant Road.

bears the letterhead "Stone House, Kendal Green." [154] When the Dwight family moved to Switzerland in the early 20th century, Stone House was rented.

In 1915 Sally Dwight sold the property to Austin and Amelia White, who called it The Cedars and used it in summer.[155] White was treasurer of Shawmut Mining Company. The stone mansion was completely gutted by fire in 1918.[156] A second fire in November 1920 destroyed two barns and damaged the early farmhouse. In 1927 Amelia White sold the 56 acres to Fiske Warren and M. Phillips Mason, Trustees of the Georgian Trust.[157] She sold them an additional 150 acres on both sides of Lexington Street just north of North Avenue that had once been part of the Warren Farm. The combined landholding of more than 200 acres was in turn transferred to Francis Goodale and John Robert Nichols, Trustees of Trapelo.[158]

In 1931, the Trustees of Trapelo sold about 150 acres to the Cambridge School Inc., with restrictions that it could be used only for educational, religious, or charitable purposes. The school kept part of the land for a new high school campus, divided off house lots along Georgian and Fairhope Roads, and kept Bear Hill in Waltham, which remained undeveloped until recent years. The Trustees of Trapelo kept a second parcel of 54 acres, which they leased to the Trapelo Golf Club for a term of 20 years beginning in 1931. The club built a clubhouse at the northeast corner of North Avenue and Lexington Streets and a nine-hole "semi-public" golf course open to both members and outsiders.[159]

Cambridge School of Weston

The history of the Cambridge School goes back to 1886, when Arthur and Stella Gilman founded the Cambridge School for Girls, a traditional college preparatory school. By 1929, enrollment had declined and the future of the school was in jeopardy. With the decision of the board to appoint John R.P. French as headmaster and to create a new upper school in Weston, the school was essentially refounded as a distinctly different institution, one that embraced the philosophy of the Progressive Education Movement.

The progressive philosophy was eloquently expressed by French in this statement of 1931:

> The progressive school teaches the child to think for himself instead of passively accepting stereotyped ideas. It keeps always in mind the fact that each child is different from every other, and that what makes an educated person useful in his particular walk of life, what makes him interesting, what makes him an individual, is not his resemblances to other people but his differences.[160]

Progressive educators focused on the needs of the individual student rather than the body of knowledge he was supposed to acquire.

French was a seasoned educator who saw an opportunity to create an experimental school to serve as a model for American education. He accepted the job with the understanding that he would develop a coeducational boarding and day high school in the country, with the elementary division remaining on Concord Avenue in Cambridge. He was later to write, "A small group of optimists undertook the complete reorganization of the school along progressive lines. . . . All we had was boundless ambition, a set of convictions about the possibilities of private secondary education and the need for drastic changes."[161]

The fact that the school was coeducational was as revolutionary as French's progressivism. In the 1930s, the Cambridge School was the only coeducational independent school in the Boston area and one of only a few such schools in New England.

French explored the outskirts of Boston and, with the help of his friend Fiske Warren, he found the site he wanted in Weston. The Trustees of the Trapelo enclave, together with Fiske Warren, made a generous offer of 25 acres, together with the White Farm house and barn, for $30,000. Although located just 12 miles from Boston, the land was distinctly rural. Fiske Warren loaned the school $75,000 toward the $87,707 construction cost of the original classroom building.

In his book *Individuals and Community: The Cambridge School: The First Hundred Years,* George St. John says that without the interest and generosity of Fiske Warren, the Weston campus could not have been acquired. Warren was a highly successful businessman and investor who lived a spartan lifestyle so that he could give generously to social causes. He embraced the theories of land reformer and economist Henry George, whose book *Progress and Poverty* (1879) proposed a single tax on the intrinsic value of land but not on improvements. According to St. John, Warren established several single-tax colonies in the United States and overseas

Figure 10-72. John R.P. French was a progressive educator who established the Cambridge School in its Weston location and developed it as a coeducational high school. French had three major aspirations for his students: to understand and support democracy, to set their own goals, and to follow their own convictions.

to implement the theory. The land sold to the Cambridge School had been part of such an enclave.[162] Fiske Warren's admiration for Henry George inspired the street name Georgian Road.

Cambridge School in the 1930s and 1940s

The upper school opened in Weston in September 1931 with a new building and 106 pioneering students. On the first day, they climbed the stairs to a big loft in the converted barn to hear French talk about his hopes for the school, then followed him down to the athletic field to pull weeds. The "athletic field," a rough peat bog in a patch of woods, was a symbolic place to begin instilling the philosophy of working together toward a common goal.

The Kendal Green campus had only minimum facilities, but French saw this as an opportunity to give students experience working with tools. In February 1932, the *Christian Science Monitor* carried a story and pictures of students erecting a hobby shop for woodworking and crafts:

> Red-cheeked girls and husky boys are swinging axes, pounding nails, sawing wood, and planing boards these days at the Cambridge School in Kendal Green. They are building a Hobby Shop as part of their progressive educational training. And the shop is fast nearing completion at the hands of the students under the supervision of Mr. Alfred Hulst, instructor in hobbies and mechanical engineering at the school.[163]

The first winter, students cut ski trails through the woods. The school received nationwide publicity from a winter photograph showing two girls with axes standing by trees weighed down by snow. The picture was sent over the AP wire and appeared in newspapers from Alabama to Wisconsin, one of which carried the explanatory caption "Lumber jills fell trees."[164]

Central to the school day was a two-hour morning period of self-directed study, during which students could research projects of their choice. Teachers were expected to tailor their subjects to the individual's ability to master the core curriculum or go beyond it. In an effort to avoid competition or incentives, the school had no honor roll, no grades, and no prizes.

The school struggled financially during the Depression and war years and had trouble raising money for capital projects. In 1934 it published a fund-raising brochure that explained the philosophy of the school and what had been accomplished. By that time, students and teachers had built a classroom building and biology laboratory as well as school furniture and equipment, a tennis court, an astronomy observatory, a stage, and gardens. During the war years, the school had its own farm where students kept poultry and pigs, planted vegetable gardens, and operated a dairy that supplied milk and butter.

French began his effort to build a gymnasium and assembly hall in 1937. Again, fund-raising proved to be a problem, and it took 14 years to complete the building. In 1945 French noted the underpaid faculty and facilities inferior to other schools, adding, "While at first our primitive conditions had a certain romantic appeal, the tendency of late has been for parents and visitors to become increasingly critical."[165] To make things worse, a fire in 1946 destroyed the red barn across from the White farm house, which had been used as a dormitory and dining room. To replace the dining room, the school purchased an army surplus Quonset hut as a "temporary" solution that lasted a decade.

In 1946 the executors of the will of Fiske Warren sold the former Trapelo Golf Club property to the Cambridge School, which moved the clubhouse to

Figure 10-73. M. Adolphus Cheek Jr., headmaster of Cambridge School from 1951 to 1968, greatly increased enrollment and built new facilities, in part with the help of students. Cheek wrote, "When our students become adults we want them to realize they don't have to take things as they find them in their community."

its campus and remodeled it into a girls dormitory called Trapelo House. Part of the golf course was turned into soccer and hockey fields.

Cambridge School after 1950

Under the leadership of M. Adolphus Cheek Jr., headmaster from 1951 to 1968, the Cambridge School experienced a renaissance. Enrollment increased from 128 students in 1950–51 to 300 in 1965, including 140 boarders. The school added seven buildings, three tennis courts, and an outdoor swimming pool. The new buildings were simple and functional.

The Science Wing was built in 1953–56 by students, who surveyed the land, cleared the site and did the construction. Using student labor greatly decreased costs, but to Dolph Cheek, the real value was educational:

> We should be thinking of creating many new schools not just from the tax dollar but from citizens working together and giving services and materials. More of the spirit of pioneers, hewing through the wilderness, is needed. . . . When our students become adults we want them to realize they don't have to take things as they find them in their community. They can creatively improve and build.[166]

The 1954 yearbook said of the Science Wing: "From one Spring to another it has grown, and, with the faint echo of medieval faith, become a symbol of community effort toward a community goal."[167]

Major buildings constructed over the next decade were not built by students for several reasons, including the technical nature of the construction and the death of building supervisor Jim Annett. Architect Hugh A. Stubbins Jr. designed the 1957 dining hall, which was destroyed by fire in 1974 and rebuilt the following year.[168]

Kendal Common

In 1949, the Cambridge School sold the lower 40 acres of the former Trapelo Golf Club to Kendal Common Inc. The group's progressive views on "community building" mirrored the philosophy of headmaster John R.P. French, after whom French Road is named. Kendal Common was incorporated in 1948 in Cambridge by a group of young married academics and scientists who shared a common vision of the kind of place they wanted to live and raise their children. They didn't want their proposed development to look like a typical subdivision and were ready to experiment with new architectural concepts. They were environmentally conscious, with strong concerns about preserving wildlife and the natural landscape. Above all, they wanted to create a sense of community.

Kendal Common was organized as a semi-cooperative. Each lot owner was (and still is) a shareholder in the corporation, with voting rights and shared responsibility for maintaining common land. The group planned to have a children's playground, pool, tennis court, and common house for social activities, but only the playground was built. Later, Kendal Common provided partial funding for a swimming pool at the Cambridge School in return for rights to use the pool and tennis courts. Planting plans for the edges of roads were done by a landscape architect, who chose plantings like highbush cranberry and honeysuckle to attract birds and wildlife.

Founding members took care of legal work, engineering, and record-keeping for the new development. Some members worked on the construction of their own houses, with help from neighbors on carpentry or electrical work. The neighborhood had its own version of the "lawn party," where everyone labored to remove rocks from a front yard, then graded and seeded it. Communal work was encouraged not just to save money but also to build ties within the community.

All but one of the 22 houses in Kendal Common were built between 1950 and 1960. Prospective buyers had to agree to use certain architects and have their plans approved by the Kendal Common board

Figure 10-74. Pictures and headlines on this page were taken from a marketing brochure prepared about 1952 for Kendal Common. The text begins as follows:

"Four short years ago, Carl Koch invited a group of families interested in modern architecture to investigate the possibility of buying and developing the old Trapelo Golf Course in Weston as a cooperative community. Eight of those present were so enthused of the idea that they pooled their resources, their wisdom, their efforts . . . to make possible the dream they called Kendal Common.

"THE LAND consists of a 45 acre rolling meadow divided into 24 lots from one to three acres in size. One portion of this tract was retained by the corporation as a recreation area, another at the pond for the proposed community house.

"THE IDEA was an ideal; modern homes with all their freedom and color and sun . . . among neighborly people who appreciate the advantages of doing things together."

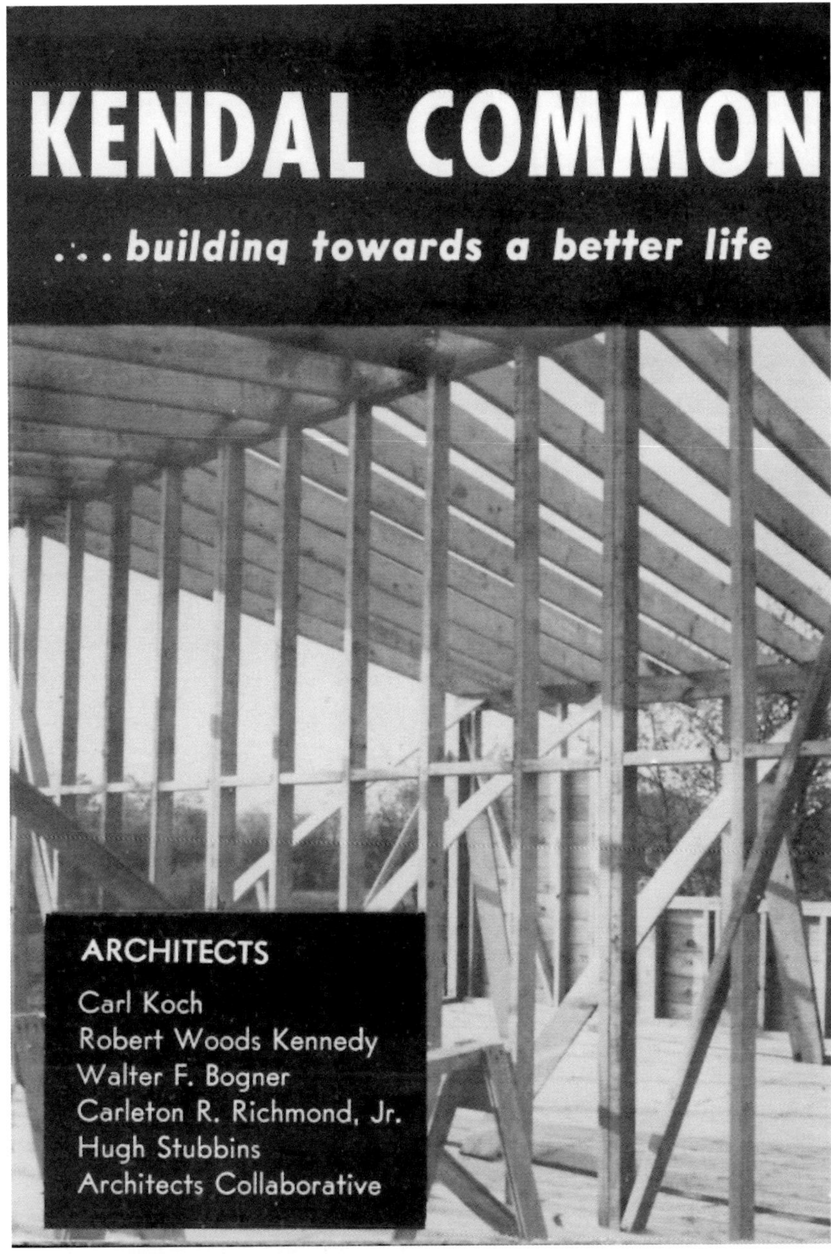

Santa Comes To Kendal Common

Paper Bags Become Hallowe'en Costumes

Our Bus Party for "Grown-ups" Was A Delightful Experience

KENDAL COMMON: LAND + COMMUNITY ACTIVITIES

The Kendal Common brochure was prepared as a community service by Dan Fogel, who was in advertising. The Fogels were among the first families to build in the neighborhood and lived there until 1996. Kendal Common was one of several similar enclaves in suburban Boston. They were started after the war by younger people interested in modern art and architecture and seeking a new way to live and a house they could afford. Fogel described it as an "adventure in living."

Figure 10-75. Buyers of land in Kendal Common were required to build houses in the Modern style. The Kendal Common marketing brochure from about 1952 shows drawings and photographs of proposed and completed houses.

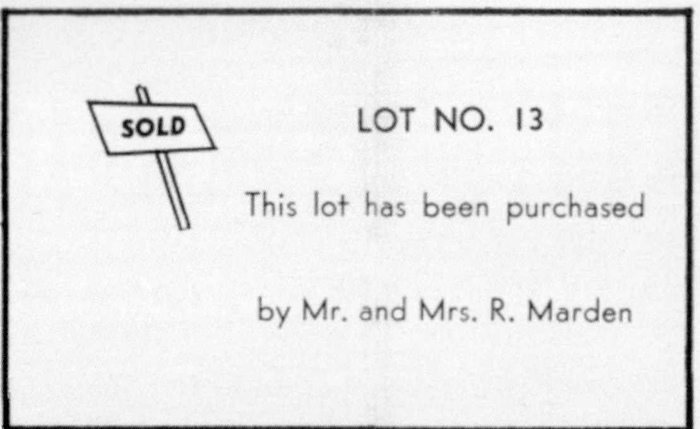

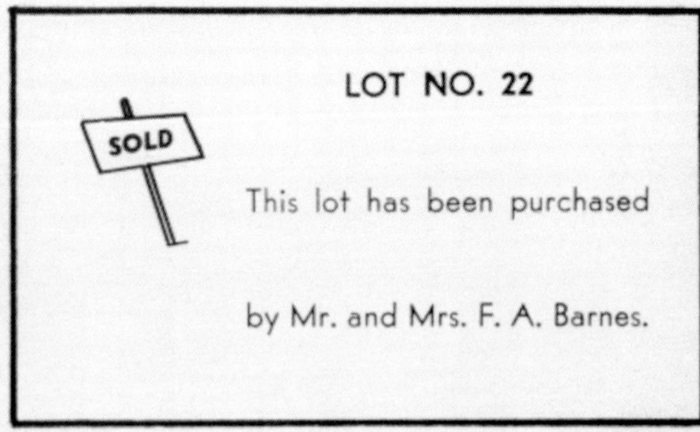

of directors. Carl Koch was involved from the beginning. After a few years, the group drew up a panel of architects that included not only Carl Koch and Associates but also Robert Woods Kennedy, Carleton R. Richmond Jr., Hugh A. Stubbins Jr., The Architects Collaborative, Compton and Pierce, and Morehouse and Chesley, an impressive group of leaders within the modernist movement in Boston.

Postwar Land Conservation and Development

The postwar building boom and construction of Route 128 spelled the end for the cornfields of Kendal Green. The land behind the Drabbington Lodge was subdivided into 13 house lots with frontage on the newly created Drabbington Way. Harold Coburn's farmland was sold for development of what is now Whitney Tavern Road and the north end of Drabbington Way. In 1951, the executors of the will of Anna C. Hastings sold most of the Hastings property to Louis J. Kirsch for $60,000. Kirsch sold off the workers' cottages and subdivided the rest of the land. After Samuel Philip Miller's death in 1956, 28 acres of his farm were subdivided into Hobbs Brook and Forest Ridge Roads.[169] The Dean property was sold for development around 1960. A man-made pond was created by the Valley Pond Association in Lincoln, which dammed the stream and sold off house lots around the new pond.

Along with the increase in development came the movement to preserve open space around Cat Rock, which was reportedly named for the wildcats or bobcats that once frequented the area. The story of Cat Rock and the Eighty Acres begins in 1947, when local skiers established the Cat Rock Ski Club, a nonprofit organization with membership limited to Weston residents.[170] The club cut down trees to create an open ski slope and wooded trail and set up a rope tow that operated on weekends and holidays. Lift tickets cost $1. With no artificial snowmaking, the season was usually short. In 1957, the private Cat Rock Trust sold 64 acres, including Cat Rock Hill, to the town for well below market value.[171] Weston Recreation Department ran the ski slope for the next two decades. It was crowded each weekend when conditions were good.

In the 1950s, the Tyler Farm was sold to Albert and Frances "Peg" Hunt and Frederick C. "Buck" Jr. and "Pit" Dumaine, two couples who were close friends. They repaired and rented the 18th-century house, which was nearly in ruins, and kept the "Eighty Acres"

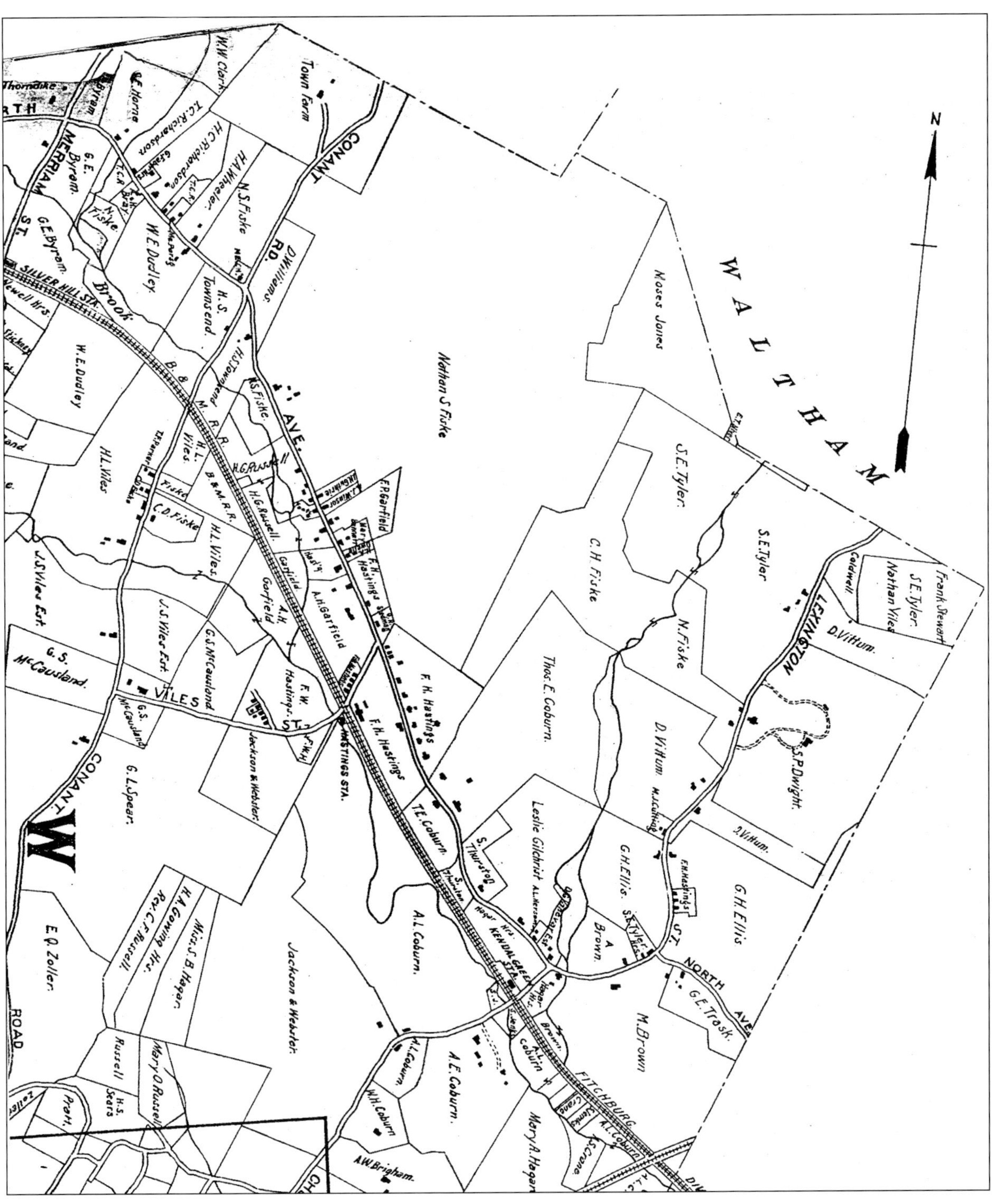

Figure 10-76. This detail from the 1908 Atlas of Middlesex County *shows Kendal Green and part of the Church Street area discussed in the next chapter. Notice the size of the Fiske Farm, which was eventually developed as the King's Grant neighborhood.*

Brief Hobbs Family Genealogy

Josiah Hobbs (1684–1779) [Bought land in Weston, 1729]
  Ebenezer (1709–1762) [oldest son,* m. Eunice Garfield in 1734. Had nine children.]
    Isaac [oldest] (1735–1813) m. Mary Sanderson of Waltham in 1757
      Ebenezer II [second child] (b. 1762). Had eight children, including
        Susan—first wife of Isaac Fiske
        Sophronia—second wife of Isaac Fiske
      Isaac Jr. [third son] (1765–1834), m. Mary Baldwin in 1790
        Abigail (b. 1791)
        Isaac (b. 1793)
        Ebenezer (b. 1794)
        Capt. Samuel (b. 1795) m. Abigail Kendal in 1834
        Abigail [6th child] (b. 1801) m. John Flagg
        Mary Ann [8th child] (b. 1805) m. Nathan Hagar in 1832
    Capt. Matthew [sixth son] [Revolutionary War captain of Weston company]
      Capt. Henry (1784–1854) [harness and carriage maker]
    Samuel [eighth child] [tanner and currier]

* "ancestor of all the Hobbs family in Weston"

for their own recreational use. Both men liked wielding chain saws and splitting wood. They harvested apples from the orchard, planted winter rye to attract deer, and raised baby quail. In the late 1950s, Hunt and Dumaine hired Melone & Sons to build a dam on Hobbs Brook and dredge the marsh grass from the swamp, creating the present Hobbs Brook Pond (also referred to as Cat Rock Pond). They stocked the pond with brown trout, and Peg Hunt organized the Eighty Acres Fishing Club, which gave out fishing badges to anyone who paid a small fee. In the 1970s, the Hunt/Dumaine land was subdivided and about 60 acres conveyed to the town as conservation land, including the pond and adjacent meadow.[172] Together with the 64 acres previously sold to the town by the Cat Rock Trust, the land is now part of one of Weston's largest open space preserves.

Houses in the North Avenue and Lexington Street Area

75 to 87 Brook Road: By 1895, these six houses on White Lane housed organ factory employees.

200 Church Street (Kendal Green Station): Labeled Weston Depot on the 1875 map, this station was on the Fitchburg (later Boston & Maine) railroad line. It was renamed after the Central Massachusetts Railroad—which also had a "Weston Station"—opened in the 1880s. On the 1889 map, the station is labeled Kendall (sic) Green or Weston. The depot was remodeled in 1904.[173]

216 Conant Road (c. 1785). On the 1794 Kingsbury map, this Federal-style house belonged to Nathaniel Bemis.

217 Conant Road (1934): Colonial Revival.

254 Conant Road (c. 1847–48): Greek Revival house built for farmer Jesse Sumner Viles, son of Jesse and Sally Viles, on land owned by the Viles family.

300 Conant Road (1895): Queen Anne house built for dairy farmer Henry Lewis Viles. His grandson and namesake, who still lives in the house, has a copy of the original bill from builder Herbert M. Gregg for $5,631.25, a substantial sum that included the dairy barn and milk-processing building (dairy shed) still on the property. The property includes a pond where ice was cut in winter to supply the dairy.

312-318 Conant Road (late 19th century): Four-family house built by Henry L. Viles for his dairy workers. The house had no indoor plumbing until it was sold after World War II.

326 Conant Road (c. 1900): Queen Anne cottage.

440 Conant Road (1860–61): Although an 18th-century house once stood in this location, the present Greek Revival dwelling was built in the early 1860s as the town poorhouse. The 1862 town report contains the first complete report of the Overseers of the Poor and discusses the new building.

15 Ellis Road (1959–60): Built by Jeanne and Norman Saunders as part of the Kendal Common community, this early solar house was included in the 1980 book *Solar Houses for a Cold Climate.* Norman Saunders, a professional engineer and inventor, named the house Experimental Manor. The plan was based on an original Gropius design modified for them

Kendal Common: There are 22 houses in the Kendal

Common development, on 40 acres, plus common lands and a common playground. Addresses are as follows: **Kendal Common Road:** 3, 4, 16, 17, 23, 30, 40, 45, 46, 49; **French Road:** 7, 8, 11; **Main Street, Waltham** (continuation of North Avenue): 1481, 1485, 1489; **North Avenue:** 1, 31; **Ellis Road:** 3, 9, 12, 15.

17-19, 23, and 27 Lexington Street (1887): Three houses built by Francis Henry Hastings for workers at the Hook & Hastings organ factory.

39 Lexington Street: Site of the Elisha Warren house, built 1743, destroyed by fire November 9, 1920.

62 Lexington Street (c. 1852–56): Greek Revival house built for single woman Eliza DeRehbender and later owned by Marshall Cutting.

71 Lexington Street (18th century): Traditionally known as the John Warren homestead, this house is among the oldest in Weston and was owned by Warren descendants into the 20th century. Until about 1774, Lexington Street passed to the east side of the house, and what is now the rear faced onto the road. John Warren Jr. and his wife, Abigail, had a daughter Cynthia (b. 1780), who married John Cutting Jr. in 1799. Their son, John Warren Cutting (1800–1873), married Cynda Lane in 1823 (see 178 Lexington Street). A younger son, Marshall Cutting (1818–1889), married Lucinda Wallis in 1840. Marshall Cutting's daughter, Ellen, married Darius Vittum, who later shared the house with the family of their son, Walter, and his wife, Ethel. Their daughters, Lillian and Mae, were the last of the Warren-Cutting descendants to occupy the homestead, selling it in 1970.[174]

95 Lexington Street (pre-1750): This Colonial house with Colonial Revival alterations is known as the White farmhouse and is used as a student dormitory for the Cambridge School of Weston.

143 Lexington Street (1936): Built by police office Harlan Berry using lumber from the demolished Hook & Hastings factory.

178 Lexington Street (before 1768): Built for farmer Abraham Sanderson and subsequently owned by John Warren Cutting (until 1873), Sidney E. Tyler, and his son, Herbert "Bert" Tyler, who farmed here until the mid-20th century.

34 North Avenue (c. 1865): Built by farmer William H. Floyd and purchased in the early 1870s by George E. Trask, a wholesale butcher who had a large slaughterhouse on the property. Trask had two sons: Guy, who is listed in the 1906 directory as station agent and postmaster at Stony Brook, and Robert, who is listed in the 1909 directory as station agent at Kendal Green.

46 North Avenue (1916): Built for farmer Samuel Phillip Miller.[175]

70 North Avenue (c. 1878): Italianate summer house built for Edward J. Brown, a Boston wool merchant who lived in Cambridge during the winter. The original covered entrance porch and uncovered wraparound porch have been removed.

87 North Avenue (c. 1761, with additions and an earlier section): The Isaac Hobbs House is listed on the National Register of Historic Places. According to the nomination form, the north wing may have existed when Josiah Hobbs purchased 122 acres of land in 1729, with several houses included. Josiah established the tannery as early as 1730 and his descendants operated it until 1860. The house passed to Josiah's son Ebenezer. In 1758, when Ebenezer's son Isaac (Sr.) married Mary Sanderson, Ebenezer gave him one third of the house. Isaac built a large addition to the south by 1761, after which it was always referred to as the "double house." His grandson, Samuel, married Abigail Kendal, the daughter of Rev. Samuel Kendal of First Parish Church. Abigail left the property to her nephew Gen. James F.B. Marshall, who moved here about 1884. In 1889 General Marshall enlarged and remodeled the house, adding the central gable, entrance porch, small wing to the south, and terrace at the southwest corner. He owned the house until his death in 1891. The tannery site is east of the house on conservation land conveyed to the town by the Miller family.

88 North Avenue (c. 1786 with addition): The Georgian-style Hobbs-Hagar house was originally five bays wide with a center chimney. Within a few years, three bays and a second entrance were added to the east. Visually, the two parts were united using decorative details like the corner quoins, lintels over the windows, dentil cornice, and doorway surrounds with fluted pilasters. Inside, details include a fine Federal-style elliptical staircase. The house was built by Isaac Hobbs for his sons Isaac (Jr.) and Ebenezer II, both of whom worked at the family tannery across the street. In 1832 Nathan Hagar Jr. married Mary Ann Hobbs, daughter of Isaac Jr. After Isaac's death a few years later, Nathan moved into the house at No. 88 and about the same time formed the partnership of Hobbs and Hagar for the manufacture of shoes. According to Lamson, the "shoe factory" was located in a building that stood on the southeast corner of the property.[176]

99 and 107–9 North Avenue: These two adjacent houses were originally rear ells of the Hobbs-Hagar house at No. 88. Map evidence suggests they were moved across the street between 1852 and 1866. The house at No. 99 is known as the Hersum house because of its long history of ownership by the family of plumbing contractor Arthur Hersum, who also served as one of Weston's first water commissioners.

No. 107–9 North Avenue (Brodrick's Store) was used as a general store and post office. A weighing scale for wagons stood outside; later a filling station was here.

121 North Avenue: Traditionally thought to have been built by Ebenezer Hobbs, eldest son of Josiah, at the time of his marriage in 1734. The house was originally one-over-one in plan, with the oldest section being the three bays on the east side.

135 North Avenue (1899): The Drabbington Lodge was built by George and Sarah Thurston to replace an earlier farmhouse that they had converted into an inn. That building was destroyed by fire. The signed and dated plans by architect Frank W. Weston for the new Shingle-style hotel are located in the Massachusetts Archives.

147 North Avenue (1904): The rustic log Thurston Bungalow, also referred to as the Drabbington Annex, was designed by architect George E. Strout for George and Sarah Thurston, owners of the Drabbington Lodge. Late-19th- and early-20th-century bungalows came in all sizes and styles and were often inspired by exotic architecture. One book divides American examples into nine types, of which two are relevant here: the "retreat or summer house" and the "Adirondack lodge" built of logs.[177] This house has the characteristic wide overhanging eaves, show rafters, eave braces, and triangular pediment marking the main entrance. The popularity of the form stems from the work of the Greene brothers in California, who pioneered the Craftsman style.

153 North Avenue (1902): The Shingle-style Thurston Cottage was designed by architect George E. Strout for the owners of the Drabbington Lodge and was rented to guests.

161-163 North Avenue (c. 1823): This Federal-style farmhouse was built for farmer Converse Bigelow (c. 1785–1858) and then owned by Kendall H. Stone. In 1881, the 70-acre working dairy farm was purchased for Thomas Coburn, who added the ell.[178] His son Harold (Sr.) continued dairy operations until after World War II. The house is now owned by Harold W. Coburn Jr. The estimated construction date is based on strong similarities between this house and 199 North Avenue.

Kendal Green Fire Station (1908): Kendal Green was Weston's first fire station. The rare example of all-concrete construction is unique in Weston. The simple classical styling is the work of architect Alexander S. Jenney, and the builder was Aberthaw Construction Co. of Boston. (See chapter 5.)

171 North Avenue (c. 1707–08): The Whitney Tavern is thought to have been built for William Whitney, who married Martha Peirce in 1706, and was taxed in Weston as early as 1708.[179] In the late 19th century, the house was owned by Kendall H. Stone and then by Thomas Coburn, both of whom lived next door at No. 163 and used the former tavern for boarding farmhands. In 1894, Francis Hastings wrote that the Whitney Tavern had been a "commonplace tenement house for seventy-five years or more." The house retains its original exterior appearance, including the distinctive saltbox shape.

189 North Avenue (1891): This Shingle-style house was built by Francis Henry Hastings for his caretaker/gardener. Like many of its contemporaries, it was originally painted with a dark wood-colored paint or stain.

190 North Avenue (1885): Seven Gables is a fine example of the Shingle style designed by Boston architects Hartwell and Richardson for organ factory owner Francis Henry Hastings. Hastings married Anna Coburn in 1899. After his death in 1916, her niece Anna Hall came to live with her. After Anna Hastings's death in 1950 at age 97, Anna Hall remained at Seven Gables until her death in 1978 at age 101.

191 North Avenue (1885): Built as the stable for Seven Gables across the street, No.191 was probably also designed by Hartwell and Richardson.

199 North Avenue (1823): The Hastings homestead was built by Jonas Hastings (1784–1865), a "cordwainer," or shoemaker, who acquired property on both sides of North Avenue over a period of about 30 years, from 1805 to 1834. An 1823 agreement between Jonas Hastings and Phinehas Conant of Stow to build the present house is recorded at the Middlesex Registry of Deeds (250/67).[180] Conant was to receive $527 to build a house 40 feet long, 18 feet wide, and two stories high, with one chimney and three "fire places." The description includes other specific details of construction and indicates that an "old house" was to be taken down. The present barn is thought to have been built several years before the house. About 1833, the west end was occupied by Jonas's son, Francis Hastings, who married that year. This Francis Hastings made boots in a shed behind the house and farmed the land alongside his father. His son, the organ manufacturer Francis Henry Hastings, was born and brought up in the old homestead. The house remained in the Hastings family until 1914, when Francis Henry Hastings sold it to Norman Jacobson, a longtime key employee at Hook & Hastings Co. After the organ factory closed down, Norman Jacobson and his two siblings ran an antique shop in the barn, which closed after the death of the last brother, Harold, about 1955.

In a short history of Hastings homestead written in 1893 by Mary Giddings, sister of Francis Henry

Hastings, she writes that before the Hastings house was built, the farm had belonged to Deacon Barrett, who had a home in Charlestown and lived in Weston only part of the year. After he died, "an old negro slave, or servant, Nancy Budge, was allowed to make it her home for several years" and for this reason it was also referred to as the Budge place. When the earlier house was torn down to make way for the Jonas Hastings house, some of the doors and window sashes were reused.

221 North Avenue: Site of District Schoolhouse #4, built in the early 1850s and demolished in the 1940s.

225, 227, and 231 North Avenue (1893): Three Shingle-style houses built by Francis Henry Hastings for workers at the nearby organ factory.

237 North Avenue (1880): Mansard cottage built in 1880 by George Stedman (also spelled Steadman), who is listed in the 1887 directory as a foreman at "Waltham band." This name may refer to the American Waltham Watch Band Company, one of three companies in Waltham that manufactured watch bands.

241-247 North Avenue: Ranch houses built on site of Jonathan Warren house.[181]

248 North Avenue (demolished mid-1990s): Site of the Weston Dog Ranch, established about 1926 by Alfred Lederhos, treasurer and superintendent of the R.T. Ryan Iron Works in Allston and a canine lover who operated the veterinary as a second business. The metal arched gateway that once stood at the entrance to the driveway was designed and manufactured by Lederhos. The gateway was put up for auction in the mid-1990s, when the property was sold for development.

256 North Avenue (1889): Built by Hiram Garfield's son, Alfred, as a rental house, on land he purchased from his father.

260 North Avenue (1890): Francis Henry Hastings bought the lot from Hiram Garfield in 1888 and built the house for one of his employees. In 1909 it was sold to Joseph Gilson, a mechanic at the factory, whose family remained here for several generations.

263 North Avenue: This house appears to have been built in stages, with the earliest part of the house possibly dating about 1875. Owner Samuel Patch Jr. had a shop, which still remains behind the house.

266 North Avenue (1891): Francis Henry Hastings bought the lot from Hiram Garfield in 1888. The house was built by organ factory employee Frank Gowell three years later.[182]

269-271 North Avenue (c. 1859–61): Hiram Garfield, another son of George W. Garfield, purchased land from his father in 1852. This Italianate house was probably begun about 1859, when Hiram sold the family homestead at No. 277 to his brother Daniel. In 1887 Hiram sold the house to Hiram Bennett, a house painter who built the wing to house his wife's maiden aunt.

272 North Avenue (1843–44): Originally Greek Revival in style, this house was altered with the addition of two peaked gables in the Gothic Revival mode. The original owner, George W. Garfield Jr., was a wheelwright whose father built the house at No. 277.

273 North Avenue (1930): Built by Earle F. Foote, who ran the general store across the street together with his brother. Weston building permit #249 lists the architect as Small House Service Bureau.

276 North Avenue (1927): Built by Mrs.William Otto, granddaughter of Ebenezer Tucker (see No. 306). Mrs. Otto also built No. 270 as her retirement home in 1947.

277 North Avenue (c. 1821): This Federal-style house was built for George W. Garfield Sr., who bought a total of 10 acres on both sides of North Avenue from Nathan Fiske in 1820. Garfield, who came from Lincoln, married Rebecca Weston in March 1819. In 1821, he was assessed for "1 shop within or adjoining to dwelling house, 2 acres tillage land, 3 acres English mowing and 3 acres pasture." Garfield had three sons and six daughters. The three sons—George (1820–1905), Hiram (1829–1889), and Daniel (1833–1905)—all settled nearby. The house remained in the Garfield family until 1906, when it was sold to Waltham merchant Jeremiah Cronin, father of Grover Cronin.

282 North Avenue: Approximate location of the Garfield/Foote blacksmith shop (since demolished).

293 North Avenue (1891–92): John Guthrie, an organ factory employee, bought the lot from the Fiske family in 1891. He was taxed that year for one unfinished house, which is Queen Anne in style.

297 North Avenue (c. 1892–96): George N. Stevens, an organ factory employee, bought this lot from the Fiskes in 1890 and built a house that was later destroyed by fire. He subsequently built the present well-detailed Queen Anne house and sold it in 1896.

306 North Avenue (c. 1838): This Greek Revival house was built by Ebenezer Tucker, who grew vegetables and raised hay and also had a forge where he made tools. He took the tools to Boston and sold them to a company that later became Brecks.

337 North Avenue (1926): Charles J.R. Cahill built

this Colonial Revival house after he bought the Fiske farm from W.F. Schrafft. Weston building permit #55 lists William Haines of Waltham as the architect. The old Fiske farmhouse (since demolished), built by Alonzo Fiske about 1845, was located next door, approximately where the Dairy Joy parking lot is now.

360 North Avenue (18th century with alterations): The oldest part of this house is said to have been built about 1740 by Bradyll Smith, a prominent citizen who held many political offices including representative to the General Court. It was later owned by Joseph Hickson, from about 1780 to 1796, and retired sea captain Robert Calef and later Calef's widow, from 1796 to 1834. The house has been much altered.

377 North Avenue (1971–72): The present Weston United Methodist Church, designed by architect Peter Thomas, is the third church on the site.

399 North Avenue (c. 1927): Colonial Revival

405 North Avenue (c. 1903): Gable-front farmhouse with fieldstone front porch.

406 North Avenue (c. 1870s): Built for a member of the William Dudley farm family.

413 North Avenue (1850): The first parsonage for the nearby Methodist church was built on land purchased for $100 from Capt. S. Fiske.

415 North Avenue (c. 1835): Late Federal house with notable barn.

419 North Avenue (c. 1834): Built for Samuel Patch Sr.

431 North Avenue (c. 1834, remodeled 20th century): Known as the Park-Boyce house. Boyce was a blacksmith. His son sold the property to George W. Faber of Lincoln in 1884. George and Thomas Faber built a ropewalk to make "Hand made Linen Window, Garland, Dumbwaiter Cord." The ropewalk was located 10 to 15 feet from the road just north of the house and extended beyond the spring, where they bleached and finished off the cord.[183] By 1900, machine-made sash cord drove them out of business and the ropewalk was torn down. Before the house was remodeled, it had Gothic-style windows.

479 North Avenue and higher numbers: See chapter 12.

126-128 and 130-134 Viles Street (1887): Two double houses built by Francis Henry Hastings for workers at the nearby organ factory, which was under construction at that time.

Notes

1. 1874 *TR.* The stone trough was later replaced by a decorative cast-metal trough identical to the one in front of First Parish Church. It was moved out of the way of traffic sometime during World War II and subsequently disappeared. Some say it was used for scrap metal and others that it is buried in the dump.
2. Coburn scrapbook #2, 32 (c. 1897).
3. In the early 1860s, the only larger property in Weston was the 419-acre Boylston farm then owned by out-of-town resident Charles Francis Adams and later bought by Gen. Charles Jackson Paine. The Boylston farm is now the site of Weston High and Middle School. See 1861 Weston tax records.
4. The extent of the land is outlined on the 1875 *Middlesex County Atlas* map of Weston.
5. MCRD 7/18, Thomas and Magdalen Underwood to Nathan Fiske, 1673. See also Pierce's *Fiske and Fiske Family,* cited below, 92, and Weston chapter in Hurd's *History of Middlesex County,* 503, for a brief summary of Fiske descendants in Weston. Lawyer Isaac Fiske was a descendant.
6. Pierce, Frederick Clifton, *Fiske and Fisk Family* (published by the author), 496.
7. Bond's *History of Watertown,* 1028.
8. The 1794 Kingsbury map shows the John Warren house (71 Lexington Street), Nathaniel Warren house (39 Lexington Street, destroyed by fire), and T. Warren house (Lexington and North Avenue, no longer extant).
9. MCRD 30/118, John Cheney Jr. to Josiah Hobbs, October 1729, 122 acres "together with the Houses Orchards Fences Trees Improvements and Water Courses." The land had once been part of the Warren Farm. Cheney's father had purchased it in 1724 from Ensign J. Warren. See also WHC files. Sources vary as to the date the tannery was established. Lamson says that "so far as can be gathered by records, the tannery was started between 1750 and 1760." See Lamson's account in *HTW,* 158–59, and his chapter in *History of Middlesex County,* 504, for information on Hobbs family members. See also the brief Hobbs genealogy in this chapter.
10. Lamson chapter, *History of Middlesex County,* 495.
11. Marshall, Francis V., "The Hobbs Tannery," *WHSB,* July 1990, 4.
12. Middlesex County Probate #11618, Estate of Isaac Hobbs Jr., 1834.
13. Barber, John Warner, Historical Collections (Dorr, Howland & Co., Worcester, 1839). In comparison, Wayland manufactured 230 pairs of boots and 29,666 pairs of shoes, valued at $22,419, according to Barber.
14. Fiske, Charles H., "1876 Centennial Oration," 26.
15. The Waltham press printed dimensions of each building after the fire of October 25, 1884. See also H. Bentley Crouch's unpublished history of the Weston Fire Department. Physical evidence of the shoddy mill remains on the east side of Church Street at Stony Brook.
16. The mill and millpond appear on the 1880s layout of Church Street, Town Engineers Office.
17. MCRD 220/390, Habakkuk Stearns to Town of Weston, April 1817. The 1794 map shows a house on the property belonging to Stearns; however, the architecture of the present house at 440 Conant Road and the history of the poor farm indicate that this house was replaced in 1860.
18. Lamson, *HTW,* 137, includes this quote from the 1860 town report.
19. A committee examined several sites including the farms of John A. Lamson, Henry J. White, and Nathan Barker. As none of these properties was considered suitable, no action was taken. Lamson, *HTW,* 148.
20. 1876 *TR.*
21. 1878 *TR,* 22.
22. 1897 *TR,* 33.
23. 1915 *TR,* 79.
24. Kennedy, Donald G., "James Marshall, Part II," *WHSB,* May 1985 (issued January 1987).
25. Weston's Thomas Marshall has been described incorrectly as "a member of George Washington's staff." Washington had on his

staff another Col. Thomas Marshall, from Virginia.
26. Kennedy, op. cit., 3.
27. Kennedy, Donald G., "James Marshall, Part I: Booker T. Washington, and the Hampton–Weston Connection," *WHSB,* March 1985 (issued January 1987).
28. See also "A Letter from Tuskegee" by Booker T. Washington, *The First Parish Calendar,* vol. II, no. 3, January 17, 1895.
29. No. 89, 99, 107-109, and 121 North Avenue. See "Plan of Estate of J.F.B. Marshall, Kendal Green, Weston, Mass., January 1889," MCRD, Plan Book 67, Plan 51, May 1891. Some of this property was purchased by Marshall rather than inherited.
30. Tax records of 1886 show Marshall owning a store, indicating that the post office–general store date from that time.
31. "Robin Hood Played Part in Naming KENDAL GREEN," *WHSB,* January 1980, 7. Quotes much of a letter owned by Miss Anna Hall and apparently written by Marshall as a letter to the editor.
32. Kennedy, op. cit., part II, 5.
33. Ochase, Orpha, *The History of the Organ in the United States* (Indiana University Press, Bloomington & London, 1975), 124. See also Ayars, Christine M., *Contributions to the Art of Music in America by the Music Industries of Boston, 1640–1936* (New York: The H.W. Wilson Co., 1937), 168–75.
34. Coburn, Philip, "Weston's Hook-Hastings Organ Factory," *WHSB,* October 1983, 2.
35. Ochase gives the date of partnership as 1870, while Philip Coburn reports the May 1866 date. Coburn appears to have had access to articles of co-partnership from 1866, which say that to become a partner Hastings gave the Hook brothers a note for $6,666 payable at $1,000 yearly with semiannual interest. After becoming a co-partner, Hastings also paid $2,200 rent per year on buildings and land valued at $30,000. The second articles of co-partnership in 1871 were drawn up after the agreed-upon five years. See Coburn, "Weston's Hook-Hastings Organ Factory," op. cit., 2.
36. Van Pelt, William T., compiler, *The Hook Opus List, 1829–1916 in Facsimile, with a Compiled List of Organs 1916–1935 and Facsimiles of Promotional Publications* (Richmond, VA: The Organ Historical Society, 1991), 6.
37. Ochase, op. cit., 219.
38. Ayars, op. cit., 172.
39. Extract from *Church Music Review,* as quoted in a Hook & Hastings brochure, "Console of Organ, First Church of Christ, Scientist (Mother Church), Boston, Massachusetts" (Hook & Hastings scrapbook, WHS).
40. Vogel, Susan Maycock, "Hartwell and Richardson: An Introduction to Their Work," *Victorian Architecture in Boston,* May 1973 issue of the *Journal of the Society of Architectural Historians,* vol. XXXII, no. 2, 132.
41. Kennedy, Donald G., "Francis Hastings' Labor Experiment," *WHSB,* January 1984.
42. Hastings's diary has been lost but excerpts copied from it by Miss Anna Hall are preserved in WHS files.
43. MCRD 1683/198, Francis Hastings to Francis Warren Hastings, October 1884.
44. In 1885, Francis Warren Hastings was taxed for one dwelling and one stable with combined value of $8,000.
45. MCRD 1712/358, Francis Hastings to Francis Warren Hastings, 15 acres. This was the "woodlot" of the old Budge farm, sold by Jonathan Warren to Jonas Hastings in 1817.
46. MCRD 1741/256, Francis Hastings to Francis Warren Hastings, March 1886, "remaining portions of my farm."
47. MCRD 1760/588, Henry S. Milton to Francis Warren Hastings. For a picture of this Warren house, see Lamson's *HTW,* 127 f.
48. MCRD 1788/49, Francis Buttrick to Francis Warren Hastings, March 1887, 3.5 acres. In the 1893 directory, "Butterick House" is listed as a "hotel," and many men boarded there.
49. MCRD 1788/53, Hanford A. Warner to Francis Warren Hastings, March 1887.
50. Note that the three Lexington Street houses were built in 1887, not a decade later, as reported in the January 1984 issue of *WHSB.* The society printed a correction in the March 1984 bulletin.
51. "Church Organs," undated Hook & Hastings Co. brochure, c. 1889, WHS scrapbook.
52. Brochure for First Church of Christ, Scientist, Hook & Hastings scrapbook, WHS.
53. Ayars, Christine, op. cit., 170. According to Ayars, the organ built for New Haven's Trinity Church, finished in 1866, used pneumatic action, as did the Shawmut Congregational Church organ in Boston, built in 1866.
54. According to Ayars, op. cit., 174, the company was among the first firms to use electric action successfully.
55. Van Pelt, op. cit., 6.
56. Ibid., 262. See facsimile of c. 1912 company brochure.
57. "Organ Factory Information Wanted," *WHSB,* January 1982, 6–7, includes a list of the 71 employees who signed an engraved testimonial for Francis Henry Hastings's 70th birthday. Thirty-five are listed with Weston addresses. In 1900, more than 30 organ factory employees are listed in U.S. census records for Weston; in 1920, there were 27.
58. Kennedy, "Francis Hastings' Labor Experiment," op. cit., 4.
59. The *Boston Herald* article is reprinted in its entirety in Kennedy, "Francis Hastings' Labor Experiment," op. cit., 2–9.
60. "Fortunate Workmen: An Employer Who Looks Out for His Employees," *Danvers Mirror,* reprinted in *Waltham Free Press,* c. 1891, Coburn scrapbook #4, 160.
61. *Boston Sunday Herald,* July 13, 1890, as reprinted in Kennedy, "Francis Hastings' Labor Experiment," op. cit., 3.
62. Ibid., 4.
63. Ibid., 4–5.
64. Ibid., 8.
65. Ibid., 5.
66. Ibid.
67. Probably *Waltham Free Press,* c. 1892, Coburn scrapbook #3, 29.
68. *WDFPT,* January 5, March 23 and 30, 1906. Partially destroyed by fire in 1960 and then torn down.
69. *WDFPT,* November 18, 1904.
70. Gilson, Arthur, letter to *Town Crier* published under the headline "Weston Man, 86, Recalls Organ Factory Fire Department," August 26, 1965.
71. Crouch, H. Bentley, "History of the Weston Fire Department" (unpublished manuscript, undated).
72. Gilson, op.cit.
73. The land was bought from George and Sarah Thurston (MCRD 3379/231, 4,042 square feet, June 1908). Longtime Weston residents claim that the station was built to impede efforts to extend street railway service along North Avenue.
74. Total production taken from Van Pelt's *The Hook Opus List,* which lists all known organs. Information about size and cost from Ethelyn J. Russell, "Organs" (unpublished manuscript, c. 1907, owned by Betty Rafuse).
75. Oft-mentioned organs sent outside Massachusetts include the following: Plymouth Congregational Church, Brooklyn (1865); First Presbyterian Church, Pittsburgh (1870); Union Park Congregational Church, Chicago (1871); Church of the Holy Communion, Philadelphia (1873); Holy Cross Cathedral, Cincinnati (1875); Industrial Exposition, Milwaukee (1881); St. John's Cathedral, Denver (1881); Central Congregational Church, Philadelphia (1883); Lafayette Avenue Presbyterian Church, Brooklyn (1886).

Important organs made after the factory moved to Kendal Green included the following: St. Mary's Cathedral of San Francisco (1889); St. Joseph's Cathedral, Hartford (1890); St. Ann's Roman Catholic Church, Philadelphia (1893); Epworth Methodist Episcopal Church in Norfolk (1895); Trinity P.E. Church, Buffalo (1896); Trinity Episcopal Church, San Francisco (1896); St. Patrick's Cathedral, Baltimore (1898); Temple Emanuel,

San Francisco (1898); St. Patrick's, Elizabethport, N.J. (1899); St. Agnes Church, New York (1899); New York University Chapel (1899); Music Hall, St. Louis (1899); St. Lawrence Church, Cincinnati (1899); Second Presbyterian Church in St. Louis (1900); Theological Seminary, Chicago (1900); Third Church of Christ, Scientist, Chicago (1900); Walnut Street Baptist Church, Louisville (1901); St. John's M.E. Church, St. Louis (1902); Lake Avenue Baptist Church, Rochester (1902); Presbyterian Church, Kingston, Pa. (1917); Presbyterian Church, Englewood, N.Y. (1917); Fourth Church of Christ, Scientist, New York (1917); First Baptist Church, Flint, Mich. (1919); First Church of Christ, Scientist, St. Paul, Minn. (1919); First Baptist Church, Troy, N.Y. (1919); Congregational Church, Gloversville, N.Y. (1920); Masonic Temple, St. Charles, La. (1920); Sacred Heart Church, Wichita Falls, Texas (1921).

76. Historic Boston Inc., *HB Insights*, fall of 1999, 3.

77. Van Pelt, op. cit., 55.

78. Coburn, Philip, op. cit., 5.

79. "Fine Organ Goes to Washington/The 2000th Completed by Hook-Hastings Company at Weston/The Occasion Observed by Recital, Banquet and Presentation," undated newspaper clipping probably *WDFPT*, about March 3, 1904, Hook & Hastings scrapbook, WHS.

80. "His Birthday/Employees and Friends of Mr. Hastings/Assemble to Honor His 70th Anniversary/A Notable and Enjoyable Occasion in the Organ Builder's Life," undated newspaper clipping, probably *WDFPT*, 1906, Coburn scrapbook #2. Includes names of 71 employees who signed the testimonial.

81. Ayars, op. cit., 173.

82. Harold Vincent Milligan, organist and choir director at Riverside Church, to Hook & Hastings Co., January 13, 1913, reprinted as a company advertisement (WHS).

83. Coburn, op. cit., 8.

84. 1890 *Boston Herald* article, as reprinted in Kennedy, "Francis Hastings' Labor Experiment," op. cit., 8.

85. Undated clipping, probably *Waltham Free Press*, Coburn scrapbook #3, 89.

86. Parents of children attending District Schoolhouse #5 on South Avenue also resisted pressure to close their neighborhood school, but #5 was more sparsely attended and was closed in World War I as an economy measure.

87. Information in this section from Weston United Methodist Church, "The History of Methodism in Weston" (1989 version), and Lamson's *HTW*, 173–75.

88. According to "The History of Methodism," cited above, this was the fifth Methodist church building in Massachusetts and the seventh in New England.

89. Lamson's *HTW*, 173. See page 175 for construction details of 1828 church.

90. Organ given by Mrs. George Harrington; see Lamson's *HTW*, 176.

91. Designed by George Strout after the initial architect, G.F. Newton, didn't work out, according to the 1989 church history. The new church was dedicated on January 20, 1901, and is described in a *WDFPT* article of January 25, 1901, "The First Methodist Church at Weston Completed/Appropriate Exercises Held Sunday—the Event Largely Attended." The auditorium was 35 feet by 40 feet and seated 150. The church had stained-glass windows and cost $5,520 including furnishings.

92. The earliest recorded summer resident was Deacon Samuel Barrett, whose house was torn down by Jonas Hastings in 1823.

93. 70 North Avenue.

94. The Tiffany windows at First Parish Church were given in memory of Henry A. Gowing by his wife in 1899. See also 1949 *TR*, 131.

95. Undated newspaper clipping, Coburn scrapbook #1, 389.

96. Undated newspaper article, November 1898, Coburn scrapbook #2, 69. See also *Pung*, 61.

97. MCRD 2553/22, Gowing to Thurston, April 1897. The name Drabbington appears in the town death records as the birthplace of Sarah Thurston.

98. Plans at Massachusetts Archives. Builder was J.C. MacDonald.

99. "New Hotel/Drabbington Lodge Just/Opened at Kendal Green/A Modern House/Conveniently Arranged with/Nicely Furnished Rooms," 1899 newspaper article, Coburn scrapbook #2, 105.

100. Ibid.

101. *WDFPT*, February 2, 1900. The stable was destroyed by fire in 1928.

102. *WDFPT*, about November 1, 1901, "Work has been begun upon a pretty cottage of stone and wood," and May 23, 1902, "[the house] commands a delightful view and under the direct care of Mrs. Thurston has been elegantly furnished and appointed." Early-20th-century newspaper articles indicate it was rented as a single house.

103. The term *bungalow* was used when the house was under construction (see *WDFPT*, December 11, 1903), when completed (May 13, 1904), and in subsequent newspaper articles. The bungalow was reportedly also used as the Thurston family winter home.

104. Advertisement, Friendly Society program, "Sweethearts," April 24–25, 1925, 5.

105. *WDFPT*, August 21, 1908.

106. *WDFPT*, July 5, 1913.

107. *WDFPT*, July 5, 1912, and August 30, 1912.

108. *Pung*, 58.

109. *WFP*, November 1898, in Coburn scrapbook #2, 72.

110. *WDFPT*, April 20, 1906.

111. *WDFPT*, May 27, 1910.

112. MCRD, 5909/373, Brooke-Skinner sale of a gymnasium to Posse-Nissen School for $3,900, February 12, 1935. The Posse School is mentioned in the 1941 *TR*, 44. In 1942, L. Thurston applied for permission to operate the building as an apartment house (1942 *TR*, 15–16) but did not complete the application process.

113. The Posse Institute was using the lodge on May 10, 1940, when a newspaper article in the *Weston News Review* reported a fire.

114. *Massachusetts Magazine*, vol. 2, 1909, 137.

115. 1889 newspaper clipping, *WFP*, Coburn scrapbook #4, 32.

116. WDFPT, March 31, 1899. According to town records, Brodrick was born in Roxbury and his father was from Nova Scotia.

117. *WDFPT*, December 11, 1903.

118. 1893 directory.

119. MCRD 2885/17, April 1901. Daniel Garfield sold the property for $1,600 to James's brother, William H. Foote, together with the buildings and "all the water power and machinery attached hereto." William sold to James in 1903.

120. Story from Elsie Foote Cooke, daughter of James Foote, also related in *Pung*, 62.

121. *WDFPT*, December 2, 1904.

122. *WDFPT*, March 7, 1919. Foote had his cider analyzed at a laboratory.

123. James Foote's daughter, Elsie Foote Cooke, believes this gas pump was the first in Weston.

124. PWF, interview with Elsie Foote Cooke; also Ben Crouch to PWF.

125. "James Thomas Foote," *Middlesex County and Its People*, vol. IV, 368.

126. *WDFPT*, November 19, 1915.

127. *WDFPT*, February 12 and 19, 1915.

128. *WDFPT*, March 7, 1919.

129. *WDFPT*, October 8, 1920.

130. The land, which was all on the west side of Lexington Street, was sold to Tyler by Emily Cutting Kenney, daughter of John Warren Cutting and wife of school furniture manufacturer Oliver N. Kenney (MCRD 1291/68. $7,000, 1874). Oliver Kenney met his future wife while working for her father. According to descendant Eloise Kenney, one of Oliver's jobs was to take the wagon into the Back Bay and cut saltmarsh hay to bring back to the farm in Weston.

131. *WDFPT*, June 24 and August 12, 1904. An item on September 16, 1904, called Tyler's place "Kendal Green Farm."

132. *WDFPT,* 1897 (fire was September 21), Coburn scrapbook #2, 25.
133. Their home was at 254 Conant Road. See also "Viles Family of Weston, 1790–1980," handwritten manuscript, WHS.
134. 1919 *TR* , 47-52.
135. 300 Conant Road.
136. For a history of the family, see M.V. Washburn's "Viles Family of Weston: 1790–Now, 1908" (unpublished manuscript, WHS). The author was Henry's daughter. The nine children of Jesse Sumner Viles and Lany Ann Viles were Mary, Olive, Elizabeth, Emma, Jesse Sumner Jr., Henry, William, Ella, and George.
137. MCRD 4501/53, Town of Weston to Woodward, March 1922, $7,000. Woodward to Dean, 4825/152, March 1925.
138. Crouch, op. cit., 28.
139. MCRD, Registered Land, Book 23/309, April 9, 1912. Includes plan.
140. MCRD, Registered Land, 99/241, January 1923. Notes indicate that the property was foreclosed on May 10, 1941, and subsequently sold.
141. "Charles John Read Cahill," *Middlesex County and Its People*, vol. IV, 506.
142. Advertisement, Cedar Hill Farm, 1924 (in scrapbook owned by Jean Tierney, granddaughter of Charles J.R. Cahill).
143. The "sales stand" first appears in town tax records in 1928. The ice cream was made in the back of the boardinghouse, and Lois Cahill did a lot of the cooking. The Cahill dairy stand is now the Dairy Joy.
144. PWF interview with Jean Tierney.
145. MCRD Registered Land, 376/361, June 1945, bought by Trustees of Kendal Green Realty, formed under Declaration of Trust dated June 1, 1945. PWF interview with Aimo Teittinen, January 25, 1999.
146. Information from H. Bentley Crouch, Weston Fire Department historian.
147. "Showy Fire Levels Weston Barn," *Waltham News-Tribune,* October 22, 1949.
148. MCRD, Registered Land 547/130, November 1954.
149. "Techbuilt," brochure printed by Techbuilt, 127 Mt. Auburn Street, Cambridge (undated, probably late 1960s).
150. According to an article in the January 23, 1958, *Town Crier,* the company was formed "for the purpose of creating a new residential area of architect designed, custom built homes of a character befitting the unusual settings." Corporate officers of Weston Land Company were Fred Ruland of Waltham, president; Leonard H. Dowse of Weston, Eric Reissner of Weston and G. Arnold Haynes of Wellesley, vice presidents; Edward M. Dickson of Weston, treasurer; and Roger Ela of Wayland, clerk of the corporation. J. Irving Connolly represented the company in the sale of homesites.
151. Hobbs Brook Road. See letter from Franklin W. Hobbs, president of Techbuilt Inc., to John Cederholm, September 25, 1969 (BPL Fine Arts Department, Techbuilt file).
152. MCRD 2648/152, Edwin Bradbury to Sally Dwight, March 1898, 56.73 acres on east side of Lexington Street. See map of 1892 in Plan Book 74/50.
153. Whitehill, Walter Muir, *Boston Public Library, A Centennial History* (Harvard University Press, Cambridge, MA, 1956), 129–130. Whitehill describes Dwight as a "versatile genius." He served as librarian of the Department of State in Washington, D.C., and archivist for the extraordinary Adams family collection in Quincy before being appointed librarian of the Boston Public Library in 1892. He was granted a leave of absence two years later because of "poor health and inability to stand the cares and responsibilities of the office."
154. Dwight's letterhead read "Stone House, Kendal Green" (Francis Blake Papers, letter of June 18, 1899, 65.931, MHS).
155. For a description at time of sale, see *WDFPT,* July 30, 1915. The name The Cedars appears on a postcard in the E.B. Sears Collection, WPL history room, announcing a winter carnival on January 8, 1916, for the benefit of the American Fund for French Wounded.
156. Date of fire was April 19, 1918.
157. MCRD 5092/63, May 2, 1927 (Plan Book 74/50). The Georgian Trust was formed by a declaration of trust dated September 3, 1920 (Worcester Registry of Deeds, 2227/73, amended March 5, 1923, Book 2293/196).
158. Goodale and Nichols formed the trust in May 1927 (MCRD 5103/393). The various subdivisions can be followed in Registered Land books beginning with 184/581, Original Certificate of Title, June 7, 1929, Fiske Warren et al., Trustees of the Georgian Trust, transfer of Lot E to Goodale and Nichols, March 31, 1931 (218/325). Same-day transfer of Lot E to The Cambridge School Inc. (218/329). Transfer of Lot D to The Cambridge School, December 31, 1946, and then lot D-2 to Kendal Common Inc., Book 449/57, June 15, 1949.
159. "Trapelo Golf Club Is Seeking Increased Membership Quota of 150," *Weston News Review,* April 14, 1939.
160. St. John, George Jr., *Individuals and Community: The Cambridge School: The First Hundred Years* (Windflower Press: Cambridge, MA, 1986), ix.
161. Ibid., 21.
162. Ibid., 191.
163. *Christian Science Monitor,* February 1932, as quoted in St. John, 24.
164. St. John, op. cit., 25.
165. Ibid., 78.
166. Ibid., 96.
167. Ibid., 97.
168. Stubbins's son attended Cambridge School in the mid-1950s, as did the son of architect Carl Koch.
169. MCRD 10434/270, heirs of S. Phillip Miller to Prestige Realty Associates Inc., December 1963. See also Plan 1771 of 1963.
170. 1948 *TR,* 145.
171. Cat Rock Trust was formed under a Declaration of Trust dated November 22, 1950 (7673/527). The trust conveyed the property in October 1957 to a group of Weston residents who then conveyed 64 acres to the town, including Cat Rock Hill. See MCRD "Plan of Cat Rock Trust Property," July 19, 1957, Plan 1527 of 1957. See also 1957 *TR,* 145–46.
172. From Frederick C. Dumaine Jr., 6.5 acres in 1975, 9.23 acres in 1974, and 8 acres in 1976 including half of the pond. From Albert and Francis Hunt, 36.45 acres, November 1976, including other half of pond, small pond, and meadow northwest of pond.
173. *WDFP,* February 26, 1904. The newspaper item says, "The Boston & Maine R.R. Co. is making extensive improvements at the station in cleaning and renovating and newly painting and varnishing the interior. It looks as good as new."
174. From "The Warren Family in Watertown and Weston," undated typescript (WPL, E.B. Sears papers).
175. *WDFPT,* August 25, 1916, says, "Philip Miller is building a house on land he recently bought of the E.J. Brown estate."
176. Lamson, *HTW,* 159.
177. Whiffen, Marcus, *American Architecture since 1780: A Guide to the Styles* (Cambridge: MIT Press, 1969) and Saylor, H.H., *Bungalows: Their Design, Construction and Furnishing* (New York, 1917).
178. MCRD 806/241, Gowing, admistrator for estate of Converse Bigelow, to John Bent, 1858; 185/519, Bent to Kendall H. Stone, 1859; and 1583/513, Stone to Edward Coburn, November 1881, for $9,000.
179. Peirce, Mary F., *Town of Weston: Births, Deaths, and Marriages,* 580.
180. "More About the Jonas Hastings Homestead," *WHSB,* March 1980, 3. Includes text from deed.
181. Photo of this Warren house in Lamson's *HTW,* opposite page 111.
182. Coburn scrapbook #4, 179. "Kendall (sic) Green column," 1891.
183. Letter from Daisy S. Faber to Mrs. Nettie O'Toole.

Figure 11-1. Described as "one of the oldest and most highly respected citizens of Weston," Edward Coburn celebrated his 80th birthday in June 1900. His house at 171 Church Street was decorated with "roses and masses of forget-me-nots artistically arranged." One hundred and twenty-five relatives and friends attended and family members posed for this photograph.

CHAPTER 11

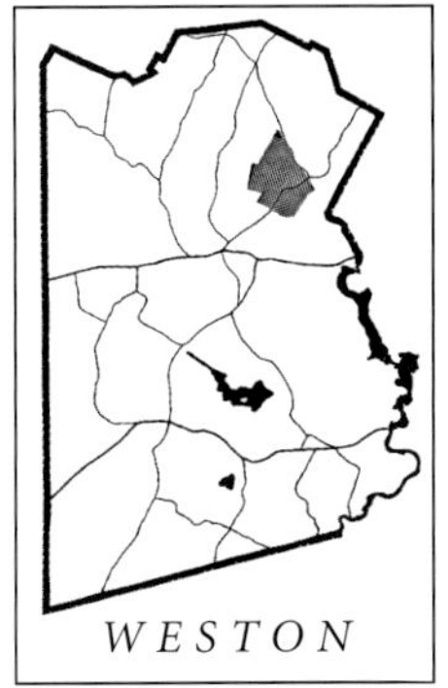

Church Street and Webster Hill

The Coburn Family

Few areas in Weston are more closely identified with a single family than Church Street and the Coburns. For almost 200 years, from 1801 until 1997, the family owned the white clapboard farmhouse that stands at the bend in Church Street. Across the street is the monumental red Coburn barn, one of the town's most beloved landmarks. For generations Coburns farmed the land and cooperated on seasonal tasks like cutting ice and driving cattle to summer pastures.

For the vignettes of everyday life found in this chapter, the author is indebted to Philip Coburn's memoir Growing Up in Weston.[1] *Coburn (1899–1983), a lifelong resident of the town, was a star football player at Harvard in the early 1920s and later a textile engineer and executive.*[2] *He records the Church Street neighborhood as it changed in the first two decades of the 20th century. On the west side of the street was the nine-hole Weston Golf Club, where early golf enthusiasts stepped gingerly through cow pastures that doubled as fairways. On Webster Hill, the rustic summer "hunting lodge" built by Frank Webster in 1898 was joined in the 1910s and '20s by handsome Colonial Revival homes for businessmen and professionals. On what is now Coburn Road was the Filene estate, a carefully tended 40-acre property that belonged to Boston department store owner A. Lincoln Filene, the only Jewish estate owner in Weston.*

For those nostalgic for life on the farm, Growing Up in Weston *describes the backbreaking work and marginal profits. Children performed many daily and seasonal tasks. Philip Coburn's after-school chores included sawing and chopping wood for the kitchen stove, cleaning the henhouse, watering and feeding the hens and ducks, taking the ashes out of the cellar, mowing the lawn, and weeding the garden. In summer he raked the "scatterins" and trod hay in the barn. This tedious job was performed under hot and dusty conditions and was difficult because the hay was so spongy he could hardly lift his legs high enough to pack it down. In fall, Coburn and the other children picked up the windfalls from the early apple trees, which were taken to Foote's to be made into cider or given to P.J. McAuliffe's horses.*

Coburn's memoir also conveys the joy of his childhood. His first sentence, "Imagine a playground of 16.8 miles," captures the freedom of children to roam the town on foot or bicycle. With his siblings and friends, Coburn built rafts and floated them in ponds and fished for pickerel and perch in Stony Brook. In the fall the boys played pickup football against the "Warren Avenue gang" or the "Silver Hill gang" and hunted for pheasants, partridges, and deer in season. They skated and played hockey on the ice ponds. When the ice melted around the edge of the pond and the boys lost a puck, they could make two more by sawing in half the hard wooden stopple of a milk can. Boys started trapping when they were 13 or 14 years old, each within his own territory. They wrapped the furs in brown paper and took a train to Leburger & Asher, Boston furriers. The price paid—perhaps a dollar for muskrat and $2.75 for most skunks—seemed like good pay for what, to a boy, was pleasure.

The Homestead on Church Street

The first Coburn to live in Weston was John, whose 18th-century farmhouse once stood at the bend of Chestnut Street.[3] In 1801 his oldest son, Jonas (1773–1836), paid $4,400 for a 120-acre farm on Church Street that had belonged to the Whittemore family since 1726.[4] The property included a sturdy farmhouse facing exactly south, built with heavy hand-hewn oak timbers and a large central chimney. In 1804 Jonas married Susannah Viles of Lexington, and of their nine children, seven survived into

Figure 11-2. In 1801, Jonas Coburn purchased a 120-acre farm on Church Street, including the Colonial house at No. 153 (at right). His son Isaac built the barn in 1841. Descendants owned the house and barn until 1997–98.

Figure 11-3. Anna Coburn (1853–1950), known as "Miss Annie" to her students, taught in the Weston schools until 1899, when she married organ factory owner Francis Henry Hastings.

Figure 11-4. William Herbert Coburn Sr. (1857–1909) was a banker. He worked closely with his friend Horace Sears in the up-building of First Parish Church. Coburn built the house at 119 Church Street in 1896–97.

Figure 11-5. Arthur Leslie Coburn (1860–1931) farmed the Church Street property until 1897, when he became superintendent at the nearby Hook & Hastings organ factory. He took over leadership of the company after the death of his brother-in-law Francis Henry Hastings.

adulthood. To understand the development of the Coburn homestead over almost two centuries, it is important to follow the history of two of these children: the second son, Isaac, and youngest son, Edward.

The Isaac Coburn Family

When Jonas Coburn died in 1836, the farm passed to Isaac (1811–1875). In 1841, Isaac married Julia Ann Cutter, a hometown girl from Cutter's Corner. That same year, he built the red barn across from the family farmhouse.[5] Following Coburn family tradition, Isaac and Julia Ann had a large family, eight in all: Isaac, Harriet Ann, Thomas, Julie Anna, Anna, Edith Laura, William Herbert, and Arthur Leslie. The two oldest children moved away from Weston as adults and the next two died at an early age, leaving the last four siblings living together in the family homestead. When the youngest, Arthur, was only 14, his mother died, followed by his father four years later. William left the job he loved at the bank and returned to help "Artie" manage the farm. Anna started teaching when just out of high school and Edith kept the house and raised watercress and forget-me-nots for market.[6] The two brothers and two sisters formed a close-knit group, living and working together until, eventually, three were married.

Figure 11-6. Anna, Edith, Will, and Arthur Coburn lived together in the family homestead until three of them married. The large central chimney and 8-over-12 window sash seen in this postcard are characteristic of the early 18th century. The c. 1726 house is now protected by a preservation restriction.

Figure 11-7. The three children of William Herbert Coburn—Pauline, Philip and William Jr.—camp out about 1909. In later years, Philip Coburn wrote Growing Up in Weston.

Anna, known as "Miss Annie" to her students, was valedictorian of the Weston High School Class of 1871. She taught at the high school and intermediate school until 1880, when she took over an unruly class of 57 "scholars" at District School #4 on North Avenue. After just one term, the school committee reported steady progress in scholarship, discipline, and morale, noting that the school now "stands before the town as one of our most reliable and progressive schools."[7]

Anna taught at the North Avenue School until 1899, when, at age 46, she married Francis Henry Hastings. He was 62 and well known in town as owner of the nearby organ factory. Anna's sister Edith moved in with the couple, leaving the family homestead in care of the farm foreman. In 1904, Edith was killed by a train in the early hours of the morning as she wandered in her nightdress down the Fitchburg railroad tracks. Her death was attributed to suicide, brought on by grief at the murder only eight days earlier of her dear friend Mabel Page.

William Herbert eventually returned to banking. He was active in First Parish Church affairs and worked closely with his friend Horace Sears in organizing First Parish activities, such as the Friendly Society, E.H. Sears Guild, and choir. When William married Maude Fairbairn in 1896, he built his own house on three acres just south of the family homestead.[8] What is now the front lawn was an orchard planted with peach and apple trees and grapevines. William and Maude had three children who survived into adulthood: William Jr., Philip, and Pauline. In 1909, when he was just 52, William Herbert Coburn died suddenly of typhoid fever.[9]

Arthur Leslie continued farming until 1897. That year he went to work at the organ factory, first as secretary of the corporation and superintendent and then as president after the death of Francis Hastings. When he married in 1898, he built his own Shingle-style house on Webster Hill.[10] Arthur continued to run the farm, although it had long since ceased to be profitable. He raised corn and other vegetables and kept about a dozen cows, selling the milk wholesale. He rented the old homestead and built a small cottage next to the barn for his tenant farmer.

According to his son "Bud," Arthur Leslie did not have the temperament to be a businessman. For example, when churches turned off their heat, he would feel obligated to send men out to tune their organs, which did not adapt well to extremes of temperature. When he took over, the organ factory was already in its declining years, and it closed only a few years after his death in 1931. His widow and children moved back to the homestead on Church Street.

The Edward Coburn Family

Isaac's brother Edward (1820–1904), the youngest child of Jonas and Susannah, was only 16 when his father died. He stayed home to help on the farm for a few years and then moved to Boston to learn the meat business.[11] At 21, he returned to Weston and purchased part of the family homestead from his older brother, Isaac. Edward built a fine Greek Revival house on a rise overlooking one of the hay fields.[12] In the first of his successful business ventures, he set himself up in the meat business, slaughtering cattle on the farm and selling the meat from a wagon that he drove himself through Weston, Wayland, and Lincoln. He was the only provision dealer in the area for almost three decades.

When his first wife, Dolly Bennett, died in 1854, he married her cousin Hannah Bennett. They had five children: Thomas, Albert, Caroline, Florence, and Oscar. When the Civil War broke out, he had a young family to support and hired a substitute to fill his place in the service. His meat business flourished. In 1871 he sold it and started a large dairy operation

Figure 11-8. Edward Coburn (1820–1904) was a successful butcher who later started a prosperous dairy farm. He owned a business block in the town center, which burned in 1893. After the fire, the First Parish Calendar *noted, "That admirable representative of what is best in New England life, Mr. Edward Coburn, with true New England courage and determination has already begun to restore the largest building . . ."*

described as one of the best in Weston.[13] He invested in property in Weston Center, where he built two houses and the town's first commercial block.[14] Unlike many farmers of his day, Edward had the means to acquire luxury items like a buggy and fine driving horses, which carried him around town.

Edward served as selectman for 14 years, treasurer of First Parish for 10 years, and state legislator for a year, in 1876. "He was a great lover of his town and never more happy than when in its service," wrote one biographer.[15] The esteem of his fellow townsmen is evident in this description of Edward as an old man: "His tall, medium figure, his dignified walk, his erect head covered with snow-white hair were, so to say, like a magnet and drew to him the friendship of all, both young and old."[16]

Figure 11-9. Three young riders from the Kendal Green Riding Stables make their way through the former Edward Coburn property toward Church Street in this 1968 photograph. At left is the Jonas Coburn house; behind it is the cupola of the red barn.

As his children reached adulthood, Edward provided well for them. When his oldest son, Thomas, married in 1881, his father bought him a 70-acre working dairy farm on North Avenue. Edward's second son, Albert Eugene, worked on his father's farm and settled in a cottage on the property.[17] Caroline or "Carrie," Edward's oldest daughter, married Louis Briggs in 1893. Edward provided a home for the couple in one of his houses in the town center. His youngest daughter, Florence, was an enthusiastic suffragette who never married. She took care of her parents and later traveled extensively. Edward's youngest son, Oscar, was killed in 1889 in a tragic fire that destroyed two large barns and his father's entire stock of 17 cows. According to newspaper reports, 22-year-old Oscar died trying to lead a valuable Guernsey out of the barn.[18]

Cooperative Farming

In the years before World War I, the extended family of Coburn brothers and cousins pooled their resources and shared seasonal chores. In winter, driveways were plowed by those who had equipment. Ice cutting was done cooperatively, as described by Phil Coburn in *Growing Up in Weston*:

> Every winter about the middle of February the three families of Coburns who kept cows would get together to cut ice for the milk can coolers . . . on the ice pond behind what is now 170 Church St. For home ice chests, they bought from George Foote. . . . [T]he ice house was about 15 feet by 15 feet and stood close to the pond. It had three five-foot doors, one above the other. After the pond had been cleared of any snow, it was scored with lines two feet apart, using a horse drawn marker for the purpose, then the process was repeated at right angles to mark off squares. An ice saw was used to cut the blocks by means of a pick pole pushed into the channel to the conveyor. Grappling hooks were placed behind them and the horse would haul them up as far as the ice house door where the cake would be pushed onto another conveyer to take it inside. Two men with what were called cant dogs would lift the cake into place. When one layer was completed it would be covered with sawdust which had been brought over from Kenney Bros. and Wolkins chair factory by pung. There were about fifteen layers of ice when the house was full.[19]

Each household was called in advance to determine its winter requirements of stove and furnace coal. Coburn men would work together to haul coal in hay wagons from Kendal Green Station to Brodrick's store, where it was weighed on the large platform scale. Frances Hastings billed each family for its share.

Figure 11-10. Harold Coburn Sr., son of Thomas Coburn, drives a team of workhorses.

Various Coburns would be designated to drive the heifers up North Avenue to pasture in Stow each May and bring them back in the fall. This trip took about half a day, with one man driving the horse and buggy and the others walking behind the heifers to keep them from running down the railroad tracks at grade crossings. The cattle drivers took the pregnant cows also, as they didn't need to be milked. The farmers would check on them periodically to see if they were ready to calve. This custom continued until after World War I, when motorized trucks came into use.

The Coburns maintained a cranberry bog near Hastings Station. After the main crop had been harvested and sent to Faneuil Hall, the family would pick what was left over for home consumption. According to Brian Donahue's *Reclaiming the Commons,* Weston had 14 acres of cranberry bogs in 1865, a number that dwindled to two by 1905.[20]

In *Growing Up in Weston,* Philip Coburn describes how, at the age of 11, he was old enough to "ride horse" for his cousin Albert:

> He [Albert] planted corn in what used to be the Riding Stable field and every once in a while he would holler at me and say, "Ride straight; you know if the rows are crooked the relatives will see them on their way to church."[21]

Early Days of the Weston Golf Club

From its formation in 1894 until 1916, Weston Golf Club was located on the west side of Church Street on land leased from Arthur Leslie Coburn and his neighbors. Golf got its start in Weston when Rev. Charles F. Russell, minister at First Parish, returned from England with a set of clubs and began hitting balls into nearby pastures. His infatuation quickly spread to friends and parishioners and a club was organized within a year. The Weston Golf Club was one of the earliest in the nation. In Massachusetts, only four golf courses had been built before Weston's was completed in 1894.[22]

The initial all-male membership roster reads like a local social register. Brenton H. Dickson served as first president; Charles J. Paine and William E. Russell as vice presidents; Albert Thorndike as secretary-treasurer; and Arthur L. Coburn, Rev. Charles F. Russell, Francis H. Hastings, J. Bertram Williams, and Robert Winsor as directors.[23] William Herbert Coburn was a charter member. The initiation fee the first year was $10 and the annual assessment, $5. Membership was limited to 100 and averaged about 65 during the Kendal Green years.

The nine-hole course initially measured about 2,000 yards and over the years was increased to

Figure 11-11. Weston Golf Club was originally located on Church Street. The club was founded here after the Rev. Charles Russell came back from England with clubs and began hitting balls across the cow pastures.

Figure 11-12. This late-19th-century photograph shows Gen. Charles Jackson Paine, wearing his legendary red suspenders, driving from the first tee at the newly formed Weston Golf Club. The caddy house is on the right and the Coburn barn is in the distance.

2,444.[24] Holes varied in length from about 160 to 400 yards and had names like Orchard, Song, Far, Oak, Hill, Bank, Bunker Hill, and Punch Bowl, which was down in the hollow. Some of the greens were surrounded by pipe fences to keep off the cows, but the third fairway was a cow pasture, and golfers had to watch their step. One of the caddies' jobs was to drive cows out of the golfers' way. After this, the course crossed Viles Street to a fairway on the present Brook Road playground. The sixth fairway headed back east along what is now Valley View Road. The eighth hole consisted of four fields separated by stone walls converted into bunkers by covering them with earth and grass.

Entrance to the club was between the red Coburn barn and the adjacent farmer's cottage. The driveway extended due west about 200 yards to a clubhouse built in 1896. This rustic, one-story structure was about 30 by 50 feet and had a wide porch along the west side. Inside were lockers, lavatories, and dressing rooms as well as a large room with a fireplace at the east end, built-in benches with cushions, and a central table where refreshments were served during tournaments. The club provided a full schedule of men's and women's golf tournaments. Members had the use of two tennis courts rented from property owners on Webster Hill.

A pipe from a spring on Webster Hill supplied water to the clubhouse and greens, which were watered by hand from a barrel transported on wheels. Mowers were drawn by horses wearing leather shoes to minimize damage to the turf.

During the summer and fall, local boys would caddy on Saturdays. Phil Coburn recounts the experience in *Growing Up in Weston:*

> [The groundskeeper, "Hornet" Bartlett,] . . . earned this nickname because he was always chasing caddies off the course when they practiced golf shots while waiting for someone to hire them. Waiting was always boring and to while away the time we sometimes rolled cigarettes from tissue paper and filled them with sweet fern, cedar bark, corn silk and occasionally the butt of an old cigar or cigarette that someone had tossed aside.[25]
>
> I received twenty cents a round for caddying which amounted to about ten cents an hour, as it took two hours to play nine holes. My brother was more fortunate. When he caddied for Mr. Batchelder, one of the better players, he received forty cents for the nine holes. This was well worth Mr. Batchelder's while because he used Spaulding "Glory Dimple" balls that cost a dollar apiece, and my brother had an extraordinarily good eye.[26]

During the years at Kendal Green, members were never allowed to play on Sundays. An 1894 edition of the *Waltham Free Press* suggests that, in 1894 at least, Sunday sports were not only discouraged but also against the law:

> We believe that as a rule people in Weston do—and very properly—object to the playing of sports and games within the corporate limits of the town on Sunday. It is with surprise that they learned of Sumner Paine and Edward A. Wilkie arrested for playing "golf" on the Lord's Day. If there is any virtue in birth, education and wealth, it should lead the possessor to be an exemplary

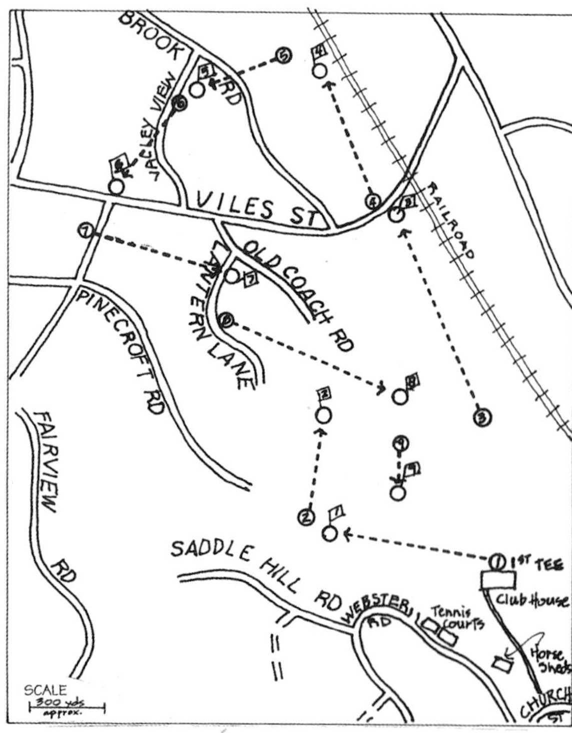

Figure 11-13. This map, adapted from the Weston Historical Society Bulletin, *shows the nine holes of the original Weston Golf Club.*

> citizen. There is not the excuse that these parties were ignorant of the law. They acted deliberately and sought of themselves to break down the barriers that New England custom has raised between the probity and morality of a typical New England township and the immorality of France, the most licentious of nations and the one with the least respect for the sanctity of the Sabbath.[27]

The reporter added, "The fine, we believe, was fittingly applied."

Although customs changed over the next two decades, A.L. Coburn, who owned much of the land, believed in a day of worship and rest and always refused permission for Sunday play. When leases were being renegotiated in 1916, another owner wanted to sell his land to a home builder. The club looked for other locations and chose 50 acres on what is now Meadowbrook Road, offered on generous terms by estate owner Robert Winsor. After the golf club moved, the A.L. Coburn family sometimes rented its Webster Road house in the summer and lived in the old clubhouse, as the job heading the organ factory was bringing in only a marginal income.

The A. Lincoln Filene Estate

In general, the Coburns on the north side were descended from either Isaac or Edward. Frank Jonas Coburn, whose property became part of the Filene estate, was an exception. Frank was a well-to-do wool broker whose father, Jonas (Jr.), was the older brother of Isaac and Edward. In 1886 Frank bought some of A.L. Coburn's land on what is now Coburn Road and built the house and stable that later were sold to Albert W. Bingham and then to A. Lincoln Filene.[28]

Abraham Lincoln Filene (1865–1957) was the son of William Filene, a German immigrant who built up a chain of small women's clothing stores in Boston and New England in the late 19th century.[29] On William's retirement in 1890, his son Edward became president and Lincoln, general manager in charge of personnel. Lincoln became known for innovations in the field of employee relations; for example, Filene's was one of the earliest stores to establish a minimum wage and five-day, 40-hour work week. Lincoln Filene later became president and chairman of the board. In 1929 he was a leader in organizing Federated Department Stores. Among many honors, he received the gold medal of the National Retail Dry Goods Association as America's outstanding merchant in 1949.

Lincoln and his wife, Theresa, had two daughters, Catherine (b. 1895) and Helen (b. 1899). In 1909 Filene purchased a total of 40 acres in Weston. The sale included the former Frank Coburn property, which had a house, stable, and several small outbuildings.[30] Ten-year-old Philip Coburn watched from next door as Filene had Frank Coburn's house lifted off its foundation, cut in half, and moved one half to the left and the other to the right, leaving a large space for several new rooms.[31] The woodshed was raised on wooden rollers and moved through the gap and down the hill to the southeast corner of what is now Coburn Road and Church Street, where it was joined with an old henhouse to create a "gatehouse," where the chauffeur lived.

Figure 11-14. Department store owner A. Lincoln Filene purchased 40 acres in Weston in 1909. His Tudor-style mansion stood on what is now Coburn Road until it was demolished in 1937.

The remodeled mansion was a sprawling Tudor, set on a knoll, with stucco and decorative half-timbering, a hip roof, and a wide, glass-enclosed piazza across the front and side. In the living room was a fieldstone fireplace large enough to stand in, with a raised hearth and built-in benches on either side. Opening off the living room was a solarium. On the other side of the entrance hall was a dining room and a kitchen with Dutch tiles, copper utensils, and a square French oven for baking.

The driveway from Church Street was edged with gutters lined with smooth beach stones. The area enclosed by the present Coburn Road was maintained as a four- or five-hole golf course. Two more golf holes were located behind the house near the railroad tracks. A rose-covered fence surrounded a clay tennis court. Behind the stable was a squash court. The stable housed carriages in the upper level and horses, cows, sheep, and pigs below. Later, it was converted to a garage with a gas pump out front. It housed beautifully kept automobiles taken out for Sunday drives. In addition to a Packard, Mr. Filene had a red two-seater American Traveler and Mrs. Filene Sr., who lived with her son, had a Pierce-Arrow driven by a second chauffeur.

In *Growing Up in Weston,* neighbor Phil Coburn recalled the hospitality of the family, their custom of entertaining 25 to 30 guests on weekends, and his experiences working for the Filene gardener as a young man:

> We were invited to use their toboggan, skis and snowshoes on the slope in front of their house—week days only because they entertained in a large way on weekends. In the summer they invited us to use their tennis court. . . . I feel sure that the many kind deeds of the Filene family had quite an influence in our formative years. Several years later I worked two summers for their gardener. My work entailed sweeping the large porch every morning, filling wood boxes in all 23 rooms—the huge living room fireplace burned four foot logs— watering, raking and rolling the tennis court every Friday so that it would be in tip top shape for the weekend, and mowing the entire front lawn with a horse drawn mower, the lawn being a part of their private golf course. I also weeded and raked the long driveway.[32]

The south end of the present Coburn Road was not built until the 1920s, after the Filene girls were married or in college. At that time, Filene apparently enlarged or rebuilt a second house on the property referred to in tax records as the "bungalow." This building was sited high on a ledge south of the stable. From the front it looked like a modest one-story shingled structure, but in back, the house grew to a full three stories with a large servants wing later removed. In 1925 Filene hired Olmsted Brothers to design plantings along the new section of driveway.[33] When the new house was complete, Filene offered the old mansion for sale as a nursing home. The idea did not work out, and the house was demolished about 1937.

The Filenes were one of the first Jewish families in Weston. Although they undoubtedly experienced the anti-Semitism widespread in all communities at the time, Filene was an avid golfer who was accepted as a member of the Weston Golf Club. Club historian Ray Heist recalls that when the golf club moved to Meadowbrook Road, members were not allowed to play on Sundays until after church. Filene would stand on the first tee and wait until he saw Robert Winsor's car go by on the way home from First Parish. Filene was also an early member of the Weston Saddle and Bridle Club.

Theresa Filene was well known for her charity work. The Filenes entertained groups like the Boston newsboys, who were treated to a Saturday in the country with outdoor sports, lunch, and music. She held fundraisers for the Boston Music School Settlement and sponsored free concerts by its pupils. One year the Filenes treated 100 children from the North End settlement to a day at Norumbega Park. After the First World War, Mrs. Filene was "a tireless worker on behalf of returning servicemen," initiating dances to provide recreation and hospitality to help ease the men back into civilian life. About 1919 she was appointed chairman of the Central Bureau of Entertainments of the Boston War Camp Community Service. In this capacity, she was described as a woman with a "marked degree of executive ability" and "striking individuality . . . distinguished in manner and beauty." [34]

After World War II, Filene sold the Weston property to a developer and moved some of the staff to his other estate in Marstons Mills on the Cape.[35] The outbuildings were converted to private homes snapped up by young couples looking for a place to live at a time of postwar housing shortages.

Webster Hill

Webster Hill takes its name from Frank G. Webster, a banker with the firm of Kidder Peabody in Boston and a close friend of Frank Coburn.[36] About 1898, Frank Webster built a rustic summer cabin sometimes referred to as a hunting lodge.[37] Webster's wife, Mary, owned 77 acres on the hill in partnership with Hannah Coburn [Jackson], wife of Frank Coburn and, after his death, of Fred W. Jackson.

Until 1909, the only houses on the hill were the Webster cabin and Arthur L. Coburn's shingled house on lower Webster Road. That year, Mary Webster and Hannah Jackson sold 6.5 acres to Alice B. Eliot, who with her husband, landscape architect George W. Eliot, built a handsome Colonial Revival house on Church Street designed by Samuel Mead.

The following year, Webster and Jackson sold land

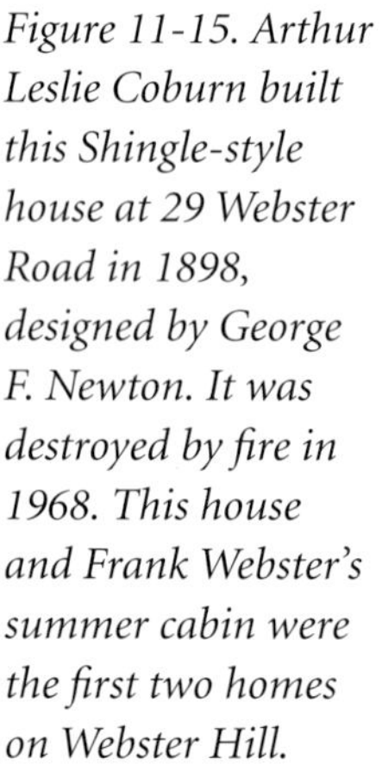

Figure 11-15. Arthur Leslie Coburn built this Shingle-style house at 29 Webster Road in 1898, designed by George F. Newton. It was destroyed by fire in 1968. This house and Frank Webster's summer cabin were the first two homes on Webster Hill.

to Paul Winsor, brother of estate owner Robert Winsor. Paul was an MIT graduate who became chief engineer of Motive Power and Rolling Stock with the Boston Elevated. According to family tradition, he was awarded a patent for a street railway braking device and used the income from the invention to build his unique concrete house. With its hard southern yellow pine beams, concrete walls, asbestos shingle roof, expensive handmade green floor tiles in the family area, and plain Venetian red tiles in the large servants wing, the house was fireproof and virtually indestructible.[38] The layout was planned for Paul's semi-invalid wife, Jesse, and their two small boys. Jesse's activities were limited but did include caring for plants in a conservatory designed especially for her. Paul Winsor apparently overextended his finances in the construction and had to sell after only a few years.

Development on the hill continued as Webster and Jackson sold land to Mary A. Plumer and her husband, Boston businessman and machinery manufacturer Charles S. Plumer. The couple built a house in 1910–11, also designed by Samuel Mead. They subdivided the land within the loop of what they called Plumer Road, a name that fortunately didn't stick. In all, about half a dozen houses were built on Webster Hill between 1910 and the beginning of World War I, followed by another building cycle in the mid-1920s. At that time, Warren Campbell's fieldstone house was designed by reform-minded New York architect Ernest Flagg.

In *Growing Up in Weston,* Phil Coburn recalls the early days of the automobile, when Webster Road, which was then just a gravel road, was a testing ground to see whether a car could "make the grade." The tests were usually carried out on weekends, and watching them provided a form of entertainment for young boys. Any car that didn't make it up the hill would back down and try again. In those days, muffler cutouts were not forbidden, and Coburn recalls that "the noise was wonderfully loud."

Webster Hill had quieter attractions as well. The children picked lady's slippers and partridgeberries in the pine woods and cowslips near the deep spring hole where the earliest skunk cabbage and jack-in-the-pulpit grew.[39] Quarts of blueberries from the slope made their way into Coburn pies and muffins.

Children of Thomas Coburn

Thomas Coburn had four children: Edward, Harold, Raymond, and Mildred Elizabeth. Two of the three boys took up farming. Edward graduated from Burdett College and worked on his father's farm until 1912, when he married and purchased 82 acres just north of Weston on what is now Tower Road in Lincoln. Edward enjoyed the independent life of the farmer and, until the mid-1960s, ran a diversified operation that included raising high-grade livestock and dairying.[40] Some of Edward's fields were later developed as the Coburn Farms subdivision in Lincoln. Edward's younger brother Harold took over management of their father's dairy farm on North Avenue when Thomas died in 1916.

Raymond Coburn graduated from Harvard College in 1910 and trained as a highway engineer. He began working for the state in 1911 and in 1923 became construction engineer for the Massachusetts Department of Public Works.[41] In this position, he was responsible for the construction or reconstruction of all state roads, including the Route 20 bypass in Weston. Coburn also served the town as selectman and longtime member of the school committee.

Recent Years

James Dolan worked for Arthur Leslie Coburn as farm manager from the mid-1920s until Coburn's death in 1931. After that, Dolan continued to live in the farmer's cottage and to work the land as a tenant farmer. He kept an average of 14 dairy cows, raised chickens, and grew acres of potatoes, along with hubbard squash, corn, tomatoes, and other market vegetables. Some produce was sold at a farm stand on Church Street but most was taken by a trucker to Faneuil Hall market and sold for whatever the market would bring. Some years, a season of hard work yielded only a subsistence income.[42]

In 1974, the children of Arthur L. Coburn sold the 44-acre Coburn meadow to the town. Beginning in 1997, the 23-acre property at 171 Church Street was developed under an agreement that preserved the Edward Coburn house and protected part of the property with conservation easements. At Town Meeting of 1997, voters agreed to purchase the c. 1726 Coburn homestead, to be resold with preservation restrictions, and the adjacent meadow, to be preserved as conservation land. Through these efforts, the pastoral Church Street landscape remains largely intact as a reminder of Weston's agricultural heritage.

Houses in the Church Street/Webster Hill Area

22 Church Street (1755): The Elisha Jones house is one of the most sophisticated, high-style examples of Georgian architecture in Weston. It may be the town's first example of the use of twin chimneys instead of a center chimney. The builder, housewright Jeduthan Baldwin, took full advantage of the twin-chimney plan to create a wide, spacious central hallway with handsome staircase. The house was among the first in Weston to be built with a four-over-four rather than the more common two-over-two room plan. Georgian exterior features such as the pedimented window lintels and corner quoins are rarely seen in Weston. The house was originally located on Highland Street and was moved twice by Charles H. Fiske. (See chapters 16 and 18.)

36 Church Street: According to "The Weston Meeting House Common and Its Neighbors," a printed lecture (c. 1900) by Charles H. Fiske, this house was originally a store that stood next to First Parish Church. It was purchased by George W. Cutting Sr., who moved it to the corner of Boston Post Road and School Street and continued to use it as a store. After Cutting took possession of another store on what is now the town green, the earlier store was remodeled and enlarged into his residence. In the last years of the 19th century, the site was sold to the town for a library. The house was purchased by Charles H. Fiske Jr., who moved it to its present location just beyond the house Fiske's father had moved. (see photo in chapter 15).

39-43 Church Street (1891): Three-family house built for Patrick J. McAuliffe and his brother, John. P.J. McAuliffe, one of Weston's best-known and loved citizens, ran the stable, served as Weston's first police chief, and was also an undertaker. The livery stable was built in 1902 after a disastrous fire that destroyed the earlier stable, along with many horses and valuable carriages. At the time of that fire, McAuliffe had 22 horses, plus 4 being boarded.[43]

51 Church Street (1897–98): Andrews-Woodworth house. See chapter 14.

Church Street (c. 1881): Weston Station. Picturesque Stick-style railroad station built for the Massachusetts Central Railroad (see chapter 3) from designs by an unknown architect. The well-detailed board-and-batten structure has wide overhanging eaves to shelter passengers, large decorative truss brackets, and carved ornaments on window and door lintels. The depot was moved east to the other side of Church Street about 1912, when the present overpass was built. In 1975 it was one of only six original depots still extant along the railroad line, the others being in Wayland, Waltham Highlands, Gilbertville, Bondsville, and Amherst. Stations came in only two basic designs. The most important stations, including Weston, utilized a gable-on-hip roof, while subordinate stations had a conventional gable. Depots built after 1887 had a hip roof. Weston Station had a built-in freighthouse and a telegraph office.

72 Church Street (c. 1857 with additions): According to an early-20th-century house history, Alpheus Cutter tore down an existing house and built this one. His son Edwin remodeled it in 1870, and probably added the mansard roof at this time. In 1902 the house was purchased by George and Lillian Pushee, who owned it until 1942. About 1917 they added a large Colonial Revival front porch (since removed), leaded-glass ellipical fanlight, and modillion block cornice. Pushee's business, D.C. Pushee and Sons, manufactured brushes. In a 1909 series of short biographical sketches, the *Boston Herald* wrote that George Pushee "is a fine type of the progressive New England manufacturer. . . . He has an enviable reputation as a golfer and his friends claim that he was never known to flub a tee shot or hook a ball."[44]

96 Church Street (1910): Colonial Revival house built for Alice B. and George W. Eliot (1861–1921), a landscape designer, from designs by architect Samuel Mead.

119 Church Street (1896–97): Colonial Revival house built for banker William Herbert Coburn.

120 Church Street (1925–26): Built for engineer Warren D. and Elizabeth M. Campbell from designs by New York architect Ernest Flagg (1857–1947), designer of the Corcoran Art Gallery, Naval Academy in Annapolis, and Singer Building in New York City, and author of *Construction of Small Houses.* Flagg developed a technique of building masonry houses by filling an 18-foot space with rubble fieldstone and pouring in concrete to bond the stones. He was an urban reformer interested in construction of multiple-family dwellings and economical small houses. His early training at the École des Beaux-Arts in Paris is reflected in the French influences in this house.

153 Church Street (c. 1726): Three generations of Whittemores lived here between 1726 and 1801, including Jeremiah; his son Capt. Isaac Whittemore, who served in the Revolutionary War; and Isaac's son Aaron. The house was sold to Jonas Coburn in 1801, with 120 acres, for $4,400. In the early 20th century, Mrs. Arthur Leslie Coburn invited the founder of SPNEA, William Sumner Appleton, to visit the homestead. After crawling around the attic examining the structure, he theorized that the west parlor and sleeping quarters above had been built later than the east side. The woodwork in the west side is more finished, with the corner posts boxed in and simple paneling below the windows.

154 Church Street (1841): Built by Isaac Coburn, the monumental red barn is a well-loved Church Street landmark. The nearby cottage, demolished in 1999, was built by Arthur Leslie Coburn for his tenant farmer in 1902.

171 Church Street (1841): This Greek Revival house was built by Edward Coburn and occupied by his descendants into the 1990s. The house was remodeled and the ell rebuilt in 1999 as part of the Coburn's Barn subdivision. The present small stable was preceded by two larger barns, the first built in 1841 and destroyed by fire in 1889 and a second destroyed by fire in 1954. The latter was the location of the Kendal Green Riding School.

179 Church Street: Post Civil–War Second Empire cottage built by Edward Coburn and rented to Fred Hall, owner of the nearby shoddy mill along Stony Brook. The mansard-roofed house was later occupied by Edward's son, Albert, until his death in 1920, and then by Albert's nephew, Raymond Coburn, from 1922 to 1977.

Kendal Green Pumping Station (1911): This small fieldstone pumping station, notable for its quality craftsmanship, was built by the private Weston Water Company. The company was incorporated in 1896 and was taken over by the town in 1921. The Kendal Green facility was the town's major water resource for many years and remained in use until the early 1970s.

Kendal Green Station: See chapters 6 and 10.

27 Coburn Road: A. Lincoln Filene's second house.

31 Coburn Road: Filene estate caretaker's cottage. The house was connected by wire to the main house so the Filenes could ring for the caretaker. The living room is said to have been built as a playroom for the Filene girls. After the first caretaker/gardener moved in, the playhouse was enlarged and used only as a residence. One of the longtime caretakers, David Stark, was Scottish, as was his wife. All the Scots in the area used to gather here for picnics on weekends.

32 Coburn Road: Modern one-story house designed by Carl Koch in 1949 and enlarged by the same firm in 1962. The house appeared on the cover of *House Beautiful* in 1949. The issue included an article by Koch and photographs by noted architectural photographer Ezra Stoller.

37 Coburn Road: Stable converted to a garage by A. Lincoln Filene and then to a residence after the estate was subdivided.

43 Coburn Road: Site of A.L. Filene's Tudor-style mansion, demolished about 1937.

64 Coburn Road: "Gatehouse" and chauffeur's residence for the Filene estate. The structure was formed out of two outbuildings built by Frank Coburn and moved by A. Lincoln Filene from the area that is now Carroll Circle to the corner of Coburn Road and Church Street. After World War II, the house was moved back from the road.

19 Gypsy Trail (1898, 1913): Built by Frank G. Webster, a banker at Kidder Peabody, as a simple cabin, valued at only $600 in tax records. Around 1911, the Webster hunting lodge was rented for the summer to author Arthur Stanwood Pier, who wrote for the *Youth's Companion* and was instrumental in promoting the Boy Scouts. It was purchased about 1913 by Margaret and Francis Goodale, who enlarged and remodeled the cabin as a year-round residence.

161-163 North Avenue: Thomas Coburn house. (See chapter 10.)

16 Saddle Hill Road (1912): All-concrete house built for Paul and Jesse Winsor.

23 Webster Road (1911): This Colonial Revival house was designed by Samuel Mead for Charles and Mary Plumer. After Charles Plumer's death in 1912, the house was rented, then purchased in 1915 by architect and engineer Archibald Monks, who owned it until 1957. He sold it to Granton H. Dowse Jr., who lived here until the end of the century.

29 Webster Road: Site of Arthur Leslie Coburn's Shingle-style house, which was built in 1898 and destroyed by fire in 1968.

37 Webster Road (1927): Colonial Revival house built for manufacturer Benjamin P. Whitney and his wife, Barbara, from designs by Samuel Mead.

38 Webster Road (1913): Stucco Colonial Revival house built by salesman Homer Lockwood and his wife, Mary, in 1913.

58 Webster Road (1920–21): Paul Winsor sold 30 acres and his concrete house at 16 Saddle Hill Road to John M. and Virginia C. Lilly in 1920. They built this well-detailed Colonial Revival house on the large property.[45]

60 Webster Road (1925–26): Colonial Revival house designed by architect Walter Macomber for lawyer Robert A. Warren and his wife, Grace. Macomber also designed No. 64.

64 Webster Road (1925–26): Georgian Colonial house built for lawyer Waldo Noyes and his wife, Evelyn. It was designed by Evelyn's brother, Walter Macomber, a Virginia architect who worked on the restoration of Williamsburg. The builder, John Macomber, was Evelyn's father.

74 Webster Road (1913–14): Stucco Colonial Revival built by physician Jonathan R. Powell and his wife, Lalia.

78 Webster Road (1925): Colonial Revival house built by Hudson shoe manufacturer Lawson T. Hill and his wife, Florence.

83 Webster Road (1914): Built for Edith H. and Edward P. "Ted" Ripley and completed in December 1914.[46] Ripley, brother of teacher Emma Ripley, was an "orchardist" whose family owned apple orchards extending from Ripley Lane into Wayland. (See chapter 12.)

Coburn Family
(partial genealogy—does not include all spouses or all children in each generation)

John Coburn (1747–1796)
- Jonas Coburn (1773–1836), m. Susannah Viles
  - Emily (1808–1870)
  - Jonas (1810–1889)
    - Frank Jonas (1853–1894)
  - Isaac (1811–1875), m. Julia Ann Cutter in 1841
    - Isaac Emery (1842–1907)
    - Harriet Ann (1844–?)
    - Thomas (1846–1853)
    - Julie Anna (1851–1852)
    - Anna Cutter (1853–1950), m. Francis Henry Hastings in 1899
    - Edith Laura (1854–1904)
    - William Herbert (Sr.) (1857–1909)
      - William Herbert (Jr.) (1897–?)
      - Philip Fairbairn (1899–1983) (wife Natalie, no children)
      - Pauline Austin (1900–1943), never married
    - Arthur Leslie (1860–1931), m. Helen Haines in 1898
      - Arthur Jr. "Bud"
        - Frederick
        - Arthur III
        - Lawrence
      - Anne Cutter
      - Mary Chapman [Hazard]
  - Susan Ann (1814–1910)
  - Lucy (1816–1843)
  - Harriet (1816–?)
  - Edward (1820–1904), 1) m. Dolly Bennett (d. 1854);
    2) m. Hannah Bennett (1830–1917) in 1854
    - Thomas Edward (1855–1916), m. Harriet Sherman in 1881
      - Edward Sherman (1882–1976), m. Minnie Meyer in 1912
        - Elizabeth
        - Florence [Smith]
        - Marion
      - Harold Winthrop (1885–1953), m. Christine Dennis
        - Harold W. Jr.
        - Thomas
      - Raymond Willard (1887–1977), m. Marian Wetherbee in 1921
        - Barbara
        - Edward "Ted"
        - Helen
        - Frank
        - Raymond W. Jr.
      - Mildred Elizabeth (1895–1986), m. Earl West
        - Thomas C.
        - Harriet Elizabeth
    - Albert Eugene (1857–1920)
      - Albert Charles
    - Caroline Bennett (1867–1954), m. Louis Briggs
    - Florence Mabel (1869–1936)
    - Oscar Bennett (1871–1889)
- John Coburn (1775–?)
- Abijah Coburn (1787–1861), m. 1) Lydia Hastings; 2) Sophia Hastings
  - Abijah (1816–1907) unmarried
  - John (1823–?)
- William Coburn (1790–1832)

Notes

1. Coburn, Philip, *Growing Up in Weston* (Copigraph Inc., 1981).
2. Obituary: "Philip F. Coburn, 84, was textile engineer, Harvard football star," *Boston Globe*, June 1, 1993.
3. Genealogical information in this chapter from *Genealogy of the Descendants of Edward Colburn-Coburn*, published in 1913 (Silas R. Coburn, editor) and reprinted in 1978. John Coburn's 18th-century house burned in 1928 and was replaced a few years later by a house on the same foundation close to Chestnut Street. That house (No. 85) was demolished in 2001. With his second wife, John Coburn had two other sons: Abijah, who made his home on South Avenue, and William.
4. MCRD 144/366, Aaron Whittemore to Jonas Coburn, November 1801.
5. Coburn, Arthur Leslie, "The Coburn Homestead" (three-page history, privately printed, 1912). Written for Weston's Bicentennial, with footnotes added by his daughter, Anne Cutter Coburn, in 1977.
6. Hazard, Mary Coburn, "My Second Home" (presented to the Saturday Morning Club, March 7, 1992), 6.
7. 1881 *TR*, 48–49.
8. MCRD 2465/598, A.L. Coburn to W.H.C., May 1896 (119 Church Street).
9. In 1918, William Herbert Coburn's sister, Anna Coburn Hastings, donated an organ to First Parish Church in memory of her husband, Francis Henry Hastings. Horace Sears paid for an enlarged choir loft and new transept dedicated to the memory of William Herbert Coburn.
10. This house was designed by George F. Newton. The preliminary grading plan was done by the Olmsted firm (Library of Congress, File #2067, correspondence of May–November 1898). Photographs at WHS.
11. "Biographical Portrait, Edward Coburn" (typescript by unknown author, early 20th century), 2.
12. 171 Church Street.
13. Newspaper report on Edward Coburn's 79th birthday, Coburn scrapbook #2, 104.
14. Edward bought what is now 436 Boston Post Road and built the house next door at No. 426. His business block included three buildings directly west of No. 436, all "closely connected to appear as one," according to a newspaper report at the time they were destroyed by fire in 1893. The Coburn Block was rebuilt as a single unit. After their marriage in 1893, Edward's daughter, Caroline (Carrie), and her husband, Louis Briggs, lived at 436 Boston Post Road, which was divided into two living units.
15. "Biographical Portrait," op. cit., 4.
16. Ibid., 1.
17. Albert married in 1884 and had one child, Albert Charles, in 1885. The house is at 179 Church Street.
18. "Tragic Death, Oscar Coburn While Trying to Save Cattle," unknown newspaper, November 16, 1889.
19. Coburn, *GUIW*, 26–27. The ice pond was probably behind 171 Church Street.
20. Donahue, 200.
21. Coburn, *GUIW*, 11.
22. The first course in Massachusetts was constructed in 1892 on the Warren Farm in Brookline. The Country Club was second, in 1893, followed by the Essex Country Club and Prides Crossing Golf Links. Weston and Myopia were both ready for play in 1894. In the United States, 11 courses were operative by 1893 and 20 more were built in 1894. (Figures from Ray Heist's "The Weston Golf Club—A History," undated typescript.)
23. "Weston Golf Club, By-laws, adopted October 3, 1894," MHS (Francis Blake Papers, 53:755). See also *WHSB*, March 1981, 4–5. The following is a list of the first 50 members of the Weston Golf Club (1894): Grafton S.L. Abbott, S.C. Bennett, H.L. Brown, Arthur S. Burrage, Arthur L. Coburn, Wm. H. Coburn, Algernon Coolidge Jr., Livingston Cushing, Brenton H. Dickson, Brenton H. Dickson Jr., Edward Dickson, Andrew Fiske, Augustus H. Fiske, Charles H. Fiske, Charles H. Fiske Jr., Edward Fiske, Lyman Gale, Harrison C. Hall, Francis H. Hastings, George Haven, John O. Henshaw, Albert Hews, John Hitchcock, Charles W. Hubbard, Charles C. Kenney, Charles Merriam 2nd, Herbert Merriam, William Munroe, W. Putnam Page, Charles J. Paine, Grant M. Palmer, Edmund M. Parker, George S. Perry, Chandler Robbins, T.H. Robbins, Arthur J. Russell, Charles F. Russell, William E. Russell, Horace S. Sears, William D. Swan, John B. Thomas, Albert Thorndike, Sturgis H. Thorndike, Henry E. Warner, Joseph B. Warner, J. Bertram Williams, Robert Winsor, W. McM. Woodworth, B.L. Young.
24. The following description of the course combines material from Phil Coburn's *Growing Up in Weston* and "A History of the Weston Golf Club," op. cit. For a layout of the course, see *WHSB*, May 1981, 6.
25. Coburn, *GUIW*, 23–24.
26. Ibid., 25.
27. *WDFP*, 1894, as quoted in *WHSB*, March 1983, 5.
28. MCRD 1740/97, Arthur L. Coburn to Frank Coburn, 10 acres, $1,200, March 1886. House and stable appear on town tax records in 1887.
29. Gorman, Babette, *All About Filene's and the People Who Made It Grow* (Filene's Marketing Department, 1979), 2–16.
30. MCRD 3430/521, Brigham to Filene, two parcels of 10 and 5 acres, April 1909. Also 3459/282, Hiram Logan, trustee, to Filene, 23.94 acres, July 1909.
31. Coburn, *GUIW*, 14.
32. Ibid., 15.
33. Records of the Olmsted Association, Reel 380, Library of Congress.
34. *WDFPT*, July 11, 1919.
35. MCRD 7054/384, Lincoln Filene to Henry J. O'Meara, 39.62 acres, $42,000, August 29, 1946. Subdivision plan shows existing buildings.
36. Frank G. Webster is listed in Boston directories in 1898 and subsequent years as a banker with Kidder Peabody & Co. He lived at 232 Newbury Street, just down the street from Frank Coburn.
37. The cabin was valued in tax records at $600, a low sum suggesting a very modest structure.
38. Winsor family letters collected by Henry S. Reeder, current owner of the house (16 Saddle Hill Road).
39. Letter, Anne Cutter Coburn to Margaret Phillips, undated.
40. *Middlesex County and Its People*, vol. IV, 493.
41. "Testimonial, Raymond W. Coburn," Commonwealth of Massachusetts Department of Public Works brochure, printed for testimonial dinner in Cambridge, March 21, 1957. See also *Middlesex County and Its People*, vol. IV, 493.
42. PWF telephone interview with Jim Dolan (Jr.), December 1998.
43. *WDFPT*, February 4, 1902. See also April 18, 1902.
44. *WDFPT*, May 7, 1909 (quoted from the *Boston Herald*).
45. MCRD 4343/590, Paul Winsor to Lilly, April 1920, buildings and 31 acres. Note that Lilly appears in tax records of 1921 as owner of one house (the Paul Winsor house) and in 1922 as owner of two houses, both valued at $10,000 (the Paul Winsor house and a new house). See also *WDFPT*, April 30, 1920, and August 20, 1920.
46. MCRD 3854/47, Francis Goodale to Edith H. Ripley, January 1914. House appears on tax records in 1915. See also *WDFPT*, April 10 and December 26, 1914.

Figure 12-1. This massive barn stood behind the Stratton homestead at 420 Concord Road. Compared to estate barns such as Herbert Merriam's, pictured later in this chapter, the Stratton barn was a utilitarian structure with few architectural embellishments. Notice the windmill, which pumped water to the water tower at left. On top of the windmill is 10-year-old Ernest Jones. Generations of Strattons farmed this property from the 1730s until 1903. (Photo c. 1885)

CHAPTER 12

The Northwest

Concord, Merriam, and Sudbury Roads

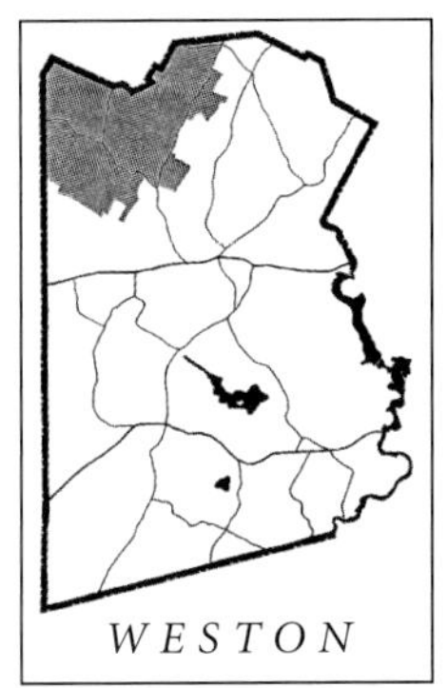

The history of the northwest section begins with the early farmers. Men like William Smith on Sudbury Road and Jonathan Stratton on Concord Road sustained large families by raising livestock, growing grain and corn, cutting hay, and planting apple orchards.

"Gentlemen farmers" bought up their farms after the Civil War. Some, like Herbert Merriam, built new mansions. Others restored dilapidated farmhouses. Weston resident and early preservation advocate Joseph S. Seabury was inspired by the Stratton farmhouse when he wrote in The House Beautiful *in 1913:*

> *No house on a country road is so interesting or so charming as the old structure that grew up, as it were, with the elms that shade it, the apple orchard beside the barn, or the old inhabitant across the way. A new stucco dwelling with graded lawns and imported shrubbery and a neat garage is surely far from home on this country road of ours.*[1]

In 1905, the Weston Land Association inaugurated a new type of land use in the northwest—the subdivision. Silver Hill and Westland Roads developed into a distinctive neighborhood of middle-class houses convenient to the Silver Hill stop on the Fitchburg Railroad line. At the time it was laid out, Silver Hill was the largest subdivision in Weston.

Up to this point, the historical pattern is familiar and predictable. The purchase of the Grant Walker estate by the Jesuit order introduced a unique element that profoundly influenced future growth in this remote corner of town. In the early 1920s, a pioneering group of three priests, 40 students, and four brothers became the first residents at the newly established Jesuit "house of studies" at Fairview. One of the early fathers later recalled his thoughts in first coming to Weston:

> *There had been rumors telling us that our new neighborhood would be strongly Unitarian, and as we strode along over the crisp and hardened snow, many faces peered from behind curtained windows to see 'if the young priests really had horns,' as popular report had it.*[2]

At the bend of Concord Road, the Jesuit fathers built the largest building ever constructed in Weston. Their multimillion-dollar "scholasticate," completed in 1927, was 340 feet long and four stories high, plus a cellar and sub-cellar. Limestone columns at the end of each wing stood 50 feet high.

Despite the initial skepticism of Weston residents, Weston College proved to be a good neighbor. Seminarians taught neighborhood children to skate on College Pond. Scientific research at the seismographic observatory brought the town widespread recognition. The college purchase of the Merriam Farm in 1930 kept that land from being developed. Finally, when Weston College closed and the land was no longer needed, the Jesuit fathers sold the town more than 200 acres, including College Pond, the surrounding conservation and recreation land, and the municipal-purpose land where the Merriam Village elderly housing was later constructed.

Yankee Farm Families: Concord Road and Upper North Avenue

In the 1730s, Jonathan Stratton settled on upper Concord Road and built a house that was probably

Figure 12-2. This 1898 photograph of the Stratton house at 420 Concord Road was the work of Alvah and George Howes, natives of the western Massachusetts village of Ashfield. Notice the doghouse. During their active years as professional photographers, from 1886 to 1906, the Howes brothers traveled through rural New England taking pictures of farms, factories, shops, and schools, along with anyone willing to pose. Their Weston images are all dated 1898. Some 20,000 Howes glass-plate negatives survive today.

Figures 12-3 and 12-4. These 1898 photographs by the Howes brothers show the house and barn built for the Cheney family at 455 Concord Road.

just one room on the ground floor with a bedroom above.[3] Stratton and his wife, Dinah Bemis, had 12 children, a fact that perhaps inspired the expansion of his house to a symmetrical two-over-two room plan sometime between 1780 and 1800. Although his farm of about 48 acres was not exceptionally large, Stratton's yields of hay and grain were high. Tax records consistently show him to be one of the wealthiest residents in the period before the War for Independence. His descendants continued the farm until about 1903, the year George H. Stratton died of a heart attack at age 77 while taking his vegetables and eggs by carriage to Waltham.[4]

In 1765, prominent Boston merchant Samuel Phillips Savage (1718–1797), who was then 47 years old, bought a farm at the corner of North Avenue and Lincoln Street, where he lived the rest of his life. Savage has been called "Weston's most prominent patriot" because of his leadership role in the Revolutionary War.[5]

Jesse Cheney (1754–1827) bought 74 acres on upper Concord Road in 1795.[6] His only son, Joseph, was a farmer and shoemaker who married the girl next door, Sukey Stratton, in 1804. Their son, Gilbert, is thought to have built the present Greek Revival house.[7] When the last of the Cheney farmers, George G., died in the 1890s, his obituary notes that, although living in Weston, he was identified with the people of Lincoln in its business, religious, and social affairs.

By about 1679, Lt. John Brewer had established a gristmill in the far northwest corner of Weston, powered by the headwaters of Stony Brook.[8] This was the beginning of what Lincoln historian John C. MacLean has called a Weston-Lincoln network of mills, ponds, dams, and streams that formed an important milling complex for more than a century.[9] By the early 19th century, John Dudley had built a house on North Avenue near the Lincoln town line and was taxed for a grist- and sawmill.[10] In the late 19th and early 20th centuries, George F. Harrington was operating a grist- and sawmill in Lincoln just over the town line.[11] Known as the Jenkins-Harrington Mill, it stood by the millpond until it was destroyed by fire about 1929–30.[12] Harrington also owned a large farm in Weston and Lincoln and improved his dairy stock by taking cows to breed with select bulls on the farm of the wealthy Codman family in Lincoln.[13]

Figures 12-5 and 12-6. Nahum Smith (1824–1911), the fifth generation of the family to live on Sudbury Road, was a farmer and longtime school committee member. The accompanying portrait is his wife, the former Susan Daggett (1824–1910).

Yankee Farm Families: Sudbury Road

The Smith land grant of 1670, reportedly written on sheepskin parchment long since lost, totaled 160 acres on both sides of Sudbury Road. The Smiths were living in Weston by 1675–76, when Indians burned one of their barns in the only Weston incident of King Philip's War. Of the four important early houses on Sudbury Road, two were built by the Smith family and occupied by successive generations into the 20th century.

The house at 111 Sudbury Road was built for William and Mary Hobbs Smith, who were married in 1714 and had completed the original one-over-one west section by the time their first child, Bradyll, was born in 1715. Bradyll was active in Weston political affairs and served as a colonel in the Revolutionary War. His brother Josiah built the tavern that still stands on the town green. The youngest son, James, took over the family farm, which passed to his son Samuel and then to his son Samuel Jr., who married Martha Stratton in 1819.

Samuel Jr. is thought to be the builder of the second Smith house, now 89 Sudbury Road. The construction in about 1826 may have been prompted by the birth of a son, Nahum, two years earlier. Nahum's aunt Lucy married Boston merchant George Babcock and Nahum inherited their wealth, allowing him to travel extensively to England and Scotland to visit the villages of his ancestors.[14] He and his wife, Susan, updated their house with a central peaked gable and other Italianate details and added a windmill over the well and a tank so that water could be delivered to the house and barn. Nahum served on

Figure 12-7. William and Mary Smith are thought to have built 111 Sudbury Road as a "one-over-one" house in time for the birth of their son Bradyll in 1715. When this photograph was taken, in 1940, the house had been more than doubled in size and the bay window and door hood had been added. Members of the Smith family still live nearby.

Figure 12-8. Nahum Smith's grandchildren, Lincoln (left), Carl and Sylvia, were raised on Sudbury Road.

the school committee in the late 19th century during the pivotal transition to centralized schools.

Nahum's sons, Charles Edward and Walter Leslie, continued farming the family homestead. Charles was born in 1849 but didn't marry until 1907, when he was 58. His biographical sketch in *History of Middlesex County* describes him as a "skilled agriculturalist and . . . able business man" who engaged in general farming and market gardening.[15] His three children, Lincoln, Sylvia, and Carl, were raised on Sudbury Road and continued to own land there until recent years.

Down the street from the Smith property are two other early farmhouses. No. 45 Sudbury Road is traditionally thought to have been built in 1731 for John Bemis, brother of Dinah Bemis Stratton. The property continued in use as a farm until the late 19th century. Louis Roberts bought what was known as the Childs Farm at 63 Sudbury Road in 1873 and ran a dairy called Strebor, which is Roberts spelled backwards. Roberts had a herd of Guernsey cattle and delivered milk in Weston into the early decades of the 20th century. His daughter, Helen, ran the dairy in the 1930s, doing all the milking, bottle washing, and delivery with the help of one hired man. She was an active Girl Scout leader and had a campground for overnights on a knoll on the east side of Ripley Lane.[16] The end of Strebor farm came with the great hurricane of 1938, when the barn caved in under the weight of a fallen tree. Not long afterward, the livestock was sold, ending more than 50 years of Roberts dairy operations.

Ripley Lane

Off Sudbury Road on what is now Ripley Lane was another large farmstead, purchased in the late

Figure 12-9. The Roberts dairy farm (63 Sudbury Road) was called Strebor, which is Roberts spelled backwards. Louis Roberts and then his daughter, Helen, ran the dairy for more than 50 years, from 1873 to the late 1930s.

1870s by Francis B. "Frank" Ripley (1841–1939), a Civil War veteran with a colorful and romantic war record. During his service in the Grand Army of the Republic, Ripley was severely wounded in the Battle of Antietam and left on the field for dead. He spent seven months in an improvised hospital in Chambersburg, where he was nursed back to health by his future wife, Laura Ritner. After the war, Ripley returned to Pennsylvania to marry Miss Ritner. In 1879 he gave up his job in Boston, bought the farm on Ripley Lane, and "retired" to Weston. His land totaled just over 100 acres and extended to the Wayland town line.[17] The property, which they named Lawnfield, was known for its orchards. The couple ran a dairy farm and took in summer boarders. Laura's mother came to help, along with her two sisters: Emma, who married neighbor Louis Roberts, and Ella, whose daughter, Anna Harlow, married neighbor Charles Edward Smith.

Figure 12-10. Francis B. Ripley (1841–1939) was the inspiration for this oil painting by Gertrude Fiske of an aging soldier in his blue Union uniform. When he died at age 98, Ripley was Weston's last Civil War veteran. He is pictured clutching a cane with a gilded head, thought to be the now lost Boston Post *cane that was once passed consecutively to the town's oldest inhabitant.*

In 1891 the Ripleys held an elaborate 25th wedding anniversary party. A lengthy newspaper account described the winding carriage drive "that sometimes narrows to a mere bridle path" and the "broad acres of orchard, meadow, tillage, hills and pasture forming a perfect pastoral picture."[18] On the night of the party, the residence was decorated with hundreds of Chinese lanterns, their "fantastic colorings producing strange, foreign effects." By the 1890s, the house had acquired mythic status as the Revolutionary War–period home of "Dr. Wheaton," the Tory who allegedly hid Weston's celebrated British spy, John Howe. Subsequent research has failed to substantiate this and other details of the spy story.[19]

As an old man, Frank Ripley loved to receive callers, who were seated by the antique fireplace and regaled with Civil War stories. He was the only Civil War veteran left in Weston when he died in 1939 in his 98th year. He was survived by his unmarried daughter, Emma, and two sons, Edward Pearson Ripley, known as Ted, and Ernest. Emma taught school in Weston for 42 years and authored the 1961 book *Weston: A Puritan Town.* Ted operated the family farm and Ripley Ridge Orchard just over the town line in Wayland. His dedicated service to the town included terms as overseer of the poor, moth superintendent, tree warden, measurer of lumber, wartime fuel administrator, water commissioner for 21 years, and assessor for 31 years.[20]

Charles Merriam:
Beginnings of the Family Fortune

In the early 19th century, Weston was something of a shopping mecca. Women came each spring or fall from as far as the New Hampshire and Vermont lines to shop at Daniel S. Lamson's dry-goods store, stayed overnight at a tavern, and returned home the next day with enough cloth to last the entire year. According to descendant and Weston historian Col. Daniel S. Lamson, "No one ever thought of going to Boston to buy goods."[21]

Figure 12-11. In 1879, the 18th-century farmhouse at 44 Ripley Lane was purchased by Francis Ripley, who operated a dairy and extensive orchards. By the 1890s, when this picture was taken, the roof had been raised and the porches and central wall dormer added.

It was at Lamson's store that Charles Merriam (1803–1865) laid the foundation for the family fortune. Merriam was born in Concord and moved to Weston in 1821, when he was just 18. He worked at Lamson's store and proved to be such a popular and enterprising merchant that he took over the business after Lamson's death in 1824.[22] He married Caroline Ware of Newton about 1829 and built a house on Central Avenue in the town center across from the store.[23] By the mid-1830s, the popularity of Weston as a retail center was beginning to falter. Merriam shifted his focus and in 1836 formed a partnership with merchant Henry Sayles in a Boston firm later known as Sayles, Merriam & Brewer.[24]

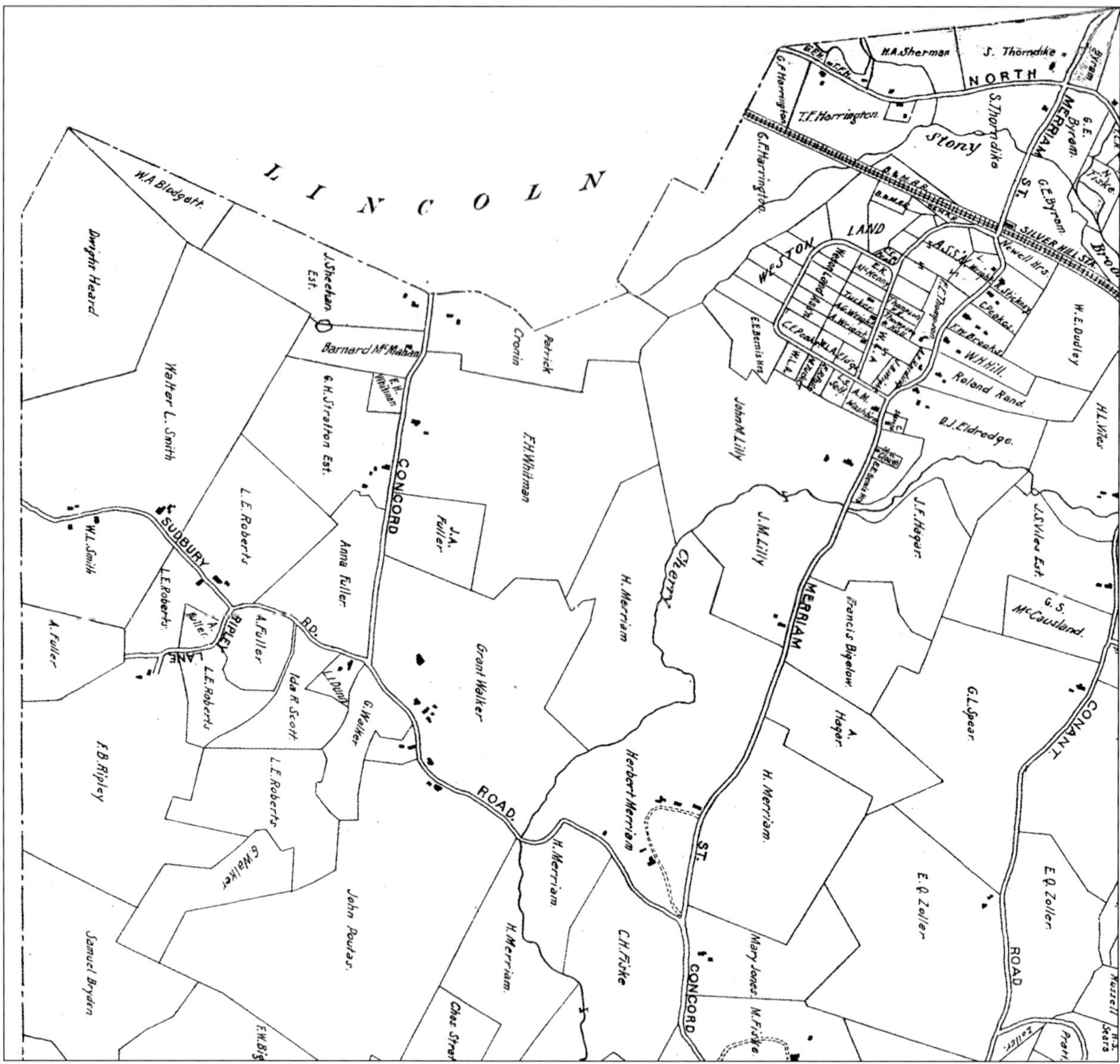

Figure 12-12. Detail from the 1908 Atlas of Middlesex County.

Merriam moved to the city and became quite wealthy, but he always retained his ties to Weston. In 1859 he donated $1,000 for the purchase of books for the new town library, the first gift of money for a permanent trust fund. In 1865 Merriam made a second gift of $1,000, this time to establish what came to be known as the Merriam Fund for the Benefit of the Silent Poor of Weston. His letter to the selectmen makes it clear who was to benefit:

> And I desire that the interest and income shall be paid over, not to the paupers, but to that class of honest, temperate men and women, who work hard or are prudent and economical, and yet find it difficult to make both ends meet. To such, a load of groceries, or a little flour or meal, will always be of great service.[25]

The disposition of the money was to be entirely private.[26]

Charles Merriam met an accidential death later that year. The sorrow of the town was expressed in a resolution passed by the town meeting:

> That we have heard with sincere regret and sorrow of the accident by which the valuable life of Charles Merriam, Esq., formerly a citizen of this town, and a noble-hearted and liberal benefactor to it, was terminated. By his generous gift for the foundation of a public library, and also by a similar generous gift for the relief of the "silent poor" of Weston, he had enshrined himself in the hearts of the people, and secured grateful remembrance for his name in all future years.[27]

Herbert Merriam, "Gentleman Farmer"

Charles and Caroline Merriam had seven children, including Charles (b. 1832), who became a successful Boston merchant; Waldo, who was killed in the Civil War; and their fifth child, Herbert (1841–1926), who was born in Boston but later returned to Weston and established Cherry Brook Farm.

Herbert served in the 44th Massachusetts Volunteer Infantry in the Civil War, married Fanny Hawes of Boston, and settled in Weston in the early 1870s. He bought 150 acres at the junction of Concord Road and Merriam Street (then called Lin-

Figure 12-13. Herbert Merriam (1841–1926), a rugged individualist, was extremely proud of his long gray beard.

coln Road) and built a large frame mansion (1875) and monumental red barn (1876).[28] The barn, one of the largest in Middlesex County, had entrances on three levels, including a ramp to the hayloft. One of the three cupolas atop the barn housed a rotary windmill used to pump water into a large tank under the roof. In later years, the structural beams supporting the tank gave way, and it fell through two floors into the basement, killing several cows.

Merriam was a member of the Union Club of Boston and the Boston Athletic Association, a charter member of the Weston Golf Club, and a member of The Country Club in Brookline. He had three children who survived into adulthood: Charles 2nd, Caroline, and Jesse, who married Edward Fay.[29] We know the Merriams traveled. An item in the *Waltham Daily Free Press Tribune* of April 14, 1905, informed the community that "Mr. and Mrs. Herbert Merriam & Miss Caroline Merriam have gone south to remain until May. The winter has been spent by them in Lenox."

Figure 12-14. The main house for Herbert Merriam's Cherry Brook Farm was built in 1875 at the intersection of Concord Road and Merriam Street.

Figure 12-15. The 1876 Merriam barn was one of the largest in Middlesex County, until it burned to the ground in October 1926. The foundation is still visible next to the brush dump.

Figure 12-16. Mrs. Charles Merriam (center) played the role of "Weston" in the 1913 Bicentennial pageant. Adults, from left: Miss Elizabeth Hubbard as "Present," Mrs. J.D. Nichols as "Ceres," Mrs. Charles Merriam, Miss Rosamond Bennett as "Future," and Miss Barbara Bennett as "Past."

Tragedy at the Merriam Barn

Beginning in 1904, the farm was managed by Herbert's son Charles 2nd (1871–1915), who introduced modern scientific methods and turned the dairy into a model of efficiency and a reported commercial success.[30] A graduate of Harvard, class of 1893, Charles was an ardent sportsman who hunted, fished, and played golf. He was married in 1902 and had a son, Charles Jr., and two daughters.[31] Before abandoning textiles for agriculture, Charles was superintendent of the Lyman Mills in Holyoke, a cotton manufacturing firm.

By 1916, the Merriam farm totaled 231 acres of woodland, hayfields, pastureland, and even a quarter-mile tract where Herbert Merriam exercised his trotting horses. He owned District Schoolhouse #3 at the junction of Concord and Merriam Streets, which he purchased in 1901 after the town began to phase out the one-room schoolhouses.[32]

Herbert and his son, Charles, were serious gentlemen farmers who took great pride in their livestock. Thus it was all the more tragic when the "fancy-bred" cattle fell victim to a foot-and-mouth epidemic that struck New England in 1915. The extremely contagious and fatal sickness had been known in Europe since the 16th century, but was first seen in the United States in 1870. An outbreak that began in Russia in 1910 reached America in 1914. The *Waltham Daily Free Press Tribune* reported on its spread through neighboring communities in 1915:

> . . . the foot and mouth disease in this city and vicinity has become alarming and despite efforts of State and National forces . . . spread continues. . . . In addition to the discovery of a new case here [in Waltham], the disease was found among a herd of 60 cattle at the Charles Merriam farm on Merriam Road, Weston, and quarantine [was instituted]. . . not only [on] the premises but also [in] the entire town with reference to the transportation of cattle.[33]

Every cow on the Merriam farm had to be killed. A long trench was dug in a field below the barn, and the entire herd driven into the trench and shot one by one. When Charles Merriam died not long afterward at age 44, the official cause was listed as Ludwig's angina and septicemia. Some said he died of a broken heart from seeing his outstanding livestock suddenly obliterated.[34]

Herbert Merriam outlived his son by more than a decade. In *Once Upon a Pung,* Brenton H. Dickson describes the old man, who was popularly known as Grampa, as a "rugged individualist" with a "sumptuous white beard." According to Dickson, when Grampa walked to the nearby Cherry Brook Station, his family was never sure whether he'd be back that day or weeks later. The story goes that he once left for a trip around the world "with only a toothbrush and a celluloid collar or two packed in a grocery bag."[35]

As others adopted 20th-century advances, Grampa fiercely resisted:

> [He was] . . . a man of the old school when grandfathers were patriarchs whose words and opinions went undisputed; a man who condemned everything modern from automobiles to plumbing, not only for their uselessness but for the unnecessary expense of maintaining them. [36]

Dickson writes that the Merriam house was comfortable in every way except that Grampa would not allow indoor plumbing and felt that two indoor privies, one upstairs and one downstairs, were quite adequate. Automobiles were allowed on the Merriam farm only on a temporary basis, never overnight. [37]

Herbert Merriam died in January 1926 at age 84. Nine months later, fire broke out in the landmark barn. Farmhands first on the scene led horses and cows to safety. Weston's first motorized pumping engine rushed to the scene but there were no hydrants nearby, so the fire truck drove to College Pond and stretched a 2½-inch hose back to the barn. By then, flames had engulfed the entire structure, and the barn was a total loss. [38]

After the death of Herbert Merriam, the estate land was sold to the Trustees of Boston College, who, with the Society of Jesus of New England, transferred the entire 204 acres to Weston College in 1930.[39]

Figure 12-17. Samuel G. Snelling was a Boston mechant who established a summer home in Weston after the Civil War. He bought the 18th-century house once owned by Revolutionary War patriot Samuel Phillips Savage and added the front section shown in this 1890s photograph. Snelling's addition burned down at the beginning of the 20th century, but the early part of the house remains at 479 North Avenue.

Figure 12-18. This Shingle-style mansion (now 10 Cherry Brook Road) was built in 1893 for Boston businessman William Munroe. Later owners John M. Lilly and William G. Renwick kept the 100-acre estate intact. Beginning in the late 1950s, the property was subdivided into the Cherry Brook Road neighborhood.

Estate Development: 1880s and 1890s

In addition to the Merriam farm, a number of country places were established in the northwest in the last two decades of the 19th century. Perhaps because of the remoteness from the town center, owners of these properties were not as active in Weston affairs and are less well known than their counterparts in the center and south.

In the mid-1870s, Boston merchant Samuel G. Snelling and his wife, Anna, bought the farm formerly belonging to Samuel Phillips Savage for use as a summer residence. Snelling added a large gambrel-roofed addition in front with a generous veranda.[40] In 1887 Anna Snelling sold the property to Samuel Lathrop Thorndike (1830–1911), a "descendant of Revolutionary stock" and well-known Boston attorney.[41] The property remained in the Thorndike family until 1929, when the heirs of Sturgis H. Thorndike sold it to Edward Merritt.[42] At that time, a map of the estate shows 71.71 acres on both sides of North Avenue and extending across the Lincoln line.[43] Merritt began building a mansion on the hill in Lincoln, but as it neared completion, it was struck by lightning and leveled in a major fire.[44] A handsome brick Colonial Revival house was erected on the foundation and occupied by Merritt and later by the Beebe family. The old farmhouse was converted to a residence for staff and remained part of the estate until 1950. Stone posts at the corner of North Avenue and Lincoln Road still mark the entrance into the property.

In 1893, William Munroe established his country estate on 100 acres on Merriam Street and what is now Cherry Brook Road, where he constructed a fine Shingle-style mansion.[45] Munroe was president of Stone and Downer Co., customhouse brokers and import/export agents with offices on State Street in

Boston. The *Waltham Daily Free Press Tribune* described the "valuable country place" when Munroe sold it 12 years later to John M. Lilly of Indianapolis:

> The estate contains about 100 acres of land, with frontage of nearly 2300 on the street and adjoins the estates of Herbert Merriam and Grant Walker. The buildings consist of a large modern house, stable and various outbuildings, which have cost, with other improvements, more than $30,000.[46]

Lilly sold the property in 1914 to William G. and Mary Renwick, who carried on the estate tradition for another generation. Renwick was a lawyer and well-known gun fancier who added a room for his extensive collection. On the property were small houses for the longtime caretaker, Ralph Benotti, and a chauffeur.[47]

In 1895 the Cheney farm on upper Concord Road was sold to Francis H. Whitman, a Boston lawyer whose principal residence was in Cambridge. His sons, Edward and Henry, were the ones who used the farm, which they called Gofam, an acronym for "gift of father and mother."[48] Ernest Jones, who had grown up on the Stratton farm, became the caretaker. He married Marie Zimmermann, a Swiss girl who worked for the family, and the couple raised their five children on the Whitman farm. Ernest Jones put in formal gardens, planted apple trees, mowed the fields for hay, and built a baseball field, where his sons and neighborhood boys played baseball.

In 1897, Daniel Sharpe Ford, owner of the magazine *Youth's Companion*, bought a 99-acre farm on Concord Road from George W. Dunn and chose an elevated site for his new summer home, described as "so large and of such striking architectural design that from a distance is may well be compared to a baronial castle."[49] Photographs show a sprawling white clapboard Colonial Revival house with porches extending in all directions. Here Ford spent much of his time as his health began to fail, still actively overseeing the publishing and editorial departments of the magazine he had made into the leading juvenile publication in the country. He died in December 1899.

Grant Walker Estate, "Fairview"

In 1900, Grant Walker (1851–1920) purchased the former Daniel Ford estate, which he called Fairview.[50] Little is known about the Boston-born Walker except that he was a graduate of Harvard College, class of 1873, and amassed a substantial fortune investing in textiles. At his death, he was described as a "prominent figure in mill circles."[51] Walker lived on Beacon Street in Boston and came to Weston only in the summer.

The frame mansion built by Ford burned to the ground on May 11, 1910, with damage estimated at $20,000. Walker hired architect Samuel Mead and spared no expense in constructing an 18-room brick mansion with 10 bathrooms, completed in 1912 on the same site.[52] Later, visitors who entered the foyer described the "virile simplicity of design worked out in the richest and most tasteful materials."[53] Walker made lavish use of fine woods such as Brazilian satinwood, mahogany, oak, bird's-eye maple, and cypress, in floor-to-ceiling paneling. A double staircase led up to four large chambers, each with private bath. On the second floor was a glass sun parlor and, directly beneath it, a broad piazza, red tiled and framed by white Doric columns. On a clear day, the tower of Boston College was visible in the distance.

Figure 12-19. Grant Walker is pictured in front of the frame Colonial Revival mansion he purchased in 1900 from the heirs of Daniel Ford. Walker made his fortune investing in textile mills. This house burned down in 1910.

Figure 12-20. Architect Samuel Mead designed Grant Walker's new brick Colonial Revival mansion, Fairview, which still stands at 319 Concord Road. After his death, the property was purchased by the Society of Jesus and became the site for Weston College, a Jesuit seminary.

The grounds were carefully laid out with well-kept lawns, shade trees, and a succession of flowering shrubs. In front of the present seminary building was an apple orchard. On the property were three frame houses, a fine carriage house, greenhouse, cattle barn, hay barn, and henhouse.[54] Water for the estate was pumped from a well to a 10,000-gallon water tower on the south side of Concord Road.

Grant Walker died in April 1920. Although never an active participant in Weston affairs, he remembered the town with a generous bequest of $10,000, with the income to be used to buy library books. In 1921 his wife, Mabel, the grandniece of a Jesuit priest, sold the 120-acre property to the Society of Jesus for $110,000 for a "house of studies." [55]

Figure 12-21. Rev. Edward P. Tivnan (1882–1937) was the first rector of Weston College, from 1924 to 1931.

Jesuit Scholasticate at Fairview

In the first two decades of the 1900s, the Roman Catholic Church in the United States was expanding rapidly to serve an increasingly large Catholic population. Many young men educated at Jesuit high schools entered the order founded in 1540 by Ignatius of Loyola. The Jesuits placed a high priority on education. Until the mid-1960s, students were required to study three years of philosophy followed by four years of theology. After graduation, they were assigned to posts throughout the world, with those in New England often teaching at Jesuit schools such as Boston College High School, Boston College, Fairfield University, and The College of the Holy Cross.[56]

With scholastics entering the order in increasing numbers, the seminary in Woodstock, Maryland, became overcrowded and the order began searching for a site in New England. A decision was made to build a House of Philosophy in New England and use Woodstock as a Theologate. The Walker estate was selected from more than 20 properties.[57] In the winter of 1921–22, the first group of 40 first-year philosophy students and faculty arrived in Weston. An Irish railroad hand who escorted one of the advance corps to its new home was heard to remark: "Well, if some of the 'Blue Bloods' could only see what I am bringing home to them!"[58]

Figure 12-22. In the early years of Weston College, before construction of the monumental brick "scholasticate," every foot of space in the former Walker mansion was put to use. From 1922 to 1927, as many as 137 people ate meals daily in the dark and crowded cellar dining room. Notice the white tablecloths.

The former summer estate was quickly adapted to new uses. The dining room in the brick mansion became the first chapel, the cellar was partitioned off for a dining room, two drawing rooms were used as classrooms, and students were crowded three or four to a room in the master bedrooms and attic servants quarters. Walker's carriage house was remodeled into classrooms and a dormitory and his hay barn became the recreation hall. The Rev. Francis J. McNiff, S.J., was the first Superior at Fairview, as the facility continued to be called until 1927.

The society hired the Boston firm of Maginnis and Walsh to draw plans for its new building. Senior partner Charles D. Maginnis was the leading Roman Catholic architect in the United States during this period of expanding Catholic facilities. The nationally recognized Boston firm specialized in both Gothic and Classical church design. Their work in the Boston area includes buildings at Boston College, Emmanuel College, and scores of churches including St. Julia in

Figure 12-23. The Walker carriage house, renamed Bapst Hall, was remodeled to provide temporary living quarters, classrooms, and a science laboratory.

Weston. Near the end of his life, Maginnis was awarded the Gold Medal of the American Institute of Architects, the highest award the institute confers.

Charles Maginnis and many at Fairview favored a site farther removed from Concord Road, about 200 yards east of the present building, which would have given the monumental Beaux Arts structure a proper setting. Expediency prevailed and a site was chosen close to the Walker mansion because the community dining room was initially located in the mansion.

An early plan to have cloisters around the building was ruled out, to the regret of those who later tried to find a place to walk in winter. Because of funding constraints, the authorities decided to construct only one third of the building, and the architects made last-minute changes so that the north wing could stand alone. Ground-breaking ceremonies were held on April 9, 1924.[59]

Later that year, the Rev. Edward P. Tivnan, S.J., arrived to replace Father McNiff, becoming the first rector of Fairview. A native of Salem, Tivnan attended Boston College, taught chemistry there and at Fordham, and served as president of Fordham before coming to Weston.[60] Tivnan was instrumental in building the new facility and shaping institutional life.

Hollow tile was used to temporarily close the end of the north wing after it was completed in 1925. It was clear, however, that increasing numbers of scholastics would present a problem within two years. With the cost of building increasing each year, leaders pressed ahead to complete the entire building. At the last minute, a decision was made to build a scholasticate, which was a combined house of philosophy and theology, for the New England Province, rather than a House of Philosophy for both provinces. One wing would be used for the philosophers, another for the theologians, and in between, a third wing housed the faculty and library. The rotunda formed a "divide" between the two levels of students, who were not allowed to commingle.

An article in the *Boston Globe* in May 1927 announced the opening of the new scholasticate, which was "believed to be the largest in the country devoted to the preparation of young men for the priesthood."[61] The four-story structure was 340 feet long and contained an estimated 180,000 to 200,000 square feet of space, including the upper basement level.[62] All functions of the seminary were housed here, including eating, sleeping, educational, spiritual, and recreational facilities.[63] The most elaborate space, the chapel, extended upward for three floors. The *Boston Globe* reported that the building had 400 rooms and a library of 100,000 volumes.

In 1928, the scholasticate at Weston housed 21 faculty, 219 seminarians, and six brothers for a total of 246, making it also the largest house in the society in population, by a small margin.[64] The cost of the new building, including furnishings and equipment, was $2,253,024.[65] Philosophy students received bachelor and master of arts degrees from Boston College and theologians received seminary degrees from Gregorian University in Rome.

The 1927 *Globe* article announced three days of tours, after which the public would not have ready access to the interior. On the weekend of May 19–21, throngs of curious visitors arrived, an estimated 12,000 on Sunday alone. Automobiles were parked along the roads as far down as Weston Center, as Catholics and non-Catholics inspected the building and were reported to be "delighted."[66]

The setting of the scholasticate in an outlying corner of a rural town was not a disadvantage. Students were restricted in their contacts with the outside world. They were not allowed to have cars and rarely took the train into Boston. Some philosophers were known to hide in the basement of the workmen's house and listen to the only radio on the property.

Father Edward Tivnan, writer of a firsthand account of the early years of Weston College, talks of the initial attitudes of the people of Weston toward the college:

> Weston had always been famous as a very exclusive place. No streetcar lines were allowed to pass through the town. Restrictions of all kinds were imposed which kept the place in the condition of a real old, narrow New England town. Thus the consternation of the natives can easily be imagined when it was announced that Grant Walker's "Fairview" had been purchased by the Jesuits. Rumors of all kinds were immediately set afloat. It was to be an orphan asylum, school for boys,

college, etc. Approaches were made at the State House to prevent the usual exemption from taxes. The feeling against us was very bitter.[67]

Tivnan's memoir describes how the feelings of the townspeople gradually changed:

> But once we were established here, the quiet behavior of the scholastics as they passed through the town on holiday walks, had the desired effect and the townspeople began to wonder what manner of young men the newcomers were. Shortly after our arrival, a grass and brush fire which seriously threatened the house of a neighbor, very hostile to us, was extinguished by the scholastics—another conquest. Little by little, the hostility was changed to friendliness.[68]

In 1928 the rector was invited to address the members of First Parish Church on "The Jesuits and Their Work." Father Tivnan's history records their reaction:

> They seemed very much pleased and extremely cordial. . . . The beauty of the building has added much to the beauty of Weston and of this the people are very proud. Finally, when we chose the legal title, "Weston College," which was done at the request of the people themselves, there was great satisfaction . . .[69]

After the college was made a Collegium Maximum, the full title became Collegium Maximum Westonionse Sancti Spiritus.

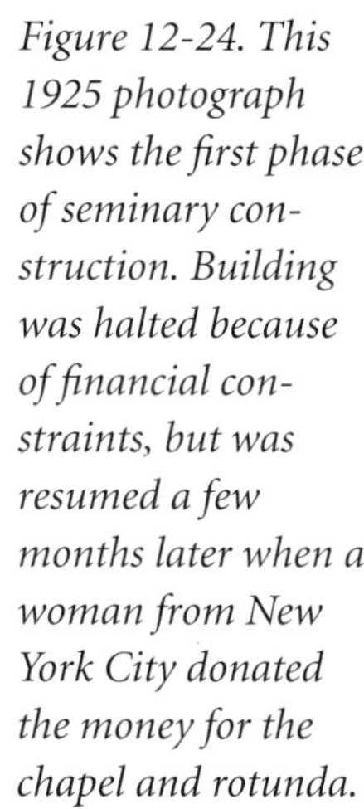

Figure 12-24. This 1925 photograph shows the first phase of seminary construction. Building was halted because of financial constraints, but was resumed a few months later when a woman from New York City donated the money for the chapel and rotunda.

Development of Weston College

Just east of the seminary was the Merriam farm, which was owned by Herbert Merriam until his death in 1926. In the early 1920s, the Jesuit fathers approached him about exchanging properties. Father Tivnan recorded the elderly Merriam's opposition:

> . . . [the old man] was enamored of his farm despite the fact that he was running it as a losing proposition. He intended to die there, so he informed the reverend visitors, and when he did die, he expected that his grandson and his posterity to the end, would carry the burden and continue to feed the white elephant.[70]

When Merriam died, the farm lay fallow for two years and his heirs pressed for a sale. New uses were

Figure 12-25. Weston College was designed by the nationally known firm of Maginnis and Walsh and cost more than $2 million. This aerial view was taken in 1927, the year the building was completed.

Figure 12-26. The chapel design has been praised as "the most distinguished example of 20th-century Classicism in Greater Boston."

Figure 12-27. Recreational facilities on the Weston College property included a golf course, swimming pool, baseball diamond, and skating pond.

explored—a Catholic academy for girls (not a good idea, according to the Jesuit fathers), a housing development, and a truck farm with the possibly of a "roadhouse." Permission was quickly secured from Rome to buy the property for $75,000. Soon afterward, the college rejected a proposal to use some of its land on Merriam Street as an amateur aviation field.

Purchase of the Merriam estate brought the total acreage to 360. This description of the outdoor facilities was written in 1930:

> Looking out from the back of the house we see broad acres that assure fresh farm products and healthy recreation. A [seven-hole] golf course whose shorn fairway gives the effect of a lawn, rolls for several hundred yards down from the terraces where the building stands. Beyond this are the baseball field with its new grandstand built by the Theologians . . . the tennis courts, the wooden handball court, the pond, and finally on the neighboring hill, the large Merriam Farm, now our property.[71]

Under the supervision of a local farmer, seminarians raised chickens and planted, weeded, and harvested extensive vegetable gardens. The Jesuits moved the old District Schoolhouse #3 into the woods, where they practiced preaching until it was taken down in 1931.

The society later declined to purchase a farm on the south side of Concord Road, as it was not considered necessary to protect the integrity of the church property. For many years this farm had belonged to John Poutas, a farmer, stonecutter, and granite dealer. It was sold to Francis Bowker, who established the Pine Tree poultry farm. Bowker let his chickens range free through the Jericho swamp, protected by six to eight foxhounds, while awaiting the day when real estate in the neighborhood would gain in value.

Figure 12-28. Father Kilroy, Provincial of the Jesuits in New England, and Father Tivnan, rector of Weston College, are seated in this 1928 photograph of one of the first ordination classes.

Figure 12-29. This photograph of an ordination ceremony in the Weston College chapel shows several of the 12 stained-glass windows, which are the work of Earl Edward Sanborn of Boston.

Other changes made at Weston College over the years include the addition of a cemetery, a step that initially caused controversy among Weston residents. Although the planned burial plots were to be screened from view, the proposal was defeated several times at Town Meetings beginning in 1937. Finally an agreement was reached to permit the cemetery in return for allowing townspeople to use College Pond for skating. A total of 348 burials took place here through 1981, when this cemetery was filled and an adjacent plot prepared for future interments.

Until the college closed in the late 1960s, the fields were plowed and the grounds carefully tended. Local residents recall the priests in their long black robes strolling along Concord Road to the railroad tracks each evening on their after-dinner walk.

In the mid-1960s, philosophers at Weston College began taking their courses at Boston College, commuting there by bus. In 1969 the philosophers moved to Boston College and the theologians to a new facility in Cambridge called the Weston School of Theology. The future of Weston College was uncertain. Over the next decade, the town was able to acquire more than half the land. In 1975 the Society of Jesus undertook the remodeling of the former seminary building as a retirement home, the first and only such facility in New England for Jesuit priests. The renamed Campion Center houses 75 men on two floors of assisted living units and a 33-bed licensed nursing facility, as well as a separate retreat center for groups and individuals.

Weston Observatory

In 1928 Weston College set up the Weston College Seismological Laboratory in the basement of the former Grant Walker mansion, using equipment donated by Georgetown University. The college registered its first earthquake in January 1931.[72] From these humble beginnings, the renamed Weston Observatory has become an internationally known facility for earthquake detection and geological studies. The observatory was connected to Boston College informally until 1947, when it was accepted as the Graduate Department of Geophysics at the school, offering courses in geophysics and geology. In the 1970s, ownership of the building and land was transferred to Boston College.

The choice of seismology as a field of study was not a coincidence. Jesuits have contributed so much to the development of seismology that it has been called "the Jesuit science."[73] In the mid-1920s, the Jesuit Seismological Association had 19 member stations at Jesuit colleges and universities across the country.

Father Tivnan led the initial efforts to establish a seismology laboratory at Weston and appointed

Figure 12-30. Rev. Daniel Linehan, S.J., an internationally known expert on earthquakes, checks the seismograph at Weston College about 1965.

the first director, Rev. Henry M. Brock, S.J., who served from 1928 to 1935. Under the leadership of the Rev. Michael J. Ahern, S.J. (1877–1951), director of the Weston Observatory from 1940 to 1950, the laboratory constructed the present 15-room Weston Observatory in 1947–49. The building had a geological museum, library, instrument rooms, and an electronic laboratory. Ahern was well known as a leading proponent of Jesuit scientific research and founder of the American Association of Jesuit Scientists in 1921. As director from 1929 to 1950 of the Catholic Truth Hour, he was also one of the most influential spokesmen for American Catholicism.

His successor, Daniel Linehan, S.J. (1904–1987), founded the Graduate Department of Geophysics and directed the Weston Observatory from 1950 to 1972. Linehan was a pioneer in observational seismology, geomagnetism, engineering geophysics, and geoarchaeology, as well as a renowned scientist-explorer. He applied principles of geophysics to engineering problems like helping Weston locate two new water sources: the Nickerson and Fitzgerald wells. Linehan participated in expeditions to the Arctic, where he located a new position for the magnetic North Pole, and the Antarctic, where the Linehan Glacier is named for him.

Father Linehan was followed by yet another dynamic leader, James W. Skehan, S.J., director of the observatory from 1973 to 1993. Skehan founded the undergraduate Department of Geology at Boston College in 1957 and has led geological expeditions throughout North America.

Seismologists at Weston Observatory record, locate, and compute the magnitude of the 50-plus earthquakes that occur in the New England area each year, and can also record significant earthquakes worldwide. Seismic instruments detect ground vibrations generated by nuclear tests and thus play an important role in the surveillance of nuclear weapons sites. The observatory also participates in regional geologic and plate tectonic studies documenting the movement of continents over millions of years and identifying fault zones.[74]

"Little Cork Village"

At the turn of the century, the far corner of Weston near the Lincoln line acquired the name Little Cork Village because three Irish immigrant families had settled there: the Cronins, Sheehans, and McMahons. Patrick and Daniel Cronin bought 36 acres on the Lincoln town line in 1877.[75] For about 50 years, the family ran a small dairy farm, grew vegetables, and raised chickens.[76] Patrick had five children: James, who ran the farm after his father died; Jerry, who drove the town school bus; John, who worked as caretaker for Weston College; Louise, who became a nun; and Margaret.

Figure 12-31. Joseph Sheehan Sr. with baby hawks.

John Joseph Sheehan came to Weston in the 1880s and is listed in the 1887 town directory as a wholesale butcher living on Wellesley Street. According to his descendants, Sheehan ran the "slaughter shop" that appears on the 1875 map at the intersection of Wellesley and Ash Streets.[77] Slaughterhouses were smelly operations in this era of limited refrigeration, and this one would have been directly across from the estate of James Brown Case. Sheehan descendants speculate that town pressure influenced John Joseph's decision to sell that property and buy 25 acres in the far northwest corner in 1890.[78]

To get his permit, Sheehan promised to do little or no slaughtering from May to October and to stay at least 1,000 feet from Concord Road.[79] In 1892 the board of health noted, "The site of the slaughter house is well retired and not in sight from the road. Many years must elapse before it will be the cause of annoyance to any one."[80] The Cambridge Water Board inspected to ensure that it would not contaminate their water supply.

Sheehan built a Victorian frame house with small rooms in the rear where his workers could board. He employed five or six men, including herdsmen to feed and tend the cattle, butchers to kill and dress the

12-32. Margaret McMahon lived with her three children in a small house on Concord Road near the Lincoln town line.

meat, and a driver to take it into Faneuil Hall, where Sheehan had a market stall.[81] John Joseph died in 1898 at the age of 35. He left a widow, Catherine Reardon Sheehan, and six children, the oldest just 10 years old. Catherine Sheehan continued to apply for the slaughterhouse permit until 1916. Their son Anthony became Weston's postmaster and their daughter Mary Sheehan [Berry] was town clerk. The house built by Sheehan the butcher is now occupied by his great-grandson Joseph P. Sheehan Jr.

The third Irish immigrant family to settle in Little Cork Village was the McMahons.[82] The three unmarried siblings, Barney, Mary, and Francis, and their elderly parents lived in a mansard cottage that, like many in Weston in the early 20th century, had no indoor plumbing until after the last McMahon left. The family had a strawberry patch and vegetable garden and Mary worked at the Statehouse in Boston. Every day she walked from Concord Road to the Silver Hill depot to take the train to work.

Although stone walls line most of Concord Road, there are none in front of the Sheehan and Cronin properties. The two families were founding members of St. Julia Church and donated their walls for the facade of the new church building.

The Stratton Farm in the 20th Century

On May 12, 1905, an item in the Weston column in the *Waltham Daily Free Press Tribune* reported, "We understand that the estate of the late Geo. H. Stratton on Concord Street is for sale. It will make a fine gentleman's place, as it is so prettily situated." But the farmstead proved difficult to sell and stood vacant for six years. The story of how the house was finally purchased can be found in a 1913 article in *The House Beautiful,* a magazine that regularly featured stories about Colonial houses. This particular article, entitled "Adding New Life to Old Houses," was written by Joseph Stowe Seabury, a resident of Weston and an eloquent advocate for preserving old houses and making them "as home-like and convenient as new ones."

In his typically dramatic fashion, Seabury tells the story of the Stratton house:

> Not far from my home in Massachusetts there is a house which for six years has been begging on the market. It contained all the characteristics and rare interior features of the eighteenth century. A hundred times I have passed on warm summer days and in beating snowstorms, and always it had the same promising expression. Half of the time it was unoccupied and lonely. It seemed to say "Look at my great center chimney, my doorway, my big oven and my view. Take me and doctor me up, and then see if I won't keep you warm and make you happy." The old house seemed to crowd closer and closer to the road to waylay the passerby. I used to go in and wander through the vacant rooms.[83]

Seabury describes the contrasting reactions of two "city men," the kind of outsiders who had been buying up farmland in Weston for decades:

> In November, 1911, there suddenly and simultaneously appeared two city men unknown to each other, who were looked upon as serious buyers. The first examined the premises and said it was "impossible" and "only suitable for a chauffeur," while he himself would build on the knoll across the street. The second was a man after my own heart. He quietly enthused over points that only such a structure could possess . . .[84]

Seabury describes his pleasure as the two men began to bid, and "at last one of our dear old-fashioned places was in keen demand":

> The No. 2 secured it—and at a higher price than the owners were asking. The work on the alteration has just been completed, and how gratifying it is to see the historic gem, standing white and beautiful among the ancient trees, good for another hundred years. An old-fashioned garden across the road, with its rustic arbor, renders the house more fittingly placed. . . . There are bathrooms, electric fixtures and old furniture in exquisite taste, rooms thrown together, long rambling ells and awnings.[85]

Figure 12-33 and 12-34. Charles Peakes, shown here in his Masonic uniform, was one of two original trustees of the Weston Land Association, which developed Silver Hill and Westland Roads. His wife, Mabel, was the sister of Winslow Washburn, another of the original Weston Land Association organizers.

The buyers were Boston residents Alice L. Anthes and Horace J. Phipps. Phipps was a gentleman artist in stained glass who worked in the style of Louis Comfort Tiffany, and Anthes was his secretary and later his wife.[86] They named their 45-acre farm Pine Rest. For the restoration, Phipps hired Boston architect Frank Chouteau Brown, who later achieved prominence as one of the country's leading architectural historians specializing in early New England buildings. The Stratton house is one of his earliest known residential commissions.[87] "Before" and "after" pictures published in Seabury's book *New Homes under Old Roofs* show a large rear addition to accommodate servants and a new entrance porch adorned with a latticework trellis.[88]

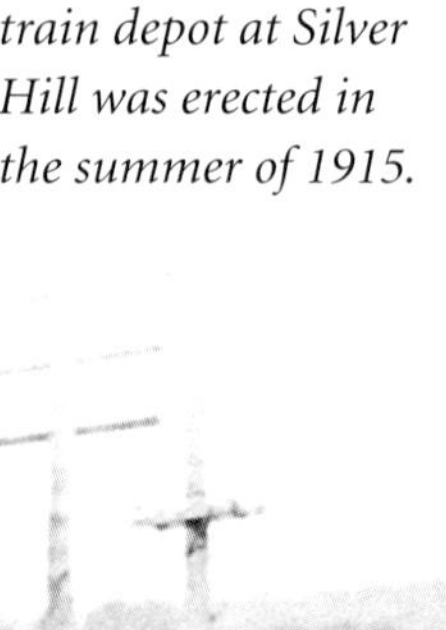

Figure 12-35. This train depot at Silver Hill was erected in the summer of 1915.

Silver Hill

No one knows, for sure, the origin of the name Silver Hill. Two stories have been handed down from generation to generation, one that Captain Kidd came out from Boston with his "chest of silver" and buried it at the top of the hill, and the other that the name referred to a stand of silver birches.[89] Several "diggings" atop the hill have failed to uncover any treasure. The name appears on the 1875 map, which shows the Silver Hill stop on the Fitchburg Railroad. Although the railroad had come through three decades earlier, most of the land south of the tracks was still part of long-established farms on each side of what is now Merriam Street.

In 1895 Frank H. Brooks and his wife, Carrie, purchased 10 acres on the east side of Merriam Street, where he built a handsome Colonial Revival house across from Carrie's sister Fannie Thompson. Brooks, who worked in Boston as a dealer in Oriental carpets, had a large chicken and duck farm on the property, with three or four long poultry houses out back. The birds produced 15–20 bushels of eggs a day, which his nephew, Raymond Washburn,

Figure 12-36. Raymond Washburn (1899–), one of four children of Winslow and Alice Washburn, became an automobile dealer and appraiser. He was still driving a car at age 101.

Figure 12-37. The 1905 Washburn house at 198 Merriam Street was one of the first in the Silver Hill subdivision. By building their own substantial houses at prominent corners, Washburn and his brothers-in-law set the architectural tone for the development. Raymond Washburn's 1956 Packard is in the driveway.

packed in boxes after school, wrapping each egg separately in brown paper. Raymond's father, Winslow Washburn, would carry the eggs in two large suitcases on the train to his job at the Waltham Watch Company, where he sold them to fellow employees.

About 1900, Brooks sold three acres along Merriam Street to his widowed mother, Arvilla Stickney, who built a Queen Anne house with corner tower. At the same time, he deeded two acres to his brother-in-law, Charles E. Peakes, treasurer of F.E. Atteaux & Co. of Boston, manufacturer and importer of dyes and chemicals. Peakes built a fine Colonial Revival house with matching barn and garden shed.

Until the late 19th century, new house lots in Weston were generally subdivided from larger lots in a casual, as-needed basis reflecting minimal demand for middle-class "suburban" housing in what was basically a rural, agricultural community. Brooks saw the potential for more-intensive real-estate development in the Silver Hill area and organized to tap the emerging market for house lots convenient to rail transportation.

Family relationships are important in this story, particularly the relationship between Carrie Washburn Brooks and her four siblings: Mabel (Mrs. Charles Peakes), Cora (Mrs. Edmund McKenney), Fannie (Mrs. Frederick Thompson), and Winslow Washburn. In April 1905, the Weston Land Association was formed, with Frank Brooks and Charles Peakes as trustees and Winslow Washburn as clerk.[90] The unincorporated joint stock association sold 500 shares, each valued at $100, to raise the $50,000 needed to purchase land and construct roads.

The trustees bought 30 acres bounded on the north by the railroad tracks and east by Merriam Street. Their subdivision plan for Silver Hill shows 89 lots.[91] Roadwork was under way by late April, when the local newspaper columnist noted that the association had planted "some fine sugar maple trees" on the new Silver Hill Road.[92] Lots sold fast, with many purchasers buying double lots for a total of about 60,000 square feet. The May 26, 1905, issue of the *Waltham Daily Free Press Tribune* reported that the association had sold 380,000 square feet of land in 10 days. The Silver Hill Road lots were largely sold by 1915, while lots on Westland Road were still for sale into the next decade.

To set the standard for new house construction, Washburn, Peakes, and McKenney built three of the first houses in the neighborhood, all located at prominent corners. The Washburn house at 198 Merriam Street and the McKenney house at 40 Silver Hill Road are both "Four Squares" with high fieldstone foundations. They were designed by architect George Strout and are nearly identical. The substantial house built by Peakes at 44 Silver Hill Road directly across from McKenney was a two-family residence used as a rental property.

The association had its own water system. Behind

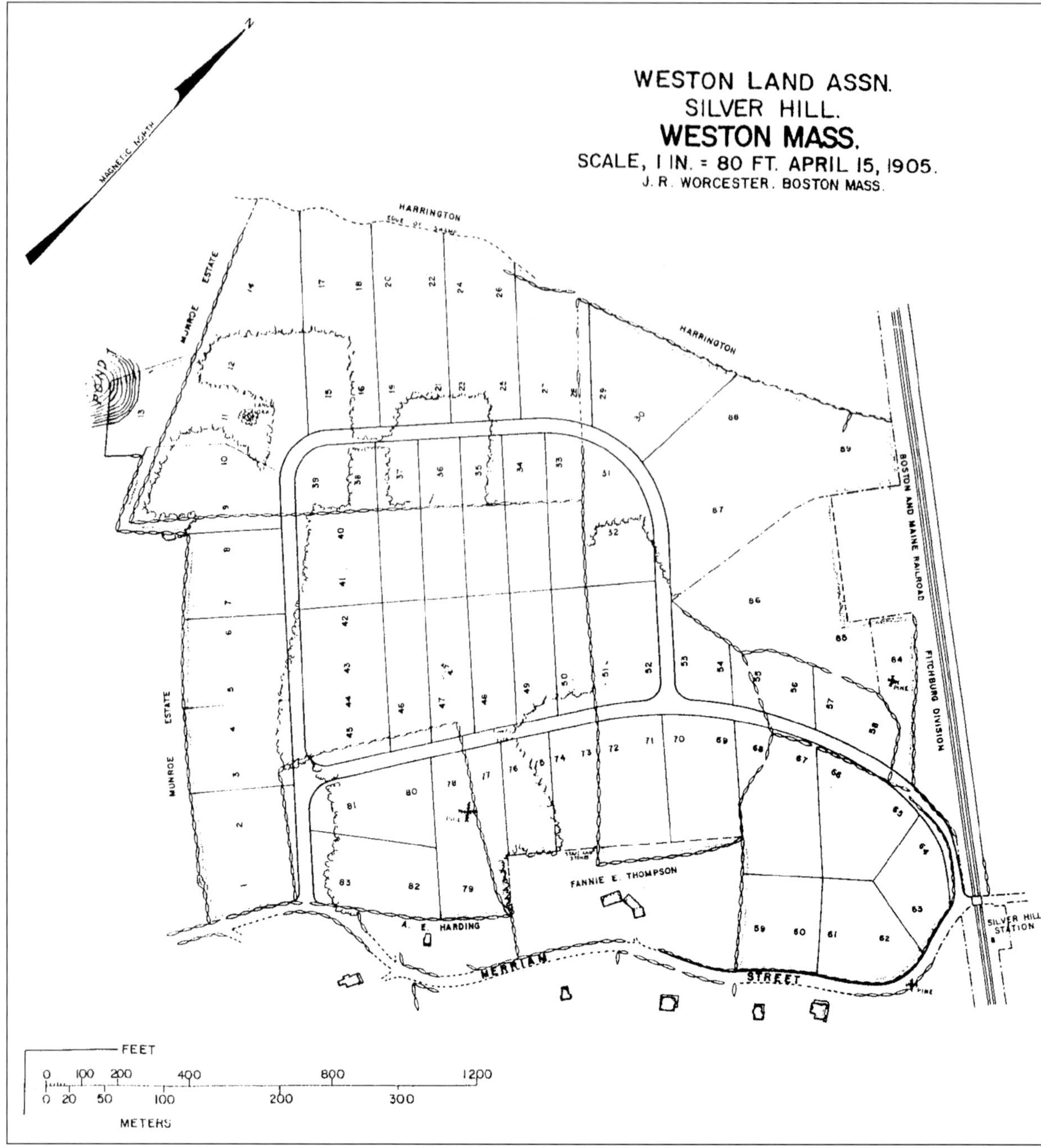

Figure 12-38. A newspaper reporter wrote this about the 1905 Silver Hill subdivision: "Mother nature has done more for this charming spot than money could accomplish, the rolling surface, partly wooded and partly cultivated, with curved steets winding through the trees, making it resemble a natural park."

Peakes's house on Silver Hill Road was a well with a full-size pump house that pumped water into a tank on the top of the hill opposite the railroad station. Carrie Brooks walked here from her house on Merriam Street every day to turn on the pump. The water system served 32 houses in the neighborhood until the town took it over in the 1920s.[93]

Mink Farming in Weston

The part of Weston bordering Lincoln was so remote that a Newton resident, George Rose, operated a small mink farm there in relative obscurity for more than 30 years, from the early 1930s into the 1960s.[94] At its peak in the late 1950s, Rose had 400 to 500 minks, including 100 females kept year-round for breeding. The animals lived in 250 to 300 small pens in the woods along Stony Brook and were fed ground-up livers and lungs from the Brighton abbatoir and later fish parts from Gloucester and horsemeat from Maine. While no other mink ranches are known to have existed in Weston, Sudbury and Maynard had much larger mink-breeding operations.

Houses in the Northwest

10 Cherry Brook Road (1893): Shingle-style mansion built for William Munroe, a Boston custom-house broker. His estate of 100 acres included a stable and other outbuildings, which have not survived. The entrance was off Merriam Street. Munroe sold the property in 1905 to John M. Lilly, who sold it in 1914 to William G. and Mary Renwick. The Renwicks called it Ravenswood and kept the estate intact until it was purchased for development by Edward Sweidler in the late 1950s. Part of Renwick's gun collection was given to the National Museum of American History in Washington, D.C., in 1972. The Cherry Brook Road subdivision plan, designed by the landscape architecture firm of Shurcliff and Merrill, was approved in September 1959.

302 Concord Road (1894–95): Well-detailed Queen Anne house built by carpenter Frank Murdock. During the Weston College era, it was occupied by John Cronin, who had been the caretaker for the Grant Walker estate. [*Note*: When the Jesuits built Weston College, they moved the Walker caretaker's house (an old farmhouse) and a barn across the street to a new site behind No. 302. The house, which is no longer extant, became known as the Workhouse and was a residence for men who worked on the property.]

319 Concord Road: 1) Fairview, a Georgian Revival brick mansion designed by Samuel Mead for Grant Walker and completed about 1912. 2) Weston College: a brick Beaux Arts seminary building constructed for the Society of Jesus in 1924–27 from designs by Maginnis and Walsh.

420 Concord Road (oldest section c. 1735–40): Constructed for farmer Jonathan Stratton, the house remained in the Stratton family until purchased about 1911 by Alice Anthes. Her friend Horace Phipps hired Frank Chouteau Brown to remodel and enlarge it. The next owners, the Speares, removed Brown's lattice front porch and added a pedimented doorway, which was in turn removed in 1989. They subdivided the property and donated some of the land for conservation. The property cannot be further subdivided and sight lines have been protected.

455 Concord Road (c. 1850): Jesse Cheney bought the 74-acre farm in 1795. His grandson Gilbert N. Cheney (1807–1880) married Amanda Adams in 1831 and was probably the builder of the present Greek Revival house. Gilbert's son, George G. Cheney (b. 1836), was the last of the Cheney farmers. His widow, Mary Cheney Gowell, sold the house to lawyer Francis H. Whitman. In late 1928, Whitman's son, Henry, sold 70 acres to Frances M. Frazier. She added a ballroom for entertaining and hired an Italian mason from Lincoln to build a brick serpentine wall inspired by a Jeffersonian wall at the University of Virginia.[95] Neighborhood baseball enthusiasts were pleased when she sold to Eddie Collins, a Hall of Fame baseball player who was then general manager of the Red Sox. Ted Williams, Bobby Doerr, Jimmy Foxx, and Roger Cramer visited the house. Eddie Collins is remembered fondly for giving baseball tickets to kids on the street.

484 Concord Road (1891): Queen Anne house built by butcher John Joseph Sheehan. The family has a promissory note for $2,500 borrowed to build it.

27 Lincoln Street (mid-19th century): Greek Revival house.

173 Merriam Street (c.1928): Colonial Revival house.

181 Merriam Street (c. 1902): Queen Anne house.

198 Merriam Street (1905): "Four Square" house built for Winslow A. and Alice Olney Washburn in 1905, designed by George Strout and built by H.D. Beardsley of Waltham. The Washburns had four children: Olney, Raymond (b. November 12, 1899), Florence, and Marion. Raymond was still living in the house on his 100th birthday in November 1999. The house retains its original brown shingles, trim, and interior features.

204 Merriam Street (c. 1911): Brick Colonial Revival house built for a Mr. Howard, who died before the house was completed. His widow, Ruby Howard, lived there for many years with her four children.

213 Merriam Street: Owned by dairy farmer Dennis Eldridge in the early 20th century.

222 Merriam Street (c. 1895): Queen Anne house built about 1895 for Albert E. Harding, who worked at the organ factory.

227 Merriam Street (c. 1892): Queen Anne house built in 1892 for Roland Rand, organ builder at the Hook & Hastings factory.

230 Merriam Street (c. 1926): Dutch Colonial cottage.

231 Merriam Street (c. 1896): Queen Anne house built for Waldo C. Hill, a watchmaker.

245 Merriam Street (1901): Colonial Revival house built for Frank H. and Carrie Brooks.

251 Merriam Street (1921): Built for Frank and Carrie Brooks's daughter, Mabel.

254 Merriam Street (1911): Shingled cottage built for Martha Kenyon.

255 Merriam Street (1901): Colonial Revival house built for Charles and Mabel Peakes.

261 Merriam Street (1901): Queen Anne house built in 1901 for Arvilla Stickney, mother of Frank Brooks.

268 Merriam Street (1908): Built in 1908 for Lyman Wright as part of the Silver Hill subdivision.

Merriam Street: Silver Hill Station (1915, demolished 1973). For many years, the stove was kept stoked by Albert Wright, who lived a few houses away on Merriam Street. It had been partially destroyed by fire when it was demolished.

324 Merriam Street: Nineteenth-century mansard cottage that at one time housed the caretaker on the Thorndike estate. Members of the Thorndike family added a section where they could stay in winter to enjoy cross-country skiing and sports. The house was still part of the 70-plus acre Thorndike estate in 1929, when it appears on a map prepared at the time of the sale to Edward Merritt.[96]

479 North Avenue: Colonial house owned by Revolutionary War patriot Samuel Phillips Savage and later by Capt. Thomas Bigelow, Samuel G. Snelling (who extensively remodeled it), and Samuel Lathrop Thorndike and his descendants.

541 North Avenue (c. 1796–98): Federal house constructed for John Dudley, who is referred to in deeds as a "housewright." By 1811 Dudley was taxed for a gristmill and sawmill located on the nearby pond at the northwestern edge of Weston near the Lincoln line. The property stayed in the Dudley family until the late 19th century, when it was sold to Thomas F. Harrington. In 1890, it was sold to farmer Herbert Sherman.

North Avenue: Johnny's Fudge Stand. Site of the George F. Harrington house, which stood partly in Lincoln and partly in Weston until it burned in the 1930s. Barn foundation still visible.

44 Ripley Lane (mid-18th century): Sometime after this Colonial farmhouse was purchased by Francis B. Ripley in 1879, the roof was raised and the central wall dormer added. An early photograph shows the original windows, which had 8/12 sash and shutters and extended to the cornice line. The picturesque rural setting for the house and large red barn is enhanced by hay fields, stone walls, and a flock of sheep.

15 Round Hill Road, Lincoln (also numbered 31) (1929): Brick Colonial Revival mansion built on the former Thorndike estate in 1929 for Edward and Elizabeth Merritt and later owned by the Beebe family (Beebe was a wool broker) and by Gerald Blakeley.

4 Silver Hill Road (1906): Notable one-story bungalow built in 1906 for farmer Dennis Eldridge, who lived nearby at 213 Merriam Street and probably never moved to Silver Hill Road.

14 Silver Hill Road (1907): Colonial Revival house built for Edward Parkhurst.

24 Silver Hill Road (1906): Queen Anne house built about 1906 for Arabella G. and Almon Wright.

31 Silver Hill Road (1911): Colonial Revival house built for Walter Reed, a bookkeeper in Boston.

37 Silver Hill Road (1909): Built for Grace Carr in late Queen Anne style.

40 Silver Hill Road (1909): "Four Square" house built for Edmund K. and Cora McKenney in 1909. McKenney is listed in the 1906 directory as a "traveling man" and in the 1909 directory as a mechanic. A newspaper article said he was associated with J.M. Mossman of New York, manufacturers of safes and bank vaults.

44 Silver Hill Road (1906): Built for Charles Peakes, probably as a rental property and as an example of the size and scale of houses he wanted to see in the new Silver Hill subdivision.

49 Silver Hill Road (1910–1911): Colonial Revival house built in 1910–11 for Henry J. and Amy F. Lawrence.

54 Silver Hill Road (c. 1935): Colonial Revival.

55 Silver Hill Road (c. 1940): Colonial Revival.

61 Silver Hill Road (c. 1940): Tudor/Colonial Revival.

4 Stony Brook Road (c. 1929 with alterations): Brick caretakers house built about the same time as the brick mansion at 15 Round Hill Road. Moved down the hill to its present location after the estate was subdivided in 1965.

Sudbury Road corner Concord Road: The White House. One of three frame secondary dwellings on the Grant Walker estate, this house was reportedly used by the Walkers when their mansion burned. Later owned by Weston College.

45 Sudbury Road: Colonial house with central chimney and two-over-two plan, built by early members of the Bemis family of farmers. Daniel Bemis was the owner at the time of the 1795 map. In the late 19th and early 20th centuries, the house was owned by the Fuller family. Their daughter married Roland B. Rand, a prominent local surveyor.

63 Sudbury Road: The 1794 map shows a house in this approximate location belonging to Samuel Lawrence. On the 1830 map, the house belonged to "Mr. Childs." It was owned by the Childs family until at least 1866. In 1873, Louis E. Roberts bought the farmhouse and two parcels of land, 34 and 38 acres, for $4,300. His family operated the property as a dairy well into the 20th century.

74 Sudbury Road (1934): International-style house designed by Edwin B. "Ned" Goodell for Richard and Caroline Field (see chapter 8).

89 Sudbury Road (c. 1826): Federal house with two-over-two center-hall plan built for Samuel Smith Jr. and updated in the mid-19th century with an Italianate-style central peaked gable and other Italianate features added by his son, Nahum.

102 Sudbury Road (c.1940): International-style house designed by Edwin B. "Ned" Goodell for Hassler Whitney (see chapter 8).

111 Sudbury Road (c. 1715): One of the oldest houses in Weston, the original one-over-one section was built for William and Mary Smith and is thought to have included the left three bays. Except for a brief period, members of the Smith family lived and farmed here until 1940, a period of 225 years.

12 Westland Road (1911–12): Colonial Revival house built for Percy Rand.

18 Westland Road (1939–40): Colonial Revival house built for Charles Cahill.

Notes

1. Seabury, Joseph S., "Adding New Life to Old Houses," *The House Beautiful,* vol. XXXIV, June 1913, 2.
2. "Fairview: The Founding of the New House of Studies at Weston, Mass.," in *The Woodstock Letters: A Record,* vol. LI, October 1922, 227.
3. The Stratton farmhouse is now 420 Concord Road. For information on the house and family, the author is indebted to Ellie Reichlin's unpublished typescript "A Little Bit of House History: 420 Concord Road" (undated, WHC files).
4. George Stratton had three daughters—Susan, Florence, and Edith—and three sons—Erwin, Dexter, and Byron. In addition, he raised Ernest Jones (b. 1875), who went to live with the family when he was 10 years old. Ernest was the father of Harry Jones, a lifelong resident who served the town in many capacities including town clerk and town accountant.
5. For further information on Savage, see Lawrence Park, *Major Savage and His Descendants* (1914, WHC files), and "Weston's Most Prominent Patriot," a lecture at the Weston Historical Society, January 1975 (WHC files). In 1803 the farm was sold to Capt. Thomas Bigelow.
6. Edward Adams to Jesse Cheney, March 1975, Book 119/21. See also Book 2376/566, Mary Gowell (wife of the late George G. Cheney), to Francis H. Whitman, 1895.
7. 455 Concord Road.
8. Lamson, *HTW,* 160 (footnote).
9. MacLean, John C., *A Rich Harvest* (Lincoln Historical Society, 1987), 176.
10. Dudley's house still stands at 541 North Avenue. See WHC records and 1811 tax records.
11. Some 19th-century maps show the two millponds. Information provided by Clifford Harrington Jr.
12. PWF interview with Clifford Harrington Jr., great-grandson of George. See also MacLean, op. cit., 178.
13. Information provided by Clifford Harrington Jr.
14. On his death, the *WDFPT* of September 22, 1911, wrote, "For 31 years he went regularly to Europe every fall . . ."
15. *Middlesex County and Its People,* vol. IV, 456–57.
16. Information provided by John Cronin.
17. MCRD, Charles Washburn to FBR, 20 acres of land formerly belonging to Wm. Roberts (Book 1122/339, April 11, 1870). John Carter to FBR, 70 acres + 4 acres (Book 1523/500, October, 1879) and Benjamin March to FBR, 9 acres (1208/100). For a description of the property, see the article on the Ripley 25th anniversary party, in Coburn scrapbook #3, 1.
18. Undated newspaper clipping, probably 1891, Coburn scrapbook #3, 1. This article also tells about Ripley's brush with death at Antietam.
19. Harold Travis, editor of the *Weston Historical Society Bulletin* in the mid-1970s, carefully investigated the idea that the Ripley house was the home of "one Wheaton" and concluded from deed and other research that no Wheaton had ever owned the Ripley house. See "Venerable Landmark on Ripley Lane: The House of 'Doctored' History," by Harold Travis, *WHSB,* January 1974; also March 1975, "The Spy That Hid in Weston."
20. 1953 *TR,* 138.
21. Lamson, 155.
22. *History of Middlesex County,* 509.
23. Merriam built the house (since demolished), which later belonged to E.O. Clark and then served for a time as the St. Julia parsonage (see 1889 map detail, chapter 15).
24. *History of Middlesex County,* 494.
25. See full text of letter in *History of Middlesex County,* 494.
26. In the Francis Blake papers at the MHS is a letter from Daniel Lamson to FB (64.916) March 1895, requesting anonymity for the silent poor, adding that disclosing the help defeated the purpose of Merriam in establishing the fund, which Lamson believed was the first of its kind in the state.
27. Lamson, 144.
28. MCRD, Louis Roberts to H. Merriam, October 2, 1873, Book 1278/287, $3,000, 50 acres. William M. Roberts to HM, October 2, 1873, Book 1278/298, $5,000, 80-acre and 20-acre parcel (total 150 acres). The property included three houses, two barns, and a henhouse.
29. Pope, Charles H., *Merriam Genealogy in England and America* (Boston: Charles H. Pope, 1906), 300.
30. HUA, obituaries, 1915.
31. See *Middlesex County and Its People,* vol. IV, 343, for information about Charles Merriam (b. 1904), son of Charles Merriam and grandson of Herbert Merriam. Says he was "prominent among the business men of Weston . . . who are well known and thoroughly well established." Managed the Weston branch of the Waltham Trust Company. Family home was on Central Avenue. He had two children, Charles (b. 1926) and Robert (b. 1927). In later years, this Charles Merriam settled in California.
32. MCRD, Book 5178/481, gives history of the building. The quarter-acre lot was bought by the town in January 1853 and sold with the schoolhouse by authorization of Town Meeting March 25, 1901. Merriam bought the parcel for $300.
33. *WDFPT,* February 17, 1915.
34. "The Three Spires of the Merriam Barn," *WHSB,* vol. XVII, no. 2, January 1981, and "The Foot and Mouth Disease" (same issue) from newspaper accounts assembled by Homer C. Lucas, ed. by B.H. Dickson III.
35. Dickson, *RR,* 108.
36. Dickson, *Pung,* 35.
37. Dickson, *RR,* 108.
38. Crouch, H. Bentley, "The Merriam Barn Fire," *WHSB,* vol. XVII, no. 1, October 1980, 3, and *Waltham News-Tribune,* October 30, 1926. The loss was estimated at $35,000, including farm and dairy equipment.
39. MCRD, Trustees under the will of Herbert Merriam (trustees were John Merriam and Charles S. Pierce) to Boston College, December 13, 1927, Book 5178/482, 204 acres, includes listing of each parcel and from whom Merriam bought it.
40. See Lamson, opposite page 127, for a picture of the house with this addition, which was later destroyed by fire.
41. "S. Lothrop Thorndike Dead at 82," unknown newspaper, Coburn scrapbook #2,

347. Thorndike, who died in June 1911, was a member of the Harvard class of 1852 and director or trustee of numerous railroads, mills, and Boston charitable organizations. See also *WDFPT,* June 23, 1911.
42. MCRD, Anna Snelling to Samuel Lathrop Thorndike, 1887 (Book 1800/587), Anna L. Thorndike, widow of SLT, to Albert Thorndike of Weston, Sturgis H. Thorndike of Boston and Mary Fiske, wife of Charles H. Fiske Jr. of Weston, 1911 (3652/43). Albert and Mary conveyed their shares to SHT in 1916. See also Albert H. Thorndike to Edward and Elizabeth Merritt, 1929 (5337/166). Albert inherited the property in the will of SHT, who died in 1928 (probate #166236).
43. MCRD, Plan 241 of 1929, Book 5337/166.
44. Bentley Crouch, in his unpublished typescript on the history of the Weston Fire Department, 28, reports the damage as $20,000.
45. Now 10 Cherry Brook Road. MCRD, George A. Keller to Helen Munroe, Book 2172/521, January 1893. Also Munroe to John M. and Virginia Lilly, Book 3170/579, June 1905.
46. *WDFPT,* July 7, 1905.
47. PWF interview with Teresa Zamprogno, daughter of Ralph Benotti, November 6, 1999.
48. PWF interview with Harry Jones, son of Ernest and Marie Zimmerman Jones, March 1999.
49. Quote from obituary of Daniel Ford, undated clipping in Coburn scrapbook #3, 126. Information on George W. Dunn can be found in the *Waltham Daily Free Press Tribune,* May 26, 1905: Dunn was born in Templeton in 1821, moved to Weston early in life, married Abigail Viles, was a prominent man in Weston affairs, serving as road commissioner, member of the school board, and selectman. His seven children were Alphonso, Herbert R., Mrs. Horace Hews, Mrs. Frank Murdock, Mrs. I.W. Hastings, and Misses Lillie and Mara. Died in May 1905.
50. MCRD, executors of D.S. Ford to G. Walker, Book 2825/424, $43,000, 98-plus acres in three parcels, one on the north side of Concord Road and two on the south side. See Plan Book 106/34 "Plan of land in Weston known as the George W. Dunn Farm, April 20, 1897."
51. Walker had a large financial interest in the Danvers Bleachery & Dye Works and directorships at the Androscoggin Mills, Bates Manufacturing Company, Naumkeag Cotton Company, and Warwick Mills. See obituaries, *Boston Herald* and *Boston Transcript,* April 5, 1920.
52. *WDFPT* June 16 and December 29, 1911. In 1913 the house was valued at $40,000.
53. *The Woodstock Letters,* op. cit., vol. LI, 229.
54. 1917 Weston assessor's records. The henhouse was valued at $1,000 and Walker was assessed for 300 fowl.
55. MCRD, Book 4473/590. November 1921. Histories of the college usually recount the bargaining that brought down the asking price of $175,000.
56. Arnoldy, Ben, "Campion Center," *Weston Town Crier,* July 30, 1998.
57. "The New Scholasticate at Weston," *Woodstock Letters,* vol. LI, 99. For further details on the early years of the college, see Father James L. Burke, S.J., *Jesuit Province of New England: The Formative Years* (c. 1976, written for the 50th anniversary of the New England Province).
58. "Fairview," *Woodstock Letters,* vol. LI, 224.
59. The general contractor was J.P. Keating of Westboro.
60. Also instrumental in establishing the facility were Father Rockwell, provincial of the New England/New York jurisdiction and purchaser of the property; Father O'Gorman, who was in charge of New England under Father Rockwell and suggested the purchase of the property; and Father Kilroy, who succeeded Father O'Gorman and was the first provincial of the New England Province, in charge of overseeing construction. Funding for the chapel and for the later purchase of the Merriam farm came from Mrs. Helen Grant.
61. *Boston Globe,* May 19, 1927.
62. Weston assessor's office records 140,132 square feet in the upper four floors and 39,596 square feet in the basement. The 1970 town report listed the square footage as about 200,000.
63. The main public activities were focused on the first floor—the location of the chapel, several parlors, recreation rooms, the infirmary, and the physical laboratory and lecture room. The second floor contained classrooms and bedrooms off the central corridors. On the third floor were more than 80 small bedrooms. The "basement," which was largely above ground level, contained the biology and chemistry labs, lecture rooms, refectory, clothes room, grocery room, vegetable room, butchers meats, and ice-cream room, according to notations on plans that have been preserved at the Massachusetts Archives.
64. In 1928 the population at Weston was 246 and at Woodstock, 243.
65. "Cost of Establishing the Scholasticate at Weston" (unpublished typescript, undated, NEPA).
66. Tivnan, Edward P., S.J., "History of Weston [College]" (unpublished typescript, 1928), 10 (NEPA).
67. Father Edward P. Tivnan, op. cit., 12.
68. Ibid., 12.
69. Ibid., 13.
70. Ibid.
71. *The Woodstock Letters, A Record,* vol. LIX (Woodstock College, June 1930), 221.
72. Macelwane, James Bernard, S.J., ed., *Jesuit Seismological Association: 1925–1950,* 25th Anniversary Commemorative Volume (Central Station: St. Louis University, 1950).
73. "Seismology, the Jesuit Science: Some Jesuits and Their Geophysical Observatories," information prepared by Joseph MacDonnell, S.J., at Fairfield College and distributed via the Internet at www.faculty.fairfield.edu/faculty/jmac/sj/geophysics.htm.
74. In 1961, when the Coast and Geodetic Survey (C & GS) undertook the development of a Worldwide Network of 125 Standard Seismograph Stations, Weston Observatory was among the first of these installations to be established. Through a contract with the C & S, the observatory established the New England Seismic Network in 1962.
75. MCRD, John S. Williams to Daniel and Patrick Cronin, November 20, 1877, Book 1458/181. The original house on the property later burned to the ground.
76. Information provided by Cronin and Sheehan family members.
77. Sheehan's deed (MCRD, Sumner F. Davis to John Sheehan, Book 1842/452, March 23, 1888, $1,500, 30 acres) does not specifically mention the slaughter shop.
78. MCRD, Waltham Savings Bank to John Sheehan, Book 2007/330, November 4, 1890, $400, 24.62 acres (conveyed to bank by John S. Williams in 1887).
79. 1891 *TR,* 25–26.
80. 1892 *TR,* 58.
81. Information provided by Joseph P. Sheehan Sr. and Jr.
82. In the 1887 directory, Barney McMahon is listed as a farmer on Concord Road. The McMahon property was at 474 Concord Road.
83. Seabury, Joseph S., "Adding New Life to Old Houses," *The House Beautiful,* vol. XXXIV, June 1913, 2.
84. Ibid.
85. Ibid.
86. Horace J. Phipps first appears in Boston directories as working in stained glass in 1888 and is so listed until 1923. Firm names included Phipps, Slocum and Co. (with William S. Slocum); Horace J. Phipps and Co.; and Phipps, Ball, Burnham Co., with Walter G. Ball and Wilbur H. Burnham. Ref: BPL Fine Arts Department, architectural file.
87. Later Brown served as an editor of "The White Pine Series of Architectural Monographs," staff architect for SPNEA, and, in the 1930s, Massachusetts director of the Historic American Buildings Survey, a federal project

to inventory early buildings.

88. Seabury, Joseph S., *New Homes Under Old Roofs* (New York, 1916), Plates XXIV and XXV.

89. Cooke, Elsie, "Silver Hill" (undated typescript, WHC files).

90. MCRD, Articles of Association, recorded April 20, 1905, Book 3156/107.

91. MCRD, plan of Weston Land Association, Silver Hill, May 2, 1905, Plan Book 154/34.

92. *WDFPT,* April 21 and 28, 1905.

93. 1920 *TR,* 58–59.

94. In 1941 the mink farm had a permit from the board of health (1941 *TR,* 93). The 1961 assessor's report (*TR,* 63) lists 200 mink in the Table of Aggregates.

95. MCRD, Book 5308/232 (Whitman to Frazier, December 11, 1928).

96. MCRD, Plan 241 of 1929 in book 5337/166.

Figure 13-1. Workers at the Massachusetts Broken Stone quarry line up for a group photograph in 1933. In the background is the main screening tower, where crushed stone was separated by size into compartments for loading into trucks. Superintendent Bill Bourget is at the far right. As many as 50 men worked at the Weston quarry in the early days, when the work was very labor intensive. Many of the quarrymen were immigrants from Canada or Italy and lived in Waltham. Some worked for "Mass. Broken Stone" all their lives.

CHAPTER 13

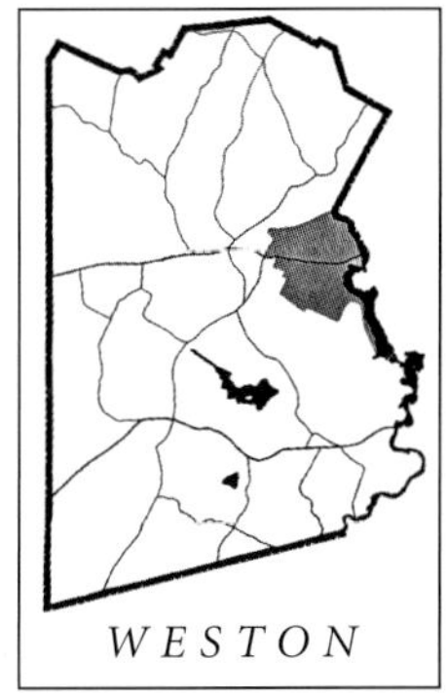

Boston Post Road (East)

Stony Brook to Crescent Street

Stony Brook is the largest tributary of the Charles River and forms part of the boundary between Weston and Waltham. Traditionally, the name refers not only to the brook but also to the area where the brook intersected the Great Country Road, now Boston Post Road. Historian Daniel Lamson was unusually poetic in recalling the beauty of the landscape just a stone's throw from the present Route 128:

> *[There was] a little cañon, enclosing the pool out of which the cascade fell. From above, the waters of the brook came down the rapids white with foam, the banks covered with mosses and ferns, the oaks and hemlocks overarching the stream. Altogether it formed one of the most beautiful bits of natural scenery to be seen this side of the White Mountains, the delight of artists and the admiration of all beholders.*[1]

Lamson writes that "Snake Rock at Stony Brook," also known as "Devil's Den," on the north side of the post road, was once "a place of refuge and deposit for thieves and their plunder."[2] *Legend has it that highwaymen would hide in the den and swoop down on unsuspecting stagecoaches.*

By the mid-19th century, Sibley's machine shop at Stony Brook was the town's most important industrial site. By the turn of the century, the rock ledges across the street at Devil's Den were being quarried; and within the next decades, Massachusetts Broken Stone Company was operating what would become Weston's largest 20th-century industrial site. On Crescent Street, the waters of Three Mile Brook powered mills used for more than 250 years to manufacture everything from flour to window screens.

Today a busy Mobil Gas Station stands on land once part of the Sibley mills. Plans are under way to develop a large office building at Devil's Den, which was still owned by Massachusetts Broken Stone in the year 2000. In dramatic contrast, the site of the former chair factory on Crescent Street has been preserved as town conservation land. Those who walk the land can still find the foundations of the mill and trace the outlines of the millpond and canal that fed water to a large undershot wheel.

In 1993, by vote of Town Meeting, Crescent Street became Weston's first Local Historic District, a designation that aims to preserve the character of the street by reviewing proposed architectural changes.

Figure 13-2. Stony Brook was dammed to provide power for Weston mills. The date and exact location of this photograph are unknown.

The Mills at Stony Brook

Lamson's *History of the Town of Weston* records that Stony Brook was an important mill site as far back as 1679, when Richard Child erected a corn mill and later a sawmill, which produced lumber to build the early houses of Weston.[3] In 1831 Henry Coolidge, Nathaniel L. Sibley, and Joseph Treat, all machinists from Waltham, bought 155 acres on both sides of the post road from Abraham Bigelow, along with a dwelling house, sawmill, gristmill, cider mill, two barns, an icehouse, cattle shed, and piggery. Coolidge, Sibley, and Treat erected a machine shop and operated the gristmill along with a mill for the manufacture of cotton yarns. For many years, the machine shop specialized in cotton machinery and looms for textile cities like Lowell and Lawrence, as well as door locks and steel and iron hardware.[4] Company growth was encouraged by the construction, in 1844–46, of the Fitchburg Railroad, later the Boston and Maine, with a station at Stony Brook.

Nathaniel L. Sibley (1805–1890) became sole

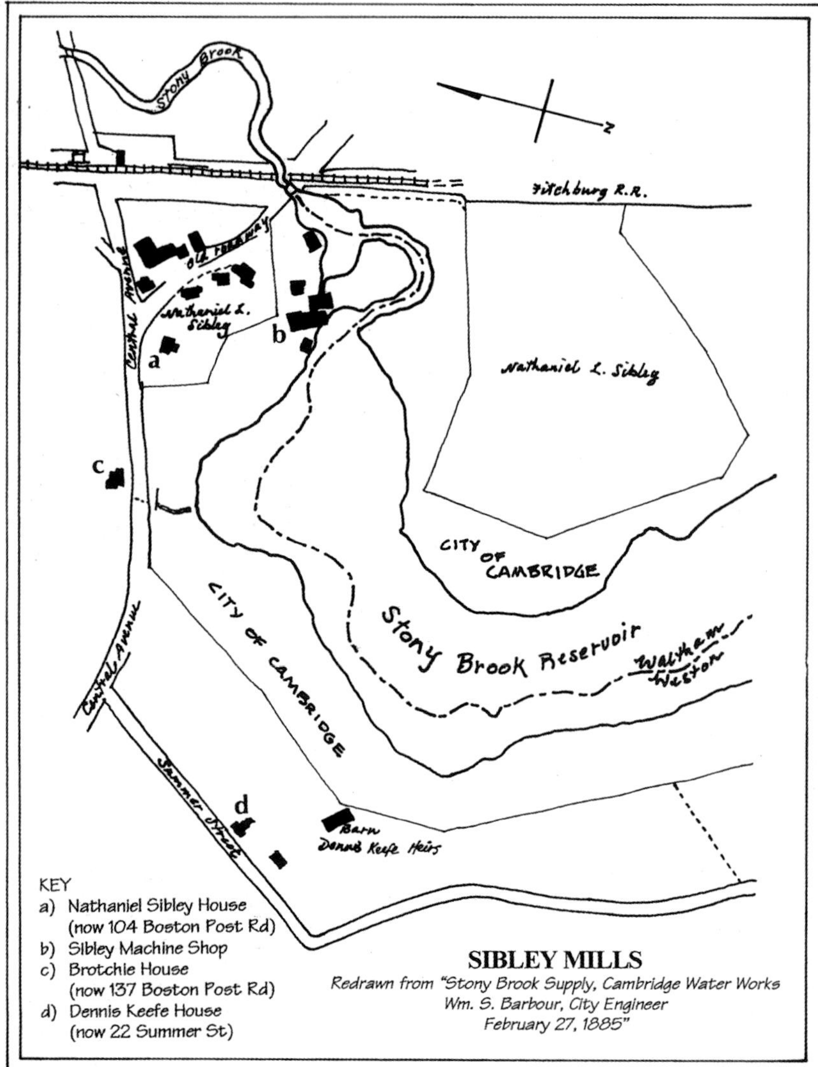

Figure 13-3. This map, adapted from an 1885 plot plan of the entire Stony Brook Reservoir, shows the extent of the Sibley mill complex before the City of Cambridge was given rights to the waters of Stony Brook.

owner of the mills in 1850. He built himself a new house set on a rise and embellished with the latest Italianate details.[5] About the same time, Sibley sold a half-acre lot across the street with the stipulation that the lot could never be conveyed "to any foreigner whether naturalized or not."[6]

In 1859 Sibley began making wood planing machines, the Sibley dovetailer, and Sibley pencil sharpeners sold to schools "from Maine to Alaska," according to Lamson's history. He was taxed two years later for 73 acres with water privileges, five dwellings, two barns, a blacksmith shop, store house, two machine shops, and a carriage house.[7] At $11,000, the taxable valuation was one of the highest in Weston. The 1860 U.S. census lists 14 machinists living in a boardinghouse on the property.

A newspaper article in the 1880s describes the "small hamlet" of Stony Brook:

> . . . as picturesque and weirdly romantic a spot as can be found in all the country around and shows none of the marks that denote an advancing civilization and contains nothing to indicate that it ever communes with the thriving towns . . . [to] the east. Skirting this local "sleepy hollow" . . . courses a murmuring brook that for four generations has leaped at the huge, old-fashioned water wheel of "Sibley's mill."[8]

Mills on Three Mile Brook, Crescent Street

What is now Crescent Street was part of the Great Country Road until the early 1850s, when the road was widened and straightened. The improvement left a short loop of the original narrow roadway. Behind Crescent Street is Three Mile Brook, which drains the eastern end of the town center and flows into a series of three man-made millponds. Waterwheels provided power to a succession of small industries.

The first mill site was located behind 293 Boston Post Road at the junction of the present bypass. The dam and mill pond appear to have been created in the early 19th century by Alpheus Cutter. At the time of the town's Bicentennial in 1913, Mrs. Francis B. Sears collected the following information from his daughter, Miss Mollie Cutter:

Figure 13-4. Sometime after 1839, manufacturer Samuel H.F. Bingham built this handsome Greek Revival house (now 39 Crescent Street) next to his mill and mill pond.

Figures 13-5 and 13-6. These 1898 photographs show the Charles A. Freeman screen factory, which operated behind 39 Crescent Street from the 1890s to 1933. Use of screens increased during this period, as scientists established the link between insects and disease transmission. Construction of the Boston Post Road bypass in the early 1930s interfered with the water flow of Three Mile Brook and led to closing of the factory.

> Mr. Alpheus Cutter had been employed in some manufacturing enterprise in Watertown. When he married he came to Weston, bought the premises which Mrs. Sears now owns, with a considerable additional tract farther to the eastward. He soon got tired of farming and built a dam to develop a water power [sic] and began the fulling of cloth. After a time he changed his machinery and began the manufacture of cotton batting. There was quite a demand for his goods, and the business was successful in a small way. [9]

The second mill site, behind the present 39 Crescent Street, was the location of an early gristmill. In 1838 the water privilege was purchased by machinist Samuel H.F. Bingham, who made machinery for the manufacture of coarse woolen goods.[10] According to Lamson, he also invented the butter and cheese drill, an item said to be "in such demand that he had difficulty in filling his orders."[11] Bingham prospered, and sometime after 1839 he built the fine Greek Revival house that still overlooks the pond.

The property passed to machinist Henry Bowen and later to Charles A. Freeman. From the 1890s to

Figure 13-7. No. 21 Crescent Street was built in 1812 by farmer Luther Harrington. Later owners included David Perry, his son George, Francis B. Sears Jr., and his son Edwin (Buck).

about 1933, Freeman operated a factory here that produced window and door screens and weatherstripping. The mill was originally powered by an old-fashioned turbine waterwheel, replaced in the late 1890s by a "breast" wheel about 15 feet in diameter with a small supplemental gasoline engine.[12]

The third mill site was located 500 to 600 feet north of the Federal-style "brick-ender" built by farmer Luther Harrington at what is now 21 Crescent Street. In 1854 Samuel Shattuck established a school furniture factory here. The main products were desks and chairs sold to primary schools through his brother, Boston dealer William G. Shattuck, and later through A.G. Whitcomb & Son.[13]

In the early 1880s, A.G. Whitcomb was bought by George Springer Perry (1855–1904), who changed the name to Geo. S. Perry & Company and added school supplies and slate blackboards to the list of products distributed by the Boston-based firm. George was one of four children of David Perry, who had purchased the Harrington homestead in 1866. George continued to make school desks and chairs in Weston.[14] In 1883, he and his new bride built their own house at the corner of Crescent Street and Boston Post Road.

In the 1880s, manufacturing responsibilities at the school furniture factory changed hands when an employee of Shattuck, Oliver N. Kenney, purchased that part of the business. He was succeeded by his sons George and Ralph, in 1895, although George retired soon after. In December 1901, Ralph and another brother, Charles, along with Henry Wolkins, bought out George Perry and formed a new partnership under the name of Kenney Bros. & Wolkins.[15] A few months later, the *Waltham Daily Free Press Tribune* reported that "Kenney Bros. are working on an order of 1500 intermediate desks for Washington, D.C."[16]

Power for the chair factory was originally supplied by a turbine waterwheel, replaced in the late 1890s by a 28-foot-diameter undershot waterwheel, which was more efficient but a headache in winter months. Ice would form on one side and cause it to run unevenly. A small steam engine was used during the summer when water was low. The wheel was destroyed in a disastrous fire of May 21, 1905, thought to have been of incendiary origin, which razed the original mill.[17] A one-story frame structure

Figure 13-8. Henry Perry's daughter, Marion, with Peter Pony, by the barn at 21 Crescent Street. Notice that the barn has been remodeled and shingled. (c. 1910s photo)

Figure 13-9. George Springer Perry (1855–1904), one of David Perry's three sons, took over distribution of school furniture made at the factory behind his Crescent Street home.

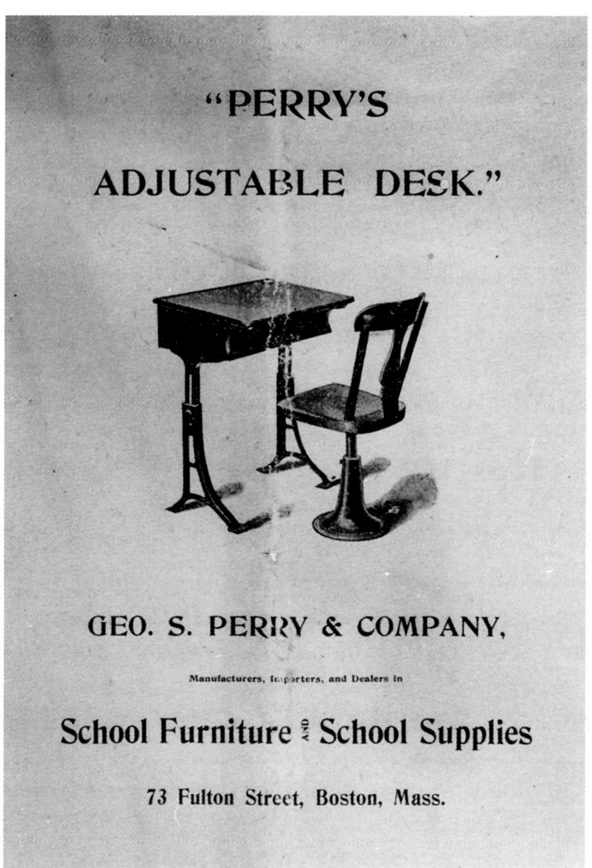

Figure 13-10. This catalog dates to the early 1880s, when Perry took over the previous firm of A.G. Whitcomb.

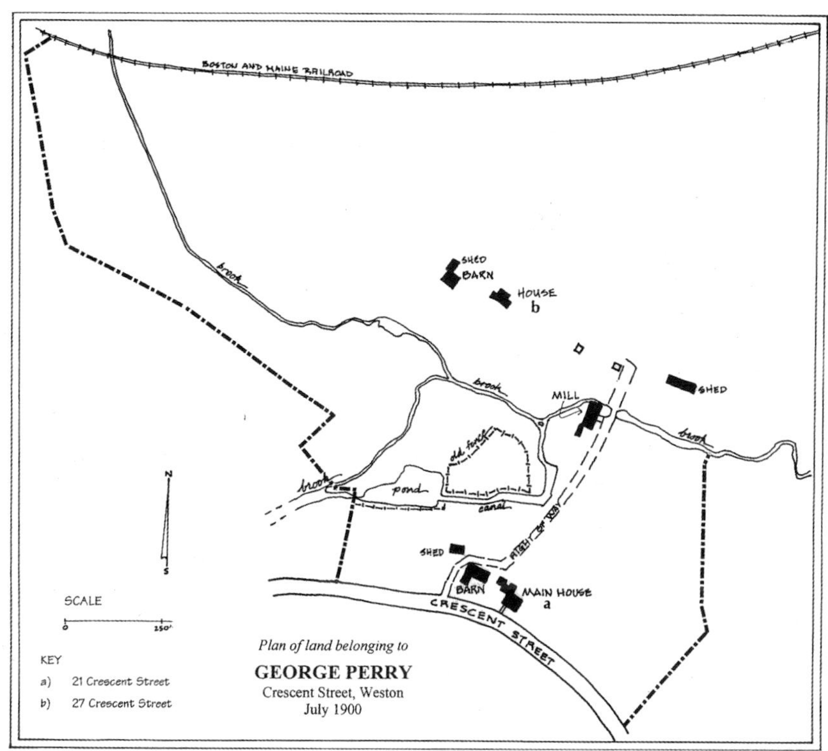

Figure 13-11. The chair factory was located just north of Crescent Street. It was powered by water from Three Mile Brook, channeled through the mill pond shown on this 1900 plot plan. Traces of the mill site still remain on what is now the Sears conservation land.

was quickly rebuilt on the same site, with new machinery.[18]

No finishing was ever done in Weston. The desk boxes and seat tops were hauled on a two-horse cart to Boston, where they were finished and packed for shipment all over New England and New York state. A Kenney descendant described the trip to the Fulton Street warehouse:

> Once a week and two or three times a week during the summer months, the "hill team" with its load of furniture on the way to Boston was a familiar sight on the Post Road. The load was made up in the afternoon and promptly when the whistle blew at 7 o'clock the next morning the team started up the hill, turned left on Crescent St. to the Post Rd. . . . Gus Upham drove the team for many years and he was so regular that it is said old timers used to set their watches when he passed their doors.[19]

Figure 13-12. The mill wheel remained standing long after the chair factory closed in 1917. Waterwheel fans came from distant places to see it and take pictures. This image was taken by noted Wayland photographer Alfred Wayland Cutting, probably in the mid-1910s.

Figure 13-13. The Queen Anne house at 225 Boston Post Road was built in 1883 for George Perry and his wife, Charlotte.

Figure 13-14 (above). After the death of her brother George, Hattie Perry (center) inherited the house at 225 Boston Post Road and lived there until 1946. In Weston: A Puritan Town, *Emma Ripley describes her as "New England at its best."*

The chair factory remained in Weston until 1917, when Kenney Bros. & Wolkins purchased a larger factory in Baldwinsville.[20] The next year, the executors of George Perry's estate sold 66 acres on Crescent Street to Horace Sears.[21]

Stony Brook Reservoir

Meanwhile, back at the Sibley Mills, manufacturing had ceased in the mid-1880s when the Massachusetts State Legislature granted water rights to Stony Brook and its tributaries to the City of Cambridge.[22] The 1884 Act to Provide a Further Supply of Water for the City of Cambridge gave the city the right to raise the height of Roberts Mill dam on River Street by 20 feet to create the Stony Brook Reservoir. The act required Cambridge to pay for damages and for measures to maintain water purity.[23] When completed three years later, Stony Brook Reservoir covered 75 acres and extended a mile and a half along the Weston/Waltham border south of Boston Post Road.[24] The well-crafted brick gatehouse, which still stands atop the dam at the southern end, was built by Cambridge mason and contractor Marshall N. Stearns and completed in 1887.[25]

Cambridge expanded the system in 1894–97 with the addition of Hobbs Brook Reservoir in Lincoln. They added regulations on disposal of household waste water, garbage, and manufacturing waste, use of manure, and location of stables, pigsties, animal yards, burial places, hospitals, tanneries, slaughterhouses, and sewerage and drainage facilities.

Weston was not the first community to experience

Figure 13-15. Stony Brook Reservoir was created by raising the existing milldam at Roberts Mill on River Street. This engraving of the gatehouse and dam appeared in the 1887 annual report for the City of Cambridge.

General View of Stony Brook Basin, showing the Dam, Abutments and Gate House.

Figure 13-16. This aerial photograph from about 1950 shows the size of Stony Brook Reservoir as compared to the nearby Massachusetts Broken Stone quarry pit. Also visible are the Fitchburg Railroad tracks and Cedar Hill subdivision in Waltham. Route 128 had not been constructed.

the political clout of the growing Boston metropolitan area in its quest for a pure drinking water supply. In 1846, the state legislature had authorized the City of Boston to take the waters of Lake Cochituate. By the 1870s, when the subject of additional water supplies for Boston was raised, communities bordering watercourses raised strong objections, declaring the "right of inhabitants of the town to use their own water for domestic and manufacturing purposes."[26] In the 1872 session, the state legislature had petitions from 27 cities and towns to take water from various rivers and ponds.[27] Serious public discussion at the time focused on two subjects relatively new to public consciousness: the need for a metropolitan approach to services and the belief that pollution of watercourses made them unfit water supplies and potential hazards to public health. Cambridge chose to develop its own water supply system, while most other greater Boston communities eventually became part of the metropolitan system.

Weston's hostile reaction to the taking of water rights and subsequent closure of the Sibley Mills was expressed by historian Daniel Lamson:

> All the available portions of this valuable plant have now been completely destroyed by the Cambridge water board, who have seized the mills and rendered its future usefulness as a factory impossible. This act of the Cambridge authorities wipes out all this important factory privilege and destroys the taxable value of this industry for the town. It is time our people should realize the immense injury to farms and manufactories which the free and easy grants of the legislature of late years to water companies are doing. They are giving away for the asking the control of springs and waterways, which bids fair to destroy the value of our farms and property.[28]

Brenton H. Dickson III recalled the effect on recreation in the town. Swimming was forbidden almost everywhere in the center because the brooks flowed into the reservoir, although "you could swim in the reservoir, or anywhere else for that matter, providing you weren't caught."[29] Fishing in the water basin was also taboo. Dickson tells of his father, who was town clerk, and Police Chief P.J. McAuliffe smuggling fishing poles down to the Stony Brook Reservoir, "all of which goes to show that 'Bloody Alonzo's' dealings were resented by the old as well as the young."

Massachusetts Broken Stone Company: Early Years

This picturesque description of the Devil's Den property appeared in a Waltham newspaper of the 1880s:

> . . . rising almost perpendicularly to an altitude of nigh three hundred feet, is a hill of some forty acres composed of immense boulders, deep and perilous chasms, and all covered with a venerable growth of oak and walnut. A hundred feet back from, and perhaps sixty above the grade of the country road leading to Weston, is the entrance to the "Devil's Den"—a huge subterranean cavern under this hill which tradition says was the abiding place of the evil one in the days when "Old Nick" is supposed to have perambulated this mundane planet . . .[30]

The reporter added that a recital of deeds attributed to Old Nick would "curdle the blood of youth and cause a shiver to steal over the frame of age."

At the turn of the century, town leaders became concerned about the future of Devil's Den. In May 1899 Henry J. Jennison wrote fellow selectman Francis Blake urging quick action to prevent the City of Cambridge from placing a stone crusher there. He concluded his letter by saying, "I think it would be a grand scheme for us as selectmen in connection with our Park Commissioners . . . to petition the Metropolitan Park Commission to take this for park purposes and thus avoid this nuisance, as well as to reserve one of the natural beauties of the place."[31] The petition, printed in the 1899 town report, added that the land "has been for many years . . . an objective point for excursions from many surrounding cities and towns, as well as a resort for landscape artists in the practice of their profession."[32]

Figure 13-17. Massachusetts Broken Stone Company was formed in the 1890s. The firm took over the Waltham Trap Rock Company quarry at Devil's Den in 1916.

The Metropolitan Park Commission heard the petition to make the site a public park. Its ruling is not recorded in town reports, but according to a newspaper account of March 1900, the commission was willing to help provided the town would pay its share.[33] About the same time, Blake received a letter from Stony Brook resident Dr. Walter E. Hobbs expressing his desire to avoid a quarry even though such a use might increase the value of his property:

> My dear sir: The den property here is again in danger of being turned into an unsightly quarry with a surrounding population of foreign quarrymen. Any influence that you can bring to bear with the Park Commission if done at once will hinder and I hope prevent the consummation of this nefarious scheme. . . . Our land interests will rather be made more valuable as we shall sell more smaller house-lots. We would rather keep a higher plane of development even at a loss.[34]

The park plan never materialized. In early 1900, the *Waltham Daily Free Press Tribune* reported that the property had been purchased for a quarry, and by 1901 Waltham Trap Rock Company was operating a stone crusher there.[35] In 1916, the operation was leased to the Massachusetts Broken Stone Company. Known as Mass. Broken Stone, the company had been founded in the 1890s and incorporated in 1908

Figure 13-18. This 1946 aerial view shows the front quarry, with Boston Post Road in the foreground. In the early 1950s, the company opened a second quarry pit.

by Arthur J. Wellington, a pioneer in the development of the crushed-stone business in the state.[36] He was the first in the industry to use heavy machinery, large primary crushers, power shovels, and diesel engines. His company operated other quarries, including Roberts Quarry in Waltham. Mass. Broken Stone took title to the Weston property in 1926.

Initially, the principal product was crushed stone. It was much in demand for road building, as early-20th-century macadam roads were made with layers of crushed stone sprayed with bitumen. The front quarry pit, once the location of the Devil's Den cave, was excavated first, to an initial depth of 150 feet. To transport stone and other materials, the company used the Fitchburg (later Boston and Maine) Railroad, which had a siding on site. To provide water for stone crushers and steam boilers, the company built a dam along Three Mile Brook, creating the present Quarry Pond, also known as the Duck Pond.

Later History of Massachusetts Broken Stone

Henry O. Robinson began working for Massachusetts Broken Stone Company in the early 1920s, and his son Richard later served as treasurer and president. The family acquired the Wellington share of the business in 1967. Over the years, the Robinsons contributed men and equipment to plow snow at town properties, fight forest fires, build a horse ring, move boulders, and black-top church parking lots.

As road-building methods changed, the company adapted its products so that by the early '30s they were making bituminous concrete and by the '50s, Portland cement concrete. In the 1940s Mass. Broken Stone acquired nearby houses previously owned by Nathaniel Sibley, Amos Crane, and Andrew K. Brotchie. The Brotchie house had been used for many years as a combined residence and grocery.

In the early 1950s, the company opened the rear quarry pit, which was eventually excavated to a depth of 385 feet. The operation reached peak activity in the interstate-highway era of the 1950s and '60s. By 1962, concern about depletion of rock reserves in Weston influenced the company to organize the Berlin Stone Company, located on the Massachusetts Central Division of the Boston and Maine Railroad. Plans to bring carloads of stone by rail from Berlin to Weston were blocked by adverse zoning rulings, which also enjoined other types of manufacturing at the Weston site.[37] Despite the cost of mining aggregate stone to a great depth within a small area, the company decided to reopen the 12-acre front quarry pit, which was taken down to 425 feet. In the early 1980s, as the cost of mining increased with the depth of the pit and real-estate values soared, Mass. Broken Stone decided to develop the property. They discontinued quarrying but maintained production of "hot-top" asphalt. Once

Figure 13-19. The man in the center of this mid-20th-century photograph is Tony Fucci.

Figure 13-20. The Massachusetts Broken Stone Company produced crushed stone needed for road building.

Figure 13-21. Detail from the 1908 Atlas of Middlesex County.

the quarry pits were no longer pumped, it took seven years for rain and groundwater to fill them to the top.

In 1988, after several years of legal battles over zoning, Town Meeting voted to accept a settlement agreement with Mass. Broken Stone. In exchange for rezoning the entire 75-acre site for business, the owner agreed to limit development to 350,000 square feet of office space.[38] A real-estate down cycle and continued legal disputes delayed development into the next century.

The Francis B. Sears Estate

Beginning in the late 19th century, the history of Crescent Street was influenced by three generations of the Sears family. Francis Bacon Sears (1849–1914), one of three sons of the Rev. Edmund Hamilton Sears, moved to Weston as a young man when his father became pastor of First Parish Church. He began his career as a bank teller and rose to the position of president at Third National Bank and later chairman of the board of directors of National Shawmut Bank. Described as a "Puritan without the Puritan angularities," Sears was reputed to be "one of the best known bankers in Boston."[39]

In 1875 he married Mary Elizabeth Sparhawk, whose family owned the landmark house at 293 Boston Post Road. This house had been built in 1795 for the Rev. Dr. Samuel Kendal and enlarged over the course of the 19th century.[40] He and Mary Elizabeth had three children, Edmund H. II, Francis B. Jr., and Katherine (Mrs. William Endicott Jr.). The family lived in Boston and used the Kendal/Sparhawk house and surrounding 20 acres as a summer place convenient to the home of Francis's widowed mother and younger brother, Horace. In 1906 the house burned to the ground. The site stood vacant until 10 years later, when Mary Elizabeth, then a widow, hired architect Samuel Mead to design the present Neoclassical mansion with its imposing two-story portico.

Francis "Frank" B. Sears Jr. (1882–1943) graduated from Harvard in 1905 and began his career

Figure 13-22. The wedding of Francis B. Sears Jr. and Marian Buckingham was held in the Unitarian church in Wayland. The bridesmaids wore "dainty gowns of embroidered mull over white silk [and] white leghorn hats with long white plumes." The maid of honor was Miss Katherine Sears and ushers were Robert Winsor Jr., Mr. Barrett, and Charles Richardson. (1906 photo)

Figures 13-23 and 13-24. The family of Francis B. and Mary Elizabeth Sparhawk Sears spent summers in this imposing house on Central Avenue (left), until it was destroyed by fire in 1906. It was replaced by the present Neoclassical mansion (now 293 Boston Post Road), which Samuel Mead designed for the widowed Mrs. Sears in 1916.

working for his uncle Horace. After almost 20 years in the dry-goods business, he retired from the field and was elected president of Waltham National Bank.[41] Frank and his brother Edmund married two sisters: Leslie Buckingham, who married Edmund in 1904, and Marian, who married Frank in 1906. The girls had excellent social credentials. Since childhood they had summered in an antique house in Wayland with their unmarried aunt and their bachelor uncle, Alfred Wayland Cutting, an antiquarian and photographer of the disappearing New England landscape. Frank and Marian had three children, Francis B. III, Rosamund, and Edwin Buckingham. In 1921 the family purchased the 66-acre Crescent Street property from Horace Sears and began operating it as a gentleman's farm.[42]

Frank Sears, always the thrifty Yankee, dismantled the abandoned chair factory and used the lumber to build the shingled cottage at 29 Crescent Street for his chauffeur, Isaac Comeau. Comeau kept the family automobiles in a nearby heated garage and also cared for the great carriages stored in the homestead barn. On the property was a tenement that had once housed workers at the chair factory.[43] This building was virtually abandoned until 1933, when it became the home of the Melone family.

The Melone Family

Guiseppe "Joseph" Melone (1892–1979) came to the United States from Penne, Italy, in 1921, settling in Waltham. His brother Antonio worked at Mass. Broken Stone. Joseph found work as a landscape gardener with a regular Weston clientele including the Fiskes, Robert Winsor, and Dr. Fresenius Van Nuys. He was part of the workforce that completed the new town green. In 1924 he returned to Italy to bring back his wife, Maria Anna, and young son, Vincent. When they arrived at the port in Naples, he found that their visas had expired, and he had to return to the United States without them. Five years passed before the family was finally reunited in 1929. Joseph and Maria Anna rented a third-floor flat in Waltham, and Joseph rode his bicycle each day to Weston. As the country sank into the Depression, the Melones struggled to provide for their growing family.

While working for Dr. Van Nuys, Joseph Melone discovered the former chair factory tenement, vacant and in disrepair. One room was filled with rotten apples placed there for storage and abandoned; other rooms were overgrown with weeds and infested with snakes. At the urging of Van Nuys, Francis and Marian Sears agreed to allow the Melones to live in the house if they repaired it themselves and assisted with work on the estate. For a number of years, the house had no electricity, central heat, running water, or indoor plumbing. But there was plenty of food from their extensive vegetable gardens, and a nearby barn full of cows, pigs, goats, and chickens. Joseph kept a team of horses for plowing and haying and a pony to pull the hayrake and a little red pung for the children.[44]

Figure 13-25. The Melone family is pictured here in a 1956 Town Crier *article. The eight children earned record honors at Weston High School for excellence in scholarship, athletics, and citizenship. Back row: Vincent, John, Daniel, Anthony, and William. Front row: Cecelia, Maria Anna (Mrs. Joseph), Joseph, and Anna.*

Their daughter Anna recalls a "two-class system in Weston . . . not just old Yankee and immigrant as might be expected, but also the wealthy and the workers. Each had respect for the other in their respective places."[45] The eight Melone children excelled at Weston High School. Vincent, William, Anthony, Josephine, John, Daniel, Anna, and Cecelia graduated with outstanding records in scholarship, sports, and citizenship and worked diligently as alumni to support the Weston Boosters and high school athletic programs.[46]

Joseph Melone Landscaping began in 1935 with a single Ford truck. J. Melone and Sons, formed in 1946, has become a large corporation dealing in sand, gravel, cement, road construction, and property development. The former chair factory tenement, occupied by the Melone family from 1933 until 1990, is now owned by the town and officially designated The Melone Homestead.

Edwin "Buck" Sears

Francis and Marian Sears both died in 1943. Because Francis III had committed suicide at age 20, the estate became the property of the two younger children. Rosamund had enjoyed a brief career as a

Figure 13-26. Edwin B. Sears (1911–1987) was the youngest child of Francis B. Jr. and Marian Sears. Buck, as he was called, was an amateur artist and musician also deeply interested in historic preservation. In 1975 he gave the Town of Weston his half-interest in 61 acres now known as the Sears conservation land. This 1983 pastel is by Ralph Ayer.

sculptor, and Edwin, known as Buck or Bucky, was a competent "gentleman" painter and musician who loved New England history, architecture, and antiquarianism.[47] Both suffered from mental difficulties. Buck has been described as a timid, reclusive, and cautious man, set in his ways. Neither he nor Rosamund ever married, and both required the services of a legal guardian in their later years because of failing competency.

Buck maintained residences in Weston, Boston's Back Bay, and Camden, Maine.[48] He visited Weston only sporadically but refused to sell the estate or change anything. The property was left virtually abandoned from the 1960s until the early 1990s. Buck cared deeply for the land and didn't want it developed. Perhaps he had seen a 1933 plan, now preserved in the files at the Society for the Preservation of New England Antiquities (SPNEA), for a 28-lot subdivision called Millbrook on the land behind Crescent Street. Instead, in 1975, Buck Sears conveyed to the town his one-half interest in 61.47 acres, for a price of $1. His sister's half-interest in what is now the Sears conservation area was purchased as part of the Uyterhoeven-Germeshausen land acquisition plan.

Edwin "Buck" Sears died in 1987, leaving the main house, barn, and chauffeur's house to the Society for the Preservation of New England Antiquities and Trustees of Reservations.[49] SPNEA archivists sorted through hundreds of letters, books, photographs, and memorabilia found scattered everywhere in trunks, drawers, and boxes, both in Weston and in Camden. Odds and ends included Edwin's daily undated chronicles penciled on small notepads assembled with string or rubber bands or placed randomly in envelopes. Many papers were covered with mold because the Weston house had not been heated for years. On one of these papers, Buck Sears wrote that he would be remembered for having saved everything.[50]

Residential Development, Boston Post Road

Houses along the east end of Boston Post Road between Stony Brook and No. 293 exemplify the change from farming community to residential suburb. Farmhouses include the Derby house (228 Boston Post Road, Federal-style), Horatio Fiske house (11 Rolling Lane, Greek Revival), and Jacob Hagar house (158 Boston Post Road, Colonial Revival).

In the early 19th century, a small farmhouse was expanded into the three-story Federal-style house now owned by the Gifford School. The owner at that time, Jeptha Stearns, reportedly planned to use the building as a tavern. He added two large front rooms and a wide hall on the ground floor, along with a second-floor hall for dancing. The expense was so great that Stearns had to sell the building before ever opening his tavern.

Figure 13-27. In 1926, when this photograph of Stony Brook Station was taken, there was a grade crossing on the Boston Post Road and the station was on the east side of the tracks. In the distance is a small freight house. The original color of the 1880 station was probably cream with dark red trim. The Stony Brook Post Office was located here from November 1897 to July 1934. In 1930, when a bridge was built over the tracks, the station was relocated to the west side and the freight house was removed. The station was demolished in 1951 when Route 128 was built.

Over the years, the house passed to several distinguished owners including the Hon. James Lloyd, onetime senator from Massachusetts, and John Mark Gourgas (1766–1846), descendant of a family of French Huguenot nobles. Gourgas bought the approximately 70-acre property in 1821 and maintained it as a gentleman's farm. His younger brother, John James Joseph Gourgas (1777–1865), spent summers in Weston in his declining years. J.J.J. Gourgas was a founder of the Ancient Accepted Scottish Rite of Freemasonry and served as first Grand Secretary General.[51] His daughter married her cousin, John Louis (or Jean Lewis) III, the youngest of the seven children of John Mark Gourgas. They built the house across the street at 178 Boston Post Road in 1842.

When John Mark died, the house at No. 177 was sold to a Boston coin broker, John G. Ellis, whose family owned it for more than 60 years. Another Boston merchant, William T. Farley, a dealer in dry goods, restored the house in 1913 and added Colonial Revival embellishments including the two-story porch columns and a balustrade that has since been removed. In 1971 the 26-acre property was purchased by the Gifford School, which had been established in 1964 in Cambridge. The school provides integrated educational and clinical services for nearly 100 special-needs students whose lives are complicated by emotional, behavioral, or academic problems. The students range in age from 8 to 20 and come from more than 50 cities and towns in eastern Massachusetts and New Hampshire.

Beginning after the Civil War, the Boston Post Road—then called Central Avenue—became a location for fashionable new houses. The Stick-style house at 215 Boston Post Road was built in 1867 by Edward "Ned" Fiske, scion of one of Weston's oldest families.

Figure 13-28. In the early 19th century, a small farmhouse was expanded into the three-story Federal house now owned by the Gifford School. When this picture was taken in 1898, it belonged to Boston coin broker John G. Ellis, whose family owned it for more than 60 years. Another Boston merchant, William T. Farley, bought the house in 1913 and added the present two-story porch columns.

Figure 13-29. This picture was taken about 1938 from the ledge at Massachusetts Broken Stone looking east along Boston Post Road. The bridge over the Boston and Maine Railroad tracks was completed in 1930. Behind the small white house is Stony Brook Station, which had been moved to the west side of the tracks. The sign for the Amoco gas station is visible at the lower right. Behind the station and railroad tracks is the future location of Route 128.

Edward graduated from Harvard in 1853, practiced law in his father's Boston office for a few years, then retired due to poor health. According to Brenton Dickson III's account in *Random Recollections,* he "created quite a stir" by marrying one of the servants in his mother's household, Adelaide Frost. She came from Maine and the couple lived in Maine until Augustus Fiske's death in 1865, when they moved back to Weston. Fiske purchased five acres from David Perry in 1866 and built the house at 215 Boston Post Road. The tax valuation—$9,000—was for several years the highest of any house in Weston. Fiske died of consumption in 1870 at age 37, only a short time after the house was completed. In 1887, his widow bought seven more acres and built an impressive carriage house, later converted to the residence at No. 205.

In 1910–11, George Frank Blake and his wife, Alice, built Olde Fieldstone at 270 Boston Post Road (now 18 Skating Pond Road). Blake, who was not related to estate owner Francis Blake, was president of A.M. McPhail Piano Company, a Boston piano manufacturer. He was also a great friend of Robert Winsor and lived for a time in the Bryden farmhouse on the Winsor estate before purchasing this property in 1903. The house was not built until 1910. It was designed by Hubert G. Ripley, who had worked with the nationally known firm of Peabody and Stearns before joining in partnership with Weston resident A.J. Russell and then practicing alone at the time Olde Fieldstone was built. In September 1911, four photographs of the stone house appeared in *American Architect,* indicating its interest to the architectural profession.[52]

The last of the grand houses along this stretch of the Post Road was Cedarhurst at the corner of Boston Post Road and Rolling Lane. The well-appointed brick Georgian Revival was built in 1921–22 for George W. Bentley, president of a wholesale grocery company. Some years earlier, the architect, Clifford Allbright, had married Bentley's daughter Caroline. Allbright continued to live with the family even after Caroline died in childbirth in 1918. He also designed houses for Bentley's other two daughters, Grace, at 41 Summer Street, and Ruth, at 222 Boston Post Road. The Bentley house, matching garage, and 22 acres remained in the fam-

Squabs

and

Homer Pigeons

for sale by

E. A. Brotchie

Stony Brook

Figures 13-30 and 13-31. At the turn of the century, Andrew K. Brotchie operated a grocery store at 137 Boston Post Road. His son Everett sold the "homer pigeons." (c. 1995 photo)

ily until 1945. The land was subdivided in the late 1940s to create the Rolling Lane neighborhood.

Buildings: Stony Brook to Crescent Street

Boston Post Road at Route 128. Site of the Stony Brook Railroad Station, built about 1880 at the Stony Brook stop on the Fitchburg Railroad, probably replacing an earlier structure. For many years, the station housed the Stony Brook Post Office. It was originally located south of Boston Post Road on the east side of the tracks, but was rotated 180 degrees and moved to the west side of the tracks when the grade crossing bridge was built on Boston Post Road in the early 1930s. In the 1940s, the station was still being heated by coal-burning stove for the comfort of passengers.[53] It was used as a contractor's office when the Weston section of Route 128 was under construction, and then demolished after the roadway opened in late 1951.

104 Boston Post Road (1854). Built for prosperous mill owner Nathaniel Sibley. Up-to-date Italianate details such as the decorative porch posts and paired brackets were used to modernize the basic Greek Revival-style main block.

137 Boston Post Road (c. 1853). Probably built for George W. Rand but generally known as the Andrew K. Brotchie house. Brotchie, who was born in Scotland, bought the house in 1897 and operated a grocery here. Either he or an earlier owner added decorative Queen Anne details to the simple mid-century structure. Brotchie's unmarried daughter, Ella, lived here until 1945, when the property was sold to Massachusetts Broken Stone.

158 Boston Post Road (c. 1904). Colonial Revival house built by farmer Jacob F. Hagar.

161 Boston Post Road (1897). Queen Anne/Colonial Revival house built for Amos S. Crane, "export traffic manager" for the Boston and Maine Railroad; later occupied by Massachusetts Broken Stone president Richard Robinson.

177 Boston Post Road (c. 1807). Three-story Federal house with a history of distinguished owners (see text). Now Gifford School.

Figure 13-32. Beginning after the Civil War, Boston Post Road became a favored location for fine homes built by Weston's new elite. One of the first was built in 1867 for Edward "Ned" Fiske at 215 Boston Post Road. For a few years, it had the highest valuation of any home in Weston. The carriage house at right is now a residence at No. 205.

Figure 13-33. George Frank Blake (1856–1938) was president of the Boston piano manufacturing firm of A.M. McPhail.

Figure 13-34. The comfortable living room of Olde Fieldstone had a stone fireplace, which later owners replaced with a brick version.

178 Boston Post Road (1842). Built for John Louis Gourgas III, gentleman farmer, who bought the land from his father, John Mark Gourgas, who lived across the street at No. 177. John Louis owned it until his death in 1883. For much of the early 20th century, it was owned by the Spaulding family.

193-195 Boston Post Road. The Hobbs family lived in a house on this site for generations, until the homestead was sold in the early 1920s to settle the estate. The present house, although traditionally

Figure 13-36. Nineteen-twenties silhouette of Alice Weston Blake (1866–1934).

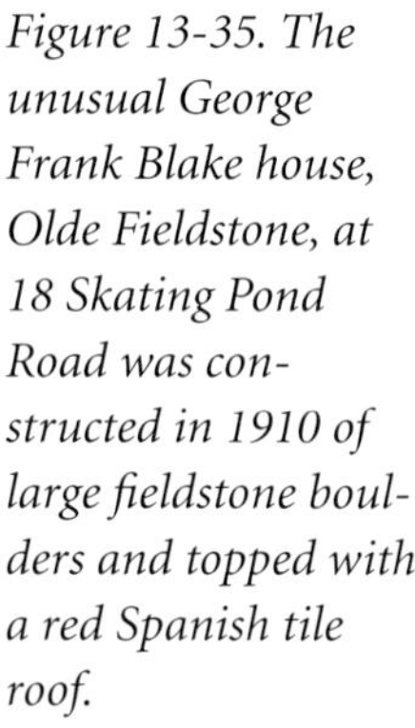

Figure 13-35. The unusual George Frank Blake house, Olde Fieldstone, at 18 Skating Pond Road was constructed in 1910 of large fieldstone boulders and topped with a red Spanish tile roof.

known as the Amos Hobbs house, is largely Colonial Revival in style and dates primarily from the early 20th century. A 1920 item in the Waltham *Daily Free Press Tribune* notes, "The old Hobbs house on Central Avenue has undergone many changes. . . . The house has been modernized in many respects . . ."[54]

205 Boston Post Road (1887). Carriage house for No. 215, built by Adelaide Fiske, converted to a residence in 1984.

214 Boston Post Road (1897). Queen Anne/Colonial Revival house built by Susan H. and Edward Fiske Jr., probably for rental. The two siblings lived with their widowed mother across the street.

215 Boston Post Road (1867). Well-detailed Stick-style house built for Edward "Ned" Fiske (see text).

222 Boston Post Road (1925–26). Tudor house designed by architect Clifford Allbright for his sister-in-law, Ruth (Bentley) Havlin, and her husband, Arthur, an executive at Boston Edison.

225 Boston Post Road (1883; stable 1887–88). Queen Anne house designed by Ernest N. Boyden, architect of the James Case house, for George S. and Charlotte "Lottie" Perry. The Perrys had no children and the house was inherited by George's unmarried sister, Hattie, who lived there until her death in 1946. A later owner, Anthony Melone, subdivided the land in the early 1970s to create Hillcrest Road.

228 Boston Post Road (c. 1798). Built for farmer John Derby Sr., who owned about 52 acres. Several generations later, Annie Derby married Henry J. Jennison (1842–1916), a principal in the real-estate partnership of Train & Jennison. Jennison represented Weston in the House of Representatives and served as selectman from 1890 to 1900. The house stayed in the Derby/Jennison family until 1923.

247 Boston Post Road (c. 1899). Built by George S. Perry for his farmworkers. In the 1930s and 1940s, it was the home of Faith L. Meserve, the town's first female physician.

248 Boston Post Road. See chapter 20.

251 Boston Post Road (c. 1846). Built by machinist Luther Harrington Jr., who purchased three-quarters of an acre from Alpheus Cutter in late 1845 for $75 and sold it a decade later for $2,100, including the house and an additional quarter acre.[55] The Greek Revival house originally had a porch across the front. In 1858, the house came into the ownership of Horatio A. Hagar. Ten years later it was conveyed to his wife, Lois, "to her sole and separate use, free from the interference of her said husband and not liable for his debts."[56] It remained in the Hagar family until 1940.

255 Boston Post Road (1909–10). Two-family house built for J.J. Cassidy, who is listed in the 1911 directory as a laborer.[57]

277 Boston Post Road. Built as the coachman's house for No. 293. This house was subdivided from the rest of the property in 1938.

280 Boston Post Road. See chapter 20.

293 Boston Post Road (1916). Prominent Neoclassical house designed by architect Samuel Mead for Mary Elizabeth Sparhawk Sears, widow of Francis B. Sears Sr. The property includes a notable barn and a mill site in the rear.

10 Crescent Street (1922). Colonial Revival house designed by architect Harold Graves for Henry W. Perry, son of David Perry (the elder). Henry, who was in the boot and shoe business, lived here only a few weeks before dying of a heart attack in July 1922.[58] After his death, the house was occupied by his wife, Mary, and two children, Marion and David A. After David was married, he brought up his family at 10 Crescent Street until his aunt Hattie died, when they moved to 225 Boston Post Road. David was a member of the school committee and later a founder of Weston Boosters. The David A. Perry Memorial Scholarship is named for him.[59]

21 Crescent Street (1812). Handsome Federal-style, brick-end house built by farmer Luther Harrington Sr. The date "1812" is carved into the attic posts. In later years, the farm was owned by two generations of the David Perry and Francis B. Sears Jr. families. The property includes a large and distinctive shingled barn.

27 Crescent Street. The early history of 27 Crescent Street is not known. The house has evolved over time and has been the subject of much speculation. The front section is earlier in date and has corner posts and wide floorboards. Examination of the framing indicates that the front two-over-two section once stood alone (without the rear rooms and wings) and that there was once a door in the center of the north facade. Additions to the structure appear to date from the mid- to late-19th century. At that time, the structure appears to have been adapted for multifamily use. Entrances were built at the two gable ends and the early section was divided with a double wall. Framing members visible from the basement suggest the building may have been moved to its present site at that time. The present chimneys are small and the remodeled house was heated by stoves.

A letter written by William Stimpson to the Weston selectmen on July 31, 1863, gives the history of a dispute between Stimpson and William G. and Samuel Shattuck, previous owners of his property at

21 Crescent Street. In the letter Stimpson complains, "In the year 1859, W.G.S. hired a Dwelling House in Brook's pasture . . . at the end of W.G.S. land and put into it two or three families who constantly used my Farm-Road." It has been speculated that the renters worked at the nearby chair factory managed by Samuel Shattuck. No. 27 Crescent Street was occupied from 1933 to 1990 by the family of Joseph and Maria Anna Melone and has been officially designated by the town as The Melone Homestead. It is presently owned by the town and leased to Land's Sake.

29 Crescent Street (1924). Colonial Revival saltbox built by Francis B. Sears Jr. for Isaac and Theresa Comeau. Comeau was from Nova Scotia and worked for Sears as a chauffeur.

39 Crescent Street (c. 1839). Well-detailed Greek Revival house built by successful mill owner Samuel H.F. Bingham, who purchased the house lot in 1839. Later owners included machinist Henry Bowen and/or his wife, Mary, from 1869 to 1895; Charles A. Freeman, 1895 to 1944; and Howard Gambrill Jr. and/or his wife, Mary, 1946 to 1998.

49 Crescent Street (c. 1804, 1850). The age and evolution of this house are uncertain but it is thought to have been built for Abraham Sanderson Jr., who bought the property in 1804. Sanderson managed an existing gristmill on the property. Other stylistic features date from the mid-19th century.

Gatehouse Lane (1887). Red-brick gatehouse for Stony Brook Reservoir, built by Marshall N. Stearns, owned by the City of Cambridge.

8 Rolling Lane, formerly 190 Boston Post Road (1921–22). Built for wholesale grocer George W. Bentley from designs by Clifford Allbright.

11 Rolling Lane, formerly 208 Boston Post Road (c. 1839). Greek Revival house built by Horatio N. Fiske, a cordwainer, or shoemaker, who also farmed the 18 acres. The rear ell is earlier in date. The property was later owned by the Downing family and, beginning in 1928, by Weston Real Estate Trust, which subdivided off the house.

18 Skating Pond Road, formerly 270 Boston Post Road (1910–11). Olde Fieldstone. Built for piano manufacturer George Frank and his wife, Alice, from designs by architect Hubert G. Ripley.

12–68 Summer Street. The land on the east side of Summer Street off the Boston Post Road was owned by Dennis and Bridget Keefe, Irish immigrants who purchased 26 acres in 1851 and built the Italianate house at **22 Summer Street**, which appears on town tax records in 1861. The couple had 11 children, seven of whom survived. Frank and Cornelius (1854–1902) became grain dealers and used the large barn that still stands behind 26 Summer Street to store grain from a gristmill at Stony Brook. Cornelius ran a grain store in the town center for 15 years. When he died at age 47, his obituary cited his "enviable reputation for honesty and fair dealing."[60] The business was sold to J. Cushing of Fitchburg, large shippers of grain, hay, and feed.

Members of the Keefe family built the twin Queen Anne houses at **12 and 16 Summer Street** (c. 1895) as well as the house behind No. 12 (**14 Summer Street**, 1902). A daughter, Joanna, married William F. Sherburne (1843–1931), a local farmer who shook up his family by becoming Catholic. About 1912, the Sherburnes built the brown-shingled house at **42 Summer Street** where William raised vegetables and kept a few cows and chickens. His son Frank, who worked as a clerk for the Boston and Maine Railroad in Boston, built the house next door at **30 Summer Street** (c. 1923). When Frank's son, Bill, was a boy in the Depression days, his biggest thrill was to run down after school to the Boston and Maine Railroad tracks and watch the "steamers" go by. In 1958, Bill Sherburne became the fourth generation to build a house here, at **50 Summer Street**, on a field previously used to raise nursery trees. The property at **26 Summer Street** was also part of the Keefe homestead at one time. In 1926 dentist Ernest Wells rebuilt an existing Keefe barn into the present Colonial Revival house.

The west side of the street was the Hobbs cow pasture. Development began about 1910, when the Hobbs heirs sold a quarter-acre lot at **51 Summer Street** to Clarence "Fleetwood" Mosher, who, like his father, was a gardener at the Case Estates. That year, Mosher built a simple brown-shingled house remembered for its beautiful garden. His brother, Harold, lived down the street at **68 Summer Street** (c. 1925) and worked as the groundskeeper at the Riverside Golf Links. Herman E. Hobbs sold 1.25 acres to Charles W. Robbins for **33 Summer Street** (1912), a high-style Colonial Revival house more typical of Robbins's previous house in Brookline than of this country street populated by homes of farmers and tradesmen. In the 1920s, other Hobbs land was purchased and resold by the Weston Real Estate Trust, which placed restrictions that no buildings could be erected without the written consent of the trust.[61] In this way, Robert Winsor and his three children, who served as trustees, maintained some control over the type of houses built on the perimeter of their Meadowbrook Road holdings.

120 Summer Street. The following summary is based on three sources: 1) a 1963 house history written using information from Margaret Dorothy Martin Sewall, who was born in the house in 1875 and is a descendant of James McCann; 2) a 1963–64 report

Genealogies

Sears Family
(*Note*: Fourth generation not listed except for children of Francis Jr. and Marian Sears.)

Rev. Edmund Hamilton Sears (1810–1876), m. 1839 to Ellen Bacon (1811–1897)
  Katherine (died young)
  Francis Bacon (1849–1914), m. 1875 to Mary Elizabeth Sparhawk (1846–1923)
    Edmund Hamilton II (1878–1946), m. 1904 to Leslie Buckingham
    Francis Bacon Jr. (1882–1943), m. 1906 to Marian Buckingham (1879–1943)
      Francis B. III (1907–1928), unmarried
      Rosamond (1910–1980s?), unmarried
      Edwin Buckingham (1911–1987), unmarried
    Katherine, m. William Endicott Jr.
  Edmund Hamilton Jr.
    married, children, lived in St. Louis
  Horace Scudder (1855–1923), unmarried

Perry Family (three generations)

David Perry (1814–1872), m. Sophia Kenniston
  Frank (1849–1915), m. Sarah Loring
    (probably no children)
  George Springer (1855–1904), m. Charlotte Johnson,
    no children
  Henry William (1857–1922), m. Mary Drew
    Louise (1891–1968), m. Everett Brotchie
    Marion (1894–1984), m. Frederick Kenney
    Eleanor (1896–1959), m. George Winslow Henderson
    David A. (1902–1954), m. Alice Johnson
  Hattie (1852–1946), unmarried

Kenney Family (3 generations)

Oliver N. Kenney (originally Canney) (1834–1895)
 m. 1859 to Emily Cutting, daughter of John Warren Cutting of Lexington Street
  Ralph (1864–1942)
    Walter S.
    Karl E.
    Grace
  Charles Cutting (1860–1945), m. 1885 to Clara Frances Stimpson (1861–1923)
    William Oliver (1888–1970), unmarried
    Elizabeth Cutting (1889–1983), unmarried
    Frederick Stimpson (1892–1988), m. Marion Perry
    Winthrop Warren (1894–1964), m. Harriet Morris
    Horace Sears (1895–1996), m. Elsie Clark
  George W. (1866–1900), m. Ethelyn,
    no children
  Emily (1872–1961), m. Joseph Leavy,
    no children
  Oliver (Weston firefighter, died at a young age)

by Philip W. Baker based on structural examination; and 3) information provided to the author by Katherine and Thomas Peebles, who restored the house in the early 1970s.

According to Mrs. Sewall's history, Edward Garfield purchased 28 acres on Summer Street in 1687. He continued to live in Watertown but built a small house to be used when he farmed the land in Weston. This house was more like a simple shelter, according to Philip W. Baker, whose firm specialized in Early American buildings. His report described the original section of No. 120 as a one-story, one-room structure "of a very primitive nature" that may not have had any windows. Baker dates this part of the present house to about 1690—a date probably based in part on the Sewall history. He notes that the molding on the wide pine board sheathing indicates a date range between 1680 and 1720. These boards, some up to 18 inches in width, are installed horizontally on two of the walls. According to Baker, the second (north) room was added about 1790 and the attic was probably finished between the mid- and late 19th century. About 1810, a straight run of stairs was added to reach the attic, which was previously accessible only by ladder.

On the 1794 Kingsbury map, the house is shown as belonging to the Widow Garfield, a descendant of Edward. About 1840, the property was purchased by James McCann, an Irish immigrant who had previously lived in Waltham. For several years, Cooper Garfield, an elderly descendant of the original owner, lived with the McCanns and provided them with the background information on the house. One of McCann's seven children, Sarah, married John M. Martin in 1871 (see 168 Summer Street). Martin farmed the land at No. 120. A large barn was torn down about 1916.

120 Summer Street is notable for its "First Period" architectural elements, which were carefully preserved by the Peebles family and left visible so they can be examined. As Baker summarized, ". . . [this is] a very unique, primitive and original building. . . . The various stages . . . tell an interesting and comprehensive story, which would be lost if tampered with."

168 Summer Street. (Photo in chapter 4.) This 18th-century house is the only remaining Weston example with a one-over-one room plan that was never enlarged to two-over-two. Beginning about 1870, it was occupied by John Martin, an Irish immigrant who worked as a tenant farmer for the Loring estate. Martin married the daughter of James McCann (see 120 Summer Street) and the couple had eight children. Their son Charles, a foreman on the Winsor estate, bought No. 168 from the Loring estate in 1925. The house was not wired for electricity until the 1930s, and the first indoor bathroom was installed in 1938. Note that when Summer Street was straightened, the house was no longer right on the road.

Notes

1. Lamson, *HTW,* 161.
2. Ibid., 21. According to Richard Robinson at the Mass. Broken Stone Company, the den was 30–40 feet above road level and was removed as part of the quarry operations on the front pit.
3. Ibid., 160.
4. Ibid., 160–161.
5. 104 Boston Post Road.
6. MCRD 629/455, N. Sibley to George W. Rand, 1852 (137 Boston Post Road).
7. Three early buildings associated with the Sibley mills survived until the mid-20th century. A large, gambrel-roofed house said to have been built by Abraham Bigelow was later used as a boardinghouse for mill employees. This house was destroyed by fire. A second house collapsed from age and decay, and a third house near the present gas station was torn down when Route 20 was redesigned in 1961.
8. "Suicide?" undated newspaper probably *WFP,* Coburn scrapbook #1, 229.
9. Francis B. Sears to Samuel C. Bennett, June 10, 1913 (Weston Town Hall vault). This information came from Alpheus's daughter, Miss Mollie Cutter. In his *History of the Town of Weston,* Lamson wrote: ". . . it is claimed that here he [Alpheus Cutter] made the first cotton batting in this country, and then cotton cloth, later moving to Waltham and starting the industry there." (Picture caption opposite page 15.)
10. MCRD 369/210, J.H. Gowing, J. Hill to Bingham, land with water privilege, $1,450, January 1838. On January 1, 1839, Bingham also bought the adjacent one-acre house lot from Charles Bigelow (379/513). See also Lamson's *HTW,* 158 (footnote).
11. Lamson's *HTW,* 157. According to Weston resident Elmer Jones, the drill was used to take a core sample from a tub of butter or cheese to check for quality.
12. Information on the screen factory from an undated letter from Bill Kenney, who at that time was living in Sarasota, Florida (WHC files).
13. Samuel Shattuck purchased 100 acres in 1853 from Nathan Barker and Dr. Otis Hunt (653/259), who had bought it the year before from the administrator of the estate of the late Isaac Harrington (639/519). In 1854, Samuel Shattuck sold certain rights to the land to his brother William, a "chair dealer," for $1,000 (707/370). In this deed, Samuel conveys the dam across the brook, a 3.5-acre piece of land with a pond, and the right to use the farm road. In June 1855, Samuel Shattuck sold the rest of the farm to William C. Stimpson. William Shattuck retained his right to dam the brook and to use the road to reach his 3.5-acre parcel, which is where the chair factory was located. The arrangement caused considerable conflict between Stimpson and the Shattuck brothers, as indicated by a petition from Stimpson to the Weston selectmen, dated July 31, 1863, and found in the town vault. The petition details numerous grievances. The document states, "In the year 1859, WGS [Wm. Shattuck] hired a Dwelling house in Brooks pasture about 12 rods from the Bar-way at end of WGS land and put into it two or three families who constantly used my Farm Road, notwithstanding my protest." This dwelling house is thought to be the house now No. 27 Crescent Street. Shattuck later bought this house at auction. According to Stimpson, "The travel through my Road to this place was very annoying, heavy teams of manure, lumber &c, cutting up the Road which I had to repair." The selectmen solved the controversy by turning the farm road into a private way, which

Shattuck and others could use to reach Shattuck's land, and awarding Stimpson damages of $500 (July 18, 1863).

See also Lamson, *HTW,* 161. Also report of R.G. Dun & Co. (1875–79), vol. 74, 147, Harvard Business School, Baker Library. Their credit report says that Amasa G. Whitcomb worked for William G. Shattuck for 25 years before succeeding him in business.

14. Perry kept the same offices at 73 Fulton Street. He also had factories in East Boston and Roxbury. See Bill Kenney's letter, already cited, and *In Memoriam, George Springer Perry,* a booklet made at the time of Perry's death and including a biographical sketch (collection, Eloise Kenney).

15. This account is largely taken from an undated letter from Oliver Kenney's grandson Bill Kenney, written from Sarasota, Florida. Kenney differs slightly from Lamson, who says that Oliver Kenney succeeded Shattuck in 1875. Eloise Kenney, great-granddaughter of Oliver, has a collection of company catalogs and business papers including the partnership agreement of December 14, 1901. As an interesting sidelight, the Perry and Kenney families were united when Frederick Kenney, son of Charles and grandson of Oliver, married Marion Perry, daughter of Henry W. and niece of George Perry.

16. *WDFPT,* February 7, 1902.

17. "$6000 Fire at Weston," *WDFPT,* May 22, 1905. Says mill was "old wooden structure" two stories high, 30 feet by 50 feet, valued at $2,000, with stock valued at $4,000.

18. *WDFPT,* June 9 and 30, July 28, and November 3, 1905.

19. Letter from Bill Kenney, op. cit.

20. Kenney Bros. & Wolkins continued into the 1950s or '60s under successive generations of the Kenney family. During the Depression, the company was run out of Charles Kenney's home at 315 Boston Post Road while the factory remained in Baldwinsville.

21. MCRD 4197/347. See also "Plan of land in Weston belonging to George S. Perry," July 1900. John S. Rice, surveyor (copy at SPNEA).

22. Chapter 256 of the Acts of 1884.

23. MCRD 1712/325, July 10, 1885. See lengthy legal report on Stony Brook Reservoir in 1914 *TR,* 100, "Report of Committee on Cambridge Watershed," includes copy of Chapter 256 of the Acts of 1884 and Chapter 510 of the Acts of 1897 and also the 1899 Rules and Regulations on Stony Brook Reservoir and Tributaries.

24. For extensive construction and water-supply details, as well as an account of the opening of the reservoir in late 1887, see *City of Cambridge Annual Documents, 1887* (Cambridge, Harvard Printing Co., 1888), 233–56. According to the report, the enabling act was obtained on May 21, 1884, ground was broken January 13, 1885, and the work was completed November 3, 1887. Some 70,000 cubic yards of mud were removed. When finished, the depth of water at the dam was 30 feet and the reservoir held 360,000,000 gallons. See also Arthur J. Krim, *Report Five: Northwest Cambridge* (Cambridge Historical Commission, 1977), 25–27, and MCRD "Cambridge Water Works Showing Stony Brook Supply, Land Taken at Roberts Basin," February 27, 1885, Filed Plan 19.

25. The gatehouse is 25 feet by 31 feet and one story in height, but beneath it are five chambers extending to a depth of 38 feet, according to *The Mayors Address* . . . (ibid.).

26. *Boston Journal,* March 15, 1872, reprinted in "The Water Supply System of Metropolitan Boston, 1845–1947," by Martha H. Bowers and Jane Carolan, Louis Berger & Associates Inc., Wellesley, Massachusetts, 1985, II–6.

27. *Boston Daily Advertiser,* March 7, 1872. See also Bowers & Carolan, op. cit.

28. Lamson, op. cit., 161.

29. Dickson, Brenton H. III, "Of Pungs and People," *WHSB,* December 1988, 3–4. Dickson gives no other information on the identity of "Bloody Alonzo."

30. "Suicide?" op. cit.

31. Henry J. Jennison to Francis Blake, May 27, 1899 (Francis Blake Papers, MHS, 65.931).

32. 1899 *TR,* 27–28.

33. *WDFPT,* March 9, 1900. See also February 2, 1900.

34. Dr. Walter E. Hobbs to Francis Blake, February 3, 1900 (Francis Blake Papers, MHS, 67.973).

35. *WDFPT,* February 2, 1900.

36. Robinson, Richard, "Massachusetts Broken Stone Company, Weston, Massachusetts" (unpublished manuscript, c. 1969).

37. 1963 *TR,*199–202.

38. 1988 *TR,* 193–203.

39. WDFPT, August 28, 1914. The obituary also notes that he was a director of the Boston YMCA and one of the prime movers in promoting the erection of its Huntington Avenue building. See also "F.B. Sears Dies Suddenly After Short Illness," undated newspaper clipping, 1914, Coburn scrapbook #2.

40. There have been three houses on the site of 293 Boston Post Road. The first belonged to Benjamin Peirce, who kept a tavern there. After Peirce's death, it was purchased by Rev. Dr. Samuel Kendal, minister of First Parish. This first house burned in 1791 and parishioners helped Kendal rebuild. This second house was being used as a summer house by the Francis B. Sears family when it burned in 1906. The present house was built in 1919.

41. Harvard University archives, 10th and 25th reunion reports, class of 1905. See also *Middlesex County and Its People,* vol. III, 26.

42. MCRD 4447/12,13, July 1921.

43. 27 Crescent Street—see also house listings at end of chapter.

44. Melone (Pollock), Anna, "Recreation on the Melone Homestead, Weston, 1940s," *WHSB,* spring 1998.

45. PWF interview with Anna Melone (Pollock), July 1998.

46. "Melone family honored at Boosters awards night," *Weston Town Crier,* June 5, 1997. Also "8 Melones Set Family Record for Weston High Activities," *The Town Crier,* December 20, 1956.

47. "Earliest Recollections: Furnishings from the Family of Edwin B. Sears," exhibit catalogue, SPNEA, Boston, May 1983–July 1984, 9.

48. Sears left the Camden house to SPNEA in 1982.

49. The heirs also benefited by subdividing off an extra lot (15 Crescent Street) in a way Edwin Sears did not anticipate.

50. Quote from archival description of "Papers of Edwin B. Sears, Weston, Mass. Received 1988," SPNEA.

51. He was also third Sovereign Grand Commander from 1832 to 1851. J.J.J. Gourgas was credited with reviving the rite after the great anti-Masonic agitation and serving as "the backbone of the Scottish Rite in the United States." The Gourgas Medal is the highest award that can be conferred by the Northern Masonic Jurisdiction.

52. "House of Mr. G. F. Blake, Weston," *American Architect,* September 20, 1911, vol. 100, #1865.

53. Bentley Crouch to PWF. In the 1940s, Crouch was hired to tend the fire at Stony Brook Station. He went there every morning to build the fire and every afternoon after school to add more soft coal.

54. *WDFPT,* December 8, 1920.

55. Harrington bought the .75 acre in October 1845 for $75, with no buildings (MCRD 476/102). Three years later, he paid $20 for an additional piece of land, about a quarter acre, from Luke Brooks (544/547, May 1848). The new parcel was described as "near the dwelling house of the said Harrington," indicating that the house had been built in the interim.

56. MCRD 1039/214, May 1868.

57. *WDFPT,* May 14, October 15, 1909, March 4, 1910.

58. PWF interview with Eloise Kenney, granddaughter of Henry Perry.

59. Coburn, Philip, "Don't Forget David Perry," letter to the editor, *Weston Town Crier,* April 26, 1982.

60. Obituary for Cornelius Keefe, Coburn scrapbook #2, 183. Obituary for Bridget Keefe, *WDFPT,* December 30, 1904.

61. For example, see MCRD 4929/117.

Figure 14-1. The Horace S. Sears estate, Haleiwa, stood on Boston Post Road just east of First Parish Church. This picture was probably taken in early 1905, before the landscaping was completed. Sears, the son of the minister at First Parish Church, had only a high school education but made his fortune in textile manufacturing. The mansion was designed by Joseph Everett Chandler, who is best known for his work in the Colonial Revival style. The Italian gardens were the work of noted landscape architect Arthur Shurtleff (later Shurcliff). Alhough the mansion was torn down after World War II, Horace Sears's generosity and civic leadership left a lasting legacy in Weston.

CHAPTER 14

The Horace Sears Estate, Haleiwa

An Italian Villa in Weston

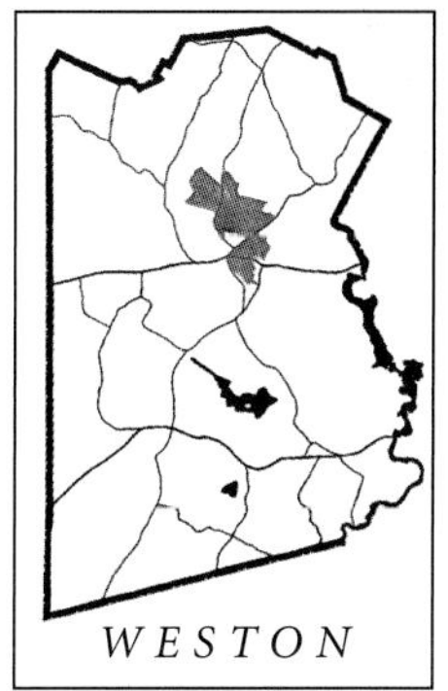

The period between the Civil War and World War I has been described as the Age of Elegance, a time when "the millionaire was the American hero."[1] Those with money to spend on architecture were free to borrow from great artistic traditions of the past to construct their own French palace, English manor house, or Italian villa transplanted to American soil. They could indulge any desire for fantasy and escape from the problems brought about by rapid industrialization, immigration, overcrowded cities, poverty, and disease. As America rushed toward the modern age, those who could afford it looked back to the great civilizations of Europe.

In New England towns like Weston, lavish displays of wealth were less common, tempered, as they were, by the New England Puritan conscience. The Sears estate was an exception. Between 1898 and 1903, Horace Scudder Sears (1855–1923) developed Haleiwa, pronounced Hal-e-e-wa, *a Hawaiian word meaning "beautiful place" or "the perfect home."[2] Located on a hill on the north side of Central Avenue (now Boston Post Road) just east of First Parish Church, the mansion was the most ornate ever built in Weston. What makes the estate particularly unusual is the sophisticated use of the Italian villa theme. With stucco, red roof tiles, fountains, and statuary, Sears brought the magic of Italy to a New England hillside.*

We do not know why Horace Sears, a minister's son of charitable, public-spirited nature, chose to build in a manner so flamboyant. A reporter for the Boston Evening Transcript *tried to explain it this way in a lengthy article about Haleiwa written in 1919:*

> *Long before in Weston I had been intrigued when told that this red-roofed villa was the realization of a boy's dream to build, a dream unforgotten and undimmed when to Horace Scudder Sears arrived the hour wherein dreams could be translated in stone and wood. It is this which makes Haleiwa exceptional—so few boyish dreams are exploited!—among the stately homes of New England.3*

Because of his business success, Sears had the money to make his boyhood dream a reality. Because of his upbringing in an environment of books and learning further cultivated by travel, he had the education and artistic sensitivity to demand something special from his architect.

The Sears mansion survived for only half a century, but many landscape elements remain along the 300 block of Boston Post Road. Lion salients with shields still guard the entrance drive. The textured concrete walls and ornamental iron gates remain, along with fountains, terraces, balustrades, and the elegant "tennis house."

But the Sears legacy is much greater than these architectural fragments. Horace Scudder Sears was Weston's greatest benefactor. His vision for Weston found physical expression in the stone church of 1888, the town common, the new library, the fire station, and Town Hall, all made possible in part because of his leadership and financial generosity. He made substantial gifts to the schools, the library, and First Parish. He supplied a house for Weston's teachers, contributed land for the town's first swimming pool, and organized the Friendly Society. In his will he left trust funds to plant and care for the town's trees, maintain the common, provide prizes and scholarships for high school students, and assist library employees.

The author is particularly indebted to Sears for his role in publishing Col. Daniel Lamson's History of the Town of Weston. *Lamson died in 1912 with his manuscript still incomplete. Sears arranged for the book to be edited, printed, and distributed free to 100 households. It was Weston's first history.*

Early Life

Horace Sears moved to Weston at age 10 when his father, the Rev. Dr. Edmund Hamilton Sears, became minister at First Parish. The Reverend Sears was a distinguished figure best known as the author of the Christmas hymn "It Came Upon a Midnight Clear." A graduate of Union College and Harvard Divinity School, he was ordained in the First Parish Church in Wayland in 1839, the same year that he married Ellen Bacon. The following year he accepted a call to Lancaster, where his daughter, Katherine, was born. The demands of the large church took a toll, and Sears, suffering from mental exhaustion, resigned in 1847. He returned to Wayland, where he recovered from his depression and served as

Figure 14-2. Horace Sears's father, Rev. Dr. Edmund Hamilton Sears (1810–1876), was pastor of First Parish Church after the Civil War. He has been described as a "quiet country minister, with the heart of a mystic." Reverend Sears is best known for his Christmas hymn "It Came Upon a Midnight Clear."

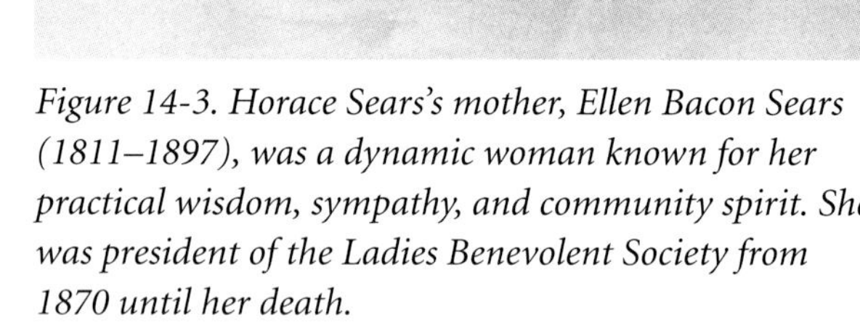

Figure 14-3. Horace Sears's mother, Ellen Bacon Sears (1811–1897), was a dynamic woman known for her practical wisdom, sympathy, and community spirit. She was president of the Ladies Benevolent Society from 1870 until her death.

minister at First Parish for 17 years. Reverend Sears wrote three of his seven books in Wayland.[4] His three sons, Francis Bacon, Edmund Hamilton Jr., and Horace Scudder, were born there, and young Katie died of scarlet fever.

At the close of the Civil War, Edmund Sears resigned his pulpit to devote himself to writing. He began to preach occasionally at First Parish in Weston, and in 1865 accepted the call to the Weston church. Edmund purchased a clapboard Italianate house on 10 acres just east of the church. This property later became the core of his son's estate. Horace Sears eventually moved the family home across the street, where it stands today.[5]

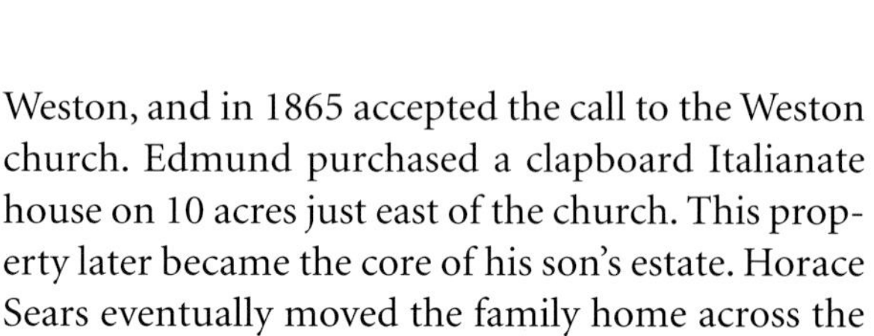

Horace Sears ended his formal education in 1871 at age 16, when he graduated in a class of seven from Weston High School. With the principal and a few enthusiasts, he organized the high school alumni association that year.[6] For the next few years, Sears apparently traveled and worked as a clerk in Boston. He moved back to Weston in 1875 to help care for his father, who had fallen out of a tree and never fully recovered. Reverend Sears died in January 1876, when Horace was just 20. In the late 1870s, Sears worked as assistant treasurer to Gen. James F.B. Marshall at the Hampton Normal and Agricultural Institute in Virginia, a school founded at the close of the Civil War to educate black teachers.[7] Several other Weston residents had a strong connection to the school including Horace's brother Edmund Jr., who taught history and natural sciences at Hampton for a year after his graduation from Harvard College. In the early 1880s, Sears returned to Weston to live with

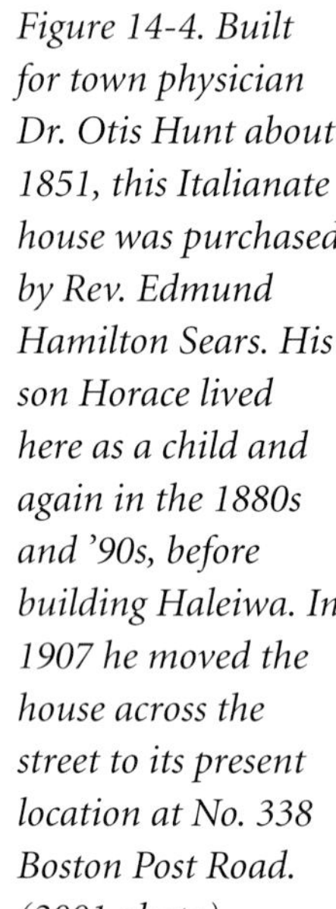

Figure 14-4. Built for town physician Dr. Otis Hunt about 1851, this Italianate house was purchased by Rev. Edmund Hamilton Sears. His son Horace lived here as a child and again in the 1880s and '90s, before building Haleiwa. In 1907 he moved the house across the street to its present location at No. 338 Boston Post Road. (2001 photo)

his widowed mother, and their home became the center of parish social life.

Business Career

In 1880 Sears became bookkeeper at the venerable Boston firm of N. Boynton & Co., which had its origins as a ship chandlery.[8] By the 1880s, N. Boynton was a major selling agent for the heavy cotton canvas or "duck" cloth used to make not only sails but also awnings, tents, wagon covers, flags, bunting, heavy clothing, and shoes. The company developed ties with the West Point Manufacturing Company in Georgia. After six years as an accountant, Sears was taken into the firm and elected treasurer of West Point.

N. Boynton & Co. continued to build and manage mills into the 1890s. The company furnished money to build the Lanett Mill near West Point, Georgia, the Lanett Bleachery and Dye Works, and the Chattahoochee Valley Railroad to carry cotton and goods to and from the mills. It began managing the Brookside Mills, and in 1896 invested in the Warwick Mills in Rhode Island, becoming the selling agent. This mill manufactured fine fabrics, a great departure from the heavy duck cloth that had been the company's mainstay.

In 1900 Eleazar Boynton retired. William H. Wellington, Horace Sears, and Edward Boynton formed a new partnership, Wellington, Sears & Co., with headquarters on Franklin Street in Boston. William Wellington was a brilliant salesman, naturally optimistic. He entered enthusiastically into the building of mills and was always pushing to improve and expand.[9] Sears was quiet and precise and had a complete grasp of financial matters. His skills complemented the vision and daring of Wellington, who would never make a move without consulting his partner. To Wellington's charge that he was a pessimist, Sears would reply, "I'm merely presenting things to you as they are."[10]

Figure 14-5. Horace Scudder Sears (1855–1923) moved to Weston when he was 10 years old and graduated from Weston High School in 1871.

Figure 14-6. Sears (fourth from left) was a founder and first president of the First Parish Friendly Society, which was established in 1885 to help raise money for a new church building.

Civic Contributions: 1880s and 1890s

As his business career advanced, Horace Sears began a long tradition of public service in Weston. A strong supporter of all civic improvements, he devoted particular attention to Weston schools, the Weston Public Library, and First Parish Church. He was elected to a term on the school committee when he was just 24 years old.[11] As the high school outgrew its quarters, he was instrumental in securing a convenient parcel of land for a new high school in the mid-1890s.

Although his own education did not extend past high school, Sears was a cultivated man known for his extensive book collection. In 1887 he was elected trustee of the Weston Public Library, a position his father had held before his death and which Horace held for 34 years. With estate owner Francis Blake and others, Sears was an important advocate for a new library building.

Throughout his life, Horace Sears was devoted to First Parish Church. He was instrumental in raising money and influencing the design of the stone church, one of the architectural treasures of the town. To help with fund-raising, the First Parish Friendly Society was formed in January 1885, with Horace Sears as president. His role in the overwhelming success of the Friendly Society cannot be overestimated. He was a natural showman who gathered around him a coterie of talented friends. To provide a suitable performance space, Sears later built a theater attached to his estate mansion.

In 1895, Sears was one of the founders of the Village Improvement Society, a group devoted to town beautification and improved services. One outgrowth of the society was the formation of the Weston Electric Light Company, with Sears as its longtime treasurer.

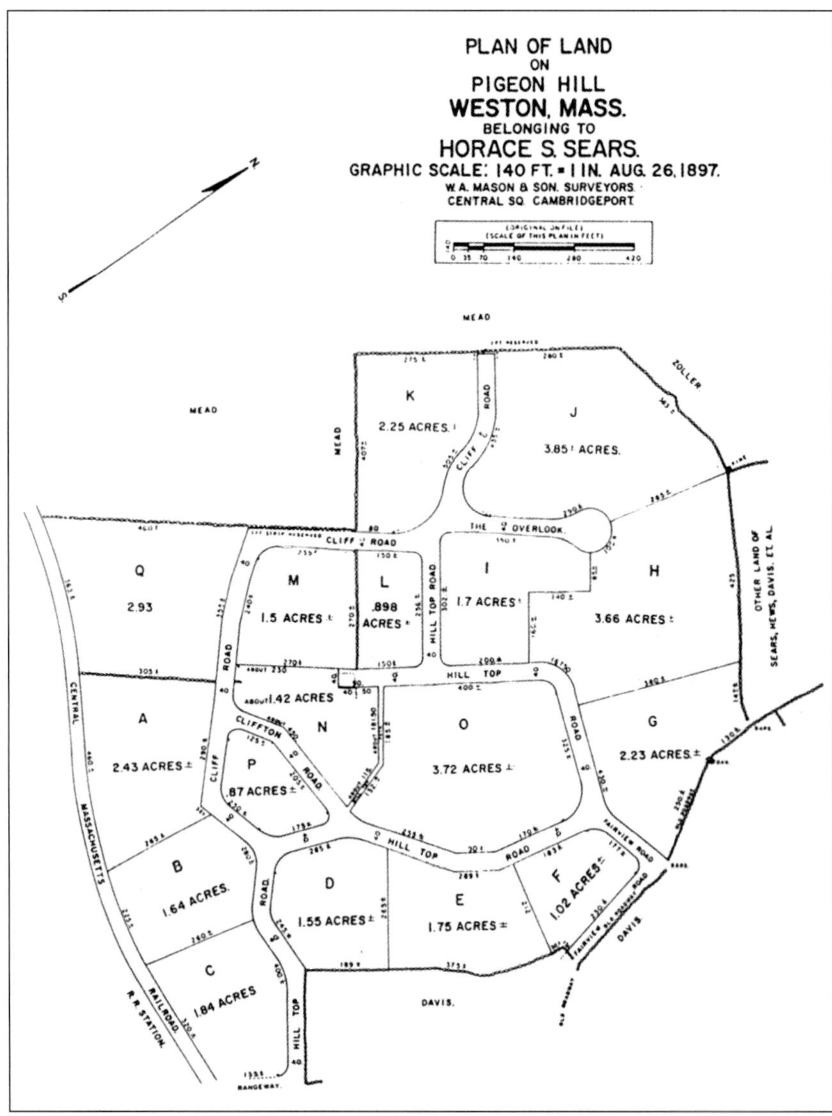

Figure 14-7. Beginning in 1897, Horace Sears developed the Pigeon Hill neighborhood, Weston's first planned subdivision.

Pigeon Hill

The year 1897 was a turning point for Horace Sears. His mother died in April. Sears purchased his brothers' share of her real estate, giving him control of the hillside on which he would shortly build his estate mansion.[12] In July he sold a lot on Church Street to Abbie B. Andrews, who hired architect Joseph Everett Chandler to plan her handsome Colonial house.[13] A few years later, Chandler would design the Sears mansion.

In the fall of 1897, Sears began selling lots on Pigeon Hill, on 46 acres purchased from the Lamson family.[14] The 17 parcels were laid out with a sophisticated plan of winding streets and culs-de-sac new to Weston. One of the attractions was proximity to the Central Massachusetts Railroad, which had a station at the foot of the hill. In 1903 Robert Winsor purchased one of the Sears lots for Weston's first private school, known as the Pigeon Hill School until it moved to the Meadowbrook Road area. By 1908, eight new houses had been built.

The names of Pigeon Hill residents appear over and over in Friendly Society programs as they joined the Sears social circle. Two of the first lots were sold to Alexander S. Jenney, architect of the town library and later the fire stations at Kendal Green and the town center. Architect A.J. Russell, son of First Parish minister Charles Russell, was an early buyer, as was lawyer Grant Palmer. Palmer took the Central Massachusetts Railroad into his Boston office every day until he was 90 years old. Others who built on Pigeon Hill included W.B. Clarke, a Boston bookseller, and town physician Dr. Frederick Hyde. Architects Samuel Mead and Harold S. Graves lived on the hill just outside the Sears development.

Olmsted Brothers: Planning the Sears Estate

In 1898, at age 43, Sears began the long process of developing Haleiwa. His first step was to consult Olmsted Brothers, the nationally known Brookline firm, which at that time included landscape architects John Charles Olmsted, his stepbrother

Figure 14-8. In 1903, Boston bookseller W.B. Clarke built this house on Pigeon Hill (now 45 Hill Top Road). Clarke's design was clearly influenced by the nearby Sears mansion.

Frederick Law Olmsted Jr., and Arthur A. Shurtleff (later Shurcliff). The firm produced 26 plans for the Sears property between April and September 1898.[15] Although these drawings have been lost, index cards list them as topographical maps, studies for the location of the drive and for a general plan, planting notes, and plans for treatment of the principal view.

A letter from Horace Sears to Olmsted Brothers, dated August 1, 1898, indicates how Sears approached the task of planning his house and land:

> The partial suggestions which you make do not meet my requirements. What I want is a full and comprehensive plan for the laying out of my whole estate, showing the grades, roads, shrubbery, flowers, etc; then I can work upon it by degrees as I feel inclined. . . . The approximate location of any house I may build is well understood, and the road, as you have just laid it out, seems to be all right. But it is quite probable I may not decide to build a new house for some years; but meantime I want to be working on the grounds, particularly planting out shrubs and trees, constructing the road, and changing the grade of my old tennis courts.[16]

Within weeks Sears had plans for more than 80 flower or shrubbery beds with some 4,200 individual plants. Olmsted Brothers was hired to oversee building the drive and creating the beds. Except for a follow-up visit one year later, the involvement of the firm ends in the fall of 1898.

"Fit for a King"

Construction of the palatial mansion commenced in 1899. Although the principal architect was Joseph Everett Chandler, the first phase was a 200-seat

Figure 14-9. The main entrance to Haleiwa was on the north facade, shown here. The Sears mansion illustrates many features typical of the second Italian Renaissance Revival. The wall surface was stucco, which imitated the masonry surfaces of the original Italian models. Windows were graduated in height and banding was used to set apart the upper story. Also characteristic were the pedimented portico, wide overhanging eaves with brackets, hipped roof, and red clay roof tiles.

Figure 14-10. The Sears mansion was the most elaborate in Weston, a town where comfort generally took precedence over elegance in estate design.

Figure 14-11. This photograph by Alfred Wayland Cutting shows the dining room at Haleiwa. (Photo c. 1907–08)

theater designed by Harold Graves and opened in 1901. The partially completed "villa" was described in a 1902 *Boston Sunday Herald* article headlined "Weston Has Become the Lenox of the East":

> Horace Scudder Sears is building a magnificent house, Italian in style of architecture, which is usually shown to every newcomer. Indeed . . . it occupies such a commanding position that he can hardly fail to notice it. It is located on Central Avenue but, turn as one will, for a radius of a mile it peeps out from many vistas, its red tile roof reflecting the sunlight. [17]

The main entrance was located on the north side, where steps led up to an open porch guarded by marble lions copied from Italian originals. On the porch, a massive sculptured marble table and marble benches offered a place of repose in front of the imposing dark green door with Florentine bronze knocker and bosses.[18] The south facade faced the garden and was dominated by three high arched windows that illuminated the entrance hall and second-floor stair landing.

Only superlatives like "breathtaking" and "fit for a king" were ever used to describe the interior of the Sears mansion. Visitors entered a "great front hall with . . . marble balustrades and pillars capped with gold filigree."[19] The imposing white Italian marble fireplace had been purchased by Sears on his European travels. A broad stairway led up to a spacious landing used for dancing. On the landing was another elaborate Italian marble fireplace carved with the inscription:

THE BEAUTY OF THE HOUSE IS ORDER
THE BLESSING OF THE HOUSE IS CONTENTMENT
THE CROWN OF THE HOUSE IS GODLINESS
THE GLORY OF THE HOUSE IS HOSPITALITY.[20]

The arched windows offered choice views across the gardens and beyond.

On the west side of the stair hall was a drawing room with tooled-leather wallpaper and gilded furniture, beyond which was the entrance to the theater. On the east side was a dining room with high ceilings and oversized furniture, and next to it a living room, "lined to the ceiling with fine bindings, polished and dusted."[21] The east wing included the kitchen and service area.

The main library on the third floor was approached through the long, narrow "Napoleon gallery," with a curved ceiling and walls lined with bookshelves. Sears was an admirer of Napoleon and fashioned the gallery to exhibit busts, bas-reliefs, chairs, books, and mementos of the French ruler. The wood-paneled main library had another massive Italian marble fireplace and two levels of bookshelves filled with the "choicest editions" on a wide variety of subjects. A 1919 article about the Sears estate claimed that Sears owned more than 7,000 volumes, with at least 6,000 in perfect bindings, exquisitely tooled.[22]

The house had two bowling alleys, a billiards room, and a master bathroom with sunken tub draped with yellow curtains.[23] A Star Room, described in a newspaper account as "one of the extraordinary features of the place," had a large gold "indicator" that extended straight through the roof to a ship weather vane. Inside, the indicator was surrounded by prominent stars correctly positioned and illuminated by electricity onto the "heavenly blue" ceiling.[24]

"Italy Delightfully Blended with New England"

The design of the Sears estate was inspired by Italian Renaissance country villas and gardens that captured the imagination of educated Americans beginning in the 1890s. The 1919 newspaper article in the *Boston Evening Transcript* said of the estate:

> Its "note" throughout is Italian, the note of a hundred villas in Italy. Mr. Sears was first attracted to Italy by reading about it, then by travel there. No man with a receptive mind can see Italy and come away unenthusiastic over its charm.[25]

The article adds that the Sears house and gardens were not copied from any particular garden or villa in Italy but rather the effort was to have "Italy delightfully blended with New England."

One of the surprises of the Sears story is his choice of Joseph Everett Chandler (1864–1945) to design the main house.[26] By the late 1890s, Chandler was launched on a distinguished career specializing in the restoration of historic New England houses and the design of new ones based on Colonial prototypes. For Horace Sears, Chandler produced something

Figure 14-12. This photograph by Alfred Wayland Cutting is labeled "Dr. Sayward of Wayland on the grounds of Haleiwa" and was taken about 1907–08.

completely different but possessed of the same exuberance.

Chandler's inspiration appears to have been the Villa Lante, considered by some to be the most complete example of the villa form.[27] It was highlighted in the important 1894 publication *Italian Gardens* by Charles Platt, a noted artist, landscape architect, and architect for the well-to-do. Platt's book was the first illustrated study in English of the Italian Renaissance garden and the first in an avalanche of writing on Italian landscape design that continued through the 1920s.[28] The Villa Lante was also the subject of two articles in architectural magazines in 1897 and 1898, just at the time that Sears was formulating his estate plan.[29] The Sears tennis house is a copy of the "casino," or summer house, at the Villa Lante, and the mansion has many design similarities.

The Gardens, "Land of Frill and Fantasy"

In the years between 1902 and 1910, short items in the *Waltham Daily Free Press Tribune* chronicle the development of the Sears garden. In December 1902, workmen began terracing the grounds and constructing an ornamental colonnade. The following May, they laid out walks and "beauty spots." The paper predicted, "When his plans are entirely worked out he will have one of the handsomest properties in eastern Massachusetts."[30]

In August 1903, Horace Sears held a formal dedication and reception. The newspaper account speculated that "Mr. Sears has been profuse in his invitations and it would seem as though every one had been accepted." The article added these details about the grounds:

> Those present had every opportunity to thoroughly examine the beauties of the place, both interior and exterior. The landscape features are beautiful, the display of flowers being very handsome. The show of begonias was pronounced remarkable.[31]

In April 1904, the newspaper reported that Sears was building artificial ponds, which probably refers to the marble pool close to the house.

Sears was not finished yet. On May 12, 1905, the *Waltham Daily Free Press Tribune* reported, "A wall, steps and columns of fieldstone and concrete, forming an architectural feature of great beauty, are being constructed on the estate of Horace Sears," and in October 1905, wrote, "Mr. H.S. Sears is having a handsome concrete bank wall put in along the line of the street." On May 1, 1908, the newspaper columnist noted that "when the four rows of trees recently planted by H.S. Sears opposite his estate have attained a good growth he will have a strikingly beautiful vista." That August, he was beautifying the south side of Central Avenue, where "an artificial pond is to be one the attractions there which will be seen from the mansion down an avenue of trees." This lagoon, which was destroyed in building the State Road Bypass, was narrow but extended almost 600 feet in length.[32] In 1910 Sears added the concrete wall and ornamental gates on the south side of Central Avenue and extended the wall on the north side.[33]

The Haleiwa garden design has traditionally been

Figure 14-13. This postcard of the south facade exemplifies one of the principles of Italian garden design: the unity of the house with the surrounding countryside. Large windows took advantage of hilltop views. Landscape features like the lion's-head fountain in the foreground lined up along a north–south axis that extended to a distant lagoon.

considered the work of prominent landscape architect Arthur A. Shurtleff (later Shurcliff), who had opened his own office in late 1904. Evidence of his involvement includes this diary citation written on the day of his wedding to Margaret Nichols, on April 17, 1905:

> [I woke early and] immediately I took the early train to Weston to the Horace Sears estate where I took charge of setting out the avenue of horse chestnut trees. My mind was naturally rather divided in its interests only being held to the tree work by pressing need of seeing it completed in season for the spring leaves.[34]

Because 1905 was the year when the garden's major architectonic features were being constructed, the fact that Shurtleff was supervising tree planting on the day of his wedding is a clear indication that he was responsible.

The Italian Garden at Haleiwa was a wonderful creation, conceived with grand vision and an expansive sense of space. The plan of the house and garden is oriented to the scenic vistas rather than to the road, a European idea that resulted in the entrance being on the north side away from Boston Post Road.

The architectural elements of the Sears garden were constructed of poured concrete, with exposed aggregate stone giving the surface texture and irregular coloration. Improved techniques for working with concrete allowed builders at the turn of the century to effectively and cheaply imitate masonry surfaces.

Sears was still working on the grounds on November 1, 1907, when the *Waltham Daily Free Press Tribune* reported, "The general appearance of the beautiful estate of Horace S. Sears is much enhanced by the removal of the homestead house to the south side of Central Avenue." So popular was the Sears garden that by 1909 Sears had to limit the public to specified visiting hours, as explained in this newspaper item:

> H.S. Sears has put up a neat bronze tablet on the main entrance gate to his estate on Central Avenue announcing that the property is private grounds but that the public is welcome there on Wednesday and Saturday afternoons between 3 and 6 o'clock.[35]

Theater and Entertainments at Haleiwa

The theater wing at Haleiwa was the first part of the house to be completed. In January 1901 Sears held a reception at his new "casino," attended by an estimated 150 to 200 neighbors and friends.[36] A more formal opening took place in November 1901. One newspaper account described Sears as "one of the popular bachelors in Boston society, with great wealth, artistic tastes, and assured position." The

Figure 14-14. Sears was a man of medium height, with a closely clipped mustache and beard. His office demeanor at Wellington Sears Company was quiet but precise. He was particular about having things done right.

writer gave the following description of the performance:

> There is a great interest in society in the opening next Friday evening of H.B. [sic] Sears' beautiful theater on his country estate here. The interest does not all centre in the building itself, but extends to the performance, for which much has been promised. Beatrice Herford, one of the entertainers, will give her new monologue, and a pickaninny scene from a New York production by society buds will be another feature, and as a piece de resistance a society girl will do a novel dance. There will be a one-act comedy, "A Country Romance." . . . It is entirely a subscription affair, and quite exclusive.[37]

As with many Sears entertainments, the affair was chaired by one of his inner circle, Robert Winsor's sister, Jane (Mrs. Lyman Gale), and raised money for charity.

In the first decades of the 20th century, the *Waltham Daily Free Press Tribune* frequently included reports such as this one of May 5, 1905: "There were more than 70 performers in the musical and operatic entertainment by the Ellis Memorial club at Mr. Sears's Casino. The event was eminently successful."

Not all parties at Haleiwa were exclusive. Sears reportedly invited the whole town to dances at his mansion, attended by local farmers in their best dress-up clothes. Until the new town hall was built in 1917, the theater at Haliewa was used regularly for

Figure 14-15. Sears purchased this house (now 334 Boston Post Road) across from his estate mansion and turned it into a "Teachers' Lodge." From 1913 until the 1950s, it provided a home for unmarried female teachers, who often had difficulty finding places to board. (2001 photo)

THIRTY-SEVENTH ANNUAL REUNION

Weston High School Association

"Haleiwa"

Friday evening, June the 12th

MCMVIII

Figure 14-16. Horace Sears helped establish the Weston High School Association and hosted the 37th annual reunion in July 1908 at Haleiwa.

Friendly Society programs widely attended by town residents.[38] Horace Sears was always at the door to greet his guests. In the spring of 1915, the Friendly Society put on its first musical at Haleiwa. The operetta was such a success that the society produced *The Red Mill* in 1919 at Sears's theater.

Sears also made his private bowling lanes available for tournaments. In 1914 the "Ladies Committee" sent a notice: "On the nights of the Bowling Tournament at Haleiwa, the ladies in the families of the bowlers are invited throughout the season to join in a game of Bridge Whist for which tables will always be arranged."[39]

Civic Contributions: 1900–1923

Sears contributed in other ways to the life of the community. He was instrumental in establishing the town's first swimming pool in 1906 on a small piece of his land on School Street. In 1913 he set up the Teachers' Lodge. As a member of the Town Improvement Committee in 1911, he influenced the choice of his own landscape architect, Arthur Shurtleff, to redesign the town center. To oversee construction, he served as chairman of the three-member Park Commission from 1917 until his death. One obituary called the town common "largely the plan and gift of Mr. Sears."[40] Sears was also chairman of the committee that constructed and furnished the new town hall. He donated $20,000 to the $75,000 town appropriation and made sure that the building had a suitable meeting hall/theater. After *The Red Mill,* Friendly Society plays were held in the new town hall.

Later Estate Development

A plan of the Sears estate in 1913 shows a property of nearly 56 acres extending from Church Street almost to Maple Road.[41] The mansion, formal gardens, and greenhouses were located on the north side of Central Avenue. By 1913, Sears also owned two houses across the street, along with an overseer's lodge on School Street and gardener's lodge and adjacent staff house on Wellesley Street.

A path extended through the estate to the train depot on Church Street. Brenton Dickson's book *Once Upon a Pung* explains its purpose:

> The Central Avenue contingent cut through Mr. Horace Sears' woods where a well-maintained path saved them nearly half a mile of walking. This path was illuminated from dusk until after the arrival of the midnight train. When the midnight train passengers had time to walk the length of the path, Mr. Sears' butler turned off the lights, all of which illustrates the neighborhood spirit that prevailed.[42]

Sears made three important land transactions in the

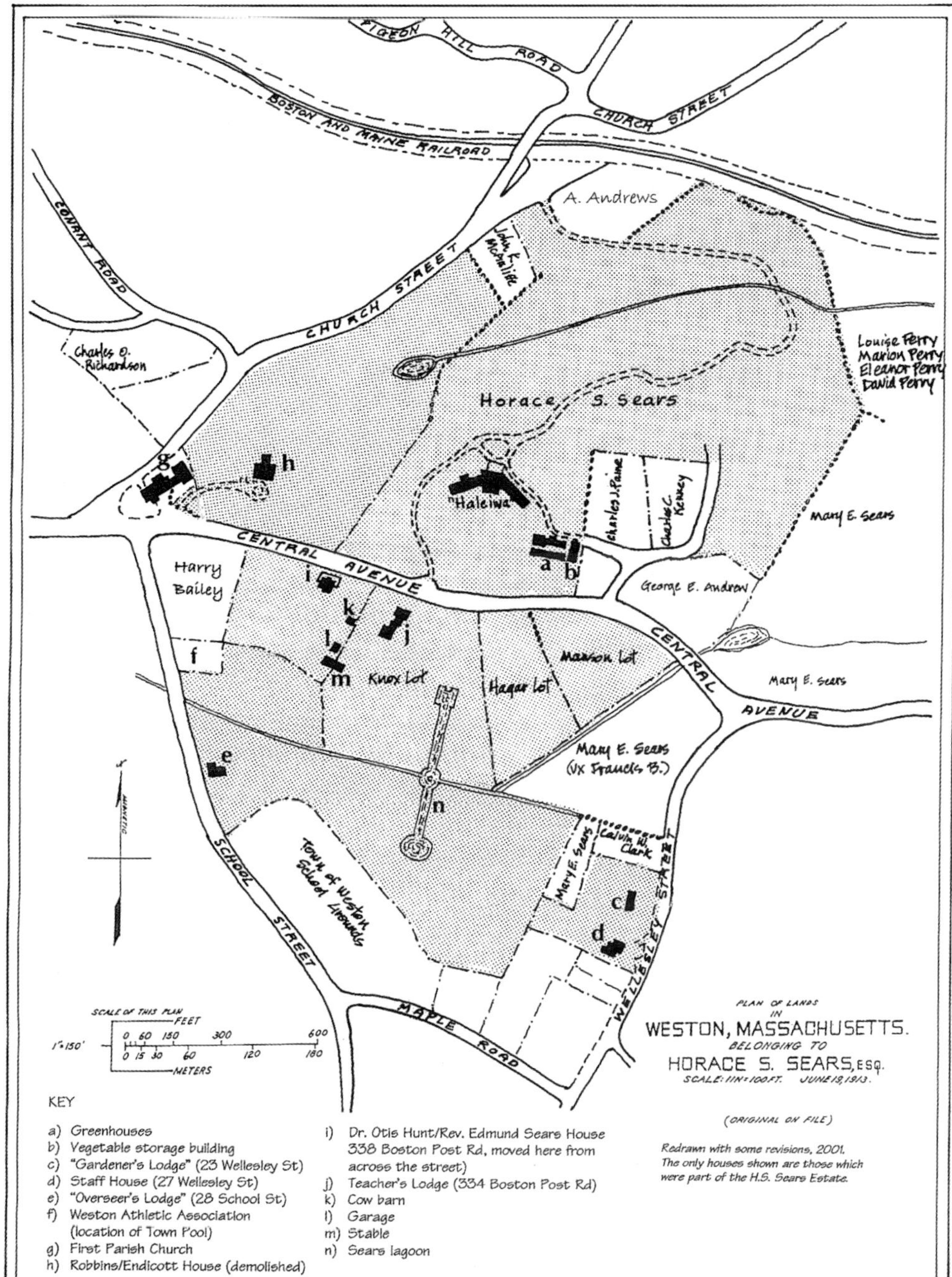

Figure 14-17. This map of the Sears estate is based on a plot plan of 1913. The estate extended north to the Central Massachusetts Railroad tracks and south almost to Maple Road. Notice the shape of the lagoon on the south side of Central Avenue (now Boston Post Road).

five years before his death. Two of these involved the children of his brother Francis. He purchased 66 acres on Crescent Street from the George S. Perry estate in 1918 and sold it three years later to his nephew Francis B. Sears Jr. In 1920, Sears gave First Parish Church 3.3 acres and a house just east of the church, subject to life tenancy by his niece, Mrs. Katharine Endicott. The Endicott house was torn down in 1967 to make way for the present Sunday school building.[43]

In the third land deal, Sears purchased the 90-acre Zoller Farm on Conant Road in 1919.[44] He remodeled the old farmhouse and built a large modern dairy barn. In October 1920 the newspaper reported that, as soon as the new barn was completed, Sears planned to move his choice cows from

Figure 14-18. Horace Sears built this English Country house for his gardener about 1912–13. Designed by Harold Graves, it still stands at 23 Wellesley Street.

Figure 14-19. No. 118 Conant Road dates back to about 1740, when John Walker built the central-chimney farmhouse in two sections. In 1778 his granddaughter Thankful married Oliver Conant, whose name was given to the town road that split the farm. About 1903, when this picture was taken, the property belonged to Henry and Elizabeth Zoller.

his farm in Cotuit to Conant Road.[45] Two months later, he deeded the entire property to Helena R. Bailey, wife of his business colleague and protégé, Harry Bailey.

Death of Horace Sears and Later History of Haliewa
Horace Sears died in 1923 at age 68. At his funeral, the chancel of the church was massed with flowers, "more than had ever been seen at a funeral by many present."[46] The eight male servants from Sears's Weston home acted as pallbearers.

Probate records reveal an estate valued at more than $2.5 million.[47] The mansion and surrounding 35 acres were valued at almost $94,000. Sears left bequests to relatives and friends, to each employee of Wellington Sears & Co., and to each member of his estate staff, noting, "The summer seasons are to be considered as full years with the Italian laborers who have worked so cheerfully and so faithfully for me year after year."[48] He left money to the town for changes and repairs to the town hall ($15,000). He set up permanent funds to assist library employees ($8,000), maintain the town common ($10,000), maintain the Teachers' Lodge or for general educational purposes ($10,000), plant and care for trees and shrubs in public places ($5,000), maintain an athletic field ($5,000), buy books for the library ($3,000), award high school graduation prizes ($3,000), and provide college scholarships to male Weston High School graduates without regard to race, religion, or denomination ($14,000).

First Parish Church got $35,000 to build the present Parish House, a project that had been under way before Sears's death. He left money in permanent funds for First Parish and other Unitarian causes and bequests to charitable institutions including Waltham Hospital and the Hampton Institute.[49]

To his business colleague Harry L. Bailey, Sears left all his real estate in Weston and on the Cape. This included contents from livestock and automobiles to the wine in Sears's wine cellars, later reported to be of only "modest" value.[50] Each of the three trustees, Harry L. Bailey and Charles O. Richardson, both of Weston, and Joseph M. Jackson

Figures 14-20 and 14-21. Henry Zoller (1839–1912) was the son of German immigrants. In Growing Up in Weston, *Phil Coburn describes the old farmer plowing his driveway, with his mustache covered with icicles and his coat tied around the waist with a rope to take the place of the missing buttons. These pictures of Henry and his wife, Elizabeth, were taken about 1903.*

of Roslindale, received $75,000. The remaining money was divided into three trusts, with a maximum of $150,000 each, for his two nephews and niece, with any money left after that to be divided between his brother Edmund and sister-in-law Mary E. Sears. Although the nephews and niece were hardly "cut off" as reported in tabloid accounts, Brenton Dickson wrote that they had expected more from their rich bachelor uncle. Reportedly, they did not talk to the Baileys for years.

Charles O. Richardson

Harry Bailey and Charles O. Richardson were protégés of Sears. Both were bright young men with no college education who, like Sears, began at the bottom and through intelligence and enterprise rose to the highest levels of business success. Sears helped advance their careers and influenced them to settle in Weston.

Charles O. Richardson (1871–1963) began work as an office boy at Wellington Sears when his widowed mother was unable to afford to send him to Harvard despite his acceptance. From sweeping floors and lighting stoves, he rose to partner in 1917 and eventually became treasurer of the company. Horace Sears was instrumental in persuading Richardson and his mother to move to Weston. They lived for a time in his mansion before Sears arranged for Richardson's move to a nearby house at the corner of Conant Road and Church Street. In 1914, the 43-year-old Richardson married young Laura Woodworth, daughter of neighbor Ralph Woodworth and a frequent participant in Friendly Society productions.

Richardson was an active member of First Parish Church. He worked to ensure that Sears's wishes for the Parish House were carried out. In 1949 he purchased the Teachers' Lodge and adjoining land from Harry Bailey and gave about 1.8 acres to St. Peter's Church, with the provision that the church build there within ten years.[51] The new building was completed by the end of the allotted decade and provides an important visual focus for the intersection of Boston Post Road and the bypass. Richardson maintained the Teachers' Lodge into the 1950s, when it was no longer needed.

Harry and Helena Bailey and Colchester Farm

Harry Louis Bailey (c. 1878–1962) began work in 1898 as a mill operative in the Stark Mills in New Hampshire. He was first employed at Wellington, Sears & Co. in 1901 as a clerk, at age 23. Described as "the handsomest and most attractive young man around—a dashing man," Bailey was also a shrewd businessman.[52] About 1910 he met the delicate and vivacious Helena Ravie, reputed to be a talented singer and minor member of the Italian nobility. Ravie was staying in Weston as a long-term house guest of Lyman and Jane Gale.[53] Within six months, the couple were married. They settled across the street from Horace Sears, at the corner of Boston Post Road and School Street. Bailey became a partner at Wellington Sears in 1917, president in 1931, and chairman of the board from 1944 until 1946, the year the company was purchased by West Point Manufacturing Company.[54]

Figure 14-22. Horace Sears is in the front seat of his Panhard car, to the right of the driver. In the back are his close friends and colleagues Charles O. Richardson, Harry L. Bailey, and Charles C. Kenney. At left is the north facade of Haleiwa. Note the marble lions.

As mentioned earlier, Horace Sears deeded the 90-acre Zoller Farm to Helena Bailey in 1920. The Baileys developed Colchester Farm, a dairy advertising Guernsey milk and cream.[55] Their caretaker lived in the Zoller farmhouse. The Baileys built several cottages along Conant Road for the dairymen. Their stucco barn with its slate roof was of immense proportions and was valued at $24,500, a huge sum for a nonresidential structure. Harry Bailey founded the Weston Saddle and Bridle Club and added two riding rings at its Colchester Farm headquarters. The landmark barn was demolished after the club closed in the early 1950s. The Weston Saddle and Bridle Club site was developed into houses on Sears, Colchester, Hamilton, and Laurel Roads.[56]

The question of why Horace Sears willed his house and remaining real estate to Harry Bailey has never been fully explained. Robert Winsor's nephew Winsor Gale dismissed any hidden motives. His simple answer was that Bailey was like a son to Sears, who had no children of his own.[57] The Sears will was a rich source of gossip and speculation. The *Boston American,* a tabloid not known for its accuracy, had a field day with the bequest to Bailey, which they incorrectly reported as $1 million. The account points the finger at Bailey's wife, Helena:

Figure 14-23. Newlyweds Harry and Helena Bailey lived in this house at 348 Boston Post Road from about 1911 until they inherited Haleiwa. The transitional Queen Anne/Colonial Revival-style house was built in 1888–89 for Dr. Frederick Jackson, the town's resident physician in the late 19th century. (1996 photo)

> The story of how a beautiful Italian girl, who landed in this country practically penniless, secured fame and fortune for herself and her husband, was revealed today with the announcement of a bequest of more than $1,000,000 to Harry L. Bailey of Weston. The bequest has created great surprise in the town of Weston . . . . While Bailey and his wife are provided with more valuable real estate than they can ever hope to enjoy, relatives of their benefactor, including a brother in St. Louis, were practically cut off.[58]

The story goes on to talk about how the wealthy philanthropist extended a helping hand to a deserving young man and was later lured away from his old friends by a beautiful woman.

The Baileys lived for a time in the Sears mansion. Helena Bailey ripped out the marble balustrades and leather wallpaper, replacing them with wrought iron and plain stucco. The gold furnishings, including the gilded piano, were shipped to New York for auction.[59] In later years, the Baileys moved to New York City and left the house vacant. In the fall and winter of 1949–50, the mansion was demolished by a wrecking company, which reportedly assigned 10 experienced workmen to scientifically tear it down and salvage hard-to-get building materials. A newspaper article describing the demolition reveals the mores of the postwar era:

> Taxes, upkeep costs and rising land values are fast bringing to a close the era of estate and mansion development in suburbs generally and particularly in the Weston-Wellesley areas. Soon most of the tremendous homes and estates will be but memories as their wide acres are redeveloped with neat, modern, low up-keep residences.[60]

As predicted, a modest, one-story ranch house was built on the site in 1951.

Buildings in the Sears Estate Area

320 Boston Post Road (1957–59). St. Peter's Episcopal Church was designed by Hoyle, Doran & Barry and built on land formerly part of the Sears estate. The cost was reported at more than $500,000. The present Georgian Colonial design was chosen after a more contemporary design ran into opposition from church members. Stained-glass windows in the chapel were moved from the former church building at 439 Boston Post Road.

309 and 311 Boston Post Road. See chapter 20.

315 Boston Post Road (1895). Queen Anne house built for Charles C. Kenney, friend of Horace Sears and principal in the firm of Kenney Bros. & Wolkins, on land purchased from Ellen Sears.

317 Boston Post Road. See chapter 18.

321 Boston Post Road. Location of Sears greenhouses (demolished) and a cold storage building (c. 1910–15) that still remains. Sometimes called the "mushroom house," the latter was built into the hill and constructed entirely of random rubble fieldstone.

327 Boston Post Road. Site of the Sears mansion and remaining landscape elements including the marble pool, lion's-head fountain, terrace, and grand staircase. Present ranch house built in 1951 and occupied for decades by Victor and Marjorie Harnish.

334 Boston Post Road (mid-19th century). Greek Revival house built for Sophia Marshall, daughter of Rev. Samuel Kendal. Sold by the heirs of her daughter, Elizabeth Knox, to Horace Sears in 1907. In 1913, Sears turned it into the Teachers' Lodge.

335 Boston Post Road. Location of the Sears tennis house and tennis court.

338 Boston Post Road (c. 1851). Italianate house built for Dr. Otis Eugene Hunt (1822–c. 1904), town physician from 1848 to 1864. Sold in 1869 to Rev. Dr. Edmund Hamilton Sears, minister of First Parish Church. An addition probably dates to the late 1880s, when Horace Sears was living with his widowed mother. It includes a sitting room and bedroom with fine decorative woodwork and also a bathroom, reputed to be the earliest in Weston, which still retains its copper tub and original vanity and fixtures. Horace Sears moved the house across the street in 1907.[61] A newspaper item noted, "It looks a little odd to see the old Sears mansion painted a light color. If we are not mistaken, it had retained its dark shade for 40 years or more."[62] Sears made the house available as the home and office for town physician Dr. Frederick Hyde and sold it in 1921 to town physician Dr. Fresenius Van Nuys.

348 Boston Post Road (1888–89). Built for Dr. Frederick W. Jackson, probably with financial assistance from Ellen Sears. Jackson, a graduate of Long Island Medical School, was a physician in Weston from 1885 to about 1900. Harry L. Bailey, protégé and business partner of Horace Sears, purchased the house from

Figure 14-24. This aerial view of the Sears property was taken not long after Haleiwa was demolished. It shows the ranch house built in 1951 on the site of the mansion, the remains of the axial landscape plan, the tennis house—which still stands to the left of the circular driveway—the remains of the greenhouses, and the vegetable storage building (lower right), which still stands at 321 Boston Post Road. At the far right is 317 Boston Post Road.

the Jackson family in 1911 and lived here at least until the death of Horace Sears, when Bailey and his wife, Helena, inherited the Sears mansion.

51 Church Street (1897–98). This gambrel-roofed Colonial Revival residence was designed by Joseph Everett Chandler for Abbie B. Andrews. It was inspired by the Hancock house, which once stood on Beacon Street next to the Massachusetts Statehouse. Because of the controversy surrounding its demolition in 1863, the Thomas Hancock house became America's most widely imitated Colonial building by the 1890s. Beginning in 1908, 51 Church Street was rented to Ralph Woodworth Sr., a Boston lawyer who purchased it in 1913. Woodworth's daughter, Laura, married Sears's protégé Charles O. Richardson. His son, Ralph Jr., World War II ace and musician, later lived here.

6 Conant Road (c. 1900; remodeled c. 1916). This shingled house was purchased by Horace Sears from Charles F. Richardson and later sold to Charles O. Richardson. After C.O. Richardson married Laura Woodworth in 1914, the couple hired Joseph Everett Chandler to enlarge and remodel the house, which still features the hand-blocked French scenic wallpaper added at that time. The interior is a good example of Chandler's flamboyant decorative style, which has been described this way: "If one molding is good, then two must be better."

118 Conant Road (c. 1740). This Colonial saltbox was built for farmer John Walker, owned by his descendants including Oliver Conant, and later purchased by farmer Henry Zoller, a descendant of German immigrants. Sears bought the farm from the Zoller family and transferred it to Helena (Mrs. Harry) Bailey, who used it as the caretaker's house for Colchester Farm. The house was rented and subsequently purchased by Kenneth and Rosanna Bennett in the 1940s.

Figure 14-25. The Sears estate walls and gates, grand staircase, fountains, and retaining wall with balustrade still remain in the 300 block of Boston Post Road just east of First Parish Church. (2000 photo)

111, 115, and 119 Conant Road (1921). Built for staff at Colchester Farm. Attributed to Harold Graves.

7 Hill Top Road (c. 1926). Dutch Colonial.

11 Hill Top Road (c. 1927). Colonial Revival.

21 Hill Top Road (1898). Colonial Revival saltbox built for Catherine and Herbert Everett.

38 Hill Top Road (1936). Colonial Revival house designed by the Boston firm of Kilham, Hopkins and Greeley for Mr. and Mrs. E. Olsen Field.

42 Hill Top Road (1898–99). Asymmetrical clapboard house with Shingle-style massing and Colonial Revival details, built for Mary Q. Thorndike and her husband, Albert, who worked for the Boston firm of Jackson & Curtis, stock brokers.

44 Hill Top Road (1898). Colonial Revival house built by architect Alexander S. Jenney as his own residence.

45 Hill Top Road (1903). Built for Maria and William Butler Clarke, owner of W.B. Clarke Co., booksellers on Tremont Street. Original design takes inspiration from the Italian Renaissance tradition.

46 Hill Top Road (1919). Frame Tudor attributed to architect Alexander Jenney.

17 Old Road. C.J. Paine Jr., son of Gen. Charles Jackson Paine, lived here in a house that has since been demolished.

23 Old Road (c. 1910). Not part of the Sears subdivision. The Colonial Revival house was designed by architect Harold Graves as his own residence and occupied by his descendants into the 1990s, when it was purchased and remodeled.

27 Old Road (c. 1790). Small Federal house built by Thomas Bigelow. Moved to its present location sometime between 1909 and 1911, when the railroad overpass was built.

10 Pigeon Hill Road (1904; 1925–26). Built as Pigeon Hill School, the building was converted to a residence in the mid-'20s, after the school moved to Meadowbrook Road.

13 Pigeon Hill Road (c. 1925). Distinctive bungalow.

20 Pigeon Hill Road (1900). Shingle-style house built for Arthur J. Russell, son of First Parish Church minister Charles Russell and architect with the Boston firm of Brainerd, Leeds and Russell.

26 Pigeon Hill Road (1899–1900). Colonial Revival house built for lawyer Grant Palmer and his wife, Marian. According to the oral history of their son, Grant Jr., when the Palmers were about to be married in 1891, they would take a horse and buggy and go from town to town to see where they would like to live. On one of these occasions they visited Weston and decided this was the place. They rented several houses before buying a lot on Pigeon Hill.

50 Pigeon Hill Road (1891). Architect Samuel Mead built this fine Shingle-style house as his own residence. The property includes a carriage house and greenhouse. Of interest on the 15-acre site is the collection of rhododendrons, beech trees, and other species planted by Mrs. Mead, who was an avid horticulturist. Their son, Charles, left the property to the Arnold Arboretum, which later sold it with conservation restrictions.

56 Pigeon Hill Road (1906). This unusual stucco house with its distinctive two-story entrance porch and Colonial Revival detailing was built for town physician Dr. Frederick T. Hyde. He lived here only a few years before moving back to his former residence on Central Avenue. The builder was Howard L. Cooper.[63]

28 School Street (mid-19th century). Picturesque Italianate house purchased by Ellen Sears and used as the gardener's lodge and later the overseer's lodge for the Horace Sears estate.

23 Wellesley Street (1912–13). Designed by architect Harold Graves in the English Country style as the gardener's lodge for the Horace Sears estate.

27 Wellesley Street. Colonial Revival double house thought to have been built or remodeled for Sears estate staff about the same time as the adjacent No. 23.

Notes

1. Andrews, Wayne, *Architecture, Ambition and Americans: A Social History of American Architecture* (New York, 1978), 144.
2. Balch, W.R., "Haleiwa," *Boston Evening Transcript,* July 12, 1919. Balch gives the translation "perfect home." The translation "beautiful place" comes from a note by Edwin "Bucky" Sears in Album 12 of the Alfred Wayland Cutting albums, SPNEA. Pronunciation courtesy of Winsor Gale.
3. Ibid.
4. Kennedy, Donald G., "Edmund Sears: Pastor, Poet, Mystic," *WHSB,* January 1983, 6.
5. MCRD 1086/172. Moved to present location at 338 BPR in 1907.
6. "Horace Scudder Sears: 1855–1955," tribute printed in the 1954 town report on the 100th anniversary of his birth, 3.
7. Kennedy, Donald G., "James Marshall, Part I: Booker T. Washington and the Hampton–Weston Connection," *WHSB,* March 1985, 5.
8. Richardson, Mabel, *Wellington Sears Company: Its First Hundred Years, 1845–1945* (unpublished manuscript, 1945).
9. William Wellington did not live in Weston and should not be confused with the Wellingtons at Gateways Farm.
10. Richardson, op. cit., 46
11. Sears also served as president of WHS Alumni Association in 1877–78, 1907–09, and 1917–18.
12. MCRD 2592/115, Francis B. and Edmund H. Sears to HSS, September 1897.
13. MCRD 2577/23, HSS to A.B. Andrews, July 1897 (51 Church Street).
14. MCRD 2525/511, 41 and 5 acres (January 1897). See also Plan Book 107/16, August 26, 1897.
15. Frederick Law Olmsted National Historic Site, 99 Warren Street, Brookline. Relevant files include index file cards and plant list of August 1898.
16. Library of Congress Manuscript Division, microfilm reels, Job #2060 (correspondence, 1898, and field report, August 1899).
17. "Weston Has Become the Lenox of the East," *Boston Sunday Herald* magazine section, May 11, 1902.
18. Balch, op. cit.
19. Dickson, *RR,* 86, and *Pung,* 70.
20. Balch, op. cit.
21. Ibid.
22. Ibid. While the Balch article is undoubtedly

exaggerated, it is clear that the book collection was large and of high quality.

23. Dickson, *RR*, 87.

24. Newspaper article in scrapbook owned by Marjorie Harnish, date and name of publication cut off (c. 1949).

25. Balch, op. cit.

26. The attribution to Chandler comes from two sources: 1) Edwin "Bucky" Sears, great-nephew of Horace and devotee of architecture, attributes the building to Chandler in a note inserted into Album 12 of the Alfred Wayland Cutting albums at SPNEA. This note describes the five interior photographs taken by Cutting and states, "The house was designed by Joseph Everett Chandler." 2) Mabel Richardson, daughter of Sears protégé Charles Richardson, recalled to PWF that "it was a tradition that Chandler designed that house—I do believe that he did." Chandler was a well-known figure in the Richardson household and designed a major addition to their house in 1916. Mabel Richardson recalls going to Chandler's house in Sudbury and seeing his garden, which was "sort of Italian." Chandler's name appears in 1904 and 1906 lists of Friendly Society participants and on its 1913–14 membership roster.

27. Platt, Charles A., *Italian Gardens* (New York: Harper & Brothers, 1894), 13 ff. The Villa Lante was located in Bagnia just north of Rome.

28. Morgan, Keith N., *Charles A. Platt: The Artist as Architect* (Architectural History Foundation and MIT, 1985).

29. Platt's book was serialized in *Harper's Magazine* in July and August 1893; and the villa was the subject of articles in *American Architect and Building News* in December 1897 and *Architectural Record* in October–December 1898. Sears and Chandler could also have been familiar with Faulkner Farm in Brookline, designed by Charles Platt for prominent lawyer and politician Charles Sprague and completed about 1899. The garden included a small outbuilding modeled after the same casino. Faulkner Farm was the subject of numerous articles in the first years of the new century and was universally praised by critics, who called it a "new model for American gardens and for a new American life, that of the country villa." (See Emmet, Alan, "Faulkner Farm: An Italian Garden in Massachusetts," *Journal of Garden History*, vol. 6, no. 2, 174. (Later called the Brandegee estate.) See also Griswold, Mac and Weller, Eleanor, *The Golden Age of American Gardens: Proud Owners, Private Estates, 1890–1940* (New York: Harry N. Abrams Inc., in association with the Garden Club of America), 46.

30. *WDFPT*, May 15, 1903.

31. *WDFPT*, September 4, 1903.

32. The shape can be seen on the 1913 plot plan. There is also a photograph in the 1919 *Boston Evening Transcript* article.

33. *WDFPT*, July 8, September 2, and November 11, 1910.

34. Shurtleff, Arthur A., *Journals*, vol. 5, April 27, 1905, 83. Shurtleff (later Shurcliff) married Margaret Homer Nichols on April 27, 1905. Her family had a home on Beacon Hill and a summer house in Cornish, New Hampshire. Charles Platt also had a home in Cornish, where he designed important examples of the Italian garden style. See also Rebecca Davidson's chapter "Charles A. Platt and the Fine Art of Landscape Design" in Keith Morgan's *Shaping an American Landscape: The Art and Architecture of Charles A. Platt* (Hanover, NH, 1995), 75 ff.

35. *WDFPT*, July 9, 1909.

36. *WDFPT*, January 11 and 18, 1901.

37. "Society People in Vaudeville," newspaper clipping, about November 26, 1901 (Francis Blake Papers, MHS, vol. 43).

38. In 1906–07, for example, 6 of 14 Friendly Society programs were held at Haleiwa. That year, Sears hosted "The Wisdom of Solomon," "The Weston Press," two dramatic programs, a card party, and the season finale.

39. Typed notice dated January 12, 1914 (E.B. Sears papers, WPL history room).

40. Obituary, "Horace Scudder Sears," undated 1923 clipping, Coburn scrapbook.

41. MCRD, Plan Book 219/5A and B, 1913. This acreage does not include the 10-acre parcel directly east of First Parish Church that in 1913 was held by Charles O. Richardson and later belonged to Sears himself.

42. Dickson, *Pung*, 11–12.

43. Before the Endicotts, this house had belonged to Chandler Robbins and before that to David Lane.

44. Elizabeth Q. Zoller to HSS, June 1919, 4268/131. Farmhouse at 118 Conant Road.

45. *WDFPT*, October 13, 1920.

46. Obituary, "Horace Scudder Sears," *Waltham Evening News*, April 25, 1923.

47. His partnership share in Wellington, Sears & Co. was valued at over $1 million and textile mill stocks at another million. Value of real estate was as follows: mansion and 35 acres between Church Street and Central Avenue (almost $94,000); land and two houses on Wellesley Street ($18,500); summer property in Cotuit ($58,000).

48. Middlesex Probate #141547, 4. The amount willed to company employees was $200 each, with an additional $100 for each five years of service. Staff received $100 each, $100 additional for each five years of service.

49. For example, $25,000 was willed to Weston Point Manufacturing Company to erect a memorial building, library, or church in Langdale, Alabama: "I request that this building be located in Langdale . . . the oldest and most central of all the mill villages. But I wish this bequest to be considered as an evidence of my equal esteem, affection and high regard for the workers of all four villages whose faithful and efficient labors have built up one of the finest industrial textile plants in the country" (Probate #141547).

50. "Wonderful Sears' Estate Left H.L. Bailey, But He Won't Live There/Priceless Art Treasures, Autos, Wine Cellar and Hall—His Employees Left $100 Each" (undated newspaper clipping in scrapbook owned by Mrs. Victor Harnish).

51. MCRD 7445/109, June 22, 1949. The deed specifies that if St. Peter's did not meet the conditions, the land would be conveyed to the town for general municipal purposes.

52. PWF interview with Winsor Gale, August 5, 1998.

53. Different sources spell the name "Ravie" or "Ravi." In an interview with Winsor Gale (1901–2000), he recalls "Senorita Ravi" when she stayed at the Gale house. The *Waltham Free Press* reported in May 1911, "A reception was given by Horace S. Sears at his residence Friday to announce the engagement of H.L. Bailey to Senora Helena Ravi."

54. "Harry Louis Bailey, 84, Dead: Ex-Wellington Sears Chairman," *New York Times*, May 28, 1962.

55. Advertisement, Friendly Society program for "Sweethearts," April 24 and 25, 1925.

56. Parts of Aberdeen, Sunset, and Montvale Roads were also built on former Zoller farmland.

57. Winsor Gale to PWF, August 5, 1998. As a young man, Gale played bridge with his uncle Robert and Horace Sears.

58. "Sears Gave Friend's Wife $75,000/Romance in $1,000,000 Bequest/Love Story of Beautiful Italian Girl Revealed by Will of Horace S. Sears," *Boston American*, April 28, 1923.

59. Dickson, *RR*, 88.

60. Undated newspaper article, c. 1949, in scrapbook belonging to Mrs Victor Harnish. The wrecking company was the Marshall C. Spring company of Newton Lower Falls.

61. See *WDFPT*, September 6, October 11, and November 1, 1907, for reports on moving the house across the street.

62. *WDFPT*, January 31, 1908.

63. *WDFPT*, January 26, March 9, November 23, 1906, and May 1, 1908.

Figure 15-1. The "Town Square" at Church Street and Boston Post Road was the heart of the community. At left is the first town hall. The metal watering trough was installed about 1897, shortly after the Weston Water Company was organized. The trough was a coppery black color and had a pipe up the middle and a drain to prevent the water from overflowing. It was set on a small circle of cobblestones level with the road surface. An identical trough stood at the intersection of Church Street and North Avenue. (Photo c. 1913)

CHAPTER 15

Evolution of the Town Center

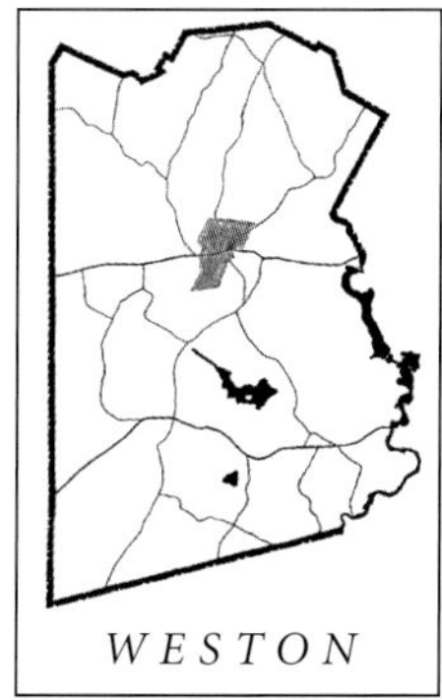

Weston Center has always been the heart of the town's religious, civic, and commercial life. While businesses have changed over the years from blacksmith shops to gift shops, their location has remained roughly the same. In the late 19th century, Weston, like other New England towns, turned its attention to "village improvement." As early as 1892, a plan was published in the annual town report showing a new layout for the "town square" at the intersection of Church Street, Boston Post Road, and School Street. Two decades later, Weston adopted a more sweeping plan to create a town green out of swampland and build a new town hall and fire station.

What is remarkable here is the ability of town leaders to think ahead, to think big, and to rally public support for the spending of tax dollars on a major civic improvement project. These leaders brought in outstanding talent to do the design, most notably landscape architect Arthur Shurtleff (who later changed the spelling of his name to Shurcliff). In his 1917 speech dedicating the new town hall, Selectman Benjamin Loring Young hailed the achievement of the town in working steadily and persistently toward its goal:

> *Six years ago, Mr. Shurtleff told us that "the execution of the Town Improvement Plan would give Weston a Town Common of remarkable individuality and in many respects the finest open space of its kind in the Commonwealth." That prophecy seemed a vision and a dream, but it has come true. The seed planted in good soil has grown to the ripe fruit.*
>
> *Six years ago we had no fire station, no Town Common, no adequate Town Hall. To-day we have all these things—not for ourselves alone, but for our children and our children's children . . .*[1]

The Town Improvement Plan was carried out during a period of widespread nostalgia for America's colonial past. Creating a New England town green and surrounding it with red-brick Colonial Revival town buildings was part of a celebration of the past that, at the same time, brought Weston into the modern era.

Figure15-2. At the second meetinghouse of 1722, the men sat on benches on the west side and the women on the east, with seating assigned according to "estate" and age. Permission to build family pews along the walls was granted from time to time to the "highest payers." The bell tower at left was added in 1799–1800.

Early History of the Town Center

Weston has one of the best preserved segments of the Great Country Road, later known as Central Avenue and, since the 1920s, as Boston Post Road. At one time, this was the most important transportation route west from Boston. In 1695, when the settlers in the Farmers' Precinct of Watertown got permission to build their own church, they chose a location on the post road in the geographical center of The Farms.[2] The original 30-foot-square meetinghouse and its 1722 replacement were used for both religious services and town meetings.

The second meetinghouse was built on what is now the town green and originally looked like a Colonial house.[3] It was remodeled in 1799 and a bell tower added at the west end. A new bell was purchased from Revere & Sons.[4] The noted firm, headed by Revolutionary War patriot and silversmith Paul Revere, cast church bells for meetinghouses throughout New England.[5] Their 997-pound creation now hangs in the steeple of the present First Parish Church.[6]

Over the course of the 18th century, church members received permission to build carriage sheds on town land adjacent to the meetinghouse. These shelters, which provided protection for horses and carriages during long church services, were constructed with private funds and reserved for the use of their builders.[7]

Across from the second meetinghouse, Josiah Smith (1722–1782) built a tavern in 1757.[8] The original structure had a gambrel roof and central entrance facing north onto the post road. In 1763 Smith added a large kitchen and another taproom on the east side, along with a second-floor ballroom with a curved ceiling. The Josiah Smith Tavern was one of the most popular of the inns along the post road.

Josiah Smith served as selectman from 1766 to 1779 and was a leading figure during the Revolutionary War period. In 1775, he and Samuel Phillips Savage were delegates to the Provincial Congress at Concord, presided over by John Hancock. After Josiah's death in 1782, his son Joel, also a well-known "Liberty man," succeeded him as landlord. After Joel died in 1817, the tavern was run for a decade by his son-in-law, George Washington Peirce. The opening of other east–west routes, the early-19th-century temperance movement, and the growth of railroad transportation all contributed to the decline of the tavern business. The old hostelry closed in 1838. In 1842 the property was sold to John and Marshall Jones, whose family used it as a residence for more than a century.[9]

The Lamson Family

John Lamson (1686–1757) was the first of the family to settle in Weston, in 1709.[10] He purchased a large tract extending from the town center north and east to Pigeon Hill, including the site of the present town green and town hall.[11] Until its demolition in the early 20th century, the 1765 Lamson homestead was a well-known landmark.[12]

John's son Samuel (1736–1795) is best known as the captain of the Weston militia company that marched to Concord with more than 100 men on April 19, 1775. Later, Samuel was active in town affairs and rose to the rank of colonel in the Third Middlesex Regiment. His third son, Isaac (1765–1806), ran a store in Weston from the 1780s to 1806 on the site where Cutting's Store later stood.[13]

Samuel's ninth child, John (1791–1855), in partnership with New York City merchant David Lane, established the mercantile house of Lane, Lamson & Co. According to family history, the firm was "the first French importing house in the United States," with branches in Boston, New York, Paris, and Lyon. John retired from business in 1853 and, with his wife, Elizabeth Turner Kendall, took up residence in the homestead in Weston.[14] David Lane married Caroline Lamson and purchased property in the town center just east of First Parish, where he built the house later occupied by the Rev. Chandler Robbins and subsequently by Katherine Sears Endicott.[15]

Samuel's 10th child, Daniel S. Lamson (1793–1824), was a lieutenant colonel of the Third Middlesex Regiment and kept a dry-goods store in Weston. According to his nephew and namesake, the historian Daniel S. Lamson, this store became one of the most important in Middlesex County:

> The business was very extensive, taking in all the towns west of us to the Vermont and New Hamp-

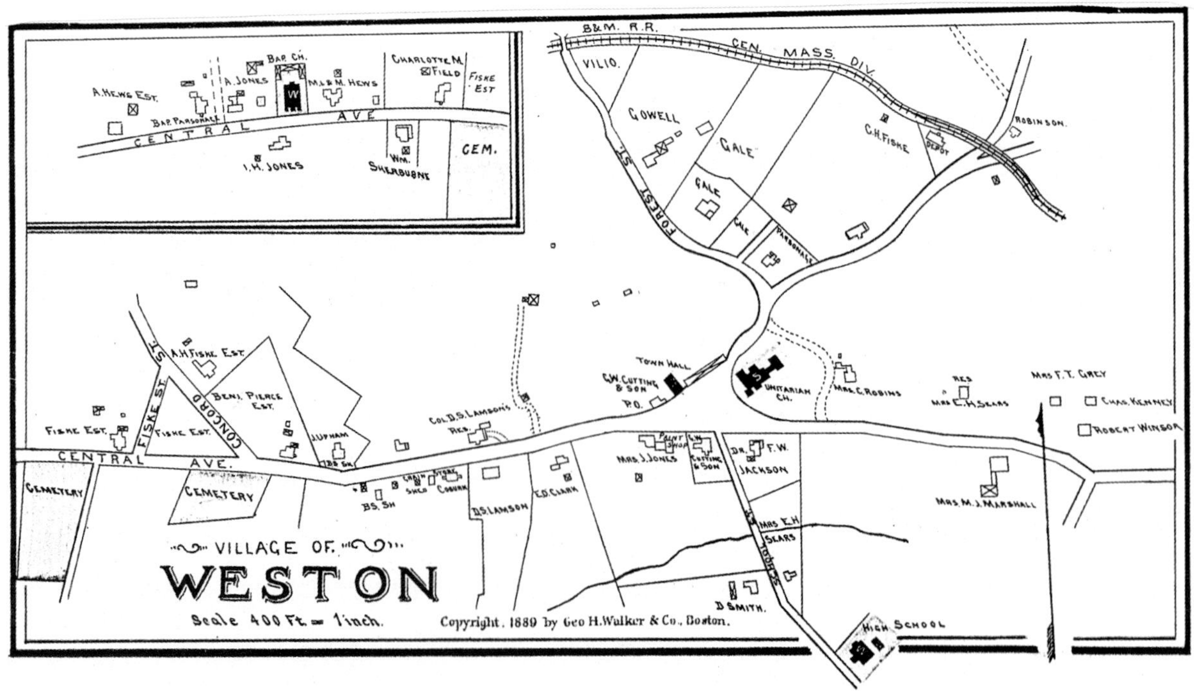

Figure 15-3. The 1889 Middlesex County Atlas *included this detail map of Weston town center. Note the location of the Lamson property in the heart of today's commercial district.*

shire line. It was the custom in old times for women to make their purchases in the spring or fall for the whole year. They would drive down from long distances in their "one-horse shay," put up over night at the tavern, returning home the next day. No one ever thought of going to Boston to buy goods. Waltham ladies came to Weston to buy. Cloths of all sorts were to be had. But, complaint being made that there was no one to make up the cloths, Mr. Lamson built the little shop about 1817, and installed a tailor. Mr. Lamson died in 1824, leaving what was considered a handsome fortune in those days, all of which he had made in Weston.[16]

Figure 15-4. Rev. Joseph Field (1788–1869) was minister at First Parish for half a century, the longest in church history. Field was Weston's first "distinctively Unitarian" minister. He kept the congregation together during a period of financial and doctrinal crisis and presided over construction of a new church building.

Lamson was succeeded by Charles Merriam and then by Henry W. Wellington, both of whom left Weston for the greener pastures of Boston. With the departure of Wellington in 1838, the prestige of the dry-goods store declined.

Other distinguished Lamsons could be mentioned, but in Weston history, the most important was Daniel Sanderson Lamson (1828–1912), grandson of Samuel and son of John.[17] Lamson studied law and was admitted to the bar in 1854, although he never practiced. Following the family tradition of military service, he organized a home guard even before the outbreak of the Civil War to drill troops for the impending conflict. By 1861 he had been commissioned major of the 16th Regiment of Massachusetts Volunteers, the successor to the Third Middlesex Regiment. He rose to the rank of lieutenant colonel in 1863 but was discharged for disability in 1864. The colonel was the last of the Lamsons to occupy the family homestead. His *History of the Town of Weston, 1630–1890* was published posthumously in 1913.

Colonel Lamson's two sons, Joseph Fenwick ("Fenny") and George H.D. Lamson, took control of the family land in 1908.[18] George, a well-known horseman, bought out his brother in 1921. He farmed and managed the real estate into the 1930s.[19] In the history of the town center, the Lamsons figure prominently as the principal landowners in what would become the commercial and institutional heart of the town.

Figure 15-5. In 1840 First Parish built this Greek Revival temple-front church to replace the 1722 meetinghouse. The handsome colonnade was an afterthought, added after the building was completed. Even nonmembers contributed to the subscription fund for this embellishment. This picture dates before 1875, when a clock was placed in the tower.

Construction of the 1840 First Parish Church

The first five ministers at First Parish Church served the congregation for more than a century and a half. Joseph Mors was minister from 1702 to 1706, William Williams from 1709 to 1750, Samuel Woodward from 1751 to 1782, Samuel Kendal from 1783 to 1814, and Joseph Field from 1815 to 1869.

Field's ministry had a rather inauspicious beginning on February 1, 1815, when, according to Lamson, "the thermometer . . . was eight degrees below zero, and the refreshments provided for the occasion . . . froze on the tables, the fruit being hard as stones."[20] Under his leadership, First Parish Church weathered two major challenges. The first was the doctrinal upheaval that took place throughout Massachusetts beginning in the mid-1820s. The organization of the American Unitarian Association by the Rev. William Ellery Channing in 1825 transformed the liberal reform wing of Congregationalism into a separate Unitarian denomination. First Parish became Unitarian in 1825 with the formation of the

Figure 15-6. Tromp-l'oeil painting was used to give the interior of the 1840 church a more distinctive architectural presence.

Unitarian Society as a religious society separate and independent from the town. Weston's was one of only 15 churches in the state where the embrace of Unitarianism did not lead to a split and formation of another church.[21] Field was the first distinctly Unitarian minister in Weston, but his cheerful, happy spirit kept the church together:

> The salient points of his life and character were the exceedingly practical cast of mind and the overflowing goodness of his heart. . . . Doctrines he cared little about except in their most general and comprehensive summary . . . once having settled the main points, he did not think it worth while to keep debating them over again.[22]

The second challenge was a financial restructuring, which took place when the church voluntarily separated from the town and moved to a system of contributions from its own members.[23] Prior to this, despite years of vigorous protests from the town's Baptists and Methodists, all Weston residents were taxed for the expenses of First Parish unless they could produce a certificate testifying that they had paid the tax to support their own church. The transition to contributions, which were harder to collect than compulsory taxes, was eased in 1830 by the creation of a ministerial fund of $1,500, which laid the foundation for the present church endowment. In 1833, in a final settlement to what had been an ongoing controversy, Massachusetts adopted the eleventh amendment to the state Constitution severing the connection between church and state.[24]

From 1814 to 1835, the Female Cent Society at First Parish collected one cent a week from its members in support of missionaries and other good works. The first Sunday school was established in 1827 and the First Parish Ladies' Benevolent Society in 1841.

During the Reverend Field's tenure, the imposing wooden Greek Revival church was constructed in 1840 on a small piece of land only one quarter of an acre, donated by Clarissa Smith. In front of the church was a scruffy patch of land known as the common. The present stone church stands slightly forward from the site of the 1840 building. To fund construction, church leaders auctioned off pews for amounts between $75 and $125. Thirty-eight of the 58 pews were sold, raising most of the $3,800 cost.

Not everyone liked the new church. In his history, Col. Daniel Lamson expressed his strong preference for the historic 1722 meetinghouse:

> There are persons still living who can remember the old church with its high-backed pews, sounding-board and pulpit. There was an air of solemn dignity, an emphasis on religious fervor, which this old church typified, that impressed the beholder with a reverence its successor never succeeded in doing. The destruction of this old landmark, built of solid oak, and replaced by a monstrosity which only a nineteenth century architect could devise, shows both lack of reverence and the decay of faith, a marked trait in our times.[25]

The name used at the 1840 dedication ceremony was Congregational Parish. The term The First Parish was first used in 1837 on the warrant for a parish meeting.[26]

The plan to build a new church created a problem for the town, which had been holding town meetings at First Parish since the town was incorporated in 1712. On May 4, 1840, at the last town meeting held in the old meetinghouse, a committee reported that it had made an agreement with the church to include a convenient place for town meetings and other public purposes in the new building. The town proposed to pay the cost of a basement with a large hall and rooms for the selectmen and town assessor. This space was to be conveyed to the town, which would save money by combining with the church rather than erecting a separate structure. Town residents voted to accept this plan, but the basement was never built. After 1840, church and town were, finally, separate not only in financial and administrative matters but also in physical space.

Figure 15-7. Looking south on Church Street toward the town square, this picture shows the 1840 church, horse sheds, and rear of the old town hall. What is now the town green was a bog used by Colonel Lamson as a cow pasture. This picture was taken before 1888.

The 1847 "Town House" and Founding of the Weston Public Library

From 1840 to 1847, Town Meetings were held at the former Josiah Smith Tavern. In 1847, the first "Town House" was erected on the site of the 1722 meetinghouse. The Greek Revival building with its grand two-story Doric colonnade was completed in December 1847 at a cost of $4,078.[27] To inaugurate the new hall, Weston residents were invited to a Union Ball a few months later. Charles H. Fiske later wrote that "individuals attended even from Boston" and "It was the brilliant event of the season, and the Hall was resonant with revelry."[28]

The town voted to use the rooms on the lower floor for school purposes. Plans were devised for a high school but no action was taken until 1854, when $150 was granted and a room finally fitted up.[29] The high school remained here until 1878, when a separate building was constructed on School Street.

In the winter of 1856–57, citizens met at the town hall and decided by vote that "the general intelligence of the Town could be most economically and effectually secured by a free public library."[30] A committee of three men—Isaac Fiske, Dr. Otis E. Hunt, and First Baptist Church minister Rev. Calvin H. Topliff—led volunteers in securing donations totaling about $500 in cash and $70 in books. With funds in hand, the library was officially established at Town Meeting in November 1857. The first bylaws stated that borrowers had to be at least 16 years old and that the library would be open every other Saturday from 3 to 5 P.M. and every Saturday night from 7 to 9 P.M.

John Coburn was chosen as the first librarian and filled the office for 36 years, from 1857 to 1893. The library published its first catalog in 1859, listing 1,100 books.[31] The fledgling organization got its first major endowment gift that same year, when Charles Merriam donated $1,000. The original space was too small from the beginning. Trustees reported that there was hardly enough space for everyone to stand in the room on library days, adding, "A library room is not only for delivery of books, but also for social intercourse and friendly greeting, and should be furnished with settees enough to accommodate all who desire to sit."[32]

Figure 15-8. The 1847 Weston Town Hall was the first home of the high school, library, and fire department. The monumental Greek Revival style was well suited to this type of institutional building.

Immediately after the Civil War, the town hall was enlarged at the west end.[33] The new "Memorial Hall" met the need of the library for more space and provided a fitting location for a handsome white marble tablet bearing the names of soldiers killed in the conflict. An item in the *Waltham Sentinel* of 1867 commented on the "nice library room" with its "costly carpet," furniture, and kerosene chandelier.[34] The reading area was kept well supplied with the leading magazines and newspapers of the day.

In the 1861 catalog, books were classified under the following divisions: Agriculture, Biography, Fiction, History, Juvenile, Religious and Moral, Scientific, and Travels. That year the trustees' report contained the following comment on reading of fiction:

Figure 15-9. The second floor of the 1847 Town House had a large hall used for town meetings and community events. It is not known what entertainment is pictured in this rare interior view.

Figure 15-10. John Coburn (1823–c. 1893) was the town's first librarian.

> . . . fiction is more generally read than any other division of the Library. . . . In selection of these books, the Committee have used considerable discrimination. We believe that most of these novels have literary merit, and exert a salutary, elevating influence, while none of them are directly immoral or vitiating. Let fictitious works have their proportion of time, and they refine, amuse, and instruct; let them absorb the entire attention, and they debilitate the mind, morbidly excite the sensibilities, and render their devotee nervous and impractical. We caution readers against their disproportionate use.[35]

The warning was repeated again in 1871:

> The market is flooded with works of fiction. . . . Sometimes a work is called for which is making a sensation in reading circles, and it is worth while to buy it and read it for the sole purpose of learning what the popular taste is and on what thin pabulum its cravings are satisfied. . . . We doubt whether such reading tends to any other result than confirmed moral indolence and emptiness of both heart and brain.[36]

In 1881, space within the town hall was altered to provide a book room 14 by 32 feet, holding 5,000 volumes. That year, the library was opened on Wednesdays from 1 to 5 P.M. The additional space soon proved inadequate, and in 1889 the trustees advised that the library would soon outgrow its quarters.

In addition to housing the library and town offices, the Town House had a second-floor meeting room used frequently for singing programs, lectures, or discussions "on any subjects which are intended to diffuse useful knowledge in the community." At the opening of the Civil War, a drill corps used the upper hall for a drill room and armory.

Beginning in the early 1890s, Town Hall provided space for yet another fledgling town institution, the fire department. The first hook-and-ladder truck was housed in the basement, which opened out to ground level at the rear. P.J. McAuliffe's stable down on Church Street supplied the horses. Fire apparatus was stored here until the present brick fire station was constructed in 1914.

Cutting's Store

Lamson's history traces the general store in the town square back to 1804, when Joel Smith's son, George W. Smith, opened a grocery. The store changed hands and was moved before being bought in 1833 by George Warren Cutting Sr. (1805–1885), who had come to town some years earlier to work as a store apprentice.[37] In addition to being young and ambitious, Cutting was an amiable man known for his strict integrity. His store prospered. In 1856 he leased a building next to the town hall that had been built in 1852 by John Lamson. In 1859 Cutting was appointed postmaster, an office he held until his death. In 1875 Cutting purchased the store building from the Lamson family.

G.W. Cutting Sr. and his wife, Elizabeth, had eight children. Their oldest son, George Warren Jr. (1834–1923), succeeded his father in the store and as postmaster from 1885 to 1917. He served as town clerk for 54 years and was honored at his retirement with this tribute to his "sturdy New England character":

> His administration of the office was not only notable for its length of service, almost unequalled by any in the annals of the Commonwealth, but it was notable also for the fidelity, courtesy and scrupulous exactness which characterized his work.[38]

G.W. Jr. and his wife, the former Josephine M. Brown, had six children. Their oldest daughter, Sarah, married Arthur B. Nims, who worked as a clerk at her father's store. The oldest son, Alfred Leslie (1868–1926), attended commercial school before opening a grocery on North Avenue in 1888, at age 20. Another son, George W. Cutting (1877–1942), was referred to as "Junior" after his grandfather died. Trained as a civil engineer, this G.W. Cutting was also the town treasurer. When he died in 1942, his wife, Helen Warren Cutting, took over the treasurer's job. She served until 1964, making a total of 98 consecutive years that a member of the Cutting family served as a town official.

After the death of George W. Cutting Sr. in 1885, G.W. Jr. took his son Alfred Leslie and son-in-law A.B. Nims into partnership. For a time, they ran both the central store and the Kendal Green branch, which was later turned over to George W. Brodrick.

An 1888 newspaper article "A Massachusetts Town: Scenes in Cutting's Store at Weston" explains the importance of Cutting's to the community:

Figure 15-11. John Lamson erected a store in the town square in 1852 and four years later leased it to George W. Cutting. Three generations operated the well-known general store. The flat-roofed section to the right was the first of several additions.

Figure 15-12. George Warren Cutting Sr. (1805–1885) founded Cutting's Store and was Weston's postmaster from 1859 until his death. In the early 20th century, the store issued several historically oriented promotional calendars, including this one in 1909 showing the family patriarch and the 1840 church.

Figure 15-13. George W. Cutting Jr. (1834–1923) succeeded his father as proprietor of G.W. Cutting & Sons and as postmaster, a position he held from 1885 until 1917. He was town clerk for 54 years. His oldest son, Alfred L. Cutting, and son-in-law, Arthur B. Nims, helped operate the thriving general store. His second son, another George W. Cutting (referred to as 2nd or Jr.), was a civil engineer and Weston town treasurer.

Figure 15-14. Arthur B. Nims (left) with Cliff Cooker and Jared Heard are pictured with some of the stock of the country general store.

It became a central spot, a sort of focus for the social and business interests of the place. Here twice each day the lumbering old stage coach which until recently supplied the only means of conveyance for travellers between Sudbury and Stony Brook drew up with a great flourish to take and leave passengers, as well as papers and mail matter. This stage started in the early part of the day from South Sudbury, went to Sudbury Centre thence through Wayland and Weston to Stony

Figure 15-15. Cutting's delivery wagon was photographed at the 1913 Bicentennial parade.

Figure 15-16. Cutting's Store sold dry goods, grain, woodenware, agricultural tools, and "virtually everything that the average farm and household needed" except perishable items. (Photo c. 1913)

> Brook, where connection was made with Fitchburg railroad to Boston. . . . Its arrival at Cutting's store was an event of prime importance to the good people, for it formed the connecting link between them and the great, active, busy world.[39]

The article tells how farmers gathered at Cutting's each evening. With the excuse of getting the mail or evening paper, they would ride two miles to the village. To give their old mares a rest, they sat on boxes or barrels for an hour or more, telling "quaint" stories and talking about the crops, the weather, and town affairs. The reporter reflected, "It was wonderful how well informed they kept by this mutual interchange of thought and opinion."

As to what Cutting carried in merchandise, the reporter declined to attempt a list:

> If there is anything you want ask for it and it will be forthcoming, for what appears to the spectator inextricable confusion is a blessed realm of order to the storekeeper who knows just where everything is placed. Do you desire a list of articles? Even Mr. Cutting's intellect fails in attempting to enumerate them.[40]

Brent Dickson in *Once Upon a Pung* provides a few details on the stock and atmosphere of the country general store:

> Without being too nostalgic about Cutting's, we might recall the hand-driven coffee grinder with its red cast iron wheels that kept spinning after the job was done, and the aroma of coffee that temporarily filled the air; the bins behind the counter from which sugar, rice, dried fruits and other staples were scooped onto the scales; and finally the oily smell in the back room from kerosene that had slopped over while the customers' gallon cans were being filled. There was always a box of small potatoes beside the kerosene drum which were used for sealing off the spouts, preventing leakage on the way home.[41]

Figure 15-17. George Fiske was photographed in January 1901 walking west along Boston Post Road at the edge of what is now the town green. Notice the elm trees lining the roadway and the small tailor shop erected by the Lamson family about 1817. In the early 20th century, it was used as a harness shop. When the present town green was created, this building was moved west to the commercial center.

Dickson described the goods as primarily groceries but also a great variety of nearly everything else except cigarettes, which were "for city dudes—not for genuine down-to-earth Yankees like we raised in Weston!"

This description of George W. Cutting comes from the 1888 newspaper article:

> Behind the counter, bustling from place to place to meet the wants of different customers, is a rather stout, well-built man, bare-headed, dressed in shirt sleeves and overalls . . . his features are finely molded, his face is friendly, good-looking and intelligent, with a clear pathway along the top of his head as if a snowplough had gone through there.

The same clerks wore the same faded linen coats year after year. Everyone's credit was honored, a policy that many considered the direct cause of the store's subsequent downfall.

The esteem felt by the community toward George W. Cutting was felt also for his son Alfred Leslie Cutting, who was a selectman for 25 years and held state and county offices. His obituary paid tribute to his long service to the community:

> Simple in his habits, genial in manner, with a quiet humor that lightened the day's work for others as well as for himself, he was possessed of a fund of sound common sense which made him valuable to the town of Weston, with which he was identified throughout his life, and to the county which he served intelligently and well.[42]

First Parish Church, 1865–1885

Rev. Edmund Hamilton Sears (1810–1876) came to First Parish as an associate pastor in 1865 and took over after Joseph Field's death in 1869. During his tenure, the church constructed a combined chapel and parish hall behind the 1840 church, used from 1873 until the present parish hall was constructed in 1924. In 1866, the First Parish Benevolent Society was established on the foundation of an earlier charitable society.[43] The clock in the steeple was installed in 1875. It was a donation from Gen. Charles Jackson Paine to the town, which voted to place it in the most conspicuous place, providing, of course, that the church agreed.[44]

After Edmund Sears's death in 1876, his wife, Ellen Bacon Sears, continued to work tirelessly on behalf of First Parish for the next 21 years. She shared her house just east of the church with her son, Horace, who perhaps more than any other single parishioner influenced the history of the church and provided the impetus for every building improvement from the 1880s through the 1920s.

In 1877, the church finally built a parsonage. After the short ministries of Rev. Francis B. Hornbrooke and Rev. Hobart Clark, the church called Charles F. Russell, an energetic leader who served from 1882 to 1916. Russell was interested in civic as well as church affairs and added his influential support to progressive reforms of the late 19th and early 20th centuries. He headed the Village Improvement Society and was a member of the school committee, where he was a prime mover behind the

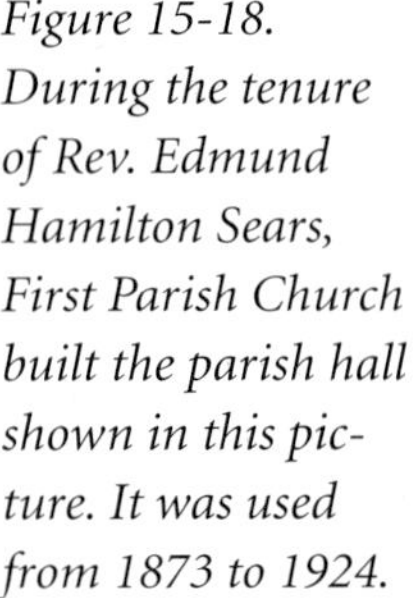

Figure 15-18. During the tenure of Rev. Edmund Hamilton Sears, First Parish Church built the parish hall shown in this picture. It was used from 1873 to 1924.

centralization of Weston's schools and the development of a system of wagons to transport the children. He helped establish the Weston Golf Club and town swimming pool. The E.H. Sears Guild (organized in 1892), volunteer choir (organized in 1895), and Women's Alliance (organized in 1898) were founded during his ministry. *The First Parish Calendar* was printed monthly from 1893 to 1896. Its motto was "That we may all be one" and it functioned not only as a source of church news but also as a way for Russell, as editor in chief, to explain and promote town improvements.

One of the first problems addressed during the Russell ministry was the question of repairing the wooden church, which, according to building committee records, "had become very shabby and its appearance . . . not at all creditable to the intelligence and zeal of the society."[45] The church considered the cost for repairs and decided instead to build something new. In 1884, after prolonged debate, the congregation voted that "the parish build a new church edifice of stone, its cost not to exceed $10,000, provided $8,000 are pledged during the ensuing year and the full amount of $10,000 before the building is begun."[46]

Figure 15-19. Rev. Charles F. Russell came to First Parish in 1882. In his 33 years of dynamic leadership, the present stone church was built, the E.H. Sears Guild and Friendly Society were established, and the monthly First Parish Calendar *was published, with Russell as editor in chief. He organized a vocal quartet, which became the genesis of the present choir. His wife, Mary Rogers Russell, was an enthusiastic worker and founder of the Women's Alliance.*

Figure 15-20. The influence of Rev. Charles Russell (rear, with beard) extended to the larger community. He was involved in building the town's first swimming pool, founding the Weston Golf Club, and promoting the Village Improvement Society. He served from 1891 to 1898 on the Weston School Committee, where he was a strong advocate for centralized schools. Pictured with him in this 1890s photograph are Emma Ripley (second row, third from left), Alice Jones (fourth), and Rebecca McKenna (eighth).

Why a stone church? Church tradition holds that Horace Sears, with William H. Coburn, had traveled to England in 1883 and must certainly have seen the stone church at North Hinksey near Oxford. Sears used his considerable influence to persuade fellow parishioners to build a stone church despite protestations that such a structure was in the Anglican, not the Unitarian, tradition.

Horace Sears, William H. Coburn, and Miss Elizabeth Gowing were appointed to solicit contributions and given a year to raise $8,000. According to church records, "It was easy to obtain a few large subscriptions at first from the friends of the enterprise but there were periods when it seemed well-nigh impossible to arouse any sustained interest in the parish at large."[47] At the end of the year, the committee had raised $8,070, just $70 over the threshold needed to begin.

Founding of the First Parish Friendly Society

One outgrowth of the fund-raising was the formation of the First Parish Friendly Society in January 1885. As the fund-raising committee was approaching its April deadline to meet the initial $8,000 goal, 13 church members responded to an invitation to meet at the Sears home to form a social organization for First Parish.[48] Horace Sears was elected president; Mrs. E.O. Clark, vice president; Robert Winsor, treasurer; and Miss Ellen Jones, secretary. All four lived within a few hundred yards of the church. The Friendly Society's objective was "to encourage friendly relations among members of the First Parish of Weston and to promote the growth and prosperity of said Parish."[49]

At its first meeting, the society pledged $300 toward the building campaign. Two years later, in the Friendly Society's first formal report, organizers noted that this pledge had been given "at a critical period of that enterprise":

> The subscription committee can undoubtedly testify to the moral support and impetus given to the movement at a time when the faith of the few was being shaken and the doubts of the many developing into open and conscientious opposition.[50]

The report added, "We confidently claim that this formative period has been with us an exceptionally brilliant one."

Subsequent entertainment served the dual purpose of increasing social and cultural opportunities and raising money for the new church building. Soon the society was offering twice-monthly events including theatricals, lectures, variety shows, holiday parties, dances and games, poetry readings, and debates. The active organization added greatly to the social life of the town.

Architecture of the Stone Church

Once the initial fund-raising goal was reached, the church appointed a building committee consisting of Horace Sears, Edward Coburn, Justin Gale, Everett O. Clark, and Mrs. Charles Jackson Paine. Someone offered a prize of $25 for a design of moderate cost,

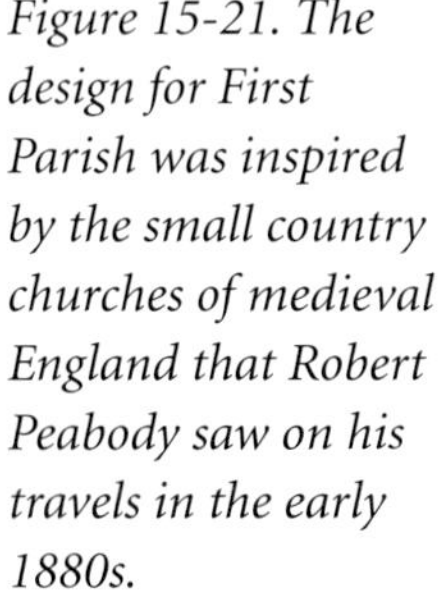

Figure 15-21. The design for First Parish was inspired by the small country churches of medieval England that Robert Peabody saw on his travels in the early 1880s.

but the results evidently did not please the committee, which voted at its first meeting to employ Peabody and Stearns. Not only was Robert Peabody an eminent Boston architect, but he was also the son of the Unitarian minister at King's Chapel in Boston. The reasons for the choice are clearly stated in the record:

> *First,* no architects in Boston stand higher in their profession than Peabody and Stearns. Their work is specially characterized by its solidity, strength and simple elegance.
>
> *Secondly:* Mr. Peabody read a paper before the last Unitarian National Conference in which he laid special stress upon the feasibility of building simple and inexpensive country churches that at the same time should be pretty and attractive. This idea ran exactly in the line of our wishes.
>
> *Thirdly:* Mr. Peabody might feel a deeper personal interest in the work from his relations with some individual members of the committee, being a college classmate of one and a personal friend of another.
>
> *Fourthly,* owing to the comparatively small amount of money to be expended, any church that will be built would contain features and limitations that would elicit criticism more or less severe. It would thus be of obvious advantage to be able to fall back upon the authority of an architect of recognized preeminence in his profession, in questions or arrangements and good taste. [51]

As a result of his own travels to England in 1882, Peabody had acquired an interest in the small country churches of medieval Britain. The picturesque design for First Parish was an early example of the more archaeological type of church that became popular in this country at the turn of the century.[52] Another example by Peabody and Stearns, considered by some to be their finest, is Christ Church on Main Street in Waltham, built about 10 years later.

First Parish is not a copy of a particular English country church but rather contains elements that could be labeled Anglo-Saxon, Gothic, Norman, Romanesque, Queen Anne Revival, and even American Colonial. It was Peabody's genius that he was able to take different stylistic elements and put them together in a way that was uniquely his. The result was a totally original design that suited the site, the building requirements, and the church's pocketbook.

One of the design problems was where to put the clock, as the tower—for economical reasons—had to be low. The record states that "at length [Peabody] submitted a plan which he felt contained the best work he could do under the circumstances and with which he was satisfied both from an artistic and economical point of view."[53]

The final design didn't satisfy everyone. One point of contention was the location of the building on the site. Most church members wanted it set farther back from the street than was the 1840 church. Instead, Peabody placed it slightly forward. The committee stood behind its architect:

> . . . Mr. Peabody's judgment was the best possible authority in the matter and . . . it would be most unwise to run any risk of seriously injuring the architecture . . . by striving to meet a popular demand founded more upon sentiment than upon calm and unbiased judgment.[54]

Peabody's placement increased the visual impact of the building.

The building committee stayed with the original design even as estimates came in far above the $10,000 limit. Committee members tried to save money. They asked the builder for a credit for any stone provided by the church. They hired a workman to deliver stones from the land of several Weston residents, including James Case and Gen. C.J. Paine. Thus the story that local people provided stones from their fields is true, to some extent. Also true is the story about children gathering stones at the seashore. A newspaper item reported, "A party of twelve went to Nahant Wednesday to gather pebbles for the vestibule of the church. They got 25,000. Another trip will be made to Gloucester in order to procure other colors. All interested are invited to assist. About 25,000 more are wanted."[55]

In the end, the committee was able to get the funds it needed. Indeed, in one report members wrote, "We wish most emphatically to deny the oft repeated assertion that we have more money than we want."[56] They noted that generous contributions had enabled them to build a "far handsomer church than hoped for at first," but a few hundred dollars more would still be useful to beautify the interior. The largest individual contributors, for amounts over $500, were Mr. and Mrs. James B. Case, Charles H. Fiske, Ellen Bacon Sears, Horace Sears, Mrs. Charles Jackson Paine, and General Paine himself. Francis Henry Hastings, owner of the Hook & Hastings Company, donated the original organ. The fact that First Parish was able to build such a fine church is a reflection of the increasing wealth of the parish in the late 19th century. The church was justly proud of its accomplishment, as stated in the church records:

> The new church will be a much finer building than we originally thought it possible or wise to erect. . . . [T]he church will be a credit to our parish and town. Its erection will undoubtedly prove quite a stimulus to the denominational

Figure 15-22. This photograph shows the interior of First Parish as originally constructed. The choir loft had a green curtain and brass rail to hide the choir and organist. The stained-glass window was later replaced.

> interests in our conference and state, [and] will attract favorable comment from many quarters.[57]

Many parishioners objected to the brick interior finish, feeling it would be damp and unhealthy. The building committee countered that, on the contrary, it would be dry and warm in winter and cool in summer, and that the artistic effect was, of course, a matter of taste. Again the committee held its ground. Both of the original stained-glass windows were eventually replaced. The Tiffany window at the southwest end, one of the church's prized possessions, was installed in 1899.[58]

Pews were still assigned in the new church, although they were rented rather than owned. A committee report of 1892 explained that the church was not yet ready to give up assigned seating because "the old custom of family occupancy and privacy at church has too strong a hold upon the society to be abrogated."[59] Free pew seating was not adopted until 1917.

The stone church was completed in 1888. To landscape the site, the church chose Charles Eliot, who, at age 28, was well launched on a short but brilliant career as a landscape architect and champion of open space preservation. Eliot's landscape plan called for native plants appropriate to the rural setting:

> ... the gentle slopes ... are as yet only grassed, but the next planting season will see masses of Mountain Laurel, and of wild Roses, Sumacs, and Barberries, set about the foot of the walls—native plants beside the native boulders.[60]

In a letter, Eliot writes that "chance and nature" fixed the crossroads in this unusual pattern but "wise design" placed the church upon the rise of ground and built it of the "rough stones of the New England fields." He concludes, "Many a village, both within and without this New England, might draw a useful lesson from Weston."[61]

Building the New Library and Planning for an Improved Town Center

By the late 1880s, town leaders were gathering support for a new library to accommodate a collection that had grown to nearly 8,000 volumes. Influential proponents included Horace Sears, who became a library trustee in 1887, and estate owner Francis Blake, who was first elected to the board of selectman in 1890 and every year donated his salary as a board member to the library.

Blake put his brother-in-law, Charles Wells Hubbard, on the committee to select a site. The committee's report of 1892 pointed to the need for an overall plan for the town center:

> . . . before erecting such a building, the town should have some comprehensive plan for laying out its central group of public and private buildings; and some general idea of the style of architecture to be used. So that, when the plan is fully

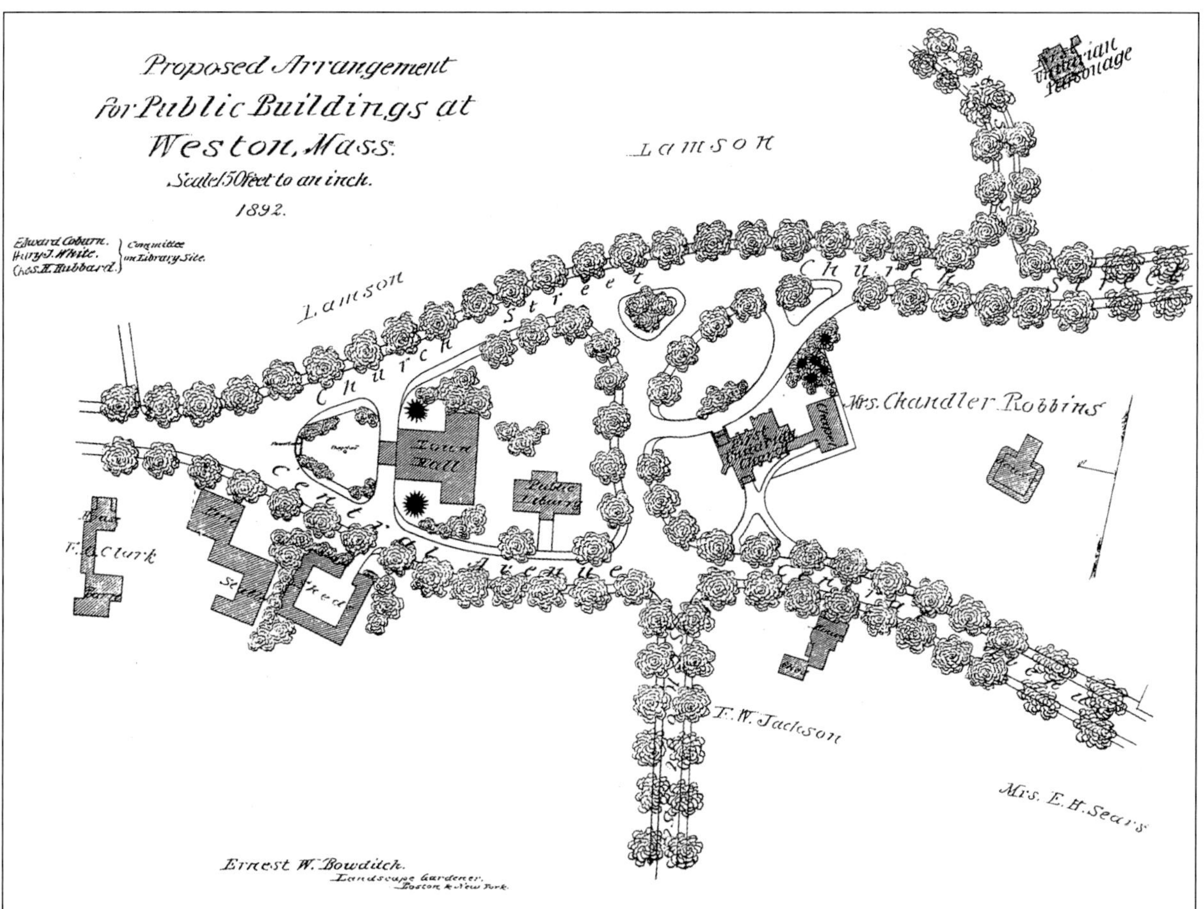

Figure 15-23. This plan by landscape gardener Ernest W. Bowditch appeared in the 1892 town report. It represents the first attempt to redesign the town center and find sites for a new town hall and library. Bowditch was related by marriage to estate owners Charles W. Hubbard and Francis Blake.

> developed, we may have our public and semi-public buildings so arranged as to best minister to the needs of the town, and foster our pride in Weston.[62]

Because the town was going to need both a library and a new town hall, the committee employed Ernest W. Bowditch to prepare a master plan and warned that "unless such action be soon taken, the harmonious grouping of our future buildings, and the beauty of their surroundings, may be made impossible."

The selection of Bowditch was undoubtedly influenced by Hubbard and Blake, as Bowditch was Hubbard's brother-in-law and the landscape architect for the Blake estate. Bowditch presented several plans, one of which was published along with the 1892 report. The Bowditch plan anticipates the more elaborate Shurtleff plan of two decades later. Bowditch showed a small common in front of First Parish Church, sited the new library and new town hall within the common, and included a suggested site for an inn. Notice the nostalgia in this rationale for including an inn:

> By locating a village inn upon the plan, your Committee does not mean to suggest that the Town should go into the hotel business. But they do believe that a pretty wayside inn, after the manner of New England fifty years ago, would be an advantage to the Town so that Weston may be able to entertain man and beast, instead of obliging them to move on to the next town.[63]

Figure 15-24. The Cutting family lived at the corner of School Street and Boston Post Road across from their general store. When Charles H. Fiske Jr. heard that the house was to be demolished to make way for the new library, he bought it from the town and moved it to its present site at 36 Church Street.

The 1892 committee report called for buying two houses at the corner of School Street and Boston Post Road, one of which was the historic Josiah Smith Tavern. The town adopted a more conservative approach and in early 1894 purchased just the George W. Cutting house.[64]

Plans for the new library were delayed by the need for a new high school, constructed in 1895–96. Supporters like the Rev. Charles Russell continued to call public attention to the problems of the library, as in this eloquent plea in the March 1896 issue of the *First Parish Calendar:*

> Now the town has bought a fitting and, I think we

> will all agree, the most desirable site. But, behold! What with a new high school house, increased yearly expenses, and the acknowledged need of a town hall, the prospects of a new library building in the near future are not bright. And yet the need is imminent. Already the present accommodations are crowded, and with the future rate of increase in books will be severely taxed at an early date. The extraordinarily narrow escape of two or three years ago only emphasizes the great and constant danger of the destruction of all our books by fire. . . . But, whatever happens, let us hope that the library will not be tucked into the rear of a new town hall. . . . Never, never, let our library creep into our town life through the back door. Dignify it, ennoble it, enthrone it. At any cost make it the great centre of intellectual life, the university of our town—free, accessible, beautiful. [65]

Because of the debt created by the new school, a special committee recommended in early 1899 that the town postpone building a library to avoid an increase in the tax rate "for the reason that such an increase would check that beneficent growth of the town which is due to the advantages it presents to persons of wealth who are in search of suburban homes."[66] But behind the scenes, town leaders overcame objections and the town voted to proceed. Francis Blake, James B. Case, Theodore F. Dwight, Albert H. Hews, and Oliver R. Robbins were appointed to the library building committee.

Rather than hold an architectural competition, a technique that had been used successfully in Wayland, the committee hired Fox, Jenney and Gale on the basis of a letter from Herbert Putnam, former librarian of the Boston Public Library, strongly commending the Boston firm. Two of the three young principals, Thomas A. Fox and Alexander S. Jenney, had been associated with Charles McKim in the construction of the Boston Public Library. [67] The fact that Jenney was a Weston resident undoubtedly worked in the firm's favor.

The building committee was pleased with the design:

> The skill of the Architects is apparent in the beauty of the general design; the peculiar ingenuity with which it has been made to fit most advantageously the irregular topography of the library site and interior arrangements for economical but effective administration. [68]

At a special town meeting on August 24, 1899, residents voted 42 to 8 to authorize borrowing $40,000 for the new building.[69] Work on the library commenced in November 1899 and was completed exactly one year later. By that time, the library contained 12,423 volumes and was open six days a week.

An article in the *Waltham Daily Free Press* after the opening on November 17, 1900, described the new library as a "simple brick and stone structure" that had "the character of old New England Architecture, without following any particular style."[70] In

Figure 15-25. The Weston Public Library moved from its original location in the 1847 town hall to its new building in November 1900. The architectural firm of Fox, Jenney and Gale included local resident Alexander S. Jenney, who is credited with the Jacobethan design.

fact, the style is a variety of English Tudor now referred to as Jacobethan, based on formal English building traditions of the late medieval period. The stone trim is Indiana limestone.

On the first floor, the large reading room was lighted on three sides by mullioned windows and featured exposed oak beams and walls tinted green with bands of white and red. The children's alcove was to the right of the main entrance and bookshelves were located in the rear ell. Basement space was allocated for future book storage and a fireproof storage room for town records. Above the children's room was a small office for the trustees.

The new library had an open stack system where patrons could browse and choose their own books. The Dewey decimal system was adopted to help patrons locate their own books. The newspaper article noted that book capacity was lower with an open stack system, thus explaining what to some was the excessive cost of the building. In the 1900 town report, library trustees noted that "it hardly seems natural to close this report without asking for a new Library building as has been their invariable custom for the last ten years. But the munificent action of the Town has now forever removed this necessity."[71]

Miss Elizabeth S. White, who succeeded librarian John Coburn in 1893, oversaw planning and construction. At her death in 1903, she was praised for her unfailing courtesy and kindness, remarkable efficiency, and literary judgment. She was succeeded by her assistant, Miss Maude M. Pennock, who served from 1903 to 1939 and was considered "a principal factor in bringing the Library to an outstanding position as a small-town library."[72]

The library had a Kendal Green branch in the vestry of the Methodist church from 1912 to about 1927. Books were replaced from time to time and delivered on request. At the main library, the children's alcove became so popular that in 1912 the trustees called for its enlargement. Space in the lower level became available in 1918 when the town clerk moved to the new town hall. Encouraged by a gift of $5,000 from library trustee Miss Louisa Case, the space was remodeled in 1922 into a children's room named for her niece, Rosamond Freeman. Margaret E. Mosher was the first children's librarian, a position she held for 42 years, until 1962. Another service provided by the library, beginning in 1901, was the display of picture collections circulated by the Massachusetts Library Art Club.

The Ellen Sears Fund was set up in the will of long-time library trustee Horace Sears, who died in 1923. The income was to be spent "for the assistance of the Librarian or Librarians or her or his assistants in case of sickness or for vacation expenses as an addition to and never a part of their regular salaries." [73]

Figure 15-26. The interior walls of the new reading room were tinted green with bands of white and red.

Figure 15-27. Miss Elizabeth White succeeded John Coburn as librarian in 1893. At her death in 1903, at the young age of 38, the library committee wrote: "Her judgment of books . . . [was] almost unerring. . . . She was never so happy as when serving others and assisting them in their search for the book that would best meet their requirements."

The Jones House and Businesses in the Town Center (1850–1915)

In discussing development in Weston Center, it is important to note that, until World War I and even later, the center included a mixture of residential, commercial, and institutional uses. In the era before zoning regulations, houses were adapted for business use and sometimes converted back to residences. Also of note is the fact that the commercial center lies between a granite ridge on the north side and a large peat bog to the south, a problem that has influenced its development from the early days to the present.

Businesses came and went. This section will focus on those that were better known in the decades before the redesign of the town center. Cutting's

Figure 15-28. Originally constructed by Josiah Smith, this historic mid-18th-century tavern was purchased in 1842 by John and Marshall Jones. John's son, Theodore, painted and trimmed carriages in the adjacent barn. Theodore married George W. Cutting's sister Sarah, and their two unmarried daughters, Alice and Ellen, were well known in town.

Figure 15-29 (above). The Jones family and neighbors relax on the porch of the Jones house (Josiah Smith Tavern) in the late 19th century: from left, Emma L. Cutting, Ellen M. Jones, Harriet F. Stimpson, John Jones Jr., Theodore Jones, and Alice E. Jones.

Store moved in mid-century to the prime location next to the town hall. Just west of Cutting's was a small tailor shop owned by the Lamson family and later used as a harness shop and millinery store.

On the south side of the town square, John and Marshall Jones purchased the former Josiah Smith Tavern in 1842.[74] The brothers owned a prosperous paint and harness-making business down the street and were men of considerable wealth.[75] The historic tavern passed to John's son, Theodore, whose carriage painting and trimming operation was housed in the barn. Theodore married George W. Cutting's sister Sarah, and their two daughters, Alice and Ellen, were well known in town. According to Brenton H. Dickson III, in *Once Upon a Pung*, Miss Ellen was quiet and shy and wore dark spectacles that made her look more severe than she really was, while Miss

Figure 15-30 (left). Joel Upham built this house next to his blacksmith shop in 1855. The rear ell is earlier in date. Joel's daughter, Carolyn, married Arthur Stoddard Burrage, and the house is still occupied by members of the Burrage family. The 1898 photograph shows the original porch and front yard. When Boston Post Road was widened in the late 1950s, part of the front yard was taken and the present high stone retaining wall constructed.

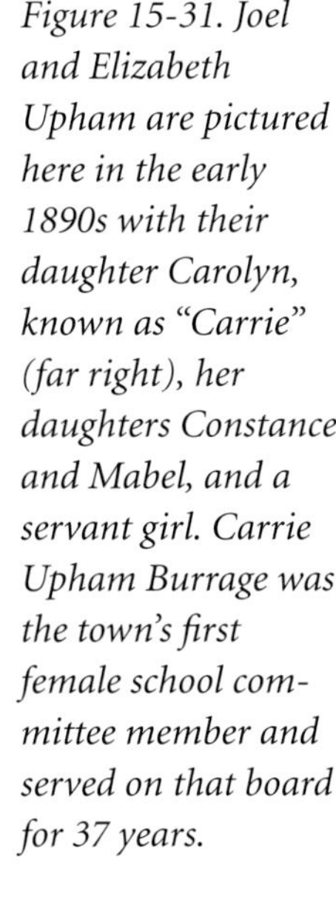

Figure 15-31. Joel and Elizabeth Upham are pictured here in the early 1890s with their daughter Carolyn, known as "Carrie" (far right), her daughters Constance and Mabel, and a servant girl. Carrie Upham Burrage was the town's first female school committee member and served on that board for 37 years.

Figure 15-32. Philip, youngest child of Carrie and Arthur Burrage, had an established Saturday Evening Post *route in the center and won several prizes for the number of magazines he sold, according to Phil Coburn's* Growing Up in Weston.

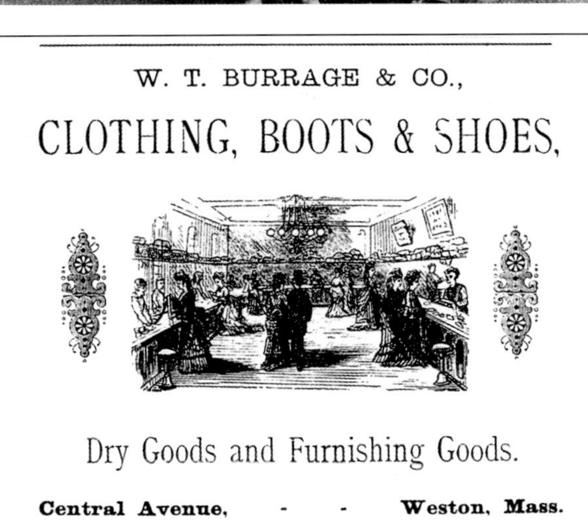

Figure 15-33. William T. Burrage operated a dry-goods store in the Coburn block from 1885 until 1917. The family lived above the store.

Alice was small, lively, and extroverted. Alice was involved in nearly every civic and social event in town, and, according to Dickson, "those . . . who didn't know her could be counted on the fingers of one hand."[76]

Farther west in what is presently the commercial center, Joel Upham took over a blacksmith shop formerly operated by Ebenezer Brackett and practiced his trade for 57 years, from 1830 to 1887. His obituary called him "the best known smithy between Boston and Worcester."[77] The shop was demolished in 1889 and another blacksmith across the street took up the business. After Upham's death in 1895, his house was left to his daughter, Carolyn "Carrie" Elizabeth Upham, and her husband, Arthur Stoddard Burrage. Carrie Burrage was the first female member of the Weston School Committee. She served for 37 years, from 1894 to 1931, including 30 years as chairman.[78]

Arthur's older brother, William T. Burrage, ran a dry-goods store across the street. Burrage's store, which advertised its founding date as 1885, continued in business until his death in 1917. He sold boots and shoes, clothing, "gent's furnishing goods," and "dry and fancy goods." The family lived above the store.

W.T. Burrage & Co. was located in the Coburn Building, a group of three connected stores built after the Civil War by farmer Edward Coburn on his four acres on the south side of Boston Post Road. In the early 1890s, the stores were occupied by Burrage, C.L. Keefe, who was a hay and grain dealer, and harness maker William Wark.[79] A fire in 1893, said to be the largest in the history of the town, destroyed the business block, with damage estimated at $21,300. Townspeople were troubled because this and another fire two months earlier were deliberately set. Despite a posted reward of $500, the identity of the arsonist was never discovered.[80]

Coburn rebuilt the stores as a single business block, which housed a variety of stores over the years

Figure 15-34. Weston Hand Laundry advertised "Fine Hand Work of All Kinds Done Promptly." This picture was taken about 1915 at the Hersum block on Boston Post Road. The storefronts of this commercial building were changed in the 1920s and the entire building was extensively remodeled in 1989.

Figure 15-35. The Coburn building, Weston's first "business block," is shown here about 1895–96. At that time the three storefronts were occupied by a grocer, the W.T. Burrage dry-goods store, and W.G. Wark, harness maker. The building still stands at 450-456 Boston Post Road.

including a drugstore, grocery, and combined ice-cream parlor and lunchroom. In 1898 Benjamin R. Parker started selling hardware, paints and oils, seeds, and bicycles and bicycle sundries. Parker also repaired bicycles and, as early as 1905, was busy with automobile repairs as well. A 1906 newspaper item noted that "Mr. Parker's automobile garage is so full that the next one that comes will have to go on the roof."[81] Later his brother, Horace, ran an auto and small appliance repair place in back.[82] For many years Parker's had a Socony gas pump. As with other gasoline pumps at the time, the fuel was pumped into a glass ball at the top of the dispenser and then was gravity-fed into the car gas tank.

Redesign of the Town Center

In 1911, with the approach of Weston's Bicentennial, town pride was running high. Benjamin Loring Young, an influential proponent of town planning, succeeded his uncle Francis Blake as selectman. Young later described the impetus behind the town improvement plan:

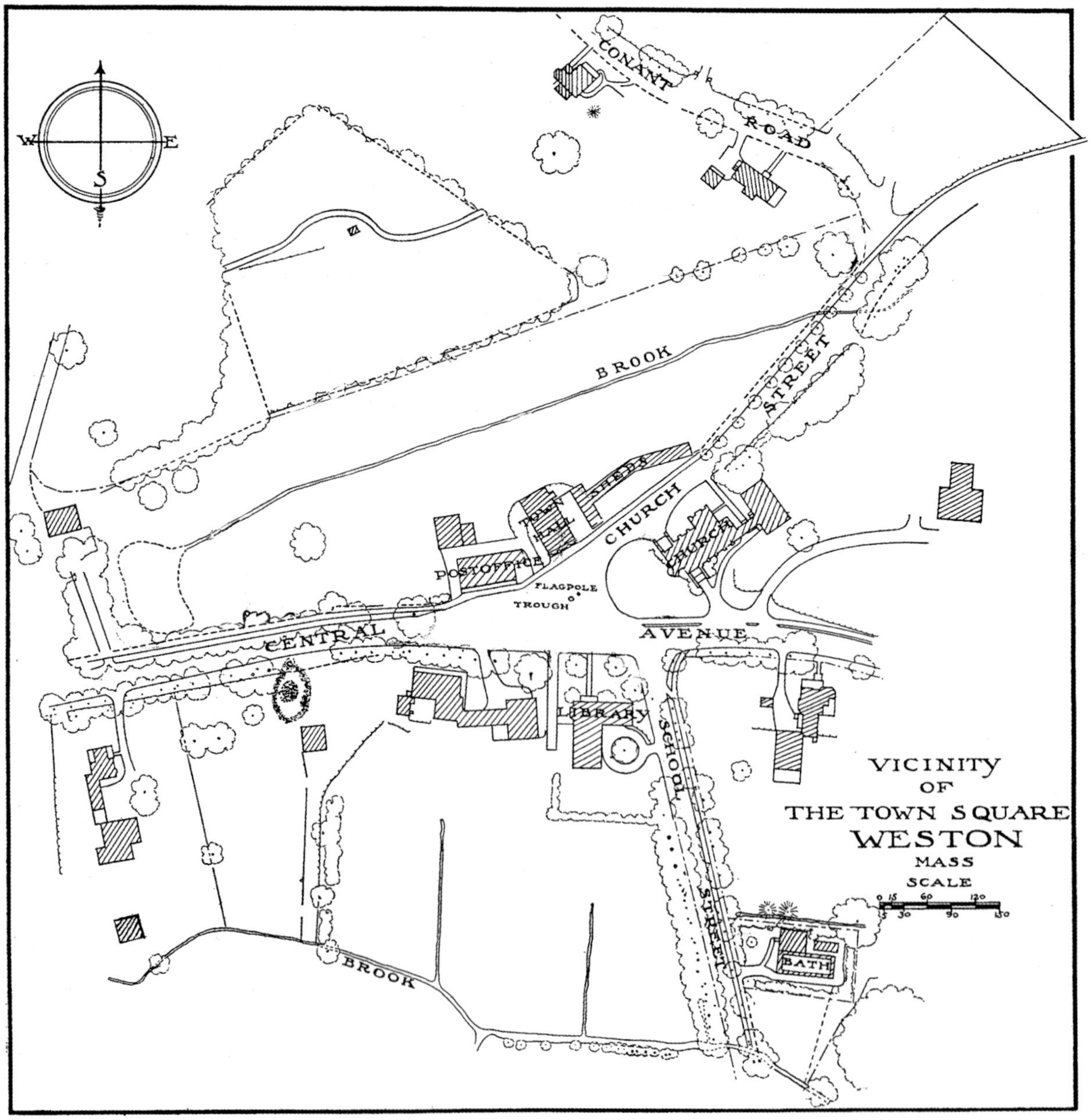

Figure 15-36. This map was prepared about 1911 to allow residents to submit their own ideas for an improved town center. Note the location of the town pool, labeled "Bath."

> There was no desire to disturb the rural simplicity of the town, but many persons felt that we should anticipate future growth and so arrange the centre of Weston that its beauty could never be marred by squalor or congestion. Towns are bound to expand and develop, municipal buildings must be built, open spaces, commons, or parks provided. The people of Weston decided to make plans in advance, believing that by so doing they could avoid incongruous growth and assure a sound and consistent evolution.[83]

Another prime mover was Alfred L. Cutting, chairman of the board of selectmen in the early 1910s. Because Cutting's Store was the only major business to be displaced, his support was critical. Horace Sears was also a leader in creating the new town common and building the new town hall.

At Town Meeting in 1911, a Committee on Improvement of the Center of the Town of Weston was formed, consisting of Charles F. Richardson, B.H. Dickson Jr., Alexander S. Jenney, Benjamin S. Blake, and B.L. Young.[84] They sent out maps of the town square, asking residents to ponder the needs and present their ideas. The committee expressed its goals as follows:

> 1st. Changes in roads . . . to reduce or avoid the dangers and noises incident to the use of motor vehicles. 2nd. The attainment of a village common or green, always found in the best types of old New England villages. 3rd. The provision of suitable locations for Town Buildings . . . each . . . surrounded by generous open spaces. 4th. The resolution of all the above problems . . . into one simple, reasonable, beautiful, lasting scheme.[85]

The town improvement committee hired Arthur Asahel Shurtleff (later Shurcliff), who by that time was well established as a landscape architect. Shurtleff (1870–1957) was born in Boston and graduated from MIT in 1894 with a degree in engineering. He did two years of graduate work in architecture, landscape architecture, and civil engineering before joining the firm of Frederick Law Olmsted in 1896. In 1898 he took the first of many study tours in Europe urged by his mentor, Charles Eliot, in order to familiarize himself with European design and planning.[86] In 1900 he aided Frederick Law Olmsted Jr. in establishing the first four-year landscape architecture program in America at Harvard University, where he taught until 1906. Shurtleff was one of the earliest members of the American Society of Landscape Architects, a professional society founded in 1899 by Olmsted and other pioneers in the field, and was made a fellow of the society in 1905. He opened his own office in November 1904. One of his first commissions was the Italian garden at the Horace Sears estate, Haleiwa. Sears was undoubtedly influential in the choice of Shurtleff for the Weston project.

During his long and distinguished career, Shurtleff did major work in the fields of town planning, engineering, and landscape and park design. He worked for the Metropolitan District Commission on development of the Quabbin Reservoir and for the Metropolitan Planning Board in Boston. He was chief landscape architect for the restoration at Colonial Williamsburg from its inception in 1928 until

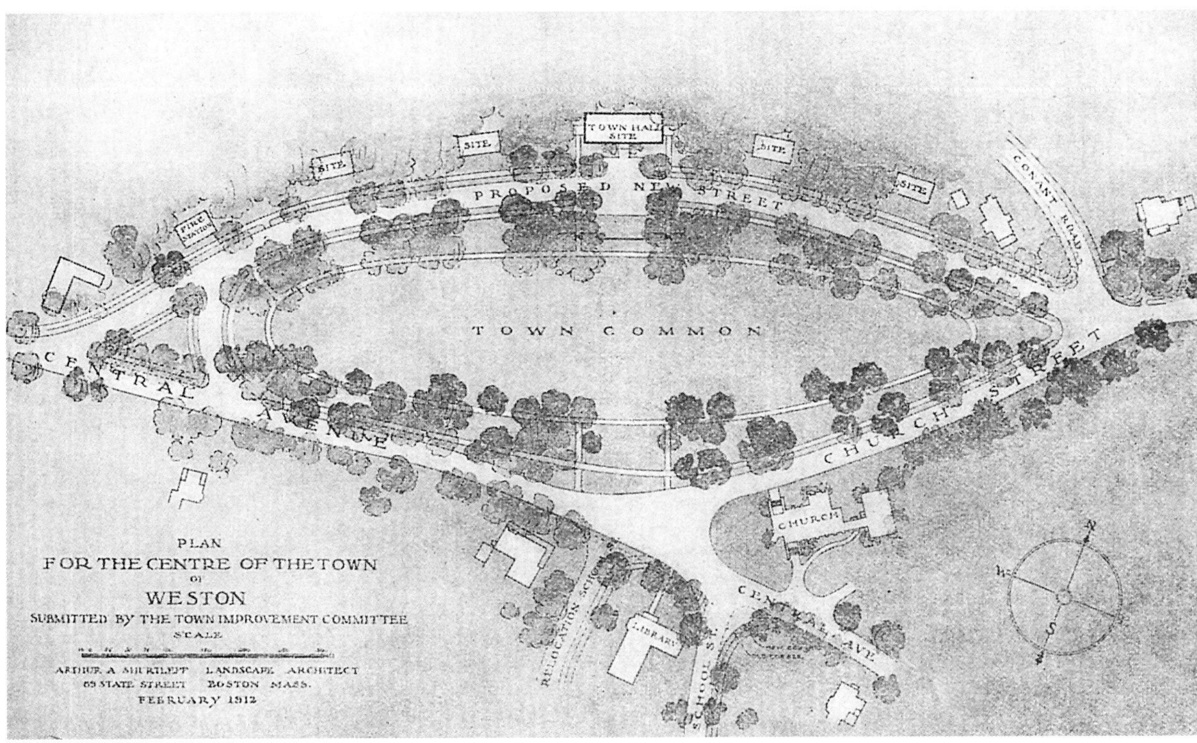

Figure 15-37. Landscape architect Arthur Shurtleff (who later changed his last name to Shurcliff) submitted this preliminary plan for the town center in February 1912. It shows six sites for buildings around a proposed town common.

1941, and did the original layout for Old Sturbridge Village. After a trip to England in 1929, he changed the spelling of his name to the more Anglican "Shurcliff."

Reflecting the influence of Frederick Law Olmsted Sr., the Shurtleff town common plan preserves the natural contours of the land, creates an open greensward surrounded by scattered groves of trees, and uses native trees, shrubs, and ground covers to create a naturalistic environment. Plantings included common barberry, dogwood, common hazelnut, witch hazel, viburnums, and woodbine.[87] The plan demonstrates Shurtleff's practical nature and engineering training. By moving a stream underground, he was able to dry out the existing swamp. A new road improved traffic circulation and isolated the four-acre common as a distinct entity.

Shurtleff helped convince town residents of the need for the town common plan. In a letter published in the 1912 *Town Report,* he expressed his enthusiasm:

> In my opinion, the execution of this scheme would give Weston a Town Common of remarkable individuality and in many respects the finest open space of its kind in the Commonwealth.[88]

To this positive vision he added a warning:

> This plan would also guard the town against congestion at the centre and also avoid further traffic dangers, and at the same time head off the growth of a slum district in the wet land behind the present Town-hall.[89]

The selectmen, always mindful of attracting new residents with new taxable property, embraced the notion of creating the finest town common in Massachusetts. Still, fiscal conservatism is evident in their comment that the plan "will not entail the erection of a new and expensive Town-house." Since the present town hall was "entirely adequate for our needs," it could be moved, renovated, and repainted white.[90] In 1912–13, the town adopted the Town Improvement Plan and began the taking by eminent domain of 11 acres held by eight different owners including Horace Sears, Charles F. Richardson, and members of the Lamson family.

Figure 15-38. As part of the Town Improvement Plan, a central fire station was constructed in 1914. In choosing the Georgian Revival style, architect Alexander Jenney carried out the New England village theme.

The "Engine House" and "Town House"

With the Town Improvement Plan complete and the land secured, the town voted in 1914 to build the much needed "engine house." The fire department was eager to proceed so it could buy a motorized fire truck to replace the outdated, horse-drawn version stored in the basement of the 1847 town hall. The new three-stall brick firehouse was designed by Alexander S. Jenney, who earlier had designed the new library. Jenney used the Georgian Revival style to carry out the ideal of the New England village. Some $16,500 was spent for the building, which was completed in late 1914.

In 1915 the town appointed a new town improvement committee consisting of Horace S. Sears, chairman; and David W. Lane, Frank W. Knowlton, B. Loring Young, and Everett A. Brotchie. Brotchie's place was later taken by B.H. Dickson Jr. This committee oversaw the work of draining the swamp in 1915 and building the new town hall in 1916–17.

For the design of the town hall, the committee chose Boston architects Bigelow and Wadsworth. The firm was headed by Henry Forbes Bigelow (1867–1929), a leading architect in Boston and designer of distinguished commercial buildings as well as city and country houses for well-known clients.[91] The $95,000 appropriation included a $20,000 contribution from Horace Sears. To keep from going over budget, Sears donated additional funds for lighting fixtures, seating, and even draperies for the new auditorium, which was given the name Sears Hall.[92]

The new Weston Town Hall was dedicated on November 27, 1917, in a ceremony to which all town residents were invited. In his speech, B. Loring Young recognized the role of Sears:

> I cannot close this account of our doings without a word of gratitude to the man who has so greatly helped to make possible the achievement of our ideal. Did I not believe that it would be distasteful to his natural modesty I would attempt to recount his many services, his munificent gifts to the town. Suffice it to say that except for his bounty, this Town-house, had it been built at all at this time, which is doubtful, would not now be lighted by these beautiful electric fixtures, nor would you ladies and gentlemen be seated in those comfortable chairs. For his kindness of heart, for his public spirit and generosity, for his

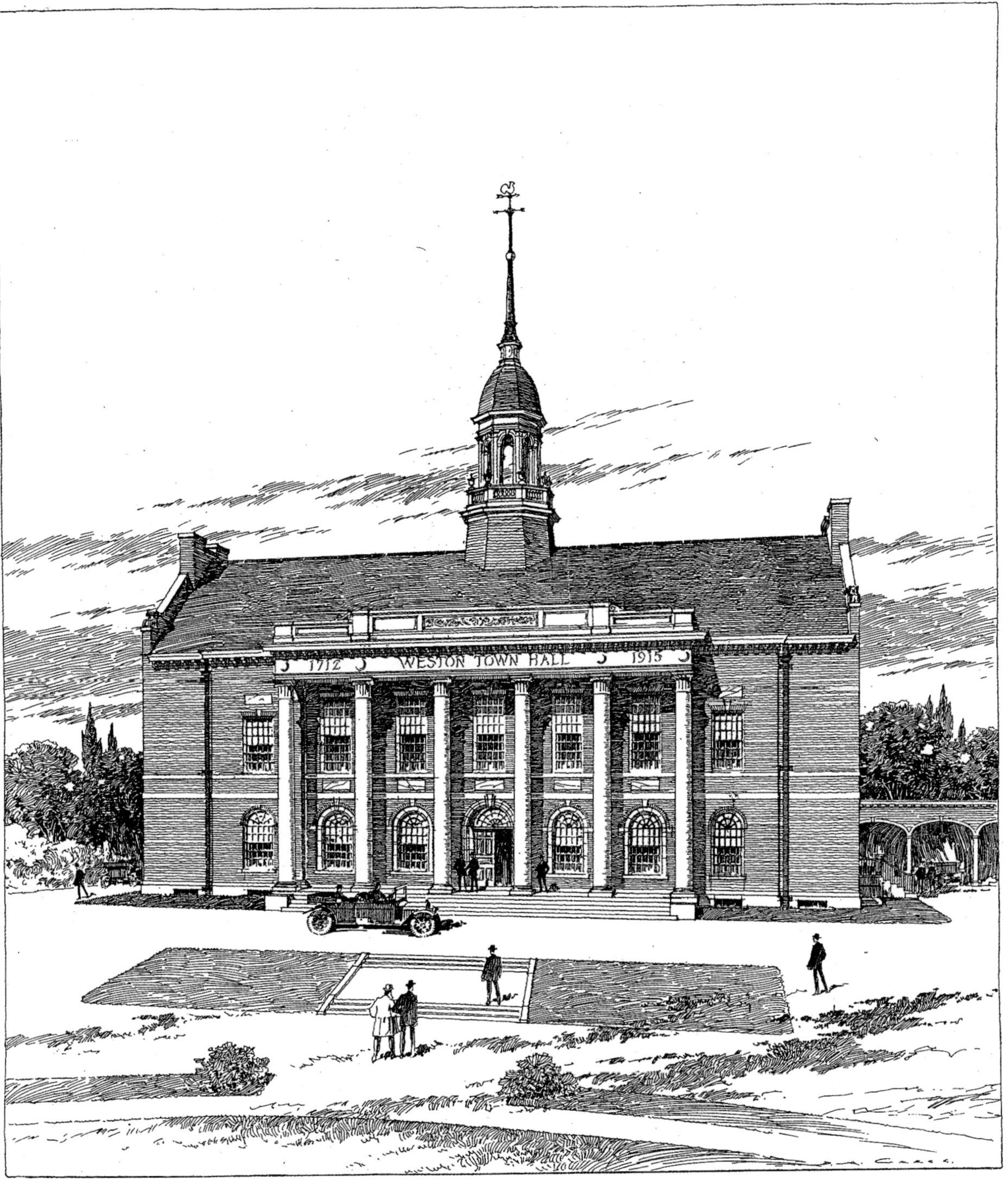

Figure 15-39. Like the fire station, the 1917 Weston Town Hall uses the Georgian Revival style and is built of brick. The Boston architectural firm of Bigelow and Wadsworth designed the new administrative building as the centerpiece of the Town Improvement Plan.

> devoted service to us and our town, we owe to Horace Scudder Sears a debt of love and of gratitude which we shall always remember and which we can never repay. [93]

The Hon. Calvin Coolidge, then lieutenant governor of the Commonwealth, gave the keynote address, in which he praised Weston for looking beyond the utilitarian:

> We are coming to see in these modern days that . . . we need not only utilitarian motives, but that we need to give some time, some thought and attention to the artistic in life; . . . that we need to pay some attention to that which is beautiful as well as to that which is merely useful. [94]

Creating the Town Green

To ensure that the town common plan was executed to his satisfaction, Horace Sears in 1917 secured an appointment as one of three park commissioners. They hired Arthur Shurtleff to prepare additional plans after removal of the old town hall and horse sheds in June 1919. An account in the newspaper remarked that ". . . the razing of the old buildings is opening up a wonderful view from the library, across the Common to the site of the new Hall . . ."[95] Using existing stone retaining walls, Shurtleff created a terrace and overlook on the site of the horse sheds. At the same time, he designed the path across the common, the rectangular bed of trees in front of Town Hall, and the island to the east. The flagpole was

Figure 15-40. While town leaders had initially planned to save money by moving the 1847 town hall and painting it white, that idea was discarded in favor of a new building. This photograph was taken when the venerable old "town house" was demolished in 1919.

moved to the island. New horse sheds were erected on Church Street next to First Parish Church on land belonging to Horace Sears.

In 1919 the park commissioners reported that most of the work on the common had been completed. The loss of the town hall prompted this poignant comment:

> It was with a certain tinge of sadness that the citizens of the town watched the demolition of the old Town Hall with all its precious associations and memories—of merrymakings and parties—of the schoolroom which it sheltered long ago, with its happy school life, exhibitions, and graduation exercises—of the pleasant library room when the library was in its small beginnings—and of patriotic and philanthropic meetings when the walls echoed with eloquent and moving appeals.[96]

Over the years, the town common has been maintained in accordance with the philosophy expressed in the report of the park commissioners in December 1921: "It is our interpretation of the wishes of the Town that it desires a Town Common and not a public Park, and our work has been based upon that understanding." Town officials have guarded against the encroachment of ancillary structures like bandstands and monuments.

Weston gained regional and even national attention for its new "civic center." In the early 1920s, an economist from the Office of Rural Life in the U.S. Department of Agriculture was assigned to prepare a publication showing country villages how to modernize their town centers.[97] He was referred to Arthur Shurtleff, who showed him the Weston plan. "Before" and "after" sketches were published in an article in the USDA *Farmers' Bulletin* called "Re-Planning the Rural Village."[98] In 1929 the town was awarded one of 100 Centennial Silver Medals minted by the Massachusetts Horticultural Society in honor of its 100th anniversary. The award was for "raising the standard in the design and planting of town commons. The common and the colonial town hall which overlooks it are considered models."[99]

In 1926, park commissioners successfully petitioned the town to acquire one more parcel to protect the integrity of the town common. The town appropriated $5,000 to purchase 1.8 acres on the north side of Town House Road from George H.D. Lamson.[100] The old Lamson stable and barn were removed, and since then Lamson Park has been part of the open space that frames Weston Town Hall.

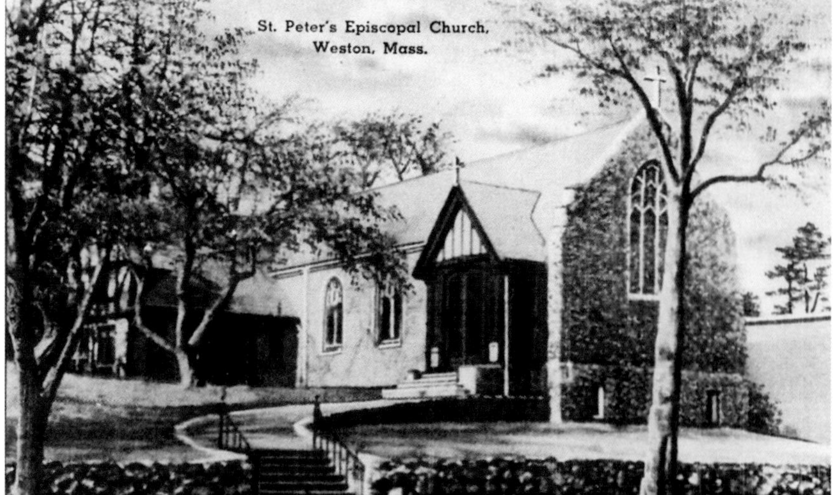

Figure 15-41. St. Peter's Episcopal Church constructed its first building in the town center in 1917. It was purchased by the Church of Christ, Scientist, when St. Peter's moved to its present location.

St. Peter's Episcopal Church and the Christian Science Society of Weston

Episcopal services were first held in Weston in the late 19th century. According to "An Informal Early History of St. Peter's Episcopal Church, Weston," the moving force behind these services was Mary Gilman Lamson (Mrs. Daniel S. Lamson), who was born in England and confirmed in the Anglican Church. Although she attended services at First Parish, the introduction of Unitarian theology weakened her association with that venerable establishment and she began working to form an Episcopal parish.

Discussions and informal prayer services were held at the Schoolhouse on the Rock, formerly District Schoolhouse #1 on Boston Post Road, which was leased from the town for several years.[101] After the schoolhouse was sold in 1901, services were again held in homes including Laxfield, the home of Mrs. George Fiske on Concord Road. The congregation was made up largely of women and people of English origin. The first pastor, Father Papineau, came to Weston about 1902 and served until 1915. He was also pastor at St. George's Church in Maynard. He has been described as "an extremely high churchman, who might even be called a zealot, but everyone liked him within and beyond the Parish."[102] By 1905 the congregation had grown and services were being held in the 1847 town hall once a month in winter and twice in summer.[103]

Figure 15-42. The St. Peter's congregation rejected a contemporary design in favor of this classic New England village church, erected in 1959 at 320 Boston Post Road. (2001 photo)

In 1915, Rev. Frederick Arthur Reeve became priest-in-charge. Although the congregation had contemplated building its own church as early as 1913, the idea gained momentum when it came time to demolish the old town hall. The Lamson family conveyed a portion of land on Boston Post Road just west of their homestead.[104] The church building was designed by Brigham, Coveney and Bisbee to meet the congregation's desire for something "perpendicular Gothic in style, of the type of smaller English parish churches of the fourteen and fifteenth centuries." The cornerstone was laid on November 25, 1917, and services were first held in the still uncompleted building on September 15, 1918.[105] In 1921, St. Peter's Church acquired a rectory at 650 Boston Post Road.

In 1949, Charles O. Richardson, a member of First Parish Church, gave St. Peter's a parcel of land on Boston Post Road near the intersection of the bypass to be used for a new and larger church. Designed by Hoyle, Doran & Barry in a traditional Georgian Colonial style, the new brick building was dedicated in 1958. The congregation sold its original church to the Christian Science Society of Weston, which had been holding services in town since 1950.

St. Julia Roman Catholic Church

The earliest reference to Weston Catholics, in the *History of the Archdiocese of Boston,* lists the town as one of the missions of the new Saxonville parish of 1848. The date coincides with the mid-century emigration of thousands of young men and women from famine-stricken Ireland to New England, where they found work in the homes of prosperous farmers and merchants. At the turn of the century, Weston Catholics wishing to celebrate Mass had to take the train or drive by carriage to Waltham (St. Mary's Church) or Wayland (St. Zepherin's, with St. Ann's as its mission). Two hundred worshipers reportedly attended the first Catholic Mass in Weston, celebrated in Weston Town Hall in 1912. Rev. Timothy Brosnahan, pastor of St. Mary's Church in Waltham, led the service.[106] From 1914 to 1919, St. Mary's maintained a mission in Weston and provided a priest every Sunday to say Mass at services in the town hall.

In 1919, when membership had reached about 100, a parish was established in Weston under Father William J. Foley. Father Foley boarded with a family in the parish and, as there was no Sunday school, walked to houses around town where children gathered for religious instruction. He labored two years to raise money for a church. A building lot was purchased from George W. Cutting Jr. next to the relocated Cutting's Store.[107] Sometimes conflicting stories are told of the involvement of three civic-minded Unitarian estate owners—Horace Sears, Charles Jackson Paine, and Robert Winsor—in helping build a church for their Catholic employees. Protestants joined in fund-raising events like fairs and whist parties and, according to one history, "everyone in town seemed eager to get the Church built."[108] A newspaper item of November 1919 noted:

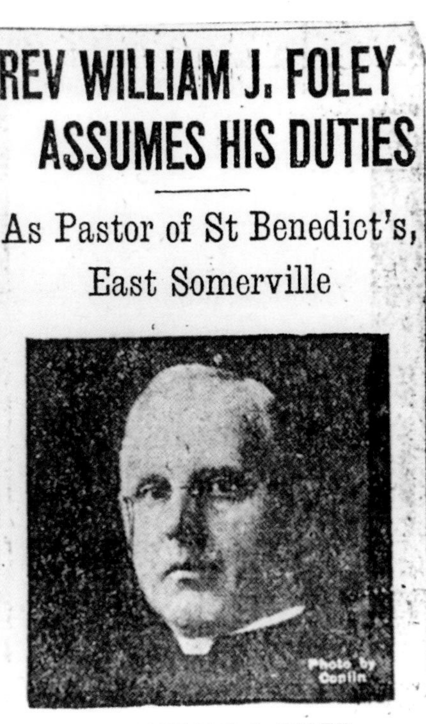

REV WILLIAM J. FOLEY ASSUMES HIS DUTIES

As Pastor of St Benedict's, East Somerville

Photo by Conlin

REV WILLIAM J. FOLEY

Figure 15-43. Father William J. Foley was the first pastor of St. Julia Parish, which was established in 1919. Under his leadership, Weston's Roman Catholics built their own church.

Figure 15-44. St. Julia Church was designed by Maginnis and Walsh, architects of Catholic churches and institutional buildings throughout the country. The first Mass was conducted in the new building on Christmas Day 1921. An addition in 1961–62 increased the length and added a wing off the back.

> . . . the construction of a church building in Weston will be a great convenience to many people and those for whom it is to be built are not over supplied with the world's goods, so help them out.[109]

The "Norman-Gothic" structure was designed by Maginnis and Walsh, a Boston architectural firm nationally known as designers of Catholic churches and institutional buildings. Men of the parish transported local fieldstone by horse and cart from the Cronin farm on Concord Road and the Arthur Coburn land on the north side.[110]

The original church seated 300 and cost $50,000. Father Foley selected the name St. Julia in memory of his mother. According to a church history, St. Julia in Weston may be the only Catholic Church in the country to bear that name. The sculpture over the front door was chiseled from a picture of Julia Foley. The first Mass was conducted at the church on Christmas Day 1921 and the building was officially dedicated in 1922. A two-story house moved to the rear of the church was used as the rectory. Daily Mass was held here in the early years because the sanctuary was heated only on Sundays.

The Holy Name Society was active by the 1940s and the Ladies Sodality, formed in 1942, was reestablished after a wartime hiatus. Under the leadership of Father Frank M. Graf, who served as parish administrator from 1956 to 1960 and then pastor until 1965, the church built a major addition in 1961 designed by Maginnis, Walsh and Kennedy. Stonework was carefully matched, making it difficult to tell exactly where the addition begins at the back of the original building.

The modern era of St. Julia Parish began with the conclusion of Vatican II and the arrival in 1965 of Monsignor Francis Rossiter, who assumed the difficult task of guiding the parish through the turbulent period of Vatican II changes. He organized the St. Julia Women's Club in 1965 to promote cultural and social activities among women of the church. The Thrift Shop, founded by Father Graf, has flourished since 1965 for outreach to the needy in the area. Monsignor Rossiter built a new rectory in 1971–72 and wanted to build a parish center; but most new construction in the archdiocese had been halted at the time because of debt accumulated during the building boom of the 1960s. Under the leadership of Rev. Robert Tyrrell, who was assigned to St. Julia Parish in 1992, the church experienced revitilization and growth, as evidenced by the construction of a new parish center in 1995–96.

Later History of First Parish Church

In 1912, fire struck the 1877 First Parish parsonage. A new residence was completed by 1913, designed by architect and church member Harold Graves. The following quote is from the building committee, composed of Horace Sears, Louisa Case, and Amos S. Crane:

> The plans provide for a plain but attractive house on very simple but pleasing colonial lines. . . . In the service end there are modest accommodations for one, or, if desired, two servants, which

Figure 15-45. (left) In 1877 the church constructed this parsonage, first occupied by Rev. Francis B. Hornbrooke. It stood at the corner of Church Street and Conant Road until it was destroyed by fire in 1912.

Figure 15-46. (right) The First Parish parsonage was rebuilt in 1913 in the Colonial Revival style from designs by Harold S. Graves. The house still stands at 3 Conant Road, although the porches have been removed.

are all that would ever be required for a house of this size, and there has never been any suggestion or thought of providing for more.[111]

In 1918, a Hook & Hastings organ was given to the parish by Anna Coburn Hastings in memory of her husband, Francis Henry Hastings. Horace Sears paid for the changes required to enlarge the choir loft and install the organ within a new transept dedicated in memory of his friend William Herbert Coburn, who was Anna's brother.

In 1922, Horace Sears offered to fund the building of a new parish hall. Although he was involved in the planning, Sears did not live to see completion of the addition by the Boston firm of Appleton and Stearns, successors to Peabody and Stearns. In his will, Sears left $35,000 to complete the project, as well as $30,000 as a permanent fund for First Parish Church. In 1930 the church added the Sears Memorial Chapel, named after the Rev. Edmund Hamilton Sears. The architect was Weston resident Harold Willis, of the firm Allen and Collens, which is best known for the medieval-style Cloisters and Riverside Church in New York City.[112] The last major building project at First Parish was the construction of a modern Sunday school building in 1967–68, designed by Pierce and Pierce.

Businesses in the Town Center (1915–1950)

The redesign of the town center and construction of the town common had a corresponding impact on commercial life. In late 1917, G.W. Cutting & Sons was moved, building and all, to the south side of Boston Post Road, where it stood just east of the new fire station. A short item in the *Waltham Daily Free Press Tribune* observed that "the removal of the

Figure 15-47. The Sears Memorial Chapel at First Parish Church, designed by Harold B. Willis, was dedicated in 1930. Money was provided by the will of Horace S. Sears in memory of his father. The Hook & Hastings organ in the chapel was a memorial to Rev. Charles Russell, the chancel was given by the Case sisters, and the organ screen honored five generations of the Field family.

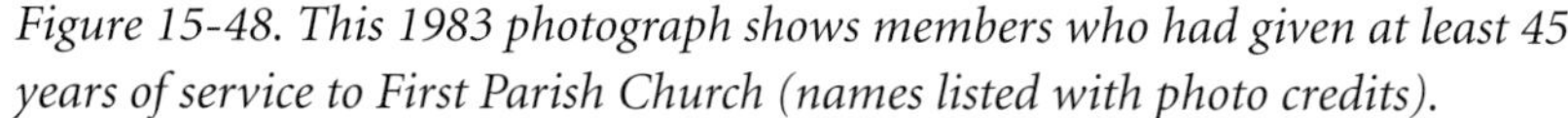

Figure 15-48. This 1983 photograph shows members who had given at least 45 years of service to First Parish Church (names listed with photo credits).

Figure 15-49. To implement the Town Improvement Plan, Cutting's Store was moved in 1917 to a lot just east of the fire station. The old-fashioned general store finally closed in 1939.

piazza uncovered a mine of wealth to the small boys of the neighborhood who dug up pennies, nickels, and even an occasional quarter."[113]

The post office moved to its own building in the emerging commercial center near the Coburn block. Anthony Sheehan was appointed postmaster, a position that had been held since 1859 by two generations of Cuttings. Sheehan's dedication to the job is legendary among residents, who recall how he made it from upper Concord Road even after the heaviest snowstorms.

George W. Cutting Jr. died in 1923 and his son Alfred Leslie Cutting in 1926. The store continued in operation under longtime partner Arthur B. Nims. Cutting's was never modernized and retained the look of a country store through the 1920s and '30s. The wood floors and heavy wooden barrels remained, along with the smell of freshly ground coffee beans. Customers could still buy grain, dry goods, and farm tools and get their molasses jugs filled from a barrel in the back room. Peanut butter was dipped from a vat, spread on a sheet of brown paper, wrapped, and weighed, to be transferred to a jar at home. Cheese was cut from a large wheel. Children bought penny candy and five-cent ice-cream cones.

Many residents liked the old-fashioned atmosphere and would have deplored modernization, but times were changing. Competition from small local food markets like the Colonial Market and Weston Quality Market and new "supermarket" chains like the First National and A&P helped bring an end to Weston's renowned general store after more than a century of operation.[114] George W. Cutting & Sons closed for business in June 1939. St. Julia Church purchased the property and tore down the building. A flagpole was placed in the center of the newly landscaped grounds, now the location of the rectory and parish hall.[115]

Another vestige from a passing era was the last village smithy, run by Oliver Patriquin in the town center beginning about 1918. His son, Calvin, remembers it as a "a very busy shop, with the ringing of hammers striking the anvils and horses milling around waiting to be shod."[116] Old-timers gathered there and shared stories. Patriquin was known for ornamental ironwork custom-made for estate owners, architects, and house restorers. He fashioned garden gates, iron stair railings, door hardware, fireplace andirons and screens, and plant holders in all sizes and shapes. When business dropped off dur-

Figure 15-50. This photograph from the 1940s shows the Hersum block at right, built by plumbing contractor A.L. Hersum in the late 19th century.

ing the Depression, Patriquin moved to the corner of Love Lane and Boston Post Road, where his former shop still stands.

In the decade after redesign of the town center and construction of Town House Road, the 18th-century Lamson homestead was razed and a new Mediterranean-style commercial block was built in its place. James H. McManus opened a popular ice-cream parlor at the east end of the block, with tables and a soda fountain inside and outdoors an eating area covered with an awning. High school boys in the 1930s brought their dates here for sundaes and banana splits made with McManus's own ice cream.

The following is a list of businesses in Weston Center taken from suburban directories of 1915, 1926, 1936, 1946, and 1949. Although some businesses may have been inadvertently omitted, the compilation is useful in charting the growth in the number of businesses and the change in goods and services available.

Businesses in Weston Center (1915 directory)

Wm. T. Burrage & Co., dry goods
G.W. Cutting & Sons, general store and post office
Benjamin R. Parker, hardware, and auto and bicycle repairing
Benj. H. Shaw, general repairing and machine work, harnesses, bicycle shoes, stable and poultry supplies
Weston Hand Laundry

Businesses in Weston Center (1926 directory)

Colonial Motor Sales, autos and repairs
Colonial Market
Colonial Tailors and Furriers
G.W. Cutting & Sons, general store
Abel J. Colpitts, plumber
The Ginter Co., groceries
Marie R. Haynes, insurance and real estate
Hillcrest Market, vegetables
Hillcrest Tea House
Benjamin R. Parker, hardware
Oliver Patriquin, blacksmith
"Madam Subelia's" dry goods, needles and thread, fabric, knickknacks (Marie Subelia)
Warren Twombley, undertaker
Weston Quality Market
U.S. Post Office

Businesses in Weston Center (1936 directory)

North Side, Boston Post Road

First National Stores, 399
Charbonneau's (druggist), 401
Weston Spa (lunchroom), 407
Francis Bowker (real estate and insurance), 409
Vera Chase Beauty Salon, 411
John H. Benson (real estate and insurance), 483
Great Atlantic and Pacific Tea Co. (address not given)
James McManus, ice-cream manufacturer (address not given)

South Side, Boston Post Road

G.W. Cutting & Sons, 378
Benjamin R. Parker Hardware, 450
U.S. Post Office, 462
Weston Quality Market, 464
Ye Weston Thread & Needle, 466
Weston Center Barber Shop, 476
Post Road Press Inc., 478 (published newspapers including the *Weston News Review*)
Abel Colpitts (plumber), 544
Colonial Motors, 596

Businesses in Weston Center (1946 directory)

North Side of Boston Post Road

John W. Boyd (insurance) and L. Davenport Boyd (real estate), 395
Weston Pharmacy (Warren Eaton, proprietor), 397
First National Stores, 399
Central Tailors, 401
Village Hair Stylist, 405
Weston Spa (restaurant), 407
Colonial Tailors & Furriers Inc., 413

South Side of Boston Post Road

Parker's Garage and Benjamin R. Parker (hardware), 450
Weston Gift Shop, 452
Carver's (soda fountain, ice cream, sandwiches, candy, snacks), 456
U.S. Post Office, 462
Weston Market, 464
Weston Center Barber Shop, 476
Weston Sports Shop (refrigerators, washing machines, electrical appliances, sporting goods), 478
Village Book Stall, 494
A.J. Colpitts (plumber), 544
Weston Studio (upholsterers), 582
Colonial Motors and Wheelock Oil Co., 596

Businesses in Weston Center (1949 directory)

North Side of Boston Post Road

L. Davenport Boyd and John W. Boyd (real estate), 395
Weston Pharmacy, 397
First National Stores, 399
Central Tailors, 401
Village Hair Stylist, 405
Weston Spa, 407
Colonial Tailors & Furriers Inc. 413-15
Weston Taxi (waiting room), 483

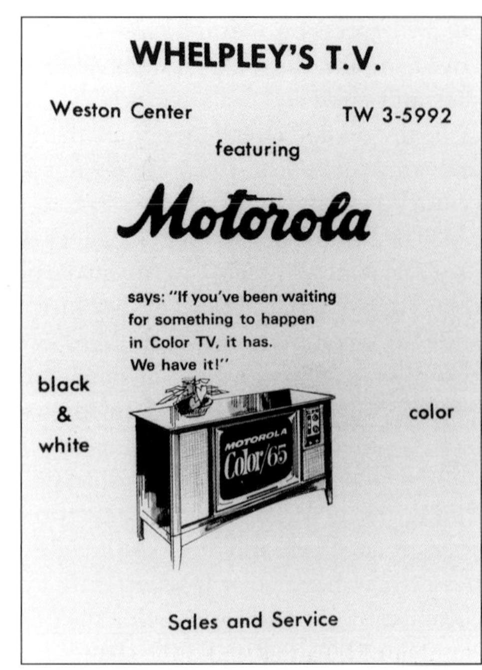

Figure 15-51. These advertisements were taken from the Weston High School yearbooks of 1955, 1960, and 1961. Ye Olde Cottage Restaurant has been in its current location since 1952. Patrons at Carvers could have ice cream or sandwiches and wait for the bus, which ran along Route 20 from Hudson into Boston during commuter hours. Whelpley's sold radios, televisions, electrical appliances, and records. Bickford's was a "5 and 10 cent store."

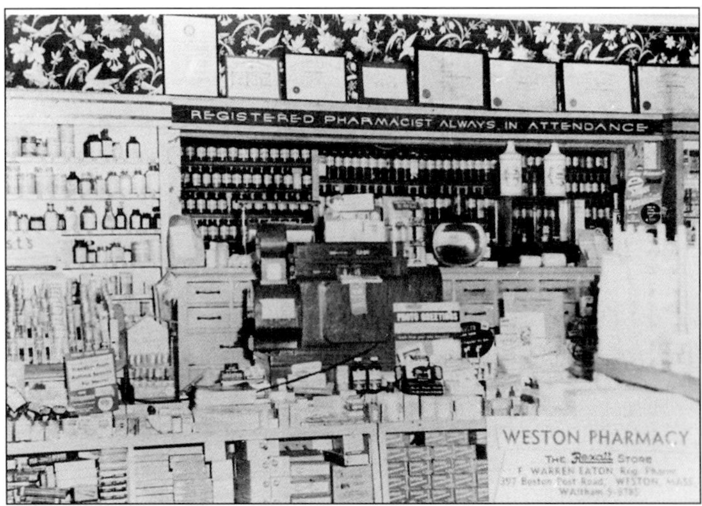

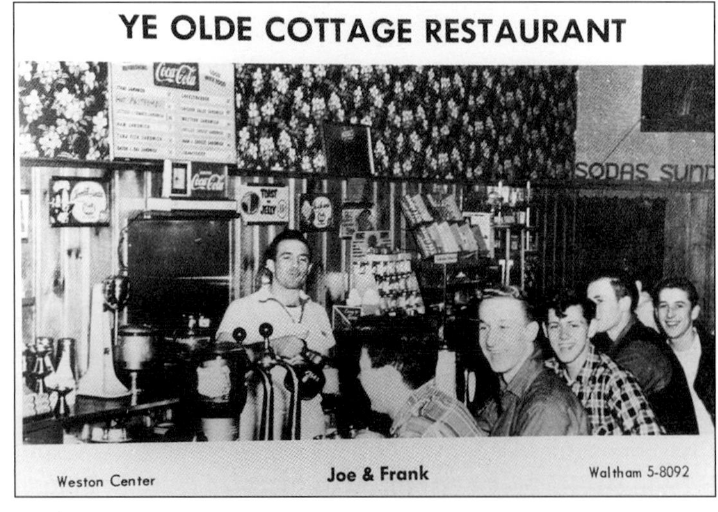

Figure 15-52. This photograph of the commercial block at 391-407 Boston Post Road shows the trees that once made parking more challenging.

South Side of Boston Post Road
Benjamin R. Parker, 450
Weston Gift Shop, 452
Carvers (variety store), 456
Newton-Waltham Bank & Trust Co., 458
U.S. Post Office, 462
Weston Market (fresh meats, fish, frozen foods, vegetables, free delivery), 464
Art's Taxi, 468
Whelpley Radio Service (complete radio and television sales and service, electrical appliances), 478
Village Book Stall, 494
Bernice Caffrey (gift shop), 508
Weston Sports Shop (athletic equipment, clothing), 512
A.J. Colpitts (plumber), 544
Weston Studio (upholsterers), 582
Colonial Motors and Wheelock Oil Co., 596

The Town Center after 1950

In the early 1960s, planning began for the largest commercial building in Weston Center, designed to accommodate an expanded Triple A supermarket and more stores. The cornerstone was laid in 1966. The structure was built within an extensive peat bog on piles up to 45 feet deep.[117] A parking lot was created by laying down a base of sawdust and cinders topped with bituminous concrete. This process of stabilizing wetlands for construction and development was allowable before passage of the Wetlands Protection Act. According to one estimate, some 60 percent of Weston's business district is in the wetlands, and its development could not take place today.[118]

Permits for the new development were granted based on town plans for a central sewerage district—plans that were later rescinded. For more than 30 years, sewerage was pumped several times a week from a temporary holding tank. State environmental regulations passed in the mid-1990s proved to be the catalyst for owners of commercial properties on the south side of Boston Post Road to join together in building a solar aquatic wastewater-treatment plant and greenhouse, which opened in the 1990s.

Colpitts Road was developed in the 1960s and '70s to accommodate increased demand for office space. The post office was built in 1965, medical building in 1967, and office building in the early 1970s, all designed by architect and Weston resident Marjorie Pierce. Developer David Colpitts was a grandson of Abel J. Colpitts, who came to Weston in the 1920s from Nova Scotia and started a successful plumbing and heating business located for decades at the corner of Boston Post Road and what is now Colpitts Road.

The Jones sisters lived in the historic Josiah Smith Tavern until Alice died in 1948 and Ellen in 1950. They left the house and contents to the Society for the Preservation of New England

Figure 15-53. In 1967, a 25,000-square-foot commercial building opened with the Triple A supermarket as the principal tenant. The building was constructed in wetlands, which was allowed before passage of the federal Wetlands Protection Act. (1965–66 photo)

Figure 15-54. Laying the cornerstone of Weston's first large commercial building (21 Center Street) are, from left, Ward Carter, Francois Comeau, Henry Comeau, Henry Acconcia, David Bradley, Lucy Boyd, Jack Boyd, Arthur Brooks (architect), Herman "Bud" Koester (selectman), and Ernest Comeau. (1966 photo)

Antiquities (SPNEA) "in order that the house . . . may be preserved for posterity as a place of historical and educational interest."[119] For the next 33 years, SPNEA leased the property back to the town. After approval from the Probate Court, the Town of Weston purchased the building in 1983 and assumed the obligation to preserve the house.[120] The barn was renovated by the Women's Community League as a Bicentennial project in the mid-1970s and since then has been used for the Clothing Exchange as well as exhibitions, parties, and other events.

In 1951, the Weston Public Library added a collection of phonograph records that could be borrowed. By its 100th anniversary in 1957, the Weston Public Library housed more than 40,000 volumes, was open 60 hours a week, and had a circulation of 84,722 volumes. Staff consisted of five full-time librarians assisted by six part-time employees. The library had greatly expanded its role as a community center, a role that has continued to grow in its second century.

By the late 20th century, town institutional buildings in the center were becoming outdated. In 1986 the fire station was closed for two years for remodeling and enlargement. New vehicle entrances were constructed at the rear, and the original front openings were permanently closed. In 1987 a library building committee was established to consider on-site expansion. After thorough study, the committee recommended new construction. In 1995, after nearly a century in the town square, the library moved to a new building on School Street designed by the architectural firm of Galliher and Baier. In the year 2001, construction is under way to restore and enlarge the 1917 town hall.

Buildings in the Town Center Area

349 Boston Post Road (1887–88). First Parish Church. Designed by Robert Peabody and originally landscaped by Charles Eliot.

356 Boston Post Road (1899–1900). Weston Public Library. Designed by Fox, Jenney and Gale in the Jacobethan style and constructed in brick with limestone trim.

358 Boston Post Road (1757, enlarged 1763). Josiah Smith Tavern. Georgian gambrel-roofed tavern built with a central-chimney plan. The 1757 rooms retain their original fabric, including Georgian raised-field paneling and trim. The 1763 addition, also well preserved, includes a second chimney, two first-floor rooms, and a second-floor ballroom. The building was used as a tavern until 1838, purchased in 1842 by Marshall and John Jones, and occupied by their descendants until 1950. For this reason it is often referred to as the Jones House.

374 Boston Post Road (1921). St. Julia Roman Catholic Church. Gothic Revival fieldstone structure designed by Maginnis and Walsh and built by John Capobianco. Anthony M. Zottoli and Brothers sculpted the stone carving on the exterior tympanum and Cascuri and Disascari did the wood carvings in the sanctuary.[121] Rectory built 1971–72. Parish Hall of 1995–96 designed by the Sudbury firm of Dion & Sokol.

394 Boston Post Road (1914). Weston Fire Station. Brick Georgian Revival design by Alexander Jenney constructed as part of the Town Improvement Plan.

391-407 Boston Post Road (1920s). Mediterranean-style cast-stone commercial block constructed on the site of the 18th-century Lamson homestead. In the 1930s it was known as the McManus block, after the best-known tenant. Weston Pharmacy was established here about 1939.

409-415 Boston Post Road (1933–34). Built on former Lamson land, this brick business block had offices on the second floor and two apartments at the back.[122]

426 Boston Post Road (1897). Queen Anne house built for Edward Coburn, for either rental or use by family members.[123] The house remained in the Coburn family until 1957, when it was acquired by the L. Davenport Boyd real-estate company along with the adjacent residence at No. 436. The company added the brick storefront. The Chestnut Shop opened in the rear in 1964.

430 Boston Post Road (c. 1897). This four-stall horse barn was originally part of the property at No. 426 and was located directly behind that house. It was moved to the present site in the 1960s, when the supermarket was constructed. Leiby's began in 1949 as Norumbega Nursery at 181 South Avenue. The company was primarily a landscape business. It moved to the barn in 1958, and the name was changed to Arthur Leiby's Nursery & Garden Shop.

436 Boston Post Road. Thought to have been built in the early 1800s by Joel Smith for his eldest son, Capt. George Washington Smith. In 1810 Captain Smith married Clarissa Lamson, daughter of Col. Samuel Lamson, thus uniting two of Weston's most distinguished families. The house was originally located just east of First Parish Church but was moved by David Lane to its present site about 1845. The house was acquired by the Coburn family and used as a two-family, one side of which was occupied for many years by Edward Coburn's daughter, Caroline Coburn Briggs, and her husband, Louis. The Briggs family sold the house to John and Lucy Boyd in 1957 and it was converted for office use. Local architect Marjorie Pierce designed the alterations for both No. 426 and No. 436.

439 Boston Post Road (1917–18). Gothic Revival stone church designed by Brigham, Coveney and Bisbee for St. Peter's Episcopal Church and sold to the Christian Science Society of Weston in 1958. They remodeled the sanctuary and held services there beginning in February 1959. The Christian Science Reading Room, complete with study and sales rooms, was first opened in May 1959 and remodeled in 1969–70. The Sunday school wing, designed by Arthur H. Brooks Jr. & Associates of Cambridge, was added in 1977–80.

450-456 Boston Post Road (1893–94). Coburn block. Frame commercial block constructed by Edward Coburn after his earlier commercial block was destroyed by fire. One storefront has been occupied since 1898 by a hardware dealer (originally Benjamin R. Parker, now Puopolo Hardware).

458 Boston Post Road (1926). Used as a combined bank and post office until the post office built its own separate facility, after which the facade was remodeled. The bank was a branch of the Waltham Trust Company until 1933, when the branch was not authorized to reopen after Roosevelt's "Bank Holiday." It later reopened as the Newton-Waltham Bank and is presently Fleet Bank.

464-478 Boston Post Road (c. 1890). Hersum block. Until 1989, this frame commercial block was two stories with a flat roof and retained its decorative cornice treatment and early-20th-century storefronts. At that time the present third story was added and the facade completely remodeled. Businesses located here over the years include *Weston News,* a weekly newspaper once published here, Whelpley's radio and television store, Sammett's Card Shop, Pop Miller's Market, a shoe-repair shop, a barbershop, and a beauty shop (now the Gift Gallery and Florentine Frames).

483 Boston Post Road (1964) This commercial building was designed by Marjorie Pierce. The west wing was originally a freestanding, Federal-style, hip-roofed tailor shop built by Daniel Lamson about 1817 as an adjunct to the family dry-goods store on what is now the town green. In its first century, the shop was reportedly also used as a clothing store for men and boys, barbershop, and harness shop. The original location is shown on the "Plan of Land Taken for Public Park," May 20, 1913 (MCRD Plan Book 227/16). When the town green was created about 1917, the building was moved onto Lamson land in the commercial area, where it was used as a taxi office and news dealership. Marjorie Pierce remodeled it for Bernice Caffrey, who had a gift and interior design shop there. The shop was later moved a second time and incorporated into the new building at No. 483.

486 Boston Post Road. Site of a blacksmith shop, which was set back from the road. The last smithy, Oliver Patriquin, moved to a smaller shop at Love Lane and Boston Post Road by the mid-1930s. The present brick building was built in 1953 for the Weston Post Office, which moved about a decade later to Colpitts Road. From about 1964 to 1974, No. 486 was the office for Sweidler building company (now Weston Pediatric Physicians).

494 Boston Post Road Originally the barn for No. 510, this structure was remodeled in 1919 as headquarters for the newly formed Women's Community League, which opened The Willow Plate as a combined tearoom and salesroom for baked goods and handicrafts made by local women.[124] From 1921 to 1934, Marian Case sold produce here from Hillcrest Gardens. The building was later occupied for many years by the Village Book Stall. The three-ton circular stone now placed upright in front was unearthed by the bookstore owner about 1963 and identified as a wheelwright's stone used by the neighboring blacksmith (now Cambridge Trust Company).

505 Boston Post Road (1855–56). Frame late-Greek Revival house with earlier ell, built for blacksmith Joel Upham (1803–1895), oldest of 12 children of blacksmith Abijah Upham. Joel Upham's blacksmith shop, which he operated beginning about 1828–30, stood near the road. The house was left to his daughter, Carolyn (Carrie), and her husband, Arthur Stoddard Burrage, whose sudden death in 1895 left her with three young children: Constance (1885–1973), Mabel (1886–1986), and Philip. Constance attended Radcliffe

College and became a teacher at Weston High School. The two sisters lived in the house until their deaths. It is now occupied by descendants of Philip.

510 Boston Post Road (1765; 1824). Built for potter Abraham Hews and substantially remodeled in the Federal style in 1824 by Marshall Jones (1791–1864). According to Lamson's history, when Jones acquired the dilapidated house, it had never been painted. Jones established a paint and harness business on the property, taking into partnership his brother, John. The house itself was used as a residence. In later years, Dr. Fresenius Van Nuys rented half the house, from about 1909 to 1918. In 1948 it was acquired by John and Lucy Boyd and remodeled as medical and dental offices with apartments upstairs.

527 Boston Post Road (1920–21). Colonial Revival house built for Milton T. Coffin.[125]

542 Boston Post Road (c. 1924). Small wooden Colonial Revival office built for A.J. Colpitts Plumbing & Heating. It was originally located closer to the corner of Colpitts Road and was moved in the mid-1970s. A.J. Colpitts established his own business in 1920 after working some 20 years for plumber A.L. Hersum.[126]

543 Boston Post Road. See chapter 16.

544 Boston Post Road (1927). Built for Abel J. and Harriet Colpitts as their residence, from designs by Harold Graves.

For numbers above 544, see chapter 16.

Center Street (1966). Large brick commercial building designed by Arthur Brooks and originally housing the Triple A Market.

Church Street. See Chapter 11.

1 Colpitts Road (1972). Colonial Revival house built for David Colpitts as his residence.

5 Colpitts Road (1938). Colonial Revival house built for Abel Colpitts and moved here from Boston Post Road.

Colpitts Road (1965). U.S. Post Office. Until the post office was built, Colpitts Road was just a driveway.

3 Conant Road (1913). First Parish Church Parsonage. This Colonial Revival house, designed by Harold Graves, replaced the 1877 parsonage, which had been destroyed by fire.

6 Conant Road (1905, 1916). Built for lawyer Charles F. Richardson on land purchased from Col. Daniel S. Lamson. The 1905 portion was designed by Samuel

Cutting Family (3 generations)

George Warren Cutting Sr. (1805–1885), m. Elizabeth Lord, 1830
- Caroline Elizabeth (1831–1911), m. George Willis, 1853
- Sarah Lord (1833–1863), m. Theodore Jones, 1857
  - Ellen (1857–1950), unmarried
  - Alice (1861–1947), unmarried
- George Warren Jr. (1834–1923), m. Josephine Maria Brown, 1865
  - Sarah (1866–1947), m. Arthur B. Nims
  - Alfred Leslie (1868–1926)
  - George Warren Jr. (1877–1942), civil engineer
  - Bessie Brown (1874–1876)
  - Ellie Mabel (1880–?)
  - Edmund Eugene (b. and d. 1882)
- Harriet Fenno (1838–1923), m. William Cutter Stimpson, 1860 (d. 1864)
  - Clara Frances (1861–1923), m. Charles Cutting Kenney, 1885
  - Charlotte Elizabeth (1862–1863)
  - Charles Hall (1864–1946)
- Margaret Lord (1842–1907), m. Isaac Emery Coburn, 1871
- Emma Louisa (1844–1922), unmarried
- Ellen Marion (1846–1849)
- Edward Leslie (1850–1942), m. Caroline Keniston, 1879

Sarah Cutting Jones, wife of Theodore Jones, died at age 30 in 1863, leaving two young daughters, Ellen and Alice. Their aunt, Harriet Cutting Stimpson, and her children went to live in the Jones house and took care of the two girls (the Jones sisters). Harriet's husband, William Cutter Stimpson, was killed in the Civil War at Poplar Spring, Virginia, in 1864.

Mead and built by J.C. Macdonald.[127] In 1916, it was enlarged and remodeled by well-known Colonial Revival architect Joseph Everett Chandler for Charles O. Richardson, a friend of Horace Sears and a partner at Wellington Sears beginning in 1917. The Chandler addition includes a dining room important for its paneling and French scenic wallpaper.

8 Conant Road (1931). Tudor house built for Lester and Elizabeth Flint.

15 and 17 Conant Road (1880). Stick-style house built for Justin E. Gale, Weston High School principal and later treasurer of Brookside Mills. According to family tradition, the builder was neighbor William N. Gowell. The barn was converted to a house at No. 17.

12 Conant Road (1905). Built for Mary L. Hubbard.

18 Conant Road (after 1894). Built for Ellen P. Hubbard.

22 Conant Road (c. 1895). Colonial Revival house built for Lyman Gale, son of Justin Gale. Lyman married Robert Winsor's sister, Jane, and worked at Kidder, Peabody & Co. Jane Gale was the first president of the Women's Community League.[128]

25 Conant Road (c. 1873). Built for William N. Gowell, one of Weston's best-known carpenter-builders.

33 Conant Road (1892–93). Queen Anne house built for Benjamin R. Parker, who at that time worked at the school furniture factory on Crescent Street and later opened a hardware store on Boston Post Road.

One Town House Road (1929). Brick Georgian Revival mansion designed by Harold Willis for Kenneth and Margaret Lyman Parsons. It was inspired by the 1729 plantation house Westover on the James River in Virginia.

Town House Road (1917). Weston Town Hall. Brick Georgian Revival design built as part of the Town Improvement Plan, using Bigelow and Wadsworth, architects; the firm of Densmore & LeClear, engineers; Leighton-Mitchell Company, contractor; and Arthur A. Shurtleff, landscape architect.[129]

Notes

1. 1917 *TR,* 110–11.

2. The first meetinghouse was located just south of the present First Parish Church, where the church parking lot is today.

3. The covenant with housewrights Randall Davis and Benjamin Rand remains among the records in the town vault and provides some construction details.

4. Mary Peirce wrote in 1893 that the bills for the repairs, amounting to more than $3,000, and for the bell, with Paul Revere's signature, "are filed with the town papers." These repairs included the building of a tower and spire on the west side, and two porches, one on the east and one on the south. The stairs for entering the gallery were moved from the body of the church to the porch on the east side and the tower on the west. The windows were lowered, and the ground floor was covered with pews. The sale of pews helped defray the expense of repairs. See *First Parish Calendar,* November 15, 1893, vol. 1, no. 2. The 200th anniversary history of the church says the square pews were removed at that time and long ones substituted.

5. In 1801 the parishioners raised $420.24 toward the cost of a larger bell for the bell tower. They were allowed a credit of $72.88 for their small Canadian bell, which had been brought to Weston by local soldiers either in an expedition against the French and Indians or during the Revolutionary War. The church also hired a Boston blacksmith to make a "spindle, Vane and scroll" for the top of the bell tower. This weather vane was lost when the meetinghouse was demolished in 1840. (Reference: letter from town historian Mary Francis Peirce to Selectman Francis Blake in 1894, Blake papers, MHS.)

6. According to the firm's stock book, Weston's bell was number 44. Only five Revere bells older than this exist today. According to church history, in 1792 Revere cast his first bell, which is still located in a church in North Cambridge. Revere consistantly improved the quality of the metal, so the Weston bell has a fine, mellow tone.

7. In a petition considered at the 1799 town meeting, a group of church members asked permission to erect a stable for carriages between the stable owned by Capt. Isaac Jones and that of Enoch Greenleaf.

8. Smith was the son of William Smith of Sudbury Road (see chapter 12). For 20 pounds, he bought land from Joseph Bigelow Jr. on December 9, 1756. He bought an additional 20 acres from Joseph Bigelow Jr. on March 24, 1757, for 50 pounds (MCRD Book 54/592.) On the tax list of 1757 (the earliest remaining tax list), Josiah Smith is taxed for property valued at 26 pounds and real estate valued at 70 pounds.

9. MCRD 415/145, John Warren to Marshall Jones, gentleman, and John Jones, Esquire, $2,800, March 12, 1842.

10. Daniel S. Lamson, "Weston," chapter XXXIII in *History of Middlesex County, Massachusetts,* 506. See also *Descendants of William Lamson of Ipswich, Mass., 1634–1917,* by William J. Lamson (New York, Tobias A. Wright, Printer and Publisher, 1917).

11. In 1861 Elizabeth Lamson was taxed for the 113-acre "homestead" and John A. Lamson Jr. for 87 acres.

12. The Lamson homestead was located on the north side of Boston Post Road at the intersection of the present Town House Road, behind what is now the pharmacy at 397 Boston Post Road. A picture can be found in *Descendants of Wm. Lamson* (op. cit.) It was torn down when the present commercial block was constructed. A second Lamson house, which was smaller and later in date, was located just west of what is now the Christian Science Church at 439 Boston Post Road. This Italianate frame building was built into the hill and survived until the 1940s.

13. "Lamson Family," *The Massachusetts Magazine,* vol. 2, 1909, 138.

14. John and Elizabeth were married in 1814. In 1861 (six years after John's death), Elizabeth was taxed for the following: two dwellings (valued at $3,000 and $300), two barns, shop, store (valued at $2,000), wagon house, icehouse, cow barn, and 113 acres. John A. Lamson Jr. was taxed for a dwelling, barn, and 87 acres.

15. The Lane/Chandler/Endicott house was torn down to make way for the First Parish Sunday school building. See deed from George Smith, trader, and Mary Ann and Ellen Smith, singlewomen, to David Lane of New York City, merchant, 8.5 acres with dwelling house, store, barn, and other buildings, on north side of the great road, bounded by land of Dr. Otis Hunt and also by the meetinghouse, also 10.5 acres on the south side of Boston Post Road (MCRD, Book 656/349, July 1853). The property on the north side of the road is now owned by First Parish Church. Katherine Sears

Endicott was the daughter of Francis Bacon Sears and the niece of Horace Sears.
16. Lamson, *HTW,* 155.
17. A second branch of the family in Weston, descendants of Samuel's brother, John Lamson (b. 1724), produced Alvan Lamson, who was raised on the family farm, studied at Phillips Academy and Harvard, and in 1818 became minister of First Church and Parish in Dedham, one of the oldest churches in the state, presiding over the church during a period of conflict as the church made the transition to Unitarianism.
18. MCRD, 3374/85 and 3374/467.
19. "Funeral Services for George H. Lamson, Sportsman . . ." *Weston News Review,* August 11, 1939.
20. Lamson, *HTW,* 15.
21. Ripley, Emma F., "The First Parish in Weston, 1698–1948," 13.
22. "Dr. Field, of Weston," obituary clipped from unknown newspaper, 1869.
23. According to *The First Parish in Weston,* the last assessment by the town for taxes to support the church was made in 1824, and the first record of the payment of the ministerial salary on the church book is May 5, 1826, for the year ending May 1, 1826. See also Lamson, *HTW,* 178, for an example of the Baptist Society exemption certificate.
24. Hart, ed., *Commonwealth History of Massachusetts,* vol. IV, 12–13.
25. Lamson, *HTW,* 11.
26. Coburn, Elizabeth S., "History of the First Parish, Weston, Massachusetts," written for the Women's Alliance, April 18, 1921.
27. 1917 *TR,* 105. To give an idea of the speed with which public policy decisions could be made and implemented, the vote to build the town hall took place in May 1847 and the job was completed by December. The builder was Albert Higgins of Concord, Massachusetts, according to Charles H. Fiske (see note 28).
28. Fiske, Charles H., "The Weston Meeting House Common and Its Neighbors," a paper presented to the Friendly Society on January 7, 1909, and then issued in printed form, 8–9. The Committee of Arrangement consisted of the following: Samuel Hobbs, S.H.F. Bingham, Nathan Hagar, Luke Brooks, Isaac Coburn, Benjamin Pierce Jr., Leonard L. Brown, John Coburn, and J.Q.A. Harrington. Floor managers were George Smith, James H. Wright, and Benjamin Pierce Jr.
29. "A History of Weston Schools," undated typescript, WHC files.
30. Ripley, Emma F., *Weston Town Library History: 1857–1957* (booklet printed for the 100th anniversary), 1.
31. The First Parish Calendar, March 15, 1896, vol. III, no. 5.
32. Ripley, *Weston Town Library History,* op. cit., 2.
33. Lamson, *HTW,* 144–45.
34. *Waltham Sentinel,* April 26, 1867, as quoted in *WHSB,* October 1966. The 1866 enlargement, which increased the size of other parts of the building as well, reportedly cost $4,120, which included $525 for the marble memorial tablet. In "The Weston Meeting-House Common and Its Neighbors,"cited above, Charles H. Fiske says that the town hall was enlarged in 1860-62 by cutting it in half, moving the northerly half back 30 feet, and then reconnecting the two exposed ends. This information is not corroborated by Lamson or other sources.
35. Ripley, *Weston Public Library History,* op. cit.
36. Ibid., 3.
37. "Cutting Family," *The Massachusetts Magazine,* vol. 2, 1909, 136. Cutting bought the grocery from Jonathan P. Stearns. See also *Waltham Free Press,* May 8, 1885, and "Weston's Oldest Store Stock Was Sold at Auction Tuesday" in the *Weston News Review,* July 14, 1939.
38. 1918 *TR,* 229.
39. Ibid.
40. Ibid.
41. Dickson, *Pung,* 3–4.
42. Obituary, newspaper clipping, unknown newspaper and date.
43. *The First Parish Calendar,* October 16, 1893, vol. 1, no. 1, 2.
44. 1876 *TR* (year ending March 15, 1876), 30–31. Paine had the tower clock made especially for the town and paid the entire cost of installation.
45. "Records of the Inception, Building & Dedication of the New Church Edifice for the First Parish (Unitarian) of Weston, Mass., 1884–1886" (meeting notes, unpublished manuscript, First Parish Church archives). Quote from record of first meeting, April 1883.
46. Ibid., vote at First Parish Church annual meeting, April 7, 1884.
47. Ibid., 4.
48. Those present on January 12, 1885, were as follows: Mrs. Charles F. Russell, Mrs. Robert Winsor, Miss Anna C. Coburn, Miss Edith L. Coburn, Miss Hattie Sanderson, Mr. Horace S. Sears, Mrs. E.O. Clark, Miss Hattie S. Perry, Miss Alice E. Jones, Miss Georgiana Buchanan, Miss Ellen M. Jones, Mr. Robert Winsor, and Mr. William H. Coburn. See "Records of the First Parish Friendly Society of Weston, organized January 12, 1885, vol. I" (unpublished manuscript).
49. Friendly Society Bylaws.
50. "Records of the First Parish Friendly Society of Weston, organized January 12, 1885," vol. I.
51. "Records of the Inception, Building & Dedication of the New Church Edifice . . ." op. cit., July and August 1884.
52. Holden, Wheaton A., "The Peabody Touch: Peabody and Stearns of Boston, 1870–1917," *Victorian Architecture in Boston,* the May 1973 issue of *The Journal of the Society of Architectural Historians,* vol. XXXII, no. 2, May 1973, 119 (includes watercolor illustration).
53. "Records of the Inception, Building & Dedication of the New Church Edifice . . ." op. cit.
54. Ibid., March 26, 1887.
55. Coburn scrapbook #1, 244
56. "Records of the Inception, Building & Dedication of the New Church Edifice . . ." op. cit., April 4, 1887.
57. Ibid.
58. A gift of Mrs. Henry Gowing in memory of her husband.
59. Standing Committee Notes, 1892 (FPC archives).
60. Eliot, Charles W., *Charles Eliot, Landscape Architect* (Boston and New York: Houghton, Mifflin & Co., Riverside Press, 1903), 226–27. Letter of September 18, 1888.
61. Ibid.
62. *1892 TR,* 97.
63. Ibid., 99.
64. MCRD, Book 2254/519, March 1, 1894.
65. *The First Parish Calendar,* March 15, 1896, vol. III, no. 5.
66. Report of the Committee on a New Library Building, March 6, 1899, in 1898 *TR,* 58.
67. Letter, Herbert Putnam to Francis Blake, June 9, 1899 (MHS, Blake Papers, 65.931).
68. Draft report of the committee on new building, about September or October 1899 (MHS Blake Papers, 65.932).
69. See letter from Theodore Dwight to Francis Blake reporting on the town meeting of August 24, 1899. Blake was vacationing in the mountains (MHS, Blake papers, 65.933).
70. *WDFPT,* November 19, 1900.
71. 1900 *TR,* 61.
72. 1964 *TR,* 182–83. Miss Pennock died in September 1963.
73. Ripley, op. cit., 10.
74. MCRD, Book 415/144, March 12, 1842. $2,800 for 11 acres with buildings.
75. Lamson, *HTW,* 156, 161–62, 213.
76. Dickson, *Pung,* 6.
77. Joel was the oldest son of Abijah Upham, also a blacksmith. His grandfather, also named Abijah, was a prominent town leader. The quote comes from his obituary, probably from the *Waltham Free Press* (Coburn scrapbook

#3, 206). See also 505 Boston Post Road at end of chapter.

78. The May 15, 1894, issue of *The First Parish Calendar* greeted the appointment in this way:

> "The town has this year made an innovation upon the usual custom in appointing a woman a member of the school board. Of course, such a progressive town as ours would very soon awake to the advantages which attend such a course. . . . It is the mothers who keep abreast of their children, and know most nearly what is happening. So we welcome the new lady member, and wish her success in the task she has undertaken."

See also 1913 *TR,* 44.

79. MCRD, Book 992/100, October 13, 1866 (heirs of Benjamin Peirce to Edward Coburn).

80. *WDFP,* October 23, 1893, "Loss of $21,300: Weston Visited by Largest Fire Known There." Also insurance statement of loss by fire, October 23, 1893: two-story building on Central Avenue occupied as dwelling and store, value $3,000. Grain storage building owned by Edward Coburn, $1,000. Grain Store owned by Edward Coburn, $800. Grain belonged to C.L. Keefe, valued at $8,500. Also in fire was W.C. Burrage & Co, value of contents in Coburn building $4,821. Value of stock of W.G. Wark, $1,000. See also Ben Crouch's unpublished manuscript on the history of the Weston Fire Department, 5.

81. *WDFPT,* December 2, 1906.

82. *WDFPT,* May 5 and 19, 1905.

83. 1917 *TR,* 108. Speech at the dedication of the new town hall.

84. The mission of the first committee: "To consider the improvement and development of the center of town and secure proper building sites." To study the details and financial implications of the proposed plan, a second committee was later appointed, consisting of Henry L. Brown, Horace S. Sears, Robert Winsor Jr., Warren P. Adams Jr., and Charles H. Fiske Jr.

85. Letter "To the Citizens of the Town of Weston." The map was to be returned no later than January 9, 1912 (Town Hall vault).

86. Eliot was a member of the Olmsted firm before his untimely death in 1897.

87. *1919 TR,* 75.

88. Letter, Arthur A. Shurtleff to C.F. Richardson, March 5, 1912, in 1912 *TR,* 119.

89. Ibid.

90. 1912 *TR,* 40.

91. Among his works, designed under the firm name of Winslow, Wetherell & Bigelow or Bigelow & Wadsworth, were the Hotel Touraine, new Parker House, Tremont Building, Shreve Crump & Low on Tremont Street, Steinert Building, Oliver Ditson Building, Walker Building, library at Radcliffe College, and Kidder, Peabody & Company offices. Closer to home, the firm of Winslow and Bigelow also designed the Needham Town Hall in 1902. [Ref: Withey, *Biographical Dictionary of American Architects (Deceased),* 57.]

92. 1917 *TR,* 291–92. A note of interest: The *Waltham Daily Free Press Tribune* reported that the new auditorium was closed from June to August 1919 to correct the acoustic properties. (June 20 and August 15, 1919)

93. 1917 *TR,* 110.

94. 1917 *TR,* 116.

95. *WDFPT,* June 20, 1919.

96. 1919 *TR,* 72–73.

97. "Weston's Civic Center Has Won National Fame," newspaper clipping (name and date cut off), 1925 (Weston Town Hall vault).

98. *Farmers' Bulletin* No. 1441 of 1923, according to "The Federal Government Describes Weston's Town Green," *WHSB,* October 1981, 4–5.

99. 1929 *TR,* 22.

100. See 1926 *TR,* 24, and MCRD, Plan Book 390/19, March 24, 1927. See also "Plan of Land to Be Taken by the Town of Weston for Park Purposes," February 26, 1927 (copy at Weston Historical Commission).

101. Now 280 Boston Post Road. WHS has a picture of the school building with a cross on top.

102. Quoted in Emma Ripley, *Weston: A Puritan Town,* 110.

103. *WDFPT,* February 10, 1905. See also April 7, 1905.

104. "Plan of Land in Weston, Mass., a part of the Lamson Estate," MCRD plan (1917) by Henry F. Beal, Engineer, Book 4111 (end), copy, WHC files. Shows location of Lamson house. See also 4111/327.

105. As the parish grew, the building was enlarged. Plans were drawn by architect and church member Clifford Allbright, and by 1930 the church had added to the chancel, added a sacristy (vestry), and increased seating capacity. In the 1940s, Allbright sketched a conceptual drawing for a parish house extending west from the vestry, but this addition was never constructed.

106. *WDFPT,* March 22, 1912.

107. MCRD 4375/119, GWC Jr. to Roman Catholic Archbishop of Boston, August 3, 1920.

108. "Historical Notes," a history of St. Julia Roman Catholic Church compiled under the direction of Mr. and Mrs. Stephen Riley by the Golden Jubilee Historical Committee, 1969 (typescript, June 1, 1970).

109. *WDFPT,* November 7, 1919.

110. "Historical Notes," op. cit.

111. "Preliminary Report by the Building Committee for the New Parsonage," October 31, 1912.

112. A full description of the interior of the chapel and memorials can be found in "Service of Dedication, Memorial Chapel, First Parish in Weston," May 25, 1930.

113. *WDFPT,* November 16, 1917. The same was also true when the store was torn down in the early 1940s.

114. The Colonial Market advertised in the Friendly Society program "Sweethearts" April 24–25, 1925, 2, as follows: "It is my constant desire and effort to merit and retain the friendly regard of the members of the Friendly Society in Weston as well as all others. It is my business to supply you with the best of fresh meats, green vegetables, groceries, and fruit, delivered at your convenience in order that you may be assured of a sure and constant source of supply. Telephone your orders to Waltham 2658, H.H. Young, Prop."

115. "Historical Notes," op. cit. Note that in later years a new rectory was built on the site.

116. Letter, Calvin Patriquin to PWF, January 27, 2001.

117. Information provided by David H. Bradley.

118. PWF interview with David Bradley.

119. Alice Jones, Registry of Probate #280645, Ellen M. Jones, #298510 (died August 15, 1950, in Waltham). The bequest to SPNEA is specified in both wills.

120. 1983 *TR,* 24. The town paid $48,542 and received endowment funds in the amount of $97,084, which were placed in a trust fund with the income to be used for maintenance.

121. WHC files.

122. *Weston News Review,* September 13, 1933.

123. *WFP,* February 12, 1897.

124. *WDFPT,* July 11, 1919.

125. *WDFPT,* August 6 and October 20, 1920.

126. *WDFPT,* July 23, 1920.

127. *WDFPT,* July 14 and 21, 1905, and January 19, 1906.

128. See *WDFPT,* November 24, 1911.

129. Published in *American Architect,* vol. 114, no. 2241, December 4, 1918, plates and plan.

Figure 16-1. Isaac Fiske and Rev. Joseph Field were next-door neighbors and longtime friends.

CHAPTER 16

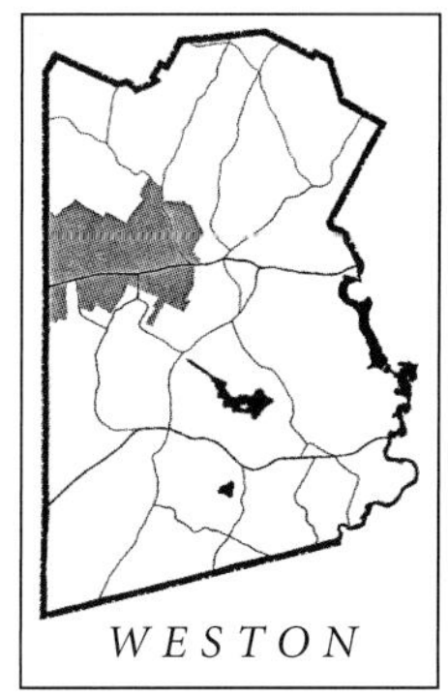

Boston Post Road (West)

Concord Road to Wayland

This chapter tells the story of families who lived along Boston Post Road and Concord Road just west of the town center. Some, like the Joneses, Hewses, Fiskes, and Peirces, settled in Weston before the Revolutionary War and still owned land a century later. The Hews pottery grew from a small family business on Boston Post Road to a North Cambridge company known throughout the country for everything from humble flowerpots to art pottery.

The old families were joined by hardworking immigrants like the Foote brothers, Beriah Ogilvie, and Cyrus Clark, all of whom came from the Canadian maritime provinces in the late 19th and early 20th centuries. With the help of their wives and children, they built businesses that served the needs of the growing community.

The history of Isaac Jones and the Golden Ball Tavern is told in greater detail in The Tavern and the Tory *by Howard Gambrill Jr. and Charles Hambrick-Stowe. The book follows Isaac during the political upheavals leading up to the Revolutionary War and also tells the remarkable story of how the former tavern was restored as a museum in the 1960s.*

The Jones Family and Golden Ball Tavern

Josiah Jones was one of the first settlers in Weston and one of two original deacons at First Parish Church. The Jones land was located on the southeast side of Highland Street and the Great Country Road. Josiah's descendants were men of consequence in the town's business and political life, especially Elisha (1710–1776) and Isaac (1728–1813), two cousins who both left important architectural legacies.

Elisha Jones was a successful merchant, aristocrat, colonel in the colonial militia, and prominent town leader. He was also an outspoken Loyalist who fled to Boston to be under British protection in the politically charged years before the Revolutionary War. His house on Highland Street, undoubtedly the grandest in Weston when it was built in 1755, was moved to its present site on Church Street in Weston's most dramatic 19th-century preservation saga.[1]

In 1765–68, his cousin Isaac built an inn identified by the "sign of the golden ball." It was praised by an 18th-century Englishman as ". . . the most convenient inn of any of the road" and "equal to most in England, the rooms commodious, provisions good, servants attentive."[2] The transformation of the landmark Georgian-style tavern into a museum was Weston's 20th-century preservation triumph.

Figure 16-2. The landmark tavern at the "sign of the golden ball" was built in 1765–68 by Isaac Jones. The house stayed in the Jones family until the 1960s. (c. 1870 photo)

By the early 1770s, Isaac Jones was one of the wealthiest men in Weston and owner of the prestigious front pew at the meetinghouse. But like his cousin Elisha, Isaac was a political conservative. The Golden Ball Tavern became known for Tory activity. Delegates to the Worcester Convention in 1775 denounced Isaac and urged those who opposed British rule to shun his house and "treat him with the contempt he deserves."[3] Isaac's role in harboring General Gage's spies is one of Weston's most popular Revolutionary War stories.[4] He later joined the Patriot cause and regained his leadership position in the community. He served 10 years as a selectman and operated the inn until 1793.

Isaac's older son, Isaac Jr., died in 1780, leaving him with one other son, William Pitt Jones, and eight daughters. In 1803 Isaac deeded half of his 141-acre farm to William. A few years later William married Abigail Abrams, and the couple had 13 children, 10 of whom lived to maturity. They lived in the east half of the house, while Isaac, his wife, Mary, and his two unmarried daughters lived in the west half. To provide additional space for a kitchen, Isaac moved an existing building and attached it to the west end. In later years, three of William Pitt's most enterprising sons headed west to seek their fortune. Others stayed in Weston but never equaled their illustrious ancestor in wealth or prestige.

Abraham Hews and Hews Pottery

About the time Isaac Jones was building his new tavern, Abraham Hews (1741–1818) began manufacturing earthenware pottery just down the road. The Hews pottery occupies a unique place in the history of ceramics. It was the only one of all the early redware shops to grow into a major business and the only pottery known to have manufactured redware products for more than a century and a half without interruption.[5] At one time, the Hews pottery company was the oldest in continuous operation in the United States.

Figure 16-3. These cups and jugs were made by the Hews pottery, one of the oldest redware producers in New England.

THE PRISCILLA SHOP, 651 BOSTON POST ROAD, WESTON, MASS.

Figure 16-4. Abraham Hews Jr., potter and town postmaster, built this house at 651 Boston Post Road about 1794. The fanlight over the door is characteristic of the Federal style. This house is one of only two brick-enders in Weston.

Although the company used 1765 as the official date of its founding, researchers have suggested 1769 as a more likely date, as Abraham was first taxed as a new resident in 1768. His ledger, preserved at Baker Library at the Harvard Business School, begins in the mid-1770s. Here he records the chamber pots, porringers, mugs, and milk pans sold to Weston residents in the period during and after the Revolutionary War.

When Abraham Hews Jr. (1766–1854) joined his father in business, the pottery became known as Abraham Hews & Sons. In her book *Early New England Potters and Their Wares,* Lura Watkins calls the Hews family "true executives, better suited than the average craftsman to build up an industry."[6] In 1814, the second Abraham is described in deeds as a "gentleman." He built a fine Federal-style house, one of the few "brick-enders" in Weston, and relocated the pottery workshop nearby.[7] In addition to managing the business, Abraham Jr. was appointed the town's third postmaster by President Madison in 1812 and held the office until his death in 1854.[8]

Of Abraham Jr.'s dozen children, six were sons. Horace (b. 1815) served as town treasurer for 29 years. George became known as a musician and piano-maker, and the other four—Marshall, Samuel, Abraham III, and Horatio—were involved in the pottery business. Horatio and his son Albert Horatio provided the leadership that enabled the company to grow from a small local shop to a nationally known company in the years after the Civil War.

Hews Pottery after the Civil War

The timeworn account book of Abraham Hews does not record when the Hews pottery made its first flowerpot, but by the 1860s flowerpots had replaced the jugs and milk pans as the company's most important product. In a speech to the Cambridge Citizens' Trade Association in 1895, Albert Horatio Hews (1844–1903) explained how the company feared it might have to close in the first year of the Civil War. Business was depressed and flowerpots were more a luxury than a necessity.

But orders continued, and post–Civil War manufacturing improvements led to a phenomenal increase in production of the company's specialty. In his 1895 speech, Hews explained that until about 1864 or 1865, common flowerpots had always been made by hand on the potter's wheel. Hews recalled the excitement "when some of the boys in the old pottery 'broke the record' by making one thousand three-inch pots in ten hours."[9] In 1863 the Hews company purchased two of the earliest patented "pot machines," along with the exclusive right to use them in Massachusetts.[10] They improved the machines, and before long a smart boy without any previous experience could make 3,000 in the same 10-hour day.

Another change described by Hews concerned preparation of the clay:

> The hundred years from 1765 to 1865 saw no

Figure 16-5. The Hews letterhead from the 1890s shows the small Weston manufactory at left, contrasted with the North Cambridge facility built in 1871. For a time in the late 19th century, A.H. Hews & Co. was the world's largest manufacturer of flowerpots.

GARDEN VASE AND PEDESTAL.

No. 38.

No. 39.

There being a great variety of vases in the market, we can offer but two particular advantages of this over any other kind of Garden Vase. Plants thrive better in Earthen than any other material. It makes a very superior vase for Parlor use during the Winter, being much lighter to handle than iron or stone. Size, Vase 23-inches high, 16-inches diameter. Pedestal, 21-inches high, 14-inches diameter

Electrotypes for Nos. 38 and 39 united, $1.60, post paid.

A. H. Hews & Co , North Cambridge, Mass. 17

Window Boxes and Domestic Wares

SPITTOON.

No. 20. Parlor Spittoon. Finished variety of colors.

No. 22. Cuspadore. Finished in Vermillion, Green and Maroon.

No. 20.

NEW PATTERN WINDOW BOX. Very Attractive.

CUSPADORE.

No. 21.

No. 22.

CROCUS POTS. Finished in imitation of Rough Stone, Scotch and White Granite.

LOG HANGING POT.

No. 23.

No. 24.

No. 24 may be used as a Hanging Pot or Window Box, the Base, or Saucer being separate from the Log. Furnished in three sizes—9, 12 and 15 inches.

WINDOW BOX, 15 INCHES LONG.

Electrotypes of Nos. 21, 24, 25—65 cent, post paid.

Electrotypes of Nos. 20, 22, 23, at 50 cents each, post paid.

No. 25.

Figure 16-6. The 1878 catalog illustrated some of the garden and domestic items produced by A.H. Hews & Co. The firm was famous for its art pottery.

improvement in the process of preparing clay. It was ground in a wooden tank or tub, propelled by an ox. There is even a tradition to the effect that sometimes when the ox was busy a cow was substituted in his place. Personally I cannot vouch for such a statement; but the old horse in the mill I shall never forget. When I had reached the mature age of six years I was considered old enough to go to the factory, before and after school, and drive that horse to grind clay.[11]

One reason for the company's later choice of a site in North Cambridge was proximity to superior-quality clay. By the 1890s, the company was able to produce 100 tons of sifted clay per day.[12]

The process of drying and firing the pottery was still as crude in 1865 as it had been a century earlier. In his 1895 trade association speech, A.H. Hews noted that "the capacity of our flower pot drying rooms of today far exceeds the entire product of any one year prior to 1865."[13] Before 1865, wood was used for firing. It took three cords of white pine and from 30 to 40 hours of labor to thoroughly fire a small furnace. By 1895, three tons of bituminous coal could fire five times as much pottery in 15 hours.

In 1871 the rapidly growing business, renamed A.H. Hews & Co., moved to a large factory on Crescent Street in North Cambridge, where it was closer to central markets and could expand its facilities. According to Lamson's history, the Hews payroll went from 15 in 1871 to between 85 and 100 in 1889. In 1871 the company produced 800,000 pieces. By 1889, the number had increased to 7,000,000.[14] At one time, the factory manufactured more flowerpots than any other ceramic manufacturer in the world. According to an article in the *Cambridge Chronicle* of 1892, A.H. Hews & Co. was "the largest and leading pottery of its kind in the country."[15]

In addition to the humble unglazed flowerpot, the company moved into the manufacture of ornamental "jardinieres" and art pottery. Where previously Americans had imported such wares, A.H. Hews & Co. began producing new shapes and copying ancient glazes. Among its products were "some of the most beautiful specimens of American Art Pottery."[16] A catalog issued by A.H. Hews & Co. about 1876 shows urns, vases, and art ware imitating Greek and Etruscan pottery. The company made copies of Chinese and Japanese works that compared favorably with those of Oriental master potters.[17] The Hews exhibition at the Philadelphia Centennial was praised by that city's newspaper, which called the garden articles much superior in quality and style to those offered by other potteries, both domestic and foreign. The company was awarded the only medal given for American-made "antique" pottery.[18]

A.H. Hews also sold undecorated chinaware and boxes of prepared colors for those interested in painting their own dishes. Some of their pottery, better known as the Albert and Albertine ware, was decorated with floral designs in high relief and sold in the biscuit stage, before glazing. The company also sold veranda boxes, cuspidors, lamp bases, and

Figure 16-7. Company president Albert Horatio Hews built his Stick-style house in 1880 on family land on Boston Post Road. The house still remains at No. 699, although the porch and other architectural features have been altered over the years. This photograph appeared in the 1897 book Boston, Massachusetts, *by George W. Englehardt.*

umbrella stands and, according to one newspaper article, "If one feels disposed towards cremation Messrs Hews & Co. can furnish an urn, at a very moderate price, that should satisfy the most aesthetic purchaser."[19]

In Weston, Albert Horatio Hews built a handsome Stick-style house in 1880 on family-owned land on what is now Boston Post Road. The mansion, which was pictured in George Englehardt's 1897 book *Boston, Massachusetts,* was within a few hundred yards of the pottery started by his great-grandfather. When he died in 1903, A.H. Hews was praised for his civic-minded contributions to Weston, including his role as director of the fledgling electric light company.

A.H. Hews and his wife, Mary, had no children. After his death the company was reorganized as a corporation. It was renamed Lockwood Products in 1959 and moved to Leominster in 1980. The company made clay pots until the late 1950s, when polypropylene plastic began to be used extensively.[20]

First Baptist Church

The history of the Baptist church in Weston goes back to 1772, when Oliver Hastings was baptized in Framingham. He brought the new faith back to his home on the south side of Weston, where the "reformation," as it was called, gradually took hold. In 1784, four young men in the small Baptist Society—Justus Harrington, Samuel Train Jr., James Hastings, and Joseph Seaverns—built a crude frame meetinghouse on South Avenue east of Wellesley Street.[21] The Baptist Church of Christ in Weston was officially formed in 1789.[22] The distinguished Charles Train, who later became a state representative, began preaching in Weston in 1806. He divided his time between the Framingham and Weston churches, which voted to be known as the Baptist Church of Christ at Weston and Framingham. In 1825, the Framingham church separated from its parent.

Baptists were the first alternative religion in Weston, but before long they were joined by Methodists in regularly protesting "illegal assessments for ministerial tax, ringing bell, providing wood [and] repairing the meeting house" for the established parish church.[23] From 1812 through 1824, a certified list of Baptists, Methodists, and, by 1824, Episcopalians was required for exemption from the ministerial tax.[24]

According to church histories, members of the early church were generally "poor in this world's goods" and "subject to their full share of opprobrium" because of their beliefs.[25] Still, the congregation gradually increased and by the late 1820s the old meetinghouse was inadequate and in disrepair. Because the location on South Avenue was inconvenient, the church purchased a quarter-acre lot on what is now Boston Post Road, where they built a church 44 by 55 feet in size.[26] The 1828 building committee consisted of Deacon Isaac Jones, Josiah Smith, Otis Train, Deacon Uriah Gregory, and Amos Lamson. Timbers from the old meetinghouse were reportedly reused to build a parsonage in 1833.[27] Adult believers were baptized by full immersion in the "Baptismal Pond," located behind what is now the Weston Highway Department. The four-ton "Baptist rock" marking the spot was moved to the church grounds in 1986.[28]

The Rev. Calvin H. Topliff, who served the church during the Civil War years, was one of three men appointed in 1856 to start a public library for Weston. He was a library trustee from 1857 to 1866 and also served as a member of the school committee for at least seven years. A prominent supporter of the Civil War, the Reverend Topliff worked to secure volunteers, "inducing men to enlist to preserve the country from the impending overthrow."[29] It was Topliff who traveled south on behalf of the town to bring back the body of 17-year-old Ralph Abrams Jones, great-grandson of the builder of the Golden Ball, who was killed in the battle of Antietam. According to oral history, the minister brought back rhododendrons and planted them by the wrought-iron gates to the Central Burying Ground in memory of those who had given their lives.[30]

By the last year of Reverend Topliff's ministry, in 1867, the church was prosperous enough to buy an organ and paint the building. For two years after he left, seminary students shared the pulpit and the church experienced a revival called "one of the most extensive, powerful and uplifting revivals of religion that this town has ever known."[31] Fifty members were added in two years.

Figure 16-8. Rev. Amos Harris presided over the rebuilding of First Baptist Church in the early 1880s and the 100th anniversary celebration of 1889.

Figure 16-9. First Baptist Church moved from its original location on South Avenue to Boston Post Road in 1828. No pictures have been found of the 1828 structure, which was completely rebuilt in 1881 in the Victorian Gothic mode.

Figure 16-10. This interior view of the First Baptist Church sanctuary shows the type of stenciling and ornamentation popular when the church was rebuilt in 1881.

Figure 16-11. First Baptist Church also built a new parsonage during the post–Civil War period. The Italianate house still stands at 683 Boston Post Road. The barn at right was converted to a house at No. 681. (Photo c. 1904–09)

Under the leadership of Rev. Amos Harris, the church was "thoroughly renewed" in 1881 and enlarged "with a spacious audience-room as its main sanctuary . . . and a large and beautiful vestry with desirable rooms adjoining."[32] The addition of a baptistry brought an end to outdoor baptisms. Although the building was never called a new church, the Victorian Gothic style and high cost of renovation (reported as $9,000 to $10,000) make it clear that the church was essentially rebuilt.[33] The parsonage was also rebuilt during this period of post–Civil War prosperity. In the early 20th century, a tennis court was added next door "for the young people."[34]

The Reverend Harris served as pastor from 1875 to 1891. During his tenure, the Young People's Union was formed and in 1889 the church celebrated its 100th anniversary. In the previous century, 368 people had been baptized into the church and 138 received by letter. Membership had reached 162. At the anniversary celebration, a stagecoach and four horses carried guests from the railroad station to the church. Speeches filled a 70-page book.[35]

Rev. Joseph Edmund Perry, Ph.D., was minister in 1922 when the congregation decided to replace the aging wooden church. The building committee, chaired by estate owner Charles H. Jones, wanted a site closer to the town center but was unsuccessful in buying land from the Lamsons. Horace Sears offered a lot on Boston Post Road near Wellesley Street, and the building committee recommended that the church accept his offer and build a stone church there. Church members evidently preferred the existing location but extended their gratitude for his neighborly offer.[36]

The first set of plans for a stone or brick church proved too expensive. Church minutes record that "Mr. Jones proposed that we build a white colonial building which he was sure could be built for $50,000. He offered, if we did this, to pay one half the cost."[37] The design eventually used was drawn by Boston architect Charles B. Dunham. The cornerstone, laid on July 15, 1923, had space for a small box containing a church history, the 1922 town report, and a sermon by Dr. Perry. The new building, reported to have cost $56,000 including furnishings, was dedicated on June 1, 1924.

In 1926, the church built a new parsonage for Dr. Perry.[38] Again, Charles H. Jones was chairman of the building committee. In 1961 the Baptist church purchased Whittemore House from the estate of Homer Whittemore for use as a nursery, kindergarten, and Sunday school. The church has operated the weekday Whittemore House Nursery School since 1972.

Whittemore House had been built as a church, although the present structure retains few traces of the Shingle-style original. It was constructed for the Congregational Society, which first met in January

Figure 16-12. Rev. Dr. Joseph E. Perry, minister at First Baptist from 1916 to 1928, was one of Weston's most popular clergymen. In 1917, he started the town's first Boy Scout troop. In 1918, when this photograph was taken, Dr. Perry was given a three-month leave of absence to serve as a military chaplain.

Figure 16-13. During Reverend Perry's tenure, First Baptist replaced its 19th-century wood-frame church with this brick Georgian Revival structure designed by Boston architect Charles Dunham and completed in 1924.

Figure 16-14. This frame church was constructed in 1892 for the newly formed Congregational Society, which disbanded less than a decade later. In 1927, Homer F. Whittemore remodeled it into a house that presently is used as a Sunday school for First Baptist Church and a weekday nursery school (now 670 Boston Post Road).

1891. Later that year, the group called a minister, Robert Gordon, and purchased a lot from Albert Horatio Hews.[39] The first service in the new "chapel" was held in December 1892. After 10 years, the congregation had not increased in size, finances were strained, and the Congregational Society disbanded. Congregationalism was not revived in town until the formation of the present Congregational Church of Weston in 1959–60.

The Fiske Family: Isaac Fiske, Esq.

Isaac Fiske (1778–1861) was a descendant of Watertown farmer Nathan Fiske, one of Weston's earliest settlers. He was born on the Fiske homestead on North Avenue in 1778 and graduated from Harvard College in 1798. In 1802 his marriage to Sukey Hobbs, daughter of tannery owner Ebenezer Hobbs, united these two prominent north-side families. The couple lived in one of the Hobbs family houses on North Avenue until about 1805, when they built a fine house in the Federal style, which still stands at 639 Boston Post Road. Isaac trained in the law under Artemas Ward Jr. and practiced in a small freestanding office across the street from his home. In January 1816 he sold his house to the new minister at First Parish, his friend Rev. Dr. Joseph Field, and bought the ancient Baldwin Tavern next door.[40] After the death of his first wife, Fiske married her sister, Sophronia, in 1832.

Isaac practiced law, traded in real estate, and served 7 years as selectman, 11 years as town clerk, and 4 years as representative to the General Court. In 1820 he was a delegate to the Constitutional Convention. Fiske was Registrar of Probate of Middlesex County from 1817 to 1851. After Artemas Ward Jr. moved his law practice to Concord, Fiske took Alpheus Bigelow Jr. under his tutelage and trained him in the law. Later, Bigelow built his own house and law office on Boston Post Road near the Wayland town line. In 1851 Fiske and Bigelow were two of six Weston men listed in *The Rich Men of Massachusetts,* which described Isaac as "a man of excellent character. Benevolent."[41] Isaac Fiske died in 1861 and was buried in the Central Burying Ground across from his home.

In 1890 the Baldwin Tavern, which had been home to Isaac, his son Augustus H., and several of his eight grandchildren, was consumed by flames in a major fire that broke out in the early hours of the morning. Neighbors and friends worked through the night to save the furniture and keep the blaze from spreading. The total destruction of this "relic of colonial times" galvanized the public. At a special town meeting a few months later, residents finally voted to purchase fire-fighting equipment and take steps to establish a fire department.

Figure 16-15. The 1805 Isaac Fiske/Rev. Joseph Field house was altered a century later by Samuel Mead, who rebuilt the wing, raised the roof, and added dormers and a roof balustrade that was later removed. The house still stands at 639 Boston Post Road.

Augustus H. Fiske and His Children

Although Isaac and Sukey Fiske had nine children, seven died young. Of the remaining two, only Augustus Henry (1805–1865) had children of his own. After graduating from law school, Augustus lived and worked in Boston, where he was "a most thoroughly read lawyer, and his practice was extensive, almost without a parallel in Boston."[42] In 1848 he bought the Rev. Samuel Woodward house on Concord Road across from his boyhood home for use as a summer residence.[43] Because of the newly established Fitchburg Railroad, the hard-driving Fiske was able to commute into Boston. The parson's house remained in the Fiske family until 1972.

Although he "began with small means," by mid-century Augustus H. Fiske was the second richest man in Weston, according to the 1851 publication *The Rich Men of Massachusetts,* which listed his assets at $150,000 and his attributes as follows:

Figure 16-16. Members of the Fiske family sit on their stone wall to protest plans to tear down the wall and widen Concord Road. In the background is the Fiske house, Dudeville, at 19 Concord Road, originally built for Rev. Samuel Woodward. From left are Andrew and Gertrude Fiske; William, Thomas, and Chandler Robbins; Gertrude Fiske (Jr.); and Ned Dickson.

> A man of knock-down logic, keen sarcasm, and the most varied and thorough literary acquirements, with a memory that can clench a thousand new facts with greater ease than it can let go a single old one. Generally handles witnesses without gloves.... In reference to benevolence—although it is our rule to be silent where we cannot praise—we must hazard the suggestion, that whoever seeks an engagement with Augustus H. Fiske in modern financiering is bound to come off "second best." [44]

Augustus was always a frugal liver. But according to B.H. Dickson III, "when he died at age 59 and his widow and children began to enjoy the fruits of his labors, frugality was no longer a consideration. They all set about enjoying themselves . . ."[45]

The oldest of the eight children, Edward ("Ned"), practiced law in his father's Boston office for a few years, retired due to poor health, and then married one of the servants. Their union "created quite a stir," according to Dickson. He and his bride, the former Adelaide Frost, retired to Maine until the death of Augustus in 1865, when they moved back to Weston and built a stylish house right on Boston Post Road.[46] For several years, it had the highest tax valuation of any house in Weston. Not long after the house was finished, Fiske died of consumption, leaving the property to his widow and two children.

The romantic entanglements of Ned's younger brother, George, also kept the family on their toes. George sowed his wild oats in Europe after college but eventually settled down with his second wife, Mary, and started to build Laxfield. The brick mansion on Concord Road near Cherry Brook Station was said to resemble its namesake, the Fiske ancestral manor house in England. George died of pneumonia in 1902, before the house was completed, but Mary finished it and lived there for many years.

Sarah Fiske married the Rev. Chandler Robbins, who was many years older and had adult children of his own. To complicate the family tree, one of his children married Sarah's brother, Charles H. Fiske. The Rev. Chandler Robbins family lived in a house just east of First Parish Church that was demolished in later years to make way for the present Sunday school building. According to Dickson, his aunt Sarah was very tender-hearted. Among her kind deeds, he relates that she would purchase fly traps full of flies from Cutting's Store and then release the flies out in the woods.

Charles H. Fiske: Moving the Jones-Marshall House

Charles Henry Fiske (1840–1921), the fourth of Augustus Fiske's eight children, took over his father's law practice. Of his many contributions to civic life, he is best remembered as Weston's first preservationist. A great admirer of Colonial architecture, he was particularly fond of the Elisha Jones house on Highland Street, also known as the Marshall house. When its owner, Gen. Charles Jackson Paine, decided he wanted to build something new, he offered the stately old edifice to Fiske. At a reported cost of $1,000, Fiske moved it to family land on Boston Post Road. For five years, from 1883 to 1888, it stood between the Reverend Field house

Figure 16-17. The Fiskes host an afternoon of tennis at their country home at 39 Concord Road, which appears in the background. Back row: Mrs. Andrew Fiske, Miss Louisa Case, Mary Dickson, B.H. Dickson Jr., ___, Margaret Slade, and several unknown guests. Front row: Edward Fiske, Charles Merriam, ___, Ned Dickson, ___ Paine, and G.R. (?) Payson.

Figure 16-19. Members of the Fiske family enjoy a summer afternoon at their country place at 39 Concord Road.

and Isaac Fiske's Baldwin Tavern, overlooking the cemetery. [47]

To give the house a more advantageous setting, Fiske purchased land at what is now 22 Church Street and arranged to move it again.[47a] Leaving trees ruined in its wake and traffic in chaos, the house got only as far as Concord Road when it became apparent that it would have to be cut in two. The first half resumed its journey through the town center, but the other half continued to block the main road. Wagon teams had to be rerouted. To compound the problem, on March 12, 1888, New England was hit with its worst blizzard in years. Finally, after four weeks and considerable public outcry, the house reached its destination. The landmark structure still stands as testimony to Fiske's determination.

In the 1890s, Charles Fiske's only son, Charles Jr., rescued another early house from the wrecking ball. The town had purchased the lot at the corner of Boston Post Road and School Street as the site for the new library. Fiske Jr. moved the old Cutting house from there to a hillside location just east of the first transplant, where it became his home. Charles Jr. was the fourth generation of the family to become a lawyer.

Figure 16-19. This portrait of lawyer Andrew Fiske was painted by his daughter, noted artist Gertrude Fiske.

The Andrew Fiske Family: Gertrude Horsford Fiske

Andrew Fiske, the youngest child of Augustus, became a successful lawyer, trustee, and onetime partner in the Boston firm of Hale & Fiske, now Hale & Dorr. He married Gertrude Horsford, whose father, Eben Norton Horsford, was the wealthy scientist-inventor and amateur archaeologist who built Norumbega Tower. The couple spent their winters on Commonwealth Avenue in the Back Bay, spring and fall at the family's Weston estate, Stadhaugh, on Concord Road (since demolished), and summers at Cataumet. Andrew and Gertrude had five children: Gertrude, Augustus, Gardiner, Cornelia ("Posey"), and Hannah.

Figure 16-20. Three of the five children of Andrew and Gertrude Horsford Fiske are pictured here, probably in the 1930s, along with two spouses: from left, Gardiner H. Fiske, Harold B. Willis Sr., Cornelia "Posey" Fiske Willis, Connie Morss Fiske (Mrs. Gardiner Fiske), and Miss Gertrude Horsford Fiske (Jr.). Another daughter, Hannah, had died in 1919, and Augustus is not in the photo.

Their oldest daughter, Gertrude Horsford Fiske

Figure 16-21. Gertrude Horsford Fiske has been described as a major artist of the Boston School, which was active in the early 20th century. She went beyond conventional subject matter in paintings like this one of 1917 called The Weston Quarries, *which now hangs in the Weston Public Library. It was given to the town by the artist's nephew Harold B. Willis Jr.*

(1878–1961), participated in the proper social events for young ladies, including the customary debut.[48] She was a good athlete and avid golfer who one year won the Massachusetts Golf Championship. In her mid-20s, Gertrude turned her attention away from athletics and Boston society to pursue a career as a professional painter. She enrolled in the School of the Museum of Fine Arts in Boston, where she was among a relatively small group of pupils who completed the full seven-year museum school curriculum. She began training about 1904 under Edmund C. Tarbell, Frank Benson, and Philip Hale and completed her studies in 1912.

Her early work was strongly influenced by the Boston academic tradition, which embraced light, color, and attention to detail. Like her contemporaries, she portrayed the elegant and privileged lifestyle that many of the Boston painters shared. But Fiske went beyond these conventions. She painted portraits of tradesmen and the elderly and emphasized modern utilitarian intrusions like telephone poles in her paintings of rural towns. She captured the industrial landscape of the Massachusetts Broken Stone quarry in a work that now hangs in the Weston Public Library.

Figure 16-21A. Gertrude Fiske painted this well-loved view of the Coburn barn on Church Street.

Fiske's unique artistic expression won praise from the critics of her day. The following review in the Boston *Sunday Herald* of February 1916 gives evidence of her early success:

> Largeness and serenity of vision mark the work of this painter, only a few years out of the art school and already hailed as a probable celebrity. What a brilliant emotionality can accomplish when . . . added to right technique is proved in several of her works which are making even jaded gallery trotters take notice.[49]

By her late 30s, she was considered the leading woman painter of Boston. In more recent years, she has been described as "a major figure of the Boston School" and was included in the 1986 Boston Museum of Fine Arts exhibition "The Bostonians: Painters of an Elegant Age: 1870–1930."[50]

Gertrude Fiske's independent financial status gave her freedom to paint where she wished. In Boston, she maintained studios at various times in Copley Hall, Riverway, and Fenway Studios. She had a large studio on the top floor of the barn at the family's Weston home and spent summers at her second home in Ogunquit. Here she painted the rocky Maine coast and beaches and studied with Charles H. Woodbury, whose "bold, aggressive and painterly visions of nature" were to have an influence on her throughout her artistic career. [51]

By 1935 she had exhibited in over 10 one-woman shows, won more than 18 prestigious awards, and was represented in major museums nationwide. With Woodbury, she founded the Ogunquit Art Association. She was also a founding member of the prestigious Guild of Boston Artists and the Concord Art Association. In 1922 Fiske was elected an associate member of the National Academy of Design and that same year was named the first and only woman on the Massachusetts State Art Commission. She was also active in civic affairs in Weston, serving as a trustee of the Weston Public Library for more than 35 years. She was remembered by her family as a "passionate, frugal, loving and very strong-willed person" who remained "a fairly shy person despite her social involvements."[52] Gertrude Fiske was living year-round in Weston and still painting in her studio in the barn when she died in 1961 at age 82. A few years later, the Fiske summer house was torn down.

Harold B. Willis

In 1920, Cornelia ("Posey") Fiske married architect Harold Buckley Willis (1890–1962), a graduate of the Harvard class of 1912 and a decorated war hero known for his service in the French Flying Corps.[53] The couple had three children: Harold Buckley "Bus" Jr., Andrew Fiske, and Hannah Bradford. Halfway up the driveway of the Fiske country place in Weston, Willis built a house patterned after the late-17th-century Parson-Capen House in Topsfield. According to family tradition, he bought a condemned house in Sudbury and utilized the paneling, hand-hewn beams, and staircase.[54] Willis later collected architectural fragments for reuse in his flamboyant Hammond Castle in Gloucester and well-known Cloisters Museum, where a stone cloister was shipped from Europe and reassembled. Salvaged Delft and Islamic tiles from Willis's collection made their way into Fiske family houses along Concord Road.

As an independent architect and later member of the firms of Allen and Collens and Collens, Willis and Beckonert, Willis was involved in the design of buildings throughout the Northeast. His work in Weston is further described in chapter 8. He was later to write: "My greatest kick out of life is from architecture, which is a grand game," and "Too bad there isn't any real money in architecture."[55]

Figure 16-22. In the early years of World War I, Harold B. Willis Sr. (1890–1962) volunteered as an ambulance driver in France. He became a pilot in the French Flying Corps (Lafayette Escadrille), was shot down and captured, and escaped to France after 14 months in a German prison camp. His war decorations included the Legion of Honor and the French Military Medal.

Mary Frances Peirce

In 1836, Benjamin Peirce (1819–1872) bought the house on the corner of Boston Post Road and Concord Road that had once belonged to lawyer Artemas Ward Jr.[56] The house, which he called Lilac Farm, remained in the Peirce family for 78 years.

Mary Francis Peirce (1831–1914), seventh of his 10 children, holds a special place in Weston history. She graduated from Framingham State Normal School and worked for 33 years at Cambridge Latin School, where she taught everything from algebra, geometry, physics and trigonometry to French, Greek, Latin, history, and political economy.[57] When her health failed, she retired to the family homestead and spent the next 28 years researching, sorting, and publishing the records of the Town of Weston.

Without the aid of copiers, computers, or even a typewriter, Mary Francis Peirce organized and edited the early Weston records into four volumes published by the town. Her zeal for perfection was greatly admired by her contemporaries and by historians and genealogists who still rely on her work today. In 1893, Arthur C. Goodell, editor of the Commission on Publication of the Province Laws, wrote to the selectmen:

> I cannot refrain from expressing my admiration of the extreme fidelity with which the work appears to have been performed. . . . Weston is exceptionally fortunate to have one so admirably qualified to do this kind of work perfectly, as the modest editor of these records has shown herself to be.[58]

After her death, the house was rented and then sold to Joseph Stowe Seabury, who in 1920 moved it 200 feet back from the road.[59] Seabury was a real-estate agent for Poole & Seabury, "brokers in City and Country Homes," and a strong advocate for preserving Colonial houses.[60]

Cyrus Clark

Thus far this chapter has chronicled the "old families," descendants of Weston's early settlers. In the late 19th century, a new group of settlers arrived, determined to make their way in a new land. They came from Ireland, Italy, Scandinavia, and, most important to this chapter, Nova Scotia and the Canadian maritime provinces.

Figure 16-23. No. 543 Boston Post Road was built about 1785 and purchased in 1789 by eminent lawyer Artemas Ward Jr. Later owners included town historian Mary Francis Peirce and old-house enthusiast Joseph S. Seabury, who moved it back from the road.

Figure 16-24. Cyrus Clark (1864–1964) came to Weston from Prince Edward Island as a young man and went into the dairy business. His wife, Emma, is in the background.

Figure 16-26. In 1921, the Fiske barn was moved from its original site at 625 Boston Post Road to its present location at No. 582, where it was converted to shops.

Cyrus Clark grew up on Prince Edward Island and immigrated to New England as a young man. When he first came to Weston in the early part of the century, Cyrus was a stableman for the Dicksons. His wife, Emma, also worked for the family. In 1906 he bought an acre of land from the great-grandson of Isaac Jones and built a simple clapboard farmhouse on Golden Ball Road.[61] Cyrus and Emma had four children, John (b. 1905), Bessie (b. 1907), May (b. 1911), and Gladys (b. 1913). In later years, other houses on Golden Ball Road were built by Clark family members.

Clark began cultivating Concord Road land that belonged to the Dickson cousins, the Fiskes. They allowed him to use a large barn at the corner of Boston Post Road and Fiske Lane that had been saved in the Baldwin Tavern fire of 1890. Clark built up his own dairy and kept horses for contracting and hauling. But in 1920, a relative of the Fiskes, Dr. Chandler Robbins, arranged to build a house on the hill next to the barn.[62] Clark lost his lease and sold the contents of the barn at auction. A printed broad-

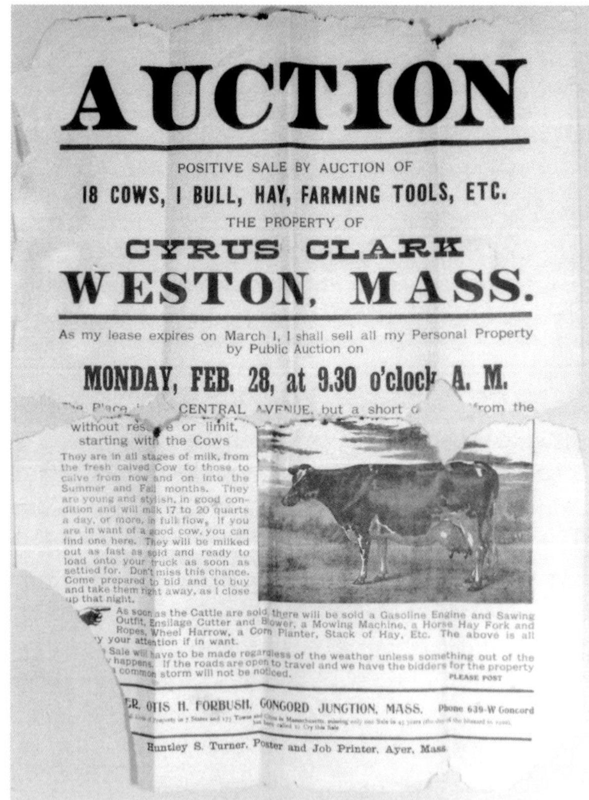

Figure 16-25. In 1920 Cyrus Clark lost his lease on the Fiske barn, where he had kept his cows and equipment. He sold the contents of the barn at auction, including 18 cows advertised as "in all stages of milk" and "young and stylish." Clark built his own barn behind his house on Golden Ball Road and restarted his dairy business there.

side advertised 18 cows, one bull, and assorted farming implements:

> [The cows] are in all stages of milk from the fresh calved cow to those to calve from now and on

> into the summer and fall months. They are young and stylish, in good condition, and will milk 17 to 20 quarts a day or more, in full flow. If you are in want of a good cow, you can find one here. They will be milked out as fast as sold and ready to load onto your truck as soon as settled for. Don't miss this chance. Come prepared to bid and to buy and take them right away, as I close up that night.
>
> As soon as the cattle are sold, there will be sold a Gasoline engine and Sawing outfit, ensilage cutter and blower, a mowing machine, a horse, hay fork and ropes, Wheel Harrow, a Corn Planter, Stack of Hay, etc. [63]

The barn was moved a few hundred feet east to a site across the street, where it was converted to shops.[64] Clark started up his dairy operation again on his own property on Golden Ball Road. He built a barn with stalls for 20 cows and a small dairy building with equipment for sterilizing bottles and pasteurizing milk. Cyrus took care of the cows, which had to be milked twice a day by hand, while his son, John, who hated cows, was in charge of milk processing. When they first went into business, the family and their one hired man washed and sterilized the glass milk bottles manually. Later, they got a bottle-washing machine and an automatic capping machine, but the bottles still had to be placed in the machine by hand. John Clark's son, Jim, recalls climbing inside the pasteurizing tank to clean it.

Everyone in the family worked hard. Although he owned only one acre on Golden Ball Road, Cyrus Clark maintained extensive vegetable gardens on the Fiske land and later on land belonging to Ralph Jones at the end of Golden Ball Road. Emma Clark and her young daughters weeded long rows of carrots and picked beans. They made beer, ginger beer, and elderberry wine. As a young adult, Gladys began working for the Willis family. John supplied wood to the Fiske house in Boston for use in winter. At night he would take his rifle and coonhounds and hunt raccoons in the woods of Weston. Until the advent of artificial fur, he sold the skins for \$20 to \$30 to be fashioned into raccoon coats.

In the early 1950s, Cyrus Clark stopped keeping cows. His barn was torn down and the Clarks began processing milk produced by other dairy farmers. Even before John's son Jim was old enough to drive legally, one of his jobs was to pick up milk from the Miller and Tyler farms in Kendal Green and from Walter Harrington in Wayland. In the 1950s and '60s, Clark's Dairy had two trucks, which delivered milk and cream, ice cream, bacon and eggs, orange juice, and other items to houses in Weston, Wayland, Sudbury, and Lincoln.

Figure 16-27. Cyrus Clark maintained extensive vegetable gardens on land belonging to the Fiske family and Ralph Jones. Here he uses a combination of machine and hand labor to plow fields located approximately where Davenport Road is today.

Figure 16-28. Cyrus Clark's son, John, earned extra money hunting raccoons and selling the pelts for raccoon coats. He is pictured here with his coon hound.

Figure 16-29. Because John Clark hated cows, his father put him in charge of milk processing. In this 1934 picture, John is at the wheel of the delivery truck. The glass milk bottles had to be sterilized, filled, and capped.

Figure 16-30. In 1911, Mr. and Mrs. James Lawson Foote celebrated their 50th wedding anniversary at the old homestead in Woodville, Nova Scotia. All eight sons and one daughter were present for this family portrait, including several who had settled in Weston. Back row: William, Cherith, Hartley, Harvey, James T., Frank, and George Foote. Front row: Irad, James L. and Anna McNair Foote, and Ida Foote Bezanson.

The dairy on Golden Ball Road operated on an honor system. When no family member or employee was present, patrons could help themselves to milk, juice, or whatever else they needed and write down what they took on a pad of paper, along with their name. People would sometimes write down what they took and forget to write their name, and their slips would be hung on the bulletin board until people recognized the handwriting. The dairy wasn't locked up until 9 or 10 o'clock at night.

Cyrus Clark died in January 1964 at age 99-½. He was active, together with his son John, in the operation of the dairy business until just before his death. Not long after, Clark's Dairy closed its doors. In 1968, Cyrus Clark's grandson Jim began working as a barber in the town center.

George A. Foote: Dealer in Coal and Ice

At the turn of the century, times were hard in Nova Scotia. The children of farmers like James L. Foote came to New England in search of jobs and a better life. Of his nine children, six settled in Weston for at least part of their lives: James, George, Cherith, Irad, William, and Frank. [65] None had more than an elementary school education. James and George were among the Weston residents profiled in *Middlesex County and Its People,* a 1927 four-volume history that included short biographical entries of well-known members of the community.[66] James had a prosperous blacksmith shop and cider mill on North Avenue. George's success as a dealer in coal, wood, ice, and building supplies is described below. Cherith worked over the years as a florist, teamster, wood dealer, and milkman who sold milk in square glass bottles from his dairy on Warren Avenue. Irad was a carpenter and William worked as a painter and chair maker before moving to Waltham. Frank came to Weston to help James run Foote's Spa at the west end of the relocated Fiske barn on Boston Post Road. The spa, which operated in the 1920s, sold ice cream, soda, and meals cooked by Frank's wife, Alice.

George Albert Foote (1867–1944) came to Weston in 1884. According to the 1927 history, he was "able and energetic" and built up "an enterprise which came to be known as one of the leading concerns of its kind in this section."[67] In 1895 he purchased land on Concord Road next to the Cherry Brook Railroad Station, one of only two stops in Weston on the Central Massachusetts Railroad and a good location for off-loading freight.[68] Foote set up supply yards and an office on the east side of Concord Road south of the tracks and in 1905 built his house there. In 1911 he advertised as a "dealer in best quality coal, wood, ice, lime, brick, cement, flue lining and tile pipe, etc."[69] Another company located at Cherry Brook beginning about 1904 was J. Cushing & Co., wholesale dealers in grain, flour, feed, hay, straw, and salt.[70]

By 1915, Foote's business had grown so large that he sold off the coal and building-supply dealership to the Waltham Coal Company and concentrated on ice. Except for farmers and estate owners who cut and stored their own ice, Foote was the only local supplier. He "harvested" ice from Foote's Pond on Warren Avenue, where the water level was raised by damming the stream.[71] Winters were colder then and the pond froze each year, enough for one, two, and sometimes even three harvestings, as in the winter of 1903–04. Each winter, the *Waltham Daily Free Press Tribune* kept readers informed about the thickness of the ice, which varied between about 9 and 12 inches.

Foote's ice harvest was a community event. The ice was cut by hand or with horse-drawn cutters, later replaced by machine cutters. As many as 25 men were needed. Sections of about 20 blocks would be partially cut and then floated like small icebergs over to the shore. The individual ice cakes, each about one foot thick, were then split apart with a spear and directed onto an inclined ramp, where they could be pulled out of the water by rods attached on each side with a pulley chain. When the ice cakes reached the top of the ramp, they would slide down a sluiceway to a platform between Foote's two large wooden icehouses. Here men would pack the blocks into the houses in layers separated by sawdust and insulated with hay.

After the ice was harvested and the pond refroze, children were welcome to skate on Foote's Pond, which was a popular gathering place. At one time the town maintained a floodlight and warming hut. Dozens of neighborhood children played Snap the Whip and Fox and Geese, competed in hockey games, or skated through the meadow and out to the railroad tracks.

Foote's employees delivered ice around town in yellow delivery trucks with a scale at the rear. Drivers chipped off chunks of ice to be weighed and carried to the customer's "ice box." After the two icehouses were destroyed by fire in 1936, Foote built a new one on his Concord Road property and had ice brought in by rail. Not long after, electric refrigerators brought an end to the ice business.

The Footes were connected, both by marriage and in business, with another family from Nova Scotia who settled in the area. In 1900 Cherith Foote married Orinda Ella Ogilvie, sister of Beriah Ogilvie. In 1910 Cherith sold part of his land on Warren Avenue to Beriah Ogilvie, whose business still supplies the needs of Weston residents at the turn of the 21st century.[72]

B.L. Ogilvie & Sons: A Family Company

Beriah Lemont Ogilvie (1877–1951) was born in Kings County, Nova Scotia, the son of a sea captain. Like the Foote brothers, he had only a limited primary school education before coming to Weston in 1894. After working as foreman at J. Cushing's feed store for 13 years, Ogilvie organized his own business in 1919. He began with teaming and before long was selling hay, grain, building materials, wood, coal, cement, and farm implements. An advertisement for B.L. Ogilvie's in a Friendly Society program of 1925 illustrates the diversity of the business after only six years:

Figure 16-31. Beriah Ogilvie came to Weston from Nova Scotia and worked at Cushing's feed store before starting his own business in 1919. This picture shows his first truck, fashioned from a Model T Ford. Beriah's son Harold stands at left alongside his mother and younger brother, Raymond.

Figure 16-32. This 1939 office picture shows cashier Raymond Ogilvie standing behind the register at B.L. Ogilvie & Sons Inc., with John Loring (center) and Harold Ogilvie (right).

> Contracts for lumber filled. Coal bins filled. Grain orders promptly attended to. Fertilizers and seeds to suit your needs. Hay, flour, lime, cement and bricks. Sawdust, shavings, straw and poultry litter. Equipment for all kinds of trucking. Oak wood and pine kindling. Biscuits and Kibbles for dogs. [73]

The company acquired a fleet of trucks in order to plow Weston's roads and driveways. By 1927, Ogilvie's biographical sketch in *Middlesex County and Its People* reported that, despite postwar financial fluctuations, Ogilvie had made his business an "unqualified and lasting success."[74] He had increased the business from one truck to six, was employing 10 men, and had taken his place as "one of the financial leaders of this section."

Beriah Ogilvie's success was due in part to the hard work of his large extended family. In 1900 Ogilvie married Mary Elizabeth Arrington, a Salem girl who was working as a nursery maid for a local family. The couple had five children: Harold (1902–1965), Gladys "Dolly" (Mrs. Francis Whittemore Jr.),

Figure 16-33. Employees at the annual B.L. Ogilvie & Sons dinner in 1941, with Beriah Ogilvie (seated, third from left).

Figure 16-34. The Ogilvie family built up a fleet of trucks that were painted bright blue with BLUE TRUCK DELIVERY *in yellow letters. Here Gus Lawson and Ray Foote deliver coal in 1938.*

Delcia "Pearl" (Mrs. Julius Pickering), Myrtle "Vina" (Mrs. Vernon MacLeod), and Raymond (b. 1912). Everyone worked in the business. Bookkeeping was done by Mary Elizabeth and later by all three daughters. The five presidents of the company have all been family members: Beriah Ogilvie, his sons Harold and Raymond, Dolly's son Alden Whittemore, and Alden's brother-in-law Kenneth Sutherland. Beriah's nephew Frederick Foote was also one of the cornerstones in the business in the early years. In 1910, Beriah built a house on Warren Avenue next to where he later located his business. In the 1920s

Figure 16-35. The grain room and lumberyard of B.L. Ogilvie & Sons in 1941.

Figure 16-36. Percy Warren (1865–1917) was president and manager of Weston Water Company and Weston's first superintendent of streets. He used modern methods to bring town roads up to the standards needed in the automobile age.

and 1930s, members of the family built houses on the south side of Warren Place.

To supply local needs for lumber, Ogilvie built a sawmill and cut trees from the family woodlot on Sudbury Road into rough lumber used for building. Farmers could bring their own logs to be cut to order. The sawmill was the closest to Boston and cut logs from as far away as Weymouth. Custom sawing proved a problem, as farmers would return when the store was closed on Sundays and take what they thought was their wood. In later years, the sawmill was discontinued and Ogilvie's began supplying hardware and lumber.

When Beriah Ogilvie started on Warren Avenue, there was no store, just a barn where he kept horses for teaming and hauling. Beginning in 1928, the company had a yard and railroad siding at the end of Warren Avenue where coal and supplies could be unloaded. Hay, peat moss, and wood shavings were stored here in a cement-block garage. Later, when trucks replaced horses, Ogilvie took out the stanchions in the barn and put up pegboard for hanging farm implements. As coal furnaces became obsolete, the company began selling oil burners and heating oil. It became known for its "Blue Truck Delivery" fleet, driven by employees in blue uniforms. In 1953–54, B.L. Ogilvie & Sons constructed an office in front of the barn, and in 1975 the company tore down the barn and built a 5,000-square-foot hardware and garden building behind the office. The large metal lumber storage building in the rear was constructed in 1992. Gradually, the business shifted from supplying farmers to supplying suburbanites moving into Weston.

John Edward Lingley and Sons

John Edward Lingley came to Weston from Port Williams, Nova Scotia, and initially obtained work as a chauffeur for General Paine. In 1924 he bought a Model T truck and started picking up rubbish door to door. People separated out garbage and table scraps, which were fed to pigs. Lingley dug foundations, took care of yards, cut ice for George Foote, and was reportedly the first to mow the town common with a power mower.[75] His wife, Hilma, did ironing for Chandler Robbins. They had four sons—John, Ted, Henry, and Harold—three of whom settled around Warren Avenue. Harold was a sergeant on the Weston police force and Ted kept a poultry farm at the end of Warren Avenue. Henry delivered coal for Ogilvie's, worked in the sawmill, continued his father's trash business, moved furniture, supplied wood, sold loam and gravel, and slaughtered livestock in the woods behind Warren Lane. As he was later to say, "If there was a nickel in it, we'd do it."

Percy and Harry Warren and the Development of Warren Avenue

What is now Warren Avenue does not even appear on the 1875 map. The area took on increased importance when the Central Massachusetts Railroad began service in 1881, allowing for convenient freight delivery. In 1896, private investors formed the Weston Water Company and Weston Electric Light Company. They built a small brick building on the still unnamed road, initially shared by both companies.[76] Power for the steam generators and water pumps was supplied by coal unloaded at a railroad siding.

Percy Warren (1865–1917) was president and

Figure 16-37. In the early 20th century, the Weston Rod and Gun Club operated a skeet-shooting club on what is now Gun Club Lane.

manager of the Weston Water Company, and his brother Harry (1876–1958) worked for the Weston Electric Light Company and its later owner, Edison Electric Illuminating Company. Both were public-spirited men instrumental in introducing new services to the town. Percy graduated from Weston High School and Northeastern University and took post-graduate courses in engineering at MIT. In addition to running the water company, he served as Weston's first superintendent of streets and developed a system of construction and maintenance that made liberal use of machinery to improve roads to modern standards. Percy built his house at the end of Warren Avenue across from the water and electric company headquarters.

In 1905, the *Waltham Daily Free Press Tribune* reported that William Whittemore and Percy Warren were building houses on the road to the pumping station, known as Ice House Road but not yet formally christened:

> When these houses are finished there will be 11 dwellings, the pumping station and the ice house on this road. It is a much used road, but has not yet any name. "Water Street" has been suggested as appropriate.[77]

Public sentiment apparently favored the name "Warren," which was given to all three streets in the neighborhood: Warren Avenue, Warren Lane, and Warren Place. [78]

Percy Warren was yet another neighborhood resident profiled in *Middlesex County and Its People,* in 1927:

> The picture that will ever remain warm in the hearts of his host of friends and admirers in Weston . . . is that of Mr. Warren driving his automobile through the streets, usually with a group of Italians going to or from work, or children whom he loved so well, or neighbors whom he was taking to their homes. . . . Few men have devoted their lives and activities to the general welfare of their community and for the promoting of the progress and development of their city as had Mr. Warren . . .[79]

When he died in June 1917, he was remembered as "one of Weston's best loved citizens."[80]

Golden Ball Hotel

By the late 19th century, the former Golden Ball Tavern had passed into the hands of George H. Jones, great-grandson of Isaac. He and his wife, the former Lettie Frost, had three children: George Jr. (1870–1899), Mary Caroline "Mae" (1873–1957), and Ralph Frost (1881–1963).

Sometime in the early 1880s, the family began taking in boarders. Mae, who was a young girl at the time, later wrote a short "Sketch of the Boarders & Inhabitants of Jones's Golden Ball Hotel."[81] She recalled the first two brothers from St. John, New Brunswick, who came to earn their living and support the family back home. For two summers, the treasurer of the Galveston Railroad in Galveston, Texas, vacationed here with his wife. The Joneses boarded the men who were remodeling C.J. Paine's house and the men building the

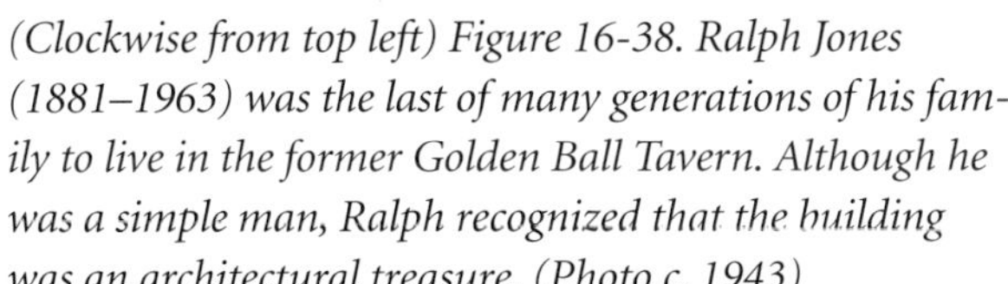

(Clockwise from top left) Figure 16-38. Ralph Jones (1881–1963) was the last of many generations of his family to live in the former Golden Ball Tavern. Although he was a simple man, Ralph recognized that the building was an architectural treasure. (Photo c. 1943)

Figure 16-39. This photograph of the former Golden Ball Tavern exemplifies one of the landscape conventions of the turn of the century, the profusion of vines around the doorway. In addition to farming, the Jones family earned extra income taking in boarders.

Figure 16-40. Rather than restore the Golden Ball Tavern to reflect a single time period, the museum shows the "layers of history" and interprets the house as it evolved over time.

Figure 16-41. Since 1968, the Golden Ball Tavern Museum has been sponsoring an outdoor antique show to raise money for museum maintenance and programs. (Photo c. 1978)

Figure 16-42. Howard Gambrill, shown here with his wife, Mary, led the community-wide effort to preserve the Golden Ball Tavern and turn it into a museum.

new First Parish Church. And then there were the "cat boarders":

> The Angelic and the cranky ones all get mixed and sure enough we find a little of both mixed up in Mr. and Mrs. Gerry or better known at the Golden Ball as the cat boarders. For with them came two monstrous cats weighing about twenty pounds and when the mistress called for Sir Thomas he walks dignified down into the breakfast room where he eats with his dear master & mistress.[82]

In the kitchen, Lettie Jones and her daughter were assisted by servant girls including "the pale-faced girl from Nova Scotia" and "our jolly Stella." Also living in the house at that time were two sons of William Pitt Jones: Charles (1824–1899) and William (1826–1904), neither of whom married.[83] When Mae married Harry Warren, the couple lived in the house as well.

In his entire life, Ralph Frost Jones rarely spent even a night away from the house. He was a lean, small man, very taciturn. He kept three or four cows, raised chickens, hayed his fields, and raised market crops like strawberries and asparagus. He made egg deliveries. Neighbors would come by with milk containers to be filled. A hired man lived out back and helped with the chores. Whenever Mae or Ralph needed money, they would sell off land or antique furniture from the house.

Ralph regarded himself as caretaker of the historic tavern. He and Mae resisted Harry Warren's suggestion to sell it because it was so expensive to heat and maintain. Ralph knew the house was special. For years, a class from Harvard came out to Weston every year to study the structure of the unusual double gambrel roof.[84] He had hoped to leave the Golden Ball to his niece, Alice Warren, but she and her parents all died before Ralph.

Figure 16-43. The Fiske Law Office, shown here at the time of the 1976 Bicentennial parade, was constructed about 1805 and has been used over the years as a law office, playhouse, cemetery department office, housing for veterans, and historical society headquarters.

Golden Ball Tavern Museum

The story of how the 18th-century Golden Ball Tavern became a museum begins with Weston's 250th anniversary celebration in 1963. Howard Gambrill Jr., a recently retired Gillette Company executive, was chairman of the committee charged with awarding plaques to the 50 oldest houses in Weston. Gambrill had always been interested in early houses and served as a board member of the Society for the Preservation of New England Antiquities and a trustee of Historic Deerfield. He called on the elderly Ralph Jones, who gave him a tour of the house where his family had lived for six generations. Gambrill's reaction has been described as "love at first sight."

When Ralph Jones died shortly thereafter, the house and six acres were placed on the market.[85] Development appeared inevitable. To save what he recognized as a town treasure, Howard Gambrill bought the property and made a proposition to the people of Weston. If they demonstrated that they, too, cared about the tavern by raising $100,000 to restore and endow it, the Gambrills would donate the entire property to a museum trust.[86] Gambrill felt the tavern should not be tax-supported. He encouraged widespread, grassroots support for a building that would provide for a better understanding of earlier generations and serve as a focus for unified community spirit. He was committed to a careful and well-endowed preservation effort meeting the highest standards of authenticity.

Saving the Golden Ball was a group effort that over the years has involved hundreds of Weston residents as donors and volunteers. The original trustees included Gambrill as chairman, his wife and co-preservationist Mary Butler Gambrill, Brenton H. Dickson III, Alice Perry [Lucas], Alfred Thomas, Lawrence H. Pexton, and Margaret "Pit" Dumaine. Dumaine is credited with suggesting the idea of the outdoor antique show, first held in 1968. Homer C. Lucas was an early stalwart who was instrumental in raising the endowment money.

By May 1964, the Gambrills had established the Golden Ball Tavern Trust and the public got their first look at the inside of the house. The next year, visitors were invited to vote on whether to restore the house to its 18th-century appearance or leave it as it was in 1965, showing changes that had taken place over 200 years. Voters opted to show the layers of history.

A search of the attic made clear the extent to which Ralph Jones had acted as custodian of the family history. The space was crammed with two centuries of artifacts including furniture, ceramics, mirrors, kitchen utensils, surveying gear, and an old loom. Among the family papers was a book of unsigned tickets from the Watertown Bridge lottery, which Isaac Jones, Ralph's great-great-grandfather, had the franchise to sell. Architectural fragments such as 18th-century window sash and wood-panel sliding shutters were found in the attic, allowing for more accurate restoration. Ralph even saved the gilded wooden "golden ball," which now hangs in the museum.

Later History of the Fiske Law Office

Although Isaac Fiske was the first of many generations of Fiske lawyers, he was the only one to conduct business from the quaint two-room office on Boston Post Road. An article in the *Boston Globe* of 1916 shows a picture of the "little old law office" then being used as a playhouse where Fiske children could give parties, play games, and dress their dolls.[87] In 1920, when the Fiske heirs divided their Weston property, Charles H. Fiske Jr. got the law office. He enlarged it by adding a rear ell.[88] In 1928, Charles Jr. gave the building to the Town of Weston with the stipulation that if the town ever wanted to tear it down, Fiske heirs would have the right to purchase and move it.[89]

The building was used as the cemetery office until 1936, when it was turned over to the five-year-old Weston Historical Committee as a respository for its growing collection of historical records and relics. Miss Gertrude Fiske was chair of the original committee, which also included Alice Jones and Edward P. Ripley. When the Jones sisters died and left the former Josiah Smith Tavern to the Society for the Preservation of New England Antiquities, the town's collection was moved to the tavern. The Fiske Law Office was pressed into service for rental to World War II veterans. Plumbing was simple and adequate, but "insulation was conspicuous by its absence" and tenants had trouble keeping warm.[90]

When the last tenant died in 1965, the newly formed Weston Historical Society offered to restore and maintain the building as its headquarters. Headed by President Harold Travis and Restoration Chairman F. Leslie Ford, the society leased the building in 1966. Members put in hundreds of volunteer hours restoring it over the next four years. Beginning in the 1970s, the society moved parts of its collection to the Josiah Smith Tavern. In the early 1990s, they returned responsibility for the Fiske Law Office to the town.

Boston Post Road from Highland Street to Wayland

On the north side of Boston Post Road just west of Highland Street was the John Flagg Tavern, which gained fame when President George Washington spent the night there on October 23, 1789, on his journey to New England. Lamson reports that Colonel Marshall and town officials welcomed him the next morning and "his progress through the towns of New England was one uninterrupted ovation, the people far and near flocking along his route."[91] President John Quincy Adams dined at the Flagg Tavern in 1798.[92] It was for many years the principal stopping place for New York mail coaches and continued in use well past 1830, reportedly longer than any other tavern in Weston.

Figure 16-44. George Emerson lived in a dilapidated shack on the site of the Flagg Tavern, which had burned in 1902. His yard was filled with charred remains from the fire, along with rubbish and junk of every description. Emerson raised and trained gamecocks and was known for the illegal cockfights held in his barn.

By 1875 the former tavern had been purchased by farmer Charles Emerson, whose family owned it when it burned to the ground in 1902. The two charred brick chimneys weren't demolished until decades later and, in the interim, served as the principal landmark in Weston for early motorists traveling by automobile to New York.[93] George W.D. Emerson, Charles's son, lived beyond the cellar hole in a dilapidated shack surrounded by rubbish and junk. He was, in the words of Brenton H. Dickson III, "as ungroomed as his surroundings."[94] To illustrate his eccentric style, one resident recalled the year Emerson's horse died in his front yard during the winter and he refused to move the body until spring.[95]

Emerson was a poultryman who specialized in raising and training gamecocks. He and his birds are mentioned occasionally in the Weston column of the *Waltham Daily Free Press Tribune*. For example, his Bantivia Jungle gamecock, a native of India

Figure 16-45. District School #2 was located on Highland Street until the bypass was constructed in the early 1930s. At that time, it was moved to its present site at 700 Boston Post Road.

named Murderer, "seemed to have a decided antipathy to anything religious" and to be "possessed of an evil spirit."[96] Emerson had another specialty as well. Before his barn became too dilapidated for safety, gentlemen would congregate there for illegal cockfights often raided by local police.[97]

In 1919 George Emerson leased a half-acre to the Paul Revere Garage for a filling station later known as the Flagg Tavern Filling Station. The station was there into the 1940s. In 1921 Emerson leased land to another firm to construct and maintain "golf links" for 10 years on any part of his 65 acres. [98]

Most of the 18th-and early-19th-century houses along the west end of Boston Post Road were originally farmhouses on large tracts of land. Beginning in the late 19th century, some of this land was sold for country estates. In 1891–92, wool merchant Lorenzo N. Kettle purchased land from Edward H. Sibley, whose family homestead was located across the street. Kettle's land extended to Love Lane and included all of what is now Claridge Drive and Sutton Place.[99] His 1892 Colonial Revival frame mansion was designed by Samuel Mead, a talented young architect who had moved to Weston only a year before. A 1902 newspaper article in the *Boston Sunday Herald* described the estate:

> A fringe of elms protects the house from a view of the street, except at one point, and a winding driveway through the trees leads to the mansion on the hill. There are 45 acres in this estate, and from the hilltop, where the house stands, there is a fine view of the distant hills, and of the estate of Grant Walker . . .[100]

Kettle maintained a Boston residence at 687 Boylston Street as well as a "cottage" in Bar Harbor.[101] He died in 1910, and the property was sold in 1919 to Walter H. Walker, who was also in the wool business. At that time, it included the house, stable, garage, barn, foreman's cottage, and 46 acres of "finely developed land," according to the newspaper, which added, "The avenues, constructed at great expense and extending through the grounds for nearly a mile, together with lawns, gardens, shrubs and decorative shade trees, are valuable and attractive features of the estate."[102] The property continued in use as a gentleman's farm until after World War II. Francis P. Kirk, who bought it from Walker in 1938, sold "Massachusetts grade" apples "grown and packed by F.P. Kirk at Stonyridge."[103] Louis DeVito, longtime caretaker of the estate and manager of the large apple orchard, came to Weston from Italy in 1923, at age 18.

Figure 16-46. This photograph of 787 Boston Post Road was taken from a field across the street. Architectural details such as the corner quoins are typical of the late Georgian period, while the hip roof and delicate porch columns are characteristic of the Federal style, which became popular after the Revolutionary War.

Across the street, another early farmstead was purchased in 1922 by Miss Marion B. Farnsworth, who named it Exmoor Farm. Miss Farnsworth was a serious gentlewoman farmer who maintained an apple orchard and kept Jersey cows, poultry, and two Exmoor ponies said to be the first of the breed in this country. The property included a Colonial farmhouse that she moved in 1935, along with its sprawling ells, wings, and porches, over the apple orchard to a site 700 feet back from the road, where she doubled it in size. Eleanor Raymond was the architect for the additions and for a Colonial Revival house built on the old foundation. Miss Farnsworth acquired the 65-acre Emerson property in 1931 and eventually owned a total of 150 acres. About 40 acres across the railroad tracks in the Jericho Forest were conveyed to the town in the late 1950s as conservation land. In 1954, the property was purchased by Frank B. Carter Jr. and his wife, Lucy, who renamed it Woodleigh and maintained it as a working farm.

In 1920, the Trustees of the Charles Jackson Paine Estate purchased 33 acres of the former Livermore Farm extending from Boston Post Road to Highland Street adjacent to the Paine estate. The property, which includes a mid-century Greek Revival farmhouse on Boston Post Road, remains undeveloped.[104]

For much of the 19th century, the land that is now Weston Estates belonged to the Brown family. They farmed it for several generations until the death of market gardener and prominent town leader Henry L. Brown (1840–1912). In 1917, the 125-acre farm in Weston and Wayland was sold to Louis Dean (1879–1960), who lived in the farmhouse on Boston Post Road.[105] Dean ran a dairy, raised vegetables, and kept a large piggery at the end of what is now Buckskin Drive and extending into Wayland. This piggery was one of several in Weston, the others being at South Avenue and Winter Street and on Dean's other farm, on Conant Road near the Lincoln town line. After the war, the dairy farm was discontinued. Dean Dairy still operated an ice-cream stand there and in Waltham, selling sundaes, banana splits, and other ice-cream treats to carloads of eager customers.

In 1966 Louis Dean's son, Wendall, sold the farm to Weston Estates Corporation. The 1966 subdivision agreement, signed by Ernest Comeau, created more than 50 lots in Weston on Buckskin Drive and parts of Westerly Road and Whispering Lane.[106] The main house was moved to one of the newly created lots and the hired hands' house was enlarged and remodeled to fit in with the new development.[107] Lots in Weston Estates were targeted to an upscale market and sold with restrictions like prohibiting the hanging of clothes out to dry and the storage of boats within sight of the street. The first home, a sales model designed by Scholtz Homes, was completed by the Comeau construction company at 61 Buckskin Drive in 1968.[108]

Figure 16-47. Alpheus Bigelow Jr. built this Federal-style law office about 1827 across the street from his elegant residence. The office is similar in style to that of Bigelow's mentor, Isaac Fiske. (Photo c. 1930s)

Figure 16-48. This photograph of the Ephraim Cutting house conveys the simple beauty of the rural landscape. The house, which stood at 829 Boston Post Road, was torn down in 1928.

Next to the Dean property, Paul Clifford, who was in the wool business in Boston, purchased land from the Bigelow heirs in 1920. Clifford maintained the approximately 30 acres on the south side of the street as an apple orchard. Blanche Bigelow, the last of her family to live in Weston, was later to write about what might have happened to this property:

> In 1919, before the days of zoning, my Father's children had a very high offer from an Air Plane Co. for the land on which the Orchard now stands. While we did not want to accept the offer ... we were not in a position to refuse such a large sum. In the perplexity, my Uncle ... sent for Mr. Clifford who at once took the matter into his own hands. By offering us a fine price for the land and by turning it into an orchard, he preserved the residential character of the region.[109]

The property was sold in 1949 and subdivided into 19 lots on Apple Crest Road.[110]

The size of homes and lots in the post–World War II period contrasted with a 13-lot subdivision of 1930, Irvington Court, at the corner of Boston Post Road and Highland Street. This land, which had belonged to the Hews family, was developed by J. Irving Connolly with small Colonial Revival houses on lots generally 10,000 to 16,000 square feet.[111]

Many families on the north side of Boston Post Road contributed to the creation of the Jericho Town Forest between the mid-1950s and mid-1970s. The largest gift, from Blanche T. Bigelow, was a bit more than 100 acres donated in 1957. Marion Farnsworth made major contributions. Parcels over 10 acres were also given by Sweidler Building Company; Paul and Lula Bartlett; Brenton H. Dickson III, trustee; and the estate of Gertrude H. Fiske.

Buildings: Boston Post Road (West)

3 Applecrest Road. Alpheus Bigelow Jr. Law Office (see 863 Boston Post Road).

543 Boston Post Road (c.1785). This Georgian-style house was built for the brothers Daniel and Ebenezer Eaton, who were leather dressers. In 1789, it was purchased by eminent lawyer Artemas Ward Jr., who was the son of Gen. Artemas Ward of Shrewsbury, the first commander in chief of the Continental Army under George Washington. Notable details include corner quoins and a delicate portico on the outside and wood paneling, overmantels, and imported fireplace tiles in the well-preserved interior rooms. The Benjamin Peirce family lived here for 78 years, until the death of Mary Francis Peirce in 1914. In 1920, Joseph S. Seabury moved the house back from the road to its present site.

Boston Post Road, corner Concord Road. Soldiers Field Park, given to the Town of Weston after World War I by the descendants of Isaac and Augustus Henry Fiske in memory of Charles Henry Fiske 3rd, U.S. Infantry, who died in France in 1918. Harold Willis designed the monument, which was built in 1931.

Boston Post Road. Farmers' Burying or Burial Ground. Oldest cemetery in Weston, established 1703.

Boston Post Road. Central Cemetery (originally Central Burying or Burial Ground). The 1.5 acres was conveyed to the town by Isaac Jones on January 1, 1790, and the first burial was May 7, 1792. A stone wall delineates the boundaries. In 1937 the town received a gift of $5,000 from Miss Josephine Merriam of Minneapolis to build the wrought-metal and stone gateway, which was designed by Allen, Collens and Willis.

Boston Post Road. Linwood Cemetery, established in 1873 on nine acres purchased from Marshall Hews. First burial, July 1874. Enlarged in 1904 and again in 1951; now 50 acres.

582 Boston Post Road. Barn moved in 1921 from the Fiske property at No. 625 and converted to shops. Among the businesses once located here were Foote's Spa, Weston Studio of Upholstery, Young's Market, Chaplin's ice-cream store and lunch counter, and Orth Chevrolet Sales and Service.[112]

596 Boston Post Road. From the early 1920s until 1957, Charles Wheelock owned and operated a service station here. Known as Colonial Motors, it was always a busy station handling primarily auto service and repair but also pumping gas and towing. At one time a wrestling ring was underneath the garage and wrestling matches were held once a week. This ended when too many outsiders, described as "a rough crowd," started to attend. Edward Abbott operated the station from 1957 to 1982.

625 Boston Post Road. Site of the 18th-century Baldwin Tavern, which was purchased by Isaac Fiske about 1815 and lived in by Fiske family members until it burned in 1890. The site remained vacant, except for the large barn, until the present house was built in 1921–22 for Chandler Robbins and Laura (Foster) Robbins. Robbins's father, also named Chandler, was married to Sarah Fiske, granddaughter of Isaac Fiske. Before the new house was built, the Fiskes moved the barn to a new location across the street at No. 582.

626 Boston Post Road (c. 1805). Fiske Law Office. Although the builder and the construction date of the law office have been the subject of some debate, a 1973 report by the Weston Historical Commission stated that "no one has questioned the fact that Isaac Fiske used the Law Office after 1805."[113] The hip roof is typical of the Federal style.

639 Boston Post Road (c. 1805). Fiske-Field House. Built for lawyer Isaac Fiske. (The house has been attributed to Salem architect Samuel McIntire but no documentation exists for this claim.) The Federal-style house has a gracious center hall and four-over-four room plan. In 1815, Fiske sold it to Rev. Joseph Field, who occupied the house until his death in 1869. In 1907 the house was remodeled under the direction of architect Samuel Mead, who enlarged and renovated the east wing, raised the hip roof to create a third story, and added dormers and a decorative balustrade that was later removed. Before and after photographs were printed in Joseph Seabury's 1916 book *New Homes Under Old Roofs*.

646 Boston Post Road (c. 1887). Transitional Italianate/Queen Anne house built about 1887 for farmer William F. Sherburne, who purchased his half-acre lot from a member of the Jones family.[114]

647 Boston Post Road (c. 1863). Mansard cottage built about 1863 for a member of the Hews family.

649 Boston Post Road (1906). The east wing of the neighboring Hews house at No. 651 was removed to make way for this house, built by contractor H.L. Cooper for Mrs. Horace Hews.[115]

650 Boston Post Road (1909–10). "Four Square" house built for Edward A. Jones, who is listed in the 1911 directory as a publisher in Boston. The builder was John C. Macdonald. In 1921 the house was sold to the Protestant Episcopal Church of the Diocese of Massachusetts and served as the rectory for St. Peter's Church until the congregation moved from its original location at 439 Boston Post Road.

651 Boston Post Road (c. 1794). Built for Abraham Hews Jr., who succeeded his father in managing the family pottery. The house is one of only two brick-enders in Weston. The dormers were added later. Both interior and exterior have been carefully preserved. Hews was the town's third postmaster. The post office was located in the wing on the west side of the house.

657 Boston Post Road (1923–24). First Baptist Church. Brick Georgian Revival church designed by Charles P. Dunham and built by Charles H. Mead.

661 Boston Post Road (c. 1854).

662 Boston Post Road (1765–68). Golden Ball Tavern. Built for Isaac Jones, the tavern has been called "the most beautifully proportioned example of Georgian architecture" in Weston. The housewright has never been identified. The house has a finely detailed center doorway and double-hipped roof, which in the northern and middle colonies occurred primarily on high-style examples. The room plan is four-over-four with a central hallway. Interior woodwork, paneling, and fireplaces are remarkably well preserved. The former tavern is a museum open to the public.

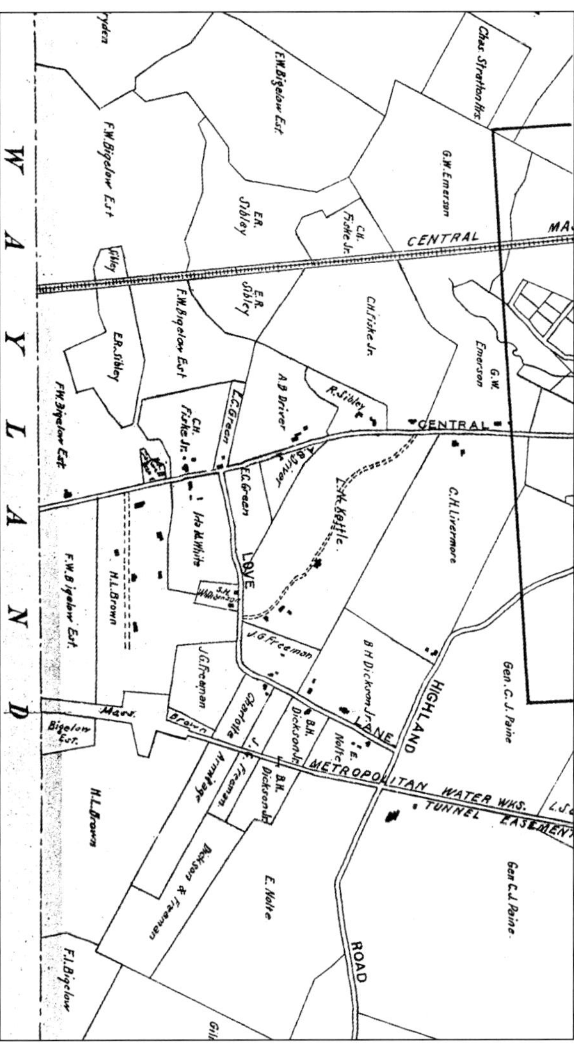

Figure 16-49. This detail from the 1908 Atlas of Middlesex County *also includes the Love Lane area.*

663 Boston Post Road (c. 1840s, enlarged and remodeled, 2000–01)

669 Boston Post Road. Deed records suggest that this house was built by Andrew Jones, grandson of Isaac Jones, between 1891 and 1896. The charm of this well preserved late-19th-century dwelling is enhanced by the matching 1½-story barn. Beginning in 1913, the house was occupied for many years by George Welcome.

670 Boston Post Road (1892). Built as a Shingle-style church for the short-lived Congregational Society, Homer F. Whittemore greatly altered the deteriorating building when he bought it in 1927 to use as a residence. It now belongs to the Baptist church and is called Whittemore House.

674-676 Boston Post Road. Well-preserved late-19th-century house occupied for many years by the Sherman family.

681 Boston Post Road. Originally the barn for the First Baptist parsonage next door, this building was converted to a house about 1912. The garage was added in late 1990s.

Jones Family
(* indicates a family member who made his or her home at the Golden Ball Tavern throughout his or her life)

Captain Josiah Jones (1640–1714)
- Josiah (1670–1734), m. Abigail Barnes
    - Elisha (1710–1775)
    - other children
- James (1680–1770), m. Sarah Moore
    - *Isaac (1728–1813)
        - m. Anna Cutler in 1753 (first wife)
            - Isaac Jr. (1754–1780)
            - Elizabeth (b. 1757)
            - Lucy (1759–1812)
            - infant
        - m. Mary Jones Willis (second wife)
            - Hepzibah (1762–1817)
            - Mary (1764–1786)
            - *William Pitt (1766–1854), m. Abigail Abrams
                - William Pitt Jr. (1806–1825)
                - Stephen Abrams (1807–1893)
                - *Isaac Henry (1809–1889), m. Caroline Whittemore
                    - Isaac Henry Jr. (b. 1838)
                    - Mary Jane
                    - *George H. (1842–1909), m. Lettie Frost c. 1869
                        - *George Jr. (1870–1899)
                        - *Mary "Mae" Caroline (1873–1957)
                            - m. Harry Warren
                                - Alice Warren (1905–1962)
                        - *Ralph Frost (1881–1963): last Jones to live in GBT
                    - Ralph Abrams (1845–1862), killed in Civil War
                - Abigail (1811–1893)
                - Edward (1814–1882)
                - Andrew (Edward's twin brother) (1814–1902)
                - *Charles (1824–1899)
                - *William (1826–1904)
                - *plus five children who died as infants*
            - Sarah (1769–1824)
            - *Martha (1771–1853), never married
            - *Anna (1774–1817), never married
            - Eunice (1777–1860)

683 Boston Post Road (c. 1880). This Italianate-style residence replaced the earlier Baptist parsonage on the same site. The church built a tennis court nearby about 1906.

687 Boston Post Road (1926). This Colonial Revival house was built to replace the parsonage at No. 683, which was then sold to a private owner. No. 687 was a parsonage until 1989.

699 Boston Post Road (1880). This Stick-style house was built for pottery manufacturer Albert Horatio Hews. A photograph appeared in *Boston, Massachusetts* by George W. Englehardt (Boston, 1897). The house remained in the family until 1927. Probably sometime thereafter, it was decreased in size and altered with the addition of the present Colonial Revival porch.

700 Boston Post Road (1852). Built as West Center District Schoolhouse #2, this one-room schoolhouse was used until 1893–94, after which it was converted to a residence. The building was moved from its original location on the east side of Highland Street about 1931 to make way for the Boston Post Road bypass.

Fiske Family

Isaac Fiske (1778–1861)
- Augustus H. (1805–c. 1865), m. Hannah Bradford
  - Edward, m. Adelaide Frost
    - Edward, m. Ethel Kidder, no children
    - Susan H., unmarried
  - Margaret, m. William Watson, no children
  - Sarah, m. 1. Sidney Willard, no children
    2. Chandler Robbins, three children
    - William B., m. Marian S. Bennett
    - Thomas H., m. Alice Ames
      - Thomas H. Jr.
      - William B.
    - Chandler, m. Laura Foster
      - Chandler Jr.
      - Joseph F.
      - Laura
  - Charles H. (1840–1921), m. Cornelia Robbins
    - Charles H. Jr., m. Mary D. Thorndike
      - Cornelia
      - Charles H. 3rd (died in World War I)
      - Rosanna
  - Lucy, m. Frank Morison, no children
  - Mary, m. Brenton H. Dickson Sr.
    - Brenton H. Jr., m. Ruth W. Bennett (see chapter 17)
    - Edward, unmarried
  - George, m. 1. Johanna ?, no children
    2. Mary Rood, no children
  - Andrew, m. Gertrude H. Horsford in 1878 (she died in 1920)
    - Gertrude, unmarried
    - Augustus H., m. Esther W. Bennett
      m. Ruth Sterry, no children
    - Gardiner H., m. Constance Morss, no children
    - Cornelia (Posey), m. Harold B. Willis
      - Harold B. Jr.
      - Andrew F.
      - Hannah B.
    - Hannah B., unmarried (d. 1919)

734 Boston Post Road (c. 1846). This Greek Revival house was built by Daniel Livermore after he inherited the property from Amos Harrington in 1846.[116] In 1920, the 33-acre Livermore farm was sold to John Bryant Paine and the trustees of the Charles J. Paine Estate.

725 Boston Post Road. Approximate site of the John Flagg Tavern.

745 Boston Post Road (1937). Built in 1937 by Marion Farnsworth on the site of an earlier Colonial farmhouse that she moved back from the road (now No. 751). Designed by architect Eleanor Raymond, who also designed additions to the Colonial farmhouse after the move. Raymond, who practiced from 1919 to 1973, has been described as a "pioneer in contemporary architectural design, energy conservation, environmental compatibility, technical innovation and coloration" and "among the first women architects in the United States to make significant contributions to the built environment."[117]

751 Boston Post Road (c. 1721, enlarged, moved). The earliest part of the house is thought to have been built about 1721 for farmer James Mirick. It was owned in the late 19th century by the Hastings family and from 1913 to 1922 by Mrs. V.P. Blanchard, who moved and enlarged it in 1913–14. In 1922, it was purchased by Miss Marion B. Farnsworth, who named it Exmoor Farm. In 1935, she moved the entire house again, this time well back from the street to its present location. Eleanor Raymond was the architect for alterations at that time. The large property was purchased in 1954 by Frank B. Carter Jr. and his wife, Lucy, who called it Woodleigh. Lucy Carter still maintains it as a working farm.

761 Boston Post Road (c. 1840). This Greek Revival house was built for Mark C. Sibley, a farmer who owned 101 acres on both sides of the road. In 1868 he sold the farm to his son, Edward, also a farmer, who owned it until his death in 1915.

770 Boston Post Road (1892). Architect Samuel Mead designed this Colonial Revival mansion for Boston wool merchant Lorenzo N. Kettle. Until 1997–98, the barn and carriage house were still standing near the corner of Love Lane and Claridge Drive.

787 Boston Post Road (c. 1775–85). This important late Georgian/Federal house is sometimes known as The Vineyard. It has fine exterior and interior detailing and a notable east wing and barn.

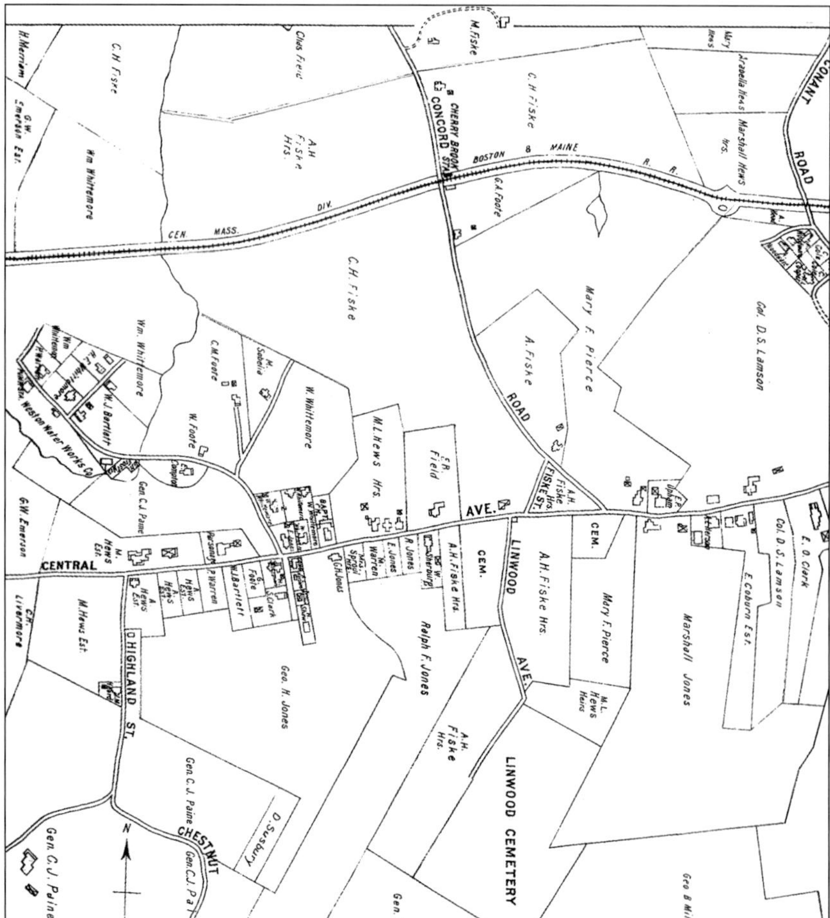

Figure 16-50. Detail from the 1908 Atlas of Middlesex County.

811 Boston Post Road. The Federal-style house probably dates to the early 19th century. Ralph Abrahams kept a store on the property from 1802 to 1821; then Oliver Shed kept a grocery and retail liquor store here until 1830, when the store was destroyed by fire.[118] In the early 20th century the property was owned by farmer Edward Green. His son, Edward Jr., was a mechanic and chauffeur and by 1926 had opened a garage for automobile repairing known as Green's Garage.

820 Boston Post Road (c. 1848). The Greek Revival "temple-front" design, the only one of this particular version in Weston, clearly dates the front portion of the house to the mid-19th century, the height of Greek Revival fashion. It was built for farmer Albert Hobbs, a member of the prominent North Avenue family, who purchased the eight-acre property in 1848. The rear ell is earlier.

823 Boston Post Road (c. 1750). The Colonial house was built for farmer Joseph Livermore, a member of one of Weston's early families. He reportedly operated a malt house on the property, which today includes a rare surviving ensemble of well-preserved early outbuildings.

863 Boston Post Road (1827). This gracious, amply proportioned late Federal residence was built for lawyer Alpheus Bigelow Jr. (b. 1784). The interior is the finest example in Weston of high-style Federal detailing. Bigelow married Mary Ann Hubbard Townsend in 1811. In 1851, the publication *Rich Men of Massachusetts* lists his worth at $200,000—the most of any man in Weston at the time—with the explanation, "Received by marriage." Blanche Bigelow, granddaughter of Alpheus Jr. and Mary Ann, was the last of the family to live here, until the 1940s. Alpheus Bigelow Jr.'s Federal-style law office still stands across the street at what is now 3 Applecrest Road.

6 Buckskin Drive (mid-19th century). This farmhouse was built for the Brown family. Elijah and Simeon Brown purchased the 143-acre Ephraim Livermore farm in 1834. The farm passed from Elijah to Simeon in 1850 and remained in the family until sold by the heirs of Henry L. Brown to Louis W. Dean in 1917 (then 125 acres). The farmhouse was moved to its present location when the property was subdivided into Weston Estates in the 1960s. It originally faced the street and was turned 90 degrees and moved to the east.

24 Buckskin Drive. Dean Dairy farmworkers lived in a small house that was enlarged and remodeled when the property was developed.

19 Concord Road (1752). Built for Rev. Samuel Woodward, pastor of First Parish Church, this central-chimney Colonial house is highly significant for its intact quality and architectural features, including remarkable Georgian paneling in both first- and second-floor rooms. In a 1974 report, Abbott Lowell Cummings noted that "in its character and trim [the house] suggests the status of an important local figure such as a minister. . . . The overriding importance of this house . . . is the trim of the early portion which . . . is both first-class, unspoiled, and wonderfully representative of its period." The house also has a notable Victorian addition built as a billiards room or ballroom, with palm capitals and an early crystal chandelier. Later owners included Dr. Amos Bancroft and John Jones. Augustus Fiske bought it in 1848 and the house remained in the Fiske family until 1972. It was owned or rented at various times to family members Dr. Chandler Robbins, Gardiner Fiske, and, finally, Hannah Wilkinson, granddaughter of Augustus Fiske, who lived here for 25 years. Listed on the National Register of Historic Places.

49 Concord Road (1919–20). This Colonial Revival version of a 17th-century "First Period" house was designed by the young architect Harold B. Willis for himself and his bride, Posey Fiske, and built on Fiske estate land. The house reuses oak paneling and other architectural details salvaged from an early New England house.

71 Concord Road (1905). "Four-Square" house built for ice and coal dealer George A. Foote.

Concord Road overpass. (1912). Built over the Central Massachusetts Railroad tracks to eliminate the grade crossing.

83 Concord Road. The entrance into the George and Mary Fiske estate, Laxfield, was through the stone posts in front of this house, which was on the estate grounds and was used at times by Fiske family members.

Golden Ball Road. *No. 7:* Farmhouse built for Cyrus Clark in 1906. *No. 9:* Built by his son John on the site of the Clark cow barn. *Nos. 53, 57 and 61:* Built by Cyrus Clark. *No. 59:* Built by William Compton for himself and his wife, Bessie Clark Compton. *No. 47:* May Clark Davidson house.

2 Laxfield Road (1902). Laxfield. The brick mansion was built for George and Mary Fiske. The property included 23 acres later subdivided into the Laxfield Road development.

3 Plain Road (by 1750). Probably built for James Livermore, who married Elizabeth Hastings in 1750, this house once had a much larger wing and was located near the site of the present 863 Boston Post Road. It was moved to its present location in 1811. Alpheus Bigelow Jr. and Mary Ann Hubbard Townsend set up housekeeping here after they were married in October 1811.

25 Warren Avenue (early 20th century). Built for Cherith Foote, who operated a dairy here until about 1940. Cows grazed in a pasture next to the house.

30 Warren Avenue (c. 1898). Owned since 1900 by the Compton family. Edward Compton came from England and worked as a coachman and hostler on the Paine estate.

39 Warren Avenue (1910–11). Built for Beriah Ogilvie, founder of B.L. Ogilvie & Sons.

71 Warren Avenue (1905). Built for Percy Warren, who bought the land from William Whittemore.[119] The house was later sold to the town. Superintendents of the water department are required to live here to be available for emergencies.

Notes

1. Now 22 Church Street. See later in this chapter for story of the moving. See also chapter 18.
2. This evaluation came from a British officer, a prisoner of war, in 1777. See Howard Gambrill Jr. and Charles Hambrick-Stowe, *The Tavern and the Tory: The Story of the Golden Ball Tavern* (Weston: Golden Ball Tavern Trust, 1977), 6. The quote is originally from Lt. Thomas Anbury, *Travels Through the Interior Parts of America* (London: William Lane, 1789, and later printings), vol. 2, 57–58.
3. Lamson, 189, quote from the resolution of 1775.
4. Accounts of the spy story vary. In the archives of the Golden Ball Tavern is one account written by Ensign D. Berniers about his journey with Captain Brown and his servant, John, on the orders of General Gage. Another account from the *Journal of John Howe* (published in 1827 and reprinted in part in Lamson's *History of the Town of Weston*, 76–78) is a more exciting but probably apocryphal version.
5. See Watkins, Lura Woodside, *Early New England Potters and Their Wares* (Cambridge: Harvard University Press, 1950), 43, and MacSwiggan, Amelia, "The Hews Pottery—An 18th Century Enterprise," *Antiques Journal*, November 1953, 36–37.
6. Watkins, op. cit., 43.
7. The house still stands at 651 Boston Post Road. The pottery was just to the east.
8. At that time, he was the oldest postmaster in the service and had served the greatest number of years.
9. "Flower Pots and Their Manufacture," *Cambridge Chronicle*, January 26, 1895 (text of a speech by A.H. Hews).
10. The Pottery Molding Machine was invented in 1861 by William Linton of Baltimore, Maryland, according to the article "The Hews Company and Its Contribution to the Culture of Flowerpots" by Hazel H. Lathrop in *WHSB*, fall 2000, 9.
11. Ibid.
12. Ibid.
13. Ibid.
14. Lamson, *HTW*, 156.
15. "An Old Concern: Something about Hews & Co.'s Celebrated North Cambridge Pottery," *Cambridge Chronicle*, May 21, 1892.
16. "A Cambridge Pottery," *Cambridge Chronicle*, February 11, 1888.

17. MacSwiggan, op. cit., 36
18. *Cambridge Chronicle,* February 11, 1888. The award for excellence was pictured in an 1878 catalog page reproduced in the October 1975 issue of the *Weston Historical Society Bulletin* (vol. XII, no. 1), which also includes a short article by Barbara Teller on "The Hews Pottery: A Progress Report," a follow-up to her article in the bulletin the previous year.
19. *Cambridge Chronicle,* February 11, 1888.
20. "Pots from the 'Plastic City,'" *Boston Globe,* May 30, 1983.
21. The location, which was on the north side of South Avenue, appears on the "Plan of the Gill Farm in Weston Belonging to Ward N. Boylston, Esq.," drawn in 1820 (copy owned by Thomas Paine.) The same location is marked on the 1794 Kingsbury map.
22. The church separated off from Medfield.
23. For text of the 1822 protest, partly quoted here, see Lamson, *HTW,* 179.
24. In F.V. Marshall's typescript "Samuel Train & the Baptist Society of Weston," dated 1976, she reviews the history of taxation of Baptists and other religious groups in Weston. According to Marshall, although there may have been some exemptions of Baptists in the early years, it was not until 1794, three years after the ratification of the 10 original amendments to the U.S. Constitution (including Article 1 on freedom of religion) that the Weston tax lists show citizens exempt from the minister's tax. In that year, eight Baptists and seven Methodists were listed "no Minister's Tax," "no Parish Tax," or "Independent." From 1812 to 1824, Marshall found that certified lists were required for exemption, with the last such list made in 1825. The 1825 list included 33 Baptists, 33 Methodists, and 14 Episcopalians (as there was no Episcopal church in Weston, the 14 Episcopalians would have had to be attending church out of town). After 1825, the list was unnecessary, as a voluntary separation of church and state had finally taken place in Weston.
25. "The Weston Baptists and Their Church, 1789–1939" (First Baptist Church, Weston, 1939), 5.
26. MCRD, Josiah Smith to Baptist Church of Weston, Uriah Gregory and Isaac Jones, Deacons, one-quarter acre for $50, March 26, 1828, Book 283/475. This land was not donated by the Hews family, as is written in some church histories. In 1881 Horace Hews did give the First Baptist Society a piece of land 10 feet wide along the east side of their lot and extending back the whole length (ref. church meeting records, April 6, 1881).
27. Digest of "An Historical Survey of the Beginning and Progress of the Baptist Church in Weston," given Sunday, June 16, 1913, at the Baptist church by the pastor, James M. Lent.
28. *Town Crier,* April 17, 1986. According to this article, faint markings were still visible on the rock.
29. "The Weston Baptists and Their Church," op. cit., 10.
30. *Town Crier,* October 19, 1989.
31. "The Weston Baptists and Their Church," op. cit., 10.
32. "History of the First Baptist Church in Weston, Mass., Historical Discourses and Addresses Delivered on the Occasion of Its Centennial Anniversary, July 14, 1889" (Boston, Edward A. Jones, 1890), 20. The quote, included within the history, is from the Baptist paper, the *Watchman.*
33. The striking design was the work of an unsung artist referred to in church minutes only as "the Architect." See church minutes of March 9, 1881, and November 23, 1881 (First Baptist Archives).
34. *WDFPT,* May 18, 1906: "There has been some talk of laying out a tennis court for the young people near the Baptist parsonage." Photos of the tennis court can be found in FBC archives.
35. "The Weston Baptists and Their Church," op. cit., 12.
36. First Baptist Church Records, May 31, 1922, 206 (FBC archives).
37. Records of the First Baptist Church, entry for May 8, 1922. See also May 31, 1922; March 27, 1923; and July 15, 1923 (FBC archives).
38. Perry served the Weston congregation for 12 years, from 1916 to 1928, "shepherding his flock with wisdom, sympathy and humor," according to church history.
39. See Lamson's *HTW,* 180–81.
40. MCRD 214/430, Fiske to Field, January 4, 1816. Fiske's new home, the Baldwin Tavern, stood on the site of the present 625 Boston Post Road. For background on this tavern see *WHSB,* March 1973, 1–3, and *WHSB,* March 1974, 4–5.
41. Forbes, A. and Greene, J.W., *The Rich Men of Massachusetts* (Boston: W.V. Spencer, Publisher, 1851), 125.
42. Obituary, *Boston Advertiser,* July 19, 1865.
43. 19 Concord Road.
44. Forbes & Greene, op. cit., 124. Fiske is listed as being worth $150,000. The only Weston resident with a higher net worth was lawyer Alpheus Bigelow, with $200,000.
45. Dickson, *RR,* 4.
46. Now 215 Boston Post Road. See also chapter 13.
47. The cost is given in the *Waltham Free Press,* August 17, 1883. See also August 10, 1883.
47a. See typescript of diary of B.H. Dickson Jr., 1888, and other materials in 22 Church Street file, WHC. Also *Waltham Free Press,* March 2 and 16 and May 4, 1888.
48. "Gertrude Fiske (1878–1961)," exhibition catalogue prepared by the Vose Galleries of Boston Inc. for an exhibit held October 1 to December 31, 1987. Includes bibliography, list of exhibitions and awards.
49. *Boston Sunday Herald,* February 1916.
50. The quote is from Vose Galleries catalog, op. cit., 9. See also the MFA exhibition catalog, Trevor J. Fairbrother, *The Bostonians, Painters of an Elegant Age, 1870–1930* (Boston: Museum of Fine Arts, 1986), 207.
51. Vose Gallery catalog, op. cit., 5
52. Ibid., 6.
53. "Willis Breaks From Prison Amid Fusillade of Shots," *Boston Sunday Globe,* January 12, 1919 (lengthly article). Willis was flying for the French "Lafayette Escadrille" when his plane was shot down in 1917. He was held as a prisoner for 14 months in a number of different German prison camps before successfully escaping in 1918 and making his way to Switzerland. See also obituaries after Willis's death on April 17, 1962, and records of the Harvard class of 1912, Harvard University Archives.
54. 49 Concord Road.
55. Harvard College class of 1912, *25th Anniversary Report,* 789–91.
56. 543 Boston Post Road.
57. Harold G. Travis, "The Untold Story of Mary Frances Peirce," *WHSB,* May 1978, 1, 4, 5.
58. Ibid., 5.
59. For the original plot plan, see "Plan of Land in Weston, Mass. owned by J.F. and G.H.D. Lamson to be conveyed to Marian B. Seabury" June 25, 1918, MCRD Plan Book 268/6. (Lamson had bought the house from the Peirce heirs.)
60. Advertisement from Friendly Society program "Sweethearts," April 24 and 25, 1925.
61. 7 Golden Ball Road. MCRD, George H. Jones to Cyrus Clark, Book 3209/28, January 1906.
62. The present 625 Boston Post Road.
63. Broadside owned by members of the Clark family.
64. 582 Boston Post Road. The move took place in 1921.
65. The nine children were William, Cherith, Hartley, Harvey, James, Frank, George, Irad, and Ida. Information supplied by Elsie Cooke, daughter of James T. Foote.
66. *Middlesex County and Its People,* vol. IV, 368 (entry for George A. Foote).
67. Ibid.
68. MCRD, Book 2371/553, June 8, 1895. Edward & Mary Peirce to GAF.
69. Advertisement, 1911 directory, 4.

70. See *WDFPT,* September 12, 1902, and January 1, 1904. Also advertisement, 1915 directory, 9.
71. One year, the *WDFPT* reported, "To insure good clear ice for next winter, Mr. Foote is pumping his pond dry and will give the bottom a thorough cleaning" (September 29, 1911).
72. MCRD, Book 3531/377, C. Foote to B.L. Ogilvie, April 12, 1910.
73. "Sweethearts," April, 1925, op. cit.
74. Middlesex County and Its People, vol. IV, 367.
75. Interview, PWF with Henry Lingley, son of John Lingley, July 1999.
76. 71 Warren Avenue.
77. *WDFPT,* May 12 and October 13, 1905.
78. The name Whittemore Lane appears in the 1908 town report but was changed to Warren Avenue in the 1909 report (see assessor's list).
79. *Middlesex County and Its People,* vol. IV, 515.
80. *Waltham Daily Free Press Tribune,* June 29, 1917. See also 1918 town report, 221.
81. Unpublished manuscript in Golden Ball Tavern Museum archives.
82. Ibid.
83. Charles "was of a gentle and kindly disposition and delighted in a quiet life, reading and meditating much," according to his obituary.
84. Information in this and the next paragraph from an audiotape by Raymond W. Jones Jr. of Illinois (Golden Ball archives).
85. In his will (Probate #385639), Ralph directed his executor to set up a trust fund to benefit his faithful housekeeper, Madeline J. Caulfield. After her death, the money in the trust was to go to the Weston Public Library, which eventually received about $34,500.
86. The $100,000 goal was reached by October 1969 and the property transferred to the ownership of the Golden Ball Tavern Trust.
87. *Boston Globe,* January 1, 1916.
88. Weston Historical Society bulletins of January 1966 and March 1970 give different accounts of whether this was a new addition or an old shed off the Fiske barn moved in 1920.
89. MCRD Book 5240/527, June 1928. Price of building not to exceed $500.
90. See *Weston Historical Society Bulletin* of January 1966, May 1967, March and May 1970, and March 1978. Quote from March 1970, 3.
91. Lamson, *HTW,* 112–13.
92. Ibid., 116.
93. "The Ruins of the Flagg Tavern," *WHSB,* May 1972, 1.
94. Dickson, Brenton H. III, "Travel and Transportation Through Weston," *WHSB,* May 1969.
95. Telephone conversation with Douglas Henderson, October 1999. See also Brenton Dickson, *Once Upon a Pung,* 30–31.
96. *WDFPT,* January 18, 1907.
97. For a description of a raid, see "Police Fooled/Cocking Man Held in Weston/Officers Were Told It Was an Auction," *WDFPT,* April 5, 1901. Emerson was standing on guard, and when police came, participants fled. Emerson claimed he had invited the men to his farm to attend an auction of gamebirds. According to the article, "there is intense feeling in the town against Mr. Emerson . . ."
98. MCRD Book 4314/88 (1919, to Paul Revere Garage for filling station) and 4484/284 (1921, to Cunningham Brothers for golf links). The lease allowed the brothers to build the "Flagg Tavern Tea Room" and "it is agreed that . . . [Emerson] shall have all the garbage made on the premises free of charge." In 1930 Marion Farnsworth, who held mortgages on Emerson's property, foreclosed for breach of condition, and when Emerson died shortly thereafter, the administrator of his estate granted the 65 acres to Farnsworth (Book 5523/104 and 5547/538).
99. See "Plan Showing the Land of Lorenzo N. Kettle," July 1896, Plan Book 274/5 (recorded June 27, 1919, MCRD).
100. "Weston Has Become the Lenox of the East," *Boston Sunday Herald,* May 11, 1902.
101. *Waltham Free Press,* June 27, 1902.
102. *WDFPT,* July 2, 1919. See also MCRD 4269/135 and Plan Book 274/5.
103. Text on cardboard box found in the Kettle barn before it was demolished about 1998.
104. 734 Boston Post Road. See MCRD, Book 4328/61, March 8, 1920 (Livermore to Paine Trustees).
105. MCRD, Book 4126/436, April 2, 1917, Harriet E. Brown to L.W. Dean.
106. MCRD, Book 11037/77, Wendell Dean and Boston Safe Deposit and Trust Co. to Weston Estates Corp., January 24, 1966. Subdivision plan, page 75 of same book.
107. 6 Buckskin Drive (main house) and 24 Buckskin Drive.
108. Madden, Nick, "Elite on Common Ground," unpublished manuscript, April 1998.
109. Blanche T. Bigelow to Mrs. Paul Clifford, October 10, 1946 (WHC files).
110. MCRD, 7506/413, November 15, 1949, Clifford to Sullivan; subdivision plan of January 6, 1950, 7588/537. The Sullivans reserved the right to approve building plans (see, for example, 7588/537).
111. "Plan of Irvington Court, A Restricted Subdivision in Weston, Mass., owned and developed by Irving Connolly," June 1930, Plan 674 of 1930, recorded at end of Book 5473.
112. Raymond Ogilvie's oral history, Weston Public Library. See also *WDFPT,* December 10, 1920.
113. It is difficult to be exact about the date and difficult to completely rule out the theory that it was built somewhat earlier by Artemas Ward Jr., who practiced law in Weston and mentored young Fiske before moving to Charlestown about 1800.
114. MCRD, Charles Jones to WFS, January 1886, Book 1735/125.
115. *WDFPT,* May 18, 1906.
116. MCRD, Ellen C. Livermore, & al. to C.J. Paine & al., Trustees, March 8, 1920, and will of Amos Harrington, allowed February 10, 1846.
117. Cole, Doris, *Eleanor Raymond, Architect* (Philadelphia: The Art Alliance Press), 1981.
118. Lamson, *HTW,* 157.
119. *WDFPT,* October 27, 1905.

Figure 17-1. Members of the Schwartz family enjoy a picnic in the woods. This photograph probably dates to the late 1880s. John Schwartz (center, with beard) came to the United States from Germany. In 1864, he purchased a 70-acre farm at the southwest corner of Love Lane and Highland Street, where he and his family worked hard to make a living from the land.

CHAPTER 17

Love Lane

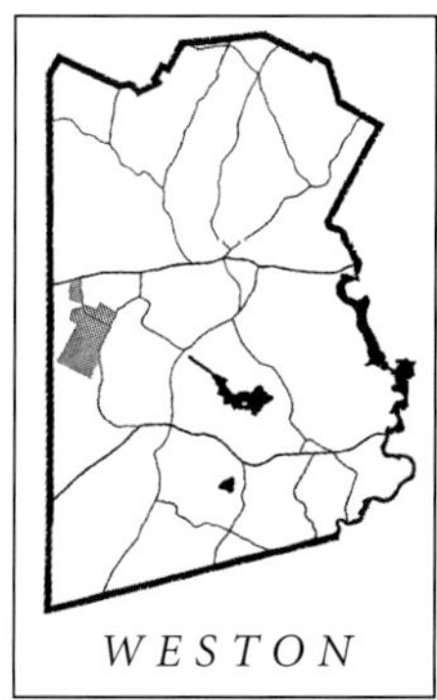

Love Lane, known as Elm Street until the beginning of the 20th century, appears on the earliest Weston maps. The history of Love Lane exemplifies the major change in land use that took place in Weston in the late 19th and early 20th centuries, as family farms became gentlemen's farms. By 1910, all the land from the present Claridge Drive to Highland Street was part of four small estates belonging to Lorenzo Kettle, James Freeman, Brenton H. Dickson Jr., and George Nolte. The Kettle estate fronted on Boston Post Road and is discussed in chapter 16.

James Freeman and his wife, the former Caroline Case, lived on Love Lane only in the summer. Nolte developed a dairy farm operated by a resident caretaker and built a rustic bungalow for his family's summer use. Brenton H. Dickson Jr. lived in his rambling brown-shingled house year-round, commuting regularly by train into the city. A century later, the entire Dickson complex, including the house, cow and horse barns, horse paddocks, and even the chicken coop and corn crib, has remained intact. Sometimes, no more than a fieldstone wall separates these historic structures and their landscape of hayfields and woodlands from the late-20th-century mansions of a new generation of successful entrepeneurs.

Jonas Sanderson and the Weston Beacon

Of the early farmers in the area, the best known is Jonas Sanderson, who captured the imagination of later generations because of his role in maintaining the military signal beacon during the Revolutionary War.[1] Family history records that the beacon light came from lanterns hung in the topmost branches of an elm that towered above Sanderson's house at the southwest corner of Highland Street and Love Lane.[2] The Weston beacon was one of only three on the outskirts of Boston, to be guarded day and night in case of British attack and set afire only in response to a signal from Beacon Hill. At that time, Boston would have been visible from this high point in Weston, whereas today the view is obscured by second-growth forest on land once cleared for farm fields.

The Sanderson homestead consisted of a house, barn, and about 70 acres. There were extensive apple orchards, a few pear and cherry trees, about 20 tillable acres, and enough pasture to support a dozen cows. In 1864 the property was sold to John Schwartz, a German immigrant who came to America in 1845 at age 18 and initially worked as a saw sharpener in the lumber boom town of Bangor, Maine.[3] The job paid well but was bad for his lungs, and Schwartz moved to Weston in search of a healthier way to make a living and a more wholesome environment for his children. While in Bangor, Schwartz painted a bucolic picture of farm life. His children soon learned that to eke out a living from a "rock infested" Weston farm meant long hours of backbreaking work.

Figure 17-2. The three-story house owned by Jonas Sanderson and later by John Schwartz stood at the southwest corner of Highland Street and Love Lane until it burned to the ground in 1897.

The children were expected to do their part. As young teenagers, John Melvin Schwartz and his brother, Everett, were given responsibility for marketing the produce. They would leave for Boston about six o'clock in the evening, arrive some four hours later, line up the horse and wagon in a row with others along the sidewalk, and catch a few hours of sleep before early-morning buyers arrived to inspect their offerings and bargain for the best prices.

Recreational opportunities were few. When not doing farm chores or going to school, the boys played baseball, although to get into a game meant a walk of two miles each way. Often in the evening the family would sing together, sometimes joined by Mr. Laws, the traveling fruit tree salesman, who stayed at the Schwartz house while in Weston and could play the violin, albeit badly.

Descendants of Jonas Sanderson continued to

Figure 17-3. Farmer John Schwartz hays his fields on Highland Street near the corner of Love Lane.

Figure 17-4. The summer house built by the Freemans at 55 Love Lane began as a four-room cottage. It had been considerably enlarged when this photograph of the rear facade was taken about 1913.

own land on Love Lane until the early 20th century. George Sanderson, grandson of Jonas, built his own house in the 1850s using the then popular Greek Revival style. George specialized in raising "small fruits," probably strawberries and raspberries, and E.E. and W.B. Sanderson are listed in directories as florists.[4] In March 1905 the *Waltham Daily Free Press Tribune* reported that "George Sanderson & Son have a beautiful display consisting of 200,000 fine pansy plants of good colors."[5] Traces of their five greenhouses still remain.

The Freeman/Paine Estate

James and Caroline Case Freeman were among the first "summer people" to move to Love Lane in the late 19th century. James Goldthwaite Freeman (1848–1912), described as "one of Boston's best known real estate men and an expert in the value of properties," was a partner in the firm of Codman and Freeman and later Freeman and Lawrence.[6] He also served in both branches of the Massachusetts legislature. His marriage in 1888 to Caroline Case, oldest of four daughters of estate owner James Brown Case, was one of the first celebrated in the new First Parish Church. In 1891 the couple purchased on the east side of Love Lane seven acres that had belonged to the Sanderson family.[7] They built a small summer house here in 1903, designed by the well-known Boston architectural firm of Fehmer and Page. This house, which had only three rooms on the first floor and one on the second, became the core of a much larger mansion created in a series of expansions undertaken between 1908 and 1911 by the same architectural firm.[8] In 1910 the Freemans purchased land across the street with a small mid-19th-century house, which they used as a farmer's cottage.[9]

Caroline shared the Case family interest in horticulture. The property was noted for its "superb lawns," variety of shrubs and fruit trees, and perennial and rose gardens.[10] Large specimen trees include a Sargent's weeping hemlock on the front lawn said to be the oldest example of this unusual tree in the United States. Along the street is a stone wall of single

Figure 17-5. Caroline Case Freeman (1856–1919) was the oldest of the four daughters of estate owner James B. Case. She established the Rosamond Freeman Fund at the Weston Public Library in memory of her daughter, who died of scarlet fever.

boulders called a "hen's tooth" or "balancing wall." The only similar wall in Weston is on the Wellesley Street property formerly belonging to Caroline's sister Marian, now the Case Estates.

The Freemans used the Love Lane house only in summer. Caroline had a buoyant personality even in the face of the adversity that marked her life. Several children died in infancy and a daughter, Rosamond, died of scarlet fever in 1902 at age nine. In 1913, after the death of her husband, she sold the estate to her sister Louisa. When Caroline died in 1919 at age 63, she left to the Weston Public Library a fund of $10,000, known as the Rosamond Freeman Fund, with income to be applied to the purchase of books, preferably for the children's department.[11]

The Paine Trustees bought the property in 1920 for Georgina Paine Fisher, daughter of Gen. Charles Jackson Paine. Seven years earlier, Georgina had married Richard Thornton Fisher, a forester and first director of the Harvard School of Forestry in Petersham, Massachusetts. The couple had five children: Richard, Anne, Faith, Charles Paine, and John Bryant. In her book *Flotsam & Jetsam, Memories from My Childhood*, Anne Fisher Tatlock describes the elegant living room, with its floor-length, dusky purple Japanese silk curtains and a painting by the artist Frank Benson over the fireplace.[12] Cedars lined the driveway, and in the rear, luxuriant wisteria festooned down three stories to the brick terrace. Every morning Luke Brennan, an elderly Irishman, arrived by jitney bus from Waltham to Love Lane to tend the Fishers' large vegetable garden. Tatlock describes riding progressivly more challenging horses at the Dickson stables. Richard Fisher died in 1934 and Georgina later married writer Llewellyn Howland. She lived in the house on Love Lane until her death in 1989 at age 101.

The Nolte Family

By the late 1890s, the landmark 18th-century house once belonging to Jonas Sanderson was deteriorating but still much admired for its architecture and fine location. Many people tried to buy the property, including George Henry Nolte (1864–1954), who often came out to Weston on pleasant Sunday afternoons to picnic in the country.[13] At that time, Nolte lived on Bay State Road in Boston and worked at the Boston Stock Exchange.[14]

In 1897, the Sanderson house caught fire and burned to the ground.[15] When Nolte read about the fire in the morning papers, he took the first train from Boston and agreed to purchase the property on the spot. His daughter would later write that the property was a gift to his wife, Evelyn, as a summer home and "the source of a little income."[16] Nolte set up a dairy farm with a caretaker's house, large barn with root cellar and ice vault, two-story chicken house, cow barn with special stall for the bull, storage house, corn crib, woodshed, and "engine house" with equipment to pump water from the cistern all the way to the family bungalow. There were six

Figure 17-6. George Henry Nolte (1864-1954) bought the property at the southwest corner of Love Lane and Highland Street after the fire of 1897. The family spent summers in a rustic bungalow with a huge stone fireplace. The chimney still survives on conservation land given to the town by the Nolte family.

Figure 17-7. George Nolte set up a dairy farm and built this house at 16 Love Lane for the caretaker.

hayfields, three apple orchards, an ice pond, kitchen garden, cornfields, brook, and a big swamp. Until about 1916, the farm sold two or three wagonloads of apples in Waltham each season. Nearby was a cranberry bog.

In the early years of the 20th century, the farm was run by caretaker George Welcome. The Nolte family spent May to September at a cabin called "the bungalow" built in 1904 at the south end of the property.[17] Nolte's daughter describes idyllic summers there:

> The Bungalo [sic], which was on a pine covered hill some distance from the farm house, was a rambling rustic structure with wide porches wonderful for trikes and red wagons. There were tall French doors in the living room and in the guest suite. Back of the kitchen and laundry were two rooms for help plus a toilet and basin. We connected with the Welcomes by wind-up telephone. Our drinking water came from a cool, clear brook just part way down the hill. Kerosene lamps provided light. To us children it was a dream house, and it broke our hearts when it had to be demolished about 1918 when it became a hang-out for tramps in the winter.[18]

After the Boston Stock Exchange failed in 1906, the family moved to New York, where George Henry Nolte worked as treasurer of the private banking house of Flint & Co. The farm continued as a working dairy until the Welcomes retired in 1915. Evelyn Nolte enlarged the farmhouse, which she called Dutch Cottage, and moved there for a few years with her three younger children to be near the oldest son, George Francis, who was enrolled at Harvard. Evelyn was a liberal who marched in the suffragette parade of 1916, to the consternation of her neighbor Ruth Dickson, who didn't approve of women's suffrage. She was also a Christian Scientist in a community where everyone seemed to belong to the Unitarian church. Because of her religious beliefs, she would not allow her children to be vaccinated. For this reason, the Noltes' daughter Dorothea was not able to attend public school.

The Dickson and Nolte children played together in a little playhouse and tree house on the property and used the corn crib as a theater. In one of their plays, Teddy Dickson decided they needed smoke and brought over a vacuum cleaner to blow out dust at the appropriate moment. Despite living next to the horse-loving Dicksons, the Nolte children never learned to ride. Their only horse, Major, was a 20-year-old nag. The Dicksons' Shetland pony regularly threw off the children and Ruth Dickson finally gave up. In his last years, old Major couldn't do much more than make it to the train station, and when he died in 1917 the family got a car, opening up new worlds like Revere Beach and the Cape.

George Francis Nolte (1895–1960) became a vice president at National City Bank in New York City and lived in the city with his mother, devoting himself to her needs. He remained a bachelor all his life. Evelyn Nolte returned to Weston every summer until she died in 1959. In 1960, George retired from the bank and moved back to the farm in Weston, intending to restore the property. After only about a week at the old homestead, he developed pneumonia and died without signing a will outlining his intention to leave the land for conservation as a memorial to his mother. Nolte's siblings concurred with this wish. In 1970, his brother Whitney sold the town more than 40 acres as town forest and recreation land and donated an additional five-acre section as the Evelyn White Nolte Forest.[19] The farm buildings and three fields were sold to Edward Dickson, who continued to preserve the land and the Dutch Cottage. Hikers still stumble upon the massive stone chimney from the Nolte summer bungalow.

The Dickson Family

In 1899 another Boston businessman, Brenton H. Dickson Jr. (1868–1946), purchased 22 acres across from the Nolte farm. Two years later, Dickson and his bride, Ruth Bennett, moved into their new Shingle-style house, Ivy Abbey, which was a wedding present from Dickson's father. [20] The house was designed by Pigeon Hill resident A.J. Russell, son of First Parish minister Charles Russell and an architect with the Boston firm of Brainerd, Leeds and Russell. The younger Dickson worked with his father at B.H. Dickson & Co. on Milk Street, procuring southern cotton for mills in the Northeast. The house name referred to the picturesque ivy cover and original

Figure 17-8. B.H. Dickson Jr. and his wife, the former Ruth Bennett, enjoy a Sunday horseback ride. Ruth Dickson's life revolved around horses. In her eyes, a horse was a superior being that could do no wrong.

cross shape, which was altered over the years to accommodate a growing family of seven children: Mary, Brenton III, Teddy, Anna, Edward, William, and Ruth (Babe). Mary died of diabetes just before insulin was discovered, and Teddy died young of a brain tumor.

Brenton Dickson Jr. served as town clerk from 1918 to 1943 and selectman from 1926 to 1943. According to his son, Edward, he deserves at least some credit for changing the street name from Elm Street to Love Lane. The two street names were used alternately from the 1890s to the 1920s, with Dickson expressing his strong preference for Love Lane by removing the town's Elm Street signs and storing them in his basement. The name was officially changed at Town Meeting in 1906.[21]

Dickson Jr. was "an individualist." His son and namesake describes how cousin Grady Fiske introduced his father to John Marquand:

> So he took John up to my family house and into the smoking room where my father was sitting. The smoking room was a terrible mess, furniture all threadbare and stacks of this, that and the other thing. You couldn't see any walls because there were all sorts of pictures and newspaper clippings and photographs pinned all over them, and my father was in his usual old clothes, using safety pins for buttons. Whenever Grady Fiske and my father got together they always talked about the hard times they were having, and wondered how . . . they were going to make ends meet. . . . On the way home John Marquand said "I suppose you have to help your cousin out once in a while?" Grady said "Hell, no! He's the richest member of the family."[22]

Figure 17-9. Mary Fiske, daughter of Augustus H. Fiske, married Brenton H. Dickson Sr. They are pictured here about 1865–66. Dickson and his son B.H. Jr. worked as cotton brokers in Boston.

Life in this remote section of town in the early decades of the 20th century has been described by Brenton H. Dickson III in his two books, *Once Upon a Pung* and *Random Recollections.* He tells how his father traveled 20 minutes by carriage to Weston

Figure 17-10. Built for the newly married B.H. Jr. and Ruth Dickson, Ivy Abbey was so named because it was originally shaped like a cross and covered with ivy.

Station in the morning to catch the Central Massachusetts into Boston. No other commuter lived so far from the station. Family errands and shopping were done in Boston, unless the item could be bought at Cutting's Store. The Dicksons began using an automobile for these trips beginning in 1912.

Ruth Dickson's life revolved around horses, which she kept in the large barn still standing on Love Lane. She was particularly interested in Morgans and used the family farm in Vermont for raising this special breed. Her son Brenton recalled her philosophy that a horse is a superior being, and when a rider was thrown off, it was never the horse's fault. She told girls that she wouldn't take them riding if they were wearing lipstick because they were thinking more of themselves than of their horse.[23] In the winter, she took gangs of children for pung rides on a large open sledge pulled by her team of workhorses. Peter, a huge gray Great Dane, accompanied Mrs. Dickson everywhere. Like all animals, he could do no wrong in her eyes.

The Dickson property was operated as a small-scale farm where food was raised primarily for family and staff. The hired men grew vegetables, maintained an orchard with apple and pear trees, and kept two cows, a few pigs, poultry, and guinea hens, which were "particularly obnoxious" because of their constant squawking. The cook made butter in a wooden churn in the kitchen and one of the men made ice cream every Sunday.

In the early years of the 20th century, country families could obtain many food items from dealers who made regular rounds through the town. Brenton Dickson III describes these traveling merchants:

> Once a week Foppiano's fruit wagon came past our driveway. You always knew when he was coming because you could hear him calling out his wares from a long way off, and as his decrepit old horse, all skin and bones, shuffled along very slowly, there was ample warning of his approach. He would stop at the end of our driveway while we bought peanuts and any fruit the cook happened to need. Russell's butcher cart, a wagon with an arched white canvas top, came all the way from Wayland once or twice a week, and as the horse stood patiently, swishing away the flies with its tail, the butcher would lower the rear panel, select a cut of meat, weigh it and trim it and throw the scraps aside for our dogs. Mr. Russell had excellent meat. . . . Looking very much

Figure 17-11. Children of B.H. Jr. and Ruth Dickson with their St. Bernard, Tober I, in 1909. From left, B.H.D. III, Anna, Mary, and Teddy.

Figure 17-12. Brenton Dickson Jr. drives his wife, Ruth, and her sister, Esther, in their 1908 Corbin. The motor was air-cooled and often caught fire.

Figure 17-13. Brenton H. Dickson III and Helen Paine were married September 15, 1928. Pictured here in the wedding portrait are, from left, Louise, Chattie, Julia, Carol, Sally, and Helen Paine; Brenton H. Dickson III; Theresa Winsor; Alice Sherburne; Anna Dickson; Ruth Dickson (child); and Sally Warren.

like Russell's cart was Mr. Heard's fishwagon that came by every Thursday. Then there were Mr. Foote's ice carts, painted a bright yellow, with scales dangling out behind. Mr. Foote also dealt in coal, which he delivered in very dirty wagons that came lumbering up our hill every autumn.[24]

In 1905 and 1907, George Sanderson's unmarried daughter, Lizzie, sold the Sanderson farmhouse to Brenton H. Dickson Jr. His parents fixed up and furnished the place but did not enjoy summering there, and in subsequent years the house was occupied by farm help. In 1931 it was enlarged and remodeled as a year-round home for Brenton H. Dickson III (1903–1988) and his wife of a few years, Helen Paine, granddaughter of Gen. C.J. Paine.

The main house was inherited by Edward Mellen Dickson (1912–2000), third son of Brenton H. Dickson Jr. Edward graduated from Harvard in 1934 and served as a naval lieutenant in World War II. He devoted much of his life to public service. He was town clerk from 1951 to 1971, selectman from 1954 to 1968, and state representative for 14 years. He was an ardent supporter of the METCO program. In 1998, Dickson and his wife, Polly, donated 10 acres on Highland Street for the mixed-income development Dickson Meadow.

Arthur Hunt and the Golden Soap Company

At the other end of Love Lane, in about 1897, Ida White built a house near the corner of Boston Post Road. Fifteen years later, she sold it to Arthur Hunt, who operated a business with the fine-sounding name Golden Soap Company. He collected grease, fat and bones, and garbage from schools and institutions, made soap from the grease, and fed the garbage to his pigs.[25] He would cut off a hunk of his soap to pay people for their grease. The pigs were kept under the barn and fed through a trapdoor. Needless to say, the smell from the pigs was not pleasing to the neighbors. Until the 1930s, some of the rendering of fat was done in vats in the barn. Hunt lived on Love Lane until about 1966.

Figure 17-14. Edward M. Dickson (right) and his grandniece Lee Fernandez, in front of the Dickson barn on Love Lane.

Next door was a summer house built in 1904 by Sarah Williamson, whose husband, Boston lawyer William Williamson, died the year before the house was completed. The Williamsons had a winter home on Marlboro Street in Boston. The Federal Revival design is the work of noted Colonial Revival architect Joseph Everett Chandler. In October 1904, the *Waltham Daily Free Press Tribune* reported, "The new house now building for Mrs. Williamson on Elm Street

Figure 17-15. Arthur Hunt lived at 106 Love Lane for more than 50 years. He collected grease to make soap and garbage to feed his pigs, which were kept under the barn.

Figure 17-16. Oliver Patriquin (1882–1972) was born in Nova Scotia and came to Boston, alone, at age 12. German ornamental iron workers took him in and taught him the blacksmithing trade. When the influenza epidemic struck in 1918, Patriquin moved his young family to Chestnut Street in Weston. He had a blacksmith shop in Weston for 38 years, first in the town center and then on Love Lane. In this photograph from about 1962, he holds a ship's candleholder.

. . . will be a conspicuous object in that part of town, it being a large house, three stories in height and on elevated ground." In 1909 the property was sold to lawyer and cotton manufacturer John S. Farlow and his wife, Edith. The Farlows, who lived here until 1936, hired architect Samuel Mead to enlarge the house and add a wing to the north side in 1911. Initially, at least, the Farlows used the house only in the summer. Their comings and goings were recorded in the local papers.

Houses in the Love Lane Area

109 Highland Street (c. 1757). Built for farmer Moses Harrington. Converted to a two-family house by 1827. Sold in 1899 to Brenton H. Dickson Jr. along with 22 acres of land and since then maintained as a rental house.

125 Highland Street (1900–1901). Ivy Abbey was designed by A.J. Russell for Brenton H. Dickson Jr. and his bride, Ruth Bennett Dickson. To accommodate their seven children, the west wing was added in 1910 and the east wing, designed by Samuel Mead, in 1927.[26] The house has been occupied continuously by the Dickson family, in later years by Edward M. Dickson, his wife, Polly, and their four children.

16 Love Lane (c. 1898). The Dutch Cottage, so named because of its Dutch Colonial design, was built by banker George Henry Nolte for the caretaker of his dairy farm.

26 Love Lane (c. 1850–56). Built for farmer George Sanderson and remodeled and enlarged in 1931 for Brenton H. III and Helen Paine Dickson.

55 Love Lane (1903, 1908–11). Begun as a small summer house for James and Caroline Case Freeman and enlarged many times by the Freemans. In 1920 the Paine trustees purchased it for Gen. Charles Jackson Paine's daughter, Georgina Paine Fisher (Howland), who lived here until 1989. Enlarged and renovated in the 1990s by Cheryl and Joseph Dempsey.

98 Love Lane (1904). Federal Revival summer house designed by Joseph Everett Chandler for Sarah Williamson and built by Howard L. Cooper. Lawyer John Farlow and his wife, Edith, owned the house from 1909 to 1936 and added the wing in 1911. From 1937 to 1964 it was owned by Lillian and Charles Hills, who was general manager for General Radio Co.

106 Love Lane (c. 1897–98). Built for Ida White and owned by Arthur Hunt from 1912 to about 1966. The house was originally shingled and has been extensively remodeled, most recently in 1999.

99 and 107 Love Lane. Brick Tudor houses built about 1929 and 1930, respectively.

Corner, Love Lane and Boston Post Road. Oliver Patriquin had his blacksmith shop in the town center until the 1930s, when he moved to this small shop at the corner of Boston Post Road and Love Lane. He is listed in the 1936 directory under the name Weston Shoeing Forge.

Notes

1. For more information on the beacon, see Harold G. Travis's "The Beacon on Sanderson Hill," *WHSB,* October 1974. The other two beacons were in Stoughton and Malden, according to the Travis article. See also *WHSB,* October 1976.

2. Schwartz, Melvin H., "John Schwartz" (unpublished manuscript,1964), provided to the author by Jean Dowell, a great-granddaughter. The Schwartz family bought the property from the Sandersons. Note that at the time of the town's Bicentennial, the elm was well known enough to have a name: the Washington Elm. Note also the following article in the *WDFPT* of June 13, 1913:

> We hear that Mrs. Jackson and sister are of the 4th generation of Sandersons in Weston, that their great-grandfather, Jonas Sanderson 1st, lighted and tended the "Beacon Light" at his home. . . . The light was hung from a tall elm tree and could be seen at Acton, also [sic] loaned money to assist in the Rebellion, and served on War Committee, was member of "First Church." They have his silver shoe buckles, warming pan, tea table, and old deed 1770. . . . Also old deed of Josiah Coolidge, of whom he bought . . . [in 1748].

See also *WDFPT Anniversary Edition,* 5, for item on the "Washington Elm Tree House."

3. Ibid.

4. 1893 directory.

5. *WDFPT,* March 31, 1905.

6. *WDFPT,* November 28, 1919.

7. MCRD 2065/194, Charles H. Fiske to Freeman, 1891. See also 3778/584, Freeman to Louisa Case, 1913, and 4388/161, Case to Paine Trustees, 1920s.

8. Plans in possession of owner. On June 23, 1911, the *WDFPT* reported, "From twelve to fourteen men have been at work since last November rebuilding Jas. G. Freeman's house on Elm St. The work has been in charge of J.J.Brown [contractor] . . ."

9. 46 Love Lane, house and barn demolished in 1996.

10. *WDFPT,* October 8, 1920. The landscape plan—said to have been drawn about 1903 by a former student of Frederick Law Olmsted—has been lost.

11.1955 *TR,* 82.

12. Tatlock, Anne Fisher, *Flotsam & Jetsam, Memories from My Childhood* (Northampton, MA: Annex Press, 1999), 2.

13. Dickson, *Pung,* 29.

14. *WDFP,* February 12, 1897, reported on the sale to Nolte, who was described as a banker with the firm of F.R. Cordley and Co. of Boston.

15. For a description of the fire, see *WDFP,* January 22, 1897.

16. Letter, Dorothea Nolte Kelley of Dallas, Texas, to Dorothea Thomas, January 4, 1997.

17. *WDFPT,* April 22, 1904, "G.H. Nolte is building a log cabin on Highland Street."

18. Letter, Dorothea Nolte Kelley to PWF, February 10, 1997.

19. Records, Weston Conservation Commission. Money from the sale to the town was used to pay inheritance taxes.

20. Dickson information from interviews with Edward Dickson and from Brenton H. Dickson III's books, *Once Upon a Pung,* 13, and *Random Recollections,* 45–77.

21. 1906 *TR,* 204.

22. Cheek, Jeannette, "Weston, A Community" (quote from Brenton H. Dickson oral history), *WHSB,* December 1988.

23. Tatlock, op. cit., 12.

24. Dickson, *RR,* 68–69.

25. Letter from Peggy Hunt to Mary Perriello, undated.

26. *WDFPT,* December 2, 1910, "Brenton H. Dickson, Jr. has just completed an annex to his home for the benefit and pleasure of the children."

Figure 18-1. Sumner (left) and John Bryant Paine, oldest of the seven children of Charles J. and Julia Paine, are pictured with a toy sailboat in 1879. Their father had recently taken up yacht racing, and six years later would win his first America's Cup.

CHAPTER 18

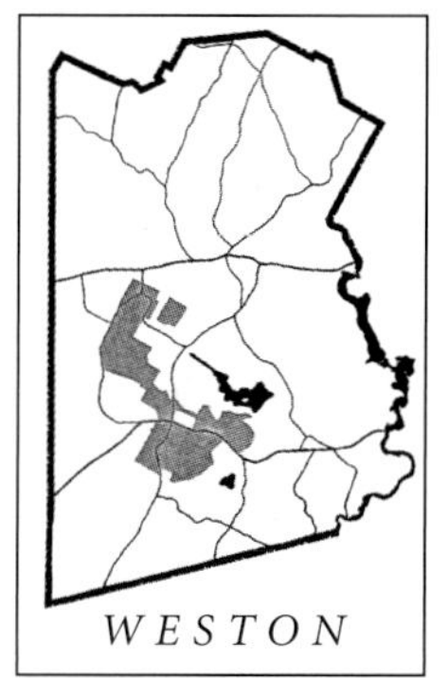

General Charles Jackson Paine

"The Modern Discoverer of Weston"

In 1902, the Boston Sunday Herald *magazine section proclaimed Weston "the Lenox of the East" and Gen. Charles Jackson Paine "the modern discoverer of Weston"—a kind of socially prominent explorer who had scouted out this backwater farm town 30 years before and found it eminently suitable for a "country place."*[1] *By building a house that was, to quote the* Herald, *"roomy and comfortable, rather than outwardly magnificent," Paine set an unpretentious tone for estate development to come. And he acquired land, hundreds of acres of land, so that by 1907 the estate had reached its maximum size of 758 acres.*[2] *Even if he had accomplished nothing else, Paine would be important in Weston history because of the size of his landholdings, which were the largest in Weston from 1882 until after World War II. As late as 1950, the family trust still managed more than 700 undeveloped acres.*

But Charles Jackson Paine was also a well-known figure outside of Weston, a man described at his death as representing "an earlier generation of Bostonians famous for the honors they brought their native city and their Nation in sports, finance and war."[3] *At age 31 he was among the youngest to attain the rank of general in the Civil War. He was the nation's most celebrated yachtsman in a period when the sport of sailing reached its high point of public interest.*[4] *Three times he successfully defended the America's Cup in boats designed and built in Boston. He was a power among Boston capitalists, a "pioneer railway promoter . . . who laid the steel bands across the desert and mountains that first bound the East to the great West."*[5] *His shrewd investments in steel, textiles, mines, and utilities also paid off handsomely, and at his death in 1916 his estate was valued at nearly nine million dollars.*[6]

Despite his wealth and fame, Paine was a modest man who avoided any kind of display. One reporter covering the America's Cup races noted the contrast between Paine's "old straw hat and plain garb" and the elaborate yachting outfits of less famous and less wealthy owners.[7] *"He was democratic to the last degree, with no nonsense about him," wrote another reporter, who added, "to be a plain American citizen is good enough for him."* [8]

A portrait by John Singer Sargent and bronze bust by Boston sculptor Bela Lyon Pratt capture the general's aquiline nose, hollow cheeks, drooping mustache, and sharp Yankee chin.[9] *A newspaper reporter who interviewed Paine at the height of his fame following the third America's Cup race gives the following verbal portrait:*

> *An impassive, yet kindly countenance; the face of a student, of a recluse. . . . The form tall and spare, and slightly bent. A low voice, one that you must listen to acutely. A man who answers your question in the fewest words, who stops when he has answered it; whose great pleasure in life is not, most decidedly, in hearing himself talk. In short, a quiet man, unostentatious, retiring, utterly devoid of self-consciousness. . . . "A man of steady nerves," says one who knew him in youth; "he was a good billiard player. Always plucky and persistent, quiet and reserved . . . he was an iron boy, as he has shown himself an iron man."*[10]

The story of Gen. Charles Jackson Paine and his progeny is told in the family history Growing Paines.[11] *There the reader can savor many details of everyday life "snatched from oblivion" by the author, great-grandson Thomas Paine.*

Early Life and Civil War Service

Charles Jackson Paine (1833–1916), eldest of nine children of Charles Cushing Paine and Fanny Cabot Jackson, was born in Boston to a distinguished family that included great-grandfather Robert Treat Paine, signer of the Declaration of Independence, and brother Robert Treat Paine, the lawyer and philanthropist whose estate in Waltham still bears his name.[12] Educated at Boston Latin School and Harvard College, class of 1853, Paine was the fifth generation in his family to graduate from Harvard. He studied law with Rufus Choate and was admitted to the bar in 1856. After a two-year family grand tour of Europe, he practiced law for a short time in St. Louis and Boston before the outbreak of the Civil War.

The war provided a kind of direction Paine had not found in law, which he practiced reluctantly and with little success. In a letter to his father in the spring of 1861, Paine described Boston overtaken with war fever:

Figure 18-2. During the Civil War, Charles Jackson Paine rose rapidly through the ranks. In 1864 he was appointed brigadier general in command of a regiment of black soldiers. Throughout his life, Paine was referred to as "the General."

> Thousands of flags are waving from every window, horses carry them on their heads, every street is filled with little boys, with small drums & shouldered broomsticks, & uniforms are almost as common in the streets as citizen's dress.[13]

That September, Paine was authorized to recruit a company of volunteers. He rose quickly from captain of the 22nd Massachusetts Volunteers to major of the Eastern Bay State Regiment to colonel of the Second Louisiana Regiment under Gen. Benjamin Butler. In one Louisiana battle, he was reported killed in action. Several days later, news of his good health reached Boston:

> NOT DEAD, BUT LIVING. It now appears that the notices of the noble career of Colonel Charles J. Paine of the Second Louisiana, which have been printed within the last day or two, were all true, except as regards the alleged death of the gallant subject. The latest advices from New Orleans inform us that Colonel Paine lives to read his own "obituary notice."[14]

Paine later wrote that he was "entertained at seeing accts of my death," adding that reports of the battle "were all bosh" and "the fight was fearful and so were the descriptions, that is the only resemblance."[15]

In July 1864, Paine was appointed brigadier general and assigned command of an all-black division. His initial skepticism about how his troops would perform in battle was dispelled outside Richmond that September when they stormed Newmarket Heights and captured enemy defenses. Newspaper accounts of courage added greatly to the prestige of the black troops.[16] Paine's respect for his black soldiers and concern for their future in the postwar South is evidenced in his Civil War letters to his father:

> I think the negro suffrage question is one of a great deal more importance than the N.Y. papers do; all questions, that is, bearing on the status of the negro; if negroes thr [sic] the South are not put into a fair position of equality according to their intelligence and ability with white people, there will be outbreaks everywhere . . .[17]

Paine was promoted to major general in 1865. This letter from a colleague, written after the war, suggests the reasons for his military success:

> General Paine was a deep and laborious student in the art of war; of very quiet and retiring disposition . . . ; a cheerful tent and mess mate; a kind and generous comrade; and one of the coolest men under fire I ever saw. His image often appears to me . . . sitting on that old bay horse at the Battle of Plains Store, about the only field officer mounted, with that inseparable short black pipe in his mouth, only removing it to give some order in a cool, collected manner, while his men were falling around him in scores . . . calm in defeat, calm in success.[18]

During four years of war, Paine dreamed of buying a farm in the country. He wrote to his father, "Farming is the only occupation I fancy," and in another letter proposes a joint venture:

> An interest in farming gives one of the greatest attractions of a country place. Find a good big one South of Boston somewhere & North of Washington & when the war is over . . . we will go into farming jointly. In the summer, I'll raise colts & you pigs—we'll halve the carrots & compare the balance sheets at the end of the year. I'm not joking about this.[19]

In 1865, as the war was drawing to a close, he directed his sister Mamie to take his photographs, "write on the back of them 'wants a wife' and send them round to all the rich and pretty girls you know." He pondered his future in this letter to his father:

> Then comes the question of what I am going to do when the war is over. . . . Now what is there? Politics I can't endure under any circumstances . . . Farming is my fancy . . . a large farm *to make*

> *money.* Now as you consider that rather a poetical or lunatical idea, can you suggest anything better. I'm open to advice . . . & I'd like it soon; for the time may come without warning when I must decide what respectable occupation, lucrative & influential, is begging for my services?[20]

In thinking about the end of the war, Paine wrote that he was sure of one good thing at least, that "cigars will be cheaper."[21]

Marriage and Business Success

In retrospect, Paine need not have worried about finding the right girl. In 1867, at age 34, he married 20-year-old Julia Bryant (1847–1901). Not only did Miss Bryant have a sweet disposition, but also her social position was without equal and she was heir to a substantial fortune through her grandfather John Bryant, founder of the Far East trading firm of Bryant and Sturgis. Julia had lost both her parents and grandparents and was alone in the world except for a companion. She brought to the marriage a seaside cottage in Nahant and a large and magnificently furnished brick town house at 87 Mt. Vernon Street on Beacon Hill, designed by Charles Bulfinch.[22]

Paine abandoned the practice of law, a career more his father's choice than his own, and devoted his attention to managing his money. He multiplied his own inheritance and the larger fortune of his wife by investing in railroads at a time when Boston capital was financing western railroad expansion. For years he served as director of the Chicago, Burlington & Quincy; the Atchison, Topeka & Santa Fe; and the Mexican Central Railway. One railroad president was quoted as saying, "When, on an important question, I can convince Charles Paine of my view, I know that I am right."[23] A memoir about Paine's lifelong friend, Henry Lee Higginson, includes this description of Paine at work:

> [He] was reputed to be one of the ablest men on the C[hicago], B[urlington] and Q[uincy] Board of Directors. He sat also habitually in the office of Lee, Higginson & Co, where he could be seen almost any forenoon ensconced in a comfortable armchair, handsome, silent, puffing at a cigar which seemed never to have had a beginning and certainly never had an end.[24]

Nor did he ignore the potential for growth in gas and electric power companies and the expanding need for materials like steel, copper, and chemicals.

Paine's stature in the Boston financial community led to his 1897 appointment by President McKinley to a three-member commission on international bimetallism, which went abroad to ascertain the views of the governments of France, Great Britain, and Germany. McKinley was a leading proponent of bimetallism, a monetary standard based on the use of two metals, traditionally silver and gold, rather than just gold.[25]

Figure 18-3. C.J. Paine (standing, second from left) and Miss Julia Bryant (third from left, seated) were photographed with friends and relatives in late summer 1866.

Figure 18-4. Julia Bryant had a sweet disposition and unmatched social credentials. She was the only child of John Bryant Jr., whose father was founder of the Far East trading firm of Bryant & Sturgis and one of Boston's early millionaires.

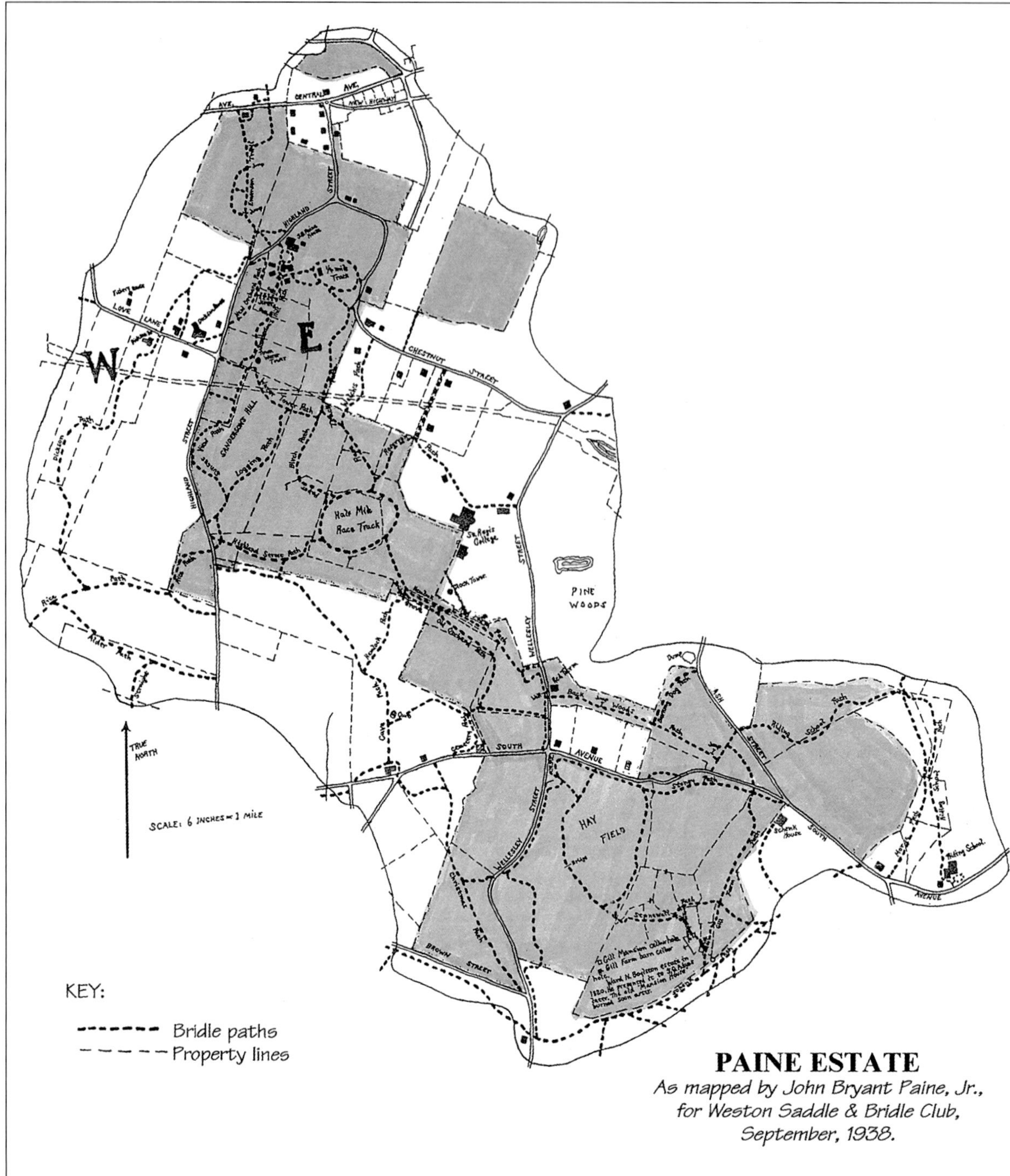

Figure 18-5. In 1868, Charles Jackson Paine bought his first 120 acres in Weston. Four decades later his "farm" reached its maximum size of 758 acres. Using trails marked on this Weston Saddle and Bridle Club map, members of the family could ride on their own land almost all the way to the Ferndale Farm barn on South Avenue.

The Farm in Weston

Charles Jackson Paine did not forget his dream to own a farm. One year after his marriage, he bought his first 120 acres in Weston.[26] The property at Highland and Chestnut Streets included an unusually large and elaborate Georgian mansion built in 1755 for wealthy merchant Elisha Jones. The house came with an unusual history, as Elisha was a leading Tory sympathizer during the Revolutionary War and in 1774 he was forced to flee to Boston, where he died some months later. The Weston property was confiscated and sold at auction after the war to a general on the winning side, Thomas Marshall, from whom it passed to other notable owners before Paine acquired it in 1868.

Paine immediately began buying more land. He purchased 58 acres from Isaac Jones in 1869 and a total of 80 acres from farmer John Dunn in the 1870s and '80s.[27] Dunn continued to live in his 18th-century farmhouse on Wellesley Street until his death. In 1882, the general made his largest Weston purchase, the 345-acre Gill Farm, later known as the Bolyston Farm, which included the site of the present Weston high and middle schools, as well as land directly to the north, east, and west.[28] At this point, Paine could ride horseback on his own land from his house on Highland Street to the corner of South Avenue and Ash Street.[29]

The antique Elisha Jones house on Highland Street lacked modern conveniences, particularly in

Figure 18-6. Charles and Julia Paine added the mansard-roofed section at right to the original 18th-century house on Highland Street. In 1883 the antique house was moved off the property to make way for the large addition at left. The resulting structure was known as the Big House. (Photo c. 1900)

the kitchen. Within a few years of moving to Weston, the Paines added a major addition known as the ell, with a large new kitchen, "back kitchen," large dining room, four bedrooms, servants' quarters, and a dairy and laundry in the basement.[30] In the early 1880s, as the family grew, the general decided to replace the 1755 portion of the house. He offered the historic structure to Charles H. Fiske, preservation-minded member of an old Weston family, who moved it in 1883 and again in 1888 to its present location at 22 Church Street.

On the site of the old house, Paine built an addition designed by Boston architect Carl Fehmer. The resulting structure, affectionately known as the Big House, had somewhere between 30 and 44 rooms, depending on who counted. The tower joining the old and new sections helped, to some extent, to distract the eye from the awkwardness of the design and also functioned as a water tower and a high point from which to view the distant skyline of Boston. The house was probably always painted gray.

Figure 18-7. The entrance hall had green wallpaper in a bold pattern and a hunting trophy over the mantel. In this c. 1904 photograph it was decorated for a party, with yachting pennants and chrysanthemums from the greenhouse. The open stairwell reached up to the third floor.

Regardless of its aesthetic merits, the family finally had enough room not only for the children but also for guests who frequently stayed weeks at a time. Visitors could relax on the wide piazza that wrapped around the north and west sides of the house or meander through interior rooms with 10-foot ceilings, dark oak paneling, pressed-brick fireplaces, and heavy moldings. The grand oak staircase was set within an open stairhall, three stories high and 18 by 40 feet wide, papered with green wallpaper and lit by a skylight and banks of windows and glazed doors. A cabinet full of yachting trophies and cups won by the general and his sons stood in the great hall. In later years, the walls were adorned with mounted African game heads of all sizes including antelope, zebra, and a large Cape buffalo. On the first floor was a large parlor, dining room, back parlor or library, and C.J. Paine's office. The rug in the den was a spread-eagled lion complete with foot pads, claws, and a snarling head. In the dining room opposite the marble fireplace hung General Paine's Civil War brigade flag, a black fort against a faded red field. The stairs led to six bedrooms on the second floor and an attic that was initially unfinished except for the billiard table corner. There were no bathrooms in Fehmer's addition and only one "w.c." in the ell.

The exterior walls were insulated with brick to keep the house cool. When the house was electrified around the late 1890s, the wiring was left exposed rather than buried in the walls. Over time, wooden moldings were placed over wires connecting primitive switches to converted gas chandeliers and sconces.

Development of the Estate Grounds

In December 1883, Paine wrote to the renowned landscape architect Frederick Law Olmsted at his Brookline office:

> My Dear Sir:
> I should be glad to have your advice about the position of an avenue to my house here, if you will kindly come out here for so small a matter. We shall be here a few days longer before moving to Boston . . .[31]

The result of Olmsted's visit was a simple sketch of house and barns connected by a great circular drive. The general was apparently satisfied with this minimal plan until September 1894, when the successor firm of Olmsted, Olmsted and Eliot was hired to landscape the immediate vicinity of the house. The planting list was spartan compared to those prepared by the firm for fellow Weston estate owners Charles Jones and Horace Sears.

In its prime, the estate grounds had extensive apple, peach, and pear orchards. The vegetable garden was originally located on the west side of Highland Street. Large greenhouses provided flowers all year long. Behind the Big House was a barn complex arranged around a quadrangle. The large main barn housed about 15 cows and 15 to 20 horses, tended by a foreman and two or three hired men. Riding paths

Figure 18-8. Chrysanthemums, orchids, lilies, and roses were grown in the greenhouses. (1917 photo)

Figure 18-9. The Paine barn complex pictured in this 1917 photograph was converted to an unusual residence in 1970.

Figure 18-10. Paine built an art studio for his daughters, Helen and Georgina, who were talented painters. One side was entirely glass, to capture the north light prized by artists. Inside was a cozy fireplace under a balcony. The studio was demolished in the late 1990s. (1918 photo)

were developed through the estate land, and trotting racetracks of a quarter mile and a half mile were cut into the woods behind the house. Sporting facilities also included a lawn tennis court and a two-lane bowling alley housed in a long, narrow clapboard outbuilding. In 1909 General Paine built a studio for his artistic daughters at the edge of the back lawn.[32] The small, classical structure was constructed with slabs of exposed aggregate concrete cast on the ground and then hoisted into place.

Figure 18-11. Swedish-born Maria von Gerber was 26 when she was hired as a wet nurse for baby Helen. "Mimi" became the Paine housekeeper and expertly managed the household staff and care of the children. She was remembered for her strength of character and high principles.

Family Life

By the early 1880s, the family had grown to five children: Sumner (1868–1904), John Bryant (1870–1951), Mary Anna Lee "Molly" (1873–1967), Charles Jackson Jr. (1876–1926), and Helen (1881–1947). Two later additions, Georgina (1888–1989) and Frank Cabot (1890–1952), arrived by 1890. The large family was a challenge enjoyed by Julia Paine:

> Julia loved family life, and very much ran the Paine household. She knew her own mind, and was quick with her words. She was unpretentious, retiring, selfless, ever generous, and of "sweet philosophy."[33]

Julia was devoted to First Parish Church, to which she gave generously. In the 1870s she donated money for the new parsonage and a clock for the church steeple, later transferred to the present stone church. She read widely and pursued her artistic talents by studying anatomy and drawing at the Boston Museum School. She rode horses and enthusiastically took up bicycle touring with her children. She and her husband shared a passion for traveling.

The Paines came to Weston in the spring, left in July and August for Nahant or, after 1902, for Cataumet, and returned in the fall. They headed back to Beacon Hill only when the weather got cold, which could be as late as early December. To orchestrate packing of the caravans of wagons needed for each move, the family relied on a large household staff headed by housekeeper Maria (Mimi) von Gerber. Mimi was a Swedish immigrant who had sailed to America with her new husband, young and full of plans for the future, only to find herself a penniless widow with a newborn child. She came to the Paines as a wet nurse for baby Helen and over the years took on increasing responsibilities, keeping three houses in order, running the kitchens, overseeing canning of jelly in jars by the hundreds, and caring for the children.

Mimi's half sister, Elna, came from Europe as the family seamstress and laundress. In 1895 she married Carl Anderson, and the couple spent winters at the Paine house in Weston, raising their five children in a second ell added in back of the kitchen. For additional household help like the cook, her assistant, the upstairs maid, and perhaps a nurse for the children, Mimi hired mainly Swedish women, perhaps four at any one time, who lived on the third floor of the original ell. Every Sunday the Paines' coachman would take Mimi and the four maids to the Lutheran church in Waltham.

The Paines had no butler. Sam, the "house man," sharpened knives, made fires, and stoked the coal furnace. One man tended the orchards while another took care of the greenhouses, assisted by one or two hired men of Italian descent who potted plants. Another hired man worked the vegetable garden, two men in the barn prepared harnesses and carriages, and at times the family employed two chauffeurs.

The Weston house had a schoolroom behind the grand staircase where the children did their lessons in the spring and fall. In the 1880s the older boys went to Mr. Hopkinson's school in Boston before going on to Harvard. Much later, the youngest, Frank, attended Middlesex School. The headmaster, Frederick Winsor, was married to Frank's sister Molly. Helen went to boarding school in New York and Nina to Miss Winsor's school, in the charge of Frederick Winsor's sister. The two girls were artistically inclined and were encouraged to study at the Boston Museum School and with local artists of renown.

The family entertained at dinner parties. Nina later wrote of the strain of such social occasions:

> Papa endured these dinner parties because in theory he approved of social life, but he was much too shy to enjoy them for their own sake. Mamma . . . used to tell us how the French dancing teacher of his day had pronounced him "a leetle timide." He transmitted this shyness to his children. . . . We were a shy lot, all of us.[34]

The general was very attached to sweets, but candy was not allowed in the house because he wanted his children to have good teeth. He was also fond of cigars. According to his great-grandson Thomas, he used only one match a day to light his first cigar and after that chain-smoked until day's end.

Paine was a longtime member of the Somerset Club and the Union Club and a member of the Corporation, or governing board, at Harvard and MIT. He endowed the Charles J. Paine Scholarship, which allowed one young man each year from Weston High School to pursue his education at either Harvard or MIT. He was the first president of the board of trustees of the Middlesex School, and the Bryant Paine dormitory is named for Charles and Julia.[35]

Figure 18-12. C.J. Paine and J. Malcolm Forbes formed a syndicate to build the Puritan, *shown here on the cover of the popular* Harper's Weekly. *The innovative design gained them national attention when the yacht won the America's Cup in 1885.*

Yacht Racing and the America's Cup

In the mid-1880s, Charles Jackson Paine achieved his greatest fame as the country's foremost yachtsman, known for the "dashing manner in which he upheld American's supremacy on the sea" as winner of three straight America's Cup races.[36]

Paine had sailed since he was a child; but it was not until the late 1870s, when his railroad investments began paying off, that he took up racing. In 1878 he bought the schooner *Halcyon* and by altering the design turned a slow vessel into a star performer. He joined the Eastern Yacht Club in Marblehead and later the New York, New Bedford, and Beverly Yacht Clubs.

In 1885, Paine and J. Malcolm Forbes headed a syndicate that built the *Puritan* and successfully defended the America's Cup against a British challenger, the *Genesta.*[37] In the two succeeding years, General Paine assumed the entire costs of building the *Mayflower,* which defeated the *Galatea,* and the *Volunteer,* which defeated the Scottish yacht *Thistle* to become his third vessel to win the prestigious America's Cup.

Although Paine employed a yacht designer and an experienced skipper, he was involved in every detail of design and race strategy. His designer, the well-known Edward "Ned" Burgess, credited Paine with their success:

> From the beginning General Paine has thought out the effect of every line, and every detail of construction and rig, and directed all, so as to secure him the possession of the fastest yacht in the world. These large racing sloops are most complicated and delicate machines, and only the most skillful engineer can hope to run them with success. I have been simply his executive officer.[38]

The general's son John Bryant recalls his father doing everything he could to lighten up the *Volunteer* before the race and to increase her speed in light weather, "even to the extent of planing off a quarter of an inch of her deck simply to save a few hundred pounds of weight."[39]

After the victory of the *Volunteer* in October 1887, the mayor of Boston held a public reception for Paine and Burgess at Faneuil Hall, attended by a reported 7,000 people who thronged to hear tributes and shake the hands of the honored guests.[40] The *Boston Transcript* reported on the gala affair:

> Old Faneuil Hall rang all evening with cheers for both the owner and designer. It was a gathering that has seldom been seen, the men coming from

Figure 18-13. Charles Jackson Paine won his third America's Cup race in 1887 with the yacht Volunteer. *Like his previous winners, the boat was designed and built by Edward "Ned" Burgess. This photograph shows the boat after its racing days were over and the mast had been modified.*

> every section of New England to do honor to the one man who, through his liberality and his energy, brought home to Boston three successful cup defenders.[41]

Speeches were recorded in the elaborate commemoration volume *A Testimonial to Charles J. Paine and Edward Burgess from the City of Boston, 1887,* printed by the city.

The Town of Weston also held a reception for General and Mrs. Paine at the town hall on October 26, 1887. The newspaper printed this report:

> Weston does not claim to be much of a yachting town, although some of its coming voters do own a few boats on the raging (?)[sic] Charles River. . . . But its citizens do know how to appreciate perseverance and Yankee pluck and skill, and when General Charles J. Paine—their summer townsman—won such a decisive victory over the Scotch sloop, their pleasure was as great as though the proud Volunteer floated within their midst.[42]

Town Hall was adorned with flags, bunting, and yacht pennants, along with broad banners with the names *Volunteer, Puritan,* and *Mayflower.* Outside, a row of colored lanterns lit up the motley array of vehicles belonging to local farmers and estate owners. Everyone who lived within the limits of the town was invited, and few were not present to pay their respects.

Edward Burgess died before the next America's Cup race of 1893, when Paine's entry, the *Jubilee,* was eliminated in the trials. Paine retired from America's Cup racing and enthusiastically took up golf, which had been introduced into Weston by First Parish minister Rev. Charles Russell in 1894. Into his 80s, he could be seen on the links wearing his legendary red suspenders. Paine served as president of the Weston Golf Club and was a founder of The Country Club in Brookline.

Second Generation—Sumner and John Bryant Paine and the 1896 Olympic Games

Charles Jackson Paine's oldest son, Sumner, enrolled at Harvard but did not graduate. He later received a medical degree from Denver Medical College, studied in Germany for two years, and then opened an office in Cambridge, "but he never applied himself to his profession, and he did not care to follow in the footsteps of his father, as he had no taste for financial affairs."[43] His main interests were athletics and military affairs. Both he and his younger brother John Bryant served in the Massachusetts Regiment during the Spanish-American War, although they did not see combat. John Bryant, Harvard class of 1891, continued on at the law school but did not

Figure 18-14. The Boston Athletic Association was the only U.S. club to accept an invitation to the first modern Olympics in Athens, Greece, in 1896. The eight BAA representatives included Sumner and John B. Paine (seated, holding pistols), both of whom won first-place medals in pistol shooting.

complete his degree. Although their interests in sports and the military were similar, the personalities of the two were quite different, as pointed out in an article in the *Boston Record*:

> Sumner Paine apparently would like to be thought quite a man of the world . . . and enjoys life as well as the next young man. John B. is quite like his father. He is a very modest young man and belongs to an entirely different set.[44]

Sumner and John were among 13 self-appointed U.S. delegates to the first modern Olympic games, held in April 1896 after a lapse of 1,500 years. Eight of the athletes were members of the Boston Athletic Association (BAA), the only club in the United States to accept the invitation of the newly formed International Olympic Committee to send a team.

The story of how the brothers won three first-place medals in revolver and pistol contests is told by Sumner Paine in an 1896 article in the magazine *Shooting and Fishing*. He was living in Paris and got an unexpected visit from his brother:

> I came home to lunch one day and found my brother, Lieutenant John B. Paine, sitting in my office. I had not the slightest idea that he was on this side of the pond.
>
> "When does the next train start for Athens?" said he.
>
> "I don't know," said I.
>
> "Well," said he, "find out, and get your revolvers and we will go there, for the Boston Athletic Association (of which we are both members) has sent a team over, and as there are two revolver matches we may be able to help out the Americans."[45]

Thousands of Greeks poured into Athens for the games, filling the newly renovated 40,000- to 50,000-seat stadium and standing in crowds on the surrounding hillsides. The Paine brothers reached the city just in time for their match the next day. John won easily with a score of 442, Sumner was second with 380, and the next closest score was below 200. The next day, by prior agreement between the brothers, the first day's winner did not participate. Sumner won easily with a score exactly the same as his brother's the previous day. After the games "it was one continual round of pleasure," as the athletes were honored with receptions, picnics, and a state luncheon with the king of Greece.

Sumner's skill with a revolver came under public scrutiny in less favorable circumstances five years later, when he came home unexpectedly and discovered his wife with his daughter's music teacher in compromising circumstances.[46] He was arrested for brandishing a weapon and firing it repeatedly into the air in his pursuit across Boston Common. His close friend Brenton H. Dickson Jr. testified at the court hearing, "That man is the best shot in the world and if he wanted to he could have hit the man."[47] Because of this scandal and other problems, Sumner was a disappointment to his father. When he died in 1904 at the young age of 35, his father gave up drinking because of its pernicious effects on his oldest son.

John was a skilled yachtsman. A "chip of [sic] the old block," wrote one newspaper reporter, who added that "yachting is second nature to the Paines."[48] John joined his father in the three triumphant America's Cup races. The year after the victory of the *Volunteer* in 1887, the 18-year-old designed and built the first of at least five sloops. Aboard the *Jubilee* with his father in the cup race of 1893, the *New York Times* called him "the very incarnation of ideal young Boston" and the *Boston Globe* commented on his fashion and habits, so like his father's:

> He is no dude. He is not fastidious in his dress, wears old clothes when yachting, and never owned a yachting suit. He has never liked society, and it is told of him that some years ago . . . his mother offered him $25 a dance for every one which he attended. . . . He is the youngest of the designers of the present field of cup defense.[49]

John and his father were similar in many ways. It was not just the mustache, modest demeanor, and passion for sailing but also their life pattern: law training, early restlessness, military service, marriage, and finally management of the family fortune. In 1900, at age 30, John married Louise Rue Frazer, an art student and friend of his sister. The couple settled in Weston in a clapboard house off Boston Post Road that the general had built in 1884.[50] The garage

Figure 18-15. Helen Paine [Kimball] painted her brother John about 1910.

Figure 18-16. Helen, fifth of Charles Jackson Paine's seven children, was an accomplished artist.

had a machine shop where John, his hands covered with grease, tinkered with the automobiles that were his second passion after sailing.

Molly, Charlie, Helen, Nina, and Frank

In 1894 the general's third child and oldest daughter, Mary Anna Lee "Molly" Paine, married Frederick Winsor, who taught for several years before founding the Middlesex School in 1901. The wedding was something of a disaster. Two special trains hired to bring guests from Boston to Weston were stranded en route. When the wedding party arrived at First Parish Church and learned that only 60 of their expected 400 guests had arrived, they remained outside in their carriages, "under the roasting rays of the afternoon sun and the curious gaze of the townspeople who had turned out to see the society people." Guests from one train finally appeared, the ceremony was performed, and everyone returned to the Big House. The parlor was draped with 600 yards of asparagus fern, interspersed with countless roses. On the mantels, General Paine's great silver trophy cups brimmed with roses.[51]

The general's third son, Charles J. Paine Jr., was well known as a college baseball pitcher at Harvard, where he was class of 1897. After graduation he was employed by Lee, Higginson & Co. and later pursued business interests in lumber, coal, and copper. He was married in 1902 and lived in Weston in a house off Old Road.

Helen and Georgina were the artists of the family. Helen studied with noted portraitist Charles Hopkinson and maintained a studio at Charles and Chestnut Streets in Boston. She married Rev. Thatcher R. Kimball of Boston, assistant curate of St. Stephen's Church and a dedicated worker among the poor of the South End.[52] Georgina married Harvard forestry professor Richard Thornton Fisher in 1912 and settled on Love Lane. She reportedly played golf every morning from the time she was nine.

Figure 18-17. General Paine's youngest daughter, Georgina, was photographed with her horse Harlequin in 1901.

Frank Cabot Paine graduated from Harvard in 1912 and, after a brief stint selling bonds at Lee, Higginson, went on to become a noted yachtsman, naval architect, and founder of the boatbuilding firm of Burgess, Swasey & Paine. His yacht *Yankee* set the

Figure 18-18. Charles Jackson Paine died in 1916. His estate, valued at nearly nine million dollars, was placed in trust for his descendants.

all-time record for speed over a 30-mile America's Cup course and was a three-time candidate in the cup races of 1930, 1934, and 1937.[53] Frank married Virginia Low in 1915 and the couple settled at Greenways, a Federal Revival house on several hundred acres on the Sudbury River in Wayland.

Death of Julia and C.J. Paine

Julia Bryant Paine died unexpectedly in 1901 at age 54, a blow from which the general never recovered. Sumner died just a few years later, and Charlie's marriage, like Sumner's, ended in divorce. In 1904, Charles Jackson Paine set up several trusts for his children and grandchildren. The Paine Trust continues to hold and sell land in Weston for the benefit of the general's descendants.

Paine descendants saved a copy of C.J. Paine's tax return for the year ending December 31, 1914, the first year the Internal Revenue Service collected a tax on income. Paine had a gross income of $315,562, including $204,327 in dividends, and paid a total of $9,823. Of his property in Weston he wrote that "expenses of a farm for pleasure were much in excess of the receipts and neither receipts nor expenses are included."[54]

Gen. Charles Jackson Paine died on August 12, 1916, just 10 days shy of his 83rd birthday. Rev. Charles F. Russell, minister of First Parish Church, wrote an eloquent letter to the editor of the *Boston Transcript,* lamenting the end of "a life so rich in notable achievements in deed and character as to demand more than a mere passing notice." Russell praised Paine as "soldier, statesman, sportsman and financier and notable in each" and a man whose life was based "not only on force and courage, but on truth, on honor, on public spirit, on soberness and modesty, on consideration for others."[55]

An inventory after his death valued the farm in Weston, with an estimated 750 acres, at $97,250. His total real-estate holdings were valued at $229,555 and his total personal estate, largely in stocks and bonds, at $8,679,960. Under the will, the bulk of the estate was put into a large trust fund to be divided into six equal shares from which his six children could receive income. The sons could withdraw half their share after age 30, but the daughters' portions had to remain in trust.

John Bryant Paine at the Big House

After the general's death, John Bryant Paine moved into the Big House with his wife, Louise, his oldest son, John Bryant Jr. (1901–1976), and his six daugh-

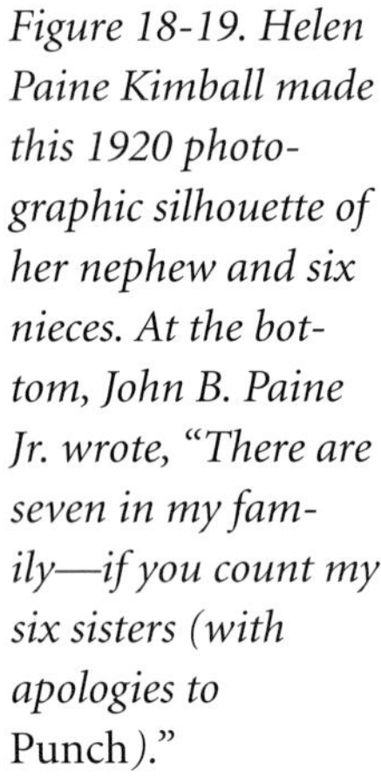

Figure 18-19. Helen Paine Kimball made this 1920 photographic silhouette of her nephew and six nieces. At the bottom, John B. Paine Jr. wrote, "There are seven in my family—if you count my six sisters (with apologies to Punch*)."*

Figure 18-20. John Bryant Paine had a passion for automobiles. He built his own engine, a "self-starter," and put it into a Packard body. His daughter Helen drives the car he made for his children. (1909 photo)

Figure 18-21. Three-year-old Carol Paine stands next to the family car in 1909.

ters: Helen (b. 1904), Caroline "Carol" (1906–2000), Julia (1909–1943), Louise (b. 1911), Charlotte "Chattie" (1913–1966), and Sarah "Sal" (b. 1919). Except for winterizing the house, he made few changes. Large tracts of the estate land were leased to the Mezzit family, whose rapidly expanding Weston Nurseries was located in Weston until after World War II. The stable remained full of horses and cows and the old bowling alley was converted into a chicken coop.

During the 1920s, various members of the J.B. Paine family traveled to Europe, the American West, and, most ambitiously, to Nairobi and the Serengeti Plain. They returned from Africa after five months with hundreds of photos and the heads and skins of gazelles, lions, a water buffalo, dik-dik, giraffe, and leopard later mounted in the great hall of the Big House. A newspaper gossip column commented on the trip:

> Can you imagine Mrs. John Bryant Paine of Weston with PEARLS. She enjoys a different side of life such as she had last year when she took her entire family to Africa to shoot tigers. One of the daughters has a superb leopard coat made of the skin of the animal shot by Mr. Paine. This form of sport is about the most expensive known but who thinks of expense in the same sentence as the Paine fortune.[56]

John Bryant Paine pursued his later avocations with the same energy earlier devoted to sailing and automobiles. In addition to hunting and fishing, he loved photography and maintained a darkroom in the Big House. He took elaborate home movies and in 1932 created several three-reel productions with Brent Dickson as actor and scriptwriter. In the '30s and '40s, he took up furniture making. With the assistance of his wife, who did the carving, he produced fine reproductions of classic Early American furniture in a workshop in the attic. He made leatherwork purses and albums and built a model airplane with a five-foot wingspan. In the late 1930s he experimented with audio recording. He also kept a collection of springer spaniels.

Figure 18-22. In the fall of 1927, the J.B. Paine family embarked on a five-month African safari.

The Third Generation

John Bryant Paine Jr. (1901–1976), known as Jack, was the eldest of seven and the only boy. He attended Pigeon Hill School and later Middlesex, where he was embarrassed to be "the boss's nephew."[57] Like his father and grandfather, he took his hobbies seriously.

Figure 18-23. John Bryant Paine relaxes with his Brittany spaniels in 1939.

His first collection, butterflies and moths, eventually included 712 specimens, nearly every known North American variety. Later he became an avid collector of minerals, books, and records. He was a compulsive diary writer whose 37 volumes of daily memoirs were willed to the Massachusetts Historical Society. J.B. Jr. was the seventh generation of Paines to attend Harvard, from which he graduated in 1923. For years after graduation he lived with his parents in the Big House, which was comfortable and well suited to his creative pursuits.

Figure 18-24. Georgina Paine Fisher painted this portrait of her nephew John Bryant Paine Jr.

His first job was a low-paying position in the statistical department of Old Colony Trust Company, at a salary of $600 a year. After successfully predicting the stock market crash of 1929 and other market upheavals, he moved into financial planning. In his leisure time, he cleared brush from the trails and cut new ones through the estate property, all of which he named and mapped for the Weston Saddle and Bridle Club. Among his most legendary creations was a Lionel train layout that took over the third-floor landing. Brenton Dickson III painted the Alpine scenery, his mother and sister Chattie made houses, and his father filmed a 16 mm color movie on the set, culminating in a mock train wreck.

Five of his six sisters married well before Jack, and most of them stayed close to home. Helen and family friend Brenton H. Dickson III were wed in 1928 and remodeled an old farmhouse on Love Lane. Julia, who married Kennard Wakefield about a year later, died in 1943 at age 34, the day after giving birth to her fourth daughter. Carol and her husband, Charles Ganson, settled in a house on the estate. Ganson was made a Paine trustee and set up the law practice of Taylor, Ganson and Perrin, which handled the family's legal business. Chattie, who never married, lived with her parents in the Big House. The two girls who left Weston were Louise, who married A.W. "Bill" Erickson and lived for

Figure 18-25. J.B. Paine Jr.'s many hobbies are reflected in this 1941 photograph of his study in Weston. Here he kept his mineral and butterfly collections.

many years in the Bahamas, and Sal, who ran a ranch in Wyoming with her husband, Waldo Forbes.

Finally, in the midst of World War II, Jack and his longtime friend Rita Nash were married. After the war, they moved into the 18th-century Dunn farmhouse, which had been carefully restored by John B. Sr. and Louise Paine. In 1948 Jack took advantage of a sluggish real-estate market to buy Barnstable House on Orchard Avenue.[58]

After World War II, farm operations dwindled on the Highland Street property. The orchards were let go and fields became overgrown. John Bryant Paine died in 1951. His widow, Louise Frazer Paine, moved into a smaller house on the property in 1967 and died the following year. The Big House was left

Figure 18-26. The wedding of Sally Paine and Waldo Forbes. (Names with photo credits)

Figure 18-27. John Bryant and Louise Frazer Paine pose in the art studio with six of their children, six spouses, and 17 grandchildren. (c. 1945–46 photo; names with photo credits)

vacant. Efforts to sell it were unsuccessful. Because of its size, tax liability, and operating costs (there were 11 fireplaces, none with a damper, and two large coal-burning furnaces), the house was finally demolished in 1972, just as the historic preservation movement was gaining momentum nationwide.

In 1950, the Paine Trust still owned more than 700 acres. John Bryant Paine Jr. was instrumental in establishing the Highland Town Forest with over 150 acres of Paine land deeded to the town in 1955. One of his pet projects before his death in 1976 was clearing trees that had grown up on the west side of Highland Street since his youth and blocked the views of sunsets behind Mount Wachusett and Mount Monadnock.[59]

In 1959, some 62 acres were sold to the town for a new high school, and in 1968 the adjacent 41 acres were sold for a junior high. The trust still owned 247 acres in 1977, 137 acres in 1987, and about 75 acres in 1999. Undivided interests in the land have passed from the general's six children to his 21 grandchildren and 63 great-grandchildren.

Houses Associated with the Paine Family and Houses in the Highland/Chestnut Street Area

317 Boston Post Road (1884). Stick-style house built for Gen. Charles Jackson Paine and originally occupied by Mrs. F.T. Gray and her children. According to Thomas Paine, in *Growing Paines,* the house was constructed by William N. Gowell using designs of Morris Dorr, at a cost of $4,511. After his marriage in 1900, C.J. Paine's son John Bryant Paine lived here with his young family. In later years, it was rented to other family members in need of housing, including the Wentworths and Ericksons.

734 Boston Post Road. See chapter 16.

One Chestnut Street. See chapters 1 and 19.

27 Chestnut Street (1933). Colonial Revival house designed by Boston architects Mowll and Rand for Mrs. Sarah A. Gordon.

34–40 Chestnut Street. Blacksmith Oliver Patriquin purchased land on Chestnut Street and, over time, built four houses.[60] William Henderson was builder for the first (No. 40, c. 1920) and William Compton for the second (No. 38). The third (No. 36) was constructed by Patriquin with the help of several carpenters and included a wrought-iron stair railing that he designed. The fourth house (No. 34) was "more like a summer camp" where the family lived in the early years of the Depression. The roof and walls were covered with heavy tar paper. The house had minimal plumbing and a single large woodstove that provided enough heat to warm three small bedrooms. A large oil lamp was suspended from the open rafters. Later Patriquin finished this house, where he lived in his later years. He had a blacksmith shop on the property. (See also chapters 15 and 17.)

44–74 Chestnut Street. Amri and Mary Barker, the two children of farmer Nathan Barker, were largely responsible for the development of the houses between 44 and 74 Chestnut Street. Amri inherited the main farmhouse and barn, located at what is now No. 52. This structure burned in the mid-20th century. No. 44, built about 1895, was a tenant house for the Barker farm. No. 74 was built in 1885 for Mary Barker when she married Oliver L. Sherburne. In the 1887 directory, Sherburne is listed as foreman for C.J. Paine. No. 70, built about 1913 and remodeled in the 1980s, was built by Mary and her daughter-in-law, Mrs. Nathan Sherburne, after Oliver died.

78 Chestnut Street. Home of builder William Henderson, who constructed the houses at Nos. 40, 70, 72, and 85 Chestnut Street.

85 Chestnut Street. In 1911 the old John Coburn/Luther S. Upham homestead with about 20 acres was sold to Boston lawyer E. Sohier Welch, who used it as a summer house and gentleman's farm. The Colonial farmhouse burned and was replaced in 1931 by a Colonial Revival house built using the old foundation and central chimney. This house was demolished in 2001 after the present house was completed. The old barn still stands next door at No. 81.

109 Chestnut Street (1870). Built in 1870 for Luther F. Upham, a farmer whose family homestead was located just down the street. In 1892 Upham sold the property to General Paine, who used it to house his farm manager and later Mr. Corrigan, the family chauffeur.

115 Chestnut Street (1956). Colonial Revival house designed by architect Marjorie Pierce.

118 Chestnut Street (c. 1870). Built as an ell extending from the Paine estate mansion, this structure was moved to its present site sometime in the late 19th century. It was occupied by the estate gardener and later by Charles M. Ganson and Caroline Paine Ganson, daughter of John Bryant Paine.

140 Chestnut Street. Complex of barns and outbuildings, with some framing timbers in the main barn thought to date to the 18th century. The main barn was converted to a residence in 1970 by General Paine's great-granddaughter the poet Carol Ganson and her husband, James Burnes. Architect Richard Trenaglio, professor at MIT School of Design, was the "idea person"; the design and the work itself was done by Trenaglio, his students, the Burneses, and their friends.

150 Chestnut Street (1967). Built for Louise Frazer Paine, widow of John Bryant Paine, so that she could move out of the Big House. Later occupied by grandson Charles M. "Mac" Ganson Jr.

22 Church Street (1754–55). Built for prominent merchant Elisha Jones, this exceptionally fine Georgian house was originally located on the Paine property on Highland Street. The construction date is documented in Elisha Jones's ledger, and the name of the housewright, Jeduthan Baldwin, is also known. Elisha Jones was a third-generation member of one of the first families to settle in Weston. By 1747 he had established a store, the earliest recorded in Weston. He was active in town government for 28 years, holding numerous key positions including selectman. But because he was a prominent Tory, Elisha was forced to leave Weston in September 1774 and took refuge in Boston with the British troops. His property was confiscated in 1779 and his homestead, along with 75 acres of his land, was sold at auction in 1782 to Gen. Thomas Marshall.

Marshall sold the property in 1801 to John Clark, a Cambridge physician, who conveyed it to his mother-in-law, Ruth Mackay. Her son, Capt. John Mackay, was a sea captain who, with Jonas Chickering, founded the firm of Mackay and Chickering for the manufacture of pianos. The ivory for the keys was bleached on the farm in Weston. In 1838 John Mackay sold the 100-acre property, which changed hands several more times before the sale to C.J. Paine in 1868.

In 1883 Paine gave the house to Charles H. Fiske on the condition that it be relocated. He moved it to Boston Post Road (where No. 633 is today) and in 1888 he moved it again, to 22 Church Street. (See chapter 16.)

316 Wellesley Street (c. 1773). Built for Joel Smith, son of Josiah Smith, who owned the well-known tavern on Boston Post Road. The house is thought to date from 1773 because that is the year Joel was married and the year he was granted a liquor license as a retailer "in his new house." No. 316 was originally on the west side of Wellesley Street but the road was straightened, leaving the house on the east side. Beginning in 1843, the property was owned by John Dunn, a farmer who appears to have gotten into financial difficulties. To satisfy his creditors, the house and part of the land were sold in 1882 to Gen. C.J. Paine, for $4,500. Dunn continued to live in the house until his death, after which it was occupied by Paine's foreman, Oliver L. Sherburne, along with other tenant farmers. In 1946 it was extensively remodeled by Mrs. John Bryant Paine Sr., who reportedly loved the old house and fixed it up for her son and daughter-in-law, who lived there until 1948.

Abbreviated Paine Genealogy

Charles Cushing Paine (1808–1874), m. Fanny Cabot Jackson (1812–1878)
  Gen. Charles Jackson Paine (1833–1916), m. Julia Lee Bryant (1847–1901)
    Sumner (1869–1904), m. Salome Brigham
    John Bryant (1870–1951), m. Louise Rue Frazer
      John Bryant Jr. (1901–1976), m. Henrietta "Rita" Nash
      Helen (1904–), m. Brenton H. Dickson III
      Caroline "Carol" (1906–2000), m. Charles M. Ganson
      Julia Lee (1909–1943), m. George Kennard Wakefield
      Louise (1911–), m. Arioch Wentworth Erickson
      Charlotte "Chattie" (1913–1966)
      Sarah "Sal" (1919–), m. Waldo E. Forbes
    Mary Anna Lee (1873–1967), m. Frederick Winsor
    Charles Jackson Jr. (1876–1926), m. Edith M. Johnson
    Helen (1881–1947), m. Thatcher R. Kimball
    Georgina (1888–1989), m. 1. Richard Thornton Fisher (d. 1934)
      2. Llewellyn Howland
    Frank Cabot (1890–1952), m. Virginia Marie Low
  Capt. William Cushing Paine
  Robert Treat Paine
  Frances Cabot Paine
  Sarah Cushing Paine
  Marianne Paine
  Sumner (Edward Jackson) Paine
  Helen Paine
  Cary Paine

Notes

1. "Boston Has Become the Lenox of the East," *Boston Sunday Herald,* May 11, 1902.
2. The taxable acreage list under C.J. Paine's name in the town records varies with the years as follows: 1870 (118), 1880 (176), 1883 (577), 1900 (739), 1907–08 (758), 1910 (640), 1916 (657). The Paine Trust still owned 694 acres in 1950.
3. "Gen C.J. Paine to Be Laid to Rest," unknown newspaper, about August 17, 1916 (Coburn scrapbook #2).
4. Paine is one of only a few Weston residents profiled in the *Dictionary of American Biography,* which made the following assessment of Paine's yachting contributions: "his practical skill and conspicuous fairness were influences on American yacht design and international sport" (vol. II, 147).
5. "Gen C.J. Paine to be Laid to Rest," op. cit.
6. Inventory of Charles J. Paine, filed April 11, 1917, shows personal estate of $8,679,960 and real estate of $229,555, for a total of $8,909,515.
7. *Dictionary of American Biography* (New York: Scribners, 1932), vol. II, 147.
8. "Men Who Love the Water—Sketches of Some of Boston's Leading Yachtsmen," *Boston Herald,* January 26, 1890.
9. The portrait, done in 1904, was donated by the family to the Boston Museum of Fine Arts in 1954. The Pratt bust was sculpted in 1905 and is still owned by a member of the family.
10. *Boston Transcript,* October 5, 1887.
11. The full title of the book is *Growing Paines: Paternal Patterns and Matrimonial Matters in a Family Boston Born & Bred,* by Thomas M. Paine (privately printed, Wellesley, MA, 1991). The author drew on this source for much of the family history contained in this chapter and is indebted to author and family archivist Tom Paine for making available his extensive photograph collection and research materials.
12. Paine, Sarah Cushing, *Paine Ancestry: The Family of Robert Treat Paine, Signer of the Declaration of Independence,* edited by Charles Henry Pope (Boston, printed for the family, 1912), 3.
13. CJP to his father, April 30, 1861, as quoted in *Growing Paines,* 98.
14. *Boston Daily Advertiser,* June 10, 1863.
15. *Paine Ancestry,* 252 (letter of June 25, 1863).
16. Ibid., 258 (quoted from the *New York World*).
17. Ibid., 266.
18. Charles A.R. Dimon to *Boston Transcript* editor, October 6, 1887, as quoted in *Growing Paines,* 103.
19. CJP letters to his father, January 28, 1863, as quoted in *Growing Paines,* 100. Also letter of January 8, 1863, on page 99.
20. CJP to his father, March 12, 1865, as quoted in *Growing Paines,* 104–05.
21. CJP to Mamie, March 6, 1865, as quoted in *Growing Paines,* 104.
22. This house remained in the estate of Charles Jackson Paine until the mid-1950s, when Georgina Paine bought the property from the trust, generously endowed it, and presented it to the Colonial Society for its headquarters.
23. Higginson, Henry L, "Charles J. Paine," *Boston Transcript,* August 14, 1916.
24. "Henry Lee Higginson," *Massachusetts Historical Society Proceedings,* February 1920, 117.
25. For further information on the commission, see *The Commercial and Financial Chronicle,* New York, April 17, 1897, vol. 64, no. 1660.
26. MCRD 1032/535 (William M. Roberts to CJP, March 1868), $9,000.
27. Paine purchased 26 acres of woodland and pasture from John Dunn in May 1876

(MCRD, 1394/582), 2.64 acres in October 1876 (1414/587), and 52 acres, plus the house at 316 Wellesley Street and barn, in June 1882 (1601/272 and Plan Book 38, plan 55). A letter from Dunn's brother, now owned by Thomas Paine, expresses his appreciation that Dunn could continue to live in the house: "I wish you to know the gratitude I have in my heart towards you for the kindness you showed my poor brother in permitting him to remain in his former home till he was called to his eternal home."

28. MCRD 1608/215, William C. Johnson & al to CJP (August 21, 1882) and Plan Book 38, plan 56. The plan shows five lots totaling 345 acres. Sale price $11,500. Map owned by Tom Paine shows "Plan of the Gill Farm in Weston Belonging to Ward N. Boylston, Esq. 1820." The history of this property is told in *WHSB* (January 1973, 3–4). According to this article, when Ward Boylston died in 1828, he left the property to his personal friend John Quincy Adams, sixth president of the United States. His son, Charles Francis Adams, made frequent trips to inspect the farm, which was let to tenant farmers. The property remained in the Adams family until sold to CJP.

29. Note that one major landholding of the Paine family, the so-called Livermore purchase, including the house at 734–736 Boston Post Road and 43 acres, was acquired in 1920, after the general's death, by the trustees of his estate.

30. The name "Mr Dorr" is handwritten on the sheet covering the roll of plans, suggesting that he was the architect or builder.

31. Olmsted Papers, Library of Congress, Reel 65, Job #1396, letter of December 3, 1883. Also Frederick Law Olmsted National Historic Site, Brookline, Massachusetts, Job #1396, #2–4, Plan of Grounds, December, 1883.

32. *WDFPT,* April 2, 1909. J.C. Macdonald, builder. The art studio was demolished in 1998.

33. *Growing Paines,* 108.

34. *Growing Paines,* 138, as quoted from Georgina Paine's memoir, *Afterthoughts.*

35. *Growing Paines,* 140.

36. "Gen. C.J. Paine to Be Laid to Rest," op. cit. The America's Cup is one of the oldest and best-known trophies in international sailing yacht competition.

37. An additional source on the 1880s America's Cup races is Joseph E. Garland's *The North Shore* (Commonwealth Editions, Beverly, MA, 1998), 77–87.

38. *Paine Ancestry,* 241.

39. *Growing Paines,* 125.

40. "Paine-Burgess Testimonial," issued by the City of Boston, as quoted in *Paine Ancestry,* 241.

41. "The Late General Paine, 'America's Cup Defender,'" *Boston Evening Transcript,* August 16, 1916, 14 (includes illustration of Faneuil Hall decorated for the reception of 1887).

42. "Another Hearty Reception: General and Mrs. Charles J. Paine Receive the Congratulations of the People of Weston," unknown newspaper, about October 28, 1887 (Coburn scrapbook #4). See also "Reception for Gen. and Mrs. Paine," *Waltham Free Press,* October 28, 1887.

43. *Paine Ancestry,* 269, and obituary in *WDFPT,* April 22, 1904.

44. *Boston Record,* October 18, 1890.

45. This account of the Olympics comes from two sources that vary slightly in detail. One is a letter by Sumner Paine in the May 1896 issue of *Shooting and Fishing* quoted in part in B.H. Dickson's article "Weston's Olympic Medalists," *WHSB,* January 1983, and the other is Jonathan Shaw's "The Unexpected Olympians: How Harvard Dominated the First Modern Games—In Spite of Itself." *Harvard Magazine,* July–August 1996, 37–45.

46. *WDFPT,* May 31, 1901.

47. *Growing Paines,* 156.

48. "John Paine, Yachtsman—Looks Almost Boyish, and Is a Chip of [sic] the Old Block," undated clipping from unknown newspaper, Harvard University Archives, file of John B. Paine, class of 1891.

49. *Boston Globe,* August 6, 1893 (quoted in *Growing Paines,* 181).

50. 317 Boston Post Road.

51. "Winsor-Paine—Daughter of the General the Fair Bride—Brilliant Ceremony in a Weston Church—Striking Decorations in Country House—Unpleasant Delay of Trains From Boston," Boston newspaper report after the wedding of June 18, 1894.

52. "Paine's Daughter Weds," *Boston Herald,* December 28, 1905, and *WDFPT,* December 29, 1905.

53. See Frank Paine's obituary in *Yachting Magazine,* December 1952.

54. Collection of Thomas M. Paine.

55. Russell, Charles F., letter to the editor, *Boston Transcript,* August 18, 1916, on the death of Charles Jackson Paine.

56. As quoted in *Growing Paines,* 193.

57. *Growing Paines,* 214.

58. Tom Paine reports the purchase price as $40,000 for the house (140 Orchard Avenue) and 8 acres.

59. At the time of the nation's bicentennial in 1976, a bronze plaque was placed on a boulder at a high point of land on the east side of Highland Street, reading as follows: "This memorial was erected by the Town of Weston and the Weston Forest and Trail Association on land donated to the town in 1955 by the Charles Jackson Paine family so that the view to the west might be enjoyed by the future generations."

60. Information on these four houses from a letter from Calvin Patriquin to PWF, received March 2001.

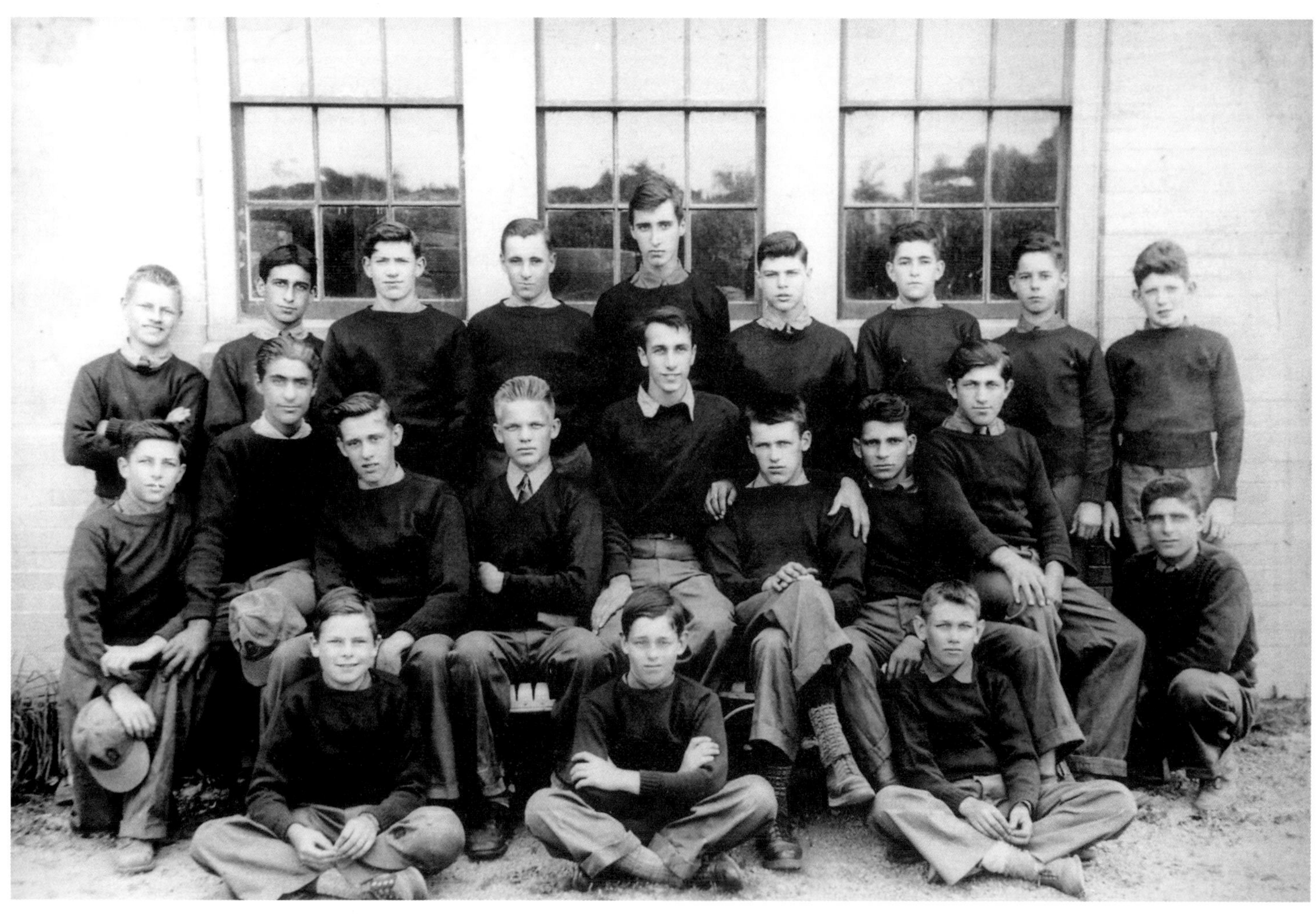

Figure 19-1. Hillcrest Farm, later renamed Hillcrest Gardens, was the unique creation of Marian Roby Case. She conceived it as "an experimental farm" devoted not only to scientific agriculture but also to "train[ing] the American boy to a love of the soil." Her "Hillcrest boys" had uniforms, attended weekly lectures, and were required to keep journals of their nature observations. Miss Case's enterprise should be viewed in the historical context of the early-20th-century progressive movement, when reformers worked to address the problems created by urbanization, industrialization, and immigration. (Photo c. 1938. Names listed with photo credits)

CHAPTER 19

Case's Corner

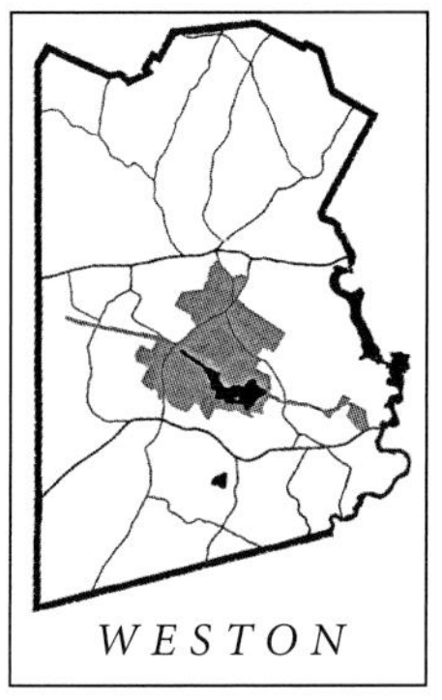

"Case's Corner" tells the story of the James Case estate, Marian Case's Hillcrest Farm, the Demmon-Morrison estate (now Regis College), and the Weston Aqueduct and Reservoir. The Case and Demmon-Morrison estates are discussed together not only because of their geographical proximity but also because of the many interesting parallels. Both estates were established by Boston businessmen, maintained and improved by strong, independent-minded daughters, and eventually turned over to nonprofit institutions.

The two central figures, Fannie Demmon Morrison and Marian Case, were born within a few years of each other and raised in the same genteel society. Their fathers died within a year of each other, when both women were in their 40s. Both established their own identities and pursued their personal interests and social goals with energy and commitment. Fannie Morrison has been described as "an eccentric independent woman" and "a forthright individual who abhorred bigotry in any form."[1] Marian Case's vision of a model farm staffed by boys learning to love nature provoked "knowing grins" from contemporaries who viewed her as "somewhat flighty" and her dress as "mannish." [2] She persevered despite initial failures, once writing, "At Hillcrest we have run our plough through rough, uncultivated land. It has caught in many a stubble, but it has been hitched to the stars."[3]

Both women were deeply involved in horticulture. In Weston, Fannie Morrison's expertise was overshadowed by that of Marian Case, who was a leading member of the Massachusetts Horticultural Society and whose Hillcrest property was a center for plant experimentation and display. In Pasadena, California, where the Morrisons spent the winters and eventually moved year-round, Fannie Morrison's garden was described as among the most beautiful in the city. [4] In 1938 she gave the money to build the Fannie E. Morrison Horticultural Center, home of the spring and fall flower shows.[5]

There were rumors of a competitive spirit between Fannie Morrison and the Case sisters, Marian and Louisa. According to local legend, improvements on one property would be followed immediately by improvements on the neighboring estate. While this personal rivalry cannot be documented, it is indeed true that both women made substantial improvements to their respective holdings, especially during the 1910s.

Today, the Regis College campus retains many of the features of the Demmon-Morrison estate. The dignified brick mansion, now the Regis College president's house, still stands on the hill. Nearby is the fieldstone tower that Fannie Morrison called her "special delight." The expansive lawn and allée of trees lining the drive convey something of the formal, manicured grounds that she created out of what was once a hayfield.

The Case Estates land remains undeveloped. The farmhouses, yellow-brick barn, and red schoolhouse remain as Marian Case arranged them for Hillcrest. Whether the land and buildings will be preserved in the future remains a question. Marian Case once made this plea for the preservation of beautiful places, which is as relevant today as it was when she wrote it in 1916:

> *But am I asking too much of you to help to make the world a place in which gardens can be planted and woodland walks enjoyed. We can keep the world beautiful if we all earnestly desire it to be so and will look for the way.*[6]

Early History of the Area

The flat and fertile land around Case's Corner was used for agriculture from the earliest days of settlement into the 20th century. At the corner of Wellesley and Chestnut Streets stands the Abel Allen house, traditionally dated to 1696 and long considered the oldest remaining house in Weston. Allen was one of 19 men who gathered in 1710 to elect the first two deacons of what is now First Parish Church.[7] The house remained in the Allen family until about 1760. The next owner, Thomas Rand, was a housewright, Revolutionary War patriot, and prominent civic leader. At his death, Rand owned 112 acres, along with the "mansion house," barns, a cider mill, and a carpenter shop.[8] One of his dozen or so children, Thomas Jr., built a farmhouse on Wellesley Street just north of the family homestead.[9]

Weston's first minister, Joseph Mors, lived on Wellesley Street at the intersection of the present Maple Road. Mors was called to the newly established church in 1702. To encourage him to settle in this remote precinct, town fathers agreed to build

Figure 19-2A. The 1853 Marshall L. Upham house was on the east side of Ash Street, across from the early-18th-century Upham Homestead. After the Weston Reservoir was built, it became the home of the water board caretaker. The house was moved in 1916 to its present site at 207 Newton Street. (1901 photo)

Figure 19-2. A later owner added the decorative Connecticut River Valley-style doorway to the c. 1740 Upham farmhouse at 208 Newton Street. (2001 photo)

him a house 40 feet by 20 feet.[10] Mors was unpopular and in 1706 the congregation asked him to leave. They agreed to buy his house and farm, which became the home of the second minister, William Williams. He has been described as "an ideal country minister, liberal in thought and open minded . . . [with] a reputation abroad as a preacher of talent."[11] But in 1750, after 41 years, Williams was also dismissed, for reasons unknown. He remained in the former parsonage until his death in 1760.

The Upham family was the largest landowner in the area. Thomas Upham Jr., his brother, Abijah, and their widowed mother came to Weston in 1719 and settled on Ash Street. Their Colonial farmhouse with its saltbox roof was the subject of many nostalgic photographs before it was demolished to make way for the Weston Aqueduct and Reservoir. A cousin, William, arrived a few years after Thomas Jr. and bought a large farm on Newton Street adjoining Thomas's land.[12] About 1740, Thomas Upham III and his uncle, Abijah, built a house at the northern end of Newton Street. For many years, members of the family operated a blacksmith shop across the street.

At the time of the 1794 Kingsbury map, the town's "work house" was located approximately where Field School is today. In the early 19th century, the town bought a new poor farm in a remote northside location.

James Brown Case

James Brown Case (1826–1907) was one of the first Boston businessmen to summer in Weston. Case was a dry-goods commission merchant who began his career selling fabric for mills and later organized the firm of Case, Leland and Company.[13] He was president of the Bates Manufacturing Company in Lewiston, Maine, and an officer in the Edwards Manufacturing Company of Augusta, Maine, a firm that produced shoe flannel. After his retirement, he shifted his focus to banking and for several years was president of the National Bank of Redemption.

An obituary in the *Boston Globe* described him as "widely known in banking circles."

His wife, Laura Williams (1833–1918), was the daughter of a wealthy and prominent Boston family. She was proud of her ancestry and, when the couple built their mansion on Wellesley Street in 1889, she used the Williams coat of arms to ornament one of the fireplaces. James and Laura Case had four daughters: Caroline Sumner (1856–1919), Mabel (1858–1883), Louisa Williams (1862–1946), and Marian Roby (1864–1944). Their Boston home at 468 Beacon Street was used in the winter months when the family was not traveling.

In 1863, Case purchased 46 acres in Weston from his wife's uncle Charles White.[14] On the property was a gambrel-roofed Colonial house previously owned by Caleb Hall and by Gen. Daniel Derby.[15] The Cases used it as their summer home until it was destroyed by fire in September 1882.[16] Seven years later, in 1889, Case built a distinctive Shingle-style residence designed by architect Ernest N. Boyden.[17] At the time, it was one of the three most expensive houses in town, the others being the mansions of Charles Wells Hubbard and Francis Blake. The large "living hall," with its polished oak paneling, built-in benches, and Romanesque brownstone fireplace, clearly reflects the influence of the great 19th-century architect H.H. Richardson, who died just three years before the house was built. The inscription over the fireplace reads "East or west, home is best," with "east" referring to the family's Boston house and "west" to the house in Weston.

The large boulder in the front yard may have inspired the estate name, Rocklawn. Case planted fine specimen trees and maintained part of his land as hayfields. He purchased an Italianate cottage across the street for the caretaker.[18] By 1905 he owned 121 acres, including the Country, Woodland, and Field School sites and the land now farmed by Land's Sake. His property did not include most of what is now known as the Case Estates.

In these early years of the estate era, summer residents like James Case were not always welcome. A letter from Case to selectman and fellow estate owner Francis Blake in 1897 reveals Case's frustrations with the town. His anger was triggered by a dispute over the triangular piece of land within the roadway at Case's Corner, which Case contended belonged to him. When he decided to fence it, the town stepped in to block him, prompting this letter to Blake:

> . . . if it could be wrested from me you can readily see what a terrible menace it would be to my residence. As ownership carries the right to use or be built upon, a mart for the sale of old horses and carriages could be established or a pig pen built that would impair the value of my house

Figure 19-3. Merchant and banker James Brown Case built this Shingle-style house in 1889 as a summer residence. It has been owned by the town since 1946 and is used as school administration offices. The original porte cochere has been removed.

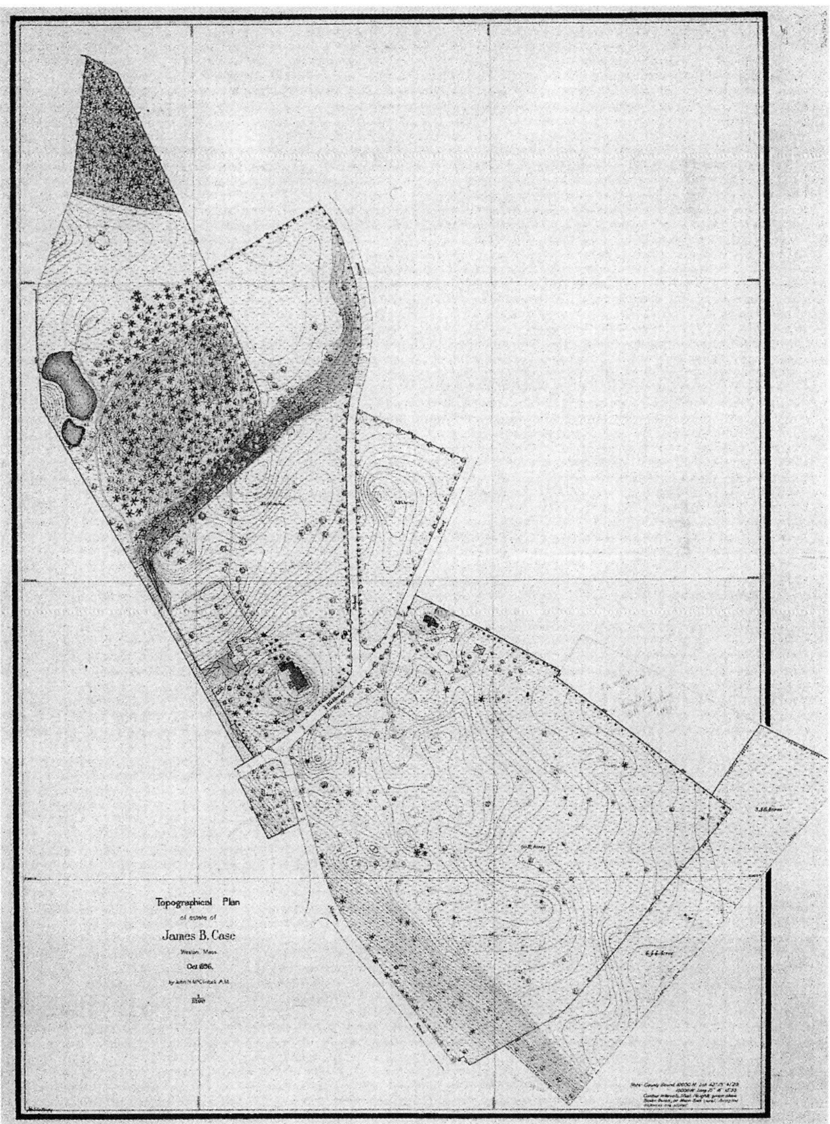

Figure 19-4. Most of the James Case estate is now owned by the Town of Weston. His 121 acres are the site of Country, Woodland, and Field Schools, the town pool, the Scout House, and Case Park. Case also owned the 35-acre field purchased by the town in 1986. (1896 map by John McClintock)

Figure 19-5. The main Case barn stood behind the house until April 4, 1947, when it was destroyed by fire. The new Weston Community Center is close to the site. At right is the cow barn, built in 1916.

Figure 19-6. The James Case estate had extensive greenhouses behind the house.

> and in fact make it wholly undesirable to occupy.[19]

Case goes on to vent a litany of frustrations with the town and mentions yet another fire:

> It seems as if I had to fight for existence in Weston. In "63" I bought my place and began . . . changes when in "76" from jealousy or cussidness my house was burnt. Still I kept on making changes attributing my loss to deviltry. But I have been "under fire" ever since. Telephone poles granted to others refused to me. . . . Another thing I will mention. Taking land for road widening without asking and without offering to pay for it. . . . It has been my pleasure to mow the grass on the road sides and keep it clean. Now! The day I left home . . . my man while cleaning the road in front of the house and bordering the triangle was ordered off by Upham. This order I consider tantamount to forbidding me to continue the pleasure of keeping the road tidy and indicating a preference for neglect and sloveness . . .[20]

Case concludes, "I am sorry to see such hostile feeling as it lessens my interest in the town."

The dispute over ownership of the triangle dragged on. More than a year later, with Case threatening to abandon Weston as his legal residence, Francis Blake sent a masterful letter crafted to soothe his feelings. He reminded Case of the tax advantages of Weston: ". . . I have diligently sought to steer our Town on a course which should make her a safe and desirable transport over the sea of taxation for just such men as yourself."[21] Blake, always a town booster, concluded his lengthy letter this way:

> Now when all this is done and when those of us who are "of your kind" have expressed our regret for all that has gone before why shouldn't you . . . help us in promoting the prosperity of the town?

Daniel Demmon, "The Copper King"

Daniel Lake Demmon (1831–1908) was a contemporary of James Case, although he came to Weston more than 25 years later.[22] Known in financial circles as the "copper king," Demmon was a self-made man whose substantial fortune came from shrewd investments in copper, coal, railroad expansion, and real estate. In 1856 he married Fannie Kimball, who died giving birth to a daughter, also named Fannie (1857–1941). In later years, his daughter would become his constant companion. Demmon remarried in 1859, but his second wife died two years later after giving birth to two more children, about whom little is known.

In 1889, the same year James Case built Rocklawn, Demmon purchased the Hosea Davis farmhouse, barn, and 104 acres on Wellesley Street for $8,000.[23] Like Case, he was a gentleman farmer, maintaining horses and a few cows, raising vegetables, and keeping apple orchards. Demmon and his daughter Fannie used the farmhouse from early May until as late as Thanksgiving. In the winter, they lived near the Cases on Beacon Street in the Back Bay.[24] While still in her teens, Fannie Demmon began serving as her father's hostess and interacting with his business associates, which may have helped cultivate her astute business sense.

Just before the turn of the century, Daniel Demmon purchased four more parcels contiguous to the original farm, including the hillside where his estate mansion would be constructed. The purchase included the Deavale (Deavall)-Kellen homestead, where Fannie lived in the summer of 1899. That year she married Barnabas "Barna" Thacher Morrison, a manager of the Reading Rubber Company. Both he and Fannie were over 40 at the time of their marriage. While the couple were on their honeymoon in Europe, Daniel Demmon began building a new

Figure 19-7. Daniel Demmon, known in financial circles as the "copper king," purchased 100 acres on Wellesley Street in 1889 and built this frame Colonial Revival house a decade later. His daughter, Fannie Morrison, later updated the facade by encasing it in brick. The Demmon-Morrison estate is now the Regis College campus.

house on the highest point of land, facing east toward Boston. The frame clapboard house was typical of the Colonial Revival style popular at the turn of the century.

Over the years Demmon embellished the grounds, refined the rough farmers' walls, and added practical improvements such as a windmill to generate electricity and a wooden water tower.[25] He lived here each summer, joined by his daughter and son-in-law. In the winter, the Morrisons lived at 53 Chestnut Street on Beacon Hill. In 1902, birth of a stillborn child ended prospects for a family.

The Demmon estate was among those pictured in the May 1902 *Boston Sunday Herald* article entitled "Weston Has Become the Lenox of the East," which included this brief description:

> Mr. Demmon's estate comprises 179 acres, and is approached by a winding driveway leading to the main residence, crowning the hilltop. It is a large wooden house, with fine terraced gardens sloping down to the stables and to the lodge.[26]

An account in the *Sunday Globe* the next month describes "extensive flower and vegetable gardens and thickets of woods which make it diversified and attractive."[27] On the east side of Wellesley Street was a large man-made pond with a stone wall around it.

The Maple Road/Wellesley Street Neighborhood

Meanwhile, in the 1880s and 1890s, a new neighborhood was developing on Wellesley Street just north of the Case property. The middle-class enclave was located within easy walking distance of the town center and Weston Station. Indeed, in this pre-automobile era, before the construction of the post road bypass, this area was as convenient as a similar neighborhood emerging at the same time just west of the commercial center.

The pivotal figure in the development was Henry Jackson White (1828–1915), known as Deacon White because of his leadership position at First Baptist Church. White moved to Weston from Taunton in the 1860s and became a successful market gardener. He sold his first house, an Italianate cottage at 84 Wellesley Street, to James Case, and it became the home of Case's superintendent. In 1869,

Figure 19-8. "Deacon" Henry J. White (1828–1915) was a mainstay at First Baptist Church and a well-loved civic leader. At his death he was remembered as "unspoiled, sweet, generous and humane."

Figure 19-9. Deacon White (left) and high school principal Charles M. Eaton are pictured in front of White's farmhouse, now 3 Maple Road, about 1895.

Figure 19-10. Beginning in the 1890s, Henry J. White sold off lots along the newly created Maple Road. This view looking east from the corner of School Street shows two new homes set within the deforested landscape.

White moved up the street to the house at the corner of Wellesley Street and what is now Maple Road.[28] It faced south onto farm fields until Maple Road was cut through. A prominent man in Weston town affairs in the late 19th century, White served as selectman from 1881 to 1889, assessor from 1882 to 1889, and town treasurer and collector from 1890 to 1913.[29] He was Weston's representative to the General Court in 1883 and superintendent of the Baptist Sunday school for 18 years. That he was held in high esteem is clear from tributes like this one:

> He was the soul of honor. All who came in contact with him admired him and loved him. Tempering

a cool head with a warm heart, he became a friend to all, whether their rank was high or low.[30]

Beginning in 1885, White began subdividing his property into house lots averaging one-quarter to one-half acre. Maple Road, originally referred to as White Place, was laid out through the property in 1891 and completed by 1896. By 1897 White had sold more than a dozen lots.[31] Many early owners were local tradesmen, among them four carpenter-builders, a house painter, a truckman, and a blacksmith. George W. Cutting, proprietor of Cutting's general store, bought land from White and built a house, as did his son Alfred L. Cutting and son-in-law Arthur B. Nims.

On the perimeter of the neighborhood were estates owned by Horace Sears, Robert Winsor, and the Cases. All three men maintained houses on Wellesley Street for their estate staff and influenced neighborhood growth in other ways. Winsor's competition for the design of houses backing up to the golf course is described in chapter 20.

Water Supply System of Greater Boston

The Weston Aqueduct and Reservoir, constructed between 1901 and 1903, cut a swath across the town and brought dramatic change to more than 200 acres of fields and low-lying meadows just south of Case's Corner. This major public works project was part of a regional plan designed to supply water to the Boston metropolitan area.

The evolution of Boston's public water supply prior to 1950 proceeded in four well-defined stages, the last two involving major construction projects in Weston.[32] The initial stage (1825–48) resulted in the development of Boston's first public water supply, brought by aqueduct from Lake Cochituate in Natick to the Brookline Reservoir.[33] In the second stage (1871–95), Boston's system was extended to reservoirs on the Sudbury River. The third stage (1895–1926) involved creation of the Metropolitan Water District and further westward expansion of the system. The Weston Aqueduct and Reservoir date from this period. The fourth phase (1926–47) was dominated by the construction of Quabbin Reservoir. A second aqueduct, now known as the Hultman, was built through Weston along with a second reservoir, the Norumbega. This fourth phase is discussed in chapter 28, which includes a map of the system.

Water supply development was prompted by the phenomenal physical growth of Boston, which had a major impact on surrounding communities. From 1790 to 1860, the urban population grew 870 percent, from 18,320 to 177,840. Officials filled in the Back Bay and annexed neighboring communities but still could not provide for all public services and land-use needs within the city's own boundaries. Surrounding towns objected when Boston proposed to divert their water supplies for the use of city dwellers. In Weston, the battle over control of water rights was played out, not with Boston, but with the City of Cambridge, which gained control over water from Stony Brook and its tributaries in the 1880s.

While some advocates called for additional annexation, others proposed creation of special agencies operating on a metropolitan scale to develop and maintain services for communities, which would keep their own separate identities. In 1895, the state board of health issued a landmark report that became the blueprint for the development of the metropolitan water supply system. The report investigated rivers throughout the region and proposed using the south branch of the Nashua River near Clinton as an additional source. It proposed building a very large reservoir, now known as the Wachusett, which would contain a full year's supply even if Boston's water use doubled. This reservoir would be connected by a 12-mile aqueduct to Reservoir #5, now called the Sudbury Reservoir, then under construction by the city. From there, the water would be conveyed through the Sudbury Aqueduct to the main distribution facilities at Chestnut Hill in Brookline. The report also predicted that another aqueduct directly from the Sudbury Reservoir would be required within a decade and specified a 13-mile conduit to the town of Weston. The comprehensive building program was expected to provide sufficient water supply for the metropolitan area for 20 years.

To implement the program, the Metropolitan Water Act was passed in 1895, establishing a Metropolitan Water District that initially included seven cities and six towns in the Boston area. The Sudbury Reservoir and Wachusett Aqueduct were completed in 1898, the Wachusett Reservoir was built between 1897 and 1905 and raised to full level in 1908, and the Weston Aqueduct and Reservoir were constructed in 1901–03.

In 1901, water supply and sewerage disposal functions were consolidated with the creation of the Metropolitan Water and Sewerage Board. In 1919 this board was consolidated with the Metropolitan Parks Commission to create the Metropolitan District Commission (MDC).

Weston Aqueduct and Reservoir

The Weston Aqueduct extends 13.5 miles from the Sudbury Reservoir to the Weston Terminal Chamber off Loring Road.[34] The aqueduct is 13 feet wide and 12 feet high and has a capacity of 300 million gallons a day. Several conduit types were used, including over two miles of tunnel and nine miles of "cut and cover," or embankments. Most sections have concrete bases and side walls lined with a single ring of

Figure 19-11. In 1902 the Waltham press described the construction of the Weston Aqueduct this way: "It was quite an interesting sight . . . to watch the six immense wagons drawn by three and four horses each, loaded with huge iron pipes, on their way to the Metropolitan Basin. No one has any idea of the magnitude of this great work, unless they visit the tunnel. . . . There is no cessation of work, a day and a night force being constantly employed."

brick, while some portions are fully lined with three rings of brickwork.

Just east of Wellesley Street, the tunnel section terminates in a 1,500-foot open channel leading to a holding and equalizing reservoir. The straight channel, which is lined with formal rows of conifers, contrasts with the naturalistic contours of the adjacent Weston Reservoir. The reservoir covers approximately 66 acres to a maximum depth of 28 feet. At the east end, a 900-foot curved earthen embankment was built with a concrete core wall designed to appear like the other shores. It contains a chamber with wood and metal screens to catch debris entering the final tunnel segment. The last stretch ends at the terminal chamber. From this large concrete well, water flowed through one of four distribution mains leading to either Chestnut Hill or Spot Pond.

Surrounding land was acquired to protect the water from pollution. Of the original 237 acres taken for the project, 143 acres belonged to members of the Upham family.[35] The early-18th-century Upham farmhouse on the west side of Ash Street was torn down. The Marshall L. Upham house across the street was used as the water board's caretaker house until about 1916, after which it was moved to Newton Street.[36]

Landscaping and Construction

Chief Engineer Frederic P. Stearns is considered the "architect" of the Metropolitan Water Supply System, which has been praised as an engineering masterpiece.[37] A hallmark of Stearns's work was his belief that technology and nature could thrive together provided that attention was paid to aesthetics as well as engineering.[38]

Stearns was responsible for bringing in the eminent Brookline landscape firm of Olmsted Brothers to develop the 150 acres surrounding the reservoir.[39] The 1900 town report described the goal:

> Under their direction, the excavated material will be formed into natural looking masses: and the entire surrounding of the reservoir will be so treated as to give it the appearance of a natural lake, with islands and wild wooded shores, irregular and marked by rough ledges.[40]

The area was planted with conifers and arborvitae to

inhibit soil erosion and create a parklike character. Conifers were chosen because they drop their needles onto the ground rather than producing leaves, which would blow into the reservoir.

The Metropolitan Water and Sewerage Board contracted with another important Boston firm, Shepley, Rutan and Coolidge, to design aboveground structures. Except for the head chamber in Southborough, all are variations of the same basic theme: a simplified Renaissance Revival design executed in tan granite with pink granite trim and a red clay tile roof. Of the 10 chambers, the Weston Terminal Chamber is the most decorative.

Construction of the reservoir and aqueduct involved daily employment of several hundred men and use of hundreds of tons of high explosives, which rattled nearby houses and shook dishes off their shelves.[41] Construction continued around the clock, using workers divided into three crews, each laboring eight hours a day. Several men were killed in accidents during construction.

Workers were housed in shacks along Ash Street referred to as the "Italian camp." The shacks remained in use even after the project was completed.[42] In 1901, the weekly Weston column in the *Waltham Daily Free Press Tribune* reported on a police raid:

> [Three Weston policemen] . . . raided the Italian camps at both ends of the tunnel, and secured nearly six half barrels of lager, twenty or twenty-five empty half barrels, 77 bottles of lager, over 100 empty bottles and two bottles empty whiskey jugs. . . . The goods seized are stored in the Town House and present quite a novel appearance for a town the character of Weston.[43]

In 1902 police raided the "negro camp" at the west end of the tunnel, again seizing a quantity of liquor. On March 6, 1903, gangs working from the east and west ends reached each other and broke into noisy celebration.

Figure 19-12. The Weston Aqueduct and Reservoir were constructed to bring water from the Sudbury Reservoir to greater Boston. In this photo of May 1903, the open channel off Ash Street was close to completion.

Figure 19-13. Hundreds of men labored with steam shovels and hand tools on the water supply project. Several men were killed during construction. Workers were housed in shacks along Ash Street referred to as the "Italian camp" (see photo in chapter 4).

Figure 19-14. The 13.5-mile Weston Aqueduct terminates off Loring Road. This handsome Renaissance Revival terminal chamber and all other above-ground structures were designed by the distinguished Boston architectural firm of Shepley, Rutan and Coolidge. (1903 photo)

Town reports make it clear that leaders considered this "metropolitan reservation" and reservoir to be a valuable addition to Weston, a value that might be greatly increased by its ultimate development as a public park.[44] Proponents of the metropolitan park system, which was being developed almost simultaneously, also praised the project. They saw it as providing significant open space to substitute, in part, for the large public reservation that had been proposed but never created in the Waltham/Weston area.[45]

Until 1977, when the controversial fence was erected, the reservoir was physically accessible but legally off-limits to the community. Every summer, the foreman at the Metropolitan Water Works had to chase would-be fisherman of two types, "boys who like the sport and to whom the chance of getting caught adds [to] the element of sport and older persons who find the excellent fish an addition to their tables."[46] The newspaper reported, "While loath to bring to court men who in other respects are good citizens, the Board feels the necessity of enforcing the law."[47] Arrests were made and fines imposed.

Use of the aqueduct and reservoir has changed over time.[48] By 1985, the Weston Aqueduct was the oldest of the Metropolitan Water Supply aqueducts still in active service. The Weston Reservoir and Aqueduct and its associated structures are listed on the National Register of Historic Places.

Fannie Edson Morrison

Daniel Demmon died in 1908 at age 76. Fannie, always her father's closest companion, inherited most of his assets, valued at nearly two million dollars. She immediately set out to improve the Weston property.[49] After traveling through Europe in 1909, she was inspired to line the drive with poplar trees like those she had seen in Normandy and Lombardy.[50] To keep the 144 trees in perfect shape, she supervised the trimming herself. In more recent years, the poplars have been replaced by Katsura trees, which do not have the same upright, columnar form.

Her next project was to construct a fieldstone tower copied from a medieval Norman tower in Chartres, France. Designed by local architect Harold Graves, the structure served as a water tower and housed a clock and a set of Westminster chimes. Ninety-four steps led to the top of the 61-foot-high structure, which had views from Boston to the church spires of Worcester. This is how Fannie Morrison described her creation:

> When my father died and left me the place, it was all a hayfield from the wall in front of the Mansion House to the street. To me that was not consistent with the estate, so I set to work pulling the rocks out to make a lawn. Then what to do with the rocks? I had always wanted a clock-tower. In English stories there is usually one on the stable. We also needed a water-tower, for the old wooden tank my father had built on the hill was most unsightly. So I combined the two—and added the chimes. . . . Well, they were beautiful. Often I have seen people halt their autos in the road to listen to them.[51]

Figure 19-15. Fannie Demmon Morrison inherited her father's estate on Wellesley Street in 1908. One of her first projects was to build this fieldstone tower, inspired by a trip to France. It housed a water tower, clock, and set of Westminster chimes. (1933 photo)

Figure 19-16. In 1914 Fannie Morrison updated her father's clapboard house with a new brick exterior designed by Samuel Mead. A comparison of this photograph with one earlier in the chapter shows the extent of the transformation. Even the stone wall was replaced with brick. (1934 photo)

The tower was built on a ledge, with foundations blasted out of solid rock. Of the finished product she wrote: "I used to say it would stand for a thousand years, and the races of the next century would have legends as to who erected it . . ."[52]

In the winter of 1913–14, Fannie undertook what must be the most dramatic home improvement in Weston history. She hired Weston's other leading architect, Samuel Mead, to transform her father's house into a more formal Georgian Revival mansion. A brick veneer was placed directly over the 1899 clapboard structure, which retained its original interior. Even the stone retaining wall was rebuilt in brick. Mead is thought to have designed the matching brick coach house.

In the winter of 1911, the Morrisons took their first trip to California, where their French-made Renault caused quite a stir:

> Automobile men of California will be much interested in Mr. Morrison's magnificent car which . . . is of the famous Renault make, and was bought in Paris. Mr. Morrison imported it for his own use, and a French chauffeur along with it. The car cost $12,000, and is one of the best ever seen on the Pacific Coast.[53]

Later that year the Morrisons embarked on a world tour that took them to China, Japan, and India. As usual, their travels were followed in the local paper, which reported that Fannie brought back two miniature Japanese dogs, weighing about five pounds each, and 10 exotic "India" birds.[54] Always a lover of animals, she furnished her home with silver water bowls and cushioned baskets for the comfort of her six small dogs.[55]

The visit to California was the beginning of a new seasonal pattern for the Morrisons. They spent summers in Weston and winters in Pasadena, where they purchased an estate in 1913. In 1915 Barnabas Morrison suffered a "stroke of apoplexy" and was declared incapable of caring for his property. During the years before and after his death in 1921, Fannie traveled each fall by private railway car to Pasadena, taking her personal maid, cook, and chauffeur and leaving behind a fully staffed house in Weston. She became involved in Pasadena's social life and gave generously to the humane society, horticultural society, and community playhouse. In 1930 she was awarded a medal for distinguished civic service. Describing her as "uncommonly self-effacing and reserved," Pasadena newspapers noted that she declined to have her picture taken or printed in the newspaper.

In 1927 Fannie Morrison sold her estate in Weston for $225,000 to the Sisters of St. Joseph of Boston for use as a resident Catholic women's college. The melodious chimes of the bell tower reportedly

Figure 19-17. In September 1927, the Demmon-Morrison estate was purchased for the newly established Regis College. Fannie Morrison's furniture and decorative arts came with the mansion, which was used as a residence hall and dining room for the first Regis students. It is now the home of the Regis College president.

clinched the sale.[56] For the next 14 years she spent most of her time in California, where she died in 1941 at age 84. The fortune she left far surpassed what she had inherited, despite federal income taxes and years of economic depression. She left most of her money to the Massachusetts General Hospital and Massachusetts Society for the Prevention of Cruelty to Animals, but also made bequests of $50,000 to Regis College, which had taken such devoted care of her estate, and $10,000 to the Weston Public Library.

Regis College

Rev. Mother Mary Domitilla Buttimer, C.S.J., the founder of Regis College, had originally planned to

Figure 19-18. College Hall was the first building constructed for Regis. In this 1929 photograph of the first two graduating classes, the chapel wing had not yet been built.

Figure 19-19. The founder of Regis College was Rev. Mother Mary Domitilla Buttimer of the Congregation of the Sisters of St. Joseph.

Figure 19-20. Regis students wore uniforms until 1936. In the early years, each class had a different design. Class officers in 1933 were Julie Saunders, president; Dorothea Fennell, vice president; Margaret Donovan, secretary; and Esther Donohoe, treasurer.

Figure 19-21. This aerial view shows the tree-lined driveway of the former Demmon-Morrison estate as well as the mansion, carriage house, fieldstone tower, College Hall (1928–30), O'Connell Science Building (1938), and St. Joseph Hall (1947).

locate the college in Newton. State proceedings delayed the opening for one year, during which time the Morrison estate became available. The 1927 purchase included the mansion and brick carriage house, a caretaker's house at the foot of the hill, and two staff houses on Ash Street.

The Catholic liberal arts college for women was named in honor of Mother Mary Regis Casserly, C.S.J., the first Superior of the Congregation of the Sisters of St. Joseph of Boston. Initial financial backing came from the congregation and area Catholic businessmen. The sisters embraced Fannie Morrison's medieval tower as a "historic link to Le Puy, France," where the Sisters of St. Joseph had been founded in 1650.[57]

Regis College was established to provide young women with the facilities and advantages of higher education. As stated in the initial issue of the catalog, its aim was to send forth students "whose character, culture, and efficiency will enable them to uphold the noblest ideals of Catholic womanhood." These ideals were nurtured and strengthened by Sister M. Finbarr Barry, C.S.J., the first dean, who continued in this position until 1946.

In September 1927 the mansion house, still furnished with Mrs. Morrison's furniture, tapestries, and oil paintings, became the residence hall and dining room for the first 47 students of Regis College.[58] A glass-enclosed conservatory was remodeled as the first chapel, and the elegant ballroom on the upper floor served as an assembly hall and the scene of student entertainments. One of the small estate buildings was remodeled to house the library, laboratories, and gymnasium and the other to accommodate classrooms.

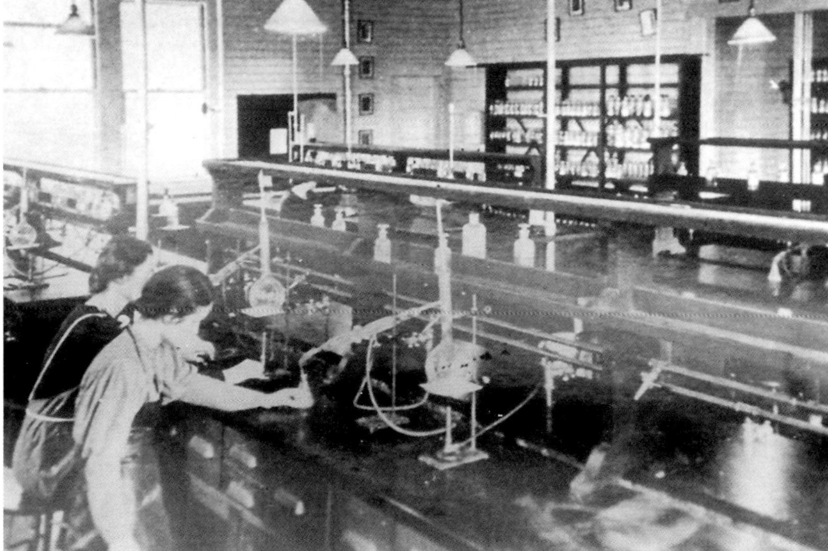

Figure 19-22. The chemistry laboratory was housed in the former carriage house, now known as Walters Hall, prior to construction of the O'Connell Science Building in 1938.

Construction on the first section of the five-story brick and granite College Hall was completed by September 1928 and the second wing two years later. Designed by Boston architect T. Edward Sheehan, College Hall served as the main administrative and classroom building and centerpiece for the emerging

Figure 19-23. Undergraduate students form an honor guard of "daisy chains" for graduating seniors to walk through. (1943 photo)

campus. Later buildings included the Cardinal O'Connell Science Building (1938), St. Joseph Hall (1947), Regis Library (1955), four dormitories, a student union (1962), an athletic complex (1982), and the Fine Arts Building and Auditorium (1993).

Initially, curriculum centered on the study of English, the classics, modern languages, religion, philosophy, mathematics, biology, chemistry, physics, history, sociology, and education. By the 1990s, Regis offered 19 departments of major concentration, more than 300 courses of study, a continuing education program, bachelor of science and master of science degrees in nursing, and a master of arts in teaching. Enrollment in 1995–96 was 1,336, of which about 700 were full-time, traditional undergraduate students.

Figure 19-24. Louisa Case sponsored a May Day party in 1933 for the benefit of the First Parish Church music committee. Among the activities were donkey rides, a fortune-teller, a Maypole dance, and a baby show.

In 1948, Francis Cardinal Spellman gave his important stamp collection to the Sisters of St. Joseph. Sister Fidelma Conway, C.S.J., opened the Cardinal Spellman Room in the new Regis College Library in 1955. Five years later, the collection was merged with a Philadelphia stamp museum to form the Cardinal Spellman Philatelic Museum. The independent, educational organization constructed a museum building, which opened in 1963 on the Regis campus. It houses more than two million stamps and a premier philatelic library.[59]

The Case Family, Second Generation: Louisa Williams Case

The four Case sisters spent their childhood summers in Weston. In 1883, the year after their farmhouse burned to the ground, the family summered in Bar Harbor, where 25-year-old Mabel was killed in a carriage accident.[60] Only the oldest sister, Caroline, ever married.

The death of James Case in 1907 brought major changes to the family. They sold the house at 468 Beacon Street and Louisa lived with her mother in Weston. In 1912, the year Louisa turned 50, she purchased a small cottage across the street.[61] She enlarged it and used the kitchen for canning and the barn for boarding horses and storing farm equipment. She built a potting shed with attached greenhouse and a large fieldstone garage with space for five automobiles and quarters for the chauffeur above. In the backyard, Louisa planted gardens that provided a graceful setting for lawn parties such as her May Party of 1933, which included a pet and hobby show, baby show, and fashion show, all for the benefit of the Music Committee of First Parish Church.

After the death of her mother in 1918, Louisa inherited the Case family mansion and continued to live in the style of her parents. She was remembered as a "perfect lady in all respects," shy and retiring, known for her kindness and thoughtfulness.[62] She has also been described as "conservative, someone who everybody listened to and respected" and "down-to-earth, as opposed to Marian."[63] Her lifestyle is suggested by this recollection of Brenton Dickson III:

> Perhaps the most impressive sight of a summer afternoon was watching the Misses Case drive by—Miss Marian and Miss Louisa. They had a beautiful black carriage drawn by perfectly groomed black horses. A black coachman sat on the elevated front seat while the Misses Case sat behind amid luxurious upholstery.[64]

Louisa maintained a winter house on Commonwealth Avenue in Boston. In Weston she was a gentlewoman farmer who kept a herd of Guernseys, a bull, and a team of driving horses. About 1921,

Louisa built a house behind the earlier caretaker's house so that her gardener, John Mele, didn't have to ride his bicycle from Waltham every day. Mele worked for Louisa for more than 40 years, running two greenhouses to provide her with vegetables and flowers year-round. During the winter, Louisa would send her chauffeur out to Weston to pick up milk and produce from the farm.

Louisa Case was a director of the Massachusetts Horticultural Society and member of the Visiting Committee of the Arnold Arboretum of Harvard University. She was an active participant in town organizations including First Parish Church, the Women's Community League, the Weston Garden Club, and the Weston Public Library.

In the late 1930s, Louisa donated one acre to the Weston Scouts for a meeting house and the adjacent two acres at the Wellesley/School Street intersection to the town as a permanent park in memory of her parents. In 1942, at the age of 80, Louisa gave the family mansion and 59 acres to the Arnold Arboretum.[65] She gave an additional 41 acres in 1946, for a total of 100. Just before her death in 1946, the Town of Weston needed land for new school buildings and Louisa Case and Harvard officials agreed to sell the town 46 acres, including the Case mansion, barn, and greenhouses. When the large barn burned nearly to the ground on April 3, 1947, leaving only the stone foundation opposite the cow barn on Alphabet Lane, the insurance settlement was nearly double the $10,000 that the town had paid for the entire 46 acres. A new high school, now Field School, was built on Louisa's land in 1950, followed by Country School in 1955. The present town pool, originally two ponds on her property, opened in 1951. In 1958 an additional 31 acres of former Case land was taken by eminent domain for the building of Woodland School.

Marian Roby Case

Marian Case was not as pretty or ladylike as her sister Louisa. Because of her unconventional ideas, she has been described as "sort of the odd stick in the family" but also as "exceedingly kind and helpful to others."[66] She had a pronounced lisp. After her father's death, Marian, then age 45, embarked on a career combining farming and education, calling herself a "farmerette." She was later to explain that she purchased the farm as a cure for bronchitis:

> Realizing that I could not continue to spend my winters among the east winds of Boston, I took a cottage in Weston for the winter, and with horseback riding and other out-of-doors exercise, kept well. About this time the land next to our old family estate in Weston came into the market. I then felt that if I were to live in the country, it would be well to have my interest there . . .[67]

Figure 19-25. Marian Case (1864–1944), youngest daughter of James B. Case, established a model farm just south of her father's estate. She was well known in horticultural circles and won awards for her educational programs.

Figure 19-26. Marian Case purchased 102 Wellesley Street in 1909 and named it Appletree Cottage. She lived here until her death in 1944.

Figure 19-27. Between 1909 and 1912, Marian Case also purchased the three farmhouses at 101, 131, and 137 Wellesley Street. The Thomas Rand Jr. house at No. 131, shown here, was built about 1790. Thomas Jr. was one of three men in his family who marched to Concord at the beginning of the Revolutionary War. In the Hillcrest era, farm superintendent Tom Park lived here for many years.

Marian Case had a strong affection for the disappearing farm landscape.[68] To preserve the pastoral setting around her, in 1909 she began buying land just south of her father's estate. Her initial purchases included 23 acres and three houses. One of these, which she called Appletree Cottage, became her home until her death in 1944.[69]

One result of these land acquisitions was to stop development of houses planned for the land between Wellesley and Ash Streets. One already under construction was purchased and moved across the street, where it was converted to the clubhouse for Miss Case's Hillcrest Farm. The original foundation was covered and used for winter storage of apples and vegetables. Miss Case would later write that "the farmers in Weston were amused at my having purchased the land with the thought of growing fruit and vegetables on it."[70]

"The Most Perfect Farm in New England"

In 1909, Marian Case established Hillcrest Farm, which she described as "an experimental farm where we wish to work up the scientific side of agriculture as well as to employ boys of the town through their long summer vacation."[71] The next year, Miss Case published the first of a series of annual reports nicknamed the "green books," which carefully chronicle each summer's events. Her wry sense of humor can be seen in the very first sentence: "The land was bought in the spring of 1909, but the first summer was spent in taking stones out of the ground, a crop with which the Town of Weston is rich . . ."[72] The green books paint a clear picture of Marian Case as an idealist. Her initial vision of Hillcrest as a model farm is described by one of the Hillcrest boys:

> Miss Case has said that we want to make this the most perfect farm in New England, to grow the best quality of fruit, to inspire New Englanders to return to the soil, and not let the people of Oregon beat New England in growing fruit. [73]

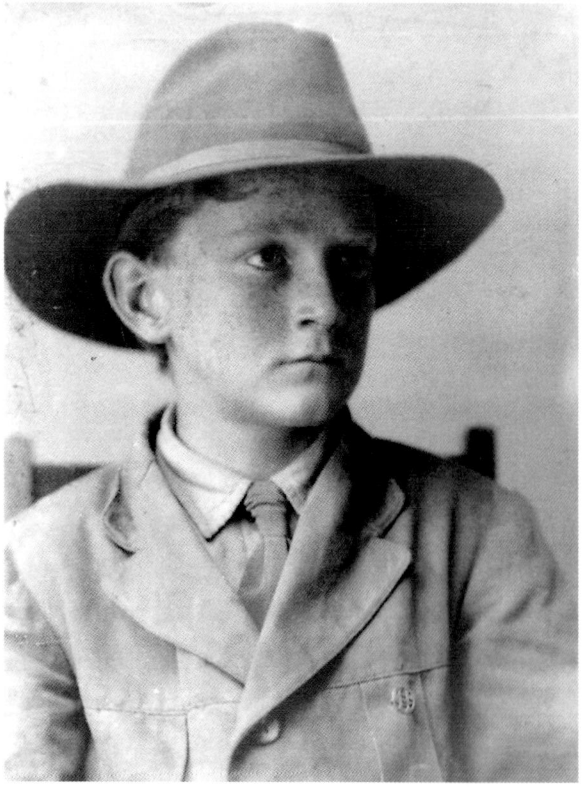

From 1910 to 1919, Hillcrest operated as a truck farm. A 1917 article lists 50 vegetables grown here, of which potatoes and corn were the most important. The farm sold cherries, pears, plums, apples, peaches, and grapes, along with 10 varieties of berries. Income from sales never equaled the cost of operating the property in Miss Case's unique manner, although she never gave up hoping that the farm would become self-supporting.

Part of what made Hillcrest unique was the source of labor, provided by the "Hillcrest boys." The first summer, eight boys worked here and in later years up to 20. The boys were generally 12 to 18 years old, although some were younger. For the first few years, only Weston boys were eligible. When others wished to take part as well, Miss Case enlarged the program and took boys who commuted from Waltham and Auburndale. Beginning about 1919, a few participants from Boston and other communities boarded on the property.[74]

The boys were given uniforms that initially consisted of a khaki jacket and trousers, a silk tie, and a Stetson hat with a silver Hillcrest pin. The uniform changed over time and later included a khaki shirt and pants and a green sweater with the embroidered monogram H-C for Hillcrest. Miss Case set her pay scale at a dollar a week for the first two years of training, during which the boys worked from eight to noon each morning. In the third year, "they have the privilege of working all day for $20 a month." Wages were low even for that time, when day workers on estates were earning about two dollars a day. In *Growing Up in Weston,* Phil Coburn, who was a Hillcrest boy, tells how his brother decided against working there when he figured out that he would be earning four cents an hour, and he could make ten cents an hour working as a farmhand for his uncle. Not only that, but Marian Case was a tough taskmaster who expected the boys to do their work and do it right.

But being a Hillcrest boy was more than just a job. As one boy was to write, ". . . she [Marian Case] wants us to make something of ourselves and to benefit us," adding, "We learn to work at Hillcrest. You may say that is easy enough, but at Hillcrest we learn to work scientifically."[75] In her account of the annual ritual of picture-taking, Marian Case reveals an intense pride in "her boys" and their development:

Figure 19-28. The Hillcrest uniform and pin were among the many similarities between Miss Case's program and the Boy Scout movement, which was founded in England in 1908 and brought to the United States in 1910. Although Miss Case emphasized agriculture while Scouting stressed camping and outdoor life, both focused on adolescent boys and sought to build character, instill moral values, encourage fitness and self-improvement, and foster national pride.

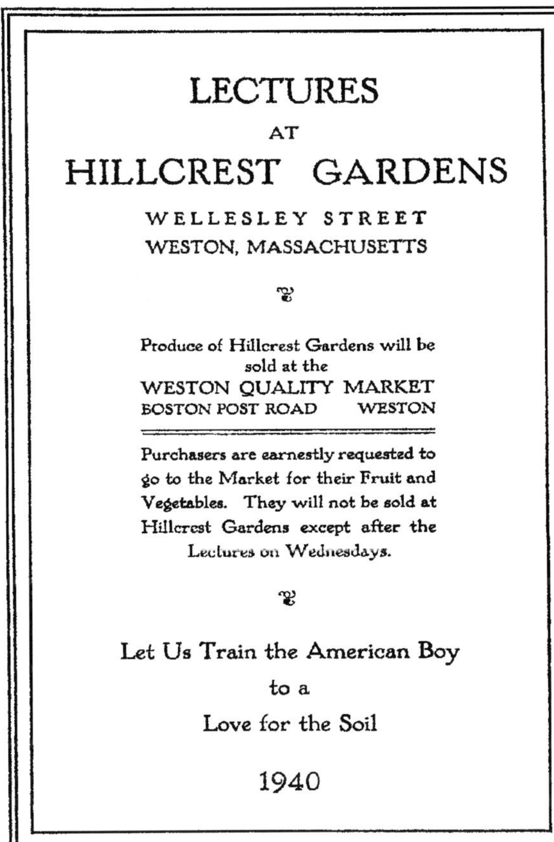

LECTURES
AT
HILLCREST GARDENS
WELLESLEY STREET
WESTON, MASSACHUSETTS

Produce of Hillcrest Gardens will be sold at the
WESTON QUALITY MARKET
BOSTON POST ROAD WESTON

Purchasers are earnestly requested to go to the Market for their Fruit and Vegetables. They will not be sold at Hillcrest Gardens except after the Lectures on Wednesdays.

Let Us Train the American Boy
to a
Love for the Soil

1940

Figure 19-29. Weekly lectures at Hillcrest Gardens introduced the Hillcrest boys to a wide range of topics. In 1912, for example, speakers discussed insect pests, fungus enemies of insects, native plants, peaches, and "The Ascent of Mount Rainier."

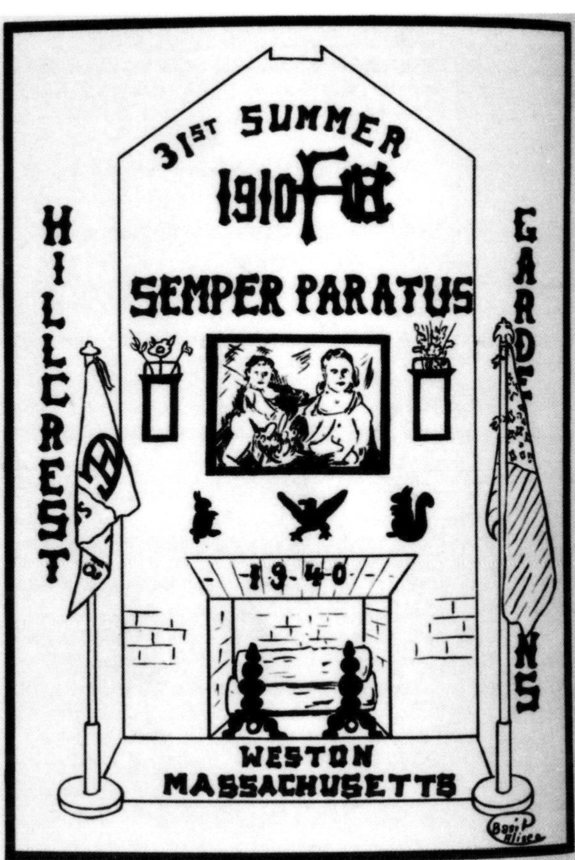

Figure 19-30. The Hillcrest motto, Semper Paratus *("Always Prepared") was similar to the Boy Scout motto, "Be Prepared." (1940 illustration)*

> During the summer I asked the different boys to my studio and there took their photographs . . . so that each boy has his portrait hanging in the hall. . . . The taking of these photographs also shows how the boys develop. One boy in coming to my studio this year . . . asked me if I thought he had grown since last summer. I was able to tell him that I thought he had grown in everything that makes a boy worth while.[76]

Hillcrest functioned as a kind of "practical school of agriculture." Miss Case set aside a daily study hour when the boys were required to keep a journal of their activities and nature observations.[77] To keep in touch with the latest in agriculture and to interest the boys in nature, Miss Case planned summer lectures by specialists. Topics ranged from "Fungus Enemies of Insects" to "The Forests of Germany" to stereopticon slides of American, European, or Japanese gardens. During some 30 years of lectures, 115 men, including college presidents, outstanding scientists, and former Hillcrest boys, appeared on the program.[78] Lectures took place in the clubhouse, where the upper room was furnished with folding chairs and a stereopticon curtain. Friends and neighbors were invited to attend. As soon as Miss Case and her two sisters had been seated in their armchairs up front, the boys would march upstairs with the dark green and gold Hillcrest flag.

To broaden their exposure to the ideals embodied in great literature, Miss Case read aloud to her charges. She was a sentimental person and sometimes came close to tears. Her favorite poems were Wordworth's *Happy Warrior,* Lowell's *Vision of Sir Launfal,* Sill's *Opportunity,* and Longfellow's *Fiftieth Birthday of Agassiz,* and she once wrote, "When they grow to be men I want them to connect these four poems with Hillcrest."[79] The motto of Hillcrest was *Semper Paratus* meaning "Always prepared." Miss Case felt that, with their training at Hillcrest, the boys would be ready for anything they were called upon to do. The Hillcrest theme song reinforced the values of public service and citizenship:

> Only Hillcrest farm boys, we'll soon be
> Hillcrest men,
> True and trusted citizens, we'll work for Weston
> then.
> Bound to make her greater far than she has
> ever been.
> We are the farm boys of Weston.

Because "boys need amusement as well as work," Miss Case organized annual outings to places like Walden Pond; Nantasket Beach and Paragon Park; Salem; Benson's Wild Animal Farm; Franklin Park; and Ringling Brothers Circus. In 1911 she took them to Buffalo Bill's Wild West Show for his final appearance in Boston. Phil Coburn recalled driving to Wenham in Miss Case's seven-passenger Lozier to visit the Proctor estate, where the caretaker pointed out the shrubs and flowers. On the third summer, a drum corps was formed. Outfitted with six snare drums, one base drum, eight fifes, and a pair of cymbals, the Hillcrest drum corps marched proudly in the town's Bicentennial parade of 1913. Sometimes the boys themselves would plan special programs. One year they had a mock town meeting with each boy playing the part of a town official. The clubhouse was the social as well as educational hub of Hillcrest and served as the location of games, spelling bees, parties, teas, picnics, and Red Cross sales.

The "Green Books"

Each Labor Day, the season ended with a picnic, to which each boy could ask a girl. In the afternoon, parents and friends came to watch the awarding of prizes and silver Hillcrest pins and to hear reports that each boy had written about the farm. These papers were a required part of the Hillcrest program. Topics included the history of Hillcrest, agricultural practices, weather data, hurricane damage, monthly flowering lists of herbaceous plants, lists of birds and wildflowers, and records of plant introduction trials. The student reports have been evaluated as "generally of high quality and lasting value."[80] They provide data that is useful in documenting the age of certain plants at the Case Estates and determining the date of introduction and persistence in New England of exotic plant introductions. The Labor Day papers were published in the annual green books, along with special reports by such well-known horticulturists and botanists as John G. Jack, Elmer D. Merritt, W.H. Wilson, and John Wister.

The boys often used their essays to express appreciation to Marian Case. The following quotation is from a 1913 essay written by Harold Weaver, a black youth whose father was Miss Case's cook. Harold was a Hillcrest boy for several years and during the school year attended a state normal school in North Carolina:

> Who else is doing for boys in Weston what Miss Case is doing? I answer no one, then why should we not help her, by not causing her to worry, by doing our duty to the best of our ability. . . . Let us honor and appreciate our Hillcrest Farm.[81]

Another of the boys wrote, "The future is before us . . . every boy that has ever been one of the band at Hillcrest will turn his thoughts back here many times and be ready to return thanks to Miss Case for her patience and generous treatment of each one of us."[82]

Marian Case used the green books to share her hopes, dreams and frustrations. In 1917 she pondered whether her efforts were appreciated by the people of Weston:

> Sometimes I wonder if the good people of Weston who buy these vegetables at low market prices delivered at their doors, ever stop to wonder who pays for raising them and the berries, plums, apples and peaches which three times a week are sent around the town.[83]

She added this musing in which she writes of herself in the third person: "She can have boys trained to teach other boys to grow food for the people. Is she willing to pay the cost? She needs the interest and appreciation of her neighbors." Shortly after publication of this issue, Miss Case received a petition signed by 64 neighbors, expressing their thanks and urging that the farm's produce continue to be distributed in Weston.[84]

For many years, Miss Case awarded prizes for the best essays written by students in the Weston schools. The best overall essay was often printed in the annual green book. She assigned a different topic each year: for example "Forest and Flower Preservation in America," "Ten Greatest Americans," "Roads of Weston," "Government of Weston," and "Stone Walls and Fences of Weston." For each grade from 7 to 12, she gave out one $10 gold piece, two $5 gold pieces, and four $2.50 gold pieces, for a total of 42. Miss Case handed out the awards at a full school assembly that was one of the major events of the year. The essay contest helped Miss Case promote the values of patriotism, civic responsibility, and appreciation of nature and the New England landscape to young people throughout the town.

Included in the green books are wonderful bits of philosophy. For example, this comment was written by 13-year-old E. Stanley Hobbs Jr., who went on to

Figure 19-31. Each year, beginning in 1911, Marian Case published a small book with a green cover recording the development of Hillcrest and including reports and observation papers written by the boys. Miss Case distributed the "green books" to libraries as far away as the Royal Horticultural Society in England. Cover designs were drawn by the boys or by visitors to Hillcrest.

became a supervisor at Hillcrest and later a dental surgeon:

> The first thought that came to me as I cast about me for a subject was the realization of how small a space even a human being occupies in this wonderfully complete moving picture of growing and living things that the creator has placed each of us in. The first feeling was one of deep responsibility and humility that I should be allowed to act even in a small way as a steward to help care for my part of God's creation, all of which is so fearfully and wonderfully made.[85]

The next year, Hobbs commented on another of nature's creations:

> They say that every form of plant was made for a purpose and has a value in itself if we could only know how to apply it, but we found it necessary to wage a continuous warfare on a large array of vegetation known as weeds . . .[86]

Development of Hillcrest Farm

The first year, fruits and vegetables were delivered by "bicycle express."[87] The farm received an order and the items were picked and delivered in a box strapped to the handlebars by one of the boys. The second year, the Weston route was covered by a horse-and-wagon team that included the draft horse Pluck and his companion, Win. But the chief means of distribution, beginning in 1913, was a Ford automobile truck. Along with the wagon, it was used to carry produce on regular routes through Weston, Auburndale, West Newton, and Waltham, as well as into Somerville or even Faneuil Hall Market if the farm had extra. Hillcrest catered to its customers, planting the varieties of vegetables that they preferred. By 1920, merchants were willing to come to the farm for produce and it was no longer necessary to deliver. From 1921 to 1933, Miss Case operated the Hillcrest Market in the town center, where fresh vegetables, perennials, and bulbs were sold in season.[88] In subsequent years, produce was sold directly to the Weston Quality Market.

Each year, improvements were made to the property. In 1911 masons built a stone wall with battlemented top, 10 feet high, 6 feet thick, and 200 feet long. The massive structure has been described as "the largest free-standing dry wall in New England," a claim that has never been carefully substantiated.[89] The inspiration for the wall reportedly came to Marian Case on a visit to Tokyo, where she was impressed with a scene of pine trees towering over gray stone walls. In his oral history, longtime Arnold Arboretum director Richard Howard said the wall was supposed to have been a birthday present to Marian from her sister, Louisa, who built it while Marian was away for the winter.[90] The wall gave rise to the nickname The Sentinels for the nearby house, because the pine trees rose like sentries behind it. It proved useful for the protection of fruit trees, especially peaches.

In the winter of 1912–13, a wall of three- and four-foot-high boulders, referred to as a "hen's tooth" or "balancing" wall, was built from the clubhouse to the The Sentinels. By 1912, Miss Case had planted perennial gardens, wildflower gardens, and roses around Appletree Cottage. That same year, another Greek Revival house and about 40 acres of farmland were purchased from George Milton, who had summered in Weston for more than four decades and retained life tenancy to the house.

Figure 19-32. The Case farm pond was fed by springs and never froze solid. For this reason, town leaders chose it in 1951 as the site for the new town pool.

Part of the Milton land was used to plant a vineyard with 800 grape plants producing 40 varieties of grapes.

In 1913 Marian Case installed the Skinner system of irrigation, which carried water in adjustable pipes located 8 to 10 feet above the ground, so that the water descended like rain. This was the first use of the Skinner overhead system in Massachusetts. The pipes were taken down in the winter. Richard Howard would later say, "... the methods of cultivating plants were very, very good. She was always seeking something better ..."[91]

In 1916 Marian Case built the cow barn as an adjunct to the main Case barn. Designed by the architectural firm of Fox and Gale, the stucco building became the center of dairy operations for Hillcrest Farm. Cows roamed the adjacent pasture and were watered at a farm pond that was fed by springs and never froze solid. A second pond was used for skating and cutting ice. In summer, the ponds were surrounded by blueberry bushes, and a muskrat house sat in the middle of the water. The narrow strip of land between the two ponds was removed when they were adapted for use as the town pool.

In 1917 Marian Case purchased five more acres between Ash and Wellesley Streets from George and Isaac Hastings, brothers who lived in mirror-image houses on the east side of Wellesley Street. The Hastings land was cultivated to supply food urgently needed during World War I. That year, Miss Case reflected on the future direction of the farm:

> As long as the war lasts we feel that Hillcrest must do its part towards raising food. After that, I wonder! ... From the varied lay of our land at Hillcrest we have an exceptional opportunity for making ... a garden.[92]

Hillcrest Gardens: 1920 to 1944

Hillcrest Farm/Hillcrest Gardens was established during the heyday of American estate gardening, which began about 1890 with the Italian garden movement and continued until World War II. The eclectic architecture of the period was complemented by a wide variety of garden and landscape treatments inspired by European and Far Eastern prototypes. Marian Case's Hillcrest operation did not fit the typical mode. Her source of labor, the Hillcrest boys, and her emphasis on their education and character development, was unusual. She started Hillcrest as a model farm, with an emphasis on preserving the New England agricultural tradition, and only gradually developed ornamental gardens. These gardens were not intended to complement a grand mansion but rather to be of value in the scientific study of horticulture.

Figure 19-33. Because of her health and horticultural interests, Marian Case often traveled to the Mediterranean in winter. She had contacts in Italy, Greece, and Egypt and arranged to have seeds of potentially useful ornamentals sent to Weston for trial. This picture was taken in Naples in 1929.

By the 10th summer, about 1920, Marian Case reported with pride on the growing prestige of her enterprise:

> Hillcrest is no longer only a Weston institution, for it is well-known in Washington, having received many plants for propagation from the Bureau of Plant Industry. Professor Sargent has sent us a hundred shrubs from the Arnold Arboretum, besides seventeen cherries and twenty-seven lilacs from his greenhouse.[93]

Hillcrest sent representatives to South Africa, Labrador, China, and other countries to collect plant specimens. In 1924, Miss Case became a member of Britain's Royal Horticultural Society and began receiving seeds from Kew Gardens.

A shift in emphasis from farming to horticulture is reflected in the 1920 name change from Hillcrest Farm to Hillcrest Gardens. Miss Case attributed the change to the influence of Charles Sargent and John Jack of the Arnold Arboretum. Her pride in the variety of species on the property is demonstrated in the 1920 annual green book, which lists all the indigenous and planted trees and hardy shrubs at Hillcrest, including their botanical names. Horticultural development increased in the 1920s primarily through the work of John C. Wis-

Figure 19-34. This 1937 photo of the Hillcrest boys includes Miss Case (center, rear) and Tom Park in the shirt and tie. Park was one of the first group of Hillcrest boys and became foreman in 1930, replacing Peter Mezitt.

ter, secretary of the Pennsylvania Horticultural Society and president of the American Iris Society, and also Arthur Williams, who became Miss Case's gardener about 1922. Wister first came to Hillcrest as a lecturer. In 1923 he planned roads and paths, a special woods garden, and a test garden for the Iris Society, which eventually included more than 700 cultivars. Wister also suggested the peony garden, which was planted in alphabetical order with double-blossomed varieties in the outside beds and singles in the center. Art objects were included in the garden designs, most notably the 1935 statue of a Hillcrest boy incorporated into a fountain and birdbath made by Hugh Bigelow. In carrying out the garden plans, Arthur Williams had a "deft touch with plants," which, together with his constant search for better growing methods, "produced the outstanding horticultural specimens for which Hillcrest became known."[94]

As an active and influential member of the Massachusetts Horticultural Society, Marian Case offered Hillcrest prizes as early as 1911, when the award was for improvement in blueberry cultivation.[95] In 1920 she gave $1,000 to the society for prizes named for Hillcrest Farm. Hillcrest medals for children's gardens were awarded from 1918 to 1933.[96] In 1927, 37 bronze medals were awarded to children who prepared outstanding exhibits or gardens. She contributed substantial sums to help establish the magazine *Horticulture* and regularly wrote articles and short observations, 30 alone in 1920. In 1921, Miss Case was elected a trustee, a post she held for more than a decade.

In 1926, Marian Case was awarded a gold medal by the Massachusetts Horticultural Society and presented with the following citation:

> Since 1910, Miss Case has financed and energetically conducted a vocational gardening school for boys between the ages of nine and eighteen. Equipped with this knowledge in the art and practice of raising first-class flowers, fruits and vegetables and taught to appreciate the book of Nature, these boys go forth worthy, capable and practical. Miss Case's deep love of Nature has found expression in this most useful work and in her the art of garden craft has a staunch and generous friend.[97]

In 1930 she received the society's Centennial Gold Medal for her educational work within the society itself.

Miss Case was in close association with the Arnold Arboretum and received many plants from the Arboretum for trial in Weston. In 1922 she was appointed to the Overseers Committee of the Botanic Gardens of Harvard University. She was an active member of the Women's National Farm and Garden Association and served as its president in 1927–28, when the national organization met at Hillcrest.

Hillcrest received many prizes for the quality of its produce. For example, in 1920 Hillcrest and Miss Case received 97 awards and votes of thanks from the Massachusetts Horticultural Society and in 1922, 52 awards from the Weston Grange.

The last addition to the Hillcrest physical plant was the yellow-brick barn of 1927, which replaced an earlier barn on the Milton property. Designed by Samuel Mead, the Hillcrest barn incorporated

Figure 19-35. Hillcrest won many awards for produce displays like this one at the Massachusetts Horticultural Society fall show in 1921.

advances in design in the cold rooms for fruits and vegetables and special facilities for the storage of manure. The horse stalls had electric lights and steam heat. An attached greenhouse was used for starting seedlings and overwintering. For fertilizer, Marian Case mixed manure collected in the barn with potash created by burning brush in the nearby fieldstone incinerator, which she constructed in 1921.[98] She also had an area in the barn where chemical fertilizers were stored.[99]

The Hillcrest improvements and programs could not have been carried out without the help of dedicated supervisors such as Tom Park, Jack Williams, and Dennis Crowley. Park was the son of Miss Case's coachman and Williams the son of her gardener. All three began as Hillcrest boys, Park in the very first season. All combined a knowledge of agriculture with the patience to work with boys. Another supervisor, Peter Mezitt, worked here from 1917 until the 1920s, when Marian Case helped him establish Weston Nursery. Mezitt's son, Edmund, was a Hillcrest boy. Supervisors lived in the farmhouses on the property, which were also used to house boys boarding from out of town.

Hillcrest Gardens flourished in the 1930s, at least until September 1938, when a disastrous hurricane swept the area. Some 2,500 pines, 500 oaks, and 250 maples were lost, along with more than 100 fruit trees. Many of the fine specimen trees were damaged. The "sentinel" pines standing guard behind the high stone wall were toppled.[100]

Many former Hillcrest boys attended a celebration held in 1939 in honor of Hillcrest's 30th anniversary. Dennis Crowley reported that more than 200 boys had benefited from the program. Harold Mosher, one of the original Hillcrest boys, was by that time superintendent of the Riverside Golf Course and remarked that never a day passed but that he found occasion to use the knowledge gained at Hillcrest. Another reported that the lessons of hard work and enjoyment of the world of living things had given him a much wider view of life. One "graduate" wrote

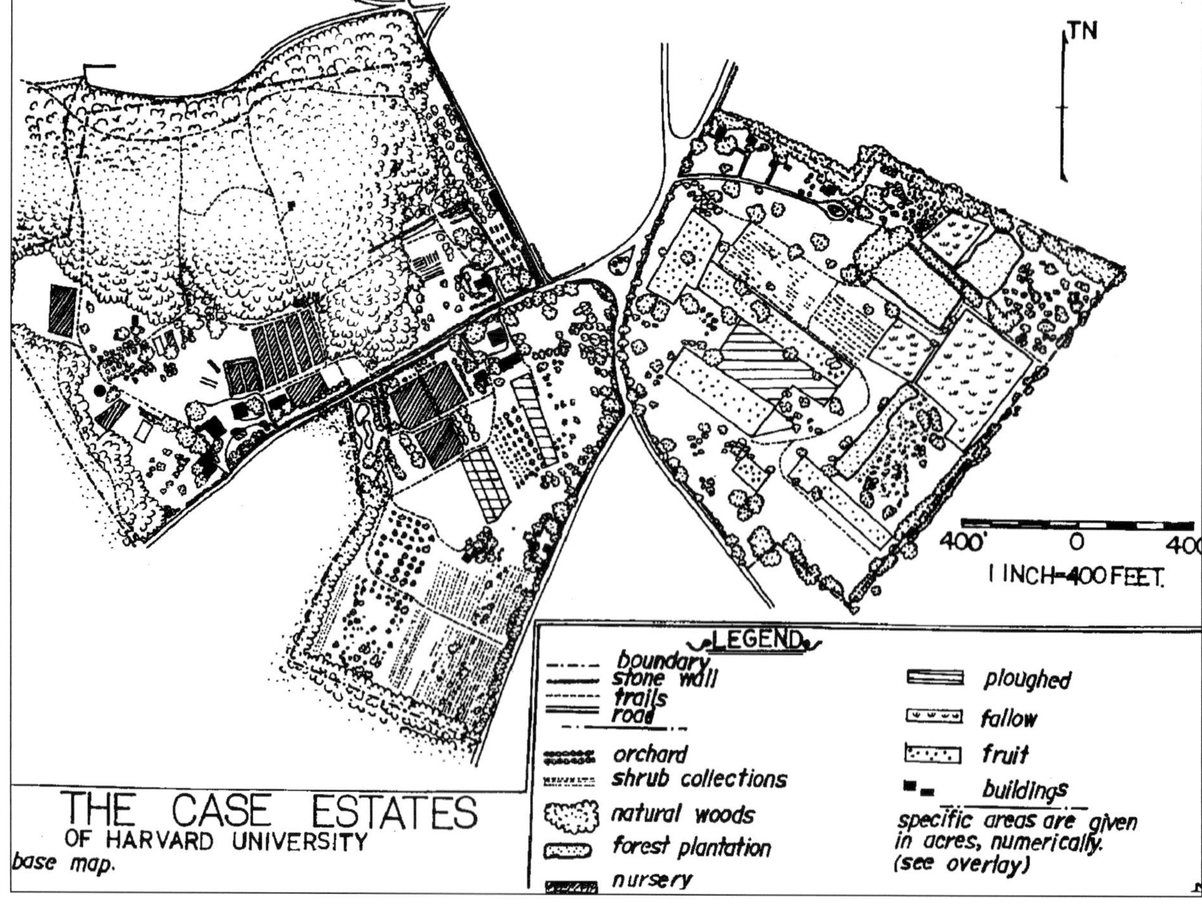

Figure 19-36. The Arnold Arboretum of Harvard University operated an active program at the Case Estates. This map shows how the arboretum used the land.

on his questionnaire: "The only trouble with Hillcrest Gardens is that not enough people know about it."[101]

In his after-dinner speech at the 1939 celebration, John C. Wister pondered the future of Hillcrest Gardens. One suggestion, which he dismissed, was that the land be turned into a town or metropolitan park. Continuing the school was more difficult, according to Wister, as it required additional money and a teaching staff. The Massachusetts Horticultural Society, Harvard University, and Wellesley College were suggested as organizations that might be able to continue the program.[102] Wister concluded, "We cannot lay down exact programs for the future. All Miss Case can do is to express her wish that her present work should continue."[103] Hillcrest operated through 1942, although reduced in size and scale due to the war and Miss Case's ill health.

The Arnold Arboretum

Marian Case died on July 4, 1944. She left Hillcrest Gardens to the Arnold Arboretum in her will, which reads as follows:

> I impose no restrictions whatever except that the land or its proceeds . . . shall be used for the general purposes of the Arnold Arboretum. It is, however, my earnest hope that the estate may be maintained. . . . it is my earnest desire that the summer work in agriculture for boys be continued in the manner developed at "Hillcrest" during the past thirty years.[104]

Marian's bequest of 102 acres is said to reflect the influence of her sister, Louisa, who wanted the family property to remain intact. Altogether, the gift of the two sisters to the arboretum totaled 202 acres, of which 75 acres were transferred to the Town of Weston in 1947 and the late 1950s for school construction.

The Arboretum renamed the property Case Estates and operated it as an educational facility and place for plant propagation and experimentation. Because Weston was colder than the arboretum in Jamaica Plain, plants could be tested for hardiness. Special displays of ground covers, shrubs for perennial gardens, and small street trees were established. A rhododendron garden was developed by the Massachusetts Chapter of the American Rhododendron Society beginning in the 1970s. Three arboretum directors lived on the property: Donald Wyman, Richard Howard, and Peter Ashton. In 1982 Howard wrote, "Hillcrest Gardens established a standard of excellence . . . which the Case Estates of the Arnold Arboretum hope to maintain."[105]

In 1986 the arboretum sold the 35.65-acre field across from Case House to the town as municipal purpose land. The town leases the field to Land's Sake, a nonprofit organization that, in the tradition of Marian Case, provides fresh produce and opportunities for young people to work in the fields and learn about the land. In 1990, the arboretum determined that the Case Estates was no longer central to its mission, and over the next few years most of the houses were sold to private owners. The Arnold Arboretum still owns more than 60 acres of open fields and woodlands that are among the town's most prized open spaces.

Figure 19-37. This photograph of the Arnold Arboretum's popular annual plant sale was taken in September 1988. In the background is the clubhouse, where Marian Case held lectures and study hours for the Hillcrest boys.

Houses in the Case's Corner Area

102 Ash Street (c. 1901). Colonial Revival house built about 1901 for a member of the Upham family.

221 Ash Street. Colonial-period house dismantled and moved from 42 Milk Street in Newburyport by Helen E. Kelsey in 1923.[106] The house was reassembled on the foundation of an earlier house that had burned. Miss Kelsey, an enthusiastic student of old houses, paid $700 for the structure, plus $200 to Stone Brothers of Boston to move it to Weston in four trips. Miss Kelsey was a member of the Wellesley College class of 1895. For a time, she taught English and mathematics and worked as registrar at her alma mater before becoming a businesswoman in New York City.

226 Ash Street (by 1908). Purchased by Marian Case in 1913 as a residence for her chauffeur, George Olson. Enlarged and remodeled in 1999.

229 Ash Street (c. 1894). Built for Eli Brock, a native Englishman and well-known local poultryman.

233 Ash Street (c. 1847). Once one of three Rand family houses grouped together on upper Ash Street, this Greek Revival example was built for wheelwright Willard Rand.

One Chestnut Street (c. 1696). The earliest section was built for Abel Allen (1669–1756) and has long been considered the oldest remaining house in Weston. The original one-over-one room house consisted of the two 18-foot-square southwest rooms, a massive chimney with smoke chamber, and an entryway and stair on the east. About 1720, a lean-to was added on the north with a large fireplace incorporated into the existing stack. In 1750 the house passed to Abel's son, David, who was killed in a military expedition to Canada in 1759 or 1760. Col. Elisha Jones became administrator of the estate. Frances Marshall, who researched the house extensively in 1977, believed the house passed about that time to Thomas Rand, although no deed has been found.[107] The house underwent major reconstruction about 1760, which she believed was done by Rand, a skilled builder. Two rooms, one-over-one (13 feet by 14 feet), were added to the east. The 1720 lean-to was removed and replaced with a larger one extending across the north side containing a kitchen and borning room and giving the house its present saltbox form. At the east end of the new lean-to were added three small rooms of equal size (6 feet by 6 feet), one over the other, the lowest being a milk room with stone floor placed three feet below grade. These rooms were connected by a winding stair. The front stair was removed at this time.

Thomas Rand (1727–1805) was a prominent citizen, housewright, and patriot who held many town offices including selectman in the critical years 1773–77. Rand was called on repeatedly for town work like repairing schoolhouses and remodeling the meetinghouse in 1800. The house at One Chestnut Street remained in the Rand family until 1903, owned by descendants Benjamin Rand, Clarissa and Henry Robbins, and Oliver J. Robbins. In 1903 it was sold to William H. and Caroline Rogers Hill of Brookline, who used it as a summer house called Barberry Lodge. Subsequent owners were Ralph Slayton, Thomas and Virginia Scott (1961 to 1976), and Theodore and Barbara Alfond (1976 to the present). The Scotts directed a major restoration in the early 1960s using Philip W. Baker. The Alfonds have made sensitive additions while carefully preserving the antique structure. Listed on the National Register of Historic Places.

3 Maple Road (structural frame 1704, house c. 1830–50). The present house stands on the site of the 40- by 20-foot house built for the town's first minister, Joseph Mors, in 1703–04 as an inducement for him to settle in Weston. The second minister, William Williams, lived here from 1710 until his death in 1760. The house ceased to be a parsonage after 1750, when Williams was dismissed from his position and the next minister built a home closer to the town center. By the time of the 1795 map, the former parsonage was occupied by Deacon Samuel Fiske, who still lived there in 1813 at the time of Reverend Kendal's Centennial sermon. Several church histories written after Kendal's sermon say the parsonage was torn down. Structural analysis suggests that the framing posts and beams were retained when the house underwent a complete rebuilding sometime between 1813 and the mid-19th century. The original central chimney was removed and replaced with twin chimneys. New fireplaces were installed on the north wall of each front parlor, with up-to-date Federal-style mantels. The center entrance was updated with sidelights and fluted pilasters. Windows, doors, and trim also date from this rebuilding. From 1833 to 1837, the house and 26 acres were owned by Francis Dudley, a housewright. It had several subsequent owners before 1869, when it was purchased by farmer and town leader Henry J. White. He sold off the farmland beginning in the 1880s to create the present Maple Road/Wellesley Street neighborhood. White lived here until his death in 1915.

5 Maple Road. Originally an outbuilding connected to 3 Maple Road, it was converted to a separate house about 1891 and remodeled to its present appearance in 1948–49.

9 Maple Road (1898). Queen Anne house built for Kate and Alphonso H. Dunn, a "truckman."

10 Maple Road (1894). Transitional Queen Anne/Colonial Revival house built for George A. Hirtle, who advertised himself in the 1893 directory as a "practical horseshoer" with "particular attention to over-reaching and interfering horses." He sold the house in 1903 to Milledge E. Crouse, also a blacksmith, who sold it about four years later to coachman Patrick J. Connors.

13 Maple Road (1894). Colonial Revival house built for Alberta and Sidney B. Ross, a carpenter later listed as a contractor and builder.

14 Maple Road (c. 1893). Queen Anne house built for Arthur B. Nims, son-in-law of George W. Cutting. Nims worked with other members of the family at Cutting's Store.

20 Maple Road (1893). Queen Anne house built for Alfred Leslie Cutting, who worked with his father at Cutting's Store and was active in local and regional politics.

Newton Street. See chapter 24 for No. 131 and lower numbers.

138 Newton Street (1908). Built for farmer Franklin G. Cooper.[108] Like several of his neighbors on Newton Street, Cooper raised strawberries. This item appeared in the June 21, 1912, *Waltham Daily Free Press Tribune:* "If a town exhibition of strawberries were to be made, F.G. Cooper would certainly take the first prize for the size and eating quality of his berries."

181 Newton Street. Built for a member of the Upham family and owned by Uphams until 1911. In

1920, the Waltham paper printed the following item about the house:

> ". . . a large farmhouse built about 1768 and known as the James Upham Place. The old dwelling was restored and improved in 1912 under the architectural direction of Little & Brown, by C. Eliot Ware, the owner at that time. The house is the center chimney type, with many old fireplaces and early features."[109]

201 Newton Street (1922). Colonial Revival house built for William and Marian Conant on former Upham family land. Designed by architect Guy Lowell.

205 Newton Street (c. 1890). Queen Anne house built for a member of the Upham family.

207 Newton Street (1853). Built for Marshall L. Upham (1824–1909) in a transitional Greek Revival/Italianate style. The youngest of 12 children of Abijah Upham, Marshall was a farmer and Weston road commissioner who also was in charge of music at the First Baptist Church for 64 years. Two of his children, Frank H. and Augustus M. Upham, also settled in Weston. This house originally stood on the east side of Ash Street. The Metropolitan Water Board used it as its caretaker's residence until 1916, when it was sold and moved to the present location.[110]

208 Newton Street (1740). Colonial house built for Thomas Upham III at the time of his marriage. Since the property was owned by his uncle Abijah, it has also been called the Abijah Upham House. Both men were important citizens of the town who served as selectmen and deacons of First Parish Church. The house was occupied successively by the families of Thomas Upham III, John A. Lamson and his wife Elizabeth (Upham), George and Nathan Upham, and Augustus M. Upham and his daughter Anna M. Upham. The blacksmith shop of George and Nathan Upham was located across the street for many years. Mr. and Mrs. F. William Aseltine Jr. purchased the house in 1953 from the Upham family. In his booklet about the house called *The 1740 Mansion*, written in 1963 for the town's 250th anniversary, Aseltine Jr. writes:

> In its final restoration by Mr. and Mrs. F. Wm. Aseltine Jr. . . . the greatest emphasis was on authenticity, and thereby reverting the house and its component details (e.g. main entrance treatment, dentil detail, etcetera) in character, form and feeling to its noble past position. In this quest, and after research, the program was entirely completed in 1963.[111]

Aseltine's "authentic restoration" included the addition of an ornate Connecticut River Valley doorway. Similarly, some of Aseltine's historical information is of dubious authenticity. According to Upham descendant Gilbert M. Upham, the result is "a buildup . . . of a very ordinary farm and farmhouse into something completely out of character for that era."[112] While neither original nor appropriate to Weston, Aseltine's doorway has won its own place among local lovers of architecture and decorative arts.

27 School Street (c. 1852–56) Greek Revival house built by housewright John Parradee.

28 School Street. See chapter 14.

44 School Street. Building A (1895) was built for Weston High School from designs by Samuel Mead of Cabot, Everett and Mead. **Building B** (1908, 1911) was built as a one-story, two-room school designed by architect J. Williams Beal for the four primary grades. The building was too small almost immediately and was expanded to two stories in 1911 under the direction of Alexander Jenney. **Building C** (1932) was built for Weston High School, from designs by Ralph Harrington Doane. The Georgian Revival structure suffered a major fire in 1948 and the original gambrel roof was never rebuilt. Doane was born in Nova Scotia and educated at MIT. He was considered an expert in school design and was a member of the National Advisory Council of School Building. Rindge Technical High School in Cambridge is another example of his work. His outstanding achievement, however, was the 1927 Motor Mart Garage in Park Square, for which he received the Harleston Parker award of the Boston Society of Architects.[113] Now Brook School Apartments elderly housing. (See chapters 5 and 8 for photos of Buildings A, B, and C.)

47 School Street (by 1856). Originally owned by housewright John Parradee. Sold by James Keyes in 1863 to Oliver N. Kenney, who managed the school furniture factory on Crescent Street. The original Italianate detailing was removed in a 20th-century remodeling.

68 School Street (c. 1891). Built for George W. Cutting, postmaster and owner of George W. Cutting & Sons general store.

86 School Street (1941). Weston Scout House. See chapter 8.

17 Wellesley Street (by 1908). Shown on the 1908 *Middlesex County Atlas* as belonging to John B. Fiske, who was a gardener at the James Case estate.

18 and 22 Wellesley Street. See chapter 20.

23 and 27 Wellesley Street. See chapter 14.

35 Wellesley Street (c. 1895). Queen Anne house

probably built for carpenter Sidney B. Ross and then sold to Gustavus Smith, a retired farmer who moved here from 138 Wellesley Street.

39 Wellesley Street (1892). Queen Anne house built for Merrill French, the town auditor.

40, 44, 56, 60, 64, 70 Wellesley Street. See chapter 20.

49 Wellesley Street (c. 1893). Queen Anne house.

51 Wellesley Street (1892). Queen Anne house built for carpenter-builder John C. Macdonald and his wife, Mary Eliza, who is listed in the 1893 directory as a bookkeeper. Macdonald was the builder for the Drabbington Lodge on North Avenue and the fire station on Boston Post Road.

55 Wellesley Street (c. 1891). Queen Anne house built for Carrie L. Smith, who resold it in April 1892 to E.W. Russell, a housepainter, and his wife, Fannie.

59 Wellesley Street (1892). Transitional Queen Anne/Colonial Revival house built for carpenter John J. Brown, who is later referred to as a contractor and builder.

63 and 67 Wellesley Street. Colonial Revival houses from the mid-1920s.

74 Wellesley Street. Transitional Greek Revival/Italianate house which first appears on the town map of 1889.

76 Wellesley Street (c. 1862). Transitional Greek Revival/Italianate house probably built for farmer James W. Moore.

80 Wellesley Street (1862). This house was originally similar to the adjacent No. 76, also built by carpenter Fitz A. Robinson. Robinson lived at No. 80 until his death. In 1912, his widow sold the house to Louisa Case, who enlarged it and built a fieldstone garage with quarters upstairs for her chauffeur, Arthur J. Horrigan. Also remaining on the property is the Robinson barn and a potting shed once attached to a greenhouse built by Miss Case.

84 Wellesley Street (c. late 1850s). This Italianate cottage was probably built for Henry J. White. White married Lydia Morse in September 1856 in Weston and may have built the house shortly thereafter. It does not appear on the 1857 map but was in place by the 1866 map, under White's ownership. By the early 1870s he had sold it to James Case and moved up the street to 3 Maple Road. Case used No. 84 for his estate staff. Beginning in 1907, it was occupied by the farm superintendent, Allen Mosher, then by his daughter, Margaret, who in Louisa Case's will was granted life tenancy. The house is presently owned by Margaret's great-nephew Robert Mosher Jr. and his wife, Denise, who restored and enlarged it.

86 Wellesley Street (c. 1921). Built by Louisa Case for her gardener, John Mele.

89 Wellesley Street (1889). Originally called Rocklawn, this Shingle-style estate house was built for James Brown Case from designs by Ernest N. Boyden and was the home of two generations of the Case family. The hexagonal room over the north entrance was added about 1913 as a sunroom for Mrs. James B. Case. The house was deeded to the Town of Weston about 1946. The porte cochere at the front (south) entrance has been removed. The kindergarten addition was added in 1951. The large barn adjacent to the house burned in April 1947.

101 Wellesley Street (c. 1843). The Sentinels. Greek Revival house built for farmer Nathan Barker, who owned it until 1896. The house was purchased in 1909 by Marian Case, who named it The Sentinels and used it for Hillcrest staff. In 1922, her gardener, Arthur Williams, moved here with his family, including his son, Jack. Some Hillcrest boys who boarded for the summer stayed with the Williams family.

Wellesley Street and Alphabet Lane (1916). The cow barn was designed by Fox and Gale for Mrs. James Brown Case, who owned this land until her death in 1918. The barn contained stalls, tool storage, a milk room, washroom, coal heater, hay storage, and a manure pit. It was the center of dairy operations for Hillcrest Farm.

102 Wellesley Street (1897). Queen Anne house built for carpenter-builder Howard L. Cooper. Marian Case purchased it in 1909, remodeled it, called it Appletree Cottage, and made it her home until her death. During her tenure, the house was surrounded by gardens. Nearby, the field referred to as Crosslots was perhaps the most fertile on the farm and was devoted to market crops including vegetables and berry bushes. Also on this side of Wellesley Street was the five-acre Hastings Field purchased from the Hastings estate in 1917. After the property was transferred to the Arnold Arboretum, No. 102 became the home of the arboretum director, Donald Wyman.

131 Wellesley Street (c. 1790). Federal-style house with later additions built for farmer and housewright Thomas Rand Jr., whose father was also a housewright (see One Chestnut Street above). Rand heirs sold the house to farmer Josiah Hastings in 1817; his descendants sold it to Marian Case in 1909. Her farm supervisor, Tom Park, lived here for many years.

132 Wellesley Street (1893). Queen Anne house built for Isaac W. Hastings, member of a family who owned land on both sides of Wellesley Street from 1817 until the early 20th century. Isaac worked as city engineer for Newton. (See also No. 134.)

133 Wellesley Street (1909). Hillcrest Clubhouse (later referred to as the Red Schoolhouse). This house, originally owned by Frank Mulock, was under construction across the street when it was purchased by Marian Case in 1909. She moved it in January 1911 and remodeled it for use as the educational and social center of Hillcrest.[114]

134 Wellesley Street (1893). Queen Anne house built for George Hastings, brother of Isaac, using a plan that is almost a mirror image of No. 132. The two houses both appear on town tax records in 1894, valued at $2,200.

135 Wellesley Street (1927). Hillcrest Barn. Yellow-brick barn designed by Samuel Mead and constructed by William Kellar for Marian Case and used as the center of operations for the Hillcrest agricultural program. The first floor had cow and horse stalls, a packing room for washing and packing fruits and vegetables, and an office. The second floor was for hay storage and the cellar for storage of farm equipment and manure pits. There was a feed room, tool room, and harness room. A greenhouse extended off the back.

Behind 135 Wellesley Street. Fieldstone incinerator built in 1921 to burn brush and debris and secure ashes for fertilizer.

137 Wellesley Street (c. 1847). Greek Revival house built for farmer Otis Train. George Milton, a merchant from Boston, purchased the property in 1869 and used it as a summer place for more than 40 years before selling to Marian Case in 1912. Milton retained life tenancy and lived here until his death in 1918. In subsequent years, the house was occupied by Theodore Chandler and his wife, Mary Williams Chandler, who was a relative of Miss Case. Hillcrest boys boarded here. After Mrs. Chandler's death in 1956, the house was used as a residence by Arnold Arboretum directors Dr. Richard Howard and Peter Ashton.

138 Wellesley Street (c. 1855–59). Greek Revival house built for farmer Otis Train, who purchased about four acres in 1855. In 1859 he sold his other house and land across the street (see No. 137).

142 Wellesley Street (c. 1905).

163 Wellesley Street (1924). Tudor Revival house designed by architect R. Clipston Sturgis.

235 Wellesley Street (1900, 1914). Originally a frame Colonial Revival built for estate owner Daniel Demmon, the mansion was remodeled in 1914 by his daughter, Fannie Morrison. Samuel Mead designed the more formal Georgian Revival exterior executed in brick veneer. A sunroom was added at that time to make the house more symmetrical. An item in the *Waltham Daily Free Press Tribune* of March 27, 1914, told of the lucky man who won the contract to haul 90 tons of frieze stone from Boston. The porte cochere was removed in the 1950s. The house and estate property were sold in 1927 to the Sisters of St. Joseph, who originally used the house for classroom and residence space for their new Regis College and now use it as the president's house. On the property is a matching brick carriage house, as well as a 1911 fieldstone water and bell tower designed by Harold Graves.

Notes

1. Meade, Catherine M., CSJ, "The Demmon-Morrison House, 235 Wellesley Street, Weston, MA, 1900, 1914," (unpublished manuscript, May 1981), 11.
2. Kennedy, Donald G., "The Case Family Legacy to Weston," *WHSB,* May 1982, 8.
3. Case, Marian, *The Eighth Summer at Hillcrest Farm,* 1917, 6.
4. *Pasadena Star-News,* April 22, 1941.
5. "Fannie E. Morrison, Who Donated Large Sums to Institutions Here and in East, Dies While Asleep," *Pasadena Star-News,* April 21, 1941.
6. Notebook of Marian Roby Case, 1916, Series 1A, Box 1, Folder 5, Library of the Arnold Arboretum.
7. Lamson, *HTW,* 7.
8. "Abel Allen House," nomination form, National Register of Historic Places, 1977.
9. Because Thomas Jr. died in 1794, his house, now numbered 131 Wellesley Street, is shown on the 1794 Kingsbury Map as belonging to the Widow Rand.
10. Kendal, Rev. Samuel, D.D., "A Sermon, Delivered at Weston, January 12, 1813, on the Termination of a Century, since the Incorporation of the Town" (Cambridge: Hilliard and Metcalf, 1813). According to Kendal, the house was raised in 1703. (See also entry for 3 Maple Road at the end of this chapter.)
11. "The First Parish in Weston: 1698–1948, Weston, Massachusetts," 250th anniversary publication for First Parish Church, 1948, 9.
12. Upham, Gilbert M., "Debunking the 1740 Mansion," unpublished typescript, November 30, 1991. Upham says that William Upham's land stretched all the way to the Charles River. See also Upham, F.K., *Descendants of John Upham of Massachusetts* (Albany: Joel Munsell's Sons, 1892).
13. Kennedy, Donald G., "The Case Family Legacy to Weston," *WHSB,* May 1982, 1. According to Kennedy, the name of the Case firm later changed to Case, Dudley, and Battelle and finally Battelle, Hurd, and Company—all in the dry-goods brokerage business.
14. MCRD 913/372, White to Case, September 1863, four parcels of 30, 13, 3, and under 1 acre for a total of 46-plus acres.
15. The following obituary for Nathan Barker recounts some history of the Derby family in Weston (*WDFPT,* May 16, 1902): "In the death of the venerable Nathan Barker . . . we have to record the demise of the oldest citizen of Weston. Mr. Barker was born in 1808 and was 93 years old. When a young man he was in the employ of General Daniel G. Derby, a man of mark in this generation, and of the Derby family of Salem. The Colonial residence of General Derby was situated where now stands the house of James B. Case. He was noted for his lavish hospitality and here gathered men of note of their day: among these were Commodores Perry, Decatur and Bainbridge. Mr. Barker's account of some of these festivities was very amusing. Upon the settlement of the General's estate, he having died in Weston in 1843, Mr. Barker purchased a good deal of the land . . ." Barker sold part of this land to

Charles White in 1845 (457/32).

16. For an account of the fire, see *WFP*, September 9, 1882, and "A Mystery Solved . . . and an Accident," *WHSB,* May 1983, 10. This fire was apparently the second for the Case family, the first being in 1876.

17. Undated plans for the house, with architect's name, are owned by the Weston School Department. Construction date from town tax records.

18. 84 Wellesley Street, probably built in the late 1850s and later acquired by Case.

19. Letter, James Case to Francis Blake, September 13, 1897 (Blake Papers, MHS 64.925). See also 1898 *TR,* 23–27.

20. Ibid. The fire in 1876, referred to in this quotation, did not destroy the house.

21. Letter, Francis Blake to James Case, December 21, 1898 (Blake Papers, MHS 65.928).

22. The author is indebted to Sister Catherine M. Meade, C.S.J., whose unpublished 1981 research paper, "The Demmon-Morrison House," cited above, is the principal source for this section.

23. MCRD 1946/6. Plan of the estate drawn by John McClintock in 1896 shows the farmhouse and barn complex close to Wellesley Street (Regis College Archives).

24. The Demmon house was at 128 Beacon Street; James Case was at 468 Beacon Street.

25. *WDFPT,* May 26, July 14, 1899, and May 4, 1900.

26. "Weston Has Become the Lenox of the East," *Boston Sunday Herald,* May 11, 1902.

27. *Boston Sunday Globe,* June 1902, reprinted in *WDFPT,* June 27, 1902.

28. MCRD, 1083/103, Otis Hunt to White, 1869.

29. For more details on White, see "A Fatal Ride: Sad Death of Mrs. Henry J. White of Weston," July 1893 (White was injured and his wife and son killed by a train at a railroad crossing near Kendal Green), and "Death of Henry Jackson White," *WDFPT,* April 9, 1915.

30. Obituary, *WDFPT,* April 9, 1915.

31. Grading and sidewalk construction for Maple Road was done in 1896 (1896 *TR,* 38). For lot sales and deed references, see "Maple Road/Wellesley Street" Area Form H, prepared by Pamela W. Fox for WHC and MHC, June 15, 1994.

32. Bowers, Martha H. and Carolan, Jane, "The Water Supply System of Metropolitan Boston, 1845–1947," prepared for the Metropolitan District Commission, Boston, under the auspices of the Cultural Resource Group, Louis Berger & Associates, Inc., 1985. The author is indebted to Bowers and Carolan for much of this information on the water supply system.

33. Prior to this first cycle, city dwellers obtained their water from springs, wells, and ponds, or from small, privately financed water companies.

34. In addition to the Bowers and Carolan report, cited above, details about the project can be found in annual reports of the Metropolitan Water and Sewerage Board, 1902–09. See also "The Water Supply System of Metropolitan Boston, Thematic Multiple Properties Submission," nomination form for the National Register of Historic Places, 1989, as well as accompanying MHC inventory forms for the Weston Reservoir, Weston Aqueduct, Weston Channel Chamber, and Weston Terminal Chamber. The aqueduct passed through the Weston property of Henry L. Brown, Mrs. Charlotte Armitage, George Sanderson, Mrs. Evelyn Nolte, Gen. C.J. Paine, Luther Upham, Oliver Sherburn, Amri Barker, and Daniel Demmon before joining the channel and reservoir.

35. "Commonwealth of Massachusetts Metropolitan Water Works Plan No. 127 of Land Takings," January 23, 1902 (Plan Book 134, Plan 43A and B), shows land taken from Marshall L. Upham (41.9 and 35.5 acres), James M. Upham (45.6 acres), Nathan E. Upham (14.6 acres), and Albert G. Upham (5.6 acres)

36. Lamson's *HTW* pictures the first Upham house (c. 1720) opposite page 191. The mid-19th-century Marshall L. Upham house was moved in November 1916 to 207 Newton Street.

37. Bowers and Carolan, op. cit., v–13.

38. The *Boston Evening Transcript* in 1919 noted that Stearns "combined in rare degree both scientific attainment and a love of the beautiful, as the result of which his achievements adorned as well as served in a utilitarian sense the communities for which he worked." (December 2, 1919, 4, as quoted in Bowers and Carolan, V–13)

39. According to MHC inventory form #803, 26 plans dated from October 1900 to March 1905 still exist at the Olmsted National Historic Site in Brookline. The Library of Congress Manuscript Division contains correspondence and memos regarding the reservoir, primarily from F.L. Olmsted Jr. and Arthur Shurtleff, who was a member of the firm at the time. The archival material indicates that unusual attention was given to conservation of natural features, forest improvement, and choice of appropriate plantings.

40. 1900 *TR,* 24.

41. 1903 *TR,* 51–52.

42. Metropolitan District Commission Record Series #EN4.12/889X, Wachusett volumes, Weston Reservoir, Section 1, August 4, 1902, Photo #4467. See *WDFPT,* August 27, 1915, for account of ruffians destroying "a garden belonging to one of the Italians in the camp on Ash Street."

43. *WDFPT,* October 11, 1901.

44. 1903 *TR,* 52.

45. "A New Public Reservation Results from the Work of the Metropolitan Water Board/Opportunity Presented for Beautifying the Region about Weston—The Basin will Make a Charming Lake, with Two Islands—Growth of a Great Park System," *Boston Herald,* February 25, 1901.

46. *WDFPT,* July 2, 1919.

47. Ibid.

48. After 1940, the aqueduct was generally supplied directly from Shaft 4 of the Hultman Aqueduct. The Sudbury Reservoir remained in active use until 1978 and sometimes supplied water during dry years. Beginning in 1951, Weston Aqueduct Supply Mains (WASMs) #3 and #4 extending from the Weston Terminal Chamber received their water from a branch of the high- pressure Hultman Aqueduct. After that, the Weston Aqueduct supplied an average of about 45 million gallons per day to low-lying land in Boston via WASM #1 and #2. MWRA water supply projects under construction at the turn of the 21st century will change the use of the Weston Aqueduct and Reservoir. Once the MetroWest Tunnel is completed in 2003, a branch of this new water supply tunnel will connect to the branch of the Hultman Aqueduct that now extends to Loring Road. Water from this connection will flow at high pressure into WASM 3 or will flow at reduced pressure into covered storage tanks constructed off Loring Road in 1998–2000 and from there into WASM 1 and 2. WASM 4 can be operated at either high or low pressure as the situation warrants.

49. Demmon's second daughter, who lived outside the country, received a small annuity. See "Over a Million Willed by Demmon," undated newspaper clipping, Coburn scrapbook #2. See also Meade, op. cit., 8. Meade's paper lists Demmon's real estate holdings, largely in Boston, valued at $1,643,200.

50. Letter, Fannie Morrison to Sister Patrice, December 2, 1935 (see appendix VII in Meade's "The Demmon-Morrison House"). The poplars were planted in the spring of 1910.

51. Ibid.

52. Ibid.

53. *Pasadena Star,* January 11, 1911. Quoted in *WDFPT,* January 20, 1911.

54. *WDFPT,* May 17, 1912. See also October 20, 1911; January 5, March 22, and May 3, 1912, for trip reports.

55. Meade, op. cit., 11.

56. Fannie Morrison to Sister Patrice, op. cit.
57. "Regis College History," Office of Public Information press release, 1990.
58. McQueeney, Katherine, "The Regis Heritage," *The Regis Quarterly,* Jubilee Issue, February 1952. Other accounts give the number of students the first year as 55.
59. "The Spellman Museum of Stamps & Postal History Facing the 21st Century," *WHSB,* fall 1999.
60. "The Accident at Northeast Harbor," *Mt. Desert Herald,* August 2, 1883, reprinted in *WHSB,* May 1983, 11.
61. 80 Wellesley Street.
62. Lofty, Elizabeth, "Looking back at the history of the Case Estates," *The Wayland-Weston Town Crier,* August 22, 1985, 1.
63. Kennedy, "The Case Family Legacy to Weston," op. cit., 8.
64. Dickson, *RR,* 69. The Weston house was staffed by a laundress, a cook, a second maid, and two men in the greenhouses, in addition to the caretaker, two farmhands in the barn, and part-time help.
65. For deed references in this paragraph, see MCRD 6651/113, 7026/111, 9211/548 and Plan Book 280/15 (James Case land in 1919) and Plan 1140 of 1946 in 7026/111 (plan of land proposed for new school site, 1946).
66. First quote from Margaret Mosher in Lofty, op. cit., second quote from Kennedy, "The Case Family Legacy to Weston," op. cit., 8.
67. Case, Marian Roby, *Hillcrest Gardens, Weston, Mass., the 20th Summer,* 1929.
68. In later years she prepared a lecture on New England Landscape and Farm Scenery with slides taken by local photographers.
69. Nos. 101, 102, and 131 Wellesley Street were the first three houses. Appletree Cottage was No. 102.
70. Case, *Hillcrest Gardens,* 1929, op. cit., 9.
71. Case, Marian Roby, *The Second Summer at Hillcrest Farm,* 1911, 4.
72. Ibid., 3.
73. Weaver, Harold, "Hillcrest, Past and Present," *The Fourth Summer at Hillcrest Farm,* 1913, 20.
74. Crowley, Dennis, "Why I am at Hillcrest Gardens," in *Hillcrest Gardens: The 13th Summer,* 1922, 7.
75. Weaver, Harold, "The Reason Why," *The Third Summer at Hillcrest Farm,* 1912, 4–5.
76. Case, Marian Roby, *The Second Summer at Hillcrest Farm,* 1911, 4.
77. In his oral history (WPL, 1986), Jack Williams recalled that Miss Case ran the study hour like a class, with the following schedule: Monday, drawing; Tuesday, public speaking; Wednesday, guest lecturer; Thursday, write report on lecture; and Friday, write observation paper on something seen during the week. On Labor Day, prizes were given for drawings and observation papers as well as reports.
78. Howard, Richard A., "The Hillcrest Gardens, Weston, Massachusetts," in *Arnoldia,* bulletin of the Arnold Arboretum, vol. 20, no. 9–10, December 23, 1960.
79. 1920 "Green Book," 57.
80. Howard, Richard A., "Bibliographic Data on the Hillcrest Gardens Books, 1911–1941," *Journal of the Arnold Arboretum,* vol. XLI, 1960, 318–19.
81. Weaver, "The Reason Why," op. cit., 5.
82. Hobbs, E. Stanley Jr., "Why I Am at Hillcrest," *The Fifth Summer at Hillcrest Farm,* 1914, 6.
83. Case, Marian Roby, *The Eighth Summer at Hillcrest Farm, Weston,* 1917, 45.
84. Howard, Richard A.,"The Hillcrest Gardens," *WHSB,* October 1982, 2.
85. Hobbs, Stanley, "Pears," *The Second Summer at Hillcrest Farm, Weston,* 1911. For more about Stanley Hobbs, see *Middlesex County and Its People,* vol. III, 169.
86. Hobbs, Stanley, "Diary of the Third Year at Hillcrest," *The Third Summer at Hillcrest Farm, Weston,* 1912, 16.
87. Information in this section from Marian Case's annual reports, the "green books," which describe farm operations and improvements.
88. Burke, George Murray Jr., "Hillcrest Through the Years," *Hillcrest Gardens,* 1940, 12. The shop was at 494 Boston Post Road. See also oral history of Richard Howard (Weston Public Library Oral History Project, 1980s).
89. "Louisa's Wall: Largest? Longest? A treasure in any case," *Harvard Magazine,* July–August, 1998, 92.
90. Richard Howard oral history, op. cit., 41.
91. Ibid., 40.
92. Case, Marian Roby, *The Eighth Summer at Hillcrest Farm,* 1917, 42.
93. Case, Marian Roby, *The Tenth Summer at Hillcrest Farm,* 1919, 11.
94. Howard, Richard A., "The Hillcrest Gardens," *WHSB,* October 1982, 5.
95. Benson, Albert E., *History of the Massachusetts Horticultural Society* (Boston: Massachusetts Horticultural Society, 1929), 455.
96. Howard, Richard, "The Hillcrest Gardens," *WHSB,* May 1982, 10.
97. Ibid.
98. "The History of Hillcrest for 1921," in *Hillcrest Gardens, Weston, Mass., the 12th Summer,* 12.
99. Richard Howard oral history, op. cit., 40.
100. The 1938 "green book" has a complete report on hurricane damage, 69–74.
101. *Hillcrest Gardens, the 30th Summer,* 1939, 28.
102. The Massachusetts Horticultural Society declined Miss Case's offer of the property, an offer that had stipulated that the society would keep up the gardens and the school. (See letter from John C. Wister, landscape architect, Swarthmore College, to Dr. Richard A. Howard, Arnold Arboretum, April 9, 1960, Arnold Arboretum Archives.)
103. Wister, John C., "The Future of Hillcrest Gardens," *Hillcrest Gardens, the 30th Summer,* 1939, 32.
104. Middlesex County Probate #257650. The letter from Wister to Howard, cited above, states that Miss Case wanted a written agreement from Harvard not to sell the property and to keep up the gardens and the school. Her lawyer informed her that Harvard lawyers were never willing to accept a gift with such stipulations. Her lawyer stated that "as Miss Case had confidence in the good faith of the Harvard representatives . . . she ought to take their assurance that they intended to keep up the gardens and the school . . ."
105. Howard, "The Hillcrest Gardens," *WHSB,* October 1982, 12.
106. *WHSB,* May 1974.
107. Rand bought 33 acres of the Allen farm at auction in 1781 but Marshall believed this was land only. See Frances V. Marshall, "The Abel Allen House, Number One Chestnut Street, Weston, Mass." (typescript, April 10, 1977). See also "Weston's Allen House Restores Its 17th Century Tone," *The Town Crier,* December 14, 1961; "Property Report" by Philip W. Baker, August 28, 1961 (WHC files); and Brenton H. Dickson III, "The Scott House," *WHSB,* March 1966.
108. *WDFPT,* February 14, 1908.
109. *WDFPT,* August 13, 1920.
110. *WDFPT,* July 14, October 20, and November 10, 1916.
111. Aseltine, F. William Jr., *The 1740 Mansion* (privately printed, 1963), 18.
112. Upham, Gilbert M., "Debunking the 1740 Mansion," unpublished typescript, November 30, 1991.
113. Withey, Henry and Elsie, *Biographical Dictionary of American Architects (Deceased),* 176.
114. *WDFPT,* June 25, 1909, and January 20, 1911 (Miss Case moving the Mulock house).

Figure 20-1. This photograph of investment banker Robert Winsor was taken at the 1913 Weston Bicentennial. By that time he was the town's second largest landowner, with well over 400 acres. Under his leadership, the Weston Golf Club moved from Church Street to its present location within Winsor's Meadowbrook Road estate.

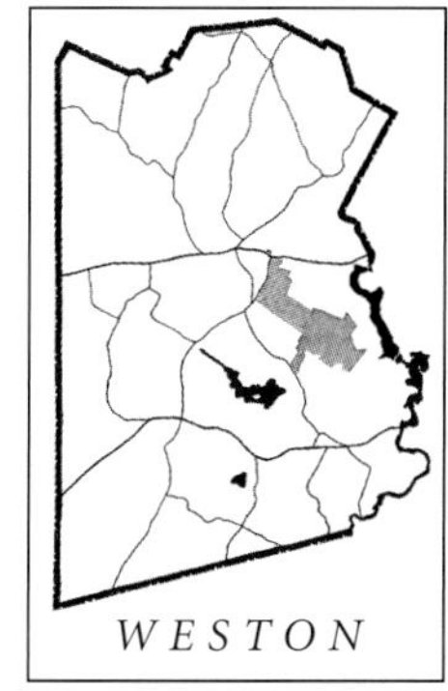

CHAPTER 20

Robert Winsor
The "J. P. Morgan of Boston"

Robert Winsor settled in Weston in 1883. He was a young Harvard graduate with just a few years of experience at Kidder Peabody & Co., where he began his career as a clerk. Nearly a half century later, when he died in 1930, he was the firm's senior partner. Under his leadership, Kidder Peabody developed from an eminently respectable investment bank of little more than local influence to one of the greatest banking institutions in the world.[1] *Newspaper articles lauded him as "the J.P. Morgan of Boston" and "one of the country's leading bankers."*[2] *He was praised as a man of foresight who had anticipated the need for improved transportation, utilities, banking, and communications.*

In Weston, too, Winsor was a man with vision. Over the course of 35 years, he purchased more than 472 acres, making him the town's second largest landowner. His holdings included much of the land bordered by Boston Post Road, Summer Street, Loring Road, Doublet Hill Road, Newton Street, and Wellesley Street. Other Boston businessmen also amassed extensive landholdings in Weston, but Winsor was the first to make large-scale plans for the future development of his entire estate. Relocating the Weston Golf Club and Meadowbrook School onto his property proved to be the catalyst in transforming hundreds of acres of farm fields and woodlands into the prime residential community centered along Meadowbrook Road.

Early Life and Education

Robert Winsor (1858–1930) was born in Salem, Massachusetts, the oldest son of Dr. Frederick Winsor (1829–1889) and Anne Bent Ware (1830–1907).[3] His father, a much loved physician, served as a medical officer in the Civil War and then practiced first in Salem and later in Winchester. His mother was a teacher whose character and commitment to education are evident in the achievements of her seven children. She was the daughter of Henry Ware Jr., well-known Unitarian minister and antislavery advocate. She started a private girls school in Boston and later a school for her own children in her home, supplementing the family income by taking in additional pupils. Anne and Frederick Winsor also established a Unitarian church in Winchester.[4]

After preparing for college at Phillips Exeter, Robert graduated from Harvard in 1880. An all-around athlete, he played for three years on the varsity football team, where he was known as the "prince of goal kickers."[5] He was also an exceptional baseball player, serving as captain of the team the year he graduated. He became something of a sports legend because of one game where he played catcher against Yale without benefit of mask, catcher's mitt, or other protection except for a piece of rubber held between this teeth. Although described as a "keen student," an article written after his death suggests that Winsor was not a scholar:

> Mr. Winsor is of the type of men who are leading athletes in college, and who put their abundant energy into their business careers after graduation, with results that sometimes surprise those who go through college devoting their entire time to their studies.[6]

Immediately after his graduation, he secured employment at Kidder Peabody & Co. at a salary reported in one account to have been $100 a year and in another to have been under $1,000.

Career Success and First Two Decades in Weston

In 1883 Robert Winsor married Eleanor May Magee of Winchester. The couple built the house still standing on a hill overlooking Boston Post Road at the corner of Hemlock Road. The Shingle-style house was the first in Weston designed by Samuel Mead, a young architect who himself settled in Weston a few years later.

The story of how Winsor came to live in Weston is told in part in an 1883 letter from Horace Sears to Andrew Fiske in which he describes Winsor as a "great gain":

> He is a young fellow about my age who is in Kidder Peabody & Co.'s employ & whose connections are of the very best. . . . He has not much money I judge & has built a little box of a house but that makes no difference. I am sure you will like him & I am rejoiced that he came to Weston, being attracted there thro' Mr. Russell, who is an old friend of the family. Winsor was married

Figure 20-2. Robert and Eleanor Magee Winsor had six children, only four of whom survived into their teenage years. Judging from the distinctive "leg-o'-mutton" sleeve on the dress, this photograph was taken about 1894–96.

> about two weeks ago to a very charming girl & only came to his new house last week. He could not find a lot upon which to build at any reasonable price & we were so anxious to secure him that Mother bought all the Davis pasture containing about 20 acres next to our land & sold him a lot there.[7]

First Parish Church, where "Mr. Russell" was minister, was to benefit greatly from Winsor's settlement in Weston, as the young man was an ardent Unitarian and became one of the church's most generous supporters.[8]

Winsor was quickly recognized at Kidder Peabody for his business acumen. In his obituary, a longtime friend is quoted as saying that Winsor's first-year Christmas bonus "was larger than the bonus of any other employee of the firm, because they believed he had been the most useful man they had."[9] In 1894 he was admitted into partnership; and in 1904 the *Boston Post* proclaimed him one of the "Men of the Hour on State Street."[10]

This was a period of reorganization and consolidation in American industry, and Winsor was a leading figure in this process. On the Sunday after his death, the *Boston Sunday Post* ran a front-page story entitled "Energetic Eighties Produced Group of Men, College Friends, Who Built Banking, Telephone and Transportation Interests of City, State and Nation." The reporter analyzes this illustrious group, most of them classmates in the Harvard class of 1880, including Theodore Roosevelt, Robert Bacon, William A. Gaston, Richard Saltonstall, and Josiah Quincy. The author summarizes Winsor's role as follows:

> Perhaps Robert Winsor was the greatest of the '80's great young men, at least in the business world. . . . He conceived great projects. . . . Winsor had the insight that saw the transportation needs of the last four decades. He saw the needs of and the demand for illuminating and heating gas. He saw the demand for communication. . . . Robert Winsor saw these things. He grasped their importance and he . . . found the men to develop them. Not only did he find the men, but he found the money, millions of money, for the developments.
>
> Robert Winsor, self-effacing, publicity-shy, hiding his activities under a firm name, that of Kidder, Peabody & Company, was one of those extraordinary men whom professors of biological sciences will tell you happens only when nature wishes to create a Gladstone, a Wilson, or a Morgan.[11]

His first "coup" was the reorganization, with classmate William A. Gaston, of the old West End Street Railway into the Boston Elevated Railway Company, thus consolidating the city's new subway system with existing surface transportation to form one company. Winsor merged several greater Boston gas companies into the Boston Consolidated Gas Company. He and Gaston consolidated nine existing banks to establish the National Shawmut Bank, one of the largest in New England. Winsor and his firm became the representative of the Morgan interests in New England, and he was one of three or four men in the country called upon when Morgan wanted to put over a national or international deal. He was involved in the financing of the expanding American Telephone and Telegraph and United States Steel Companies. He served as a director of dozens of companies and for a time exerted strong influence in the affairs of three large New England railways.

Described as a man of "forceful personality and constructive mind," Winsor was blessed with "far sightedness, broad vision, ability, conscientiousness and natural leadership."[12] He was interested in the industrial development of New England and was a "most constructive force for her betterment."[13] This sentiment was echoed by another writer:

> From his athletic days at Harvard until the day of his death, he was essentially a fighter. He loved the winning more than the prize that the winner earns. He loved power, but the power which he sought was only a means to an end. He felt strongly that with it he could accomplish what was best for his city, New England and the country.[14]

Figure 20-3. Anne Ware Winsor poses with her seven children and 17 grandchildren in front of 10 Winsor Way about 1906. When asked how it was that the entire family had assembled for such a photograph, Winsor Gale (then a boy, at the far left) replied, "Uncle Robert knew how to get things done." Among the group are Mary Pickard Winsor, founder of the Winsor School, and Frederick Winsor, founder of the Middlesex School. (Names listed with photo credits)

In Weston, he was highly respected, but no one knew him well. He worked hard. His nephew described him as a "hard man to be fond of."[15] He was not socially active and didn't go to clubs or participate often in golf or other sports.

Winsor and His Siblings

With business success came financial prosperity. Within a few years of his move to Weston, Winsor began purchasing additional property. Between 1887 and 1890, he acquired land at the corner of Wellesley Street and Boston Post Road, laid out what is now Winsor Way, and built two houses.[16] One became the residence of his widowed mother, Anne Ware Winsor, who moved to Weston along with five of Robert's younger siblings. By 1900, all the children except Mary were married.

Robert Winsor's first loyalty was his family. Although this was a family with many superstars, Robert was the one who made the money; and many family members worked for him in some way. He assisted his siblings as they became established in homes and careers.

His sister Mary Pickard Winsor (1860–1950) was two years younger. In 1886 she was asked to teach a group of Beacon Hill girls, and thus began one of Boston's most distinguished private schools. In 1910 Miss Winsor's establishment was incorporated as the Winsor School. Robert was actively involved as an original incorporator, longtime member of the Executive Committee, and active fund-raiser in the effort to build a girls school as fine as any available for boys. Mary Pickard Winsor lived with her mother until Anne Winsor's death in 1907. Her accomplishments were all the more remarkable given the fact that she became deaf and used a horn and later a "black box" to aid her hearing.

The next sibling, Paul (1863–1936), along with his wife, Jessie, and sons Paul and Felix, lived next door to his mother in the former one-room schoolhouse sometimes known as the Schoolhouse on the Rock. Robert had purchased the building in 1900 when it was no longer needed by the town and hired Samuel Mead to convert it into a residence. In 1912, Paul built his own concrete house on Webster Hill.

Sisters Annie (1865–1955) and Elizabeth (1870–1960) also followed family tradition in starting schools. Annie married Joseph Allen and moved to White Plains, New York, where she established a private coeducational school. Elizabeth, who married MIT English professor Henry Pearson, started the Eliot Pearson School for nursery school teachers at Tufts University, said to be one of the first of its kind.[17]

Jane Winsor (1868–1952) married Lyman Whitman Gale in 1895, and the couple built a house on Conant Road. For many years, Lyman Gale worked as a broker for Kidder Peabody on the Boston Stock

Exchange. Jane directed Friendly Society productions and was a founder of the Toy Theatre in Boston and of the Women's Community League in Weston. The couple had three children: Priscilla, Emma, and Winsor.

The youngest sibling, Frederick (1872–1940), married Mary Anna Paine, daughter of estate owner Charles Jackson Paine. Frederick graduated from Harvard in 1893. He taught for several years, organized a school in Baltimore, then came to Concord to carry out his dream of founding a boarding school dedicated to "liberality, honesty, simplicity, and undenominational Christianity." In founding Middlesex School in 1901, he had the backing of Boston men of affairs including his brother and father-in-law, two of the original six trustees. The original 235 acres of land were given by General Paine. Frederick was headmaster for 37 years and Robert served as treasurer for 24 years.[18]

Development of Chestnut Farm

In 1898 Winsor made his first large land purchase, the 83-acre Bryden farm, for which he paid $24,000.[19] The property included much of the land that would become the Weston Golf Club, along with the Greek Revival Bryden farmhouse, which still remains on Meadowbrook Road. The Bryden barn was struck by lightning and burned to the ground in 1899.

Winsor set out to develop his estate, Chestnut Farm. His Tudor-style mansion has been attributed to architect A.J. Russell, son of Rev. Charles Russell, and was completed by 1902.[20] The two-and-a-half-story dark-shingled house was set on a small hilltop and had a plan shaped like a W, with picturesque gables facing in all directions. Because the house was just one room in width, all the principal rooms had windows on both north and south sides. The wide entrance hall had a sweeping staircase. There was a living room with two large green velvet sofas and a piano, a morning room with desk and telephone, a dining room, billiard room, kitchen, and large porch on the south side overlooking the open fields. There were carved ceilings and mammoth carved fireplaces. Upstairs there was a master bedroom, children's rooms on the west side, and an attic story with servants' rooms.

The Winsor estate was the third, after Paine and Sears, to be described in the 1902 *Boston Sunday Herald* article headlined "Weston Has Become the Lenox of the East":

> This, too, occupies a hilltop position, from which there is a magnificent outlook. Mr. Winsor's estate comprises 112½ acres, and the country house, built after the English style, is approached by a magnificent woodland drive.[21]

A newspaper article in 1903 described it as "a beautiful estate, where comfort, not lavishness, is the keynote."[22]

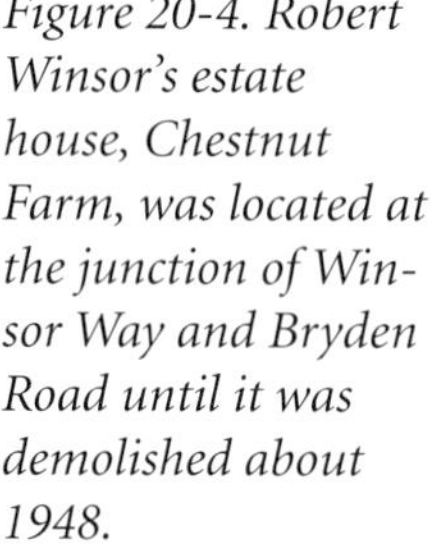

Figure 20-4. Robert Winsor's estate house, Chestnut Farm, was located at the junction of Winsor Way and Bryden Road until it was demolished about 1948.

Figure 20-5. The rambling Tudor house was completed by 1902. A newspaper article described it as "a beautiful estate, where comfort, not lavishness, is the keynote." Like many turn-of-the-century Weston houses, it was covered with dark brown shingles.

Figure 20-6. Robert and Eleanor Winsor lunch on the porch of Chestnut Farm with two of their sons.

Detailed 1904 and 1905 plans by Aspinwall & Lincoln, civil engineers, show the layout of roads and buildings in the early years.[23] One entrance drive, now Winsor Way, passed by the home of Winsor's mother on the way to the main house. A second driveway off Wellesley Street passed by a pond, apple orchard, and grass tennis court. A few small staff houses were located along Wellesley Street.

Robert Winsor wanted his children to grow up in an unpretentious farm atmosphere, although this was not easy to provide, given his power and influence. The estate was run as a gentleman's farm and supplied fresh food for the family. Buildings were generally simple and utilitarian in style. The main barn or stable, rebuilt after the 1899 fire, was a substantial structure, more than 200 feet long, with stalls for horses and cows, a cellar for vegetable storage, and a hayloft. Nearby was a henhouse and a duck house. In 1910 Winsor built a cottage on Boston Post Road for his superintendent, Philip R. Spaulding.[24]

Over the next two decades, Winsor bought additional land. One major purchase was the Hagar farm, a total of 149 acres acquired in 1903 and 1906.[25] By 1918, Winsor was taxed for 472 acres. Only Charles Jackson Paine owned more land in Weston.

As early as 1910, it is clear that Winsor was thinking about future subdivision. That year, he hired the nationally known Brookline firm of Olmsted Brothers to make a general plan for the property. Frederick Law Olmsted Jr. was the principal partner involved in the Winsor job and recorded the following meeting with the couple on March 20, 1910:

> He wants to keep place quiet and natural. Does not want to go in for any large expenditures; but wants to build some woods-roads and gradually improve the place with the idea in mind of subdividing it as time goes on, in 10 or 25 or 50 years, into smaller places of (say) ten acres and upwards. He had recently built a crude pond and wants it brought to a finish. . . . He wants advice about vicinity of house . . .[26]

Winsor asked the firm to lay out a road system that would be convenient for his own use and of value when the property was subdivided. He wanted them to design the edge of the new skating pond and to enhance the natural scenery by clearing, thinning, and adding plantings.[27]

In a field report that fall, Olmsted representative F.A. Hammond expressed concern that the pond be fashioned in a naturalistic manner:

> [Mr. Spaulding] wished me to go with him to the swamp in the woods, where all the undergrowth and trees have been removed preparatory to excavating for the pond. He said he was afraid Mr. Winsor would make a mistake if he went too far with the work before having some advice or plans. . . . Judging from the area cleared, I thought that there was danger of their making the pond too formal in outline to look well in that location.[28]

Figure 20-7. The four-acre artificial pond on what is now Skating Pond Road was constructed out of swampland beginning in late 1909. The following year, 75 laborers were reported to be at work removing enough muck to make it deep enough for swimming.

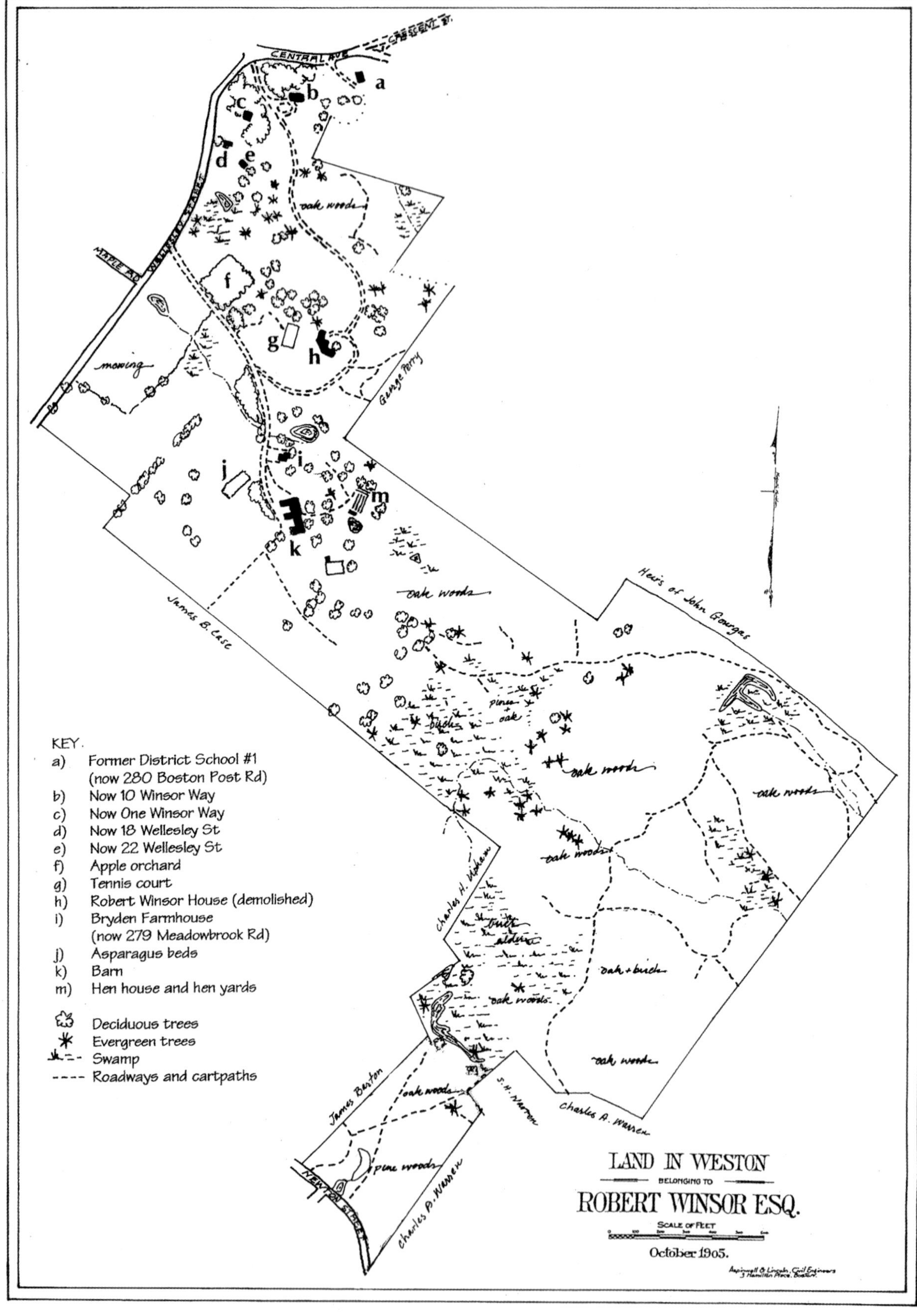

Figure 20-8. This map is a simplified version of a 1905 map by Aspinwell & Lincoln, civil engineers. At that time, the Winsor estate was about 200 acres, or less than half its eventual size.

Winsor was firm in his desire for a pond deep enough for swimming. The Olmsted firm staked out the outline, and in the winter of 1910–11, the pond was dug out and the muck deposited on the farm fields.

The landscape architects made recommendations for the grounds in the immediate vicinity of the mansion house, including broad areas of lawn, a large flower garden and greenhouse, and a shrubbery garden for plants of special botanical interest. But unlike Winsor's immediate neighbors, Marian Case and Horace Sears, Winsor had limited interest in cultivating specimen plants or creating the type of formal garden popular in the early 20th century. There is no evidence that he followed through with any of the key suggestions. The firm might have guessed his priorities from one of its first field reports, when a representative reported that Mr. Winsor would not consider closing a gap in the stone terrace because the children coasted through the opening in winter.

In December 1910 the firm provided a plan showing prime house sites on hilltops throughout the estate and a road plan with "practically all roads which could reasonably be called for in case the property is cut up into lots."[29] Road construction did not begin in earnest until late 1916.[30] The line of Meadowbrook Road had to be changed, in part because Winsor was unable to purchase the Kingsbury property on Loring Road.

The beauty of the Meadowbrook Road area is clearly the result of this careful planning process. The plans demonstrate the continued influence of the naturalistic design principles advocated by Frederick Law Olmsted Sr., father of American landscape architecture. Olmsted Brothers located roadways and house lots based on topographical and geological features, taking advantage of any irregularity.

Interestingly enough, at the same time Winsor was planning his own property, he was also involved in creation of a "utopian" community of affordable workers housing in the Forest Hills section of Jamaica Plain. Winsor is credited as the chief sponsor of the 30-acre Woodbourne development, which was laid out about 1912 by Olmsted Brothers and involved several prominent architectural firms. Winsor reportedly sent emissaries to Europe to study housing and searched carefully for a site convenient to transportation. Woodbourne has been described as a "child of idealism" and a "city neighborhood with the virtues of country life."[31]

Family Life

Chestnut Farm was the Winsors' primary residence. The family initially summered in Cataumet, in a house they built overlooking Buzzards Bay. When the children had families of their own, they began going to Mt. Desert Island, to a rustic camp with a series of cabins. The Winsors had a house on Marlborough Street in Boston, a warm-weather getaway in Bonita, California, and an old farmhouse and barn on a hill in New Boston, New Hampshire, which was accessible by train for winter weekends.[32]

The mansion in Weston reflected Winsor's prosperity and accommodated his growing family. Four children survived into early adulthood: Robert Jr. (1884–1944), Philip (1893–1918), Alexander "Sandy" (1894–1966), and Mary P. "Bud" (Trumbull; 1896–1968). Another son, Frederick, died at age 6 and a sixth child in infancy. Winsor devoted considerable attention to the needs of his children as they were growing up. To provide convenient private schooling for the three youngest, he was instrumental in establishing the Pigeon Hill School, predecessor to Meadowbrook School.

Figure 20-9. Robert and Eleanor Winsor with their oldest son, Robert Jr., and three younger children, Philip, Alexander, and Mary "Bud," who were all born between 1893 and 1896. In the background is the Winsor's first house, now 309 Boston Post Road.

The Winsor skating pond was a local landmark. Early photographs show girls skating in leisurely fashion in their long flowing dresses and boys practicing hockey in a center section, set off by long boards. In *Growing Up in Weston,* Philip Coburn describes hockey games with the stars of the 1915 Harvard team, who were friends of the Winsor boys. At the west end of the pond was a curling rink "where a horse drawn plane made the ice as smooth as glass." Coburn writes, "On Sunday afternoons you could hear the players, clad in scotch plaid jackets and tam-o-shanters, calling out 'Sweep it, sweep it.' These were the same men who bowled at Mr. Sears' at night during the week."[33] With the flick of a switch on a nearby tree, anyone wishing to skate in the evening could turn on lights.

Next to the pond was a log shelter with log benches for putting on skates and a fireplace that burned four-foot logs. Here, according to Coburn, "Mrs.Winsor sat in front of a table, serving hot coffee and tea to the grown-ups and marshmallows and cocoa to the children."[34] This pleasant custom continued until the Winsor boys went into the service in 1917. Brenton H. Dickson III recalled Mrs.

Figure 20-10. The Winsor skating pond was divided into areas for skating, ice hockey, and curling. In February 1912, newspapers reported an estimated 100 people, young and old, enjoying the fun one Sunday afternoon. The date of this panoramic photograph is unknown.

Figure 20-11. The Weston High School football team practiced on the Winsor property. In the background is the large barn later converted to a clubhouse for Weston Golf Club.

Winsor ladling out steaming hot soup from a large urn. He added that the Winsors' reputation for hospitality brought an influx of strangers from outside the community and the pond had to be closed to the public.

In summer, children dove into the water from the top of the skating pond shelter. The young Winsors also had a 10-foot raft. Other ponds within the golf club were off-limits for swimming, according to Brenton Dickson III's *Once Upon a Pung*. He tells the story of how Robert Winsor's nephew Felix and a friend, Weston Blake, went swimming without permission in the pond by the eighth green. To teach them a lesson, the Winsor foreman confiscated their clothes. They were able to walk to their homes on Boston Post Road without seeing anyone or being seen, an indication of how sparsely populated the town was in the early decades of the 20th century.

In the fall, boys played informal football games on the sheep pasture, where the second fairway of the golf club is today. After the game, the players would go into the barn for a glass of milk fresh from the pail.

At the Bicentennial celebration of 1913, the Winsor estate was the location of athletic contests and the historical pageant, which was the highlight of the three-day event. Newspapers reported that fully 3,000 people entered the estate that day to attend the performance:

> They found in the upper section of "Chestnut Farm" a natural open air theatre that could not be better laid out for a performance of this kind. . . . The natural theatre could not have been completed without the waterway, for a part of the performance called for the landing of Lief Erickson and his band of Norsemen in their Viking ship. . . . [I]t was an impressive scene when the early settlers from the far North made their landing . . . [35]

The pond used for the Bicentennial pageant is thought to be the one on Willow Road, another artificial pond created by dredging swampland and building a small dam.

The Winsor boys had difficulties following in the footsteps of their illustrious father. All three attended Harvard, classes of 1905 (Robert), 1915 (Philip), and

Figure 20-12. Two of the children of Alexander "Sandy" Winsor enjoy a sleigh ride. In the background is 37 Skating Pond Road (1917), built for Sandy at the time of his marriage and demolished in the late 1990s.

Figure 20-13. Family portrait in the early 1920s. Back row: Alexander "Sandy" Winsor, Walter Trumbull, Mary "Bud" Winsor Trumbull, and Robert Winsor Jr. Middle row: Hope Bancroft Winsor (Mrs. Alexander), Eleanor Magee Winsor, Robert Winsor, and Susan Baker Winsor (Mrs. Robert Jr.). Grandchildren: Elise Winsor, Philip Trumbull, Alexander Winsor Jr., and Robert Winsor III.

1916 (Sandy), although Sandy left during his junior year and did not graduate.[36] Philip, an exceptionally good amateur golfer, died of pneumonia in France in November 1918 while serving as an ambulance driver for the American Field Service.

When Sandy married Elizabeth Hope Bancroft in 1916, his father built the young couple a picturesque shingled house in the English Revival style just down the road from the skating pond. Robert Jr. married Susan Baker in 1919, and Winsor built them a Colonial Revival house on Winsor Way. The couple later divorced. Robert Jr. and Sandy joined Kidder Peabody and were made partners in the late 1920s. Robert stayed at the firm throughout his career, managing the Back Bay office. Sandy left Kidder Peabody in the early 1930s, spent some time as an insurance salesman, and then, beginning about 1936, worked exclusively for the family real-estate trust.

Robert Winsor's daughter, Mary Pickard Winsor II (nicknamed Bud or Buddy), married Walter H. Trumbull Jr. in 1919. He also joined Kidder Peabody and became a partner. Winsor built the newlyweds a house on Meadowbrook Road.

Figure 20-14. Laborers with hand tools are pictured here in 1923 constructing the present sixth hole of the Weston Golf Club.

Weston Golf Club and Weston Real Estate Trust

The Weston Golf Club was founded in 1894 and originally located on Church Street on land leased from several owners. The early history is discussed in chapter 11. Robert Winsor was one of the original founders and served as president from 1914 to 1925.

In 1916 the club was looking for a new home. Minutes of the Executive Committee record three possibilities: 1) renting new land adjacent to the existing Kendal Green course; 2) uniting with a new country club in the process of being organized, to be located on the Bigelow estate on the Weston/Wayland line; and 3) "land which Mr. Winsor has in mind which would make a suitable 9-hole course."[37] In March 1916, the club voted to accept the Winsor proposal. The Weston Golf Club Inc. was organized, and by 1917 a new nine-hole course had been completed along with two clay tennis courts.[38]

In November 1918, Robert Winsor made a dramatic change in ownership of his land. He turned over 422 acres to the newly formed Weston Real Estate Trust "for the purpose of holding, managing, and selling certain real estate . . ."[39] Winsor and his three surviving children were designated as trustees and owned most of the 3,000 shares. He retained 16 acres for his own use and deeded 50 acres to the Weston Golf Club.[40]

Contrary to popular belief, Winsor did not donate his property to the Weston Golf Club. The deed makes it clear that he financed the land purchase and renovations by holding a $38,500 mortgage, payable with interest. He included a clause in the deed stating that "the granted premises shall be used only for a golf course or country club" and if this purpose were to change, the property would revert to himself or his heirs.

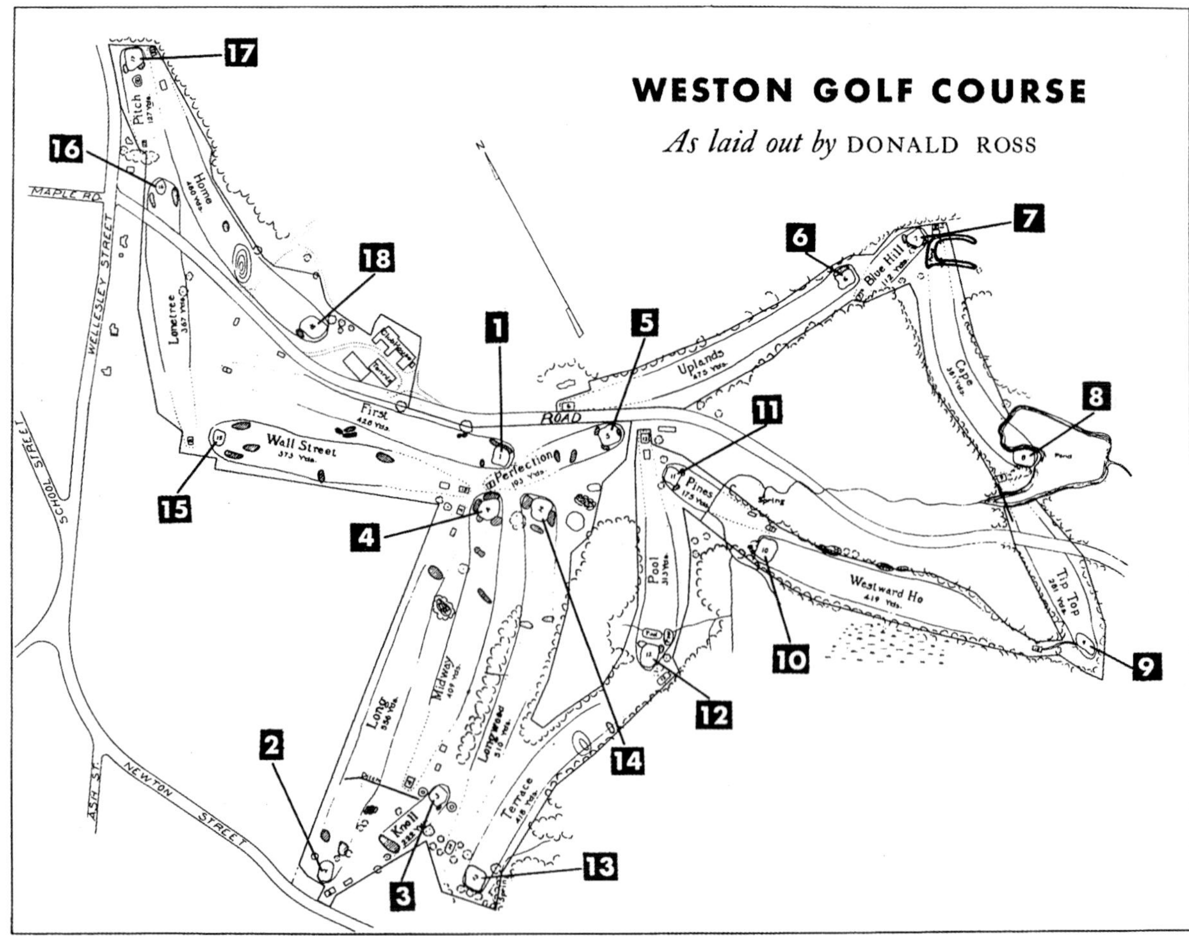

Figure 20-15. The Weston Golf Club was laid out by Scotsman Donald C. Ross, who was renowned for his course designs.

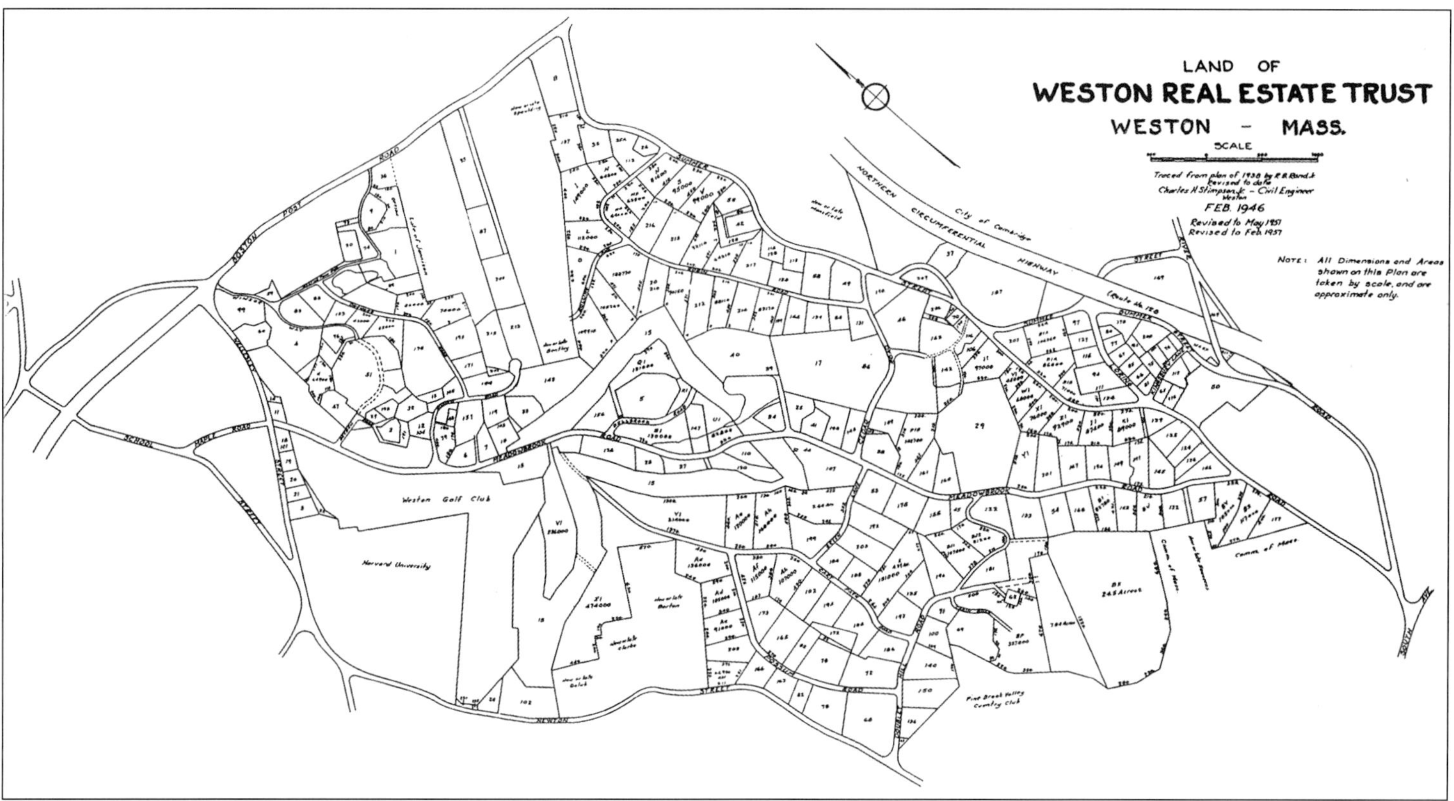

Figure 20-16. In 1910, Robert Winsor hired the Brookline landscape design firm Olmsted Brothers to lay out a road system within his estate and identify prime house sites. Eight years later he turned over 422 acres to the newly formed Weston Real Estate Trust, which sold the land gradually over the next 70 years. This map of 1946 shows house lots created up to that point within the property, which extended from Wellesley Street east to Summer Street.

After Winsor sold the land to the golf club, he moved his farm operations to the other end of the estate. The large barn was renovated into a clubhouse designed by Harold Graves, a member of the club who offered his services free of charge. Graves's design featured a graceful colonnaded porch flanked by two wings. On the second level of one wing was an open terrace covered in the summer by canvas awnings. The ell where Winsor once kept his string of Morgan horses became the ladies' dressing rooms, and another ell where the Guernseys once stood in stanchions became the men's locker room. Four bowling alleys were created on the ground floor in the former sheep pens. Here young men who caddied during the summer worked as pin setters on winter evenings. Directly in front of the clubhouse was a putting green.

The Weston Golf Club was fortunate to secure the services of Donald C. Ross to design and supervise the building of the new course. Ross, a Scotsman, has been described as "one of the world's outstanding golf architects." Horse-drawn vehicles were used for earth moving, and construction was done by men with picks and shovels. Seeding and watering were done by hand. The original nine holes included the first three and last four of the present 18-hole course. An additional nine holes, also designed by Ross, were completed in 1923, again financed by a mortgage from Winsor.

The dues schedule for the new club included an entrance fee of $30 and annual dues of $50 per family, plus a yearly golf fee of $10 per person. Golf and tennis were permitted on Sunday only after church. Not until 1929 was the Sunday rule suspended.

Ray Heist, Weston Golf Club historian, has pointed out how Winsor's resettlement of the golf course onto his land enhanced its residential value, allowing him to transform ordinary farmland into desirable residential lots. The Meadowbrook Road area is among the first examples in the country of a residential community developed around a golf course, making full use of the fairways as design elements. Heist also noted the importance of Weston Golf Club as a social center for the leaders of Weston. For many years, it was the only club in Weston at which members could have dinner. Christmas parties, dances, and organized social and athletic events brought together the town's business and professional elite.

Meadowbrook School

A second institution that enhanced the value of the Winsor land was Meadowbrook School, which moved to its present site in 1924 and changed its name from Pigeon Hill School at that time. As with the golf course, Winsor made his land available for purchase by an institution on which he and his family exerted great influence, at a time when its original location proved unsuitable. Winsor's daughter, Mary Trumbull, was president of the school's Executive Committee in 1924 and his daughter-in-law, Mrs. Alexander (Sandy) Winsor, was also a member.

The first Meadowbrook School building was designed by Allen and Collens with Harold Willis as associate architect.[41] The school originally included kindergarten through eighth grade but by 1932 had

Figure 20-17. In 1924, the Pigeon Hill School moved to a larger site within the Winsor estate and was renamed Meadowbrook School.

changed to preschool through sixth grade. When ground was broken for Meadowbrook School, the road from Wellesley Street was extended and renamed Meadowbrook Road.

The Weston Golf Club initiated a winter sports program using the school facilities. The club installed lighting on the pond for skating, built a warming shack, and used the school kitchen to prepare warm drinks and snacks. Sections of the pond were reserved for different types of skating, and "mechanical music provided an air of festivity."[42] The main event of the season was a winter carnival. The hill from Meadowbrook Road to the school property was used for sledding. Winsor built a "first class" toboggan chute with a high wooden stand at the top of the hill.[43] Toboggans holding four or five people would shoot down the hill and sweep out at the bottom. Winsor even arranged to have the slide iced. The toboggan chute was used for only a few years, in the mid-1920s.

Residential Development

Development of the Meadowbrook Road area began in earnest in the 1920s. The Weston Roads Trust was formed to build roads. All property owners were required, and are required even today, to become members of the Roads Trust and contribute to the maintenance and plowing of the roads, which are still privately owned. In 1994 the Weston Roads Trust had 185 members, assessed at $100 per acre. The trust maintains 8.25 miles of roads, including Meadowbrook, Doublet Hill, Cart Path, Possum, Green, Cedar, Farm, Robin, Dellbrook, Bryden, Dogwood, Hidden and Skating Pond Roads, and Winsor Way.

In 1922 the Weston Real Estate Trust invited architects and draftsmen from New England and New York to enter a competition for the design of a "small house in the country." The "programme" explained the goals:

> The type of house they have in mind is for a family of two where the wife does the housework, and it is assumed that both are used to refined surroundings and simple, dignified living. The character of the land is informal. . . . Factors entering into the selection will be cost, economy of operation, convenience, beauty and opportunity of enlargement.[44]

More than 100 sets of drawings were received. The judges, Robert Winsor and his three children, awarded the first prize of $1,000 to Stanley B. Parker of Boston. None of the 10 winners was a Weston resident.

Weston architect Harold S. Graves wrote about the contest in a series of articles in the *Boston Evening Transcript.* Graves noted that changes in lifestyle had changed perceptions as to what was necessary in a house:

> The majority of families in the last few years have reduced the overhead expense of housekeeping by managing without a maid servant, seeking more compact living quarters and by less entertaining of guests. Many who lived in kitchenette suites during the war are returning to the country, and experience has taught them that they can manage very comfortably with compact quarters, but, without exception, the demand is for a good-sized living room with fireplace.[45]

In his memoir *Growing Up in Weston,* Philip Coburn says the competition was designed to attract young married couples to live around the golf course. Publishing the exterior sketches and floor plans in the *Transcript* gave the Winsor development additional publicity. According to Coburn, the six houses on the golf-club side of Wellesley Street resulted from the competition.[46] At least one of these, No. 60, was designed by Harold Graves.[47]

The Weston Real Estate Trust had a small dark green–painted sales office on Meadowbrook Road and published a brochure entitled "Sites in WESTON for Large or Small Houses." This dignified, soft-sell promotional piece reflects Winsor's desire to protect the rural character of the land:

> The owners are very anxious to preserve the appearance and the atmosphere of the Country. No lots of less than two acres are sold. A very pleasant neighborhood has developed. . . . No restrictions are made in regard to the cost or size of houses built on the land. It is felt that large and small houses have the same chance for beauty, and that the people who come to this community have the perception to adapt houses to the natural beauty of the surroundings.[48]

Under a full-page picture of a waterfall is the caption "The path along the brook is open to the neighborhood but is not for sale." Pointing proudly to the two institutions that formed the core of the new neighborhood, the copy reads, "Nearly 500 acres of land surround that of the Weston Golf Club and the Meadowbrook School." The price of land was $3,000 an acre. The brochure adds, "Before land is shown, it is asked the name of prospective buyers be given the Trust." The trust has been described as "choosy" about who was allowed to purchase lots in the new development. Prospective buyers had to be of the accepted socioeconomic and religious background.

Some lots within the former Winsor estate are less than one acre, but in general Winsor voluntarily subdivided his property into parcels larger than required even under present-day regulations. The restrictions he placed on development of his estate had an influence beyond the immediate Meadowbrook area. Together with other prominent citizens, Winsor is credited with encouraging the town to adopt protective zoning. His son Sandy was on the fledgling planning board in 1924, the year the board hired prominent landscape architect Arthur A. Shurtleff to make recommendations for the first zoning ordinances.

The pace of development was slow in the 1920s. Among the earliest buyers were Thomas Cabot and his wife, Virginia Wellington Cabot, who built a stone Colonial Revival house in 1928 on Farm Road, and oil heiress "Babs" Macy Lewis, who built a house that year on Willow Road, later owned by Brandeis University.

Robert Winsor: Later Years

In his irreverent local history *Random Recollections*, Brenton H. Dickson III says that First Parish services were attended by many Kidder Peabody "young hopefuls" who had built houses in Winsor's new development. Dickson's father referred to them as "Mr. Winsor's slaves" and maintained that he could see Winsor "checking his list every Sunday to make sure they were all present."[49]

As he got older, Winsor turned increasingly to religion. In 1919 he joined with other prominent Unitarian men to found the Unitarian Laymen's League, serving on the first Executive Council. The organization of the league was completed at a convention in Springfield, Massachusetts, in April 1919. Weston sent the second largest delegation, a group of 11 men including Winsor, his son-in-law Walter H. Trumbull Jr., and Horace Sears. [50]

In 1923 Winsor contacted artist N.C. Wyeth to create a series of paintings to illustrate a book of 40 parables from the Bible. In his correspondence, Wyeth writes that "the book is to be made the best money can buy, and an edition of 10,000 to be printed to be given away to all Unitarian churches. . . . He is willing to spend $15,000 on this project."[51] The book, *Parables of Jesus,* containing the N.C. Wyeth illustrations, was finally published in 1931. In 1956, family members donated two of the Wyeth paintings to First Parish Church, where they now hang in the Parish Hall.

In the early 1920s, Kidder Peabody & Co. was involved in a major lawsuit known as the Willett-Sears Case. George W. Willett and Edmund H. Sears sued various banking firms, including Kidder Peabody, claiming they had been deprived of their controlling interest in certain companies by means of an unlawful conspiracy. The trial was closely followed in Weston because of the involvement of both the Sears and Winsor families and was a major embarrassment to Winsor, who was called upon to testify. At the time, some people thought of Winsor as sharp, if not dishonest, while others felt that he was unusually upright and loyal to family, friends, and business associates.[52]

Eleanor Winsor died in 1924. Sometime after her death, Winsor added a tower to his estate house, reached by an elevator. The one- or two-room addition was largely glass windows, allowing for panoramic views. Winsor used it as a retreat, but his

Figure 20-18. Thomas and Virginia Wellington Cabot were among the early buyers in the Meadowbrook Road area. Their home on Farm Road, called Hidden Hearth, was constructed in 1928.

Figure 20-19. By the 1920s, Robert Winsor was a senior partner at Kidder Peabody & Co., where he started his career as a clerk. At his death in 1930 it was written, "New England has suffered the loss of one of the leading bankers of the country."

Figure 20-20. Walter and Mary "Bud" Trumbull, Robert Jr. and Susan Winsor, and Alexander and Hope Winsor with their children in the 1920s.

grandchildren were allowed up there on occasion and would be rewarded with a stick of gum.[53]

The stock market crash of October 1929 was devastating to Winsor and his firm, where he was the senior active partner. Less than three months later, on January 7, 1930, Robert Winsor died of a heart attack in New York City at age 71. The governor of Massachusetts was among the many dignitaries who attended the funeral at First Parish Church. Winsor is buried in Linwood Cemetery.

The Depression brought land sales almost to a halt. A 1939 map shows that only 43 residential parcels, including those belonging to the family, had been carved out of the former estate at that time. Many of the interior roads were not completed until after World War II.The mansion was demolished about 1948. Arthur L."Bud" Coburn purchased the "broom swept cellar hole" and built a brick house on the foundation. Coburn's house was later used as the Canadian Consulate. In 1998, the Coburn house was demolished to make way for a mansion more than twice the size of Winsor's, set on a lot of less than four acres. John Winsor, Sandy's son, converted the garage on Bryden Road for his family, using doors and other materials salvaged from the main house. The connection between Winsor Way and Bryden Road was closed by planting trees.

Figure 20-21. Sport Fest at the Weston Golf Club in the mid-1920s.

The Weston Real Estate Trust was managed by Sandy Winsor until his death in 1967 and thereafter by Philip Trumbull, son of Winsor's daughter, Mary. Lots were sold by word of mouth rather than advertising. In 1986, after nearly 70 years of operation, the Winsor estate land had all been sold and the Weston Real Estate Trust was dissolved.

Later History of the Weston Golf Club

During the prosperous 1920s, the Weston Golf Club expanded its course from 9 to 18 holes, added a squash court, enlarged the clubhouse, and added living quarters for club staff.[54] Membership declined after the 1929 stock market crash and dues were harder to collect. It was difficult to attract new members, as few could afford the luxury of a country club or an expensive game like golf. A low point came at the beginning of 1933, when the club had only 195 members on active status, along with 96 on leave of absence. Dining room service was curtailed, staff reduced, and greens fees lowered.

Still struggling to survive the financial squeeze, the club suffered another setback when, on December 3, 1938, fire started in the upper level of the clubhouse. The stubborn two-alarm blaze destroyed the third floor and did substantial damage to the second. The roof collapsed and the front porch was beyond salvaging.[55] The board decided not to replace the third-floor living quarters or the porch, resulting in a less attractive building that did, however, have a new room with a ceiling high enough for a badminton court. Badminton became a popular club sport for many years.

With the U.S. entry into World War II, members resigned to enter the service. Membership again sank below 200. Not only were gasoline, tires, and various foods rationed, but there was also a severe shortage of tennis and golf balls. As an inducement to membership, the initiation fee was waived in 1944. As servicemen returned home in 1945, membership climbed to 333 and soon reached full capacity of 400. In 1953, the flourishing club paid off its last mortgage and built a much needed swimming pool, the first of many improvements. Two new golf holes and a practice area were completed in 1965. In 1966 the club discontinued the winter sports program, and the following year, paddle tennis was added to the athletic program.

Houses in the Winsor Estate Area

248 Boston Post Road (1910). Cottage built for Winsor estate superintendent Philip Spaulding and then sold in 1916 to hide-broker Owen Howe and his wife, Charlotte. The house was doubled in size in the mid-1920s with an addition by Harold Graves.

280 Boston Post Road (1851; remodeled c. 1900). Built as District School #1 and later known as the Schoolhouse on the Rock, the building was sold in 1900 to Robert Winsor and remodeled by Samuel Mead into a house used by Winsor's brother, Paul, and his family.

309 Boston Post Road (1883). Designed by Samuel Mead for the young Robert Winsor. The exterior of the house was originally covered with the dark-stained wood shingles popular in Weston at the turn of the century.

311 Boston Post Road (1892). Carriage house built by Robert Winsor and converted to a house about 1910. Preserves its original Shingle-style appearance.

4 Bryden Road. Winsor garage, built after 1911, converted to a house in 1947.

18 Cedar Road (1928). Built for Edmund Billings from designs by Harold S. Graves.

22 Conant Road (1895). Colonial Revival house built for Lyman W. Gale and his wife, Jane, who was Robert Winsor's sister.

8 Farm Road. Mid-19th-century Greek Revival farmhouse probably built for a member of the Hagar family and later part of the Winsor estate.

31 Farm Road (1928). Hidden Hearth. Stone Colonial Revival house built for Thomas D. and Virginia Wellington Cabot from designs by Winthrop Aldrich.[56] Enlarged and remodeled, 2000–01.

4 and 8 Hidden Road. Based on study of early estate maps and discussions with local residents, it appears that the Winsor duck house and henhouse were converted into the houses at 4 and 8 Hidden Road, respectively.

121 Meadowbrook Road (1929). Tudor house designed by architect Thomas Bird Epps for Vernon and Phyllis Tallman.[58]

143 Meadowbrook Road (1928–29). Built for Harold Allen from designs by architect Harold S. Graves.[59]

209 Meadowbrook Road (c. 1923, addition 1928). Frame Tudor house built by Robert Winsor for his daughter, Mary "Bud" Winsor, and her husband, Walter H. Trumbull Jr., from designs by Harold S. Graves.

279 Meadowbrook Road. This mid-19th-century Greek Revival house may have been built by John A. Lamson, who owned the farm from 1847 to 1858, or his son John Jr., who owned it from 1858 to 1864. It is generally referred to as the Bryden farmhouse after Christopher H. Bryden, farmer and milkman, who had a dairy there in the late 19th century. Bryden sold the 83-acre farm to Robert Winsor in 1898 for $24,000.

Figure 20-22. A major fire at the Weston Golf Club on December 3, 1938, destroyed the front porch and third floor. The clubhouse was rebuilt without some of the architectural amenities.

283 Meadowbrook Road. This house has become known as the Winsor Duck House. The name is puzzling because Winsor estate maps show the henhouse and duck house standing close to each other on what is now Hidden Road, where there was a small pond at the time.[60]

16 Saddle Hill Road (1911). Built for Robert Winsor's brother, Paul, and his wife, Jessie. See chapter 11.

33 Skating Pond Road. Built for Sandy Winsor's oldest son, Bancroft. On the property is a playhouse built for his mother, Hope Bancroft Winsor, when she was a child and later moved from Beverly to Skating Pond Road.

37 Skating Pond Road (c. 1917, demolished 1990s). Site of the house built by Robert Winsor for his son Alexander "Sandy" and Hope Bancroft at the time of their marriage.

18 and 22 Wellesley Street (by 1905). Houses in these locations appear on the 1905 Aspinwall and Lincoln map of the Winsor estate and were probably occupied by staff.

40, 44, 56, 60, 64, and 70 Wellesley Street. Colonial Revival houses built in the 1920s on Winsor estate land. See description of design contest in this chapter.

Partial Winsor Genealogy
(N.B.: Spouses and children in third generation listed only for Robert Winsor's children.)

Frederick Winsor (1829–1889), m. Anne Bent Ware (1830–1907), 1857
- Robert (1858–1930), m. Eleanor May Magee (1855–1924), 1883
  - Robert Jr. (1884–1944), m. Susan Revere Baker, 1919
    - Robert
    - Edith
    - Elizabeth Ware
    - Faith
  - Frederick (1889–1894)
  - Philip (1893–1918)
  - Alexander "Sandy" (1894–1966), m. Elizabeth Hope Bancroft, 1916
    - Alexander
    - Elise Hope
    - Robert Hale Bancroft
    - John Milligan
    - Philip
  - Mary Pickard "Bud" (1896–1968), m. Walter H. Trumbull Jr., 1919
    - Philip Winsor
    - Eleanor
    - Gertrude
    - Walter Henry
    - Hope
  - ____ Winsor (b. and d. 1900)
- Mary Pickard Winsor (1860–1950), unmarried
- Paul Winsor (1863–1936), m. Jessie Baldwin, 1888
  - Paul (b. 1900)
  - Felix (1901–1961)
- Annie Ware (1865–1955), m. Joseph Allen, 1900
  - Dorothea Teulon Allen (b. 1901)
  - Annie Winsor Allen (b. 1902)
  - Joseph Allen (b. 1905)
  - David Allen (b. and d. 1906)
- Jane Loring (1868–1952), m. Lyman Whitman Gale, 1895
  - Priscilla Gale (b. 1896)
  - Emma Whitman Gale (b. 1900)
  - Winsor (b. 1901)
- Elizabeth Ware (1870–1960), m. Henry Greenleaf Pearson, 1898
  - Anne Winsor Pearson (b. 1899)
  - Theodore Pearson (b. 1903)
  - Mary Pearson (b. and d. 1906)
  - Robert Winsor Pearson (b. 1910)
  - Henry Greenleaf Pearson Jr. (b. 1912)
- Frederick Winsor (1872–1940), m. Mary Anna Lee Paine, 1894
  - Charles Paine Winsor (1895–1951)
  - Dorothy Winsor (b. 1896)
  - Frederick Winsor (1900–1958)
  - John Bryant Winsor (1903–1919)
  - Theresa Winsor (b. 1904)

60 Wellesley Street (1925). Colonial Revival house designed by Harold Graves for Elliott Greene 3rd, who was an engineer.

4 Willow Road (1928). Brick and stone mansion built for Burnham and "Babs" Macy Lewis from designs by architect Eric Kibbon. Estimated cost listed on Weston building permit No. 70 was $100,000.

One Winsor Way (c. 1889). Colonial Revival house constructed for Robert Winsor, who built No. 10 about the same time. Winsor deeded this house to his mother in 1893.

10 Winsor Way (c. 1889). Late Queen Anne/Colonial Revival house constructed for Robert Winsor. Robert's father, Frederick Winsor, died in 1889; and his widowed mother, Anne Bent Ware Winsor, and siblings moved from Winchester to this house. Winsor deeded No. 10 to his mother in 1890. The 1893 directory lists five siblings—Mary, Annie, Elizabeth, Frederick, and Jane—living with his mother at Central Avenue (now Boston Post Road) and Wellesley Street.

29 Winsor Way. Site of the house built about 1920 by Robert Winsor Sr. for his son Robert Jr. and his wife, Susan Baker Winsor, and demolished about 1987–88.

63 Winsor Way. Site of the Robert Winsor mansion, demolished about 1948. Present house, the third on the site, was built in 2000–01.

Notes

1. Haven, Charles P., "Energetic Eighties Produced Group of Men, College Friends, Who Built Banking, Telephone and Transportation Interests of City, State and Nation," *Boston Sunday Post,* January 12, 1930.
2. "Robert Winsor: Hub Leader Was World Figure for 50 Years," *Boston American,* January 7, 1930, and "Robert Winsor," *Transcript,* January 7, 1930 (obituaries).
3. "Descendants of Rev. Henry Ware, Jr." (typescript, 1965).
4. Lyman, Mrs. Arthur, "Mrs. Frederick Winsor, an address made to the Older Classes in Miss Winsor's School, Monday, May 27, 1907" (privately printed, 1907).
5. "Funeral Services Will be Held Tomorrow for Winsor," *Boston Herald,* January 8, 1930.
6. "Men of the Hour on State Street," *Boston Post,* January 10, 1904.
7. Horace Sears to Andrew Fiske, 1883, as quoted in *WHSB,* March 1984, 3. Winsor's purchase is recorded in MCRD 1643/350. He purchased 20 acres from Davis and sold most of it back to Ellen Sears, reserving a house lot for himself.

8. Robert Winsor's nephew Winsor Gale, who years later served as church treasurer, recalled that every year expenses would exceed income and the deficit would be picked up by Winsor, Horace Sears, and one other estate owner whose identity he could not recall.
9. "Funeral Services Will be Held Tomorrow for Winsor," *Boston Herald*, January 8, 1930.
10. *Boston Post*, January 10, 1904.
11. *Boston Sunday Post*, January 12, 1930.
12. "Funeral Services Will be Held Tomorrow for Winsor," *Boston Herald*, January 8, 1930.
13. Ibid.
14. "Robert Winsor," *Boston Herald*, January 8, 1930.
15. PWF interview with Winsor Gale, December 1995.
16. MCRD 1784/237 (Francis B. Sears to RW, 1887) and 1783/129 (Hiram Logan to RW, 1887). Also Plan Book 9B, plan 57, "Plan of the heirs of Luke Brooks" (1859). The two houses are now numbered 10 Winsor Way (Anne Ware Winsor's house) and One Winsor Way (which was originally accessed from Wellesley Street).
17. Oral history by Winsor Gale, Weston Public Library, 10.
18. Middlesex School archives.
19. MCRD 2686/180 (C.H. Bryden to RW, 1898) and Plan Book 112/32 (1898). The Bryden farmhouse remains at 279 Meadowbrook Road.
20. Attribution to Russell from WHC files.
21. *Boston Sunday Herald*, May 11, 1902.
22. 1903 newspaper article (no publication name or date), Harvard University Archives, #B5122 (Robert Winsor file).
23. Frederick Law Olmsted National Historic Site, Brookline, Massachusetts, Job #3994, #4, Sheet 1, "Topographical Plan of Land in Weston owned by Robert Winsor, Esq.," January 1904; additions June 1914.
24. Olmsted Papers, Library of Congress, Job #03994, Microfilm Reel 232, September 25, 1910, and November 23, 1916.
25. MCRD 3028/552. Plan Book 142/39. Also 3246/62. Plan Book 162/1.
26. Olmsted Papers, op. cit., March 20, 1910.
27. According to newspaper reports, Winsor began constructing the four-acre artificial pond in November 1909 (*WDFPT*, November 19, 1909).
28. *WDFPT*, November 16, 1910.
29. *WDFPT*, December 13, 1910. In the last major communication from Olmsted Brothers to Winsor, in August 1912, the firm provided a plan designating prime house sites on topographical high points, adding that "we have not indicated house sites for the lowland areas because those areas offer little attraction for high class residences" and could be developed later without difficulty (August 19, 1912).
30. A follow-up report in the Olmsted files, dated November 23, 1916, notes that Spaulding was opening up the main roadways along the center lines specified in the Olmsted plans of six years earlier.
31. Campbell, Robert, "Forgotten Utopias," *Boston Globe Magazine*, May 21, 1995. See also *WDFPT* December 22 and 29, 1911, on the newly organized Boston Dwelling House Company:

> "The proposition is neither a charity nor a money-making venture. It is an honest, consistent effort to help people who cannot pay . . . a high rent, nor [buy] homes to bring up their families in an environment that will conduce (sic.) to good citizenship." 12/29/11

32. Interview with Philip Trumbull, January 1996.
33. Coburn, Philip, *Growing Up in Weston*, 36.
34. Ibid.
35. *WDFPT*, Weston Anniversary Edition, June 15, 16, 17, 1913, 4.
36. Biographical information on the three Winsor boys from Harvard University Archives, reports of classes of 1905, 1915, and 1916.
37. Minutes, Weston Golf Club Executive Committee. For a complete history of the Weston Golf Club, see also Ray Heist's "A History of Weston Golf Club" (several typescripts, undated, and a printed version, undated).
38. When incorporated in 1916, officers were Robert Winsor, president; B. Loring Young, vice president; F. Winthrop Batchelder, secretary; and Brenton H. Dickson Jr., treasurer.
39. MCRD 4239/481–86 and 4276/202.
40. MCRD 4200/225, 227, 228 and Plan Book 266/13.
41. Olmsted National Historic Site Job #3994, includes plans for Meadowbrook School dated February 4, 1924, and January 23, 1926.
42. Heist, Ray, "A History of Weston Golf Club," op. cit.
43. PWF interview with Winsor Gale, December 1995.
44. Graves, Harold S., "A Prize Plan for Those Interested in 'A Small House in the Country,'" *Boston Evening Transcript*, June 24, 1922, part 4, page 3. See also July 1 (2nd-prize winner) and July 8, 1922 (3rd-prize winner), and December 20, 1924.
45. Ibid.
46. Coburn, *GUIW*, 56. Coburn puts the number of houses at seven because Winsor sold seven lots. However, only six houses were built, now numbered 40, 44, 56, 60, 64, and 70 Wellesley Street. One house, No. 64, is built on a double lot. All these houses were built between about 1922 and 1926. See also MCRD, Plan Book 321, Plan 37 (for lots at 56–70 Wellesley Street).
47. Plans in possession of owner.
48. Weston Golf Club archives, undated brochure.
49. Dickson, *RR*, 145. According to Dickson, the Kidder Peabody contingent shrank noticeably in size after Winsor died.
50. *The Christian Register*, April 17, 1919, and *Unitarian Year Book*, American Unitarian Association, July 1, 1919, to June 30, 1920.
51. Wyeth, Betsy James, ed. *The Wyeths, The Letters of N.C. Wyeth*, 1901–1945 (Boston, 1971), 696–97 and 721. In another letter, dated 1926, Wyeth describes meeting with Winsor to discuss the book, which was published in 1931 by David McKay Co. of Philadelphia and was called *Parables of Jesus*, with S. Parkes Cadman as author.
52. The jury trial in 1923–24 resulted in a judgment of more than $10 million for the plaintiffs. In the end, however, only one dollar was paid because of a release signed when the original deal was made. Although Kidder Peabody was legally protected from paying damages, the company was branded as guilty of unethical conduct. Robert Winsor's nephew Winsor Gale has pointed out that rules of business practice were different then, and businessmen made money in ways that would be illegal today.
53. Interview with Philip Trumbull, op. cit.
54. Heist, Ray, *op.cit.*
55. Waltham newspaper, as quoted in Ray Heist's "The Depression, the fire and a war," part of his history of the Weston Golf Club, op. cit.
56. Cabot, Thomas, *Beggar on Horseback: The Autobiography of Thomas D. Cabot* (Boston: David Godine, 1979), 51. Estimated cost of the house listed on Weston building permit #153 was $60,000.
57. Town of Weston building permit #149 of November 1928, Roland B. Rand, builder, $12,000 estimated cost listed.
58. Town of Weston building permit #96 of March 1928, lists the estimated cost at $30,000.
59. Plans dated March 1928. Estimated cost listed on Weston building permit #112 was $20,000.
60. Maps located at the Frederick Law Olmsted National Historic Site in Brookline. A possible explanation for the name is suggested in the oral history by Weston Blake, who lived in the nearby Bryden farmhouse until about 1912. Blake recalled a "duck house" where his father, George Frank Blake, "hung the ducks that he'd shot down in North Carolina with Charlie and Johnny Paine and Dr. Van Nuys, and hung them up for the winter . . ." Interview with Weston Blake, January 30, 1983 (Oral History Project, WPL), 3.

Figure 21-1. Hundreds of canoes gathered at the Boston Athletic Association boathouse about 1904 for the annual field day for water sports. As leisure time increased and public transportation improved, the Lakes District in Weston, Newton, and Waltham became a major recreational resource for the Boston metropolitan area. By 1920, the Metropolitan District Commission estimated that there were 6,000 canoes berthed along this stretch of the Charles River.

CHAPTER 21

Down by the Riverside

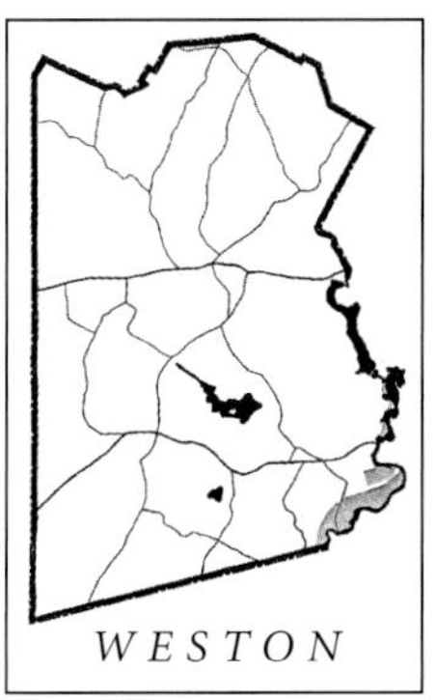

Public perception of the Charles River has changed over the centuries, as people with different economic needs and social values have used it to provide food, drinking water, transportation, waterpower, and recreation. In his history of Weston, Lamson reports that the Indians had their settlements along the banks of the Charles River, although according to Lamson these settlements were located not in Weston but farther up along the shore. Early settlers farmed the fertile valleys and logged the riverbanks. Beginning in the late 1700s, dams were built in neighboring towns to provide waterpower for new industries. One of these, the Moody Street dam in Waltham, flooded land upstream to create the Lakes District in Weston and Newton. Histories of the Charles River note the total lack of concern during this period for the ecological health of the waterway.

In the late 1800s, as the river's economic value for farmers and manufacturers declined, its importance as a scenic and recreational resource was fast increasing. The need to preserve open space within the rapidly growing urban environment was recognized beginning in the 1870s with the creation of the Boston park system. In the 1890s, the Metropolitan Park Commission was established and the Charles River Reservation created. Over the next 40 years, the river was heavily used for canoeing, boating, swimming, and fishing. So active was the Riverside area of Weston and Auburndale that it inspired a popular song, "Down by the Riverside," based on the old Negro spiritual "I'm gonna lay down my sword and shield, down by the riverside."[1]

Between 1930 and 1970, as development increased rapidly throughout the region, the Charles River suffered a decline. Sewage and industrial wastes polluted the water. The concrete ramps and overpasses of Route 128 and the Massachusetts Turnpike exemplify mid-century priorities. Recreational facilities at Riverside and Norumbega Park closed. Fortunately, the Charles River Reservation was a direct beneficiary of the environmental movement, which began in the early 1970s. Through the efforts of public agencies and private groups such as the Charles River Watershed Association, water quality has been significantly improved and recreational use of the river is increasing. Canoes can be rented on the Newton side of Weston Bridge. Boats still leave from the Moody Street bridge for regular trips through the Lakes District—a unique way of looking at Weston and one of its most significant natural resources.

Figure 21-2. This portrait of Rachel Alden Kingsbury was taken in 1889 when she was 90 years old.

Early History of the Area

In the late 18th and early 19th centuries, most of Weston's riverfront land was part of three large farms belonging to the Kingsbury, Seaverns, and Slack families. Elijah Kingsbury (1751–1831) took over the former Thomas Upham farm on Loring and River Roads about 1780.[2] He married Sarah Lamson in 1797 and had four children, including a son, John (1803–1859), who inherited the farm. John's son, Otis Kingsbury (b. 1835), built his own house on Loring Road sometime after mid-century, along with a second small residence, a barn, and a workshop where he built a buggy every winter to earn extra cash.[3]

In 1814 the Boston Manufacturing Company built the Moody Street dam in Waltham to provide power for a new kind of textile mill, the first in America to perform all the operations necessary to convert raw cotton into finished textiles.[4] The dam was raised in 1815, creating a higher millpond and flooding more acreage upriver. Kingsbury hayfields

Figure 21-3. Otis Kingsbury is pictured here with his wife, Sarah, and daughter, Emma. His farm was along the Charles River. In 1912, he made it into the newspaper for producing a vine of eight squash weighing 96 pounds.

HERBERT SEAVERNS,
Florist
202 MOODY STREET, - - WALTHAM.
Plants and Fancy Pottery-ware. *Seeds and Bulbs.*
Decorations for all occasions.
GREENHOUSES, EAST NEWTON STREET, - - WESTON.

Figure 21-5. As the Seaverns farmland along the river was gradually sold off, some members of the family began growing fresh flowers in greenhouses. Such perishable items were profitable and required little land.

became Kingsbury Cove, one of a series of coves and inlets along a bulge in the Charles River that became known as the Lakes District.

A second large farm along the Charles, shown on the 1794 Kingsbury map as belonging to J. Seaverns, stayed in the Seaverns family for another century. When the Boston & Worcester (later Boston & Albany) tracks were laid in 1834, Samuel Seaverns was so opposed to trains passing through his land that he could not be persuaded to enter a railroad car and would turn his back on the trains as they passed. As town historian Daniel Lamson put it, "The compensation he received . . . was not considered by him as an equivalent for the intrusion upon his property."[5]

Seaverns's son Manley must have overcome his father's distaste for the omnipresent railroad, as he built his own house on Park Road abutting the tracks and worked as a conductor for the B & A. Manley and his brothers, Ralph and Stanley, inherited Samuel's 75-acre farm.[6] After much of their land was taken as part of the metropolitan park system, the Seavernses raised flowers in greenhouses next to their homes. Another piece of the original Seaverns

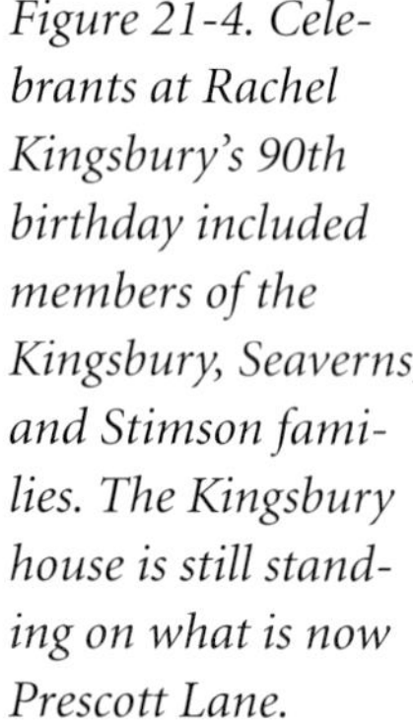

Figure 21-4. Celebrants at Rachel Kingsbury's 90th birthday included members of the Kingsbury, Seaverns, and Stimson families. The Kingsbury house is still standing on what is now Prescott Lane.

farm was sold to Francis Blake, son-in-law of Charles Townsend Hubbard. Blake bought 69 acres along South Avenue and Park Road from William Seaverns in 1887 to expand his Keewaydin estate, which is described in chapter 23.[7]

The Slack farm was located along the river near the Wellesley town line. Manufacturer Charles Townsend Hubbard bought the 214-acre farmstead in 1867 to use as a country retreat. Information on the Hubbard estate can be found in chapter 22.

Metropolitan Park Movement

In the early 1890s, C.T. Hubbard's son, Charles Wells Hubbard, and his brother-in-law and fellow conservationist, Francis Blake, became involved in a movement to protect the Charles River as part of a proposed metropolitan park system serving the greater Boston area. During this period, growing industrialization and urbanization throughout the country fueled public support for parks, which were viewed as a necessary contrast to the artificiality of city life. Parks provided urban residents with a place to escape from the crowded and stressful environment of the city. They were also promoted for their public health benefit in protecting a pure drinking water supply. The parks movement coincided with the increasing interest among all classes in outdoor sports such as sailing, bicycling, baseball, and lawn tennis. Hand in hand with the new athleticism came an appreciation of the beauty of the natural environment, fueled by the work of landscape painters and the popularity of the camera as a way to record the visual landscape.

Proposals for a metropolitan Boston park system date back at least to 1869, when Robert Morris Copeland outlined a park system that extended west as far as Newton Corner. The push to establish a metropolitan system was continued by Ernest W. Bowditch, his associate and the future brother-in-law of Charles Wells Hubbard. Bowditch, an engineering graduate of MIT, took over Copeland's landscape gardening practice after Copeland's death in 1874.[8] The following year, the 24-year-old Bowditch published a two-page pamphlet, "Rural Parks of Boston," which included a plan for a metropolitan system. The Bowditch plan has been called "a most impressive achievement and one that was not equaled—in metropolitan planning, at least—until 1893."[9] Over the next two decades, however, public officials concentrated on construction of parks within the Boston city limits, including Frederick Law Olmsted's famous "emerald necklace." When the city park system was close to completion, public attention was again directed to the need for coordinated regional action.

In the 1890s, the push for a metropolitan park system was led by landscape architect Charles Eliot (1859–1897), son of Harvard President Charles William Eliot and graduate of the Harvard class of 1882. Eliot apprenticed with the Olmsted firm from 1883 to 1885, traveled in Europe for a year, and in 1886 opened his own office practicing the infant profession of landscape architecture. From 1893 until his death in 1897, Eliot practiced with Frederick Law Olmsted and his son, John Charles, in the partnership of Olmsted, Olmsted and Eliot.

By the early 1890s, Eliot was publicly urging lovers of nature to rally to preserve open spaces near their doors. Eliot identified sites "in daily danger of utter destruction" and warned that the larger metropolitan region threatened shortly to become "a vast desert of houses, factories and stores, spreading over and overwhelming the natural features of the

Figure 21-6. The landmark 1893 Boston Metropolitan Park Report included this photograph of the Charles River taken by Weston estate owner Charles Wells Hubbard.

landscape."[10] He argued that open space was as important to urban communities as sewage treatment, water, or highways:

> Local breathing spaces, and the existence of pleasant features of natural scenery in the neighborhood, are really as essential to the moral and physical health of a community as the absolutely utilitarian improvements that are usually given the precedence.[11]

In 1891 Eliot founded the Trustees of Public Reservations, now called the Trustees of Reservations, a nonprofit conservation organization that has since protected more than 2,500 acres in the Charles River Valley.[12] In 1891, the trustees brought together Boston park officials, leaders of neighboring towns, and organizations such as the Appalachian Mountain Club. The meeting spawned the Metropolitan Park Commission and the first metropolitan system of parks in America.[13] Along with journalist Sylvester Baxter, Eliot is considered the father of the Metropolitan Park Commission and served as its landscape architect until his death at the young age of 37.

Charles W. Hubbard and Francis Blake were key landowners in the area of the future Charles River Reservation and were involved, early on, in lobbying on behalf of preservation. After the Metropolitan Park bill authorizing appointment of a temporary study commission was passed in the legislature in the spring of 1892, Charles Eliot contacted Blake for help in illustrating the commission's report:

> . . . I am in hopes that you will . . . allow the use of some of your plates of scenery near Boston. Anything on Charles River will be particularly welcome. It is the commission's purpose to show . . . something of the good things which still exist near town.[14]

Figure 21-7. This photograph was taken from Charles W. Hubbard's home on Orchard Avenue. In the foreground, hidden by a row of evergreens, are the tracks of the Boston and Albany Railroad. Between the tracks and Park Road is the 19-acre parcel that Hubbard donated to the town in late 1892. The gift protected Hubbard's view but also began the process of preserving the banks of the Charles River for public use.

A photograph of the river credited to Hubbard appears in the landmark 1893 report. A few years later, in 1896, Blake was asked to testify in favor of the bill authorizing the Metropolitan Park Commission to purchase open space along the river.[15]

Weston Park

Hubbard and Blake also donated or sold at discounted prices large tracts of their own land along the river for park and recreation purposes. The first transfer occurred in late 1892, when Hubbard offered the town of Weston 19 acres bordering the Charles for a town park. Weston Park was the first major public open space in this small country town and the largest ever designated as parkland. The deed imposed restrictions lasting 1,000 years, during which time no buildings, viaducts, embankments, or any other structures were to be erected above ground level within the park, except for the usual park structures. The benefit to the neighbors was clearly spelled out:

> . . . .in order that...Francis Blake, Livingston Cushing and Robert D. Andrews . . . [and successor owners] . . . may have benefit . . . for light, air, prospect and every other advantage that may be derived from the . . . land being so kept open.[16]

Weston Park was accepted at a special town meeting held on Saturday, December 31, 1892, at 4 P.M. Critics at the time questioned the timing and motivation of Hubbard's gift. An article in the *Boston Herald* on January 1, 1893, suggested the reason:

> The move is taken as a checkmate to the plans of the Boston and Albany Railroad Company, which intended crossing this land, and, by the construction of an embankment from 40 to 60 feet high, ruining the view from the many fine estates and disfiguring the banks of the river.[17]

The next day's Boston *Traveller* provided further details, including the prominent role of Francis Blake, then one of three selectmen. At the meeting, Blake noted that the railroad tracks could be rebuilt along another route that would not spoil this beautiful bit of river scenery.[18] The railroad threatened to contest the park as illegal because of insufficient notice to voters and "manifest collusions" to prevent the railroad from using a course already filed with the railroad commission. Blake countered by offering to personally pay any legal costs incurred by the town in accepting the gift.

Blake objected to charges that the park was a boondoggle for the benefit of adjacent property owners. In a letter of January 3, 1893, to F.T. Fuller, author of the *Traveller* article, Blake defends his honor:

> My only regret in the matter is that you should believe me capable of using my influence for the

furtherance of a scheme which was not for the general benefit of the Town and State as well as for the particular benefit of a few of your fellow townsmen.[19]

Also speaking at the December 31 town meeting was Sylvester Baxter, influential journalist for the *Boston Herald* and secretary of the temporary metropolitan park commission. A few days later, Baxter wrote an article for the *Boston Herald* entitled "Preserving Charles River Scenery" in which he praised the town's acceptance of the gift of land as a "notable beginning" toward the goal of public ownership of the banks of the Charles.[20]

Hubbard continued his own personal preservation campaign by selling a total of 42 acres to the City of Newton in 1893, at a price reported to be half its assessed value.[21] This land, which included a mile of riverfront just across the Park Street bridge from Weston, is now part of the Leo J. Martin Golf Course.

Metropolitan Park Commission in Weston

Many Weston residents were considerably less enthusiastic about the metropolitan park plan and the implications of public ownership of sizable expanses of parkland. In April 1893, while the bill to establish the Metropolitan Park Commission was still pending before the legislature, Weston voted to oppose its passage at a hotly contested town meeting. A subsequent newspaper article entitled "Weston Wants State Parks, But Not the Metropolitan Plan" explained concerns about taxes and interference with local self-government.

Despite Weston's lack of support, the Metropolitan Park Commission (MPC) was permanently established by an act of the legislature in June 1893. The original bill provided that Boston, Cambridge, 10 other cities, and 23 towns including Weston be part of the Metropolitan Park District. One of Eliot's recommendations, never implemented, was for a major wilderness reservation along the Charles River and Stony Brook from Prospect Hill in Waltham to Doublet Hill in Weston.[22]

The first step in implementing the metropolitan system was the opening of the public reservations at Middlesex Fells and Blue Hills. By 1895 the MPC began to focus on the Riverside area of the Charles, because the western sector had not yet been provided with a large and accessible public open space. These four miles of the Charles were already heavily used for boating and, in winter, ice skating. In 1896, the Metropolitan Park Commission filed a plan for the taking of land in Weston for the Charles River Reservation.[23]

In general, the takings consisted of a strip of riverbank from Waltham to Wellesley, of sufficient width to preserve the natural beauty of the river view. But at the south end of Weston, the reservation was expanded to include all of the Seaverns farmland between the Boston and Albany Railroad tracks, Park Street, and the Charles River. Thirty years later, this property became part of the golf course. The total area of Metropolitan Park takings was 77 acres.[24] Of Weston's 2.7 miles of riverfront, more than two miles were included within the reservation.[25]

By 1903, the Metropolitan Park Commission had acquired more than 9,000 acres throughout the region.[26] A report that year by its landscape architects, Olmsted Brothers, stated that the commission had been remarkably successful in acquiring the reservation land recommended a decade earlier, except for important gaps like Doublet Hill in Weston. They noted that Doublet Hill had acquired additional significance because it linked the Charles River Reservation to the holdings of the Metropolitan Water Board, which had just completed building the Weston Aqueduct and Reservoir. The park commission was never successful in acquiring either Doublet Hill or Prospect Hill in Waltham for a wilderness reservation in the western district comparable in size to Blue Hills or Middlesex Fells.

Weston Bridge

For decades, local leaders protested that the tax burden of the metropolitan system fell disproportionately on Weston. The town's point of view was clearly expressed in the controversy over whether the town should contribute toward a wider bridge needed to relieve the traffic congestion generated by the popularity of the Charles River Reservation.

The 1903 town report recounts the history of Weston Bridge beginning in 1849, when Newton and Weston jointly built a stone bridge across the Charles at South Avenue. Not long afterward, the Weston half of the bridge collapsed and was replaced by a wooden structure. In 1889 the town appropriated money to rebuild the bridge, and a committee recommended that Newton and Weston join together to build a completely new structure for the convenience and safety of those who passed under it by canoe, as well

Figure 21-8. In the mid-19th century, Newton and Weston joined together to build a stone bridge across the Charles River at what is now South Avenue. The Weston side of the bridge collapsed and was replaced by a wooden structure.

Figure 21-9. Weston later rebuilt its side of the bridge in stone. Photographs of Weston Bridge like this one in 1892 show a clear difference in the stonework.

as over it. The City of Newton decided that its side of the bridge might well stand another 40 years and declined the offer. Weston proceeded to reproduce its half of the original stone bridge.[27]

The 1903 town report pointed out that the 21-foot-wide bridge was still in perfect condition and wide enough for normal weekday use. The problem was that on Sundays and holidays in the boating season, special police officers had to be employed to keep the bridge from being blocked by pedestrians who paused to enjoy the view of river life:

> . . . there are about four thousand canoes berthed in the various public and private boat-houses between Riverside and Waltham. It is therefore

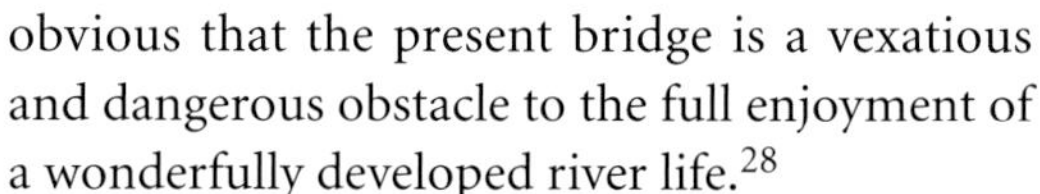

> obvious that the present bridge is a vexatious and dangerous obstacle to the full enjoyment of a wonderfully developed river life.[28]

Proposals to build a new bridge paid for by Newton and Weston were opposed by both communities. They argued that the bridge was in good condition and sufficiently wide for ordinary teaming, driving, and foot traffic, and furthermore, the vast majority of those hanging around the bridge on Sundays were nonresidents. Lawyer Samuel C. Bennett, a South Avenue resident who argued the case for the town, asserted that Weston was already contributing more than its share, per capita, to the metropolitan park system.[29] Not only that, but the town had a population of only 1,834 inhabitants in nearly 17 square miles, or more than 5.5 acres for every man, woman, and child; therefore, "Weston does not need the Metropolitan Park System . . ."[30]

The town's argument must have been heard because the picturesque 19th-century stone arched bridge stood until 1916. That year, a reinforced concrete triple-arched bridge was opened to traffic.[31] An unusual feature of the design was the overhanging sidewalks, which projected over eight feet beyond the spandrels to provide plenty of room for Sunday spectators.

Recreational Facilities along the Charles: the Boston Athletic Association

Between 1893 and 1897, three major recreational facilities were established along the Charles River in

Figure 21-10. The picturesque stone bridge was replaced in 1916 by a reinforced concrete version shown in this photograph of canoeist Hazel Kingsbury. The concrete bridge has since been replaced. (c. 1924 photo)

Weston and Newton. Norumbega Park on the Newton side of the river was devoted to amusements, while the two facilities in Weston emphasized organized sports and physical fitness. These "recreation grounds" can be seen as an outgrowth of the turn-of-the-century progressive movement and have similarities to "reform parks" established in cities during this period.[32] The principal purpose was to organize the increasing leisure time of urbanites and to encourage them to participate in sports and games as an antidote to the physical inactivity of office and factory work.

In March 1893, Francis Blake agreed to sell the Boston Athletic Association (BAA) 20 acres along the Charles River in Weston, reportedly at a favorable price, to be used as a summer outdoor sporting facility. The amount of land was later increased to almost 25 acres.[33] Blake was an outdoorsman, athlete, and early supporter of the association, which had been organized in 1887 "to encourage all manly sports, and promote physical culture." By 1892, the private, all-male, distinctly upper-class club had 2,250 members, a clubhouse at the corner of Blagden and Exeter Streets in Boston, and a boathouse at the foot of Chestnut Street on Beacon Hill. The BAA is perhaps best known as the sponsor of the annual 26-mile Boston Marathon, an event initiated just after the first modern Olympic Games in Athens, Greece, in 1896.

Initial plans for the outdoor facility in Weston were drawn by Ernest W. Bowditch and published in the *Boston Journal* in early 1893.[34] They show a football field, baseball diamond, bowling green, quarter-mile bicycle and running track, grandstand, boathouse, tennis courts, bathhouses, and a clubhouse pavilion. By 1894, the boathouse was open for members, who

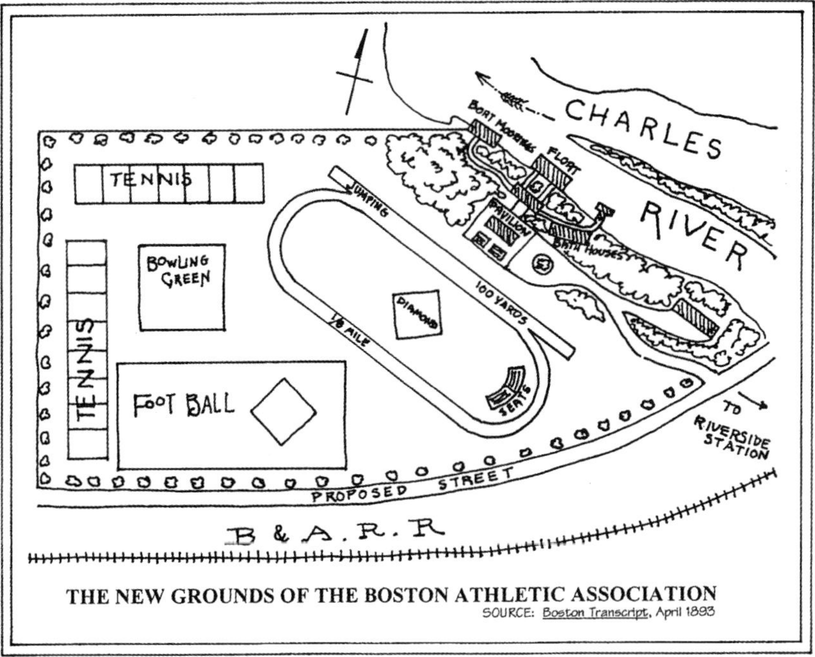

Figure 21-11. In 1893, the Boston Athletic Association bought land along the Charles River in Weston to be used as an outdoor recreation grounds for its members. This plan shows facilities for tennis, lawn bowling, football, baseball, track, and boating.

Figure 21-12. Boston University purchased the Boston Athletic Association property in 1927 and renamed it Nickerson Field. It was used by BU for home football games until 1953. Football players lived here and commuted by train to classes in Boston.

Figure 21-13. The Boston Athletic Association later built a gun club house for trapshooting.

could berth their canoes here for $2 a year.[35] By the early 20th century, the BAA had a gun club house used for trap shooting on Saturdays and holidays.

The property lay across the river from Riverside Station and was connected by a footbridge. Carriages had to use the bridge at South Avenue to reach any of the Auburndale train stations, a driving distance of at least a mile. In 1896, using mostly private funds, Blake constructed a substantial steel-truss bridge from the BAA property to Newton. At the same time, he built Riverside Road, which ran from the bridge to the entrance of his estate.[36]

In 1927 Boston University purchased the Boston Athletic Association property and renamed it Nickerson Field.[37] Varsity football players lived here and were given five round-trip tickets a week to take the train into Boston to attend classes.[38] Bleachers were erected in 1930 and the field was used for BU home games until 1953, when the school purchased Braves Field in Allston.[39] During their last season in Weston, football players reportedly dismantled the vacant boathouse and used the wood for bonfires before each home game.[40]

Riverside Recreation Grounds: Early Years, 1896–1914

In 1896 Charles W. Hubbard proposed a plan "to foster Outdoor Sport" by providing "Youth of the Metropolitan District with a Splendid Reservation on the Banks of the Charles for All Forms of Athletic Exercise."[41] His idea was to build athletic fields, a swimming pool, and a boathouse and operate the recreation grounds as an association of clubs, each with 20 to 40 members united by school or social affiliation.

In support of the elaborate plan, Hubbard enlisted the endorsement of prominent Boston leaders including the mayors of Boston, Cambridge, and Newton; the presidents of Harvard, MIT, and Boston University; the heads of Boston and suburban schools districts; and the chairman and secretary of the state board of health.[42] He wanted the Metropolitan Park Commission to acquire the land and work with him in developing the facilities. The MPC declined to participate and Hubbard proceeded at his own expense, acquiring 40 acres with a half mile of riverfront from the Seaverns family.[43] Riverside Recreation Grounds, popularly known as The Rec, opened on September 25, 1897, with a swimming and diving contest refereed by Hubbard himself.[44] The next year, Hubbard offered to sell the facility at cost to the Metropolitan Park Commission but again his proposition was declined.[45]

The main building at The Rec was a U-shaped, shingled structure. Both legs of the U were two stories high, while the base was three stories. The 50-meter swimming pool was surrounded on three sides by this building. The restaurant, dance pavilion, two bowling alleys, and dressing rooms for the pool were located on the ground floor. By 1900, there were storage racks for 300 boats. Upstairs were more dressing rooms and lockers, 14 bedrooms, 16 club rooms (meeting rooms rented to local canoe clubs by the year), and a 200-foot balcony overlooking the river. Patrons could dine on the balcony while watching canoeists and steam trains on the B & A's High-

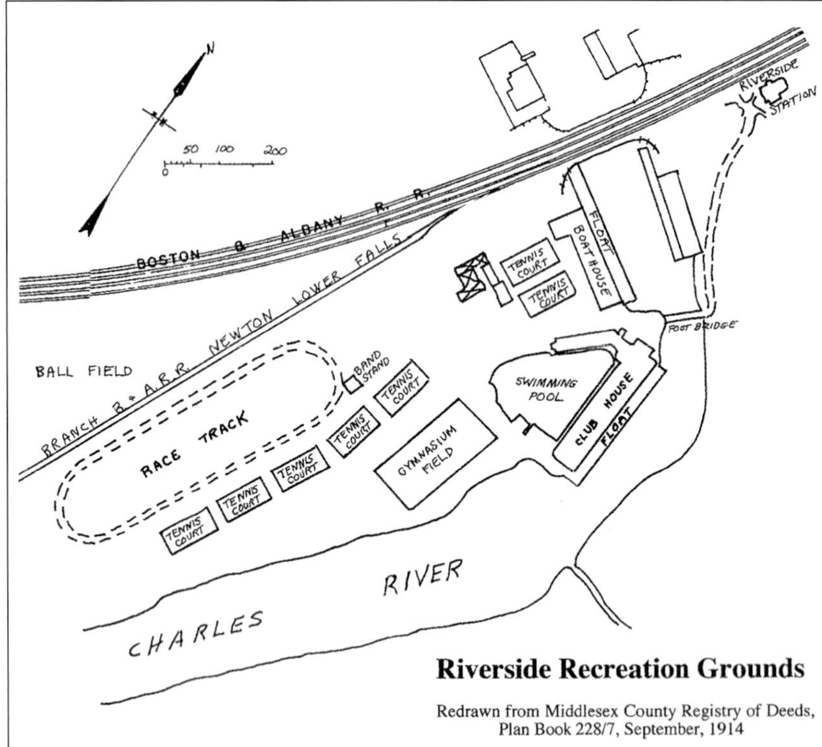

Figure 21-14. Charles W. Hubbard developed Riverside Recreation Grounds, which had tennis courts, ball fields, a boathouse, a track, and one of the largest swimming pools in New England. This plan dates to 1914, when Hubbard gave The Rec to the Metropolitan District Commission.

Figure 21-15. The main Riverside Recreation Grounds clubhouse is shown here about 1904. Canoes could be rented for 20 cents an hour and boat racks for five dollars a year. Notice the 11-man canoe in the foreground.

land Branch line. A separate boathouse was available for junior members, and an annex included racks for 120 more boats.

In the early years, annual memberships cost $10, or $5 for students. Single-day tickets were available for 25 cents.[46] Bathing suits and towels could be rented for 10 and 5 cents. Patrons could berth their own boats here by the year or rent canoes, rowboats, and even a 17-paddle, 10-passenger war canoe. Bedrooms could be rented for 35 cents a night or $3 a week. At the turn of the century, The Rec was managed by James B. Knowlton, with Herman Boos, the gymnastics instructor at MIT, as director of games and sports.

The swimming pool was equipped with springboards and a diving tower with platforms at 5, 10, 15, and 25 feet above the water.[47] The spring-fed pool was pumped out frequently and refilled with clear, cool water flowing in through the gravel bottom. An 1898 promotional brochure boasted of six gravel tennis courts commanding a beautiful view of the river and informed subscribers that they could invite ladies to play on Court No. 1. The brochure lists other amenities: a quarter-mile cinder track; fields for match and practice games of football, baseball and basketball; a large field for pole vaulting, jumping, and putting shot; and an open-air gymnasium. Instruction was available in gymnastics and swimming. The restaurant at Riverside could accommodate 100 diners. The 1898 brochure promised that, during the warm weather, a 50-cent table d'hôte dinner would be served in the evenings and also at lunchtime on weekends. On Saturday

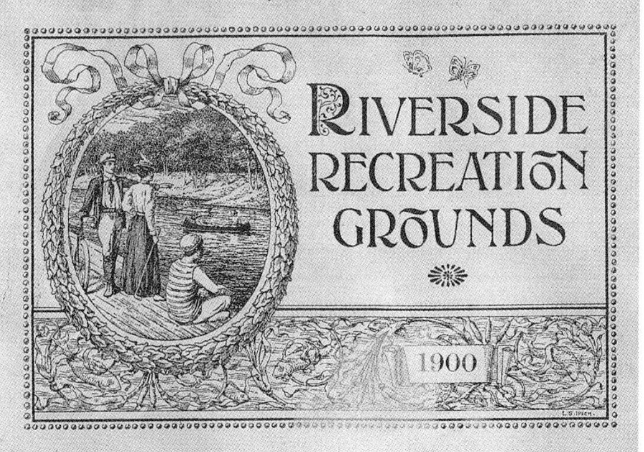

Figure 21-16. The 1900 promotional brochure includes this statement of goals: "These grounds have been laid out . . . not as a business venture, but with the view of preserving and developing a section of country most admirably adapted for recreation and athletics.

Figure 21-17. This postcard from before 1927 shows the rustic interior of The Rec boathouse.

Figures 21-18. The Riverside Station (left) on the Boston and Albany Railroad was across the Charles River from the Boston Athletic Association and Riverside Recreation Grounds. The building on the Weston side of the river is Partelow's boathouse, which later moved to the Newton side.

Figures 21-19. In its heyday in the early 20th century, Riverside Recreation Grounds was "one of the best-known recreational sites in the United States," according to historian Robert Pollack. The New England Amateur Athletic Union used it for track meets and in the 1920s the world's record in the 100-meter dash was set here.

evenings, visitors could enjoy band music and "occasional illuminations of the river."

The new recreation grounds were easily accessible by public transportation. The site was directly across the Charles from Riverside Station on the Boston and Albany Railroad and could be reached by a short path and a single-truss iron footbridge, which still remains at Riverside Park. According to one brochure, the railroad ran 13 trains out to Riverside in the afternoon. The Rec was also just a short walk from the electric trolleys that operated along the center of Commonwealth Avenue. A double track from Lake Street in Boston to the Weston Bridge was completed by the spring of 1896.

One of Hubbard's goals was for Riverside Recreation Grounds to become a place for athletic training, competitive meets, and field days. A 1900 brochure proudly mentioned that the running track and athletic fields had already been used for championship meets, including the Amateur Athletic Union national championships. This was the first time this annual event was ever held in New England. In the 1920s, the world record for the 100-meter dash was set at Riverside.[48]

Another goal expressed in early promotional literature was for Riverside Recreation Grounds to function as a "popular country club," offering social as well as sporting opportunities for young businessmen. Mary Hubbard French was later to say that Hubbard's plan for Riverside Recreation Grounds was inspired by The Country Club in Brookline, where both Hubbard and Blake were members. Membership at The Rec was granted to those who presented "written applications with endorsements (recommendations) satisfactory to the Management."[49] In the early years, single-use (nonmember) tickets could also be purchased at city and university clubs, including the Boston Athletic Association; Cambridge Golf and Country, Puritan, Technology, Algonquin, Somerset, Union Boat, and University Clubs; and Bank Officers' Association.

Figure 21-20 and 21-21. The Rec was a popular location for company picnics with cookouts, games, and athletic contests. In the evening, picnickers moved on to Norumbega Park, which was just over half a mile away. These pictures from about 1912 are labeled "Ladies' Potato Race" and "Edison Field Day, Lunch for 3500."

Figure 21-22. This photograph was one of a series taken in 1914, when Charles Wells Hubbard gave the 41-acre Riverside Recreation Grounds to the Metropolitan Park Commission.

The grounds could be rented for private company picnics featuring cookouts, sports, and games. In the evening, picnickers would move on to Norumbega Park. Among the groups using Riverside for annual outings were Boston City Hospital, the Appalachian Mountain Club, the Gillette Company, and the Bank Officers' Association of Boston.[50] A brochure of about 1912 shows a picture labeled "Edison Field Day, Lunch for 3500."[51]

It is difficult to gauge the extent to which Riverside Recreation Grounds was used by residents of Weston. A 1905 article in the *Waltham Daily Free Press Tribune* reported that neighbors objected to the playing of lawn tennis on Sundays, an activity subsequently barred by the town.[52] Interviews with children of estate owners, estate caretakers, and farmers growing up in the southeast corner of the town in the 1910s and '20s suggest that most did not go to The Rec and were only vaguely aware of its existence. Weston children generally swam at the town pool on School Street. Riverside Recreation Grounds appears to have attracted residents from the greater Boston area, who came by train and trolley, and later children from Auburndale and Waltham.

Hubbard had always intended to place Riverside Recreation Grounds under public control. In 1914 his report to the board of trustees indicated a firm desire to make it part of the public recreational system:

> The Grounds were started by me twenty years ago to meet what I thought was a public need—athletic fields and recreation facilities for the young men of Boston and Suburbia. . . . Since then, the Metropolitan Parks System . . . has been developed at public expense. Yet in my opinion the Riverside Recreation Grounds by their location on the river still offer exceptional advantages for the purposes for which they were intended. I am also convinced that their usefulness would be very much increased were they operated by some public association, as was my original expectation. . . . The two public organizations that suggest themselves are the YMCA and the Metropolitan Park Commission.[53]

In November 1914, C.W. Hubbard gave Riverside Recreation Grounds, valued at "$200,000 or more," to the Metropolitan Park Commission. The gift included 41 acres of land, two large wooden buildings, and a wide and expensive variety of recreational and athletic facilities.[54] The park commission's initial approach to the facility was cautious, and from the beginning, reports expressed concern about maintenance.[55]

Figure 21-23. Norumbega Park was established in 1897 to help increase patronage on the new Commonwealth Avenue trolley line. It was an immediate success, attracting more than 12,000 on opening day. This poster from 1905 shows the arrangement of the pleasure grounds, which featured a merry-go-round, open-air theater, restaurant, penny arcade, and a zoo that, for a time, was the largest in New England.

Norumbega Park

Riverside Recreation Grounds and the Boston Athletic Association emphasized physical education and sport. For amusement, the place to go was about a half-mile downriver in Newton, where Norumbega Park opened in June 1897, just three months before The Rec. Norumbega was developed by Newton native Adams Claflin and fellow directors of the Commonwealth Avenue Street Railway, who felt that an amusement park at the end of the line would increase trolley patronage. Named after Eben Horsford's Norumbega Tower, the park was an immediate success. A reported 12,000 people came on opening day. The railway company had to purchase new trolleys to handle huge crowds flocking to Norumbega Park on summer weekends.[56]

Fun seekers could ride the merry-go-round, explore the penny arcade, take a canoe out on the Charles River, swing on huge wooden swings, or picnic on the extensive grounds, which featured an electric fountain with brightly colored spotlights. There were free band concerts, open-air movies, and gymnastics exhibitions. One summer, a performance starred a pair of white diving horses. The park had a fine restaurant, penny arcade, and vaudeville theater. In the early years, the Pavilion Restaurant, the largest structure, accommodated 250 diners, who enjoyed the creations of a talented chef. By 1901, seating capacity had increased to 500.

As the park expanded, the management added a zoo that for a time was the largest in New England. For years it was run by noted animal expert John T. Benson, who later founded Franklin Park Zoo in Boston and Benson's Wild Animal Farm in Hudson, New Hampshire. Here Weston children got their first look at African lions, bears, bisons, camels, wild boars, wolves, monkeys, and a golden eagle.[57] Weston historian Alice Fraser recalled that on Mondays the lions were not fed, and their roaring could be heard all the way to her farm at Cutter's Corner. Except for the bears, the zoo animals were sold off in the early 1940s because they were too expensive to feed year-round. By keeping the hardy bears, which could eat almost anything and hibernated in the cold weather, manager Roy Gill could continue to advertise live animals.[58]

Boating on the Charles

In his autobiographical notes, Charles Wells Hubbard recalled that when his family first came to Weston, there were no more than 20 boats on the river between the Hubbards' country place and Waltham.[59] This number soon increased dramatically. Bostonians were drawn to Riverside because the lower basin of the Charles was still tidal and thus unsuitable for recreation until construction of the Charles River Dam in 1910. During the late 19th century, mass production of wood and canvas canoes was perfected and two well-known manufacturers, Robertson and Partelow, had factories and rental facilities in the Lakes District.[60] Trains and, by the 1890s, trolleys provided excellent transportation. Private clubs and public "boat liveries" were constructed near rail lines, making it possible for city residents to rent or store canoes in the days before the automobile.

King's Handbook of Newton, published in 1889, devotes a chapter to Riverside, described in these idyllic terms:

> It is to be doubted whether any other large city in the civilized world has, within easy access to its heated human masses, a reach of river at once so attractive and so quiet as the Charles River between Waltham and Newton Lower Falls. The entire river has its delights, but below the dam at Watertown the navigator is subject to the exigencies of the tide, and, moveover, the shores are not of the wooded sort that the boatman loves to see as he floats along. Beginning at the watch works at Waltham, there is a stretch of river four or five miles long, taking in the windings, that is without rival anywhere for pleasure-boating purposes.[61]

King's Handbook describes the *White Swan,* a small "side-wheeler" steamboat that made several trips daily in summer from the Moody Street bridge in Waltham to Riverside. Launched in 1873, the pleasure boat held 150 passengers.[62] For 16 years the *White Swan* was the queen of the river and leader in

Figure 21-24. This detail from an early-20th-century print of the Charles River shows the prominent bulge known as the Lakes District. The image is oriented with the north (Waltham) side at the bottom.

impressive illuminated flotillas such as this one described in King's guidebook:

> Occasionally, in September, a spectacle is presented here that not even Venice in her palmiest days could have far surpassed. On an appointed night the steamer White Swan starts up river from Waltham, followed by upwards of 400 boats, of every variety, from leaky yawls and crazy rafts to costly cedar shells and aboriginal canoes and the kerosene steamers of the newspaper reporters. Every boat is belted with lines of lanterns and filled with joyous monarchs of the wave; and from sundry islands and moored rafts salvos of artillery, rockets, golden rain, Japanese fires, fiery colored starts and other pyrotechnics flame across the black sky, while the great estates along the shores . . . are brilliantly illuminated. On the river there are thousands of people . . . and the music of military bands is taken up from point after point, as the magnificent cortege moves up to Fox Island and Islington, following the White Swan, as its Bucentaur [sic], Newton Boat Club, Boston Canoe Club, Arlington Canoe Club, Somerville Boat Club, Waltham Canoe Club, Upper-Charles-River Boat Club, Aurora Canoe Club, Harvard Club, and others, each with from a dozen to fifty boats in massed column, their oars and paddles keeping time to the sweet music of the bands and the choruses of the rowers, whose charming boat-songs reverberate from the forested banks and the island thickets.[63]

When the new Prospect Street bridge opened in Waltham in 1889, the sturdy vessel could not go under it safely, and it passed into legend.

Among the earliest boating facilities were the Newton Boat Club, organized in 1875, and the

Figure 21-25. This 1904 photograph shows the narrow Weston Bridge crowded with spectators enjoying a day at the river. The Norumbega Park boathouses (far left), Riverside Recreation Grounds, and Robertson's were the three largest canoe liveries in the state.

Figure 21-26. Canoeists saluted the national anthem by raising their paddles to a vertical position. This image is part of a panorama taken at the Fifth Annual Gala Day sponsored by the Auburndale-Riverside Canoe Association on August 23, 1919. The canoe was one of the few places where young men and women could be together without a chaperon.

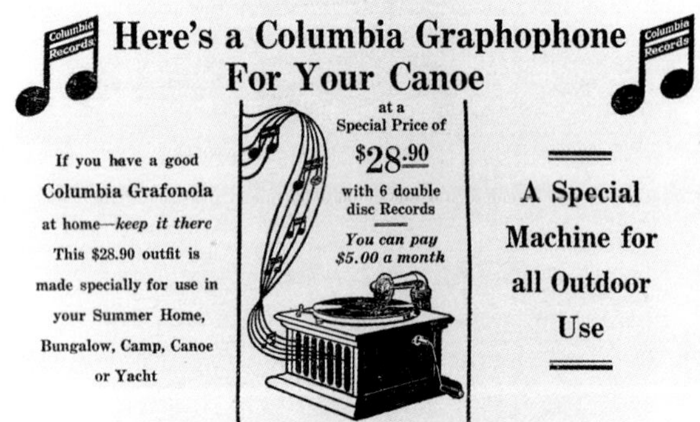

Figure 21-27. Music added to the canoeing experience. Bands performed in the evening at riverside bandstands, glee clubs sang, and canoeists played guitars or banjos. The less talented could buy a crank-type phonograph especially designed for outdoor use.

Partelow and Robertson boathouses. By the turn of the century, the three largest liveries were Riverside Recreation Grounds, Norumbega Park, and Robertson's.[64] At that time, an estimated 4,000 to 5,000 canoes were stored along the six-mile Lakes District.[65] In 1902 the superintendent of the Metropolitan Park Commission was quoted in the *Boston Globe* as saying, "More canoeing is done on this stretch of the river than is done on all the rivers in the rest of Massachusetts put together."[66] A 1903 Boston guidebook notes that "on a pleasant afternoon or evening the water is often so densely covered that one might almost cross the stream by stepping from one canoe to another."[67]

Around the turn of the century, a young Auburndale man's first major purchase was likely to be a canoe, according to Newton historian Robert Pollock. A canoe provided more than just wholesome recreation. It was also one of the few places where a young man and young woman could be together without a chaperon. Photographs show young men paddling from the stern and young ladies facing them, holding open books and parasols. In 1903 the metropolitan park police posted strict rules for canoeists. Couples were forbidden to recline side by side in a canoe. One couple was arrested for kissing, and the Boston press gleefully reported on their trial:

> The canoeist arrested for kissing his sweetheart at Riverside was fined $20. At that rate it is estimated that over a million dollars' worth of kisses are exchanged at that popular canoeing resort every fine Saturday night and Sunday.[68]

A police detachment was formed with officers deputized by both Weston and Newton. The Metropolitan Police station, which opened in 1904 on the Newton side of the river, included a mounted spyglass to observe canoeists from a distance.[69]

Bands like the popular 25-piece American Waltham Watch Company Band played at bandstands at Norumbega, Riverside, or Fox Island, where as many as 1,000 canoes might be in attendance, along with hundreds of "automobilists and excursionists." On hot nights, canoe enthusiasts would sleep in their canoes, protected by mosquito netting and burning joss sticks. A 1900 brochure from the Riverside Recreation Grounds designated certain "illumination nights," when canoeists were urged to carry Japanese lanterns. Arrangements could be made for music by guitars and mandolins on moonlit nights in June, July, and August. The Canoeists' Illumination Association sponsored yearly illuminations and special events such as the 1906 Floral and Novelty Parade for decorated canoes.[70] The association was composed of members from each club and boathouse from Waltham to Riverside.

The most extravagant events were the Charles River carnivals, which originated about the mid-1880s. These spectacles were held periodically and sometimes coordinated with special occasions such as the GAR (Grand Army of the Republic) Encampment in Boston in August 1904 and the Governors' Conference in August 1915.[71] Attendance at the 1904 event was said to be 155,000.[72]

Canoeing on the Charles River continued to be highly popular through the 1920s. Its decline has been attributed to the automobile, which came into increasing use during that decade. The automobile gave young couples the same opportunity for privacy with-

Figure 21-28. A war canoe from the Waltham Canoe Club is paddled by nine men including "Duck" White at the stern, John Sunderhauf (third from left), and Ollie Kingsbury (seventh from left).

out the risk of capsizing. Canoes could be carried atop cars, so boathouses began to lose their importance. Recreation sites that were not accessible by public transportation provided novel destinations. Ironically, the construction of Route 128 to handle increased automobile traffic dealt a severe blow to the beauty and tranquillity of the Charles in the early 1950s.

Flood, fire, and the Depression also combined to bring an end to the golden years of canoeing. During early-spring storms in March 1936, the Charles River reached its highest level ever recorded. A gauge at Riverside measured more than 44 feet above sea level, or approximately four feet higher than normal.[73] The raging torrent flooded many of

Figure 21-29. This photograph from about 1906 shows the Weston Bridge (left) and a refreshment stand on the Newton side of the river.

THE

Heinz River Luncheon

MAKES A

DAINTY REPAST

Some of **The 57**

Heinz Tomato Soup

Heinz Baked Beans

Heinz Sweet and Sour Pickles

Heinz Preserved Fruits

LUNCHEONS PUT UP AT THE OFFICE OF

The Weston Country Club

Figure 21-30. In a souvenir booklet from about 1904, the Weston Country Club advertised the "Heinz River Luncheon." One newspaper printed this advice concerning food: "The lunch should be the last thing put in the canoe. You can never tell when you get into a canoe just where you are going to land, and to sit down suddenly on a huckleberry pie tends to mar the joy of what otherwise would be a perfect day."

the boathouses, and huge ice chunks carried by floodwaters wiped out the floating platforms. Few of the damaged boathouses were rebuilt. During the Depression, many people kept their canoes in the backyard rather than pay an annual storage fee. Fire destroyed the boathouses at Riverside Recreation Grounds in May 1959, after The Rec had closed its doors. The last of the grand shingled boathouses at Norumbega Park burned to the ground on June 1, 1966.

Today the picturesque Metropolitan Park Commission boathouse in Newton, built for waterborne police, is occupied by the Charles River Canoe and Kayak Service, which rents boats and offers instruction. Next door, the building originally used for public rest rooms now houses the offices of the Charles River Watershed Association, established in 1965 to protect the river and promote its recreational use.

Figure 21-31. Alden Kingsbury's business card shows the type of handmade wooden canoes that he later made in Weston.

Kingsbury Family and Canoe Making in Weston

After H.V. Partelow moved across the river to Auburndale in the early 1890s, most canoe manufacturers were located on the Newton side of the river. Alden "Ollie" Kingsbury, great-grandson of Weston farmer Elijah Kingsbury, was a canoe builder who learned his trade at Robertson's at the turn of the century. David Kingsbury, Ollie's son, reminisces that when Robertson refused to raise his pay by $1 a week, Ollie quit and paddled down to Emerson's, where he immediately got another job. Beginning in 1914, Ollie built canoes in a shop on the property of his father, Otis, on Loring Road. In the early years of World War I, he ran all the concessions at The Rec with the help of his wife, Esther, who laundered the bathing suits and towels at home. After the Loring Road property was sold about 1922, Ollie Kingsbury built his own house and boatbuilding shop, which still remains on River Road. He continued to make canoes until demand fell off during the Depression.

In 1946 and 1947, Ollie and David went back to building canoes. In a six-month period they made about 36 and sold them for $135 each to Norumbega Park and the Riverside Recreation Grounds.[74] According to David, they needed about 2½ days to build a canoe from start to finish, using white cedar from northern Maine and Canada to make the ribs and planking, spruce for the gunnels, white oak for the keels and stems, and mahogany for the wales and seats. (The wale is the finished piece of wood that extends the length of the canoe along the top edge.) The Kingsburys shaped their canoes over a mold, first steaming the ribs to go around the mold to form the frame, then nailing ⅛-inch planking into the ribs with brass clinch nails. Canvas was then stretched over the planking and tacked all around. Ollie Kingsbury, like other canoe builders, used his own special formula for the canvas filler that was painted on to fill the cloth pores. After smoothing the entire canvas surface with a pumice stone, the canoes were given one coat of paint and two coats of varnish. As part of the final finishing, David Kingsbury caned the seats. Ollie Kingsbury's original handmade canoe molds are still being used by a canoe manufacturer in New Hampshire who is making "Kingsbury Canoes" by the same handcrafted method.

Riverside Recreation Grounds After World War I and Leo J. Martin Golf Course

In 1919, the Metropolitan District Commission (MDC) was formed by combining the park commission with the previously merged sewer and water commissions. Over the next decades, the agency

Figure 21-32. Employees at The Rec relax in the summer of 1917 or 1918. Back row: Pauline Young, Louis Young, Harold Young, and Ollie Kingsbury. Front row: Dave Gan and Clarence Chaisson.

faced the recurring dilemma of how to continue operating the popular Riverside Recreation Grounds while lacking funds to properly maintain it. Charles Hubbard continued to take a strong interest until his death in 1933 at age 77. In a letter to Hubbard, James A. Bailey, first commissioner of the MDC, expressed concern about costs:

> . . . there will be required, from year to year, to keep those buildings in repair, a very considerable sum, and I am of the opinion that it is not a wise expenditure of public moneys to keep indefinitely in repair these large and costly buildings.[75]

But the popularity of The Rec overruled the commissioner's judgment.

Administrative policies changed gradually under public ownership. The atmosphere of a male-only club gave way to a more welcoming attitude toward women. The management could no longer require membership applications. In 1923 they stopped leasing the grounds to private parties for their exclusive use. In 1929, after passage of the state "Sunday Sports" law, the MDC allowed the tennis courts to be used on Sundays.

In 1926, the Metropolitan District Commission was directed to investigate the feasibility of constructing one or more public golf courses within the metropolitan park system.[76] At that time, Boston had only one public course, at Franklin Park. Two new courses, at Riverside and the larger Ponkapoag course at Blue Hills, were built as a result of this report. The first nine holes were laid out on Riverside Recreation land and within the 19-acre Weston Park, which was transferred to Commonwealth control under a long-term lease. The course was probably designed and constructed using in-house MDC personnel.

Riverside Golf Course, also referred to as Riverside Public Golf Links, opened on May 1, 1930.[77] Despite the Depression, 50,000 rounds of golf were played in 1931 at a cost of a dollar per morning or afternoon on Saturdays, Sundays, and holidays. An additional nine holes on the south side of the Charles River were ready for use in 1932. The facility included a one-story Colonial Revival clubhouse. The course sold 477 seasonal memberships to regular users in 1933.[78]

Figure 21-33. Riverside Golf Course opened in 1930. The locker building, shown here in 1934, stood until the 1960s, when additional land was taken for widening Route 128.

Figure 21-34. The Riverside Recreation Grounds swimming pool was the largest in New England. Measuring 50 by 35 meters, it had a gravel bottom and was spring fed. (1950 photo)

In 1934, the first Massachusetts Golf Association tournament was held at Riverside. In 1936 an irrigation system using water from the Charles River was installed with labor provided by the Works Progress Administration. In 1945, an act of the legislature was passed to name the course in honor of Leo Jerome Martin, former state amateur golf champion and member at Riverside who was killed in World War II. A memorial bronze plaque attached to a massive boulder was placed on the clubhouse grounds in Martin's honor.[79]

Beginning in the mid-1930s, the MDC considered the impact of a proposed new highway encircling the metropolitan area. Route 128 cut directly across the Riverside Recreation Grounds, forcing the agency to give up 4.5 acres including several tennis courts. Within a few years of its opening in 1951, the highway required major reconstruction to accommodate heavy traffic demand. In the early 1960s, the Public Works Department (PWD) took additional land, and the MDC and PWD feuded over the cost of moving or replacing the 1930s clubhouse, redesigning the course layout, and building a new parking lot.[80] The present modern clubhouse, designed by the Boston firm of Desmond and Lord, was completed in 1963.

The most recent major change at the Leo J. Martin facility was the introduction of cross-country skiing in 1975. Lincoln Guide Service ran the ski operation and offered instruction, lighted touring tracks, and man-made snow when necessary. That same year, an additional building was constructed with private funds to house a golf museum displaying mementos of Francis Ouimet and providing offices for the Massachusetts Golf Association and Women's Golf Association.

From the 1930s to the 1950s, Riverside Recreation Grounds continued in operation. While attendance patterns varied over the decades, The Rec continued to draw from the greater Boston area as well as from nearby Auburndale. From about 1947 to 1952, it was also used by the Newton YMCA for a summer camp. By the 1950s, the general character of the area and the use of the grounds were changing, due in part to the negative impact of Route 128. Welfare and community services used the site for summer day camps run by religious or community groups and attended by underprivileged children.[81]

Conflict developed over whether to assist these welfare organizations despite the growing expense of maintaining the facility.

Riverside Recreation Grounds never reopened after the 1958 season. In 1959, the acting MDC commissioner deemed the buildings a safety hazard and public health menace too costly for repairs. On May 10, 1959, three months before their scheduled demolition, the two remaining 60-year-old wooden structures burned to the ground in a fire attributed to boys playing with matches. The charred remains were leveled and the pool filled in. Today the area, known as Riverside Park, has been reduced to about 10 acres accessible from Recreation Road and Route 128 north. In 1970, the MDC considered building a new recreational facility on the site, but the proposal was never implemented. The iron footbridge still spans the Charles River.

Later History of Norumbega Park

The history of Norumbega Park closely parallels that of Riverside Recreation Grounds. Both opened in 1897 and reached their peak of success around 1920. Declines in attendence during the '20s and the Depression were reversed during World War II, when proximity to public transportation again became critical. After the war, neither facility was well maintained, and changing lifestyles meant fewer patrons.

The Totem Pole at Norumbega Park was one of the largest and best-known ballrooms during the 1930s, when dancing to popular bands attracted large crowds seeking inexpensive entertainment. In 1936 a new manager, Roy Gill, prohibited liquor except for beer and wine in the restaurant. He instituted a dress code at the ballroom requiring jackets and ties for men and banning slacks and bobby sox for women. Neither men nor women could attend "stag," and jitterbugging was prohibited. Gill refurbished the room with new sofas and expensive carpeting and hired the top bands in America. Broadcasts from the Totem Pole were heard all over the United States. With the advent of World War II, musicians and their audiences joined the Armed Forces. The big bands enjoyed a brief revival after the war, but the automobile, along with the newly invented television, contributed to the decline of interest in ballroom dancing.

By 1953, only a few rides were left at Norumbega Park. One of the last was "Davy Crocket's nightmare," the park's one and only "dark ride," featuring phosphorescent skeletons that dimly illuminated what had once been one of the two Norumbega boathouses. The park closed in 1963 and the Totem Pole Ballroom in 1964. In 1966, Marriott Corporation arranged to build the present hotel on the site.

Figure 21-35. Despite the optimistic claim that "all roads lead to the Totem Pole," Route 128 also made it easier for patrons of the famous Totem Pole Ballroom to head for the beach or the mountains.

Eben Norton Horsford and "Viking Mania"

One of the most curious chapters in the history of the Charles River in Weston was the building of Norumbega Tower, a tall fieldstone structure that resembles the remains of a medieval fortress. This unique monument commemorates an event that never happened, the settlement of the Vikings in Watertown and the Charles River basin. It was erected in 1889 by Eben Norton Horsford (1818–1893), well-trained chemist and Harvard professor who lost his scientific objectivity in the search for the fabled "Lost City of New England."

Horsford was born in upstate New York, where his father was a missionary to the Seneca Indians.[82] Because of his upbringing, he had a familiarity with Indian languages and was interested in cultures predating the English settlement in North America. In 1838, at age 19, he graduated from Rensselaer Polytechnic Institute in New York as a civil engineer. He went to Germany in 1844 to study analytical chemistry under the noted professor Justus von Liebig, thus becoming one of the first German-trained American chemists. In 1847 he married Mary Gardner, a poet, who died less than a decade later leaving four daughters. A few years later, he married her sister, who bore him another daughter.

In 1847 Horsford was appointed Rumford Professor and Lecturer on the Application of Science to the Useful Arts at Harvard University, but was almost immediately transferred to the newly established Lawrence Scientific School, where he remained for 16 years. He is credited with installing the school's first chemistry laboratory, one of the first of its kind in the country, and "won renown for his thoroughness, empiricism and pragmatic cast of mind."[83] While serving as Rumford Professor, Horsford reportedly obtained more than 30 patents for chemical compounds. He was keenly interested in the chemistry of foods, as shown by his 1861 pamphlet *The Theory and Art of Breadmaking* and his development of processes for manufacturing condensed milk and baking powder, which was a new and highly profitable form of artificial yeast.

In 1863, he resigned his teaching post to direct the Rumford Chemical Works in Providence, Rhode Island, a company founded to commercialize his discoveries. Horsford became a wealthy man and well-known member of the Cambridge intelligentsia. During the Civil War, he formulated marching rations for the Union Army and was appointed by the Massachusetts governor to draw up plans for defense of Boston Harbor in case of Confederate attack. Horsford was a frequent and liberal benefactor of the newly founded Wellesley College. He served as chairman of the Board of Visitors from the early years until his death, helped to endow the library, provided funds for scientific apparatus, and set up a "sabbatical" system and pension fund for professors.[84]

Eben Horsford credited his interest in the "Northmen" to popular Norwegian violinist Ole Bull, who visited Cambridge in 1870 and suggested that a statue of Leif Erikson be erected in Boston.[85] Despite opposition by the Massachusetts Historical Society, which contended that the Norse presence in Boston had not been proved, the statue was completed in 1887 and stands today on Commonwealth Avenue. Horsford gave the address at the unveiling and then turned his attention to finding the Lost City of New England, called Norumbega, shown on some ancient maps of the New World.

A few years earlier, in 1884, Horsford had "discovered" the remains of a fort at the junction of Stony Brook and the Charles River in Weston. At first he thought his "fort" might be of French origin, but in a series of lavishly printed volumes dating between 1886 and 1893, Horsford proclaimed it to be Fort Norumbega, site of a Norse settlement and extensive fisheries dating to 1000 A.D.[86] In his publications, which are replete with photographs and maps, Horsford describes how he had pored over ancient maps and carefully analyzed the Norse sagas. Then, says Horsford, "... when I had eliminated every doubt

Figure 21-36. Eben Norton Horsford (1818–1893) was a chemist, Harvard professor, and successful entrepreneur before he got caught up in "Viking mania."

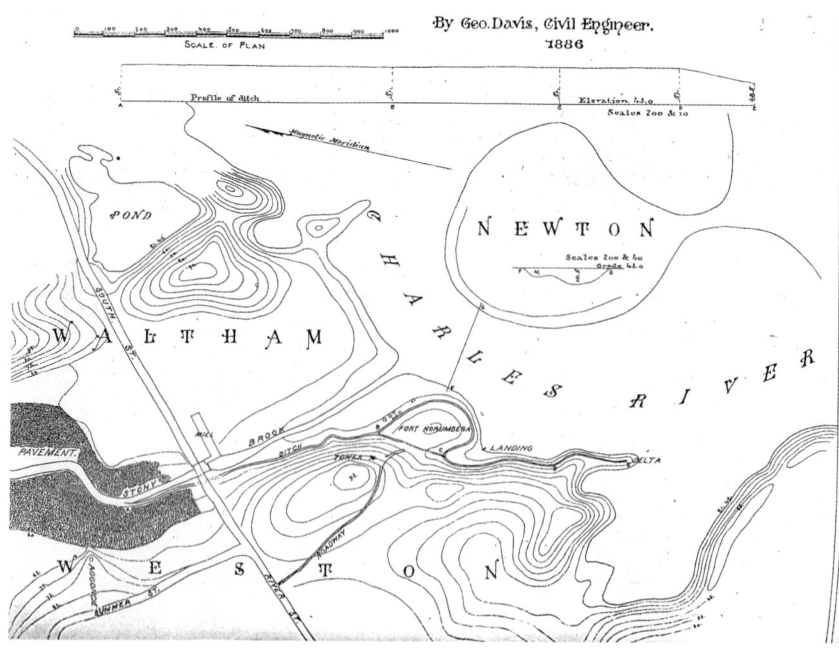

Figure 21-37. In 1886, Horsford commissioned this map showing what he felt was the site of the Viking "Fort Norumbega," just a few hundred feet from where he later built his tower.

of the locality that I could find, I drove with a friend through a region I had never before visited, of a topography of which I knew nothing, nine miles away, directly to the remains of the Fort."[87] He immediately had the area surveyed by a civil engineer, but no archaeological excavations were ever carried out. Near where Norumbega Tower now stands, Horsford did find a "great stone mortar, such as the Northmen used in very early times to grind their grain," which he incorporated into the tower design.[88]

Horsford had supreme faith in this methodology. On finding the "fort," he writes, "In a certain sense there was, in this discovery, the fulfillment of a prophecy. On the basis of the literature of the subject, I had predicted the finding of Norumbega at a particular spot. I went to the spot and found it. No test of the genuineness of scientific deduction is superior to this."[89]

Horsford followed the same line of reasoning in looking for the remains of Leif Erikson's house. He predicted where it would be located, dug three small test pits, and announced that he had, indeed, found evidence of two long log huts that must have belonged to the great Norse adventurer. The site was conveniently located on the Charles River near Mount Auburn Hospital, just a few blocks from Horsford's Craigie Street home. A granite commemorative tablet still marks the spot.

To publicize his findings, Horsford wrote *The Discovery of America by Northmen* (1888), immediately followed by *The Discovery of the Ancient City of Norumbega,* presented to the American Geographical Society at a special session in Watertown, November 21, 1889. Two hundred and fifty numbered copies were distributed by the author. At the 1889 special session, Horsford announced the "discovery of Vinland," including the site of an entire ancient City of Norumbega, located under present-day Watertown. He explained that he had erected the tower "where I first found remains of the work of the Norsemen." Subsequently, he had found traces of Norse settlement everywhere:

> The canals, ditches, deltas, boom-dams, ponds, fish-ways, forts, dwellings, walls, terraces of theatre and amphitheatre, scattered throughout the basin of the Charles are the memorials I had in mind when I said there was not a square mile draining into the river that lacked an incontestable monument to the presence of the Northmen.[90]

To Horsford, the Indian place-name Norumbega was further proof of the Norse occupation, as Horsford theorized that the name was derived from the ancient word for Norway, *Norbegia* or *Norobega,* used by the natives as meaning "belonging to Norway."[91]

Horsford was remarkably confident in his ability to describe the civilization of the early Northmen. The City of Norumbega on the Watertown site had "shops for barter, and dwellings for all classes, and, necessarily, with the culture of the Northmen, provision for amusement, for public worship, and for the wants of government."[92] He explained that the principal industries included not only fisheries, furs, and agriculture but also extensive cutting of trees for masur wood, or burl, used in the production of fine wooden objects. According to Horsford, the Viking civilization flourished until 1347, the date of the final ship in the masur trade. He summarized, "I have sought the birthplace of the earliest European colony on our shores, and something of its course as a people. I have to-day sketched the results of my labors."[93]

Norumbega Tower

The 1889 Watertown special session coincided with the dedication of Norumbega Tower, which Horsford constructed with his own funds on a bluff overlooking the Charles River in Weston. The Norman-style tower stands an estimated 35 to 40

Figure 21-38. Eben Horsford built Norumbega Tower in 1889 as a monument to his discoveries.

feet tall. The focal point is a large polished gray granite tablet with a carved inscription of the history of the site, as interpreted by Horsford. The tower was designed by Thomas Tyron, a native of Hartford who trained at MIT and practiced in New York City with Arnold W. Brunner.[94] Norumbega is one of two fieldstone towers in Weston. The second, on the Demmon-Morrison estate (now Regis College), was built several decades later.

Schools were closed on the day of the dedication, and Watertown Town Hall was "well filled with an appreciative audience," according to newspaper accounts.[95] Each person received an envelope with the program, a sketch of the tower, a copy of the tablet, maps, a poem, and other commemorative materials. A Scandinavian quartet sang a Norse song. In the official remarks, Professor Horsford was likened to Moses, Abraham, and Noah, because he was a man with new ideas who "had faith in Norumbega."

Horsford's ideas were attacked from the beginning. His critics denied the presence of Northmen in the Charles Valley or felt that, if they had touched New England, they left behind no trace of human handiwork. Horsford devoted himself to getting his ideas accepted. His next book, *The Problems of the Northmen* (1889), was written in response to Justin Winsor, the Harvard librarian whose monumental work *Narrative and Critical History of America* had dismissed Horsford's theories completely. Winsor had written, "Nothing could be slenderer than the alleged correspondences of languages; and we can see in Horsford's *Discovery of America by Northmen* to what a fanciful extent a confident enthusiasm can carry it."[96] Winsor also commented on Horsford's "incautious linguistic inferences" and "uncritical cartographical perversions."

Horsford countered by questioning Winsor's capabilities in geographical research and reiterating the value of his unique method of scientific deduction. In the next few years Horsford wrote three more books defending his theories: *The Defenses of Norumbega and a Review of the Reconnaissances* (1891), *The Landfall of Leif Erikson,* A.D. *1000, and Site of His Houses in Vineland* (1892), and *Leif's House in Vineland and Graves of the Northmen* (1893), the latter written in part by his daughter Cornelia, who followed her father's methods exactly.

How could someone like Horsford, a man with a strong scientific background and distinguished career as a university professor, become so misguided? Stephen Williams, Peabody Professor Emeritus of North American Archaeology at Harvard, has written about Horsford in his book *Fantastic Archaeology: The Wild Side of North American Prehistory,* which includes a chapter on 19th- and 20th-century "Viking mania." In an interview, Williams referred to Horsford as a "rogue professor" who lost all ability to analyze data.[97] According to Williams, the ditches, canals, and dams that Horsford was seeing were built by English settlers, but he convinced himself they were Norse. Once he had committed himself to this view, he became a fanatic. Williams also points out that Horsford didn't realize how different the past was. He looked at the Charles River and thought that the riverbed and landforms must have been exactly the same nearly a millennium earlier.

Horsford continued to defend his work until his sudden death from a heart attack in 1893. His obituary hailed him as "Leif Erikson's Champion," a man "Known the World Over for His Norse Researches," and "A Great Name in the World of Chemistry."[98] At the time of his death, Horsford was cooperating with Elizabeth Shepard on a *Guidebook to Norumbega and Vineland,* published in 1893. This delightful book instructed the archaeologically curious how to go by streetcar to the Norse sites in Cambridge, Watertown, and Weston. For 20 cents, the visitor could take the Fitchburg train to the Roberts station in Waltham, walk from there to the tower, and mount the tower steps to view the gently rolling countryside and the river. In the days before the building of Route 128, it must have been a beautiful site.

A 1903 Boston guidebook lists Norumbega Tower as "the most generally interesting spot" in the Weston area. The author of this guidebook was more skeptical of Horsford's findings:

> He elaborately carried out his identification of Watertown with the Vinland of the Northmen, and traced their wharves, canals, docks . . . the site of their stronghold, where may still be seen—at least the professor saw them—the remains of the moat and dam which the Northmen constructed.[99]

The tower could be reached by canoe, and, according to a 1906 newspaper article, thousands of canoeists visited the spot each year. The article describes the trip with the usual turn-of-the-century superlatives:

> To the canoeist who has never visited the Tower the trip is ideal, for it furnishes an opportunity to paddle his canoe into the remote corner of the stream and it is in one of these corners that lies the proper landing place to the "Tower" in what is known to the canoeists as "Lovers' Retreat."[100]

The article praises the "magnificent view" from the tower, declaring that "there is no other spot on the Charles that appeals more to the visitor to our city than Norumbega Tower."

In the late 1890s, the land around the Norumbega Tower was taken by the Metropolitan Park Commission as part of the Charles River Reservation. Horsford's heirs received permission to retain the tower and a small piece of land around it, which they owned until it was given to the Metropolitan District Commission in 1922.[101] In 1935, the MDC repointed the tower, recut the stone tablet, erected a new bronze tablet, and made other improvements to put the historic tower in good condition. The upper two thirds of the structure was taken down and rebuilt in 1973.[102]

Today, Viking scholars generally agree that Viking ships reached only to the northernmost tip of Newfoundland.[103] The only firm evidence of a Viking settlement in North America was discovered there in 1960 at L'Anse-aux-Meadows, where Norwegian archaeologists found foundations of turf-built houses resembling Norse buildings in Greenland and Iceland, along with Norse artifacts.[104] In 1965 a map was discovered, apparently dating from the 15th century, showing "Vinland" lying to the west of Greenland. This map is now generally held to be a 20th-century forgery.[105] The discovery of a single Norse coin in Maine is considered to be evidence of trading rather than local settlement.

When Norumbega Tower was dedicated, the ceremony included poetry readings.[106] The final lines of the last poem, "Envoy," provide a way of looking at the meaning of Norumbega Tower, which can be viewed as a monumental folly or as a quest, albeit misguided, for knowledge and truth about the past:

This tower to her folk we rear,
A beacon to Discovery—
Since ever truth shall make us free—
That our free thought may wax the freer
That we may welcome aye the new
Patient to try if it be the true
Nor say there is no more to hear.

Figure 21-39. The Cobb sisters explore the inlets of the Charles River in the 1890s.

Houses in the Riverside Area

119 Park Road (1864). Built for Manley Seaverns and owned by his descendants until 1954.

55 Loring Road (now Prescott Lane). Built for farmer Otis Kingsbury after the mid-19th century.

127 River Road. Location of Alden Kingsbury's boatbuilding shop.

River Rd. The handsome stone entrance posts on the east side of River Road once marked the entrance into the turn-of-the-century estate of Arthur A. Brigham.

Notes

1. Pollock, Robert F., "Down by the Riverside," in *Historic Auburndale* (Auburndale Community Association, 2nd ed., 1996), 19.
2. This history is put together from several sources. *Births, Deaths and Marriages* records that Deacon Thomas Upham married Martha Williams in 1772 and died in 1780 at age 63. Information on the Kingsbury family comes from an interview with David Kingsbury, January 1998. According to Lamson's *HTW,* the Widow Upham's house, which appears on the 1794 Kingsbury map, was one of the houses selected in 1791–92 as a "pesthouse" and "place for inoculation" during a smallpox epidemic, perhaps because of its isolated location. This house was later moved and attached to the rear of 168 Summer Street.
3. The Otis Kingsbury house remains at 55 Loring Road (now Prescott Lane).
4. Within a decade, the same investors would expand to Lowell to take advantage of the far greater waterpower of the Merrimack River.
5. Lamson, Daniel S., "Weston," *History of Middlesex County, Mass.,* D.H. Hurd, ed. (Philadelphia, 1890), vol. 1, chapter XXXIV, 511.
6. MCRD 594/131, 1848 (recorded 1850). In this very personal deed, Samuel admonishes his three sons to "take good care and provide for their mother and give her a good support in sickness and health." Most of the farm was located on the east side of Park Road south of the railroad tracks.
7. MCRD 1789/481 and Plan Book 51/48 (1887). This land is now the location of the Mass Pike interchange.
8. Zaitzevsky, Cynthia, *Frederick Law Olmsted and the Boston Park System* (Harvard University Press, 1982), 227–28.
9. Ibid., 41.
10. As quoted in *Enhancing the Future of the Metropolitan Park System* (final report and recommendations of the Green Ribbon Commission, May 1996), 13.
11. Ibid., 14.
12. The word *Public* in the organization name was later dropped. Figures on land preservation from Max Hall, *The Charles: The People's River* (Boston, David Godine, 1986), 43.
13. For a more detailed description of Eliot and the founding of the metropolitan parks system, see Norman T. Newton, *Design on the Land: The Development of Landscape Architecture* (Harvard University Press, 1971), 318–36.
14. Letter, C. Eliot to F. Blake, November 28, 1892 (Blake Papers, MHS, 23.339). A photograph of the Charles River provided by Hubbard appears on page 53 of the 1893 *Boston Metropolitan Park Report.*
15. The Blake papers at MHS include a copy of

House Bill No. 836 of 1896 authorizing purchase of open space along the Charles, with the following personal note from G. Langford to Blake: "I shall depend upon your being present at this hearing and desire that you advise the Committee as from Weston."
16. MCRD 2155/590.
17. *Boston Herald,* January 1, 1893 (Blake Papers, MHS, vol. 42).
18. "A Sharp Move," *Boston Traveller,* January 2, 1893. This article was pasted into Francis Blake's scrapbook with his notation that it was written by F.T. Fuller (Blake Papers, MHS, vol. 42).
19. Letter, F. Blake to F.T. Fuller (Blake Papers, MHS, 63.909).
20. *Boston Herald,* January 3, 1893. This article is pasted in Francis Blake's scrapbook with the notation "Sylvester Baxter" (Blake Papers, MHS, vol. 42). The text was reprinted in the 1893 *TR,* 39.
21. The land was conveyed in two parcels of 32.31 and 10.14 acres (MCRD 2291/534 and Plan Book 83/34).
22. Eliot's 1893 report is quoted at length in an article entitled "A New Public Reservation" in the *Boston Herald,* February 25, 1901 (Blake Papers, MHS, 65.940).
23. MCRD Filed Plan 187, September 1, 1896.
24. 1899 *TR,* 27.
25. 1903 *TR,* 41.
26. *Enhancing the Future of the Metropolitan Park System,* op. cit., 15.
27. See also 1890 *TR,* 44–45.
28. *1903 TR,* 38.
29. The town was already incurring extra costs because 77 acres of Weston parkland, with an assessed value of $72,000, was no longer taxable; and in addition, Weston was maintaining the 19-acre town park "which for all practical purposes is part of the Charles River Reservation." Furthermore, Weston's per-capita contribution to the cost of the Metropolitan Park System, based on its annual assessment, was $1.58 per year per person, compared to $1.06 for Newton, 76 cents for Wellesley, and 36 cents for Waltham.
30. 1903 *TR,* 43.
31. The builder was T. Stuart & Company of Newton. See Public Document #48, *Report of the Board of Metropolitan Park Commissioners,* December 1916 (Boston, Wright & Potter Printing Co., 1917), 56–60. The bridge opened to traffic on November 24, 1916. Ten percent of the approximate $50,000 cost was borne by the town of Weston.
32. For more information on reform parks, see Galen Cranz, *The Politics of Park Design: A History of Urban Parks in America* (MIT Press, 1982), chapter 2.
33. MCRD 2192/326 and Plan Book 81; also 2386/82 and plan at end of Book 2386. The initial 20 acres were sold for $9,200.
34. "Outdoor Campus: The B.A.A. Purchases Property at Riverside," *Boston Journal,* March 29, 1893 (Blake Papers, MHS, vol. 42).
35. Flyer, Boston Athletic Association Riverside Grounds, c. 1894 (Blake Papers, MHS, 53.755). Later, canoes could also be rented here for $2 a day (see BAA Constitution, Bylaws, House Rules, Athletic Events, May 1896).
36. Riverside Road was paid for with $8,000 in private funds and $2,000 in town funds. On the Newton side, Blake bought land and constructed a private way to Charles Street. Blake's initial efforts to build the bridge itself were opposed by the Newton Boat Club, which argued it would obstruct their views of the river. Blake and Hubbard were members of the club and eventually prevailed. For details about the controversy with the Newton Boat Club and the bridge and road building, see Blake Papers, MHS, 69.987–89. The bridge was closed to vehicular traffic in the 1930s (1934 *TR,* 24–25) and was replaced in the 1990s by a narrow footbridge on the same pilings. The building of the Mass Pike and Route 128 has completely changed this area.
37. MCRD 5166/86, September–October 1927, $50,000.
38. Bob Pollock to PWF.
39. Pollock, Robert, op. cit., 24.
40. Bob Pollock to PWF.
41. *Boston Sunday Herald,* March 15, 1896 (later reprinted as a circular). Includes map (WHS).
42. "Riverside Recreation Grounds 'The Popular Country Club,'" 1898 flyer.
43. The 40-acre parcel included 12 acres bought from Ralph Seaverns in 1895 and 7 in 1896, and 4 and 17 acres bought from Manley Seaverns in 1899 (see CWH to Commonwealth of Mass., 1914, 3923/515).
44. The contest featured competitors from Newton, Brookline, and Roxbury high schools, the Newton Boat Club, and BAA, according to Robert Pollock's article "The 'Rec' Turns 100," printed in *Centennial Celebration, Riverside Recreation Grounds,* September 27–28, 1997.
45. Minutes, Metropolitan Park Commission, September 26, 1898 (vol. 3, 434).
46. In his article for the Riverside Recreation Grounds Centennial, cited above, Robert Pollock makes the following price comparison: "Castile soap was selling for two cents a bar, good quality cotton towels were three cents, boys' knee-pants were nineteen cents, a handmade shirt sold for a dollar . . ."
47. "Riverside Recreation Grounds, 'The Popular Country Club,'" op. cit.
48. Pollock, Robert, "Riverside Recreation Grounds Centennial: September 25, 1997" (unpublished manuscript).
49. "Riverside Recreation Grounds, 1900," brochure (NHS/JH).
50. Pollock, "Riverside Recreation Grounds Centennial," op. cit.
51. "Riverside Recreation Grounds, Auburndale, Mass.," undated brochure, c. 1912–13 (NHS/JS)
52. *WDFPT,* May 26, 1905.
53. Report to the trustees of the Riverside Recreation Grounds in early 1914, as quoted by Jonathan Mann in "The Riverside Recreation Grounds" (unpublished manuscript, 1966, WHS).
54. Letter from Mr. Gray of Ropes, Gray, Boyden and Perkins to the secretary of the MDC, March 31, 1926, as quoted by Jonathan Mann in "The Riverside Recreation Grounds" op. cit.
55. Report of the Board of Metropolitan Park Commissioners, 1915 (Boston, 1916), 11.
56. Pollock, "Down by the Riverside," op. cit.
57. For additional information on Norumbega Park, see Pollock chapter in *Historic Auburndale,* op. cit., 17–31.
58. Pollock, "Down by the Riverside," op. cit., 27.
59. Hubbard, Charles W., "Autobiographical Notes" (unpublished manuscript, undated), 5. Copy obtained by the author from Stanley French Jr.
60. McAdow, Ron, *The Charles River* (Marlborough, MA, 1949). According to David Kingsbury, who built boats in Weston with his father, Alden ("Ollie"), in a three-mile stretch of river there were several other boat shops that operated at different time periods: Joseph Emerson, Kingsbury, Waltham Canoe, Arnold, and Mose Colen.
61. Sweetser, M.F., *King's Handbook of Newton, Massachusetts* (Moses King Corporation, Boston, 1889), 211.
62. See also Travis, Harold G., "Steamboat on the Charles, 'The White Swan' 1873–1889," *WHSB,* May 1978.
63. Ibid., 214.
64. Bob Pollock has identified the following liveries in the Lakes District where you could rent a canoe in the late 19th or early 20th century: Riverside Recreation Grounds (Weston, two sections, burned 1959); Partelow's/Robertson's (Newton, damaged in 1936 flood); Auburndale Boat House/Grays/Gray and Frost/Jack Frost (Newton, probably damaged in 1936 flood); Newton Boat Club (Newton, damaged in 1936 flood); Terminal Boat House (Newton, where Lasell's Stoller Boat House is now, on Charles Street. The trolley spur line terminated here); Boston Athletic

Association/BU Boathouse (Weston, burned); Emerson's/Metropolitan (Newton, burned about 1911); Norumbega Park (Newton, two sections, burned, 1966); WawbeWaWa (Newton, named for white goose in Longfellow's "Hiawatha," exists today as private residence); Waltham Boat and Canoe Club (Waltham, Purgatory Cove); Arnold's (Waltham, Woerd Avenue); Waltham Canoe Club (Waltham, Woerd Avenue); Nutting's (Waltham opposite watch factory. Nutting's boathouse dated back to the 1880s; the ballroom opened on the street level above the boathouse in 1914).

65. The 1903 *TR,* 38, gives the figure 4,000. Robert Pollock has estimated as many as 5,000.

66. *Boston Globe,* May 6, 1902.

67. Bacon, Edwin M., *Boston: A Guide Book* (Ginn & Co., Boston, 1903), 116.

68. *Boston Herald,* August 1903, as reported in Pollock, "Down by the Riverside," op. cit.

69. Ibid., 21.

70. "Charles River Canoeists' Illumination Association Has Plans Nearly Completed," *WDFPT,* May 19, 1906, and "Thousands Attend the Opening Concerts on the Charles River," June 4, 1906.

71. Souvenir programs for the Charles River Carnival Governors' Night and G.A.R. Encampment (Waltham Public Library Archives).

72. Elliott, Janice, "River Carnival Major Waltham Event in 1904," *The [Waltham] News-Tribune,* July 8, 1964.

73. *Newton Graphic,* March 20, 1936.

74. David Kingsbury to PWF, January 1998.

75. Letter, James A. Bailey to C.W. Hubbard, March 25, 1920, as quoted in Mann, "The Riverside Recreation Grounds," op. cit.

76. House . . . No. 150, "Special Report of the Metropolitan District Commission Relative to the Feasibility of the Construction of Public Golf Courses in the Parks of the Metropolitan District," December 10, 1926.

77. Information on the early years of Riverside Golf Course in *Annual Reports of the Metropolitan District Commission* (Public Document No. 48), 1929 to 1947.

78. Ibid. (1933 report). Other statistics for 1933 are that 25,191 people played the course during the year, 243 rented lockers, 5,116 rented towels, and 351 was the largest number playing on a single day.

79. Chapter 357, Acts of 1945. See also *MDC Annual Report,* December 1947, 59.

80. "Riverside Golf Club Feud Flares," *Boston Traveler,* February 16, 1961.

81. In 1955, the camp was used by 264 full-time campers with five organizations. Some 1,260 children from 15 other organizations used it on an irregular basis.

82. Information about Horsford's life comes primarily from the following five sources: Harvard University archives; Rensselaer Polytechnic Institute archives; Stephen Williams, *Fantastic Archaeology: The Wild Side of American Prehistory* (University of Pennsylvania Press, 1991), 206–10; Richard John, "Vita: Eben Norton Horsford," *Harvard Magazine,* September–October 1988, 44; and "Prof. Horsford; Leif Erikson's Champion Dies Suddenly," *Boston Transcript,* January 2, 1893.

83. John, "Vita, Eben Norton Horsford," op. cit.

84. Glasscock, Jean, ed. *Wellesley College, 1875 to 1975, A Century of Women* (Wellesley College, 1975), 18–21, and "Scheme Matured and Adopted by the Trustees in 1886 on the basis of a bequest made to Wellesley College in 1878 by Eben Norton Horsford," January 1, 1886. This document explains how Horsford wished his large gift to be apportioned.

85. Williams, op. cit., 207.

86. Horsford, Eben Norton, *John Cabot's Landfall in 1497 and the Site of Norumbega* (1886); *The Discovery of America by Northmen* (1888); *The Discovery of the Ancient City of Norumbega, A Communication to the President and Council of the American Geographical Society at their Special Session in Watertown, November 21, 1889* (Cambridge: privately printed, 1889); *The Problem of the Northmen: A Letter to Judge Daly, President of the American Geographical Society* (Cambridge, privately printed, 1889); *Watertown: The Site of the Ancient City of Norumbega* (1890); *Sketch of the Norse Discovery of America* (1891); *The Defenses of Norumbega and a Review of the Reconnaissances* (Boston and New York, 1891); *The Landfall of Leif Erikson, A.D. 1000 and Site of His Houses in Vineland* (Boston, 1892); and *Leif's House in Vineland* (printed with Cornelia Horsford's *Graves of the Northmen,* Boston, 1893).

87. Horsford, *Problem of the Northmen,* op. cit., 12.

88. Horsford, *Discovery of the Ancient City of Norumbega,* op. cit., 44.

89. Horsford, *Problem of the Northmen,* op. cit., 12.

90. Horsford, *Discovery of the Ancient City of Norumbega,* op. cit., 25–26.

91. Ibid., 19.

92. Ibid., 37.

93. Ibid., 45.

94. "The Norseman," *WFP,* July 26, 1889. This article gives the firm name Brunner & Tyron. Horsford's book credits "Mr. Tryon."

95. "Norumbega: The Memorial Tower Dedicated," *WFP,* November 29, 1889.

96. Winsor, Justin, ed., *Narrative and Critical History of America,* vol. II (Boston and New York, 1889), 98.

97. Stephen Williams to PWF, January 21, 1997.

98. "Prof. Horsford, Leif Erikson's Champion Dies Suddenly," *Boston Transcript,* January 2, 1893.

99. Bacon, Edwin M., *Boston: A Guide Book* (Ginn & Co., Boston), 1903, 117.

100. "Charles River Canoeists' Illumination Association Has Plans Nearly Completed," *WDFPT,* May 19, 1906.

101. Metropolitan Park Commission minutes (vol. 5, June 29, 1900) and Metropolitan District Commission minutes (vol. 2, August 10, 1922).

102. For the 1935 improvements, see MDC Commission annual report, February 1936, 6. For 1973 rebuilding, see "1889 Norumbega Memorial Tower 1973 Restoration," *WHSB,* October 1973.

103. Graham-Campbell, James, ed., *Cultural Atlas of the Viking World* (Oxfordshire, England, 1994), 175–80, and Else Roesdahl, *The Vikings* (London, 1987), 274–76.

104. "Ancient Site Offers Clues to Vikings in America," *New York Times,* March 9, 2000, D1. See also *Time,* May 8, 2000.

105. Ibid., 178–79.

106. Horsford, *Discovery of the Ancient City of Norumbega,* op. cit. 63.

Figure 22-1. Members of the Hubbard family enjoy a carriage ride in the country in the 1880s. The patriarch, Charles Townsend Hubbard, sits in the rear seat. Four of his five children lived in Weston for at least part of the year. Driving the coach is his only son, Charles Wells Hubbard, who married Anne Swann and lived in the estate mansion, Ridgehurst, on Orchard Avenue. C.T. Hubbard's daughter Charlotte married Benjamin Loring Young and had a summer home on what is now Young Road. Elizabeth married Francis Blake and lived next door to her father and brother. Anne married Bancroft Davis and settled across the street from Ridgehurst. The Davises are in the middle seat. The large extended family owned much of the land in the southeast corner of Weston.

CHAPTER 22

The Hubbard Estate and Orchard Avenue

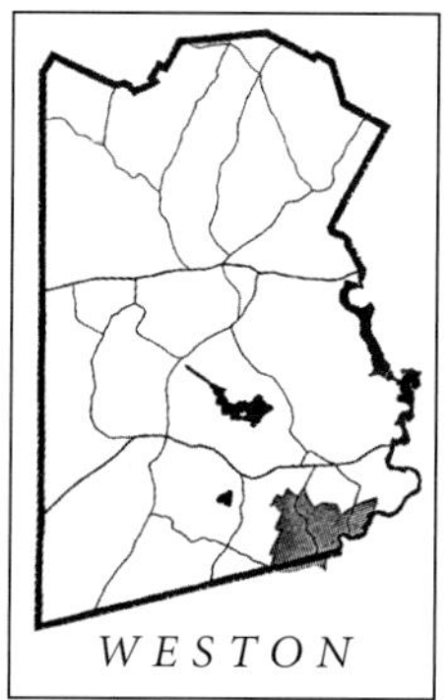

Imagine a picturesque valley of meadow and upland, woodlands and farm fields, traversed by the meandering Charles River. Beginning in 1834, Boston and Albany Railroad trains wind their way between Riverside and Wellesley Farms stations. Later, estate houses and formal gardens are built along the hilltops. Route 128 and the Massachusetts Turnpike have not yet engineered a broad swath of destruction across the peaceful countryside.

Three generations of Hubbards influenced the development of this valley. Charles Townsend Hubbard was one of the first Boston businessmen to choose Weston as the location for a country home. Over the next half century, he and his children and grandchildren bought hundreds of acres and built graceful mansions in the Orchard Avenue area. His only son, Charles Wells Hubbard, was particularly important in shaping the property with an eye toward its natural beauty.

Charles Wells Hubbard's interests and vision extended well beyond simply improving his own estate. Hubbard was a major force in preserving the land along the Charles River as public open space. He established the Riverside Recreation Grounds to provide affordable recreational opportunities for an increasingly urban population. He also expanded housing opportunities in Weston by creating Chiltern Hundreds, one of Weston's first major subdivisions.

This chapter tells the story of the Hubbard family, their business enterprises, and the evolution of Hubbard land on Orchard Avenue. Charles Wells Hubbard's role in supporting the metropolitan parks movement and creating Riverside Recreation Grounds is detailed in chapter 21.

Figure 22-2. Charles Townsend Hubbard bought the 214-acre Slack Farm along the Charles River in 1867. His family used the existing farmhouse as their country home for more than 15 years. The section to the right was an addition.

Purchase of the Slack Farm

John Slack had a large farm in Weston and Wellesley beginning in the late 18th century.[1] In 1867 his descendants could no longer pay the mortgage, and the 214 acres along the Charles River were sold at public auction to Charles Townsend Hubbard, the highest bidder at $5,800. The deed reserved the right of Elizabeth Slack to occupy part of the house for her lifetime and to keep a cow.[2] Mary Hubbard French, granddaughter of C.T. Hubbard, was later to say, "Miss Slack and her companion went with the house."[3] The Slack farmhouse was located off a dirt road between what is now Orchard Avenue and Intervale Road, near the railroad tracks. Here Charles T. Hubbard brought his young family for the summer, devoting the last 20 years of his life to improving and beautifying the property.[4]

Charles Townsend Hubbard: Business and Family Life

Charles Townsend Hubbard (1817–1887), son of Henry and Mary Hubbard, could trace his lineage back to the earliest English settlers in Ipswich. Because of his father's heavy losses in New Hampshire cotton mills, Hubbard had to leave school at an early age.[5] He began work as a commission merchant, purchasing southern cotton, tobacco, and sugar for northern markets. In 1845 he married Louisa Bowman Sewall, daughter of Benjamin Sewall, who was the senior partner in the old Yankee ship-owning and cordage-manufacturing firm of Sewall Day & Co. That year, Hubbard wrote a letter to his new father-in-law describing two disastrous seasons of shipwrecks and dropping prices. He concluded with a fresh optimism and eagerness to begin again, which undoubtedly contributed to his later business success, as did the Sewall family connection.[6] In 1848, with his father-in-law's assistance, Hubbard started the Boston Flax Mills in

Figure 22-3. This unusual double portrait suggests the strong degree of affection between manufacturer Charles Townsend Hubbard (1817–1887) and his son, Charles Wells. (1871 photo)

Figure 22-4. Elizabeth Wells (1822–1890), the second wife of Charles Townsend Hubbard, was a quiet, reserved woman who was a good mother to her children and stepchildren.

East Braintree, a venture that proved profitable in processing flax and hemp.

Charles T. and Louisa Sewall Hubbard had four daughters: Louisa, Mary, Elizabeth, and Charlotte.

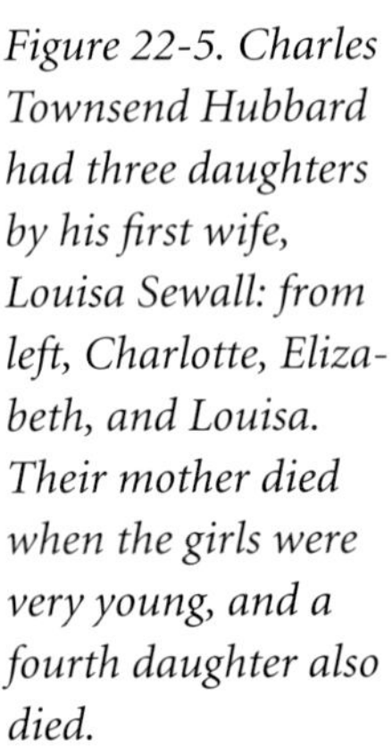

Figure 22-5. Charles Townsend Hubbard had three daughters by his first wife, Louisa Sewall: from left, Charlotte, Elizabeth, and Louisa. Their mother died when the girls were very young, and a fourth daughter also died.

Mary died at a young age and the other girls were still young when Louisa Sewall Hubbard also died. With three small children to take care of, Charles Townsend Hubbard soon married again, in 1855. With his second wife, Elizabeth Wells (1822–1890), of Hartford, he had two more children, Charles Wells (1856–1933) and Anne (1858–1946).

In his unpublished autobiography, young Charles described his mother and his own attitudes toward society:

> I do not believe there was much romance about this marriage—but she made a good mother to her children and step children. My mother's grandparents were all born in England and my mother might have been an Englishwoman—She had a very quiet reserved and dignified and conscientious character and coming from a distant city and living the first part of her married life in the country—and having no relatives in Boston; she made few friends there. My own younger sister Annie while she had a great many strong personal friends did not care at all about general society and would take no trouble to cultivate it in any way—owing to these handicaps and my own want of sociability—my own social acquaintance in Boston was unusually small.[7]

When Charles Wells was born, the family was living in Newton and C.T. Hubbard was treasurer and general manager of the Boston Flax Mills and also a junior partner at Sewall Day & Co. The business prospered during the Civil War, and in succeeding years the family spent winters on Beacon Hill while continuing to develop the country place in Weston.

In his autobiography, Charles described summers at the Slack farm like this:

> In the early days when all my sisters were at home the old farm house was well filled with our guests—and we had at times 8 or 9 carriage and saddle horses. I believe the people passing on the R.R. thought we kept a boarding house and livery stable. In addition to our driving and riding we had boats on the river—which at that time could not have had more than 20 boats between our place and Waltham. In short we lived under ideal conditions for having a good time with our friends—one of my old friends . . . said he remembered sitting down with twenty at breakfast.[8]

Charles recalled how the children put on theatrical productions in an outbuilding used as the laundry:

> One summer when I was about 14 I fitted up a rough stage, and we children gave a little play. My father was so much interested that he had the building enlarged putting in quite a complete little stage—in the fitting of which I had a chance to exercise my love of carpentry.
>
> Each summer of 1871, 72, 73 we gave several plays in this theatre and there are now in my library two bound volumes of these plays. I have always felt that this amateur acting had an educational value—our company consisted of Carrie and Mabel Case who lived about three miles away and Will and Walter Bush. Their older sister Fanny our acting manager—my sister Annie and myself—with now and then a guest at the house to help out. I remember one amusing incident. Old Mr. Sewall like other slightly deaf people sometimes made audible comments—and in a scene where I was playing the lover he remarked—"Does it pretty well does he not—looks as if he really meant it."[9]

The family also spent time in the summer in the White Mountains, where C.T. Hubbard owned property in Intervale and had plans for a house, which he never built. Charles W. and his sister Anne later donated the land to the town as a park reservation. About 1873, young Charles took the first of what he called "tramping" trips. These hunting, camping, and canoeing expeditions in New Hampshire, Maine, and the Adirondacks included hikes up Mount Washington with his brother-in-law, Francis Blake.

Homes for C.T. Hubbard's Daughters

In the 1870s, C.T. Hubbard purchased nearly 200 additional acres including the Ichabad Pierce farm, Jonas Cutter farm, Charles Cutter farm, and Bush homestead, along with land belonging to Benjamin Cutter, Daniel Seaverns, and the Livermore family.[10] In 1879, he was taxed for 404 acres in Weston.[11]

When his three oldest daughters married, he gave them each land near the Slack farmhouse. Their grandfather, Benjamin Sewall, contributed money for each young couple to build a house. The oldest daughter, Louisa, and her first husband, John Cotton Jackson, chose the French Academic style, with a mansard roof and dark wood interiors. Mary Hubbard French called it a "very ugly Victorian," and the family must have agreed, as it was torn down in the next generation and replaced by a granddaughter's house.[12]

In 1873, Hubbard's daughter Elizabeth married scientist and inventor Francis Blake, who commissioned the young architect Charles McKim to design their house.[13] Blake made his own fortune with the 1878 invention of the Blake telephone transmitter. A story passed down in the family alleges that Elizabeth's stepbrother, Charles Wells Hubbard, knew of the device but decided not to invest in any of "Frank Blake's half-baked schemes."[14] Blake purchased additional land and worked with landscape gardener Ernest W. Bowditch to develop his property into a formal showplace.

Figure 22-6. Anne Hubbard (1858–1946) married Bancroft Chandler Davis in 1882. Her brother once wrote that "while she had a great many strong personal friends, [she] did not care at all about general society and would take no trouble to cultivate it in any way . . ." (1881 photo)

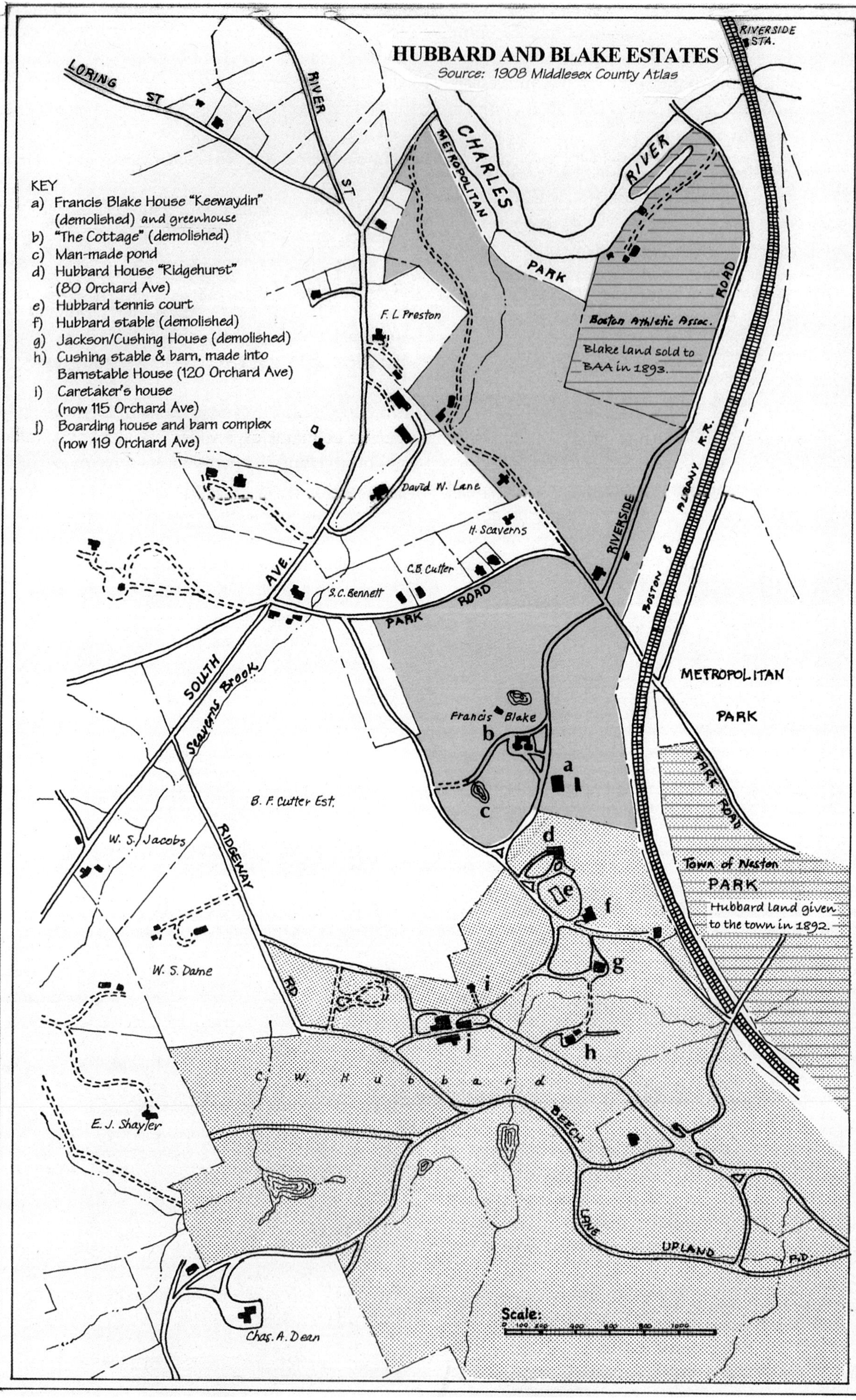

Figure 22-7. This map of the Hubbard and Blake estates is based on the 1908 Atlas of Middlesex County. *Also shaded is the land that Hubbard gave to the Town of Weston in December 1892 and the land that Blake sold to the Boston Athletic Association in 1893.*

The Blake estate is discussed in detail in the next chapter. Of interest here is the fact that, in 1880, Blake decided to enlarge his house and erect a multipurpose secondary building. When McKim was unable to do the design, Blake turned to the Boston firm of Cabot and Chandler, who soon afterward were brought in to design the main house, Ridgehurst, on the Hubbard estate.[15]

In September 1875, C.T. Hubbard's third daughter, Charlotte, married businessman Benjamin L. Young at St. Mary's (Episcopal) Church in Newton Lower Falls in a ceremony performed by Rev. Phillips Brooks. The two Beacon Hill families were referred to in the newspaper as "the elite of the city."[16] Hubbard sold the Youngs 50 acres on South Avenue and Newton Street, where they built a large shingled summer house.[17]

The youngest child, Anne, married Bancroft Chandler Davis at First Church in Boston in November 1882. Davis, scion of another socially prominent Boston family, was trained as a lawyer but spent much of his life as a serious gentleman farmer in Weston, building up the Ferndale Farm dairy discussed in chapter 24. The Davises started planning their house, The Pines, on Orchard Avenue in the spring before their marriage. In her diary, Elizabeth Wells Hubbard writes: "Bancroft has brought out some architectural papers and Anne is amusing herself making plans for her lot by the Pines." In another entry she writes: ". . . Bancroft brought a sketch of a house for Anne [that] Mr. Emerson has drawn, but we were not much pleased with it. Our plan by Mr. Cabot was brought out and Charlie made a sketch from it, very much smaller which pleased me."[18] By August 1882, the cellar was nearly dug out. A cottage was built in back for the Davis gardener and an apartment over the garage for the chauffeur.

Charles Townsend Hubbard's only son, Charles Wells Hubbard, was not married until 1889. By that time, C.T. Hubbard had built Ridgehurst, where he lived until his death in 1887.

Building Ridgehurst

In 1878 Charles Townsend Hubbard merged his company with a struggling cotton mill in Ludlow to form the Ludlow Manufacturing Company, for which he served as treasurer until his death. He moved the Braintree operation to Ludlow, initiating a period of major expansion including new mills and housing for mill operatives. Charles Wells Hubbard would later write: "It was my father's wish to have these do credit to the village and to afford good living conditions to the operators."[19] In the U.S. census of 1880, Ludlow was one of three New England towns mentioned as having the best housing conditions for mill workers.[20] Landscape work at the mills and throughout the village was supervised by Ernest Bowditch.[21]

In 1880, with the death of his father-in-law, Benjamin Sewall, and increased business success, C.T. Hubbard was so well off that he took his family to Europe for a year. When he returned in 1881, at age 64,

Figure 22-8. Ridgehurst was constructed in 1883 for Charles Townsend Hubbard and is Weston's finest example of Shingle-style architecture. (1904 photo)

Figures 22-9 and 22-10. Ridgehurst took a year and a half to build and cost $65,000. Fine craftsmanship is evident in these interior photographs.

he began building his own stylish mansion on Orchard Avenue, nestled between the homes of his daughters. The Shingle-style house, set on a ridge with panoramic views south over the Charles River to the distant hills, took a year and a half to build and cost $65,000, a staggering sum at the time.[22]

Details about the construction are related in a letter from C.T. Hubbard's daughter-in-law, Anne Swann Hubbard, to a later owner. She credited the design to "Professor Chandler." Francis Chandler (1844–1925) was associated with Edward C. Cabot until 1888, when he withdrew to become professor and later head of the department of architecture at MIT. She praised the unnamed mill builder, who had never before constructed a residence:

> Mr. Hubbard's father insisted on having the builder who had done mills so successfully for Ludlow (& Braintree) & he certainly did a wonderful job "by the day." It is the best built house I ever was in.[23]

She added that details such as the English and Chinese fireplace tiles "were felt to be 'a touch beyond.'" As to the origin of the name Ridgehurst, Anne Swann Hubbard writes, "I think it was connected with the lovely old town of Lavenham in the English Midlands where the Hubbards came from."

Pink granite trimmed with brownstone was used for the lower story. Shingles on the upper stories were originally painted a dark base color with dark trim. To the side and rear is an expansive veranda. Originally, stained-glass windows brought light into the stair tower and "living hall," which features Minton tiles and a fireplace with intricately carved wooden faces. The walls were originally covered with embossed leather, later changed to the present Chinese tea paper imported in small squares.

Family tradition holds that Frederick Law Olmsted himself was involved in the landscaping. Mary Hubbard French recorded the following quote from a lost diary of her mother, Anne Swann Hubbard: "When they were building Ridgehurst, Mr. Olmsted came out to see about the planting around the house."[24] The layout of Orchard Avenue, with its smooth serpentine curves, may reflect Olmsted's influence. The road follows the natural topography as it sweeps around what the Hubbards called Gaiety Hill.

Charles Townsend Hubbard died suddenly in 1887 at the age of 70, bringing to a close the first chapter of the development of the Hubbard estate. A newspaper article, doubtless exaggerated, summarized the status of the estate about 1888, still well before the height of the estate building boom in Weston:

> The locality known as Hubbard's Corner . . . pays nearly one-third of the whole town tax. The late Charles T. Hubbard, an extensive cordage maker who accumulated piles of money in the war time, resided there. . . . The locality is delightful and overlooks the Charles River. . . . The Hubbard Corner bank and corporation stocks and other property yield a rich harvest to jolly Mr. Hews, the tax gatherer.[25]

Charles Wells Hubbard:
Education and Business Experience

Charles Wells Hubbard was 30 years old when his father died, and well prepared to take his place at the Ludlow Manufacturing Company and as patriarch of the family estate in Weston. Hubbard had prepared for college at "Mr. Noble's," later Noble and Greenough School, and, after taking time off because of failed eyesight, entered Harvard, where he graduated in the class of 1878.

Young Charles began his career as a day laborer at the Ludlow Manufacturing Company and was later amused when people at the mill would say he "never did a day's work." He related his experiences in his 50th college reunion report:

> First I went into the works as a day laborer, taking down machinery in an old mill and setting it up in a new one. This was very hard and dirty work, and occupied eleven hours a day, but I enjoyed it. It gave me an intimate knowledge of the intricate parts of all machines, and put me in touch with the mill workers. After this job was done, I studied the machines in operation. Our mills were then lighted by kerosene lamps, and there was no system of caring for the dust—such conditions would not be tolerated now—but we did away with them as fast as we learned how.[26]

He was moved to the Boston office, acting as his father's assistant and taking over as treasurer after his father's death.

Hubbard was always interested in tools, machinery, and mechanical inventions. He and brother-in-law Francis Blake both tinkered with the newly invented telephone, working on how to ring up one subscriber without disturbing others on the same line. In the process, Hubbard invented a form of hotel communication that was patented, won a silver medal at the Paris Exposition of Electricity in 1880, and was used in a White Mountain hotel.[27] Although he had to abandon his experiments to attend to the Ludlow business, he would later say that his mind was constantly busy studying improved methods and machinery. Because of its use of the latest modern technology, Ludlow Manufacturing Company cornered the market in jute manufacturing.

Figure 22-11. Charles Townsend Hubbard started the Ludlow Manufacturing Company, which made twine, upholstery webbing, and other products from a coarse fiber called jute. Father and son worked to make Ludlow a model factory town.

During the 25 years under C. W. Hubbard's leadership, the Ludlow Manufacturing Company experienced exponential growth. The company made yarn for the foundations of carpets, coarse bagging for cotton bales, twines of all sizes and strength, and upholstery webbing. These products were all fashioned predominantly of jute, a fiber grown 10,000 miles away in the Bengal (Calcutta) region of India. In 1902 the company was reorganized as the Ludlow Manufacturing Associates, run by nine trustees including Ernest Bowditch and Francis Blake. In 1909, sales were reported to be in excess of $6 million annually.[28] The company employed 3,500 operatives and owned most of the town of Ludlow, including 1,400 acres of land and hundreds of houses rented to employees.[29]

Like his father, Charles Wells Hubbard wanted Ludlow to be a model village, a place where workers felt an "esprit de corps" about the company and community. Immediately after his father's death, he began his own series of improvements with the building of the Hubbard Memorial Library, dedicated in 1888. The company built the Ludlow Hospital, Textile School, and Stevens Memorial Building, which housed a gymnasium, swimming pool, bowling alley, reading room, and other leisure facilities. It maintained a large athletic field and two parks. In his autobiography, C.W. Hubbard writes:

> The welfare of the men, women and children thus brought to our village was a matter of great concern to us—and much more than other manufacturers at that time we felt responsible for their welfare. I think we were many years in advance of public opinion in this matter—and that we were considered by some as sentimental enthusiasts.[30]

These major employee welfare efforts, carried out in a spirit of progressive paternalism, did not prevent the company from experiencing a major strike in 1909. Hubbard was later to write:

> I never myself felt that such welfare work was certain insurance against strikes—but I did feel that while humanity and patriotism required it of employers it was also a good business investment—that if it did not avoid it would soften strikes.[31]

This proved to be the case during the four-month period of conflict and unrest, which did not result in violence.

Charles Wells Hubbard: Marriage and Family Life
In 1889 Charles Wells Hubbard married Anne Laurens Swann, who at age 22 was 11 years younger. They met at Isle au Haut, an island off the coast of Maine where Hubbard was a guest of Ernest Bowditch and his wife, Margaret, who was Anne's sister.[32] Bowditch had established a summer colony of friends and family at Isle au Haut, described as a place for "more rustic rusticating" than nearby Bar Harbor.

Anne Swann Hubbard was as an intelligent woman who, like so many women of her era, was unable to reach her full potential. Her grandson described her wide-ranging pursuits:

Figure 22-12. The three oldest children of Charles W. and Anne Swann Hubbard pose outside Ridgehurst in this turn-of-the-century photograph.

Figure 22-13. Anne Swann was 22 years old when she married 33-year-old Charles Wells Hubbard. She was widely read and widely traveled, with a lively interest in world affairs and Western culture.

> She was an anglophile, very intelligent, widely travelled in Great Britain and Western Europe with a wide interest in traditional Western culture. I remember a number of times as a child being surprised at grandma's trenchant comments about life and the then current trend of world affairs. Grandma was an avid photographer and gardener. She was quite wealthy and enjoyed all the benefits attendant to such fortune. But she was uneasy in the role of grand dame. The Victorian Era mold of what constituted the proper role for womanhood was confining and never allowed her to make full use of the intelligence and various talents she possessed.[33]

One of her contemporaries, a male relative by marriage, is reported to have said of her: "She has a mind like a man."

During the years their children were growing up, the estate in Weston provided a country retreat and constant thread in a life that otherwise did not follow a set pattern. For a time, the couple wintered in Weston. When their children reached school age, they hired homes in the city; and in

Figure 22-14. Charles W. and Anne Swann Hubbard are pictured on the veranda at Ridgehurst about 1912, with their son Charles W. Jr. (left), daughter-in-law Dorothy (lower left), and daughters Mary, Elizabeth (center) and Anne, who was called Nancy. Mary was nine years younger than her closest sibling.

Figure 22-15. Charles W. (back right) and wife Anne play mixed doubles on the grass court next to Ridgehurst, about 1910.

Figures 22-16 and 22-17. Anne Swann Hubbard stands in front of the "camp wagon," which her daughter claimed was the first of its type in the country. Designed by Charles Wells Hubbard, it included a bunkroom, chemical toilet, and small galley kitchen. The sides pulled out to form two additional rooms. The camp wagon was shipped by rail to the station nearest the intended campsite, then was hauled the rest of the way by six strong horses. After several years on Lake Winnipesaukee, Hubbard purchased land on Meredith Neck with three miles of lakefront.

Figure 22-18. This 1888 photograph of the Hubbard farm buildings shows the former Slack barn (right; since demolished), which Charles W. moved to this location, and the boardinghouse for workers (left), now 119 Orchard Avenue.

1902–03, Hubbard built an elegant town house facing the Charles River on Bay State Road.[34] Summers were spent at a family cottage on Isle au Haut, at Cataumet, on the North Shore, and later camping on Lake Winnipesaukee, where Hubbard bought land on Meredith's Neck. Family scrapbooks show Charles and Anne Hubbard in their old clothes roughing it on the shores of the lake. They camped in an early horse-drawn, wooden version of the "RV" copied from the real Gypsy wagons that sometimes encamped on the shores of the Charles River in Weston. The family also had a house in Jamestown, Rhode Island, where they headed in spring and fall to watch yachting races and go duck hunting in season.

Charles W. and Anne Swann Hubbard had four children: Charles Wells Jr. (1890–1966), Elizabeth (1894–1991), Anne Swann Jr., who was called Nancy (1896–1978), and Mary Greene (1905–1993). The girls attended Winsor School. Hubbard was the first treasurer of the school's executive committee and was instrumental in establishing the private girls school in its present Longwood location.

Conservation and Recreation

The concern for public welfare and community development evidenced in Hubbard's business practices in Ludlow can be seen in his involvement with the upbuilding of Weston beginning in the 1890s. It was in the area of land conservation that he made his largest and most lasting contribution to future generations of Weston residents. As described in greater detail in the previous chapter, Hubbard was instrumental in preserving more than 100 acres along the Charles River for public use and enjoyment. In 1892 he donated 19 acres for the town's first public park. In 1893 he sold the City of Newton 42 acres of riverfront for park purposes. A few years later, he purchased land along the Charles for the construction of Riverside Recreation Grounds, an outdoor sporting facility that he later donated to the Metropolitan Parks Commission. The Weston and Newton parkland and most of the former Riverside Recreation Grounds are now used for the Leo J. Martin Golf Course, a public recreational resource made possible through Hubbard's conservation initiatives. In 1972, the Metropolitan District Commission was asked to rename Riverside Park in honor of Charles W. Hubbard. The MDC voted instead to erect a Hubbard memorial tablet.[35]

Development and Operation of the Hubbard Estate 1888–1919 and the Italian Gardens

From Charles Townsend Hubbard's death in 1887 until the end of World War I, the Hubbard land on the Orchard Avenue side of the railroad tracks remained largely undeveloped. Occasionally, a house lot was carved out for a relative or friend. In 1888, C.T. Hubbard's daughter, Louisa Jackson, sold her mansard-roofed house to a family friend, Livingston Cushing (1856–1916), who used it in the summer until his death in November 1916. Louisa later sailed off to France.

Livingston Cushing was a well-known Boston

lawyer who practiced in partnership with Samuel C. Bennett, another member of the Hubbard/Blake inner circle, who lived nearby at South Avenue and Park Road. Cushing, Bennett, and Hubbard were contemporaries at Harvard, where Cushing was captain of the varsity football team for three years.[36] In the 1890s, when Hubbard proposed his plan for Riverside Recreation Grounds, Cushing and two other former Harvard team captains served on the executive committee. Shortly after Livingston Cushing bought the Orchard Avenue house, Charles W. Hubbard sold to his congenial new neighbor an additional 12 acres, on which Cushing built a combined stable and barn later converted into the dwelling known as Barnstable House. He hired lumberjacks from Canada to build an authentic-looking log cabin on the property. Cushing relatives recalled eating Thanksgiving dinner in the log cabin, their food brought over from the main house on huge trays.[37]

Hubbard moved his other farm buildings down Orchard Avenue to the bend in the road, where he developed a complex of wood-frame barns and outbuildings. He had a caretaker's house, dormitory for unmarried outdoor help, dairy barn, and another large barn with sections for carpentry and repairs. The Hubbards kept six or seven saddle horses and five workhorses, two pairs and one single. Nearby was a shed and a blacksmith shop known as The Forge. Between the main house and the Jackson/Cushing property was a tennis court and a large stone stable later adapted as a garage, with an apartment for the coachman or chauffeur.

Elsewhere on the estate was a sawmill, used at one point to clear chestnut trees killed by the blight. The pigpen was on Ridgeway Road.[38] The Hubbard pond, located west of Ridgeway Road, was created by damming up the brook and was used for cutting ice in winter and swimming in summer. At one time there were bathhouses along one side.

During this period, Hubbard sold only a few parcels to non-family members. Fellow Harvard graduate Frederick Blake Holder bought land at Orchard Avenue and Oxbow Road in 1892 and built a house called Ridgeways.[39] S.F. Denton bought on Oxbow Road in 1899 and built a shingled house, and Gordon Donald bought on Bullard Road in 1917 but died before completion of his brick Tudor.[40]

In the 1902 *Boston Sunday Herald* article "Weston Has Become the Lenox of the East," the writer describes the important estates in Weston, including the Hubbard and Blake estates, which he praises in his concluding remarks:

> Perhaps the most notable feature of the town is the great park on the south side, in which are located the residence of Charles W. Hubbard, Francis Blake, and others. This park is thrown open to visitors on Saturday afternoons, and a drive through it is a popular event.[41]

Figure 22-19. Although dairy cows were given up sometime after Charles Wells Hubbard's death in 1933, the hill on Orchard Avenue retains its pastoral appearance because of conservation restrictions. The gap in the trees at the upper left is where the reservoir for the Blake estate water system was located.

Figure 22-20. About 1910, Charles W. built a billiards room at the back of Ridgehurst (right). The addition was later detached and moved closer to Orchard Avenue, where it became a separate residence at No. 74.

The Blake estate was the more formal, while the Hubbard property was maintained in a natural style except in the immediate vicinity of the main house.

In the fall of 1910, C.W. Hubbard contacted Olmsted Brothers to design the grounds around Ridgehurst and to integrate a billiards room added for Charles Jr. and his college friends.[42] Olmsted Brothers extended a stone retaining wall east toward the adjacent Blake house and introduced a formal Italian garden measuring about 55 by 80 feet. The space was enclosed by a colonnade and vine-covered pergola and featured two hip-roofed grottoes and a fountain.

Interior space was divided into two square perennial flower beds and a grassed center. The geometric layout and architectonic quality are typical of the Italian garden style popular at the turn of the century. Plans still on file at the Olmsted office in Brookline show that the Hubbards were offered an alternate choice with the same basic layout but with Japanese-style pagodas and a statue of Buddha.[43] The Italian garden was constructed in early 1912. Photographs show the abundant use of plant materials common in an era when plants were inexpensive and a full-time Italian gardener was on staff in season.

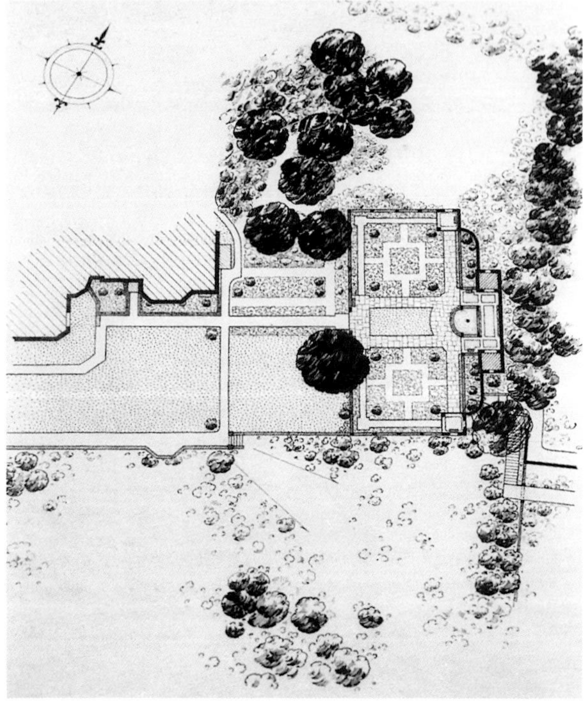

Figure 22-21. Olmsted Brothers, successor firm to the great 19th-century landscape architect Frederick Law Olmsted, designed a formal Italian-style garden for the Hubbards in 1912.

Figure 22-22. The winter view from the upper floors of Ridgehurst shows the Italian garden, and the hills of Newton in the distance.

Charles Jr. graduated from Harvard in 1912 and married Dorothy Briggs that same year. Looking back at his early business life, he was later to write:

> Upon graduation I went into the textile mills in which my immediate forbears had been prominent and successful for two generations. This move was due solely to nepotism, against which I hereby warn all and sundry . . .[44]

In subsequent years, Charles Jr. became an investment banker and managing trustee of the estate. His sister Elizabeth married U.S. Navy career officer John Forsyth Meigs in 1913. Hubbard built them a house called The Knoll on Orchard Avenue, but after only a few years Meigs was transferred to China.[45]

As his oldest children left home, Hubbard must have taken stock of the enormous size of Ridgehurst and the number of servants needed to maintain it. Mary Hubbard French recalled that when she was a child during the pre–World War I years, the Hubbards had an indoor staff of 12. The best remembered was Amelia "Millie" Murray, an Irish nurse who was so well loved that she was buried in the Hubbard lot at Mount Auburn Cemetery. The servants' quarters were in a large wing on the north side. Around the early 1920s, the entire wing was

Figure 22-23. Charles Wells Hubbard (1856–1933) was instrumental in preserving more than 100 acres along the Charles River for public use and enjoyment, including what is now the Leo J. Martin Golf Course.

Figure 22-24. House Beautiful *published this photograph of the garden in March 1917.*

removed, placed on rollers, and pulled by horses across the fields to Ridgeway Road, where it was made into a separate house.[46] Some years later, the billiards room was also detached and moved to its current location fronting Orchard Avenue.

When the United States entered World War I, Charles and Anne Hubbard offered Ridgehurst to the Red Cross for use as a hospital and converted the Cushing stable complex into Barnstable House, a comfortable home for their smaller family. The Red Cross never used the estate mansion. After C.W. Hubbard moved out, Ridgehurst was rented or left vacant until his son, Charles Jr., lived there for a time in the 1930s.

In 1922, C.W. Hubbard deeded eight acres of former Jackson/Cushing land to his daughter Anne ("Nancy") and her husband, Boston antique dealer Edward C. Wheeler.[47] Charles had already torn down the "ugly Victorian" built by his stepsister and in its place the Wheelers erected a mid-18th-century Colonial house purchased from Israel Sack and moved piece by piece from Newmarket, New Hampshire. The house, which they called Glen Acres, was originally the home of wealthy mercantile trader John

Figures 22-25 and 22-26. These "before" and "after" photographs illustrate one of Charles Wells Hubbard's adaptive reuse projects. Livingston Cushing had built the combined barn and stable on Orchard Avenue pictured in the photo at left. In the late 1910s, Charles Wells Hubbard converted it to a residence called Barnstable House (right). The house on the left side of the lefthand picture was moved across the street, and for this reason was given the name Wendover.

Burleigh. Workmen spent six months carefully dismantling it and labeling beams, hearth tiles, clapboards, chimney bricks, Dutch tiles from two rooms, paneling, and original French scenic wallpaper—everything except plaster and shingles—17 truck loads in all.[48]

Chiltern Hundreds

In the fall of 1919, Charles Wells Hubbard turned over 155 acres to a real-estate trust similar to that formed by Robert Winsor just one year earlier. Eleanor Dean Pearse, only child of his neighbor Charles Dean, joined with Hubbard in creating Chiltern Hundreds, a subdivision recorded in 1925.[49] The term "The Hundreds" refers to the 1699 division of land in Wellesley into 100-acre tracts, and "Chiltern" is thought to be an English place-name favored by the Hubbards. According to one observer, the project was "very dear to [Hubbard's] heart," as he "felt Weston ought not to be just for the very large land-holder."[50]

Chiltern Hundreds was by far the largest subdivision in Weston up to that time. Unlike Winsor's Meadowbrook Road development, where lots were carved out individually for each purchaser, Chiltern Hundreds was laid out as a whole. One plot plan, printed in a detailed promotional brochure issued by Boston realtor Walter Channing about 1926, shows 168 lots, including several dozen across the town line in Wellesley.[51] The subdivision was the work of Arthur A. Shurtleff, who is now generally known by the last name Shurcliff, which he adopted a few years later. The eminent Boston landscape architect had designed the Weston Town Green in the 1910s, and in the mid-1920s was working on a "Town Plan" for Weston, including zoning guidelines. In Chiltern Hundreds, Shurtleff and Hubbard put into place some of the provisions later required by zoning. Deed restrictions were used to prohibit business and industrial uses and ensure that residences were single-family only.[52] Houses had to be set back a certain distance from the road and property lines. Lot sizes were relatively consistent, averaging between one-third and one-half acre.

The winding street plan encompassed the present Chiltern, Locust, Dean, Ferndale, Old Colony, Pembroke, and Columbine Roads, as well as the southern parts of Oxbow and Ridgeway Roads. Twenty acres were reserved as a "picturesque private park," including the brook valley and two ponds. Ten acres of this park could be used for future tennis courts, playing fields, and a swimming pool "or such similar use and construction as the residents of Chiltern Hundreds shall provide." Land north of the brook, now Hubbard Road, was designated for future subdivision. Three acres were reserved for a "school house and playground when needed by the town." Although the school and most of the recreational facilities were never constructed, Shurtleff's design is a model for a carefully planned residential subdivision. Not only did he preserve open space and landscape features, but he also thought about future needs and set aside land for neighborhood amenities.

The Channing promotional brochure described Chiltern Hundreds as "part of a group of large family estates" where the owners were developing "a beautiful residential section, under certain social and building restrictions" that would be "separated from the congested suburban districts." Lot sizes were large enough "such that the atmosphere of the country will always be preserved, and the feeling and appearance of crowding, so objectionable in many suburban developments, eliminated." Chiltern Hundreds was lauded as "a very healthy location," 300 feet above sea level at the highest point, with views from Arlington Heights to the Blue Hills. The brochure touted the nearby "Metropolitan Park" and four golf clubs within three miles. The minimum cost of houses was set at $10,000.[53] Hubbard's personal interest in the future of the area is reflected in this statement: "As the proprietors of Chiltern Hundreds live on their adjoining estates, and as their avenues pass through it to reach the station, this development is certain to be guarded with the greatest care."

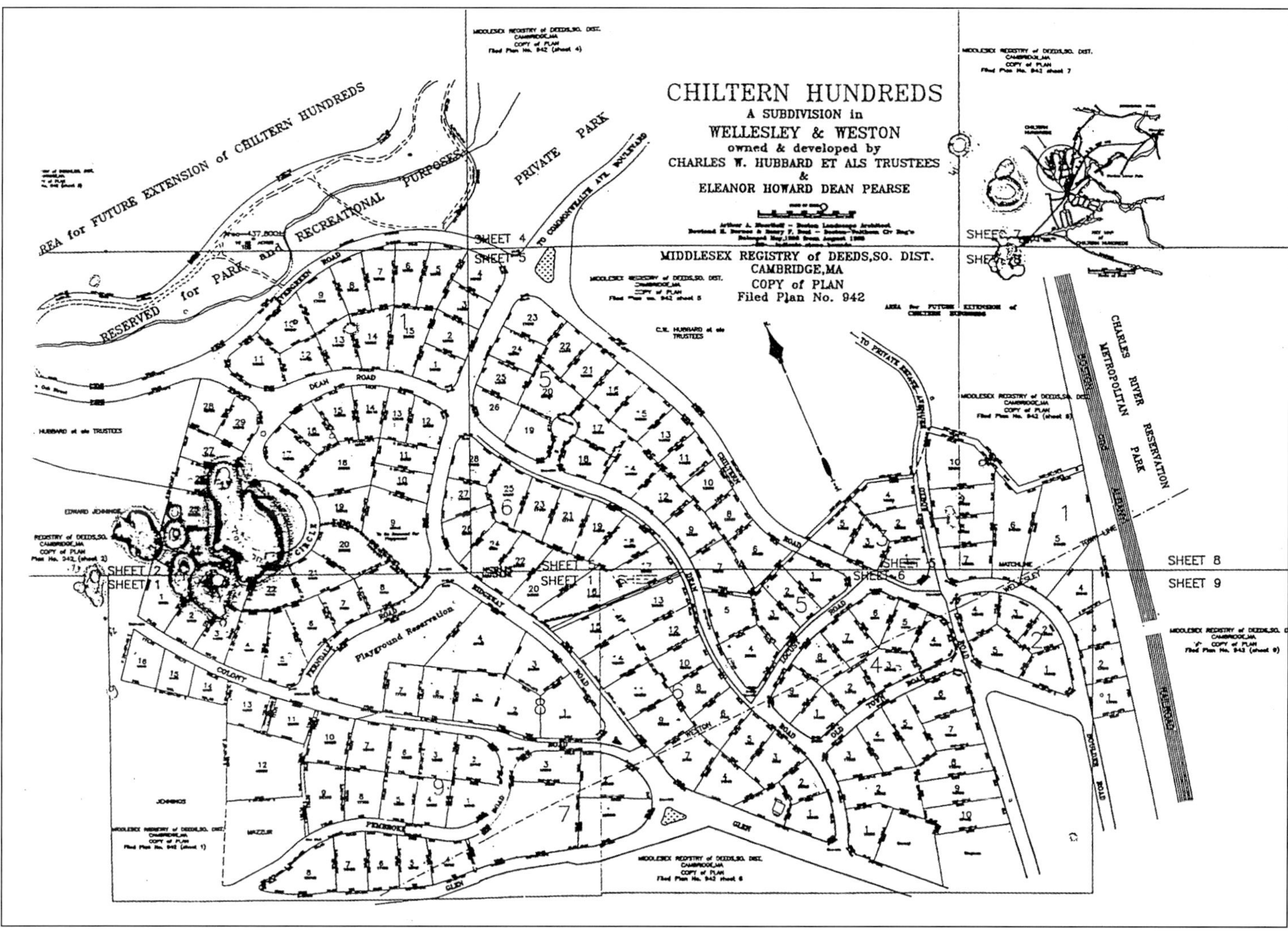

Potential buyers were informed that Wellesley Farms Station had "twenty trains a day each way, with numerous expresses, twenty-five minutes to South Station." Another selling point important in the automobile age was the proximity to "Commonwealth Avenue Boulevard," which offered a "direct, attractive, half-hour approach to Boston." Because the area was not within walking distance to stores, the brochure mentions that neighboring houses were already served by three milk routes, three laundry routes, S.S. Pierce Co., and other Boston and local stores that made deliveries.

The small wooden sales office was located at the corner of Ridgeway and Glen Roads in Wellesley. Lots closest to the train station were the first to be purchased.[54] The adoption of Weston's first zoning bylaw in 1928 made it necessary to change the size of some parcels. Lots in Chiltern Hundreds sold reasonably well until the 1929 stock market crash ushered in the Depression. It was only in the 1950s, after most of the lots had finally sold, that the real-estate market in Weston fully recovered.

The Hubbard Estate after World War I and Hubbard Water System

In 1926, C.W. Hubbard's youngest daughter, Mary, married Stanley French (1902–1969), who worked for Houghton Mifflin and later directed Riverside Press. During their married life, the couple lived in four different houses on the estate.[55] As a founding member of Weston Forest and Trail Association, French worked with Charles Wells Hubbard Jr. and the estate trustees to permanently preserve the pastoral landscape through substantial land donations, including the Hubbard Trail and the hill on the west side of Orchard Avenue.

Charles Wells Hubbard died in 1933 at age 77. His son, Charles Jr., took over the estate and moved into Ridgehurst. Dairying was abandoned at some point, but the farm staff continued to keep horses, pigs, and chickens. The working farm was managed from 1920 until his death in 1945 by Philip Bridgeman, an Englishman remembered as a patient, even-tempered, and methodical man who could do anything of a practical nature.

During the Depression, unemployed hoboes and tramps camped in the warmer months along the railroad tracks just below the Blake and Hubbard estates. The inviting pines were the last stretch of woodland before the more populated Boston suburbs. With full employment in the war years, the drifters were gradually assimilated into the work-

Figure 22-27. In the early 1920s, C.W. Hubbard put more than 150 acres of his land into a real-estate trust and hired landscape architect Arthur Shurtleff (later Shurcliff) to design the Chiltern Hundreds subdivision. The minimum cost of houses was initially set at $10,000.

force. The Boston and Albany Railroad, an important transportation link through the area since the early 19th century, became even more vital during the war. Gas was rationed and the bulk of the nation's freight and passenger traffic, including commuter traffic, moved by rail. It has been estimated that perhaps 90 trains a day passed along the four tracks of the B & A during the 1940s, among them whole trains of flatbed cars carrying Sherman tanks and military vehicles.[56]

As part of Civil Defense, the Hubbard water tower was fitted out as an aircraft observation post, complete with catwalk, field telephone, and air raid siren with a loud, wailing pitch.[57] Although the German *Luftwaffe* never threatened the eastern United States, World War II was, nevertheless, the death knell for the estate as it had existed for two generations. In the fall of 1942, a two-day auction was held to dispose of the farm equipment. Only the vegetable garden behind the caretaker's house was maintained, as a Victory Garden. In 1945, the main house was sold.

The Hubbard Water System continued to supply Orchard Avenue and Chiltern Hundreds and to serve as backup for the Jennings and Dean systems. Until the 1960s, the huge elevated tank built in the late 1890s still stood on 30-foot legs at the end of Hubbard Road on the highest elevation of the estate.[58] Water was pumped up to the tank and gravity-fed to houses. Initially, this water came from a well near the small stone pump house still standing on Orchard Avenue. When this supply proved insufficient in the early 20th century, C.W. Hubbard acquired a small parcel from the Metropolitan Parks Commission and built a pump house to tap wells near the Charles River.[59] Still later, when river pollution contaminated this source, the company arranged to purchase water from Wellesley.[60]

Family members were enlisted as water meter readers. In the late 1940s, the job fell to Stanley French. Every six months, on Saturday and Sunday, he would put on his old clothes and make the rounds. Eventually, about 120 houses were served by the Hubbard system, which grew too large to continue as the essentially amateur country utility of its origin. The system was offered free of charge to the town, which reluctantly took over 3.63 miles of Hubbard water mains in 1962.[61]

Houses in Orchard Avenue Area

33 Bullard Road (c. 1917). Brick Tudor mansion built for wool merchant Gordon Donald, partner in Hallowell, Jones & Donald Wool Co., from designs by Gordon Allen, architect, Boston.[62] After Donald's death, his widow, Alice, stayed on in the 17-room brick English country house with their three children and a staff that included chauffeur/caretaker Benjamin F. Knight, who lived with his wife in a cottage adjoining the garage.

49 Orchard Avenue (c. 1882). Caretaker's cottage for Davis house.

59 Orchard Avenue (1882). Queen Anne house built for newlyweds Bancroft C. and Anne Hubbard Davis. Sold in 1924 to Mrs. Joseph Eldredge, a widow, who later married tennis champion Raymond Bidwell.

74 Orchard Avenue (by 1910). Built as the billiards room of Ridgehurst. Moved and converted to a house around the mid-1920s.

80 Orchard Avenue (Ridgehurst, 1881–83). Shingle-style estate mansion built for Charles Townsend Hubbard from designs by noted architect Francis Chandler. The intact quality of the house is due in part to ownership by only three families in more than a century, the Hubbards (1883–1945), George N. and Anna Chamberlain Jr. (1945–80), and Harold and Paula Schwenk (1980–present). Among the many remaining original features are the butler's pantry, laundry drying racks, food pantry with marble slab for rolling pastry, dumbwaiters, bell box, speaking tubes, fire system with rack for holding hoses and an ax, and bathrooms with original plumbing fixtures.The original house was part gas and part electric, with some fixtures combining both.

86 Orchard Avenue. Site of the Hubbard tennis court. After Stanley French died in 1969, Mary Hubbard French bought the lot from the Chamberlain family and built a house designed by Marjorie Pierce.

92 Orchard Avenue (c. 1937). Built for Charles Wells Hubbard Jr. and his wife, Dorothy, on the site of the Hubbards' large stone stable/carriage house/garage.

100 Orchard Avenue (Burleigh house/Glen Acres). Mid-18th-century house moved here from Newmarket, New Hampshire, by Anne Hubbard Wheeler and her husband, Edward, about 1922. In 1937 it was sold to Clinton Biddle and his wife, Barbara, who brought up their five children here after the death of her husband the following year. According to notes from Mary Hubbard French, part of the "playhouse" in front was once a wing of the Slack farmhouse, moved here from its original location near the railroad tracks. This parcel was previously the site of Louisa Hubbard Jackson's house, which had been torn down before the Wheelers moved the Burleigh house. The Jacksons' mansard-roofed farmer's cottage, often referred to as the "yellow house" (c. 1874), remains on the property as of 2001.

115 Orchard Avenue. Estate caretaker's house later occupied by Edward "Ted" and his wife "Finch" Hubbard.

119 Orchard Avenue. The front section originally housed unmarried outdoor farmworkers. The building was red shingled with a porch on the front and side when Thomas and Virginia Rainey Scott rented it during World War II from the Hubbards for $65 a month. The Scotts later purchased the property. The rental was part of C.W. Hubbard Jr.'s contribution to the World War II effort, as housing was scarce. Still on the property is The Forge, a blacksmith shop that retains its bellows. At one time a driveway connected No. 119 to Ridgeway Road.

140 Orchard Avenue (Barnstable House). Originally built by Livingston Cushing as a combined barn and stable, it was converted to a house by Charles Wells Hubbard during World War I and occupied by the Hubbard family for many years. From 1948 to 1977, it was owned by John Bryant Paine Jr. Along the driveway is a frame outbuilding apparently used as a combination icehouse and shed. On the property is Livingston Cushing's log cabin, which has been described as an "adult playhouse." Members of the Hubbard family used to go there with friends and cook and spend the night in the cabin, with its two large fireplaces and supplementary coal furnace in the basement. Bunks came out from the wall, with mattresses. "You had the feeling (except when you heard the trains) that you were a long way from anywhere."

147 Orchard Avenue (Wendover). Hubbard coachman's house. According to Mary Hubbard French, the name Wendover derives from the fact that it was moved from across the street. The original appearance has been altered.

164 Orchard Avenue (The Knoll, c. 1913). Colonial Revival house built by Charles Wells Hubbard for his daughter, Elizabeth, about the time she married John Forsyth Meigs in 1913. Sold to the Barrons.

165 Orchard Avenue. Location of a rock carved with the initials "J.D." Known as the Davenport Stone, tradition holds that the initials were carved by Rev. John Davenport on an outing up the Charles River with Governor Winthrop in 1639.[63]

64 Oxbow Road. Built for S.F. Denton, who bought the land in 1899.

99 Oxbow Road. (Ridgeways, 1893). Built as a summer house for Boston merchant Frederick Blake Holder and his wife, Agnes. The house is nicely sited on a knoll and combines Tudor half-timbering in the gables with Shingle-style design features.

136 Ridgeway Road (Bide-a-wee). Mary Hubbard French claimed that this house was used as a retreat for tired businesswomen and secretaries, where they could go for a few days to get away from it all. Later occupied by the Stanley Frenches.

Partial Hubbard Genealogy

Charles Townsend Hubbard (1817–1887)
- m. 1. Louisa Sewall in 1845
  - Louisa, m. 1. John Cotton Jackson
    - ? children
      - m. 2. Ferdinand Canda
  - Mary (died as young child)
  - Charlotte, m. Benjamin Loring Young in 1875
    - Margaret "Daisy" (b. 1876)
    - Charlotte "Lottie" (b. 1879)
    - B. Loring Young (1885–1964)
  - Elizabeth (1849–1941), m. Francis Blake in 1873
    - Agnes (1876–?), m. Stephen Salisbury Fitzgerald in 1906
      - no children
    - Benjamin (1877–1959), m. Ruth Field in 1908
      - Francis (b. 1909)
      - Ruth (b. 1911)
      - Elizabeth (b. 1913)
      - Benjamin Jr. (b. 1915)
      - Joan (b. 1926)
- m. 2. Elizabeth Wells in 1855 (after Louisa Sewall Hubbard's death)
  - Charles Wells (1856–1933), m. Anne Swann in 1889
    - Charles Wells Jr. (1890–1966), m. Dorothy Briggs
      - Charles Wells III (b. 1913)
      - Edward "Ted" (b. 1916)
    - Elizabeth Blair (1894–1991), m. John F. Meigs
      - Charles
      - John Jr.
      - Montgomery
    - Anne Swann Jr. "Nancy" (1896–1978), m. Edward Wheeler
      - Ann
    - Mary Greene (1905–1993), m. Stanley French
      - Katherine
      - Elizabeth
      - Stanley Jr.
  - Anne (1858–1946), m. Bancroft Chandler Davis in 1882
    - Martha
    - Mabel

153 Ridgeway Road. About the early 1920s, the north wing of Ridgehurst, which had been built as the maid's quarters, was moved to this site and made into a separate house. It was enlarged by the Thayer family, who bought it about 1928. The firm of Perry, Shaw and Hepburn designed a 1934 addition. A billiards room was built in 1937.

Notes

1. The house labeled on the 1794 Kingsbury map as "formerly J. Stedman" became the Slack house.
2. MCRD 1008/103, 1009/2. See also "Historic Slack Homestead on Walnut Street Sold," *The Townsman* (Wellesley, Mass.), August 12, 1927. Gives history of Slack family in connection with another Slack house. For map of property, see MCRD, Plan Book 14/57, "Land in Weston belonging to the Heirs of Robert F. Slack."
3. Mary Hubbard French notes in WHC files.
4. According to Col. Daniel S. Lamson in the "Weston" chapter in Hurd's *History of Middlesex County*, 505, the estate was called Woodlande. When the mansion was finished in 1883, it was called Ridgehurst. The estate seems to have been commonly referred to as the Hubbard estate rather than Woodlande.
5. Noon, Alfred, ed., *The History of Ludlow, Massachusetts* (Springfield, MA, 1912), 287.
6. Letter, C.T. Hubbard to B. Sewall, July 16, 1845 (MHS, Blake Papers, 75.1092).
7. Hubbard, Charles W., "Autobiographical Notes" (unpublished manuscript, undated), 2.
8. Ibid., 5.
9. Ibid., 6.
10. CTH's major purchases, in addition to the Slack farm, were as follows: from George J. Pierce, three tracts totaling 103 acres (MCRD 1203/518, 1872); from Geo. P. Cutter & heirs of Jonas Cutter, two tracts totaling 65 acres (1206/606, 1872); estate of Chas. Cutter, three lots totaling 58 acres (1370/519, 1875); Eliz. & Frederick Bush, two tracts, 24.5 acres (1876) and 37 acres (1878).
11. In 1879 Hubbard was also taxed for five horses, eight cows, three dwelling houses, a barn, carriage house, and greenhouse.
12. Louisa Jackson was deeded 1.8 acres in 1873. Her house is described in a letter from Anne Hubbard Wheeler, dated January 1974. The Jackson house was located approximately where 100 Orchard Avenue stands today.
13. See chapter 23. The house site was not deeded to the Blakes until October 1876 (MCRD 1413/468, acreage not specified).
14. Katherine French to PWF.
15. Schiller, Ann H., "Charles F. McKim and His Francis Blake House," *Journal of the Society of Architectural Historians,* vol. XLVII, no. 1, March 1988, 13.
16. Newspaper clipping, undated, pasted into diary of Charlotte Hubbard Young (MHS, Young Papers).
17. MCRD 1533/304, C.T. Hubbard to B.L. Young, 1880, $7,500, 50 acres formerly owned by Charles Cutter and 3-acre triangular-shaped lot.
18. Diary sections transcribed by Mary Hubbard French can be found in WHC files.
19. Hubbard, op. cit. 15.
20. Ibid.
21. McChesney, Herbert L., *A History of Ludlow, Massachusetts* (Ludlow Bicentennial Committee, 1978), 225.
22. Letter, Anne Swann Hubbard to Anna Chamberlain, written between 1945 and 1960, in possession of current owner.
23. Ibid.
24. French, Mary Hubbard, transcribed diary entries for Anne Swann Hubbard (WHC files).
25. "A Massachusettts Town, Scenes in Cutting's Store at Weston," unknown newspaper, c. 1888.
26. *50th Reunion Report, Harvard Class of 1878.*
27. Hubbard, "Autobiographical Notes," op. cit., 9.
28. McChesney, op. cit., 226.
29. "The Ludlow Manufacturing Associates, Ludlow, Mass. U.S.A." (undated brochure, post-1908), Ludlow Memorial Library archives.
30. Hubbard, op. cit., 16.
31. Ibid., 20.
32. Charles W. Hubbard III to PWF, fall 1997.
33. Letter, Stanley G. French Jr. to PWF, fall 1997.
34. No. 79, now owned by Boston University. See C.W. Hubbard autobiography, 9.
35. MDC minutes, October 25, 1972 (38–151).
36. Cushing and Bennett were class of 1879. See Harvard University Archives.
37. Hubbard, C.W., op. cit., 9. Also notes of Mary Hubbard French and information from Mrs. David Little, March 2, 1971 (WHC files). The Cushings were Mrs. Little's aunt and uncle. The log cabin in still standing on the property at 140 Orchard Avenue.
38. Bates, Cynthia B., "A Study of One Square Mile in the Southeast Corner of Weston," unpublished manuscript, 1979. Reportedly Anne Swann Hubbard couldn't bear to eat the pigs, so they were kept only to eat the garbage.
39. MCRD 2138/101. Deed restrictions required that the house cost at least $10,000 and the stable $1,000 and that the buildings be set back at least 25 feet. No fences could be erected within 20 feet of the road, and no "mechanical or other trade or manufacture of any kind, and no shops, stores, or livery stables" were allowed.
40. MCRD 4137/1 and Plan Book 259/6.
41. *Boston Sunday Herald,* May 11, 1902.
42. Archives, Olmsted National Historic Site, Brookline, Massachusetts. Plans, Job #5058, reel 243. Correspondence shows that Hubbard was involved in the landscape planning and attuned to scenic views. He later sold at least one property with deed restrictions prohibiting planting of trees that might block his view. See also title search for 100 Orchard Avenue prepared by Francis N. Balch, Esq., for Professor Clinton Biddle (document owned by George and Nancy Bates).
43. National Park Service, Frederick Law Olmsted National Historic Site, Brookline, Massachusetts, Job #5058.
44. Harvard University *25th Reunion Report, Class of 1912* (1937).
45. 164 Orchard Avenue. Olmsted Brothers did a planting plan in 1916 (Frederick Law Olmsted National Historic Site, Job #5058, Plan 79).
46. Charles Wells Hubbard III to PWF.
47. MCRD 4488/349, 1922.
48. Bates, Cynthia B., "History of the Burleigh Mansion, Newmarket, New Hampshire, and Weston, Massachusetts" (unpublished manuscript, June 24, 1985).
49. MCRD, Filed Plans 824 and 942. Subdivision first recorded September 29, 1925. First sales, October 1925.
50. Cheek, Jeannette, "Weston: A Community," 275th Anniversary Address, *WHSB,* December 1988, 3.
51. "Chiltern Hundreds," brochure prepared by Walter Channing, Realtor, 50 Congress Street, Boston, dated about 1926. The number 168 represents only the number of lots shown in the brochure. Some of the lot layouts were later changed and some people bought two lots. Chiltern Hundreds also encompasses the land reserved on the plan for future development.
52. Other restrictions: 1) private garage for no more than three automobiles; 2) no part of the property could be used for mechanical, mercantile trade, or manufacturing purposes (MCRD 4894/117).
53. The minimum price of $10,000, which is mentioned in the Channing promotional brochure, was later raised to $15,000, as indicated in a letter of January 20, 1936, from one of the Channing sales agents to Harold C. Wiswall of Wellesley Hills, stating, "The biggest difficulty we are having in Chiltern Hundreds is the restriction of $15,000 but we are very anxious to get something moving.... If you find the restrictions a stumbling block, we will be very glad to receive an offer subject to our being able to secure the necessary releases to make the restrictions $12,000 above the ground." (Clarence A. Bunker Collection, Wellesley Historical Society.)
54. MCRD Plan Book 393/9, April 1927, shows lots sold. Note that some of the original 168 lots were later enlarged, and the subdivision was later expanded.

55. 74 and 147 Orchard Avenue, 99 Oxbow Road, and 136 Ridgeway Road. After Stanley French's death, Mary built the house at 86 Orchard Avenue.
56. Stanley G. French Jr. to PWF.
57. Ibid.
58. Notes in WHC files date the Hubbard water system to 1899.
59. Land for the lower pump houses was deeded from Metropolitan Park Commission in 1904. In 1908 the MPC voted to approve Hubbard's plan for a pump house designed by architect George C. Wales (letter, December 10, 1908, Hubbard file, MDC Archives).
60. Information on the water system from Charles Wells Hubbard III, who worked on the system during his college years in the 1930s.
61. The tank was dismantled after the system was taken over by the town.
62. Pictured in *Achievements of New England Architects and Engineers* (Boston: Lewis J. Hewitt, 1927), vol. 1, 255.
63. Paine, Thomas M., "John Davenport's Rock," *Old Time New England*, vol. LVIII, no. 1, summer 1967, 20–21.

Figure 23-1. Francis Blake's artistry and technical skill as a photographer are evident in this memorable image of his daughter, Agnes, taken in the summer of 1889. The monumental urns were set at intervals along the balustrade at the Blake estate, Keewaydin, in the southeast corner of Weston. Many of the photographs in this chapter were taken by Blake and provide ample documentation of both his talents and the elegance of his estate.

CHAPTER 23

Francis Blake, Keewaydin, and the Telephone

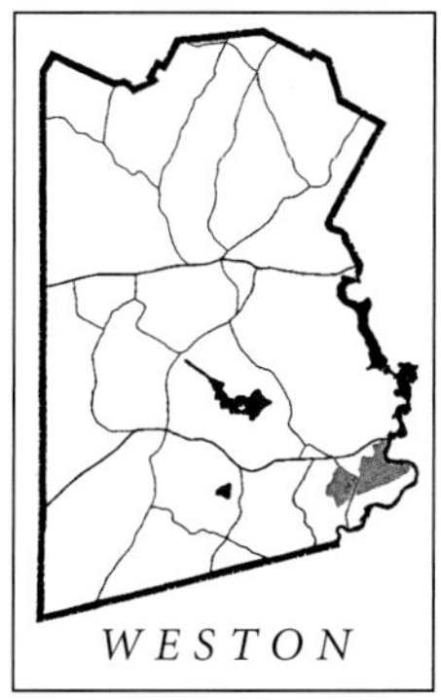

Francis Blake was one of the most famous men ever to live in Weston. His invention of the Blake Transmitter is widely credited with ensuring the success of the Bell Telephone Company during what has been called the "heroic and experimental period of early telephony." Bell's "toy" of the 1870s quickly became the key to a treasure chest. Blake and other industry pioneers saw the value of their stock increase exponentially as telephones made their way into households throughout the nation.

Blake was famous not only for his invention but also for the fabled lifestyle at his estate, Keewaydin, located in the southeast corner of Weston in the area of the present Blake and Tamarack Roads. Turn-of-the-century writers described Keewaydin in terms usually reserved for royalty. Blake's "palatial villa," an early work by the gifted architect Charles Follen McKim, was set on a hilltop surrounded by manicured lawns, formal gardens, and greenhouses.

Here Francis Blake lived the life of a true Renaissance man, pursuing interests in applied science, photography, arboriculture, politics, and outdoor sports and recreation. In 1902 he received an honorary master of arts degree from Harvard recognizing the breadth of his achievements as an "artistic mechanician, successful inventor and promotor of science." He served as Weston selectman for 20 years and at his retirement in 1910 was praised for "fidelity and sound business judgment," which helped make Weston "one of the best-governed towns in the Commonwealth."[1]

Francis Blake was very precise in everything he did. As a young man, he progressed rapidly in his work with the geological survey because he was so accurate. In later years, he calculated to the penny the cost of dinner parties and home improvements. And he saved everything. Blake's papers, preserved at the Massachusetts Historical Society, contain not only correspondence and diaries but also volumes of household receipts, newspaper clippings, photographs, and ephemera. He saved the yearly licenses for his six dogs, the water meter records for each customer of the Keewaydin Water Works, and 30 years of invitations to the Thursday Evening Club. In this collection, students of Weston history can find gems like an early sketch of the town seal, which Blake himself designed, and a letter from Daniel Lamson explaining how he came to write the history of Weston. The Blake Papers provide a unique insight into a man of uncommon talent and energy. Few traces remain from his grand Keewaydin estate, but Blake's decisions as a selectman helped shape the development of Weston to the present day.

Early Life and Education

Francis Blake was born in Needham on Christmas Day 1850, the son of Francis and Caroline Trumbull Blake and grandson of state senator and U.S. district attorney Francis Blake. He was an eighth-generation descendant of Agnes and William Blake, a colonial leader who came to Massachusetts in the early 1600s. In later years, Blake would hire a genealogist to trace his roots in England. Although the family ancestry was distinguished, the Blakes were not wealthy. Francis attended Brookline High School, where one of his teachers fostered his inclination toward applied science by organizing an after-school course in surveying.

Figure 23-2. Blake's family was distinguished but not wealthy. As he achieved financial success, Blake hired a genealogist to trace his lineage back to England. He used this crest on his bookplate.

Figure 23-3. Francis Blake made a fortune with the invention of the Blake Transmitter, for which the fledgling Bell Telephone Company paid him in stock. A true Renaissance man, Blake combined scientific precision with a strong aesthetic sensibility. He was also a community leader and served as a Weston selectman for 20 years. (1901 photo)

Figure 23-4. Elizabeth Hubbard was the daughter of manufacturer Charles Townsend Hubbard. When she married Francis Blake in 1873, her father gave the young couple some of his land on which to build a house. (Photo 1872–74)

While still a 16-year-old high school student, Blake's uncle secured him an appointment to the U.S. Coast and Geodetic Survey, where he received the training in physics and electrical communication that led to his later success.[2] During 12 years with the survey, he rose rapidly in rank and traveled widely to cities in the United States and Europe as part of his work calculating scientific location. In 1869 Blake was involved in determining the difference in longitude between Harvard College and the coastal station in San Francisco. The distance of about 3,000 miles was determined within a few feet, a measurement that would have seemed miraculous a few years earlier but could finally be accomplished using astronomical observations and the electric telegraph.

In 1870 he took leave to become an astronomer for the potentially hazardous Darien Expedition, which sailed to Central America to explore possible routes for a ship canal between the Atlantic and Pacific. In 1872 he returned to the Coast Survey and was stationed at Brest, France, the Imperial Observatory in Paris, and the Royal Observatory in Greenwich, England.

Marriage and Building of Keewaydin: 1873–1875

In June 1873, Blake married Elizabeth Livermore Hubbard (1849–1941), daughter of Weston estate owner Charles Townsend Hubbard.[3] The couple had two children: Agnes (1876–?) and Benjamin (1877–1959).

As a wedding present, her father gave Elizabeth a house lot sited on a high plateau overlooking rolling hills and valleys to the Blue Hills in the distance. Ten years later, Hubbard built his own house next door to take advantage of the same panoramic view. Money for the Blake house came from Elizabeth's grandfather, cordage manufacturer Benjamin Sewall.

Blake hired the 26-year-old architect Charles Follen McKim, who up to that time had designed only a few houses, one for a friend of Blake's. Architectural historian Ann H. Schiller writes that the house was of particular significance for Blake. Although he came from a prominent family, his father had never been successful, and Blake had put up with years of low-paying work and constant travel with the coast survey.[4] Now, thanks to his wife's father and grandfather, Blake had an opportunity both he and his architect relished.

The commission was important to McKim because Blake gave him freedom to experiment. McKim expressed his appreciation in several letters, saying that "to design a house and have your client agree with you and to let you alone is to know something about Paradise in advance."[5] McKim designed

Figure 23-5. Blake's house, shown here before the facade was encased in yellow brick, was an important early work of the young architect Charles Follen McKim. The original interior was virtually intact when the house was demolished in 1965.

Figures 23-6 and 23-7. Charles McKim designed the interior finishwork and even offered to cut his commission so that his client could afford the fine woodwork and paneling. These photographs taken by Blake himself show patterned tile on the hall floor, embossed-leather wallpaper, painted ceilings, and built-in dining room cabinets and shelves.

every detail inside and out and was so determined to have it built the way he planned that he offered to cut down on his commission rather than let Blake disappoint him in the finish of the principal rooms.[6]

The asymmetrical Queen Anne house had towers, chimneys, dormers, porches, a porte cochere, and bay windows projecting out in all directions. Schiller writes that, in the Blake house, "[o]ne can see the beginnings of what was to become a distinctively American house, sheathed in shingles with bays and towers and broad verandas, especially suited to the informality of resorts such as Newport and Bar Harbor."[7] The Blake house had an awkward, additive quality that was not present in later examples by

McKim, as he gained control of massing and became one of the acknowledged masters of American architecture of the late 19th and early 20th centuries.

Inside, the Blake house had a large rectangular "living hall" that connected every major space. On the outside a broad veranda shaded most of the main living spaces. Important rooms featured rich floor-to-ceiling oak or mahogany paneling, embossed-leather wallpaper, and beamed ceilings. Red tiles were used on some floors. Woodwork was largely unpainted and later generations remembered the inside as very dark. Photographs show ornate interiors with an abundance of patterning in the wallpaper, rugs, sofas, and draperies, along with tassels everywhere. Furniture was of golden oak with overstuffed velvet cushions. The kitchen was in the basement.

Francis Blake saved every receipt, every bill, and every piece of correspondence from potential builders, along with records of man hours and receipts for every fixture and furnishing down to the last $5 for the brass door knocker. The house cost about $20,000 to build.[8] The Blakes moved in on January 13, 1875. They called the house Keewaydin, meaning "Home of the West Wind."[9]

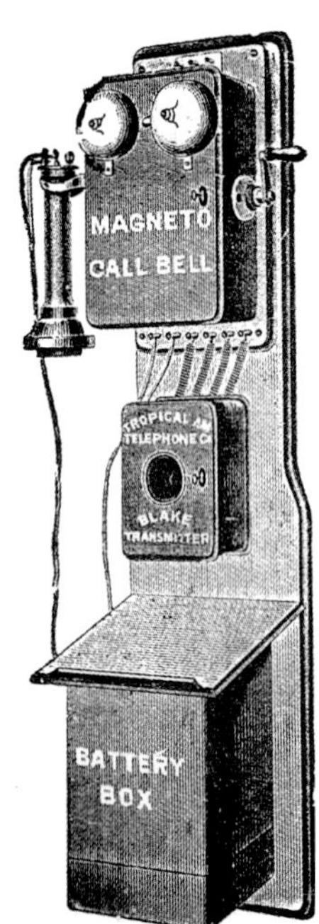

Figure 23-8. This illustration of an early telephone shows the central box labeled "Blake Transmitter." Before Blake's invention, the telephone had limited usefulness because the sound quality was so poor.

Invention of the Blake Transmitter

During his last two years with the U.S. Coast Survey, from 1876 to 1878, Blake did office work from his home in Weston and devoted leisure moments to experimental physics and electrical communication. He built a well-equipped laboratory in his home. Blake had been introduced to Bell's telephone at the Centennial Exposition of 1876, and he constructed his own set of telephones, experimenting with the proportions and materials for each component. Barely a month after his resignation from the survey in April 1878, he began a series of experiments that led to the invention of the Blake Transmitter, a device that amplified the voice so it could be heard over a telephone wire. The transmitter was purchased by the Bell Telephone Company later that year in a deal that made Blake a director of the fledgling company.[10]

In an 1886 speech, Blake gave this self-effacing account of his role in the invention of the telephone:

> Barely ten years ago—on the 25th day of June, 1876—Professor Alexander Graham Bell presented to the world his supreme invention of the art of transmitting [sounds] . . . by means of electricity. . . . Before Bell, no one had obtained results which had induced capital to lend its fostering hand for their development;—today at least a hundred million dollars are invested in the business of telephoning throughout the world. We who have entered the field opened by Bell's genius may fairly lay claim to only the working out to mechanical perfection of the broad principles first enunciated by him.[11]

But articles like "The Romance of the Telephone," written in 1900, claim that it was the Blake Transmitter that enabled Bell to succeed in an intensely competitive field. Bell's original invention didn't actually work very well:

> The Bell Telephone, as exhibited in 1876, excited only passing interest among the wonders of the Centennial. The transmitter was not reliable; you never knew whether you were going to hear a buzz, a break or a word.[12]

Bell had no money; he was sick, in debt, and fighting for his embattled company. Blake came along with a transmitter as satisfactory as the one developed by Thomas Edison for rival Western Union. Not only that, but Blake preferred to sell it for stock rather than cash. As one observer remarked, "If ever a man came as an angel of light, that man was Francis Blake."[13] The Blake Transmitter put Bell on an even footing with Western Union and encouraged capitalists to come forward while Bell pursued and won a suit for patent infringement. By 1886 there were 250,000 Blake Transmitters in use throughout the world. As for Francis Blake, his future was assured. The value of Bell Telephone stock soared and Blake began to reap his reward.

Figure 23-9. Blake probably had the first telephone in Weston. In 1880 he paid to connect his house to telephone service available in Newton Lower Falls.

Figure 23-10. This panoramic view shows the relationship between the Blake house and The Cottage, a multipurpose outbuilding.

Development of Keewaydin

In the decade immediately following his invention, Blake devoted his attention to improving Keewaydin. He enlarged and remodeled the house and obtained additional furnishings custom-made in Boston or purchased on a grand tour of Europe in 1882. North of the house across a broad sweep of rolling lawn, he built a major complex of attached outbuildings. He purchased additional land and landscaped the estate, adding a pond and formal gardens. He developed a sophisticated water supply system that eventually provided water to neighbors in the South Avenue area. Not surprisingly, Blake even installed poles from his house to Newton Lower Falls so he could have his own private telephone connection. This cost him $887.50.[14]

Money for improvements came not only from the invention of the transmitter but also from the estate of Benjamin Sewall, who died in 1879 leaving assets of over a million dollars. Sewall's business holdings included a large stake in C.T. Hubbard's Ludlow Manufacturing Company and were put into a trust fund benefiting his granddaughters.

Blake initially asked Charles McKim to design his additions; but McKim was experiencing personal problems and Blake eventually hired the Boston firm of Cabot and Chandler. Senior partner Edward Cabot is credited with the plan for The Cottage, a handsome complex of attached brick outbuildings grouped around an interior brick courtyard. There was a stable/carriage house, coachman's cottage and other staff housing, mechanical workshop, photography darkroom, two-lane bowling alley, storeroom, and gymnasium. Later a squash court was added and the gymnasium converted to a miniature theater seating 75 to 100 people and "fitted up with all the accoutrements of a first class playhouse."[15] Within this all-purpose utilitarian complex was a boiler room from which the house was heated through underground pipes. In one of the rooms, Blake had a hand printing press that he used to print invitations, dinner menus, and theater programs for Keewaydin.

The combined laboratory and workshop was described in an 1895 newspaper article:

> It might have been a corner of a very neat and well-ordered iron foundry and was not the sort of a place one would expect a scholar to fit up for his recreation and study. There were lathes, drills, vises, a small forge, anvil, and a variety of other machines of wonderful workmanship and unknown name. The motive power is supplied by a good-sized gas engine. Skilled mechanics who have visited Mr. Blake's laboratory declare that they have never seen a finer assortment of machinery in any factory.[16]

Blake developed the Keewaydin landscape in a formal style rarely employed by Weston estate owners, who, with the dramatic exception of Horace Sears's Italian garden of two decades later, generally preferred a more casual approach. The design is credited to Ernest W. Bowditch (1850–1918), landscape gardener and engineer who supervised work on the estate through the late 1890s.[17] Although

Figure 23-11. The Cottage was designed by architect Edward Cabot and included not only a stable and coachman's quarters but also a mechanical laboratory, photography darkroom, bowling alley, and theater. (1893 photo)

Figure 23-12. Blake's well-equipped and orderly machine shop included a gas-powered engine and an impressive array of tools. The inventor took these documentary photographs, which have been described as "at once accurate and elegant." (1893 photo)

Figure 23-13. Blake was one of several Weston estate owners who built private bowling alleys. The Keewaydin example had fine woodwork and light fixtures. The sign on the rafters reads "Bowlers are requested not to Lob the Balls." (1893 photo)

Bowditch has remained largely unheralded in the history of landscape architecture, he laid out many estates and suburbs in the Northeast in the late 19th and early 20th centuries including the well-known resort community of Tuxedo Park, New York. He worked for at least one other Weston estate owner, Charles Jones, before Jones came to Weston.

Bowditch was an exact contemporary of Blake and both men grew up in Brookline. After studying engineering at MIT, Bowditch joined the first Darien Expedition to explore Central America. The following year, Blake sailed with the second expedition under the same commander. Later, the two men shared common Hubbard relatives through marriage and were both major shareholders and trustees of the Ludlow Manufacturing Company.[18] By the 1890s, under Bowditch's skilled direction, the Blake estate became the finest showplace in Weston.

The estate reached its maximum size of about 100 acres in 1887, the year Blake purchased 60 acres along the Charles River from farmer William Seaverns. The acreage decreased to about 75 after Blake sold part of the Seaverns land to the Boston Athletic Association in the early 1890s. The main entrance to the Blake estate was located on East Newton Street, now Park Road, opposite the present entrance to the Massachusetts Turnpike tollbooths. The roadway has since disappeared but stone entrance posts remain, hidden behind a screen of trees and shrubs. The winding estate roads passed by a man-made "miniature lake" staked out by Bowditch in 1879. Carefully mown lawns were planted with fine specimens of the rarest conifers from all parts of the world. Down the hill near The Cottage were two grass tennis courts.

The focal point at Keewaydin was a sunken garden adjacent to the house at the edge of the ridge, from which the land sloped down to the railroad tracks. The ridge was marked by a stone balustrade with huge urns atop the posts. The garden was five feet below grade level and was surrounded by a walkway with views in all directions. Said to have been inspired by the gardens at Hampton Court in England, the sunken garden had a formal circular layout with a central sundial imported from Europe. In 1892 Blake imported 100 tubbed evergreens from England. A subsequent newspaper article reported, "During the summer months, this spot is brilliant with velvet lawns, potted plants and graceful palms and ferns."[19]

A second dramatic landscape feature was a series

Figure 23-14. The sunken garden was inspired by the gardens at Hampton Court. At the center was a sundial made by a famous London maker of scientific instruments. This garden and the adjoining terrace walk were decorated with more than 100 "choice tub plants." (1893 photo)

of three broad terraces built using massive stone walls 20 feet high. Blake excavated these terraces into the slope down from his house to the railroad tracks. The terraces could be reached by a stone-lined tunnel from the basement of the house. On the upper terrace were plum, peach, apple, and pear trees. The second terrace was covered with seasonal flowers, while the third was the location of greenhouses, which supplied roses, forced flowers, and fresh figs to the house year-round.[20]

At the foot of the terraces were the tracks of the Boston and Albany Railroad, which provided a subject for Blake's motion photography as well as an essential link to the outside world. Every morning the newspaper was thrown off the train and the butler would go down the "paper path" to retrieve it.[21] A railroad siding allowed Blake to purchase a whole carload of coal each winter.

Both Blake and his wife, Elizabeth, were interested in the grounds and gardens. The Blake Papers include long lists of plantings ordered from local nurseries as well as from the well-known Mount Hope Nurseries in Rochester, New York, run by Ellwanger & Berry. In her diary, Elizabeth Blake describes working in her lawn garden and planting wildflowers along a path at the end of the pond.

Figure 23-15. In 1886, Francis Blake took this photograph of the New York Express speeding along the Boston & Albany tracks at 48 miles per hour. It shows his skill at motion photography and also documents the construction of the stone terraces on the hillside below his house.

Figure 23-16. Blake's papers include this drawing of Spanish bantam hens he raised on the Weston property. Because the Blakes got their mail in Newton, the address is given as Newton Lower Falls.

Blake nailed identifying labels on each tree and kept a yearly record of their growth that he hoped would be of value to arboriculturists.

The Keewaydin greenhouses were famous. One well-documented example, ordered in 1891 from the celebrated Lord and Burnham Company of Irvington, New York, measured more than 127 feet long and cost close to $6,000.[22] Perhaps this was the greenhouse in which Blake raised chrysanthemums entered into an exhibition at Horticultural Hall in 1900. The *Boston Herald* reported that "Francis Blake shows a few poor plants that appear to be out of place," to which Blake replied in a letter to the editor:

> In justice to my head gardener, Mr. Frank Leith, I call your attention to the fact that these plants have been awarded the first prize offered for "Six plants grown to bush form, in not over eight-inch pots, without stakes."[23]

Blake operated a gentleman's farm at Keewaydin complete with the requisite cows, horses, pigs, and chickens. A dovecote over the entrance to the stable provided a nesting place for pigeons, which he photographed in flight. In addition to The Cottage, estate outbuildings included a cow barn, chicken houses, a root cellar, and cottages for the butler, chauffeur, teamster, and chicken man.[24]

In general, Blake was more interested in horticulture than farming, but in the 1890s he turned his attention to his dairy herd because of an outbreak of tuberculosis. He wrote a report, reprinted in the *Boston Herald,* recounting how a veterinarian examining a sick cow in his stable suspected tuberculosis and found the disease in six of his ten cows, which then had to be killed. Blake was particularly alarmed that milk from two of the worst afflicted cows had been used in his household right up to the day the disease was found. Blake pointed out the danger of transmitting tuberculosis through the milk of diseased cattle and called for action to protect public health.[25]

The last major "improvement" at Keewaydin occurred in the summer of 1893, when the northeast end of the house was extended to enlarge the schoolroom and servants' area and the entire house was encased in tan firebrick. An October 1893 entry in Elizabeth Blake's diary suggests the reason for the change:

> Francis is busy at present photographing our new home, we might call it, for the bricks give an appearance of newness and the house is charm-

Figure 23-17 This illustration appeared in the 1899 book Picturesque and Architectural New England: Architectural Features, *which featured many Boston-area estates. It shows the entrance into Keewaydin from what is now Park Road, the well-tended grounds and gardens, and the shooting water in the pond.*

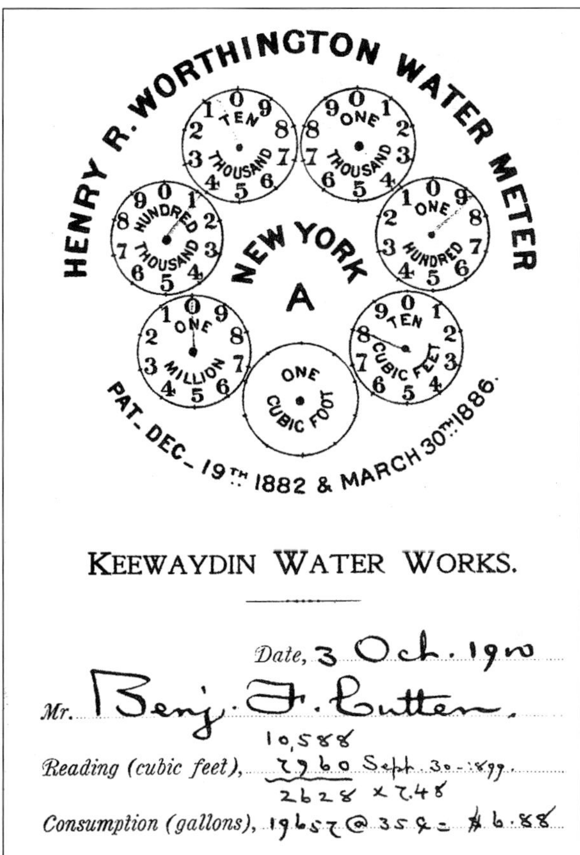
HENRY R. WORTHINGTON WATER METER
NEW YORK
PAT. DEC. 19TH 1882 & MARCH 30TH 1886.

KEEWAYDIN WATER WORKS.

Date, 3 Oct. 1900

Mr. Benj. F. Cutter.

Reading (cubic feet), 10,588 7960 Sept. 30.-1899.
2628 x 7.48

Consumption (gallons), 19657 @ 35¢ = $6.88

Figure 23-18. Francis Blake's brother, an engineer with a water works company, helped him design the water system at Keewaydin. Blake later agreed to supply some of his neighbors. He calculated to the penny the cost of the system and personally recorded the meter readings.

> ingly clean & fresh—a strong contrast to the faded and stained wood.[26]

It would be interesting to know what Charles McKim thought of the new brick facade, which completely changed the character of the 20-year-old structure and probably gave it the up-to-date appearance Blake considered suitable for a man of his wealth and position.

Keewaydin Water Works

As part of the improvements to his estate, Blake established the Keewaydin Water Works in 1880. He itemized to the penny the $10,817.61 he spent developing the water works, which were designed by his brother C.H.M. Blake, an engineer with the Central Falls and East Providence Divisions of the Pawtucket Water Works.[27] The system included a stone-lined reservoir built at a reported elevation of 227 feet at the high point of the hill on the west side of Orchard Avenue.[28] This reservoir is still extant and is marked by a plaque. A Worthington Steam Pump pumped water to the reservoir from a well 27 feet deep and 10 feet in diameter, theoretically capable of furnishing 225,000 gallons daily. According to an 1880 newspaper report, the reservoir was of sufficient pressure to throw a stream of water 80 feet high in Blake's pond at the foot of the hill.[29] The shooting water was turned on for special occasions.

Blake set up the system for his own use and later agreed to supply his brothers-in-law B.L. Young and B.C. Davis and his Hubbard in-laws, who used Blake's water as a secondary supply. In 1902 bills were rendered to the following additional subscribers generally living along South Avenue: Samuel Bennett, Benjamin Cutter, David W. Lane, Edward Dooley, Herbert Seaverns, Fred W. Smith, Mrs. Dennis Doyle, and William DeYoung Field. In 1901, total water consumption of the Blake system was more than five million gallons.[30] In 1944 the system had 18 customers and an operating revenue of $553. At that time, an engineering study recommended that the system not be accepted as part of the town water system because of its age and small-diameter pipes.[31] Keewaydin Water Works was still in operation when the Blake land was sold for development in the mid-1960s.

Although the system was engineered by his brother, Blake was clearly involved with all issues of maintenance, water quality, and billing. Notes about overhauling pumps, reading meters, and problems with freezing are all in Blake's handwriting. His files included ordinances of neighboring water systems in Wellesley and Newton as well as scientific papers concerning water quality.[32]

"An Eccentric Suburban"

By the 1890s, Blake and his estate had acquired an almost legendary status celebrated in newspaper reports lauding his achievements, lavish entertainments, and "manorial residence" in Weston. An article entitled "An Eccentric Suburban" describes him as "one of the romantically-grown-rich telephone men . . . [who] lives just out of the city . . . where he has a palace and lives like a duke." The reporter adds, "He bears his great wealth well, and is more of the type of the English country gentleman than is possible for the average new rich man to become."[33]

Public interest in the Blake estate was derived in part from its proximity to the Boston and Albany Railroad, which made it familiar to hundreds of train travelers passing by each day. The 1902 *Boston Sunday Herald* article "Weston Has Become the Lenox of the East" includes a typical reference to the railroad:

> The residences of Mr. Hubbard and Mr. Blake may be seen by passengers on the Boston & Albany railroad, just below Riverside. Doubtless the attention of many passengers has been attracted to these places by the appearance of the fine terraced gardens extending down to the railroad tracks.
>
> Mr. Blake's gardens are far-famed . . . . The trains rushing by the base of the hill testify to life and activity. Away beyond is the valley of the

Figure 23-19. The elegance of this horse and carriage suggests the "manorial" lifestyle for which Blake was justly famous.

> Charles River. Looking in the opposite direction the vista is delightful—a magnificent park, with a small pond in the middle foreground, and squirrels and rabbits frisking about. It is dreamland, and within a few hundred feet from a railroad track.[34]

Train travelers whose curiosity was piqued could return and explore the grounds more fully, as the Blake estate was open to the public. An article from 1895 noted, "At the gate which leads into the grounds is a sign welcoming visitors, with the one restriction that they shall confine their visits to certain hours of the day—a restriction which the abuse of hospitality has rendered necessary."[35] When the 1902 article was written, the Hubbard and Blake estates were open on Saturday afternoons and a drive through was described as "a popular event."

"Man Who Enjoys Life"

Part of the public fascination involved Blake's continued scientific experiments amid the elegant surroundings of wealth and leisure. One article reported that "he amuses himself as an amateur blacksmith or machinist, working in metals with his own hands at his forge."[36] In the full-page illustrated article "Man Who Enjoys Life" in the *Boston Sunday Globe* of December 1895, the reporter describes Blake the gentleman-inventor:

> The inventor was interrupted in the midst of some very absorbing experiments he was making with a new lathe, but he came forward with a cheerful word of welcome, wiping his greasy hands as he did so upon an old apron which had evidently seen long service.

Asked about his work, Blake gave this reply:

> My work for the last few years has been entirely play. Since my invention of the long distance transmitter I have not invented anything of particular commercial value. Still, I am busy in here most of the time, for I take the keenest delight in machinery and all sorts of mechanical devices.

As for his view of the future, Blake could not be prevailed upon to prophesy:

> He was very conservative in regard to the future of the flying machine, horseless vehicles, the manufacture of diamonds, telephone, or any other communication with the planet Mars, or the substitution of the elements administered in capsules for food as taken at present.[37]

In the dozen years after his invention of the transmitter, Blake received 20 patents, including one in 1885 for a more powerful version to satisfy commercial demand for long distance. The only other invention for which he is known is the 1897 Minot-Blake Precision Microtome, an improvement on an earlier precision cutting instrument used by pathologists and biological laboratories.

Blake was well known as an outdoorsman. One reporter detailed the exercise regimen that Blake followed with his usual scientific precision:

> Of the thousands of canoeists who traverse the Charles River from Riverside to Waltham from one week's end to another there is probably no more noticeable figure than Mr. Francis Blake of Weston. Mr. Blake is a great devotee of the water. Every forenoon at just 10 o'clock he can be seen paddling down from Riverside, and his trip is to the dam at Waltham. Day by day he makes the trip, rain or shine, and so regular is he that campers along the river can set their clocks by his arrival and departure.[38]

Blake was a prominent supporter of the movement to preserve the Charles River in Weston for public use. In 1893, the Appalachian Mountain Club asked him to speak to the state legislature in support of the Metropolitan Parks Bill, which established a regional park system for the greater Boston area.[39] That same year he added momentum to the parks movement by arranging for the Boston Athletic Association to purchase some of his land along the Charles River for a summer sports and recreation facility. In 1896 Blake was again asked to testify before the legislature, this time in favor of allocating funds for the Charles River Reservation. In a letter to Charles F. Sprague, chairman of the Committee on Metropolitan Affairs, he expressed his vision of the Charles River as a regional recreational resource:

> Having lived for nearly a quarter of a century in full view of one of the most beautiful stretches of the Charles River, I am impressed with the fact that it has, from year to year, made steady

> progress toward becoming, to the inhabitants of Boston and her suburbs what the upper Thames is to the inhabitants of London.[40]

Further information about the Boston Athletic Association and the parks movement can be found in chapter 21.

Blake was renowned for his discriminating taste in food and wine. His passions in this area were duly recorded—and doubtless highly exaggerated—in articles such as "Man Who Enjoys Life," which carries the subheading "He Is a Millionaire, and Paid $8000 for His Own Private Coffee Roaster . . ." The article describes Blake's latest diversion, Turkish coffee roasting:

> He has bought himself one of the latest and most approved roasters, had it brought to his home in Weston and set up, the motive power being furnished by a powerful engine which he has in his laboratory. His coffee he now buys direct from the plantations, and at the trifling expense of $8000, the cost of the plant, he is able to drink a cup of the beverage every morning, which is, in the minutest details, prepared in the most approved manner.[41]

The reporter adds that Blake's salary as a Weston selectmen, $25 a year, would just about cover the cost of his morning cup of coffee.

Francis Blake was a major consumer of fine imported foods like guavas, citrons, currants, and oolong tea, as well as expensive Havana cigars purchased from specialty shops in the city. Basic foodstuffs came from J.W. Davis, "first class family groceries," in Auburndale. Included among the formal printed bills that he carefully pasted into scrapbooks arranged by date are a few crumpled, handwritten bills from Weston farmers like George B. Cutter for 20 boxes of strawberries and S.H. Warren for eggs. In 1881, there is a formal printed bill from F.S. Browne, "dealer in choice fruits and vegetables," for strawberries, currants, raspberries, and blackberries. Browne later supplied Blake with milk, at eight cents a quart, and cream. Because Francis Blake saved all his receipts, it is possible to paint a clear picture of where the family shopped for other items as well. Clothing and dry goods, along with toys for the children, came from stores around Washington and Winter Streets in Boston.

The Blake house had a large wine cellar. Blake saved extensive correspondence with New York wine dealers regarding choice wines, ordered by the case, aged Scottish and rye whiskey, and high-class champagne.[42] He purchased wine and liquor for the Somerset Club. One of his scrapbooks is filled with pasted labels from wine bottles, along with the receipts. Blake often recorded what wines and liquors he served guests at Keewaydin and how many bottles they drank.

Among Blake's more curious avocations was word games. Perhaps nothing better illustrates his methodical and tenacious personality than his entry and follow-up to a contest sponsored by *Woman's World and Jenness Miller Monthly* in 1896, in which a prize of $250 in gold was offered to the contestant who formed the largest number of words from the word *editors*.[43] Blake entered several carefully written, alphabetical lists totaling 403 words. When he did not win, he inquired and was told that the winning list had 5,701 words. With his usual thoroughness, Blake worked out the mathematical possibilities for letter combinations and concluded that no more than 500 words in the standard dictionary could be formed from the word. He obtained a copy of the 5,701-word list and then asked for a copy of the 711 words that contest judges had allowed to pass. In one of his final letters, he offered the contest editor a challenge, in which he and the magazine would both submit a certified check for $5,000 to Harvard University, the college would judge the word lists, and if 700 or more of the words on the winning list were verified, the magazine would get its check back. Unfortunately, the correspondence ends at this point, and researchers may never know how Blake and the magazine resolved the "editors" contest.

The Photography of Francis Blake

Francis Blake took up photography in the mid-1880s and pursued it with his customary intensity and precision. According to a newspaper article of 1892, Blake became involved in the medium after he was ordered by his physician to cut back on his work:

> He labored so long and indefatigably upon this perfection of the patent and the subsequent development of his business enterprises that his eyesight began to fail, and his physician, fearing a general breakdown of his health, ordered him to abstain from everything that required continuous

Figure 23-20. With his usual scientific precision, Blake documented his photography studio in 1893.

Figure 23-21. Francis Blake's greatest contributions to the history of photography were his high-speed images, most of which were taken in the early 1890s.

> attention and mental concentration. . . . He took up amateur photography as a diversion and recreation, and it shortly developed into a passion. His inventive genius could not be held in check.[44]

Blake became an active member of the Boston Camera Club in 1886 and spent the next four years developing a shutter that would allow for quick photographic exposures. He became interested in the work of instantaneous photographers such as Edward (Eadweard) Muybridge and was soon producing pictures classified as "amateur" only because Blake did not sell his work. In all other ways, he was a consummate craftsman.

In 1892, Blake's photographs appeared at the Boston Art Club in an important exhibition of amateur photographers from around the country. He was awarded a medal, and the press proclaimed his instantaneous photography "little short of marvelous."[45] Blake demonstrated his technique by photographing lawn tennis champions smashing forehand volleys and lobs at exposures reported to be half of a thousandth of a second. He captured Boston & Albany trains moving at a speed of 48 miles per hour, pigeons in flight with their eyes and features "as sharp as if they had been standing still," and galloping horses "so finely cut that the dust thrown off from the hooves is caught and distinctly portrayed."[46] One reviewer put Blake's work into perspective:

> It is difficult for persons not thoroughly familiar with photography to appreciate the obstacles overcome by Mr. Blake, who . . . is excelled by none in the world as a scientific photographer. He is a recognized authority on lenses and shutters, having spent many years in study and experiment, and evolved a system which has enabled him to "break the record" in instantaneous photography.[47]

Figure 23-22. The Blakes encouraged their children to participate in outdoor activities. Here the family and their canine friends relax with C.N. Payson (far left) next to the grass tennis court. Because Francis Blake saved his dog licenses, we know that one year he owned a St. Bernard, three Scotch terriers, and a mastiff.

Figure 23-23. Unlike many of his fellow estate owners, Francis Blake did not have a summer house. The family traveled each year to the White Mountains of New Hampshire, where their favorite hotel was the Glen House. Blake saved the menu, shown here.

Although Francis Blake achieved considerable recognition in photography circles, he stopped exhibiting his pictures about 1893 and his work was largely forgotten. In a recent article in *The Massachusetts Historical Review,* photography historian Keith F. Davis writes, "It has taken a full century for historians to rediscover Blake's importance and begin to include him in our history books."[48] While his documentary photographs of home and family were both precise and elegant, it was in the area of high-speed photography that Blake made his greatest contribution. Davis describes these images as "[f]ull of whimsy and wonder" while at the same time "reveal[ing] aspects of reality that are completely invisible to the naked eye."[49] Davis explains the significance of Blake's work as "an original artistic vision based on a boldly modern understanding of both time and the potentials of photography."[50]

Family Life and Entertaining at Keewaydin

The Blakes' first child, Agnes, was born on January 2, 1876. With scientific exactitude, Blake noted the precise time and weather conditions in his diary: "Miss Agnes Blake came into the world, the umbilical cord being cut at 11h, 24m, 45s am. . . . It is worthy of note that the sun came out bright just as Agnes was born." A son, Benjamin Sewall Blake, was born 13 months later on February 14, 1877.

Elizabeth Blake's diaries give insight into a life that revolved around her children. She took them into the city for theater, musical concerts, and shopping. She encouraged outdoor activities like coasting, sleigh riding, and skating in winter and horseback riding, tennis, and canoeing in summer. In January 1897 she recorded in her diary that the young people took a walk up Doublet Hill, and "those with long dresses were soaking wet when they got back." July 4th was celebrated with a picnic at Nonesuch Pond and fireworks at Keewaydin. Elizabeth Blake was always worried about the children's health. Agnes had curvature of the spine, which was treated with a brace and special exercises, and Benjamin often required rest for headaches.

For a time in the early 1890s, Benjamin went by train to Mr. Hopkinson's school on Beacon Hill and Agnes went by carriage to the Dana Hall School.

Figure 23-24. Blake took this picture of his two children, Agnes and Benjamin, in the Keewaydin conservatory in April 1887.

Figure 23-25. Wide sleeves were the fashion in the mid-1890s, when young Agnes was feted at parties, teas, and luncheons in preparation for her debut into Boston society in 1895 at age 19.

Later both children were privately tutored. For Benjamin, who was not a strong student, private tutoring continued until he finally passed the requisite examinations to enter Harvard in 1897 at age 20.

The Blakes did not have a summer house and preferred to vacation with relatives on a family farm in Illinois or at White Mountain resort hotels like Intervale House in North Conway, Crawford House, and especially the Glen House. This famous 19th-century hostelry had accommodations for 500 guests. Blake was an avid mountain climber who kept careful track of his ascent times and was remembered for not allowing rest stops.[51] A newspaper item from Intervale, New Hampshire, said that Blake had reached the peak of Mount Chocorua in two hours. Fellow climbers often included his brother-in-law, Charles Wells Hubbard, neighbor Livingston Cushing, and son Benjamin. Diaries also mention trips to Nassau and the Bahamas.

As Agnes and Benjamin entered adolescence, Elizabeth Hubbard Blake became increasingly preoccupied with their social life. They attended dancing classes in Boston. Beginning about 1893, at age 17, Agnes was caught up in a whirlwind of teas, sewing circles, luncheons, and parties that led up to her debut. Elizabeth Blake's diary describes a typical event of those years, a small informal dance for Agnes at Keewaydin, in which the conservatory and window seat in the dining room were filled with ferns and yellow chrysanthemums, the library had red linen coverings on the carpets, and supper was served in the billiards room with accompanying piano and violin music.

Nineteen-year-old Agnes was formally launched into society at a ball held in Pierce Hall in Boston on January 14, 1895. Society columnists wrote in glowing terms of the "magical touch of fairyland" created with gold and white Easter lilies, roses, and carnations that reportedly took Galvin the florist and his men 24 hours to arrange. Among the 260 guests were young "belles and buds" drawn from the Boston Sewing Circle '95 and the senior and junior classes at Harvard. One article noted that, although Francis Blake lived in a palatial place in the country, "his associations and those of his family are largely in town and in the most exclusive set."[52]

Over the next years, Agnes presided over many social events held at Keewaydin for her Boston friends, such as the June hayride and picnic described in her mother's diary:

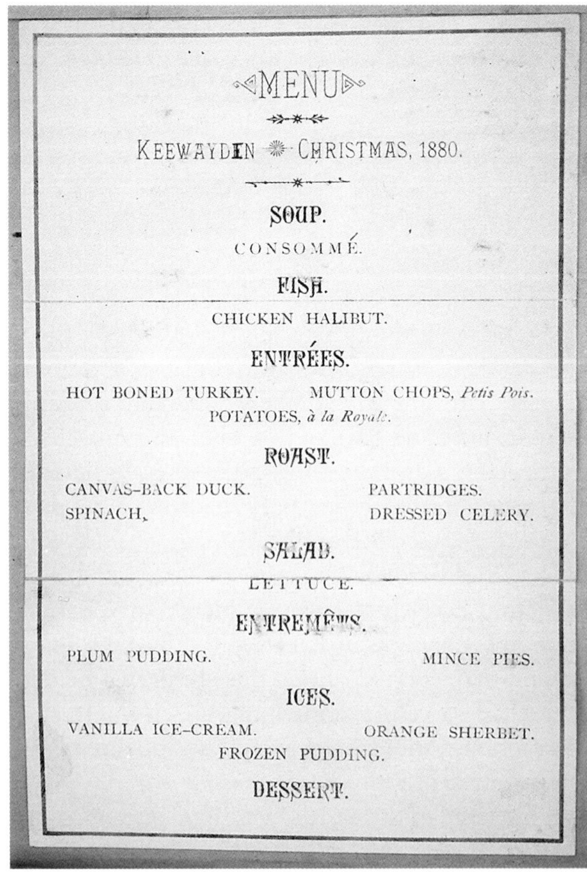

MENU

KEEWAYDIN CHRISTMAS, 1880.

SOUP.

CONSOMMÉ.

FISH.

CHICKEN HALIBUT.

ENTRÉES.

HOT BONED TURKEY. MUTTON CHOPS, *Petis Pois.*
POTATOES, *à la Royale.*

ROAST.

CANVAS-BACK DUCK. PARTRIDGES.
SPINACH. DRESSED CELERY.

SALAD.

LETTUCE.

ENTREMETS.

PLUM PUDDING. MINCE PIES.

ICES.

VANILLA ICE-CREAM. ORANGE SHERBET.
FROZEN PUDDING.

DESSERT.

Figure 23-26. Christmas Day was Francis Blake's birthday, and it was celebrated with an elaborate dinner. Blake was a connoisseur of fine food and wine. Many menus from Keewaydin have survived, some printed by Blake himself on a handpress in The Cottage.

Figure 23-27. The theater at Keewaydin held about 100 guests, who were treated to sophisticated productions put on by the Blakes and their South Avenue neighbors. (1893 photo)

> [Agnes] drove to the station for those who came by train, taking up Mrs. Lane on the way, as chaperon. The wagon was arranged with straw. . . . After a cold lunch in the woods, they drove & then had more than an hour for salad, ice cream & strawberries & champagne & some games before taking the 10:58 pm train—Lisa Wells chaperoned them to town.[53]

In January 1895, Agnes had a party for nine couples with a sleigh ride, dance in the bowling alley, and theater entertainment. In 1896 Elizabeth Blake records that new electric lights were in operation in time for yet another dance given for Agnes.

Christmas was always a special occasion, as this was Francis Blake's birthday. The entire Blake and Hubbard extended family was traditionally invited for a formal Christmas dinner followed by games. A printed menu card for Christmas dinner at Keewaydin in 1880 details the eight-course meal.

Entertaining often involved polished theatrical productions in the Keewaydin theater. Actors generally included Blake's daughter, Agnes, and members of the Field, Bush, Lane, and Tudor families on South Avenue. Blake's theater may have served as inspiration for Horace Sears, who established the Friendly Society in 1885 and constructed an even larger theater at his estate, Haliewa, at the turn of the century.

The Blake Papers include a printed program for the operetta *A Very Odd Trick* performed at Keewaydin in November 1884. An enthusiastic newspaper reviewer called the play "the best musical performance of the amateur stage":

Figure 23-28. Actors in Keewaydin plays included William DeYoung Field, Benjamin F. Field Jr., and C.G. Bush, shown here. Blake's ability to photograph at fast shutter speeds allowed him to take this kind of candid shot.

> The charming operetta "A Very Odd Trick" was repeated last Wednesday evening at the cozy little

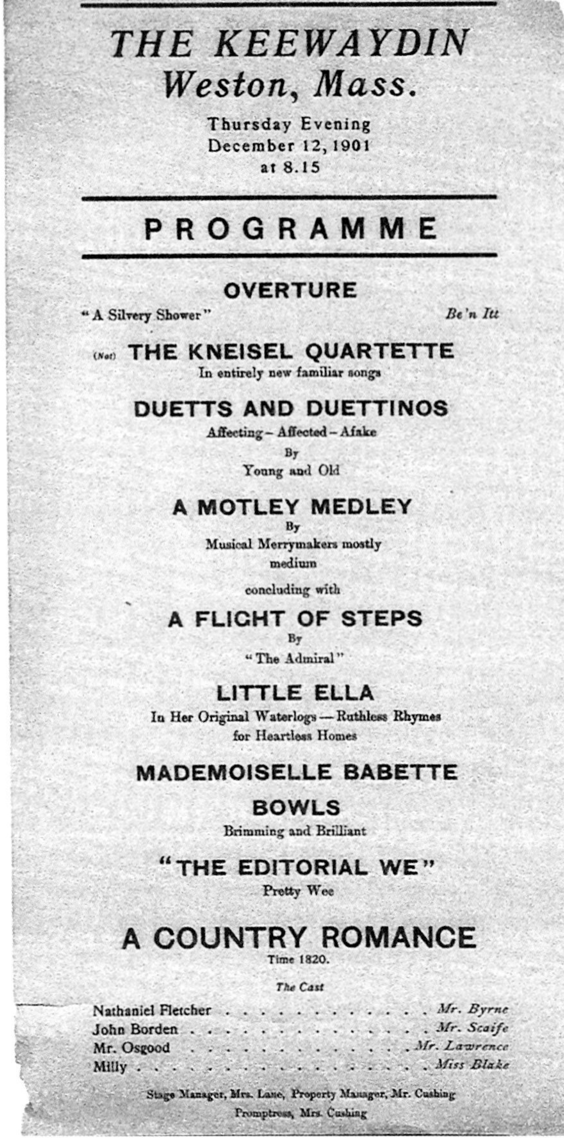

THE KEEWAYDIN
Weston, Mass.

Thursday Evening
December 12, 1901
at 8.15

PROGRAMME

OVERTURE
"A Silvery Shower" — *Be'n Itt*

(Not) THE KNEISEL QUARTETTE
In entirely new familiar songs

DUETTS AND DUETTINOS
Affecting – Affected – Afake
By
Young and Old

A MOTLEY MEDLEY
By
Musical Merrymakers mostly medium

concluding with

A FLIGHT OF STEPS
By
"The Admiral"

LITTLE ELLA
In Her Original Waterlogs — Ruthless Rhymes for Heartless Homes

MADEMOISELLE BABETTE

BOWLS
Brimming and Brilliant

"THE EDITORIAL WE"
Pretty Wee

A COUNTRY ROMANCE
Time 1820.

The Cast

Nathaniel Fletcher . . . . *Mr. Byrne*
John Borden . . . . *Mr. Scaife*
Mr. Osgood . . . . *Mr. Lawrence*
Milly . . . . *Miss Blake*

Stage Manager, Mrs. Lane, Property Manager, Mr. Cushing
Promptress, Mrs. Cushing

Figure 23-29. Agnes Blake appeared in this variety show at Keewaydin in 1901.

> theatre attached to Mr. Francis Blake's elegant residence in Weston. The audience, which was composed of many notables from Boston and vicinity, expressed unqualified admiration of the work and the talent that ably carried out the ideas of both composer and author. It is not often that so fine an amateur performance is given in private or public, the event with its brilliant social surroundings marks the gay season with a white stone.[54]

In her diaries of April 1894, Elizabeth Hubbard Blake describes small, informal Saturday-evening theatricals with Agnes playing the lead:

> Last evening was the third Saturday evening on which we have had charades in the theatre. Mr. Wm. Field & Mrs. Lane are the chief managers. . . . Last evening Lord Lovall was played; Mr. Field & Agnes taking the principal parts. The word "Kee-way-din" was acted in three syllables. Then Agnes was Joan of Arc tied to a stake wood sticks piled in front of her & red light burned behind her. It was very effective.[55]

The Thursday Evening Club

Some of the most elaborate entertainments at Keewaydin were given for the Thursday Evening Club, one of the oldest and most prestigious of the smaller clubs of Boston. The distinguished group of 100 men of social or intellectual prominence met on alternate Thursday evenings at homes of members, where papers on science, literature, or current events were read and discussed, followed by supper. Among the all-male club members were H.H. Richardson, Frederick Law Olmsted, Robert Treat Paine, Judge Oliver Wendall Holmes, Rev. Edward E. Hale, and Rev. Phillips Brooks. E.N. Horsford, builder of Norumbega Tower, was a member in the 1880s, along with the presidents of Harvard and MIT, Harvard historian Justin Winsor, distinguished botanist Asa Gray, preservationist William Sumner Appleton, and architect Robert Peabody. Blake was invited to join about 1882.

Blake entertained the group every other year, in April. On the night of the party, a special railroad car reserved for Thursday Club members was attached to the rear of the 7 P.M. Boston & Albany train, with conductors instructed not to collect tickets. The 1884 invitation advises guests that "the run to Auburndale will be made in 31 minutes, where carriages will be waiting." In the 1890s, guests were

Thursday Evening Club
24 April, 1902.

Boston & Albany Railroad Co., 140 fares,	$14.56
H. L. Lawrence Co., Turkeys & chickens,	17.35
Somerset Club, Cigars & cigarettes,	16.60
S. S. Pierce Co., Cigars,	17.00
Charles G. Tinkham, Barges,	36.00
B. Johnson, Sweetbreads,	17.50
Deerfoot Farm Co., Cream,	4.20
R. Hollings & Co., Wiring for wireless teleg.	7.17
Masten & WellsFireworks Mfg. Co., Owl Lights,	19.12
Charles Evans, Waiters,	23.80
10 Qts. Apollinaris Water,	1.80
13 " Burgundy, Chambertin 1883,	45.00
19 " Champagne, Moet 1893 Cuvee 81,	57.00
Rich & Matthews, Oysters, Salmon & Lobsters,	33.73
Philadelphia Ice Cream Co., 18 Qts.,	8.80
Isaac Locke & Co., Lettuce,	1.00
Daniel P. Wise, Cake & rolls,	2.55
Gas and electric light, (estimated-	5.00
Total:-	$328.18

81 persons present.

Figure 23-30. Blake kept a careful record of the cost of entertaining 81 members of the Thursday Evening Club in April 1902. The largest expense was for champagne and Burgundy.

transported from the station to the house in "six old red line 'busses, each drawn by four horses."[56] Blake's notes from 1902 carefully set out the timing of the event: "arrive 7:45, three speakers, fire gun 9:05, supper 9:15, leave house 10:30, leave Auburndale, 10:52." One year Elizabeth Blake recorded in her diary that red lights were strung around the pond and along the paths and "the fountain playing made it look like fairyland."[57]

Blake kept every R.S.V.P. and made a list of each member with notes next to his name like "bad health" or "came without accepting." He recorded all expenses. His total cost for the April 1902 meeting, attended by 81 members, was $328.18, which covered the Burgundy, champagne, cigars and cigarettes, turkeys and chickens, oysters, salmon, lobsters, Philadelphia ice cream, train fares, "illumination," and even the estimated expense for gas and electric light. The "illumination" was by Master & Wells, a fireworks company that provided displays such as "owl lights" for the Thursday Evening Club extravaganzas. Blake's guests appreciated the effort. One wrote, "I always consider it the one spree of the staid old Thursday club."[58]

Boston Daily Globe.

WEDNESDAY, JUNE 25, 1902

FRANCIS BLAKE,

Who Receives Honorary Degree of Master of Arts at Harvard Today.

Figure 23-31. In 1902, Francis Blake received an honorary master of arts degree from Harvard recognizing his achievements as an "artistic mechanician, successful inventor, and promotor of science."

Other Clubs and Societies

Blake was a member of more than 50 other local, regional, and national organizations that reflect the breadth of his interests.[59] He belonged to most of Boston's prestigious social clubs, held important trusteeships at many of the city's major institutions, and was an active member of countless sporting, scientific, and civic clubs. Indeed, it is easy to see why he initially declined to serve as vestryman at St. Mary's Episcopal Church in Newton Lower Falls, citing his many other humanitarian commitments. He later accepted "with the understanding that I am not to attend meetings . . . and am not to be appointed a member of any committee."[60]

Blake served on the Board of Overseers of Harvard College for more than 12 years, chairing the committee overseeing the Jefferson Physical Laboratory and Department of Physics. For over 10 years, he was a member of the MIT Corporation and chairman of the Visiting Committee for the Department of Mechanical Engineering and Applied Mechanics. He was a long-term trustee of Massachusetts General Hospital and of the Museum of Fine Arts.

Blake belonged to clubs for horseback riding, canoeing, and golf, including The Country Club in Brookline, Boston Riding Club, New Riding Club, Weston Golf Club, Amersand Golf Club, Boston Athletic Association, and Newton Boat Club. His social clubs included the St. Botolph Club, Somerset Club, Union Club, Algonquin Club, and Triangle Club as well as the Monday Whist Club, which, according to tradition, had existed since colonial days. He was a member of many scientific organizations including the American Academy of Arts and Sciences, American Geographical Society, American Institute of Electrical Engineers, Boston Society of the Archaeological Institute of America, Boston Society of Civil Engineers, Boston Electric Club, New England Meteorological Society, Massachusetts Horticultural Society, and even the American Society of Psychical Research, which was devoted to the serious investigation of hypnotism, mediumistic phenomena, apparitions, and haunted houses. His antiquarian interests are reflected in memberships in the Bostonian Society, American Antiquarian Society, American Folk Lore Society, and Colonial Society.

Blake's progressive ideology and concern for civic improvement and good citizenship are indicated by membership in organizations like the American Academy of Political & Social Science, Village Improvement Society in Weston, Massachusets Society for Promoting Good Citizenship, Citizens Association of Boston, and the Rural Club, which featured speakers on topics such as "What can we do to improve Massachusetts Agriculture?"

Politics and Service as Weston Selectman

In 1884 Blake became involved in Weston politics as part of a reform-minded faction within the Republican party that refused to support the candidacy of

Figure 23-32. As a selectman, Blake wrote his own letters in a neat and graceful hand using the Keewaydin letterhead.

James G. Blaine for president. Blake and other Weston "mugwumps" backing Democrat Grover Cleveland formed an independent Republican Club, with Blake as president and fellow estate owners Charles Townsend Hubbard, Horace Sears, and Robert Winsor as officers.[61] After Cleveland's election, Sears wrote to Blake, "We are going to 'celebrate' in a modest way next Thursday night, with a bonfire—salutes—fireworks, etc. And a few mugwumps in our vicinity will illuminate . . ."[62]

Blake was first elected to the board of selectmen in 1890, became chairman in 1900, and retired from office in 1910 after 20 years of service. During these critical decades, Weston changed from a predominantly agricultural community to a favorite location for country homes. Blake was sensitive to the problems of transition. He was a consummate diplomat, respectful of his constituents and attentive to their concerns.

The selectmen guided Weston through a progressive agenda that included centralizing the schools, building a new high school and library, improving roads, purchasing fire-fighting equipment, and installing streetlights, telephone and electric lines, and fire hydrants. Town reports from the early 1890s show an interest in town planning that undoubtedly reflects Blake's influence. The 1892 town report includes the first conceptual plan for a redesigned town center, prepared by Blake's landscape designer, Ernest W. Bowditch. Blake himself served as chairman of the library building committee and worked diligently on its design and construction.[65] Blake looked not only to the future but also to the past. In his first years in office, the town hired Mary Francis Peirce to organize town records and Blake himself designed the town seal.

Blake had the foresight to see that Weston's future growth and prosperity would come, not from industrial development or "improvements" like street railways, but by attracting people seeking quiet country homes. He worked to preserve the natural beauty of the town, introduce modern conveniences, and keep down the tax rate. The 1902 *Boston Sunday Herald* article "Weston Has Become the Lenox of the East" praises his leadership and offers this assessment of Weston's image at the turn of the century:

> He is greatly interested in the development of Weston, and has been a strong factor in its upbuilding. He . . . has directed the affairs of the town in a manner to make it attractive to those who love a country life amid surroundings which are comfortable rather than magnificent, conservative rather than pronounced, beautiful rather than gorgeous.[66]

Second and Third Generations at Keewaydin

Benjamin Sewall Blake graduated from Harvard in the class of 1901 and married neighbor Ruth Field in 1908. The newlyweds fixed up Pine Cottage, the former butler's house near where the turnpike tollbooths are today. They had five children: Francis (b. 1909), Ruth (b. 1911), Elizabeth (b. 1913), Benjamin Jr. (b. 1915) and Joan (b. 1926). The third generation grew up with the seasonal rhythm of estate life. In spring they watched the newly hatched ducklings. In summer, Benjamin Blake dammed the brook for a swimming hole, as the pond had too many leeches. In winter the children skated to Waltham on the Charles River. Ruth Blake Oliver recalled riding the barges to public school for two years and then attending Pigeon Hill and Winsor Schools. Ruth Field Blake's mother, Amelia, lived with the family and made all the children's clothes until she died in 1929.

Benjamin's sister, Agnes, married Boston lawyer Stephen Salisbury Fitzgerald in 1906. For many years the Fitzgeralds lived in the main house with Elizabeth Blake. Later, they bought the former Preston house on the south side of South Avenue near the Charles River. The couple had no children.

Francis Blake died on January 19, 1913, at age 62. His compulsive spirit must have prompted someone to tuck into his receipt book the bill from the "fur-

Figure 23-33. Benjamin Blake, pictured here as a young man, moved into the main house at Keewaydin about 1937 and maintained the lifestyle of an earlier era.

nishing undertaker" who provided the cedar casket with silver lining and engraved sterling silver plate, as well as 12 carriages to take mourners to Linwood Cemetery.[67] In his will, Blake left the Town of Weston $1,000 to establish an endowment fund for the purchase of library reference books.

Elizabeth Hubbard Blake lived on at Keewaydin until her death in 1941. Her granddaughter Ruth recalled that when she was growing up in the 1910s and '20s, the house had a cook, kitchen maid, waitress, butler, and two upstairs maids, along with a full complement of outdoor farm help.[68] The Benjamin Blake family moved to the big house about 1937, maintaining it with just a cook, waitress, and chambermaid. Benjamin Blake was an avid hunter who added his own decorative touches like mounted bear and deer heads and a small stuffed bear that stood on its hind legs, hands clasped, holding the umbrellas. No thought was given to changing the wallpaper or furnishings. The family lived the lifestyle of the past.

Benjamin Blake was a gentleman farmer and amateur arborist who experimented with planting native North American trees outside their normal range and Asian and European trees from similar climates. He was a member of the visiting committee to the Arnold Arboretum and chairman of the Weston Park Commission. For 40 years he hosted the Harvard class of 1901 during the annual reunion week. In his 50th-reunion report, he looked back on a life of contentment:

> I have never been eminent in any way myself, but get great satisfaction from the success of my sons and sons-in-law. . . . My domestic life is, I think, unusually happy. My hobbies are arboriculture, shooting, and fishing. I trust everybody, but cut the cards.[69]

Benjamin Blake died in May 1959 at age 82.

His wife kept the farm going the way he liked it, as much as she could. The small staff kept the lawns carefully mowed, raised a few chickens and vegetables, and maintained some of the greenhouses. The superintendent doubled as a chauffeur, as Ruth Field Blake didn't drive. The interiors of the big house and cottage remained frozen in time, almost as they had looked a half-century earlier, except for the layers of dust that settled over areas rarely used since Francis Blake's death. Neighbor Stanley G. French Jr. recalls his childhood impression of Blake's theater, which had a "magical ambience even though dust was deep all over everything and it had probably been decades since the stage had seen its last production."

The bucolic atmosphere of Keewaydin was changing. The Hultman Aqueduct was constructed through the property in the late 1930s. Construction of the Weston section of Route 128 in 1950 was noisy and destructive but paled by comparison to the devastating effect of the Massachusetts Turnpike five years later. Blake's granddaughter Betty remained at Pine Cottage until the bulldozers came right up to the house. The pastoral valley with its brook and duck pond was filled in and raised by an estimated 40 feet to create the site for the tollbooths and Weston–Newton interchange. Instead of the peeping noise of hundreds of tree frogs in the night, residents heard trucks changing gears on the hill. Proposals to build a professional football stadium at Nickerson Field exacerbated neighborhood concerns for years until Foxboro Stadium was constructed in 1970–71.

Figure 23-34. This aerial view shows the Weston interchange of the Massachusetts Turnpike, which was built largely on land taken from the Blake estate. Francis Blake's property once extended to the Charles River. In the 1890s, Blake sold some of his river frontage to the Boston Athletic Association. He constructed Riverside Road, which connected the main Keewaydin entrance on Park Road to the river. He built a bridge wide enough for a carriage to cross over to Auburndale, where the original Riverside Station was located. The bridge and sections of Riverside Road remain in this picture.

When Ruth Field Blake died in 1963, her children were confronted with the problem of what to do with the property. The historic preservation movement was just beginning to raise public consciousness. The public viewed the house as "colossal and rather ugly." A proposal by the Congregational church to readapt the house as a school didn't work out. Vandalism was an issue. Local teenagers remember breaking into The Cottage to bowl in the bowling alley. In 1965, the property was sold to Edward B. Swiedler, a major developer in the Metrowest area.[70] Ruth Blake Oliver recalled the overwhelming task of disposing of the contents of the house and outbuildings, the accumulation of nearly a century: "There was so much stuff. There were sleighs, old cars, wooden horse-drawn snow plows, tennis rackets, horse equipment. Nothing was ever thrown away."

In her oral history, local architect Marjorie Pierce

Figure 23-35. Keewaydin survived until the mid-1960s, when it was demolished to make way for the Blake and Tamarack Road subdivision. This photograph dates to about 1964.

expressed her view that Blake's research laboratory should have been preserved in a museum. In addition to the forge and drawers full of precision tools, the room still had a mockup of the Blake Transmitter hanging on the wall. Some of Blake's tools may have found their way into museum collections. His files and papers were donated to the Massachusetts Historical Society, where they now fill more than 70 manuscript boxes. Swiedler salvaged some wood paneling, which was stored in a shed but later destroyed by fire. Vandals took the urns from the garden and even stones from the walls. The house was demolished by a wrecking company about 1965.

The original stone entrance posts to Keewaydin remain along Park Road near the corner of Blake Road. The pond remains on the property at 11 Tamarack Road and the Keewaydin main house stood where 44 Tamarack Road is today. Swiedler Development Corporation built approximately 20 houses on Blake and Tamarack Roads and the northern portion of Orchard Avenue in the late 1960s and early 1970s. Some of the unusual specimen trees planted by Francis Blake and his son Benjamin still remain as small reminders of one of Weston's grandest estates.

Notes

1. 1910 *TR*, 265–66.
2. Blake's uncle was the distinguished commodore George Smith Blake.
3. The Blakes were married at St. Mary's Church in Newton Lower Falls. For information about Elizabeth Hubbard's family, see chapter 22.
4. Schiller, Ann H., "Charles F. McKim and His Francis Blake House," *Journal of the Society of Architectural Historians*, vol. XLVII, no. 1, March 1988, 6.
5. Ibid.
6. Blake Papers, letter of January 13, 1874, as quoted in Schiller.
7. Schiller, op. cit., 7. As with many Queen Anne houses, clapboards were used on the first floor and shingles on the second, along with a slate roof. Later Shingle-style houses have a uniform shingle covering.
8. The builder was Patrick Tracy of West Newton. Receipts are in the Blake Papers, MHS, especially Box 46.
9. This translation was provided to the author by Blake's granddaughter Ruth Blake Oliver. In the Blake Papers, Box 42, a newspaper article of 1880 entitled "A Pleasant Entertainment" says the translation was "northwest wind."
10. See footnote in the Hubbard Estate chapter for information about Gardiner Greene Hubbard, who was the father-in-law of Alexander Graham Bell and second cousin of Charles Townsend Hubbard. The author does not know what role, if any, the family connection played in Blake's development of his transmitter.
11. Draft of speech for the Thursday Evening Club meeting at his house, April 1886 (MHS, Blake Papers, Box 58.829).
12. Bocock, John Paul, "The Romance of the Telephone," in *The Munsey*, November 1900,
13. *The Sun,* August 6, 1910 (MHS, Blake Papers, Scrapbook 42). For more information about the early years of the Bell company, see *Alexander Graham Bell: The Man Who Contracted Space,* by Catherine MacKenzie (Boston and New York: Houghton Mifflin Co., The Riverside Press, Cambridge, 1928).
14. MHS, Blake Papers, vol. 3, 653 (1880).
15. Thomas M. Paine's *Keewaydin Keepsake* (Chevy Chase, 1988, unpublished typescript) provides the information about the gymnasium being converted to a theater and the addition of the squash court by the architectural firm of [Alexander S.] Jenney and [Willard] Frost.
16. "Man Who Enjoys Life," *Boston Sunday Globe,* December 15, 1895.
17. The Blake Papers at MHS indicate that Bowditch even handled disbursement of

money to contractors building The Cottage and doing landscape work (vol. 3).
18. Bowditch was married to Margaret Swann. In 1889 Charles Wells Hubbard, Blake's brother-in-law, married Margaret's sister, Anne.
19. "Man Who Enjoys Life," op. cit. Note also a clipping preserved in the Blake Papers (vol. 42, 1894), which indicates that Blake had problems overwintering the trees. He wrote to a gardening column for advice, saying that the plants were stored for winter in a 50-foot by 20-foot brick storehouse, 18 feet high, with "perfect means of controlling light and temperature." The reply offered suggestions and comments on the popularity at the time of potted plants: "For terraced gardens, these shrubs are almost indispensable."
20. Information supplied by Ruth Blake Oliver. See also H. Langford Warren, *Picturesque and Architectural New England* (Boston, 1899), vol. I, 98–99.
21. Information supplied by Ruth Blake Oliver.
22. Letter of May 2, 1891 (MHS, Blake Papers, Box 47.671). Lord and Burnham constructed a large number of conservatories and greenhouses for public parks and private gardens throughout the United States.
23. *Boston Herald,* letter to the editor, November 8, 1900 (MHS, Blake Papers, Box 67.974).
24. 1910 Weston tax records show Blake taxed for the following; residence $20,000; stable and connecting buildings $20,000; cow barn $1,000; greenhouse $1000; three dwellings at $1,500 each; another dwelling $3,500; and a barn $500. His land is listed as "lawn and garden" 18 acres; Boston and Albany RR lot 19 acres; and Seaverns place 38 acres for a total of 75 acres.
25. "Germs of Death in Milk," *Boston Herald,* February 9, 1890. Reprint of a paper delivered by Blake to the Thursday Evening Club.
26. Elizabeth Hubbard Blake diary, October 29, 1893 (MHS, Blake Papers).
27. "A Pleasant Entertainment" (unknown newspaper, undated, MHS, Blake Papers, vol. 42). A complete description of the water works is found in this 1880 newspaper article.
28. Blake bought the "Reservoir Lot" from his father-in-law, Charles Townsend Hubbard, in 1881 (MCRD, 1578/267).
29. "A Pleasant Entertainment," op. cit. Other articles give slightly different figures on the height of the water spray.
30. Letter from F.P. Stearns, chief engineer at Metropolitan Water and Sewage Board, July 31, 1902 (MHS, Blake Papers, Box 62.881).
31. 1945 *TR,* 86.
32. MHS, Blake Papers, Box 62.
33. "An Eccentric Suburban," *Boston Herald,* December 26, 1883. Note also that the multivolume *History of Middlesex County,* published in the 1890s, devotes three pages to Blake and includes an illustration of the estate.
34. *Boston Sunday Herald,* May 11, 1902.
35. "Man Who Enjoys Life,"op. cit.
36. "An Eccentric Suburban," op. cit.
37. "Man Who Enjoys Life," op. cit.
38. *Boston Post,* August 1906.
39. Letter from Francis Blake to Rosewell B. Laurence, February 15, 1893 (MHS, Blake Papers, Box 23.347). As a member of the Appalachian Mountain Club, Blake organized an outing in 1896 at which club members tried to retrace the journey of Governor Winthrop and the Rev. John Davenport in the 1630s when they came to view this part of the Charles River. The club traveled to the location where Davenport was thought to have cut his initials JD in a rock. For further information on the establishment of the Metropolitan Parks Commission, see chapter 21.
40. Francis Blake to Charles Sprague, March 14, 1896 (MHS, Blake Papers, Box 63.897).
41. Compare this quote with the entry of February 17, 1895, in Elizabeth Hubbard Blake's diary: "We have a new coffee pot. Francis has been trying Turkish coffee at the Somerset Club lately & wished to get a pot such as the Turks use. He went to Hagofo Bugigian & found exactly what we wanted. . . . A mill for grinding very fine came with it & three very small porcelain cups with metal stands."
42. MHS, Blake Papers, Box 56 and vol. 30.
43. MHS Blake Papers, Box 72.
44. "Blake's Great Feat: His Photographs of the Tennis Cracks Were Made More Quickly Than Any Ever Taken," *Record,* May 2, 1892 (MHS, Blake Papers, vol. 42).
45. Ibid.
46. "Man Who Enjoys Life," op. cit.
47. *Boston Transcript,* May 5, 1892 (MHS, Blake Papers, vol. 42).
48. Davis, Keith F., "The High Speed Photographs of Francis Blake," *The Massachusetts Historical Review,* vol. 2, 2000, 1.
49. Ibid., 6.
50. Ibid., 22.
51. Hubbard, Charles W., "Autobiographical Notes" (undated, unpublished manuscript), 7.
52. *Boston Sunday Journal,* January 20, 1895. Newspaper clippings describing the ball in MHS Blake Papers, Box 76.1105.
53. Elizabeth Hubbard Blake diary, June 9, 1895 (MHS).
54. MHS Blake Papers, newspaper clipping in vol. 45. Also, in February 1890, the *Waltham Daily Press Tribune* reported on a production of *The Fairy of the Fountain,* subtitled *Diamonds and Toads,* a musical drama in two acts starring Agnes Blake and the South Avenue contingent. The newspaper praised the fine painted scenery and performances of Ruth Field as Bo Peep and Robert Lane as Boy Blue.
55. Elizabeth Hubbard Blake diary, April 15, 1894 (MHS).
56. *Boston Herald,* April 4, 1890.
57. Elizabeth Hubbard Blake diary, April 29, 1894 (MHS).
58. Higginson to Francis Blake, April 19, 1894 (MHS, Blake Papers, Box 60.849).
59. MHS Blake Papers, Box 52.
60. Francis Blake to William P. Morse, April 15, 1903 (MHS Blake Papers, vol. 28). According to Ruth Blake Oliver, Blake was instrumental in buying a house for the rector.
61. MHS Blake Papers, Box 63.893.
62. MHS Blake Papers, Box 63.
63. Omitted.
64. Omitted.
65. Each year, Blake donated his selectman's salary to the library for the purchase of books. One year he added extra money for the purchase of *The Silva of North America,* which at $350 was the most costly set of reference works the library had ever possessed. See *Historic Homes and Places and Genealogical and Personal Memoirs Relating to the Families of Middlesex County, Massachusetts,* vol. I (New York, 1908), edited by William Richard Cutter.
66. *Boston Sunday Herald,* May 11, 1902.
67. MHS Blake Papers, vol. 28.
68. Ruth Blake Oliver to Pamela Fox, telephone interview September 28, 1997. Oliver recalled that the staff cut ice on the pond, tapped the maple trees for syrup, hayed the fields, kept cattle, raised fresh vegetables stored in root cellars for the winter, and took care of peach, apple, pear, and plum trees.
69. *Harvard Class of 1901, Fiftieth Anniversary,* 1951, 11.
70. MCRD Book 11397/229 (1965). Also Plan 1103 of 1967 recorded in Book 11397/229. Also 11622/457 (1968).

Figure 24-1. This unusual interior photograph was taken at the Cutter farm about the turn of the century. Benjamin Franklin Cutter is reading at right. The Cutters farmed in the South Avenue/Park Street area for well over a century. Benjamin's granddaughter Alice Tyler Fraser wrote about growing up in Weston. Her stories, along with photographs such as this one, help to paint a picture of everyday farm life in a small rural town.

CHAPTER 24

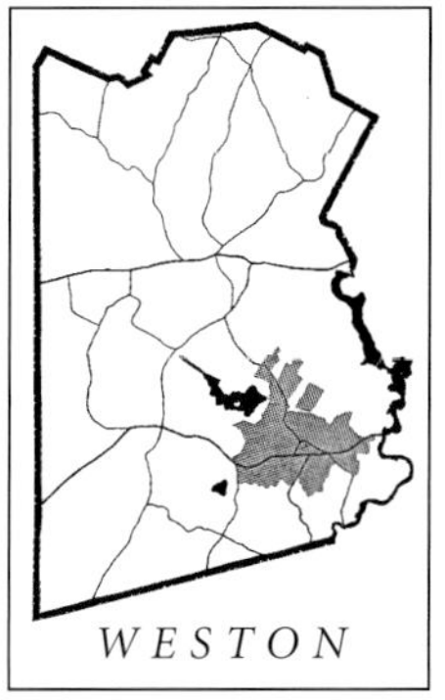

Cutter's Corner
South Avenue and Newton Street

Cutter's Corner is named for the family whose farmhouse, cider mill, and barn once stood at the intersection of South Avenue and Newton Street. This chapter looks at the development of the south end of Newton Street and east end of South Avenue. What might seem to be a random collection of farms and small country estates was actually a close-knit community with a cast of major and minor characters.

Local farm families at Cutter's Corner, including the Coburns, Cutters, and Popes, were tied together by blood and marriage. Newer and more socially prominent families like the Hubbards, Youngs, Davises, Blakes, Fields, Bushes, and Lanes were also interrelated.

These two groups remained, in many ways, quite separate. The Bushes and Fields acted in theatricals at the Blake estate, Keewaydin. The Cutters and Popes gathered on Sunday evenings to sing hymns and patriotic songs. Social and economic barriers kept them apart. But relationships also developed. The children of the neighborhood played together. Farmers supplied strawberries and eggs to the merchants and lawyers. Lawyers became gentlemen farmers. Estate owners took farm children under their wing and provided them with special experiences. Keewaydin Water Works supplied everyone's water. These interactions are detailed in an engaging series of articles, "Growing Up in Weston," written by Alice Tyler Fraser, the great-great-granddaughter of the first Cutter to settle in Weston.

Early Farms

In the late 18th century, the Spring family owned three houses in the area, two of which are important to this history.[1] The Colonial farmhouse built by Thaddeus Spring on South Avenue across from the intersection of Newton Street was sold in 1804 to Richard Cutter (c. 1756–1823). The deal included 164 acres, a cider mill, an extra woodlot, and a pew in the meetinghouse.[2] Cutter is said to have ordered 95 varieties of apple, pear, peach, plum, apricot, nectarine, and cherry trees to plant on his new farm.[3]

Jonathan Spring, older brother of Thaddeus, lived down the road at 263 South Avenue. The farmhouse that he built in 1764 remained in the family until the early 19th century, when it was sold to Abijah Coburn (1787–1861).[4] Abijah was the half brother of Jonas, who established his branch of the Coburns on Church Street. Both Abijah and his bachelor son, also named Abijah (1816–1907), were bootmakers. The house later became part of Ferndale Farm dairy.

The Morse family farmed in the area for many

Figure 24-2. Generations of the Morse family occupied the 18th-century farmhouse that still stands at the intersection of South Avenue and Oak Street. This photograph was taken in 1936, before the house was restored and the two front doors replaced by a single wide door and leaded-glass sidelights.

Figure 24-3. Eighty-one-year-old Frank Morse (left) is shown here with Winslow Pope in 1924.

years. On the 1794 Kingsbury map, the house at the corner of South Avenue and Oak Street belonged to Beniah Morse. In the 19th century, it was a two-family occupied by two cousins with the same surname. According to an article in the *Waltham Daily Free Press Tribune,* it was once home to 21 children all attending Weston schools, "a record which can hardly be paralleled."[5] In the early 20th century, the Morses were still there, just getting by. George Morse was known for his strawberries and raspberries, which he sold to the carriage trade, and for his white wine, which was primarily for his own consumption.

Figure 24-4. Charlotte Hubbard Young, daughter of Charles Townsend Hubbard, is shown here in the mid-1880s with her two oldest children, Margaret (Daisy) and Charlotte.

24-5. The large shingled mansion built by Charlotte and Benjamin L. Young is still standing at 4 Newton Street at the corner of Young Road.

On Newton Street, Samuel Child built his house on the hill in 1749.[6] By the late 19th century, it was one of several belonging to farmers Charles A. and Samuel Warren, who specialized in growing strawberries and developing new varieties.

The road from South Avenue to Newton Lower Falls was known as East Newton Street until 1904, when the name was changed to Park Road. Until the construction of the Massachusetts Turnpike, East Newton Street/Park Road intersected with South Avenue directly opposite the lower end of Newton Street.

Charles Townsend Hubbard and His Daughters

Charles Townsend Hubbard bought hundreds of acres of farmland in the southeast corner of town beginning in 1867. The land around Cutter's Corner passed into the hands of his two youngest daughters, Charlotte, who married Boston businessman Benjamin Loring Young (1849–1907), and Anne, who married lawyer and gentleman farmer Bancroft Chandler Davis (1853–1934).

The Youngs were married in 1875 and had three children, Margaret "Daisy" (b. 1876), Charlotte "Lottie" (b. 1879), and B. Loring Young (1885–1964). Their winter home was at 285 Beacon Street in Boston. In the early 1880s, the couple began developing a country place near Charlotte's father on

Figure 24-6. Bancroft C. Davis (1853–1934) was trained as a lawyer but preferred the life of a serious gentleman farmer. With his wife Anne, youngest daughter of C.T. Hubbard, he established the model dairy on South Avenue known as Ferndale Farm.

Figure 24-7. Textile manufacturer Francis A. Foster (1843–1921) was described as "widely known in mercantile and banking circles for his foresight and good judgment."

Figure 24-8. Boston architect James Kelley designed Foster's Renaissance Revival brick mansion, now the clubhouse for Pine Brook Country Club. The hip roof, wide overhanging eaves, and classical porch columns are characteristic of the style. (Howes brothers photo, 1898)

Figure 24-9. Foster's Doublet Hill mansion was pictured in the 1899 publication Picturesque and Architectural New England: Picturesque Massachusetts, *which featured many Boston-area estates.*

Orchard Avenue. Charlotte Young wrote in her diary of 1883 that "Ben calls Daisy his partner in the farm and she takes as much interest as he does in all the improvements. We have a large stock barn now building which will be a great pleasure to all of us."[7] By 1885 the Youngs were taxed for 114 acres, three dwellings, and two barns. Their Shingle-style mansion still remains, along with an impressive carriage house later converted to a residence.

Anne Hubbard and Bancroft Davis were married in 1882 and had two children, Martha and Mabel. Beginning in 1882, they built a large Queen Anne house and stable close to the Hubbards on Orchard Avenue. Anne was a strong pacifist Quaker known for her charitable nature. Bancroft was described as a witty, humorous man, widely known and loved by his many friends. The couple had a second home on Martha's Vineyard, where Davis pursued his favorite sport of yachting.

Like the Hubbards, Bancroft Davis was a member of a prominent New England family that could trace its ancestry in America back to the earliest years of settlement.[8] Davis was admitted to the Massachusetts bar in 1884 and practiced in Boston for about two years. After a serious bout with scarlet fever, he abandoned law and devoted himself to farming at Weston. In 1889, the family went to France for three years. They returned to the United States in 1892 and spent the next three decades acquiring land and developing Ferndale Farm as a model dairy described later in this chapter.

The Francis A. Foster Estate, Doublet Hill

In May 1892, Benjamin and Charlotte Young sold 49 acres to Francis Appleton Foster (1843–1921), who developed a small but "beautifully-kept" estate called Doublet Hill. The main house, a "notable example of a brick country house," was designed by Boston architect James T. Kelley and constructed in 1895–96.[9] The property included the old Stimpson farmhouse and a large new barn with living quarters for staff.

Francis Foster began his business career at age 17 after graduating from Boston English High School and studying six months of commercial law. He opened his own office in 1879 and a decade later organized the partnership of Francis A. Foster & Co. on Franklin Street in the heart of the Boston dry-goods district. In 1902, he began printing and dyeing

Figure 24-10. Foster was a breeder of fine horses and had a riding ring on his property. His foreman, George Welcome, is holding the center horse. (Howes brothers photo, 1898)

Figure 24-11. South Avenue resident Samuel C. Bennett (1858–1925), a lawyer and judge, represented the town in disputes over the Stony Brook Reservoir, Charles River Reservation, and Weston Bridge. He is pictured here in 1913, the year he gave the historical address at the town's Bicentennial.

cotton art draperies under the name Puritan Mills. He was also a director of mills in Fall River and New Bedford.[10] Foster was a lifelong bachelor.

The 1899 guidebook *Picturesque and Architectural New England: Picturesque Massachusetts* describes the estate beginning with the elevated site:

> Doublet Hill . . . which thousands ascend annually to enjoy the expansive view . . . pronounced by officers of the coast survey to be more extensive and satisfactory than that from any other hill in Eastern Massachusetts, rises from the banks of the Charles River in two picturesque summits of almost equal height, 364' and 360', separated by a broad ravine.[11]

Here, overlooking the Blue Hills 12 miles distant, Foster positioned his house for maximum dramatic effect:

> The house stands at the head of a long, open slope fronting toward Riverside and Wellesley, the steep, wooded pitch of the summit above and behind, constituting a season-varying background. The road by which the place is approached rises gradually from the river banks, and, as it nears the house, winds slightly so that it can be seen from the windows in every room.[12]

The main house, described as Italian Renaissance in style, was a sophisticated classical design executed in light cream-colored brick with terra-cotta ornamentation imported from Pennsylvania. Two wide colonnaded piazzas were connected on the south side by a tiled terrace with broad stone steps leading to the lawn and gardens. A porte cochere sheltered the main entrance, which was located on the north side. Lion heads ornamented the ends of the rafters under the wide, overhanging eaves.

Architect James T. Kelley received his training in

Figure 24-12. Frederick Thomas Bush was among the first of many business and professional men to settle in Weston beginning in the mid-19th century. This photograph of the onetime U.S. Consul to China was taken by his neighbor Francis Blake.

Figure 24-13. Bush remodeled the existing Starr farmhouse on South Avenue into a picturesque Italianate country house later occupied by his daughter, Fannie, and her husband, David W. Lane.

the office of Sturgis & Brigham and opened his own office in the mid-1880s in his home on Beacon Hill in Boston. In 1910, Kelley formed a partnership with Weston resident Harold S. Graves, although he carried on most of his work alone. He was deeply interested in the history and art of France and Italy and traveled abroad numerous times.

Francis Foster was a member of the New England Breeders Association and was much involved in breeding fine horses. According to a biographical sketch, he could often be seen in a riding ring near the road, exercising his colts; and "sometimes even on Sunday mornings, church-goers were amazed to see him working them out with a bull-whip."[13] His formidable personality was summarized as follows:

> A man of somewhat forbidding presence and exacting business conduct, he was nevertheless well-liked by many who penetrated his craggy

Figure 24-14. The F. Loring Preston house, later occupied by Stephen and Agnes Blake Fitzgerald, was on the south side of South Avenue near the Charles River. (Howes brothers photo, 1898)

Figure 24-15. Glenfeld, built by Benjamin and Elizabeth Field, was another of the fine homes at the east end of South Avenue. It was torn down and replaced by the present house at One Whitehouse Lane. (Howes brothers photo, 1898)

exterior, and he was a generous supporter of worthy causes in Weston.[14]

On his death in 1921 at age 78, Foster left $2,500 to the Weston Library for the purchase of reference books as an aid to the self-development of youth. He also bequeathed $500,000 to Wellesley College and $1 million to MIT.[15]

More New Arrivals

By the late 19th century, other business and professional men had settled around Cutter's Corner. One of the first was Frederick T. Bush (b. 1815), who served as United States Consul to Hong Kong from 1845 to 1852.[16] Frederick Bush returned to America and established the East India house of Bush and Comstock.[17] He purchased the old Starr farm on South Avenue across from what is now Whitehouse Lane and remodeled the existing early-18th-century farmhouse. His daughter Amelia married Joseph Warren Field, and their daughter Ruth married Francis Blake's son, Benjamin.

Another daughter of Frederick Bush, Fannie, married David Weston Lane in 1878. He was the son of David and Caroline Lamson Lane and was in business with his father in the firm of Lane, Lamson & Company, importers based in Boston, New York, and Paris.[18] The David W. Lanes and their four children lived on the former Bush property, which included several houses and a large barn. Every day the coachman would take Lane to the Auburndale train station in a horse and carriage, long after everyone else had bought a car. After he retired, "Uncle David" would go over to the Blake house, Keewaydin, for tea every afternoon with his sister-in-law Amelia and his niece.[19] The Lanes' coachman, Edward Dooley, lived in a small house across from the present Glenfeld East. He collected garbage and fed the food scraps to pigs, which he kept penned in the back woods.

Immediately to the west of the Lanes at Brookwood lived Samuel Crocker Bennett (1858–1925), lawyer, judge, and dean of Boston University Law School. Bennett moved to Weston in 1891. He served as school committee chairman and town counsel and was selected in 1913 to give the historical address at the Bicentennial. A lengthy tribute delivered at the 1926 town meeting after his death speaks of his "thorough knowledge of law, his judicial temperament, his common sense and unfailing courtesy," which "combined to make him an ideal magistrate and he was regarded both by the Bench and Bar as one of the ablest lawyers in the Commonwealth . . ."[20]

Just east of the Lane property was the home of F. Loring Preston, grandson of early Weston estate owner Josiah Quincy Loring. In later years, the Preston property was purchased by Francis Blake's daughter, Agnes, and her husband, lawyer Stephen Fitzgerald. They fixed up the existing house and also built a new house on the 14 acres, which was on the south side of South Avenue just west of what is now Route 128.

On the north side of South Avenue, merchant Benjamin F. Field and his wife, Elizabeth, purchased 35 acres from Frederick Bush and C.T. Hubbard in 1878.[21] The Field house, Glenfeld, was located at what is now One Whitehouse Lane but was later demolished. In 1896, the Fields' three children, Benjamin F., Fanny, and William DeYoung Field, sold the main house and most of the land.[22] William DeYoung Field, who reportedly disliked the original house, retained five acres and in 1897 built a well-detailed Colonial Revival house on what is now Nash Lane. William was in the importing business with David Lane. Not long afterward, he moved to Europe permanently, leaving his new house empty.

The remaining 30 acres of Field land were sold to the Mathews family and then to the Shaw brothers of Bath, Maine, who tried to develop one of Weston's first subdivisions. To attract buyers, the brothers may have been counting on the proximity of the new Commonwealth Avenue trolley line, which had been extended to Norumbega Park in Auburndale in 1896. Their ambitious 1898 plan for Glenfeld shows 80 house lots varying in size from about 6,000 square feet to an acre. Two Shingle-style houses remain to show what the developers had in mind, but the subdivision was a complete failure. In looking for revenue from the land, the brothers also quarried samples of granite from ledge at the rear of the property, but the stone was not good enough for mining.[23]

William DeYoung Field's house on Nash Lane was leased in 1908 and later purchased by Frederick Hapgood Nash (1874–1946), senior partner with the Boston law firm of Choate, Hall and Stuart.[24] After the Shaw subdivision failed, Nash and George Sturgis jointly purchased the Glenfeld land.[25] In

Figure 24-16. This photograph was taken looking north from what is now the Massachusetts Turnpike. It shows the rear of the Cutter farmhouse (c. 1858) and barns, all of which have been demolished. The house was torn down in the 1990s to make way for the present medical office building. (Photo c. 1900)

1921, Sturgis married Rosamond Bennett, fifth child of Judge Samuel Bennett, and the couple built a brick Colonial Revival house called The Ledges designed by Boston architect C. Howard Walker.[26]

West of Cutter's Corner were three small country estates belonging to Warren S. Dame, Dr. Abner Post, and Egbert J. Shaylor. Dame was a principal in the Boston firm of Dame, Stoddard & Co., importers and dealers in fine table and pocket cutlery. His house remained at the corner of Ridgeway Road and Corwood Drive until it was destroyed by fire in February 1960.

Egbert J. Shaylor was a wealthy gentleman and ardent horticulturist whose national reputation as a peony expert is explained in a 1905 newspaper article:

> He has drawn on England, France, Holland and Japan for new and improved sorts until he now has some 10,000 plants embracing about 400 of the best varieties in the world and forming a collection second to none in the United States.[27]

A newspaper item of 1916 announced that Shaylor would be opening his peony garden to the public for one week in June, and "his annual peony show is something everyone should see."[28] Although the Massachusetts Turnpike took a large chunk of the former Shaylor property and cut off the original entrance drive from South Avenue, Shaylor's Shingle-style estate house remains on Corwood Drive.

Cutter Farm in the Early 20th Century (1903–1920)

The Cutter house, barn, and cider mill were the dominant features of Cutter's Corner. The family had prospered in the years since Richard Cutter bought the 164 acres in 1804. Richard's son Jonas had inherited the western portion of the property, which later became Ferndale Farm. Jonas's son, George Berkeley Cutter, was married in 1845 and built a Greek Revival farmhouse on South Avenue.[29] He and his wife, Mary, had a greenhouse and raised flowers as a business.

Another of Richard's sons, Charles, had inherited the eastern section of the farm. His son, Benjamin Franklin Cutter (1827–1903), was the next to occupy the homestead at Cutter's Corner. In 1858 he tore down the Colonial farmhouse built by Thaddeus Spring and replaced it with an up-to-date three-bay Greek Revival with a porch across the front. This house stood at the prominent intersection of South

Figure 24-17. Benjamin Franklin Cutter (1827–1903) was the third generation of his family to occupy the farm at Cutter's Corner. He had four children: Franklin H., Susan, Helen, and Charles B.

Figure 24-18. Susan Cutter (1867–1935) attended normal school and worked as a teacher until she was forced to retire because of Parkinson's disease. Despite her illness, she raised her two nieces, Elinor and Alice, and later married Winslow Pope. (Photo c. 1898)

Avenue and Newton Street for nearly 140 years.[30] At the turn of the century, Benjamin owned 50 acres.

As soon as Benjamin's son Charles could manage it, his father had him getting up at 4 A.M. to take care of five horses, a flock of hens and chickens, and two cows that had to be milked twice a day. After the morning chores, Charles would come in for breakfast and rush off to the one-room schoolhouse on Ware Street.[31] After Benjamin's death, Charles Bond Cutter ran the farm and the cider and vinegar business.

Another of Benjamin's four children, Susan, was a teacher until she became ill with the "shaking palsy," which progressed slowly the rest of her life. Her sister, Helen, married Edward S. Tyler in 1901. Two daughters were born in the next two years, Elinor in 1902 and Alice on July 24, 1903, the same day that Tyler died of typhoid fever and pneumonia. Helen came home to Weston with the two baby girls, joining an extended family that also included Great-Uncle Charles S. Cutter. Helen Cutter Tyler never recovered from her husband's sudden death. She became increasingly melancholy and began to wander the countryside looking for him. Finally, when her daughter Alice was eight years old, Helen was taken to Westboro State Hospital, where she died in 1922.[32]

Alice Tyler Fraser later recorded many details of her childhood in two published articles on "Growing Up in Weston." They describe a farm family of comfortable means, with the requisite piano and Victorian furnishings and even updated plumbing and heating:

> The house had ten rooms and was heated by stoves that were set up in the fall and stored in the back shed in summer. The bathroom, which had been a bedroom, had a stove, and a fire was built in it on Saturday nights for baths. We used soapstones to warm the beds. A hot air furnace was put in about 1910 or '11, and the heat from the front hall register helped warm the two front bedrooms. The parlor was very Victorian and used only on special occasions. Elinor and I practiced on the square grand piano. Dusting the whatnot was my particular chore on Saturday mornings. The items were interesting, but I usually missed one shelf and had to go back. The Axminster carpet was taken up each spring and beaten on the clothesline. A straw matting was the summer carpet. The parlor was not used very often. Every Saturday morning Elinor and I had to

Figure 24-19. This photograph of Benjamin F. Cutter's best parlor shows the wealth of material goods available to a prosperous farm family in the late 19th century. (Photo c. 1900)

Figure 24-20. The Cutter barn and cider mill were well known. The mill had three floors, with the presses at basement level, barrel storage on the second floor, and large casks of cider aging into vinegar at level three. Benjamin Cutter also made champagne cider. (Photo c. 1900)

> clean our bedroom, and I liked taking the rugs out onto the porch roof and shaking them. It was a tin roof, and when it rained I liked to hear the sound.[33]

A covered well stood in the front yard. By the early 20th century, Francis Blake's Keewaydin Water Works was providing water piped in from the street. The family did not have electricity.

Alice spent as little time as possible in the house. Her memoirs emphasize the love of nature and freedom of children to explore their surroundings:

> I loved the farm, and we were free to roam all over it. A brook, Seaverns Brook, crossed it.... The brook was stoned up on both sides as far as a bridge that was built across it for a wagon road to the fields and orchard. East of the bridge the yard sloped to the brook, and the horses came down to drink. The cows had big tubs for water in the barnyard back of the barn. We waded in the brook in summer. We called it "Our Brook", and when it crossed under Park Road to the Bennett's land, it was called "Bennett's Brook" and then "Lane's Brook.". . . We lay on the bridge and watched water bugs and minnows.[34]
>
> We climbed the trees, went across the fields to the orchard which was up the hill on Ridgeway Road, picked cowslips in a marshy pond in one of the fields and forget-me-nots and watercress in the brook. In one pond there were snapping turtles . . .[35]

Cutter farm specialized in cider and vinegar but also produced a wide variety of foodstuffs for family consumption, as enumerated by Alice:

> Behind the house was a home orchard with Early Williams and Gravenstein and Russett apples, Bartlett and Comice pears. I used to get up early to eat apples as they fell. Off the ell of the house was an outhouse. A grapevine grew up over it, and in the fall Margaret Nash and I would climb up and gorge ourselves on grapes.
>
> Aunt Sue always had a vegetable garden. In winter carrots, cabbages, squash, potatoes, and turnips, as well as two or three barrels of apples, were kept in the cellar. She made jams and jellies and canned pears and peaches and pickles. . . . She kept a flock of hens, and each year a "setting" hen hatched new chickens. The two-year-old hens were kept for "chicken every Sunday." On Friday night the hired man would kill the hen and pluck and dress it and hang it in the cellar. I learned to pluck them.[36]

The massive cider mill and barn were directly adjacent to each other behind the house. In season, wagonloads of apples arrived daily to be crushed. Fraser described the cider-making operation:

> The mill had three floors; the big presses were in the basement. The apples, brought in barrels, were poured into the grinding hoppers on the first floor, gradually. The pulp landed on big squares of cloth, and when enough pulp had been spread all over the cloth, the sides were folded in and a big slotted board was placed on it. There were six or eight layers. Then the big presses were turned down on top of the pump, and cider came out in a wide spout. I was usually there with my mug for fresh cider. Barrels were stored on the second floor, and on the third, big casks of cider aging into vinegar. The barrels and casks were hoisted to the third floor by heavy rope pulleys.... Margaret Nash and I would pull each other up and down by the ropes at the side of the opening. Sometimes we would climb the

> stairs to the third floor and go from cask to cask, opening the spigot and tasting the vinegar.[37]

Fraser's grandfather Benjamin made champagne cider filtered through fine white sand from a beach in Ipswich. Fraser recalled Harvard boys coming to the house trying to buy some of the fermented brew.

Everyday Life at Cutter's Corner

Alice Tyler Fraser and her sister attended District School #5 at the corner of Ware and South Avenue. She recounted her personal experiences with chores and discipline:

> There was a big iron stove in the room, and a woman in the neighborhood made the fire in cold weather. In the back of the school were separate outhouses for boys and girls. Washing the blackboards and clapping the erasers was a chore we liked to do after school. When there was a bad snowstorm, Miss [Rebecca] McKenna usually stayed overnight at our house. She and my aunt were old friends. . . . She was horrified when I told her that she once made me stand in a corner when I was in first grade and once had tied me in my chair. Perhaps today I would be called an "over-active" child.[38]

In Alice's youth, the school went through grade 4. Her aunt asked permission for Alice to attend fourth grade at the grammar school on School Street, where she recalled the poetry recitations on the last Friday of each month. By that time, the number of students at District School #5 had dwindled to 10 or 12, but parental pressure kept it open until World War I.

When Alice was young, the family walked to the Congregational church in Auburndale for Sunday school. Although the Cutters had been members of First Parish for generations, Newton Street was a long, hilly road with few houses, while South Avenue was a more open, well-traveled road with sidewalks all the way to Auburndale.

Figure 24-21. Charles B. Cutter Jr., Alice Cutter Tyler [Fraser], and Margaret Nash play with Billy the goat in this 1911 photograph.

Grocery shopping was largely unnecessary, as much of the family food was either produced on the farm or purchased from traveling vendors. Mr. Heard, the fish man, came on Thursday, and the family always had fish chowder or oyster stew on Friday. Aunt Sue had oranges sent from Florida in the winter, and the children got a tangerine in their stockings each Christmas. Other traveling peddlers provided specialty items. Alice recalled that once a year, a man with a gaily decorated cart pulled by a huge Belgian horse came through town selling harness equipment and ornaments for horses.

For other items, the family often shopped in Waltham or Newton. They stopped at Clifford Cobb's dry goods on Moody Street and, for a special treat, bought ice cream at Mr. Farmer's Ice Cream Parlor next door. They bought new shoes for school each August at Tarleton's in West Newton and banked at West Newton Savings Bank.

For recreation, the children climbed Norumbega Tower, went swimming at Riverside Recreation Grounds, or crossed the bridge to Norumbega Park. Twenty-five cents purchased admission (5¢), an ice-cream cone (5¢), merry-go-round ride (5¢), and an extra 10 cents for the penny arcade or more rides on the merry-go-round to try for the brass ring. Occasionally, the family took the train to South Station and the East Boston ferry from there to Revere Beach, where MDC bathhouses were clean and well kept.

"Going calling" was one of the summer duties required of the Tyler girls. Once every summer, Aunt Sue would take them in the buggy to call on the North Side relatives, cousin Anna and Mr. Hastings, the Arthur Coburns, and cousin Maud Coburn.[39] Alice Tyler Fraser recalled, "We wore our best clothes and were on our best behavior. I remember how slippery the horse-hair furniture was. Refreshments usually made up for the long periods of sitting still. On the home trip, the horse would have a drink of water at the watering trough in the center."

In the spring and fall, Gypsies would arrive to camp in the woods on Loring Road where the entrance to Meadowbrook Road is today. Fraser remembered that the children were afraid of them but went close enough to see their wagons, horses, and ponies. The men were horse traders and the women went from house to house selling trinkets and scarves and telling fortunes. Tramps also stopped by the house and Aunt Sue always gave them a sandwich and milk and an extra sandwich to take with them. "Somehow," Fraser mused, "all the tramps seemed to know who would feed them."[40]

Fraser's account points to the social difference between longtime residents and the more affluent newcomers and how these differences were bridged. Fraser recalled the friendliness of adults like Judge Bennett, who waved to the children every morning as his coachman drove him to the station, and Mrs. B.L. Young, who invited her to have tea and play in her children's bedrooms. The Nashes took her on her first long automobile trip, to Deerfield, Massachusetts. One summer Mrs. Bancroft Davis invited Alice, Elinor, and Aunt Sue to her house in Edgartown. She engaged a crafts teacher and a dancing teacher, and Alice learned to make raffia baskets and do the Highland fling.

Neighborhood children played together. The Bennetts were generous with their baseball equipment and field next to Park Road. One summer the South Side Sox and the Valley View Bums, two scrub teams of five or six boys each, had a series of games. Tom Bennett, the youngest of the Bennett boys, was interested in sports but was not allowed much activity due to "chest weakness." He organized races for the neighborhood children like the .8-mile loop from Cutter's Corner to Ware Street, up to Newton Street, and back to the corner. Alice played with Margaret Nash. One summer they set up a lemonade stand in the triangular plot of land where Newton, South Avenue, and Park Street came together. That ended when Mrs. Nash found her sugar and lemons disappearing. Later Margaret picked corn from her father's garden and the children sold that, to her father's consternation.

Children from well-to-do families shared their advantages, recalled Fraser:

> There were six Bennett children, all older than we were. Barbara, the older daughter, was like a big sister to me. When Elinor and I were seven or eight, she came over and read the "Just So Stories" to us. She taught me rhymes and jingles and Pig Latin that she had learned, but best of all, she taught me to ride horseback. She went to the Park Riding School and to the Winsor School. She owned a lovely black saddle horse named Janice, and when I was eight years old she let me ride Janice from the Bennett's farm to Aunt Nellie's house . . .
>
> I used to stand on the stone wall and watch Barbara and her friends, Betty and Nancy Hubbard, ride by on their beautiful horses. Some years later, when Barbara had one of the western horses that had been . . . "broken" at the Loker Farm on Winter Street where Rivers School is now, she let me ride "Janice" on one of their riding parties.[41]

The Mabel Page Murder

The tranquillity of the neighborhood was shattered on March 31, 1904, when 41-year-old Mabel Page, "a woman of blameless life and high character," was found slain at her home on South Avenue. The subsequent investigation and trial attracted widespread media attention from 1904 until 1906, when Charles Tucker was put to death for the murder. The case proved to be of such intense public interest that the entire transcript of the trial and all subsequent appeals was printed in two volumes with 1,598 pages rich in detail, not only about the crime but also about life in Weston in this first decade of the 20th century.[42]

At the 1905 trial, the opening statement for the prosecution set the scene on the day of the murder. Mabel Page was a woman "attractive in appearance, beautiful in character, symmetrical to a remarkable degree in figure and form," according to the prosecutor's opening statement.[43] She lived with her elderly father, her brother, Harold, and a housekeeper. Her invalid mother had died about a year before the murder. Mabel had been devoted to her mother and had taken on the responsibilities of caring for her father, who was no longer able to work. She sold embroidery and needlework to help the family along. The prosecutor related how the virtuous Miss Page had been collecting money for her mother's tombstone, money that Tucker allegedly stole before killing her.

On the morning of the murder, her brother and father were out and the housekeeper went off to the doctor, leaving Miss Page cutting out a dress on the living room table. Her father returned in the early afternoon and found his daughter dead in her chamber.[44] Mr. Page summoned the medical examiner, who saw the cut at her throat and thought the death was suicide. There was no further medical examination until the next morning, when the undertaker found deep knife wounds in her back and police were notified.

Figure 24-22. The murder of 41-year-old Miss Mabel Page in 1904 shattered the bucolic atmosphere of Cutter's Corner. Here a reporter and a policeman wait outside the Page home on South Avenue.

Word of the shocking crime began to spread. Police questioned everyone seen in the neighborhood at the time of the murder, particularly Charles Louis Tucker, a 24-year-old youth who lived with his parents in Auburndale. Tucker was unemployed at the time. He claimed he had walked to Cutter's Corner and then to the athletic grounds to see if there was any target shooting that day. Police discovered the sheath of a hunting knife and then the knife itself, which Tucker had tried to destroy. The knife still had traces of blood on it. At that time, the blood could not be analyzed to see if it was animal blood, as Tucker claimed. On April 9, Charles Tucker was arrested and charged with murder.

Trial of Charles Louis Tucker

At the trial, the government introduced as evidence a note, found at the scene of the murder, with handwriting alleged to be Tucker's. The police claimed that $12 was missing from a downstairs bureau. A witness testified that the defendant was trying to raise money to go to St. Louis. A final piece of physical evidence was a Canadian stickpin that the prosecution claimed was missing from a pincushion in Mabel Page's room.

In his closing statement, Tucker's lawyer, James H. Vahey, argued that Tucker was arrested because of public pressure to produce a murderer. Although many people had seen him in the neighborhood at the time of the murder, they all testified that he was enjoying a pleasant stroll. Vahey protested that Tucker's knife could not have produced the fatal wounds, as it had only a single cutting edge. He argued that, as a matter of law, it was improper to show that the defendant needed money, and that poverty does not establish a motive. He noted that money was found in an upstairs bedroom, where Miss Page had probably moved it.

Vahey urged the jury to look at the motive:

> But you are not going to believe, Mr. Foreman and gentlemen, that this boy, who was cleaning up his lawn, who was helping his poor, aged, infirm father to do the work and the chores about that house, while he was working upon that lawn conceived the idea that he would go into this house and get a knife and that he would go up to that house and kill that woman who had done him no wrong.[45]

Vahey was particularly scornful of the prosecution's expert on handwriting analysis. On the question of the stickpin, the defense claimed that Tucker also had a Canadian stickpin and produced witnesses who had seen him wear it.

Tucker testified about his actions on the day of the murder:

> . . . on the thirty-first day of March I was just as happy as any boy could be; I had everything in this world to live for, a good mother and father and a good home. Gentlemen, I didn't have in my mind the Page family. . . . And I also wish to say, gentlemen, that on this day . . . I went to walk leisurely, having a smoke to pass away the time, and I went to Cutter's Corner and from there to the railroad track to see them shoot, if they were shooting, and then home. After that I went with my father to the theatre and then came home as happy as any boy could be . . .[46]

He told how he had broken up his knife because of fear that he was under suspicion.

Tucker was found guilty. Motions for a new trial were denied. The case was appealed to the Supreme Judicial Court and later to the Supreme Court of the United States, which declined to issue a writ of error. Tucker was sentenced to die. On May 22, Gov. Curtis Guild Jr. received a petition signed by 116,555 people urging executive clemency.[47] The case made daily headlines on the front page of the *Boston Globe.* The executive office was deluged with pleas for Tucker's life. Tucker steadfastly proclaimed his innocence, and headlines proclaimed his confidence that he would be saved.

On June 8, 1906, the *Globe* headline announced in four-inch-high letters, "Tucker Must Die." The governor, in declining an appeal for clemency, cited his belief that the verdict was just and that nothing in the boy's somewhat disreputable history argued for clemency. He added that "of more importance than the life of any one citizen is the . . . safeguarding of woman's chastity in the lonely farmhouse as well as in the patrolled

The Boston Daily Globe.

BOSTON. TUESDAY MORNING, JUNE 12, 1906—SIXTEEN PAGES PRICE TWO CENTS

TUCKER IS ELECTROCUTED, MEETS DEATH BRAVELY

Sentence Executed at 12:12:30 This Morning—Condemned Man Asks Warden Bridges Not to Delay Fatal Hour.

Protests His Innocence to His Counsel Up to a Very Late Hour.

Mr Vahey Issues a Statement Criticising the Governor.

Eleventh-Hour Attempt to Secure Reprieve Ends in Complete Failure.

CHARLES LOUIS TUCKER

He Reads a Statement in Which He Asks Forgiveness for All Wrong He Has Done.

Walks Quickly and Carelessly From Cell to the Chair.

TUCKER'S LAST WORDS.

Read From Slip of Paper Just Before His Death.

"I hope God will forgive me for all the wrongs I have ever done in my past life. I forgive everybody who has ever wronged me. I am at peace with my Maker. May God have mercy on my soul."

Figure 24-23. The trial and subsequent execution of Charles Tucker for the Page murder was widely reported in the Boston press. Convinced of the young man's innocence, more than 100,000 people signed a petition urging executive clemency.

streets of the city . . ."[48] President Theodore Roosevelt declined to intervene, and on June 12, 1906, Tucker was put to death by electrocution.

The Tucker case became part of Massachusetts legal history. It has been cited 148 times in Supreme Judicial Court opinions, most recently in 1996. The case is used to clarify the question of when a murder is premeditated, with "malice aforethought," and therefore punishable as murder in the first degree. Another Supreme Judicial Court case involved the *Boston Globe,* which was judged guilty of contempt of court and interference with the administration of justice for printing facsimiles of Tucker's handwriting and the note found at the murder scene, with an analysis by handwriting experts.[49]

Many Cutter's Corner residents, including Susan Cutter, testified at the Tucker trial. One result of all the media attention was that the Cutters installed a telephone. At the time of the murder, the only telephone was at the Bennetts'. With reporters constantly knocking on the door wanting to use the telephone, Aunt Sue had a "nickel-in-the-slot" phone installed.

In 1912, the town finally distributed money that had been offered as a reward for help in capturing the killer. The largest sum went to Police Chief P.J. McAuliffe, who had found the stickpin among Tucker's effects. The *Boston Herald* criticized the payouts, noting that "the principle of paying public money to those who give evidence for the prosecution is inherently wrong . . ."[50]

Development of Ferndale Farm

Bancroft and Anne Davis began development of Ferndale Farm in 1891 with the purchase of 125 acres between Newton Street and South Avenue. Between 1905 and 1909, they greatly increased their livestock. In 1910 they purchased an additional 23 acres on the west side of Newton Street, built a massive stone barn, and hired farmer Frank Pope from Vermont to manage the dairy. The barn was 225 feet long and cost a reported $60,000.[51] Pope lived in a nearby farmhouse reserved for the manager, and Abijah Coburn's old place became a boardinghouse for the hired men. By 1915, Ferndale Farm had more than 60 cows. The stone barn was expanded, increasing its tax evaluation to $15,000 and making it the largest and most expensive farm building in Weston. Pens for the heifers were located in the barn annex and a bull pen and pigpens in the back field.

Ferndale Farm has been referred to as a "model dairy." The facilities were modern, up-to-date, and very clean. Even the behavior of the hired men was exemplary. According to Alice Fraser, Pope's help never used coarse or cheap language.

In late 1915, Anne Davis purchased the Benjamin Cutter farm, bringing the Davis holdings to a high point of 213 acres. Several reasons have been put forward as to why the Cutters gave up the farm. Charles Cutter, who paid rent to the other heirs, was having difficulty obtaining apples. Labor was scarce. Glass bottles and jugs were becoming popular for cider, and the family would have needed to install new equipment to modernize the cider mill.

Figure 24-24. The enormous 1910 Ferndale Farm barn stood at 275 South Avenue until it was demolished about 1990. For many years it had the highest tax valuation of any barn in Weston.

For the next several years, haying and farming on the Cutter property was done by the Popes. Aunt Sue moved to Oak Street, where she built a small house. For the first time, the family had electric lights. The following year, Susan Cutter married Frank Pope's father, Winslow Pope, known to Alice Tyler Fraser as Grandpa. He was a lively character from North Dakota who introduced Alice to Western folk ballads and Buffalo Bill's Wild West Show.

Beginning in 1916, Alice took over a small Ferndale Farm milk route, for $2 a week, seven days a week. She described her morning routine:

> Grandpa called me at 5:30 A.M., and I dressed and ran from Oak Street across by the barn and down South Avenue to Ferndale. I harnessed "Dinah" or "Chub" to the Democrat wagon and drove around to the milk room, where Lee Turner loaded the two cases of milk and cream into the wagon. At first the route covered South Avenue, the Youngs, the Blakes, Mrs. Davis on Orchard Avenue, over Ox Bow and Ridgeway Road and up Glen Road to the Glen House . . . then back through Hubbard's woods to what is now Bullard Road and down Shaylor Lane to South Avenue . . .[52]

By 1918 and 1919, Alice added customers in Wellesley Farms and Wellesley Hills and doubled the amount of milk and cream sold. In the winter of 1919–20, when Alice was a senior in high school, only pungs could be used for six weeks because of heavy snow, and she was allowed to cut back to every other day after school.

Figure 24-25. At age 13, Alice Tyler [Fraser] took over a short Ferndale Farm milk route for two dollars a week, delivering milk to customers every morning. She is pictured here in June 1920 in her high school graduation dress. Alice lived in Weston throughout her life. She was an inexhaustible source on Weston history and served as archivist for First Parish Church and the Weston Historical Society.

In addition to managing the dairy, Frank Pope planted strawberries and beans for the Boston market. He would drive his truck around the neighborhood at 5 o'clock in the morning, picking up young people willing to pick berries for two cents a box. The wholesale price was 13 cents a quart. For years, Alice also picked blueberries on Newton Street and Ridgeway Road and in the Nonesuch Pond area.

Every Friday night, Frank Pope drove the White truck to Waltham for groceries, taking five or six young people with him to go shopping or to the movie show at the Rex Theatre on Moody Street, where admission was 10 cents. On Sunday nights, Alice, Aunt Sue, and Grandpa would go to the Popes', where Thelma Pope played the piano for hymns and World War I songs. The Popes organized sleigh rides, hayrides, and corn-husking bees, along with parlor games in winter. In 1920, Alice Tyler Fraser graduated from high school and entered Boston University.

Figure 24-26. Alice Tyler [Fraser] at Ferndale Farm in 1918.

Model Farm to Country Club

In the early 1920s, Bancroft and Anne Davis sold Ferndale Farm and moved to Washington, D.C., where Bancroft Davis died in 1934. The land between South Avenue and Newton Street was purchased by Frank Pope and Porter L. Newton of Waltham, who promptly sold 85 acres to the ABC Development Company of Boston. This company also purchased the Foster estate, leased part of the Young estate, and developed the entire property as Pine Brook Valley Golf Club. The Foster mansion became the clubhouse and the barn was used as a locker room until it was destroyed by fire in February 1947. Fairways, tees, and greens were constructed by men with picks and shovels, aided by horse-and-wagon teams. Delbert Theall, an immigrant from Calgary, Canada, was in charge of the physical construction of the golf course and served as superintendent until the early 1930s. Pine Brook opened to members about 1924 and was incorporated as Pine Brook Country Club in 1944.

Pine Brook was among the first Jewish golf clubs in the country, established in an era when Jews were discriminated against at other country clubs. It was rumored in the neighborhood that land had been sold to Pine Brook with the understanding that none of the club members would live in Weston. Even years later, real-estate agents routinely told Jewish families that they would "not be happy" living in Weston.

Frank Pope continued to operate Ferndale Farm, which combined with Willow Farm in Newtonville. Pope struggled during the Depression to keep the land, but in 1937 he was unable to make payments and it was taken over by a trusteeship including B. Loring Young.[53] For some time thereafter, the dairy was run by Albert T. Waugh Sr., who lived in the manager's house. About 20 Brown Swiss cows were still pastured behind the barn. Occasionally one of them would get through the fence and amble across the golf course. Milk trucks arrived each morning at 4:30 to unload large metal cans of Vermont milk to be pasteurized and bottled. Ferndale Dairy Inc. was still operating at mid-century, when the company advertised "The Milk for Particular People" in the Weston High School yearbook.[54]

The Ferndale boardinghouse and six acres were sold in 1937 to British-born orthopedic surgeon William Elliston and his wife, Harriet, who was trained as an anthropologist. They planted fruit trees and grapevines, developed a sizable raspberry farm, and ran an egg business with 300 laying hens housed

Figure 24-27. The 18th-century Jonathan Spring house at 263 South Avenue was purchased in 1937 by Dr. William Elliston and his wife, Harriet, who is pictured here in 1982. The Ellistons raised raspberries and flowers, which they sold at a roadside stand. The couple helped establish the Roxbury-Weston programs. Bill, who is pictured in chapter 9, was a founder of the Weston Forest and Trail Association.

in the barn. They also grew flowers as a small business and at one time had 10,000 gladioli. Harriet Elliston later recalled, perhaps with some exaggeration, that when she and her husband moved to Weston, there was only one other registered Democrat in town. Always known for her liberal views and civil rights activism, she marched with Martin Luther King Jr. on Boston Common and worked to organize the Roxbury-Weston Day Camp and Programs to bridge the social gap between suburban and inner-city children. To help raise money, the Ellistons held a raspberry festival every year. In 1955 Dr. Elliston and others founded the Weston Forest and Trail Association. After her husband's death in 1984, Harriet considered ways to preserve the land that she and her husband had worked so hard to improve. In the late 1980s, she became the first homeowner in Weston to place a restriction on her house and barn to preserve the exterior appearance for future generations.

Beginning in the late 1930s, the Ferndale Farm barn was used for the New South Avenue Riding Club. Horses could be rented, trained, and boarded here, and large indoor and outdoor riding rings were available day and night. In 1951 the Ferndale Farm trustees subdivided the land and sold the stone barn. The riding school continued for a time, and later the barn was rented for storage of everything from cars to coffins. It was razed to make way for a Florida-style mansion completed in 1991.

B. Loring Young

Benjamin L. Young died in August 1907 at age 58. The estate mansion on Newton Street remained the home of his widow, Charlotte Hubbard Young. In 1912 their son, B. Loring Young, built his own home on Young Road.

B. Loring Young (1885–1964) was Weston's most prominent 20th-century politician and a power in Republican party politics for decades. He was brilliant, handsome, and rich. He was also a man of high ideals and commitment to public service, whose egalitarian spirit is reflected in his boast of being, at one time, the only non-Jewish member of the Pine Brook Country Club.

Young graduated from Noble and Greenough School and Harvard College, class of 1907, where he lettered on the track team.[55] In later years he was very active in Harvard affairs, serving as overseer from 1922 to 1928. Young married Mary Coolidge Hall in 1908 and the couple raised four children before their divorce in 1935. After graduating from Harvard Law School, Young spent nine years with the firm of Ropes, Gray and Gorham. He was elected to the Massachusetts House in 1916 and served as chairman of the House Ways and Means Committee and Republican floor leader before being elected speaker, a position he held from 1921 to 1924. His public service included chairmanship of the state board of probation from 1927 to 1942 and federal referee in bankruptcy from 1925 to 1941. Some say

Figure 24-28. B. Loring Young (1885–1964) was a state legislator and power in Republican party politics for decades. A Weston selectman for more than 30 years, he was known for his progressive views. He is shown here with his wife, the former Mary Coolidge Hall, and their children.

B. Loring Young could have been governor, were it not for personal difficulties.

Young's influence on the development of Weston began in 1910. At the age of 25, he was elected to the Weston Board of Selectmen to fill the vacancy created by the resignation of Francis Blake. For most of the next 36 years, Young represented the south side, continuing the progressive policies of his famous uncle. Young took an enlightened view of the role of town government and spent countless hours planning for controlled growth:

> The government of that town has been my special hobby in life, and I have tried to introduce all the modern improvement in town affairs, such as zoning, planning boards, and all other legislative safeguards possible to encourage municipal beauty and comfort.

The town common and town hall were built during his tenure and "in both of these projects his genius found expression."[56]

Figure 24-29. Concrete pipes for the Hultman Aqueduct are visible in this late 1930s view of the Lane house on South Avenue.

Figure 24-30. Looking west on South Avenue toward Cutter's Corner, the Lane house, at left, is nestled in a pleasant valley that was filled in when the Massachusetts Turnpike was built.

Brenton H. Dickson III remembered Young as "a man whose use of the English language was so forceful that he could influence a whole gathering with a few well-chosen phrases":

> Any Article in the Town Warrant detrimental to the Weston way of living was promptly squelched by his persuasive tongue. The Young-Tyler-Dickson triumvirate of Selectmen ruled during a critical period in the town's history, and the majority of residents were satisfied with what they did and how they did it. [57]

Two Aqueducts and the Massachusetts Turnpike

Cutter's Corner felt the impact of major metropolitan public works projects beginning in 1901, when land was taken for the building of the Weston Aqueduct.[58] The aqueduct passed north of Cutter's Corner before entering the Terminal Chamber, a classical limestone structure dramatically sited on a hill near Loring Road. In 1939–40, the Hultman Aqueduct was constructed south of South Avenue to a tunnel under the Charles River.[59]

The construction of Route 128 and the Massachusetts Turnpike changed forever the peaceful country atmosphere of Cutter's Corner. Route 128, completed in 1951, cut off the neighborhood from the Charles River. Before it was even finished, plans were under way for a major east–west toll road. The exact route was a subject of intense speculation from about 1950 to 1954, and residents of Cutter's Corner did what they could to direct officials away from the natural valley south of South Avenue. Between 1955 and 1957, the first section of the Massachusetts Turnpike was constructed from the New York border to Weston. Harriet Elliston recalled how the hill across from her home was blasted and removed during construction. After a simple warning whistle, the rocks would fly, many landing in the Ellistons' front yard. At least four houses in the Cutter's Corner neighborhood were moved to locations south of the turnpike.

In 1979, two parcels of back land in the area were transferred to the Town of Weston as conservation land. The Weston Forest and Trail granted 9.62 acres of former Sturgis land to the town, and the Massachusetts Audubon Society transferred 15 acres of former Young land, including a large pond called Hemlock Pond.

Houses in the Cutter's Corner Area

50 Corwood Drive (1890s). Shingle-style house built for Egbert Shaylor.

60 Corwood Drive. Moved from Shaylor Lane, where it was a secondary house on the Egbert Shaylor estate.

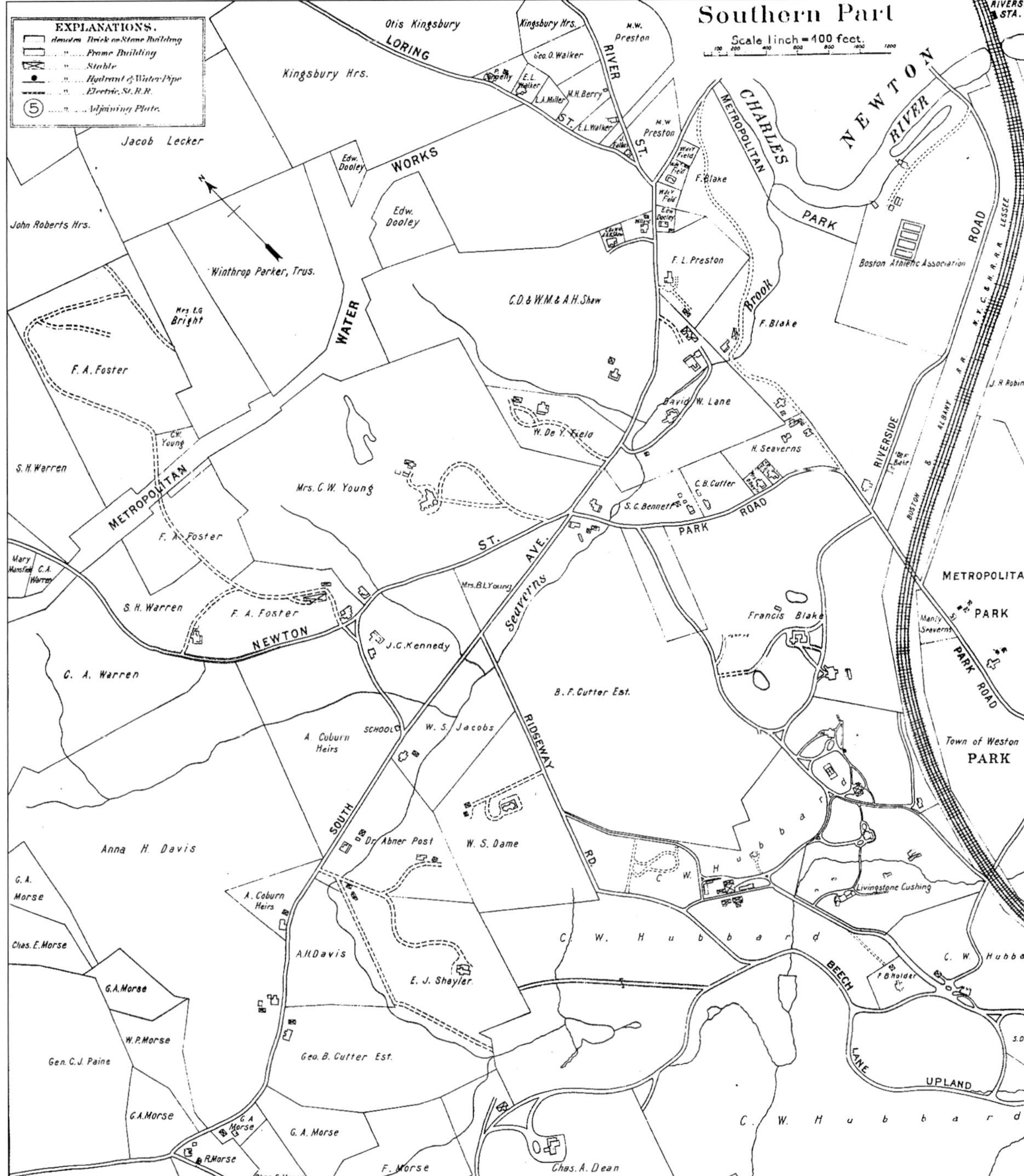

Figure 24-31. Detail from the 1908 Atlas of Middlesex County.

70 Corwood Drive (c. 1846). Greek Revival house built for farmer George Berkeley Cutter (1822–1899). Originally located at 292 South Avenue, it was moved to make way for the Massachusetts Turnpike. A well-built stone wall along South Avenue marks the original location. Cutter had a greenhouse and raised flowers as a business.[60]

Glenfeld East. Tax records suggest that turn-of-the-century developers built two Shingle-style houses on Glenfeld East as part of the unsuccessful Glenfeld development. Both houses are being renovated as part of the Cutter's Bluff development.

19 Nash Lane (1897). Colonial Revival house built for importer William DeYoung Field. The house first appears in 1897 tax records valued at $8,000, with a barn at $1,600 and 5 acres. Leased in 1908 and later purchased by lawyer Frederick H. Nash. Property subdivided in 1946.

4 Newton Street (c. 1885). Shingle-style mansion built for Benjamin L. Young and his wife, the former Charlotte Hubbard, as a summer home.

22 Newton Street. Post–Civil War house that became part of the Young estate.

26 Newton Street (c. 1860). Italianate house with characteristic central wall gable; later became part of the Foster estate. Traditionally said to have been built in the 18th century.

42 Newton Street (1895–96). Italian Renaissance brick estate mansion built for dry-goods merchant Francis A. Foster from designs by Boston architect James T. Kelley. Used as clubhouse for Pine Brook Country Club since mid-1920s.

54 Newton Street. Traditionally said to have been built for farmer Samuel Child in 1749. By the late 19th century, it was one of several houses belonging to farmers Charles A. and Samuel Warren.

125 Newton Street (c. 1870). Italianate house probably built for James Cooper, who bought the 70-acre farm in 1858 from the Keyes family.

126 Newton Street (1872). Italianate house built for farmer Marcus M. Fiske, who bought the land from James Cooper in 1871 (see also Nos. 125 and 131). In 1895, Fiske sold the 16-acre property to James Barton, a market gardener and vegetable dealer.

131 Newton Street (c. 1790). Built for farmer Josiah Hastings, this Federal-style house stayed in the Hastings family until the mid-19th century and then passed to another farmer, James Cooper, who owned it into the 20th century.

North of 131 Newton Street. See chapter 19.

59 Orchard Avenue (1882–83). Bancroft and Anne Hubbard Davis house. See chapter 22.

48 Ridgeway Road. Colonial Revival house moved here when the Mass Pike was constructed.

56 Ridgeway Road. Part of a house once belonging to David W. Lane was moved here when the Mass Pike was under construction. Local architect Marjorie Pierce incorporated it into a new house that uses floorboards, windows, and other architectural fragments from the Lane house.

134 South Avenue. Site of the mid-19th-century Benjamin Cutter farmhouse, torn down in 1994 to make way for the Gateway Medical Office building.

196 South Avenue. This farmhouse was part of the George S. Cutter property until 1881, when Elizabeth and Edward Page of Boston bought the house and 34 acres.[61]

215 South Avenue. On this property is District School #5 (1853), the only remaining schoolhouse never converted to a residence. School #5 was closed in 1917. Only #4 on North Avenue stayed in use longer. The Italianate schoolhouse was originally located closer to the corner of Ware Street and South Avenue and was moved in 1920.[62]

240 South Avenue. Caretaker's house and barn on Dr. Abner Post's country estate.

263 South Avenue (c. 1764). Built for farmer Jonathan Spring, sold to bootmaker and farmer Abijah Coburn in the early 19th century, and occupied by him and later by his son, also named Abijah (d. 1907). Purchased by Bancroft and Anne Davis in 1911 and used as the boardinghouse for the men at Ferndale Farm. When the Davises sold Ferndale, the Colonial farmhouse was purchased in 1920 by Lawrence B. Page, who remodeled the former saltbox by lifting the roof at the rear. Later, it became the home of Dr. William and Harriet Elliston.

275 South Avenue. Site of Ferndale Farm dairy barn (built 1910, demolished early 1990s).

279 South Avenue (mid-19th century). This farmhouse became the home of Frank Pope, manager of Ferndale Farm.

292 South Avenue. Site of George Berkeley Cutter house (see 70 Corwood Drive).

334 South Avenue (18th century). Home of generations of the Morse family of farmers. The double house once had two identical front doors where a single door and sidelights are now.

343 South Avenue. Civil War–era mansard house belonging to the Morse family, moved back from its original location when this stretch of South Avenue was relocated and widened in 1928.[63]

One Whitehouse Lane (formerly 99 South Avenue, 1922). Brick Colonial Revival designed by Boston architect C. Howard Walker for George Sturgis and his bride, Rosamond Bennett. Land subdivided in 1995.

44 Young Road (mid-1880s). Young estate carriage house, converted to a residence (see 4 Newton Street).

Notes

1. Little is known about one of the Spring farmhouses, located on the east side of Newton Street near South Avenue and no longer extant. Labeled as "T. Spring," it may have belonged to Thomas Spring, father of Thaddeus and Jonathan. The Thaddeus Spring house, dated 1760 in Lamson's *HTW*, 65, was purchased by Cutter and stood until the mid-19th century, when it was replaced by a house demolished in the 1990s. The Jonathan Spring house (c. 1764) passed into the Coburn family and is now 263 South Avenue.
2. MCRD 159/332.
3. Fraser, Alice Tyler, "Growing Up in Weston: 1903–1920," part I, *WHSB*, October 1984, 1.
4. The 1764 date is taken from Lamson's *HTW*, 65. See also Mary F. Pierce, *Births, Deaths and Marriages*, 40, 46.
5. *WDFPT*, November 26, 1920.
6. Ibid.
7. Diary of Charlotte Hubbard Young, October 30, 1883 (Young Papers, MHS).
8. His grandfather John Davis was governor and later a senator from Massachusetts. His uncle John Chandler Bancroft Davis served as assistant secretary of state. See *National*

Cyclopaedia of American Biography (New York: James T. White, 1937), vol. XXVI, 243.
9. Quotation from "Weston Has Become the Lenox of the East," *Boston Sunday Herald*, May 11, 1902, which pictures the Foster house. Tax records indicate that the house was still unfinished in 1895. When completed, it was valued at $20,000. Foster was also taxed for 53 acres and seven horses.
10. "Francis Appleton Foster," *National Cyclopaedia of American Biography*, op. cit., vol. XIX, 45.
11. Hale, Edward Everett, D.D., *Picturesque and Architectural New England: Picturesque Massachusetts* (Boston: D.H. Hurd & Co., 1899), vol. 2, 102–03. Includes two exterior and one interior photo, and architect's name.
12. Ibid.
13. 1955 *TR*, 82.
14. Ibid.
15. *National Cyclopaedia*, op. cit.
16. A daughter was born in China. Bush's flair for the dramatic is evident in this story of the baby's presentation to society. Frederick Bush was hosting his traditional formal New Year's Eve dinner when the butler came in with a large silver serving tray. Bush lifted the heavy cover with a flourish, revealing the newborn infant, and proclaimed, "I am announcing the birth of my daughter, Amelia DuBlois Bush." (Told to PWF by Amelia Bush's granddaughter Ruth Blake Oliver).
17. Lamson, "Weston" chapter in Hurd's *History of Middlesex County*, 501.
18. See Blake Papers, Box 76, MHS, for 1860 articles of copartnership of David Lane, Robert A. Turner, and David W. Lane under firm of Lane, Lamson & Co. and also original 1837 partnership agreement.
19. Ruth Blake Oliver to PWF.
20. 1926 *TR*, 286.
21. MCRD, 1480/236, F.T. and E.S. Bush to E.S. Field, 14.5 acres, June 1878, and C.T. Hubbard to Field, 20 acres, 1497/421, December 1878. Both transactions land only.
22. MCRD 2522/407, Field to Mathews, August 1896. See also 4197/290 (mentions deed from B.F. and Fanny Field to William DeYoung Field in 1898). The Mathewses sold the land to the Shaw brothers. Benjamin F., Fanny, and William DeYoung Field were cousins of Joseph Warren Field.
23. Robert Sturgis to PWF.
24. MCRD 3394/11, Field to Nash (lease, 1908) and 4197/290 (sale, 1918).
25. MCRD 4912/587 and 4912/591, November 1925.
26. Now One Whitehouse Lane.
27. *WDFPT*, March 31, 1905 (based on a *Boston Globe* article).
28. *WDFPT*, June 9, 1916.
29. The house was originally located just west of 292 South Avenue and was moved to its present location at 70 Corwood Drive when the Mass Pike was constructed.
30. The date of this house is taken from the oral history of Charles B. Cutter, son of Charles Cutter and grandson of Benjamin (Weston Public Library Oral History Project, November 17, 1986). Cutter says that Benjamin F. Cutter took out an insurance policy in 1858 that covered his barn, cider mill, and "a dwelling house to be built near them this summer for the insured . . ."; 7.
31. Ibid.
32. Information in this paragraph from Fraser, "Growing Up in Weston," op. cit., 1–2.
33. Ibid., 2.
34. Ibid.
35. Ibid., 3.
36. Ibid.
37. Fraser, Alice, "Growing Up in Weston: 1903–1920," part II, *WHSB*, January 1985, 3.
38. Ibid., 1.
39. Julia Ann Cutter, daughter of Charles Cutter, married Isaac Coburn, son of Jonas and Susannah (Viles) Coburn.
40. Fraser, "Growing Up in Weston," part II, op. cit., 3.
41. Fraser, "Growing Up in Weston," part I, op. cit., 4.
42. Attorney General's office, *The Official Report of the Trial of Charles Louis Tucker for the Murder of Mabel Page in the Superior Court of Massachusetts* (Boston: Wright & Potter Printing Co., 1907).
43. Ibid., 55.
44. Ibid., 58. Mr. Page found a note in her handwriting: "Have just heard that Harold is hurt and is at the Massachusetts Hospital. Have gone in 12 o'clock." In fact, Harold was not hurt, but someone apparently had deceived Miss Page into believing that he was.
45. Ibid., 1438.
46. Ibid., 1532.
47. In the book *Commonwealth History of Massachusetts*, edited by Albert B. Hart (New York: States History Company, 1930), the petitioners were disparaged as "sentimentalists," many of whom knew nothing about the case. Also on the list were "the names of entire families, including . . . children in the cradle"; 123.
48. Attorney General's office, op. cit., 1578.
49. The author would like to thank Franklin Levy for his assistance with legal research. See Supreme Judicial Court of Massachusetts, Middlesex, Commonwealth v. Charles L. Tucker (189 Mass. 457:76 N.E. 127; 1905 Mass. LEXIS 917), and Glove Newspaper Company v. Commonweath (188 Mass. 449; 74 N.E. 682; 1905, LEXIS 1198).
50. As quoted in *WDFPT*, February 16, 1912.
51. Fraser, "Growing Up in Weston," part II, op. cit., 5. See also MCRD "Plan of Land in Weston," December 1917, registered land, Book 84/465, #13416.
52. Ibid., 5.
53. MCRD, Registered Land, 274/373 (B. Loring Young and George Sturgis, Trustees, under Doc. #144866, 1937).
54. 1949 *Weston High School Yearbook*, 83.
55. See "B. Loring Young Dies, Ex-GOP Leader Was 79," *Boston Globe*, June 5, 1964, and "Benjamin Young, Lawyer, 78, Dies," *Boston Traveler*, June 4, 1964.
56. "Honorable Benjamin Loring Young, An Appreciation," 1922 *TR*, 36.
57. *Pung*, 49.
58. MCRD 132/15, "Plan No. 129 of Land Takings, Land in Weston," by Frederic P. Stearns, Chief Engineer, August 27, 1901. From Weston Reservoir, the aqueduct passed through the land of Charles and Samuel Warren, Francis Foster, Charlotte Young, the Shaws, and Edward Dooley before entering the Terminal Chamber. See also chapter 19.
59. The Hultman Aqueduct passed through property owned or formerly owned by Anne Davis, B.F. Cutter, Samuel Bennett, Agnes Blake Fitzgerald, Benjamin Blake, and others, then down by Boston University's Nickerson Field.
60. *WDFPT*, April 12, 1912.
61. MCRD 1580/597 and 598, October 13, 1881. G.S. Cutter to Eliz. D. Page, 6 acres and 28 acres, $4,000.
62. *WDFPT*, May 14, 1920.
63. MCRD, "Plan of Land in Weston belonging to Charles Morse," Plan Book 91/43, 1895.

Figure 25-1. Glen Farm, owned by Edward Jennings, was one of the largest dairies in Weston at the turn of the century. At the height of his operation, in 1903, Jennings had 112 dairy cows. The milk delivery wagons are pictured in front of the more elaborate of two large barns. In the center is Edward's son Clifton. This barn was destroyed in a major fire on December 16, 1903. Edward Jennings and his sons built many of the houses in the 200 and 300 block of Glen Road on lots that were originally part of the farm.

CHAPTER 25

Glen Road at the Four Corners

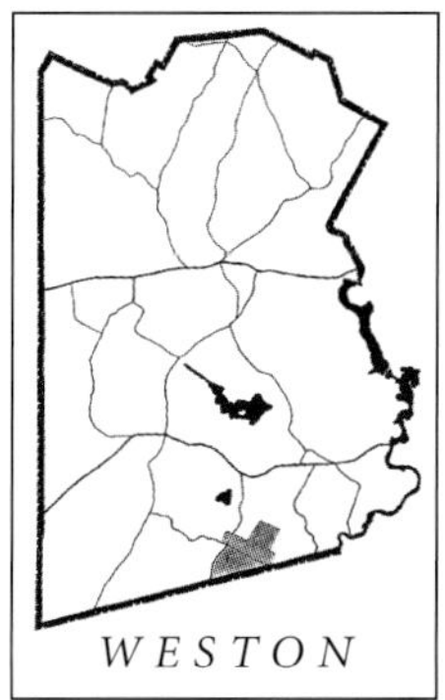

The history of Glen Road from the Four Corners at Oak Street and Cliff Road to the Wellesley town line illustrates three themes common in Weston history: longtime agricultural use of the land, the increasing attractiveness of Weston for summer vacationers, and the transition from farm to suburb. All three are illustrated in the story of two brothers, Edward and Willard Jennings, who worked hard to increase the economic value of their family farm. Edward built up a substantial dairy operation called Glen Farm. Willard opened a summer resort, Glen House, where well-to-do families could enjoy the country atmosphere within easy commute to Boston. As times changed, the brothers had to revise their business plans and, finally, cash in their major asset, the land. Edward Jennings subdivided his Glen Road street frontage into house lots and built a neighborhood with remarkable architectural unity.

This chapter also tells the story of three generations of the Wyman-McNutt family, another old Weston farm family. Their story is enhanced by photographs and the memories of centenarian Nelson McNutt, who recalls when strawberry fields and vegetable gardens made up the landscape at the Four Corners.

Edward Jennings and Glen Farm

The 1794 Kingsbury map shows only two houses on the eastern end of Glen Road. The older was built in 1732 for Nathaniel Jennison, who grew up in Watertown and was only 22 when he moved out to the sparsely settled, newly incorporated town of Weston. His house was originally located on the north side of the road, across from its present location.[1]

In 1826, the 114-acre farm was sold to Levi Jennings. When he died in 1870, the farm was left to his five grandchildren: Charlotte, Caroline, Willard (1854–1933), Edward (1856–1940), and Ellen. They each received pieces with descriptive names like "meadow lot," "peach and pear orchard," "old rye piece," "elm tree piece," "homestead and cow barn lot," "raspberry lot," "long orchard," "bog meadow lot," and "cranberry meadow."[2]

Edward decided to go into the dairy business. He was a hardworking, enterprising man whose neighbor went so far as to call him a "slave driver." He and his wife, Ella Brown Jennings, had five sons: Levi (b. 1878), Clifton Victor (b. 1879), Charles (b. 1885), Brenton (b. 1888), and Warren (b. 1890). Beginning in the 1880s, Edward bought parts of the farm owned by his siblings.[3] In building up Glen Farm, he took out mortgages and loans on his land and personal property, and for most of his life he had trouble with debt. For example, in 1879 he borrowed $800 from his sister Charlotte and secured the loan with a horse, covered milk wagon, double-runner pung, and more than 146 milk cans.[4]

Figure 25-2. The Edward Jennings family lived in this 1732 farmhouse, which had been built by Nathaniel Jennison. In 1924, Jennings moved the original part of the house across Glen Road to its present location at No. 266.

Dairying was an important farm specialty in Weston. Milk had to be delivered fresh, which gave local farmers an advantage. Jennings started out in 1880 with 12 cows, and by 1903, at the height of his operation, he owned 112. He used about 75 acres to grow "green fodder" or cattle corn, which was cut up by machine into small pieces and stored in two large silos.[5] Other fields were hayed. To take care of the cows and fields and handle milk processing and delivery, Jennings employed about 20 men.

At the turn of the century, Jennings had three or four milk wagons on the road. His trucks delivered primarily in Newton and Wellesley but traveled as far as Brighton. One of his special contracts was to furnish the entire supply of milk for what was then the Lasell Seminary in Auburndale. The drivers would start out on their routes at midnight. After returning in the morning, they would collect milk from local farmers to supplement milk produced on the Jennings farm. Jennings sold both regular milk and

Figure 25-3. This picture of the two Jennings barns was taken before a disastrous 1903 fire. Glen Road is in the foreground.

baby's milk. The baby's milk had two caps instead of one and was more expensive, although there was no actual difference in the milk itself.[6]

In August 1900, a large fire destroyed one of the Jennings barns. A fire department report noted that "on account of the delay in ringing the alarm Mr. Jennings's barn was all ablaze when the department arrived."[7] Its replacement was equipped with apparatus to fill a large number of bottles simultaneously, as well as a separator, refrigerator, and other appliances of modern dairying.

Three years later, the modern barn was also completely destroyed by fire. The blaze of December 16, 1903, was discovered in the early hours of the morning by the driver of one of the milk teams, who lived with his family in a tenement in the barn.[8] Employees and neighbors were able to save all but two calves. The town report noted that the alarm was pulled so late that the fire company could do nothing to save the building. Damage, estimated at $20,000, was covered by insurance. The horse barn and tool house were saved.

Newspaper reports speculated that the fire had been accidentally set by a tramp who had gotten into the barn for the night. Fire department historian Bentley Crouch records another theory, that the Jennings fires were deliberately set:

> It is wise, when mention is made of the Jennings fires, to bear in mind the fact that at the time it was suspected, although never proven, that they were set, for it was a known fact that the Jennings farm was not a paying proposition and that Edward had had little success in trying to sell his property.[9]

Another Jennings barn was destroyed by fire in 1906.[10]

Five months after the 1903 fire, Jennings advertised that he was selling his dairy cows:

> . . . having disposed of my retail milk business, which I have conducted for thirty years, I sell all my entire large herd of prime young cows, comprising all breeds. . . . All of them I selected personally and they are the best that money can buy.[11]

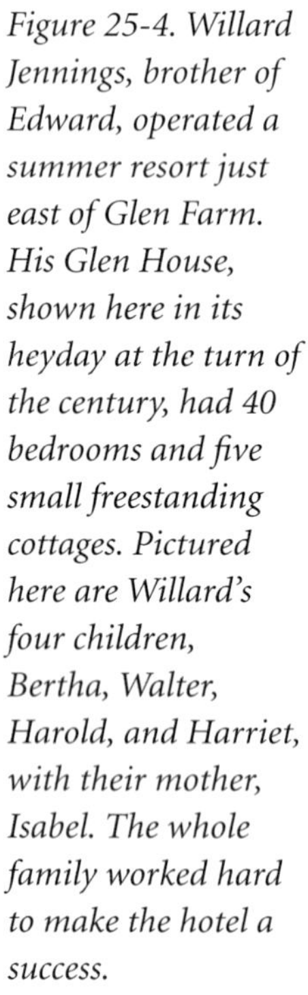

Figure 25-4. Willard Jennings, brother of Edward, operated a summer resort just east of Glen Farm. His Glen House, shown here in its heyday at the turn of the century, had 40 bedrooms and five small freestanding cottages. Pictured here are Willard's four children, Bertha, Walter, Harold, and Harriet, with their mother, Isabel. The whole family worked hard to make the hotel a success.

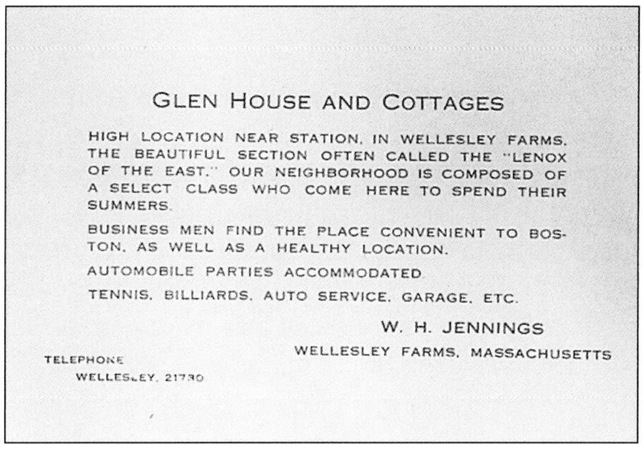

Jennings advertised a thoroughbred Durham bull weighing 1,400 pounds and "fat as a seal."

He sold his carts, barges, open two-seat carriage, and high milk wagon. After the sale Ed Jennings continued dairy farming, but the business was never as extensive as it was at the turn of the century.

GLEN HOUSE AND COTTAGES

HIGH LOCATION NEAR STATION, IN WELLESLEY FARMS, THE BEAUTIFUL SECTION OFTEN CALLED THE "LENOX OF THE EAST." OUR NEIGHBORHOOD IS COMPOSED OF A SELECT CLASS WHO COME HERE TO SPEND THEIR SUMMERS.

BUSINESS MEN FIND THE PLACE CONVENIENT TO BOSTON, AS WELL AS A HEALTHY LOCATION.

AUTOMOBILE PARTIES ACCOMMODATED.

TENNIS, BILLIARDS, AUTO SERVICE, GARAGE, ETC.

W. H. JENNINGS

WELLESLEY FARMS, MASSACHUSETTS

TELEPHONE
WELLESLEY, 21730

Figure 25-5. This advertisement for Willard Jennings's Glen House Hotel probably dates to the 1910s.

Glen House Hotel

Edward's older brother, Willard, also inherited part of the family farm in 1870. A letter from his granddaughter tells how he initially earned his living:

> [He] raised vegetables and fancy raspberries and took them to Boston with his two sons, Walter and Harold. They would load at night and start out in the middle of the night and drive a horse with the produce, arriving at dawn at the famous Boston market. After the fall work was done, Grandfather and his boys would go to Maine to gather greens and rosemary. After school, the children, even my two aunts and Grandfather and Grandmother, made Christmas wreaths and roping to trim the big churches in Boston.[12]

By the 1870s, Weston was becoming a popular place to escape the summer heat of the city. Farmers could earn extra money opening their homes to guests. About 1875, Willard built a house with a stylish mansard roof and began taking in summer boarders.

Willard's establishment prospered. With additions in the 1890s and early 1900s, Glen House grew to a 40-room hotel. Five small guest cottages were added, probably in the 1910s. According to the 1902 Wellesley publication *Our Town,* prominent professional men from "even so far away as Philadelphia" were attracted by the beauty and quiet of the spot.[13] On a clear day, guests could see the dome of the Statehouse from the upper floors, not to mention "typical New England scenery" for miles in every direction. Parents of Wellesley College students stayed at Glen House and "amused themselves on rainy days with billiards and ping pong." They set up a "barge and carriage line" between the college and hotel. Glen House had a tennis court.

Willard's granddaughter describes the hotel operation as follows:

> They had families return many summers with their chauffeurs and personal maids. They loved my Grandmother's cooking and Grandfather always had beautiful flower beds and made unusual table arrangements for the dining rooms. There was plenty of room for the children to play on the farm and the husbands could get into Boston in a very few minutes by train then. One year, the Attorney General of Mass[achusetts] at that time brought his children and a pony and pony cart. We were there at that time and I was allowed to drive the children to Wellesley and Waltham. . . . All four children of my Grandfather worked very hard with their parents to make "Glen House" a success.[14]

In a subsequent letter, she remembers the occasional problem with water supplies:

> When my grandfather was running the summer hotel their water supply came from Ed Jennings. Every once in a while the water supply was cut off for some reason. One can imagine trying to keep guests happy without water. How they ever ran the hotel with no refrigeration, no air conditioner, minimum electricity [sic]. Of course my grandfather and Uncle Ed did cut ice on the pond across the road from the hotel so they did have ice and probably an ice chest.[15]

The success of Glen House was due partly to convenient rail transportation. About 1902–03, the Boston and Albany Railroad printed a brochure called "Summer Homes," which listed vacation spots along the B & A route. The goal was to promote ridership by encouraging regular getaways from the city to country destinations like Glen House and Glen Farm, which are listed under the heading "Wellesley Farms." The pamphlet notes that the station was only 22 minutes from Boston and that "Glen Farm is probably one of the most beautiful country spots in Massachusetts." Among the health benefits also enumerated was the location "free from east winds," meaning that no unhealthy Boston air would ever trouble guests at Glen House:

> It is interesting to note that such a thickly wooded country, so like the hills of New Hampshire, can be found in such close proximity to Boston. Wellesley is considered by many of Boston's ablest physicians to be a very healthful place, it being situated in highlands and free from east winds. Glen House is situated on a high hill and the rooms are naturally cool and airy.[16]

As automobiles gained increasing popularity over the next two decades, a later advertisement noted that "automobile parties" could be accommodated, and that the hotel had auto service and a garage.

Even while he was running the hotel, Willard Jennings continued to grow small fruits on his 24-acre property. The 1902 *Our Town* article reported that he had not abandoned fruit culture and in fact had established "a system of reciprocity with Boston, by which he annually supplied Thompson's Spa with thousands of boxes of berries, while Faneuil Hall market furnishes such food material as is not produced at home."[17]

The Glen House operated into the 1920s. In February 1931 a serious fire did $10,000 in damage to the house, which was rented at the time. It was probably after the fire that the large hotel wing was removed, along with the third floor of the original house. The remodeled residence remains along with the five guest cottages, which have been converted to year-round use.[18] Willard Jennings died in 1933 at age 79.

Development of Glen Road

Edward Jennings continued dairy farming on a small scale through the 1940s. From all accounts, he was not a good businessman. His property was always heavily mortgaged and he was reportedly none too prompt in paying bills. Nelson McNutt, son of the neighboring farm family, worked for him and recalled at least one time when Ed couldn't pay his taxes. When his son Levi lent him the money, Ed used it to buy cows instead. His machinery was always broken down. He would borrow machinery from Fred Young, the Dean estate caretaker, and bring it back broken.

As Jennings needed money, he began developing his frontage along Glen Road. He and his son Warren built many of the houses in the 200 block of Glen Road with the help of local carpenters. Before long, the street was dubbed "Jenningsville" by the neighbors. In the 1920s, the pace of building accelerated and plans became more standardized. Eleven of the Jennings houses follow the same basic plan, with one of three different roof treatments.

Figure 25-6. Between 1913 and 1928, Edward Jennings and his sons built 18 new houses along Glen Road. The first was probably No. 260 (at left), built for Edward's second son, Clifton Victor Jennings.

One of the earliest houses was built for Edward's second son, stockbroker Clifton Victor Jennings, in 1913. A few years later Clifton built an almost identical house next door and moved there with his family. Houses were built for Edward's oldest son, Levi Brown Jennings, who was an interior decorator, and his third son, Charles Dudley Jennings, whose house was later destroyed by fire. Charles was in charge of milk deliveries and collections when the dairy was in operation, and he and his wife boarded four drivers. Later Charles gave up working at Glen Farm and bought a grocery store in Wellesley Hills. A fourth son, Brenton, became deaf and mute due to scarlet fever and had to be institutionalized. The youngest son, Warren, worked for his father taking care of the farm and building houses. He lived in what was originally an addition to the 18th-century family homestead. In 1924, the original Colonial house was moved across the street to its present location on the south side of Glen Road and the addition was made into a separate residence.

To service the new houses, Edward Jennings developed the Glen Farm Water Company, which eventually provided water to 32 houses in the neighborhood.[19] The system included a well, two windmills, and a large wooden water tank on the west side of Glen House Way. Early residents recall that when the Jennings property was foreclosed by various banks, the water system was also foreclosed and the water supply cut off to all houses within the system. Arthur Von Hippel, a professor at MIT and Glen Road resident, arranged to tie the neighborhood into the Wellesley water system by laying water pipes from Oak Street to Glen Brook Road in Wellesley.

Edward Jennings got into serious financial trouble during the Depression. In January 1931 another of his barns burned, a loss valued at $7,000. In October 1932 about 80 acres of Jennings land was acquired by the town for nonpayment of taxes.[20] Twenty-five of these acres are now town recreation land, including the baseball field off Gail Road originally known as Jennings Field and now called Burt Field.

Jennings's problems didn't end there. His remaining herd of cows became infected with tuberculosis in the late 1930s and had to be destroyed. He still had a chicken and egg business, which he had built up beginning in the 1920s, reaching a peak of 1,000 chickens in 1938. In the 1938 hurricane, the roof of one of the coops blew off. Arthur Von Hippel recalls seeing Jennings "sitting on the ruins of his chicken house, illuminated by lightning and frantically waving his arms to keep the chickens from following the roof which had flown down the street."[21] By this time, Jennings was more than 80 years old. He died two years later, in 1940.

Figure 25-7. George Nelson Wyman (left) and Percy Styles, a teamster who worked for the Jennings family, are pictured about 1919 hauling logs to the Hubbard sawmill. The lumber was used to build a new barn on the Wyman property.

The Wyman-McNutt Family

The 1794 Kingsbury map shows a house at the northwest corner of Oak Street and Glen Road belonging to the Pratt family. According to tradition, this house was moved across the street and became the ell of the Federal-style farmhouse constructed at the northeast corner in 1812. The Pratts lived here until 1830, when the real estate of the late Paul Pratt was sold at public auction. The farm was advertised as "between 60 and 70 acres of excellent land, well divided into mowing, pasturing, tillage, and wood land, with an excellent orchard, producing annually from 50 to 100 barrels of the best of winter apples; a good House, Barn, &c." [22]

The property passed to several owners before being purchased in 1850 by Daniel Wyman (1798–1879), who moved here from Waltham with his wife, Mary, and their six children.[23] At the time, the property included three of the four corners at Oak Street and Cliff and Glen Roads.

Daniel's son George Otis Wyman (b. 1831) lived here from 1850 until his death in 1905. He and his wife, Hannah Black, had two children: George Nelson (1863–1934) and Mary Elizabeth (1872–1932), who inherited the farm and shared the farmhouse. George Nelson never married. His nephew, Nelson McNutt, remembered him as a quiet man who kept to himself, sometimes not even answering when greeted by neighbors. In appearance, he was "like all the farmers," always dressed in work clothes with muddy knees from kneeling down and weeding the fields. He was a smart man, according to his nephew, a man who "could have amounted to something if he had the opportunity."[24]

His sister, Mary Elizabeth Wyman, met her husband, Charles McNutt, while he was working as a teamster for Ed Jennings. McNutt, who was from Nova Scotia, later worked as a caretaker for nearby estate owner Garret Schenck. The couple had five children: Ella, Charles Nelson, Edith, Florence, and Evelyn. McNutt left the family shortly after his youngest daughter was born in 1915 and the couple were later divorced.

Figure 25-8. George Otis Wyman (1831–1905), shown here, was the son of Daniel Wyman, who bought the farm on Glen Road in 1850. Their property included three of the four corners at Glen Road and Oak Street. George Otis Wyman had two children, George Nelson and Mary Elizabeth.

The Wyman-McNutt family is unusual among Weston farm families only because information and photo albums remain to document their lives. Many details have been provided by Nelson McNutt, who was born in 1899 and has lived at the same corner in Weston for most of his life. His memory, amazing even at age 100, spans the 20th century. When McNutt was growing up, sons and grandsons of farmers were still eking out a living from small family farms. Because the land had been handed down from earlier generations, farmers could manage by

Figure 25-9. Charles McNutt (center) met his future bride, Mary Elizabeth Wyman, when he was working as a teamster at the neighboring Glen Farm. The couple had five children. He is pictured here with his father-in-law and brother-in-law.

Figure 25-10. Nelson McNutt, Sophie Hamilton, Sophie's daughter May, and Florence, Evelyn, and Mary Elizabeth Wyman McNutt pose in front of 317 Glen Road in the early 1920s. Notice the mailbox at right. Sophie was the cook for Edward Jennings, who ran a boardinghouse for three or four of his milkmen and permanent help.

Figure 25-12. George Nelson Wyman raised strawberries as a cash crop and paid neighborhood children two cents a box to pick them. The children used the money to buy penny candy, or gum for five cents a pack. At right is Edith McNutt (b. 1901) with Hollis and Jack Wagstaff, sons of the Peirce estate caretaker.

Figure 25-11. George Nelson Wyman (1863–1934) was the third generation of his family to operate the farm at the Four Corners. He never married, and lived at 317 Glen Road with his sister and her family.

growing their own food and earning just enough to pay property taxes and buy a few necessities. If more cash was needed, part of the land would be sold to neighboring estate owners, who often had their eye on particular parcels.

By 1908, the Wyman farm was down to 55 acres. George Nelson Wyman had a few apple trees and raised beans, potatoes, and other crops for family use. Before World War I he kept a few cows and sold the milk to Ed Jennings. Later, Nelson would walk up the street to the Charles Jones estate to buy milk for 20 cents a quart. George Wyman's cash crop was strawberries, and much of the land at the Four Corners was given over to strawberry fields. Wyman never hired help except at harvesttime, when he paid neighborhood children to pick berries for two cents a box. He sold the strawberries locally, delivering them to customers who bought from him year after year. The children used the money to buy four candies for a penny or gum for five cents a pack.

After World War I, George Wyman decided not to

Figure 25-13. No. 317 Glen Road, constructed about 1812, has a low hip roof typical of the Federal style. The bracketed hood over the front door was added in the mid-19th century. The Ford Model T wagon was purchased in late 1919. This photograph was taken in January 1921, not long after the house had been painted.

Figure 25-14. Nelson McNutt (right) sits with Christie, an Italian laborer who worked on the Schenck estate. Christie lived on Ash Street in one of about a half-dozen shanties with tarpaper roofs.

Figure 25-15. In the early 20th century, traveling vendors delivered fresh provisions directly to Weston homes. This picture, taken about 1912–14, shows the wagon from Russell's in Wayland delivering meat and vegetables. Another truck delivered fish, and the Grand Union Tea Company brought cocoa, tea, and spices.

keep cows anymore and to replace his earlier cow barn. He cut the wood on his own property and borrowed Ed Jennings's team of horses to haul it to the Hubbard estate, where there was a sawmill near Ridgeway and Glen Roads. He built the barn with the help of relatives. About 1920, Wyman built a similar barn to house a new Model T station wagon purchased by his 21-year-old nephew, Nelson McNutt. Nelson recalled that, with delivery charges and the war tax, the cost of the car came to about $750. He saved the money from his earnings as a day laborer. Inexpensive and dependable cars like the Model T made automobile transportation widely available by the 1920s.[25]

As a young man, Nelson McNutt walked the 20 minutes to Wellesley Farms station and took the train into Boston to study automobile mechanics at the YMCA, now Northeastern University. Sometime before his 20th birthday, he went to work at the Dean estate as a "day man," chopping wood, gardening, picking apples, cutting ice, making butter, cutting hay, or doing whatever job was needed at the time. After the estate was sold to the Byrons, he worked outside Weston, served in World War II, and then was a maintenance man at Norumbega Reservoir until his retirement at age 70.

George Nelson Wyman farmed until the day he died of a heart attack in 1934. His land was divided among his nieces and nephew. Nelson McNutt's house at the northwest corner of Oak Street and Glen Road dates from 1937, when it was rebuilt following a fire. The house at the southeast corner, built for his sister Edith, dates from 1939. At the turn of the 21st century, these two modest houses were still owned by the family. When asked, as he often is, about selling his land, Nelson is reported to have said that he doesn't need the money and is very happy living the way he does. In the early 1990s, a large new shingled house was built on the northeast corner on land that had belonged to Ella McNutt Morse. No corner in Weston better demonstrates the contrast between prosperous suburban Weston in the year 2000 and the simple life of farm families in the first half of the 20th century.

Houses in the Glen Road Area

233, 235, 241, 243, and 247 Glen Road (c. 1910s). Cottages built as part of Willard Jennings's Glen House summer resort hotel.

245 Glen Road (1875, with alterations). Part of the 2½-story mansard house built by Willard Jennings. The original house was enlarged to create the Glen House Hotel. The present appearance of the house dates after a 1931 fire.

246 Glen Road (c. 1916). One of three Jennings houses from the 1910s, this stucco house utilizes design elements from the Colonial Revival and Craftsman styles.

253 Glen Road (c. 1917). Similar to No. 246 in design and use of stucco.

254 Glen Road (c. 1926). Jennings house built in Tudor style, similar to No. 265.

259 Glen Road. Home of Warren Jennings. The house was originally built as an addition to the Jennison/Jennings house (see No. 266). In 1924 it was detached from the Colonial house, which was then moved across the street. The addition was moved back and to the east and remodeled as a separate residence.

260 Glen Road (c. 1913). Probably the first house to be built on the Edward Jennings property along Glen Road, built for Edward's second son, Clifton Victor Jennings. Some years later, Clifton built an almost identical house next door at No. 262 and moved there with his family. As with the other two houses from the 1910s, No. 260 has wide overhanging eaves with show rafters and a steeply pitched hip roof.

262 Glen Road (c. 1922). See No. 260.

265 Glen Road (c. 1928). Tudor-style Jennings-built house similar to No. 254.

266 Glen Road (c. 1732). Center-chimney Colonial built for Nathaniel Jennison, one of Weston's earliest settlers, and later occupied by the Jennings family. Moved from its original location across the street in 1924. It was probably at this time that the enclosed entrance vestibule and sunroom were added. The addition made the 18th-century house look much like its 20th-century neighbors, for which it had clearly served as a model in scale and proportion. (See also No. 259.)

270 Glen Road (c. 1924). Hip-roofed version of the Jennings standard plan. In his later years, Edward Jennings lived here and had large chicken coops out back.

271 Glen Road (c. 1922). No. 271 is the only one of the Jennings-built, gambrel-roofed houses to have a central pavilion.

276 Glen Road (c. 1923). Dutch Colonial version of the Jennings plan.

277 Glen Road (c. 1923). Hip-roofed version of the Jennings plan. Home of Edward Jennings's eldest son, Levi Brown Jennings.

281 Glen Road (c. 1921). Dutch Colonial version of the Jennings plan.

284 Glen Road (c. 1924). Hip-roofed version of the Jennings plan, close in appearance to No. 294.

287 Glen Road. Site of a Jennings house built for Edward's third son, Charles, and destroyed by fire on August 11, 1958.

288 Glen Road (c. 1923). Dutch Colonial version of the Jennings plan.

291 Glen Road (c. 1925). Dutch Colonial version of the Jennings plan.

294 Glen Road (c. 1922). See No. 284.

297 Glen Road (c. 1923). Gable-roofed version of the Jennings plan.

301 Glen Road (c. 1926). Hip-roofed version of the Jennings plan.

311 Glen Road (1923). Built by Frederick Young after he left his job as caretaker of the Dean estate. Not a Jennings-built house.

317 Glen Road (c. 1812, with earlier ell). Built for farmer Paul Pratt. The part that is now the ell was moved from its original location on the northwest corner of Oak Street and Glen Road. The 1812 main block has a low hip roof typical of the Federal style. The Italianate hood molding over the front door was probably added by Daniel Wyman sometime after 1850 to give the old farmhouse a more up-to-date look. The house remained in the Wyman-McNutt family until the late 20th century.

Glen Road. For higher numbers, see chapter 27.

Notes

1. Bates, George P., "The Nathaniel Jennison House" (unpublished typescript, 1985). The Jennison house is now located at 266 Glen Road. The author is grateful to owner George Bates for the use of his invaluable history, which includes much of the information on the Jennings family related in this chapter, as well as many additional details on the early history of the house. George Bates and his wife, Nancy, have lived at No. 266 since 1961.
2. MCRD 1596/528–36 (1882).
3. On the 1885 tax records he owned 67 acres, including the family homestead. By 1903 he was taxed for an additional 65 acres.
4. Edward Jennings to Charlotte Jennings, Mortgage of Personal Property, April 7, 1879. See Bates, op. cit, insert before page 25.
5. "Weston Neighbors," *Our Town,* a monthly magazine devoted to the interests of the Town of Wellesley, vol. VI, no. 11, November 1902, 140.
6. Bates, op. cit., 28.
7. Crouch, H. Bentley (untitled, undated typescript on the history of the Weston Fire Department), 9.
8. "Fire in Weston/Serious Fire on the Jennings Farm," *WDFPT,* December 16, 1903.
9. Crouch, op. cit.
10. *WDFPT,* September 14, 1906.
11. Advertisement dated May 17, 1904, as shown in Bates, op. cit., after page 23.
12. Letter from Muriel Jennings Case (Mrs. Floyd) to George Bates, April 28, 1985, as quoted in Bates, op. cit., 21.
13. "Weston Neighbors," op. cit., 39.
14. Letter cited above from Case to Bates, April 28, 1985, as quoted in Bates, op. cit., 21.
15. Ibid., 21a.
16. "Summer Homes on the Boston and Albany," issued by the Passenger Department, Boston and Albany Railroad. Undated brochure (c. 1903), 36 (Wellesley Historical Society).
17. "Weston Neighbors," op. cit., 140.
18. The cottages were subdivided off in 1950. See "Plan of Land in Weston, Mass.," January 31, 1950, Plan 670.
19. Bates, op. cit., 25–26.
20. MCRD, 5682/499, 501, 503, 505, 507 (1932).
21. Bates, op. cit., 26.
22. "Administrator's Sale of Real Estate," notice dated January 21, 1830 (author's files).
23. Information on the Wyman family from several sources: "Descendants of Daniel Wyman" (typescript, author's files); interviews with Nelson McNutt, 1996, 1997 (author's files). See also deed from Nahum P. Warren to Daniel Wyman, MCRD 1196/226, March 30, 1850. Also probate of will of George O. Wyman (#68865) and Book 3268/35. See also research on 317 Glen Road by George P. Bates (author's files).
24. PWF interview with Nelson McNutt.
25. Several years later, Nelson bought a new Ford and sold his first car to his sister Ella. She drove it a few more years and then stored it in a shed behind the house, where it remained until it was restored in the 1990s.

Figure 26-1. In 1902, Arthur W. Clapp built this Tudor mansion on the rocky hilltop of Mt. Penal near the Wellesley town line. A bachelor, Clapp lived here with his unmarried sister. In 1909, the property was purchased by wool merchant Edward R. Peirce and his wife, Helen. After this house was destroyed by fire in 1925, it was rebuilt using almost the same floor plan. The second mansion is now known as Henderson House.

CHAPTER 26

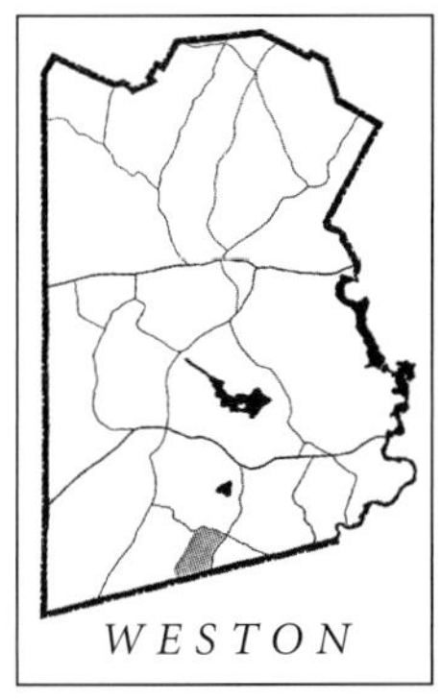

The Edward R. Peirce Estate

The History of the Henderson House

The Edward R. Peirce estate, which straddled the Weston-Wellesley town line, was once one of the largest in the area, encompassing almost 325 acres in the two towns at the time the main house was built in the mid-1920s. The Tudor mansion, now known as Henderson House, was the last of the grand Weston estate houses. The design was the work of the eminent Boston architects Coolidge, Shepley, Bulfinch and Abbott, a firm that, under various partnership names, has been in continuous existence from 1886 to the present day. At the time of construction, the Peirce house was by far the most expensive in Weston in tax valuation. The estate was one of the last in Weston to be subdivided. The extensive landholdings were privately owned and maintained through the late 1950s. Although the surrounding land has since been developed, the house itself has been carefully preserved by Northeastern University and remains a symbol of the estate era in Weston.

Arthur Winship Clapp and Mt. Penal

At the turn of the century, the country estate later owned by Edward R. Peirce was established by another Boston businessman, Arthur Winship Clapp, who first purchased land in Weston in 1901.[1] Clapp was treasurer of E.H. Clapp Rubber Co., advertised in Boston city directories as "rubber manufacturers and grinders." In 1902 he constructed a Tudor-style mansion on the dramatic hillside site known at Mt. Penal (also spelled Mt. Pennel). This house burned to the ground in 1925 but is important to the history of the present house because of strong similarities in style and floor plan.

Clapp lived at Mr. Penal with his unmarried sister, Antoinette, until his death in 1907.[2] Miss Clapp reportedly preferred the livelier social life of Wellesley to the isolation of rural Weston, and in 1909 she sold the 85-acre property to Edward R. Peirce.[3]

Figure 26-2. The Clapp mansion, Weston's finest example of early Tudor architecture, featured the characteristic wood and stucco half-timbering.

Figures 26-3 and 26-4. The interior of the Clapp/Peirce house was photographed sometime between 1909 and January 1, 1925, when it was destroyed by fire.

The Peirce Estate before the Fire of 1925

Edward Russell Peirce (1864–1951) was a prominent Boston wool merchant listed in Boston directories as one of the three principals and later treasurer of Crimmins & Peirce, "one of the best-known names in the wool industry."[4] Pierce started work in the wool business at age 16, making him one of a generation of Weston estate owners with only a high school education. Peirce and his wife, Helen (d. 1942), had no children. Local residents describe Helen as a short, stocky woman with an aristocratic bearing and Edward as a thin man with a yellow mustache. The Peirces were very private people. No photographs of the couple have yet been discovered despite the fact that they lived in Weston for more than 40 years.

Peirce called his estate Hawthorne. He immediately began a series of remodeling and construction projects designed by the firm of Shepley, Rutan and Coolidge and its successors.[5] Senior partner Charles Allerton Coolidge (1858–1936) was one of Boston's eminent architects. He began his career in the office of Henry Hobson Richardson and after the great master's death formed the partnership to continue the work of the office. The firm, known at the turn of the 21st century as Shepley Bulfinch Richardson and Abbott, is now the oldest in the city.

Between 1910 and 1927, Peirce remodeled the Clapp house (1910); built a new garage (1911); remodeled the existing barn into a "recreation building" (1911, 1915, 1919); built a new greenhouse (1917), vegetable storage cellar (1917), and staff cottage (1920s); and, in 1925–27, rebuilt the main house itself.

Although the Clapp house was less than a decade old when Peirce moved there, he evidently found it outdated and inadequate. He spent more than $90,000, a huge sum at the time, to enlarge the service wing, update interior trim and electrical wiring, and introduce modern amenities such as master-bedroom closets. Peirce then turned his attention to a common problem of the day—accommodating the automobile. His new garage had a wooden turntable 15 feet in diameter that could be rotated by hand to direct cars into one of four parking places or into a rear work area to be washed or repaired. The chauffeur and his assistant had rooms upstairs. The existing barn was remodeled into a recreation building that eventually included a bowling alley and rooms for lounging, games, dancing, and billiards,

Figure 26-5. After he bought the property, Peirce hired the nationally known Boston firm of Shepley, Rutan and Coolidge to design a series of outbuildings, including this Tudor-style garage of 1911. Inside, cars were moved around using a rotating wooden turntable. The chauffeur and his assistant lived upstairs. The garage was demolished when the estate was subdivided in the 1960s. (1916 photo)

Figure 26-6. Two members of Peirce's staff, Mr. McKuen and his sister, Mrs. Wagstaff, are pictured in the Peirce garden in 1916.

along with staff living quarters on the second floor. Flowers and grapes were grown in the new greenhouse, which had a central stone "potting house" and two glass wings extending out at right angles. The last outbuilding was a three-bedroom cottage for the butler.

Beginning about 1915, Peirce purchased additional land in Weston and just over the town line in Wellesley. By 1927, he and his wife owned 190 acres in Weston and 133 acres in Wellesley, for a total of 323.[6] The Peirce estate was one of the largest in the area. By comparison, the four largest in Weston in 1915 belonged to the Paine (658 acres), Winsor (471 acres), Hubbard (294 acres), and C.H. Jones families (259 acres).

Peirce used his Weston home in the spring, summer, and fall and spent winters in Pasadena, California, or traveling.[7] A chauffeur drove him to work at his office in the wool district in Boston. Unlike many earlier estate owners in Weston, Peirce was not a gentleman farmer. Except for a lawn around the main house and small flower and vegetable gardens, the land was kept as woods. The entrance off Cliff Road passed by a pond populated by geese, swans, and other "exotic" birds introduced by Peirce. For staff, he had a butler, chauffeur, laundress, housemaid, cook, waitress, caretaker, and seven or eight laborers hired as day men at $2 a day.

Figure 26-7. After fire destroyed the original mansion, Peirce hired Coolidge, Shepley, Bulfinch and Abbott to design a replacement. The firm logged an unusually high total of 248 drawings, including this interior elevation of the new stair hall.

Rebuilding Hawthorne

On January 1, 1925, fire broke out in the mansion, which was described in newspapers as "one of the show places of Boston and vicinity." The Peirces were in California for the winter. Fire departments from several towns faced crippling difficulties in battling the blaze. Because there was no nearby hydrant, Weston firemen had to draw water from a pond, and their pump froze in the bitter cold. Wellesley firefighters were called to another fire. The original Clapp mansion was a total loss, estimated at $200,000 to $250,000.[8]

To rebuild, Peirce hired the same firm, now Coolidge, Shepley, Bulfinch and Abbott. Apparently Peirce was a demanding client, for the architects logged an unusually large total of 248 drawings, the first dated June 1, 1925.[9] These included sketches for a possible new exterior style, floor plans, elevations, and careful pencil renderings of interior rooms. The existence of this extensive documentation adds to the architectural significance of the Peirce house. The mansion was completed in 1927 at a cost estimated by the firm at $440,819. In 1928 it had by far the highest valuation of any house in Weston, $125,000. The second highest, $56,000, was for the Horace Sears mansion on Boston Post Road.

The new house was rebuilt using virtually the same floor plan and at least part of the original foundation. The first-floor stonework is less rustic than the original and the second floor is half-timbered rather than shingled. The shape of the porte cochere was changed, as was the rear porch, which was round on the 1902 Clapp house and six-sided on its successor.

Later History of the Estate

The 1938 hurricane caused extensive loss of trees on the Peirce estate and throughout Weston. Local residents recall that in the two decades after the

Figure 26-8. The new house was a more up-to-date version of the Tudor style. The shape of the porte cochere and rear sunporch was changed and the original rustic fieldstones on the lower level were replaced with a more formal cut stone. When the house was completed in 1927, it had the highest valuation of any house in Weston. It was purchased in 1961 for Northeastern University with the financial help of trustee Ernest Henderson and is now officially named the Henderson House Conference Center.

storm, the Peirce estate was more open and manicured and appeared to be at its peak at a time when others in Weston were past their prime or already subdivided. Edward Peirce died in 1951 at age 87. Remarkably, the property remained intact for close to a decade under the ownership of Roger Ward Babson (1875–1967), known as the "father of financial forecasting" and founder of Babson College.[10] He was 76 when he moved to Weston with his wife, Grace Knight Babson. She died in 1956.

In 1960, the Babsons' only child, Edith Babson Mustard, sold the land to a group of Wellesley businessmen. They subdivided more than 300 acres into the Peirce Estates, a development characterized by large wooded lots on winding streets.[11] New roadways laid out within the former estate include Westcliff, Falmouth, Royalston, Salem, Scotch Pine, Sturbridge, and Yarmouth Roads; and Scotch Pine and Falmouth Circles.

A stone garden storage building behind the main greenhouse was incorporated into a new house on Scotch Pine Road. The new owner wanted to save the stone potting house, which had terrazzo floors, slate countertops, and wood paneling, but the 1917 structure had to be demolished because it did not conform to setback requirements.[12] The butler's cottage lay in the path of the proposed Scotch Pine Road, and the developer decided to move it just over the town line to Wellesley. The Town of Wellesley brought legal action to block the relocation because the house was small and was considered inappropriate to the expectations of the new neighborhood.[13] The town need not have worried, as the small structure was enlarged and completely altered, preserving only the Tudor-style first-floor windows.[14]

The main house proved difficult to sell and Mrs. Mustard considered tearing it down. Northeastern University President Asa S. Knowles became interested in the property as a continuing education and conference center. In 1961 Ernest Henderson, president of Sheraton Corporation and a member of the Northeastern Board of Trustees, purchased the Peirce house on behalf of Northeastern. The renamed Henderson House was renovated by the university and opened in 1962. It remains in active use for educational programs, forums, ambassadorial dinners, business meetings, and social and civic events.

Buildings Remaining from the Peirce Estate

60 Cranmore Road (Wellesley). 1920s Peirce butler's cottage. Moved to its present site in the 1960s, enlarged and remodeled.

16 Scotch Pine Road. Includes part of a garden storage building.

55 Westcliff Road (1925–27). Henderson House Conference Center. Built by Edward R. Peirce from designs by Coolidge, Shepley, Bulfinch and Abbott. Now owned by Northeastern University and named in honor of college benefactor and trustee Ernest Henderson.

Notes

1. MCRD, A.R. Clapp to Arthur W. Clapp, 30 acres (2918/138, September 12,1901), C.H. Jones to A.W. Clapp, 40 acres (2916/311, September 13, 1901); C.H. Jones to A.W. Clapp, 15 acres (2947/366, February1902). See also Plan Books 131/38–40, 135/23. Clapp first taxed in 1903 for two dwellings ($17,000 and $3,500), stable ($3,000), and three horses.
2. Clapp died April 6, 1907, at age 48. See also obituary of Antoinette Clapp, *Wellesley Townsman*, September 21, 1934.
3. MCRD, 3483/334, November 1909.
4. "Edward R. Peirce, died August 1st," *The Townsman* (Wellesley), August 9, 1951, 2.
5. Coolidge studied architecture at MIT and supplemented his early training in the office of Henry Hobson Richardson, where he remained until Richardson's death in 1886. He formed a partnership with two other members of Richardson's drafting staff to complete the work of the office and continue the practice. Shepley, Rutan and Coolidge established its own fine reputation, with commissions for the campus plan and first buildings at Stanford University; the Art Institute and public library in Chicago; and the Ames Building, Chamber of Commerce, South Station, and Harvard Medical School in Boston. In 1925 Coolidge organized a new firm, taking into partnership Henry R. Shepley, son of his former associate, along with Francis V. Bulfinch and Lewis B. Abbott. During this last phase of his career, he was identified with the design of major hospitals including the Peter Bent Brigham. After Coolidge's death, the firm reorganized as Shepley, Bulfinch, Richardson and Abbott. The archives of Shepley Bulfinch Richardson and Abbott has a list of Peirce jobs, dates, and costs, and a complete set of floor plans and elevations for most jobs. See Withey, Henry and Elsie, *Biographical Dictionary of American Architects (Deceased)*, 136.
6. By 1927, assessor's records list 92 acres in Weston owned by Edward Peirce and 98 owned by his wife, Helen, a total of 190 acres in Weston. In Wellesley, Edward owned 45 acres and his wife 88 acres, adding up to 133 acres in Wellesley and a total of 323 acres in both towns. MCRD, 2918/138, 2916/311, 2947/366, 3483/334, 3963/455, 3972/577, 4015/272, 4028/185, 4031/447. Norfolk County Registry of Deeds, Dedham. Important land transactions in Wellesley: 1309/144, 1321/237, 1339/565, 1362/623.
7. Information on the workings of the estate from 1995 interviews with Fred Campbell and Nelson McNutt, longtime Weston residents who remember the Peirce era.
8. See H. Bentley Crouch's unpublished manuscript on the Weston Fire Department and also the following article from a scrapbook belonging to Harold Coburn: "Peirce Mansion Is Burned/Show Place in Weston Is Destroyed with Estimated Loss of $200,000."

"Despite the combined efforts of the fire departments of Weston, Wellesley, Waltham and Newton, fire yesterday afternoon destroyed 'Hawthorne,' the home in Weston of Edward R. Peirce, 'one of the show places in Boston and vicinity.' The total loss is estimated at $200,000.

"The mansion, which was erected in 1902, was remodeled in 1910 at a cost of $90,000. The furniture alone was valued at $50,000. With the exception of a few chairs, nothing was saved.

"Mr. and Mrs. Peirce are spending the winter in California, and when the fire started, shortly before four o'clock, there was no one at the place with the exception of the caretaker, Archie Wagstaff. The latter first noticed smoke coming from a cellar window, and he immediately notified the Weston firemen. By the time the apparatus had made a four-mile run to the estate, the house was in flames. There were no hydrants within a mile of the house and it was necessary to pump water from a private pond in the neighborhood. The fire is believed to have started from an over-heated furnace."

9. Archives, Shepley Bulfinch Richardson and Abbott, Boston.
10. His firm, *Babson's Reports Inc.,* was the first in the country to specialize in investment counseling and stock market forecasting. In World War I, Babson was director of information and education under the U.S. Secretary of Labor. In the 1940s he ran for President as the Prohibition party candidate. See Earl L. Smith, *Yankee Genius, A Biography of Roger W. Babson* (New York, 1954), and the Babson entry in *Encyclopedia Americana.* See also "Mr. and Mrs. Roger Babson Buy Peirce Estate on Cliff Road," *Wellesley Townsman,* November 22, 1951, and "Grace Knight Babson, Wife of Roger W. Babson, Passed Away at Home on Monday, April 30," *Wellesley Townsman,* May 3, 1956.
11. "Peirce Estate Purchased by Local Group for Residential Development," *The Townsman* (Wellesley), January 21, 1960.
12. PWF telephone interview with Joseph S. Banks, owner, 16 Scotch Pine Road, 1995.
13. PWF telephone interview with John Marden of Concord, one of the developers of the Peirce Estates, 1995.
14. 60 Cranmore Road.

Figure 27-1. Charles Jones began developing his estate, Fillmore Farm, in 1901. This photograph shows the rear of the house and stable, both of which remain at 458 Glen Road. Jones had originally intended to build a simple farmhouse, which ballooned to 80 feet long. The stable yard was framed on one side by a combined boiler house, potting shed, and greenhouse. The vegetable garden in the foreground was surrounded by a fieldstone wall.

CHAPTER 27

The Charles H. Jones Estate, Fillmore Farm

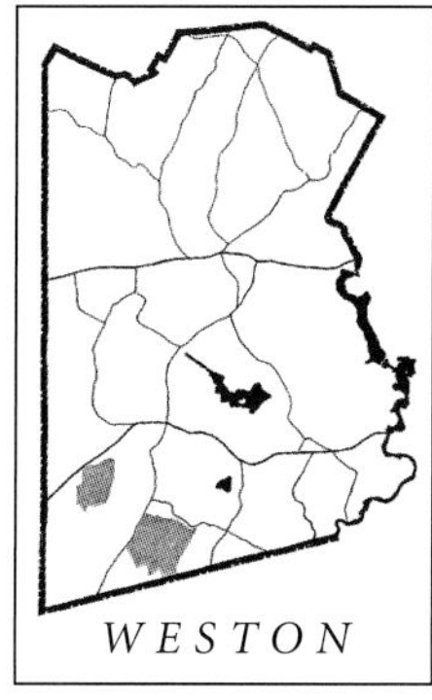

Charles Jones was an American success story. He began work in the shoe industry in his mid-teens and started his own manufacturing business at age 26. His company, Commonwealth Shoe and Leather, developed the Bostonian shoe, a brand name still associated with quality and comfort. Like others who rose to leadership positions in American companies in the late 19th century, he understood the need for more efficient production and the trend toward a more consumer-oriented society.

Jones was the most serious of Weston's gentlemen farmers. He was certainly the only Weston estate owner ever pictured on the cover of a Guernsey cattle breeders' publication. His 270-acre estate, the fourth largest in Weston, was equipped with farm buildings of every description, including a manure pit so substantial that it was valued at $1,000.[1] At least 19 buildings remain from the Charles Jones estate, among them the main house on Glen Road, staff cottages, the beagle kennel, the pump house, and one of the last remaining icehouses in Weston. Sturdy double-laid fieldstone walls and wooden gates remain along Glen Road, Wellesley Street, Shady Hill Road, Ledgewood Road, Woodchester Drive, and elsewhere within the former estate grounds.

Jones has been described as a tall, handsome man, forceful and opinionated, a great sportsman who enjoyed life. The esteem of his colleagues is clear in this tribute from the New England Shoe and Leather Industry at the time of his death:

> *There is little doubt that his advice and example have greatly helped to improve manufacturing methods in this section. Socially, he was a most delightful gentleman, interested in art, literature, education, farming, yachting and travel and imbued with a spirit of philanthropy. . . . We in the shoe industry will miss him greatly, and we feel that there may never again be another Charles H. Jones in the realm of American footwear.[2]*

Figure 27-2. Charles Henry Jones (1855–1933) founded Commonwealth Shoe and Leather Company, makers of Bostonian shoes. Jones was an avid yachtsman and serious gentleman farmer who also taught adult Sunday school classes at First Baptist Church.

Education and Business Career

Charles Henry Jones (1855–1933) was born in Ashfield in northwestern Massachusetts and educated in Boston public schools. At age 14 he entered Dartmouth College, class of 1873, but dropped out after his freshman year. As to why he left school, his grandchildren report that he "had a lot of hustle" and may have preferred bear hunting to studying.[3] Jones retained his ties to Dartmouth and was awarded an honorary master of arts degree in 1908.

Immediately after leaving college, Jones went to work in the shoe industry at a salary of $2 a week.[4] At that time, shoe uppers and bottoms were made in factories, but final assembly was still essentially a home craft. By 1875, the industry began using "bottoming machines" to perform this step in the factory. While his superiors clung to traditional production patterns, Jones saw the need to enlarge the business to accommodate change.

In his late '20s, about the time he was to begin his own business, Jones married the former Bessie

Figure 27-3. Four generations of the Jones family gather behind the Weston house on Thanksgiving in 1925. Emily Roberts, mother of Bessie Roberts Jones, is in the foreground, with Bessie, Paul, Charles H., and Ruth Jones, Paul's daughter. On the piazza is Harriet M. Jones and her great-aunt Sarah P. Cushing.

Roberts, a Boston girl described as "very much Beacon Hill." A graduate of Wheaton Seminary, she was known for her religious fervor, nurtured by a "conversion experience." The couple had four children: Paul (b. 1884), Elizabeth (b. 1900), Charles Jr. (b. 1903), and Harriet (b. 1904). In later years, Bessie became crippled with severe arthritis and was confined to a wheelchair.

In 1881, backed with $100,000 from prominent leather man Henry B. Endicott, Jones established Charles H. Jones & Co. Three years later, the company expanded and incorporated as the Commonwealth Shoe and Leather Company.[5] By 1901 it had factories in Whitman, Massachusetts, and in Gardiner and Skowhegan, Maine, as well as a Boston office at 66 Lincoln Street, in the leather district. This area of Boston had been redeveloped beginning in the 1880s for leather-related trades, a major contributor to New England's economic base.

Commonwealth became known for high-quality men's shoes that fit properly rather than simply mimicking the latest fashions. One of its best-selling lines was Bostonians, which in 1906 retailed for about $4 a pair. Its shoes were also sold under other trade names including Londons, Footsavers, and Mansfields, the latter a less-expensive line introduced during the Depression. Jones's two sons, Paul and Charles Jr., succeeded him in leadership positions. The family owned the company into the 1960s and managed it until about 1979, when it was sold to the Hanover Shoe Company.[6] The Bostonian shoe is still made, a tribute to its motto: "Fit Right—Feel Right."

Jones took an active leadership role in trade affairs, serving as director of the New England Shoe and Leather Association from 1906 to 1914 and first vice president from that time until his death.[7] He was a director of the National Boot and Shoe Manufacturers' Association. As chairman of the New England association's tariff committee, he was considered "perhaps the country's best informed expert on hides and legislation concerning hides."[8] At any hearing he could instantly cite statistics in support of untaxed raw materials for the leather industry. He was credited with winning the victory for free hides in 1909. He played an important role

Figure 27-4. Jones built his company by introducing quality products and more efficient production.

in framing major tariff acts, including the Payne-Aldrich Act of 1909, the Underwood-Simmons Act of 1913, and the Fordney-McCumber Act of 1922.

Charles Jones and Chapoquoit Island

In the early 1890s, Jones was instrumental in the development of Chapoquoit Island off Cape Cod.[9] He first came to the Cape to hunt and fish and quickly recognized the qualities that would make Chapoquoit one of the primary yachting centers on Buzzards Bay. He purchased one third of the island and joined with the only other owner in making the 36-acre island into a summer resort. Landscape architect Ernest W. Bowditch laid out the roads, and in 1891 Jones built Beachstone, one of the first two houses. The architect, J. Williams Beal, was later to design Jones's house in Weston using the same Shingle style.[10] An 1897 Falmouth history called the island's development "an illustration of the benefits of capital and cultivated taste."

Charles Jones was a devoted yachtsman who owned fast sailing boats of different classes. He built his first large boat, the *Chapoquoit,* in 1890, followed a year later by the 30-foot sloop *Ashumet,* which became champion of the Bay.[11]

Olmsted Brothers and the Development of the Estate in Weston (1901–1902)

In February 1901, Jones began purchasing land in Weston.[12] He named his property Fillmore Farm because much of the land had once belonged to the Fillmore family. In July 1901 he wrote to Olmsted Brothers asking for advice on improving his property. Two weeks later, John Charles Olmsted visited Weston, beginning nearly 30 years of association between Jones and the nationally recognized Brookline landscape firm.[13]

John Charles (1852–1920) was the son of Frederick Law Olmsted's brother, John Hull Olmsted, who died when the boy was a child. His mother later married Frederick, who adopted his nephew. At the time the Jones estate was being developed, the senior Olmsted was failing, mentally and physically, and John Charles was head of the firm. In their work on the Jones estate, the firm continued the landscape tradition of the senior Olmsted. They used native plant materials to design a pastoral landscape that appeared natural rather than man-made except for the flower garden.

Internal documents from the Olmsted firm are quoted here in some detail to provide insight into the thought process involved in the development of Fillmore Farm. On his first visit, John Charles Olmsted determined that Jones had two main goals, to create a farm operation for his own use and to develop house sites that could be sold at a profit.[14] He described the Jones property as former agricultural land "now mostly overgrown with birch and young forest growth" and surrounded by less-than-prosperous farmers:

> He [Jones] is now building pretty near the street . . . adjoining the chicken yard of his neighbor, who seems to be a small farmer. There is also another small farmhouse across the street. . . . There appears, judging from foundations, to have been a little poor old farmhouse next to where his front drive forks. . . . This part of the land was bought of some woman, the survivor of a farmer family and the place grew wild for years.[15]

When Jones first moved to Weston, he had a 17-year-old son, Paul, and seven-month-old daughter, Elizabeth. Olmsted's report indicates that Jones had some ambivalence about how the property in Weston would fit with his lifestyle:

> His present summer house is at West Falmouth, which he mostly built up himself. His winter

Figure 27-5. Jones had a summer home on Chapoquoit Island on Cape Cod, where he built and raced the 30-foot sloop Ashumet.

Figure 27-6. These stone posts still mark the Glen Road entrance to the Jones estate. In the 1950s, the owners decreased the size of the house by removing a large section of the second floor and taking off the rear porches.

home is, I understood, in Brookline. He seems to be building in Weston as an experiment. He thinks he may live there in winter but fears it may be too lonesome for his family.[16]

By the time Olmsted Brothers was consulted, construction of the house and combined carriage house/stable was already under way. John Charles was unhappy with the general plan. He reported that Jones had originally chosen another house site on a hill in the southeast corner of the property but had changed his mind, "probably because it was too lonesome for his wife." Architect J. Williams Beal chose the Glen Road site. Jones and Beal started with the concept of building a farmhouse and adjacent barn in the New England tradition. Jones intended to keep three cows for his own use and a few workhorses. Olmsted noted, "The house, however, has grown and is now rather large for a farmhouse and has several bathrooms and a carriage porch." Olmsted felt that the more stately residence did not belong next to a farm barn. Nor was the house properly oriented on the site:

> The new house is pleasantly located for a rather small, cheap place but seemed to me wrong end to, that is, the kitchen is at the south end and the reception room and sitting room are at the north end. It is also unpleasant to have the barn so near the house, as it is to have a cow and manure yard. . . . This may have been justifiable when he planned to build a real farmhouse, but he has allowed himself to drift away from that idea.[17]

On his first visit, John Charles Olmsted modified the driveway layout and suggested a boulder wall and posts to mark the entrance.

Although Olmsted was critical of his work, John Williams Beal (1855–1919) was well trained and well regarded in the Boston area. Beal studied architecture at MIT and worked in New York City as a draftsman for two of America's preeminent architectural firms, Richard Morris Hunt and later McKim, Mead & White. After travel and study in Europe, he returned to Boston in 1888 as head of his own firm.[18]

The Glen Road house is a late example of the Shingle style popular in coastal New England towns between about 1880 and 1900. Although still asymmetrical, the design is less sculptural than the earlier Jones house on Chapoquoit Island. The Weston house was accented with Colonial Revival details such as roof balustrades, some of which were later removed. The original dark brown shingles were typical of the period. Nineteen-thirties pictures show green shutters and pink-and-white-striped awnings along the rear facade. The house was enlarged by the mid-1910s and then made smaller in the 1950s. The first floor had a double living room, wood-paneled dining room, library, garden room, music room, and billiards room.

Choosing a site for the formal garden proved difficult. Jones was not pleased with Olmsted's suggested location behind the laundry yard out of sight from the main house. To put a garden directly behind the house required building up a terrace, using as much as 2,200 cubic yards of fill. Olmsted wrote,

Figure 27-7. Olmsted Brothers helped Jones create a pond in the wetlands behind his house. To the right is the carriage house; at left is a pump house.

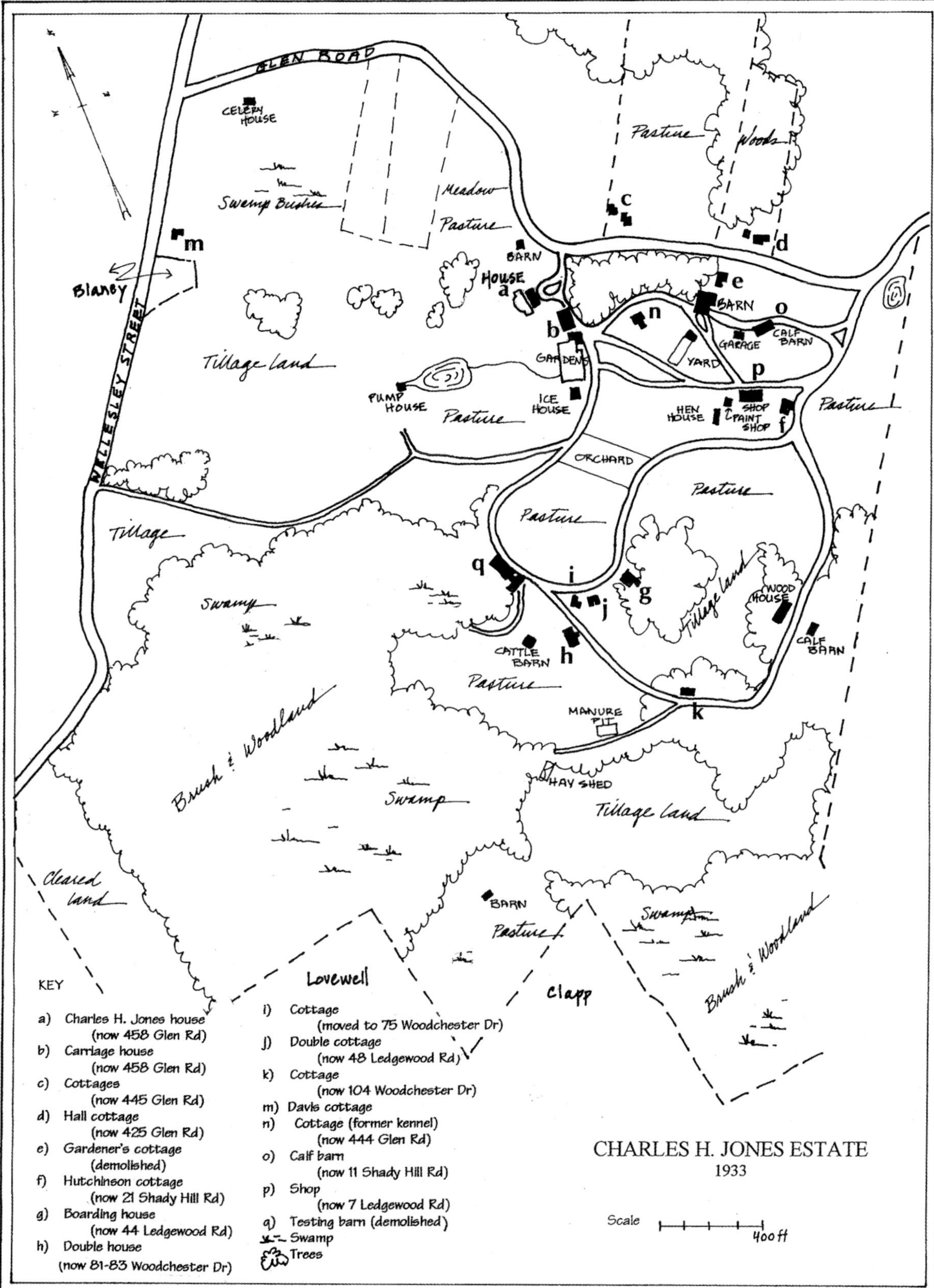

Figure 27-8. The 270-acre Jones estate was the fourth largest in Weston. More than 19 outbuildings still remain, including staff cottages, a boardinghouse for hired men, a calf barn, and a dog kennel. This map has been redrawn from a 1933 map prepared at the time of Charles Jones's death. Buildings and landscape features are generally labeled or keyed using the same words as the original. Just west of the main house is the terrace where the formal garden was located.

"This is more than we proposed in our previous plan, but it seems to us that the amount of filling . . . is of little consequence to you, as it will merely serve as a dumping place for the earth you are going to excavate to form your pond."[19] The resulting semicircular terrace was redesigned in the mid-1920s.

In November 1901, Olmsted Brothers sent Jones an extensive planting plan.[20] The cost of plant materials, including packing and freight, was about $550 for more than 1,000 individual plants. For trees, the firm suggested hawthorns, witch hazel, silver-bell trees, pin oaks, beeches, elms, white and red oaks, and several varieties of birch and dogwoods. Shrubs included honeysuckle, forsythia, elder, highbush blueberry, cranberry, winterberry, swamp azalea, barberry, pepperbush, and dwarf sumac. The plan called for flower beds full of roses, peonies, lilies, phlox, columbines, and mixed perennials. The banks of the terraces behind the house were planted with creeping roses.

Jones and his family had moved into the house by August 1902, when John Charles Olmsted again visited Weston. The civil engineer showed Olmsted a road layout and told him that Jones was thinking of building a new and larger house on a hill. He would retain use of the stable and turn over the Glen Road house to a farmer or rent it to a friend. Jones never built this second mansion, but the comment suggests that he, too, was dissatisfied. As far as Olmsted was concerned, nothing about the Jones estate was right:

> His method of proceeding without any comprehensive . . . plan . . . and asking advice after he had decided or partly executed his ideas . . . makes it impossible to arrive at any creditable result. The house is too far from the street and entrance for a gate lodge, too large and expensive for that or for a farmer, too near the stable to let, and has the kitchen wing, etc. at wrong end. The lane is a poor undignified approach to his future house and other house sites he speaks of, the vegetable garden breaks across what would have been finer as a meadow. . . . The pond has a stiff, unnatural shore. The ice-house doesn't keep ice as it should. The stable has the proportions of a farm barn but is too ornate for that and is too high and prominent for a stable.[21]

Time has proved kinder to Jones and his architect. The house and carriage house still remain. Today, having the carriage house next to the house is convenient and the combination of the two buildings is visually appealing. The setting, including meadow, pond, tool house, icehouse, and walled garden, has remained largely intact.

Operation of Fillmore Farm

Charles Jones may have initially envisioned a modest country farmhouse and three cows, but it was not long before he devised more ambitious plans. He began raising purebred Guernsey cattle, and, according to his granddaughter, "what he decided to do, he did to perfection."[22]

In 1903 Jones built his first dairy barn, a monumental five-story structure with ground-level entrances at four levels. Cows were milked here and the milk kept cool in a soapstone sink using ice from the icehouse. In the early 20th century, the milk was not pasteurized. The barn had special stalls for pregnant dairy cows, which had to be bred each year to have a calf and keep up their milk. Because farm managers didn't want these fancy cows to drop their calves in the meadow, they were brought to the "maternity" stalls to be checked once or twice a night. At the top of the dairy barn was a water tank. Water was pumped to the tank from an artesian well and pump house near the pond and from there was gravity-fed to pipes throughout the estate.

About 1914, Jones built a second large dairy barn called the test barn or testing barn, located on the south side of Woodchester Drive near the corner of

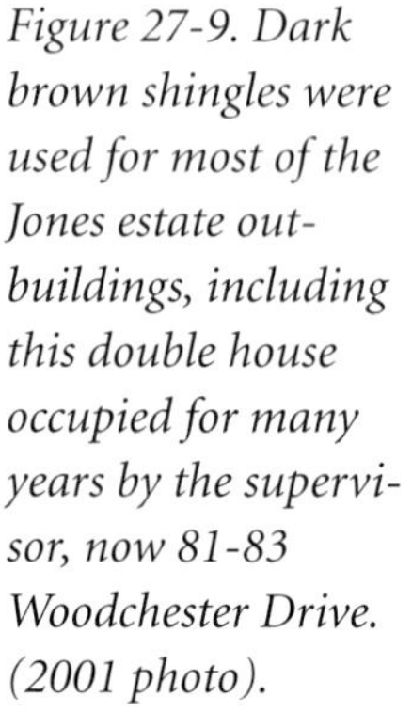

Figure 27-9. Dark brown shingles were used for most of the Jones estate outbuildings, including this double house occupied for many years by the supervisor, now 81-83 Woodchester Drive. (2001 photo).

Ledgewood Road. The purebred Guernseys were stabled here so that their daily milk output could be weighed and recorded. Local residents recall that the testing barn had shiny stainless-steel pipes and pasteurizing and bottling equipment, all kept scrupulously scrubbed and scoured.

Jones was a member and onetime president of a Guernsey cattle breeders association and, according to his granddaughter, was pictured on the cover of its publication about 1919.[23] His bulls were valuable, world-champion animals that sold for as much as $2,000. Jones held occasional cattle auctions under a tent on the hill across from the testing barn. Cows and bulls were led across a wooden platform while those in attendance sat on folding chairs rented for 25 cents.[24]

Jones also kept thoroughbred Kentucky bluegrass horses. His daughters were both accomplished horsewomen. In their teens and 20s, they would go to Lexington, Kentucky, to buy foals with good lineage to train as riding horses. In 1908 Jones purchased the old District Schoolhouse #6 at the corner of Brown and Winter Streets, where he owned 70 acres not contiguous to the Glen Road property. He converted the schoolhouse to a residence for his herdsmen and horse trainers. In 1919 he sold the old schoolhouse and some of the property to the Inter Allied airport, which transformed his horse and cow barns into an airplane hangar.[25]

By 1915, most of the major buildings on the estate had been completed.[26] That year Jones was taxed for six horses, 51 cows, 12 bulls, and 12 swine.[27] Fifteen to 20 men were employed outside, including half a dozen to take care of the cows, a few horse men, and a man to take care of the dogs.

Figure 27-10. Charles D'Intinosanto (1884–1968), an Italian immigrant, worked for the Jones family for decades, building many handsome stone walls and doing whatever was needed to keep the estate running.

Figure 27-11. In the backyard, Jennie D'Intinosanto had an outdoor oven used for baking bread and roasting peppers.

Charles D'Intinosanto

One of the longtime caretakers of the estate was Charles D'Intinosanto (1884–1968), an Italian immigrant who began working for Jones in the spring of 1921. D'Intinosanto struggled to establish his family in the United States in the years when immigration laws were becoming increasingly restrictive. He first came to America about 1909 and worked as long as he could on a temporary visa. After returning to Italy for a brief reunion with his family, he came back to the United States and found work repairing roads in Weston. Again his visa expired and he had to go back to Italy. On his third stay in the United States, D'Intinosanto was finally able to send for his wife and children. They lived with relatives in Connecticut until he was able to secure not only a job with Charles Jones but also a small home for his family on Glen Road.[28]

Charles D'Intinosanto was a "man of all trades" who did whatever was needed.[29] An accomplished stonemason, he kept the stone walls in good repair and built some of the later walls. Jones was a considerate employer. D'Intinosanto's daughter Jean recalled that "one day Mr. Jones came to visit and decided we needed a bigger place with more room for the children to play. He and my father chose a spot for a new house far out in the woods, accessible only by a narrow wagon path."[30] That house, built in 1925 on what is now Woodchester Drive, provided space for the family, which by then included six children. In the backyard was an outdoor brick oven where Jennie D'Intinosanto baked bread and roasted peppers. The children took the crusty homemade Italian bread to school and traded it for the more

Figure 27-12. This 1953 ranch house at 4 Ledgewood Road was the first to be built after the Jones estate was subdivided. The one-story, 2000-square-foot residence is typical in size and style for the decade after World War II.

Figure 27-13. This original gate from the Jones estate has been preserved on Ledgewood Road.

fashionable store-bought soft white bread brought by the Weston children.

Every year, estate workers and their families were invited to a bean supper given by Bessie and Charles Jones for staff and guests of the family. More than 100 people enjoyed the annual catered meal of ham, baked beans, brown bread, and apple pie, served from buffet tables on the front lawn. Afterward, guests joined in singing hymns.[31]

Charles Jones and First Baptist Church

In his first years in Weston, Jones started a Sunday school on his estate. He fitted up a building for the purpose, but later transferred the school to First Baptist Church and hired a barge to carry the members to and from the church and school every Sunday. Jones himself taught these classes, which demonstrated "thorough scholarly study and crystal like clearness."[32] His Baptist affiliation was unusual in a town where most estate owners attended First Parish or one of the area Episcopal churches.

When the Baptists decided to build a new church in 1923, Jones was appointed chairman of the Building Committee. When initial estimates proved too expensive, Jones suggested a new design and offered to pay half the cost.[33] He was also a trustee of the Gordon School of Theology and Missions and director of the Evangelistic Association of Missions. Bessie Jones and her sister-in-law Miss Laura Jones were among the founding members of the Weston chapter of the Women's Christian Temperance Union, which first met at the Baptist church in November 1920.[34]

The Depression and Postwar Period

Charles Jones died on January 4, 1933, at the age of 77. Probate records valued the Glen Road property at about $86,000 and Jones's total estate at more than a million dollars.[35] For a time, a resident manager operated the dairy farm under the direction of the trustees, who included Paul Jones and Charles Jones Jr. When they decided to close the dairy, the trustees sold the cattle at auction and rented the fields for hay. The two dairy barns were rented to dairy operators who had their own cows.[36] In the late 1930s and early 1940s, the testing barn was rented to Wellesley Farms Dairy, which pasteurized and bottled milk produced on the estate or brought in by truck. Milk trucks traveled along Woodchester Drive, which was then a narrow dirt road.

The trustees rented the staff cottages and converted the outbuildings.[37] Mr. Tingley, the best remembered of the resident managers, filled these houses with young married couples, who walked their babies along the quiet country roads and swam in the Jones pond.

Cows grazed in fields all around. Edwin Land, founder of the Polaroid Corporation, rented the converted beagle kennel as a summer retreat and did experiments in the five-story dairy barn.

According to Jones's grandson Paul Jones Jr., the trustees didn't want to sell the property as long as it didn't take too much time or money to maintain it. Rentals covered expenses, but gradually it became harder to get workers and difficult to keep up with new employment regulations. In 1945, the mansion and 13.5 acres were sold to Merton and Audrey Williams, who removed a reported 13 rooms on the second floor to make the house easier to manage. Later it was sold to a nonprofit organization, which installed an Olympic-size pool inside the stone garden wall (later removed).

In the early 1950s, two brothers from Newton, Merrill and E. William Nutting, purchased the rest of the land for development. Plans labeled Briarcliff Estates and dated 1952–53 show lots between one and two acres arranged along the old estate roads.[38] Lot lines were configured to accommodate existing buildings, which were saved except for the testing barn. During this postwar period, demand for housing was so great that no usable structure was wasted. The first of the Nutting houses, a one-story ranch typical of the early 1950s, was built at the intersection of Ledgewood and Shady Hill Roads. Woodchester Drive, Ledgewood, Shady Hill, Hickory, and Blueberry Hill Roads, Pond Brook Circle, and Briar and Driftwood Lanes were all developed on the former Jones estate.

Buildings Associated with the Jones Estate

96 Brown Street. See chapter 29.

425 Glen Road. When Charles Jones was alive, this house was occupied by his maiden sister, Miss Laura Jones. After the big house was sold to the Williams family in 1945, Jones's widow, Bessie, lived here until she died in October 1948 at age 86.

432 Glen Road. Site of the 1903 Jones dairy barn (demolished).

438 Glen Road. During the Jones estate era, the high stone retaining wall on this property was part of a bull-pen enclosure and formed one wall of a ramp up from an enclosed bull pen to the five-story dairy barn. An outbuilding built into the wall housed the bull barn, which held about eight prize bulls. The walls, ramps, gates, and part of the outbuilding were retained when a contemporary house was constructed here in 1967. The house, designed by architect Lawrence Partridge for his own family, was pictured in two publications: *Houses Architects Design for Themselves,* edited by Walter F. Wagner Jr. (McGraw-Hill, 1974), and *House and Gardening Remodeling Guide to Home Improvement,* spring-summer, 1970.

444 Glen Road. Built as the dog kennel. Jones and his son Paul bred beagles as a hobby, for hunting. The sound of 15 to 20 barking dogs would reverberate through the woods. Paul Jones would let a rabbit or ferret loose and send the beagles to chase after it. For some years between Jones's death and the estate subdivision, the converted former kennel was rented as a residence by Edwin Land, founder of the Polaroid Corporation.

445 Glen Road. In Jones's day, two houses stood on this property. One, occupied by a man who did general farming, burned down in February 1950. The other, which still remains, was the home of long-time gardener Edward L. Abbott.

455 Glen Road. See chapter 30.

458 Glen Road (1902). Built for Charles H. Jones from designs by J. Williams Beal. The present 2.2-acre property includes the original main house, carriage house/stable, and Olmsted Brothers garden. The carriage house had horse stalls at the lower level and a special room on the main floor for washing vehicles. The upper level was used for the estate office and storage. The building was later used for cars.

466 Glen Road. On this property is the stone ice-house and the walled vegetable garden. Ice was cut from the pond behind the main house. A combined boiler house/potting shed/tool house/greenhouse has been demolished.

492 Glen Road (early 1930s). Built for Charles H. Jones. He may have built it for one of his sons, who later decided not to live there. While under construction, it was sold to Mr. and Mrs. Gordon Grant, who owned it until about 1954. The property was landscaped by Olmsted Brothers.[39]

528 Glen Road. In front of the present ranch house is the Jones estate's "Celery House," a largely underground structure used for vegetable storage.

4 Ledgewood Road. First of the postwar subdivision houses built on the Jones estate.

7 Ledgewood Road. Referred to in tax records as the "blacksmith shop" and also called the carpenter shop, this building was used for repair and maintenance work. In front of the present house are the stone walls that enclosed a second bull-pen. Originally, the entrance to this house was from what is now the rear, from a roadway that connected Shady Hill Road to the main house. For this reason, the rear facade is of greater architectural interest than the front.

44 Ledgewood Road. Built for single men and married men who lived outside Weston, this building was called the boarding house and had a common dining room.

48 Ledgewood Road. Marked "double cottage" on the 1933 map and used as worker housing.

11 Shady Hill Road. The calf barn, for baby calves, was later converted into this residence. On this property are stone posts marking the entrance to an estate road that went past the 1903 barn, the carriage stable, and the Jones mansion and then connected to Glen Road.

21 Shady Hill Road. Referred to in Olmsted correspondence as the "farmer's house." Built about 1903 to house estate staff. Called Hutchinson House on the 1933 map because Mr. Hutchinson was renting it at that time. According to longtime residents, it was not built specifically as the bull keeper's house.

544 Wellesley Street. Arthur Davis, the Jones chauffeur and "old family retainer," got this house when the estate was broken up.

66 and 72 Woodchester Drive. Site of the cattle auctions.

75 Woodchester Drive. This worker's cottage once stood next to 48 Ledgewood Road. It was moved out of the path of the present road, turned around, and repositioned.

81-83 Woodchester Drive. Double house built for supervisory staff. At one time, one side was occupied by Mr. Tingley, overall superintendent of the Jones estate, and one side was rented by Mr. MacIllwraith, caretaker of the Peirce estate.

104 Woodchester Drive. Built about 1925 for longtime caretaker Charles D'Intinosanto. He and his wife, Jennie, lived there until the mid-1960s.

Pump house. This structure still stands at the edge of the pond.

Notes

1. The manure pit was a large rectangular space with stone walls but no roof, entered through two massive swinging doors. Wagons with loads of manure from the estate could dump it from a road at the level of the top of the stone wall. Pigs were kept at one end of the pit.
2. Obituary, *Boston Herald,* January 5, 1933.
3. PWF telephone interviews with Ruth Andrews, Paul Jones Jr., and Penelope Hare, grandchildren of Charles H. Jones.
4. Gardiner Board of Trade, *Gardiner & Bostonians: 55 Years of Progress* (Gardiner, Maine, c. 1951), chapter titled "Commonwealth Comes to Gardiner."
5. An 1884 credit report from R.G. Dun records that Commonwealth Shoe was capitalized at $175,000. The three principals, Jones, Endicott, and Charles Bigelow, held almost all the stock.
6. PWF telephone interview with Paul Jones Jr.
7. *Boston Herald,* op. cit.
8. Obituary, Dartmouth College alumni magazine, April 1933.
9. Information on Chapoquoit Island in West Falmouth comes from the following four sources: 1) Ruth M.J. Andrews, *Chapoquoit Houses, 1890–1990* (W. Falmouth, 1990); 2) Harriet M.J. Sinclair, ed., *75th Anniversary History of Chapoquoit Island, 1890–1965, and the Chapoquoit Yacht Club, 1903–1965* (Kendal Printing Co., Falmouth, MA, 1965); 3) Falmouth Historical Society; 4) "He Founded Chapoquoit," obituary of Charles H. Jones from *Falmouth Enterprise,* January 12, 1933.
10. Jones sold the property to a friend in 1895 but the house returned to family ownership in 1931. Jones built a second house but sold it shortly thereafter and moved to the family boathouse at the foot of the hill. Mrs. Jones is reported to have quipped that "they had gone steadily downhill since settling at Chapoquoit."
11. Sinclair, op. cit.,18. Both Jones and his son Paul raced the *Ashumet* extensively. Jones had a 17-foot boat, the *Kitten,* and a 21-footer, *Robin Hood,* also built in the early 1890s, and a 15-foot boat called *The Next,* designed by Nat Herreshoff and raced successfully by Paul Jones while still in his teens. Charles Jones was an early member of the Chapoquoit Yacht Club, founded in 1903. In later years he purchased a large steam yacht, the *Deborah.* The family was active in island affairs, and Jones's descendants still live on Chapoquoit. Although he spent much of his leisure time on the Cape, Jones also retreated with his hunting buddies to rugged wilderness camps in the Deep South and Nova Scotia.
12. Between 1901 and 1910, he purchased property belonging to H.A. Train and Henry J. Jennison (40 acres), J.O. Lovewell (10-plus acres), S.F. Clark (9-plus acres), J.W. Morse (18-plus acres), J.F. Wight (70 acres), the heirs of John H. Harrington (28 acres), and Edward Jennings (50 acres).
13. Letter of July 31, 1901, records of the Olmsted Association, Library of Congress, Manuscript Division, Reel 8, Record #38.
14. August 12, 1901, records of the Olmsted Association, Library of Congress, op. cit.
15. Ibid.
16. Ibid.
17. Ibid.
18. Beal's office was best known for county buildings such as the Plymouth County Hospital and Jail. They also designed buildings for the Walk-Over Shoe Company in Brockton, All Souls' Unitarian Church in Roxbury, George Brown Hall at the New England Conservatory of Music, and numerous residences throughout New England. See Withey, Henry F. and Elsie R., eds., *Biographical Dictionary of American Architects (Deceased)* (Los Angeles, 1956). Also, obituary, *Boston Herald,* July 8, 1919, and *American Architect,* August 6, 1919, vol. 116, 183, and card file, Boston Public Library Fine Arts Department, 19. On the Charles Jones job, the engineering firm was French & Bryant and the contractor was W.H. Mague (Olmsted files).
19. Ibid. August 29, 1901. Jones was willing to go to great lengths to achieve the right effect. He was dismayed to discover that his driveway was so high that only 10 inches of the stone foundation of the house would be exposed. The architect's drawing had shown two feet of underpinning, according to this field report from the exasperated John Charles: "He [Jones] said he thought that if the architect had intended to show that amount of underpinning it was a question whether he ought not to lower the drive, even if it cost two or three hundred dollars to do so." Olmsted discouraged that idea, which would have required lowering not only the drive but also the adjoining lawn.

20. Ibid.

21. August 12, 1902, records of the Olmsted Association, Library of Congress, op. cit.

22. PWF telephone interview with Ruth Andrews, April 20, 1997.

23. Ibid.

24. PWF interview with Jean D'Intinosanto Jones, June 30, 1997.

25. MHC inventory form, 96 Brown Street, June 15, 1994.

26. List of buildings from 1915 tax records: dwelling $12,000; foreman's dwelling $5,000; barn $6000; stable and garage $4,500; stove-house and blacksmith shop $3,000; heifer barn $1,500; calf barn $1,500; quarantine barn $500; pasture barn $400; hay shed $400; wood house $400; manure pit $1,000; testing barn $7,500; kennel $1,000; greenhouse $1,500; Miss Jones's Cottage $2,000; boardinghouse $4,000; new double dwelling $2,500; two cottages @ $1,250; three dwellings on Glen Road $2,100; dwelling Winter and Brown Street $1,500; dwelling Wellesley Street $600.

27. Town of Weston tax records.

28. Their first house was in front of the main house and was later torn down.

29. PWF interviews with Jean D'Intinosanto Jones (1998) and Yola D'Intinosanto Colby (1999.)

30. PWF interview with Jean D'Intinosanto Jones. Jean married Harry Jones, who is not related to the Charles Jones family.

31. PWF interview with Yola D'Intinosanto Colby, January 1999.

32. This quote is from an undated newspaper clipping in a scrapbook in the First Baptist Church archives. Carl Smith, a member of the church, recalled in his memoirs that Charles Jones and his family came to church in a Rickenbacker sedan driven by Arthur Davis, the chauffeur. The people of the Jones estate came in a Graham Brothers bus, often driven by Edward Abbott.

33. See chapter 16. First Baptist Church archives include minutes and scrapbooks with newspaper clippings and other information about Charles Jones.

34. *WDFPT,* December 3, 1920.

35. Middlesex Registry of Probate, #192621.

36. PWF interview with Paul Jones Jr., April 20, 1997.

37. In the 1940s, many of the houses that later had Ledgewood, Shady Hill, and Woodchester Road addresses bore just one address: 410 Glen Road. To differentiate the houses, the fire department assigned letters to each one (A, B, C, etc.) and distributed cards with the particular letter to the occupants to refer to in case of fire. (Information from H. Bentley Crouch.)

38. MCRD, Plan 2044 of 1952 in Book 7997 (end) and Plan 1688 of 1953.

39. Olmsted Job #9235, Olmsted National Historic Site, Brookline, Massachusetts.

Figure 28-1. This picture of Minnie Palmer Dean is from a photo album compiled by Eleanor Dean Pearse, daughter of Charles and Minnie Dean. Through photographs like this one from 1915, labeled "the ruby gown," she documents the lifestyle of her parents. The album includes pictures of the main house on what is now Byron Road, barns and other outbuildings, the grounds and gardens, family carriages and cars, her father's rustic hunting camp in Maine, the steam yacht in Florida, and even her parents' tombstones in Linwood Cemetery, labeled "Finis."

CHAPTER 28

The Dean and Schenck Estates and Norumbega Reservoir

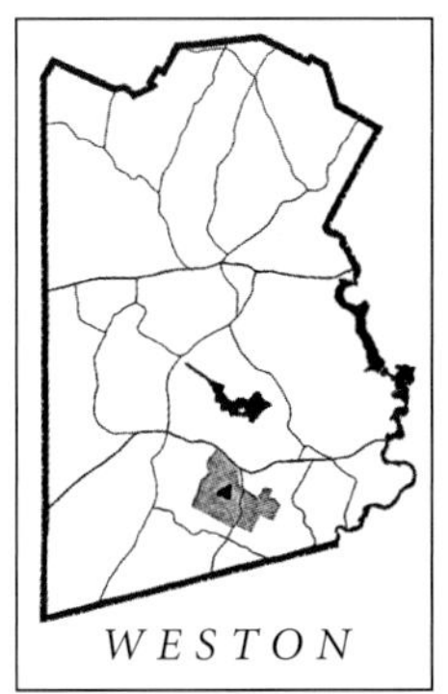

Two paper manufacturers developed adjoining estates along Oak Street at the turn of the century. Charles Dean headed Hollingsworth and Whitney, a major New England firm that merged with Scott Paper in 1954. Garret Schenck was founder and president of Great Northern Paper Company. When he died in 1928, the company had the largest payroll of any manufacturer in the state of Maine.

The two men had more in common than just business interests and shared property lines. Both were quiet, modest men known for their foresight, courage, and leadership. Neither took an active role in Weston social or political life. Although their homes were in Weston, they were better known in the mill towns of Maine, where their logging and manufacturing operations were located and where they worked to improve living conditions for their employees. Both men loved sportfishing in the ocean and in the lakes of Maine. For relaxation, they retreated to rustic camps around Moosehead Lake, in the Maine wilderness they knew and loved.

The Dean and Schenck properties bore the impact of the building of the Norumbega Reservoir in 1939–40. Almost 90 acres were taken for the 124-acre reservoir, including Schenck's Pond.

Both the Dean and Schenck mansions have been demolished. Six-foot-square granite entrance posts and a curved stone wall mark the original entrance to the Schenck property at South Avenue and Bittersweet Lane. What was once the drive into the Dean estate, now Byron Road, passes the former Dean caretaker's house and barn, the old orchard, and a fieldstone garage and frame coach house now converted to residences. Venerable old rhododendrons still line the driveway up to the mansion site.

Charles Dean: Early Life and Business Career

Charles Augustus Dean (1844–1921) was born in Shrewsbury, Massachusetts. His spirit and tenacity were apparent at an early age, when, determined to fight in the Civil War despite his youth and his father's opposition, he ran away at age 16 to join the infantry.[1] His father brought him back home but, seeing how unhappy his son was, relented and allowed Charles to rejoin the Vermont Eighth Regiment for the duration of the war. He is remembered in regimental history for accepting a dare to jump out of the trenches and grab a Confederate canteen,

Figure 28-2. Paper manufacturer Charles Dean (1844–1921) is shown here in a 1920 photo labeled "A greeting from Buck."

which he succeeded in retrieving, complete with a bullet hole from the resulting gunfire.[2]

Dean was one of a generation of self-made men who made fortunes in manufacturing and industry in the post–Civil War years. He began as a salesman for a paper company in Cincinnati in 1864. He came to Boston in 1875 as sales manager for Hollingsworth & Whitney and became president in 1899.[3] The company had offices in Boston, three mills in Winslow, Maine, and two mills in Gardiner, Maine. Gardiner was the same town where another of Dean's neighbors, Charles H. Jones, owned a shoe manufacturing plant.[4] Under Dean's direction, Hollingsworth & Whitney increased its capital by nearly tenfold and its annual production by twenty-fold to become "the largest manilla paper and paper bag manufacturing company in the United States."[5]

Dean was a slightly built man, short in stature, who sported a goatee and had sparkling eyes and a ready smile. He was a dynamic leader and man of vision who was likened to Teddy Roosevelt because of his love of the outdoors and disdain for style. According to one account, "He would never wear a silk hat and preferred to be dressed in rough clothing and was a fine pal on a hunting or fishing trip."[6] To his estate staff he was quiet and polite, never a bossy man. They remember him walking along his piazza quietly puffing on a cigar. His wife, Minnie Palmer Dean, was the bossy one. The minister's daughter and former schoolteacher was described with words like "domineering." The Deans had one daughter, Eleanor, who married Langdon Pearse.

Development of Oak Ridge

In 1896 Charles Dean began buying land in Weston, eventually acquiring 117 acres.[7] To design buildings for his estate, Oak Ridge, Dean chose the Boston architectural firm of Hartwell and Richardson. Henry W. Hartwell and William C. Richardson were popular in the 1880s and '90s for their large suburban houses for newly successful executives. Although their work was "neither forward in style nor innovative in interior planning," architectural historian Susan Maycock Vogel explains that "they could be relied upon to provide buildings which were competently designed, excellently constructed, and comfortably up-to-date in the accepted styles of the day."[8]

Between 1898 and 1900, the main house, coach house, combined caretaker's house and barn, and farm barn were constructed in the Colonial Revival style.[9] The buildings were unified visually by the use of shingles and the gambrel-roof form popular at the turn of the century.

The Dean estate was among those described in the 1902 *Boston Sunday Herald* article "Weston Has Become the Lenox of the East":

Figure 28-3. This aerial view of the Colonial Revival main house on the 117-acre Dean estate shows the formal garden in front and the barn and caretaker's house at the upper right. The estate driveway, now Byron Road, is in the foreground.

Charles A. Dean's estate on Oak [S]treet is another beautiful place. It is approached by a long driveway leading up to a prominent elevation. From the plateau on which the house stands, Norumbega Park is easily visible, and with a glass one may see Bunker Hill monument and read the time by the clock on Memorial Hall [at Harvard University], Cambridge. The house is surrounded by a fine growth of trees, and in midsummer only its roof is visible above the foliage from a viewpoint on the street.[10]

Inside, the hall, parlor, music room, and library were connected by wide openings with double

Figure 28-4. Rocking chairs are set out on the terrace in a photograph from about 1919.

Figure 28-5. The library of the Dean house about 1919.

Figure 28-6. By 1917, when this photo was taken in front of the carriage house, these horse-drawn vehicles were becoming relics of the past.

Figure 28-7. The combined caretaker's house and barn, now 14 Byron Road, was the first estate building to be constructed. This photograph from about 1901 shows caretaker Fred Young and his daughter Marie Lucy at the far left.

pocket doors. Rooms were paneled with mahogany and exotic woods and comfortably furnished with chintz-covered lounging chairs and wicker. The music room had a small pipe organ. In the dining room, Dean displayed his prize fishing catches. On the second floor was a master suite with two bedrooms, bath, and porch sitting room. In all, the house had at least 20 rooms including four bedrooms for the maids and cook. An elevator ran from basement to third floor to transport wood for the fireplaces.[11]

The coach house across the street had mahogany stalls with brass plates engraved with the names of the driving horses. Carriages and sleighs had velvet cushions and brass fittings. The butler had quarters on the first floor and the coachman and "second man" slept in bedrooms on the second floor and took their meals at the caretaker's house. Farm equipment was kept in the basement, accessible through ground-level entrances at the rear. Large coal-burning furnaces in the coach house provided heat to the main house through underground pipes.

The caretaker and his family lived in a small house attached to a carriage barn, which had space for two horses and everyday business carriages. A greenhouse at the east end was used for starting plants. Apples were stored in the cellar. Connecting the house and carriage barn was a milk room with a large ice chest. Before the advent of more modern methods, the milk was set out on shelves in shallow 12-inch metal pans. The cream would rise and was skimmed off the top to use in making butter.

Figure 28-8. The main barn on the Dean estate was located behind the caretaker's house. It housed workhorses, four or five cows, farm equipment, grain, and hay. (1928 photo)

Dean Estate Grounds and Gardens

Stone posts marked the front and rear entrances into the Dean estate. A long gravel driveway wound through farm fields before coming to the main house, which was more formally landscaped. Along the east facade was a terrace overlooking flower gardens. As was common after the turn of the century, these formal gardens complemented the classical style and symmetry of the house and were arranged along an axis extending out from the terrace. Rose gardens and perennial beds were connected by gravel paths and punctuated with bronze statuary and a sundial. There was a gazebo, a lily pond edged with rocks, and a tennis court.

Tucked away in the woods was a Japanese garden, the only one of its kind in Weston. A rustic arched wooden bridge crossed over a lotus pond. The Oriental motif was enhanced by an open pavilion, large wooden Tori gate, and stone lanterns. The Japanese garden exemplified the free borrowing from other cultures in this age of eclecticism in both house and garden design.

The estate produced most of its own food. Cows supplied fresh milk. Butter was made regularly and in winter was shipped by train to the Deans in Florida. Large vegetable gardens and orchards with apple, peach, pear, and plum trees yielded ample produce. Grape arbors and gooseberry and currant bushes were located behind the caretaker's house. A half dozen pigs were kept on the other side of Oak Street on a part of the estate used as a dump.

The Dean estate had its own water system. Water was pumped from the stone pump house next to the lotus pond to a large copper container in the attic of the main house, from which it was gravity-fed throughout the house. The estate also had a small kennel for hunting dogs.

In Dean's day, Oak Ridge was carefully manicured. Byron Road was not paved until the early 1920s. Until then, the gravel road was hand-raked every Saturday so that the first tracks would be from the family carriage traveling to church on Sunday morning.

Figures 28-9 and 28-10. Estate gardens borrowed from many cultural traditions. The exotic Japanese style was the inspiration for Dean's open pavilion, Tori gate, and rustic arched bridge over the lotus pond. (Photos c. 1919)

Workings of the Dean Estate

Frederick Young (1855–1945) was caretaker at Oak Ridge from the time the property was purchased until Dean's death in 1921. The present-day word *caretaker* does not properly convey the responsibility of his position, which involved overseeing the entire development of the property and its daily operation. Young was a boyhood friend of Dean and worked for him in Roxbury before coming to Weston. When asked about the estate, Dean would remark, "This isn't my place, this is Fred's place."[12] Young was known for his green thumb. It was probably he who planted the famed rhododendrons on the drive up to the main house, which have now reached a height of some 20 feet. Young worked right alongside his men in planting and harvesting crops, maintaining the formal gardens, cutting and storing

Figure 28-11. Frederick Young (1855–1945) was Dean's caretaker from the time the property was purchased until Dean's death in 1921. He was responsible for the development of the property and its daily operation. When asked about the estate, Dean would remark, "This isn't my place, this is Fred's place."

Figure 28-12. By the late 1910s, the Deans had three automobiles, including the 1916 Pierce Arrow shown here under the porte cochere.

Figure 28-13. Men from the Dean and Schenck estates worked together to cut ice by hand on the pond between the two properties.

Figure 28-14. When his father-in-law, Frederick Young, retired, William Campbell (above) took over as caretaker and maintained the grounds until the property was developed after World War II. This photograph was taken in the caretaker's house.

Figure 28-15. Dean built one of Weston's first three-car garages in 1917. It was converted to a house after World War II.

hay, hauling wood, and supplying the big house with milk, butter, and produce.

The coachman, William Campbell, came to the United States from Nova Scotia in the early 1910s and a few years later married the caretaker's daughter, Marie Lucy Young. Fred Campbell, the second of their four children, tells stories about his father and Mrs. Dean, two outspoken individuals who were a challenge to each other. In 1916 Charles Dean bought a Pierce-Arrow and sent Campbell to a course at the YMCA in Boston to learn how to drive and maintain it. One of Campbell's duties was to drive Dean to Wellesley Farms Station, where he took the train to work in Boston. Dean also owned a Dodge used for estate business and a Cadillac open on the sides and used principally in summer.

As many as 20 men were employed in the fields and gardens during the busy season. Some of the seasonal "day men" walked all the way from Newton Lower Falls for pay of $2 a day. Workers included first- and second-generation immigrants, mostly Irish, as well as the sons of neighboring farmers. Nelson McNutt worked at the Dean estate for many

Figure 28-16. In winter, snow was packed down on the roads and sleighs and pungs became the preferred means of transportation.

years, year-round, for $27 a week, doing whatever was needed. Longtime Weston residents have expressed the same sentiment as McNutt when he said, "There were the poor people and the rich people. The poor people worked for the rich people, and they didn't pay that well."

Although estate owners and farmers lived side by side, there was a clear dichotomy between the well-educated, well-to-do estate owners and the locals, who did not have the same money or education. Inevitably, there were clashes between the realities of farm life and the idyllic rural atmosphere that estate owners were seeking. Fred Campbell tells the story of how his father was driving Charles Dean home from the train station and they saw the neighboring farmer Edward Jennings walking along the road in his overalls. Dean had his chauffeur stop to pick up Jennings, who had been spreading manure on his fields. When Dean commented on the smell, Jennings replied, "Well, Mr. Dean, people who like the country have to like the country smells."

The Deans in Maine and Florida

The Deans lived in Weston in the spring, summer, and fall and spent winters in Florida, where warm weather helped alleviate Dean's hay fever and asthma symptoms. Florida was largely undeveloped at that time and was a haven for fishing and wildlife. Dean's first 22-foot motor launch was replaced in 1894 by a 44-foot cabin cruiser, the *Myakka*. This boat, although described as a "grand affair," was dwarfed by the 80-foot steam yacht *Aroostook* Dean acquired

Figure 28-17. The Deans went to Florida for the winter. Their yacht Aroostook*, acquired in 1903, was 80 feet long and could house the family on long trips.*

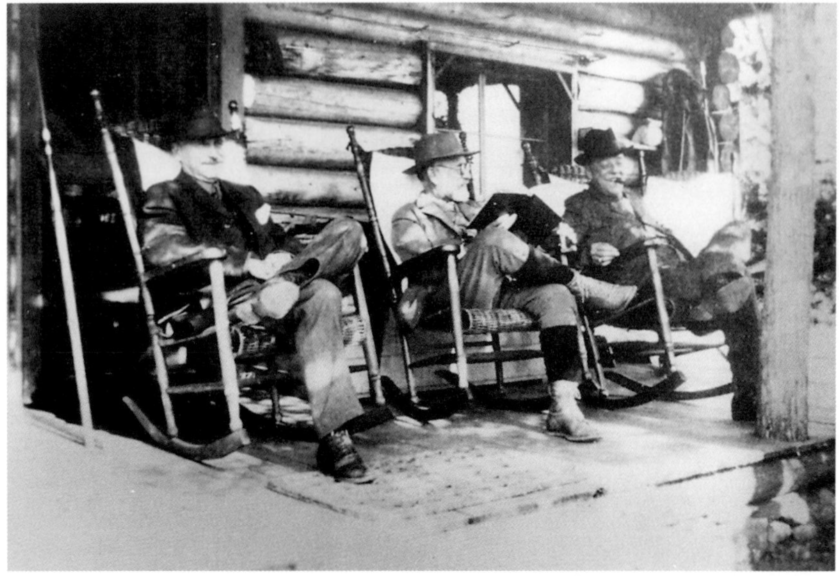

Figure 28-18. Charles Dean owned a hunting camp in Maine called Kokad-jo. (1914 photo)

in 1903. This vessel was large enough for the Dean family and crew to live comfortably for five months of the year.[13]

In summer, Dean escaped to his wilderness Camp Kokad-jo near Moosehead Lake in Greenville, Maine. In the early 20th century, this type of camp was seen as a place of rejuvenation where men could meet the challenge of nature and ward off the physical and mental decay fostered by white-collar urban life. The camp was accessible only by canoe. It has been suggested that Dean went there to get away from everything, including his wife. In the family photo album, Dean's daughter labels the picture of the rustic log cabin "All papas." Here he could relax on the porch rocking chairs with his hunting and fishing companions, who were photographed in casual dress but still wearing the ever-present felt hats. The log interior was crammed with simple wooden furniture, books, and camping gear.

Figure 28-19. Walter and Helen Byron purchased the Dean house, outbuildings, and about 60 acres of land in 1928.

Hollingsworth & Whitney had lumbering operations and offices in Greenville, and Dean was involved in improving community life. The company built a YMCA and Dean personally financed the 22-bed Charles A. Dean Hospital, which opened in 1917 and is still operating.[14] He sent produce two or three times a week by rail from his gardens in Weston to mill families in Greenville, along with crates of books for their children at Christmas.[15]

In 1913, Charles Dean established the Dean Welfare Trust to formalize his personal charities.[16] In 1915 he funded a large park in his hometown of Shrewsbury known as Dean Park. Other substantial charitable gifts, said to total in the millions of dollars, were made after his death. Charles Dean died in March 1921 at age 77 aboard the *Aroostook* while cruising his favorite fishing waters off Florida's Gulf Coast.

Later History of Oak Ridge

Minnie Palmer Dean remained in Weston until her death in 1925. In her will, she directed that the estate house be converted to a home for destitute children, but her executors concluded that the plan was impractical. Money from the sale was transferred to the Dean Foundation for Little Children, established in 1928 to support children's charities.[17]

In 1928 the main house, outbuildings, and about 60 acres were sold to Walter and Helen Byron for $75,000. Byron inherited his money from the sale of the family shoe manufacturing business in Maryland and derived his income from investments. The Byrons renamed the property Sky Meadows and brought up seven children there. The children roller-skated on the third floor of the mansion, raised rabbits in the mahogany horse stalls, and hosted their friends at debutante parties in the coach house hayloft. Although the grounds were no longer so carefully tended, the Byrons continued farm operations.

Walter Byron survived the stock market crash of 1929 but lost ownership of the property in the recession of 1937. He continued to live in the house until after World War II, even after the property had been taken over by the bank. Confidence in the economy was at such a low point during the Depression that banks could hardly give the land away. During the war, the Byrons lived in the servants quarters, which they could keep warm enough from the heat from

Figure 28-20. Andrea Byron and Bruce Campbell are pictured about 1936–37. In the background is the chicken coop that the Byrons added next to the main barn.

the kitchen. Marsha Byron Hallett, one of the children, mused: "The estate saw riches and poverty—living like kings to barely scraping by during the Depression—and finally giving up to development—c'est la vie . . ."[18]

After World War II, the property was developed under the direction of Thomas J. Diab. Buyers bought lots for about $2,000 to $2,500 and put up the one-story ranch houses popular at the time. The farm barn was torn down in the late 1940s and the other three outbuildings were made into residences. The main house was remodeled and the maid's quarters and dining room removed. Although this type of "downsizing" saved other Weston estate houses, the Dean mansion survived only until 1961, when it was replaced by a modern house with large expanses of glass. This house was torn down at the turn of the 21st century to make way for a stone mansion of contemporary design, on a lot of 4.3 acres.

Garret Schenck and Great Northern Paper Company

Garret Schenck (1854–1928) was a direct descendant of the original Dutch settlers in his hometown of Trenton, New Jersey. He began his career in a paper mill owned by his uncle, and, after mastering each step of the manufacturing process, started his own firm of Dutton & Schenck. In 1898 Schenck formed the Great Northern Paper Company and erected a paper mill in virgin wilderness near the foot of Millinocket Lake in Maine. When it opened in 1900, the mill was capable of producing 250 tons of newsprint daily and was referred to in contemporary press accounts as "the largest paper and pulp mill in the world."[19] In 1916 Great Northern built the Ripogenus Dam on the Penobscot River to supply additional power for the enlarged mill. The dam, which created a lake covering 45 square miles, was at one time the seventh largest in the world and the largest ever built by a private corporation for its own use.

Schenck headed Great Northern for 30 years until his death in 1928. At that time, the company had the biggest payroll of any manufacturer in Maine. In a lengthy tribute in the *Portland Press Herald,* the newspaper editor wrote that "Maine has lost one of its most loyal citizens and its greatest industrial leader." He added that Schenck had made Millinocket "an ideal town," and contributed "from his own means to everything that would make it a better place in which to live."[20]

Like his neighbor Charles Dean, Schenck was a keen sportsman who loved Moosehead Lake and his "Camp at Little W."[21] Although he claimed Maine as his state of residence, Schenck purchased 124 acres in Weston in 1898.[22] His three-story stucco Neoclassical mansion, completed by 1900, was designed by the Beaux Arts–trained Boston architect George F. Newton.[23] The house was pictured in the 1902 *Boston Sunday Herald* article "Weston Has Become

Figure 28-21. Garret Schenck (1854–1928) formed the Great Northern Paper Company in 1898 and erected a large paper mill in virgin Maine wilderness.

Figure 28-22. Garret Schenck's three-story stucco house (since demolished) was Neoclassical in style, with the characteristic two-story porch supported by classical columns.

the Lenox of the East."[24] Schenck lived here with his family during the winter months and had a summer cottage on Nantucket.

When Schenck couldn't get to Maine or Nantucket, he would fish in the marsh at the edge of his spring-fed pond in Weston or hunt woodcock, pheasant, and partridge in the rushes. The family rode horses and went iceboating on the pond in two-person, triangular-shaped sailboats with blades like skates that could skim across the pond at tremendous speed.[25]

One document that has survived from the Schenck estate is a complete 1926 insurance appraisal. The inventory lists the contents of every room, from the frigate model of the *Constitution* to the 541 books in the library.[26] An unusual feature was the "Radio Room" on the second floor, equipped with an Orthophonic Victrola, a DeForest portable five-tube radio set, a "Radiola super hetrodine with loop and loud speaker," and other apparatus.

Schenck and his wife, Emma, had four children: Garret Jr., who did not survive them, Caroline, Marjorie, and Hilbert. Garret Schenck died in 1928 and Emma in 1933. The entire contents of the house were sold at public auction in September 1933.[27] The house was demolished in 1938 because of tax and liability issues.

Forty acres were taken by eminent domain in 1938–39 for Norumbega Reservoir.[28] Additional land was taken for the Massachusetts Turnpike, which bisected the estate and precipitated the sale of the remaining property. In 1964, 34 acres on the north side of the Massachusetts Turnpike were subdivided into 16 lots along the newly created streets of Bittersweet Lane and Stillmeadow Road.[29]

Hultman Aqueduct and Norumbega Reservoir

The Hultman Aqueduct and Norumbega Reservoir (1938–40) was the second major engineering project built in Weston as part of the metropolitan Boston water supply system. The first was the Weston Aqueduct and Weston Reservoir (1901–03), described in chapter 19.

The Hultman/Norumbega project had its genesis in the early 1920s, when a Metropolitan District Commission (MDC) study report warned that population and per-capita water consumption were

Figure 28-23. This present-day map shows the water supply system for metropolitan Boston. Because of its elevated topography, Weston was chosen as the site for both the Weston Aqueduct and Reservoir (1901–03) and the Hultman Aqueduct and Norumbega Reservoir (1938–40). Under construction in 2001 is a deep rock tunnel that parallels the Hultman.

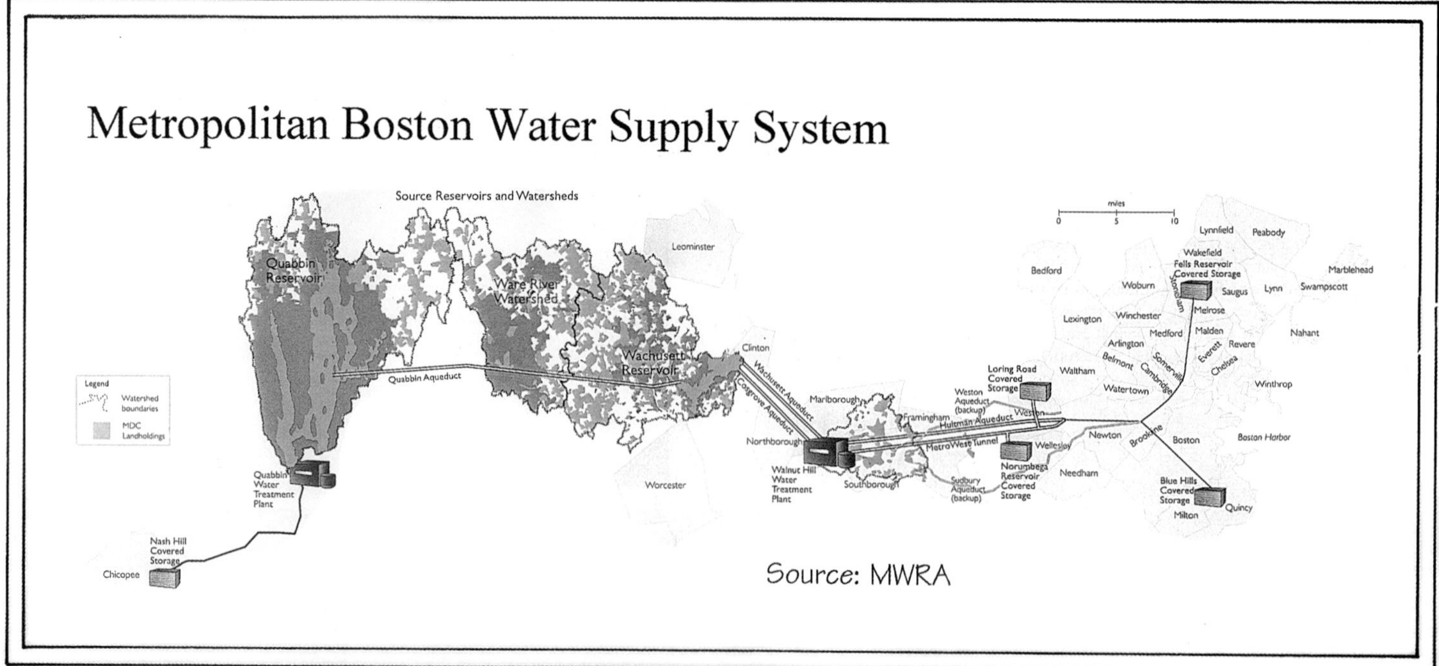

steadily increasing. With demand expected to exceed supply by 1930, the state legislature authorized extending the water supply system to the Ware and Swift Rivers and diverting Ware River water to Wachusett Reservoir.[30] The Metropolitan District Water Supply Commission was set up to design and construct two tunnels and a reservoir, which became known as the Quabbin, located 40 miles west of Weston. Chief engineer was Providence native Frank E. Winsor.

The magnitude and complexity of the Quabbin project was unprecedented. The new reservoir covered 38.6 square miles and four small country towns.[31] Land takings were on a scale previously unheard of in Massachusetts or anywhere in the United States. More than nine million dollars was spent to acquire over 90,000 acres, or more than three times the land area of the city of Boston. Property acquisition began in 1926, construction began 10 years later, and filling the reservoir took from 1939 to 1946. Quabbin has a capacity of 412 billion gallons and is metropolitan Boston's principal source of pure water.

In its annual report of 1935, the MDC suggested building a "pressure aqueduct" to bypass the Sudbury Reservoir, which was becoming difficult to protect from pollution. The proposed aqueduct would extend from Marlborough to the Charles River near the Weston Terminal Chamber.[32] It was later named for Eugene Hultman, chairman of the Metropolitan District Water Supply Commission and commissioner of the MDC at the time of construction.

Although the study committee initially favored a deep-rock tunnel, they found the cost of construction in suburban areas could be reduced by using the "cut-and-cover" method. Most of the conduit was built with reinforced-concrete steel-cylinder pipes, 11.5 feet in diameter, precast in 16-foot sections weighing 45 to 48 tons each. The pipes were made at a large plant erected for this purpose on Speen Street in Natick. The 18-mile Hultman Aqueduct was completed in October 1940.

The 1939 town report noted with concern the amount of land being removed from Weston tax rolls.[33] The pressure aqueduct required taking more than 74 acres from 27 owners.[34] Norumbega Reservoir required taking 124 acres of land from seven owners, the largest parcels being from the Dean Foundation (48 acres) and from Hilbert Schenck (41 acres).[35]

Norumbega Reservoir was built simultaneously with the aqueduct as a "high level distributing reservoir" functioning to maintain a constant flow in the conduit. It has a capacity of about 150 million gallons, which at the time of construction was one day's water supply. Norumbega covers about 50 acres to a maximum depth of some 25 feet. One of its advantages was that it was 75 feet higher in elevation than Weston Reservoir, eliminating the need for low service pumping. Schenck's Pond was kept as an emergency water supply and place for overflow runoff and storm water drainage. The Norumbega gatehouse was designed by the Boston architectural firm of Densmore, LeClear & Robbins in a style similar to other Quabbin project structures. The granite building has a hipped roof and round-arched openings fitted with hollow bronze doors.[36]

The building of the Ware-Wachusett and Swift-Ware tunnels, Quabbin Reservoir, Hultman Aqueduct, and Norumbega Reservoir took 14 years and cost $73 million. At the opening ceremony on October 23, 1940, the project was called the "greatest engineering work ever undertaken in this part of the country." Two thousand people attended a ceremony in Weston, where dignitaries headed by Gov. Leverett Saltonstall spoke at a flag-draped platform in front of the new gatehouse. As part of the celebration, Saltonstall turned the valve that opened the huge new pressure aqueduct, and within 15 minutes parts

Figure 28-24. This 1940 photo shows the spigot end of one of the Hultman Aqueduct pipes. Construction of the Hultman required land takings from 27 Weston residents. (1939 photo)

Figure 28-25. Each concrete section of pipe for the Hultman Aqueduct measured 11.5 feet in diameter and weighed 45-48 tons.

Figure 28-26. His Excellency Gov. Leverett Saltonstall spoke at the dedication of Norumbega Reservoir in October 1940.

of the reservoir floor were underwater. The governor praised the project's scale and importance:

> Fresh water now completes an underground journey to Greater Boston from 40 miles out in the heart of Massachusetts. Through tunnels big enough to let street cars pass, this water comes with such speed and purity that it assures our big cities of supplies adequate to meet every need of health and safety. . . . That is a far cry, indeed, from the old town pump.[37]

Buildings Associated with the Dean and Schenck Estates

34 Bittersweet Lane. Originally the carriage house from the Schenck estate, extensively altered when converted to residential use.

14 Byron Road (1898). Combined caretaker's house and barn designed by Hartwell and Richardson for Charles Dean and occupied until the early 1920s by Frederick Young. Enlarged and remodeled in 2000–01.

50 Byron Road (1917). Dean garage converted to a residence after World War II.

60 Byron Road (c. 1900). Combined coach house and staff quarters for the Dean estate, designed by Hartwell and Richardson and built by George Dawson. Converted to a residence after World War II, at which time the original front-facing gambrel was removed.

67 Byron Road. Site of Dean estate mansion, demolished in 1961. The second house on the site was demolished at the turn of the 21st century to make way for the present house.

Notes

1. Field, Blake H., "Charles A. Dean, Minnie Dean, 'Oak Ridge'" (unpublished manuscript, April 1978), 1.
2. Dean, Gardner Milton, *A Genealogy of the Descendants of James Dean* (Boston, 1889), 22–23.
3. Field, op. cit., 2.
4. Dean's business stationery from 1899 lists the Taconnet, Algonquin, and Mohegan Mills in Winslow, Maine, and the Cabbossee and Aroostook Mills in Gardiner, Maine (MHS Blake Papers, Box 65.933, Charles Dean to Francis Blake, September 8, 1899).
5. Field, op. cit., 2 and Carpenter, Geo. N., *History of the Eighth Regiment, Vermont Volunteer, 1861–1865* (Boston, 1886), 261.
6. Obituary, "Charles Dean Dies in Florida," unknown newspaper and date (author's files).
7. MCRD 2516/508 (Ellen V. Symonds to C.A. Dean, 44 acres, December 1896); 2652/283 (E. Jennings to M.P. Dean, 51 acres. This deed is for the portion of the Fuller farm on the west side of Oak Street). Before moving to Weston, Dean lived in Codman Square in Roxbury.
8. Vogel, Susan Maycock, "Hartwell and Richardson: An Introduction to Their Work," from *Victorian Architecture in Boston*, the May 1973 issue of the *Journal of the Society of Architectural Historians*, 132. Another example of their work in Weston is the Francis Henry Hastings house on North Avenue.
9. Dean is first listed in town tax rolls in 1901, with a residence ($23,000), stable ($10,000), dwelling and barn ($4,500), barn ($5,000), and 117 acres, for a total valuation of $59,500. The builder of the Dean house and stable was George Dawson, according to a letter of September 1899 (MHS, Blake Papers, Box 65.933).
10. "Weston Has Become the Lenox of the East," *Boston Sunday Herald*, May 11, 1902.
11. Letter to PWF from Marcia (Byron) Hallett, December 10, 1997. Describes the interior of the house and estate grounds.
12. Information in this paragraph supplied by Fred Campbell, grandson of Frederick Young.
13. Field, op. cit., 7.
14. "History of the Charles A. Dean Memorial Hospital, 1917–1959" (unpublished typescript, undated), provided by Moosehead Historical Society, Greenville, Maine.
15. Field, op. cit., 6.
16. See Field, op. cit., 5, for more detailed information on the Dean Welfare Trust and other charitable activities.
17. Ibid., part 2, 1, and part 3, 2.
18. Marcia Hallett letter, op. cit.
19. *The Northern*, published by the Social Service Division of the Great Northern Paper Company, vol. VII, no. 11, February 1928. Issue devoted to the life and achievements of Garret Schenck.
20. Ibid., 14.
21. Ibid., 12.
22. MCRD 2669/522 (Sarah A. Loker to Schenck, 124 acres, July 1898). Schenck later bought a three-acre parcel known as the Hill Piece.
23. As a young man, George F. Newton (1857–1947) was the third recipient of the coveted Rotch Traveling Scholarship, which allowed him to travel and study for two years in Europe. He completed his training at the École des Beaux-Arts. Upon returning to Boston, he went to work for Peabody and Stearns, then the city's leading architectural firm, starting as a draftsman and rising to head designer before leaving to practice independently. He retired in 1930 after a long and successful career. Newton was the designer of the First Congregational Church in Wellesley (Withey, *Biographical Dictionary*, 440).
24. "Weston Has Become the Lenox of the East," *Boston Sunday Herald*, May 11, 1902. The article mentions a deer park on the property. Schenck's grandson Garret Schenck said in a 1998 telephone interview with the author that if the information about the deer park was true, he never knew about it.
25. PWF interview with grandson Garret Schenck, 1998.

26. The appraisal included the combined caretaker's cottage, garage, and stable, as well as the pump house, icehouse, tool house, "hot beds," and chicken pens. According to Garret Schenck's grandson, also named Garret Schenck, a separate barn had been taken down by the time the assessor's report was done. The longtime caretaker on the property was George Rutherford, an Englishman famous for his World War I exploits. He took care of the estate from 1928 until his death about 1953–54.
27. The auction brochure lists more than 700 items with descriptions like "Six Initialed Bath Towels (S)." Hilbert purchased the land from his sisters in July 1935 (MCRD 5942/58).
28. MCRD 6290/54 (includes map of the takings), May 9, 1939.
29. MCRD 8967/280 (Hilbert V.N. Schenck to Dorothea Cugini, June 1957, 50 acres). See also 10715/196 for subdivision of Lawrence Cugini (subdivision map in 10715/199, December 9, 1964).
30. Chapter 375 of the Acts of 1926. The project involved constructing the Ware-Wachusett and Swift-Ware tunnels.
31. The project required relocation of 2,048 residents, moving or demolition of 1,040 buildings, and relocation of 7,500 graves in 34 cemeteries. Much of this history of the water supply system is from an excellent, comprehensive report by Martha H. Bowers and Jane Carolan, "The Water Supply System of Metropolitan Boston, 1845–1947," prepared for the Metropolitan District Commission, Boston, Massachusetts, by the Cultural Resource Group, Louis Berger & Associates Inc., Wellesley, Massachusetts, 1985.
32. Beginning at the Wachusett Aqueduct Terminal Chamber in Marlborough, the new aqueduct went to the Weston head chamber at Sudbury Dam in Southborough and from there to a new "high level distribution reservoir" called Norumbega. From there it continued on to the Charles River near the Weston Terminal Chamber. From that point, it could be extended to Chestnut Hill and Boston. Construction of the extension from the Charles River to Chestnut Hill was put on hold when the United States entered World War II. After the war, the Metropolitan District Water Supply Commission ceased to exist as a separate agency, and its functions were transferred back to the MDC, which completed the City Tunnel in 1950. Subsequent tunnel extensions to Malden (1962) and Dorchester (1974) extended the pressure system into the heart of the city.
33. The MDC was required to pay annually to the town in lieu of taxes, with the amount based on the value of property taken; however,"the valuation, once fixed, remains in force without change even though the valuation of adjoining property may be greatly increased in the future." 1939 *TR*, 27.
34. MCRD 6285/582, April 15, 1939, includes deeds and a map at end of book. Names of owners with land takings over 1 acre: Evelyn L. Wellington (10.76), John B. Paine, Trustee (3.43), Margaret W. Ranney (1.71), Hilbert Van N. Schenck (1.38), Dean Foundation for Little Children (4.24), Walter H. Byron (4.31), Abner Post estate (2.48), Marianne Charlot (1.89), J. Dallas and Margaret M. Corbiere (1.76), Samuel C. Bennett estate (2.88), Robert Lane, et al. (4.33), F. Robins and Marguerite Mitchell (5.84), Josephine S. Bidwell (3.72), Town of Weston (1.79), Agnes Blake Fitzgerald (7.78), Elizabeth Hubbard Blake (4.89), Boston University Athletic Association (8.53).
35. MCRD 6290/55, "Commonwealth of Massachusetts High Level Distributing Reservoir" taking map and deeds, May 9, 1939. Authority for the takings under Chapter 460, as amended by Chapter 501 Acts of 1938. Karl R. Kennison, chief engineer. Also taken for the reservoir was land of Olive F. Thornton (18.2 acres), Rose D. Fine (11.1), Charles H. Jones estate (3.3), estate of Franklin Morse (2.1), and Alfred H. Dean (0.5).
36. Bowers and Carolan, op. cit., v–4. Densmore, LeClear & Robbins designed a number of well-known structures in Boston including the Park Square Building, New England Telephone and Telegraph Company, and the 1919 Salada Tea Company Building, whose cast-bronze doors won a silver medal at the Paris Salon of 1927.
37. "Governor Opens Weston Aqueduct," *Waltham News Tribune*, October 23 and 24, 1940. See also Metropolitan Water Supply Commission, "A General Description of the Water Supply of the Boston Metropolitan District," October 23, 1940, published on the occasion of the opening by His Excellency Governor Leverett Saltonstall of the commission's new pressure aqueduct into Norumbega Reservoir, Weston, Massachusetts, October 23, 1940.

Figures 29-1A, 1B, and 1C. Henry Leadbetter settled in Weston in 1747. Generations later, his descendants still owned hundreds of acres in the southwest part of town. These pictures of "Ma's house" and "Pa's barn" were taken in the 1920s at the Leadbetter farm at 412 Highland Street at the corner of South Avenue. "Pa" and "Ma" are Alexander and Ida Leadbetter

CHAPTER 29

The Southwest

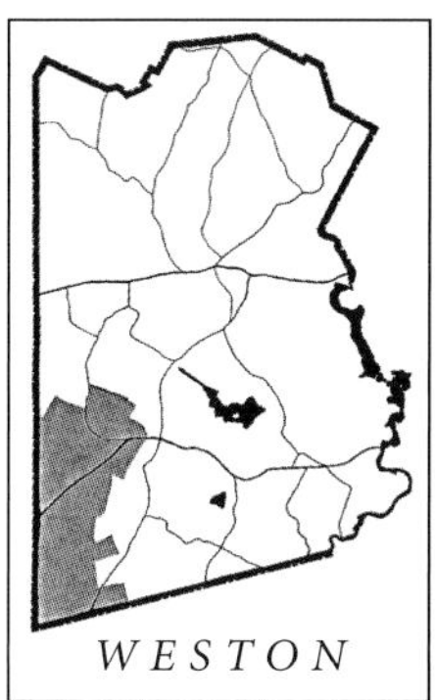

The southwest corner of Weston has always been remote from the population centers of Boston Post Road and North Avenue. During Prohibition, a few area residents used this isolation to advantage by setting up distilleries and engaging in a little rum-running. The southwest can claim as part of its heritage the town's first and only airport, where, for a few years in the early 1920s, local farmers could experience the thrill of flying. This was also the original home of Weston Nurseries, which now grows New England's largest variety of landscape plants at its Hopkinton location.

Figure 29-2. Samuel Train built this house at Winter and Bogle Streets in 1738. He and his son, Samuel Jr., helped establish the First Baptist Church.

Figure 29-3. Charles Train was the fourth generation of his family to live in Weston. He studied theology at Harvard and took charge of the Baptist congregations in Framingham and Weston beginning in 1811.

The Train and Leadbetter Families

The Train family came to Weston as early as 1662. In 1738, Samuel Train (1711–1806) and his father built the central-chimney house that still stands at the corner of Winter and Bogle Streets. Samuel and his son, Samuel Jr. (1745–1838), were active in town affairs. The family genealogy credits them with securing the town's vote to have "Five Reading & Wrighting Schools in the Winter Season."[1] The two Samuels played a key role in establishing a Baptist church in Weston and building its first meetinghouse on South Avenue just east of Wellesley Street in 1784. Samuel Jr.'s third son, Charles (1783–1849), was the church's first settled minister.

Samuel Jr.'s second son, Isaac (b. 1779), built a house at the corner of Wellesley Street and South Avenue about 1802. South Avenue was known at that time as the South County Road or Framingham Turnpike. It was less traveled than Boston Post Road but stagecoach traffic was sufficient for Train to operate a tavern here until about 1810. Business declined because of the opening of the Worcester Turnpike, now Route 9.

Also important in this corner of town were the Leadbetters, a tough old New England family known for abundant progeny and longevity.[2] Ten or 12 children per household was not uncommon, usually including at least one set of twins and a boy named Increase. The first Leadbetter in Weston, Henry (1702–1762), purchased 80 acres in 1747 and later built the farmhouse on Highland Street at the corner of South Avenue.[3] Henry's son Increase (1738–1802)

Figure 29-4. Isaac Train, son of Samuel Jr., built his house at South Avenue and Wellesley Street in 1802. It was used as a tavern for a few years, until the construction of the Worcester Turnpike (now Route 9) led to a decline in business.

sold half an acre of his field to the town for a cemetery in 1789 and is buried there along with 20 more Leadbetters and other south-side residents.[4] Eleven adult male members of the Leadbetter family are listed in the town assessor's records by 1861. Four had "homesteads": Increase (88 acres), Swift (120 acres), Increase Jr. (108 acres), and Henry (143 acres). The 1875 *Atlas of Middlesex County* shows seven Leadbetter houses in the southwest area.

Farms in the Southwest: 1875–1950

Abigail Leadbetter, one of Increase Jr.'s seven children, married Abraham Loker of Natick. Their son Andrew G. Loker purchased the 88-acre Increase Leadbetter farm located where Rivers School is today.[5] By the 1880s Andrew had built up a sub-

Figures 29-5 and 29-6. Andrew Loker took over one of the Leadbetter farms, located where Rivers School is today. In 1897, he built the bowfront Colonial Revival house at 333 Winter Street, presently occupied by Rivers Music School. His handsome dairy barn was substantially rebuilt after a major fire in 1975.

Figure 29-7. A highlight of the 1913 Bicentennial parade was the Greene ponies, trained on the Loker farm. W.A. Greene, of Auburndale, shipped 25 wild western horses by rail from Oregon. Greene hoped that the speed and endurance of these "Indian ponies" would make them excellent polo horses, but the venture proved unprofitable.

stantial dairy operation. He demonstrated his success and a fine sense of style by constructing the Colonial Revival bow-front house now used by Rivers Music School. He and his two maiden sisters, Clara and Sarah, lived here until their deaths in the 1930s and 1940s.

By 1915 Loker owned 278 acres, one of the largest landholdings in Weston. He owned much of the land along Nonesuch Pond, which was used for swimming, fishing, and camping and in later years for a small summer camp on the Natick side. In the 1910s, the farm was rented to the Greene family, who used it to break and train wild ponies brought in by the carload from the West. They built a large corral with an eight-foot fence around it. In *Growing Up in Weston,* Phil Coburn recalls riding his bicycle there on Sundays and sitting atop the fence "like rail birds," watching "real live Western cowboys" break the bucking broncos. Brenton Dickson III also had fond memories of these Wild West shows. Although it provided great pleasure to the audience, the venture proved unprofitable and was discontinued after just a few years.[6]

Figure 29-8 (above). Abijah, youngest of the four sons of Swift Leadbetter, inherited the homestead at 412 Highland Street. He is pictured with his wife, Adeline, in 1908, two years before his death. Both the house and barn are still standing.

Figure 29-9 (left). Ida Leadbetter, daughter of Abijah and Adeline, inherited the farm and managed it with her husband, Alexander Sauer. (1920 photo)

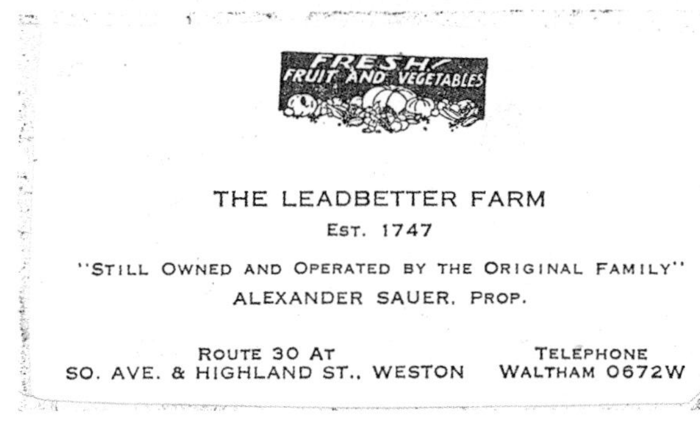

FRESH! FRUIT AND VEGETABLES

THE LEADBETTER FARM
EST. 1747

"STILL OWNED AND OPERATED BY THE ORIGINAL FAMILY"
ALEXANDER SAUER, PROP.

ROUTE 30 AT SO. AVE. & HIGHLAND ST., WESTON
TELEPHONE WALTHAM 0672W

Figure 29-10. Sauer promoted the Leadbetter heritage on his business card. Note that although the farm was established in 1747, the farmhouse itself is later in date, probably early 19th century.

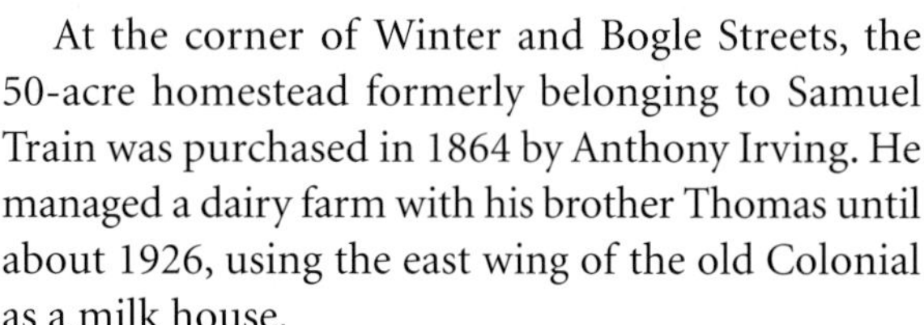

Figures 29-11 to 29-15. Everyday scenes from the Leadbetter/Sauer farm at 412 Highland Street include the roadside stand (1924), Ida and Alexander Sauer and the farm autobus (1926), Alexander Sauer with motorcycle (c. 1920), Ida Leadbetter Sauer with her cat (unknown date), and the haywagon (1940). Alexander Sauer died in 1945, and the farm was sold after nearly two centuries of family ownership.

At the corner of Winter and Bogle Streets, the 50-acre homestead formerly belonging to Samuel Train was purchased in 1864 by Anthony Irving. He managed a dairy farm with his brother Thomas until about 1926, using the east wing of the old Colonial as a milk house.

Leadbetters continued to farm in Weston until the mid-20th century. After Abijah Leadbetter died in 1910, the farm at the corner of Highland Street and South Avenue was taken over by his son-in-law Alexander Sauer, a German immigrant whose name matched his sour disposition. Sauer's business card advertised fresh fruit and vegetables at the Leadbetter Farm, "established 1747 and still owned and operated by the original family." The family had a roadside stand. Older residents recall the junk that accumulated at the Sauers', like old wagons that were falling apart and broken farm tools. When Sauer died in 1945, the farm was sold, ending two centuries of ownership by the Leadbetter family.

Across South Avenue where Pope John XXIII Seminary is today, Walter Thompson operated a farm from 1911 into the 1940s. During the Depression, he began to specialize in pigs, and by 1934 he was taxed for 300 of them. Thompson lived in a dilapidated house on the property and, like other pig farmers, spent a good part of his day on a regular route picking up garbage to feed his charges. Needless to say, the piggery smelled. Occasionally pigs would escape the confines of the broken-down wooden paddock and wander through the neighborhood. Thompson supplemented his income by disposing of dead horses and cows and selling the horsehair and skins. He kept a few cows and sold two or three cans of milk a day to the Jennings dairy.[7]

District Schoolhouse #6 and Weston Flying Field

Generations of Train, Leadbetter, and Loker children attended the one-room District School #6 at Winter and Brown Streets. The Italianate-style schoolhouse

Figure 29-16. District School #6 was used for 40 years, until the town adopted a centralized school system in 1893. The building was later converted to a two-family residence and still stands at the corner of Winter and Brown Streets.

was built in 1853, replacing a simpler 18th-century version. It remained in use until 1893, when the town adopted a centralized school system. In 1908 the vacant schoolhouse was sold to estate owner Charles Jones, who that same year acquired 95 acres along Brown and Winter Streets.[8] Jones converted the school to a two-family house for his herdsman and horse trainers and built a cow barn and horse barn in back.

According to Brenton Dickson's *Once Upon a Pung*, the tall pine forest around the schoolhouse was a favorite camping ground for Gypsies, who would "swarm over the south part of town selling baskets, telling fortunes, and scraping up cash wherever they could," prompting local residents to become more conscientious about keeping doors locked.[9] The Gypsies moved on to another camp site on Loring Road near the Charles River after Weston's first and only airport was built amid the pines.

The "flying field" or "airdrome" was built on leased land in 1919 or early 1920. Runways were cut through the forest and a U-shaped airplane hangar was fashioned by connecting the Jones cow and horse barns. Townspeople drove over to Winter Street in their Model T Fords to watch the flimsy biplanes, which looked like skeletons with canvas stretched across the frame and were cranked up by turning a single propeller by hand. Reports about the aviation field appeared frequently in the newspaper. For example, in June 1920, 75 members of the MIT class of 1914 held a reunion at the "American Aerial Corporation" field, where employees entertained the visitors with stunt flying and rides.[10] This item also appeared in 1920:

Figure 29-17. Weston had an airport for a few short years, from 1919 or 1920 through 1926. Located at Brown and Winter Streets, the airport was especially popular on Sundays. For a few dollars, local residents could take a 15-minute ride on the rickety biplanes, if they didn't mind the risk of a crash.

> A nervous passenger taking, probably, his first aeroplane trip last Sunday, became frightened as the aviator was preparing to make a landing and throwing his arms around him caused the plane to swerve with the result that it came down on top of a stone wall. No one was injured but the feelings of the aviator may be imagined.[11]

And this item:

> Mr. Walter Barton has seen the world from a new viewpoint having been a passenger in one of the airship flights on Sunday. At present prices it is a pretty expensive quarter hour but Mr. Barton says it is worth the price . . .[12]

In 1926, the Waltham *News-Tribune* reported that "the field has been an extremely popular place on a Sunday or holiday afternoon, and two planes have been kept in the air all the time, carrying passengers."[13] The planes were used for commercial business as well as pleasure flying.

Tales from Prohibition Days

Brenton Dickson III tells stories of the southwest area during Prohibition, when moonshiners considered this part of town sufficiently remote for carrying on their nefarious operations:

> One still was just off Pine Street. When neighbors observed a suspicious amount of activity in the neighborhood, Federal Agents were notified and they came out and were joined by Sumner Viles, then Chief of Police, to stage a raid. The moonshiners must have heard them coming because, although the still was hot, nobody was around. The barrels and apparatus were destroyed with axes and the operators never returned.[14]

Dickson recalls the town's finest distillery, located on Winter Street:

> New plumbing fixtures and flues were installed in a house to convert it into an efficient operation. The owners made the stupid mistake of dumping their refuse into a brook that flowed past the house. As the water became more polluted, downstream neighbors complained of the smell. Suspicion was aroused. The Federal Agents were notified and subsequently a raid was staged.[15]

Rumors abounded of rum-running at the airport, which acquired a bad reputation that led to pressure to shut it down. On Bogle Street, a "tea room" known as the Noir et Rouge, located in a converted farmhouse, was patronized almost exclusively by Wellesley College students, who were forbidden to smoke in the towns of Wellesley and Natick and were also rumored to be searching for beverages more stimulating than tea.[16] The building was the target of a self-styled reformer who threatened to blow it up. For a time, Weston police maintained constant watch, but on April 20, 1929, the watch was discontinued, and the next night the house was destroyed in a major fire.[17]

The Mezitt Family and Weston Nurseries

In 1923, Latvian immigrant Peter John Mezitt (1885–1968) purchased the property at the southwest corner of Winter and Brown Streets, including the old schoolhouse and the airport. He founded Weston Nurseries, which would become internationally known for developing new plant varieties.

Figure 29-18. Peter Mezitt (1885–1968) was a Latvian immigrant who worked for Marian Case at Hillcrest Farm before starting his own nursery at the corner of Winter and Brown Streets. His wife, Anna, worked with him to develop the renowned Weston Nurseries, which moved to Hopkinton after World War II. When he died in 1968, he was praised as "one of the nation's leading horticulturists."

Figure 29-19. Anna Mezitt is pictured in one of the Weston greenhouses about 1940.

Mezitt was born to a family of farmers in Madonna, Latvia, and studied agriculture near Moscow until he was conscripted into the Russian army. He fled Russia, working in Rumanian and Swiss gardens and making bricks in Germany to earn money for passage to America in 1911. He worked his way to New England, enrolled in a course at the University of Massachusetts at Amherst, and sent to Latvia for his bride-to-be, Anna Olga Purens. The couple was married in 1912 and had two children, Laura (b. 1913) and Edmund (b. 1915). Peter took a job as a greenhouse night watchman in Lowell, propagating and potting geraniums during the day.

In 1917 Peter Mezitt accepted a position as superintendent of Hillcrest Farm in Weston, but his heart was in nursery plants. Marian Case encouraged his talent and allowed him to use greenhouse space. Peter and Anna worked nights and weekends rooting understock and grafting fruit trees to sell to orchards. By the early 1920s, determined to become a full-time nurseryman, Peter persuaded Miss Case to help him finance the purchase of the Winter Street land.

Peter and Anna Mezitt began by raising annuals and perennials from seed while continuing to work for Marian Case and live at Hillcrest. The airport was still active when they bought the property. Because money was tight, land not used for crops was rented to the pilots. Family members recall stories of Peter Mezitt chasing planes down the runway with his truck, preventing their takeoff until the pilots had paid their rent.

The airport operated until June 1926, when a spectacular fire, quickened by a series of gas tank explosions, destroyed the hangar and 18 aircraft. An account of the fire in the *Waltham News Tribune* reported $100,000 in damage and described 14 of the planes as "under construction and practically finished."[18] The newspaper called the Weston Flying Field "one of the most important aviation centers in the state."

Growth of Weston Nurseries

After the fire, the Mezitts moved into the former schoolhouse and devoted all their time to the nursery. Peter began doing landscape jobs, and Anna and the children grew and sold perennials. By 1929, Weston Nurseries had 10 acres in production and printed its first catalog. During the Depression, they survived by responding quickly to the fashion for rock gardens, which created a demand for herbaceous perennials and rock-garden plants. They grew the business steadily by offering thousands of plant varieties suited to the New England climate and soil conditions and selling both retail and wholesale.

The main nursery, located on Winter Street just south of the schoolhouse, included barns, sheds, cold frames, and four or five greenhouses. In 1931, the Mezitts bought the former Isaac Train house at Wellesley Street and South Avenue, where they maintained an office and retail sales operation with a greenhouse on the adjacent property.[19] Plants were grown and displayed on fields at the northwest and southwest corners of Wellesley Street and South Avenue, on land leased from the Paine estate. In 1938, the Mezitts purchased the Samuel Train House and 62 acres on Winter Street from dairyman Anthony Irving.[20] They maintained extensive nursery fields in this area, including what is now Sherburn Circle. In 1940 the family purchased a house at the intersection of Brown Street and South Avenue for Edmund Mezitt, who married Wally Bralit that year.[21] Their sons, Wayne and Roger, are now the third generation to own and operate the business. By 1945, the Mezitts owned a total of 142 acres and leased additional fields from local farmers and estate owners. Rhododendrons and mountain laurel still flourish on land once part of the nursery, such as the Paine land on Highland Street across from Love Lane.

At the close of World War II, the family realized that suburban development would increasingly limit their operations, and they began to look for a new location. They had observed that the hillside locations in Weston were ideal because cold air tended to sink into the valleys, leaving the hillsides warmer and young plants less vulnerable to late-spring and early-fall frosts. Peter and Edmund found the type of land they were looking for in Hopkinton, where they purchased 300 hilly acres and began preparing roads and planting beds while continuing operations in Weston. Greenhouses and other buildings were taken down and reconstructed in Hopkinton.

May 1945 marked a pivotal moment in the history of Weston Nurseries. The previous fall, Ed Mezitt had planted several small crops on the newly purchased land, including seedlings from his first attempt at hybridizing. The new hybrid was a rhododendron created by crossing a native Carolina rhododendron growing in their yard in Weston with seeds from a Chinese variety sent by a missionary to China.[22] Edmund Mezitt later wrote about the result:

> We had all but forgotten this hybrid, until one Sunday in early May in 1945. We were just developing our nursery in Hopkinton, and were visiting it that morning, having been tied up during the busy season in Weston most of the week. My heart still skips a beat when I recall the reaction of our entire family when we saw that ribbon of brilliant pink running across the hill. My Dad was so enthusiastic about these little dwarf plants—only six to eight inches tall—in full bloom, that he immediately made the remark that this was the most spectacular rhododendron

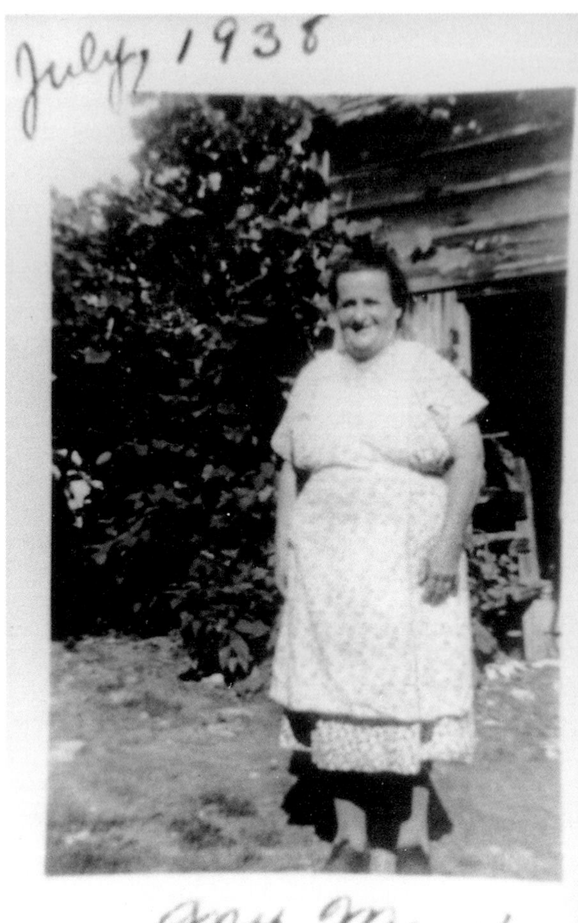

Figure 29-20. When this picture of Amelia Benotti (Mrs. Ernest) was taken at the family home on Pine Street in 1938, it was the only house on a narrow dirt road. The Benottis rented the house from the Dicksons. Ernest was one of six siblings who immigrated from Italy to Weston.

Figure 29-21. Amelia and Ernest Benotti (at left) had six girls and three boys. Pictured here about 1925–26 are Virginia, Mary, Angie, Emanuel, Anne, and Raymond.

> of our time. We named it "P.J.M." right on the spot and those of us who knew him can see the vigor, excitement and showmanship he possessed perfectly reflected in this plant.[23]

The success of the "P.J.M." encouraged Ed to continue "pollen dabbing," as he called it; and his hybrids became known throughout the horticultural world.

By 1950, all propagation and shipping facilities had been moved to Hopkinton. The Mezitts maintained a sales outlet in Weston for several more years.

The Benotti Family

In 1900, Raphael Benotti (1880–1966) became the first of six siblings to come to the United States from Cento, Italy. He and his wife, Bianca, settled in Weston, where one of his earliest jobs was on a town crew battling the prolific gypsy moths. According to one family story, he brought his brother Ernesto (1882–1940) over to help, and Ernesto's wife and oldest daughter joined the extended family in the United States. Ralph eventually settled in the northwest part of town and became caretaker of the Renwick estate. Ernesto and his family rented a small house that still stands on Pine Street. It was the only house on what was then a dirt road.

Antonio Benotti (1887–1972) and his wife, Anna, joined the brothers in 1909 and raised their family of nine children on Conant Road. The only sister, Delmina, her husband, Giuseppe Ferranti, and their children came to Weston between 1911 and 1914. Louis (1891–1968) and Joseph (b. 1878) also settled in Weston.

After working for some years as a farm laborer, Louis and his wife, Catherine, purchased eight acres on South Avenue just east of Wellesley Street. Louis built a large greenhouse and started a profitable business selling perennials, flats of annuals, and wholesale and retail cut flowers. The business continued until the mid-1950s, when the land was sold and eventually developed as High Meadow Road.

The Anza Family

Vincenzo (James) Anza (1890–1989) came to America from Sicily just before World War I.[24] After some years as an Army horse and mule tender and as a lime factory worker in Waltham, he went to work for Ralph Jones, whose farmhouse on Boston Post Road was once the Golden Ball Tavern. By 1926 Anza had saved enough money to buy horses from Jones and start his own farm. He bought 18 acres of land on Highland Street and built a small farmhouse. Once settled, he married Nellie Bianco in 1929.

James Anza worked seven days a week operating two businesses that employed as many as 20 men. He did construction work, digging cellar holes, building stone walls, and clearing land. He grew vegetables on his own property and worked fields as far away as Golden Ball Road. He sold loam and gravel from his own property. Anza was involved in the rebuilding of Route 30 in the late 1920s, loading "tip carts" of gravel by hand and hauling them with teams of horses to wetlands that needed to be filled. He used his horses to move a house at the corner of Oak Street out of the way of the new route.

James and Nellie Anza's only child, Santo, recalled the building boom of the 1950s to 1970s, which changed his neighborhood and all of Weston. Santo

Anza worked on many of the houses built on the former Jones estate on Woodchester, Shady Hill, and Ledgewood Roads. He hauled in gravel; contoured the land; built dry wells, septic systems and driveways; and then landscaped the property. Anza aimed for a rustic look by cutting down only enough trees to create space for the house and septic system. About 1988, he retired and moved back to his father's farm on Highland Street, where he began producing quality loam by composting leaves and grass clippings brought in by local landscapers. At the beginning of the new century, he was still keeping 35 beef cattle, the last herd in Weston. His cows are a familiar sight standing atop piles of loam, enjoying the heat from the decomposing organic matter and further enriching the soil with manure.

Postwar Changes

The southwest was still largely fields and woodlands until the 1960s. Sherburn Circle was developed early in that decade. On the west side of Highland Street, Black Oak and Nobscot Roads were laid out in 1961 by Country Properties, with houses constructed by Swiedler Building Corporation. Deer Path Lane and Country Drive were developed about this time as well.

Institutions moved to the area. In 1959 the core of the Loker farm was purchased by Rivers School, a private secondary school then located in Newton. The school constructed a campus on Nonesuch Pond for boys in grades 7 to 12, with buildings of Modern design. Rivers has been coeducational since 1989–90 and presently has about 325 students.

Thompson's piggery was purchased in the early 1960s by the Archdiocese of Boston for the Pope John XXIII National Seminary, the first seminary in North America for the education of men entering the priesthood in later life. Students range in age from 30 to 60 and previously worked in a wide variety of other careers.

Wightman Tennis Center was established on a 15-acre parcel once the site of the Weston Nursery barns and greenhouses. Named for tennis star Hazel Hotchkiss Wightman, the not-for-profit club was constructed in 1969 to provide indoor and outdoor tennis courts, squash courts, and indoor and outdoor swimming facilities for 300 member families.

The Church of Jesus Christ of Latter-day Saints (1967), Greek Orthodox Church of St. Demetrios (1971), and nondenominational Westgate Church (1994) were also built in the southwest during the postwar period. The mixed-income Winter Gardens development on Dickson Lane opened in September 1997, an event described in newspapers as "a milestone in Weston's 15-year effort to encourage the development of affordable housing."[25]

Houses in the Southwest

96 Brown Street (1853). Used for 40 years as District School #6. Purchased by Charles Jones in 1908 and converted to a two-family house for his herdsmen and horse trainers. Later the home of Peter Mezitt.

346 Highland Street (1897). Built for farmer John Schwartz and his wife, Sarah, who moved to this house on their son's farm in their old age after the family farmhouse at Love Lane and Highland Street burned down. (See also No. 368.)

368 Highland Street (1905). Built for farmer John Melvin Schwartz, son of John Schwartz. J.M. Schwartz had moved to an earlier house on the 57-acre farm in 1891. This first house burned to the ground in 1905 and was rebuilt on the same site.[26]

390 Highland Street (1928). Built for James Anza and later occupied by his son, Santo, who still has the plans labeled "W.M. Haines, architect, Waltham, 1928."

412 Highland Avenue (probably early 19th century). Henry Leadbetter, first of the family to settle in Weston, bought 80 acres and a house and barn in 1747—thus the property became known as the 1747 Farm. The Federal-style house, however, is later in date.[27] The house stayed in the Leadbetter family until the mid-20th century. In the 1950s it was purchased by the Woodworths, who started the 1747 Farm Horse Show here.

23 Pine Street (late 1880s). Built for farmer Lemuel Smith, who bought 37 acres from Newell Smith in 1886. The family owned the property until 1920, when it was sold to B.H. Dickson Jr. For some years the house was rented by Ernesto Benotti and his family.

461 South Avenue. Site of Mezitt greenhouses associated with the retail sales outlet next door at No. 465.

465 South Avenue (c. 1802). Isaac Train house. Federal-style house used for a few years as a tavern. Owned by the Mezitt family in the 1930s and '40s and used as a retail sales outlet.

South Avenue. South Burying Ground. The Town of Weston purchased the one-half-acre site for $5 from Increase Leadbetter in 1789. Some burials had already taken place there and it was known as the Leadbetter Cemetery.

669 South Avenue. Owned at the time of the 1875 map by Henry Leadbetter, this 18th- or early-19th-century house became the home of Edmund Mezitt after his marriage in 1940.

803 South Avenue (begun c. 1821, finished c. 1841).

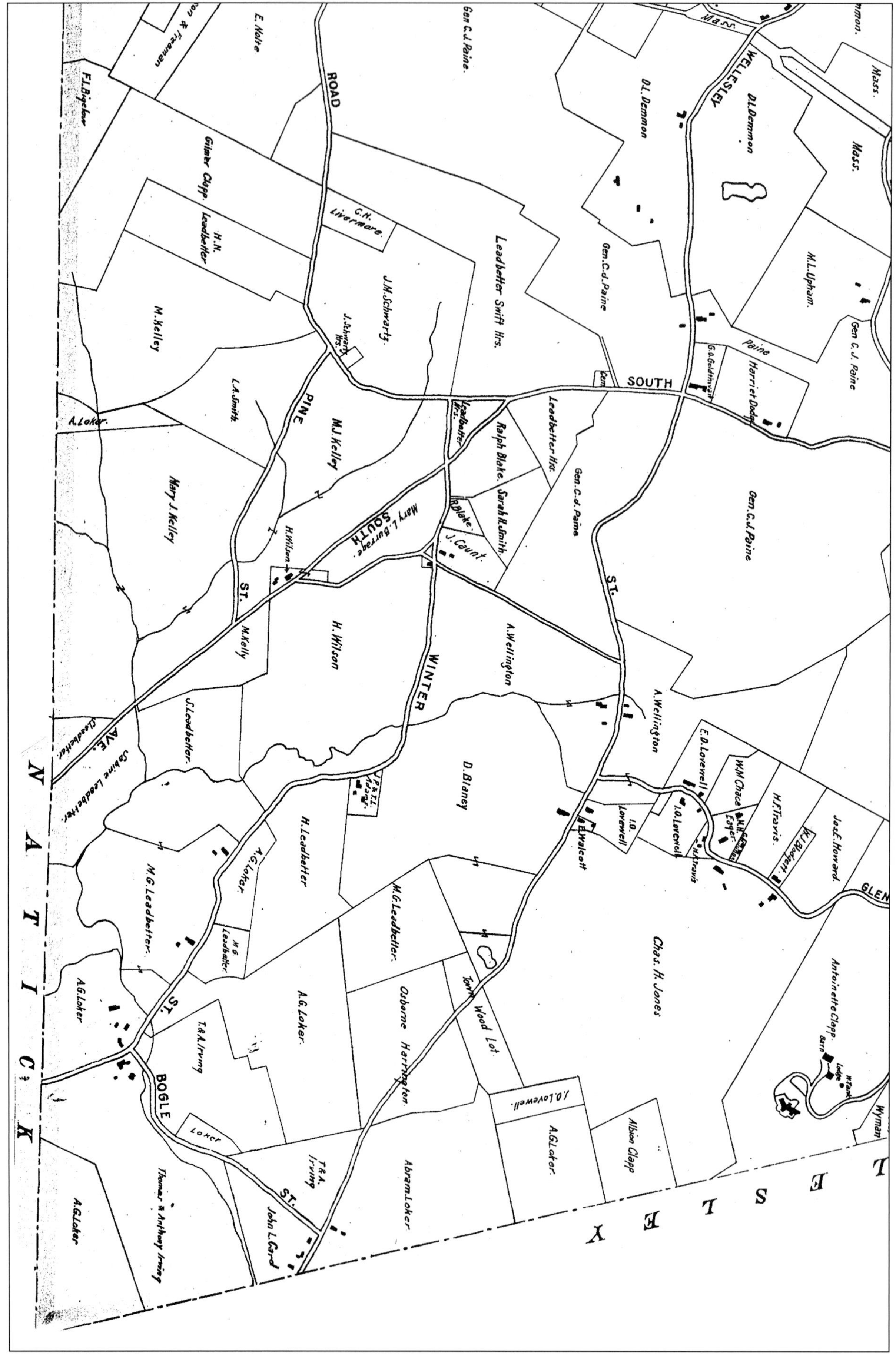

Figure 29-22. Detail from the 1908 Atlas of Middlesex County.

Federal house built for Increase Leadbetter (b. 1782), son of Increase, and later occupied by his son Sabine P. Leadbetter.[28] Not surprisingly, this house is similar on the exterior to the family homestead at 412 Highland Street.

342 Winter Street (1738). Samuel Train house. Early, well-preserved house listed on the National Register of Historic Places. Three generations of Trains, all prominent town leaders, lived here for 106 years.

285 Winter Street (c. 1877). Italianate farmhouse built for unmarried farmer Mordecai G. Leadbetter (1827–1910), fourth generation of his family in Weston. He purchased the 30-acre property about 1853 from Increase Jr. and Clara Leadbetter and sold it in 1902 to Andrew G. Loker. The house first appears on tax records in 1877.

333 Winter Street (1897). Built by dairy farmer Andrew Loker, the Colonial Revival house appears in 1897 tax records valued at $4,200, a substantial sum at the time (now Rivers Music School). The large red barn was part of the Loker farm and first appears in tax records of 1895, valued at $4,000. The barn's original gambrel roof was damaged by fire and rebuilt as a gable roof.

Notes

1. Hand, Susan Train, *John Trayne and Some of His Descendants* (privately printed, New York, 1933). The vote was in 1770.
2. Ames, J.E., *Leadbetter Records* (privately printed, 1917).
3. MCRD 49/56, Francis Fullam Jr. of Weston to Henry Leadbetter of Dorchester, for 370 pounds, 1747. Deed included a mansion house and barn; however, the present house is later in date.
4. According to one inventory form, there are 112 gravestones at South Burying Ground. The *Weston Historical Society Bulletin*, January 1978, has a list of people buried here. The 1963 *Town Report* says that Miss Polly Leadbetter, who died on January 20, 1792, was the first burial of record, adding, "Although no records prior to that time have been located, it is well known that this plot had long before been used for burials by residents of the south section. . . . In those olden days it was called 'Leadbetter Cemetery.'"
5. MCRD 1386/196, Increase Leadbetter to Andrew and Abraham Loker, March 1896. See also 1813/298, August 1887 (Andrew purchased the half interest of Abraham).
6. Dickson, *Pung*, 53, and Coburn, *GUIW*, 28.
7. PWF interview with Nelson McNutt, June 1998.
8. MCRD 3372/273, George J. Wilson estate to Charles Jones, 95 acres, June 1908; and 3403/179, Town of Weston to Jones, schoolhouse and 0.4 acre, $400.
9. *Pung*, 52.
10. *WDFPT*, June 25, 1920.
11. *WDFPT*, May 21, 1920.
12. *WDFPT*, July 23, 1920. See also February 20, March 11, May 7, May 14, July 11, and July 16, 1920.
13. *Waltham News Tribune*, June 17, 1926, 14.
14. *Pung*, 53.
15. Ibid., 54.
16. A newspaper account in the *Waltham News Tribune* after the fire of April 20, 1929, tells of Wellesley girls smoking at the Noir et Rouge.
17. Crouch, H. Bentley, history of the Weston Fire Department (typescript, undated).
18. Ibid. See also *Waltham News Tribune*, June 17, 1926, and *The News-Tribune*, August 23, 1977.
19. MCRD 5544/338, Gertrude Dimich to Mezitt, March 1931. The sales operation is described in early Weston Nurseries catalogs. Some information from interviews by PWF with Roger and Wayne Mezitt.
20. MCRD 6261/54, Irving to Mezitt, December 1938.
21. MCRD 6366/404. They sold the house (669 South Avenue) in 1950 (7583/305).
22. According to the family, Peter Mezitt never traveled to China. The family got plants through contacts made by Peter or Edmund.
23. *Weston Nurseries: Our 75th Year* (1998 catalog, Weston Nurseries, Inc.), viii. Quote was reprinted from "The Origin of Rhododendron 'P.J.M.'" by Edmund V. Mezitt, *The Rosebay*, vol. I, no. 1, 1, February 1972, Massachusetts Chapter, American Rhododendron Society.
24. PWF interview with Santo Anza, April 1998.
25. "Sold! First Affordable Housing Units Ready for Sale," *Weston Town Crier and Tab*, September 11, 1997. Six of the 24 single-family homes were priced at $90,000, with the remainder priced around $290,000.
26. Schwartz, Melvin H., "John Schwartz" (unpublished typescript, 1964).
27. The tax valuation of 1798 lists Increase Leadbetter's house at $89, compared to Oliver Conant's house (now 118 Conant Road) at $250—indicating that the Leadbetter house was a much smaller structure then.
28. Information from Linda Leadbetter, daughter of Sabine P., as quoted in WHC files.

Figure 30-1. Virginia and Linda Wellington gather hay in the fields at Gateways Farm on Wellesley Street. The girls always wore dresses, never slacks. Their father, Louis Wellington, shared the farm with his brother, Arthur, and his family. They maintained and enhanced the old-fashioned qualities of the existing house and outbuildings. Most of the Wellington photographs in this chapter were taken by Arthur's wife, Evelyn, who has been described by her granddaughter as "relentless with the Graflex."

CHAPTER 30

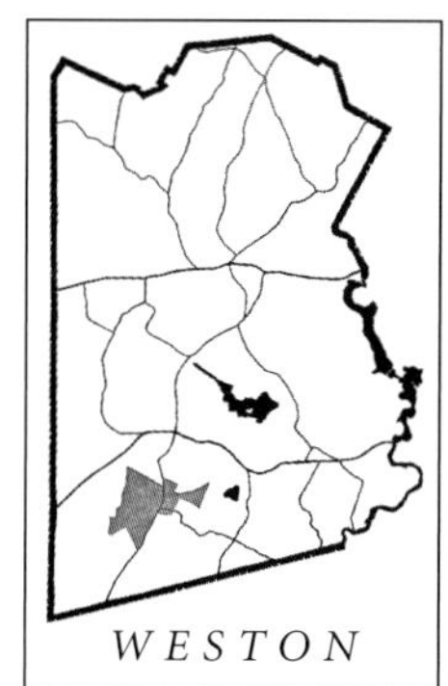

Wellington and Blaney Families

The Old-Fashioned Farm in Weston

The late 19th and early 20th centuries were a time of profound change in New England, as the traditional rural agrarian society of the old-time Yankees gave way to a world that was more urban, industrial, and ethnically and racially diverse. The advent of this "modern" age gave birth to a cultural counterforce known as antimodernism, which looked to the past as the embodiment of the wholesome values and spiritual truths on which this country was founded. The rise of the Arts and Crafts Movement, antique collecting, historic preservation, and Colonial Revival architecture were all outgrowths of this preoccupation with the past as a way of formulating identity and a sense of unity in a nation increasingly divided.

In Weston, the flowering of interest in the colonial past is exemplified in the lives of Arthur Wellington and Dwight Blaney, who purchased adjacent farms on Wellesley Street in 1907–08. Blaney and Wellington had much in common as members of long established New England families, neighbors on Beacon Hill and in Weston, and lovers of Americana. In renovating their farmhouses, the two men called upon two of New England's earliest preservation architects: Joseph Everett Chandler and George Canning Wales.

Arthur Wellington, a leather company executive, devoted much of his energy to the development of his beloved Gateways Farm as an old-fashioned summer home and gentleman's farm embodying the values of family and fellowship. Artist and antique collector Dwight Blaney used his Weston property as a country retreat and the setting for paintings that record the vanishing landscape of old-time New England.

It is a testament to the power of their vision that both the Wellington and Blaney properties have stayed remarkably untouched by time. Gateways Farm, including the Wellington farmhouse, barn, and caretaker's house, remains on about 30 acres at the corner of Wellesley Street and Glen Road. Just to the south, at 555 Wellesley Street, is the Harrington house, which Dwight Blaney bought and restored. Both properties are surrounded by conservation land that the Wellington and Blaney children sold and donated to the town to help preserve the landscape that they, too, loved so much.

Early History of the Pierce/Wellington House

The main house at Gateways Farm on Wellesley Street does not look much like an 18th-century farmhouse, but the earliest section may have been built as early as 1760 using a traditional five-bay, central-chimney plan.[1] In 1770, the owners of the 70-acre farmstead, Thomas and Mary Pierce, sold it to John Brown, and the house remained in the Brown family for nearly 130 years. Sometime between about 1800 and 1820, the original house was enlarged and updated with Federal-style mantels and woodwork.

In 1899 Samuel F. Clarke, son-in-law of the Browns, sold the farm to businessman Robert B. Blodgett.[2] A report of the sale in the Waltham *Daily Free Press Tribune* reviews the history of the property:

> Mr. Samuel F. Clarke . . . has sold his estate to a well-known Boston merchant, who intends to improve the property and occupy the same as a summer residence. It contains about 140 acres, the greater portion of which is grassland. The buildings consist of a large, old-fashioned house and barn, which have always been kept in excellent repair. Among the principal attractions of the place are the grand old maple and elm trees which were planted by Mr. Clarke over fifty years ago. . . . The estate has been in the family since 1795, being owned by Mr. Brown, the grandfather of Mrs. Clarke, who was one of the early settlers and active in town affairs. Mr. Clarke has owned and occupied it since 1847.[3]

The article added, "This has been a favorite resort for persons seeking rest and recreation during the summer season."

Robert Blodgett owned the house for about five years. He added a kitchen and service wing to the north, doubling the size of the original house.[4] The gable roof was replaced with a high gambrel, creating a full third story that gives the house its present Colonial Revival appearance. Porches and bay windows completed the transformation of the original 18th-century farmhouse into the rambling summer house purchased by Arthur and Evelyn Wellington in December 1907.

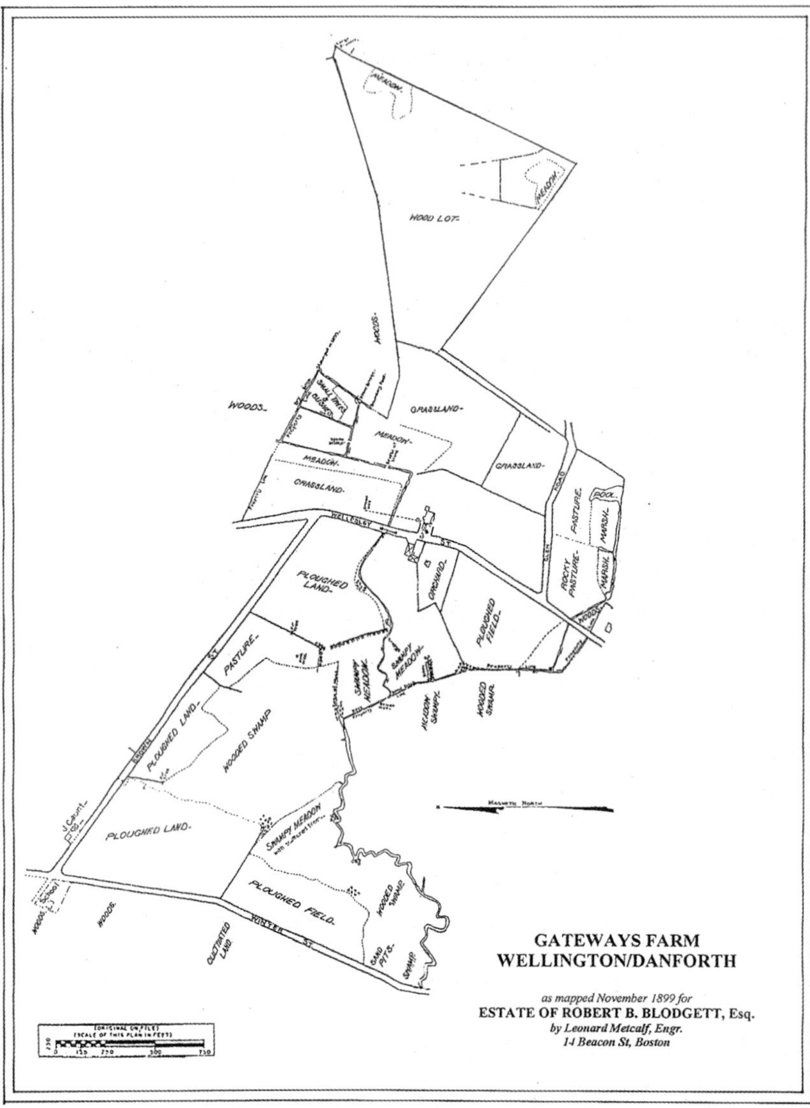

Figure 30-2. This 1899 plan of the Blodgett estate shows land use and buildings at that time. On January 3, 1908, the Waltham Daily Free Press Tribune *reported, "The William E. Barrett estate, known as the Blodgett estate . . . has been sold to a Boston party. . . . The estate comprises about 100 acres of land; largely improved by adding farm buildings and modernizing the old colonial mansion."*

Twelve gates provided access to the 107 acres of land, which extended north to Brown Street, south to Glen Road, and west to Winter Street. The Wellingtons called their farm Gateways.

The Wellington Brothers

Arthur Wellesley Wellington (1868–1938) was a handsome, vibrant man who could trace his New England ancestry back to the 17th century. His grandfather and great-uncle were dairymen who purchased the family homestead in the Wellington section of Medford.[5] Arthur was orphaned as a teenager and began his working life as a messenger boy at age 14. He joined the United States Leather Company at the time of its formation in 1893 and worked as a salesman and manager before assuming the presidency about 1918. The company advertised itself as "dealers in hemlock and union sole leather" and was located on Essex Street in Boston's leather district. At the time of his death, Wellington was described as "a prominent figure in the tanning industry."[6]

Arthur was exceptionally close to his younger brother, Louis B. Wellington (d. 1955). Louis was a partner in F.S. Moseley & Co., dealers in "commercial paper" with offices in Boston, New York, and Chicago. The two brothers married sisters, a relationship that was something of a tradition in the Wellington family. Louis was the first of the brothers

Figure 30-3. The Wellington brothers married the Lawton sisters. Arthur and Evelyn (center) were not married until 10 years after Louis and Louise (left and right).

Figure 30-4. In this early-20th-century photograph, goats Nip and Tuck pull Margaret, Linda, and Virginia, the three daughters of Louis Wellington.

to be married, in 1894 to Louise Lawton. The couple had three daughters, Margaret (b. 1896), Virginia (b. 1899), and Linda (b. 1901). Although Arthur was the older brother, he and Evelyn Lawton were not married until a decade later, with their three nieces as attendants. They sailed from New York City on the *Oceanic* for a 2½-month honeymoon in Europe.[7]

Back in Boston, Arthur and Evelyn lived with Louis, Louise, and their children. The Louis Wellingtons owned the winter home at 13 Chestnut Street on Beacon Hill in Boston and Arthur and Evelyn owned the summer house in Weston. When Arthur and Evelyn had their own child 13 years after they were married, they bought a house at 35 Chestnut Street.

When asked how the two families could live in harmony, winter and summer, a granddaughter explained that they always had fun, and the love of music acted as a bond between them. Louise played the piano and Arthur sang classical selections in his deep bass voice. Arthur was well known in musical circles. He was a regular subscriber to the Boston Symphony Orchestra and a member, from 1895 to 1937, of the Harvard Musical Association, where he was featured at least 10 times as a soloist.[8] It may have been here that he became friends with Joseph Everett Chandler, another longtime chorus member.

Arthur Wellington took pride in his family background and had a penchant for early houses and antique furnishings. The Wellington homestead in Medford, built in 1657, was among the oldest in Massachusetts. No. 13 Chestnut Street in Boston was a historic 1806 town house designed by Charles Bulfinch, Boston's premier Federal-period architect. They were filled with antiques collected or inherited by the brothers. Arthur was a member of The Trestle Board, a group of collectors interested in 17th-century furniture.[9] He relished the search for backwoods treasures, like the tole chandelier he once discovered hanging in a dilapidated farmhouse.

Figure 30-5. Members of the Wellington family spend a leisurely summer afternoon on the terrace behind Gateways.

Figure 30-6. Noted architect Joseph Everett Chandler was a good friend of Arthur and Evelyn Wellington. Evelyn took this photograph of Chandler at his Sudbury home, Manalone, in 1936. Chandler designed the Gateways garden, the caretaker's house, and the fence in front of the main house.

Joseph Everett Chandler and the Colonial Revival Style at Gateways Farm

In the years after he purchased Gateways in late 1907, Wellington hired friend and fellow antique collector Joseph Everett Chandler (1864–1945) to help create an old-time atmosphere using a skillful blend of Colonial Revival architecture, antiques, and landscape design. Chandler was one of the best known and most influential of the first generation of preservation-oriented architects who discovered, popularized, and restored Early American houses beginning in the late 19th century. Chandler was descended from old Yankee stock in Plymouth, Massachusetts, cradle of the Colonial Revival. He trained at MIT, which in 1868 had established the first school of architecture in the United States. Chandler and George Wales, who worked on the neighboring Blaney house, both graduated from MIT in 1889 as part of the first generation of architects educated in the United States in a course of study that examined Early American buildings.

Joseph Chandler is known for his work on important Massachusetts landmarks including the Old Statehouse, Paul Revere House, and Old Corner Book Store in Boston and the House of Seven Gables in Salem. He was one of a number of architects of his generation who carefully examined Colonial buildings and published photographs and measured drawings. His work has sometimes been described as "renewal" rather than "restoration."[10] In two of his best-known projects, the Paul Revere House and the House of the Seven Gables, Chandler dramatically altered the structures to heighten contrast between past and present. The resulting houses were considered highly successful in evoking the image of rugged Yankee pioneers for the edification of immigrants pouring into the North End and Salem.

Chandler was a bachelor whose home, aptly named Manalone, was in Sudbury. His social world extended to Weston, where his name appears on early-20th-century Friendly Society programs and membership rosters.[11] His first Weston project was a new house at 51 Church Street, now known as the Andrews/Woodworth house (1897–98), modeled after the Thomas Hancock House in Boston. Because of the controversy surrounding its demolition in 1863, the Hancock House became one of America's most widely imitated Colonial buildings. A few years later, Chandler designed the Horace Sears mansion, a flamboyant Italian Renaissance creation unusual for an architect almost exclusively identified with the Colonial Revival. In 1903–04, he designed the Williamson/Farlow House at 98 Love Lane using a three-story version of the Federal Revival style. Inside, the use of paneling taken from an 18th-century house

Figure 30-7. The Wellington house began as a simple 18th-century farmhouse. It was enlarged and altered several times, particularly in the early years of the 20th century, when the third floor and gambrel roof were added along with the large wing at left (later removed).

Figure 30-8. The pastoral quality of the Wellington farm is evident in this photograph looking southeast from where the Massachusetts Turnpike is today. At left is the caretaker's house; at right is the monumental dairy barn.

Figure 30-9. Joseph Everett Chandler specialized in restoring early homes and designing new ones in the Colonial style. He was also an authority on Colonial gardens. The Wellington garden was laid out in an axial pattern. Interspersed among the perennials were two large columns and objects from Evelyn and Arthur's travels.

is a Chandler trademark. In 1916, Chandler supervised the enlargement and complete remodeling of the Charles O. Richardson house at 6 Conant Road, resulting in an exuberant Georgian Revival interior enhanced with historic French scenic wallpaper.

Chandler's philosophy on the restoration of houses was very suitable to Gateways, an 18th-century farmhouse that had already been enlarged and remodeled at least twice over its long history. Chandler liked to preserve the "sum-total in 'atmosphere'" but felt free to incorporate modern conveniences.[12] Chandler also stood ready to add detailing to early houses that lacked embellishment. For the Wellingtons, he drew up plans for extensive pine paneling in the dining room.[13] While they chose not to add the paneling, they did use Chandler's design for French doors out to the back garden and a white picket fence and entrance gate on Wellesley Street. This fence was probably installed sometime after 1910, when Wellesley Street was rebuilt just west of its original route.[14] The position of the old road is marked by rows of sugar maple trees.

In 1911, Chandler drew plans for a caretaker's cottage, created by moving and realigning two or three existing farm outbuildings and adding new sections. He inserted a new garage between two of the old buildings and enhanced the picturesque effect by placing the obligatory trellis along the south side of the cottage.

Joseph Chandler brought yet another talent to Gateways—his skill as a horticulturist and landscape designer. A longtime trustee of the Massachusetts Horticultural Society, Chandler had an extensive garden at Manalone. In a chapter on colonial gardens in his 1916 book *The Colonial House,* Chandler demonstrates a familiarity with the trees, shrubs, and perennial flowers favored by early settlers. For the Wellingtons, Chandler designed a garden that relied extensively on perennial plantings and was enhanced by a lily pond, several stone-carved garden ornaments, and, most dramatically, a pair of large white fluted columns that brought architecture and nature together in a comfortable outdoor room.

Figure 30-10. This 1895 picture shows the Wellington Homestead in Medford, which dated back to 1657. Arthur Wellington (third from left) is pictured along with Louis Wellington and his future bride, Louise Lawton (second and third from right).

Arthur Wellington and SPNEA

At the turn of the century, population growth, immigration, and industrialization were changing the social makeup of New England. The rural, farm landscape was giving way to modern urban sprawl. Many early buildings were becoming tenements, if they survived at all. Traditional Yankees, fearing the loss of Anglo-Saxon identity and inheritance, argued in increasing numbers for the preservation of early buildings for their educational worth in communicating patriotic values. It was within this context that William Sumner Appleton launched a campaign to save the Paul Revere House in the North End in 1905. Appleton was a Boston Brahmin, Beacon Hill resident, and descendant of Yankee mill builder Nathan Appleton. The "restoration" of the Revere House by Joseph Chandler was among the first steps leading up to Appleton's creation of the Society for the Preservation of New England Antiquities (SPNEA) in 1910, with the goal of protecting old homes throughout New England.

Arthur Wellington purchased Gateways as a summer retreat to replace the 17th-century Wellington homestead in Medford, Massachusetts, and its fate brought Wellington and Appleton into contact. By the first decade of the 20th century, the old homestead was next to a parkway in a neighborhood of two-family homes. Part of the farm had been taken by the transit authority to expand the commuter rail line, leaving insufficient pasture for the dairy cows.[15] Wellington sold what remained of the farm to a developer with an agreement that the homestead could be occupied by members of the family for as long as they wished.[16]

Appleton first became aware of the Medford house about 1914. After a visit in 1923, he wrote to Charles Blanchard, whose ancestors had built it, stating, "The house is emphatically one of the variety that should be preserved . . ."[17] Appleton suggested raising money from families connected to the homestead. Blanchard contacted Arthur Wellington, who replied, ". . . I am the member of the family who has always been particularly interested in the old house at Wellington, as well as being an enthusiastic lover of Early American houses and furnishings."[18] Wellington added that he had considered moving the farmhouse to Weston but decided the interior was too plain and the condition of the structure too deteriorated.

William Sumner Appleton took up the cause with Wellington, writing that the Medford house had all the qualities of design and construction "that make any New England home worth while." Wellington did not share Appleton's sense of urgency. He reasoned that the family members who occupied the homestead would stay there, protecting it for the foreseeable future. It was not until almost 40 years later, long after the death of both Wellington and Appleton, that the Blanchard-Wellington house was finally demolished in 1968. Architectural fragments are now in the collection of SPNEA.

Summers at Gateways

Arthur Wellington was an active farmer who raised Brown Swiss and later Guernsey cows on a small

Figure 30-11. The Gateways barn is the largest remaining in Weston. The earliest section is at left. Several gambrel-roofed additions and a silo give the barn its present picturesque outline.

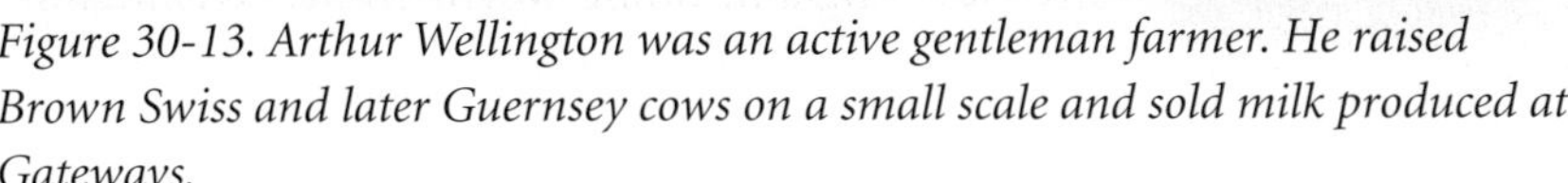

Figure 30-13. Arthur Wellington was an active gentleman farmer. He raised Brown Swiss and later Guernsey cows on a small scale and sold milk produced at Gateways.

Figure 30-12. The wedding of Margaret Wellington and Dudley P. Ranney took place at Gateways Farm in September 1916. Her sisters Linda (left) and Virginia (right) were bridesmaids.

scale, keeping careful track of their lineage.[19] By 1912 he had two riding horses and a "team," two bulls, two cows, eight heifers, and two pigs. The farm sold its extra milk to local dairymen until about 1950. Some fields were hayed while others were planted with corn and vegetables for family use or potatoes sold at market. The Wellingtons employed a caretaker, George Campbell, an assistant, and seasonal help.

The children had a pair of goats that could be hitched to a small cart. Two matched ponies, Nip and Tuck, were for riding. In the off-season, Gateways was used on weekends. In her oral history, Virginia Wellington Cabot describes begging her mother to go to Weston so she and her sisters could ride. The icy cold house was heated only by the fireplaces and a small kitchen stove.

Figure 30-14. Virginia Wellington and Thomas Cabot held their wedding reception at Gateways on May 15, 1920. (Names listed with photo credits)

Figure 30-15. In 1917, after 13 years of marriage, Arthur Wellington (right) had his first and only child, Nancy. Earlier that same year Louis Wellington (left) had his first grandchild, Louise Ranney, named for her grandmother.

Figure 30-16. Arthur introduces young Nancy to farm life at Gateways in the late 1910s.

Figure 30-17. Filling the swimming pool was a ritual marking the beginning of each summer season.

In September 1916, Margaret Wellington, oldest daughter of Louis and Louise, was married to attorney Dudley P. Ranney at Gateways Farm, with her sisters as attendants.[20] The Ranneys settled nearby on Glen Road. In 1917 they had their first child, Louise, named for her grandmother. Within a few years, the Ranneys had three more children, Virginia, Amy, and Margaret.

In August 1917, after 13 years of marriage, Arthur and Evelyn had their first and only child, Nancy. Family photographs show Arthur Wellington and Nancy together with Louis Wellington and his granddaughter Louise, who was a few months older

Figure 30-18. The family gathered to view an eclipse in the early 1930s.

than Nancy. Baby Nancy was raised in the company of the children of her first cousins as part of the large extended family.

In 1920 Virginia Wellington, second daughter of Louis and Louise, married manufacturer Thomas Cabot in a late-spring wedding at First Parish Church, with a reception at Gateways.[21] The Cabots built a house on Farm Road, where they raised their five children: Louis, Thomas, Robert, Linda, and Edmund.

In 1922 the youngest of the three sisters, Linda, married Rev. Palfrey Perkins, who was minister of First Parish Church in Weston and 18 years her senior. The Perkinses had three children: David, Arthur, and Cornelia.

The rhythm of summer life continued into the 1920s and '30s. A pool was built about 1929, and the whole family gathered each year at the beginning of the season for the traditional "filling up the pool" picture. In the 1930s, Nancy was sent to finishing school in Switzerland, and in December 1936 she married investment analyst Nicholas Danforth. Not long afterward, Arthur Wellington died of a heart attack after mending stone walls around the farm.

Figure 30-19. This 1927 photograph includes seven grandchildren of Louis Wellington, along with Arthur's daughter, Nancy. Front row: David Perkins and Robbie Cabot. Second tier: Virginia Ranney and Tom and Louis Cabot. Third tier: Amy and Louise Ranney and Nancy Wellington.

Second and Third Generations at Gateways

After World War II the Danforths moved year-round to Weston, where they raised their four children: Evelyn, Nicholas, Julie, and Nina. Louis Wellington, who lived until 1955, was like a grandfather to the Danforth children. Nearly 11 acres of the farm were taken by eminent domain for the Hultman Aqueduct in 1939. In the early 1950s, the Massachusetts Turnpike took an additional 20 acres. The Westgate Church on Winter Street was built on land once part of the farm. The north wing of the house was removed in 1959.

In 1976 the Danforths sold 44 acres to the town for conservation. Half of this acreage was west of

Figure 30-20. Nancy Wellington (center) plays with her cousins Louise (left) and Amy Ranney.

Figure 30-21. Thomas H. Jackson (center) and Gateways caretaker George Campbell include young Evelyn Danforth in the haying at Gateways Farm. (1940 photo)

the red barn. The 22 acres of conservation land on the east side of Wellesley Street was taken by the state in the late 1990s for construction of the MWRA Norumbega water storage tank. Also in 1976, the family donated land at the corner of Wellesley Street and Glen Road for conservation. Along with the previous sales, this was an important step in protecting the beauty of the historic farm and estate. In 1988, the property was listed on the National Register of Historic Places.

Figure 30-22. Nancy Wellington married Nicholas Danforth in 1936. They were photographed about 1968 in the doorway of the early-19th-century town house at 35 Chestnut Street on Beacon Hill.

Figure 30-23. Nicholas, Nancy, and Evelyn Danforth by the Gateways barn, 1946.

Figure 30-24. This 1913 relief of Dwight Blaney (1865–1944) is the work of noted sculptor Bela Lyon Pratt, who was a friend of Blaney. Pratt shows Blaney holding his artist's brushes and palette, with the rocky coastline of Maine in the background.

Figure 30-25. Edith Hill Blaney poses next to the venerable old elm in front of her house in Weston.

Today about 30 acres remain in the family. Two of the Danforth children still live at Gateways, which is one of Weston's last remaining working farms.[22] The farmstead, with its open fields and rugged stone walls, dates back to the colonial settlement. The house, barn, and caretaker's house have remained largely unchanged since the beginning of the 20th century. In 1996 the town's Open Space Plan listed Gateways as one of the most important remaining open spaces in Weston and a high priority for preservation.

Dwight Blaney: Artist, Collector, and Naturalist

The Wellingtons and their Beacon Hill neighbors enjoyed a rich social life. One acquaintance was Dwight Blaney, owner of a town house at 82-84 Mt. Vernon Street off Louisburg Square. The Blaneys and Wellingtons shared similar backgrounds and belonged to the same social and cultural milieu. Wellington scrapbooks contain photographs of the oldest Blaney child, Margaret, with Louis Wellington's three daughters, who were near her age.

It was Arthur Wellington who told Blaney about a Colonial farmhouse for sale down the street from Gateways. David Blaney recalled his father's visit to Weston to take a look. Notice the emphasis on the elm trees in Blaney's oral history. Like the spinning wheel and Revolutionary War musket above the mantel, the towering elm was a powerful symbol of old New England:

Figure 30-26. John and David Blaney play in front of their Weston house in the early 1900s.

Figure 30-27. Elizabeth, Robert, David, and John Blaney are supervised by James Scott, caretaker of the Weston property. In the background is the water tower.

> . . . Wellington said "There's an old house out here you ought to come out and see." So they got my father and my mother to come out, and the old man said . . . he went up and gave the house a push, and it didn't fall down, so he bought it. . . . I think the elm tree is what sold it to him. It was probably the largest elm in the state.[23]

Blaney acquired the house in early January 1908, less than a month after the Wellington purchase of Gateways. He called it The Old Elm.

Dwight Blaney (1865–1944) was born in Boston. He moved to Salem as a child and spent much of his boyhood exploring fields and marshes collecting bird eggs and other bits of natural history. He attended Chauncy Hall School, a socially prestigious Beacon Hill institution, graduating in 1881. His family's reduced finances meant they could not afford to send him to college. He began work as a designer in a tombstone maker's shop. One day, while sketching in the marshes of Lynn, a stranger, Robert Peabody, looked over his shoulder and was so impressed that he offered Blaney a job as a draftsman at Peabody and Stearns.[24] During his seven years with the Boston architectural firm, he worked with his school friend George Canning Wales, who was later to direct the remodeling of Blaney's houses in Boston, Weston, and Ironbound Island in Maine.

In 1891 Blaney, Wales, and another architect friend, Henry Holt, took leave from Peabody and Stearns to go abroad for two years. They lived on 10 cents each a day, traveling and sketching in England, France, and Italy on what became known as the "spaghetti and chianti" trip.[25] Dwight made more than 2,000 sketches, which he exhibited and sold on his return. While in Italy, he met wealthy heiress Edith White Hill, who was on a grand tour of Europe with her chaperone. Hill's father had owned the Eastern Steamship Company. Their marriage in 1893 made it possible for Blaney to pursue a career as a gentleman painter and financed his passion for antique collecting. Blaney is reported to have quipped that, where money was concerned, he followed the biblical teaching "I will lift mine eyes unto the Hills, from whence cometh my strength."

The Blaneys had six children: Margaret "Meg" (1898–1959), John (1900–1919), David (1902–1989), Robert (1903–1926), Elizabeth "Libby" (1905–1995), and Richard (1907–1962). In her memoirs Libby recalls nurses Annie Lynch and Mary Cronin, in blue uniforms, attending to the children's meals and weekly bath. Blaney was a demanding father with little patience. Libby recounted how she once wanted to glue shells into a cardboard box, but her father insisted that each shell be wrapped in tissue paper and labeled with a Latin name. "It was no fun," she added, "and I never looked at them again. Everything I wanted to do my way had to be done his way. Father wanted us all grown up right away . . ."[26]

Painters of an Elegant Age

Blaney was a member of the Boston School, a group of artists who reached their high point of artistic aspiration in the first three decades of the 20th century. He and fellow Weston artist Gertrude Fiske were two of 44 painters whose work was included in the 1986 Boston Museum of Fine Arts show *The Bostonians, Painters of an Elegant Age (1870–1930)*. The catalogue compares the Boston School to the more dynamic art world of New York City emerging at the same time.[27]

In the catalogue introduction, Theodore Stebbins Jr. writes that during the entire 19th century and beyond, Boston was dominated by a tightly knit "Brahmin" class whose fortunes were made in shipping and trade and later in textiles and railroads. For a time, Boston was in the forefront in literature, education, and art; but gradually this leadership faltered. By the first decade of the 20th century, Boston had lost much of its adventurous spirit in creating and collecting art.[28] The reason, according to Stebbins, lay in "satisfaction with privilege and power" combined with fear of change.

More than half the artists who made up the Boston School were at least moderately wealthy and well connected, while others, like Blaney, were Brahmins or married to Brahmins. As a result, "the pleasures of shared values and craft methods were celebrated over the taking of aesthetic risks" as "art became a social enterprise."

Fear of change arose from the rapid transition from rural to urban society experienced especially in Massachusetts, which by 1900 was the most thoroughly industrialized state in the union. Three quarters of the population lived in cities. This change had occurred in just over half a century, as Boston's population grew from 200,000 in 1850 to more than one million in the metropolitan area by 1900, intensifying issues of ethnic and class division.[29]

The Boston School, which remained dominant well into the 1930s, tended to be conservative. Fervent loyalties to past styles and traditions made it difficult for new ideas and new painters to be accepted. Blaney's work can be viewed within this traditional framework and has been described as "respected but not outstanding."[30] He had no professional training and was clearly influenced by French Impressionism and by the work of his artist friends Ross Turner, Childe Hassam, and John Singer Sargent. His work changed over the years from tight, thinly drawn renderings to free, broadly painted landscapes. He worked in both oil and watercolor. Much of his inspiration was drawn from the natural landscapes and seascapes around his country houses in Weston and Eastham, Massachusetts, and Ironbound Island, Maine.

Blaney had studios in the Fenway Studios Building in Boston and on Ironbound and exhibited his painting locally at galleries, art associations, and clubs. Blaney and Arthur Wellington, along with prominent Boston authors, lawyers, editors, artists, musicians, and preservation leader William Sumner Appleton, were members of the St. Botolph Club. In addition to being one of the city's most exclusive art clubs, St. Botolph was also one of the most sophisticated and innovative. Blaney's work was also exhibited at the Carnegie Institute, Corcoran Gallery, National Academy of Design, Cincinnati Art Museum, and Pennsylvania Academy of Fine Arts. He was awarded a bronze medal at the Panama-Pacific Exposition of 1915.

Blaney and his contemporaries in the Boston School recorded the idyllic settings in which they spent their lives. They painted the old inns, town pumps, old-time interiors, and farmhouses in small New England towns, idealized in this time of relentless industrialization. Many of their pictures depict a life of comfort and order, a commitment to home and family, and a clean and wholesome vision of American life. An example is the 1916 portrait that William McGregor Paxton painted of Elizabeth Blaney, who is depicted in the music room at Ironbound Island with objects from her father's antique collection in the background.[31] As New York artists began to render the world of ordinary people, Boston artists continued to paint this "peaceful and refined world of retreat . . ."[32]

"He Considered All Old Things as Fish to His Net"

Blaney began collecting antiques as a way of furnishing his house when he married. He found the old more pleasing than Victorian machine-made furnishings of the 1890s, and his bride-to-be must have agreed. A letter has survived from 1893 asking her to go with him to a Salem antique dealer to view three pieces he had put on reserve.[33] One of them,

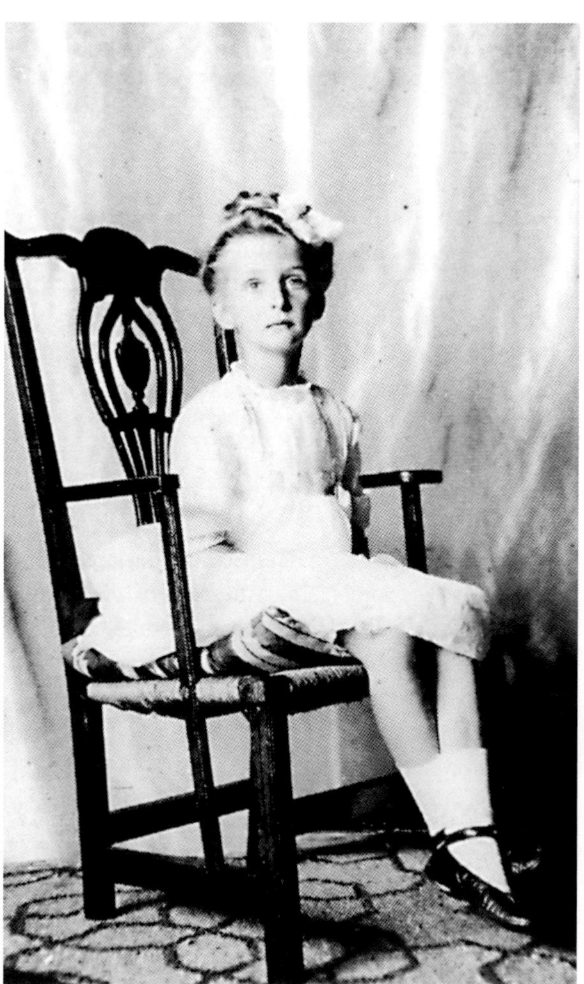

Figure 30-28. Elizabeth Blaney is pictured about 1905 seated on one of Dwight Blaney's many fine antique chairs.

Figure 30-29. This interior of The Old Elm about 1912 shows some of the Blaney collection, including a pair of double chairs flanking the fireplace, a Winsor chair, and a gateleg table.

a serpentine-front chest bought for less than $50, proved to be the only known labeled chest of drawers by Salem cabinetmaker Thomas Needham.[34] Collecting antiques was by no means an accepted or admired pastime in the 1890s, even among the upper classes. His wife's brother-in-law, the yachtsmen C.H.W. Foster, regarded Blaney's furniture contemptuously, as merely secondhand.[35]

Hunting for antiques proved exhilarating. Blaney haunted shops around Boston and collected with Israel Sack, who came to Boston in 1903 and went on to become the foremost American connoisseur and dealer in Early American furniture. Blaney encouraged Sack, who was later to write to Blaney's daughter Elizabeth: "I am ever grateful to him for the love of Americana he imbued in me."[36] Blaney focused on the period 1700–1800. His collections included silver, ceramics, pewter, brass, iron and other metal objects, Revolutionary War objects, firearms, coins, glass, needlework, enameled boxes, Japanese ivory-carved netsuke, books, and hundreds of prints and paintings. One day Blaney's son decided to count the prints and paintings actually hanging on the walls of their home on Mt. Vernon Street, Boston, excluding those stacked against the walls. He counted 600.[37] There were works by his friends John Singer Sargent and Childe Hassam and Monet's *Haystacks at Giverny,* purchased from Durand-Ruel in 1895.

In 1910 Dwight Blaney was "the first name that came to mind" when a group of antiquarians formed the Walpole Society, the first and most prestigious club for collectors of American furniture and decorative arts.[38] Named after the English antique collector Horace Walpole, the society's formation is considered a milestone in American collecting. Blaney was among the 22 original members of the all-male society and was renowned for his lusty renditions of 18th-century folk songs. Members of the Walpole Society not only had to be knowledgeable and socially compatible but also had to have the "right" background. Their exclusivity was to become apparent in the 1920s, when men like Irish Catholic Francis P. Garvan and brash businessman Henry Ford were not asked to join.[39]

In her book *The Antiquers,* Elizabeth Stillinger chronicles the lives of prominent collectors including Blaney. According to Stillinger, Blaney belonged to the second, post-Centennial generation, who began the serious classification and study of their antiques, focusing on aesthetics rather than historical significance. Some of Blaney's finest pieces were published by students of antiques like Luke Vincent Lockwood, Russell Hawes Kettell, and Clair Franklin Luther. To Blaney and his colleagues, antiques embodied the superior values and virtues of craftsmanship and home life in early America. They were looking not just for relics of famous men and events but also for objects that would "express the spirit, and shed light on the daily habits of their forefathers."[40]

A Privileged Way of Life

Blaney filled four houses with his treasures. His winter residence on Mt. Vernon Street was actually two adjacent town houses, Nos. 82 and 84, the second purchased as his family and his antique collection began to grow. According to Henry W. Kent, Blaney's Walpole Society biographer, the Boston house was "filled to overflowing with his best things of the finest period—the things he cared most for of furniture, silver, paintings and books."[41] Hand-lettered signs cautioned: "NOTICE—Do not touch or clean this DESK or anything on or in it or UNDER IT."[42] On Mt. Vernon Street, says Kent, "life was lived according to polite conventions, with art, music, friends and a distinguished cuisine."[43]

In Weston, the family lived "according to the conventions of the 18th century, more or less."[44] The Weston farmhouse had no running water and limited heat except what could be provided by the 12 fireplaces, a woodstove in the kitchen, and a small hot-air system that took the chill off a few rooms. If a milk bottle was left on the kitchen table in the winter, it would freeze by morning. Blaney once remarked that he never realized it was possible to be so uncomfortable so close to Boston.[45] The Weston house was furnished with simpler antique pieces like country furniture, farm implements, cranberry pickers and apple hovels, cheese baskets, and earthenware jugs.

The farm in Weston was used year-round on weekends and school vacations as an escape from the confinement of the city. The family would arrive at the Wellesley Farms train station, where they were met by a horse and buggy, a sleigh in winter, and later by an automobile. With them would come a "box of groceries from Brigham's Grocery Store on West Cedar Street and this sole leather trunk that had kids' clothes and all."[46] Out in the country they picnicked, played croquet, and skated and sledded in winter. When the weather was bad, the children played games indoors or chose from a large library of books and magazines.

James Scott, an Englishman, did the farmwork for the Blaneys in Weston. He and his wife, Mary, lived in the house year-round. Scott had a Cockney accent, thick glasses, and was slightly deaf. He swore like a trooper, at times prompting a scolding from Mary. The Scotts raised vegetables and potatoes, tended the apple orchard planted by Blaney, made cider using an antique cider press, and took care of the dogs and an occasional horse or cow. Mary did the cooking and was remembered for her buckwheat pancakes and tomato spaghetti with cheese and butter. As with all the meals in Weston, these were served on blue Canton china.[47]

Dwight Blaney had limited interest in farming and preferred hunting and fishing with his sporting friends at the Blaneys' third house, in Eastham on Cape Cod. This farmhouse was furnished with nautical memorabilia and located near a salt marsh with a duck blind. Among his hunting guests were Arthur and Louis Wellington. A caretaker tended the retrievers brought down from Weston, and the caretaker's wife did the cooking. While on the Cape, Blaney painted landscapes and seascapes, joined at times by artist friend Frank W. Benson.

The fourth Blaney house was on Ironbound Island, halfway between Bar Harbor and Winter Harbor, Maine. By the turn of the century, Blaney owned more than 400 acres on Ironbound. Here he lived the simple life of socially elite Maine "rusticators" of the period:

> This house was full of what you might expect in a made-over farm house of that State, whose owner was part artist, part collector, part naturalist and part fisherman. . . . [O]n Ironbound, life was spent according to natural laws from sunrise to sunset, painting and fishing.[48]

Each spring the family set off for Ironbound on the Boston boat of the Eastern Steamship Lines, with provisions and a contingent of maids to keep house and attend to the children. Their departure was noted in the newspapers. They stayed for several months and entertained lavishly, turning Ironbound into a social center for painters, musicians, naturalists, and pioneer American furniture collectors. Blaney painted the rocky coastal landscape with his friend John Singer Sargent. In 1922, on Blaney's boat, the *Irona,* Sargent painted his famous painting of his friend, *Portrait of the Artist Sketching.* Hassam painted *Sunset Ironbound: Mount Desert, Maine* in 1896, and Paxton painted *Portrait of Elizabeth Blaney* in 1916. Blaney explored Frenchman's Bay and published his shell-collecting investigations in natural history journals.[49]

Early History of the Weston Farmhouse

Antique collecting coincided with the flowering of interest in Colonial architecture, which inspired both new construction and restoration of antique houses. Like furniture and decorative arts, "ancient" houses were thought to embody the simple values and quality craftsmanship of an earlier age. It is not surprising that a collector like Blaney would also be at the forefront of the historic preservation movement. Blaney was among the first to carry out a careful and sympathetic restoration of an early Weston farmhouse.

The house he chose was significant not only because of its early date, estimated to be about 1710, but also because of its well-preserved interior and long history of association with the same family. It was beautifully sited on a low knoll facing south onto the historic road connecting Weston and Wellesley. The earliest section probably consisted of an all-purpose front room, a bedroom above, and a rear keeping room under a salt box roof.[50]

In 1714, the house with 110 acres was sold to Joseph Hastings, and it remained in the Hast-

Figure 30-30. The early-18th-century house at 555 Wellesley Street was much in need of restoration when purchased by the Blaneys in 1908.

ings/Harrington family for nearly two centuries. Sometime before the mid-18th century, a one-over-one addition to the left of the present hallway was added, along with a rear room on the first floor. Joseph Hastings's granddaughter Sarah and her husband, Stephen Harrington, bought the house in 1788 from Sarah's brother. Stephen Harrington raised the roof at the rear sometime before 1800 and was probably responsible for introducing the Federal-style fireplace mantels. In successive generations, the house was owned by Stephen's youngest son, Tyler, a well-known Methodist minister in Wellesley, then by Tyler's son John W. Harrington. The last Harringtons to occupy the homestead were John's widow, Mary, and widowed daughter, Matilda Harrington Shaw.

Blaney's 1908 purchase included more than 60 acres.[51] He acquired additional land and by 1917 owned about 120 acres. When he bought the Harrington house, Blaney paid $75 for all the remaining furniture and utensils, including a double canopy bed.[52] An old cider mill was unearthed under the shed.

George Canning Wales

To renovate the old farmhouse, Blaney hired George Canning Wales (1869–1940), fellow artist and close friend who began his professional life as an architect but later became recognized as an etcher of square-rigged clipper ships.[53] A few years after his graduation from the MIT architectural program in 1889, Wales traveled in Europe with Blaney and his future partner, Henry Holt. The firm of Wales and Holt is listed in directories from 1893 to 1907. Wales appears to have been practicing by himself when he undertook the Blaney house renovation in January 1908.[54]

The authenticity of the Wales restoration is remarkable for the period. He left most of what he found intact. What was no longer in place or could not be saved was reproduced as faithfully as possible. For example, Wales wrote this about the windows: "Frames and sash were so far gone that we put all in new, but following the old detail except that we flashed heads with copper. The old glass was used to glaze the new sash." About the door, he says, "Old door was gone. Surrounding detail was restored from what fragment remains, and a new door designed to correspond." Wales expressed pride that the house had been "restored" rather than "improved":

> I would emphasize this fact of restoration (without improvement) as being a bit unusual. We made it a keynote of all the work, even going so far as to make full size drawings of the house itself. My experience in work of this type (both my own and others') leads me to the observation that we did a good job.[55]

As part of the renovation, Blaney connected an 18th-century barn and 19th-century well house and sheds to a new garage, forming a picturesque, asymmetrical outbuilding.[56]

"A Remodeled House of Good Taste"

The Wales restoration in Weston is described in detail in a 1912 article in *House and Garden* entitled "A Remodeled House of Good Taste."[57] The author, Mary Northend, was one of the major popularizers of Colonial imagery. A native of Salem, she wrote about the "indescribable charm" of the Colonial in hundreds of magazine articles.[58] Northend employed a professional cameraman to document the Blaney house and furnishings. Her article illuminates the thought processes behind these early "restorations," which were concerned both with serious preservation and with creating the appropriate atmosphere and capturing what was deemed to be the "spirit" of the colonial forefathers.

Northend begins her *House and Garden* article by describing Blaney's search for just the right house:

> When discovered during an extended search for just such a home, it stood dilapidated and weatherbeaten, but showing unmistakable points of worth. To one unaccustomed to Colonial architecture it gave little hint of what restoration would do for it.
>
> It was admirably situated for a quiet summer home, being far removed from the bustle of city life, and showing an attractive landscape view. The old farmhouse stood just back from the road on rising ground, surrounded by a large apple orchard, while in front were two mighty elms that had stood sentinels since the house was built.[59]

Northend describes how the exterior was preserved by replacing the clapboards and painting them with a coat of "Colonial yellow paint" with white trim and green blinds. Woodbine was trained over the front porch, adding much to the "restful appearance." Not forgotten were those special touches, which completed what was viewed almost as a stage set:

> To make the scheme complete: at one side, not too far away, was placed an old well sweep, and beyond an old-fashioned garden was laid out, planted with nodding bluebells and stately hollyhocks, arranged side by side with the fragrant mignonette and heliotrope.[60]

The well sweep is mentioned again in a picture caption: "A great deal of atmosphere was preserved by retaining the old well-sweep in good condition."[61]

Northend describes the furnishings of each room and the feelings and impressions evoked—for example, by the living room, where "the old fireplace bespeaks cheer on cold winter nights. . . . An air of dignified comfort pervades this room, that is most restful."[62] The dining room offers the "impression of hospitality" and "over the fireplace the idea of the Revolutionary period is carried out by the addition of an old flint-lock and powder horn."[63] The den, a room with "well-preserved simplicity," featured a mantel shelf ornamented with powder kegs that did service in the Revolutionary War. The old kitchen "contains interesting relics of Colonial times" and still had its "old time fireplace" and brick oven, now replete with kitchen accessories. Within the room was a collection of earthenware jugs and old American-made bottles, "which are most cleverly and uniquely arranged" on wooden shelves in a side window, allowing light to show their fine coloration.

Mary Northend's article promotes the preservation of early houses by emphasizing both the spiritual benefits and the practicality of a "remodeling in good taste." Her first sentence in the 1912 *House and Garden* article sounds the theme: "It has proved to be a step in the right direction, this trend toward remodelling old-time farmhouses into summer and all-the-year homes." To Northend, the Blaney house and furnishings embodied the spiritual essence of all

Figure 30-31. In restoring The Old Elm, architect George C. Wales left most of the original fabric intact and carefully reproduced what could not be saved.

that is meant by the word *home:* "Surely no home built to-day could radiate such an inviting and home-like spirit as this with its great elms and simple vine-clad clapboards."[64] Northend ends the article with this observation about cost: "It has been urged by many house seekers that it is not economical to remodel an old house. As this one was done for two thousand dollars it proves this idea wrong."[65]

A few years later, an embossed rendition of the Blaney house was featured on the cover of another publication designed to encourage renovation of early houses. In *New Homes Under Old Roofs* (1916), Weston resident Joseph Stowe Seabury promoted "preservation" by publishing "before" and "after" pictures of formerly neglected farmhouses clothed in the dress of modern comfort. To Seabury, the added conveniences made these early houses suitable not only for historians, antiquarians, artists, and poets but also for "captains of industry, those little lords of finance who return each day to their firesides to feel again the close touch of early associations and breathe the lingering breath of far, forgotten days."[66] His book pictures simple structures transformed into large and fashionable country houses often sporting latticed porches and new decorative roof balustrades. The photograph of Blaney's house after restoration was taken by Alfred Wayland Cutting. The serious amateur photographer from nearby Wayland made "many delightful pilgrimages" with Seabury, documenting early houses and capturing the image of the disappearing rural countryside they both loved so passionately.[67]

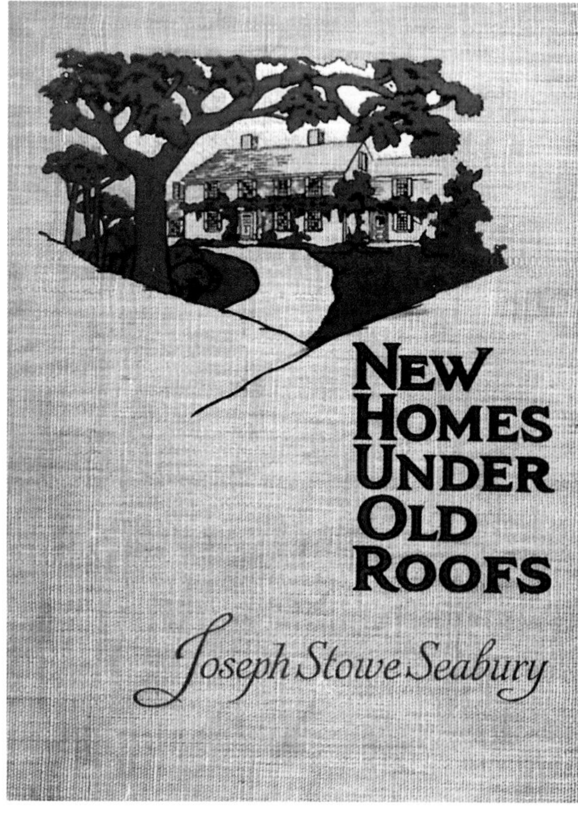

Figure 30-32. The Blaney house was featured on the cover of the 1916 book New Homes Under Old Roofs, *written by old-house enthusiast and Weston resident Joseph Stowe Seabury.*

An article in the 1917 *Boston Sunday Herald* suggests that the Blaney house continued to provide a fashionable example of the old-fashioned. Again, notice the emphasis on the old elm:

> Lovers of the picturesque and antique will be well repaid by a visit to the old-fashioned estate in Weston owned by Dwight Blaney, the artist. Near the house and towering above it is the oldest elm in Massachusetts, which is now under the care of a tree expert, who is trying to preserve the great lower limb. . . . The tree is 220 years old and in good condition.[68]

The article mentions the low ceilings, exposed beams, and other evidence of "ancient" construction that so enamored a generation that saw these as symbols of strength, security, and steadfastness. This article again shows a picture of the well sweep, that special symbol of antimodern self-reliance.

Wallace Nutting: "Bellwether of the Colonial Revival"

It is not surprising that the Blaney house was among those photographed by Wallace Nutting (1861–1941), one of the leading popularizers of the Colonial Revival in the early decades of the 20th century.[69] Ordained as a Congregational minister, Nutting began to photograph outdoor scenes as a hobby in 1897. Seven years later, he retired from the pulpit at age 43 to begin a second career as a photographer, writer, and publisher whose work is known to all lovers of Americana. He started photographing period interiors in 1904, when rain forced him indoors one day. So pleased was he with the results that he began collecting antique furniture and restoring historic houses to serve as backgrounds for his pictures. He branched out into publishing with a series of state guidebooks and books on American antique furniture. He also began manufacturing fine-quality antique reproductions. Both Nutting's famous first book, *Furniture of the Pilgrim Century* (1921), and his 1928 *Furniture Treasury* include photographs of important antique pieces owned by Dwight Blaney and Arthur Wellington.

The Blaney house was featured in two photographs by Nutting taken sometime before December 1914 and now preserved in the collection of SPNEA.[70] One shows a woman in a long dress and bonnet standing at the front door and the second the same woman leaning over the hearth. Vines trained to drape around the front doorway are typical of Nutting's images of an idyllic, back-to-nature, innocent rural life, a common theme of both the Colonial Revival and the early-20th century Arts and Crafts Movement. The hearth was another favorite image, considered the focus of the home and a symbol of warmth, protection, and family unity. Nutting's world has been described as "gentle, warm, happy, eternally serene."[71] He sold hand-colored versions of many of his photographs as works of art intended for middle-class Colonial Revival homes. A 1912 catalog explained his goal:

> These figure subjects were conceived by Mr. Nutting for the sake of preserving the historical charm of the life of our fathers. Thus we present . . . old-fashioned or "colonial" themes showing old-fashioned girls and grandsires at the center of our ancestral life, that is the hearth, and at the hospitable and beautiful front doors, and on the winding stairs and old settles of our ancestors.

Nutting included an etching of the Blaney house in his 1923 edition of *Massachusetts Beautiful.* In the 1935 edition, he added another of his trademark photos of a young woman in colonial garb standing in front of the vine-covered house.[72]

Later History of the Blaney House

Change came slowly to The Old Elm. A single flush toilet was installed after Edith Hill Blaney died in 1930. The caretaker was reported to have said, "We've been here twenty years—what are you putting a bathroom in now for?"[73] The landscape changed. Dwight Blaney planted the pine forest on what is now town conservation land behind the house. One of the two large elm trees in front had to be cut down shortly after the restoration of 1908 and the second was lost in the 1938 hurricane.

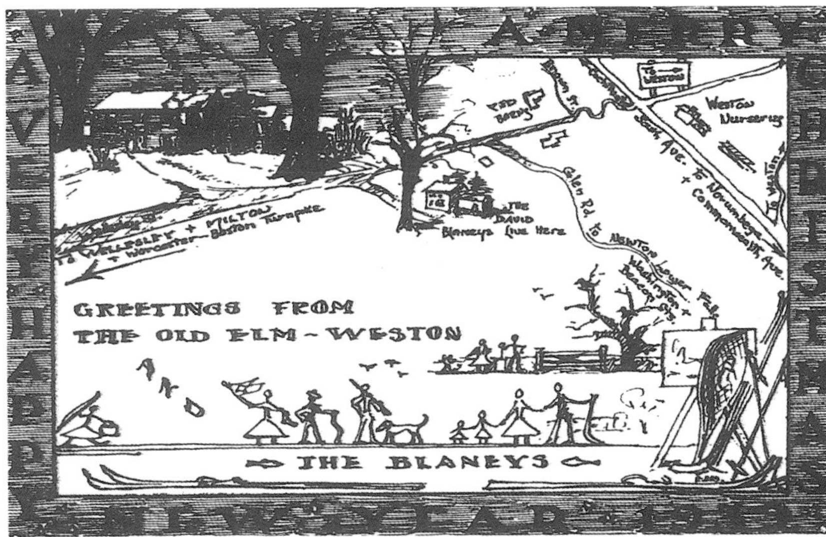

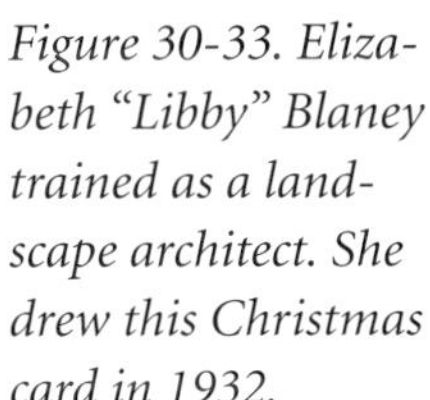

Figure 30-33. Elizabeth "Libby" Blaney trained as a landscape architect. She drew this Christmas card in 1932.

Blaney's youngest daughter, Elizabeth ("Libby"), graduated from Vassar and worked with landscape designer Beatrix Ferrand before attending the Cambridge School of Architecture and Landscape Architecture. Her senior project of 1930 was a complete plan for good development of the farm in Weston.[74] She was later to write that, when the land was divided and sold, her plan was not used and she was not pleased with the results. Libby married George Frank Cram in 1943 and the couple settled in the 1762 General Glover house in Marblehead, which she carefully restored. Her memoirs of life in Weston and Ironbound were privately printed by the family in 1992.

Figure 30-34. Wallace Nutting posed this young woman outside the vine-covered Blaney house. Nutting took these photographs to preserve "the historical charm of the life of our fathers." The "old-fashioned girl" in front of the "hospitable and beautiful front door" was one of his favorite themes. Another of Nutting's pictures of the Blaney house appeared in the 1935 edition of his book Massachusetts Beautiful. *Nutting's world has been described as "gentle, warm, happy, eternally serene." (Photo c. 1909–14)*

When Dwight Blaney died in 1944, he left his antique collection to his four surviving children. After each had taken what he or she wanted, the remainder was sold at a three-day auction. Some of the pieces made their way into major museums including the Boston Museum of Fine Arts, Winterthur, and the M.H. deYoung Memorial Museum in San Francisco.

Dwight's son David was a realtor and longtime member of the Weston Planning Board. He married Marjorie "Midge" Leatherbee in 1929, and for the first 17 years of their marriage they lived across the street from the old farmhouse. After his father's death, David purchased the house at No. 555 Wellesley Street and some 120 acres from the estate. He enjoyed farming more than his father did and raised sheep in Weston.[75] He planted vegetables, and everyone in the family participated in canning and preserving.

When the property was developed, David Blaney was careful to preserve the pastoral setting of the Blaney house, which is surrounded by conservation land. New development on the 120 acres was concentrated at the south end of the property. Radcliffe Road between Beaver Road and Wellesley Street was developed in the late 1950s. In 1966 David Blaney donated 13.6 acres to the town for conservation. He developed Sylvan Lane in the early 1970s and about the same time sold the town an additional 28 acres. The Harrington/Blaney farmhouse was listed on the National Register of Historic Places in 1976.

After David Blaney's death in 1989, his heirs held an auction on the premises to sell the remaining contents. The house itself was sold to John and Ann Sallay, who added a formal 18th-century flower garden. The garden has further enhanced the Colonial "atmosphere" so prized by Blaney, Wales, Wellington, Chandler, Northend, Nutting, and others of that generation who left their mark on Weston, New England, and the nation.

Buildings Associated with the Wellington and Blaney Farms

455 Glen Road (early 20th century). Home of Dudley Ranney, his wife Margaret Wellington Ranney (until her sudden death in 1938 at age 41 of a brain tumor), and their children, Louise, Amy, Virginia, and Margaret ("Margie") from 1928 to 1944. The Colonial Revival house was originally brown-shingled. The property included a gardener's cottage, barn for the riding horses (burned 1999), and log cabin playhouse.

487 Wellesley Street (1911). Gateways Farm caretaker's house, designed by Joseph Everett Chandler as an assemblage of existing outbuildings and new construction. Next door is the Gateways barn, one of the two most important remaining barns in Weston, a monumental structure built in sections from the 18th to the early 20th century.

500 Wellesley Street (Gateways, c. 1760, enlarged c. 1900). Remodeled Colonial farmhouse that became the Wellington family summer house.

555 Wellesley Street (The Old Elm, earliest section c. 1710). Colonial farmhouse restored by architect George Canning Wales for artist Dwight Blaney beginning in 1908.

556 Wellesley Street (1901). Built for Etta Walcott. Sold to the Blaneys in 1909 and later occupied by David and Midge Blaney and their family.

Notes

1. In the National Register nomination "Thomas Pierce House/Wellington Farm Historic District," preservation consultant Candace Jenkins theorizes that the house was built about 1760 and later considerably altered and perhaps even reoriented on the site.
2. MCRD 2716/372. Samuel F. Clarke to Robert Blodgett, 1899. [Note that Samuel F. Clark, of Weston, Yeoman, aged 27, and Louisa M. Brown, aged 23, of Weston, daughter of Marshall and Louisa Brown of Weston, were married in 1847.]
3. *WDFPT,* February 10, 1899.
4. The major 20th-century changes in the footprint of the house are documented by comparing the plan of the "Estate of Robert B. Blodgett, Esq." (November 6, 1899, filed with MCRD on January 7, 1906, as Filed Plan 399) and "Plan of Wellesley Street" 1906, recorded December 10, 1906, as Filed Plan 413 (A of 3). The latter clearly shows the new wing and porches, which were in place when the property was sold to the Wellingtons in December 1907. MCRD 3344/97 (Trustees of the late William Barrett to Evelyn L. Wellington, December 1907); see also Samuel Hudson to William Barrett (3208/138, 1906); Herbert Blodgett to Hudson, 1905.
5. SPNEA "Wellington" file (microfilm) includes typescript "Medford, Past and Present," 275th Anniversary of Medford, 1905.
6. Obituary of Arthur Wellington, *Waltham News-Tribune,* April 14, 1938.
7. Newspaper accounts "A Home Wedding in Wellington, Miss Evelyn J. Lawton Becomes the Bride of Arthur W. Wellington" and "Lawton-Wellington" from collection of Julie Hyde. These articles describe the ceremony, honeymoon, and family relationships.
8. Letter from Natalie Palme, librarian of the Harvard Musical Association, to PWF, September 2, 1997. Wellington also sang for the 25th anniversary of the Friendly Society (*WDFPT,* October 14, 1910).
9. The Trestle Board assisted the Boston Museum of Fine Arts in furnishing one of its 17th-century period rooms.
10. Denenberg, Thomas A., "Pilgrims and Progressives: The Colonial Vision of Joseph Everett Chandler, Restoration Architect" (unpublished manuscript, 1994).
11. 1906 program and 1913 roster, Friendly Society archives.
12. Chandler, Joseph Everett, *The Colonial House* (Robert McBride & Co., New York, 1924), 163.
13. The family still has these drawings, along with Chandler's blueprints from another paneled dining room and photographs of two houses with similar paneling.
14. "Plan of Wellesley St., Weston, as ordered by the County Commissioners, 1910." See also

1910 *TR*.
15. Information from Nina Danforth. The train station is still called Wellington.
16. Wellington file at SPNEA includes correspondence among William Sumner Appleton, Charles Blanchard, and Arthur Wellington regarding the Wellington homestead.
17. Ibid., May 17, 1923, WSA to CB.
18. Ibid.
19. Information in this paragraph from Julie Hyde, granddaughter of Arthur Wellington, and from 1912 town tax records.
20. See *WDFPT*, September 22, 1916.
21. The wedding took place May 15, 1920. See *WDFPT*, April 16 and May 21, 1920.
22. The main house is owned by Nicholas Danforth and the caretaker's house and barn by Julie Danforth Hyde and her husband, Peter, who moved there in 1972. In 1979, Julie Hyde began raising "Gateways" hothouse tomatoes, hydroponically, in a greenhouse on the property.
23. David Blaney, oral history (January 9 and 16, 1983), Weston Public Library, 11.
24. Morris, Anne F., *Memoirs of Elizabeth Hill Cram* (Puritan Press, Hollis, NH,1992), 4.
25. Ibid.
26. Ibid, 27.
27. Fairbrother, Trevor J., with Theodore E. Stebbins Jr., William L. Vance, and Erica E. Hirshler, *The Bostonians: Painters of an Elegant Age, 1870–1930* (Museum of Fine Arts, Boston, 1986). For further information on Blaney as an artist, see also Archives of American Art, Dwight Blaney papers, microfilm reels #4405–07. See also William H. Truettner and Roger B. Stein, *Picturing Old New England: Image and Memory* (New Haven and London: Yale University Press, 1999).
28. In regard to collecting art, Blaney was less conservative than many of his contemporaries. He was one of the first to bring back a Monet to the United States (one of the "haystack" series) and also owned several works by Prendergast.
29. Ibid.
30. Stillinger, Elizabeth, "Dwight Blaney: portrait of a collector," *The Magazine Antiques*, October 1980.
31. Fairbrother, op. cit., plate 15.
32. Ibid., 64.
33. Stillinger, Elizabeth, *The Antiquers* (Alfred A. Knopf, New York, 1980), 107.
34. "Important American Furniture, Silver, Folk Art and Decorative Arts," Christie's, New York, catalogue for sale on Wednesday, June 23, 1993, 96. Includes furniture of Elizabeth Hill Blaney Cram.
35. Stillinger, *The Antiquers*, op. cit. 108.
36. Ibid., 109.
37. Blaney, oral history, op. cit., 3,19.
38. Kent, Henry W., "Dwight Blaney, Member of The Walpole Society, 1910–1944" (Walpole Society *Note Books*, privately printed, 1944), 25.
39. Stillinger, *The Antiquers*, op. cit., 167.
40. Ibid., 44.
41. Kent, op. cit., 28.
42. Morris, op. cit., 17.
43. Kent, op. cit.
44. Ibid., 29.
45. Blaney oral history, op. cit., 3.
46. Ibid., 4.
47. Morris, op. cit., 29.
48. Kent, op. cit., 28–29.
49. Morris, op. cit., 72. See also chapter on Ironbound, 49–81. In recognition of his discovery of a previously unknown species of mollusk, scientists gave it the name *Tonicella blaneyi.*
50. The earliest section includes the front door and two windows to the east. House history courtesy of John Sallay, present owner.
51. MCRD 3345/54 (Osborn Harrington to D. Blaney, December 26, 1907) and 3346/52 (heirs of John W. Harrington to Blaney, January 1, 1908). See also 829/21 (Harrington to Harrington, 1859).
52. Copy of receipt in WHC files.
53. Obituary, "George Wales, Boston Etcher of Old Ships," *Boston Transcript*, March 22, 1940. Wales was descended from a family identified with the clipper-ship era, as was Blaney, whose father had traveled to China on a trading vessel in the early 1850s.
54. In 1912 he was entrusted with the renovation of the Samuel Fowler House in Danversport, Massachusetts, the second acquisition of the newly formed Society for the Preservation of New England Antiquities (SPNEA). (See "The Renovation of the Samuel Fowler House," SPNEA *Bulletin*, vol. III, no. 3, February 1913, Serial No. 8.) In 1917 another friend of Blaney, William Paxton, persuaded Wales to give up architecture to pursue his etching talent. According to the obituary cited above, his prints are owned by the Museum of Fine Arts in Boston, Peabody Museum in Salem, Smithsonian, British Museum, Victoria and Albert Museum, and other prestigious institutions. He was also the author of *Etchings and Lithographs of American Ships.*
55. Wales also lowered the roof of the east ell but did not change the interior rooms. Wales's notes on the restoration state that "the house was restored, not altered nor modernized, except for the East Ell of a later period, which had a high pitch roof, overtopping the main ridge." See typed notes by George Wales, WHC file on 555 Wellesley Street.
56. The 18th-century shed had been used over the years for wood storage, as a carpenter shop, and as a shoe shop for Isaac Harrington, one of Joseph's sons. See typescript "Information about the Weston House," as told to Mrs. Dwight Blaney by Mrs. Shaw (copy, WHC).
57. Northend, Mary H., "A Remodeled House of Good Taste," *House and Garden*, vol. XXII, no. 1, July 1912.
58. Marling, Karal Ann, *George Washington Slept Here: Colonial Revivals and American Culture, 1876–1986* (Harvard University Press, Cambridge, MA, and London, 1988), 167.
59. Northend, op. cit., 11.
60. Ibid.
61. Ibid., 12.
62. Ibid., 13.
63. Ibid.
64. Northend, op. cit., 13.
65. Ibid., 63.
66. Seabury, Joseph Stowe, *New Homes Under Old Roofs* (Frederick A. Stokes Co., New York, 1916), 11.
67. Preface to Seabury, ibid., 8, and "The Old Life Has Silently Passed: Photographs by Alfred Wayland Cutting (1860–1935)," brochure for Wayland Public Library exhibit, December 1989–February 1990.
68. *Boston Sunday Herald*, May 13, 1917, as reprinted in *WDFPT*, May 18, 1917.
69. For additional information, see "The Wallace Nutting Collection: A Gallery Guide, Wadsworth Athenaeum" by William H. Hosley Jr., associate curator of American Decorative Arts (August 1984).
70. SPNEA archives, #3522 (hearth) and #3518 (exterior).
71. Marling, op. cit., 172.
72. Nutting, Wallace, *Massachusetts Beautiful* (Framingham, MA, Old American Co., 1923 edition), 266. Also 1935 edition, 65, 234.
73. Blaney oral history, op. cit.
74. Morris, op. cit., 142.
75. For some years, the sheep were trucked up to Ironbound each spring and returned to Weston in the fall.

Figure C. Selectmen and former selectmen gather at the Josiah Smith Tavern in 1963 to celebrate Weston's 250th Anniversary. Standing, from left: Douglas Mercer, Richard Field, Raymond W. Coburn, William R. Dewey Jr., Charles M. Ganson, J. Robert Ayers, and Edward R. Langenbach. Seated: Stephen H. Tyng, B. Loring Young, and Edward M. Dickson.

APPENDIX

Selectmen, 1900–2000
(For a list of earlier selectmen, see appendix in Lamson's *History of the Town of Weston.*)

Francis Blake, 1890–1910
Nathan S. Fiske, 1882–1884, 1891–1912
Alfred L. Cutting 1900–1925
Benjamin Loring Young, 1910–1923, 1925–1946
Herbert E. Tyler, 1912–1948
Lawrence B. Page, 1923–1926
Brenton H. Dickson Jr., 1926–1943
Raymond W. Coburn, 1943–1950
William R. Dewey Jr., 1946–1959
J. Robert Ayers, 1948–1954
Charles M. Ganson, 1950–1956
Edward M. Dickson, 1954–1969, 1979–1982
Richard Field, 1956–1958
Douglas Mercer, 1958–1961
Edward R. Langenbach, 1959–1962
Leonard H. Dowse, 1961–1964
Stephen H. Tyng, 1962–1964
Florence E. Freeman, 1964–1968
Herman Koester Jr., 1964–1970
George M. Lovejoy Jr., 1968–1971
Thomas W. Underhill, 1969–1972
Peter A. Reiman, 1970–1973
John Paul Sullivan, 1971–1973
Harold Hestnes, 1972–1982, 2001–
Richard A. Nenneman, 1973–1974
L. Whitman Smith, 1973–1979
Joan B. Vernon, 1974–1980
Jean M. Thurston, 1980–1989
Harold B. Willis Jr., 1981–1991
Richard A. Murray, 1982–1993
Joseph W. Mullin, 1989–1998
Ann G. Leibowitz, 1991–1997
Elizabeth D. Nichols, 1993–1999
Ripley E. Hastings, 1997–
Douglas P. Gillespie, 1998–
G. William Helm, 1999–2001

Town Clerks, 1900–2000
(For a list of earlier town clerks, see appendix in Lamson's *History of the Town of Weston.*)

George W. Cutting Jr., 1864–1918
Brenton H. Dickson Jr., 1918–1944
Herman A. Dolbeare, 1944–1946
Francis Blake, 1946–1951
Edward M. Dickson, 1951–1971
Harry B. Jones, 1971–1986
Robert G. Duhaime, 1986–1989, 1990–1992
Helen V. Zolla, 1989–1990
Mary Elizabeth Nolan, 1992–

Lists prepared by Harry B. Jones, town clerk from 1971 to 1986.

WESTON
WON 7 TIED 2
UNBEATEN SPECIAL
WESTON 26 WESTWOOD 0
WESTON 0 BILLERICA 0
WESTON 13 HOPKINTON 0
WESTON 41 MEDFIELD 0
WESTON 39 WAYLAND 6
WESTON 21 ASHLAND 12
WESTON 6 FOXBORO 6
WESTON 25 MILLIS 7
WESTON 27 CAMBRIDGE 0
WESTON HIGH 1945 FOOTBALL DINNER

Figure D.

BIBLIOGRAPHY

Abbreviations

BPL: Boston Public Library
FBC: First Baptist Church
HTW: Lamson's *History of the Town of Weston*
HUA: Harvard University Archives
MHC: Massachusetts Historical Commission
MHS: Massachusetts Historical Society
MCRD: Middlesex County Registry of Deeds (South District), Cambridge
NA–NER: National Archives, New England Region, Waltham
NEHGS: New England Historic & Genealogical Society
NEPA: New England Province Archives, College of the Holy Cross
NHS/JH: Newton Historical Society/Jackson Homestead
Pung: Dickson's *Once Upon a Pung*
RR: Dickson's *Random Recollections*
SPNEA: Society for the Preservation of New England Antiquities
TR: Town of Weston annual reports
WDFPT: *Waltham Daily Free Press Tribune*
WFP: Waltham Free Press
WHC: Weston Historical Commission
WHS: Weston Historical Society
WPL: Weston Public Library
WHSB: *Weston Historical Society Bulletin*

Weston Histories and Frequently Cited Publications

(Other references listed in full in the endnotes)

Bond, Henry, M.D., *Genealogies of the Families and Descendants of the Early Settlers of Watertown, Massachusetts, including Waltham and Weston; to which is Appended The Early History of the Town* (Boston: New England Historic-Genealogical Society, 1860).

Coburn, Philip, *Growing Up in Weston* (Waltham: Copigraph Inc., 1981).

Coburn scrapbooks Nos.1–4, owned by Edward "Ted" Coburn. (These scrapbooks consist largely of newspaper clippings from the late 19th and early 20th centuries, with the date and name of the newspaper cut off.)

Conklin, Edwin P., *Middlesex County and Its People: A History*, vol. I–IV (New York: Lewis Historical Publishing Company Inc., 1927).

Dickson, Brenton H. III, *Once Upon a Pung* (Boston: Thomas Todd Co., 1963).

———. *Random Recollections* (Weston: Nobb Hill Press Inc., 1977).

Dickson, Brenton H. III and Lucas, Homer C., *One Town in the American Revolution* (Weston: Weston Historical Society, 1976).

Donahue, Brian, *Reclaiming the Commons: Community Farms and Forests in a New England Town* (New Haven: Yale University Press, 1999).

The First Parish Calendar, vol. I, nos. 1–9, October 16, 1893, to June 15, 1894; vol. II, nos. 1–8, November 15, 1894, to July 15, 1895; vol. III, nos. 1–8, November 15, 1895, to July 1, 1896 (WPL).

First Parish Church, *An Account of the Celebration by the First Parish of Weston, Massachusetts, of Its Two Hundredth Anniversary . . . 1698–1898* (Weston: The First Parish of Weston, 1900).

Fleming, Nancy N., *Weston Town Common, A History* (privately printed by the Weston Garden Club on the Occasion of Its 50th Anniversary, 1991).

Gambrill, Howard Jr. and Hambrick-Stowe, Charles, *The Tavern and the Tory: The Story of the Golden Ball Tavern* (Weston: The Golden Ball Tavern Trust, 1977).

Hart, Albert B., ed. *Commonwealth History of Massachusetts* (New York: The States History Co., 1927–28).

Harvard University Archives, reunion reports and alumni records.

Hillcrest Farm/Gardens Books, 1911–1941 (annual "Green Books" published by Marian Roby Case)

1911–1917	The [Second to Eighth] Summer at Hillcrest Farm, Weston, by the Boys for the Boys
1918–1919	. . . by the Farmers
1920–1923	Hillcrest Gardens, Weston, Mass., The [___] Summer, by the Gardeners
1924–1937	. . . by Marian Roby Case, F.R.H.S. and the Gardeners.
1938	. . . by Marian Roby Case, F.R.H.S. and the Hillcrest Boys
1939–1941	. . . by Marian Roby Case, F.R.H.S., Jack A. Williams and the Hillcrest Boys

Jones, Elmer E., *Walks on Weston Conservation Land, A Guide* (Weston: Weston Forest and Trail Press, 1999).

Kendal, Samuel, *A Sermon . . . on the Termination of a Century* (Cambridge: Hilliard and Metcalf, 1813).

Lamson, Col. Daniel S., *History of the Town of Weston, Massachusetts, 1630–1890* (Boston: George H. Ellis Co., 1913).

———. "Weston," in Hurd, D. Hamilton, ed., *History of Middlesex County, Massachusetts* (Philadelphia: J.W. Lewis & Co., 1890). vol. I, chapters 23, 24.

Lamson, Col. Daniel S. and McClintock, John N.,

"Weston," *The Massachusetts Magazine*, July 1909, vol. II, no. 3, 129.

Marsh, Lee, *Weston* (Charleston, SC: Arcadia Publishing, 1999).

Massachusetts State Census Records, located at Massachusetts State Library.

National Cyclopaedia of American Biography (New York: James T. White & Co., 1926, and subsequent volumes).

Peirce, Mary Frances, ed., *Town of Weston, The Tax Lists, 1757–1827* (Boston: Alfred Mudge & Son, 1897).

———. *Town of Weston, Births, Deaths and Marriages, 1707–1850, Gravestones 1703–1900, Church Records 1709–1825* (Boston: McIndoe Bros., 1901).

———. *Town of Weston, Records of the First Precinct, 1746–1754, and of the Town, 1754–1803* (Boston: Alfred Mudge & Son, 1893).

———. *Town of Weston, Records of the Town Clerk, 1804–1826* (Boston: Alfred Mudge & Son, 1894).

Ripley, Emma F., *Weston: A Puritan Town* (Weston: The Benevolent-Alliance of First Parish Church, 1961).

Town of Weston Annual Reports:

(*Note*: Listed below are reports available in the Town Clerk's office, Weston.)

Report of the School Committee of the Town of Weston for the year ending March 31 (1859, 1860)

Reports of the School Committee and the Town Treasurer of Weston . . . for the year ending March 1861

Reports of the Town of Weston for the year ending March 31 (1862–69)

Reports of the Town of Weston for the year ending March 15 (1870–76)

Reports of the Town of Weston for the year ending March 1 (1877–82)

Reports of the Town of Weston for the year ending February 28 (1883–92)

Town Records [1893–_____] and Reports of the Town Officers of Weston, Massachusetts for the year ending February 28 [1894–____] (1893–1913)

Town Records 1914 and Reports of the Town Officers of Weston, Massachusetts for the ten months ending December 31, 1914 (1914–15)

Town Records 1916 and Reports of the Town Officers of Weston, Massachusetts for the year ending December 31, 1916 (1916–present). Title on the cover itself varies.

Town of Weston, Birth, Death, and Marriage Records (Town Clerk's office).

Town of Weston, Assessor's Tax Records and Archival Records (Weston Town Hall vault).

United States Census Records, National Archives and Records Administration, Waltham, MA (microfilm).

Weston Historical Society, *The Weston Historical Society Bulletin* (1964–present).

Withey, Henry and Elsie, *Biographical Dictionary of American Architects (Deceased)* (Los Angeles, 1970).

Directories (listed by date)

(*Note*: Complete collection of Weston directories available at the State Library Special Collections Department at the Massachusetts Statehouse.)

Resident and Business Directory of Wayland and Weston for 1887 (Needham: Chronicle Steam Press, 1887).

Directory of Wayland, Weston & Lincoln, 1893 (Boston: Press of Brown Bros. & Co., 1893).

The Weston, Wayland, Cochituate and Lincoln, Mass., Directory, 1901–1902 (Boston: W.E. Shaw). Same title for 1904–05.

Waltham Suburban Directory, Weston, Wayland, Cochituate and Lincoln, Mass., 1911–1912 (Salem: The Henry M. Meek Publishing Co.). Same title and publisher for 1915–16, 1921–22, 1926.

Polk's Suburban (Massachusetts) Directory, 1931–32, including Weston, Wayland and Lincoln (Salem: R.L. Polk & Co.).

Weston, Wayland and Lincoln, Massachusetts, Directory, 1936 (North Hampton, NH: Crosby Publishing Co.). Same title and publisher in 1939, 1941, 1946, 1949.

Maps

Nylander, Richard, "Estates Adjoining the Great Country Road," 1775 and 1783 (WHC, 1974).

Kingsbury, Jonathan Jr., Map of Weston from surveys made in 1785, 1794, 1795, and 1796 (generally referred to as the 1794 map). This map was copied in the office of Ernest W. Bowditch in 1891 and distributed with the town report of that year.

Tower, Augustus, "Plan of the Town of Weston," 1830.

Craigie, "Map of Boston & Vicinity," 1852.

Walling, Henry F., "Map of Middlesex County, Mass." (Boston: Smith and Bumstead, 1857).

Lake, D.J., "Map of the City of Boston and Environs, from actual surveys drawn by D.J. Lake" (New York: Baker and Tilden, 1866).

County Atlas of Middlesex County, Massachusetts (Newton: J.B. Beers & Co., 1875).

Atlas of Middlesex County, Massachusetts (Boston: Geo. H. Walker & Co.) 1889, vol. I, 184–85.

McClintock, John, C.E. Map of Weston, 1903; revised and corrected to 1907 by Geo. Cutting, C.E. (shows property lines only).

Atlas of Middlesex County (Boston: Geo. H. Walker & Co., 1908), vol. 3, plates 12–13.

Eastern Middlesex County (Newton: Henry Lord & Son, 1957).

Town of Weston Assessor's Maps

Newspapers

Town Crier, Wayland-Weston Edition, October 1951 to present.

The Town Reporter, published approximately monthly by the Town of Weston. WPL has issues from 1948 to 1956 (not a complete collection).

Waltham Daily Free Press, 1888–97 (*note*: The Weston Public Library owns four volumes of newspaper clippings from various Waltham papers, dating between October 1900 and December 1920).

Waltham Daily Free Press Tribune, 1898–1924

Waltham Evening News, 1895–1914

Waltham Free Press, 1863–1900

Waltham News Tribune

Weston News Review. WPL has one issue from 1933; one from 1937; January to December 1939, 1940, and 1941; January to July 1942; September to December 1950; January to March 1951.

ILLUSTRATION CREDITS

Figure A: Courtesy of the Society for the Preservation of New England Antiquities; photo by Alfred Wayland Cutting

Figure B: Courtesy of the Weston Historical Commission; photo by Eric Wood

Figure B-1: Courtesy of the Weston Historical Society

Chapter 1

1-1. Courtesy of the Society for the Preservation of New England Antiquities; photo taken before 1916 by the Halliday Historic Photograph Co., Boston

1-2. From *Genealogies of the Families and Descendants of the Early Settlers of Watertown, Massachusetts,* by Henry Bond

1-3. From *Waltham as a Precinct of Watertown and as a Town: 1630–1884,* by Edward Sanderson (Waltham: Waltham Historical Society Inc., 1936)

1-4. Photo by Sarah B. Gilman

1-5. From *The Old Post Road,* by Stephen Jenkins

1-6. Courtesy of the Weston Historical Society

1-7. Courtesy of the Weston Historical Commission

1-8. Courtesy of John Sallay

1-9. Courtesy of the Society for the Preservation of New England Antiquities; photo by the Halliday Historic Photograph Co., Boston

1-10. Courtesy of the Society for the Preservation of New England Antiquities; photo taken before 1916 by the Halliday Historic Photograph Co., Boston. Quote from *The Tavern and the Tory,* 6

1-11. Courtesy of the Weston Historical Commission; map by Richard H. Nylander, 1974

1-12. From *The Tavern and the Tory,* by Howard Gambrill Jr. and Charles Hambrick-Stowe, 21

1-13. From "The Boston Tea Party," *New England Magazine,* vol. 8, 1893, 420. Courtesy of the Trustees of the Boston Public Library

1-14. Photo by Sarah B. Gilman

1-15. From *Town of Weston: The Tax Lists, 1757–1827* (insert)

1-16. From *An Account of the Celebration by the First Parish of Weston, Massachusetts of Its Two Hundredth Anniversary, 1698–1898*

1-17. Courtesy of The Society for the Preservation of New England Antiquities

1-18. Town of Weston archives, town vault

1-19. Courtesy of the Weston Historical Commission; from a slide by William F. Dewey Jr.

1-20. From *The History of Middlesex County,* D. Hamilton Hurd, ed., vol. I, ch. 2.

1-21. Courtesy of the Weston Historical Society

Chapter 2

2-1. Courtesy of the Weston Historical Society

2-2. Courtesy of the Weston Historical Commission (the commission has the original colored map)

2-3. From the collection of H. Bentley Crouch

2-4 and 2-5. Courtesy of the Weston Historical Society

2-6. Courtesy of the Weston Historical Society

2-7. From *Weston Historical Society Bulletin,* January 1980

2-8. Courtesy of the Weston Historical Society

2-9. Courtesy of Harold Coburn Jr.

2-10. Compiled from Palfrey, John G., *Of the Condition and Products of Certain Branches of Industry in Massachusetts for the Year Ending April 1, 1845* (Boston, 1846), and DeWitt, Francis, *Statistical Information Relating to Certain Branches of Industry in Massachusetts for the Year ending June 1, 1855* (Boston, 1856)

2-11. Courtesy of the Weston Historical Society

2-12. Courtesy of Lucy D. Boyd

2-13 to 2-16. Photos by Pamela W. Fox

Chapter 3

3-1. Courtesy of James Fraser

3-2. Courtesy of the Weston Historical Commission

3-3. Courtesy of Guy Dillaway

3-4. From *Weston Historical Society Bulletin,* October 1978 (original broadside at the Massachusetts Historical Society)

3-5. Photo by Sarah B. Gilman

3-6. Courtesy of the Coburn family

3-7. From the 1875 *Middlesex County Atlas*

3-8 to 3-10. Courtesy of the Weston Historical Society

3-11. Middlesex Registry of Deeds, South District, Plan Book 148, Plan 29; redrawn by Mary Lord

3-12. Photo by Pamela W. Fox

3-13. Courtesy of David Kingsbury

3-14. From the collection of H. Bentley Crouch

3-15. Courtesy of A. Richard Hersum

3-16. From *The Central Mass.,* published by the Boston and Maine Railroad Historical Society. Map in the collection of the Railway and Locomotive Historical Society

3-17. Courtesy of George Bates

3-18. From *Wayland and Weston Directory, 1887*

3-19. Courtesy of David Kingsbury

3-20. From Warner, Oliver, *Statistical Information Relating to Certain Branches of Industry in Massachusetts* (Boston, 1866); Wright, Carroll, *The Census of Massachusetts, 1875* (Boston, 1876); and Wright, Carroll, *The Census of Massachusetts, 1885* (Boston, 1887)

3-21. Advertisement from *Wayland and Weston Directory, 1887;* photo courtesy of the Weston Historical Society
3-22 and 3-23. Photos by Pamela W. Fox
3-24. Conjectural sketch by Thomas M. Paine of the appearance of the C.J. Paine house between 1870 and 1882
3-25. Newspaper cartoon by H. Popp, courtesy of Thomas M. Paine
3-26. From *1889 Middlesex County Atlas*
3-27. Courtesy of First Baptist Church
3-28 and 3-29. Courtesy of the Weston Historical Society
3-30. Friendly Society Archives, courtesy of Guy Dillaway
3-31. Courtesy of the Cambridge Historical Commission

Chapter 4
4-1. Courtesy of the Weston Historical Society
4-2. From the *Boston Herald*, October 18, 1897
4-3. Courtesy of the Weston Historical Society
4-4. From D. Hamilton Hurd, ed., *History of Middlesex County,* vol. I, ch. 34
4-5. Courtesy of Fred Campbell
4-6. From the Wellington family collection; photo by Evelyn Wellington
4-7. Courtesy of the Weston Historical Commission, B. Loring Young family scrapbook
4-8. Courtesy of Fred Campbell
4-9 and 4-10. Courtesy of the Wellesley Historical Society
4-11 and 4-12. Courtesy of the Society for the Preservation of New England Antiquities; photos by Lemont of Waltham, Massachusetts
4-13 and 4-14. Courtesy of Jack Martin; photos by A.W. and G.E. Howes
4-15. Courtesy of Nelson McNutt and Mildred Balanus
4-16. From the program for "Entertainment of the Weston Boys' Club," courtesy of Eloise Kenney
4-17. From Marian Case's annual reports on summers at Hillcrest (the "Green Books"), photo dated after 1915
4-18. Courtesy of Lucy D. Boyd
4-19. From *Directory of Wayland, Weston and Lincoln, 1893*
4-20 and 4-21. Courtesy of Fred Campbell
4-22. Courtesy of the Henderson House Conference Center, Northeastern University
4-23. Courtesy of the Weston Historical Society
4-24. Courtesy of Susan Graves Teare
4-25. Courtesy of First Baptist Church
4-26. Reproduced from *The History of Methodism in Weston,* Weston United Methodist Church, 1794–1994
4-27. Courtesy of the Weston Historical Society
4-28. Courtesy of the Weston Historical Society. Back row left to right: David Lane, ___, Mrs. Justin Gale, Mr. Gale, and Mr. Abercrombie. Middle row: Harrison Hall, Arthur L. Coburn, ___, Lillian Flitcroft, and Alexander Jenney. Seated: Mrs. A.L. Coburn, Miss Tucker, Henry Pearson, Mrs. Roland Rand, and Alice Flitcroft. On the floor: Charles Scott
4-29 and 4-30. Courtesy of the Weston Historical Society
4-31. Friendly Society archives, courtesy of Guy Dillaway
4-32. Courtesy of the Metropolitan District Commission Archives.

Chapter 5
5-1 and 5-2. Courtesy of the Weston Historical Society
5-3. From the program for "Sweethearts," April 1925, Friendly Society Archives, courtesy of Guy Dillaway
5-4. Courtesy of A. Richard Hersum
5-5. From *Boston American,* Sunday, February 21, 1915
5-6. Courtesy of Lucy D. Boyd
5-7. From the collection of H. Bentley Crouch
5-8. Courtesy of Eloise Kenney
5-9. From the collection of H. Bentley Crouch
5-10. Portrait hangs in Case House
5-11 and 5-12. Courtesy of the Weston Historical Society
5-13. Courtesy of the Weston Historical Society. Front row, left to right: Joe Russell, Arthur and Robert Moore, Boylston Nichols, Julia Paine, Eleanor Russell, Elizabeth Nichols, and Emily Whitney. Middle row: Mary Humphrey, Dorothy Thorndike, Harry and Louise Patterson, Rosamond Bennett, Rose Thorndike, Priscilla Gale, Irene Henderson, Mary Winsor, Gerald Henderson, Sandy Winsor, and Jack Patterson. Back row: Miss Damon, Miss Garrett, Miss Ware, Barbara Bennett, Ruth Batchelder, Nannie Whitney, Hayden and Helma (sic) Henderson, and Miss Bridges
5-14. From the collection of H. Bentley Crouch. Top row: Howard Richardson, Arthur Vittum, Herbert Lewis, Albert Brown, Jack Banford, and Fred Tucker. Second row: Nate Fiske, Everett Vittum, Roland Rand, Frank Gowell, George Stevens, John Guthrie, Harry Harding, Will Riley, Tom Coburn, and A.L.Coburn, with driver Bill Quinn
5-15. From the collection of H. Bentley Crouch
5-16 and 5-17. From the collection of H. Bentley Crouch
5-18 to 5-21 Courtesy of the Weston Historical Society
5-22. Courtesy of the Weston Historical Commission
5-23 and 5-24. From U.S. Department of Agriculture *Farmers' Bulletin* #1441, 1923
5-25. Courtesy of Weston Town Hall (town vault)
5-26. From a 1908–09 Weston Boys Club program, courtesy of Eloise Kenney
5-27. From "Souvenir of the Charles River," brochure at the Jackson Homestead, Newton, Massachusetts
5-28 and 5-29. Courtesy of the Weston Historical Society

Chapter 6
6-1. Courtesy of Nelson McNutt and Mildred Balunas
6-2 and 6-3. From the collection of H. Bentley Crouch
6-4. Courtesy of the Jackson Homestead, Newton, Massachusetts
6-5. From *Weston Historical Society Bulletin,* January 1979, 6 (original at the Waltham Historical Society in *Country Rides by Trolley*)
6-6. From *Directory of Wayland, Weston and Lincoln, 1893*
6-7. Courtesy of Weston Historical Society
6-8. Courtesy of the Massachusetts Historical Society
6-9. Courtesy of Fred Campbell
6-10. Courtesy of Lucy D. Boyd
6-11. Courtesy of the Weston Historical Society
6-12. Courtesy of Eloise Kenney
6-13. Courtesy of the Weston Historical Society
6-14. Courtesy of the Massachusetts Historical Society

6-15. Courtesy of the Weston Historical Society
6-16. Courtesy of the Massachusetts Archives, Metropolitan District Commission (MDC) collection, taken August 17, 1904
6-17. Courtesy of the Weston Historical Society
6-18. Courtesy of the Jackson Homestead, Newton, Massachusetts
6-19. Courtesy of the Weston Historical Commission, B. Loring Young family scrapbook
6-20. Courtesy of Emily Althausen
6-21. Courtesy of Nelson McNutt and Mildred Balunas
6-22. Courtesy of Emily Althausen
6-23. Courtesy of Thomas M. Paine
6-24. From *Weston Historical Society Bulletin,* March 1977
6-25. Courtesy of the Society for the Preservation of New England Antiquities
6-26. Courtesy of the Weston Historical Society, quotes from *WDFPT,* September 4, 1914
6-27. Courtesy of the Weston Historical Society
6-28. Courtesy of the Clark family

Chapter 7
7-1. Courtesy of the Weston Historical Society
7-2. Frontispiece from Lamson's *History of the Town of Weston, 1630–1890*
7-3 to 7-5. Courtesy of the Weston Historical Society
7-6. Courtesy of Eloise Kenney
7-7. Courtesy of the Society for the Preservation of New England Antiquities
7-8. Courtesy of the Massachusetts Historical Society
7-9. Courtesy of the Weston Historical Society, a gift of Miss Anna Hall (painting now hangs in the Weston Public Library)
7-10. Courtesy of the Weston Historical Society; see also *WDFPT* July 7, 1911
7-11 and 12. From *New Houses Under Old Roofs* by Joseph S. Seabury (copy at Weston Public Library)
7-13. Courtesy of The Society for the Preservation of New England Antiquities; photo by the Halliday Historic Photograph Co., Boston
7-14. Courtesy of the Weston Historical Society
7-15. Courtesy of John Sallay
7-16 to 7-27. Courtesy of the Weston Historical Society

Chapter 8
8-1. Courtesy of Eloise Kenney, photo by Webster of Waltham
8-2 and 8-3. Courtesy of the Weston Historical Society
8-4. Photo by Sarah B. Gilman
8-5. Portrait by Gertrude Fiske (hangs in Weston Town Hall)
8-6. Courtesy of the Weston Fire Department
8-7. Portrait by Gertrude Briggs (hangs in Josiah Smith Tavern); photo courtesy of Thomas Van Nuys
8-8. Courtesy of the Weston Historical Commission
8-9. Courtesy of the Society for the Preservation of New England Antiquities; photo by Arthur C. Haskell
8-10. Courtesy of the Weston Historical Society
8-11. Courtesy of the Weston Historical Society. Back row: Fred Cutler. Second row: __ Beebe, Alfred Edwards, Harold Donovan, Charles Patriquin, ____, William LeClair, and Estelle Herold. Third row: Kenneth Wilson, John Martin, Diane Sullivan, Kenneth King, Peter Carpenter, George Wheeler, and Sally Foster. Fourth row: Sandy Doyle, Franklin Johnson, Halcott Grant, Wilbur Noyes, ___ Day, James Page, Ralph__, and Lombard Sargent. Fifth (bottom) row: Catherine __, Clara Ferranti, Lorraine Comeau, Charlotte Bohlier, June Wales, Alice Shaw, Louise Benotti, and ___ D'Intinosanto.
8-12. Courtesy of the Weston Historical Society
8-13. Courtesy of the Weston Historical Society. Standing, first and last girls: Helen Eldred and Marjorie Richardson. Seated: Luis Orozco, Charles Cole, Peter Laban, Rodney Cameron, Richard Bassett, Pearson Ripley, John Chisholm, John Lingley, Arthur Jones, Frank Chaplin, and Winford Schofield.
8-14. Courtesy of Emanuel Benotti
8-15. Courtesy of the Weston Historical Society
8-16. From the 1927 town report
8-17. From the 1924 town report
8-18 and 8-19. Courtesy of A. Richard Hersum
8-20. From the collection of H. Bentley Crouch
8-21. Photo by H. Bentley Crouch
8-22. Courtesy of Fred Perkins
8-23 to 8-25. Courtesy of the Weston Historical Society
8-26. Courtesy of Jean Cahill Tierney and Jane Cahill Compton
8-27. Courtesy of the Weston Historical Commission, from a slide by William Dewey Jr.
8-28. Courtesy of Stanley French Jr.
8-29. Courtesy of Eloise Kenney
8-30. Photo by Pamela W. Fox
8-31. Courtesy of Mary Field Parker
8-32. Courtesy of the Massachusetts Archives, MDC photos (part of the 1938–40 series taken of the Hultman Aqueduct and Norumbega Reservoir)
8-33. From the Wellington family collection
8-34. Courtesy of Thomas M. Paine
8-35. Courtesy of the Weston Historical Society
8-36. Courtesy of B.L. Ogilvie & Sons
8-37. Courtesy of Mrs. Winsor Gale
8-38. Courtesy of Emanuel Benotti
8-39 and 8-40. Courtesy of the Weston Historical Society
8-41. Courtesy of the Weston Historical Society, photograph by Fairfield (for descriptions of the play, see *WDFPT,* 3/7/1919, 3/21/1919; also 11/29/1918)
8-42 and 8-43. Friendly Society archives, courtesy of Guy Dillaway
8-44. Courtesy of the Weston Historical Society
8-45. Courtesy of the Weston Historical Commission, photo by Victor Harnish
8-46. From *Weston Historical Society Bulletin,* October 1982. See also Hillcrest "Green Book" of 1938, 75.
8-47. Courtesy of B.L. Ogilvie & Sons
8-48. Courtesy of the Weston Public Library (E.B. Sears collection)
8-49. Courtesy of Weston Town Hall (town vault)
8-50 to 8-52. Courtesy of Robert and Cynthia Mosher
8-53. Courtesy of the Weston Historical Society
8-54. Girl Scout archives, courtesy of Biz Paynter
8-55. Photo by Sarah B. Gilman

Chapter 9

9-1 and 9-2. Courtesy of the Weston Historical Society
9-3. From *The Town Crier,* June 1974
9-4. Photo by Sarah B. Gilman
9-5. From *The Town Reporter,* July 1950, courtesy of the Weston Public Library
9-6. From the collection of H. Bentley Crouch
9-7. Courtesy of the Weston Public Library
9-8. Courtesy of the Weston Public Library, from *Town Crier,* April 27, 1978
9-9. Courtesy of the Weston Public Library
9-10. Courtesy of the Weston Historical Society
9-11. From *The Town Reporter,* 1952, courtesy of the Weston Public Library
9-12. Courtesy of the Weston Public Library
9-13. Courtesy of Robert and Cynthia Mosher, from Margaret Mosher's scrapbook
9-14. Courtesy of the Weston Public Library
9-15 and 9-16. Courtesy of the Weston Historical Society
9-17. Courtesy of the Weston Public Library
9-18 to 9-22. Courtesy of the Weston Historical Society
9-23. Courtesy of the Weston Historical Society; photo by Muldoon Studio, Waltham
9-24 to 9-26. Courtesy of the Weston Historical Society
9-27. From the collection of H. Bentley Crouch
9-28 and 9-29. Photos by Pamela W. Fox
9-30. Photo by Sarah B. Gilman
9-31. Photo by Pamela W. Fox
9-32. From the 1945 town report
9-33. 1955 town report insert.
9-34. Courtesy of the Weston Historical Society
9-35. Courtesy of the Weston Public Library; *Town Crier* photo
9-36. Courtesy of Lelia Orrell Elliston
9-37. Map by Hugo Uyterhoeven, February 2001, redrawn by Mary Lord
9-38. Courtesy of Hugo Uyterhoeven
9-39. Courtesy of Mrs. Kenneth (Polly) Germeshausen
9-40. Courtesy of the Weston Historical Society; see *Town Crier,* June 16, 1988
9-41 to 9-44. Courtesy of the Weston Historical Society
9-45 and 9-46. Courtesy of the Weston Public Library; *Town Crier* photos
9-47. Courtesy of the Weston Public Library, from the *Town Crier,* July 6, 1967. Front row: Tom Schofield, Brian Shuman, Mike Soper, and Dennis Kerwin. Kneeling: Steve Bright, Hadrian Mercer, Peter Grenader, and Don Campbell. Standing: Jack Crane, Vince Nishino, Steve Shaw, Doug Doane, and Wally Row.
9-48. From the collection of H. Bentley Crouch
9-49. Courtesy of the Waltham Public Library
9-50 and 9-51. Courtesy of the Weston Historical Society
9-52. From the *Boston Globe,* February 1978
9-53. Courtesy of the Weston Historical Society
9-54. Photo by Sarah B. Gilman
9-55. Photo by Pamela W. Fox
9-56. Courtesy of the Weston Historical Society
9-57. Friendly Society archives, courtesy of Guy Dillaway
9-58. Courtesy of the Weston Historical Society
9-59. Courtesy of the Weston Historical Society
9-60 and 9-61. Courtesy of the Weston Public Library
9-62. Courtesy of Weston Public Library; *Town Crier* photo
9-63. Courtesy of B.L. Ogilvie & Sons
9-64. Courtesy of the Weston Historical Society
9-65. Courtesy of the Weston Public Library
9-66. Courtesy of the Weston Public Library; *Town Crier* photo
9-67. Scout House archives, courtesy of Biz Paynter
9-68. Courtesy of the Weston Historical Society
9-69. From Margaret Mosher's scrapbook, newspaper clipping dated June 4, 1964
9-70. Courtesy of the Society for the Preservation of New England Antiquities; photo by J. David Bohl
9-71. From the collection of H. Bentley Crouch
9-72. Courtesy of the Weston Historical Society
9-73. Courtesy of John M. Gourgas
9-74. Courtesy of *Weston Historical Society Bulletin,* May 1977
9-75. Courtesy of the Weston Historical Commission; photo by Herb Randle
9-76. Courtesy of the Weston Public Library; *Town Crier* photo
9-77 and 9-78. Courtesy of the Weston Historical Society

Afterword

A-1 to A-3. Photos by Pamela W. Fox
A-4. Sketch by Ann Beha Associates Inc.

Chapter 10

10-1. Courtesy of the Weston Historical Society; photo by A.W. and G.E. Howes, 1898
10-2. Courtesy of Lucy D. Boyd
10-3. Lamson's *History of the Town of Weston,* opposite page 111
10-4. Courtesy of the Weston Historical Commission. (The bust was located in the Town Clerk's office at Weston Town Hall until early 2001, when it was moved to the historical commission office because of the renovation. Quote from the 1894 town report, 117)
10-5. Lamson's *History of the Town of Weston,* opposite page 143
10-6. From Lamson's *History of the Town of Weston,* opposite page 95
10-7. From *Weston Historical Society Bulletin,* July 1990
10-8. Courtesy of the Weston Historical Society
10-9. From the Coburn scrapbooks, undated
10-10. From *Weston Historical Society Bulletin,* May 1985
10-11. Middlesex Registry of Deeds, Plan Book 67, Plan 51 (recorded May 2, 1891)
10-12. Courtesy of Lucy D. Boyd
10-13 to 10-20. Courtesy of the Weston Historical Society
10-21. From the collection of H. Bentley Crouch
10-22. Courtesy of Betty Rafuse
10-23 to 10-25. Courtesy of the Weston Historical Society
10-26. From Van Pelt, *The Hook Opus List, 1829–1916, in Facsimile*
10-27. Courtesy of the Weston Historical Society
10-28. From a *Boston Herald* article, July 13, 1890
10-29. Courtesy of Lucy D. Boyd
10-30. Courtesy of Elsie Cooke and the Weston Market

10-31. From the *Boston Herald,* July 13, 1890
10-32. Courtesy of the Weston Historical Society
10-33. From the collection of H. Bentley Crouch
10-34. Courtesy of Betty Rafuse
10-35. Courtesy of the Weston Historical Society
10-36. Courtesy of Lucy D. Boyd
10-37 to 10-41. Courtesy of the Weston Historical Society
10-42. Courtesy of Carl Daggett Smith and Florence Coburn Smith
10-43. Courtesy of Betty Rafuse
10-44. Courtesy of Lucy D. Boyd
10-45. Courtesy of the Weston Historical Society
10-46. From the collection of H. Bentley Crouch, photo by A.W. and G.E. Howes, 1898
10-47. Courtesy of the Weston Historical Society
10-48. Courtesy of the Weston Historical Commission
10-49. Photo by Pamela W. Fox
10-50. Courtesy of the Weston Historical Commission
10-51 and 10-52. Courtesy of the Weston Historical Society
10-53. Courtesy of A. Richard Hersum, photo by A.W. and G.E. Howes, 1898
10-54. Courtesy of the Society for the Preservation of New England Antiquities
10-55. Courtesy of Elsie Cooke and the Weston Market
19-56. Courtesy of Elsie Cooke
10-57. Courtesy of the Weston Historical Society
10-58 and 59. Courtesy of Elsie Cooke and the Weston Market
10-60. From Weston High School yearbook, 1961
10-61. Courtesy of Florence Coburn Smith
10-62. Courtesy of the Weston Historical Commission
10-63. Courtesy of Harold Coburn Jr.; photo by A.W. and G.E. Howes, 1898
10-64. Courtesy of Harold Coburn Jr.
10-65. Courtesy of Florence Coburn Smith
10-66. From the collection of H. Bentley Crouch
10-67 to 10-69. Courtesy of Jean Cahill Tierney and Jane Cahill Compton
10-70. From Weston High School yearbook, 1955
10-71. Courtesy of the Boston Public Library, Fine Arts Department
10-72 and 10-73. From *Individuals and Community: The Cambridge School: The First Hundred Years,* by George St. John Jr.
10-74 and 10-75. Courtesy of Arthur and Inge Uhlir; also courtesy of Dan Fogel, who designed the brochure
10-76. From the 1908 *Atlas of Middlesex County*

Chapter 11

11-1. Courtesy of the Weston Historical Society, photo by W.A. Webster of Waltham
11-2 to 11-4. Courtesy of the Weston Historical Society
11-5. Courtesy of Edward "Ted" Coburn
11-6. Courtesy of the Society for the Preservation of New England Antiquities
11-7. Courtesy of the Coburn family
11-8. Courtesy of Edward "Ted" Coburn, quote from *First Parish Calendar,* November 15, 1893;
11-9. *Town Crier* photo, August 8, 1968, Margaret Mosher scrapbook.
11-10. Courtesy of Harold Coburn Jr.
11-11. Courtesy of the Weston Historical Society
11-12. Courtesy of Thomas M. Paine
11-13. From *Weston Historical Society Bulletin,* May 1981, redrawn by Mary Lord
11-14. Courtesy of the Weston Historical Society
11-15. Courtesy of Edward "Ted" Coburn

Chapter 12

12-1. Courtesy of Harry Jones
12-2 to 12-4. Courtesy of Harry Jones; photo by A.W. and G.E. Howes, 1898
12-5 and 12-6. Courtesy of Carl D. Smith
12-7. Courtesy of the Weston Historical Commission; from a slide by William R. Dewey Jr.
12-8. Courtesy of Carl D. Smith
12-9. Courtesy of the Weston Historical Commission
12-10. Painting by Gertrude Fiske, courtesy of the Weston Historical Society
12-11. From Lamson's *History of the Town of Weston,* opposite page 175
12-12. From the *1908 Middlesex County Atlas*
12-13. Courtesy of the Weston Historical Society
12-14 and 12-15. Courtesy of Lee Fernandez
12-16. Courtesy of the Weston Historical Society (newspaper clipping)
12-17. From Lamson's *History of the Town of Weston,* opposite page 127
12-18. Courtesy of the Weston Historical Society
12-19. Courtesy of the Weston Historical Commission
12-20 to 12-29. Courtesy of the New England Jesuit Province Archives, College of the Holy Cross
12-30. From the *Boston Sunday Globe,* April 25, 1965
12-31 and 12-32. Courtesy of Joseph Sheehan Jr.
12-33 and 12-34. Courtesy of Raymond Washburn
12-35. Courtesy of the Weston Historical Society
12-36 and 12-37. Courtesy of Raymond Washburn
12-38. From Middlesex Country Registry of Deeds, Plan Book 154, Plan 34; quote from the *Waltham Daily Free Press Tribune,* April 7, 1905

Chapter 13

13-1. Courtesy of Massachusetts Broken Stone Company
13-2. Courtesy of the Weston Historical Society
13-3. Map adapted from Middlesex County Registry of Deeds, Filed Plan 19, March 10,1885, redrawn by Mary Lord.
13-4. Photo by Pamela W. Fox, c. late 1990s
13-5 and 13-6 (including tag). Courtesy of the Weston Historical Commission, gift of Polly Gambrill Aydelott, photos by A.W. and G.E. Howes
13-7 to 13-10. Courtesy of Eloise Kenney
13-11. Map courtesy of the Society for the Preservation of New England Antiquities, redrawn by Mary Lord
13-12. Courtesy of the Society for the Preservation of New England Antiquities; photo by Alfred Wayland Cutting
13-13 and 13-14. Courtesy of Eloise Kenney
13-15. From *City of Cambridge Annual Documents, 1887,* 255, courtesy of the Cambridge Historical Commission.

13-16. From the 1950 annual report of Cambridge Water Supply, courtesy of the Cambridge Historical Commission
13-17 to 13-20. Courtesy of the Massachusetts Broken Stone Company
13-21. From the *1908 Atlas of Middlesex County*
13-22. Courtesy of The Society for the Preservation of New England Antiquities; photo by Alfred Wayland Cutting
13-23. Courtesy of the Weston Historical Society
13-24. Photo by Pamela W. Fox, 1995
13-25. Courtesy of Anna Melone
13-26. Pastel by Ralph Ayer, 1983, from *Earliest Recollections: Furnishings from the Family of Edwin B. Sears*
13-27. From the collection of H. Bentley Crouch
13-28. Courtesy of the Ashfield Historical Society; Howes Brothers photo
13-29. From the collection of H. Bentley Crouch
13-30. Photo by Pamela W. Fox
13-31. Advertisement from a 1908 Weston Boys Club program
13-32. Courtesy of the Weston Historical Commission
13-33 to 13-36. Courtesy of Joanna Blake Melone

Chapter 14

14-1. From the collection of H. Bentley Crouch
14-2. Courtesy of First Parish Church archives
14-3. Courtesy of the Weston Historical Society
14-4. Photo by Pamela W. Fox
14-5. From *Weston Historical Society Bulletin,* March 1984.
14-6. Courtesy of the Weston Historical Society
14-7. Middlesex Registry of Deeds, Plan Book 107, Plan 16
14-8. Courtesy of the Society for the Preservation of New England Antiquities
14-9. Courtesy of the Weston Historical Commission
14-10. Courtesy of the Weston Historical Society
14-11 and 14-12. Courtesy of the Society for the Preservation of New England Antiquities; photos by Alfred Wayland Cutting
14-13. Courtesy of the Weston Historical Commission
14-14. Courtesy of the First Parish Church archives
14-15. Photo by Sarah B. Gilman
14-16. Courtesy of Mrs. Victor Harnish
14-17. From Plan 5A in Plan Book 219, Middlesex County Registry of Deeds, redrawn by Mary Lord
14-18. Courtesy of Elizabeth Nichols
14-19 to 14-21. Courtesy of Mrs. Kenneth Bennett
14-22. From *Once Upon a Pung,* 68
14-23. Photo by Pamela W. Fox
14-24. Courtesy of Mrs. Victor Harnish
14-25. Photo by Sarah B. Gilman

Chapter 15

15-1. Courtesy of the Society for the Preservation of New England Antiquities; from a postcard
15-2. Courtesy of the First Parish Church archives. The author theorizes that this sketch was drawn by Mary Frances Peirce based on her interviews with town elders. This attribution is based on the similarity between this sketch and the sketch of the weather vanes, also ascribed to Peirce.
15-3. From the *1889 Middlesex County Atlas*
15-4. Courtesy of First Parish Church archives (quote from Lamson's history)
15-5 and 15-6. Courtesy of the First Parish Church archives
15-7. From *Weston Historical Society Bulletin,* May 1983
15-8. Courtesy of the Weston Historical Society; Herbert L. Brown of Waltham, photographer
15-9. Courtesy of the Weston Historical Society
15-10. Courtesy of the Weston Historical Society; photo by Webster of Waltham
15-11. Courtesy of Harold Coburn Jr.
15-12. Courtesy of the Weston Historical Society
15-13. Portrait hangs in Weston Town Hall
15-14 and 15-15. Courtesy of the Weston Historical Society
15-16. Courtesy of the Society for the Preservation of New England Antiquities; from a postcard
15-17. Courtesy of the Weston Historical Society
15-18 and 15-19. Courtesy of the First Parish Church archives
15-20. Courtesy of the Weston Historical Society
15-21. Courtesy of Eloise Kenney
15-22. Courtesy of the Weston Historical Society
15-23. From the 1892 town report
15-24 to 15-29. Courtesy of the Weston Historical Society
15-30. Courtesy of Melissa Burrage; photo by A.W. and G.E. Howes, 1898
15-31 and 15-32. Courtesy of Melissa Burrage
15-33. From *Directory of Wayland, Weston and Lincoln, 1893*
15-34. Courtesy of A. Richard Hersum
15-35. Courtesy of the Weston Historical Society
15-36. Town of Weston records, town hall vault
15-37. From the 1912 town report, 113–20.
15-38. From the collection of H. Bentley Crouch
15-39. Courtesy of the Weston Historical Commission
15-40. Courtesy of the Weston Historical Society
15-41. Courtesy of John Sallay
15-42. Photo by Sarah B. Gilman
15-43. Courtesy of St. Julia Roman Catholic Church
15-44. Courtesy of the Weston Historical Society
15-45. Courtesy of Eloise Kenney
15-46 and 15-47. Courtesy of the First Parish Church archives
15-48. Courtesy of First Parish Church archives. Front row, from left: Erlund and Beryl Field, Carol Hayes, Fanny Thomas, Helen Green, Harold Allen, and Mary and Grant "Pat" Palmer. Second row: Dick Dewey, Ed and Charlotte Hubbard, Hazel Bulwinkle, Marjory Washburn, ____, Natalie Coburn, Anne Coburn, and Cora Green. Third row: Marion Coburn, Peg Allen, Alice Perry Lucas, ___, and Meg Owen. Fourth row: ___, Jenny Kroll, ___ Margaret Mosher, Marion Stewart, Ruth Peakes, and Helen Green. Fifth row: Midge Blaney, Celeste Forbes, Ed Dickson, Alice Fraser, and Priscilla and Arthur "Bud" Coburn. Sixth row: __ Blaney, Tod Jenney, Harriet and Olsen Field, Polly and Ed Marshall, Jim and Peggy Mountz, and Howard Forbes.
15-49. Courtesy of the Weston Historical Society
15-50. Courtesy of Lee Fernandez
15-51. From Weston High School yearbooks of 1955, 1960, and 1961, courtesy of Aimo Teittinen

15-52. From *Weston Historical Society Bulletin,* March 1983
15-53 and 15-54. Courtesy of David Bradley

Chapter 16

16-1. Courtesy of the Weston Historical Society
16-2. Courtesy of the Golden Ball Tavern Museum; photo by Warren of Waltham
16-3. From *Early New England Potters and Their Wares,* by Lura Watkins; photo by Russell B. Harding
16-4. Courtesy of the Society for the Preservation of New England Antiquities (postcard)
16-5. Courtesy of the Massachusetts Historical Society, Francis Blake Papers, Box 64
16-6. From the *Weston Historical Society Bulletin,* October 1975
16-7. From *Boston, Massachusetts* by George W. Englehardt (photo c. 1897), courtesy of the Society for the Preservation of New England Antiquities
16-8. Courtesy of First Baptist Church
16-9. Courtesy of the Weston Historical Society (postcard)
16-10 to 16-13. Courtesy of First Baptist Church
16-14. Courtesy of the Weston Historical Society
16-15. From Lamson's *History of the Town of Weston,* opposite page 47
16-16. Courtesy of the Weston Historical Commission
16-17 and 16-18. Courtesy of Artemis Willis
16-19. Painting by Gertrude Fiske, courtesy of the owner
16-20. Courtesy of Artemis Willis
16-21. Painting by Gertrude Fiske, courtesy of Town of Weston and Weston Public Library
16-21A. Painting by Gertrude Fiske, courtesy of the owner
16-22. Courtesy of Artemis Willis
16-23. Courtesy of the Weston Historical Society
16-24 and 16-25. Courtesy of the Clark family
16-26. Courtesy of the Weston Historical Society
16-27 to 16-29. Courtesy of the Clark family
16-30. Courtesy of Elsie Foote Cooke
16-31 to 16-35. Courtesy of B.L. Ogilvie & Sons
16-36. From *Middlesex County and Its People* (1927), vol. IV
16-37. Courtesy of the Weston Historical Society
16-38 and 16-39. Courtesy of the Golden Ball Tavern Museum
16-40. Photo by Sarah B. Gilman
16-41 and 16-42. Courtesy of the Golden Ball Tavern Museum
16-43. Courtesy of the Weston Historical Commission
16-44. Courtesy of the Weston Historical Society
16-45. Courtesy of the Weston Historical Commission
16-46. Courtesy of Christopher Teller
16-47. Courtesy of the Society for the Preservation of New England Antiquities; photo from the Historic American Building Survey (HABS)
16-48. Courtesy of the Weston Historical Society
16-49 and 16-50. From the *1908 Atlas of Middlesex County*

Chapter 17

17-1. Courtesy of Everett Schwartz Jr.
17-2. From the *Weston Historical Society Bulletin,* January 1973
17-3. Courtesy of Everett Schwartz Jr.
17-4. From the Bicentennial Edition of the *Waltham Daily Free Press Tribune,* June 1913
17-5. Courtesy of the Weston Historical Society
17-6 and 17-7. Courtesy of Dorothea Nolte Kelley
17-8 to 17-12. From *Random Recollections,* by Brenton H. Dickson III
17-13. Courtesy of Thomas M. Paine
17-14. Courtesy of the Weston Historical Society
17-15. Courtesy of Mary Perriello
17-16. Courtesy of Calvin Patriquin

Chapter 18

18-1 to 18-6. Courtesy of Thomas M. Paine
18-7. Courtesy of the Society for the Preservation of New England Antiquities
18-8 to 18-11. Courtesy of Thomas M. Paine
18-12. *Harper's Weekly,* September 12, 1885, as reprinted in Joseph Garland's *The North Shore,* 82
18-13. Courtesy of Thomas M. Paine
18-14. From the *Weston Historical Society Bulletin,* January 1983
18-15. Painting by Helen Paine [Kimball]; photo courtesy of Thomas M. Paine
18-16. Courtesy of Thomas M. Paine
18-17. Courtesy of Lee Fernandez
18-18 to 18-23. Courtesy of Thomas M. Paine
18-24. Painting by Georgina Paine Fisher; photo courtesy of Thomas M. Paine
18-25. Courtesy of Thomas M. Paine
18-26. Courtesy of Thomas M. Paine. Back row, from left: Fred Webster, John Madden, John Forbes, Stephen Forbes, John Bryant Paine Jr., Dr. Lloyd Bacon, Elliot Forbes, Dr. Francis Moore, and Murray Pope. Front row, standing: Lucy Hulburd, Peggy Rice, Rita Nash, Sally Paine, Waldo Forbes, Chattie Paine, Virginia Morss, Charlotte Hutchins, Amelia Forbes, Alice Osborn, David Emerson (kneeling), and James Dennison (kneeling). Seated: Louise Dickson, Mary Dickson, Betsy Wakefield, Lee Wakefield, Joan Wakefield.
18-27. Courtesy of Thomas M. Paine and Lee Fernandez. Note that because the family members are not arranged in neat rows, this picture is difficult to assign names. Back row, standing: Waldo Forbes, Chattie Paine, Charlie Ganson, Betsy Wakefield, Kennard Wakefield, Lee Wakefield, Brent Dickson, Louise Dickson, Bill Erickson, Mary Dickson, and John B. Paine Jr. Seated adults: Sally Forbes, Carol Ganson, Louise Frazer Paine, John B. Paine Sr., Helen Dickson, Louise Erickson, Rita Paine. Children, upper level: Ellen Forbes, Waldo "Spike" Forbes Jr., Carol Ganson, Mack Ganson, Holly Dickson, Louise Erickson, and Lee Erickson. Children, lower level: Cherry Forbes, John Ganson, B.H. "Sandy" Dickson IV, A. Wentworth "Wentie" Erickson, Louise Erickson Jr., and Joan Wakefield

Chapter 19

19-1. Courtesy of Weston Historical Society. Back row: ____, Raymond Benotti, ____, George Olson, _____, Doug Schofield, Danny Evans, G. Murray Burke, and

_____. Middle row: Tom Williams, Sal Rizzo, _____, Elliot Leaf, Jack Williams, Maurice Subilia, Slim Gregorius, Charles Tomao, and Phil Aliseo. Front row: unknown.

19-2A. Courtesy of the Metropolitan District Commission archives

19-2. Photo by Pamela W. Fox

19-3. Courtesy of the Weston Historical Society

19-4. Courtesy of the Photographic Archives of the Arnold Arboretum, copyrighted by the President and Fellows of Harvard College

19-5 and 19-6. Courtesy of the Weston Historical Society

19-7. Courtesy of the Regis College archives

19-8. Courtesy of First Baptist Church

19-9 and 19-10. Courtesy of the Weston Historical Society

19-11. Courtesy of the Metropolitan District Commission archives (March 1902 photo), quote from the *Waltham Daily Free Press Tribune,* February 7, 1902

19-12. Courtesy of the Metropolitan District Commission archives

19-13. Courtesy of the Weston Historical Society

19-14. Courtesy of Metropolitan District Commission archives

19-15 to 19-23. Courtesy of the Regis College archives

19-24 and 19-25. Courtesy of the Weston Historical Society

19-26. Courtesy of First Baptist Church

19-27. Photo by Pamela W. Fox

19-28 and 19-29. Courtesy of the Photographic Archives of the Arnold Arboretum, copyrighted by the President and Fellows of Harvard College

19-30. From *Hillcrest Gardens, Weston, Mass., the 31st Summer,* 1940

19-31. From *Hillcrest Gardens, Weston, Mass., the 13th Summer,* 1922

19-32. From the *Weston Historical Society Bulletin,* May 1982

19-33. Courtesy of the Photographic Archives of the Arnold Arboretum, copyrighted by the President and Fellows of Harvard College

19-34. From *Hillcrest Gardens, Weston, Mass., the 28th Summer, 1937*

19-35. Courtesy of the Photographic Archives of the Arnold Arboretum, copyrighted by the President and Fellows of Harvard College. Miss Case used small copies of this photograph on the cover of the 1921 "Green Book"

19-36. Courtesy of the Photographic Archives of the Arnold Arboretum, copyrighted by the President and Fellows of Harvard College

19-37. Courtesy of the Weston Historical Society

Chapter 20

20-1 and 20-2. Courtesy of Elise Winsor Palmer

20-3. Courtesy of Mrs. Winsor Gale. Back row: Lyman W. Gale, Joseph Allen, Robert Winsor Jr., Robert Winsor, Mary Pickard Winsor, Elizabeth W. Pearson, Theodore Pearson (child), Henry G. Pearson, John Winsor (child), and Frederick Winsor. Front row: Winsor Gale, Jane W. Gale (mother), Emma W. Gale, Priscilla Gale, Dorothy Allen, Anne W. Allen (mother), Nancy Allen, Philip Winsor, Eleanor M. Winsor (mother), Alexander Winsor, Mary P. Winsor, Anne Bent Ware Winsor (grandmother), Felix Winsor, Jessie B. Winsor (mother), Paul Winsor (father), Paul Winsor, Jr., Charles P. Winsor, Frederick Winsor, Jr., Mary Paine Winsor (mother), Theresa Winsor (baby), and Dorothy Winsor.

20-4 to 20-7. Courtesy of Elise Winsor Palmer

20-8. Estate plan courtesy of National Park Service, Frederick Law Olmsted National Historic Site, redrawn by Mary Lord

20-9 to 20-10. Courtesy of Elise Winsor Palmer

20-11. Courtesy of the Weston Historical Society

20-12 and 20-13. Courtesy of Elise Winsor Palmer

20-14 to 20-16. Courtesy of the Weston Golf Club

20-17. Courtesy of Elise Winsor Palmer

20-18. From the Wellington family collection

20-19 and 20-20. Courtesy of Elise Winsor Palmer

20-21. Courtesy of Thomas M. Paine

20-22. Courtesy of the Weston Golf Club

Chapter 21

21-1. From the brochure "Souvenir of the Charles River," courtesy of the Waltham Public Library

21-2. Courtesy of David Kingsbury

21-3. Courtesy of David Kingsbury; information from *WDFPT,* November 29, 1912

21-4. Courtesy of David Kingsbury

21-5. From *Directory, Wayland, Weston and Lincoln,* 1893

21-6. From *Boston Metropolitan Park Report,* courtesy of The Jackson Homestead, Newton, Massachusetts

21-7. Courtesy of Stanley French Jr.

21-8. From the booklet *Early Days in Auburndale: A Village Chronicle of Two Centuries: 1665–1870,* published under the auspices of the Auburndale Woman's Club

21-9. Courtesy of The Jackson Homestead, Newton, Massachusetts

21-10. Courtesy of David Kingsbury

21-11. From the *Boston Transcript,* April 1893

21-12. Courtesy of Robert Pollack

21-13. Courtesy of Thomas M. Paine

21-14. "Plan of Conveyance of the Riverside Recreation Grounds . . ." September 19, 1914, Plan Book 228, Plan 7 (MCRD), redrawn by Pamela W. Fox

21-15. From "Souvenir Program of the G.A.R. Encampment, Boston, August 15–20, 1904," Waltham Public Library

21-16. Courtesy of Robert Pollock

21-17. Courtesy of the Society for the Preservation of New England Antiquities (postcard)

21-18. Courtesy of Robert Pollock

21-19 to 21-21. From a promotional brochure, c. 1912, courtesy of The Jackson Homestead, Newton, Massachusetts

21-22. Courtesy of the Metropolitan District Commission archives

21-23. Reproduction poster owned by the author

21-24. Courtesy of Cynthia Kettyle

21-25. Courtesy of The Jackson Homestead, Newton,

Massachusetts
21-26. Courtesy of David Kingsbury; photo by Fairfield
21-27. From a promotional brochure, c. 1912, courtesy of The Jackson Homestead, Newton, Massachusetts
21-28. Courtesy of David Kingsbury
21-29. Courtesy of the Society for the Preservation of New England Antiquities; photograph by Henry Peabody, c. 1906.
21-30. Advertisement from "Souvenir of the Charles River," c. 1904
21-31 to 21-32. Courtesy of David Kingsbury
21-33 and 21-34. Courtesy of the Metropolitan District Commission archives
21-35. Courtesy of The Jackson Homestead, Newton, Massachusetts
21-36 and 21-37. From *The Discovery of the Ancient City of Norumbega,* by Eben N. Horsford
21-38. From *Problem of the Northmen,* by Eben N. Horsford
21-39. Courtesy of The Jackson Homestead, Newton, Massachusetts

Chapter 22
22-1 to 22-5. Courtesy of Stanley G. French Jr.
22-6. Courtesy of Stanley G. French Jr.; quote from C.W. Hubbard's unpublished autobiography
22-7. Redrawn by Mary Lord from the 1908 *Atlas of Middlesex County*
22-8 to 22-10. Courtesy of Stanley G. French Jr.
22-11. From *Jute: An Account of Its Growth and Manufacture* (privately printed for Ludlow Manufacturing Company, 1928); courtesy of the Ludlow Memorial Library
22-12. Courtesy of Paula and Harold Schwenk
22-13. Courtesy of Charles Hubbard Meigs
22-14. Courtesy of Stanley G. French Jr.
22-15. Courtesy of Paula and Harold Schwenk
22-16. Courtesy of Charles Hubbard Meigs
22-17 to 22-20. Courtesy of Stanley G. French Jr.
22-21. Courtesy of the National Park Service, Frederick Law Olmsted National Historic Site
22-22. Courtesy of Stanley G. French Jr.
22-23. Courtesy of Charles Hubbard Meigs
22-24. Courtesy of the National Park Service, Frederick Law Olmsted National Historic Site
22-25 and 22-26. Courtesy of Thomas M. Paine
22-27. MCRD, Filed Plan 942

Chapter 23
23-1. Courtesy of the Massachusetts Historical Society; photo by Francis Blake
23-2. Courtesy of the Massachusetts Historical Society
23-3. Courtesy of the Massachusetts Historical Society; photo by William A. Webster of Waltham
23-4. Courtesy of Massachusetts Historical Society; photo by Warren Heald of Boston
23-5 to 23-7. Courtesy of the Massachusetts Historical Society; photos by Francis Blake
23-8. Courtesy of the Massachusetts Historical Society
23-9. Courtesy of the Massachusetts Historical Society; photo by Francis Blake
23-10. Courtesy of the Massachusetts Historical Society
23-11 to 23-14. Courtesy of Thomas M. Paine; photos by Francis Blake
23-15. Courtesy of the Massachusetts Historical Society; photo by Francis Blake
23-16. Courtesy of the Massachusetts Historical Society
23-17. Courtesy of the Society for the Preservation of New England Antiquities; from *Picturesque and Architectural New England: Architectural Features* by H. Langford Warren (D.H. Hurd & Co., Boston, 1899), vol. I
23-18. Courtesy of the Massachusetts Historical Society
23-19 and 23-20. Courtesy of Thomas M. Paine, photo by Francis Blake
23-21. Courtesy of the Massachusetts Historical Society; photo by Francis Blake
23-22 and 23-23. Courtesy of the Massachusetts Historical Society
23-24. Courtesy of the Massachusetts Historical Society; photo by Francis Blake
23-25 and 23-26. Courtesy of the Massachusetts Historical Society
23-27 and 23-28. Courtesy of the Massachusetts Historical Society; photos by Francis Blake
23-29. Courtesy of the Weston Historical Society
23-30. Courtesy of the Massachusetts Historical Society
23-31. From the *Boston Daily Globe,* June 25, 1902
23-32 and 23-33. Courtesy of the Massachusetts Historical Society
23-34. Courtesy of John Sallay
23-35. Courtesy of Thomas M. Paine

Chapter 24
24-1. Courtesy of the Weston Historical Society
24-2 and 24-3. Courtesy of James Fraser
24-4. Courtesy of the Massachusetts Historical Society
24-5. Courtesy of the Weston Historical Commission, B.L. Young family scrapbook
24-6 and 24-7. From *The National Cyclopedia of American Biography,* courtesy of the Massachusetts Historical Society
24-8. Courtesy of the Weston Historical Society; photo by A.W. and G.E. Howes, 1898
24-9. Courtesy of the Society for the Preservation of New England Antiquities; from *Picturesque and Architectural New England: Picturesque Massachusetts* by Edward Everett Hall (Boston: D.H. Hurd & Co., 1899), vol. II, 102
24-10. Courtesy of the Weston Historical Society; photo by A.W. and G.E. Howes, 1898
24-11. From the *200th Anniversary Edition, Waltham Daily Free Press Tribune,* June 1913
24-12. Courtesy of the Massachusetts Historical Society; photo by Francis Blake
24-13. Courtesy of the Weston Historical Society
24-14 and 24-15. Courtesy of the Weston Historical Society; photos by A.W. and G.E. Howes, 1898
24-16 to 24-20. Courtesy of James Fraser
24-21. From the *Weston Historical Society Bulletin,* October 1984
24-22. From the *Weston Historical Society Bulletin,* March 1977
24-23. From the *Boston Daily Globe,* June 12, 1906

24-24. Courtesy of the Weston Public Library, *Town Crier* photo
24-25. Courtesy of James Fraser
24-26. From *Weston Historical Society Bulletin,* January 1985
24-27. Courtesy of the Weston Public Library
24-28. Courtesy of Robert and Cynthia Mosher; from Margaret Mosher's scrapbook
24-29 and 24-30. Courtesy of the Massachusetts Archives, MDC Collection (Contract 81)
24-31. From the 1908 *Atlas of Middlesex County*

Chapter 25

25-1 to 25-5. Courtesy of George Bates
25-6. Photo by Pamela W. Fox
25-7. Courtesy of Nelson McNutt and Mildred Balunas
25-8 and 25-9. Courtesy of George Bates
25-10 to 25-15. Courtesy of Nelson McNutt and Mildred Balunas

Chapter 26

26-1 to 26-4. Courtesy of the Henderson House Conference Center, Northeastern University
26-5 and 26-6. Courtesy of Nelson McNutt and Mildred Balunas
26-7. Courtesy of Shepley Bulfinch Richardson and Abbott archives
26-8. Courtesy of the Henderson House Conference Center, Northeastern University

Chapter 27

27-1. Courtesy of Heather and Brian Bell
27-2 and 27-3. Courtesy of Ruth Andrews
27-4. Courtesy of First Baptist Church
27-5. From Harriet M.J. Sinclair, ed., *75th Anniversary History of Chapoquoit Island, 1890–1965 and the Chapoquoit Yacht Club, 1903–1965*
27-6 and 27-7. Courtesy of Heather and Brian Bell
27-8. 1933 map of the Jones estate, redrawn by Mary Lord
27-9. Photo by Pamela W. Fox
27-10 to 27-11. Courtesy of Jean D'Intinosanto Jones
27-12 and 27-13. Photos by Pamela W. Fox

Chapter 28

28-1 to 28-20. Courtesy of Fred Campbell
28-21. From *The Northern,* courtesy of Garret Schenck
28-22. Courtesy of Garret Schenck
28-23. Courtesy of the Massachusetts Water Resources Authority
28-24 to 28-26. Courtesy of the Massachusetts Archives

Chapter 29

29-1A, 29-1B, and 29-1C. Courtesy of Emily Althausen
29-2. Photo by Pamela W. Fox, c. mid-1990s
29-3. From *The Train Family,* by Russell E. Train
29-4. From *Weston Historical Society Bulletin,* spring 1994
29-5. Photo by Pamela W. Fox
29-6. From the collection of H. Bentley Crouch
29-7. Courtesy of Thomas M. Paine; quotes from *WDFPT,* December 20, 1912
29-8 to 29-15. Courtesy of Emily Althausen
29-16. Courtesy of the Weston Historical Society
29-17. From *Once Upon a Pung,* by Brenton Dickson III
29-18. From the obituary of Peter Mezitt, October 31, 1968 (possibly in the *Boston Globe*)
29-19. Courtesy of Wayne and Roger Mezitt, Weston Nurseries
29-20 and 29-21. Courtesy of Emanuel Benotti

Chapter 30

30-1. From the Wellington family collection
30-2. MCRD Filed Plan 399, recorded January 7, 1906 (plan drawn November 6, 1899), "Estate of Robert B. Blodgett, Esq."
30-3 to 30-5. From the Wellington family collection
30-6. Courtesy of Nicholas Danforth
30-7 to 30-10. From the Wellington family collection
30-11. Courtesy of the Weston Historical Society
30-12 and 30-13. From the Wellington family collection
30-14. From *Beggar on Horseback: The Autobiography of Thomas D. Cabot.* From left, Lydia Hall, Jim Cabot, Susan Baker, Henry Hall, Kitty Billings, Ralph Bradley, Linda Wellington, Jack Cabot, Virginia Wellington Cabot, Thomas Cabot, Alec Bright, Polly de Camp, Ned Billings, Margaret Ranney, Dudley Ranney, Jerome Johnson, and Eleanor Bremer.
30-15 to 30-23. From the Wellington family collection
30-24. From *The Magazine Antiques,* October 1980
30-25 to 30-27. Courtesy of Benjamin Blaney
30-28. From Christie's auction catalogue, June 23, 1993
30-29. Courtesy of Benjamin Blaney
30-30. Courtesy of the Weston Historical Commission
30-31. Courtesy of the Society for the Preservation of New England Antiquities
30-32. Cover of *New Homes Under Old Roofs,* courtesy of John Sallay
30-33. Sketch by Elizabeth Blaney [Cram] from *Memoirs of Elizabeth Hill Cram*
30-34. Courtesy of The Society for the Preservation of New England Antiquities; photo by Wallace Nutting
Figure C. Courtesy of Weston Town Hall
Figure D. Courtesy of Fred Perkins

INDEX

Abbreviations:
p: see photo or illustration caption
m: see map caption or map
c: see chart or table

ABOUT THE AUTHORS

Pamela Wilkinson Fox majored in art history at Radcliffe College and pursued her interest in architecture and historic preservation at Boston University, where she received a master's degree in preservation studies. She has worked for many years as a preservation consultant. In 1991, she and her family moved to Weston. *Farm Town to Suburb* had its genesis in a survey of the town's historic resources which she undertook for the Weston Historical Commission in 1993-94.

Sarah Bates Gilman studied photography as an undergraduate at Wellesley College and has worked for 20 years as a professional photographer. For this book, she spent hundreds of hours copying and printing photographs, and working with the author to choose the best images.

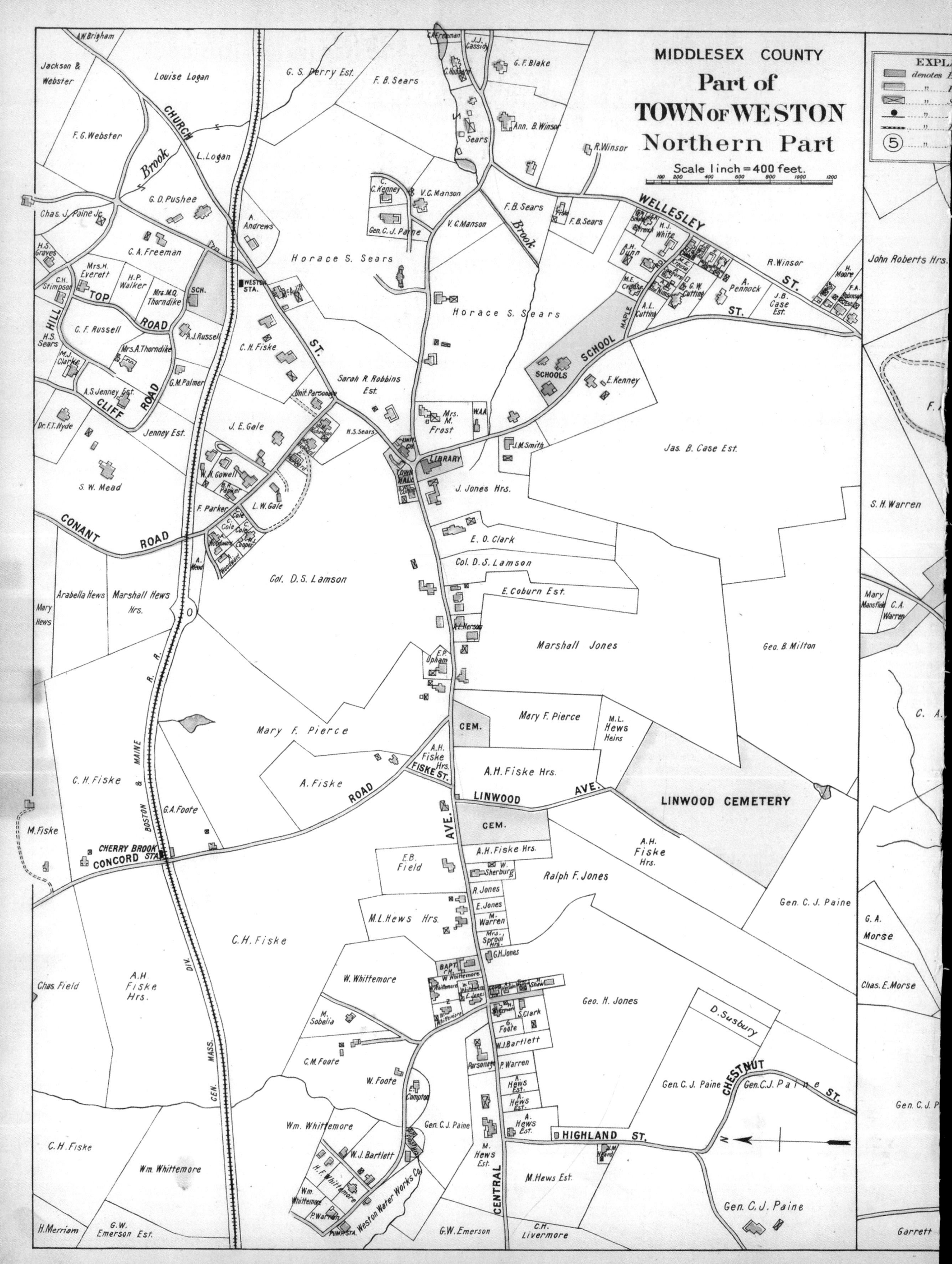
MIDDLESEX COUNTY
Part of
TOWN OF WESTON
Northern Part
Scale 1 inch = 400 feet.
WELLESLEY ST.
SCHOOL ST.
CHURCH ST.
CONANT ROAD
TOP ROAD
HILL ROAD
CLIFF ROAD
FISKE ST.
FISKE ROAD
LINWOOD AVE.
LINWOOD CEMETERY
CENTRAL AVE.
CONCORD ROAD
HIGHLAND ST.
CHESTNUT ST.
BOSTON & MAINE R. R.
MASS. CEN. DIV.
CHERRY BROOK STA.
WESTON STA.
LIBRARY
TOWN HALL
SCHOOLS
CEM.
Weston Water Works Co.
Horace S. Sears
Col. D. S. Lamson
Marshall Jones
Mary F. Pierce
Jas. B. Case Est.
Geo. B. Milton
Ralph F. Jones
Geo. H. Jones
Gen. C. J. Paine
C. H. Fiske
A. H. Fiske Hrs.
S. W. Mead
J. E. Gale
Sarah R. Robbins Est.
F. B. Sears
G. S. Perry Est.
Louise Logan
F. G. Webster
Jackson & Webster
A. W. Brigham
Arabella Hews
Marshall Hews Hrs.
W. Whittemore
Wm. Whittemore
G. W. Emerson
C. H. Livermore
H. Merriam
G. W. Emerson Est.
M. Hews Est.
John Roberts Hrs.
S. H. Warren
G. A. Morse
Chas. E. Morse
Chas. Field
M. Fiske
Garrett